EVERYMAN,
I WILL GO WITH THEE,
AND BE THY GUIDE,
IN THY MOST NEED
TO GO BY THY SIDE

GEORGE ORWELL

Essays

Edited and introduced by John Carey

EVERYMAN'S LIBRARY

242

First included in Everyman's Library, 2002
Copyright © the estate of the late Sonia Brownell Orwell
Text drawn directly from *The Complete Works of George Orwell*, edited
by Peter Davison, assisted by Ian Angus and Sheila Davison, 1998

Introduction, Bibliography and Chronology © Everyman
Publishers plc, 2002
Typography by Peter B. Willberg

ISBN 1-85715-242-5

A CIP catalogue record for this book is available from the
British Library

Published by Everyman Publishers plc,
Gloucester Mansions, 140A Shaftesbury Avenue,
London WC2H 8HD

Distributed by Random House (UK) Ltd.,
20 Vauxhall Bridge Road, London SW1V 2SA

Printed and bound in Germany
by GGP Media, Pössneck

GEORGE ORWELL

———

CONTENTS

vii

xiv

INTRODUCTION

More than the novels, more even than *The Road to Wigan Pier* or *Homage to Catalonia*, the essays and journalism are the essential Orwell. They are Orwell the man, Orwell the thinker, Orwell the political animal. The figure we meet in them is not the real-life Eric Blair. Friends remember Blair as prickly, diffident, ill at ease with ordinary people. According to his brother-in-law, who took him to pubs in working-class districts of Leeds, he was 'a skeleton at the feast' and disliked his fellow men. Those who witnessed his bids to conform to working-class manners – sucking tea noisily from a saucer in the BBC canteen, for example – saw it as an embarrassing charade. George Orwell the writer, by contrast, is confident, relaxed, open, democratic. That is not to claim that his writing misrepresents his 'true' self. You could as easily argue that the true self was masked by shyness or awkwardness in life and came out in the writing. Either way, it reminds us how much art went into the writing, for all its natural appearance.

Orwell made no secret of this. One can write nothing readable, he said in 'Why I Write', 'unless one constantly struggles to efface one's own personality'. His long-term aim was 'to make political writing into an art'. That comes as a surprise, because we do not normally think of him as an artist. He almost never praises beauty, and when he does he locates it in rather scruffy or overlooked things – a glass paperweight in a junk shop, the eye of the common toad, a sixpenny rose bush from Woolworth's. The style he developed in the essays and journalism is the verbal equivalent of these objects. It is plain and simple – or seems to be until you try to write like it yourself. It is never obscure or pretentious. English, he said, is 'the language of lyric poetry, and also of headlines' – meaning that it can be both infinitely subtle and extremely compact. His rules for writing included saying everything in the shortest possible way and using concrete words rather than abstract. Things to avoid were vagueness, hackneyed phrases, dead metaphors and decorative adjectives. He attacked pomposity, fake profundity and meaninglessness in other writers, and ridiculed jargon, especially the political kind, as when he remarked that in England the word 'bourgeois' is used almost exclusively by people of bourgeois origin.

Swift is sometimes cited as the model for his prose style. But Swift's studied, decorous irony is extremely unlike Orwell. H. G. Wells, whom he read eagerly at prep school, is a closer match. So is G. K. Chesterton, and the much less well-known Winwood Reade, author of *The Martyrdom of Man*, which he remembers reading at about seventeen. The features he picks out in Reade's writing – an insistence on the importance of economic processes, a knack of making them picturesque, an air of assured knowledge – are all distinctly Orwellian. Orwell's air of assured knowledge rests, at times, on shaky foundations. When he writes, for example, 'We live in an age in which the average human being in the highly civilized countries is aesthetically inferior to the lowest savage' the claim is so vague as to be meaningless. But the confident assertion is characteristic and stylistically essential. Surprise is an important element too. Sometimes it takes the form of unexpected opinions – as when he commends George Gissing for calling the working class savages, or, during the Second World War, challenges the view that it is worse to kill civilians than soldiers, or suggests that the first step towards a serious study of anti-Semitism would be to stop regarding it as a crime. These opinions are never just provocative – never the kind of licensed 'naughtiness' that writers in the whimsical English essay tradition used to assume. They are a sign of authentically individual thought. Surprise was one of the anti-boredom devices with which Orwell primed his prose. He could deliver an insult with the timing of a stand-up comic: 'Looking through the photographs in the New Year Honours List, I am struck (as usual) by the quite exceptional ugliness and vulgarity of the faces displayed there', or (reviewing his friend Cyril Connolly's anonymously published *The Unquiet Grave*) 'even without knowing his identity one could infer that the writer of this book is about 40, is inclined to stoutness, has lived much in Continental Europe, and has never done any real work'. Neither sentence may strike us as 'art' in the normal sense, but noticing how carefully they are constructed helps us to understand why Orwell said that writing, for him, was always an aesthetic experience.

Realism is another key Orwellian factor. One reason why he hated the Americanization of English culture was because it falsified reality. Looking through an American fashion magazine he notices that there are no references to grey hairs, fatness, middle age or death. Everything is subsumed into a fake world of eternal glamour. His own course was exactly the opposite, to strip off polish and give life back its actuality and miscellaneousness. He valued 'solid objects and scraps of useless information'. He hoarded 'petty and irrelevant' details that made the past come to life – a cabman bursting into tears in 1914, for example, because the army had commandeered his horse. From his days as a bookshop assistant in Hampstead he recalls touts from Christmas-card firms coming round as early as June – and a phrase from one of their invoices sticks in his mind: '2 doz. Infant Jesus with rabbits'. He enjoys small ads, and the pleas for partners in the *Matrimonial Post*. He notices how wartime shortages have affected the prices of alarm clocks and second-hand typewriters and scrubbing brushes. In August 1944 he watches wooden palisades going up in London squares to keep the public out, replacing the railings taken down at the start of the war. His seasonal pleasures include wallflowers, 'especially the old-fashioned brown ones', stewed rhubarb in May, and 'the endless pop-pop-pop of cherry stones as one treads the London pavements' in July.

Orwell's angle on reality adds up to more than just a zest for the commonplace. It is what made him a cultural critic. In formulating his idea of what constituted a 'culture' he did not resort to the usual exhibits – high art, civic institutions, monuments of the past. He looked, instead, at life as most people knew it. England in 1940 is the land of 'totes, dog-races, football pools, Woolworth's, the pictures, Gracie Fields, Wall's ice cream, potato crisps, celanese stockings, dart-boards, pin-tables, cigarettes, cups of tea, and Saturday evenings in the four ale bar'. Most of these things meant nothing to Eric Blair, but caring about them was part of the Orwell persona. He had an almost poetic alertness to the mundane. Coming back to England from abroad, it was the small things, he said, that made him realize he was in a different country – the coins were heavier, the beer bitterer, and the crowds with 'their mild knobbly faces, their bad teeth and gentle manners' were unlike a European crowd. His fascination with ordinariness went beyond externals. The beliefs and ideas that made up Englishness were not, for him, to be gleaned from books and broadsheet newspapers. They were the sort of thing you might overhear in the pub. He kept a list of popular fallacies – that a swan can break your leg with a blow of its wing, that powdered glass is poisonous, that bulls become infuriated at the sight of red. He catalogues these oddities with the enthusiasm of a collector. That is typical of his cultural criticism. His essays on 'Boys' Weeklies' and 'The Art of Donald McGill' – ground-breaking texts in what has since become cultural studies – both show a relish for the material under analysis even when his criticism is adverse. The *Magnet* and the *Gem* and seaside postcards, for all their political incorrectness, were elements of English life that part of Orwell was in love with. He was the first serious student of the ordinary.

He was always a political writer in that he always saw what went on around him through the perspectives of social class and economics. So in reading the essays and journalism we need to know something of how his politics developed, and what lay behind his basic assumptions. In answering the second question his essay 'Such, Such Were the Joys', about his prep-school days at St Cyprian's, Eastbourne, is a key text. There has been much debate about whether it is a fair account, with gallant Old St Cyprianites springing to the defence of the headmaster and his wife. Such interjections are beside the point. How Orwell remembered the place is what matters, not how others did. It left him with a lasting hatred of the rich and the luxuries they could afford, a distrust of authority, and a tendency to associate it with totalitarianism and persecution (both of them features of authority at the school), and a sense of himself as a victim and an outcast, unclean, unlovable, unlikely to succeed. Probably, too, thanks to 'Flip', the headmaster's repellent wife, it contributed to his difficulties in forming relationships with women.

His time at Eton reinforced some of these traits, since he was once more a poor boy among the rich. But as a scholar, living with other scholars, he was insulated to an extent from humiliating comparisons. Besides, he internalized aspects of the public-school ethos and never outgrew them. He once said that the thinking man was left-wing by conviction but right-wing by temperament. It was a shrewd piece of self-analysis and Eton, it seems, inaugurated the split. His anti-intellectualism, his homophobic scorn for the 'pansy' intelligentsia, his admiration for the 'military virtues' and his antipathy to pacifism were all prejudices that Eton encouraged, and that give us a glimpse of the Orwell who became a surprisingly keen and tough player of Eton's unorthodox form of rugby football, the Wall Game. That is not to say that they are to be wholly regretted. They allowed him to see questions from more than one angle, and achieve perceptions that would have been unavailable to a more blinkered ideologue. His observation, for example, that in prosperous countries left-wing politics are 'always partly humbug' drew on his experience of poverty abroad, but was rooted in a public-school distrust of lefty attitudinizing. His opposition to pacifism amounted to more than cheap taunts about cowardice. It was rational and considered, and his opponents' arguments were submitted to careful scrutiny. But there was also a strain in it that was simpler and suggestive of his public-school credentials. It comes out in, for example, the essay 'My Country Right or Left', which sneers at the 'boiled rabbits of the Left' whose hearts have never 'leapt at the sight of a Union Jack' and contrasts them with the young heroes 'public school to the core' who are ready to die in the cause of freedom.

Burma was the next step in his political education. It was certainly more valuable to him than university would have been. His five years there permanently widened his perspective on the world. As an officer in the Imperial Police he saw the British Raj from the inside, which means that he did not see it simply. Much as he came to hate imperialism, it was possible, he realized, to be a 'decent' person and an imperialist, as, he felt, Kipling had been. He was aware that the empire was a system of exploitation, and that it was guilty of atrocities, but he understood the pressures that drove men to commit them. As 'Shooting an Elephant' records, he knew what it was like to be hooted at by hostile crowds and surrounded by 'sneering yellow faces'. He never lost this double perspective, and he was courageous enough to admit to it. 'With one part of my mind I thought of the British Raj as an unbreakable tyranny ... with another part I thought that the greatest joy in the world would be to drive a bayonet into a Buddhist priest's guts.' At the same time, what it felt like to be a sensitive individual responsible for propping up an inhuman tyranny is unforgettably brought out in 'A Hanging'.

This persistent recourse to firsthand experience distinguishes Orwell's writing about empire from the cant of stay-at-home anti-imperialists. He insists on being realistic. In response to those who demand instant home rule for India, he argues that India is simply not ready to join the modern world: 'the whole subcontinent, in this year of 1943, is incapable of manu-facturing an automobile engine'. It is a point he returns to repeatedly: 'In the age of the tank and the bombing-plane, backward agricultural countries like India and the African colonies can no more be independent than can a cat or a dog.' These opinions did not endear Orwell to fellow Socialists. Nor did his sarcasms about Gandhi. But they too arose from his antagonism to the idea that a 'spiritual' India could somehow opt out of the modern world, as well as from his dislike of popular idols, which made him suspect that Gandhi, toying with his spinning-wheel 'in the mansion of some cotton mil-lionaire', was essentially bogus. His anti-imperialism did not stop him observing, either, that the worst barbarities Indians suffered were inflicted by other Indians, not by Europeans, and he claimed that on balance the British had done India more good than harm.

But despite these concessions he saw the poverty of India as a blatant and inexcusable injustice. The average English-man, he pointed out, spends more on cigarettes than an Indian peasant has for his whole livelihood. 'It is quite common for an Indian coolie's leg to be thinner than an average English-man's arm.' It had nothing to do with racial physique, it was due to simple starvation. To correct this injustice would mean the English, and Europeans generally, accepting a lower standard of living. Socialist propaganda had, he felt, dishonestly concealed this. The masses had been taught that Socialism would mean higher wages and better housing. Instead they should be told that, far from being downtrodden slaves, they were already living way above their income, and owed their unjust prosperity to the exploitation of coloured people. It is a lesson which the West has still to learn.

So Burma educated Orwell. It also contributed to his spiritual growth because it led to his great renunciation. When he resigned his commission in the Imperial Police he confronted years of poverty and, from his family's viewpoint, shame. Even his admirers sometimes feel that he is over-serious – 'the wintry conscience' of his generation. But his seriousness reflects the sacrifice he made, the burden of guilt he shouldered, and his determination to expiate it. Though he had renounced Christianity, this crisis and the deliberate self-abasement he undertook by mingling with social outcasts, as described in *Down and Out in Paris and London*, had the intensity of a religious conversion.

The next decisive influence on the formation of his political views was the Spanish Civil War. His decision to fight was personal as much as political. He had always felt inferior to the men who had served in the Great War, and he wanted to regain his self-respect. He did. But he also felt, for the first time, comradeship with men from far different social and cultural backgrounds. It was a revelation of how society might work if it were no longer narrowly insular and class-bound. 'I at last really believe in Socialism, which I never did before', he wrote in June 1937. Probably the biggest impact of the war, however, was to open his eyes to the ruthlessness and dishonesty of Soviet Communism. Serving with the POUM Anarchist militia against Franco's Fascists, he had imagined that he was on the same side as the Communists. In fact the Communists had no intention of allowing the Anarchists an independent role. They were proscribed and hunted down. Several of Orwell's comrades were killed or imprisoned. He and his wife were lucky to escape across the border. Quite apart from the sense of outrage this instilled, Orwell was disgusted by the cynicism with which the pro-Communist news media rewrote events. Newspaper reports, he found, bore no relation to the facts. Battles in which he had himself taken part were completely misrepresented. The very concept of objective truth seemed to him to be fading. Kingsley Martin, editor of the *New Statesman*, refused to publish his article 'Spilling the Spanish Beans' and his review of Borkenau's *The Spanish Cockpit* (they came out in the *New English Weekly* and *Time and Tide* respectively). These were betrayals he never forgave. His experience of the war in Spain lay behind his fear of totalitarianism, which is seminal to *Animal Farm* and *Nineteen Eighty-Four*, as well as to much of his later journalism. In 'Inside the Whale' (March 1940) he prophesies that Western civilization is 'almost certainly' moving into an age of totalitarian superstates, in which the autonomous individual will be stamped out of existence.

The last event that precipitated a change – or an adjustment – in his political attitudes was the outbreak of the Second World War. He had joined the Independent Labour Party in June 1938 because it was anti-war. It believed, as he did, that the impending war would be fought to preserve capitalism and imperialism, and that no Socialist could fight for such goals. It was nonsense, he wrote, to talk of opposing Fascism with capitalist democracy: they were the same thing. The only true alternative to Fascism was workers' control. When war became a reality, however, Orwell's patriotism reasserted itself literally overnight. In 'My Country Right or Left', published in the autumn of 1940, he recalls that the revelation that he would support the war, and would himself fight if possible, came to him in a dream. He now violently attacked the anti-war positions he had himself taken up. He resigned from the Independent Labour Party because its leaders persisted in calling the war a capitalist-imperialist conspiracy. He derided left-wingers who 'wailed' that it was a capitalist war and that British imperialism was fighting for loot. They had 'got their heads screwed on backwards'. The argument that democracy, as practised in England, was just the same as totalitarianism simply ignored the facts – so Orwell now insisted.

He did not, however, immediately abandon his hopes of a

Socialist revolution. When he joined the Home Guard he seems to have thought, at first, that it might develop into a people's militia – though the 'gentleness' that always came high in his list of English attributes made an armed uprising a remote possibility. His notion of what Socialism was, and what its objectives should be, itself changed during the late 1930s and early '40s. In 1939 he still believed that 'humanity must move in the direction of Communism or perish', and that the right to private property meant 'the right to exploit and torture millions of one's fellow creatures'. To a Socialist it must be apparent, he insisted, that private property and economic justice are incompatible. Defining Socialism two years later, however, he explains that it will entail state ownership of all means of production, such as land, mines, ships and machinery, but will not mean the end of private property. Rather there will be an approximate equalization of incomes, which will ensure that the highest wage or salary does not exceed the lowest by more than ten to one. Hereditary privilege, especially in education, will be abolished. So will the autonomy of the public schools and the older universities. They will be flooded with state-aided pupils chosen simply on grounds of ability. 'Private' education will cease. These measures will, Orwell trusts, ensure the disappearance of the class system. Further, Socialism's ultimate aims will be not merely insular but global. The Orwellian goal is a world state of free and equal human beings.

The problem for Orwell was how these radical social reforms could be brought about democratically. What if the majority of people did not want them? How could they be reconciled with freedom? Could the freedom to exploit others, which was the incentive behind capitalism, be terminated while preserving freedom of thought and expression? Writing in May 1941 he observes that free capitalism is coming to an end in country after country and is being replaced by totalitarian systems. This, he fears, means the end of individual liberty, not just economic liberty or the liberty to choose one's own work or travel where one likes, but intellectual and emotional liberty as well. 'The totalitarian state tries ... to control the thoughts and emotions of its subjects at least as completely as it controls their actions.' That the Socialist world he wanted could never be brought about democratically was a fear that dogged Orwell to the end. The greatest difficulty, he writes in July 1947, is 'the apathy and conservatism of people everywhere'. He still insists desperately that democratic Socialism can surely be made to work 'somewhere or other'. Perhaps the whole of Europe and Africa might combine in a 'Socialist United States'. But he admits it is not a 'hopeful objective'. A better form of society might arise in India or China, he speculates, but it would take too long. Only in Europe could democratic Socialism become a reality quickly enough to prevent the superstates destroying themselves in an atomic war. As things are, though, no such redeeming development seems likely, and he admits reluctantly that he would 'give odds against the survival of civilization'. The dawn of the atomic age had brought a similar pessimism to many people of course. But Orwell had a more personal reason for feeling hopeless – he was a democrat committed to aims that could not be achieved democratically.

The essays and journalism establish Orwell as the most incisive literary critic of the twentieth century, and that too is a consequence of his politics. Not just his politics, admittedly. He was enormously widely read, especially in out-of-the-way authors and 'good-bad books'. He had sharp aesthetic sensitivity and a rapid intelligence that could outpace most literary scholars. His brief essay on Milton says more, and more acutely, than many lifelong Milton specialists have managed. But politics are nevertheless crucial in his literary criticism. His masterly essay on Charles Dickens is distinctive because it asks political questions that no one had thought of asking, and notices quite simple things that everyone else had missed – that Dickens writes endlessly about food but never about agriculture, that he had no ideal of work, his London is a city of consumers. Orwell's challenging nomination of Gissing as the best English novelist is, again, flagrantly political. His point is that no other writer knew the swarming recesses of the late-nineteenth-century underclass as intimately as Gissing, or portrayed them as accurately. Both claims are true, though they do not make Gissing a great novelist unless you approach the question from a purely political angle. The originality of Orwell's criticism comes, also, from being unstuffy, and from admitting what most intellectuals would not admit – that *The Brothers Karamazov* is 'heavy going', that everyone likes to read about murder. With the same lack of highbrow inhibition he predicts that *Uncle Tom's Cabin* will outlast the complete works of Viginia Woolf. These unorthodoxies were themselves political, in a sense, in that they endorsed Orwell's allegiance with the common man against the highly-educated.

With politics coming so high on his critical agenda, Orwell was naturally forced to confront the question of whether a work of art could be successful aesthetically but, at the same time, politically unacceptable. His answer was yes. Greatness in art, he decides, has nothing to do with political correctness. There are good writers whose opinions would, in any age, be rejected as 'false and silly', and Swift's *Gulliver's Travels* is sufficient proof that a world-view that is barely sane can produce a great work of art. It is a deadly sin to say 'X is a political enemy: therefore he is a bad writer'. Given the vehemence with which he expressed these opinions, it is easy to assume that he would have opposed political censorship of art or literature, since obviously it might mean the suppression of aesthetic masterpieces. But his essay on Salvador Dali suggests otherwise. He has no difficulty reaching the conclusion that Dali was both a good draughtsman and a disgusting human being. But the more worrying issue arises of whether his pictures should be allowed on public display. Orwell seemingly thinks not. They are obscene and degrading and, in effect, criminal, since 'encouraging necrophilic reveries', as, he contends, Dali does, is as harmful as ordinary crime. That they have artistic merit is beside the point: 'it should be possible to say, "This is a good book or a good picture, and it ought to be burned by the public hangman."' In fact he quickly goes on to deny that Dali's pictures should be suppressed. Instead, he decides, they should be analysed and their perversions exposed. But his hesitation is understandable. He was firmly opposed to the notion of 'art for art's sake' and to the related idea that artists are exempt from moral responsibility. Art and literature, he believed, could and should make people morally better. Commenting on the news that a number of scientists had refused to work on the atomic bomb, because they foresaw what use would be made of it, he celebrates them as sane men in a world of lunatics, and feels sure that they must have had some cultural education – in literature and the arts – not just a scientific training.

Orwell's concern with the moral effects of culture alerts us to the fact that all his political opinions – his desire for social justice, his belief in universal freedom and equality – were in essence moral. He was a moralist even before he was a politician. 'Decency', a key term in his writing, is moral in its force. It reverberates with public-school notions of fair play ('I don't think it's awfully decent of you to behave like this', says Flip in 'Such, Such Were the Joys'). But it also means being concerned about other people, especially the deprived and the victimized. 'Everyone who cares for decency', Orwell says, will be grateful for a recently published book that exposes the sexual deprivations suffered by men in prison. It is also a democratic term. Orwell writes of 'the native decency of the common man', with the implication that there is a basic human goodness that binds people together. 'One has a right to expect ordinary decency even of a poet', he remarks of Ezra Pound. The inherent decency of the English – the common people even more than the educated classes – comes out, for Orwell, in their tendency to side with the underdog, and their hatred of bullying, terrorism and violent crime. It also has a sexual side. Though the English masses refuse to knuckle down to middle-class Puritanism, 'almost no one in England', Orwell believes, 'approves of prostitution'. His essay 'Raffles and Miss Blandish' contrasts the innocent, old-style English thriller with American crime fiction and pulp magazines. The staple ingredient of this 'poisonous rubbish', he finds, is sexual sadism. Criminals, particularly violent criminals, are the heroes. There is no suggestion that their crimes are reprehensible. On the contrary, they are glorified, so long as they are successful. The English pro-underdog mentality is quite alien to the culture these publications reflect. For Orwell this has political implications. He relates sexual sadism to

American power-worship. Though James Hadley Chase's *No Orchids for Miss Blandish* never mentions politics it is, in effect, 'pure Fascism', in that it offers a daydream appropriate to a Fascist mentality. Orwell never went to America and knew, so far as we can tell, little about American history and civilization. His attempt to read America's mind through a few sordid publications is plainly unsatisfactory. But his development of a political argument to justify his moral disgust is characteristic.

Self-reliance, 'masculine' hardness, and contempt for bodily comfort were moral determinants in his life as well as his writing. Public-school education was 'five years in a lukewarm bath of snobbery'. He despised fashionable 'simple-lifers' of the sort George Bowling runs into in *Coming Up for Air*, but his own ideals were not so different. He seems to have thought modern conveniences sybaritic, if not sinful. Dependence on machines was degenerate: 'the logical end of mechanical progress is to reduce the human being to something resembling a brain in a bottle'. The cottage he moved to with Eileen after their marriage had no electricity and the privy was at the bottom of the garden. The smallholding on the island of Jura he rented towards the end of his life was still more primitive. His diaries reveal that horticulture was not his strong point. Weather and pests played havoc with his vegetables. Nevertheless he struggled to be self-sufficient. In part this was a battle against his own physical decline. But it reflected a hatred of luxury that reached right back to his prep-school experiences. Friends believed that he actually relished the shortages and discomforts of the war. He was 'enormously at home' in the Blitz, said Cyril Connolly. He welcomed clothes rationing, and longed for the time when moths would have devoured the last dinner-jacket – even if it meant everyone wearing dyed battle-dress in the interim. Food did not interest him much. He pronounced wartime canteen fare 'really very good', and once ate a dish of boiled eels Eileen had cooked for the cat. The cat had Orwell's shepherd's pie in compensation.

These privations could easily be seen as religious, and Orwell, though he mocked the Christian heaven ('choir-practice in a jeweller's shop'), had something of the hermit's rigour. Mere hedonism was, he saw, self-defeating as well as ignoble. 'Men can only be happy when they do not assume that the object of life is happiness.' Hitler's great strength was that he had realized this. He had grasped the falsity of the hedonistic attitude to life, and recognized that human beings wanted 'struggle and self-sacrifice'. Though Christianity was, in Orwell's estimate, irrevocably dead, it had left, he realized, an enormous gap in Western culture. 'The real problem for our time is to restore the sense of absolute right and wrong when the belief that it used to rest on – that is, the belief in personal immortality – has been destroyed.' Modern relativism would regard Orwell's attachment to absolute right and wrong as naive. But it was inseparable from his hopes for Socialism, for Socialism meant worldwide recognition that it was right to eliminate poverty and to distribute resources evenly. Such a belief could not be logically justified. It required, said Orwell (in a review of Alfred Noyes's *The Edge of the Abyss*), 'faith, which is a different thing from credulity'. Faith in *what?* Noyes might have asked. Faith in the decency of the common man, Orwell would presumably have replied, and faith in that decency ultimately prevailing.

In his writing career his code of decency demanded that he should be independent, and not seek a leg-up from old school friends with literary connections. In the early years he suffered severely. He remembers how he would light a candle to warm his hands when they were too numb to write. No one would publish his work, and in Paris, in the autumn of 1929, he was reduced to getting a job as a dishwasher in a hotel. His first breakthrough came when Richard Rees accepted his essay 'The Spike' for publication in the *Adelphi* magazine. Orwell did not know Rees, but had subscribed to the *Adelphi* when he was in Burma, propping it against a tree and shooting at it with his rifle when it annoyed him. In August 1935 he began a regular 'Recent Novel' column for the *New English Weekly*. This paid poorly but at least he got copies of the books, which he could sell. It also extended his reading, introducing him to Henry Miller's *Tropic of Cancer*, a text that continued to intrigue him

When Victor Gollancz commissioned a book on the industrial north (*The Road to Wigan Pier*) for his Communist-dominated Left Book Club in January 1936, the £500 advance temporarily eased Orwell's money troubles. But even when he was launched on his journalistic career, he was nearly always hard up. Financial security came only at the end of his life, with the success of *Animal Farm*. He put principle before payment, preferring to write for journals whose political stance he approved of, even if the material reward was negligible. Some articles were written for nothing – 'Looking Back on the Spanish War' was one, published in the Socialist yearly anthology *New Road*. Approached by more upper-crust periodicals he was studiously offhand. When Jonathan Lehmann requested a piece for his fashionable *New Writing* in 1936, Orwell responded that 'without seeing a copy of *New Writing* I can't tell what sort of stuff it uses'. In the event, he sent 'Shooting an Elephant', which Lehmann wisely accepted. Adopting these principles, he had to keep up a punishing schedule of articles and reviews, as his Payment Notebooks confirm. In 1944, for example, he wrote almost 100,000 words for a return of just £597 19s. It was not only financial need and political responsibility that drove him. A Puritanical work ethic was part of his make-up. 'There has literally been not one day', he confessed quite late in life, 'in which I did not feel I was idling.'

With the outbreak of war many little magazines closed down and the life of the freelance literary journalist became harder. Orwell moved to London to be with Eileen and started a weekly column on theatre and film for *Time and Tide*. In 1940 he began regular reviewing for *Tribune*, and for the first time felt confident enough to write his reviews straight onto the typewriter with no preliminary drafts. He also became a regular contributor to Cyril Connolly's new cultural monthly *Horizon*, which printed some of his best essays including 'The Art of Donald McGill' and 'Raffles and Miss Blandish'. Less successful were his intermittent 'London Letters', commencing in 1941, for the left-wing but anti-Communist *Partisan Review*, published in New York. The American readership was an unknown quantity and spoke a foreign language. His style, accordingly, becomes flat and wordy, bringing home how much he usually depended on English idiom and familiarity with English culture. His workload increased when he joined the Overseas Service of the BBC in 1941, having been rejected for military service on medical grounds. He was responsible for writing a weekly news commentary for India, a job he disliked and considered a waste of time – correctly, as it transpired, since most of the intended audience did not have radios and those who did were generally too disaffected with Britain to listen. He stuck this for two years, then resigned and was appointed literary editor of *Tribune* in November 1943. The directors were George Strauss and Aneurin Bevan, left-wing Labour MPs, but critical of Soviet policy. Orwell called it 'the only existing weekly paper that makes a genuine effort to be both progressive and humane – that is, to combine a radical Socialist policy with a respect for freedom of speech and a civilized attitude towards literature and the arts'. It was for *Tribune* that he wrote his eighty 'As I Please' columns, the most personal of all his writing. Despite his new responsibilities he also began in December 1943 a weekly column about books for the *Manchester Evening News*. In the same month the occasional contributions to the *Observer* that he had begun in March 1942 were put on a regular fortnightly footing. After Eileen's death, needing money for a child-minder, he added to his already packed programme a series of short pieces for the *Evening Standard*, including his famous essay on how to make a cup of tea. Despite these professional commitments he continued to write for other outlets, when the subject or the editor's politics attracted him enough. 'Notes on Nationalism' and 'Politics vs. Literature: An Examination of *Gulliver's Travels*' were among the essays he contributed to Humphrey Slater's *Polemic*, founded in 1945. Slater, a Communist journalist in the 1930s, had, like Orwell, fought in Spain and became disillusioned with Party, and he was a leading light in the Home Guard. 'The Lion and the Unicorn' was written for Searchlight Books, which Orwell and Tosco Fyvel founded 'to criticize and kill what is rotten in Western civilization'.

When Eric Blair died on 21 January 1950, one of the brightest brains of the twentieth century cooled and darkened. They buried Blair in a country churchyard in Berkshire, but George Orwell, the character he created, did not die. He remains a personal presence in his writings, more so than almost any other English writer. 'Orwellian', like 'Dickensian' has become a word in the language. But whereas 'Dickensian' stands for an area of the imagination, the dark side of Victorian London, 'Orwellian' stands for an attitude to life. It is composed of many strands, as the reader of the essays and journalism can alone appreciate. There is the plain-speaking, the down-to-earth style, the hatred of all luxury and pretentiousness and showing-off. There is the honesty with which he dissects his own contradictions and prejudices. There is the determination to get at the facts and to experience life as others – coal miners, down-and-outs, soldiers – live it. Allied to this, there is the impatience with prating lefties who have never known anything tougher than public school and university. There is the love of books and the commitment to the art of writing, and, at the same time, the insistence on manual work, on growing one's own food, keeping goats, not being just a pampered drone. Above all there is 'decency' and Englishness and faith in the common man. The virtues and values of our present civilization – wealth, consumerism, celebrity – were not Orwell's. For Orwell they stank. Against them, he offers an example of how to think and live – and write.

John Carey

SELECT BIBLIOGRAPHY

THE WORKS

Fiction

Down and Out in Paris and London, Gollancz, 1933.
Burmese Days, Gollancz, 1934.
A Clergyman's Daughter, Gollancz, 1935.
Keep the Aspidistra Flying, Gollancz, 1936.
Coming Up for Air, Gollancz, 1939.
Animal Farm, Secker, 1945.
Nineteen Eighty-Four, Secker, 1949.

Non-Fiction

The Road to Wigan Pier, Gollancz, 1937.
Homage to Catalonia, Secker, 1938.
Inside the Whale, Gollancz, 1940.
The Lion and the Unicorn, Secker, 1941.
Critical Essays, Secker, 1946.
Shooting an Elephant, Secker, 1950.
England Your England, Secker, 1953.

Letters, Biographies, Memoirs

Collected Essays, Journalism and Letters, 4 vols, edited by Sonia Orwell and Ian Angus, Secker and Harcourt, Brace, Jovanovich, 1968. Though invaluable in their time these volumes have now been superseded by volumes 10–20 of *The Complete Works of George Orwell*, edited by Peter Davison, assisted by Ian Angus and Stella Davison, Secker, 1998, which contain much previously unpublished material. Volumes 1–9 of this edition (1986–7) reprint all Orwell's other works, restoring where possible exactly what Orwell wrote and eliminating the interference of publishers and editors. The second edition was published 2000–02.

CRICK, BERNARD, *George Orwell*, Secker, 1980 and Little Brown, 1981. The invaluable standard biography, which contains almost everything it is essential to know about Orwell as man and writer. Particularly good on the political development, which is traced in detail.

SHELDEN, MICHAEL, *George Orwell*, Heinemann and Harper Collins, 1991. Lighter and more easily readable than Crick, adding some personal details and correcting him on minor points. Better on the personality than the politics.

MEYERS, JEFFREY, *Orwell, Wintry Conscience of a Generation*, Norton, 2000. Outstanding. The first biography to make use of the new material in the Secker *Complete Works*.

DAVISON, PETER, *George Orwell: A Literary Life*, Macmillan, 1996. Has points not found in either Shelden or Meyers.

STANSKY, PETER, and ABRAHAMS, WILLIAM, *The Unknown Orwell* and *Orwell: The Transformation*, Constable, 1972 and 1979. Interesting on Orwell's life in Burma, but limited in value because of refusal by the Orwell etate to permit quotation from letters and other material.

WADHAMS, STEPHEN, *Remembering Orwell*, Penguin, 1984, and COPPARD, AUDREY, and CRICK, BERNARD, BBC, 1984. Recollections from many people, the first based on a radio biography put out by Canadian Broadcasting, the second on the BBC's *Arena* programmes on TV.

BUDDICOM, JACINTHA, *Eric and Us*, Frewin, 1974.

HOLLIS, CHRISTOPHER, *A Study of George Orwell*, Hollis & Carter, 1956.

FYVEL, T. R., *George Orwell, a Personal Memoir*, Weidenfeld, 1982. Three memoirs by people who knew him, respectively in his boyhood, at Eton, and in his days at *Tribune* and later.

LEWIS, PETER, *George Orwell, the Road to 1984*, Heinemann, 1984. Excellent short biography, well illustrated.

Criticism

WOODCOCK, GEORGE, *The Crystal Spirit*, Cape, 1967. Like much of the criticism this also contains biographical material. Woodcock, an anarchist who knew Orwell in his last decade, offers penetrating comments on the work from a Left viewpoint.

ATKINS, JOHN, *George Orwell*, Calder, 1954. The first book-length study, stressing the importance of 'decency' and morality in Orwell.

WILLIAMS, RAYMOND, *Orwell*, Collins, 1971. Short book by well-known social critic influenced by Orwell in youth, who decided he had succumbed to a mistaken belief in 'capitalist democracy'.

The World of George Orwell, edited by Miriam Gross, Weidenfeld, 1971. Collection of essays and articles, mostly about the life and background, some highly critical. Contributors include Raymond Carr (on Orwell and Spain), William Empson (life at the BBC in wartime), Malcolm Muggeridge, John Wain, Ian Hamilton.

RODDEN, JOHN, *The Politics of Literary Reputation*, Oxford University Press, 1989. Fascinating study of the growth of Orwell's reputation in several countries, including the Soviet Union and Germany. Much detailed information not to be found elsewhere.

ORWELL, the War Broadcasts and ORWELL, the War Commentaries, edited by W. J. West, Duckworth/BBC, 1985. Details of Orwell's work at the BBC during World War II, and the texts of the war broadcasts, some literary and others giving an account of wartime events. Mostly written, and some delivered on air, by Orwell.

CHRONOLOGY

DATE	AUTHOR'S LIFE	LITERARY CONTEXT
1903	Birth of Eric Arthur Blair in Motihari, Bengal, son of Richard Walmsley Blair, employed in the Opium Department of the Government of India, and Ida Mabel Limouzin, daughter of a French teak merchant from Moulmein, Burma.	Moore: *Principia Ethica.* Wells: *Mankind in the Making.* Shaw: *Man and Superman.* Butler: *The Way of All Flesh.* Conrad: *Typhoon.* London: *The Call of the Wild*; *The People of the Abyss.*
1904	Goes back to England with his sister Marjorie, five years his elder, and his mother.	Henry James: *The Golden Bowl.* Shaw: *John Bull's Other Island.*
1908		Forster: *A Room with a View.* W. H. Davies: *The Autobiography of a Super-Tramp.*
1911	Sent to St Cyprian's (of which his account, 'Such, Such Were the Joys', was considered too libellous to print in England until 1968). Cyril Connolly is a contemporary at both St Cyprian's and Eton.	Lawrence: *The White Peacock.* Mansfield: *In a German Pension.* Wharton: *Ethan Frome.* Pound: *Canzoni.* Wells: *The Country of the Blind and other Stories.*
1913		Proust: *Swann's Way.*
1914	His first patriotic poem appears in a local Henley newspaper.	Joyce: *Dubliners.* Tressell: *The Ragged Trousered Philanthropists.* Chesterton: *The Wisdom of Father Brown.* Lawrence: *The Prussian Officer.*
1915		Madox Ford: *The Good Soldier.* Lawrence: *The Rainbow.*
1916		Joyce: *A Portrait of the Artist as a Young Man.*
1917	Goes to Eton as a King's Scholar but is not a great academic success.	T. S. Eliot: *Prufrock.* Yeats: *The Wild Swans at Coole.* Kipling: *A Diversity of Creatures.* Freud: *Introduction to Psychoanalysis.* Jung: *Psychology of the Unconscious.*

HISTORICAL EVENTS

Emmeline Pankhurst founds Women's Social and Political Union. *Entente Cordiale* between France and Britain. Joseph Chamberlain begins Tariff Reform campaign. Wright brothers' powered flight.

Russo-Japanese War (to 1905). Harmsworth founds *Daily Mirror*.

Asquith Prime Minister (to 1916). First production of model T Ford car of which 15,000,000 were to be sold.

George V announces transfer of capital of India from Calcutta to Delhi. In England, strikes of dockers, miners, railwaymen, transport workers. Suffragette riots. Parliament Act reduces power of House of Lords; payment of MPs introduced. Amundsen the first man to reach the South Pole.

Woodrow Wilson President of USA. First Charlie Chaplin film. Irish Home Rule Act. Assassination of Archduke Franz-Ferdinand at Sarajevo; World War I begins. First Zeppelin raid takes place. Completion of the Panama Canal. Marconi transmits wireless telephone messages between Italian ships fifty miles apart.

Battle of Ypres. Blockade of Britain. Einstein's General Theory of Relativity.

Verdun; the Somme. Allies evacuate from Gallipoli. Battle of Jutland. Lloyd George becomes Prime Minsister. First tank in operation. Dadaist movement begins in Zürich. Easter Rising in Dublin. Passchendaele. Balfour declaration: Jewish National Home in Palestine. Establishment of Ministry of Labour. USA declares war on Germany and sends expeditionary force to Europe. Russian Revolution in March. Nicholas II abdicates. October Revolution: Bolsheviks seize control.

DATE	AUTHOR'S LIFE	LITERARY CONTEXT
1919		John Reed: *Ten Days that Shook the World.* Shaw: *Heartbreak House.*
1921	Leaves Eton.	Huxley: *Crome Yellow.* Strachey: *Queen Victoria.* Lawrence: *Women in Love.* Pirandello: *Six Characters in Search of an Author.*
1922	Joins the Indian Imperial Police until 1927 as a subdivisional officer in Burma. Occupies various positions. His boredom soon leads to hatred of his work and at the same time of what he called 'imperialist oppression'.	Joyce: *Ulysses.* Woolf: *Jacob's Room.* Wells: *A Short History of the World.* T. S. Eliot: *The Waste Land.* Galsworthy: *The Forsyte Saga.* Sinclair Lewis: *Babbitt.* Mansfield: *The Garden Party.*
1924		Madox Ford: *Parade's End* (to 1928). Forster: *A Passage to India.*
1925		Kafka: *The Trial.*
1926		Kafka: *The Castle.*
1927	Resigns from the Indian Imperial Police and returns to England. In London, spends time living with tramps.	Hemingway: *Men Without Women.* Woolf: *To the Lighthouse.*
1928	Goes to Paris where he hopes to write; takes on a series of ill-paid jobs and lives in a state of 'fairly severe poverty'.	Lawrence: *Lady Chatterley's Lover.* Woolf: *Orlando.* Waugh: *Decline and Fall.* Brecht: *The Threepenny Opera.* Bulgakov begins *The Master and Margarita* (to 1940).
1929	Returns to England at Christmas.	Faulkner: *The Sound and the Fury.* Hemingway: *A Farewell to Arms.* Graves: *Goodbye to All That.* Woolf: *A Room of One's Own.*
1930	His work is accepted by *The Adelphi* and he becomes a regular contributor until 1935.	Shaw: *The Apple Cart.* Auden: *Poems.* Bulgakov: *A Cabal of Hypocrites (Molière)* (to 1936).
1931		

CHRONOLOGY

Treaty of Versailles between the Allies and Germany. Lady Astor becomes first woman MP. German Republic adopts Weimar constitution. Civil war in Russia (to 1921). Allied intervention against Bolsheviks fails. League of Nations founded. Maynard Keynes: *The Economic Consequences of the Peace.*
Irish Treaty ends rebellion. Southern Ireland given Dominion Status. First Fascist parliamentary representation in Italy. Establishment of Soviet Commissariat of Internal Affairs, and of Secret Police. Famine in Russia. German reparations fixed at £6,000,000,000. First Birth Control Clinic opens in London.
Resignation of Lloyd George; end of Coalition government. Irish civil war. Mussolini leads Fascist march on Rome and is made Italian Prime Minister. Hyper-inflation in Germany. British Broadcasting Corporation, a private monopoly under charter, makes first broadcasts for entertainment in the world.

First Labour Goverment under Ramsay Macdonald. Death of Lenin.

Pensions Act in Britian provides Old Age Pensions, Widows' Pensions and Orphans' Pensions. Nazi Party in Germany reconstituted.
General Strike in Britain (1–12 May).
Trades Disputes and Trade Union Act: general strikes made illegal; repression of trade union activity (repealed 1945). Trotsky expelled from Russian Communist Party. Lindbergh makes first solo flight over Atlantic.
The first 'talkie' (motion picture with sound): *The Jazz Singer.*
Fifth English Reform Act: votes given to women on same terms as men. Fleming discovers penicillin. First Mickey Mouse cartoon.

Wall Street crash. Beginning of world depression. Second Labour government under Ramsay Macdonald. First English woman cabinet minister, Margaret Bondfield, Minister of Labour. BBC begins experimental television programmes. Trotsky expelled from the USSR by Stalin.
India granted Dominion status. Term 'apartheid' first used at Kroonstad, South Africa.
Destruction of Russian kulaks; enforced collectivization. In England, Housing Act tackles slum clearance.

Financial crisis in Britain; formation of National Government. Gold Standard abandoned.

DATE	AUTHOR'S LIFE	LITERARY CONTEXT
1932	Writes 'A Scullion's Diary', which is rejected by, among others, T. S. Eliot. Reluctantly becomes a teacher in a private school.	T. S. Eliot: *Sweeney Agonistes*. Hemingway: *Death in the Afternoon*. Huxley: *Brave New World*. Waugh: *Black Mischief*. Faulkner: *Light in August*.
1933	Publication by Victor Gollancz, a left-wing publisher, of his first book under the pseudonym of 'George Orwell': the autobiographical *Down and Out in Paris and London*, a comment on the reality of deprivation. Sells badly despite good reviews.	Malraux: *La Condition humaine*. García Lorca: *Blood Wedding*. Spender: *Poems*. Mann: *Joseph and his Brothers* (to 1943). Greenwood: *Love on the Dole*. Wells: *The Shape of Things to Come*.
1934	Publication of his first novel, *Burmese Days,* by Harper Bros. of New York and later Victor Gollancz. Working at a Hampstead bookshop. Becomes involved with the Independent Labour Party (ILP).	Coward: *Private Lives*; *Design for Living*. Huxley: *Beyond the Mexique Bay*. Priestley: *English Journey*. Fitzgerald: *Tender is the Night*. H. Miller: *Tropic of Cancer*.
1935	Publication of his second novel, *A Clergyman's Daughter*. Begins regular 'Recent Novel' column in the *New English Weekly*. Meets Eileen O'Shaughnessy.	Graham Greene: *England Made Me*. Auden (with Isherwood): *The Dog Beneath the Skin*. Isherwood: *Mr Norris Changes Trains*.
1936	In January, the Left Book Club – publishing venture founded by Gollancz, John Strachey and Harold Laski – commissions Orwell to write a book about unemployment and proletarian life in Lancashire. Spends two months in Wigan, Barnsley and Sheffield, living with ordinary people. Publication of *Keep the Aspidistra Flying*. Marries Eileen O'Shaughnessy. Leaves London for Spain, stopping in Paris to visit Henry Miller. In Barcelona, joins an independent, non-Stalinist, Marxist group, the POUM (Partido Obrero de Unificación Marxista).	T. S. Eliot: *Collected Poems*. Rattigan: *French Without Tears*. Dylan Thomas: *Twenty-Five Poems*. Bernanos: *Le Journal d'un Curé de Campagne*. García Lorca: *The House of Bernarda Alba*. Hemingway: *The Green Hills of Africa*. Steinbeck: *In Dubious Battle*. Faulkner: *Absalom, Absalom!* Auden: *Look Stranger!* García Lorca executed.

CHRONOLOGY

HISTORICAL EVENTS

Unemployment in Britain reaches 2,947,000. Import Duties Act (Neville Chamberlain): full-scale protection reintroduced into Britain; free trade abandoned. Great Hunger March of unemployed to London. British Union of Facists founded by Mosley. Nazis single largest party in German Reichstag. Roosevelt elected President of the USA.

Prohibition repealed in the USA. Foundation of Falange in Spain (Spanish Fascist Party). Hitler appointed Chancellor of Germany. German Catholic and Democratic Parties suppressed. Reichstag fire in Berlin; Communists accused. Concentration camps start in Germany.

Stavisky affair: suicide of shady financier involves French polititians. France, supported by Britain and Italy, opposes German terms for re-armament. Stalin begins purges of Communist Party in USSR.

Resignation of Ramsay Macdonald; succeeded by Baldwin, Prime Minister for third time. Nuremberg Laws deprive Jews of citizens' rights. Persecution of Jews. US Labor Relations Act gives workers the right to organize freely; Social Security Act introduces unemployment benefit and old-age pensions. British Council established. Sidney and Beatrice Webb: *Soviet Communism: A New Civilization?*
Death of George V; accession of Edward VIII. Constitutional crisis (December): abdication of Edward VIII and accession of George VI. In France the Front Populaire and French Left Parties' union form government under Léon Blum. Churchill demands re-armament. Outbreak of Spanish Civil War (July): revolt of Falange, led by General Franco, is supported by Germany and Italy. Republican government moves from Madrid to Valencia. Construction of Germany's west wall, the Siegfried line, begins. Maynard Keynes: *General Theory of Employment, Interest and Money.*

DATE	AUTHOR'S LIFE	LITERARY CONTEXT
1937	Publication of *The Road to Wigan Pier* which displeases his sponsor Gollancz, whose introduction warns readers against the provocative second half where Orwell appears as 'devil's advocate for the case against Socialism'. Orwell is wounded in the throat by a Fascist sniper. Returns to London via Paris. Becomes a regular contributor to *Time and Tide* until 1943.	Steinbeck: *Of Mice and Men*. Cronin: *The Citadel*. Hemingway: *To Have and Have Not*. Auden and MacNeice: *Letters from Iceland*.
1938	Tubercular haemorrhage in lung (March). In hospital until August. *Homage to Catalonia*, which marks his decisive break with Stalinism, is refused by Gollancz and published by Secker and Warburg. Orwell is vilified by the fashionable and sentimental Left in England. Goes to Morocco with Eileen for his convalescence.	Elizabeth Bowen: *The Death of the Heart*. Graham Greene: *Brighton Rock*. Sartre: *La Nausée*. Stefan Zweig: *The Dangerous Pity*. Waugh: *Scoop*. Emlyn Williams: *The Corn is Green*. Bernanos: *Les Grands Cimetières sous la Lune* (polemic against Franco).
1939	Returns to England as the Spanish Republic surrenders to Franco. *Coming Up for Air* brought out in June by Gollancz, who agrees to publish Orwell's fiction but not his documentaries. Death of his father. The alliance between Hitler and Stalin shakes him out of his pacificism, on the grounds that one has to defend 'the bad against the worse'. Attempts to enlist but is rejected on medical grounds.	Auden and Isherwood: *Journey to a War*. T. S. Eliot: *The Family Reunion*. Joyce: *Finnegans Wake*. Mann: *Lotte in Weimar*. H. Miller: *Tropic of Capricorn*. Isherwood: *Goodbye to Berlin*. Spender: *The Still Centre*. Steinbeck: *The Grapes of Wrath*. Cary: *Mister Johnson*.
1940	Publication of *Inside the Whale*, first collection of essays. Begins regular reviewing for the Socialist weekly *Tribune*.	Graham Greene: *The Power and the Glory*. Hemingway: *For Whom the Bell Tolls*. Yeats: *Last Poems*. Dylan Thomas: *Portrait of the Artist as a Young Dog*.

CHRONOLOGY

Marriage of Duke of Windsor (formerly Edward VIII) with Mrs Simpson, American divorcée. British government announces re-armament policy. Resignation of Baldwin; Neville Chamberlain Prime Minister. Fall of Blum government in France; collapse of the Front Populaire. Guernica, Spain, bombed by German planes. Rome–Berlin Axis formed. First elections under new Russian constitution – only one list of candidates. Disney's first full-length cartoon, *Snow-White and the Seven Dwarfs*. Picasso paints *Guernica*. The Golden Gate Bridge of San Francisco is completed.

Chamberlain signs Munich Pact. Estimated that one-third of British families live below poverty line. Eire becomes independent but retains Commonwealth membership. Italian Manifesto: statement of Fascist racialist ideology. First anti-Jewish measures in Italy. German *Anschluss*: Hitler annexes Austria. *Picture Post,* British illustrated weekly, first published.

Germans occupy Czechoslovakia. Nazi–Soviet pact. German invasion of Poland and occupation of Danzig starts World War II; Britain and France declare war on Germany; Warsaw surrenders. Otto Hahn and Fritz Strasmann discover nuclear fission in uranium. Balloons used as barrage to protect Britain against aircraft attack. Ministry of Information established in Britain for duration of the war. Barcelona captured by Franco's Nationalists. Surrender of Madrid. End of Spanish Civil War.

Resignation of Chamberlain; Coalition ministry under Winston Churchill (to 1945). Evacuation of Dunkirk by British. Battle of Britain. Home Guard formed. Rationing introduced. President Roosevelt elected in the USA for third term. Paris occupied by Germans; Marshal Pétain becomes French Prime Minister; Franco-German armistice signed at Compiègnes. Government of unoccupied France moves to Vichy. Trotsky assassinated in Mexico.

DATE	AUTHOR'S LIFE	LITERARY CONTEXT
1941	Publication of *The Lion and the Unicorn*. V. S. Pritchett compares Orwell to Defoe and Cobbett for his 'lucid conversational style' and his 'subversive, non-conforming brand of patriotism'. Orwell writes foreword to Joyce Cary's *The Case for African Freedom*.	Cary: *A House of Children*. Cronin: *The Keys of the Kingdom*. Fitzgerald: *The Last Tycoon*. Brecht: *Mutter Courage und Ihre Kinder*. Coward: *Blithe Spirit*.
1942	Works for the Indian Service of the BBC with, among others, T. S. Eliot and William Empson. Publication of 'Looking back on the Spanish War'.	T. S. Eliot completes *The Four Quartets*. Camus: *L'Étranger*.
1943	Death of his mother. Becomes literary editor of *Tribune* (to 1945). Resigns from the BBC.	Saint-Exupéry: *The Little Prince*.
1944	Completes the fable *Animal Farm*, a satire on Stalinism, in February. Britain now being in alliance with Stalin, no publisher is prepared to take it on. Adopts a baby boy (June).	Anouilh: *Antigone*. Sartre: *Huit-Clos*. Tennessee Williams: *The Glass Menagerie*. Shaw: *Everybody's Political What's What?*
1945	Becomes war correspondent for *The Observer* in Paris and Cologne. Meets Hemingway (another war correspondent) in Paris. Death of Eileen. In August, *Animal Farm* is finally published by Secker and Warburg and makes Orwell world-famous overnight.	Camus: *Caligula*. R. Wright: *Black Boy*. Connolly: *The Unquiet Grave*. Carlo Levi: *Christ Stopped at Eboli*. Hesse: *The Glasss Bead Game*. Waugh: *Brideshead Revisited*. Henry Green: *Loving*.
1946	Publication of *Critical Essays*. Leaves London for the island of Jura in the Inner Hebrides with his son and a nurse. Starts working on *Nineteen Eighty-Four*. Health deteriorates.	Henry Green: *Back*. Rattigan: *The Winslow Boy*.
1947	Spends seven months in hospital near Glasgow.	Camus: *La Peste*. Sartre: *The Roads to Freedom* (to 1950). Tennessee Williams: *A Streetcar Named Desire*. Mann: *Doctor Faustus*.

CHRONOLOGY

Addis Ababa recaptured from Italians by British. Battle for Crete. Germans invade Russia. Siege of Leningrad. Russo-Japanese neutrality pact. Japanese air attack on US Pacific fleet at Pearl Harbor. Orson Welles' *Citizen Kane*.

Allied landings in French North Africa. Germans capture Sebastapol; battle of Stalingrad begins. Germans enter unoccupied France. Construction at Chicago University, of the world's first nuclear reactor.

Italian government surrenders to Allies. Casablanca Conference: Churchill and Roosevelt agree 'unconditional surrender' terms for Germany.

Allied landings in Normandy: D Day (6 June). Liberation of Paris and Brussels. Women's suffrage introduced in France. France regains Lorraine, seized by Germany in 1940. Bunker bomb plot against Hitler fails. Roosevelt elected President of the USA for the fourth time.

Yalta Conference. Mussolini shot by partisans. Germany overrun by the Allies; suicide of Hitler; unconditional surrender of Germany (8 May). Atomic bombs detonated over Hiroshima and Nagasaki, Japan. End of World War II. General election in Britain: Attlee's Labour government (to 1951). Death of Roosevelt. End of Third Republic in France. Opening of Nuremberg War Crimes Tribunal. Establishment of United Nations Organization (UNO).

Churchill's 'Iron Curtain' speech. Execution of William Joyce ('Lord Haw Haw') for anti-British broadcast propaganda. Fourth Republic in France accepted by referendum. Fourth Five Year Plan announced in Russia. UNESCO established. Opening of London Airport (now Heathrow).

Indian Independence Act: India partitioned into two Dominions, India (Hindu) and Pakistan (Moslem). Breakdown of London Four Power Conference of Foreign Ministers on Germany. Communist government established in Poland. Marshall Plan: USA aid for European postwar recovery. Christian Dior opens his salon in Paris and immediately revolutionizes ladies' fashion with his 'New Look'.

DATE	AUTHOR'S LIFE	LITERARY CONTEXT
1947 *cont.*		Publication of the *Diary of Anne Frank*.
		Primo Levi: *If this is a man*.
1948	Returns to Jura in July. Unable to find a typist for *Nineteen Eighty-Four*, he types it himself. Health continues to deteriorate.	Graham Greene: *The Heart of the Matter*.
		Mailer: *The Naked and the Dead*.
		Paton: *Cry, the Beloved Country*.
		Pound: *Pisan Cantos*.
1949	Enters sanatorium in Gloucestershire in January. *Nineteen Eighty-Four is* published in June by Secker and Warburg. It is an instant success. Admitted to University College Hospital (September). Marries Sonia Brownell (October).	A. Miller: *Death of a Salesman*.
		Simone de Beauvoir: *The Second Sex*.
		Pasternak: *Selected Writings* published in England.
1950	Publication of *Shooting an Elephant*. Final haemorrhage on 21 January; dies immediately. According to his wishes, he is buried in a country churchyard in Berkshire.	Graham Greene: *The Third Man*.
		Hemingway: *Across the River and into the Trees*.
		Spender: *World Within World*.

HISTORICAL EVENTS

Assassination of Gandhi, leader of Indian independence movement. Burma becomes independent. South African government adopts *apartheid* as official policy. XIV Olympic Games in London. USSR stops traffic between Berlin and the West. Airlift begins. Communist coup in Czechoslovakia. Zionist Jews declare independent state of Israel.

Republic of Ireland recognized as having left the Commonwealth. Federal Republic in West Germany; Konrad Adenauer first Chancellor; Bonn capital. Devaluation of the pound sterling. First Russian atomic explosions recorded. Communist People's Republic proclaimed in China under Mao Tse-tung.

General election in Britain: Labour government returned without overall majority. North Korean forces invade South Korea. McCarthy Committee of Enquiry into Un-American Activities begins work. India declares herself an independent republic.

ESSAYS

1928-37

A Farthing Newspaper

G.K.'s Weekly, 29 December 1928

The *Ami du Peuple* is a Paris newspaper. It was established about six months ago, and it has achieved something really strange and remarkable in the world where everything is a "sensation," by being sold at ten centimes, or rather less than a farthing the copy. It is a healthy, full-size sheet, with news, articles, and cartoons quite up to the usual standard, and with a turn for sport, murders, nationalist sentiment and anti-German propaganda. Nothing is abnormal about it except its price.

Nor is there any need to be surprised at this last phenomenon, because the proprietors of the *Ami du Peuple* have just explained all about it, in a huge manifesto which is pasted on the walls of Paris wherever billsticking is not *défendu*. On reading this manifesto one learns with pleased surprise that the *Ami du Peuple* is not like other newspapers, it was the purest public spirit, uncontaminated by any base thoughts of gain, which brought it to birth. The proprietors, who hide their blushes in anonymity, are emptying their pockets for the mere pleasure of doing good by stealth. Their objects, we learn, are to make war on the great trusts, to fight for a lower cost of living, and above all to combat the powerful newspapers which are strangling free speech in France. In spite of the sinister attempts of these other newspapers to put the *Ami du Peuple* out of action, it will fight on to the last. In short, it is all that its name implies.

One would cheer this last stand for democracy a great deal louder, of course, if one did not happen to know that the proprietor of the *Ami du Peuple* is M. Coty, a great industrial capitalist, and also proprietor of the *Figaro* and the *Gaulois*. One would also regard the *Ami du Peuple* with less suspicion if its politics were not anti-radical and anti-socialist, of the good-will-in-industry, shake-hands-and-make-it-up species. But all that is beside the point at this moment. The important

5

questions, obviously, are these: Does the *Ami du Peuple* pay its way? And if so, how?

The second question is the one that really matters. Since the march of progress is going in the direction of always bigger and nastier trusts, any departure is worth noticing which brings us nearer to that day when the newspaper will be simply a sheet of advertisement and propaganda, with a little well-censored news to sugar the pill. It is quite possible that the *Ami du Peuple* exists on its advertisements, but it is equally possible that it makes only an indirect profit, by putting across the sort of propaganda wanted by M. Coty and his associates. In the above mentioned manifesto, it was declared that the proprietors might rise to an even dizzier height of philanthropy by giving away the *Ami du Peuple* free of charge. This is not so impossible as it may sound. I have seen a daily paper (in India) which was given away free for some time with apparent profit to its backers, a ring of advertisers who found a free newspaper to be a cheap and satisfactory means of blowing their own trumpet. Their paper was rather above the average Indian level, and it supplied, of course, just such news as they themselves approved, and no other. That obscure Indian paper forecast the logical goal of modern journalism; and the *Ami du Peuple* should be noticed, as a new step in the same direction.

But whether its profits are direct or indirect, the *Ami du Peuple* is certainly prospering. Its circulation is already very large, and though it started out as a mere morning paper it has now produced an afternoon and late evening edition. Its proprietors speak with perfect truth when they declare that some of the other papers have done their best to crush this new champion of free speech. These others (they, too, of course, acting from the highest altruistic motives) have made a gallant attempt to have it excluded from the newsagents' shops, and have even succeeded as far as the street-corner kiosks are concerned. In some small shops, too, whose owners are socialists, one will even see the sign "Ici on ne vend pas *l'Ami du Peuple*" exhibited in the windows. But the *Ami du Peuple* is not worrying. It is sold in the streets and the cafés with great vigour, and it is sold by barbers and tobacconists and all kinds of people who have never done any newsagency before. Sometimes it is simply left out on the boulevard in great piles, together with a tin for the two-sou pieces, and with no attendant whatever. One can see that the proprietors are determined, by hook or by crook, to make it the most widely-read paper in Paris.

And supposing they succeed – what then? Obviously the *Ami du Peuple* is going to crowd out of existence one or more of the less prosperous papers – already several are feeling the pinch. In the end, they will presumably either be destroyed, or they will survive by imitating the tactics of the *Ami du Peuple*. Hence every paper of this kind, whatever its intentions, is the enemy of free speech. At present France is the home of free speech, in the Press if not elsewhere. Paris alone has daily papers by the dozen, nationalist, socialist, and communist, clerical and anti-clerical, militarist and anti-militarist, prosemitic and anti-semitic. It has the *Action Française*, a Royalist paper and still one of the leading dailies, and it has *Humanité*, the reddest daily paper outside Soviet Russia. It has *La Liberta*, which is written in Italian and yet may not even be sold in Italy, much less published there. Papers are printed in Paris in French, English, Italian, Yiddish, German, Russian, Polish, and languages whose very alphabets are unrecognizable by a western European. The kiosks are stuffed with papers, all different. The Press combine, about which French journalists are already grumbling, does not really exist yet in France. But the *Ami du Peuple*, at least, is doing its gallant best to make it a reality.

And supposing that this kind of thing is found to pay in France, why should it not be tried elsewhere? Why should we not have our farthing, or at least our half-penny newspaper in London? While the journalist exists merely as the publicity agent of big business, a large circulation, got by fair means or foul, is a newspaper's one and only aim. Till recently various of our newspapers achieved the desired level of "net sales" by the simple method of giving away a few thousand pounds now and again in football competition prizes. Now the football competitions have been stopped by law, and doubtless some of the circulations have come down with an ugly bump. Here, then, is a worthy example for our English Press magnates. Let them imitate the *Ami du Peuple* and sell their papers at a farthing. Even if it does no other good whatever, at any rate the poor devils of the public will at last feel that they are getting the correct value for their money.

ERIC A. BLAIR

The Spike
The Adelphi, April 1931

It was late afternoon. Forty-nine of us, forty-eight men and one woman, lay on the green waiting for the spike to open. We were too tired to talk much. We just sprawled about exhaustedly, with home-made cigarettes sticking out of our scrubby faces. Overhead the chestnut branches were covered with blossom, and beyond that great woolly clouds floated almost motionless in a clear sky. Littered on the grass, we seemed dingy, urban riff-raff. We defiled the scene, like sardine-tins and paper bags on the seashore.

What talk there was ran on the Tramp Major of this spike. He was a devil, everyone agreed, a tartar, a tyrant, a bawling, blasphemous, uncharitable dog. You couldn't call your soul your own when he was about, and many a tramp had he kicked out in the middle of the night for giving a back answer. When you came to be searched he fair held you upside down and shook you. If you were caught with tobacco there was hell to pay, and if you went in with money (which is against the law) God help you.

I had eightpence on me. "For the love of Christ, mate," the old hands advised me, "don't you take it in. You'd get seven days for going into the spike with eightpence!"

So I buried my money in a hole under the hedge, marking the spot with a lump of flint. Then we set about smuggling our matches and tobacco, for it is forbidden to take these into nearly all spikes, and one is supposed to surrender them at the gate. We hid them in our socks, except for the twenty or so per cent. who had no socks, and had to carry the tobacco in their boots, even under their very toes. We stuffed our ankles with contraband until anyone seeing us might have imagined an outbreak of elephantiasis. But it is an unwritten law that even the sternest tramp majors do not search below the knee, and in the end only one man was caught. This was Scotty, a little hairy tramp with a bastard accent sired by cockney out of Glasgow. His tin of cigarette ends fell out of his sock at the wrong moment, and was impounded.

At six the gates swung open and we shuffled in. An official at the gate entered our names and other particulars in the register and took our bundles away from us. The woman was sent off to the workhouse, and we others into the spike. It was a gloomy, chilly, limewashed place, consisting only of a bathroom and dining room and about a hundred narrow stone cells. The terrible Tramp Major met us at the door and herded us into the bathroom to be stripped and searched. He was a gruff, soldierly man of forty, who gave the tramps no more ceremony than sheep at the dipping pond, shoving them this way and that and shouting oaths in their faces. But when he came to myself, he looked hard at me, and said:

"You are a gentleman?"

"I suppose so," I said.

He gave me another long look. "Well, that's bloody bad luck, guv'nor," he said, "that's bloody bad luck, that is." And thereafter he took it into his head to treat me with compassion, even with a kind of respect.

It was a disgusting sight, that bathroom. All the indecent secrets of our underwear were exposed; the grime, the rents and patches, the bits of string doing duty for buttons, the layers upon layers of fragmentary garments, some of them mere collections of holes held together by dirt. The room became a press of steaming nudity, the sweaty odours of the tramps competing with the sickly, sub-fæcal stench native to the spike. Some of the men refused the bath, and washed only their "toe rags", the horrid, greasy little clouts which tramps bind round their feet. Each of us had three minutes in which to bathe himself. Six greasy, slippery roller towels had to serve for the lot of us.

When we had bathed our own clothes were taken away from us, and we were dressed in the workhouse shirts, grey cotton things like nightshirts, reaching to the middle of the thigh. Then we were sent into the dining room, where supper was set out on the deal tables. It was the invariable spike meal, always the same, whether breakfast, dinner or supper – half a pound of bread, a bit of margarine, and a pint of so-called tea. It took us five minutes to gulp down the cheap, noxious food. Then the Tramp Major served us with three cotton blankets each, and drove us off to our cells for the night. The doors were locked on the outside a little before seven in the evening, and would stay locked for the next twelve hours.

The cells measured eight feet by five, and had no lighting apparatus except a tiny, barred window high up in the wall, and a spyhole in the door. There were no bugs, and we had bedsteads and straw palliasses, rare luxuries both. In many spikes one sleeps on a wooden shelf, and in some on the bare floor, with a rolled up coat for pillow. With a cell to myself, and a bed, I was hoping for a sound night's rest. But I did not get it, for there is always something wrong in the spike, and the peculiar shortcoming here, as I discovered immediately, was the cold. May had begun, and in honour of the season – a little sacrifice to the gods of spring, perhaps – the authorities had cut off the steam from the hot pipes. The cotton blankets were almost useless. One spent the night in turning from side to side, falling asleep for ten minutes and waking half frozen, and watching for dawn.

As always happens in the spike, I had at last managed to fall comfortably asleep when it was time to get up. The Tramp Major came marching down the passage with his heavy tread, unlocking the doors and yelling to us to show a leg. Promptly the passage was full of squalid shirt-clad figures rushing for the bathroom, for there was only one tub full of water between us all in the morning, and it was first come first served. When I arrived twenty tramps had already washed their faces. I gave one glance at the black scum on top of the water, and decided to go dirty for the day.

We hurried into our clothes, and then went to the dining room to bolt our breakfast. The bread was much worse than usual, because the military-minded idiot of a Tramp Major had cut it into slices overnight, so that it was as hard as ship's biscuit. But we were glad of our tea after the cold, restless night. I do not know what tramps would do without tea, or rather the stuff they miscall tea. It is their food, their medicine, their panacea for all evils. Without the half gallon or so of it that they suck down a day, I truly believe they could not face their existence.

After breakfast we had to undress again for the medical inspection, which is a precaution against smallpox. It was three-quarters of an hour before the doctor arrived, and one had time now to look about him and see what manner of men we were. It was an instructive sight. We stood shivering naked to the waist in two long ranks in the passage. The filtered light, bluish and cold, lighted us up with unmerciful clarity. No one can imagine, unless he has seen such a thing, what pot-bellied, degenerate curs we looked. Shock heads, hairy, crumpled faces, hollow chests, flat feet, sagging muscles – every kind of malformation and physical rottenness were there. All were flabby and discoloured, as all tramps are under their deceptive sunburn. Two or three figures seen there stay ineradicably in my mind. Old "Daddy", aged seventy-four, with his truss, and his red, watering eyes: a herring-gutted starveling, with sparse beard and sunken cheeks, looking like the corpse of Lazarus in some primitive picture: an imbecile, wandering hither and thither with vague giggles, coyly pleased because his trousers constantly slipped down and left him nude. But few of us were greatly better than these; there were not ten decently-built men among us, and half, I believe, should have been in hospital.

This being Sunday, we were to be kept in the spike over the week-end. As soon as the doctor had gone we were herded back to the dining room, and its door shut upon us. It was a lime-washed, stone-floored room, unspeakably dreary with its furniture of deal boards and benches, and its prison smell. The windows were so high up that one could not look outside, and the sole ornament was a set of Rules threatening dire penalties to any casual who misconducted himself. We packed the room so tight that one could not move an elbow without jostling somebody. Already, at eight o'clock in the morning, we were bored with our captivity. There was nothing to talk about except the petty gossip of the road, the good and bad spikes, the charitable and uncharitable counties, the iniquities of the police and the Salvation Army. Tramps hardly ever get away from these subjects; they talk, as it were, nothing but shop. They have nothing worthy to be called conversation, because emptiness of belly leaves no speculation in their souls. The world is too much with them. Their next meal is never quite secure, and so they cannot think of anything except the next meal.

Two hours dragged by. Old Daddy, witless with age, sat silent, his back bent like a bow and his inflamed eyes dripping slowly on to the floor. George, a dirty old tramp notorious for the queer habit of sleeping in his hat, grumbled about a parcel of tommy that he had lost on the road. Bill the moocher, the best built man of us all, a Herculean sturdy beggar who smelt of beer even after twelve hours in the spike, told tales of mooching, of pints stood him in the boozers, and of a parson who had peached to the police and got him seven days. William and Fred, two young ex-fishermen from Norfolk, sang a sad song about Unhappy Bella, who was betrayed and died in the snow. The imbecile drivelled about an imaginary toff who had once given him two hundred and fifty-seven golden sovereigns. So the time passed, with dull talk and dull obscenities. Everyone was smoking, except Scotty, whose tobacco had been seized, and he was so miserable in his smokeless state that I stood him the makings of a cigarette. We smoked furtively, hiding our cigarettes like schoolboys when we heard the Tramp Major's step, for smoking, though connived at, was officially forbidden.

Most of the tramps spent ten consecutive hours in this dreary room. It is hard to imagine how they put up with it. I have come to think that boredom is the worst of all a tramp's evils, worse than hunger and discomfort, worse even than the constant feeling of being socially disgraced. It is a silly piece of cruelty to confine an ignorant man all day with nothing to do; it is like chaining a dog in a barrel. Only an educated man, who has consolations within himself, can endure confinement. Tramps, unlettered types as nearly all of them are, face their poverty with blank, resourceless minds. Fixed for ten hours on a comfortless bench, they know no way of occupying themselves, and if they think at all it is to whimper about hard luck and pine for work. They have not the stuff in them to endure the horrors of idleness. And so, since so much of their lives is spent in doing nothing, they suffer agonies from boredom.

I was much luckier than the others, because at ten o'clock the Tramp Major picked me out for the most coveted of all jobs in the spike, the job of helping in the workhouse kitchen. There was not really any work to be done there, and I was able to make off and hide in a shed used for storing potatoes, together with some workhouse paupers who were skulking to avoid the Sunday morning service. There was a stove burning there, and comfortable packing cases to sit on, and back numbers of the *Family Herald*, and even a copy of *Raffles* from the workhouse library. It was paradise after the spike.

Also, I had my dinner from the workhouse table, and it was one of the biggest meals I have ever eaten. A tramp does not see such a meal twice in the year, in the spike or out of it. The paupers told me that they always gorged to the bursting point on Sundays, and went hungry six days of the week. When the meal was over the cook set me to do the washing up, and told me to throw away the food that remained. The wastage was astonishing; great dishes of beef, and bucketfuls of bread and vegetables, were pitched away like rubbish, and then defiled with tea leaves. I filled five dustbins to overflowing with good food. And while I did so my fellow tramps were sitting two hundred yards away in the spike, their bellies half filled with the spike dinner of the everlasting bread and tea, and perhaps two cold boiled potatoes each in honour of Sunday. It appeared that the food was thrown away from deliberate policy, rather than that it should be given to the tramps.

At three I left the workhouse kitchen and went back to the spike. The boredom in that crowded, comfortless room was now unbearable. Even smoking had ceased, for a tramp's only tobacco is picked-up cigarette ends, and, like a browsing beast, he starves if he is long away from the pavement-pasture. To occupy the time I talked with a rather superior tramp, a young carpenter who wore a collar and tie, and was on the road, he said, for lack of a set of tools. He kept a little aloof from the other tramps, and held himself more like a free man than a casual. He had literary tastes, too, and carried one of Scott's novels on all his wanderings. He told me he never entered a spike unless driven there by hunger, sleeping under hedges and behind ricks in preference. Along the south coast he had begged by day and slept in bathing machines for weeks at a time.

We talked of life on the road. He criticised the system which makes a tramp spend fourteen hours a day in the spike, and the other ten in walking and dodging the police. He spoke of his own case – six months at the public charge for want of three pounds' worth of tools. It was idiotic, he said.

13

Then I told him about the wastage of food in the workhouse kitchen, and what I thought of it. And at that he changed his tune immediately. I saw that I had awakened the pew-renter who sleeps in every English workman. Though he had been famished along with the rest, he at once saw reasons why the food should have been thrown away rather than given to the tramps. He admonished me quite severely.

"They have to do it," he said; "if they made these places too pleasant you'd have all the scum of the country flocking into them. It's only the bad food as keeps all that scum away. These tramps are too lazy to work, that's all that's wrong with them. You don't want to go encouraging of them. They're scum."

I produced arguments to prove him wrong, but he would not listen. He kept repeating:

"You don't want to have any pity on these tramps – scum, they are. You don't want to judge them by the same standards as men like you and me. They're scum, just scum."

It was interesting to see how subtly he disassociated himself from his fellow tramps. He had been on the road six months, but in the sight of God, he seemed to imply, he was not a tramp. His body might be in the spike, but his spirit soared far away, in the pure æther of the middle classes.

The clock's hands crept round with excruciating slowness. We were too bored even to talk now, the only sound was of oaths and reverberating yawns. One would force his eyes away from the clock for what seemed an age, and then look back again to see that the hands had advanced three minutes. Ennui clogged our souls like cold mutton fat. Our bones ached because of it. The clock's hands stood at four, and supper was not till six, and there was nothing left remarkable beneath the visiting moon.

At last six o'clock did come, and the Tramp Major and his assistant arrived with supper. The yawning tramps brisked up like lions at feeding time. But the meal was a dismal disappointment. The bread, bad enough in the morning, was now positively uneatable; it was so hard that even the strongest jaws could make little impression on it. The older men went almost supperless, and not a man could finish his portion, hungry though most of us were. When we had finished, the blankets were served out immediately, and we were hustled off once more to the bare, chilly cells.

Thirteen hours went by. At seven we were awakened, and rushed forth to squabble over the water in the bathroom, and bolt our ration of bread and tea. Our time in the spike was up, but we could not go until the doctor had examined us again, for the authorities have a terror of smallpox and its distribution by tramps. The doctor kept us waiting two hours this time, and it was ten o'clock before we finally escaped.

At last it was time to go, and we were let out into the yard. How bright everything looked, and how sweet the winds did blow, after the gloomy, reeking spike! The Tramp Major handed each man his bundle of confiscated possessions, and a hunk of bread and cheese for midday dinner, and then we took the road, hastening to get out of sight of the spike and its discipline. This was our interim of freedom. After a day and two nights of wasted time we had eight hours or so to take our recreation, to scour the roads for cigarette ends, to beg, and to look for work. Also, we had to make our ten, fifteen, or it might be twenty miles to the next spike, where the game would begin anew.

I disinterred my eightpence and took the road with Nobby, a respectable, downhearted tramp who carried a spare pair of boots and visited all the Labour Exchanges. Our late companions were scattering north, south, east and west, like bugs into a mattress. Only the imbecile loitered at the spike gates, until the Tramp Major had to chase him away.

Nobby and I set out for Croydon. It was a quiet road, there were no cars passing, the blossom covered the chestnut trees like great wax candles. Everything was so quiet and smelt so clean, it was hard to realise that only a few minutes ago we had been packed with that band of prisoners in a stench of drains and soft soap. The others had all disappeared; we two seemed to be the only tramps on the road.

Then I heard a hurried step behind me, and felt a tap on my arm. It was little Scotty, who had run panting after us. He pulled a rusty tin box from his pocket. He wore a friendly smile, like a man who is repaying an obligation.

"Here y'are, mate," he said cordially, "I owe you some fag ends. You stood me a smoke yesterday. The Tramp Major give me back my box of fag ends when we come out this morning. One good turn deserves another – here y'are."

And he put four sodden, debauched, loathely cigarette ends into my hand.

A Hanging
The Adelphi, August 1931; reprinted in *The New Savoy*, 1946

It was in Burma, a sodden morning of the rains. A sickly light, like yellow tinfoil, was slanting over the high walls into the jail yard. We were waiting outside the condemned cells, a row of sheds fronted with double bars, like small animal cages. Each cell measured about ten feet by ten and was quite bare within except for a plank bed and a pot for drinking water. In some of them brown silent men were squatting at the inner bars, with their blankets draped round them. These were the condemned men, due to be hanged within the next week or two.

One prisoner had been brought out of his cell. He was a Hindu, a puny wisp of a man, with a shaven head and vague liquid eyes. He had a thick, sprouting moustache, absurdly too big for his body, rather like the moustache of a comic man on the films. Six tall Indian warders were guarding him and getting him ready for the gallows. Two of them stood by with rifles and fixed bayonets, while the others handcuffed him, passed a chain through his handcuffs and fixed it to their belts, and lashed his arms tight to his sides. They crowded very close about him, with their hands always on him in a careful, caressing grip, as though all the while feeling him to make sure he was there. It was like men handling a fish which is still alive and may jump back into the water. But he stood quite unresisting, yielding his arms limply to the ropes, as though he hardly noticed what was happening.

Eight o'clock struck and a bugle call, desolately thin in the wet air, floated from the distant barracks. The superintendent of the jail, who was standing apart from the rest of us, moodily prodding the gravel with his stick, raised his head at the sound. He was an army doctor, with a grey toothbrush moustache and a gruff voice. "For God's sake hurry up, Francis", he said irritably. "The man ought to have been dead by this time. Aren't you ready yet?"

Francis, the head jailer, a fat Dravidian in a white drill suit and gold spectacles, waved his black hand. "Yes sir, yes sir", he bubbled. "All iss satisfactorily prepared. The hangman iss waiting. We shall proceed."

"Well, quick march, then. The prisoners can't get their breakfast till this job's over."

We set out for the gallows. Two warders marched on either side of the prisoner, with their rifles at the slope; two others marched close against him, gripping him by arm and shoulder, as though at once pushing and supporting him. The rest of us, magistrates and the like, followed behind. Suddenly, when we had gone ten yards, the procession stopped short without any order or warning. A dreadful thing had happened – a dog, come goodness knows whence, had appeared in the yard. It came bounding among us with a loud volley of barks, and leapt round us wagging its whole body, wild with glee at finding so many human beings together. It was a large woolly dog, half Airedale, half pariah. For a moment it pranced round us, and then, before anyone could stop it, it had made a dash for the prisoner, and jumping up tried to lick his face. Everyone stood aghast, too taken aback even to grab at the dog.

"Who let that bloody brute in here?" said the superintendent angrily. "Catch it, someone!"

A warder, detached from the escort, charged clumsily after the dog, but it danced and gambolled just out of his reach, taking everything as part of the game. A young Eurasian jailer picked up a handful of gravel and tried to stone the dog away, but it dodged the stones and came after us again. Its yaps echoed from the jail walls. The prisoner, in the grasp of the two warders, looked on incuriously, as though this was another formality of the hanging. It was several minutes before someone managed to catch the dog. Then we put my handkerchief through its collar and moved off once more, with the dog still straining and whimpering.

It was about forty yards to the gallows. I watched the bare brown back of the prisoner marching in front of me. He walked clumsily with his bound arms, but quite steadily, with that bobbing gait of the Indian who never straightens his knees. At each step his muscles slid neatly into place, the lock of hair on his scalp danced up and down, his feet printed themselves on the wet gravel. And once, in spite of the men who gripped him by each shoulder, he stepped slightly aside to avoid a puddle on the path.

It is curious, but till that moment I had never realised what it means to destroy a healthy, conscious man. When I saw the prisoner step aside to avoid the puddle, I saw the mystery, the unspeakable wrongness, of cutting a life short when it is in full tide. This man was not dying, he was alive just as we were alive. All the organs of his body were working – bowels digesting food, skin renewing itself, nails growing, tissues forming – all toiling away in solemn foolery. His nails would still be growing when he stood on the drop, when he was falling through the air with a tenth-of-a-second to live. His eyes saw the yellow gravel and the grey walls, and his brain still remembered, foresaw, reasoned – reasoned even about puddles. He and we were a party of men walking together, seeing, hearing, feeling, under-standing the same world; and in two minutes, with a sudden snap, one of us would be gone – one mind less, one world less.

The gallows stood in a small yard, separate from the main grounds of the prison, and overgrown with tall prickly weeds. It was a brick erection like three sides of a shed, with planking on top, and above that two beams and a crossbar with the rope dangling. The hangman, a grey-haired convict in the white uniform of the prison, was waiting beside his machine. He greeted us with a servile crouch as we entered. At a word from Francis the two warders, gripping the prisoner more closely than ever, half led half pushed him to the gallows and helped him clumsily up the ladder. Then the hangman climbed up and fixed the rope round the prisoner's neck.

We stood waiting, five yards away. The warders had formed in a rough circle round the gallows. And then, when the noose was fixed, the prisoner began crying out on his god. It was a high, reiterated cry of "Ram! Ram! Ram! Ram!" not urgent and fearful like a prayer or a cry for help, but steady, rhyth-mical, almost like the tolling of a bell. The dog answered the sound with a whine. The hangman, still standing on the gal-lows, produced a small cotton bag like a flour bag and drew it down over the prisoner's face. But the sound, muffled by the cloth, still persisted, over and over again: "Ram! Ram! Ram! Ram! Ram!"

The hangman climbed down and stood ready, holding the lever. Minutes seemed to pass. The steady, muffled crying from the prisoner went on and on, "Ram! Ram! Ram!" never faltering for an instant. The superintendent, his head on his chest, was slowly poking the ground with his stick; perhaps he was counting the cries, allowing the prisoner a fixed number – fifty, perhaps, or a hundred. Everyone had changed colour. The Indians had gone grey like bad coffee, and one or two of the bayonets were wavering. We looked at the lashed, hooded man on the drop, and listened to his cries – each cry another second of life; the same thought was in all our minds: oh, kill him quickly, get it over, stop that abominable noise!

Suddenly the superintendent made up his mind. Throwing up his head he made a swift motion with his stick, "Chalo!" he shouted almost fiercely.

There was a clanking noise, and then dead silence. The prisoner had vanished, and the rope was twisting on itself. I let go of the dog, and it galloped immediately to the back of the gallows; but when it got there it stopped short, barked, and then retreated into a corner of the yard, where it stood among the weeds, looking timorously out at us. We went round the gallows to inspect the prisoner's body. He was dangling with his toes pointed straight downwards, very slowly revolving, as dead as a stone.

The superintendent reached out with his stick and poked the bare brown body; it oscillated slightly. "*He's* all right", said the superintendent. He backed out from under the gallows, and blew out a deep breath. The moody look had gone out of his face quite suddenly. He glanced at his wrist-watch. "Eight minutes past eight. Well, that's all for this morning, thank God."

The warders unfixed bayonets and marched away. The dog, sobered and conscious of having misbehaved itself, slipped after them. We walked out of the gallows yard, past the condemned cells with their waiting prisoners, into the big central yard of the prison. The convicts, under the command of warders armed with lathis, were already receiving their breakfast. They squatted in long rows, each man holding a tin pannikin, while two warders with buckets marched round ladling out rice; it seemed quite a homely, jolly scene, after the hanging. An enormous relief had come upon us now that the job was done. One felt an impulse to sing, to break into a run, to snigger. All at once everyone began chattering gaily.

The Eurasian boy walking beside me nodded towards the way we had come, with a knowing smile: "Do you know, sir, our friend (he meant the dead man), when he heard his appeal had been dismissed, he pissed on the floor of his cell. From fright. – Kindly take one of my cigarettes, sir. Do you not admire my new silver case, sir? From the boxwalah, two rupees eight annas. Classy European style."

Several people laughed – at what, nobody seemed certain.

Francis was walking by the superintendent, talking garrulously: "Well, sir, all hass passed off with the utmost satisfactoriness. It wass all finished – flick! like that. It iss not always so – oah, no! I have known cases where the doctor wass obliged to go beneath the gallows and pull the prissoner's legs to ensure decease. Most disagreeable!"

"Wriggling about, eh? That's bad", said the superintendent.

"Ach, sir, it iss worse when they become refractory! One man, I recall, clung to the bars of hiss cage when we went to take him out. You will scarcely credit, sir, that it took six warders to dislodge him, three pulling at each leg. We reasoned with him. 'My dear fellow', we said, 'think of all the pain and trouble you are causing to us!' But no, he would not listen! Ach, he wass very troublesome!"

I found that I was laughing quite loudly. Everyone was laughing. Even the superintendent grinned in a tolerant way. "You'd better all come out and have a drink", he said quite genially. "I've got a bottle of whisky in the car. We could do with it."

We went through the big double gates of the prison, into the road. "Pulling at his legs!" exclaimed a Burmese magistrate suddenly, and burst into a loud chuckling. We all began laughing again. At that moment Francis' anecdote seemed extraordinarily funny. We all had a drink together, native and European alike, quite amicably. The dead man was a hundred yards away.

ERIC A. BLAIR

Clink

[August 1932]

This trip was a failure, as the object of it was to get into prison, and I did not, in fact, get more than forty eight hours in custody; however, I am recording it, as the procedure in the police court etc. was fairly interesting. I am writing this eight months after it happened, so am not certain of any dates, but it all happened a week or ten days before Xmas 1931.

I started out on Saturday afternoon with four or five shillings, and went out to the Mile End Road, because my plan was to get drunk and incapable, and I thought they would be less lenient towards drunkards in the East End. I bought some tobacco and a "Yank Mag" against my forthcoming imprisonment, and then, as soon as the pubs opened, went and had four or five pints, topping up with a quarter bottle of whisky, which left me with twopence in hand. By the time the whisky was low in the bottle I was tolerably drunk – more drunk than I had intended, for it happened that I had eaten nothing all day, and the alcohol acted quickly on my empty stomach. It was all I could do to stand upright, though my brain was quite clear – with me, when I am drunk, my brain remains clear long after my legs and speech have gone. I began staggering along the pavement in a westward direction, and for a long time did not meet any policemen, though the streets were crowded and all the people pointed and laughed at me. Finally I saw two policemen coming. I pulled the whisky bottle out of my pocket and, in their sight, drank what was left, which nearly knocked me out, so that I clutched a lamp-post and fell down. The two policemen ran towards me, turned me over and took the bottle out of my hand.

They: " 'Ere, what you bin drinking?" (For a moment they may have thought it was a case of suicide.)

I: "Thass my boll whisky. You lea' me alone."

They: "Coo, 'e's fair bin bathing in it! – What you bin doing of, eh?"

I: "Bin in boozer 'avin' bit o' fun. Christmas, ain't it?"

They: "No, not by a week it ain't. You got mixed up in the dates, you 'ave. You better come along with us. We'll look after yer."

I: "Why sh'd I come along you?"

They: "Jest so's we'll look after you and make you comfortable. You'll get run over, rolling about like that."

I: "Look. Boozer over there. Less go in 'ave drink."

They: "You've 'ad enough for one night, ole chap. You best come with us."

I: "Where you takin' me?"

They: "Jest somewhere as you'll get a nice quiet kip with a clean sheet and two blankets and all."

I: "Shall I get drink there?"

They: "Course you will. Got a boozer on the premises, we 'ave."

All this while they were leading me gently along the pavement. They had my arms in the grip (I forget what it is called) by which you can break a man's arm with one twist, but they were as gentle with me as though I had been a child. I was internally quite sober, and it amused me very much to see the cunning way in which they persuaded me along, never once disclosing the fact that we were making for the police station. This is, I suppose, the usual procedure with drunks.

When we got to the station (it was Bethnal Green, but I did not learn this till Monday) they dumped me in a chair & began emptying my pockets while the sergeant questioned me. I pretended, however, to be too drunk to give sensible answers, & he told them in disgust to take me off to the cells, which they did. The cell was about the same size as a Casual Ward cell (about 10 ft. by 5 ft. by 10 ft. high), but much cleaner & better appointed. It was made of white porcelain bricks, and was furnished with a W.C., a hot water pipe, a plank bed, a horsehair pillow and two blankets. There was a tiny barred window high up near the roof, and an electric bulb behind a guard of thick glass was kept burning all night. The door was steel, with the usual spy-hole and aperture for serving food through. The constables in searching me had taken away my money, matches, razor, and also my scarf – this, I learned afterwards, because prisoners have been known to hang themselves on their scarves.

There is very little to say about the next day and night, which were unutterably boring. I was horribly sick, sicker than I have ever been from a bout of drunkenness, no doubt from having an empty stomach. During Sunday I was given two meals of bread and marg. and tea (spike quality), and one of meat and potatoes – this, I believe, owing to the kindness of the sergeant's wife, for I think only bread and marg. is provided for prisoners in the lock-up. I was not allowed to shave, and there was only a little cold water to wash in. When the charge sheet was filled up I told the story I always tell, viz. that my name was Edward Burton, and my parents kept a cake-shop in Blythburgh, where I had been employed as a clerk in a draper's shop; that I had had the sack for drunkenness, and my parents, finally getting sick of my drunken habits, had turned me adrift. I added that I had been working as an outside porter at Billingsgate, and having unexpectedly "knocked up" six shillings on Saturday, had gone on the razzle. The police were quite kind, and read me lectures on drunkenness, with the usual stuff about seeing that I still had some good in me etc. etc. They offered to let me out on bail on my own recognizance, but I had no money and nowhere to go, so I elected to stay in custody. It was very dull, but I had my "Yank Mag", and could get a smoke if I asked the constable on duty in the passage for a light – prisoners are not allowed matches, of course.

The next morning very early they turned me out of my cell to wash, gave me back my scarf, and took me out into the yard and put me in the Black Maria. Inside, the Black Maria was just like a French public lavatory, with a row of tiny locked compartments on either side, each just large enough to sit down in. People had scrawled their names, offences and the lengths of their sentences all over the walls of my compartment; also, several times, variants on this couplet –

> "Detective Smith knows how to gee;
> Tell him he's a cunt from me."

("Gee" in this context means to act as an agent provocateur.) We drove round to various stations picking up about ten prisoners in all, until the Black Maria was quite full. They were quite a jolly crowd inside. The compartment doors were open at the top, for ventilation, so that you could reach across, and somebody had managed to smuggle matches in, and we all had a smoke. Presently we began singing, and, as it was near Christmas sang several carols. We drove up to Old Street Police Court singing –

"Adeste, fideles, laeti triumphantes,
        Adeste, adeste ad Bethlehem" etc.
which seemed to me rather inappropriate.

At the police court they took me off and put me in a cell identical with the one at Bethnal Green, even to having the same number of bricks in it – I counted in each case. There were three men in the cell beside myself. One was a smartly dressed, florid, well-set-up man of about thirty five, whom I would have taken for a commercial traveller or perhaps a bookie, and another a middle-aged Jew, also quite decently dressed. The other man was evidently a habitual burglar. He was a short rough-looking man with grey hair and a worn face, and at this moment in such a state of agitation over his approaching trial that he could not keep still an instant. He kept pacing up and down the cell like a wild beast, brushing against our knees as we sat on the plank bed, and exclaiming that he was innocent – he was charged, apparently, with loitering with intent to commit burglary. He said that he had nine previous convictions against him, and that in these cases, which are mainly of suspicion, old offenders are nearly always convicted. From time to time he would shake his fist towards the door and exclaim "Fucking toe-rag! Fucking toe-rag!", meaning the "split" who had arrested him.

Presently two more prisoners were put into the cell, an ugly Belgian youth charged with obstructing traffic with a barrow, and an extraordinary hairy creature who was either deaf and dumb or spoke no English. Except this last all the prisoners talked about their cases with the utmost freedom. The florid, smart man, it appeared, was a public house "guv'nor" (it is a sign of how utterly the London publicans are in the claw of the brewers that they are always referred to as "governors", not "landlords"; being, in fact, no better than employees), & had embezzled the Christmas Club money. As usual, he was head over ears in debt to the brewers, and no doubt had taken some of the money in hopes of backing a winner. Two of the subscribers had discovered this a few days before the money was due to be paid out, and laid an information. The "guv'nor" immediately paid back all save £12, which was also refunded before his case came up for trial. Nevertheless, he was certain to be sentenced, as the magistrates are hard on these cases – he did, in fact, get four months later in the day. He was ruined for life, of course. The brewers would file bankruptcy proceedings and sell up all his stock and furniture, and he would never be given a pub licence again. He was trying to brazen it out in front of the rest of us, and smoking cigarettes incessantly from a stock of Gold Flake packets he had laid in – the last time in his life, I dare say, that he would have quite enough cigarettes. There was a staring, abstracted look in his eyes all the time while he talked. I think the fact that his life was at an end, as far as any decent position in society went, was gradually sinking into him.

The Jew had been a buyer at Smithfields for a kosher butcher. After working seven years for the same employer he suddenly misappropriated £28, went up to Edinburgh – I don't know why Edinburgh – and had a "good time" with tarts, and came back and surrendered himself when the money was gone. £16 of the money had been repaid, and the rest was to be repaid by monthly instalments. He had a wife and a number of children. He told us, what interested me, that his employer would probably get into trouble at the synagogue for prosecuting him. It appears that the Jews have arbitration courts of their own, & a Jew is not supposed to prosecute another Jew, at least in a breach of trust case like this, without first submitting it to the arbitration court.

One remark made by these men struck me – I heard it from almost every prisoner who was up for a serious offence. It was, "It's not the prison I mind, it's losing my job." This is, I believe, symptomatic of the dwindling power of the law compared with that of the capitalist.

They kept us waiting several hours. It was very uncomfortable in the cell, for there was not room for all of us to sit down on the plank bed, and it was beastly cold in spite of the number of us. Several of the men used the W.C., which was disgusting in so small a cell, especially as the plug did not work. The publican distributed his cigarettes generously, the constable in the passage supplying lights. From time to time an extraordinary clanking noise came from the cell next door, where a youth who had stabbed his "tart" in the stomach – she was likely to recover, we heard – was locked up alone. Goodness knows what was happening, but it sounded as though he were chained to the wall. At about ten they gave us each a mug of tea – this, it appeared, not provided by the authorities but by the police court missionaries – and shortly afterwards shepherded us along to a sort of large waiting room where the prisoners awaited trial.

There were perhaps fifty prisoners here, men of every type, but on the whole much more smartly dressed than one would expect. They were strolling up and down with their hats on, shivering with the cold. I saw here a thing which interested me greatly. When I was being taken to my cell I had seen two dirty-looking ruffians, much dirtier than myself and presumably drunks or obstruction cases, being put into another cell in the row. Here, in the waiting room, these two were at work with note-books in their hands, interrogating prisoners. It appeared that they were "splits", and were put into the cells disguised as prisoners, to pick up any information that was going – for there is complete freemasonry between prisoners, and they talk without reserve in front of one another. It was a dingy trick, I thought.

All the while the prisoners were being taken by ones & twos along a corridor to the court. Presently a sergeant shouted "Come on the drunks!" and four or five of us filed along the corridor and stood waiting at the entrance of the court. A young constable on duty there advised me –

"Take your cap off when you go in, plead guilty and don't give back answers. Got any previous convictions?"

"No."

"Six bob you'll get. Going to pay it?"

"I can't, I've only twopence."

"Ah well, it don't matter. Lucky for you Mr Brown isn't on the bench this morning. Teetotaller he is. He don't half give it to the drunks. Coo!"

The drunk cases were dealt with so rapidly that I had not even time to notice what the court was like. I only had a vague impression of a raised platform with a coat of arms over it, clerks sitting at tables below, and a railing. We filed past the railing like people passing through a turnstile, & the proceedings in each case sounded like this –

"Edward-Burton-drunk-and-incapable-Drunk?-Yes-Six-shillings-move-on-NEXT!"

All this in the space of about five seconds. At the other side

26

of the court we reached a room where a sergeant was sitting at a desk with a ledger.

"Six shillings?" he said.

"Yes."

"Going to pay it?"

"I can't."

"All right, back you go to your cell."

And they took me back and locked me in the cell from which I had come, about ten minutes after I had left it.

The publican had also been brought back, his case having been postponed, and the Belgian youth, who, like me, could not pay his fine. The Jew was gone, whether released or sentenced we did not know. Throughout the day prisoners were coming and going, some waiting trial, some until the Black Maria was available to take them off to prison. It was cold, and the nasty faecal stench in the cell became unbearable. They gave us our dinner at about two o'clock – it consisted of a mug of tea and two slices of bread and marg. for each man. Apparently this was the regulation meal. One could, if one had friends outside, get food sent in, but it struck me as damnably unfair that a penniless man must face his trial with only bread and marg. in his belly; also unshaven – I, at this time, had had no chance of shaving for over forty eight hours – which is likely to prejudice the magistrates against him.

Among the prisoners who were put temporarily in the cell were two friends or partners named apparently Snouter and Charlie, who had been arrested for some street offence – obstruction with a barrow, I dare say. Snouter was a thin, red-faced, malignant-looking man, and Charlie a short, powerful, jolly man. Their conversation was rather interesting.

Charlie: "Cripes, it ain't 'alf fucking cold in 'ere. Lucky for us ole Brown ain't on to-day. Give you a month as soon as look at yer."

Snouter (bored, and singing):

"Tap, tap, tapetty tap,
I'm a perfect devil at that;
Tapping 'em 'ere, tapping 'em there,
I bin tapping 'em everywhere –"

Charlie: "Oh, fuck off with yer tapping! Scrumping's what yer want this time of year. All them rows of turkeys in the

27

winders, like rows of fucking soldiers with no clo'es on – don't it make yer fucking mouth water to look at 'em. Bet yer a tanner I 'ave one of 'em afore tonight."

Snouter: "What's 'a good? Can't cook the bugger over the kip-'ouse fire, can you?"

Charlie: "Oo wants to cook it? I know where I can flog (sell) it for a bob or two, though."

Snouter: "'Sno good. Chantin's the game this time of year. Carols. Fair twist their 'earts round, I can, when I get on the mournful. Old tarts weep their fucking eyes out when they 'ear me. I won't 'alf give them a doing this Christmas. I'll kip indoors if I 'ave to cut it out of their bowels."

Charlie: "Ah, *I* can sling you a bit of a carol. 'Ymns, too. (He begins singing in a good bass voice) –
>   "Jesu, lover of my soul,
>   Let me to thy bosom fly –"

The constable on duty (looking through the grille): "Nah then, in 'ere, nah then! What yer think this is? Baptist prayer meeting?"

Charlie (in a low voice as the constable disappears): "Fuck off, pisspot. (He hums) –
>   "While the gathering waters roll,
>   While the tempest still is 'igh!
You won't find many in the 'ymnal as I can't sling you. Sung bass in the choir my last two years in Dartmoor, I did."

Snouter: "Ah? Wassit like in Dartmoor now? D'you get jam now?"

Charlie: "Not jam. Gets cheese, though, twice a week."

Snouter: "Ah? 'Ow long was you doing?"

Charlie: "Four year."

Snouter: "Four years without cunt – Cripes! Fellers inside'd go 'alf mad if they saw a pair of legs (a woman), eh?"

Charlie: "Ah well, in Dartmoor we used to fuck old women down on the allotments. Take 'em under the 'edge in the mist. Spud-grabbers they was – ole trots seventy year old. Forty of us was caught and went through 'ell for it. Bread and water, chains – everything. I took my Bible oath as I wouldn't get no more stretches after that."

Snouter: "Yes, you! 'Ow come you got in the stir lars' time then?"

Charlie: "You wouldn't 'ardly believe it, boy. I was narked – narked by my own sister! Yes, my own fucking sister. My sister's a cow if ever there was one. She got married to a religious maniac, and 'e's so fucking religious that she's got fifteen kids now. Well, it was 'im put 'er up to narking me. But I got it back on 'em *I* can tell you. What do you think I done first thing, when I come out of the stir? I bought a 'ammer, and I went round to my sister's 'ouse and smashed 'er piano to fucking matchwood. I did. 'There', I says, 'that's what you get for narking me! You mare', I says" etc. etc. etc.

This kind of conversation went on more or less all day between these two, who were only in for some petty offence & quite pleased with themselves. Those who were going to prison were silent and restless, and the look on some of the men's faces – respectable men under arrest for the first time – was dreadful. They took the publican out at about three in the afternoon, to be sent off to prison. He had cheered up a little on learning from the constable on duty that he was going to the same prison as Lord Kylsant. He thought that by sucking up to Lord K. in jail he might get a job from him when he came out.

I had no idea how long I was going to be incarcerated, & supposed that it would be several days at least. However, between four and five o'clock they took me out of the cell, gave back the things which had been confiscated, and shot me into the street forthwith. Evidently the day in custody served instead of the fine. I had only twopence and had had nothing to eat all day except bread and marg., and was damnably hungry; however, as always happens when it is a choice between tobacco and food, I bought tobacco with my twopence. Then I went down to the Church Army shelter in the Waterloo Road, where you get a kip, two meals of bread and corned beef and tea and a prayer meeting, for four hours' work at sawing wood.

The next morning I went home, got some money, and went out to Edmonton. I turned up at the Casual Ward about nine at night, not downright drunk but more or less under the influence, thinking this would lead to prison – for it is an offence under the Vagrancy Act for a tramp to come drunk to the Casual Ward. The porter, however, treated me with great consideration, evidently feeling that a tramp with money enough to buy drink ought to be respected. During the next few days I made several more attempts to get into trouble by begging under the noses of the police, but I seemed to bear a charmed life – no one took any notice of me. So, as I did not want to do anything serious which might lead to investigations about my identity etc., I gave it up. The trip, therefore, was more or less of a failure, but I have recorded it as a fairly interesting experience.

Common Lodging Houses

The New Statesman and Nation, 3 September 1932

Common lodging houses, of which there are several hundred in London, are night-shelters specially licensed by the LCC. They are intended for people who cannot afford regular lodgings, and in effect they are extremely cheap hotels. It is hard to estimate the lodging-house population, which varies continually, but it always runs into tens of thousands, and in the winter months probably approaches fifty thousand. Considering that they house so many people and that most of them are in an extraordinarily bad state, common lodging houses do not get the attention they deserve.

To judge the value of the LCC legislation on this subject, one must realise what life in a common lodging house is like. The average lodging house ("doss house", it used to be called) consists of a number of dormitories, and a kitchen, always subterranean, which also serves as a sitting-room. The conditions in these places, especially in southern quarters such as Southwark or Bermondsey, are disgusting. The dormitories are horrible fetid dens, packed with anything up to a hundred men, and furnished with beds a good deal inferior to those in a London casual ward. Normally these beds are about 5 ft 6 in. long by 2 ft 6 in. wide, with a hard convex mattress and a cylindrical pillow like a block of wood; sometimes, in the cheaper houses, not even a pillow. The bed-clothes consist of two raw-umber-coloured sheets, supposed to be changed once a week, but actually, in many cases, left on for a month, and a cotton counterpane; in winter there may be blankets, but never enough. As often as not the beds are verminous, and the kitchens invariably swarm with cockroaches or black beetles. There are no baths, of course, and no room where any privacy is attainable. These are the normal and accepted conditions in all ordinary lodging houses. The charges paid for this kind of accommodation vary between 7d and 1/1d a night. It should be added that, low as these charges sound, the average common lodging house brings in something like £40 net profit a week to its owner.

Besides the ordinary dirty lodging houses, there are a few score, such as the Rowton Houses and the Salvation Army hostels, that are clean and decent. Unfortunately, all of these places set off their advantages by a discipline so rigid and tiresome that to stay in them is rather like being in jail. In London (curiously enough it is better in some other towns) the common lodging house where one gets both liberty and a decent bed does not exist.

The curious thing about the squalor and discomfort of the ordinary lodging house is that these exist in places subject to constant inspection by the LCC. When one first sees the murky, troglodytic cave of a common lodging-house kitchen, one takes it for a corner of the early nineteenth century which has somehow been missed by the reformers; it is a surprise to find that common lodging houses are governed by a set of minute and (in intention) exceedingly tyrannical rules. According to the LCC regulations, practically everything is against the law in a common lodging house. Gambling, drunkenness, or even the introduction of liquor, swearing, spitting on the floor, keeping tame animals, fighting – in short, the whole social life of these places – are all forbidden. Of course, the law is habitually broken, but some of the rules are enforceable, and they illustrate the dismal uselessness of this kind of legislation. To take an instance: some time ago the LCC became concerned about the closeness together of beds in common lodging houses, and enacted that these must be at least 3 ft apart. This is the kind of law that is enforceable, and the beds were duly moved. Now, to a lodger in an already overcrowded dormitory it hardly matters whether the beds are 3 ft apart or 1 ft; but it does matter to the proprietor, whose income depends upon his floor space. The sole real result of this law, therefore, was a general rise in the price of beds. Please

notice that though the space between the beds is strictly regulated, nothing is said about the beds themselves – nothing, for
instance, about their being fit to sleep in. The lodging-house
keepers can, and do, charge 1/- for a bed less restful than a heap
of straw, and there is no law to prevent them.

Another example of LCC regulations. From nearly all
common lodging houses women are strictly excluded; there
are a few houses specially for women, and a very small number –
too small to affect the general question – to which both men
and women are admitted. It follows that any homeless man who
lives regularly in a lodging house is entirely cut off from female
society – indeed, cases even happen of man and wife being
separated owing to the impossibility of getting accommodation
in the same house. Again, some of the cheaper lodging houses
are habitually raided by slumming parties, who march into
the kitchen uninvited and hold lengthy religious services. The
lodgers dislike these slumming parties intensely, but they have
no power to eject them. Can anyone imagine such things being
tolerated in a hotel? And yet a common lodging house is only a
hotel at which one pays 8d a night instead of 10/6d. This kind of
petty tyranny can, in fact, only be defended on the theory that a
man poor enough to live in a common lodging house thereby
forfeits some of his rights as a citizen.

One cannot help feeling that this theory lies behind the
LCC rules for common lodging houses. All these rules are in
the nature of interference-legislation – that is, they interfere,
but not for the benefit of the lodgers. Their emphasis is on
hygiene and morals, and the question of comfort is left to the
lodging-house proprietor, who, of course, either shirks it or
solves it in the spirit of organised charity. It is worth pointing
out the improvements that could actually be made in common
lodging houses by legislation. As to cleanliness, no law will ever
enforce that, and in any case it is a minor point. But the sleeping
accommodation, which is the important thing, could easily be
brought up to a decent standard. Common lodging houses are
places in which one pays to sleep, and most of them fail in their
essential purpose, for no one can sleep well in a rackety dormitory on a bed as hard as bricks. The LCC would be doing an
immense service if they compelled lodging-house keepers
to divide their dormitories into cubicles and, above all, to

provide comfortable beds; for instance, beds as good as those in the London casual wards. And there seems no sense in the principle of licensing all houses for "men only" or "women only", as though men and women were sodium and water and must be kept apart for fear of an explosion; the houses should be licensed for both sexes alike, as they are in some provincial towns. And the lodgers should be protected by law against various swindles which the proprietors and managers are now able to practise on them. Given these conditions, common lodging houses would serve their purpose, which is an important one, far better than they do now. After all, tens of thousands of unemployed and partially employed men have literally no other place in which they can live. It is absurd that they should be compelled to choose, as they are at present, between an easy-going pigsty and a hygienic prison.

ERIC BLAIR

Review of *Caliban Shrieks* by Jack Hilton
The Adelphi, March 1935

This is the first review to be signed 'George Orwell.'

This witty and unusual book may be described as an autobiography without narrative. Mr. Hilton lets us know, briefly and in passing, that he is a cotton operative who has been in and out of work for years past, that he served in France during the latter part of the War, and that he has also been on the road, been in prison, etc., etc.; but he wastes little time in explanations and none in description. In effect his book is a series of comments on life as it appears when one's income is two pounds a week or less. Here, for instance, is Mr. Hilton's account of his own marriage:

"Despite the obvious recognition of marriage's disabilities, the bally thing took place. With it came, not the entrancing mysteries of the bedroom, nor the passionate soul-stirring emotion of two sugar-candied Darby and Joans, but the practical resolve that, come what may, be the furnisher's dues met or no, the rent paid or spent, we – the wife and I – would commemorate our marriage by having, every Sunday morn, ham and eggs for breakfast. So it was we got one over on the poet with his madness of love, the little dove birds, etc."

There are obvious disadvantages in this manner of writing – in particular, it assumes a width of experience which many readers would not possess. On the other hand, the book has a quality which the objective, descriptive kind of book almost invariably misses. It deals with its subject *from the inside*, and consequently it gives one, instead of a catalogue of facts relating to poverty, a vivid notion of what it *feels* like to be poor. All the time that one reads one seems to hear Mr. Hilton's voice, and what is more, one seems to hear the voices of the innumerable industrial workers whom he typifies. The humorous courage, the fearful realism and the utter imperviousness to middle-class ideals, which characterise the best type of industrial worker, are all implicit in Mr. Hilton's way of talking. This is one of those books that succeed in conveying a frame of mind, and that takes more doing than the mere telling of a story.

Books like this, which come from genuine workers and present a genuinely working-class outlook, are exceedingly rare and correspondingly important. They are the voices of a normally silent multitude. All over England, in every industrial town, there are men by scores of thousands whose attitude to life, if only they could express it, would be very much what Mr. Hilton's is. If all of them could get their thoughts on to paper they would change the whole consciousness of our race. Some of them try to do so, of course; but in almost every case, inevitably, what a mess they make of it! I knew a tramp once who was writing his autobiography. He was quite young, but he had had a most interesting life which included, among other things, a jail-escape in America, and he could talk about it entrancingly. But as soon as he took a pen in his hand he became not only boring beyond measure but utterly unintelligible. His prose style was modelled upon *Peg's Paper* ("With a wild cry I sank in a stricken heap," etc.), and his ineptitude with words was so great that after wading through two pages of laboured description you could not even be certain what he was attempting to describe. Looking back upon that autobiography, and a number of similar documents that I have seen, I realise what a considerable literary gift must have gone to the making of Mr. Hilton's book.

As to the sociological information that Mr. Hilton provides, I have only one fault to find. He has evidently not been in the Casual Ward since the years just after the War, and he seems to have been taken in by the lie, widely published during the last few years, to the effect that casual paupers are now given a "warm meal" at mid-day. I could a tale unfold about those "warm meals." Otherwise, all his facts are entirely accurate so far as I am able to judge, and his remarks on prison life, delivered with an extraordinary absence of malice, are some of the most interesting that I have read.

Review of *Tropic of Cancer* by Henry Miller; *The Wolf at the Door* by Robert Francis

New English Weekly, 14 November 1935

Modern man is rather like a bisected wasp which goes on sucking jam and pretends that the loss of its abdomen does not matter. It is some perception of this fact which brings books like *Tropic of Cancer* (for there will probably be more and more of them as time goes on) into being.

Tropic of Cancer is a novel, or perhaps rather a chunk of autobiography, about Americans in Paris – not the monied dilettante type, but the out-at-elbow, good-for-nothing type. There is much in it that is remarkable, but its most immediately noticeable and perhaps essential feature is its descriptions of sexual encounters. These are interesting not because of any pornographic appeal (quite the contrary), but because they make a definite attempt to get at real facts. They describe sexual life from the point of view of the man in the street – but, it must be admitted, rather a debased version of the man in the street. Nearly all the characters in the book are habitués of the brothel. They act and describe their action with a callous coarseness which is unparalleled in fiction, though common enough in real life. Taken as a whole, the book might even be called a vilification of human nature. As it may justly be asked what good is done by vilifying human nature, I must amplify the remark I made above.

One result of the breakdown of religious belief has been a

sloppy idealization of the physical side of life. In a way this is natural enough. For if there is no life beyond the grave, it is obviously harder to face the fact that birth, copulation, etc., are in certain aspects disgusting. In the Christian centuries, of course, a pessimistic view of life was taken more or less for granted. "Man that is born of woman hath but a short time to live and is full of misery," says the Prayer Book, with the air of stating something obvious. But it is a different matter to admit that life is full of misery when you believe that the grave really finishes you. It is easier to comfort yourself with some kind of optimistic lie. Hence the tee-heeing brightness of *Punch*, hence Barrie and his bluebells, hence H. G. Wells and his Utopiæ infested by nude school-marms. Hence, above all, the monstrous soppification of the sexual theme in most of the fiction of the past hundred years. A book like *Tropic of Cancer*, which deals with sex by brutally insisting on the facts, swings the pendulum too far, no doubt, but it does swing it in the right direction. Man is not a Yahoo, but he is rather like a Yahoo and needs to be reminded of it from time to time. All one asks of a book of this kind is that it shall do its job competently and without snivelling – conditions that are satisfied in this case, I think.

Probably, although he chooses to describe ugly things, Mr. Miller would not answer to the name of pessimist. He even has passages of rather Whitmanesque enthusiasm for the process of life. What he seems to be saying is that if one stiffens oneself by the contemplation of ugliness, one ends by finding life not less but more worth living. From a literary point of view his book is competent, though not dazzlingly so. It is firmly done, with very few lapses into the typical modern slipshoddy. If it attracts critical attention it will no doubt be coupled with *Ulysses*, quite wrongly. *Ulysses* is not only a vastly better book, but also quite different in intention. Joyce is primarily an artist; Mr. Miller is a discerning though hardboiled person giving his opinions about life. I find his prose difficult to quote because of the unprintable words which are scattered all over it, but here is one sample: –

"When the tide is on the ebb and only a few syphilitic mermaids are left stranded in the muck the Dome looks like a shooting gallery that's been struck by a cyclone. Everything is slowly dribbling back to the sewer. For about an hour there is a death-like calm during which the vomit is mopped up.

Suddenly the trees begin to screech. From one end of the boulevard to the other a demented song rises up. It is the signal that announces the close of the exchange. What hopes there were are swept up. The moment has come to void the last bagful of urine. The day is sneaking in like a leper. . . ."

There is a fine rhythm to that. The American language is less flexible and refined than the English, but it has more life in it, perhaps. I do not imagine that in *Tropic of Cancer* I have discovered the great novel of the century, but I do think it a remarkable book, and I strongly advise anyone who can get hold of a copy to have a look at it.

With *The Wolf at the Door* we are on more familiar ground. In a way it is the exact opposite of *Tropic of Cancer*, for it comes under the heading of "literature of escape." The question always is, of course, where are you escaping to? In this case it is to the fantastic but very detailed universe inhabited by a small child. The story, which Mr. Havelock Ellis, who contributes an introduction, declared to be essentially "a dream," is about a peasant girl, child of desperately poor parents, in northern France soon after the war of 1870. I can best indicate its quality by a quotation: —

"I placed my books, *The Office of the Dead* and *Selected Thoughts from Bossuet*, in front of my seat, and as we knelt the little board reached level with my teeth. Should prayers last too long, I would suck the red off the *Selected Thoughts*, and my lips coloured themselves crimson. That Sunday I bit the wood, I remember particularly the taste of that Chantecroix wood, smacking of resin and covered with the grease of our little hands — and I broke one of my front teeth. . . ."

This kind of thing goes on, in a monstrous turbid stream almost without paragraphs, [for] four hundred pages. There are two things that strike one. First, that one would not expect such a shapeless book from a French writer; second, that shapeless or no it has undoubted power in it. On every page and almost in every line there are little touches like that of the child sucking the colour off the prayer-book, and as a whole the book is a marvel of imaginative reconstruction. Those who like the atmosphere-of-childhood stuff (nothing soppy, either — no tinkling through the Wendy glades) will revel in it. It is hard not to feel that the author could do better if he would trouble to cut and revise. But

I am nervous of saying this, partly because all the French critics seem to have hailed the book as a masterpiece, partly because I have not read it in the original.

As to the translation, except for the dialogue, that never-escaped pitfall, it reads so unlike a translation that one may presume it to be a very good one.

Rudyard Kipling
New English Weekly, 23 January 1936

Rudyard Kipling was the only popular English writer of this century who was not at the same time a thoroughly bad writer. His popularity was, of course, essentially middle-class. In the average middle-class family before the War, especially in Anglo-Indian families, he had a prestige that is not even approached by any writer of to-day. He was a sort of household god with whom one grew up and whom one took for granted whether one liked him or whether one did not. For my own part I worshipped Kipling at thirteen, loathed him at seventeen, enjoyed him at twenty, despised him at twenty-five and now again rather admire him. The one thing that was never possible, if one had read him at all, was to forget him. Certain of his stories, for instance *The Strange Ride*, *Drums of the Fore and Aft* and *The Mark of the Beast*, are about as good as it is possible for that kind of story to be. They are, moreover, exceedingly well told. For the vulgarity of his prose style is only a surface fault; in the less obvious qualities of construction and economy he is supreme. It is, after all (see the "Times Literature Supplement"), much easier to write inoffensive prose than to tell a good story. And his verse, though it is almost a by-word for badness, has the same peculiarly memorable quality.

> "I've lost Britain, I've lost Gaul,
> "I've lost Rome, and, worst of all,
> "I've lost Lalage!"

may be only a jingle, and *The Road to Mandalay* may be something worse than a jingle, but they do "stay by one." They remind one that it needs a streak of genius even to become a by-word.

What is much more distasteful in Kipling than sentimental plots or vulgar tricks of style, is the imperialism to which he chose to lend his genius. The most one can say is that when he made it the choice was more forgivable than it would be now. The imperialism of the 'eighties and 'nineties was sentimental, ignorant and dangerous, but it was not entirely despicable. The picture then called up by the word "empire" was a picture of overworked officials and frontier skirmishes, not of Lord Beaverbrook and Australian butter. It was still possible to be an imperialist and a gentleman, and of Kipling's *personal* decency there can be no doubt. It is worth remembering that he was the most widely popular English writer of our time, and yet that no one, perhaps, so consistently refrained from making a vulgar show of his personality.

If he had never come under imperialist influences, and if he had developed, as he might well have done, into a writer of music-hall songs, he would have been a better and more lovable writer. In the rôle he actually chose, one was bound to think of him, after one had grown up, as a kind of enemy, a man of alien and perverted genius. But now that he is dead, I for one cannot help wishing that I could offer some kind of tribute – a salute of guns, if such a thing were available – to the story-teller who was so important to my childhood.

Review of *The Fate of the Middle Classes* by Alec Brown

New English Weekly, 30 April 1936

Aristocracy can only exist while aristocratic poverty is thinkable. Hence the phrase "nor no poor knight" in that strangely accurate prophecy in "King Lear." Once it is taken for granted that a knight must have at least £1000 a year or stop being a knight, aristocracy gives way to plutocracy.

In England, for centuries past, our so-called aristocracy has been recruited by successive waves of scoundrels who have enriched themselves upon the current swindle and whose position depends solely upon money. The typical member of the House of Lords is a money-lender disguised as a crusader, with a stout wadding of bank-notes under his coat of mail. But a little lower in the social scale the money-principle has not altogether triumphed, and throughout sections of the middle class there has lingered the notion of *gentility* as something superior to and not purchasable by money. This is a point that the Communist, with his eyes glued to "economic realities," is inclined and perhaps wants to miss. Mr. Brown, as an orthodox Communist, explains class solely in terms of money and thus lumps into the middle class everyone who lives neither on dividends nor on a weekly wage. By this definition everyone from the successful professional man to the village cobbler is "middle class," the only differences between them being differences of income; and (for instance) a clergyman, a retail butcher, a sea-captain and a bookie would all have approximately the same attitude to life if their incomes happened to be the same. Actually, as everyone knows, men of similar economic status may differ enormously if they are differently affected by the concept of *gentility*. Thus, in England, an Army officer with £600 a year would die rather than admit a grocer of the same income to be his equal. It is this particular form of snobbery which, when the middle class have learned to act together, may pave the way for some form of Fascism.

For the rest, Mr. Brown's is an interesting book, written in a lively though rather slapdash style, and containing a masterly account of the change-over from industrial capitalism to finance-capitalism.

Review of *The Rock Pool* by Cyril Connolly
New English Weekly, 23 July 1936

As Mr. Cyril Connolly is almost the only novel-reviewer in England who does not make me sick, I opened this, his first novel, with a lively interest.

The usual thing to say about a first novel is that it shows great promise but the author has not got his subject-matter completely under control. With Mr. Connolly's novel I should say it is just the other way about. The treatment is mature and skilful – the book looks as if it had been worked at over a period of years – but the subject-matter, especially considering that this is a first novel, is tiresome. The story is a kind of modernization of the myth of Hylas. A young Englishman of the su-superior, monied and cultured type, an Old Wykehamist and a thoroughly ineffectual ass – a 1930 version, really, of the Bernard Shaw Englishman – lands up in one of those dreadful colonies of expatriates calling themselves artists which were dotted all over France during the nineteen-twenties. He decides that he will study them in a detached, scientific way, as one might study the fauna of a rock pool. But behold! detachment is not so easy as he thinks. Almost instantly he has fallen into the pool and been dragged down to the level of its inhabitants, or even lower if that were possible. Before long he is drinking, cadging and lechering exactly like the rest of them, and on the last page he is left gazing at the world through a mist of Pernod but dimly feeling that his present degradation is better than respectable life in England.

There are two reasons why subject-matter such as this is unsatisfactory. In the first place one can hardly approach a novel about artists' colonies on the Mediterranean without reflecting that Norman Douglas and Aldous Huxley did that kind of thing a long time ago and probably better. A more serious objection is that even to want to write about so-called artists who spend on sodomy what they have gained by sponging betrays a kind of spiritual inadequacy. For it is clear that Mr. Connolly rather admires the disgusting beasts he depicts, and certainly he prefers them to the polite and sheeplike Englishman; he even compares them, in their ceaseless war against decency, to heroic savage tribes struggling against Western civilization. But this, you see, only amounts to a distaste for normal life and common decency, and one might equally well express it, as so many do, by scuffling beneath the moulting wing of Mother Church. Obviously, modern mechanized life becomes dreary if you let it. The awful thraldom of money is upon everyone and there are only three immediately obvious escapes. One is religion, another is unending work, the third is the kind of sluttish antinomianism – lying in bed till four in the afternoon, drinking Pernod – that Mr. Connolly seems to admire. The third is certainly the worst, but in any case the essential evil is to think in terms of *escape*. The fact to which we have got to cling, as to a lifebelt, is that it *is* possible to be a normal decent person and yet to be fully alive. Mr. Connolly seems to suggest that there are only two alternatives: lie in bed till four in the afternoon, drinking Pernod, or you will infallibly surrender to the gods of Success and become a London social-cum-literary backstairs-crawler. The orthodox Christian tries to pitchfork you with a very similar dilemma. But both dilemmas are false and unnecessarily depressing.

I criticize Mr. Connolly's subject-matter because I think he could write a better novel if he would concern himself with more ordinary people. But I do not mean to imply that this book is not worth reading. Actually, during the past year I have only read about two *new* books that interested me more, and I doubt if I have read even one that was more amusing. Presumably it was refused publication in England because of the law of libel – there is no indecency in it. The Obelisk Press do a great service by publishing the books that cannot be published over here. It is a pity they think it necessary to pretend in their blurbs and catalogues that they are specialists in pornography...

Shooting an Elephant
New Writing, 2, Autumn 1936

In Moulmein, in Lower Burma, I was hated by large numbers of people – the only time in my life that I have been important enough for this to happen to me. I was subdivisional police officer of the town, and in an aimless, petty kind of way anti-European feeling was very bitter. No one had the guts to raise a riot, but if a European woman went through the bazaars alone somebody would probably spit betel juice over her dress. As a police officer I was an obvious target and was baited whenever it seemed safe to do so. When a nimble Burman tripped me up on the football field and the referee (another Burman) looked the other way, the crowd yelled with hideous laughter. This happened more than once. In the end the sneering yellow faces of young men that met me everywhere, the insults hooted after me when I was at a safe distance, got badly on my nerves. The young Buddhist priests were the worst of all. There were several thousands of them in the town and none of them seemed to have anything to do except stand on street corners and jeer at Europeans.

All this was perplexing and upsetting. For at that time I had already made up my mind that imperialism was an evil thing and the sooner I chucked up my job and got out of it the better. Theoretically – and secretly, of course – I was all for the Burmese and all against their oppressors, the British. As for the job I was doing, I hated it more bitterly than I can perhaps make clear. In a job like that you see the dirty work of Empire at close quarters. The wretched prisoners huddling in the stinking cages of the lock-ups, the grey, cowed faces of the long-term convicts, the scarred buttocks of the men who had been flogged with bamboos – all these oppressed me with an intolerable sense of guilt. But I could get nothing into perspective. I was young and ill-educated and I had had to think out my problems in the utter silence that is imposed on every Englishman in the East. I did not even know that the British Empire is dying, still less did I know that it is a great deal better than the younger empires that are going to supplant it. All I knew was that I was stuck between my hatred of the empire I served and my rage against the evil-spirited little beasts who tried to make my job impossible. With one part of my mind I thought of the British Raj as an unbreakable tyranny, as something clamped down, in saecula saeculorum, upon the will of prostrate peoples; with another part I thought that the greatest joy in the world would be to drive a bayonet into a Buddhist priest's guts. Feelings like these are the normal by-products of imperialism; ask any Anglo-Indian official, if you can catch him off duty.

One day something happened which in a roundabout way was enlightening. It was a tiny incident in itself, but it gave me a better glimpse than I had had before of the real nature of imperialism – the real motives for which despotic governments act. Early one morning the sub-inspector at a police station the other end of the town rang me up on the phone and said that an elephant was ravaging the bazaar. Would I please come and do something about it? I did not know what I could do, but I wanted to see what was happening and I got on to a pony and started out. I took my rifle, an old .44 Winchester and much too small to kill an elephant, but I thought the noise might be useful in terrorem. Various Burmans stopped me on the way and told me about the elephant's doings. It was not, of course, a wild elephant, but a tame one which had gone 'must.' It had been chained up as tame elephants always are when their attack of 'must' is due, but on the previous night it had broken its chain and escaped. Its mahout, the only person who could manage it when it was in that state, had set out in pursuit, but he had taken the wrong direction and was now twelve hours' journey away, and in the morning the elephant had suddenly reappeared in the town. The Burmese population had no weapons and were quite helpless against it. It had already destroyed somebody's bamboo hut, killed a cow and raided some fruit-stalls and devoured the stock; also it had met the municipal rubbish van, and, when the driver jumped out and took to his heels, had turned the van over and inflicted violences upon it.

The Burmese sub-inspector and some Indian constables were waiting for me in the quarter where the elephant had been seen. It was a very poor quarter, a labyrinth of squalid bamboo huts, thatched with palm-leaf, winding all over a steep hillside. I remember that it was a cloudy stuffy morning at the beginning of the rains. We began questioning the people as to where the elephant had gone, and, as usual, failed to get any definite information. That is invariably the case in the East; a story always sounds clear enough at a distance, but the nearer you get to the scene of events the vaguer it becomes. Some of the people said that the elephant had gone in one direction, some said that he had gone in another, some professed not even to have heard of any elephant. I had almost made up my mind that the whole story was a pack of lies, when we heard yells a little distance away. There was a loud, scandalized cry of 'Go away, child! Go away this instant!' and an old woman with a switch in her hand came round the corner of a hut, violently shooing away a crowd of naked children. Some more women followed, clicking their tongues and exclaiming; evidently

44

there was something there that the children ought not to have seen. I rounded the hut and saw a man's dead body sprawling in the mud. He was an Indian, a black Dravidian coolie, almost naked, and he could not have been dead many minutes. The people said that the elephant had come suddenly upon him round the corner of the hut, caught him with its trunk, put its foot on his back and ground him into the earth. This was the rainy season and the ground was soft, and his face had scored a trench a foot deep and a couple of yards long. He was lying on his belly with arms crucified and head sharply twisted to one side. His face was coated with mud, the eyes wide open, the teeth bared and grinning with an expression of unendurable agony. (Never tell me, by the way, that the dead look peaceful. Most of the corpses I have seen looked devilish.) The friction of the great beast's foot had stripped the skin from his back as neatly as one skins a rabbit. As soon as I saw the dead man I sent an orderly to a friend's house nearby to borrow an elephant rifle. I had already sent back the pony, not wanting it to go mad with fright and throw me if it smelled the elephant.

The orderly came back in a few minutes with a rifle and five cartridges, and meanwhile some Burmans had arrived and told us that the elephant was in the paddy fields below, only a few hundred yards away. As I started forward practically the whole population of the quarter flocked out of the houses and followed me. They had seen the rifle and were all shouting excitedly that I was going to shoot the elephant. They had not shown much interest in the elephant when he was merely ravaging their homes, but it was different now that he was going to be shot. It was a bit of fun to them, as it would be to an English crowd; besides, they wanted the meat. It made me vaguely uneasy. I had no intention of shooting the elephant – I had merely sent for the rifle to defend myself if necessary – and it is always unnerving to have a crowd following you. I marched down the hill, looking and feeling a fool, with the rifle over my shoulder and an ever-growing army of people jostling at my heels. At the bottom, when you got away from the huts, there was a metalled road and beyond that a miry waste of paddy fields a thousand yards across, not yet ploughed but soggy from the first rains and dotted with coarse grass. The elephant was standing eighty yards from the road, his left side towards us. He took not the slightest notice of the crowd's approach. He was tearing up bunches of grass, beating them against his knees to clean them and stuffing them into his mouth.

I had halted on the road. As soon as I saw the elephant I knew with perfect certainty that I ought not to shoot him. It is a serious matter to shoot a working elephant – it is comparable to destroying a huge and costly piece of machinery – and obviously one ought not to do it if it can possibly be avoided. And at that distance, peacefully eating, the elephant looked no more dangerous than a cow. I thought then and I think now that his attack of 'must' was already passing off; in which case he would merely wander harmlessly about until the mahout came back and caught him. Moreover, I did not in the least want to shoot him. I decided that I would watch him for a little while to make sure that he did not turn savage again, and then go home.

But at that moment I glanced round at the crowd that had followed me. It was an immense crowd, two thousand at the least and growing every minute. It blocked the road for a long distance on either side. I looked at the sea of yellow faces above the garish clothes – faces all happy and excited over this bit of fun, all certain that the elephant was going to be shot. They were watching me as they would watch a conjuror about to perform a trick. They did not like me, but with the magical rifle in my hands I was momentarily worth watching. And suddenly I realized that I should have to shoot the elephant after all. The people expected it of me and I had got to do it; I could feel their two thousand wills pressing me forward, irresistibly. And it was at this moment, as I stood there with the rifle in my hands, that I first grasped the hollowness, the futility of the white man's dominion in the East. Here was I, the white man with his gun, standing in front of the unarmed native crowd – seemingly the leading actor of the piece; but in reality I was only an absurd puppet pushed to and fro by the will of those yellow faces behind. I perceived in this moment that when the white man turns tyrant it is his own freedom that he destroys. He becomes a sort of hollow, posing dummy, the conventionalized figure of a sahib. For it is the condition of his rule that he shall spend his life in trying to impress the 'natives,' and so in every crisis he has got to do what the 'natives' expect of him. He wears a mask, and his face grows to fit it. I had got to shoot the elephant. I had committed myself to doing it when I sent for the rifle. A sahib has got to act like a sahib; he has got to appear resolute, to know his own mind and do definite things. To come all that way, rifle in hand, with two thousand people marching at my heels, and then to trail feebly away, having done nothing – no, that was impossible. The crowd would laugh at me. And my whole life, every white man's life in the East, was one long struggle not to be laughed at.

But I did not want to shoot the elephant. I watched him beating his bunch of grass against his knees, with that preoccupied grandmotherly air that elephants have. It seemed to me that it would be murder to shoot him. At that age I was not squeamish about killing animals, but I had never shot an elephant and never wanted to. (Somehow it always seems worse to kill a *large* animal.) Besides, there was the beast's owner to be considered. Alive, the elephant was worth at least a hundred pounds; dead, he would only be worth the value of his tusks – five pounds, possibly. But I had got to act quickly. I turned to some experienced-looking Burmans who had been there when we arrived, and asked them how the elephant had been behaving. They all said the same thing: he took no notice of you if you left him alone, but he might charge if you went too close to him.

It was perfectly clear to me what I ought to do. I ought to walk up to within, say, twenty-five yards of the elephant and test his behaviour. If he charged I could shoot, if he took no notice of me it would be safe to leave him until the mahout came back. But also I knew that I was going to do no such thing. I was a poor shot with a rifle and the ground was soft mud into which one would sink at every step. If the elephant charged and I missed him, I should have about as much chance as a toad under a steam-roller. But even then I was not thinking particularly of my own skin, only of the watchful yellow faces behind. For at that moment, with the crowd watching me, I was not afraid in the ordinary sense, as I would have been if I had been alone. A white man mustn't be frightened in front of

47

'natives'; and so, in general, he isn't frightened. The sole thought in my mind was that if anything went wrong those two thousand Burmans would see me pursued, caught, trampled on and reduced to a grinning corpse like that Indian up the hill. And if that happened it was quite probable that some of them would laugh. That would never do. There was only one alternative. I shoved the cartridges into the magazine and lay down on the road to get a better aim.

The crowd grew very still, and a deep, low, happy sigh, as of people who see the theatre curtain go up at last, breathed from innumerable throats. They were going to have their bit of fun after all. The rifle was a beautiful German thing with cross-hair sights. I did not then know that in shooting an elephant one should shoot to cut an imaginary bar running from ear-hole to ear-hole. I ought therefore, as the elephant was sideways on, to have aimed straight at his ear-hole; actually I aimed several inches in front of this, thinking the brain would be further forward.

When I pulled the trigger I did not hear the bang or feel the kick – one never does when a shot goes home – but I heard the devilish roar of glee that went up from the crowd. In that instant, in too short a time, one would have thought, even for the bullet to get there, a mysterious, terrible change had come over the elephant. He neither stirred nor fell, but every line of his body had altered. He looked suddenly stricken, shrunken, immensely old, as though the frightful impact of the bullet had paralysed him without knocking him down. At last, after what seemed a long time – it might have been five seconds, I dare say – he sagged flabbily to his knees. His mouth slobbered. An enormous senility seemed to have settled upon him. One could have imagined him thousands of years old. I fired again into the same spot. At the second shot he did not collapse but climbed with desperate slowness to his feet and stood weakly upright, with legs sagging and head drooping. I fired a third time. That was the shot that did for him. You could see the agony of it jolt his whole body and knock the last remnant of strength from his legs. But in falling he seemed for a moment to rise, for as his hind legs collapsed beneath him he seemed to tower upwards like a huge rock toppling, his trunk reaching skyward like a tree. He trumpeted, for the first and only time. And then down he came, his belly towards me, with a crash that seemed to shake the ground even where I lay.

I got up. The Burmans were already racing past me across the mud. It was obvious that the elephant would never rise again, but he was not dead. He was breathing very rhythmically with long rattling gasps, his great mound of a side painfully rising and falling. His mouth was wide open – I could see far down into caverns of pale pink throat. I waited a long time for him to die, but his breathing did not weaken. Finally I fired my two remaining shots into the spot where I thought his heart must be. The thick blood welled out of him like red velvet, but still he did not die. His body did not even jerk when the shots hit him, the tortured breathing continued without a pause. He was dying, very slowly and in great agony, but in some world remote from me where not even a bullet could damage him further. I felt that I had got to put an end to that dreadful noise. It seemed dreadful to see the great beast lying there, powerless to move and yet powerless to die, and not even to be able to finish him. I sent back for my small rifle and poured shot after shot into his heart and down his throat. They seemed to make no impression. The tortured gasps continued as steadily as the ticking of a clock.

In the end I could not stand it any longer and went away. I heard later that it took him half an hour to die. Burmans were arriving with dahs and baskets even before I left, and I was told they had stripped his body almost to the bones by the afternoon.

Afterwards, of course, there were endless discussions about the shooting of the elephant. The owner was furious, but he was only an Indian and could do nothing. Besides, legally I had done the right thing, for a mad elephant has to be killed, like a mad dog, if its owner fails to control it. Among the Europeans opinion was divided. The older men said I was right, the younger men said it was a damn shame to shoot an elephant for killing a coolie, because an elephant was worth more than any damn Coringhee coolie. And afterwards I was very glad that the coolie had been killed; it put me legally in the right and it gave me a sufficient pretext for shooting the elephant. I often wondered whether any of the others grasped that I had done it solely to avoid looking a fool.

GEORGE ORWELL

Bookshop Memories
Fortnightly, November 1936

When I worked in a second-hand bookshop – so easily pictured, if you don't work in one, as a kind of paradise where charming old gentlemen browse eternally among calf-bound folios – the thing that chiefly struck me was the rarity of really bookish people. Our shop had an exceptionally interesting stock, yet I doubt whether ten per cent of our customers knew a good book from a bad one. First edition snobs were much commoner than lovers of literature, but oriental students haggling over cheap textbooks were commoner still, and vague-minded women looking for birthday presents for their nephews were commonest of all.

Many of the people who came to us were of the kind who would be a nuisance anywhere but have special opportunities in a bookshop. For example, the dear old lady who "wants a book for an invalid" (a very common demand, that), and the other dear old lady who read such a nice book in 1897 and wonders whether you can find her a copy. Unfortunately she doesn't remember the title or the author's name or what the book was about, but she does remember that it had a red cover. But apart from these there are two well-known types of pest by whom every second-hand bookshop is haunted. One is the decayed person smelling of old breadcrusts who comes every day, sometimes several times a day, and tries to sell you worthless books. The other is the person who orders large quantities of books for which he has not the smallest intention of paying. In our shop we sold nothing on credit, but we would put books aside, or order them if necessary, for people who arranged to fetch them away later. Scarcely half the people who ordered books from us ever came back. It used to puzzle me at first. What made them do it? They would come in and demand some rare and expensive book, would make us promise over and over again to keep it for them, and then would vanish never to return. But many of them, of course, were unmistakeable paranoiacs. They used to talk in a grandiose manner about themselves and tell the most ingenious stories to explain how they had happened to come out of doors without any money – stories which, in many cases, I am sure they themselves believed. In a town like London there are always plenty of not quite certifiable lunatics walking the streets, and they tend to gravitate towards bookshops, because a bookshop is one of the few places where you can hang about for a long time without spending any money. In the end one gets to know these people almost at a glance. For all their big talk there is something moth-eaten and aimless about them. Very often, when we were dealing with an obvious paranoiac, we would put aside the books he asked for and then put them back on the shelves the moment he had gone. None of them, I noticed, ever attempted to take books away without paying for them; merely to order them was enough – it gave them, I suppose, the illusion they were spending real money.

Like most second-hand bookshops we had various sidelines. We sold second-hand typewriters, for instance, and also stamps – used stamps, I mean. Stamp-collectors are a strange silent fish-like breed, of all ages, but only of the male sex; women, apparently, fail to see the peculiar charm of gumming bits of coloured paper into albums. We also sold sixpenny horoscopes compiled by somebody who claimed to have foretold the Japanese earthquake. They were in sealed envelopes and I never opened one of them myself, but the people who bought them often came back and told us how "true" their horoscopes had been. (Doubtless any horoscope seems "true" if it tells you that you are highly attractive to the opposite sex and your worst fault is generosity.) We did a good deal of business in children's books, chiefly "remainders." Modern books for children are rather horrible things, especially when you see them in the mass. Personally I would sooner give a child a copy of Petronius Arbiter than *Peter Pan*, but even Barrie seems manly and wholesome compared with some of his later imitators. At Christmas time we spent a feverish ten days struggling with Christmas cards and calendars, which are tiresome things to sell but good business while the season lasts. It used to interest me to see the brutal cynicism with which Christian sentiment is exploited. The touts from the Christmas card firms used to come round with their catalogues as early as June. A phrase from one of their invoices sticks in my memory. It was: "2 doz. Infant Jesus with rabbits."

But our principal sideline was a lending library – the usual "twopenny no-deposit" library of five or six hundred volumes, all fiction. How the book thieves must love those libraries! It is the easiest crime in the world to borrow a book at one shop for twopence, remove the label and sell it at another shop for a shilling. Nevertheless booksellers generally find that it pays them better to have a certain number of books stolen (we used to lose about a dozen a month) than to frighten customers away by demanding a deposit.

Our shop stood exactly on the frontier between Hampstead and Camden Town, and we were frequented by all types from baronets to bus-conductors. Probably our library subscribers were a fair cross-section of London's reading public. It is therefore worth noting that of all the authors in our library the one who "went out" the best was – Priestley? Hemingway? Walpole? Wodehouse? No, Ethel M. Dell, with Warwick Deeping a good second and Jeffery Farnol, I should say, third. Dell's novels, of course, are read solely by women, but by women of all kinds and ages and not, as one might expect, merely by wistful spinsters and the fat wives of tobacconists. It is not true that men don't read novels, but it is true that there are whole branches of fiction that they avoid. Roughly speaking, what one might call the *average* novel – the ordinary, good-bad, Galsworthy-and-water stuff which is the norm of the English novel – seems to exist only for women. Men read either the novels it is possible to respect, or detective stories. But their consumption of detective stories is terrific. One of our subscribers to my knowledge read four or five detective stories every week for over a year, besides others which he got from another library. What chiefly surprised me was that he never read the same book twice. Apparently the whole of that frightful torrent of trash (the pages he read every year would, I calculated, cover nearly three-quarters of an acre) was stored for ever in his memory. He took no notice of titles or authors' names, but he could tell by merely glancing into a book whether he had "had it already."

In a lending library you see people's real tastes, not their pretended ones, and one thing that strikes you is how completely the "classical" English novelists have dropped out of favour. It is simply useless to put Dickens, Thackeray, Jane Austen, Trollope, etc., into the ordinary lending library; nobody takes them out. At the mere sight of a nineteenth-century novel people say "Oh, but that's *old*!" and shy away immediately. Yet it is always fairly easy to *sell* Dickens, just as it is always easy to sell Shakespeare. Dickens is one of those authors whom people are "always meaning to" read, and, like the Bible, he is widely known at second hand. People know by hearsay that Bill Sykes was a burglar and that Mr. Micawber had a bald head, just as they know by hearsay that Moses was found in a basket of bulrushes and saw the "back parts" of the Lord. Another thing that is very noticeable is the growing unpopularity of American books. And another – the publishers get into a stew about this every two or three years – is the unpopularity of short stories. The kind of person who asks the librarian to choose a book for him nearly always starts by saying "I don't want short stories," or "I do not desire little stories," as a German customer of ours used to put it. If you ask them why, they sometimes explain that it is too much fag to get used to a new set of characters with every story; they like to "get into" a novel which demands no further thought after the first chapter. I believe, though, that the writers are more to blame here than the readers. Most modern short stories, English and American, are utterly lifeless and worthless, far more so than most novels. The short stories which *are* stories are popular enough, *vide* D. H. Lawrence, whose short stories are as popular as his novels.

Would I like to be a bookseller *de métier*? On the whole – in spite of my employer's kindness to me, and some happy days I spent in the shop – no.

Given a good pitch and the right amount of capital, any educated person ought to be able to make a small secure living out of a bookshop. Unless one goes in for "rare" books it is not a difficult trade to learn, and you start at a great advantage if you know anything about the insides of books. (Most booksellers don't. You can get their measure by having a look at the trade papers where they advertise their wants. If you don't see an ad. for Boswell's *Decline and Fall* you are pretty sure to see one for *The Mill on the Floss* by T. S. Eliot.) Also it is a humane trade which is not capable of being vulgarised beyond a certain point. The combines can never squeeze the small independent bookseller out of existence as they have squeezed the grocer and the milkman. But the hours of work are very long – I was only a part-time employee, but my employer put in a 70-hour week, apart from constant expeditions out of hours to buy books – and it is an unhealthy life. As a rule a bookshop is horribly cold in winter, because if it is too warm the windows get misted over, and a bookseller lives on his windows. And books give off more and nastier dust than any other class of objects yet invented, and the top of a book is the place where every bluebottle prefers to die.

But the real reason why I should not like to be in the book trade for life is that while I was in it I lost my love of books. A bookseller has to tell lies about books, and that gives him a distaste for them; still worse is the fact that he is constantly dusting them and hauling them to and fro. There was a time when I really did love books – loved the sight and smell and feel of them, I mean, at least if they were fifty or more years old. Nothing pleased me quite so much as to buy a job lot of them for a shilling at a country auction. There is a peculiar flavour about the battered unexpected books you pick up in that kind of collection: minor eighteenth-century poets, out of date gaze-teers, odd volumes of forgotten novels, bound numbers of ladies' magazines of the 'sixties. For casual reading – in your bath, for instance, or late at night when you are too tired to go to bed, or in the odd quarter of an hour before lunch – there is nothing to touch a back number of the *Girl's Own Paper*. But as soon as I went to work in the bookshop I stopped buying books. Seen in the mass, five or ten thousand at a time, books were boring and even slightly sickening. Nowadays I do buy one occasionally, but only if it is a book that I want to read and can't borrow, and I never buy junk. The sweet smell of decaying paper appeals to me no longer. It is too closely associated in my mind with paranoiac customers and dead bluebottles.

Review of *Walls Have Mouths* by W. F. R. Macartney, with Prologue, Epilogue and Comments on the Chapters by Compton Mackenzie
The Adelphi, November 1936

This very valuable and absorbingly interesting book – a record of ten years' penal servitude in Parkhurst Prison – brings out two facts about prison life which are not generally appreciated. The first is that the evil thing about the English prison system is not the abuses but the system itself. When you talk to a man who has been in prison, he generally lays emphasis on the bad food, the petty injustices, the cruelty of individual warders, etc., giving the impression that if these minor evils were rectified our prisons would become tolerable, supposing that any prisons could be that. Actually, the cold, rigid discipline of a modern English jail, the solitude, the silence, the everlasting lock-and-key (all of it the work of prison reformers, among the first of whom was Torquemada), is more cruel and far more demoralising than the barbarous punishments of the Middle Ages. Worse than the loss of liberty, worse even than sexual deprivation, is boredom. Mr. Macartney has a good eye for significant detail, and he rubs this fact well home. It is quite usual, he says, at the week-end, to be left in utter solitude for forty-four hours with nothing to read. As a result, the tiniest distractions assume colossal importance. Apparently many of the men in Parkhurst Prison used to procure scraps of glass and secretly grind them into lenses – this must take months to do – and then, with tubes of brown paper, make telescopes with which to look out of their cell windows. Only men who were half mad with boredom would take all that trouble, incidentally risking bread and water for doing so.

The other fact Mr. Macartney makes clear is that in our prison system, as in other departments of English life, all real power is in the hands of one-eyed, permanent officials, who take no notice either of the Government of the moment or of public opinion. Even a prison governor, apparently, is almost powerless against the "screws" who have inherited a brutal system and go on administering it by rule of thumb. It is rather amusing to read about the efforts of the Parkhurst officials to censor the prison library. They were desperately anxious to prevent the convicts getting hold of "subversive" literature, but were far too illiterate to know which books were "subversive" and which were not. The only Home Secretary who seems ever to have made a fight against the cruel inertia of the prison system is Winston Churchill. Clynes, the Labour Home Secretary, actually exerted himself to take away a few of the convicts' privileges. No wonder that most long-term convicts are Tories!

The most dreadful chapter in this book is the one entitled "Notes on Prison Sex Life." It gave me a shock when I read it, for it suddenly revealed to me the meaning of a conversation of years earlier. I once asked a Burmese criminal why he disliked going to jail. He answered with a look of disgust and the single word, "Sodomy." I thought then that he merely meant that among the convicts there were a few homosexuals who pestered the others, but what Mr. Macartney makes clear is that in prison, after a few years, almost *every* man becomes homosexual, in spite of putting up a fight against it. He gives a horrible account of the way in which homosexuality gradually overwhelmed himself, first of all through the medium of his dreams. In a convict prison homosexuality is so general that even the jailors are infected by it, and there are actually cases of jailors and convicts competing for the favours of the same nancy-boy. As for masturbation, it is "referred to openly and indifferently." That is what you condemn a man to when you send him to prison for a long term. And this is the achievement of the dear good reformers (see Charles Reade's *It Is Never Too Late To Mend*) who did away with the promiscuity of the eighteenth century jails.

This is a remarkable book. It is formless and badly written, but packed full of the kind of details that matter. The author is an exceptionally brave, sharp-witted and good-tempered person. He is a Communist (he was given his savage sentence for some ineffectual espionage in the service of the Soviet Government), but not, I fancy, a very orthodox one; he will perhaps not be pleased when I say that he is too decent a human being to be "ideologically" sound. Mr. Compton Mackenzie's prologue and comments might appear at first sight to be unnecessary, but actually they have the effect of pulling the book together and supplying useful corroboration. Probably without Mr. Mackenzie's help the book would not have been published, in which case everyone who cares for decency must be deeply grateful to him.

In Defence of the Novel

New English Weekly, 12 and 19 November 1936

It hardly needs pointing out that at this moment the prestige of the novel is extremely low, so low that the words "I never read novels," which even a dozen years ago were generally uttered with a hint of apology are now *always* uttered in a tone of conscious pride. It is true that there are still a few contemporary or roughly contemporary novelists whom the intelligentsia consider it permissible to read; but the point is that the ordinary good-bad novel is habitually ignored while the ordinary good-bad book of verse or criticism is still taken seriously. This means that if you write novels you automatically command a less intelligent public than you would command if you had chosen some other form. There are two quite obvious reasons why this must presently make it impossible for good novels to be written. Even now the novel is visibly deteriorating, and it would deteriorate much faster if most novelists had any idea who reads their books. It is, of course, easy to argue (*vide* for instance Belloc's queerly rancorous essay) that the novel is a contemptible form of art and that its fate does not matter. I doubt whether that opinion is even worth disputing. At any rate, I am taking it for granted that the novel is worth salvaging and that in order to salvage it you have got to persuade intelligent people to take it seriously. It is therefore worth while to analyse one of the main causes – in my opinion, *the* main cause – of the novel's lapse in prestige.

The trouble is that the novel is being shouted out of existence. Question any thinking person as to why he "never reads novels," and you will usually find that, at bottom, it is because of the disgusting tripe that is written by the blurb-reviewers. There is no need to multiply examples. Here is just one specimen, from last week's "Sunday Times": "If you can read this book and not shriek with delight, your soul is dead." That or something like it is now being written about *every* novel published, as you can see by studying the quotes on the blurbs. For anyone who takes the "Sunday Times" seriously, life must be one long struggle to catch up. Novels are being shot at you at the rate of fifteen a day, and every one of them an unforgettable masterpiece which you imperil your soul by missing. It must make it so difficult to choose a book at the library, and you must feel so guilty when you fail to shriek with delight. Actually, however, no one who matters is deceived by this kind of thing, and the contempt into which novel-reviewing has fallen is extended to novels themselves. When *all* novels are thrust upon you as works of genius, it is quite natural to assume that all of them are tripe. Within the literary intelligentsia this assumption is now taken for granted. To admit that you like novels is nowadays almost equivalent to admitting that you have a hankering after coconut ice or prefer Rupert Brooke to Gerard Manley Hopkins.

All this is obvious. What I think is rather less obvious is the way in which the present situation has arisen. On the face of it, the book-ramp is a quite simple and cynical swindle. Z writes a book which is published by Y and reviewed by X in the "Weekly W." If the review is a bad one Y will remove his advertisement, so X has to hand out "unforgettable master-piece" or get the sack. Essentially that *is* the position, and novel-reviewing has sunk to its present depth largely because every reviewer has some publisher or publishers twisting his tail by proxy. But the thing is not so crude as it looks. The various parties to the swindle are not consciously acting together, and they have been forced into their present position partly against their will.

To begin with, one ought not to assume, as is so often done (see for instance Beachcomber's column, *passim*), that the nov-elist enjoys and is even in some way responsible for the reviews he gets. Nobody *likes* being told that he has written a palpitat-ing tale of passion which will last as long as the English lan-guage; though, of course, it is disappointing not to be told that, because all novelists are being told the same, and to be left out presumably means that your books won't sell. The hack-review is in fact a sort of commercial necessity, like the blurb on the dust-jacket, of which it is merely an extension. But even the wretched hack-reviewer is not to be blamed for the drivel he writes. In his special circumstances he could write nothing else. For even if there were no question of bribery, direct or indirect, there can be no such thing as good novel-criticism so long as it is assumed that *every novel is worth reviewing*.

A periodical gets its weekly wad of books and sends off a dozen of them to X, the hack-reviewer, who has a wife and family and has got to earn his guinea, not to mention the half-crown per vol. which he gets by selling his review copies. There are two reasons why it is totally impossible for X to tell the truth about the books he gets. To begin with, the chances are that eleven out of the twelve books will fail to rouse in him the faintest spark of interest. They are not more than ordinarily bad, they are merely neutral, lifeless and point-less. If he were not paid to do so he would never read a line of any of them, and in nearly every case the only truthful review he could write would be: "This book inspires in me no thoughts whatever." But will anyone pay you to write that kind of thing? Obviously not. As a start, therefore, X is in the false position of having to manufacture, say, three hundred words about a book which means nothing to him whatever. Usually he does it by giving a brief resumé of the plot (inci-dentally betraying to the author the fact that he hasn't read the book) and handing out a few compliments which for all their fulsomeness are about as valuable as the smile of a prostitute.

But there is a far worse evil than this. X is expected not only to say what a book is about but to give his opinion as to whether it is good or bad. Since X can hold a pen he is probably not a fool, at any rate not such a fool as to imagine that "The Constant Nymph" is the most terrific tragedy ever written. Very likely his own favourite novelist, if he cares for novels at all, is Stendhal, or Dickens, or Jane Austen, or D. H. Lawrence, or Dostoievski – or at any rate, someone immeasurably better than the ordinary run of contemporary novelists. He has got to start, therefore, by immensely lowering his standards. As I have pointed out elsewhere, to apply a decent standard to the ordinary run of novels is like weighing a flea on a spring-balance intended for elephants. On such a balance as that a flea would simply fail to register; you would have to start by constructing another balance which revealed the fact that there are big fleas and little fleas. And this approximately is what X does. It is no use monotonously saying, of book after book, "This book is tripe," because, once again, no one will pay you for writing that kind of thing. X has got to discover something which is *not* tripe, and pretty frequently, or get the sack. This means sinking his standards to a depth at which, say, Ethel M. Dell's "Way of an Eagle" is a fairly good book. But on a scale of values which makes "The Way of an Eagle" a good book, "The Constant Nymph" is a superb book, and "The Man of Property" is – what? A palpitating tale of passion, a terrific, soul-shattering masterpiece, an unforgettable epic which will last as long as the English language, and so on and so forth. (As for any *really* good book, it would burst the thermometer.) Having started with the assumption that all novels are good, the reviewer is driven ever upwards on a topless ladder of adjectives. And sic itur ad Gould. You can see reviewer after reviewer going the same road. Within two years of starting out with at any rate moderately honest intentions, he is proclaiming with maniacal screams that Miss Barbara Bedworthy's "Crimson Night" is the most terrific, trenchant, poignant, unforgettable, of the earth earthy and so forth masterpiece which has ever, etc., etc., etc. There is no way out of it when you have once committed the initial sin of pretending that a bad book is a good one. But you cannot review novels for a living without committing that sin. And meanwhile every intelligent reader turns away, disgusted, and to despise novels becomes a kind of snobbish duty. Hence the queer fact that it is possible for a novel of real merit to escape notice, merely because it has been praised in the same terms as tripe.

Various people have suggested that it would be all to the good if no novels were reviewed at all. So it would, but the suggestion is useless, because nothing of the kind is going to happen. No paper which depends on publishers' advertisements can afford to throw them away, and though the more intelligent publishers probably realise that they would be no worse off if the blurb-review were abolished, they cannot put an end to it for the same reason as the nations cannot disarm – because nobody wants to be the first to start. For a long time yet the blurb-reviews are going to continue, and they are going to grow worse and worse; the only remedy is to contrive in some way that they shall be disregarded. But this can only happen if somewhere or other there is decent novel-reviewing which will act as a standard of comparison. That is to say, there is need of just *one* periodical (one would be enough for a start) which makes a speciality of novel-reviewing but refuses to take any notice of tripe, and in which the reviewers *are* reviewers and not ventriloquists' dummies clapping their jaws when the publisher pulls the string.

It may be answered that there are such periodicals already. There are quite a number of highbrow magazines, for instance, in which the novel-reviewing, what there is of it, is intelligent and not suborned. Yes, but the point is that periodicals of that kind do not make a speciality of novel-reviewing, and certainly make no attempt to keep abreast of the current output of fiction. They belong to the highbrow world, the world in which it is already assumed that novels, as such, are despicable. But the novel is a popular form of art, and it is no use to approach it with the "Criterion-Scrutiny" assumption that literature is a game of back-scratching (claws in or claws out according to circumstances) between tiny cliques of highbrows. The novelist is primarily a story-teller, and a man may be a very good story-teller (*vide* for instance Trollope, Charles Reade, Mr. Somerset Maugham) without being in the narrow sense an "intellectual." Five thousand novels are published every year, and Ralph Straus implores you to read all of them, or would if he had all of them to review. The "Criterion" probably deigns to notice a dozen. But between the dozen and the five thousand there may be a hundred or two hundred or even five hundred which at different levels have genuine merit, and it is on these that any critic who cares for the novel ought to concentrate.

But the first necessity is some method of *grading*. Great numbers of novels never ought to be mentioned at all (imagine for instance the awful effects on criticism if every serial in "Peg's Paper" had to be solemnly reviewed!), but even the ones that are worth mentioning belong to quite different categories. "Raffles" is a good book, and so is "The Island of Dr. Moreau," and so is "La Chartreuse de Parme," and so is "Macbeth"; but they are "good" at very different levels. Similarly, "If Winter Comes" and "The Well-Beloved" and "An Unsocial Socialist" and "Sir Lancelot Greaves" are all bad books, but at different levels of "badness." This is the fact that the hack-reviewer has made it his special business to obscure. It ought to be possible to devise a system, perhaps quite a rigid one, of grading novels into classes A, B, C and so forth, so that whether a reviewer praised or damned a book, you would at least know how seriously he meant it to be taken. As for the reviewers, they would have to be people who really cared for the art of the novel (and that means, probably, neither highbrows nor lowbrows nor midbrows, but elastic-brows), people interested in technique and still more interested in discovering what a book is *about*. There are plenty of such people in existence; some of the very worst of the hack-reviewers, though now past praying for, started like that, as you can see by glancing at their earlier work. Incidentally, it would be a good thing if more novel-reviewing were done by amateurs. A man who is not a practised writer but has just read a book which has deeply impressed him is more likely to tell you what it is *about* than a competent but bored professional. That is why American reviews, for all their stupidity, are better than English ones; they are more amateurish, that is to say, more serious.

I believe that in some such way as I have indicated the prestige of the novel could be restored. The essential need is a paper that would keep abreast of current fiction and yet refuse to sink its standards. It would have to be an obscure paper, for the publishers would not advertise in it; on the other hand, once they had discovered that somewhere there was praise that was real praise, they would be ready enough to quote it on their blurbs. Even if it were a very obscure paper it would probably cause the general level of novel-reviewing to rise, for the drivel in the Sunday papers only continues because there is nothing with which to contrast it. But even if the blurb-reviewers continued exactly as before, it would not matter so long as there also existed decent reviewing to remind a few people that serious brains can still occupy themselves with the novel. For just as the Lord promised that he would not destroy Sodom if ten righteous men could be found there, so the novel will not be utterly despised while it is known that somewhere or other there is even a handful of novel-reviewers with no straws in their hair.

At present, if you care about novels and still more if you write them, the outlook is depressing in the extreme. The word "novel" calls up the words "blurb," "genius" and "Ralph Straus" as automatically as "chicken" calls up "bread sauce."

Intelligent people avoid novels almost instinctively; as a result, established novelists go to pieces and beginners who "have something to say" turn in preference to almost any other form. The degeneration that must follow is obvious. Look for instance at the fourpenny novelettes that you see piled up on any cheap stationer's counter. These things are the decadent off-spring of the novel, bearing the same relation to "Manon Lescaut" and "David Copperfield" as the lap-dog bears to the wolf. It is quite likely that before long the average novel will be not much different from the fourpenny novelette, though doubtless it will still appear in a seven and sixpenny binding and amid a flourish of publishers' trumpets. Various people have prophesied that the novel is doomed to disappear in the near future. I do not believe that it will disappear, for reasons which would take too long to set forth but which are fairly obvious. It is much likelier, if the best literary brains cannot be induced to return to it, to survive in some perfunctory, despised and hopelessly degenerate form, like modern tombstones, or the Punch and Judy show.

Review of *The Novel To-Day* by Philip Henderson

New English Weekly, 31 December 1936

Mr. Philip Henderson's book, "The Novel To-Day," is a survey of the contemporary novel from a Marxist standpoint. It is not a very good book, in fact it can be described as a weaker version of Mirsky's "Intelligentsia of Great Britain," written by someone who has got to live in England and cannot afford to insult too many people, but it is of some interest because it raises the question of art and propaganda which now rumbles like a sort of "noises off" round every critical discussion.

On the last occasion when "Punch" produced a genuinely funny joke, which was only six or seven years ago, it was a picture of an intolerable youth telling his aunt that when he came down from the University he intended to "write." "And what are you going to write about, dear?" his aunt enquires. "My dear aunt," the youth replies crushingly, "one doesn't write *about* anything, one just *writes*." This was a perfectly justified criticism of current literary cant. At that time, even more than now, art for art's sake was going strong, though the phrase itself had been discarded as ninety-ish; "art has nothing to do with morality" was the favourite slogan. The artist was conceived as leaping to and fro in a moral, political and economic void, usually in pursuit of something called "Beauty," which was always one jump ahead. And the critic was supposed to be completely "impartial," *i.e.*, to deal in abstract aesthetic standards which were completely unaffected by his other prejudices. To admit that you liked or disliked a book because of its moral or religious tendency, even to admit noticing that it *had* a tendency, was too vulgar for words.

This is still the official attitude, but it is in process of being abandoned, and especially by the extremists at the opposite poles of thought, the Communist and the Catholic. Both the Communist and the Catholic usually believe, though unfortunately they do not often say, that abstract aesthetic standards are all bunkum and that a book is only a "good" book if it preaches the right sermon. To the Communist, good literature means "proletarian" literature. (Mr. Henderson is careful to explain, however, that this does not mean literature written by proletarians; which is just as well, because there isn't any.) In Henri Barbusse's "One Looks at Russia," for instance, it is stated almost in so many words that a novel about "bourgeois" characters cannot be a good novel. So expressed this is an absurdity, but in some ways it is not a bad position to take up. Any critic who stuck to it consistently would at least do useful work by dragging into the light the (often quite unaesthetic) reasons for which books are liked or disliked. But unfortunately the notion of art for art's sake, though discredited, is too recent to be forgotten, and there is always a temptation to revert to it in moments of difficulty. Hence the frightful intellectual dishonesty which can be observed in nearly all propagandist critics. They are employing a double set of values and dodging from one to the other according as it suits them. They praise or dispraise a book *because* its tendency is Communist, Catholic, Fascist or what-not; but at the same time, they pretend to be judging it on purely aesthetic grounds. Few people have the guts to say outright that art and propaganda are the same thing.

You can see this at its crudest in the so-called book-reviews in some of the Roman Catholic papers, and indeed in religious papers generally. The editorial staff of the "Church Times" gnash their false teeth and quake in their galoshes at the mention of "modern" (*i.e.*, post-Tennysonian) poetry, but strange to say they make an exception of T. S. Eliot. Eliot is a declared Anglo-Catholic, and therefore his poetry, though "modern," has got to be praised. And the Communist critic is hardly more honest. Most of the time Mr. Henderson is keeping up a pretence of strict critical impartiality, but it is strange how invariably his aesthetic judgments coincide with his political ones. Proust, Joyce, Wyndham Lewis, Virginia Woolf, Aldous Huxley, Wells, E. M. Forster (all of them "bourgeois" novelists) are patted on the head with varying degrees of contempt; Lawrence (proletarian turned bourgeois, which is worse) is viciously attacked; Hemingway, on the other hand, is treated rather respectfully (because Hemingway, you see, is rumoured to be toying with Communism); Barbusse is bowed down to; and a huge wad of mediocre stuff called "Daughters of Albion," by Mr. Alec Brown, gets pages and pages of praise all to itself, because here at last you have real "proletarian" literature – written, like all other "proletarian" literature, by a member of the middle classes.

This kind of thing is very depressing to anyone who cares for the cause of Socialism. For what is it except the most ordinary chauvinism turned upside down? It simply gives you the feeling that the Communist is no better than his opposite number. Nevertheless, these books of Marxist literary criticism have their value for anyone who wants to study the Marxist mind. The basic trouble with all orthodox Marxists is that, possessing a system which appears to explain everything, they never bother to discover what is going on inside other people's heads. That is why in every Western country, during the last dozen years, they have played straight into the hands of their adversaries. In a book of literary criticism, unlike a tract on economics, the Marxist cannot take cover behind his favourite polysyllables; he has got to come out into the open and you can see just what kind of blinkers he is wearing.

I do not recommend this particular book, which is badly written and thoroughly dull all through, but to anyone who has not yet read it I do recommend Mirsky's "Intelligentsia of Great Britain," which was published in 1935. It is a terribly malignant but very able book, and in a distorted way it performs a remarkable feat of synthesis. It is the archetype of Marxist literary criticism. And when you read it you understand – though this, of course, is not what the author intends – why Fascism arose, and why even a quite intelligent outsider can be taken in by the vulgar lie, now so popular, that "Communism and Fascism are the same thing."

Spilling the Spanish Beans
New English Weekly, 29 July and 2 September 1937

I

The Spanish war has probably produced a richer crop of lies than any event since the Great War of 1914–18, but I honestly doubt, in spite of all those hecatombs of nuns who have been raped and crucified before the eyes of "Daily Mail" reporters, whether it is the pro-Fascist newspapers that have done the most harm. It is the left-wing papers, the "News Chronicle" and the "Daily Worker," with their far subtler methods of distortion, that have prevented the British public from grasping the real nature of the struggle.

The fact which these papers have so carefully obscured is that the Spanish Government (including the semi-autonomous Catalan Government) is far more afraid of the revolution than of the Fascists. It is now almost certain that the war will end with some kind of compromise, and there is even reason to doubt whether the Government, which let Bilbao fall without raising a finger, wishes to be too victorious; but there is no doubt whatever about the thoroughness with which it is crushing its own revolutionaries. For some time past a reign of terror – forcible suppression of political parties, a stifling censorship of the Press, ceaseless espionage and mass-imprisonment without trial – has been in progress. When I left Barcelona in late June the jails were bulging; indeed, the regular jails had long since overflowed and the prisoners were being huddled into empty shops and any other temporary dump that could be found for them. But the point to notice is that the people who are in prison now are not Fascists but revolutionaries; they are there not because their opinions are too much to the Right, but because they are too much to the Left. And the people responsible for putting them there are those dreadful revolutionaries at whose very name Garvin quakes in his galoshes – the Communists.

Meanwhile the war against Franco continues, but, except for the poor devils in the front-line trenches, nobody in Government Spain thinks of it as the real war. The real struggle is between revolution and counter-revolution; between the workers who are vainly trying to hold on to a little of what they won in 1936, and the Liberal-Communist bloc who are so successfully taking it away from them. It is unfortunate that so few people in England have yet caught up with the fact that Communism is now a counter-revolutionary force; that Communists everywhere are in alliance with bourgeois reformism and using the whole of their powerful machinery to crush or discredit any party that shows signs of revolutionary tendencies. Hence the grotesque spectacle of Communists assailed as wicked "Reds" by right-wing intellectuals who are in essential agreement with them. Mr. Wyndham Lewis, for instance, ought to love the Communists, at least temporarily. In Spain the Communist–Liberal alliance has been almost completely victorious. Of all that the Spanish workers won for themselves in 1936 nothing solid remains, except for a few collective farms and a certain amount of land seized by the peasants last year; and presumably even the peasants will be sacrificed later, when there is no longer any need to placate them. To see how the present situation arose, one has got to look back to the origins of the civil war.

Franco's bid for power differed from those of Hitler and Mussolini in that it was a military insurrection, comparable to a foreign invasion, and therefore had not much mass backing, though Franco has since been trying to acquire one. Its chief supporters, apart from certain sections of Big Business, were the land-owning aristocracy and the huge, parasitic Church. Obviously a rising of this kind will array against it various forces which are not in agreement on any other point. The peasant and the worker hate feudalism and clericalism; but so does the "liberal" bourgeois, who is not in the least opposed to a more modern version of Fascism, at least so long as it isn't called Fascism. The "liberal" bourgeois is genuinely liberal up to the point where his own interests stop. He stands for the degree of progress implied in the phrase "la carrière ouverte aux talents." For clearly he has no chance to develop in a feudal society where the worker and the peasant are too poor to buy goods, where industry is burdened with huge taxes to pay for bishops' vestments, and where every lucrative job is given as a matter of course to the friend of the catamite of the duke's illegitimate son. Hence, in the face of such a blatant reactionary as Franco, you get for a while a situation in which the worker and the bourgeois, in reality deadly enemies, are fighting side by side. This uneasy alliance is known as the Popular Front (or, in the Communist Press, to give it a spuriously democratic appeal, People's Front). It is a combination with about as much vitality, and about as much right to exist, as a pig with two heads or some other Barnum and Bailey monstrosity.

In any serious emergency the contradiction implied in the Popular Front is bound to make itself felt. For even when the worker and the bourgeois are both fighting against Fascism, they are not fighting for the same things; the bourgeois is fighting for bourgeois democracy, *i.e.*, capitalism, the worker, in so far as he understands the issue, for Socialism. And in the early days of the revolution the Spanish workers understood the issue very well. In the areas where Fascism was defeated they did not content themselves with driving the rebellious troops out of the towns; they also took the opportunity of seizing land and factories and setting up the rough beginnings of a workers' government by means of local committees, workers' militias, police forces, and so forth. They made the mistake, however (possibly because most of the active revolutionaries were Anarchists with a mistrust of all parliaments), of leaving the Republican Government in nominal control. And, in spite of various changes in personnel, every subsequent Government has been of approximately the same bourgeois-reformist character. At the beginning this seemed not to matter, because the Government, especially in Cataloñia, was almost powerless and the bourgeoisie had to lie low or even (this was still happening when I reached Spain in December) to disguise themselves as workers. Later, as power slipped from the hands of the Anarchists into the hands of the Communists and right-wing Socialists, the Government was able to reassert itself, the bourgeoisie came out of hiding and the old division of society into rich and poor reappeared, not much modified. Henceforward every move, except a few dictated by military emergency, was directed towards undoing the work of the first few months of revolution. Out of the many illustrations I could choose, I will cite only one, the breaking-up of the old workers' militias, which were organised on a genuinely democratic system, with officers and men receiving the same pay and mingling on terms of complete equality, and the substitution of the Popular Army (once again, in Communist jargon, "People's Army"), modelled as far as possible on an ordinary bourgeois army, with a privileged officer-caste, immense differences of pay, etc., etc. Needless to say, this is given out as a military necessity, and almost certainly it does make for military efficiency, at least for a short period. But the undoubted purpose of the change was to strike a blow at equalitarianism. In every department the same policy has been followed, with the result that only a year after the outbreak of war and revolution you get what is in effect an ordinary bourgeois State, with, in addition, a reign of terror to preserve the status quo.

This process would probably have gone less far if the struggle could have taken place without foreign interference. But the military weakness of the Government made this impossible. In the face of Franco's foreign mercenaries they were obliged to turn to Russia for help, and though the quantity of arms supplied by Russia has been greatly exaggerated (in my first three months in Spain I saw only one Russian weapon, a solitary machine-gun), the mere fact of their arrival brought the Communists into power. To begin with, the Russian aeroplanes and guns, and the good military qualities of the International Brigades (not necessarily Communist but under Communist control), immensely raised the Communist prestige. But, more important, since Russia and Mexico were the only countries openly supplying arms, the Russians were able not only to get money for their weapons, but to extort terms as well. Put in their crudest form, the terms were: "Crush the revolution or you get no more arms." The reason usually given for the Russian attitude is that if Russia appeared to be abetting the revolution, the Franco-Soviet pact (and the hoped-for alliance with Great Britain) would be imperilled; it may be, also, that the spectacle of a genuine revolution in Spain would rouse unwanted echoes in Russia. The Communists, of course, deny that any direct pressure has been exerted by the Russian Government. But this, even if true, is hardly relevant, for the Communist Parties of all countries can be taken as carrying out Russian policy; and it is certain that the Spanish Communist Party, plus the right-wing Socialists whom they control, plus the Communist Press of the whole world, have used all their immense and ever-increasing influence upon the side of counter-revolution.

II

In the first half of this article I suggested that the real struggle in Spain, on the Government side, has been between revolution and counter-revolution; that the Government, though anxious enough to avoid being beaten by Franco, has been even more anxious to undo the revolutionary changes with which the outbreak of war was accompanied.

Any Communist would reject this suggestion as mistaken or wilfully dishonest. He would tell you that it is nonsense to talk of the Spanish Government crushing the revolution, because the revolution never happened; and that our job at present is to defeat Fascism and defend democracy. And in this connection it is most important to see just how the Communist anti-revolutionary propaganda works. It is a mistake to think that this has no relevance in England, where the Communist Party is small and comparatively weak. We shall see its relevance quickly enough if England enters into an alliance with the U.S.S.R.; or perhaps even earlier, for the influence of the Communist Party is bound to increase – visibly is increasing – as more and more of the capitalist class realise that latter-day Communism is playing their game.

Broadly speaking, Communist propaganda depends upon terrifying people with the (quite real) horrors of Fascism. It also involves pretending – not in so many words, but by implication – that Fascism has nothing to do with capitalism. Fascism is just a kind of meaningless wickedness, an aberration, "mass sadism," the sort of thing that would happen if you suddenly let loose an asylum-ful of homicidal maniacs. Present Fascism in this form, and you can mobilise public opinion against it, at any rate for a while, without provoking any revolutionary movement. You can oppose Fascism by bourgeois "democracy," meaning capitalism. But meanwhile you have got to get rid of the troublesome person who points out that Fascism and bourgeois "democracy" are Tweedledum and Tweedledee. You do it at the beginning by calling him an impracticable visionary. You tell him that he is confusing the issue, that he is splitting the anti-Fascist forces, that this is not the moment for revolutionary phrase-mongering, that for the moment we have got to fight against Fascism without enquiring too closely what we are fighting *for*. Later, if he still refuses to shut up, you change your tune and call him a traitor. More exactly, you call him a Trokskyist.

And what is a Trotskyist? This terrible word – in Spain at this moment you can be thrown into jail and kept there indefinitely, without trial, on the mere rumour that you are a Trotskyist – is only beginning to be bandied to and fro in England. We shall be hearing more of it later. The word "Trotskyist" (or "Trotsky-Fascist") is generally used to mean a disguised Fascist who poses as an ultra-revolutionary in order to split the Left-wing forces. But it derives its peculiar power from the fact that it means three separate things. It can mean one who, like Trotsky, wishes for world-revolution; or a member of the actual organization of which Trotsky is head (the only legitimate use of the word); or the disguised Fascist already mentioned. The three meanings can be telescoped one into the other at will. Meaning No. 1 may or may not carry with it meaning No. 2, and meaning No. 2 almost invariably carries with it meaning No. 3. Thus: "XY. has been heard to speak favourably of world-revolution; therefore he is a Trotskyist; therefore he is a Fascist." In Spain, to some extent even in England, *anyone* professing revolutionary Socialism (*i.e.*, professing the things the Communist Party professed until a few years ago) is under suspicion of being a Trotskyist in the pay of Franco or Hitler.

The accusation is a very subtle one, because in any given case, unless one happened to know the contrary, it might be true. A Fascist spy probably *would* disguise himself as a revolutionary. In Spain, everyone whose opinions are to the Left of those of the Communist Party is sooner or later discovered to be a Trotskyist or, at least, a traitor. At the beginning of the war the P.O.U.M., an Opposition Communist party roughly corresponding to the English I.L.P., was an accepted party and supplied a minister to the Catalan Government; later it was expelled from the Government; then it was denounced as Trotskyist; then it was suppressed, every member that the police could lay their hands on being flung into jail.

Until a few months ago the Anarcho-Syndicalists were described as "working loyally" beside the Communists. Then the Anarcho-Syndicalists were levered out of the Government; then it appeared that they were not working so loyally; now they are in the process of becoming traitors. After that will come the turn of the Left-wing Socialists. Caballero, the Left-wing Socialist ex-premier, until May, 1937, the idol of the Communist Press, is already in outer darkness, a Trotskyist and "enemy of the people." And so the game continues. The logical end is a régime in which every opposition party and newspaper is suppressed and every dissentient of any importance is in jail. Of course, such a régime will be Fascism. It will not be the same as the Fascism Franco would impose, it will even be better than Franco's Fascism to the extent of being worth fighting for, but it will be Fascism. Only, being operated by Communists and Liberals, it will be called something different.

Meanwhile, can the war be won? The Communist influence has been against revolutionary chaos and has therefore, apart from the Russian aid, tended to produce greater military efficiency. If the Anarchists saved the Government from August to October, 1936, the Communists have saved it from October onwards. But in organizing the defence they have succeeded in killing enthusiasm (inside Spain, not outside). They made a militarized conscript army possible, but they also made it necessary. It is significant that as early as January of this year voluntary recruiting had practically ceased. A revolutionary army can sometimes win by enthusiasm, but a conscript army has got to win with weapons, and it is unlikely that the Government will ever have a large preponderance of arms unless France intervenes or unless Germany and Italy decide to make off with the Spanish colonies and leave Franco in the lurch. On the whole, a deadlock seems the likeliest thing.

And does the Government seriously intend to win? It does not intend to lose, that is certain. On the other hand, an outright victory, with Franco in flight and the Germans and Italians driven into the sea, would raise difficult problems, some of them too obvious to need mentioning. There is no real evidence and one can only judge by the event, but I suspect that what the Government is playing for is a compromise that would leave the war-situation essentially in being. All prophecies are wrong, therefore this one will be wrong, but I will take a chance and say that though the war may end quite soon or may drag on for years, it will end with Spain divided up, either by actual frontiers or into economic zones. Of course, such a compromise might be claimed as a victory by either side, or by both.

All that I have said in this article would seem entirely commonplace in Spain, or even in France. Yet in England, in spite of the intense interest the Spanish war has aroused, there are very few people who have even heard of the enormous struggle that is going on behind the Government lines. Of course, this is no accident. There has been a quite deliberate conspiracy (I could give detailed instances) to prevent the Spanish situation from being understood. People who ought to know better have lent themselves to the deception on the ground that if you tell the truth about Spain it will be used as Fascist propaganda.

It is easy to see where such cowardice leads. If the British public had been given a truthful account of the Spanish war they would have had an opportunity of learning what Fascism is and how it can be combatted. As it is, the "News Chronicle" version of Fascism as a kind of homicidal mania peculiar to Colonel Blimps bombinating in the economic void has been established more firmly than ever. And thus we are one step nearer to the great war "against Fascism" (cf. 1914, "against militarism") which will allow Fascism, British variety, to be slipped over our necks during the first week.

Unpublished Response to
Authors Take Sides on the Spanish War
[3–6 August 1937]

Response to a questionnaire sent out for *Left Review* by Nancy Cunard.

Will you please stop sending me this bloody rubbish. This is the second or third time I have had it. I am not one of your fashionable pansies like Auden and Spender, I was six months in Spain, most of the time fighting, I have a bullet-hole in me at present and I am not going to write blah about defending democracy or gallant little anybody. Moreover, I know what is happening and has been happening on the Government side for months past, i.e. that Fascism is being riveted on the Spanish workers under the pretext of resisting Fascism; also that since May a reign of terror has been proceeding and all the jails and any place that will serve as a jail are crammed with prisoners who are not only imprisoned without trial but are half-starved, beaten and insulted. I dare say you know it too, though God knows anyone who could write the stuff overleaf would be fool enough to believe anything, even the war-news in the Daily Worker. But the chances are that you – whoever you are who keep sending me this thing – have money and are well-informed; so no doubt you know something about the inner history of the war and have deliberately joined in the defence of "democracy" (i.e. capitalism) racket in order to aid in crushing the Spanish working class and thus indirectly defend your dirty little dividends.

This is more than 6 lines, but if I did compress what I know and think about the Spanish war into 6 lines you wouldn't print it. You wouldn't have the guts.

By the way, tell your pansy friend Spender that I am preserving specimens of his war-heroics and that when the time comes when he squirms for shame at having written it, as the people who wrote the war-propaganda in the Great War are squirming now, I shall rub it in good and hard.

1938

Notes on the Spanish Militias

I joined the POUM militia at the end of 1936. The circumstances of my joining this militia rather than any other were the following. I had intended going to Spain to gather materials for newspaper articles etc., and had also some vague idea of fighting if it seemed worth while, but was doubtful about this owing to my poor health and comparatively small military experience. Just before I started someone told me I should not be able to cross the frontier unless I had papers from some leftwing organisation (this was untrue at that time although party cards etc. undoubtedly made it easier). I applied to John Strachey who took me to see Pollitt. P after questioning me evidently decided that I was politically unreliable and refused to help me, also tried to frighten me out of going by talking a lot about Anarchist terrorism. Finally he asked whether I would undertake to join the International Brigade. I said I could not undertake to join anything until I had seen what was happening. He then refused to help me but advised me to get a safe-conduct from the Spanish Embassy in Paris, which I did. Just before leaving England I also rang up the ILP, with which I had some slight connections, mainly personal, and asked them to give me some kind of recommendation. They sent me to Paris a letter addressed to John McNair at Barcelona. When I crossed the frontier the passport people and others, at that time Anarchists, did not pay much attention to my safe-conduct but seemed impressed by the letter with ILP heading, which they evidently knew by sight. It was this that made me decide to produce my letter to McNair (whom I did not know) and through this that I joined the POUM militia. After one glimpse of the troops in Spain I saw that I had relatively a lot of training as a soldier and decided to join the militia. At that time I was only rather dimly aware of the differences between the political parties, which had been covered up in the English leftwing press. Had I had a complete understanding of the situation I should probably have joined the CNT militia.

At this time the militias, though theoretically being recast on an ordinary army basis, were still organised in column, centuria, seccion, the centuria of about 100 men more or less centring round some individual and often being called "So-and-so's bandera". The commander of the centuria ranked more or less as captain, but below that there was no well-defined rank except corporal and private. People wore stripes etc. of rank in Barcelona but it was "not done" to wear them at the front. Theoretically promotion was by election, but actually the officers and NCOs were appointed from above. As I shall point out later this does not in practice make much difference. One peculiar feature however was that a man could choose which section he should belong to and as a rule could also change to another bandera if he wanted to. At that time men were being sent into the line with only a few days' training and that of a parade-ground kind, and in many cases without ever having fired a rifle. I had brought with me ordinary British Army ideas and was appalled by the lack of discipline. It is [of] course always difficult to get recruits to obey orders and becomes much more so when they find themselves thrust into trenches and having to put up with cold etc. which they are not accustomed to. If they have not had a chance to familiarise themselves with firearms they are often much more afraid of bullets than they need be and this is an added source of indiscipline. (Incidentally a lot of harm was done by the lies published in the leftwing papers to the effect that the Fascists were using explosive bullets. So far as I know there is no such thing as an explosive bullet, and certainly the Fascists weren't using them.) At the beginning one had to get orders obeyed (a) by appealing to party loyalty and (b) by force of personality, and for the first week or two I made myself thoroughly unpopular. After about a week a man flatly refused to go to a certain place which he declared was exposed to fire, and I made him do so by force – always a mistake, of course, and doubly so with a Spaniard. I was immediately surrounded by a ring of men calling me a Fascist. There was a tremendous argument, however most of the men took my side and I found that people rather competed to join my section. After this, for some weeks or months, both among the Spaniards and the few English who were on this front, this kind of thing recurred over and over again. Ie. indiscipline, arguments as to what was justifiable and what was "revolutionary", but in general a consensus of opinion that one must have strict discipline combined with social equality. There was always a lot of argument as to whether it was justifiable to shoot men for desertion and disobedience, and in general people agreed that it was, though some would never do so. Much later, about March, near Huesca, some 200 CNT troops suddenly decided to walk out of the line. One could hardly blame them as they had been there about five months, but obviously such a thing could not be allowed and there was a call for some POUM troops to go and stop them. I volunteered though not feeling very happy about it. Fortunately they were persuaded to go back by their political delegates or somebody, so it never came to violence. There was a lot of argument about this, but again the majority agreed that it would be justifiable to use one's rifle against men doing this if necessary. Throughout this period, ie. January–April 1937 the gradual improvement in discipline was brought about almost entirely by "diffusion of revolutionary consciousness", ie. endless arguments and explanations as to *why* such and such a thing was necessary. Everyone was fanatically keen on keeping social equality between officers and men, no military titles and no differences of food etc., and this was often carried to lengths that were rather ridiculous, though they seemed less ridiculous in the line where minute differences of comfort were very appreciable. When the militias were theoretically incorporated in the Popular Army all officers were expected to pay their extra pay ie. anything over 10 pesetas a day, into the Party funds, and everyone agreed to do so, though whether this actually happened I don't know, because I am not certain whether anyone actually began drawing extra pay before the POUM militia was redistributed. Punishments for disobedience were, however, being used even at the time when I first reached the front. It is extremely difficult to punish men who are already in the front line, because short of killing them it is hard to make them more uncomfortable than they are already. The usual punishment was double hours of sentry-go – very unsatisfactory because everyone is already short of sleep. Occasionally men were shot. One man who attempted to cross to the Fascist lines and was clearly a spy was shot. Another

caught stealing from other militiamen was sent back supposedly to be shot, though I don't think he actually was. Courts
martial were supposed to consist of one officer, one NCO and
one militiaman, though I never saw one in action.

Periodically political delegates used to be sent round by the
Party to visit the men in the line and, when possible, deliver
[some] sort of political discourses. In addition every centuria
had one or more men in its own ranks who were called its
political delegates. I never grasped what the function of these
men had originally been – they had evidently at the beginning
had some function for which there was afterwards no need.
When with the ILP English I was appointed their political
delegate, but by this time the political delegate was simply a
go-between who was sent to headquarters to complain about
rations etc., and therefore so far as the English were concerned
it was simply a question of choosing among the few men who
spoke Spanish. The English were stricter than the Spaniards
about electing officers and in one or two cases changed an
NCO by election. They also appointed a committee of 5 men
who were supposed to regulate all the affairs of the section.
Although I was voted onto the committee myself I opposed its
formation on the ground that we were now part of an army
being commanded from above in more or less the ordinary
way, and therefore such a committee had no function. Actually
it had no important function but was occasionally useful for
regulating very small matters. Contrary to what is generally
believed the political leaders of the POUM were very hostile to
this committee idea and were anxious to prevent the idea
spreading from the English to the Spaniards.

Before joining the English I was some weeks in a Spanish
bandera, and of about 80 men in it some 60 were completely
raw recruits. In these weeks the discipline improved a good
deal, and from then on till the end of April there was a slow but
fairly steady improvement in discipline throughout the militia.
By April a militia unit when it had to march anywhere still
looked like a retreat from Moscow, but this was partly because
the men had been experienced solely in trench warfare. But by
this time there was no difficulty in getting an order obeyed and
no fear that it would be disobeyed as soon as your back was
turned. Outwardly the special "revolutionary" characteristics

remained the same till the end of May, but in fact certain differences were showing themselves by this time. In May when I was commanding a section (which now meant a platoon) the younger Spaniards called me "usted". I pulled them up about it but the word was evidently coming back, and no doubt the universal use of tu in the early months of the war was an affectation and would seem most unnatural to a Latin people. One thing that seemed to stop abruptly about March was the shouting of revolutionary slogans to the Fascists. This was not practised at Huesca, though in many cases the trenches were very close together. On the Zaragoza front it had been practised regularly and probably had its share in bringing in the deserters who were very numerous there (at one time about 15 a week on a section of front held by about 1000 men). But the universal use of "camarada" and the notion that we were all supposed to be equals persisted until the militia was redistributed. It was noticeable that the first drafts of the Popular Army who came up to the line conformed with this. Between the POUM and PSUC militias, up to the time when I last saw the latter at the beginning of March, there was no perceptible difference in state of discipline and social atmosphere.

The general organisation was in some ways very good but in others quite unnecessarily incompetent. One striking feature about this war was the good food organisation. Up till May 1937 when certain things began to give out the food was always good, and it was always regular, a thing not easy to arrange even in a very stationary war. The cooks were very devoted, sometimes bringing food up under heavy fire. I was impressed by the food-organisation behind the lines and the way in which the peasants had been got to co-operate. The men's clothes were laundered from time to time, but it was not done very well or very regularly. The postal arrangements were good and letters which had started from Barcelona always got to the front promptly, though an extraordinary number of letters sent into Spain went astray somewhere on the way to Barcelona. Ideas of sanitation practically did not exist and no doubt only the dry climate prevented epidemics. There was no medical service worth mentioning till one got about 10 miles behind the lines. This did not matter so long as there was only a small trickle of casualties, but even so many lives were lost unnecessarily. Trenches were at the beginning extremely primitive but about March a labour battalion was organised. This was very efficient and able to construct long sections of trench very rapidly and without noise. Nevertheless up to about May there was not much idea of communication-trenches, even where the front line was near the enemy, and it was not possible, eg., to get wounded men away without carrying them under fire. No effort was made to keep the roads behind the line in repair, although, no doubt, the labour to do so was available. The POUM Red Aid, to which it was voluntary-compulsory to subscribe, were very good about looking after wounded men in hospital etc. In regard to stores, there was probably some peculation and favouritism, but I think extremely little. When cigarettes began to run short the little English section received rather more than their fair share, a tribute to the Spanish character. The grand and inexcusable mistake made in this war, at any rate on the Aragón front, was to keep the men in the line for unnecessarily long periods. By Xmas 1936 the war was almost entirely stationary and for long periods during the next six months there was little fighting. It should therefore have been perfectly possible to organise the four days in four days out, or even four days in two days out, system. On this arrangement men do not actually get more hours of rest but they do periodically get a few nights in bed or at any rate with the chance to take their clothes off. As it was men were sometimes kept as long as five months in the line continuously. It sometimes happened that trenches were a long way from the enemy, say 1000 yards, but this is more boring and therefore worse for morale than being at 50–100 yards. Meanwhile they were sleeping in trenches in intolerable discomfort, usually lousy and up till April almost always cold. Moreover even when one is 1000 yards from the enemy one is under rifle and occasional shell fire, causing a trickle of casualties and therefore fear which is cumulative. In these circumstances it is difficult to do more than keep on keeping on. During February–March, the period when there was little fighting round Huesca, attempts were made to train the men in various things, use of the machine gun, signalling, open-order work (advancing by rushes etc.) etc. These were mainly a failure because everyone was suffering from lack of sleep and too exhausted to learn. I myself at this time tried to master the mechanism of the Hotchkiss machine gun and found that lack of sleep had simply deprived me of the power to learn. In addition it would no doubt have been feasible to grant leave at shorter intervals, but the failure to do so probably had reasons other than incompetence. But it would have been quite easy to take the men in and out of trenches as I have indicated, and to provide some kind of amenities for the troops not in the line. Even as far back as Barbastro the life of the troops was much drearier than it need have been. With a little organisation it would have been possible to arrange immediately behind the lines for hot baths, delousing, entertainments of some kind, cafes (actually there were some very feeble attempts at these) and also women. The very few women who were in or near the line and were getatable were simply a source of jealousy. There was a certain amount of sodomy among the younger Spaniards. I doubt whether troops can simultaneously engage in trench warfare and be trained for mobile warfare, but more training would certainly have been possible if more care had been devoted to resting the men. As it was they were exhausted for nothing at a period when the war was stagnant. Looking back I see that they stood it extremely well, and even at the time it was the fact that they did *not* disintegrate or show mutinous tendencies under these intolerable conditions that converted me (to some extent) to the notion of "revolutionary discipline". Nevertheless the strain that was put upon them was partly unnecessary.

As to jealousies between the different militias, so far as the rank and file were concerned I myself did not see serious signs of these till May 1937. To what extent the Aragón front was sabotaged from political motives I suppose we shall learn sooner or later. I do not know how important the capture of Huesca would have been, but there is little doubt that it could have been taken in February or March with adequate artillery. As it was it was surrounded except for one gap about a km. wide, and this with so little artillery that preliminary bombardments were an impossibility, as they would only have served as a warning. This meant that attacks could only be surprise attacks delivered by a few hundred men at most. By the beginning of April Huesca appeared to be doomed, but the gap was never closed, the attacks petered out and a little later it became clear that the Fascist trenches were more strongly held and that they had improved their defences. At the end of June the big attack on Huesca was staged, clearly from political motives, to provide the Popular Army with a victory and discredit the CNT militia. The result was what could have been foreseen – heavy losses and an actual worsening of the position. But as far as rank and file were concerned party-feeling did not usually get beyond vague rumours that "they", usually meaning the PSUC, had stolen guns etc. meant for ourselves. On the Zaragoza front where POUM and PSUC militia were distributed more or less alternately relations were good. When the POUM took over a sector from the PSUC at Huesca there were signs of jealousy, but this I think was purely military, the PSUC troops having failed to take Huesca and the POUM boasting that they were going to do so. The Guadala-jara victory in February could be regarded as, and in fact was, a Communist victory, but everyone was unaffectedly glad and in fact enthusiastic. A little later than this one of our aeroplanes, presumably Russian, dropped a bomb in the wrong place and killed a number of POUM militiamen. Later, no doubt, it would have been said that this was "done on purpose", but at the time this did not occur to anybody. About May, perhaps following on the Barcelona trouble, relations worsened. In Lérida, where large numbers of the new Popular Army forma-tions were in training, when detachments of Popular Army marched past, I saw militiamen of I do not know what militia giving them raspberries and bleating in imitation of sheep. As to victimisation of men known to have served with the POUM, I doubt whether it began until after the alleged espi-onage discoveries. Immediately after these there appear to have been one or two serious incidents. About the end of June it seems that a detachment of PSUC militia were sent or came of their own accord to attack one of the POUM positions outside Huesca, and the men at the latter had to defend themselves with their machine guns. I have not either the exact date or more than general facts of this, but the source from which I had it leaves me in no doubt that it happened. It was no doubt the result of irresponsible statements in the press about espionage, desertion, etc., which had caused or almost caused trouble on earlier occasions.

The fact that the militias were organised by and owed loyalty to different parties had bad effects after a certain date. At the beginning, when everyone was full of enthusiasm, inter-party rivalry was perhaps not a bad thing – this impression at least I derived from those who were in the earlier fighting when Siétamo etc. were taken. But when the militias were dwindling as against the Popular Army the effect was to make every party anxious to keep its strength up at no matter what cost. I believe that this was one reason for the fact, noted above, that leave was not granted as often as it might have been. Up till about June there was in reality no way of making a man who had gone on leave rejoin his unit, and conscription into the Popular Army, if passed into law (I forget when exactly it was passed) was completely ineffective. Therefore a militiaman once on leave could simply go home, and he had the more motive to do so as he had just drawn a big wad of back-pay, or he could join another organisation, which was often done at that time. In practice most men returned from leave, but some did not, so that every spell of leave meant a dwindling of numbers. In addition, I am certain that anxiety to keep up numbers made local commanders over-anxious not to incur casualties when they could not gain eclat by incurring them. On the Zaragoza front valuable minor opportunities – the kind of thing that would not have got into the papers but would have made a certain difference – were lost owing to this, while such casualties as did occur were completely pointless. Also the useless riff-raff, amounting to five or ten per cent, who are to be found in all bodies of troops and who should be got rid of ruthlessly, were seldom or never got rid of. In January when I complained about the state of discipline a higher-up officer gave me his opinion that all the militias competed in slackness of discipline in order to detach recruits from the others. I don't know whether this was true or said owing to momentary fed-upness.

As to the personnel of the POUM militia, I doubt whether it was much different from the others. In standard of physique, which is a rough test, they were about equal to the PSUC. The POUM did not ask party affiliation from their militiamen, doubtless because being a minority party they found it hard to attract recruits. When the men were in the line efforts were made to get them to join the party, but it is fair to say that there was no kind of pressure. There was the usual proportion of riff-raff, and in addition a certain number of very ignorant peasants and people of no particular political alignment who had prob-ably joined the POUM militia more or less by accident. In addition there was a certain number of people who had simply joined for the sake of a job. The fact that in December 1936 there was already a serious bread shortage in Barcelona and militiamen got bread in plenty had a lot to do with this. Nevertheless some of these nondescripts afterwards turned into quite good soldiers. Apart from a rather large number of refugee Germans there was a sprinkling of foreigners of many races, even including a few Portuguese. Putting aside the Germans, the best soldiers were usually the machine-gunners, who were organised in crews of six and kept rather apart from the others. The fetishistic attitude which men in this position develop towards their gun, rather as towards a household god, is interesting and should be studied. A few of the machine-gunners were old soldiers who had done their service over and over again owing to the Spanish substitute system, but most of them were "good party men", some of them men of extremely high character and intelligence. I came to the conclusion, somewhat against my will, that in the long run "good party men" make the best soldiers. The detachment of in all about 30 English and Americans sent out by the ILP were divided rather sharply between old soldiers of no particular political affili-ations and "good party men" with no military experience. As I am nearer to the first type myself I am probably not prejudiced in saying that I believe the second to be superior. Old soldiers are of course more useful at the beginning of a campaign, and they are all right when there is any fighting, but they have more tendency to go to pieces under inaction and physical exhaus-tion. A man who has fully identified with some political party is reliable in *all* circumstances. One would get into trouble in leftwing circles for saying so, but the feeling of many Socialists towards their party is very similar to that of the thicker-headed type of public school man towards his old school. There are individuals who have no particular political feelings and are completely reliable, but they are usually of bourgeois origin. In the POUM militia there was a slight but perceptible tendency for people of bourgeois origin to be chosen as officers. Given the existing class-structure of society I regard this as inevitable. Middle-class and upper-class people have usually more self-confidence in unfamiliar circumstances, and in countries where conscription is not in force they usually have more military tradition than the working class. This is notably the case in England. As to age, 20 to 35 seems to be the proper age for front-line soldiers. Above 35 I would not trust anybody in the line as a common soldier or junior officer unless he is of known political reliability. As for the younger limit, boys as young as 14 are often very brave and reliable, but they simply cannot stand the lack of sleep. They will even fall asleep standing up.

As to treachery, fraternisation, etc., there were just enough rumours about this to suggest that such things happened occasionally, and in fact they are inevitable in civil war. There were vague rumours that at some time pre-arranged truces had been held in no man's land for exchange of newspapers. I do not know of an instance of this but once saw some Fascist papers which might have been procured in this manner. The stories circulated in the Communist press about non-aggression pacts and people coming and going freely between our lines and the Fascists were lies. There was undoubtedly treachery among the peasants. The reason why no attack on this front ever came off at the time scheduled was no doubt partly incompetence, but it was also said that if the time was fixed more than a few hours ahead it was invariably known to the Fascists. The Fascists always appeared to know what troops they had opposite them, whereas we only knew what we could infer from patrols etc. I do not know what method was used by spies for getting messages into Huesca, but the method of sending messages out was flash-lamp signalling. There were morse code signals at a certain hour every night. These were always recorded, but except for slogans such as Viva Franco they were always in cipher. I don't know whether they were successfully deciphered. The spies behind the lines were never caught, in spite of many attempts. Desertions were very rare, though up to May 1937 it would have been easy to walk out of the line, or with a little risk, across to the Fascists. I knew of a few desertions among our men and a few among the PSUC, but the whole number would have been tiny. It is noticeable that men in a force of this type retain political feeling against the enemy as they would not in an ordinary army. When I first reached the front it was taken for granted that officer-prisoners taken by us must be shot, and the Fascists were said to shoot all prisoners – a lie, no doubt, but the significant thing was that people believed it. As late as March 1937 I heard credibly of an officer-prisoner taken by us being shot – again the significant thing is that no one seemed to think this wrong.

As to the actual performance of the POUM militia, I know of this chiefly from others, as I was at the front during the most inactive period of the war. They took part in the taking of Siétamo and the advance on Huesca, and after this the division was split up, some at Huesca, some on the Zaragoza front and a few at Teruel. I believe there was also a handful on the Madrid front. In late February the whole division was concentrated on the eastern side of Huesca. Tactically this was the less important side, and during March–April the part played by the POUM was only raids and holding attacks, affairs involving at most two hundred men and a few score casualties. In some of these they did well, especially the refugee Germans. In the attack on Huesca at the end of June the division lost heavily, 4–600 killed. I was not in this show but heard from others who were that the POUM troops behaved well. By this time the campaigns in the press had begun to produce a certain amount of disaffection. By April even the politically uninterested had grasped that except in their own press and that of the Anarchists no good would be reported of them, whatever their actual performance might be. At the time this produced only a certain irritation, but I know that later, when the division was redistributed, some men who were able to dodge the conscription did so and got civilian jobs on the ground that they were tired of being libelled. A number of men who were in the Huesca attack assured me that General Pozas deliberately withheld the artillery to get as many POUM troops killed as possible – doubtless untrue, but showing the effect of campaigns like that conducted by the Communist press. I do not know what happened to the division after being redistributed, but believe they mostly went to the 26th division. Considering the circumstances and their opportunities, I should say that the performance of the POUM militia was respectable though in no way brilliant.

Review of *Assignment in Utopia* by Eugene Lyons
New English Weekly, 9 June 1938

To get the full sense of our ignorance as to what is really happening in the U.S.S.R., it is worth trying to translate the most sensational Russian event of the past two years, the Trotskyist trials, into English terms. Make the necessary adjustments, let Left be Right and Right be Left, and you get something like this:

Mr. Winston Churchill, now in exile in Portugal, is plotting to overthrow the British Empire and establish Communism in England. By the use of unlimited Russian money he has succeeded in building up a huge Churchillite organisation which includes members of Parliament, factory managers, Roman Catholic bishops and practically the whole of the Primrose League. Almost every day some dastardly act of sabotage is laid bare – sometimes a plot to blow up the House of Lords, sometimes an outbreak of foot and mouth disease in the Royal racing-stables. Eighty per cent. of the Beef-eaters at the Tower are discovered to be agents of the Comintern. A high official of the Post Office admits brazenly to having embezzled postal orders to the tune of £5,000,000, and also to having committed *lèse majesté* by drawing moustaches on postage stamps. Lord Nuffield, after a 7-hour interrogation by Mr. Norman Birkett, confesses that ever since 1920 he has been fomenting strikes in his own factories. Casual half-inch paras in every issue of the newspapers announce that fifty more Churchillite sheep-stealers have been shot in Westmorland or that the proprietress of a village shop in the Cotswolds has been transported to Australia for sucking the bullseyes and putting them back in the bottle. And meanwhile the Churchillites (or Churchillite-Harmsworthites as they are called after Lord

Rothermere's execution) never cease from proclaiming that it is *they* who are the real defenders of Capitalism and that Chamberlain and the rest of his gang are no more than a set of Bolsheviks in disguise.

Anyone who has followed the Russian trials knows that this is scarcely a parody. The question arises, could anything like this happen in England? Obviously it could not. From our point of view the whole thing is not merely incredible as a genuine conspiracy, it is next door to incredible as a frame-up. It is simply a dark mystery, of which the only seizable fact – sinister enough in its way – is that Communists over here regard it as a good advertisement for Communism.

Meanwhile the truth about Stalin's régime, if we could only get hold of it, is of the first importance. Is it Socialism, or is it a peculiarly vicious form of state-capitalism? All the political controversies that have made life hideous for two years past really circle round this question, though for several reasons it is seldom brought into the foreground. It is difficult to go [to] Russia, once there it is impossible to make adequate investigations, and all one's ideas on the subject have to be drawn from books which are so fulsomely "for" or so venomously "against" that the prejudice stinks a mile away. Mr. Lyons's book is definitely in the "against" class, but he gives the impression of being much more reliable than most. It is obvious from his manner of writing that he is not a vulgar propagandist, and he was in Russia a long time (1928–34) as correspondent for the United Press Agency, having been sent there on Communist recommendation. Like many others who have gone to Russia full of hope he was gradually disillusioned, and unlike some others he finally decided to tell the truth about it. It is an unfortunate fact that any hostile criticism of the present Russian régime is liable to be taken as propaganda *against Socialism*; all Socialists are aware of this, and it does not make for honest discussion.

The years that Mr. Lyons spent in Russia were years of appalling hardship, culminating in the Ukraine famine of 1933, in which a number estimated at not less than three million people starved to death. Now, no doubt, after the success of the Second Five Year Plan, the physical conditions have improved, but there seems no reason for thinking that the social atmosphere is greatly different. The system that Mr. Lyons describes does not seem to be very different from Fascism. All real power is concentrated in the hands of two or three million people, the town proletariat, theoretically the heirs of the revolution, having been robbed even of the elementary right to strike; more recently, by the introduction of the internal passport system, they have been reduced to a status resembling serfdom. The G.P.U. are everywhere, everyone lives in constant terror of denunciation, freedom of speech and of the press are obliterated to an extent we can hardly imagine. There are periodical waves of terror, sometimes the "liquidation" of kulaks or Nepmen, sometimes some monstrous state trial at which people who have been in prison for months or years are suddenly dragged forth to make incredible confessions, while their children publish articles in the newspapers saying "I repudiate my father as a Trotskyist serpent." Meanwhile the invisible Stalin is worshipped in terms that would have made Nero blush. This – at great length and in much detail – is the picture Mr. Lyons presents, and I do not believe he has misrepresented the facts. He does, however, show signs of being embittered by his experiences, and I think he probably exaggerates the amount of discontent prevailing among the Russians themselves.

He once succeeded in interviewing Stalin, and found him human, simple and likeable. It is worth noticing that H. G. Wells said the same thing, and it is a fact that Stalin, at any rate on the cinematograph, has a likeable face. Is it not also recorded that Al Capone was the best of husbands and fathers, and that Joseph Smith (of Brides in the Bath fame) was sincerely loved by the first of his seven wives and always returned to her between murders?

Why I Join the I.L.P.

The New Leader, 24 June 1938

Perhaps it will be frankest to approach it first of all from the personal angle.

I am a writer. The impulse of every writer is to "keep out of politics." What he wants is to be left alone so that he can go on writing books in peace. But unfortunately it is becoming obvious that this ideal is no more practicable than that of the petty shopkeeper who hopes to preserve his independence in the teeth of the chain-stores.

To begin with, the era of free speech is closing down. The freedom of the Press in Britain was always something of a fake, because in the last resort, money controls opinion; still, so long as the legal right to say what you like exists, there are always loopholes for an unorthodox writer. For some years past I have managed to make the Capitalist class pay me several pounds a week for writing books against Capitalism. But I do not delude myself that this state of affairs is going to last for ever. We have seen what has happened to the freedom of the Press in Italy and Germany, and it will happen here sooner or later. The time is coming – not next year, perhaps not for ten or twenty years, but it is coming – when every writer will have the choice of being silenced altogether or of producing the dope that a privileged minority demands.

I have got to struggle against that, just as I have got to struggle against castor oil, rubber truncheons and concentration-camps. And the only regime which, in the long run, will dare to permit freedom of speech is a Socialist regime. If Fascism triumphs I am finished as a writer – that is to say, finished in my only effective capacity. That of itself would be a sufficient reason for joining a Socialist party.

I have put the personal aspect first, but obviously it is not the only one.

It is not possible for any thinking person to live in such a society as our own without wanting to change it. For perhaps ten years past I have had some grasp of the real nature of Capitalist society. I have seen British Imperialism at work in Burma, and I have seen something of the effects of poverty and unemployment in Britain. In so far as I have struggled against the system, it has been mainly of writing books which I hoped would influence the reading public. I shall continue to do that, of course, but at a moment like the present writing books is not enough. The tempo of events is quickening; the dangers which once seemed a generation distant are staring us in the face. One has got to be actively a Socialist, not merely sympathetic to

Socialism, or one plays into the hands of our always-active enemies.

Why the I.L.P. more than another?

Because the I.L.P. is the only British party – at any rate the only one large enough to be worth considering – which aims at anything I should regard as Socialism.

I do not mean that I have lost all faith in the Labour Party. My most earnest hope is that the Labour Party will win a clear majority in the next General Election. But we know what the history of the Labour Party has been, and we know the terrible temptation of the present moment – the temptation to fling every principle overboard in order to prepare for an Imperialist war. It is vitally necessary that there should be in existence some body of people who can be depended on, even in face of persecution, not to compromise their Socialist principles.

I believe that the I.L.P. is the only party which, as a party, is likely to take the right line either against Imperialist war or against Fascism when this appears in its British form. And meanwhile the I.L.P. is not backed by any monied interest, and is systematically libelled from several quarters. Obviously it needs all the help it can get, including any help I can give it myself.

Finally, I was with the I.L.P. contingent in Spain. I never pretended, then or since, to agree in every detail with the policy the P.O.U.M. put forward and the I.L.P. supported, but the general course of events has borne it out. The things I saw in Spain brought home to me the fatal danger of mere negative "anti-Fascism." Once I had grasped the essentials of the situation in Spain I realised that the I.L.P. was the only British party I felt like joining – and also the only party I could join with at least the certainty that I would never be led up the garden path in the name of Capitalist democracy.

Review of *The Civil War in Spain* by Frank Jellinek

The New Leader, 8 July 1938

Frank Jellinek's book on the Paris Commune had its faults, but it revealed him as a man of unusual mind. He showed himself able to grasp the real facts of history, the social and economic changes that underlie spectacular events, without losing touch with the picturesque aspect which the bourgeois historian generally does so much better. On the whole his present book – *The Civil War in Spain* – bears out the promise of the other. It shows signs of haste, and it contains some misrepresentations which I will point out later, but it is probably the best book on the Spanish war from a Communist angle that we are likely to get for some time to come.

Much the most useful part of the book is the earlier part, describing the long chain of causes that led up to the war and the fundamental issues at stake. The parasitic aristocracy and the appalling condition of the peasants (before the war 65 per cent. of the population of Spain held 6.3 per cent. of the land, while 4 per cent. held 60 per cent. of it), the backwardness of Spanish capitalism and the dominance of foreign capitalists, the corruption of the Church, and the rise of the Socialist and Anarchist labour movements – all these are treated in a series of brilliant chapters. The short biography which Mr. Jellinek gives of Juan March, the old tobacco-smuggler who is one of the men behind the Fascist rebellion (although, queerly enough, he is believed to be a Jew), is a wonderful story of corruption. It would be fascinating reading if March were merely a character in Edgar Wallace; unfortunately he happens to be a real man.

The chapter on the Church does not leave much doubt as to why practically all the churches in Catalonia and eastern Aragon were burnt at the outbreak of war. Incidentally, it is interesting to learn that, if Mr. Jellinek's figures are correct, the world organization of the Jesuits only numbers about 22,000 people. For sheer efficiency they must surely have all the political parties in the world beaten hollow. But the Jesuits' "man of affairs" in Spain is, or was, on the board of directors of forty-three companies!

At the end of the book there is a well-balanced chapter on the social changes that took place in the first few months of the war, and an appendix on the collectivisation decree in Catalonia. Unlike the majority of British observers, Mr. Jellinek does not under-rate the Spanish Anarchists. In his treatment of the P.O.U.M., however, there is no doubt that he is unfair, and – there is not much doubt of this either – intentionally unfair.

Naturally I turned first of all to the chapter describing the fighting in Barcelona in May, 1937, because both Mr. Jellinek and myself were in Barcelona at the time, and this gave me a measure of checking his accuracy. His account of the fighting is somewhat less propagandist than those that appeared in the Communist Press at the time, but it is certainly one-sided and would be very misleading to anyone who knew nothing of the facts. To begin with, he appears at times to accept the story that the P.O.U.M. was really a disguised Fascist organisation, and refers to "documents" which "conclusively proved" this and that, without telling us any more about these mysterious documents – which, in fact, have never been produced. He even refers to the celebrated "N" document (though admitting that "N" probably did not stand for Nin), and ignores the fact that Irujo, the Minister of Justice, declared this document to be "worthless," i.e., a forgery. He states merely that Nin was "arrested," and does not mention that Nin disappeared and was almost certainly murdered. Moreover, he leaves the chronology uncertain and – whether intentionally or not – gives the impression that the alleged discovery of a Fascist plot, the arrest of Nin, etc., took place *immediately after* the May fighting.

This point is important. The suppression of the P.O.U.M. did *not* occur immediately after the May fighting. There was a five weeks' interval. The fighting ended on May 7 and Nin was arrested on June 15. The suppression of the P.O.U.M. only occurred after, and almost certainly as a result of, the change in the Valencia Government. I have noticed several attempts in the Press to obscure these dates. The reason is obvious enough; however, there can be no doubt about the matter, for all the main events were recorded in the newspapers at the time.

Curiously enough, about June 20, the "Manchester Guardian" correspondent in Barcelona sent here a despatch in which he contradicted the absurd accusations against the P.O.U.M. – in the circumstances a very courageous action. This correspondent must almost certainly have been Mr. Jellinek himself. What a pity that for propaganda purposes he should now find it necessary to repeat a story which after this lapse of time seems even more improbable.

His remarks on the P.O.U.M. occupy a considerable share of the book, and they have an air of prejudice which would be obvious even to anyone who knew nothing whatever about the Spanish political parties. He thinks it necessary to denigrate even useful work such as that done by Nin as Councillor of Justice, and is careful not to mention that the P.O.U.M. took any serious part either in the first struggles against the Fascist rising or at the front. And in all his remarks about the "provocative attitude" of the P.O.U.M. newspapers it hardly seems to occur to him that there was any provocation on the other side. In the long run this kind of thing defeats its own object. Its effect on me, for instance, is to make me think: "If I find that this book is unreliable where I happen to know the facts, how can I trust it where I don't know the facts?" And many others will think the same.

Actually I am quite ready to believe that in the main Mr. Jellinek is strictly fair besides being immensely well-informed. But in dealing with "Trotskyism" he writes as a Communist, or Communist partisan, and it is no more possible for a Communist to-day to show common sense on this subject than on the subject of "Social Fascism" a few years ago. Incidentally, the speed with which the angels in the Communist mythology turn into devils has its comic side. Mr. Jellinek quotes approvingly a denunciation of the P.O.U.M. by the Russian Consul in Barcelona, Antonov Ovseenko, now on trial as a Trotskyist!

All in all, an excellent book, packed full of information and very readable. But one has got to treat it with a certain wariness, because the author is under the necessity of showing that though other people may sometimes be right, the Communist Party is always right. It does not greatly matter that nearly all books by Communists are propaganda. Most books are propaganda, direct or indirect. The trouble is that Communist writers are obliged to claim infallibility for their Party chiefs. As a result Communist literature tends more and more to become a mechanism for explaining away mistakes.

Unlike most of the people who have written of the Spanish war, Mr. Jellinek really knows Spain: its language, its people, its

territories, and the political struggle of the past hundred years.
Few men are better qualified to write an authoritative history
of the Spanish war. Perhaps some day he will do so. But it will
probably be a long time hence, when the "Trotsky-Fascist"
shadow-boxing has been dropped in favour of some other
hobby.

[Orwell was mistaken in thinking the *Manchester Guardian* correspondent
was Jellinek. On 13 January 1939, he wrote a letter of correction to *The
New Leader*, which was printed under the heading "A Mistake Corrected."]

In my review of Mr. Frank Jellinek's *Civil War in Spain* I
stated that Mr. Jellinek had expressed certain opinions which
were in contradiction to one of his own despatches to the
Manchester Guardian. I now find that this despatch was actually
sent not by Mr. Jellinek, but by another correspondent. I am
very sorry about this mistake and hope you will find space for
this correction.

Political Reflections on the Crisis
The Adelphi, December 1938

In all the controversies over the Popular Front, the question
least often debated has been whether such a combination could
actually win an election.

It was obvious enough from the start that a Popular Front in
England would be something quite different from the French
Popular Front, which was brought into being by an *internal*
Fascist threat. If it were formed it would be, more or less
avowedly, for the purpose of war against Germany. What was
the use of saying that collective security and so forth meant
peace and not war? Nobody believed it. The point really under
debate was whether left-wingers ought to support a war which
meant bolstering up British imperialism. The advocates of the
Popular Front shouted "Stop Hitler!" and its opponents
shouted "No line-up with capitalists!" But both seem to have

taken it for granted that if a Popular Front were formed the British public would vote for it.

Then came the war crisis. What happened? It is too early to say with absolute certainty, but if the signs are worth anything the crisis revealed two things. One, that the British people will go to war if they are told to; the other, that they don't want war and will vote against any party which stamps itself as a war party. When Chamberlain came back from Munich he was not booed and execrated but greeted by miles of cheering people. And it does not greatly matter that afterwards, when all was safe, there was a certain revulsion, on the strength of which Labour may win a few by-elections. In the decisive moment the mass of the people swung over to Chamberlain's side, and if the General Election revives the spirit of the crisis, as in all probability it will, they will do the same again. And yet for two years past the *News Chronicle*, the *Daily Worker*, *Reynold's*, the *New Statesman*, and the sponsors of the Left Book Club had been deluding themselves and part of their public that the entire British nation, barring a few old gentlemen in West End Clubs, wanted nothing better than a ten-million-dead war in defence of democracy.

Why was it possible for a mistake of such magnitude to be made? Mainly because a small body of noise-makers can for a while give the impression that they are more numerous than they are. The mass of the people are normally silent. They do not sign manifestoes, attend demonstrations, answer questionnaires or even join political parties. As a result it is very easy to mistake a handful of slogan-shouters for the entire nation. At first sight a membership of 50,000 for the Left Book Club *looks* enormous. But what is 50,000 in a population of 50,000,000? To get a real idea of the balance of forces one ought not to be watching those 5,000 people who are making a noise in the Albert Hall: one ought to be watching those 5,000,000 outside who are saying nothing, but who are quite possibly thinking, and who will cast their votes at the next election. It is just this that propaganda organisations such as the Left Book Club tend to prevent. Instead of trying to assess the state of public opinion they reiterate that they *are* public opinion, and they and a few people round them end by believing it.

The net result of Strachey and Company's efforts has been to give a totally false estimate of what the English people were thinking, and to push the leaders of the Labour Party a little further on the road to war. In doing so they have gone some distance towards losing Labour the election.

(ii)

So far as one can judge from the French Press, it seems clear that nobody in France, except the Communists and M. Kerillis, seriously wished for war. I think events showed that the English people did not wish for war either; but it would be absurd to pretend that there was not in England an influential minority which wished very ardently for war and howled with disappointment when they did not get it. And by no means all of these people were Communists.

A type that seems to be comparatively rare in France is the war-hungry middle-class intellectual. Why should this type be commoner in one country than in the other? One can think of several subsidiary reasons, but the question can probably be answered satisfactorily with a single word: Conscription.

Compared with England, France is a democratic country, there are fewer privileges attaching to status, and military service is not at all easy to dodge. Nearly every adult Frenchman has done his service and has the harsh discipline of the French army well fixed in his memory. Unless he is over age or in an exceptionally sheltered position, war means to him something quite different from what it means to a middle-class Englishman. It means a notice on the wall, "Mobilisation Generale," and three weeks later, if he is unlucky, a bullet in his guts. How can such a man go about irresponsibly declaring that "we" ought to declare war on Germany, Japan and anyone else who happens to be handy? He is bound to regard war with a fairly realistic eye.

One could not possibly say the same of the English intelligentsia. Of all the left-wing journalists who declare day in and day out that if this, that and the other happens "we" must fight, how many imagine that war will affect them personally? When war breaks out they will be doing what they are doing at present, writing propaganda articles. Moreover, they are well aware of this. The type of person who writes articles for the political Left has no feeling that "war" means something in which he will actually get hurt. "War" is something that happens on paper, a diplomatic manoeuvre, something which is of course very deplorable but is "necessary" in order to destroy Fascism. His part in it is the pleasantly stimulating one of writing propaganda articles. Curiously enough, he may well be wrong. We do not yet know what a big-scale air-raid is like, and the next war may turn out to be very unpleasant even for journalists. But these people, who have been born into the monied intelligentsia and feel in their bones that they belong to a privileged class, are not really capable of foreseeing any such thing. War is something that happens on paper, and consequently they are able to decide that this or that war is "necessary" with no more sense of personal danger than in deciding on a move at chess.

Our civilisation produces in increasing numbers two types, the gangster and the pansy. They never meet, but each is necessary to the other. Somebody in eastern Europe "liquid-ates" a Trotskyist; somebody in Bloomsbury writes a justifica-tion of it. And it is, of course, precisely because of the utter softness and security of life in England that the yearning for bloodshed – bloodshed in the far distance – is so common among our intelligentsia. Mr. Auden can write about "the acceptance of guilt for the necessary murder" because he has never committed a murder, perhaps never had one of his friends murdered, possibly never even seen a murdered man's corpse. The presence of this utterly irresponsible intelligentsia, who "took up" Roman Catholicism ten years ago, "take up" Com-munism to-day and will "take up" the English variant of Fascism a few years hence, is a special feature of the English situation. Their importance is that with their money, influence and literary facility they are able to dominate large sections of the Press.

(iii)

Barring some unforeseen scandal or a really large disturb-ance inside the Conservative Party, Labour's chances of win-ning the General Election seem very small. If any kind of Popular Front is formed, its chances are probably less than those of Labour unaided. The best hope would seem to be that if Labour *is* defeated, the defeat may drive it back to its proper "line."

But the time-factor is all-important. The National Government is preparing for war. No doubt they will bluff, shuffle and make further concessions in order to buy a little more time – still, they are preparing for war. A few people cling to the belief that the Government's war preparations are all a sham or even that they are directed against Soviet Russia. This is mere wish-thinking. What really inspires it is the knowledge that when Chamberlain goes to war with Germany (in defence of democracy, of course) he will be doing what his opponents demand and thus taking the wind out of their sails. The attitude of the British governing class is probably summed up in the remark I overheard recently from one of the Gibraltar garrison: "It's coming right enough. It's pretty clear Hitler's going to have Czechoslovakia. Much better let him have it. We shall be ready by 1941." In fact, the difference between the warmongers of the right and the warmongers of the left is merely strategic.

The real question is *how soon* the Labour Party will start effectively opposing the Government's war plans. Suppose that war actually breaks out. Some of the more soft-boiled left-wing papers have recently been discussing the "conditions" on which the Labour Party should "support" the Government in case of war. As though any Government at war could permit its subjects to make "conditions"! Once war has started the left-wing parties will have the choice of offering unconditional loyalty or being smashed. The only group large enough to be capable of resisting, and perhaps even of scaring the Government away from war, is the Labour Party. But if it does not begin soon it may never do so. Two years, even a year, of tacit acquiescence in preparation for war, and its power will have been broken.

When and if Labour loses the election, the cry will be raised that if we had had a Popular Front the election could have been won. This may obscure the issue for a long time, perhaps even for two years. Hence more Popular Frontism, more brandishing of fists and shouts for a "firm line," more clamour for overwhelming armaments – in short, more pushing of the Government in the direction in which it is going. So long as Labour demands a "firm line" which entails the risk of war, it cannot make any but a sham resistance to the fascising process which war-preparation implies. What is the use of asking for a "strong" foreign policy and at the same time pretending to oppose increased working hours, reduced wages, Press censorship and even conscription? The retort will always be the same: "How can we keep Hitler in check if you obstruct rearmament?" War, and even war-preparation, can be used as an excuse for anything, and we may be sure the Government will make full use of its opportunities. In the end a perception of what is happening may drive the Labour Party back to its proper "line." But how soon will that end come?

On September 28th the National Council of Labour made one of the few sensible moves that were made during the whole war-crisis. It appealed over the radio to the German people to resist Hitler. The appeal did not go far enough, it was self-righteous in tone and contained no admission that British capitalism, like German Nazism, has its faults; but it did at least show some perception of the right method of approach. What hope is there of that method being followed up if the Labour Party continues much longer on the path of jingoism and imperialism? It may be that sooner or later the mere fact of being in opposition will drive the Labour Party back to an anti-militarist and anti-imperialist line. But it will have to be sooner and not later. If it continues much longer in its present anomalous position, its enemies will eat it up.

Review of *Gypsies* by Martin Block; translated by Barbara Kuczynski and Duncan Taylor

The Adelphi, December 1938

M. Martin Block's book deals mainly with the gypsies of southeastern Europe, who are far more numerous and evidently live at a much more primitive level than those of England. They use tents, oxen and pack animals rather than horses and caravans, never sit on chairs, are dirty beyond belief, speak Romany among themselves and follow hereditary trades such as locksmithing, bear-leading and the making of wooden spoons and basins. Rather unfortunately M. Block does not include a chapter on the Romany language, but much of the information he has compiled is profoundly interesting, and his photographs, unlike the "illustrations" in the majority of books, do really illustrate. It is a pity that, so far as I know, no one has produced an equally detailed and up-to-date book on the gypsies of England.

As a matter of fact, the existence of this primitive nomadic people, with strongly marked racial characteristics, in a crowded country like England is a very curious thing. Why do they continue being gypsies? According to all precedent they ought long ago to have been seduced by the delights of civilisation. In England the "true" gypsies probably own rather more property and live at a slightly higher level than the average farm labourer, but they can only follow their distinctive way of life by constantly breaking the law. One is obliged to conclude that they do it because they like it. A gypsy makes part of his living by begging, and consequently, when he thinks he can get anything out of you, he is offensively servile, pours out gross flatteries and exploits his picturesqueness and even his bad English. But if you happen to meet gypsies on equal terms – or, at any rate, when they have nothing to gain by flattering you – you get a totally different impression. So far from being envious of the industrial civilisation which they see about them, they are merely contemptuous of it. They despise the "gorgios" for their physical softness, their bad sexual morals and, above all, their lack of liberty. To serve in the army, for instance, seems to them merely a despicable slavery. They have preserved most of the mental characteristics of a nomadic people, including a complete lack of interest in the future and the past. Hence the curious fact that though they first appeared in Europe as late as the fifteenth century, no one knows for certain where they came from. Perhaps it is not fanciful to say that the gypsy is, in the West, the nearest existing approach to the Noble Savage. And considering their admirable physique, their strict morals – strict according to their own peculiar code, that is – and their love of liberty, one must admit that they have a strain of nobility.

They also appear to be fairly successful in surviving. M. Block estimates that the number of gypsies in the world, if one includes the gypsy tribes of India, is about five millions, and that in Europe alone, counting only "true" gypsies, *i.e.*, those who are wholly or partly of gypsy blood, the number would be from one to one-and-a-half million. There are supposed to be 18,000 in Great Britain and 100,000 in the U.S.A. Considering that any nomadic population is necessarily small, these are respectable numbers.

Will they survive? M. Block's book seems to have been originally published in 1937, but unfortunately it says nothing about the effect on the gypsies of the recent political changes in Europe. There seem to be very few gypsies in Germany proper, but there is a considerable number in Austria and also in Russia. What is Hitler doing about the gypsies? Or Stalin? It seems almost impossible that the totalitarian régimes will fail to persecute these people on the pretext of civilising them. In the past they have survived countless attempts to stamp them out. "There is no country in western or central Europe," says M. Block, "which has not tried to get rid of gypsies by means of cruelty and persecution. None, however, has succeeded." But the terrifying thing about modern methods of persecution is that we cannot be sure, as yet, that they will not succeed. The Inquisition failed, but there is no certainty that the "liquidation" of Jews and Trotskyists will fail. It may be that the wretched gypsies, like the Jews, are already serving as a corpus vile, and it is only because they do not have friends who own newspapers that we hear nothing about it. Perhaps the concentration camps are already crowded with them. If so, let us hope that they survive it. No civilised person would wish for an instant to imitate the gypsies' habits, but that is not the same as saying that one would like to see them disappear. Existing in the teeth of a civilisation which disapproves of them, they are a heartening reminder of the largeness of the earth and the power of human obstinacy.

1939

Review of *Power: A New Social Analysis* by Bertrand Russell

The Adelphi, January 1939

If there are certain pages of Mr. Bertrand Russell's book, *Power*, which seem rather empty, that is merely to say that we have now sunk to a depth at which the restatement of the obvious is the first duty of intelligent men. It is not merely that at present the rule of naked force obtains almost everywhere. Probably that has always been the case. Where this age differs from those immediately preceding it is that a liberal intelligentsia is lacking. Bully-worship, under various disguises, has become a universal religion, and such truisms as that a machine-gun is still a machine-gun even when a "good" man is squeezing the trigger – and that in effect is what Mr. Russell is saying – have turned into heresies which it is actually becoming dangerous to utter.

The most interesting part of Mr. Russell's book is the earlier chapters in which he analyses the various types of power – priestly, oligarchical, dictatorial and so forth. In dealing with the contemporary situation he is less satisfactory, because like all liberals he is better at pointing out what is desirable than at explaining how to achieve it. He sees clearly enough that the essential problem of to-day is "the taming of power" and that no system except democracy can be trusted to save us from unspeakable horrors. Also that democracy has very little meaning without approximate economic equality and an educational system tending to promote tolerance and tough-mindedness. But unfortunately he does not tell us how we are to set about getting these things; he merely utters what amounts to a pious hope that the present state of things will not endure. He is inclined to point to the past; all tyrannies have collapsed sooner or later, and "there is no reason to suppose (Hitler) more permanent than his predecessors."

Underlying this is the idea that common sense always wins in the end. And yet the peculiar horror of the present moment is that we cannot be sure that this is so. It is quite possible that we are descending into an age in which two and two will make five when the Leader says so. Mr. Russell points out that the huge system of organised lying upon which the dictators depend keeps their followers out of contact with reality and therefore tends to put them at a disadvantage as against those who know the facts. This is true so far as it goes, but it does not prove that the slave-society at which the dictators are aiming will be unstable. It is quite easy to imagine a state in which the ruling caste deceive their followers without deceiving themselves. Dare anyone be sure that something of the kind is not coming into existence already? One has only to think of the sinister possibilities of the radio, State-controlled education and so forth, to realise that "the truth is great and will prevail" is a prayer rather than an axiom.

Mr. Russell is one of the most readable of living writers, and it is very reassuring to know that he exists. So long as he and a few others like him are alive and out of jail, we know that the world is still sane in parts. He has rather an eclectic mind, he is capable of saying shallow things and profoundly interesting things in alternate sentences, and sometimes, even in this book, he is less serious than his subject deserves. But he has an essentially *decent* intellect, a kind of intellectual chivalry which is far rarer than mere cleverness. Few people during the past thirty years have been so consistently impervious to the fashionable bunk of the moment. In a time of universal panic and lying he is a good person to make contact with. For that reason this book, though it is not so good as *Freedom and Organisation*, is very well worth reading.

Review of *Russia under Soviet Rule*
by N. de Basily
New English Weekly, 12 January 1939

"Russia under Soviet Rule" falls definitely into the "anti" class of books on the U.S.S.R., but for once it is not Trotskyist. The author – an exile, of course – holds approximately the same opinions as Kerensky and the others of the Provisional Government of 1917, with which he was associated in an official capacity. He is therefore attacking the Bolshevik experiment not from a Socialist but from a liberal-capitalist standpoint, rather as Gaetano Salvemini attacks the Fascist experiment of Italy. His book might almost, in fact, be a companion-volume to "Under the Axe of Fascism." In the last analysis it is doubtful whether any liberal criticism of a totalitarian system is really relevant; it is rather like accusing the Pope of being a bad Protestant. However, as the dictators are generally dishonest enough to claim the liberal virtues on top of the totalitarian ones, they certainly lay themselves open to attacks of this kind.

The author, it should be noticed, though hostile to the Bolshevik régime, does not think that it is going to collapse in the near future. His main thesis is that it has functioned inefficiently and that the loss of liberty and enormous suffering which it has caused were largely unnecessary. The modernisation of industry and agriculture which Stalin has undertaken is, according to Mr. de Basily, simply a continuation of something that was already happening in pre-war Russia, and the rate of progress has actually been slowed down rather than advanced by the revolution. It is of course obvious that a statement of this kind cannot be finally proved or disproved. Even to begin to examine it is to sink into a bog of statistics – and incidentally this book contains more figures, mainly from Soviet sources, and longer footnotes than any book I have read for years. But it is worth being reminded that Russia was already being fairly rapidly modernised in the ten years or so preceding the revolution. It is now, perhaps, beginning to be possible to see the Russian revolution in some kind of historical perspective, and the hitherto-accepted version of a barbarous feudal country turning overnight into a sort of super-America is something that will probably have to be revised.

But is life – life for the ordinary person – any better in Russia than it was before? That is the thing that it seems almost impossible for an outsider to be certain about. Statistics, even when they are honestly presented (and how often does that happen nowadays?), are almost always misleading, because one never knows what factors they leave out of account. To give a crude illustration, it would be easy to show, by stating the figures for fuel-consumption and saying nothing about the temperature, that everyone in Central Africa is suffering from cold. Who does not know those Soviet statistics, published by Mr. Gollancz and others, in which the curve of everything except mortality goes up and up and up? And how much do they really tell one? Mr. de Basily's statistics, naturally, point a different moral, but, without in the least questioning the accuracy of his figures, I would not infer too much from them. As far as the material side of life goes, all that seems to emerge fairly certainly is this: that the standard of living was rising during the N.E.P. period, dropped during the period 1928–33, and is now rising again but is still low by western European standards. This is denied by Soviet apologists, but not very convincingly. The average wage in 1936 was only 225 roubles a month – the purchasing-power of the rouble being about threepence. Moreover, it is well-known that it is next door to impossible for a Soviet citizen, unless on some kind of official mission, to visit any foreign country – a silent admission that life is more comfortable elsewhere.

If Mr. de Basily were merely claiming that twenty years of Bolshevik rule had failed to raise the general standard of living, his criticism would be hardly worth making. After all, one could not reasonably expect an experiment on such a scale to work perfectly at the beginning. Economically the Bolsheviks have been far more successful than any outsider would have prophesied in 1918. But the intellectual, moral and political developments – the ever-tightening party dictatorship, the muzzled press, the purges, the oriental worship of Stalin – are a different matter. Mr. de Basily devotes a good many chapters to this. He is, nevertheless, comparatively optimistic, because, as a liberal, he takes it for granted that the "spirit of freedom" is bound to revive sooner or later. He even believes that this is happening already:

"The thirst for liberty, the notion of self-respect . . . all these features and characteristics of the old Russian élite are beginning to be appropriated by the intellectuals of to-day . . . The moment the Soviet élite opens its fight for emancipation of the human individual, the vast popular masses will be at its side."

But will they? The terrifying thing about the modern dictatorships is that they are something entirely unprecedented. Their end cannot be foreseen. In the past every tyranny was sooner or later overthrown, or at least resisted, because of "human nature," which as a matter of course desired liberty. But we cannot be at all certain that "human nature" is constant. It may be just as possible to produce a breed of men who do not wish for liberty as to produce a breed of hornless cows. The Inquisition failed, but then the Inquisition had not the resources of the modern state. The radio, press-censorship, standardised education and the secret police have altered everything. Mass-suggestion is a science of the last twenty years, and we do not yet know how successful it will be.

It is noticeable that Mr. de Basily does not attribute all the shortcomings of the present Russian régime to Stalin's personal wickedness. He thinks that they were inherent from the very start in the aims and nature of the Bolshevik party. It is probably a good thing for Lenin's reputation that he died so early. Trotsky, in exile, denounces the Russian dictatorship, but he is probably as much responsible for it as any man now living, and there is no certainty that as a dictator he would be preferable to Stalin, though undoubtedly he has a much more interesting mind. The essential act is the rejection of democracy – that is, of the underlying values of democracy; once you have decided upon that, Stalin – or at any rate something *like* Stalin – is already on the way. I believe this opinion is gaining ground, and I hope it will continue to do so. If even a few hundred thousand people can be got to grasp that it is useless to overthrow Tweedledum in order to set up Tweedledee, the talk of "democracy versus Fascism" with which our ears are deafened may begin to mean something.

Review of *Communism and Man* by F. J. Sheed
Peace News, 27 January 1939

This book – a refutation of Marxian Socialism from the Catholic standpoint – is remarkable for being written in a good temper. Instead of employing the abusive misrepresentation which is now usual in all major controversies, it gives a fairer exposition of Marxism and Communism than most Marxists could be trusted to give of Catholicism. If it fails, or at any rate ends less interestingly than it begins, this is probably because the author is less ready to follow up his own intellectual implications than those of his opponents.

As he sees clearly enough, the radical difference between Christian and Communist lies in the question of personal immortality. Either this life is a preparation for another, in which case the individual soul is all-important, or there is no life after death, in which case the individual is merely a replaceable cell in the general body. These two theories are quite irreconcilable, and the political and economic systems founded upon them are bound to be antagonistic.

What Mr. Sheed is not ready to admit, however, is that acceptance of the Catholic position implies a certain willingness to see the present injustices of society continue. He seems to claim that a truly Catholic society would contain all or most of what the Socialist is aiming at – which is a little too like "having it both ways."

Individual salvation implies liberty, which is always extended by Catholic writers to include the right to private property. But in the stage of industrial development which we have now reached, the right to private property means the right to exploit and torture millions of one's fellow-creatures. The Socialist would argue, therefore, that one can only defend private property if one is more or less indifferent to economic justice.

The Catholic's answer to this is not very satisfactory. It is not that the Church condones the injustices of Capitalism – quite the contrary. Mr. Sheed is quite right in pointing out that several Popes have denounced the Capitalist system very bitterly, and that Socialists usually ignore this. But at the same time the Church refuses the only solution that is likely to make any real difference. Private property is to remain, the employer–employee relationship is to remain, even the categories "rich" and "poor" are to remain – but there is to be justice and fair distribution. In other words, the rich man is not to be expropriated, he is merely to be told to behave himself.

"(The Church) does not see men primarily as exploiters and exploited, with the exploiters as people whom it is her duty to overthrow...from her point of view the rich man as sinner is the object of her most loving care. Where others see a strong man in the pride of success, she sees a poor soul in danger of hell ... Christ has told her that the souls of the rich are in special danger; and care for souls is her primary work."

The objection to this is that *in practice* it makes no difference. The rich man is called to repentance, but he never repents. In this matter Catholic capitalists do not seem to be perceptibly different from the others.

It is obvious that any economic system would work equitably if men could be trusted to behave themselves but long experience has shown that in matters of property only a tiny minority of men will behave any better than they are compelled to do. This does not mean that the Catholic attitude toward property is untenable, but it does mean that it is very difficult to square with economic justice. In practice, accepting the Catholic standpoint means accepting exploitation, poverty, famine, war and disease as part of the natural order of things.

It would seem, therefore, that if the Catholic Church is to regain its spiritual influence, it will have to define its position more boldly. Either it will have to modify its attitude toward private property, or it will have to say clearly that its kingdom is not of this world and that feeding bodies is of very small importance compared with saving souls.

In effect it does say something of the kind, but rather uneasily, because this is not the message that modern men want to hear. Consequently for some time past the Church has been in an anomalous position, symbolized by the fact the Pope almost simultaneously denounces the Capitalist system and confers decorations on General Franco.

Meanwhile this is an interesting book, written in a simple style and remarkably free from malice and cheap witticisms. If all Catholic apologists were like Mr. Sheed, the Church would have fewer enemies.

Review of *The Clue of History* by John Macmurray

The Adelphi, February 1939

The main argument of Professor Macmurray's book can be stated thus:

The necessary and inevitable movement of human society is towards world-communism. The chief obstacle is the persistence of "dualism," from which only the Jewish consciousness has shown itself free. Consequently the Jewish mind, chiefly *via* its offspring, Christianity, has been the sole agent of human progress. Fascism, especially Hitler's version, is the last effort of the western world to escape its destiny. It will inevitably frustrate itself, and Hitler's special function is to destroy the bases of western life and usher in the Jewish Kingdom of Heaven in the form of a society of free and equal human beings.

I personally would agree with Professor Macmurray that humanity must move in the direction of Communism or perish, and that in practice it will not perish. But it is impossible not to take notice of the special rôle he assigns to the Jews. This is the central theme of the book, and as at this moment it has a particular importance, it is worth pointing out what very shaky grounds it rests upon.

Professor Macmurray begins by saying that the Hebrew culture is the only example of a religious culture that the world has seen. He makes no mention of Hinduism, though clearly one can only say that the Hebrew culture was religious and the Hindu culture un-religious if one argues in a circle and adds that by "religious" one means "Hebrew." Some such argument is, in fact, necessary to Professor Macmurray, because he is also claiming that the "religious consciousness" is incompatible with acceptance of class-divisions. Obviously this would rule out Hinduism, though caste ought not to be identified with class. But here one comes on a serious difficulty. What evidence is there that the "Jewish consciousness" either is or ever has been freer from "dualism" than any other? The Palestine Jews may have been free from the familiar dualism of this world–next world; certainly there is no clear mention of an after life in the Old Testament; but in their attitude towards *this* world they seem to have been slaves to the most incorrigible dualism of all, because they saw everything in terms of Jew–Gentile. So far from having more sense of human brotherhood than most nations, they appear to have had none whatever. The Old Testament is largely a literature of hatred and self-righteousness. No duties towards foreigners are recognised, extermination of enemies is enjoined as a religious duty, Jehovah is a tribal deity of the worst type. Finally there appears the arch-heretic Jesus, whom Professor Macmurray describes as the culminating point of the "Jewish consciousness." And yet it was precisely the Jews who rejected Jesus more decisively than any of the pagan nations.

When it comes to the rôle of the Jews in modern times, Professor Macmurray seems at times to be in danger of succumbing to a kind of racial mysticism. To begin with he speaks throughout of the "Jewish consciousness," the "Greek consciousness," and so forth, as though these were entities of known worth like coins or chessmen. Moreover, he seems to be suggesting that the "Jewish consciousness" – developing, no doubt, but recognisably the same thing – has persisted from Biblical times until the present. If this is true it makes nonsense of Marxism, which Professor Macmurray seems to accept. After all, how much has a typical modern Jew, a New York solicitor, say, in common with some bloodthirsty nomad of the Bronze Age? Is there really such a thing as the "Jewish consciousness"? According to Professor Macmurray, the great truth which Hitler has discovered is that "the source of all this pressure towards progress, equality, freedom and common humanity is – the Jew." A little later he seems to contradict this by accusing the Jews of "exclusive racialism" by which they are "self-isolated from the community of mankind." But in any case, what evidence is there that the Jews have done more or less for human progress than anyone else? One might perhaps argue that the motive force behind every progressive movement has been the teaching of Jesus, and that Jesus was a Jew; but the first statement is very doubtful and the second needs a lot of qualification. There have always been Jews in the Socialist movement, and Marx was a Jew of sorts, but one could hardly call Socialism a Jewish movement. How little Russian

Communism is a Jewish movement has just been strikingly illustrated. In the middle of an atrocious persecution, the Jewish refugees show no desire whatever to go to Russia; in fact, they will go anywhere else in preference. And in this, of course, they are reacting not as Jews but as western Europeans. In fact, is not the truth about the Jews something like this: that because in the past they have been persecuted and have followed the oriental practice of not intermarrying with foreigners, they are just different enough from their neighbours to be unpopular and to make useful scapegoats?

As to Professor Macmurray's interpretation of Christianity, it is coherent in itself but hardly seems to be borne out by the recorded teachings of Jesus. Briefly, he represents Christianity as entirely *this-worldly* and seems to assert that Jesus did not believe in personal immortality, which is negatived not only by what Jesus said but still more decisively by what he failed to say. I do not know whether this matters greatly, because, in practice, every reading of the Gospels depends on an arbitrary selection of texts. But the fathering of human progress on to the Jews, because of the results which it is capable of having, is rather a different matter.

It will be seen that Professor Macmurray is saying that Hitler is right. This he readily admits. The "Jewish consciousness" is "poison" to the Aryan races and Hitler's perception of this is "the proof of his genius." The only difference is that whereas Hitler disapproves of what is happening, Professor Macmurray approves. I do not know whether it has occurred to him that if this issue really existed, or were believed to exist, nearly everyone would side with Hitler. Professor Macmurray says, "the thought of the triumph of the Jewish consciousness fills me with joyous exhilaration." It would not have that effect upon other people. If one could popularise the idea that western civilisation is being sapped away through the influence of an alien race, the result would be to make the whole world throw itself at Hitler's feet. One does not damage a theory by standing it on its head. To say that Hitler has discovered the truth but is playing the part of Lucifer is simply to encourage anti-semitism. This is the worst possible moment for airing theories about "the Jews" as a mysterious and, from a western point of view, sinister entity. Even more at this moment than at most times it is important to remind people that the Jews are human beings before they are Jews.

Of course this does not invalidate Professor Macmurray's theory. He may be right, and Hitler after his fashion may be right. But considering the evil results of saying so, I doubt whether one ought to advance a theory of this kind if one is obliged to base it on such very shadowy evidence as the "Jewish consciousness," the "Greek consciousness" and the "Roman consciousness" – things which it is impossible to define and which probably do not exist.

Democracy in the British Army
The Left Forum, September 1939

When the Duke of Wellington described the British army as "the scum of the earth, enlisted for drink," he was probably speaking no more than the truth. But what is significant is that his opinion would have been echoed by any non-military Englishman for nearly a hundred years subsequently.

The French Revolution and the new conception of "national" war changed the character of most Continental armies, but England was in the exceptional position of being immune from invasion and of being governed during most of the nineteenth century by non-military bourgeoisie. Consequently its army remained, as before, a small professional force more or less cut off from the rest of the nation. The war-scare of the sixties produced the Volunteers, later to develop into the Territorials, but it was not till a few years before the Great War that there was serious talk of universal service. Until the late nineteenth century the total number of white troops, even in wartime, never reached a quarter of a million men, and it is probable that every great British land battle between Blenheim and Loos was fought mainly by foreign soldiers.

In the nineteenth century the British common soldier was usually a farm labourer or slum proletarian who had been driven into the army by brute starvation. He enlisted for a period of at least seven years – sometimes as much as twenty-one years – and he was inured to a barrack life of endless drilling, rigid and stupid discipline, and degrading physical punishments. It was virtually impossible for him to marry, and even after the extension of the franchise he lacked the right to vote. In Indian garrison towns he could kick the "niggers" with impunity, but at home he was hated or looked down upon by the ordinary population, except in wartime, when for brief periods he was discovered to be a hero. Obviously such a man had severed his links with his own class. He was essentially a mercenary, and his self-respect depended on his conception of himself not as a worker or a citizen but simply as a fighting animal.

Since the war the conditions of army life have improved and the conception of discipline has grown more intelligent, but the British army has retained its special characteristics – small size, voluntary enlistment, long service and emphasis on regimental loyalty. Every regiment has its own name (not merely a number, as in most armies), its history and relics, its special customs, traditions, etc., etc., thanks to which the whole army is honeycombed with snobberies which are almost unbelievable unless one has seen them at close quarters. Between the officers of a "smart" regiment and those of an ordinary infantry regiment, or still more a regiment of the Indian Army, there is a degree of jealousy almost amounting to a class difference. And there is no question that the long-term private soldier often identifies with his own regiment almost as closely as the officer does. The effect is to make the narrow "non-political" outlook of the mercenary come more easily to him. In addition, the fact that the British army is rather heavily officered probably diminishes class friction and thus makes the lower ranks less accessible to "subversive" ideas.

But the thing which above all else forces a reactionary viewpoint on the common soldier is his service in overseas garrisons. An infantry regiment is usually quartered abroad for eighteen years consecutively, moving from place to place every four or five years, so that many soldiers serve their entire term in India, Africa, China, etc. They are only there to hold down a hostile population and the fact is brought home to them in unmistakable ways. Relations with the "natives" are almost invariably bad, and the soldiers – not so much the officers as the men – are the obvious targets for anti-British feeling. Naturally they retaliate, and as a rule they develop an attitude towards the "niggers" which is far more brutal than that of the officials or business men. In Burma I was constantly struck by the fact that the common soldiers were the best-hated section of the white community, and, judged simply by their behaviour, they certainly deserved to be. Even as near home as Gibraltar they walk the streets with a swaggering air which is directed at the Spanish "natives." And in practice some such attitude is absolutely necessary; you could not hold down a subject empire with troops infected by notions of class-solidarity. Most of the dirty work of the French empire, for instance, is done not by French conscripts but by illiterate negroes and by the Foreign Legion, a corps of pure mercenaries.

To sum up: in spite of the technical advances which do not allow the professional officer to be quite such an idiot as he used to be, and in spite of the fact that the common soldier is now treated a little more like a human being, the British army remains essentially the same machine as it was fifty years ago. A little while back any Socialists would have admitted this without argument. But we happen to be at a moment when the rise of Hitler has scared the official leaders of the Left into an attitude not far removed from jingoism. Large numbers of Left-wing publicists are almost openly agitating for war. Without discussing this subject at length, it can be pointed out that a Left-wing party which, within a capitalist society, becomes a war party, has already thrown up the sponge, because it is demanding a policy which can only be carried out by its opponents. The Labour leaders are intermittently aware of this – witness their shufflings on the subject of conscription. Hence, in among the cries of "Firm front!" "British prestige!" etc., there mingles a quite contradictory line of talk. It is to the effect that "this time" things are going to be "different." Militarisation is not going to mean militarisation. Colonel Blimp is no longer Colonel Blimp. And in the more soft-boiled Left-wing papers a phrase is bandied to and fro – "democratising the army." It is worth considering what it implies.

"Democratising" an army, if it means anything, means doing away with the predominance of a single class and introducing a less mechanical form of discipline. In the British army this would mean an entire reconstruction which would rob the army of efficiency for five or ten years. Such a process is only doubtfully possible while the British Empire exists, and quite unthinkable while the simultaneous aim is to "stop Hitler." What will actually happen during the next couple of years, war or no war, is that the armed forces will be greatly expanded, but the new units will take their colour from the existing professional army. As in the Great War, it will be the same army, only bigger. Poorer sections of the middle-class will be drawn on for the supply of officers, but the professional military caste will retain its grip. As for the new Militias, it is probably quite a mistake to imagine that they are the nucleus of a "democratic army" in which all classes will start from scratch. It is fairly safe to prophesy that even if there is no class-favouritism (as there will be, presumably), Militiamen of bourgeois origin will tend to be promoted first. Hore-Belisha and others have already hinted as much in a number of speeches. A fact not always appreciated by Socialists is that in England the whole of the bourgeoisie is to some extent militarised. Nearly every boy who has been to a public school has passed through the O.T.C. (theoretically voluntary but in practice compulsory), and though this training is done between the ages of 13 and 18, it ought not to be despised. In effect the Militiaman with an O.T.C. training behind him will start with several months' advantage of the others. In any case the Military Training Act is only an experiment, aimed partly at impressing opinion abroad and partly at accustoming the English people to the idea of conscription. Once the novelty has worn off some method will be devised of keeping proletarians out of positions of command.

It is probable that the nature of modern war has made "democratic army" a contradiction in terms. The French army, for instance, based on universal service, is hardly more democratic than the British. It is just as much dominated by the professional officer and the long-service N.C.O., and the French officer is probably rather more "Prussian" in outlook than his British equivalent. The Spanish Government militias during the first six months of war – the first year, in Catalonia – were a genuinely democratic army, but they were also a very primitive type of army, capable only of defensive actions. In that particular case a defensive strategy, coupled with propaganda, would probably have had a better chance of victory than the methods casually adopted. But if you want military efficiency in the ordinary sense, there is no escaping from the professional soldier, and so long as the professional soldier is in control he will see to it that the army is not democratised. And what is true within the armed forces is true of the nation as a whole; every increase in the strength of the military machine means more power for the forces of reaction. It is possible that some of our Left-wing jingoes are acting with their eyes open. If they are, they must be aware that the *News-Chronicle* version of "defence of democracy" leads directly *away* from democracy, even in the narrow nineteenth-century sense of political liberty, independence of the trade unions and freedom of speech and the press.

Marrakech
New Writing, New Series No. 3, Christmas 1939

As the corpse went past the flies left the restaurant table in a cloud and rushed after it, but they came back a few minutes later.

The little crowd of mourners – all men and boys, no women – threaded their way across the market-place between the piles of pomegranates and the taxis and the camels, wailing a short chant over and over again. What really appeals to the flies is that the corpses here are never put into coffins, they are merely wrapped in a piece of rag and carried on a rough wooden bier on the shoulders of four friends. When the friends get to the burying-ground they hack an oblong hole a foot or two deep, dump the body in it and fling over it a little of the dried-up, lumpy earth, which is like broken brick. No gravestone, no name, no identifying mark of any kind. The burying-ground is merely a huge waste of hummocky earth, like a derelict building-lot. After a month or two no one can even be certain where his own relatives are buried.

When you walk through a town like this – two hundred thousand inhabitants, of whom at least twenty thousand own literally nothing except the rags they stand up in – when you see how the people live, and still more how easily they die, it is always difficult to believe that you are walking among human beings. All colonial empires are in reality founded upon that fact. The people have brown faces – besides, there are so many of them! Are they really the same flesh as yourself? Do they even have names? Or are they merely a kind of undifferentiated brown stuff, about as individual as bees or coral insects? They rise out of the earth, they sweat and starve for a few years, and then they sink back into the nameless mounds of the graveyard and nobody notices that they are gone. And even the graves themselves soon fade back into the soil. Sometimes, out for a walk, as you break your way through the prickly pear, you notice that it is rather bumpy underfoot, and only a certain regularity in the bumps tells you that you are walking over skeletons.

I was feeding one of the gazelles in the public gardens.

Gazelles are almost the only animals that look good to eat when they are still alive, in fact, one can hardly look at their hindquarters without thinking of mint sauce. The gazelle I was feeding seemed to know that this thought was in my mind, for though it took the piece of bread I was holding out it obviously did not like me. It nibbled rapidly at the bread, then lowered its head and tried to butt me, then took another nibble and then butted again. Probably its idea was that if it could drive me away the bread would somehow remain hanging in mid-air.

An Arab navvy working on the path nearby lowered his heavy hoe and sidled slowly towards us. He looked from the gazelle to the bread and from the bread to the gazelle, with a sort of quiet amazement, as though he had never seen anything quite like this before. Finally he said shyly in French:

'*I* could eat some of that bread.'

I tore off a piece and he stowed it gratefully in some secret place under his rags. This man is an employee of the Municipality.

When you go through the Jewish quarters you gather some idea of what the medieval ghettoes were probably like. Under their Moorish rulers the Jews were only allowed to own land in certain restricted areas, and after centuries of this kind of treatment they have ceased to bother about overcrowding. Many of the streets are a good deal less than six feet wide, the houses are completely windowless, and sore-eyed children cluster everywhere in unbelievable numbers, like clouds of flies. Down the centre of the street there is generally running a little river of urine.

In the bazaar huge families of Jews, all dressed in the long black robe and little black skull-cap, are working in dark fly-infested booths that look like caves. A carpenter sits cross-legged at a prehistoric lathe, turning chair-legs at lightning speed. He works the lathe with a bow in his right hand and guides the chisel with his left foot, and thanks to a lifetime of sitting in this position his left leg is warped out of shape. At his side his grandson, aged six, is already starting on the simpler parts of the job.

I was just passing the coppersmiths' booths when somebody noticed that I was lighting a cigarette. Instantly, from the dark holes all round, there was a frenzied rush of Jews, many of them old grandfathers with flowing grey beards, all clamouring for a cigarette. Even a blind man somewhere at the back of one of the booths heard a rumour of cigarettes and came crawling out, groping in the air with his hand. In about a minute I had used up the whole packet. None of these people, I suppose, works less than twelve hours a day, and every one of them looks on a cigarette as a more or less impossible luxury.

As the Jews live in self-contained communities they follow the same trades as the Arabs, except for agriculture. Fruit-sellers, potters, silversmiths, blacksmiths, butchers, leather-workers, tailors, water-carriers, beggars, porters – whichever way you look you see nothing but Jews. As a matter of fact there are thirteen thousand of them, all living in the space of a few acres. A good job Hitler isn't here. Perhaps he is on his way, however. You hear the usual dark rumours about the Jews, not only from the Arabs but from the poorer Europeans.

'Yes, *mon vieux*, they took my job away from me and gave it to a Jew. The Jews! They're the real rulers of this country, you know. They've got all the money. They control the banks, finance – everything.'

'But,' I said, 'isn't it a fact that the average Jew is a labourer working for about a penny an hour?'

'Ah, that's only for show! They're all moneylenders really. They're cunning, the Jews.'

123

GEORGE ORWELL

In just the same way, a couple of hundred years ago, poor old women used to be burned for witchcraft when they could not even work enough magic to get themselves a square meal.

All people who work with their hands are partly invisible, and the more important the work they do, the less visible they are. Still, a white skin is always fairly conspicuous. In northern Europe, when you see a labourer ploughing a field, you probably give him a second glance. In a hot country, anywhere south of Gibraltar or east of Suez, the chances are that you don't even see him. I have noticed this again and again. In a tropical landscape one's eye takes in everything except the human-beings. It takes in the dried-up soil, the prickly pear, the palm-tree and the distant mountain, but it always misses the peasant hoeing at his patch. He is the same colour as the earth, and a great deal less interesting to look at.

It is only because of this that the starved countries of Asia and Africa are accepted as tourist resorts. No one would think of running cheap trips to the Distressed Areas. But where the human-beings have brown skins their poverty is simply not noticed. What does Morocco mean to a Frenchman? An orange-grove or a job in Government service. Or to an Eng-lishman? Camels, castles, palm-trees, Foreign Legionaires, brass trays and bandits. One could probably live here for years without noticing that for nine-tenths of the people the reality of life is an endless, back-breaking struggle to wring a little food out of an eroded soil.

Most of Morocco is so desolate that no wild animal bigger than a hare can live on it. Huge areas which were once covered with forest have turned into a treeless waste where the soil is exactly like broken-up brick. Nevertheless a good deal of it is cultivated, with frightful labour. Everything is done by hand. Long lines of women, bent double like inverted capital Ls, work their way slowly across the fields, tearing up the prickly weeds with their hands, and the peasant gathering lucerne for fodder pulls it up stalk by stalk instead of reaping it, thus saving an inch or two on each stalk. The plough is a wretched wooden thing, so frail that one can easily carry it on one's shoulder, and fitted underneath with a rough iron spike which stirs the soil to a depth of about four inches. This is as much as the strength of

124

the animals is equal to. It is usual to plough with a cow and a donkey yoked together. Two donkeys would not be quite strong enough, but on the other hand two cows would cost a little more to feed. The peasants possess no harrows, they merely plough the soil several times over in different directions, finally leaving it in rough furrows, after which the whole field has to be shaped with hoes into small oblong patches, to conserve water. Except for a day or two after the rare rainstorms there is never enough water. Along the edges of the fields channels are hacked out to a depth of thirty or forty feet to get at the tiny trickles which run through the subsoil.

Every afternoon a file of very old women passes down the road outside my house, each carrying a load of firewood. All of them are mummified with age and the sun, and all of them are tiny. It seems to be generally the case in primitive communities that the women, when they get beyond a certain age, shrink to the size of children. One day a poor old creature who could not have been more than four feet tall crept past me under a vast load of wood. I stopped her and put a five-sou piece (a little more than a farthing) into her hand. She answered with a shrill wail, almost a scream, which was partly gratitude but mainly surprise. I suppose that from her point of view, by taking any notice of her, I seemed almost to be violating a law of nature. She accepted her status as an old woman, that is to say as a beast of burden. When a family is travelling it is quite usual to see a father and a grown-up son riding ahead on donkeys, and an old woman following on foot, carrying the baggage.

But what is strange about these people is their invisibility. For several weeks, always at about the same time of day, the file of old women had hobbled past the house with their firewood, and though they had registered themselves on my eyeballs I cannot truly say that I had seen them. Firewood was passing – that was how I saw it. It was only that one day I happened to be walking behind them, and the curious up-and-down motion of a load of wood drew my attention to the human being underneath it. Then for the first time I noticed the poor old earth-coloured bodies, bodies reduced to bones and leathery skin, bent double under the crushing weight. Yet I suppose I had not been five minutes on Moroccan soil before I noticed the overloading of the donkeys and was infuriated by it. There is no question that the donkeys are damnably treated. The Moroccan donkey is hardly bigger than a St. Bernard dog, it carries a load which in the British Army would be considered too much for a fifteen-hands mule, and very often its pack-saddle is not taken off its back for weeks together. But what is peculiarly pitiful is that it is the most willing creature on earth, it follows its master like a dog and does not need either bridle or halter. After a dozen years of devoted work it suddenly drops dead, whereupon its master tips it into the ditch and the village dogs have torn its guts out before it is cold.

This kind of thing makes one's blood boil, whereas – on the whole – the plight of the human beings does not. I am not commenting, merely pointing to a fact. People with brown skins are next door to invisible. Anyone can be sorry for the donkey with its galled back, but it is generally owing to some kind of accident if one even notices the old woman under her load of sticks.

As the storks flew northward the negroes were marching southward – a long, dusty column, infantry, screw-gun batteries and then more infantry, four or five thousand men in all, winding up the road with a clumping of boots and a clatter of iron wheels.

They were Senegalese, the blackest negroes in Africa, so black that sometimes it is difficult to see whereabouts on their necks the hair begins. Their splendid bodies were hidden in reach-me-down khaki uniforms, their feet squashed into boots that looked like blocks of wood, and every tin hat seemed to be a couple of sizes too small. It was very hot and the men had marched a long way. They slumped under the weight of their packs and the curiously sensitive black faces were glistening with sweat.

As they went past a tall, very young negro turned and caught my eye. But the look he gave me was not in the least the kind of look you might expect. Not hostile, not contemptuous, not sullen, not even inquisitive. It was the shy, wide-eyed negro look, which actually is a look of profound respect. I saw how it was. This wretched boy, who is a French citizen and has therefore been dragged from the forest to scrub floors and catch syphilis in garrison towns, actually has feelings of reverence before a white skin. He has been taught that the white race are his masters, and he still believes it.

But there is one thought which every white man (and in this connection it doesn't matter twopence if he calls himself a Socialist) thinks when he sees a black army marching past. 'How much longer can we go on kidding these people? How long before they turn their guns in the other direction?'

It was curious, really. Every white man there had this thought stowed somewhere or other in his mind. I had it, so had the other onlookers, so had the officers on their sweating chargers and the white N.C.O.s marching in the ranks. It was a kind of secret which we all knew and were too clever to tell; only the negroes didn't know it. And really it was almost like watching a flock of cattle to see the long column, a mile or two miles of armed men, flowing peacefully up the road, while the great white birds drifted over them in the opposite direction, glittering like scraps of paper.

Review of *Union Now* by Clarence K. Streit
The Adelphi, July 1939

This review/article, advocating the righting of imperial injustices, was originally published with the ironic title "Not Counting Niggers."

A dozen years ago anyone who had foretold the political line-up of to-day would have been looked on as a lunatic. And yet the truth is that the present situation – not in detail, of course, but in its main outlines – ought to have been predictable even in the golden age before Hitler. Something like it was bound to happen as soon as British security was seriously threatened.

In a prosperous country, above all in an imperialist country, left-wing politics are always partly humbug. There can be no real reconstruction that would not lead to at least a temporary drop in the English standard of life, which is another way of saying that the majority of left-wing politicians and publicists are people who earn their living by demanding something that they don't genuinely want. They are red-hot revolutionaries as long as all goes well, but every real emergency reveals instantly that they are shamming. One threat to the Suez Canal, and "antifascism" and "defence of British interests" are discovered to be identical.

It would be very shallow as well as unfair to suggest that there is *nothing* in what is now called "antifascism" except a concern for British dividends. But it is a fact that the political obscenities of the past two years, the sort of monstrous harlequinade in which everyone is constantly bounding across the stage in a false nose – Quakers shouting for a bigger army, Communists waving union jacks, Winston Churchill posing as a democrat – would not have been possible without this guilty consciousness that we are all in the same boat. Much against their will the British governing class have been forced into the anti-Hitler position. It is still possible that they will find a way out of it, but they are arming in the obvious expectation of war and they will almost certainly fight when the point is reached at which the alternative would be to give away some of their own property instead of, as hitherto, other people's. And meanwhile the so-called opposition, instead of trying to stop the drift to war, are rushing ahead, preparing the ground and forestalling any possible criticism. So far as one can discover the English people are still extremely hostile to the idea of war, but in so far as they are becoming reconciled to it, it is not the militarists but the "anti-militarists" of five years ago who are responsible. The Labour Party keeps up a pettifogging grizzle against conscription at the same time as its own propaganda makes any real struggle against conscription impossible. The Bren machine guns pour from the factories, books with titles like *Tanks in the Next War, Gas in the Next War*, etc., pour from the press, and the warriors of the *New Statesman* glose over the nature of the process by means of such phrases as "Peace Bloc," "Peace Front," "Democratic Front," and, in general, by pretending that the world is an assemblage of sheep and goats, neatly partitioned off by national frontiers.

In this connection it is well worth having a look at Mr. Streit's much-discussed book, *Union Now*. Mr. Streit, like the partisans of the "Peace Bloc," wants the democracies to gang up against the dictatorships, but his book is outstanding for two reasons. To begin with he goes further than most of the others and offers a plan which, even if it is startling, is constructive. Secondly, in spite of a rather nineteen-twentyish American naïveté, he has an essentially decent cast of mind. He genuinely loathes the thought of war, and he does not sink to the hypocrisy of pretending that any country which can be bought or bullied into the British orbit instantly becomes a democracy. His book therefore presents a kind of test case. In it you are seeing the sheep-and-goats theory at its *best*. If you can't accept it in that form you will certainly never accept it in the form handed out by the Left Book Club.

Briefly, what Mr. Streit suggests is that the democratic nations, starting with fifteen which he names, should voluntarily form themselves into a union – not a league or an alliance, but a union similar to the United States, with a common government, common money and complete internal free trade. The initial fifteen states are, of course, the U.S.A., France, Great Britain, the self-governing dominions of the British Empire, and the smaller European democracies, not including Czechoslovakia, which still existed when the book was written. Later, other states could be admitted to the Union when and if they "proved themselves worthy." It is implied all along that the state of peace and prosperity existing within the Union would be so enviable that everyone else would soon be pining to join it.

It is worth noticing that this scheme is not so visionary as it sounds. Of course it is not going to happen, nothing advocated by well-meaning literary men ever happens, and there are certain difficulties which Mr. Streit does not discuss; but it is of the order of things which *could* happen. Geographically the U.S.A. and the western European democracies are nearer to being a unit than, for instance, the British Empire. Most of their trade is with one another, they contain within their own territories everything they need, and Mr. Streit is probably right in claiming that their combined strength would be so great as to make any attack on them hopeless, even if the U.S.S.R. joined up with Germany. Why then does one see at a glance that this scheme has something wrong with it? What is there about it that smells – for it *does* smell, of course?

What it smells of, as usual, is hypocrisy and self-righteous-ness. Mr. Streit himself is not a hypocrite, but his vision is limited. Look again at his list of sheep and goats. No need to boggle at the goats (Germany, Italy and Japan), they are goats right enough, and billies at that. But look at the sheep! Perhaps the U.S.A. will pass inspection if one does not look too closely. But what about France? What about England? What about even Belgium and Holland? Like everyone of his school of thought, Mr. Streit has coolly lumped the huge British and French empires – in essence nothing but mechanisms for exploiting cheap coloured labour – under the heading of democracies!

Here and there in the book, though not often, there are references to the "dependencies" of the democratic states. "Dependencies" means subject races. It is explained that they are to go on being dependencies, that their resources are to be pooled among the states of the Union, and that their coloured inhabitants will lack the right to vote in Union affairs. Except where the tables of statistics bring it out, one would never for a moment guess what *numbers* of human beings are involved. India, for instance, which contains more inhabitants than the whole of the "fifteen democracies" put together, gets just a page and a half in Mr. Streit's book, and that merely to explain that as India is not yet fit for self-government the *status quo* must continue. And here one begins to see what would really be happening if Mr. Streit's scheme were put into operation. The British and French empires, with their six hundred million disenfranchised human beings, would simply be receiving fresh police forces; the huge strength of the U.S.A. would be behind the robbery of India and Africa. Mr. Streit is letting cats out of bags, but *all* phrases like "Peace Bloc," "Peace Front," etc., contain some such implication; all imply a tightening-up of the existing structure. The unspoken clause is always "not counting niggers." For how can we make a "firm stand" against Hitler if we are simultaneously weakening ourselves at home? In other words, how can we "fight Fascism" except by bolster-ing up a far vaster injustice?

For of course it *is* vaster. What we always forget is that the overwhelming bulk of the British proletariat does not live in Britain, but in Asia and Africa. It is not in Hitler's power, for instance, to make a penny an hour a normal industrial wage; it is perfectly normal in India, and we are at great pains to keep it so. One gets some idea of the real relationship of England and India when one reflects that the *per capita* annual income in England is something over £80, and in India about £7. It is quite common for an Indian coolie's leg to be thinner than the average Englishman's arm. And there is nothing racial in this, for well-fed members of the same races are of normal physique; it is due to simple starvation. This is the system which we all live on and which we denounce when there seems to be no danger of its being altered. Of late, however, it has become the first duty of a "good antifascist" to lie about it and help to keep it in being.

What real settlement, of the slightest value, can there be along these lines? What meaning would there be, even if it were successful, in bringing down Hitler's system in order to stabilise something that is far bigger and in its different way just as bad?

But apparently, for lack of any real opposition, this is going to be our objective. Mr. Streit's ingenious ideas will not be put into operation, but something resembling the "Peace Bloc" proposals probably will. The British and Russian governments are still haggling, stalling and uttering muffled threats to change sides, but circumstances will probably drive them together. And what then? No doubt the alliance will stave off war for a year or two. Then Hitler's move will be to feel for a weak spot or an unguarded moment; then our move will be more armaments, more militarisation, more propaganda, more war-mindedness – and so on, at increasing speed. It is doubtful whether prolonged war-preparation is morally any better than war itself; there are even reasons for thinking that it may be slightly worse. Only two or three years of it, and we may sink almost unresisting into some local variant of austro-fascism. And perhaps a year or two later, in reaction against this, there will appear something we have never had in England yet – a real Fascist movement. And because it will have the guts to speak plainly it will gather into its ranks the very people who ought to be opposing it.

Further than that it is difficult to see. The downward slide is happening because nearly all the Socialist leaders, when it comes to the pinch, are merely His Majesty's Opposition, and nobody else knows how to mobilise the decency of the English people, which one meets with everywhere when one talks to human beings instead of reading newspapers. Nothing is likely to save us except the emergence within the next two years of a real mass party whose first pledges are to refuse war and to right imperial injustice. But if any such party exists at present, it is only as a possibility, in a few tiny germs lying here and there in unwatered soil.

1940

Charles Dickens

11 March 1940

I

Dickens is one of those writers who are well worth stealing. Even the burial of his body in Westminster Abbey was a species of theft, if you come to think of it.

When Chesterton wrote his introductions to the Everyman Edition of Dickens's works, it seemed quite natural to him to credit Dickens with his own highly individual brand of medievalism, and more recently a Marxist writer, Mr T. A. Jackson, has made spirited efforts to turn Dickens into a bloodthirsty revolutionary. The Marxist claims him as 'almost' a Marxist, the Catholic claims him as 'almost' a Catholic, and both claim him as a champion of the proletariat (or 'the poor', as Chesterton would have put it). On the other hand, Nadezhda Krupskaya, in her little book on Lenin, relates that towards the end of his life Lenin went to see a dramatised version of *The Cricket on the Hearth*, and found Dickens's 'middle-class sentimentality' so intolerable that he walked out in the middle of a scene.

Taking 'middle-class' to mean what Krupskaya might be expected to mean by it, this was probably a truer judgement than those of Chesterton and Jackson. But it is worth noticing that the dislike of Dickens implied in this remark is something unusual. Plenty of people have found him unreadable, but very few seem to have felt any hostility towards the general spirit of his work. Some years ago Mr Bechhofer Roberts published a full-length attack on Dickens in the form of a novel (*This Side Idolatry*), but it was a merely personal attack, concerned for the most part with Dickens's treatment of his wife. It dealt with incidents which not one in a thousand of Dickens's readers would ever hear about, and which no more invalidate his work than the second-best bed invalidates *Hamlet*. All that the book really demonstrated was that a writer's literary personality has little or nothing to do with his

135

private character. It is quite possible that in private life Dickens was just the kind of insensitive egoist that Mr Bechhofer Roberts makes him appear. But in his published work there is implied a personality quite different from this, a personality which has won him far more friends than enemies. It might well have been otherwise, for even if Dickens was a bourgeois, he was certainly a subversive writer, a radical, one might truthfully say a rebel. Everyone who has read widely in his work has felt this. Gissing, for instance, the best of the writers on Dickens, was anything but a radical himself, and he disapproved of this train in Dickens and wished it were not there, but it never occurred to him to deny it. In *Oliver Twist*, *Hard Times*, *Bleak House*, *Little Dorrit*, Dickens attacked English institutions with a ferocity that has never since been approached. Yet he managed to do it without making himself hated, and, more than this, the very people he attacked have swallowed him so completely that he has become a national institution himself. In its attitude towards Dickens the English public has always been a little like the elephant which feels a blow with a walking-stick as a delightful tickling. Before I was ten years old I was having Dickens ladled down my throat by schoolmasters in whom even at that age I could see a strong resemblance to Mr Creakle, and one knows without needing to be told that lawyers delight in Serjeant Buzfuz and that *Little Dorrit* is a favourite in the Home Office. Dickens seems to have succeeded in attacking everybody and antagonizing nobody. Naturally this makes one wonder whether after all there was something unreal in his attack upon society. Where exactly does he stand, socially, morally and politically? As usual, one can define his position more easily if one starts by deciding what he was *not*.

In the first place he was *not*, as Messrs Chesterton and Jackson seem to imply, a 'proletarian' writer. To begin with, he does not write about the proletariat, in which he merely resembles the overwhelming majority of novelists, past and present. If you look for the working classes in fiction, and especially English fiction, all you find is a hole. This statement needs qualifying, perhaps. For reasons that are easy enough to see, the agricultural labourer (in England a proletarian) gets a fairly good showing in fiction, and a great deal has been written about criminals, derelicts and, more recently, the working-class intelligentsia. But the ordinary town proletariat, the people who make the wheels go round, have always been ignored by novelists. When they do find their way between the covers of a book, it is nearly always as objects of pity or as comic relief. The central action of Dickens's stories almost invariably takes place in middle-class surroundings. If one examines his novels in detail one finds that his real subject-matter is the London commercial bourgeoisie and their hangers-on – lawyers, clerks, tradesmen, innkeepers, small craftsmen and servants. He has no portrait of an agricultural worker, and only one (Stephen Blackpool in *Hard Times*) of an industrial worker. The Plornishes in *Little Dorrit* are probably his best picture of a working-class family – the Peggottys, for instance, hardly belong to the working class – but on the whole he is not successful with this type of character. If you ask any ordinary reader which of Dickens's proletarian characters he can remember, the three he is almost certain to mention are Bill Sikes, Sam Weller and Mrs Gamp. A burglar, a valet and a drunken midwife – not exactly a representative cross-section of the English working class.

Secondly, in the ordinarily accepted sense of the word, Dickens is not a 'revolutionary' writer. But his position here needs some defining.

Whatever else Dickens may have been, he was not a hole-and-corner soul-saver, the kind of well-meaning idiot who thinks that the world will be perfect if you amend a few by-laws and abolish a few anomalies. It is worth comparing him with Charles Reade, for instance. Reade was a much better-informed man than Dickens, and in some ways more public-spirited. He really hated the abuses he could understand, he showed them up in a series of novels which for all their absurdity are extremely readable, and he probably helped to alter public opinion on a few minor but important points. But it was quite beyond him to grasp that, given the existing form of society, certain evils *cannot* be remedied. Fasten upon this or that minor abuse, expose it, drag it into the open, bring it before a British jury, and all will be well – that is how he sees it. Dickens at any rate never imagined that you can cure pimples by cutting them off. In every page of his work one can see a consciousness that society is wrong somewhere at the root. It is when one asks 'Which root?' that one begins to grasp his position.

The truth is that Dickens's criticism of society is almost exclusively moral. Hence the utter lack of any constructive suggestion anywhere in his work. He attacks the law, parliamentary government, the educational system and so forth, without ever clearly suggesting what he would put in their places. Of course it is not necessarily the business of a novelist, or a satirist, to make constructive suggestions, but the point is that Dickens's attitude is at bottom not even *de*structive. There is no clear sign that he wants the existing order to be overthrown, or that he believes it would make very much difference if it *were* overthrown. For in reality his target is not so much society as 'human nature'. It would be difficult to point anywhere in his books to a passage suggesting that the economic system is wrong *as a system*. Nowhere, for instance, does he make any attack on private enterprise or private property. Even in a book like *Our Mutual Friend*, which turns on the power of corpses to interfere with living people by means of idiotic wills, it does not occur to him to suggest that individuals ought not to have this irresponsible power. Of course one can draw this inference for oneself, and one can draw it again from the remarks about Bounderby's will at the end of *Hard Times*, and indeed from the whole of Dickens's work one can infer the evil of *laissez-faire* capitalism; but Dickens makes no such inference himself. It is said that Macaulay refused to review *Hard Times* because he disapproved of its 'sullen Socialism'. Obviously Macaulay is here using the word 'Socialism' in the same sense in which, twenty years ago, a vegetarian meal or a Cubist picture used to be referred to as 'Bolshevism'. There is not a line in the book that can properly be called Socialistic; indeed, its tendency if anything is pro-capitalist, because its whole moral is that capitalists ought to be kind, not that workers ought to be rebellious. Bounderby is a bullying windbag and Gradgrind has been morally blinded, but if they were better men, the system would work well enough – that, all through, is the implication. And so far as social criticism goes, one can never extract much more from Dickens than this, unless one deliberately reads meanings into him. His whole 'message' is one that at first glance looks like an enormous platitude: If men would behave decently the world would be decent.

Naturally this calls for a few characters who are in positions of authority and who *do* behave decently. Hence that recurrent Dickens figure, the Good Rich Man. This character belongs especially to Dickens's early optimistic period. He is usually a 'merchant' (we are not necessarily told what merchandise he deals in), and he is always a superhumanly kind-hearted old gentleman who 'trots' to and fro, raising his employees' wages, patting children on the head, getting debtors out of jail and, in general, acting the fairy godmother. Of course he is a pure dream figure, much further from real life than, say, Squeers or Micawber. Even Dickens must have reflected occasionally that anyone who was so anxious to give his money away would never have acquired it in the first place. Mr Pickwick, for instance, had 'been in the city', but it is difficult to imagine him making a fortune there. Nevertheless this character runs like a connecting thread through most of the earlier books. Pickwick, the Cheerybles, old Chuzzlewit, Scrooge – it is the same figure over and over again, the good rich man handing out guineas. Dickens does however show signs of development here. In the books of the middle period the good rich man fades out to some extent. There is no one who plays this part in *A Tale of Two Cities*, nor in *Great Expectations* – *Great Expectations* is, in fact, definitely an attack on patronage – and in *Hard Times* it is only very doubtfully played by Gradgrind after his reformation. The character reappears in a rather different form as Meagles in *Little Dorrit* and John Jarndyce in *Bleak House* – one might perhaps add Betsy Trotwood in *David Copperfield*. But in these books the good rich man has dwindled from a 'merchant' to a rentier. This is significant. A rentier is part of the possessing class, he can and, almost without knowing it, does make other people work for him, but he has very little direct power. Unlike Scrooge or the Cheerybles, he cannot put everything right by raising everybody's wages. The seeming inference from the rather despondent books that Dickens wrote in the 'fifties is that by that time he had grasped the helplessness of well-meaning individuals in a corrupt society. Nevertheless in the last completed novel, *Our Mutual Friend* (published 1864–65), the good rich man comes back in full glory in the person of Boffin. Boffin is a proletarian by origin and only rich by inheritance, but he is the usual *deus ex machina*, solving everybody's problems by showering money in all directions. He even 'trots', like the Cheerybles. In several ways *Our Mutual Friend* is a return to the earlier manner, and not an unsuccessful return either. Dickens's thoughts seem to have come full circle. Once again, individual kindliness is the remedy for everything.

One crying evil of his time that Dickens says very little about is child labour. There are plenty of pictures of suffering children in his books, but usually they are suffering in schools rather than in factories. The one detailed account of child labour that he gives is the description in *David Copperfield* of little David washing bottles in Murdstone & Grinby's ware-house. This, of course, is autobiography. Dickens himself, at the age of ten, had worked in Warren's blacking factory in the Strand, very much as he describes it here. It was a terribly bitter memory to him, partly because he felt the whole incident to be discreditable to his parents, and he even concealed it from his wife till long after they were married. Looking back on this period, he says in *David Copperfield*:

> . . . it is matter of some surprise to me, even now, that I can have been so easily thrown away at such an age. A child of excellent abilities, and with strong powers of observation, quick, eager, delicate, and soon hurt bodily or mentally, it seems wonderful to me that nobody should have made any sign in my behalf. But none was made; and I became, at ten years old, a little labouring hind in the service of Murdstone & Grinby.

And again, having described the rough boys among whom he worked:

> No words can express the secret agony of my soul as I sunk into this companionship . . . and felt my hopes of growing up to be a learned and distinguished man, crushed in my bosom.

Obviously it is not David Copperfield who is speaking, it is Dickens himself. He uses almost the same words in the autobiography that he began and abandoned a few months earlier. Of course Dickens is right in saying that a gifted child ought not to work ten hours a day pasting labels on bottles, but what he does not say is that *no* child ought to be condemned to such a fate, and there is no reason for inferring that he thinks it. David escapes from the warehouse, but Mick Walker and Mealy Potatoes and the others are still there, and there is no sign that this troubles Dickens particularly. As usual, he displays no consciousness that the *structure* of society can be changed. He despises politics, does not believe that any good can come out of Parliament – he had been a Parliamentary shorthand writer, which was no doubt a disillusioning experience – and he is slightly hostile to the most hopeful movement of his day, trade unionism. In *Hard Times* trade unionism is represented as something not much better than a racket, something that happens because employers are not sufficiently paternal. Stephen Blackpool's refusal to join the union is rather a virtue in Dickens's eyes. Also, as Mr Jackson has pointed out, the apprentices' association in *Barnaby Rudge*, to which Sim Tappertit belongs, is probably a hit at the illegal or barely legal unions of Dickens's own day, with their secret assemblies, passwords and so forth. Obviously he wants the workers to be decently treated, but there is no sign that he wants them to take their destiny into their own hands, least of all by open violence.

As it happens, Dickens deals with revolution in the narrower sense in two novels, *Barnaby Rudge* and *A Tale of Two Cities*. In *Barnaby Rudge* it is a case of rioting rather than revolution. The Gordon Riots of 1780, though they had religious bigotry as a pretext, seem to have been little more than a pointless outburst of looting. Dickens's attitude to this kind of thing is sufficiently indicated by the fact that his first idea was to make the ringleaders of the riots three lunatics escaped from an asylum. He was dissuaded from this, but the principal figure of the book is in fact a village idiot. In the chapters dealing with the riots Dickens shows a most profound horror of mob violence. He delights in describing scenes in which the 'dregs' of the population behave with atrocious bestiality. These chapters are of great psychological interest, because they show how deeply he had brooded on this subject. The things he describes can only have come out of his imagination, for no riots on anything like the same scale had happened in his lifetime. Here is one of his descriptions, for instance:

> If Bedlam gates had been flung open wide, there would not have issued forth such maniacs as the frenzy of that night had made. There were men there who danced and trampled on the beds of flowers as though they trod down human enemies, and wrenched them from the stalks, like savages who twisted human necks. There were men who cast their lighted torches in the air, and suffered them to fall upon their heads and faces, blistering the skin with deep unseemly burns. There were men who rushed up to the fire, and paddled in it with their hands as if in water; and others who were restrained by force from plunging in, to gratify their deadly longing. On the skull of one drunken lad – not twenty, by his looks – who lay upon the ground with a bottle to his mouth, the lead from the roof came streaming down in a shower of liquid fire, white hot, melting his head like wax . . . But of all the howling throng not one learnt mercy from, or sickened at, these sights; nor was the fierce, besotted, senseless rage of one man glutted.

You might almost think you were reading a description of 'Red' Spain by a partisan of General Franco. One ought, of course, to remember that when Dickens was writing, the London 'mob' still existed. (Nowadays there is no mob, only a flock.) Low wages and the growth and shift of population had brought into existence a huge, dangerous slum-proletariat, and until the early middle of the nineteenth century there was hardly such a thing as a police force. When the brickbats began to fly there was nothing between shuttering your windows and ordering the troops to open fire. In *A Tale of Two Cities* he is dealing with a revolution which was really *about* something, and Dickens's attitude is different, but not entirely different. As a matter of fact, *A Tale of Two Cities* is a book which tends to leave a false impression behind, especially after a lapse of time.

The one thing that everyone who has read *A Tale of Two Cities* remembers is the Reign of Terror. The whole book is dominated by the guillotine – tumbrils thundering to and fro, bloody knives, heads bouncing into the basket, and sinister old women knitting as they watch. Actually these scenes only occupy a few chapters, but they are written with terrible intensity, and the rest of the book is rather slow going. But *A Tale of Two Cities* is not a companion volume to *The Scarlet Pimpernel*. Dickens sees clearly enough that the French Revolution was bound to happen and that many of the people who were executed deserved what they got. If, he says, you behave as the French aristocracy had behaved, vengeance will follow. He repeats this over and over again. We are constantly being reminded that while 'my lord' is lolling in bed, with four liveried footmen serving his chocolate and the peasants starving outside, somewhere in the forest a tree is growing which will presently be sawn into planks for the platform of the guillotine, etc. etc. etc. The inevitability of the Terror, given its causes, is insisted upon in the clearest terms:

> It was too much the way . . . to talk of this terrible Revolution as if it were the one only harvest ever known under the skies that had not been sown – as if nothing had ever been done, or omitted to be done, that had led to it – as if observers of the wretched millions in France, and of the misused and perverted resources that should have made them prosperous, had not seen it inevitably coming, years before, and had not in plain words recorded what they saw.

And again:

> All the devouring and insatiate Monsters imagined since imagination could record itself, are fused in the one realisation, Guillotine. And yet there is not in France, with its rich variety of soil and climate, a blade, a leaf, a root, a sprig, a peppercorn, which will grow to maturity under conditions more certain than those that have produced this horror. Crush humanity out of shape once more, under similar hammers, and it will twist itself into the same tortured forms.

In other words, the French aristocracy had dug their own graves. But there is no perception here of what is now called historic necessity. Dickens sees that the results are inevitable, given the causes, but he thinks that the causes might have been avoided. The Revolution is something that happens because centuries of oppression have made the French peasantry sub-human. If the wicked nobleman could somehow have turned over a new leaf, like Scrooge, there would have been no Revolution, no jacquerie, no guillotine – and so much the better. This is the opposite of the 'revolutionary' attitude. From the 'revolutionary' point of view the class-struggle is the main source of progress, and therefore the nobleman who robs the peasant and goads him to revolt is playing a necessary part, just as much as the Jacobin who guillotines the nobleman. Dickens never writes anywhere a line that can be interpreted as meaning this. Revolution as he sees it is merely a monster that is begotten by tyranny and always ends by devouring its own instruments. In Sydney Carton's vision at the foot of the guillotine, he foresees Defarge and the other leading spirits of the Terror all perishing under the same knife – which, in fact, was approximately what happened.

And Dickens is very sure that revolution *is* a monster. That is why everyone remembers the revolutionary scenes in *A Tale of Two Cities*; they have the quality of nightmare, and it is Dickens's own nightmare. Again and again he insists upon the meaningless horrors of revolution – the mass-butcheries, the injustice, the ever-present terror of spies, the frightful blood-lust of the mob. The descriptions of the Paris mob – the description, for instance, of the crowd of murderers struggling round the grindstone to sharpen their weapons before butchering the prisoners in the September massacres – outdo anything in *Barnaby Rudge*. The revolutionaries appear to him simply as degraded savages – in fact, as lunatics. He broods over their frenzies with a curious imaginative intensity. He describes them dancing the 'Carmagnole', for instance:

> There could not be fewer than five hundred people, and they were dancing like five thousand demons... They danced to the popular Revolution song, keeping a ferocious time that was like a gnashing of teeth in unison... They advanced, retreated, struck at one another's hands, clutched at one another's heads, spun round alone, caught one an-other and spun round in pairs, until many of them drop-ped... Suddenly they stopped again, paused, struck out the

time afresh, formed into lines the width of the public way, and with their heads low down and their hands high up, swooped screaming off. No fight could have been half so terrible as this dance. It was so emphatically a fallen sport – a something, once innocent, delivered over to all devilry. . . .

He even credits some of these wretches with a taste for guillotining children. The passage I have abridged above ought to be read in full. It and others like it show how deep was Dickens's horror of revolutionary hysteria. Notice, for instance, that touch, 'with their heads low down and their hands high up', etc., and the evil vision it conveys. Madame Defarge is a truly dreadful figure, certainly Dickens's most successful attempt at a *malignant* character. Defarge and others are simply 'the new oppressors who have risen on the destruction of the old', the revolutionary courts are presided over by 'the lowest, cruellest and worst populace', and so on and so forth. All the way through Dickens insists upon the nightmare insecurity of a revolutionary period, and in this he shows a great deal of prescience. 'A law of the suspected, which struck away all security for liberty or life, and delivered over any good and innocent person to any bad and guilty one; prisons gorged with people who had committed no offence, and could obtain no hearing' – it would apply pretty accurately to several countries to-day.

The apologists of any revolution generally try to minimize its horrors; Dickens's impulse is to exaggerate them – and from a historical point of view he has certainly exaggerated. Even the Reign of Terror was a much smaller thing than he makes it appear. Though he quotes no figures, he gives the impression of a frenzied massacre lasting for years, whereas in reality the whole of the Terror, so far as the number of deaths goes, was a joke compared with one of Napoleon's battles. But the bloody knives and the tumbrils rolling to and fro create in his mind a special, sinister vision which he has succeeded in passing on to generations of readers. Thanks to Dickens, the very world 'tumbril' has a murderous sound; one forgets that a tumbril is only a sort of farm-cart. To this day, to the average Englishman, the French Revolution means no more than a pyramid of severed heads. It is a strange thing that Dickens, much more in sympathy with the ideas of the Revolution than most Englishmen of his time, should have played a part in creating this impression.

If you hate violence and don't believe in politics, the only major remedy remaining is education. Perhaps society is past praying for, but there is always hope for the individual human being, if you can catch him young enough. This belief partly accounts for Dickens's preoccupation with childhood.

No one, at any rate no English writer, has written better about childhood than Dickens. In spite of all the knowledge that has accumulated since, in spite of the fact that children are now comparatively sanely treated, no novelist has shown the same power of entering into the child's point of view. I must have been about nine years old when I first read *David Copperfield*. The mental atmosphere of the opening chapters was so immediately intelligible to me that I vaguely imagined they had been written *by a child*. And yet when one re-reads the book as an adult and sees the Murdstones, for instance, dwindle from gigantic figures of doom into semi-comic monsters, these passages lose nothing. Dickens has been able to stand both inside and outside the child's mind, in such a way that the same scene can be wild burlesque or sinister reality, according to the age at which one reads it. Look, for instance, at the scene in which David Copperfield is unjustly suspected of eating the mutton chops; or the scene in which Pip, in *Great Expectations*, coming back from Miss Havisham's house and finding himself completely unable to describe what he has seen, takes refuge in a series of outrageous lies – which, of course, are eagerly believed. All the isolation of childhood is there. And how accurately he has recorded the mechanisms of the child's mind, its visualizing tendency, its sensitiveness to certain kinds of impression. Pip relates how in his childhood his ideas about his dead parents were derived from their tombstones:

The shape of the letters on my father's, gave me an odd idea that he was a square, stout, dark man, with curly black hair. From the character and turn of the inscription, '*Also Georgiana, Wife of the Above*', I drew a childish conclusion that my mother was freckled and sickly. To five little stone lozenges, each about a foot and a half long, which were arranged in a neat row beside their grave, and were sacred to the memory of five little brothers of mine ... I am indebted for a belief I religiously entertained that they had all been born on their backs with their hands in their trousers-pockets, and had never taken them out in this state of existence.

There is a similar passage in *David Copperfield*. After biting Mr Murdstone's hand, David is sent away to school and obliged to wear on his back a placard saying, 'Take care of him. He bites.' He looks at the door in the playground where the boys have carved their names, and from the appearance of each name he seems to know in just what tone of voice the boy will read out the placard:

> There was one boy – a certain J. Steerforth – who cut his name very deep and very often, who, I conceived, would read it in a rather strong voice, and afterwards pull my hair. There was another boy, one Tommy Traddles, who I dreaded would make game of it, and pretend to be dread-fully frightened of me. There was a third, George Demple, who I fancied would sing it.

When I read this passage as a child, it seemed to me that those were exactly the pictures that those particular names would call up. The reason, of course, is the sound-associations of the words (Demple – 'temple'; Traddles – probably 'ske-daddle'). But how many people, before Dickens, had ever noticed such things? A sympathetic attitude towards children was a much rarer thing in Dickens's day than it is now. The early nineteenth century was not a good time to be a child. In Dickens's youth children were still being 'solemnly tried at a criminal bar, where they were held up to be seen', and it was not so long since boys of thirteen had been hanged for petty theft. The doctrine of 'breaking the child's spirit' was in full vigour, and *The Fairchild Family* was a standard book for children till late into the century. This evil book is now issued in pretty-pretty expurgated editions, but it is well worth reading in the original version. It gives one some idea of the lengths to which child-discipline was sometimes carried. Mr Fairchild, for instance, when he catches his children quarrelling, first thrashes them, reciting Doctor Watts's 'Let dogs delight to bark and bite' between blows of the cane, and then takes them to spend the afternoon beneath a gibbet where the rotting corpse of a murderer is hanging. In the earlier part of the century scores of thousands of children, aged sometimes as young as six, were literally worked to death in the mines or cotton mills, and even at the fashionable public schools boys were flogged till they ran with blood for a mistake in their Latin verses. One thing which Dickens seems to have recognized, and which most of his contemporaries did not, is the sadistic sexual element in flogging. I think this can be inferred from *David Copperfield* and *Nicholas Nickleby*. But mental cruelty to a child infuriates him as much as physical, and though there is a fair number of exceptions, his schoolmasters are generally scoundrels.

Except for the universities and the big public schools, every kind of education then existing in England gets a mauling at Dickens's hands. There is Doctor Blimber's Academy, where little boys are blown up with Greek until they burst, and the revolting charity schools of the period, which produced specimens like Noah Claypole and Uriah Heep, and Salem House, and Dotheboys Hall, and the disgraceful little dame-school kept by Mr Wopsle's great-aunt. Some of what Dickens says remains true even to-day. Salem House is the ancestor of the modern 'prep. school', which still has a good deal of resemblance to it; and as for Mr Wopsle's great-aunt, some old fraud of much the same stamp is carrying on at this moment in nearly every small town in England. But, as usual, Dickens's criticism is neither creative nor destructive. He sees the idiocy of an educational system founded on the Greek lexicon and the wax-ended cane; on the other hand, he has no use for the new kind of school that is coming up in the 'fifties and 'sixties, the 'modern' school, with its gritty insistence on 'facts'. What, then, *does* he want? As always, what he appears to want is a moralized version of the existing thing – the old type of school, but with no caning, no bullying or underfeeding, and not quite so much Greek. Doctor Strong's school, to which David Copperfield goes after he escapes from Murdstone & Grinby's, is simply Salem House with the vices left out and a good deal of 'old grey stones' atmosphere thrown in:

> Doctor Strong's was an excellent school, as different from Mr Creakle's as good is from evil. It was very gravely and decorously ordered, and on a sound system; with an appeal, in everything, to the honour and good faith of the boys ... which worked wonders. We all felt that we had a part in the management of the place, and in sustaining its character and dignity. Hence, we soon became warmly attached to it – I am sure I did for one, and I never knew, in all my time, of any boy being otherwise – and learnt with a good will, desiring to do it credit. We had noble games out of hours, and plenty of liberty; but even then, as I remember, we were well spoken of in the town, and rarely did any disgrace, by our appearance or manner, to the reputation of Doctor Strong and Doctor Strong's boys.

In the woolly vagueness of this passage one can see Dickens's utter lack of any educational theory. He can imagine the *moral* atmosphere of a good school, but nothing further. The boys 'learnt with a good will', but what did they learn? No doubt it was Doctor Blimber's curriculum, a little watered down. Considering the attitude to society that is everywhere implied in Dickens's novels, it comes as rather a shock to learn that he sent his eldest son to Eton and sent all his children through the ordinary educational mill. Gissing seems to think that he may have done this because he was painfully conscious of being under-educated himself. Here perhaps Gissing is influenced by his own love of classical learning. Dickens had had little or no formal education, but he lost nothing by missing it, and on the whole he seems to have been aware of this. If he was unable to imagine a better school than Doctor Strong's, or, in real life, than Eton, it was probably due to an intellectual deficiency rather different from the one Gissing suggests.

It seems that in every attack Dickens makes upon society he is always pointing to a change of spirit rather than a change of structure. It is hopeless to try and pin him down to any definite remedy, still more to any political doctrine. His approach is always along the moral plane, and his attitude is sufficiently summed up in that remark about Strong's school being as different from Creakle's 'as good is from evil'. Two things can be very much alike and yet abysmally different. Heaven and Hell are in the same place. Useless to change institutions without a 'change of heart' – that, essentially, is what he is always saying.

If that were all, he might be no more than a cheer-up writer, a reactionary humbug. A 'change of heart' is in fact *the* alibi of people who do not wish to endanger the *status quo*. But Dickens is not a humbug, except in minor matters, and the strongest single impression one carries away from his books is that of a hatred of tyranny. I said earlier that Dickens is not *in the accepted sense* a revolutionary writer. But it is not at all certain that a merely moral criticism of society may not be just as 'revolutionary' – and revolution, after all, means turning things upside down – as the politico-economic criticism which is fashionable at this moment. Blake was not a politician, but there is more understanding of the nature of capitalist society in a poem like 'I wander through each charter'd street' than in three-quarters of Socialist literature. Progress is not an illusion, it happens, but it is slow and invariably disappointing. There is always a new tyrant waiting to take over from the old – generally not quite so bad, but still a tyrant. Consequently two viewpoints are always tenable. The one, how can you improve human nature until you have changed the system? The other, what is the use of changing the system before you have improved human nature? They appeal to different individuals, and they probably show a tendency to alternate in point of time. The moralist and the revolutionary are constantly undermining one another. Marx exploded a hundred tons of dynamite beneath the moralist position, and we are still living in the echo of that tremendous crash. But already, somewhere or other, the sappers are at work and fresh dynamite is being tamped in place to blow Marx at the moon. Then Marx, or somebody like him, will come back with yet more dynamite, and so the process continues, to an end we cannot yet foresee. The central problem – how to prevent power from being abused – remains unsolved. Dickens, who had not the vision to see that private property is an obstructive nuisance, had the vision to see that. 'If men would behave decently the world would be decent' is not such a platitude as it sounds.

2

More completely than most writers, perhaps, Dickens can be explained in terms of his social origin, though actually his family history was not quite what one would infer from his novels. His father was a clerk in government service, and through his mother's family he had connections with both the army and the navy. But from the age of nine onwards he was brought up in London in commercial surroundings, and generally in an atmosphere of struggling poverty. Mentally he belongs to the small urban bourgeoisie, and he happens to be an exceptionally fine specimen of this class, with all the 'points', as it were, very highly developed. That is partly what makes him so interesting. If one wants a modern equivalent, the nearest would be H. G. Wells, who has had a rather similar history and who obviously owes something to Dickens as a novelist. Arnold Bennett was essentially of the same type, but, unlike the other two, he was a midlander, with an industrial and Nonconformist rather than commercial and Anglican background.

The great disadvantage, and advantage, of the small urban bourgeois is his limited outlook. He sees the world as a middle-class world, and everything outside these limits is either laugh-able or slightly wicked. On the one hand, he has no contact with industry or the soil; on the other, no contact with the governing classes. Anyone who has studied Wells's novels in detail will have noticed that though he hates the aristocrat like poison, he has no particular objection to the plutocrat, and no enthusiasm for the proletarian. His most-hated types, the people he believes to be responsible for all human ills, are kings, landowners, priests, nationalists, soliders, scholars and peasants. At first sight a list beginning with kings and ending with peasants looks like a mere omnium gatherum, but in reality all these people have a common factor. All of them are archaic types, people who are governed by tradition and whose eyes are turned towards the past – the opposite, therefore, of the rising bourgeois who has put his money on the future and sees the past simply as a dead hand.

Actually, although Dickens lived in a period when the bourgeoisie was really a rising class, he displays this characteristic less strongly than Wells. He is almost unconscious of the future and has a rather sloppy love of the picturesque (the 'quaint old church', etc.). Nevertheless his list of most-hated types is like enough to Wells's for the similarity to be striking. He is vaguely on the side of the working class – has a sort of generalized sympathy with them because they are oppressed – but he does not in reality know much about them; they come into his books chiefly as servants, and comic servants at that. At the other end of the scale he loathes the aristocrat and – going one better than Wells in this – loathes the big bourgeois as well. His real sympathies are bounded by Mr Pickwick on the upper side and Mr Barkis on the lower. But the term 'aristocrat', for the type Dickens hates, is vague and needs defining.

Actually Dickens's target is not so much the great aristocracy, who hardly enter into his books, as their petty offshoots, the cadging dowagers who live up mews in Mayfair, and the bureaucrats and professional soldiers. All through his books there are countless hostile sketches of these people, and hardly any that are friendly. There are practically no friendly pictures of the landowning class, for instance. One might make a doubtful exception of Sir Leicester Dedlock; otherwise there is only Mr Wardle (who is a stock figure – the 'good old squire') and Haredale in *Barnaby Rudge*, who has Dickens's sympathy because he is a persecuted Catholic. There are no friendly pictures of soldiers (i.e. officers), and none at all of naval men. As for his bureaucrats, judges and magistrates, most of them would feel quite at home in the Circumlocution Office. The only officials whom Dickens handles with any kind of friendliness are, significantly enough, policemen.

Dickens's attitude is easily intelligible to an Englishman, because it is part of the English puritan tradition, which is not dead even at this day. The class Dickens belonged to, at least by adoption, was growing suddenly rich after a couple of centuries of obscurity. It had grown up mainly in the big towns, out of contact with agriculture, and politically impotent; government, in its experience, was something which either interfered or persecuted. Consequently it was a class with no tradition of public service and not much tradition of usefulness. What now

strikes us as remarkable about the new moneyed class of the
nineteenth century is their complete irresponsibility; they see
everything in terms of individual success, with hardly any
consciousness that the community exists. On the other hand,
a Tite Barnacle, even when he was neglecting his duties, would
have some vague notion of what duties he was neglecting.
Dickens's attitude is never irresponsible, still less does he take
the money-grubbing Smilesian line; but at the back of his mind
there is usually a half-belief that the whole apparatus of government is unnecessary. Parliament is simply Lord Coodle and
Sir Thomas Doodle, the Empire is simply Major Bagstock
and his Indian servant, the Army is simply Colonel Chowser
and Doctor Slammer, the public services are simply Bum-
ble and the Circumlocution Office – and so on and so forth.
What he does not see, or only intermittently sees, is that
Coodle and Doodle and all the other corpses left over from
the eighteenth century *are* performing a function which
neither Pickwick nor Boffin would ever bother about.

   And of course this narrowness of vision is in one way a great
advantage to him, because it is fatal for a caricaturist to see too
much. From Dickens's point of view 'good' society is simply
a collection of village idiots. What a crew! Lady Tippins!
Mrs Gowan! Lord Verisopht! The Honourable Bob Stables!
Mrs Sparsit (whose husband was a Powler)! The Tite Barnacles!
Nupkins! It is practically a case-book in lunacy. But at the same
time his remoteness from the landowning-military-bureau-
cratic class incapacitates him for full-length satire. He only
succeeds with this class when he depicts them as mental defect-
ives. The accusation which used to be made against Dickens
in his lifetime, that he 'could not paint a gentleman', was an
absurdity, but it is true in this sense, that what he says against the
'gentleman' class is seldom very damaging. Sir Mulberry
Hawk, for instance, is a wretched attempt at the wicked-
baronet type. Harthouse in *Hard Times* is better, but he
would be only an ordinary achievement for Trollope or
Thackeray. Trollope's thoughts hardly move outside the
'gentleman' class, but Thackeray has the great advantage of
having a foot in two moral camps. In some ways his outlook
is very similar to Dickens's. Like Dickens, he identifies
with the puritanical moneyed class against the card-playing,

debt-bilking aristocracy. The eighteenth century, as he sees it, is sticking out into the nineteenth in the person of the wicked Lord Steyne. *Vanity Fair* is a full-length version of what Dickens did for a few chapters in *Little Dorrit*. But by origins and upbringing Thackeray happens to be somewhat nearer to the class he is satirizing. Consequently he can produce such comparatively subtle types as, for instance, Major Pendennis and Rawdon Crawley. Major Pendennis is a shallow old snob, and Rawdon Crawley is a thick-headed ruffian who sees nothing wrong in living for years by swindling tradesmen; but what Thackeray realizes is that according to their tortuous code they are neither of them bad men. Major Pendennis would not sign a dud cheque, for instance. Rawdon certainly would, but on the other hand he would not desert a friend in a tight corner. Both of them would behave well on the field of battle – a thing that would not particularly appeal to Dickens. The result is that at the end one is left with a kind of amused tolerance for Major Pendennis and with something approaching respect for Rawdon; and yet one sees, better than any diatribe could make one, the utter rottenness of that kind of cadging, toadying life on the fringes of smart society. Dickens would be quite incapable of this. In his hands both Rawdon and the Major would dwindle to traditional caricatures. And, on the whole, his attacks on 'good' society are rather perfunctory. The aristocracy and the big bourgeoisie exist in his books chiefly as a kind of 'noises off', a haw-hawing chorus somewhere in the wings, like Podsnap's dinner-parties. When he produces a really subtle and damaging portrait, like John Dorrit or Harold Skimpole, it is generally of some rather middling, unimportant person.

One very striking thing about Dickens, especially considering the time he lived in, is his lack of vulgar nationalism. All peoples who have reached the point of becoming nations tend to despise foreigners, but there is not much doubt that the English-speaking races are the worst offenders. One can see this from the fact that as soon as they become fully aware of any foreign race, they invent an insulting nickname for it. Wop, Dago, Froggy, Squarehead, Kike, Sheeny, Nigger, Wog, Chink, Greaser, Yellowbelly – these are merely a selection. Any time before 1870 the list would have been shorter, because the map of the world was different from what it is now, and there were only three or four foreign races that had fully entered into the English consciousness. But towards these, and especially towards France, the nearest and best-hated nation, the English attitude of patronage was so intolerable that English 'arrogance' and 'xenophobia' are still a legend. And of course they are not a completely untrue legend even now. Till very recently nearly all English children were brought up to despise the southern European races, and history as taught in schools was mainly a list of battles won by England. But one has got to read, say, the *Quarterly Review* of the 'thirties to know what boasting really is. Those were the days when the English built up their legend of themselves as 'sturdy islanders' and 'stubborn hearts of oak' and when it was accepted as a kind of scientific fact that one Englishman was the equal of three foreigners. All through nineteenth-century novels and comic papers there runs the traditional figure of the 'Froggy' – a small ridiculous man with a tiny beard and a pointed top-hat, always jabbering and gesticulating, vain, frivolous and fond of boasting of his martial exploits, but generally taking to flight when real danger appears. Over against him was John Bull, the 'sturdy English yeoman', or (a more public-school version) the 'strong, silent Englishman' of Charles Kingsley, Tom Hughes and others.

Thackeray, for instance, has this outlook very strongly, though there are moments when he sees through it and laughs at it. The one historical fact that is firmly fixed in his mind is that the English won the battle of Waterloo. One never reads far in his books without coming upon some reference to it. The English, as he sees it, are invincible because of their tremendous physical strength, due mainly to living on beef. Like most Englishman of his time, he has the curious illusion that the English are larger than other people (Thackeray, as it happened, *was* larger than most people), and therefore he is capable of writing passages like this:

> I say to you that you are better than a Frenchman. I would lay even money that you who are reading this are more than five feet seven in height, and weigh eleven stone; while a Frenchman is five feet four and does not weigh nine. The Frenchman has after his soup a dish of vegetables,

where you have one of meat. You are a different and superior animal – a French-beating animal (the history of hundreds of years has shown you to be so), etc. etc.

There are similar passages scattered all through Thackeray's
works. Dickens would never be guilty of anything of the kind.
It would be an exaggeration to say that he nowhere pokes fun
at foreigners, and of course, like nearly all nineteenth-century
Englishmen, he is untouched by European culture. But never
anywhere does he indulge in the typical English boasting, the
'island race', 'bulldog breed', 'right little, tight little island' style
of talk. In the whole of *A Tale of Two Cities* there is not a line
that could be taken as meaning, 'Look how these wicked
Frenchmen behave!' The one place where he seems to display
a normal hatred of foreigners is in the American chapters of
Martin Chuzzlewit. This, however, is simply the reaction of a
generous mind against cant. If Dickens were alive to-day he
would make a trip to Soviet Russia and come back with a book
rather like Gide's *Retour de l'URSS*. But he is remarkably free
from the idiocy of regarding nations as individuals. He seldom
even makes jokes turning on nationality. He does not exploit
the comic Irishman and the comic Welshman, for instance, and
not because he objects to stock characters and ready-made
jokes, which obviously he does not. It is perhaps more significant that he shows no prejudice against Jews. It is true that he
takes it for granted (*Oliver Twist* and *Great Expectations*) that a
receiver of stolen goods will be a Jew, which at the time was
probably justified. But the 'Jew joke', endemic in English
literature until the rise of Hitler, does not appear in his books,
and in *Our Mutual Friend* he makes a pious though not very
convincing attempt to stand up for the Jews.

Dickens's lack of vulgar nationalism is in part the mark of a
real largeness of mind, and in part results from his negative,
rather unhelpful political attitude. He is very much an Englishman, but he is hardly aware of it – certainly the thought of being
an Englishman does not thrill him. He has no imperialist feeling,
no discernible views on foreign politics, and is untouched by
the military tradition. Temperamentally he is much nearer to
the small Nonconformist tradesman who looks down on the
'redcoats' and thinks that war is wicked – a one-eyed view, but,

after all, war *is* wicked. It is noticeable that Dickens hardly writes of war, even to denounce it. With all his marvellous powers of description, and of describing things he had never seen, he never describes a battle, unless one counts the attack on the Bastille in *A Tale of Two Cities*. Probably the subject would not strike him as interesting, and in any case he would not regard a battlefield as a place where anything worth settling could be settled. It is one up to the lower-middle-class, puritan mentality.

3

Dickens had grown up near enough to poverty to be terrified of it, and in spite of his generosity of mind, he is not free from the special prejudices of the shabby-genteel. It is usual to claim him as a 'popular' writer, a champion of the 'oppressed masses'. So he is, so long as he thinks of them as oppressed; but there are two things that condition his attitude. In the first place, he is a south-of-England man, and a Cockney at that, and therefore out of touch with the bulk of the real oppressed masses, the industrial and agricultural labourers. It is interesting to see how Chesterton, another Cockney, always presents Dickens as the spokesman of 'the poor', without showing much awareness of who 'the poor' really are. To Chesterton 'the poor' means small shopkeepers and servants. Sam Weller, he says, 'is the great symbol in English literature of the populace peculiar to England'; and Sam Weller is a valet! The other point is that Dickens's early experiences have given him a horror of proletarian roughness. He shows this unmistakably whenever he writes of the very poorest of the poor, the slum-dwellers. His descriptions of the London slums are always full of undisguised repulsion:

> The ways were foul and narrow; the shops and houses wretched; and people half-naked, drunken, slipshod and ugly. Alleys and archways, like so many cesspools, disgorged their offences of smell, and dirt, and life, upon the straggling streets; and the whole quarter reeked with crime, and filth, and misery, etc. etc.

There are many similar passages in Dickens. From them one gets the impression of whole submerged populations whom he regards as being beyond the pale. In rather the same way the modern doctrinaire Socialist contemptuously writes off a large block of the population as 'lumpenproletariat'. Dickens also shows less understanding of criminals than one would expect of him. Although he is well aware of the social and economic causes of crime, he often seems to feel that when a man has once broken the law he has put himself outside human society. There is a chapter at the end of *David Copperfield* in which David visits the prison where Littimer and Uriah Heep are serving their sentences. Dickens actually seems to regard the horrible 'model' prisons, against which Charles Reade delivered his memorable attack in *It is Never Too Late to Mend*, as too humane. He complains that the food is too good! As soon as he comes up against crime or the worst depths of poverty, he shows traces of the 'I've always kept myself respectable' habit of mind. The attitude of Pip (obviously the attitude of Dickens himself) towards Magwitch in *Great Expectations* is extremely interesting. Pip is conscious all along of his ingratitude towards Joe, but far less so of his ingratitude towards Magwitch. When he discovers that the person who has loaded him with benefits for years is actually a transported convict, he falls into frenzies of disgust. 'The abhorrence in which I held the man, the dread I had of him, the repugnance with which I shrank from him, could not have been exceeded if he had been some terrible beast,' etc. etc. So far as one can discover from the text, this is not because when Pip was a child he had been terrorized by Magwitch in the churchyard; it is because Magwitch is a criminal and a convict. There is an even more 'kept-myself-respectable' touch in the fact that Pip feels as a matter of course that he cannot take Magwitch's money. The money is not the product of a crime, it has been honestly acquired; but it is an ex-convict's money and therefore 'tainted'. There is nothing psychologically false in this, either. Psychologically the latter part of *Great Expectations* is about the best thing Dickens ever did; throughout this part of the book one feels 'Yes, that is just how Pip would have behaved'. But the point is that in the matter of Magwitch, Dickens identifies with Pip, and his attitude is at bottom snobbish. The result is that Magwitch belongs to the same queer class of characters as Falstaff and, probably, Don Quixote – characters who are more pathetic than the author intended.

When it is a question of the non-criminal poor, the ordinary, decent, labouring poor, there is of course nothing contemptuous in Dickens's attitude. He has the sincerest admiration for people like the Peggottys and the Plornishes. But it is questionable whether he really regards them as equals. It is of the greatest interest to read Chapter XI of *David Copperfield* and side by side with it the autobiographical fragment (parts of this are given in Forster's *Life*), in which Dickens expresses his feelings about the blacking-factory episode a great deal more strongly than in the novel. For more than twenty years afterwards the memory was so painful to him that he would go out of his way to avoid that part of the Strand. He says that to pass that way 'made me cry, after my eldest child could speak'. The text makes it quite clear that what hurt him most of all, then and in retrospect, was the enforced contact with 'low' associates:

> No words can express the secret agony of my soul as I sunk into this companionship; compared these every day associates with those of my happier childhood . . . But I held some station at the blacking warehouse too . . . I soon became at least as expeditious and as skilful with my hands, as either of the other boys. Though perfectly familiar with them, my conduct and manners were different enough from theirs to place a space between us. They, and the men, always spoke of me as 'the young gentleman'. A certain man . . . used to call me 'Charles' sometimes in speaking to me; but I think it was mostly when we were very confidential . . . Poll Green uprose once, and rebelled against the 'young-gentleman' usage; but Bob Fagin settled him speedily.

It was as well that there should be 'a space between us', you see. However much Dickens may admire the working classes, he does not wish to resemble them. Given his origins, and the time he lived in, it could hardly be otherwise. In the early nineteenth century class-animosities may have been no sharper than they are now, but the surface differences between class and class were enormously greater. The 'gentleman' and the 'common man' must have seemed like different species of animal. Dickens is quite genuinely on the side of the poor against the rich, but it would be next door to impossible for him not to think of a working-class exterior as a stigma. In one of Tolstoy's fables the peasants of a certain village judge every stranger who arrives from the state of his hands. If his palms are hard from work, they let him in; if his palms are soft, out he goes. This would be hardly intelligible to Dickens; all his heroes have soft hands. His younger heroes – Nicholas Nickleby, Martin Chuzzlewit, Edward Chester, David Copperfield, John Harmon – are usually of the type known as 'walking gentlemen'. He likes a bourgeois exterior and a bourgeois (not aristocratic) accent. One curious symptom of this is that he will not allow anyone who is to play a heroic part to speak like a working man. A comic hero like Sam Weller, or a merely pathetic figure like Stephen Blackpool, can speak with a broad accent, but the *jeune premier* always speaks the then equivalent of B.B.C. This is so, even when it involves absurdities. Little Pip, for instance, is brought up by people speaking broad Essex, but talks upper-class English from his earliest childhood; actually he would have talked the same dialect as Joe, or at least as Mrs Gargery. So also with Biddy Wopsle, Lizzie Hexam, Sissie Jupe, Oliver Twist – one ought perhaps to add Little Dorrit. Even Rachel in *Hard Times* has barely a trace of Lancashire accent, an impossibility in her case.

One thing that often gives the clue to a novelist's real feelings on the class question is the attitude he takes up when class collides with sex. This is a thing too painful to be lied about, and consequently it is one of the points at which the 'I'm-not-a-snob' pose tends to break down.

One sees that at its most obvious where a class-distinction is also a colour-distinction. And something resembling the colonial attitude ('native' women are fair game, white women are sacrosanct) exists in a veiled form in all-white communities, causing bitter resentment on both sides. When this issue arises, novelists often revert to crude class-feelings which they might disclaim at other times. A good example of 'class-conscious' reaction is a rather forgotten novel, *The People of Clopton*, by George Bartram. The author's moral code is quite clearly mixed up with class-hatred. He feels the seduction of a poor girl by a rich man to be something atrocious, a kind of defilement, something quite different from her seduction by a man in her own walk of life. Trollope deals with this theme twice

(*The Three Clerks* and *The Small House at Allington*) and, as one might expect, entirely from the upper-class angle. As he sees it, an affair with a barmaid or a landlady's daughter is simply an 'entanglement' to be escaped from. Trollope's moral standards are strict, and he does not allow the seduction actually to happen, but the implication is always that a working-class girl's feelings do not greatly matter. In *The Three Clerks* he even gives the typical class-reaction by noting that the girl 'smells'. Meredith (*Rhoda Fleming*) takes more the 'class-conscious' viewpoint. Thackeray, as often, seems to hesitate. In *Pendennis* (Fanny Bolton) his attitude is much the same as Trollope's; in *A Shabby Genteel Story* it is nearer to Meredith's.

One could divine a good deal about Trollope's social origin, or Meredith's, or Bartram's, merely from their handling of the class-sex theme. So one can with Dickens, but what emerges, as usual, is that he is more inclined to identify himself with the middle class than with the proletariat. The one incident that seems to contradict this is the tale of the young peasant-girl in Doctor Manette's manuscript in *A Tale of Two Cities*. This, however, is merely a costume-piece put in to explain the implacable hatred of Madame Defarge, which Dickens does not pretend to approve of. In *David Copperfield*, where he is dealing with a typical nineteenth-century seduction, the class-issue does not seem to strike him as paramount. It is a law of Victorian novels that sexual misdeeds must not go unpunished, and so Steerforth is drowned on Yarmouth sands, but neither Dickens, nor old Peggotty, nor even Ham, seems to feel that Steerforth has added to his offence by being the son of rich parents. The Steerforths are moved by class-motives, but the Peggottys are not – not even in the scene between Mrs Steerforth and old Peggotty; if they were, of course, they would probably turn against David as well as against Steerforth.

In *Our Mutual Friend* Dickens treats the episode of Eugene Wrayburn and Lizzie Hexam very realistically and with no appearance of class bias. According to the 'unhand me, monster' tradition, Lizzie ought either to 'spurn' Eugene or to be ruined by him and throw herself off Waterloo Bridge; Eugene ought to be either a heartless betrayer or a hero resolved upon defying society. Neither behaves in the least like this. Lizzie is frightened by Eugene's advances and actually runs away from them, but hardly pretends to dislike them; Eugene is attracted by her, has too much decency to attempt seducing her and dare not marry her because of his family. Finally they are married and no one is any the worse, except perhaps Mr Twemlow, who will lose a few dinner engagements. It is all very much as it might have happened in real life. But a 'class-conscious' novelist would have given her to Bradley Headstone.

But when it is the other way about – when it is a case of a poor man aspiring to some woman who is 'above' him – Dickens instantly retreats into the middle-class attitude. He is rather fond of the Victorian notion of a woman (woman with a capital W) being 'above' a man. Pip feels that Estella is 'above' him, Esther Summerson is 'above' Guppy, Little Dorrit is 'above' John Chivery, Lucy Manette is 'above' Sydney Carton. In some of these the 'above'-ness is merely moral, but in others it is social. There is a scarcely mistakable class-reaction when David Copperfield discovers that Uriah Heep is plotting to marry Agnes Wickfield. The disgusting Uriah suddenly announces that he is in love with her:

'Oh, Master Copperfield, with what a pure affection do I love the ground my Agnes walks on!'

I believe I had a delirious idea of seizing the red-hot poker out of the fire, and running him through with it. It went from me with a shock, like a ball fired from a rifle: but the image of Agnes, outraged by so much as a thought of this red-headed animal's, remained in my mind when I looked at him, sitting all awry as if his mean soul griped his body, and made me giddy... 'I believe Agnes Wickfield to be as far above *you* [David says later on], and as far removed from all *your* aspirations, as that moon herself!'

Considering how Heep's general lowness – his servile manners, dropped aitches and so forth – has been rubbed in throughout the book, there is not much doubt about the nature of Dickens's feelings. Heep, of course, is playing a villainous part, but even villains have sexual lives; it is the thought of the 'pure' Agnes in bed with a man who drops his aitches that really revolts Dickens. But his usual tendency is to treat a man in love with a woman who is 'above' him as a joke. It is one of the stock jokes of English literature, from Malvolio onwards. Guppy in *Bleak House* is an example, John Chivery is another, and there is a rather ill-natured treatment of this theme in the 'swarry' in *Pickwick Papers*. Here Dickens describes the Bath footmen as living a kind of fantasy-life, holding dinner-parties in imitation of their 'betters' and deluding themselves that their young mistresses are in love with them. This evidently strikes him as very comic. So it is, in a way, though one might question whether it is not better for a footman even to have delusions of this kind than simply to accept his status in the spirit of the catechism.

In his attitude towards servants Dickens is not ahead of his age. In the nineteenth century the revolt against domestic service was just beginning, to the great annoyance of everyone with over £500 a year. An enormous number of the jokes in nineteenth-century comic papers deal with the uppishness of servants. For years *Punch* ran a series of jokes called 'Servant Gal-isms', all turning on the then astonishing fact that a servant is a human being. Dickens is sometimes guilty of this kind of thing himself. His books abound with the ordinary comic servants; they are dishonest (*Great Expectations*), incompetent (*David Copperfield*), turn up their noses at good food (*Pickwick Papers*), etc. etc. – all rather in the spirit of the suburban housewife with one downtrodden cook-general. But what is curious, in a nineteenth-century radical, is that when he wants to draw a sympathetic picture of a servant, he creates what is recognizably a feudal type. Sam Weller, Mark Tapley, Clara Peggotty are all of them feudal figures. They belong to the genre of the 'old family retainer'; they identify themselves with their master's family and are at once doggishly faithful and completely familiar. No doubt Mark Tapley and Sam Weller are derived to some extent from Smollett, and hence from Cervantes; but it is interesting that Dickens should have been attracted by such a type. Sam Weller's attitude is definitely medieval. He gets himself arrested in order to follow Mr Pickwick into the Fleet, and afterwards refuses to get married because he feels that Mr Pickwick still needs his services. There is a characteristic scene between them:

> '. . . vages or no vages, notice or no notice, board or no board, lodgin' or no lodgin', Sam Veller, as you took from

the old inn in the Borough, sticks by you, come what come may...'

'My good fellow,' said Mr Pickwick, when Mr Weller had sat down again, rather abashed at his own enthusiasm, 'you are bound to consider the young woman also.'

'I do consider the young 'ooman, sir,' said Sam. 'I have considered the young 'ooman. I've spoke to her, I've told her how I'm sitivated, she's ready to vait till I'm ready, and I believe she vill. If she don't, she's not the young 'ooman I take her for, and I give her up vith readiness.'

It is easy to imagine what the young woman would have said to this in real life. But notice the feudal atmosphere. Sam Weller is ready as a matter of course to sacrifice years of life to his master, and he can also sit down in his master's presence. A modern manservant would never think of doing either. Dickens's views on the servant question do not get much beyond wishing that master and servant would love one another. Sloppy in *Our Mutual Friend*, though a wretched failure as a character, represents the same kind of loyalty as Sam Weller. Such loyalty, of course, is natural, human and likeable; but so was feudalism.

What Dickens seems to be doing, as usual, is to reach out for an idealized version of the existing thing. He was writing at a time when domestic service must have seemed a completely inevitable evil. There were no labour-saving devices, and there was huge inequality of wealth. It was an age of enormous families, pretentious meals and inconvenient houses, when the slavey drudging fourteen hours a day in the basement kitchen was something too normal to be noticed. And given the *fact* of servitude, the feudal relationship is the only tolerable one. Sam Weller and Mark Tapley are dream figures, no less than the Cheerybles. If there have got to be masters and servants, how much better that the master should be Mr Pickwick and the servant should be Sam Weller. Better still, of course, if servants did not exist at all – but this Dickens is probably unable to imagine. Without a high level of mechanical development, human equality is not practically possible; Dickens goes to show that it is not imaginable either.

4

It is not merely a coincidence that Dickens never writes about agriculture and writes endlessly about food. He was a Cockney, and London is the centre of the earth in rather the same sense that the belly is the centre of the body. It is a city of consumers, of people who are deeply civilized but not primarily useful. A thing that strikes one when one looks below the surface of Dickens's books is that, as nineteenth-century novelists go, he is rather ignorant. He knows very little about the way things really happen. At first sight this statement looks flatly untrue, and it needs some qualification.

Dickens had had vivid glimpses of 'low life' – life in a debtors' prison, for example – and he was also a popular novelist and able to write about ordinary people. So were all the characteristic English novelists of the nineteenth century. They felt at home in the world they lived in, whereas a writer nowadays is so hopelessly isolated that the typical modern novel is a novel about a novelist. Even when Joyce, for instance, spends a decade or so in patient efforts to make contact with the 'common man', his 'common man' finally turns out to be a Jew, and a bit of a highbrow at that. Dickens at least does not suffer from this kind of thing. He has no difficulty in introducing the common motives, love, ambition, avarice, vengeance and so forth. What he does not noticeably write about, however, is *work*.

In Dickens's novels anything in the nature of work happens off-stage. The only one of his heroes who has a plausible profession is David Copperfield, who is first a shorthand writer and then a novelist, like Dickens himself. With most of the others, the way they earn their living is very much in the background. Pip, for instance, 'goes into business' in Egypt; we are not told what business, and Pip's working life occupies about half a page of the book. Clennam has been in some unspecified business in China, and later goes into another barely-specified business with Doyce. Martin Chuzzlewit is an architect, but does not seem to get much time for practising. In no case do their adventures spring directly out of their work. Here the contrast between Dickens and, say, Trollope is startling. And one reason for this is undoubtedly that Dickens knows very little about the professions his characters are supposed to follow. What exactly went on in Gradgrind's factories? How did Podsnap make his money? How did Merdle work his swindles? One knows that Dickens could never follow up the details of Parliamentary elections and Stock Exchange rackets as Trollope could. As soon as he has to deal with trade, finance, industry or politics he takes refuge in vagueness, or in satire. This is the case even with legal processes, about which actually he must have known a good deal. Compare any lawsuit in Dickens with the lawsuit in *Orley Farm*, for instance.

And this partly accounts for the needless ramifications of Dickens's novels, the awful Victorian 'plot'. It is true that not all his novels are alike in this. *A Tale of Two Cities* is a very good and fairly simple story, and so in its different way is *Hard Times*; but these are just the two which are always rejected as 'not like Dickens' – and incidentally they were not published in monthly numbers. The two first-person novels are also good stories, apart from their subplots. But the typical Dickens novel, *Nicholas Nickleby, Oliver Twist, Martin Chuzzlewit, Our Mutual Friend*, always exists round a framework of melodrama. The last thing anyone ever remembers about these books is their central story. On the other hand, I suppose no one has ever read them without carrying the memory of individual pages to the day of his death. Dickens sees human beings with the most intense vividness, but he sees them always in private life, as 'characters', not as functional members of society; that is to say, he sees them statically. Consequently his greatest success is *The Pickwick Papers*, which is not a story at all, merely a series of sketches; there is little attempt at development – the characters simply go on and on, behaving like idiots, in a kind of eternity. As soon as he tries to bring his characters into action, the melodrama begins. He cannot make the action revolve round their ordinary occupations; hence the crossword puzzle of coincidences, intrigues, murders, disguises, buried wills, long-lost brothers, etc. etc. In the end even people like Squeers and Micawber get sucked into the machinery.

Of course it would be absurd to say that Dickens is a vague or merely melodramatic writer. Much that he wrote is extremely factual, and in the power of evoking visual images he has probably never been equalled. When Dickens has once described something you see it for the rest of your life. But in a way the concreteness of his vision is a sign of what he is missing. For, after all, that is what the merely casual onlooker always sees – the outward appearance, the non-functional, the surfaces of things. No one who is really involved in the landscape ever sees the landscape. Wonderfully as he can describe an *appearance*, Dickens does not often describe a *process*. The vivid pictures that he succeeds in leaving in one's memory are nearly always the pictures of things seen in leisure moments, in the coffee-rooms of country inns or through the windows of a stage-coach; the kind of things he notices are inn-signs, brass door-knockers, painted jugs, the interiors of shops and private houses, clothes, faces and, above all, food. Everything is seen from the consumer-angle. When he writes about Coketown he manages to evoke, in just a few paragraphs, the atmosphere of a Lancashire town as a slightly disgusted southern visitor would see it. 'It had a black canal in it, and a river that ran purple with evil-smelling dye, and vast piles of buildings full of windows where there was a rattling and a trembling all day long, and where the piston of the steam-engine worked mon-otonously up and down, like the head of an elephant in a state of melancholy madness.' That is as near as Dickens ever gets to the machinery of the mills. An engineer or a cotton-broker would see it differently, but then neither of them would be capable of that impressionistic touch about the heads of the elephants.

In a rather different sense his attitude to life is extremely unphysical. He is a man who lives through his eyes and ears rather than through his hands and muscles. Actually his habits were not so sedentary as this seems to imply. In spite of rather poor health and physique, he was active to the point of restless-ness; throughout his life he was a remarkable walker, and he could at any rate carpenter well enough to put up stage scenery. But he was not one of those people who feel a need to use their hands. It is difficult to imagine him digging at a cabbage-patch, for instance. He gives no evidence of knowing anything about agriculture, and obviously knows nothing about any kind of game or sport. He has no interest in pugilism, for instance. Considering the age in which he was writing, it is astonishing how little physical brutality there is in Dickens's novels. Martin

Chuzzlewit and Mark Tapley, for instance, behave with the most remarkable mildness towards the Americans who are constantly menacing them with revolvers and bowie-knives. The average English or American novelist would have had them handing out socks on the jaw and exchanging pistol-shots in all directions. Dickens is too decent for that; he sees the stupidity of violence, and also he belongs to a cautious urban class which does not deal in socks on the jaw, even in theory. And his attitude towards sport is mixed up with social feelings. In England, for mainly geographical reasons, sport, especially field-sports, and snobbery are inextricably mingled. English Socialists are often flatly incredulous when told that Lenin, for instance, was devoted to shooting. In their eyes shooting, hunting, etc., are simply snobbish observances of the landed gentry; they forget that these things might appear differently in a huge virgin country like Russia. From Dickens's point of view almost any kind of sport is at best a subject for satire. Consequently one side of nineteenth-century life – the boxing, racing, cockfighting, badger-digging, poaching, rat-catching side of life, so wonderfully embalmed in Leech's illustrations to Surtees – is outside his scope.

What is more striking, in a seemingly 'progressive' radical, is that he is not mechanically minded. He shows no interest either in the details of machinery or in the things machinery can do. As Gissing remarks, Dickens nowhere describes a railway journey with anything like the enthusiasm he shows in describing journeys by stage-coach. In nearly all of his books one has a curious feeling that one is living in the first quarter of the nineteenth century, and in fact, he does tend to return to this period. *Little Dorrit*, written in the middle 'fifties, deals with the late 'twenties; *Great Expectations* (1861) is not dated, but evidently deals with the 'twenties and 'thirties. Several of the inventions and discoveries which have made the modern world possible (the electric telegraph, the breech-loading gun, india-rubber, coal gas, wood-pulp paper) first appeared in Dickens's lifetime, but he scarcely notes them in his books. Nothing is queerer than the vagueness with which he speaks of Doyce's 'invention' in *Little Dorrit*. It is represented as some-thing extremely ingenious and revolutionary, 'of great import-ance to his country and his fellow-creatures', and it is also an important minor link in the book; yet we are never told what the 'invention' is! On the other hand, Doyce's physical appearance is hit off with the typical Dickens touch; he has a peculiar way of moving his thumb, a way characteristic of engineers. After that, Doyce is firmly anchored in one's memory; but, as usual, Dickens has done it by fastening on something external.

There are people (Tennyson is an example) who lack the mechanical faculty but can see the social possibilities of machinery. Dickens has not this stamp of mind. He shows very little consciousness of the future. When he speaks of human progress it is usually in terms of *moral* progress – men growing better; probably he would never admit that men are only as good as their technical development allows them to be. At this point the gap between Dickens and his modern analogue H. G. Wells, is at its widest. Wells wears the future round his neck like a millstone, but Dickens's unscientific cast of mind is just as damaging in a different way. What it does is to make any *positive* attitude more difficult for him. He is hostile to the feudal, agricultural past and not in real touch with the industrial present. Well, then, all that remains is the future (meaning Science, 'progress' and so forth), which hardly enters into his thoughts. Therefore, while attacking everything in sight, he has no definable standard of comparison. As I have pointed out already, he attacks the current educational system with perfect justice, and yet, after all, he has no remedy to offer except kindlier schoolmasters. Why did he not indicate what a school *might* have been? Why did he not have his own sons educated according to some plan of his own, instead of sending them to public schools to be stuffed with Greek? Because he lacked that kind of imagination. He has an infallible moral sense, but very little intellectual curiosity. And here one comes upon something which really is an enormous deficiency in Dickens, something that really does make the nineteenth century seem remote from us – that he has no ideal of *work*.

With the doubtful exception of David Copperfield (merely Dickens himself), one cannot point to a single one of his central characters who is primarily interested in his job. His heroes work in order to make a living and to marry the heroine, not because they feel a passionate interest in one particular subject. Martin Chuzzlewit, for instance, is not burning with zeal to be an architect; he might just as well be a doctor or a barrister. In any case, in the typical Dickens novel, the *deus ex machina* enters with a bag of gold in the last chapter and the hero is absolved from further struggle. The feeling, 'This is what I came into the world to do. Everything else is uninteresting. I will do this even if it means starvation', which turns men of differing temperaments into scientists, inventors, artists, priests, explorers and revolutionaries – this motif is almost entirely absent from Dickens's books. He himself, as is well known, worked like a slave and believed in his work as few novelists have ever done. But there seems to be no calling except novel-writing (and perhaps acting) towards which he can imagine this kind of devotion. And, after all, it is natural enough, considering his rather negative attitude towards society. In the last resort there is nothing he admires except common decency. Science is uninteresting and machinery is cruel and ugly (the heads of the elephants). Business is only for ruffians like Bounderby. As for politics – leave that to the Tite Barnacles. Really there is no objective except to marry the heroine, settle down, live solvently and be kind. And you can do that much better in private life.

Here, perhaps, one gets a glimpse of Dickens's secret imaginative background. What did he think of as the most desirable way to live? When Martin Chuzzlewit had made it up with his uncle, when Nicholas Nickleby had married money, when John Harmon had been enriched by Boffin – what did they *do*?

The answer evidently is that they did nothing. Nicholas Nickleby invested his wife's money with the Cheerybles and 'became a rich and prosperous merchant', but as he immediately retired into Devonshire, we can assume that he did not work very hard. Mr and Mrs Snodgrass 'purchased and cultivated a small farm, more for occupation than profit'. That is the spirit in which most of Dickens's books end – a sort of radiant idleness. Where he appears to disapprove of young men who do not work (Harthouse, Harry Gowan, Richard Carstone, Wrayburn before his reformation), it is because they are cynical and immoral or because they are a burden on somebody else; if you are 'good', and also self-supporting, there is no reason why you should not spend fifty years in simply drawing your dividends. Home life is always enough. And, after all, it was the general assumption of his age. The 'genteel sufficiency', the 'competence', the 'gentleman of independent means' (or 'in easy circumstances') – the very phrases tell one all about the strange, empty dream of the eighteenth- and nineteenth-century middle bourgeoisie. It was a dream of *complete idleness*. Charles Reade conveys its spirit perfectly in the ending of *Hard Cash*. Alfred Hardie, hero of *Hard Cash*, is the typical nineteenth-century novel-hero (public-school style), with gifts which Reade describes as amounting to 'genius'. He is an old Etonian and a scholar of Oxford, he knows most of the Greek and Latin classics by heart, he can box with prize-fighters and win the Diamond Sculls at Henley. He goes through incredible adventures in which, of course, he behaves with faultless heroism, and then, at the age of twenty-five, he inherits a fortune, marries his Julia Dodd and settles down in the suburbs of Liverpool, in the same house as his parents-in-law:

> They all lived together at Albion Villa, thanks to Alfred ... Oh, you happy little villa! You were as like Paradise as any mortal dwelling can be. A day came, however, when your walls could no longer hold all the happy inmates. Julia presented Alfred with a lovely boy; enter two nurses, and the villa showed symptoms of bursting. Two months more, and Alfred and his wife overflowed into the next villa. It was but twenty yards off; and there was a double reason for the migration. As often happens after a long separation, Heaven bestowed on Captain and Mrs Dodd another infant to play about their knees, etc. etc. etc.

This is the type of the Victorian happy ending – a vision of a huge, loving family of three or four generations, all crammed together in the same house and constantly multiplying, like a bed of oysters. What is striking about it is the utterly soft, sheltered, effortless life that it implies. It is not even a violent idleness, like Squire Western's. That is the significance of Dickens's urban background and his non-interest in the blackguardly-sporting-military side of life. His heroes, once they had come into money and 'settled down', would not only do no work; they would not even ride, hunt, shoot, fight duels, elope with actresses or lose money at the races. They would simply live at home in feather-bed respectability, and preferably next door to a blood-relation living exactly the same life:

> The first act of Nicholas, when he became a rich and prosperous merchant, was to buy his father's old house. As time crept on, and there came gradually about him a group of lovely children, it was altered and enlarged; but none of the old rooms were ever pulled down, no old tree was ever rooted up, nothing with which there was any association of bygone times was ever removed or changed.
>
> Within a stone's-throw was another retreat, enlivened by children's pleasant voices too; and here was Kate ... the same true, gentle creature, the same fond sister, the same in the love of all about her, as in her girlish days.

It is the same incestuous atmosphere as in the passage quoted from Reade. And evidently this is Dickens's ideal ending. It is perfectly attained in *Nicholas Nickleby*, *Martin Chuzzlewit* and *Pickwick*, and it is approximated to in varying degrees in almost all the others. The exceptions are *Hard Times* and *Great Expectations* – the latter actually has a 'happy ending', but it contradicts the general tendency of the book, and it was put in at the request of Bulwer Lytton.

The ideal to be striven after, then, appears to be something like this: a hundred thousand pounds, a quaint old house with plenty of ivy on it, a sweetly womanly wife, a horde of children, and no work. Everything is safe, soft, peaceful and, above all, domestic. In the moss-grown churchyard down the road are the graves of the loved ones who passed away before the happy ending happened. The servants are comic and feudal, the children prattle round your feet, the old friends sit at your fireside, talking of past days, there is the endless succession of enormous meals, the cold punch and sherry negus, the feather beds and warming-pans, the Christmas parties with charades and blind man's buff; but nothing ever happens, except the yearly childbirth. The curious thing is that it is a genuinely happy picture, or so Dickens is able to make it appear. The thought of that kind of existence is satisfying to him. This alone would be enough to tell one that more than a hundred years have passed since Dickens's first book was

written. No modern man could combine such purposelessness
with so much vitality.

5

By this time anyone who is a lover of Dickens, and who has
read as far as this, will probably be angry with me.

I have been discussing Dickens simply in terms of his 'message', and almost ignoring his literary qualities. But every
writer, especially every novelist, *has* a 'message', whether he
admits it or not, and the minutest details of his work are influenced by it. All art is propaganda. Neither Dickens himself nor
the majority of Victorian novelists would have thought of
denying this. On the other hand, not all propaganda is art. As
I said earlier, Dickens is one of those writers who are felt to be
worth stealing. He has been stolen by Marxists, by Catholics
and, above all, by Conservatives. The question is, What is there
to steal? Why does anyone care about Dickens? Why do *I* care
about Dickens?

That kind of question is never easy to answer. As a rule, an
æsthetic preference is either something inexplicable or it is so
corrupted by non-æsthetic motives as to make one wonder
whether the whole of literary criticism is not a huge network of
humbug. In Dickens's case the complicating factor is his familiarity. He happens to be one of those 'great authors' who are
ladled down everyone's throat in childhood. At the time this
causes rebellion and vomiting, but it may have different after-
effects in later life. For instance, nearly everyone feels a sneaking affection for the patriotic poems that he learned by heart as
a child. 'Ye Mariners of England', the 'Charge of the Light
Brigade' and so forth. What one enjoys is not so much the
poems themselves as the memories they call up. And with
Dickens the same forces of association are at work. Probably
there are copies of one or two of his books lying about in an
actual majority of English homes. Many children begin to
know his characters by sight before they can even read, for
on the whole Dickens was lucky in his illustrators. A thing that
is absorbed as early as that does not come up against any critical
judgement. And when one thinks of this, one thinks of all that
is bad and silly in Dickens – the cast-iron 'plots', the characters
who don't come off, the *longueurs*, the paragraphs in blank

verse, the awful pages of 'pathos'. And then the thought arises, when I say I like Dickens, do I simply mean that I like thinking about my childhood? Is Dickens merely an institution?

If so, he is an institution that there is no getting away from. How often one really thinks about any writer, even a writer one cares for, is a difficult thing to decide; but I should doubt whether anyone who has actually read Dickens can go a week without remembering him in one context or another. Whether you approve of him or not, he is *there*, like the Nelson Column. At any moment some scene or character, which may come from some book you cannot even remember the name of, is liable to drop into your mind. Micawber's letters! Winkle in the witness-box! Mrs Gamp! Mrs Wititterly and Sir Tumley Snuffim! Todgers's! (George Gissing said that when he passed the Monument it was never of the Fire of London that he thought, always of Todgers's). Mrs Leo Hunter! Squeers! Silas Wegg and the Decline and Fall-off of the Russian Empire! Miss Mills and the Desert of Sahara! Wopsle acting Hamlet! Mrs Jellyby! Mantalini, Jerry Cruncher, Barkis, Pumblechook, Tracy Tupman, Skimpole, Joe Gargery, Pecksniff – and so it goes on and on. It is not so much a series of books, it is more like a world. And not a purely comic world either, for part of what one remembers in Dickens is his Victorian morbidness and necrophilia and the blood-and-thunder scenes – the death of Sikes, Krook's spontaneous combustion, Fagin in the condemned cell, the women knitting round the guillotine. To a surprising extent all this has entered even into the minds of people who do not care about it. A music-hall comedian can (or at any rate could quite recently) go on the stage and impersonate Micawber or Mrs Gamp with a fair certainty of being understood, although not one in twenty of the audience had ever read a book of Dickens's right through. Even people who affect to despise him quote him unconsciously.

Dickens is a writer who can be imitated, up to a certain point. In genuinely popular literature – for instance, the Elephant and Castle version of *Sweeny Todd* – he has been plagiarized quite shamelessly. What has been imitated, however, is simply a tradition that Dickens himself took from earlier novelists and developed, the cult of 'character', i.e. eccentricity. The thing that cannot be imitated is his fertility of invention, which is invention not so much of characters, still less of 'situations', as of turns of phrase and concrete details. The outstanding, unmistakable mark of Dickens's writing is the *unnecessary detail*. Here is an example of what I mean. The story given below is not particularly funny, but there is one phrase in it that is as individual as a fingerprint. Mr Jack Hopkins, at Bob Sawyer's party, is telling the story of the child who swallowed its sister's necklace:

Next day, child swallowed two beads; the day after that, he treated himself to three, and so on, till in a week's time he had got through the necklace – five-and-twenty beads in all. The sister, who was an industrious girl, and seldom treated herself to a bit of finery, cried her eyes out, at the loss of the necklace; looked high and low for it; but I needn't say didn't find it. A few days afterwards, the family were at dinner – baked shoulder of mutton, and potatoes under it – the child, who wasn't hungry, was playing about the room, when suddenly there was heard a devil of a noise, like a small hail storm. 'Don't do that, my boy,' says the father. 'I ain't a-doin' nothing,' said the child. 'Well, don't do it again,' said the father. There was a short silence, and then the noise began again, worse than ever. 'If you don't mind what I say, my boy,' said the father, 'you'll find yourself in bed, in something less than a pig's whisper.' He gave the child a shake to make him obedient, and such a rattling ensued as nobody ever heard before. 'Why, damme, it's *in* the child!' said the father; 'he's got the croup in the wrong place!' 'No, I haven't father,' said the child, beginning to cry, 'it's the necklace; I swallowed it, father' – The father caught the child up, and ran with him to the hospital: the beads in the boy's stomach rattling all the way with the jolting; and the people looking up in the air, and down in the cellars to see where the unusual sound came from. 'He's in the hospital now,' said Jack Hopkins, 'and he makes such a devil of a noise when he walks about, that they're obliged to muffle him in a watchman's coat, for fear he should wake the patients!'

As a whole, this story might come out of any nineteenth-century comic paper. But the unmistakable Dickens touch, the thing nobody else would have thought of, is the baked

GEORGE ORWELL

shoulder of mutton and potatoes under it. How does this advance the story? The answer is that it doesn't. It is something totally unnecessary, a florid little squiggle on the edge of the page; only, it is by just these squiggles that the special Dickens atmosphere is created. The other thing one would notice here is that Dickens's way of telling a story takes a long time. An interesting example, too long to quote, is Sam Weller's story of the obstinate patient in Chapter XLIV of *The Pickwick Papers*. As it happens, we have a standard of comparison here, because Dickens is plagiarizing, consciously or unconsciously. The story is also told by some ancient Greek writer. I cannot now find the passage, but I read it years ago as a boy at school, and it runs more or less like this:

> A certain Thracian, renowned for his obstinacy, was warned by his physician that if he drank a flagon of wine it would kill him. The Thracian thereupon drank the flagon of wine and immediately jumped off the house-top and perished. 'For,' said he, 'in this way I shall prove that the wine did not kill me.'

As the Greek tells it, that is the whole story – about six lines. As Sam Weller tells it, it takes round about a thousand words. Long before getting to the point we have been told all about the patient's clothes, his meals, his manners, even the news-papers he reads, and about the peculiar construction of the doctor's carriage, which conceals the fact that the coachman's trousers do not match his coat. Then there is the dialogue between the doctor and the patient. ' "Crumpets is whole-some, sir," said the patient. "Crumpets is *not* wholesome, sir", says the doctor, wery fierce,' etc. etc. In the end the original story has been buried under the details. And in all of Dickens's most characteristic passages it is the same. His imagination overwhelms everything, like a kind of weed. Squeers stands up to address his boys, and immediately we are hearing about Bolder's father who was two pounds ten short, and Mobbs's stepmother who took to her bed on hearing that Mobbs wouldn't eat fat and hoped Mr Squeers would flog him into a happier state of mind. Mrs Leo Hunter writes a poem, 'Expiring Frog'; two full stanzas are given. Boffin takes a fancy to pose as a miser, and instantly we are down among the

176

squalid biographies of eighteenth-century misers, with names like Vulture Hopkins and the Rev Blewberry Jones, and chapter headings like 'The Story of the Mutton Pies' and 'The Treasures of a Dunghill'. Mrs Harris, who does not even exist, has more detail piled onto her than any three characters in an ordinary novel. Merely in the middle of a sentence we learn, for instance, that her infant nephew has been seen in a bottle at Greenwich Fair, along with the pink-eyed lady, the Prussian dwarf and the living skeleton. Joe Gargery describes how the robbers broke into the house of Pumblechook, the corn and seed merchant – 'and they took his till, and they took his cashbox, and they drinked his wine, and they partook of his wittles, and they slapped his face, and they pulled his nose, and they tied him up to his bedpust, and they give him a dozen, and they stuffed his mouth full of flowering annuals to perwent his crying out'. Once again the unmistakable Dickens touch, the flowering annuals; but any other novelist would only have mentioned about half of these outrages. Everything is piled up and up, detail on detail, embroidery on embroidery. It is futile to object that this kind of thing is rococo – one might as well make the same objection to a wedding-cake. Either you like it or you do not like it. Other nineteenth-century writers, Surtees, Barham, Thackeray, even Marryat, have something of Dickens's profuse, overflowing quality, but none of them on anything like the same scale. The appeal of all these writers now depends partly on period-flavour, and though Marryat is still officially a 'boys' writer' and Surtees has a sort of legendary fame among hunting men, it is probable that they are read mostly by bookish people.

Significantly, Dickens's most successful books (not his *best* books) are *The Pickwick Papers*, which is not a novel, and *Hard Times* and *A Tale of Two Cities*, which are not funny. As a novelist his natural fertility greatly hampers him, because the burlesque which he is never able to resist is constantly breaking into what ought to be serious situations. There is a good example of this in the opening chapter of *Great Expectations*. The escaped convict, Magwitch, has just captured the six-year-old Pip in the churchyard. The scene starts terrifyingly enough, from Pip's point of view. The convict, smothered in mud and with his chain trailing from his leg, suddenly starts up among the tombs, grabs the child, turns him upside down and robs his pockets. Then he begins terrorizing him into bringing food and a file:

> . . . he held me by the arms in an upright position on the top of the stone, and went on in these fearful terms:
>
> 'You bring me, to-morrow morning early, that file and them wittles. You bring the lot to me, at that old Battery over yonder. You do it, and you never dare to say a word or dare to make a sign concerning your having seen such a person as me, or any person sumever, and you shall be let to live. You fail, or you go from my words in any partickler, no matter how small it is, and your heart and your liver shall be tore out, roasted and ate. Now, I ain't alone, as you may think I am. There's a young man hid with me, in compari-son with which young man I am a Angel. That young man hears the words I speak. That young man has a secret way pecooliar to himself, of getting at a boy, and at his heart, and at his liver. It is in wain for a boy to attempt to hide himself from that young man. A boy may lock his door, may be warm in bed, may tuck himself up, may draw the clothes over his head, may think himself comfortable and safe, but that young man will softly creep and creep his way to him and tear him open. I am keeping that young man from harming of you at the present moment, with great difficulty. I find it wery hard to hold that young man off of your inside. Now, what do you say?'

Here Dickens has simply yielded to temptation. To begin with, no starving and hunted man would speak in the least like that. Moreover, although the speech shows a remarkable knowledge of the way in which a child's mind works, its actual words are quite out of tune with what is to follow. It turns Magwitch into a sort of pantomime wicked uncle, or, if one sees him through the child's eyes, into an appalling monster. Later in the book he is to be represented as neither, and his exaggerated gratitude, on which the plot turns, is to be incred-ible because of just this speech. As usual, Dickens's imagination has overwhelmed him. The picturesque details were too good to be left out. Even with characters who are more of a piece than Magwitch he is liable to be tripped up by some seductive phrase. Mr Murdstone, for instance, is in the habit of ending David Copperfield's lessons every morning with a dreadful sum in arithmetic. 'If I go into a cheese-monger's shop, and buy five thousand double-Gloucester cheeses at fourpence halfpenny each, present payment,' it always begins. Once again the typical Dickens detail, the double-Gloucester cheeses. But it is far too human a touch for Murdstone; he would have made it five thousand cashboxes. Every time this note is struck, the unity of the novel suffers. Not that it matters very much, because Dickens is obviously a writer whose parts are greater than his wholes. He is all fragments, all details – rotten architecture, but wonderful gargoyles – and never better than when he is building up some character who will later on be forced to act inconsistently.

Of course it is not usual to urge against Dickens that he makes his characters behave inconsistently. Generally he is accused of doing just the opposite. His characters are supposed to be mere 'types', each crudely representing some single trait and fitted with a kind of label by which you recognize him. Dickens is 'only a caricaturist' – that is the usual accusation, and it does him both more and less than justice. To begin with, he did not think of himself as a caricaturist, and was constantly setting into action characters who ought to have been purely static. Squeers, Micawber, Miss Mowcher,[1] Wegg, Skimpole, Pecksniff and many others are finally involved in 'plots' where they are out of place and where they behave quite incredibly. They start off as magic-lantern slides and they end by getting mixed up in a third-rate movie. Sometimes one can put one's finger on a single sentence in which the original illusion is destroyed. There is such a sentence in *David Copperfield*. After the famous dinner-party (the one where the leg of mutton was underdone), David is showing his guests out. He stops Traddles at the top of the stairs:

'Traddles,' said I, 'Mr Micawber don't mean any harm, poor fellow; but, if I were you, I wouldn't lend him anything.'

'My dear Copperfield,' returned Traddles, smiling, 'I haven't got anything to lend.'

'You have got a name, you know,' said I.

At the place where one reads it this remark jars a little, though something of the kind was inevitable sooner or later. The story is a fairly realistic one, and David is growing up; ultimately he is bound to see Mr Micawber for what he is, a cadging scoundrel. Afterwards, of course, Dickens's sentimentality overcomes him and Micawber is made to turn over a new leaf. But from then on, the original Micawber is never quite recaptured, in spite of desperate efforts. As a rule, the 'plot' in which Dickens's characters get entangled is not particularly credible, but at least it makes some pretence at reality, whereas the world to which they belong is a never-never land, a kind of eternity. But just here one sees that 'only a caricaturist' is not really a condemnation. The fact that Dickens is always thought of as a caricaturist, although he was constantly trying to be something else, is perhaps the surest mark of his genius. The monstrosities that he created are still remembered as monstrosities, in spite of getting mixed up in would-be probable melodramas. Their first impact is so vivid that nothing that comes afterwards effaces it. As with the people one knew in childhood, one seems always to remember them in one particular attitude, doing one particular thing. Mrs Squeers is always ladling out brimstone and treacle, Mrs Gummidge is always weeping, Mrs Gargery is always banging her husband's head against the wall, Mrs Jellyby is always scribbling tracts while her children fall into the area – and there they all are, fixed for ever like little twinkling miniatures painted on snuffbox lids, completely fantastic and incredible, and yet somehow more solid and infinitely more memorable than the efforts of serious novelists. Even by the standards of his time Dickens was an exceptionally artificial writer. As Ruskin said, he 'chose to work in a circle of stage fire'. His characters are even more distorted and simplified than Smollett's. But there are no rules in novel-writing, and for any work of art there is only one test worth bothering about – survival. By this test Dickens's characters have succeeded, even if the people who remember them hardly think of them as human beings. They are monsters, but at any rate they *exist*.

But all the same there is a disadvantage in writing about monsters. It amounts to this, that it is only certain moods that Dickens can speak to. There are large areas of the human mind that he never touches. There is no poetic feeling anywhere in his books, and no genuine tragedy, and even sexual love is almost outside his scope. Actually his books are not so sexless as they are sometimes declared to be, and considering the time in which he was writing, he is reasonably frank. But there is not a trace in him of the feeling that one finds in *Manon Lescaut*, *Salammbô*, *Carmen*, *Wuthering Heights*. According to Aldous Huxley, D. H. Lawrence once said that Balzac was 'a gigantic dwarf', and in a sense the same is true of Dickens. There are whole worlds which he either knows nothing about or does not wish to mention. Except in a rather roundabout way, one cannot *learn* very much from Dickens. And to say this is to think almost immediately of the great Russian novelists of the nineteenth century. Why is it that Tolstoy's grasp seems to be so much larger than Dickens's – why is it that he seems able to tell you so much more *about yourself*? It is not that he is more gifted, or even, in the last analysis, more intelligent. It is because he is writing about people who are growing. His characters are struggling to make their souls, whereas Dickens's are already finished and perfect. In my own mind Dickens's people are present far more often and far more vividly than Tolstoy's, but always in a single unchangeable attitude, like pictures or pieces of furniture. You cannot hold an imaginary conversation with a Dickens character as you can with, say, Peter Bezukhov. And this is not merely because of Tolstoy's greater seriousness, for there are also comic characters that you can imagine yourself talking to – Bloom, for instance, or Pécuchet, or even Wells's Mr Polly. It is because Dickens's characters have no mental life. They say perfectly the thing that they have to say, but they cannot be conceived as talking about anything else. They never learn, never speculate. Perhaps the most meditative of his characters is Paul Dombey, and his thoughts are mush. Does this mean that Tolstoy's novels are 'better' than Dickens's? The truth is that it is absurd to make such comparisons in terms of 'better' and 'worse'. If I were forced to compare Tolstoy with Dickens, I should say that Tolstoy's appeal will probably be wider in the long run, because Dickens is scarcely intelligible outside the English-speaking culture; on the other hand, Dickens is able to reach simple people, which Tolstoy is not. Tolstoy's characters can cross a frontier, Dickens's can be portrayed on a cigarette-card. But one is no more obliged to choose between them than between a sausage and a rose. Their purposes barely intersect.

6

If Dickens had been *merely* a comic writer, the chances are that no one would now remember his name. Or at best a few of his books would survive in rather the same way as books like *Frank Fairleigh, Mr Verdant Green* and *Mrs Caudle's Curtain Lectures*, as a sort of hangover of the Victorian atmosphere, a pleasant little whiff of oysters and brown stout. Who has not felt sometimes that it was 'a pity' that Dickens ever deserted the vein of *Pickwick* for things like *Little Dorrit* and *Hard Times*? What people always demand of a popular novelist is that he shall write the same book over and over again, forgetting that a man who would write the same book twice could not even write it once. Any writer who is not utterly lifeless moves upon a kind of parabola, and the downward curve is implied in the upward one. Joyce has to start with the frigid competence of *Dubliners* and end with the dream-language of *Finnegans Wake*, but *Ulysses* and *Portrait of the Artist* are part of the trajectory. The thing that drove Dickens forward into a form of art for which he was not really suited, and at the same time caused us to remember him, was simply the fact that he was a moralist, the consciousness of 'having something to say'. He is always preaching a sermon, and that is the final secret of his inventiveness. For you can only create if you can *care*. Types like Squeers and Micawber could not have been produced by a hack writer looking for something to be funny about. A joke worth laughing at always has an idea behind it, and usually a subversive idea. Dickens is able to go on being funny because he is in revolt against authority, and authority is always there to be laughed at. There is always room for one more custard pie.

His radicalism is of the vaguest kind, and yet one always knows that it is there. That is the difference between being a moralist and a politician. He has no constructive suggestions, not even a clear grasp of the nature of the society he is attacking, only an emotional perception that something is wrong. All he can finally say is, 'Behave decently', which, as I suggested earlier, is not necessarily so shallow as it sounds. Most revolutionaries are potential Tories, because they imagine that every-thing can be put right by altering the *shape* of society; once that change is effected, as it sometimes is, they see no need for any other. Dickens has not this kind of mental coarseness. The vagueness of his discontent is the mark of its permanence. What he is out against is not this or that institution, but, as Chesterton put it, 'an expression on the human face'. Roughly speaking, his morality is the Christian morality, but in spite of his Anglican upbringing he was essentially a Bible-Christian, as he took care to make plain when writing his will. In any case he cannot properly be described as a religious man. He 'believed', undoubtedly, but religion in the devotional sense does not seem to have entered much into his thoughts.[2] Where he is Christian is in his quasi-instinctive siding with the oppressed against the oppressors. As a matter of course he is on the side of the underdog, always and everywhere. To carry this to its logical conclusion one has got to change sides when the under-dog becomes an upperdog, and in fact Dickens does tend to do so. He loathes the Catholic Church, for instance, but as soon as the Catholics are persecuted (*Barnaby Rudge*) he is on their side. He loathes the aristocratic class even more, but as soon as they are really overthrown (the revolutionary chapters in *A Tale of Two Cities*) his sympathies swing round. Whenever he departs from this emotional attitude he goes astray. A well-known example is at the ending of *David Copperfield*, in which every-one who reads it feels that something has gone wrong. What is wrong is that the closing chapters are pervaded, faintly but noticeably, by the cult of success. It is the gospel according to Smiles, instead of the gospel according to Dickens. The attract-ive, out-at-elbow characters are got rid of, Micawber makes a fortune, Heep gets into prison – both of these events are flagrantly impossible – and even Dora is killed off to make way for Agnes. If you like, you can read Dora as Dickens's wife and Agnes as his sister-in-law, but the essential point is that Dickens has 'turned respectable' and done violence to his own nature. Perhaps that is why Agnes is the most disagreeable of his heroines, the real legless angel of Victorian romance, almost as bad as Thackeray's Laura.

No grown-up person can read Dickens without feeling his limitations, and yet there does remain his native generosity of mind, which acts as a kind of anchor and nearly always keeps him where he belongs. It is probably the central secret of his popularity. A good-tempered antinomianism rather of Dickens's type is one of the marks of Western popular culture. One sees it in folk-stories and comic songs, in dream-figures like Mickey Mouse and Popeye the Sailor (both of them variants of Jack the Giant-killer), in the history of working-class Socialism, in the popular protests (always ineffective but not always a sham) against imperialism, in the impulse that makes a jury award excessive damages when a rich man's car runs over a poor man; it is the feeling that one is always on the side of the underdog, on the side of the weak against the strong. In one sense it is a feeling that is fifty years out of date. The common man is still living in the mental world of Dickens, but nearly every modern intellectual has gone over to some or other form of totalitarianism. From the Marxist or Fascist point of view, nearly all that Dickens stands for can be written off as 'bourgeois morality'. But in moral outlook no one could be more 'bourgeois' than the English working classes. The ordinary people in the Western countries have never entered, mentally, into the world of 'realism' and power-politics. They may do so before long, in which case Dickens will be as out of date as the cab-horse. But in his own age and ours he has been popular chiefly because he was able to express in a comic, simplified and therefore memorable form the native decency of the common man. And it is important that from this point of view people of very different types can be described as 'common'. In a country like England, in spite of its class-structure, there does exist a certain cultural unity. All through the Christian ages, and especially since the French Revolution, the Western world has been haunted by the idea of freedom and equality; it is only an *idea*, but it is has penetrated to all ranks of society. The most atrocious injustices, cruelties, lies, snobberies exist everywhere, but there are not many people who can regard these things with the same indifference as, say, a Roman slave-owner. Even the millionaire suffers from a vague sense of guilt, like a dog eating a stolen leg of mutton. Nearly everyone, whatever his actual conduct may be, responds emotionally to the idea of human brotherhood. Dickens voiced a code which was and on the whole still is believed in, even by people who violate it. It is difficult otherwise to explain why he could be both read by working people (a thing that has happened to no other novelist of his stature) and buried in Westminster Abbey.

When one reads any strongly individual piece of writing, one has the impression of seeing a face somewhere behind the page. It is not necessarily the actual face of the writer. I feel this very strongly with Swift, with Defoe, with Fielding, Stendhal, Thackeray, Flaubert, though in several cases I do not know what these people looked like and do not want to know. What one sees is the face that the writer *ought* to have. Well, in the case of Dickens I see a face that is not quite the face of Dickens's photographs, though it resembles it. It is the face of a man of about forty, with a small beard and a high colour. He is laughing, with a touch of anger in his laughter, but no triumph, no malignity. It is the face of a man who is always fighting against something, but who fights in the open and is not frightened, the face of a man who is *generously angry* – in other words, of a nineteenth-century liberal, a free intelligence, a type hated with equal hatred by all the smelly little orthodoxies which are now contending for our souls.

Boys' Weeklies
11 March 1940

You never walk far through any poor quarter in any big town without coming upon a small newsagent's shop. The general appearance of these shops is always very much the same: a few posters for the *Daily Mail* and the *News of the World* outside, a poky little window with sweet-bottles and packets of Players, and a dark interior smelling of liquorice allsorts and festooned from floor to ceiling with vilely printed twopenny papers, most of them with lurid cover-illustrations in three colours.

Except for the daily and evening papers, the stock of these shops hardly overlaps at all with that of the big newsagents. Their main selling line is the twopenny weekly, and the number and variety of these are almost unbelievable. Every hobby and pastime – cage-birds, fretwork, carpentering, bees, carrier-pigeons, home conjuring, philately, chess – has at least one paper devoted to it, and generally several. Gardening and livestock-keeping must have at least a score between them. Then there are the sporting papers, the radio papers, the children's comics, the various snippet papers such as *Tit-bits*, the large range of papers devoted to the movies and all more or less exploiting women's legs, the various trade papers, the women's story-papers (the *Oracle*, *Secrets*, *Peg's Paper*, etc. etc.), the needlework papers – these so numerous that a display of them alone will often fill an entire window – and in addition the long series of 'Yank Mags' (*Fight Stories*, *Action Stories*, *Western Short Stories*, etc.), which are imported shop-soiled from America and sold at twopence halfpenny or threepence. And the periodical proper shades off into the fourpenny novelette, the *Aldine Boxing Novels*, the *Boys' Friend Library*, the *Schoolgirls' Own Library* and many others.

Probably the contents of these shops is the best available indication of what the mass of the English people really feels and thinks. Certainly nothing half so revealing exists in documentary form. Best-seller novels, for instance, tell one a great deal, but the novel is aimed almost exclusively at people above the £4-a-week level. The movies are probably a very unsafe guide to popular taste, because the film industry is virtually a monopoly, which means that it is not obliged to study its public at all closely. The same applies to some extent to the daily papers, and most of all to the radio. But it does not apply to the weekly paper with a smallish circulation and specialised subject-matter. Papers like the *Exchange and Mart*, for instance, or *Cage-Birds*, or the *Oracle*, or *Prediction*, or the *Matrimonial Times*, only exist because there is a definite demand for them, and they reflect the minds of their readers as a great national daily with a circulation of millions cannot possibly do.

Here I am only dealing with a single series of papers, the boys' twopenny weeklies, often inaccurately described as 'penny dreadfuls'. Falling strictly within this class there are at present ten papers, the *Gem*, *Magnet*, *Modern Boy*, *Triumph* and *Champion*, all owned by the Amalgamated Press, and the *Wizard*, *Rover*, *Skipper*, *Hotspur* and *Adventure*, all owned by D. C. Thomson & Co. What the circulations of these papers are, I do not know. The editors and proprietors refuse to name any figures, and in any case the circulation of a paper carrying serial stories is bound to fluctuate widely. But there is no question that the combined public of the ten papers is a very large one. They are on sale in every town in England, and nearly every boy who reads at all goes through a phase of reading one or more of them. The *Gem* and *Magnet*, which are much the oldest of these papers, are of rather different type from the rest, and they have evidently lost some of their popularity during the past few years. A good many boys now regard them as old-fashioned and 'slow'. Nevertheless I want to discuss them first, because they are more interesting psychologically than the others, and also because the mere survival of such papers into the nineteen-thirties is a rather startling phenomenon.

The *Gem* and *Magnet* are sister-papers (characters out of one paper frequently appear in the other), and were both started more than thirty years ago. At that time, together with *Chums* and the old *B.O.P.*, they were the leading papers for boys, and they remained dominant till quite recently. Each of them carries every week a fifteen- or twenty-thousand-word school story, complete in itself, but usually more or less connected with the story of the week before. The *Gem* in addition to its school story carries one or more adventure serials. Otherwise the two papers are so much alike that they can be treated as one, though the *Magnet* has always been the better known of the two, probably because it possesses a really first-rate character in the fat boy, Billy Bunter.

The stories are stories of what purports to be public-school life, and the schools (Greyfriars in the *Magnet* and St. Jim's in the *Gem*) are represented as ancient and fashionable foundations of the type of Eton or Winchester. All the leading characters are fourth-form boys aged fourteen or fifteen, older or younger boys only appearing in very minor parts. Like Sexton Blake and Nelson Lee, these boys continue week after week and year after year, never growing any older. Very occasionally a new boy arrives or a minor character drops out, but in at any rate the last twenty-five years the personnel has barely altered. All the principal characters in both papers – Bob Cherry, Tom Merry, Harry Wharton, Johnny Bull, Billy

GEORGE ORWELL

Bunter and the rest of them – were at Greyfriars or St. Jim's long before the Great War, exactly the same age as at present, having much the same kind of adventures and talking almost exactly the same dialect. And not only the characters but the whole atmosphere of both *Gem* and *Magnet* has been preserved unchanged, partly by means of very elaborate stylisation. The stories in the *Magnet* are signed 'Frank Richards' and those in the *Gem*, 'Martin Clifford' but a series lasting thirty years could hardly be the work of the same person every week. Consequently they have to be written in a style that is easily imitated – an extraordinary, artificial, repetitive style, quite different from anything else now existing in English literature. A couple of extracts will do as illustrations. Here is one from the *Magnet*:

> Groan!
>   'Shut up, Bunter!'
> Groan!
> Shutting up was not really in Billy Bunter's line. He seldom shut up, though often requested to do so. On the present awful occasion the fat Owl of Greyfriars was less inclined than ever to shut up. And he did not shut up! He groaned, and groaned, and went on groaning.
>   Even groaning did not fully express Bunter's feelings. His feelings, in fact, were inexpressible.
>   There were six of them in the soup! Only one of the six uttered sounds of woe and lamentation. But that one, William George Bunter, uttered enough for the whole party and a little over.
>   Harry Wharton & Co. stood in a wrathy and worried group. They were landed and stranded, diddled, dished and done! etc. etc. etc.

Here is one from the *Gem*:

> 'Oh cwumbs!'
>   'Oh gum!'
>   'Oooogh!'
>   'Urrggh!'
> Arthur Augustus sat up dizzily. He grabbed his handkerchief and pressed it to his damaged nose. Tom Merry sat up, gasping for breath. They looked at one another.

'Bai Jove! This is a go, deah boy!' gurgled Arthur Augustus. 'I have been thwown into quite a fluttah! Oogh! The wottahs! The wuffians! The feahful outsidahs! Wow!' etc. etc. etc.

Both of these extracts are entirely typical; you would find something like them in almost every chapter of every number, to-day or twenty-five years ago. The first thing that anyone would notice is the extraordinary amount of tautology (the first of these two passages contains a hundred and twenty-five words and could be compressed into about thirty), seemingly designed to spin out the story, but actually playing its part in creating the atmosphere. For the same reason various facetious expressions are repeated over and over again; 'wrathy', for instance, is a great favourite, and so is 'diddled, dished and done'. 'Oooogh!', 'Grooo!' and 'Yaroo!' (stylised cries of pain) recur constantly, and so does 'Ha! ha! ha!', always given a line to itself, so that sometimes a quarter of a column or thereabouts consists of 'Ha! ha! ha!' The slang ('Go and eat coke!', 'What the thump!', 'You frabjous ass!', etc. etc.) has never been altered, so that the boys are now using slang which is at least thirty years out of date. In addition, the various nicknames are rubbed in on every possible occasion. Every few lines we are reminded that Harry Wharton & Co. are 'the Famous Five', Bunter is always 'the fat Owl' or 'the Owl of the Remove', Vernon-Smith is always 'the Bounder of Greyfriars', Gussy (the Honourable Arthur Augustus D'Arcy) is always 'the swell of St. Jim's', and so on and so forth. There is a constant, untiring effort to keep the atmosphere intact and to make sure that every new reader learns immediately who is who. The result has been to make Greyfriars and St. Jim's into an extraordinary little world of their own, a world which cannot be taken seriously by anyone over fifteen, but which at any rate is not easily forgotten. By a debasement of the Dickens technique a series of stereotyped 'characters' has been built up, in several cases very successfully. Billy Bunter, for instance, must be one of the best-known figures in English fiction; for the mere number of people who know him he ranks with Sexton Blake, Tarzan, Sherlock Holmes and a handful of characters in Dickens.

Needless to say, these stories are fantastically unlike life at a real public school. They run in cycles of rather differing types, but in general they are the clean-fun, knockabout type of story, with interest centring round horseplay, practical jokes, ragging masters, fights, canings, football, cricket and food. A constantly recurring story is one in which a boy is accused of some misdeed committed by another and is too much of a sportsman to reveal the truth. The 'good' boys are 'good' in the clean-living Englishman tradition – they keep in hard training, wash behind their ears, never hit below the belt, etc. etc. – and by way of contrast there is a series of 'bad' boys, Racke, Crooke, Loder and others, whose badness consists in betting, smoking cigarettes and frequenting public-houses. All these boys are constantly on the verge of expulsion, but as it would mean a change of personnel if any boy were actually expelled, no one is ever caught out in any really serious offence. Stealing, for instance, barely enters as a motif. Sex is completely taboo, especially in the form in which it actually arises at public schools. Occasionally girls enter into the stories, and very rarely there is something approaching a mild flirtation, but it is always entirely in the spirit of clean fun. A boy and a girl enjoy going for bicycle rides together – that is all it ever amounts to. Kissing, for instance, would be regarded as 'soppy'. Even the bad boys are presumed to be completely sexless. When the *Gem* and *Magnet* were started, it is probable that there was a deliberate intention to get away from the guilty sex-ridden atmosphere that pervaded so much of the earlier literature for boys. In the 'nineties the *Boy's Own Paper*, for instance, used to have its correspondence columns full of terrifying warnings against masturbation, and books like *St. Winifred's* and *Tom Brown's Schooldays* were heavy with homosexual feeling, though no doubt the authors were not fully aware of it. In the *Gem* and *Magnet* sex simply does not exist as a problem. Religion is also taboo; in the whole thirty years' issue of the two papers the word 'God' probably does not occur, except in 'God save the King'. On the other hand, there has always been a very strong 'temperance' strain. Drinking and, by association, smoking are regarded as rather disgraceful even in an adult ('shady' is the usual word), but at the same time as something irresistibly fascinating, a sort of substitute for sex. In their moral atmosphere the *Gem* and *Magnet* have a great deal in common with the Boy Scout movement, which started at about the same time.

All literature of this kind is partly plagiarism. Sexton Blake, for instance, started off quite frankly as an imitation of Sherlock Holmes, and still resembles him fairly strongly; he has hawklike features, lives in Baker Street, smokes enormously and puts on a dressing-gown when he wants to think. The *Gem* and *Magnet* probably owe something to the school story writers who were flourishing when they began, Gunby Hadath, Desmond Coke and the rest, but they owe more to nineteenth-century models. In so far as Greyfriars and St. Jim's are like real schools at all, they are much more like Tom Brown's Rugby than a modern public school. Neither school has an O.T.C., for instance, games are not compulsory, and the boys are even allowed to wear what clothes they like. But without doubt the main origin of these papers is *Stalky & Co.* This book has had an immense influence on boys' literature, and it is one of those books which have a sort of traditional reputation among people who have never even seen a copy of it. More than once in boys' weekly papers I have come across a reference to *Stalky & Co.* in which the word was spelt 'Storky'. Even the name of the chief comic among the Greyfriars masters, Mr Prout, is taken from *Stalky & Co.*, and so is much of the slang; 'jape', 'merry', 'giddy', 'bizney' (business), 'frabjous', 'don't' for 'doesn't' — all of them out of date even when *Gem* and *Magnet* started. There are also traces of earlier origins. The name 'Greyfriars' is probably taken from Thackeray, and Gosling, the school porter in the *Magnet*, talks in an imitation of Dickens's dialect.

With all this, the supposed 'glamour' of public-school life is played for all it is worth. There is all the usual paraphernalia — lock-up, roll-call, house matches, fagging, prefects, cosy teas round the study fire, etc. etc. — and constant reference to the 'old school', the 'old grey stones' (both schools were founded in the early sixteenth century), the 'team spirit' of the 'Greyfriars men'. As for the snob-appeal, it is completely shameless. Each school has a titled boy or two whose titles are constantly thrust in the reader's face; other boys have the names of well-known aristocratic families, Talbot, Manners, Lowther. We are for ever being reminded that Gussy is the Honourable Arthur

A. D'Arcy, son of Lord Eastwood, that Jack Blake is heir to 'broad acres', that Hurree Jamset Ram Singh (nicknamed Inky) is the Nabob of Bhanipur, that Vernon-Smith's father is a millionaire. Till recently the illustrations in both papers always depicted the boys in clothes imitated from those of Eton; in the last few years Greyfriars has changed over to blazers and flannel trousers, but St. Jim's still sticks to the Eton jacket, and Gussy sticks to his top-hat. In the school magazine which appears every week as part of the *Magnet*, Harry Wharton writes an article discussing the pocket-money received by the 'fellows in the Remove', and reveals that some of them get as much as five pounds a week! This kind of thing is a perfectly deliberate incitement to wealth-fantasy. And here it is worth noticing a rather curious fact, and that is that the school story is a thing peculiar to England. So far as I know, there are extremely few school stories in foreign languages. The reason, obviously, is that in England education is mainly a matter of status. The most definite dividing-line between the petite-bourgeoisie and the working class is that the former pay for their education, and within the bourgeoisie there is another unbridgeable gulf between the 'public' school and the 'private' school. It is quite clear that there are tens and scores of thousands of people to whom every detail of life at a 'posh' public school is wildly thrilling and romantic. They happen to be outside that mystic world of quadrangles and house-colours, but they yearn after it, day-dream about it, live mentally in it for hours at a stretch. The question is, Who are these people? Who reads the *Gem* and *Magnet*?

Obviously one can never be quite certain about this kind of thing. All I can say from my own observation is this. Boys who are likely to go to public schools themselves generally read the *Gem* and *Magnet*, but they nearly always stop reading them when they are about twelve; they may continue for another year from force of habit, but by that time they have ceased to take them seriously. On the other hand, the boys at very cheap private schools, the schools that are designed for people who can't afford a public school but consider the Council schools 'common', continue reading the *Gem* and *Magnet* for several years longer. A few years ago I was a teacher at two of these schools myself. I found that not only did virtually all the boys read the *Gem* and *Magnet*, but that they were still taking them fairly seriously when they were fifteen or even sixteen. These boys were the sons of shopkeepers, office employees and small business and professional men, and obviously it is this class that the *Gem* and *Magnet* are aimed at. But they are certainly read by working-class boys as well. They are generally on sale in the poorest quarters of big towns, and I have known them to be read by boys whom one might expect to be completely immune from public-school 'glamour'. I have seen a young coalminer, for instance, a lad who had already worked a year or two underground, eagerly reading the *Gem*. Recently I offered a batch of English papers to some British legionaries of the French Foreign Legion in North Africa; they picked out the *Gem* and *Magnet* first. Both papers are much read by girls,[3] and the Pen Pals department of the *Gem* shows that it is read in every corner of the British Empire, by Australians, Canadians, Palestine Jews, Malays, Arabs, Straits Chinese, etc. etc. The editors evidently expect their readers to be aged round about fourteen, and the advertisements (milk chocolate, postage stamps, water pistols, blushing cured, home conjuring tricks, itching powder, the Phine Phun Ring which runs a needle into your friend's hand, etc. etc.) indicate roughly the same age; there are also the Admiralty advertisements, however, which call for youths between seventeen and twenty-two. And there is no question that these papers are also read by adults. It is quite common for people to write to the editor and say that they have read every number of the *Gem* or *Magnet* for the past thirty years. Here, for instance, is a letter from a lady in Salisbury:

I can say of your splendid yarns of Harry Wharton & Co., of Greyfriars, that they never fail to reach a high standard. Without doubt they are the finest stories of their type on the market to-day, which is saying a good deal. They seem to bring you face to face with Nature. I have taken the *Magnet* from the start, and have followed the adventures of Harry Wharton & Co. with rapt interest. I have no sons, but two daughters, and there's always a rush to be the first to read the grand old paper. My husband, too, was a staunch reader of the *Magnet* until he was suddenly taken away from us.

It is well worth getting hold of some copies of the *Gem* and *Magnet*, especially the *Gem*, simply to have a look at the correspondence columns. What is truly startling is the intense interest with which the pettiest details of life at Greyfriars and St. Jim's are followed up. Here, for instance, are a few of the questions sent in by readers:

'What age is Dick Roylance?' 'How old is St. Jim's?' 'Can you give me a list of the Shell and their studies?' 'How much did D'Arcy's monocle cost?' 'How is it fellows like Crooke are in the Shell and decent fellows like yourself are only in the Fourth?' 'What are the Form captain's three chief duties?' 'Who is the chemistry master at St. Jim's?' (From a girl) 'Where is St. Jim's situated?' '*Could* you tell me how to get there, as I would love to see the building?' 'Are you boys just "phoneys", as I think you are?'

It is clear that many of the boys and girls who write these letters are living a complete fantasy-life. Sometimes a boy will write, for instance, giving his age, height, weight, chest and bicep measurements and asking which member of the Shell or Fourth Form he most exactly resembles. The demand for a list of the studies on the Shell passage, with an exact account of who lives in each, is a very common one. The editors, of course, do everything in their power to keep up the illusion. In the *Gem* Jack Blake is supposed to write the answers to correspondents, and in the *Magnet* a couple of pages is always given up to the school magazine (the *Greyfriars Herald*, edited by Harry Wharton), and there is another page in which one or other character is written up each week. The stories run in cycles, two or three characters being kept in the foreground for several weeks at a time. First there will be a series of rollicking adventure stories, featuring the Famous Five and Billy Bunter; then a run of stories turning on mistaken identity, with Wibley (the make-up wizard) in the star part; then a run of more serious stories in which Vernon-Smith is trembling on the verge of expulsion. And here one comes upon the real secret of the *Gem* and *Magnet* and the probable reason why they continue to be read in spite of their obvious out-of-dateness.

It is that the characters are so carefully graded as to give almost every type of reader a character he can identify himself with. Most boys' papers aim at doing this, hence the boy-assistant (Sexton Blake's Tinker, Nelson Lee's Nipper, etc.) who usually accompanies the explorer, detective or what-not on his adventures. But in these cases there is only one boy, and usually it is much the same type of boy. In the *Gem* and *Magnet* there is a model for very nearly everybody. There is the normal, athletic, high-spirited boy (Tom Merry, Jack Blake, Frank Nugent), a slightly rowdier version of this type (Bob Cherry), a more aristocratic version (Talbot, Manners), a quieter, more serious version (Harry Wharton), and a stolid, 'bulldog' version (Johnny Bull). Then there is the reckless, dare-devil type of boy (Vernon-Smith), the definitely 'clever', studious boy (Mark Linley, Dick Penfold), and the eccentric boy who is not good at games but possesses some special talent (Skinner, Wibley). And there is the scholarship-boy (Tom Redwing), an important figure in this class of story because he makes it possible for boys from very poor homes to project themselves into the public-school atmosphere. In addition there are Australian, Irish, Welsh, Manx, Yorkshire and Lancashire boys to play upon local patriotism. But the subtlety of characterisation goes deeper than this. If one studies the correspondence columns one sees that there is probably *no* character in the *Gem* and *Magnet* whom some or other reader does not identify with, except the out-and-out comics, Coker, Billy Bunter, Fisher T. Fish (the money-grubbing American boy) and, of course, the masters. Bunter, though in his origin he probably owed something to the fat boy in *Pickwick*, is a real creation. His tight trousers against which boots and canes are constantly thudding, his astuteness in search of food, his postal order which never turns up, have made him famous wherever the Union Jack waves. But he is not a subject for day-dreams. On the other hand, another seeming figure of fun, Gussy (the Honourable Arthur A. D'Arcy, 'the swell of St. Jim's'), is evidently much admired. Like everything else in the *Gem* and *Magnet*, Gussy is at least thirty years out of date. He is the 'knut' of the early twentieth century or even the 'masher' of the 'nineties ('Bai Jove, deah boy!' and 'Weally, I shall be obliged to give you a feahful thwashin'!'), the monocled idiot who made good on the fields of Mons and Le Cateau. And his evident popularity goes to show how deep the snob-appeal of this type is. English people are extremely fond of the titled ass (cf. Lord Peter Wimsey) who always turns up trumps in the moment of emergency. Here is a letter from one of Gussy's girl admirers:

> I think you're too hard on Gussy. I wonder he's still in existence, the way you treat him. He's my hero. Did you know I write lyrics? How's this – to the tune of 'Goody Goody'?

> Gonna get my gas-mask, join the A.R.P.
> 'Cos I'm wise to all those bombs you drop on me.
>> Gonna dig myself a trench
>> Inside the garden fence;
> Gonna seal my windows up with tin
> So that the tear gas can't get in;
> Gonna park my cannon right outside the kerb
> With a note to Adolf Hitler: 'Don't disturb!'
>> And if I never fall in Nazi hands
>> That's soon enough for me
>> Gonna get my gas-mask, join the A.R.P.

> P.S. – Do you get on well with girls?

I quote this in full because (dated April 1939) it is interesting as being probably the earliest mention of Hitler in the *Gem*. In the *Gem* there is also a heroic fat boy, Fatty Wynn, as a set-off against Bunter. Vernon-Smith, 'the Bounder of the Remove', a Byronic character, always on the verge of the sack, is another great favourite. And even some of the cads probably have their following. Loder, for instance, 'the rotter of the Sixth', is a cad, but he is also a highbrow and given to saying sarcastic things about football and the team spirit. The boys of the Remove only think him all the more of a cad for this, but a certain type of boy would probably identify with him. Even Racke, Crooke and Co. are probably admired by small boys who think it diabolically wicked to smoke cigarettes. (A frequent question in the correspondence column: 'What brand of cigarettes does Racke smoke?')

Naturally the politics of the *Gem* and *Magnet* are Conservative, but in a completely pre-1914 style, with no Fascist tinge. In reality their basic political assumptions are two: nothing ever

changes, and foreigners are funny. In the *Gem* of 1939 Frenchmen are still Froggies and Italians are still Dagoes. Mossoo, the
French master at Greyfriars, is the usual comic-paper Frog,
with pointed beard, pegtop trousers, etc. Inky, the Indian
boy, though a rajah, and therefore possessing snob-appeal, is
also the comic babu of the *Punch* tradition. (' "The rowfulness is
not the proper caper, my esteemed Bob," said Inky. "Let dogs
delight in the barkfulness and bitefulness, but the soft answer is
the cracked pitcher that goes longest to a bird in the bush, as the
English proverb remarks." ') Fisher T. Fish is the old-style stage
Yankee (' "Waal, I guess" ', etc.) dating from a period of Anglo-
American jealousy. Wun Lung, the Chinese boy (he has rather
faded out of late, no doubt because some of the *Magnet*'s readers
are Straits Chinese), is the nineteenth-century pantomime
Chinaman, with saucer-shaped hat, pigtail and pidgin-English.
The assumption all along is not only that foreigners are comics
who are put there for us to laugh at, but that they can be
classified in much the same way as insects. That is why in all
boys' papers, not only the *Gem* and *Magnet*, a Chinese is
invariably portrayed with a pigtail. It is the thing you recognise
him by, like the Frenchman's beard or the Italian's barrel-
organ. In papers of this kind it occasionally happens that
when the setting of a story is in a foreign country some attempt
is made to describe the natives as individual human beings, but
as a rule it is assumed that foreigners of any one race are all alike
and will conform more or less exactly to the following patterns:

FRENCHMAN: Excitable. Wears beard, gesticulates wildly.
SPANIARD, MEXICAN, etc.: Sinister, treacherous.
ARAB, AFGHAN, etc.: Sinister, treacherous.
CHINESE: Sinister, treacherous. Wears pigtail.
ITALIAN: Excitable. Grinds barrel-organ or carries stiletto.
SWEDE, DANE, etc.: Kind-hearted, stupid.
NEGRO: Comic, very faithful.

The working classes only enter into the *Gem* and *Magnet* as
comics or semi-villains (race-course touts, etc.). As for class-
friction, trade unionism, strikes, slumps, unemployment, Fascism and civil war – not a mention. Somewhere or other in the
thirty years' issue of the two papers you might perhaps find the

word 'Socialism', but you would have to look a long time for it. If the Russian Revolution is anywhere referred to, it will be indirectly, in the word 'Bolshy' (meaning a person of violent disagreeable habits). Hitler and the Nazis are just beginning to make their appearance, in the sort of reference I quoted above. The war-crisis of September 1938 made just enough impression to produce a story in which Mr Vernon-Smith, the Bounder's millionaire father, cashed in on the general panic by buying up country houses in order to sell them to 'crisis scuttlers'. But that is probably as near to noticing the European situation as the *Gem* and *Magnet* will come, until the war actually starts. That does not mean that these papers are unpatriotic – quite the contrary! Throughout the Great War the *Gem* and *Magnet* were perhaps the most consistently and cheerfully patriotic papers in England. Almost every week the boys caught a spy or pushed a conchy into the army, and during the rationing period 'EAT LESS BREAD' was printed in large type on every page. But their patriotism has nothing whatever to do with power-politics or 'ideological' warfare. It is more akin to family loyalty, and actually it gives one a valuable clue to the attitude of ordinary people, especially the huge untouched block of the middle class and the better-off working class. These people are patriotic to the middle of their bones, but they do not feel that what happens in foreign countries is any of their business. When England is in danger they rally to its defence as a matter of course, but in between-times they are not interested. After all, England is always in the right and England always wins, so why worry? It is an attitude that has been shaken during the past twenty years, but not so deeply as is sometimes supposed. Failure to understand it is one of the reasons why left-wing political parties are seldom able to produce an acceptable foreign policy.

The mental world of the *Gem* and *Magnet*, therefore, is something like this:

The year is 1910 – or 1940, but it is all the same. You are at Greyfriars, a rosy-cheeked boy of fourteen in posh tailor-made clothes, sitting down to tea in your study on the Remove passage after an exciting game of football which was won by an odd goal in the last half-minute. There is a cosy fire in the study, and outside the wind is whistling. The ivy clusters thickly round the old grey stones. The King is on his throne and the pound is worth a pound. Over in Europe the comic foreigners are jabbering and gesticulating, but the grim grey battleships of the British Fleet are steaming up the Channel and at the outposts of Empire the monocled Englishmen are holding the niggers at bay. Lord Mauleverer has just got another fiver and we are all settling down to a tremendous tea of sausages, sardines, crumpets, potted meat, jam and doughnuts. After tea we shall sit round the study fire having a good laugh at Billy Bunter and discussing the team for next week's match against Rookwood. Everything is safe, solid and unquestionable. Everything will be the same for ever and ever. That approximately is the atmosphere.

But now turn from the *Gem* and *Magnet* to the more up-to-date papers which have appeared since the Great War. The truly significant thing is that they have more points of resemblance to the *Gem* and *Magnet* than points of difference. But it is better to consider the differences first.

There are eight of these newer papers, the *Modern Boy*, *Triumph*, *Champion*, *Wizard*, *Rover*, *Skipper*, *Hotspur* and *Adventure*. All of these have appeared since the Great War, but except for the *Modern Boy* none of them is less than five years old. Two papers which ought also to be mentioned briefly here, though they are not strictly in the same class as the rest, are the *Detective Weekly* and the *Thriller*, both owned by the Amalgamated Press. The *Detective Weekly* has taken over Sexton Blake. Both of these papers admit a certain amount of sex-interest into their stories, and though certainly read by boys, they are not aimed at them exclusively. All the others are boys' papers pure and simple, and they are sufficiently alike to be considered together. There does not seem to be any notable difference between Thomson's publications and those of the Amalgamated Press.

As soon as one looks at these papers one sees their technical superiority to the *Gem* and *Magnet*. To begin with, they have the great advantage of not being written entirely by one person. Instead of one long complete story, a number of the *Wizard* or *Hotspur* consists of half a dozen or more serials, none of which goes on for ever. Consequently there is far more variety and far less padding, and none of the tiresome stylisation and facetiousness of the *Gem* and *Magnet*. Look at these two extracts, for example:

Billy Bunter groaned.

A quarter of an hour had elapsed out of the two hours that Bunter was booked for extra French.

In a quarter of an hour there were only fifteen minutes! But every one of those minutes seemed inordinately long to Bunter. They seemed to crawl by like tired snails.

Looking at the clock in Class-room No. 10 the fat Owl could hardly believe that only fifteen minutes had passed. It seemed more like fifteen hours, if not fifteen days!

Other fellows were in extra French as well as Bunter. They did not matter. Bunter did! (*Magnet*).

After a terrible climb, hacking out handholds in the smooth ice every step of the way up, Sergeant Lionheart Logan of the Mounties was now clinging like a human fly to the face of an icy cliff, as smooth and treacherous as a giant pane of glass.

An Arctic blizzard, in all its fury, was buffeting his body, driving the blinding snow into his face, seeking to tear his fingers loose from their handholds and dash him to death on the jagged boulders which lay at the foot of the cliff a hundred feet below.

Crouching among those boulders were eleven villainous trappers who had done their best to shoot down Lionheart and his companion, Constable Jim Rogers – until the blizzard had blotted the two Mounties out of sight from below (*Wizard*).

The second extract gets you some distance with the story, the first takes a hundred words to tell you that Bunter is in the detention class. Moreover, by not concentrating on school stories (in point of numbers the school story slightly predominates in all these papers, except the *Thriller* and *Detective Weekly*), the *Wizard*, *Hotspur*, etc., have far greater opportunities for sensationalism. Merely looking at the cover illustrations of the papers which I have on the table in front of me, here are some of the things I see. On one a cowboy is clinging by his toes to the wing of an aeroplane in mid-air and shooting down another aeroplane with his revolver. On another a Chinese is swimming for his life down a sewer with a swarm of ravenous-looking rats swimming after him. On another an engineer is lighting a stick of dynamite while a steel robot feels for him with its claws. On another a man in airman's costume is fighting barehanded against a rat somewhat larger than a donkey. On another a nearly naked man of terrific muscular development had just seized a lion by the tail and flung it thirty yards over the wall of an arena, with the words, 'Take back your blooming lion!' Clearly no school story can compete with this kind of thing. From time to time the school buildings may catch fire or the French master may turn out to be the head of an inter-national anarchist gang, but in a general way the interest must centre round cricket, school rivalries, practical jokes, etc. There is not much room for bombs, death-rays, sub-machine guns, aeroplanes, mustangs, octopuses, grizzly bears or gangsters.

Examination of a large number of these papers shows that, putting aside school stories, the favourite subjects are Wild West, Frozen North, Foreign Legion, crime (always from the detective's angle), the Great War (Air Force or Secret Service, not the infantry), the Tarzan motif in varying forms, profes-sional football, tropical exploration, historical romance (Robin Hood, Cavaliers and Roundheads, etc.) and scientific inven-tion. The Wild West still leads, at any rate as a setting, though the Red Indian seems to be fading out. The one theme that is really new is the scientific one. Death-rays, Martians, invisible men, robots, helicopters and interplanetary rockets figure largely; here and there there are even far-off rumours of psy-chotherapy and ductless-glands. Whereas the *Gem* and *Magnet* derive from Dickens and Kipling, the *Wizard*, *Champion*, *Modern Boy*, etc., owe a great deal to H. G. Wells, who, rather than Jules Verne, is the father of 'Scientifiction'. Naturally it is the magical, Martian aspect of science that is most exploited, but one or two papers include serious articles on scientific subjects, besides quantities of informative snippets. (Examples: 'A Kauri tree in Queensland, Australia, is over 12,000 years old'; 'Nearly 50,000 thunderstorms occur every day'; 'Helium gas costs £1 per 1000 cubic feet'; 'There are over 500 varieties of spiders in Great Britain'; 'London firemen use 14,000,000 gallons of water annually,' etc. etc.). There is a marked advance in intellectual curiosity and, on the whole, in the demand made on the reader's attention. In practice the *Gem* and *Magnet* and the post-war papers are read by much the same public, but the mental age aimed at seems to have risen by a year or two years – an improvement probably corresponding to the improvement in elementary education since 1909.

The other thing that has emerged in the post-war boys' papers, though not to anything like the extent one would expect, is bully-worship and the cult of violence.

If one compares the *Gem* and *Magnet* with a genuinely modern paper, the thing that immediately strikes one is the absence of the leader-principle. There is no central dominating character; instead there are fifteen or twenty characters, all more or less on an equality, with whom readers of different types can identify. In the more modern papers this is not usually the case. Instead of identifying with a schoolboy of more or less his own age, the reader of the *Skipper, Hotspur*, etc., is led to identify with a G-man, with a Foreign Legionary, with some variant of Tarzan, with an air ace, a master spy, an explorer, a pugilist – at any rate with some single all-powerful character who dominates everyone about him and whose usual method of solving any problem is a sock on the jaw. This character is intended as a superman, and as physical strength is the form of power that boys can best understand, he is usually a sort of human gorilla; in the Tarzan type of story he is sometimes actually a giant, eight or ten feet high. At the same time the scenes of violence in nearly all these stories are remarkably harmless and unconvincing. There is a great difference in tone between even the most bloodthirsty English paper and the threepenny Yank Mags, *Fight Stories, Action Stories*, etc. (not strictly boys' papers, but largely read by boys). In the Yank Mags you get real blood-lust, really gory descriptions of the all-in, jump-on-his-testicles style of fighting, written in a jargon that has been perfected by people who brood endlessly on violence. A paper like *Fight Stories*, for instance, would have very little appeal except to sadists and masochists. You can see the comparative gentleness of the English civilisation by the amateurish way in which prize-fighting is always described in the boys' weeklies. There is no specialised vocabulary. Look at these four extracts, two English, two American:

When the gong sounded, both men were breathing heavily, and each had great red marks on his chest. Bill's chin was bleeding, and Ben had a cut over his right eye.

Into their corners they sank, but when the gong clanged again they were up swiftly, and they went like tigers at each other (*Rover*).

He walked in stolidly and smashed a clublike right to my face. Blood spattered and I went back on my heels, but surged in and ripped my right under the heart. Another right smashed full on Sven's already battered mouth, and, spitting out the fragments of a tooth, he crashed a flailing left to my body (*Fight Stories*).

It was amazing to watch the Black Panther at work. His muscles rippled and slid under his dark skin. There was all the power and grace of a giant cat in his swift and terrible onslaught.

He volleyed blows with a bewildering speed for so huge a fellow. In a moment Ben was simply blocking with his gloves as well as he could. Ben was really a past-master of defence. He had many fine victories behind him. But the Negro's rights and lefts crashed through openings that hardly any other fighter could have found (*Wizard*).

Haymakers which packed the bludgeoning weight of forest monarchs crashing down under the ax hurled into the bodies of the two heavies as they swapped punches (*Fight Stories*).

Notice how much more knowledgeable the American extracts sound. They are written for devotees of the prize-ring, the others are not. Also, it ought to be emphasised that on its level the moral code of the English boys' papers is a decent one. Crime and dishonesty are never held up to admiration, there is none of the cynicism and corruption of the American gangster story. The huge sale of the Yank Mags in England shows that there is a demand for that kind of thing, but very few English writers seem able to produce it. When hatred of Hitler became a major emotion in America, it was interesting to see how promptly 'anti-Fascism' was adapted to pornographic purposes by the editors of the Yank Mags. One magazine which I have in front of me is given up to a long, complete story, 'When Hell Came to America', in which the agents of a 'blood-maddened European dictator' are trying to conquer the U.S.A. with death-rays and invisible aeroplanes. There is the frankest appeal to sadism, scenes in which the Nazis tie bombs to women's backs and fling them off heights to watch them blown to pieces in mid-air, others in which they tie naked girls together by their hair and prod them with knives to make them dance, etc. etc. The editor comments solemnly on all this, and uses it as a plea for tightening up restrictions against immigrants. On another page of the same paper: 'LIVES OF THE HOTCHA CHORUS GIRLS. Reveals all the intimate secrets and fascinating pastimes of the famous Broadway Hotcha girls. NOTHING IS OMITTED. Price 10c.' 'HOW TO LOVE. 10c.' 'FRENCH PHOTO RING. 25c.' 'NAUGHTY NUDIES TRANSFERS. From the outside of the glass you see a beautiful girl, innocently dressed. Turn it around and look through the glass and oh! what a difference! Set of 3 transfers 25c.,' etc. etc. etc. There is nothing at all like this in any English paper likely to be read by boys. But the process of Americanisation is going on all the same. The American ideal, the 'he-man', the 'tough guy', the gorilla who puts everything right by socking everybody else on the jaw, now figures in probably a majority of boys' papers. In one serial now running in the *Skipper* he is always portrayed, ominously enough, swinging a rubber truncheon.

The development of the *Wizard*, *Hotspur*, etc., as against the earlier boys' papers, boils down to this: better technique, more scientific interest, more bloodshed, more leader-worship. But, after all, it is the *lack* of development that is the really striking thing.

To begin with, there is no political development whatever. The world of the *Skipper* and the *Champion* is still the pre-1914 world of the *Magnet* and the *Gem*. The Wild West story, for instance, with its cattle-rustlers, lynch-law and other paraphernalia belonging to the 'eighties, is a curiously archaic thing. It is worth noticing that in papers of this type it is always taken for granted that adventures only happen at the ends of the earth, in tropical forests, in Arctic wastes, in African deserts, on Western prairies, in Chinese opium dens – everywhere, in fact, except the places where things really *do* happen. That is a belief dating from thirty or forty years ago, when the new continents were in process of being opened up. Nowadays, of course, if you really want adventure, the place to look for it is in Europe. But apart from the picturesque side of the Great War, contemporary history is carefully excluded. And except that Americans are now admired instead of being laughed at, foreigners are exactly the same figures of fun that they always were. If a Chinese character appears, he is still the sinister pig-tailed opium smuggler of Sax Rohmer; no indication that things have been happening in China since 1912 – no indication that a war is going on there, for instance. If a Spaniard appears, he is still a 'dago' or 'greaser' who rolls cigarettes and stabs people in the back; no indication that things have been happening in Spain. Hitler and the Nazis have not yet appeared, or are barely making their appearance. There will be plenty about them in a little while, but it will be from a strictly patriotic angle (Britain *versus* Germany), with the real meaning of the struggle kept out of sight as much as possible. As for the Russian Revolution, it is extremely difficult to find any reference to it in any of these papers. When Russia is mentioned at all it is usually in an information snippet (example: 'There are 29,000 centenarians in the U.S.S.R.'), and any reference to the Revolution is indirect and twenty years out of date. In one story in the *Rover*, for instance, somebody has a tame bear, and as it is a Russian bear, it is nicknamed Trotsky – obviously an echo of the 1917–23 period and not of recent controversies. The clock has stopped at 1910. Britannia rules the waves, and no one has heard of slumps, booms, unemployment, dictatorships, purges or concentration camps.

And in social outlook there is hardly any advance. The snobbishness is somewhat less open than in the *Gem* and *Magnet* – that is the most one can possibly say. To begin with, the school story, always partly dependent on snob-appeal, is by no means eliminated. Every number of a boys' paper includes at least one school story, these stories slightly outnumbering the Wild Westerns. The very elaborate fantasy-life of the *Gem* and *Magnet* is not imitated and there is more emphasis on extraneous adventure, but the social atmosphere (old grey stones) is much the same. When a new school is introduced at the beginning of a story we are often told in just those words that 'it was a very posh school'. From time to time a story appears which is ostensibly directed *against* snobbery. The scholarship-boy (cf. Tom Redwing in the *Magnet*) makes fairly frequent appearances, and what is essentially the same theme is sometimes presented in this form: there is great rivalry between two schools, one of which considers itself more 'posh' than the other, and there are fights, practical jokes, football matches, etc., always ending in the discomfiture of the snobs. If one glances very superficially at some of these stories it is possible to imagine that a democratic spirit has crept into the boys' weeklies, but when one looks more closely one sees that they merely reflect the bitter jealousies that exist within the white-collar class. Their real function is to allow the boy who goes to a cheap private school (*not* a Council school) to feel that his school is just as 'posh' in the sight of God as Winchester or Eton. The sentiment of school loyalty ('We're better than the fellows down the road'), a thing almost unknown to the real working class, is still kept up. As these stories are written by many different hands, they do, of course, vary a good deal in tone. Some are reasonably free from snobbishness, in others money and pedigree are exploited even more shamelessly than in the *Gem* and *Magnet*. In one that I came cross an actual *majority* of the boys mentioned were titled.

Where working-class characters appear, it is usually either as comics (jokes about tramps, convicts, etc.), or as prize-fighters, acrobats, cowboys, professional footballers and Foreign Legionaries – in other words, as adventurers. There is no facing of the facts about working-class life, or, indeed, about *working* life of any description. Very occasionally one may come across a realistic description of, say, work in a coal-mine, but in all probability it will only be there as the background of some lurid adventure. In any case the central character is not likely to be a coal-miner. Nearly all the time the boy who reads these papers – in nine cases out of ten a boy who is going to spend his life working in a shop, in a factory or in some subordinate job in an office – is led to identify with people in positions of command, above all with people who are never troubled by shortage of money. The Lord Peter Wimsey figure, the seeming idiot who drawls and wears a monocle but is always to the fore in moments of danger, turns up over and over again. (This character is a great favourite in Secret Service stories.) And, as usual, the heroic characters all have to talk B.B.C.; they may talk Scottish or Irish or American, but no one in a star part is ever permitted to drop an aitch. Here it is worth comparing the social atmosphere of the boys' weeklies with that of the women's weeklies, the *Oracle*, the *Family Star*, *Peg's Paper*, etc.

The women's papers are aimed at an older public and are read for the most part by girls who are working for a living. Consequently they are on the surface much more realistic. It is taken for granted, for example, that nearly everyone has to live in a big town and work at a more or less dull job. Sex, so far from being taboo, is *the* subject. The short, complete stories, the special feature of these papers, are generally of the 'came the dawn' type: the heroine narrowly escapes losing her 'boy' to a designing rival, or the 'boy' loses his job and has to postpone marriage, but presently gets a better job. The changeling-fantasy (a girl brought up in a poor home is 'really' the child of rich parents) is another favourite. Where sensationalism comes in, usually in the serials, it arises out of the more domestic type of crime, such as bigamy, forgery or sometimes murder; no Martians, death-rays or international anarchist gangs. These papers are at any rate aiming at credibility, and they have a link with real life in their correspondence columns, where genuine problems are being discussed. Ruby M. Ayres's column of advice in the *Oracle*, for instance, is extremely sensible and well written. And yet the world of the *Oracle* and *Peg's Paper* is a pure fantasy-world. It is the same fantasy all the time: pretending to be richer than you are. The chief impression that one carries away from almost every story in these papers is of a frightful, overwhelming 'refinement'. Ostensibly the characters are working-class people, but their habits, the interiors of their houses, their clothes, their outlook and, above all, their speech are entirely middle class. They are all living at several pounds a week above their income. And needless to say, that is just the impression that is intended. The idea is to give the bored factory-girl or worn-out mother of five a dream-life in which she pictures herself – not actually as a duchess (that convention has gone out) but as, say, the wife of a bank-manager. Not only is a five-to-six-pound-a-week standard of life set up as the ideal, but it is tacitly assumed that that is how working-class people really *do* live. The major facts are simply not faced. It is admitted, for instance, that people sometimes lose their jobs; but then the dark clouds roll away and they get better jobs instead. No mention of unemployment as something permanent and inevitable, no mention of the dole, no mention of trade unionism. No suggestion anywhere that there can be anything wrong with the system *as a system*; there are only individual misfortunes, which are generally due to somebody's wickedness and can in any case be put right in the last chapter. Always the dark clouds roll away, the kind employer raises Alfred's wages, and there are jobs for everybody except the drunks. It is still the world of the *Wizard* and the *Gem*, except that there are orange-blossoms instead of machine-guns.

The outlook inculcated by all these papers is that of a rather exceptionally stupid member of the Navy League in the year 1910. Yes, it may be said, but what does it matter? And in any case, what else do you expect?

Of course no one in his senses would want to turn the so-called penny dreadful into a realistic novel or a Socialist tract. An adventure story must of its nature be more or less remote from real life. But, as I have tried to make clear, the unreality of the *Wizard* and the *Gem* is not so artless as it looks. These papers exist because of a specialised demand, because boys at certain ages find it necessary to read about Martians, death-rays, grizzly bears and gangsters. They get what they are looking for, but they get it wrapped up in the illusions which their future employers think suitable for them. To what extent people draw their ideas from fiction is disputable. Personally I believe that most people are influenced far more than they would care to admit by novels, serial stories, films and so forth, and that from this point of view the worst books are often the most important, because they are usually the ones that are read earliest in life. It is probable that many people who would consider themselves extremely sophisticated and 'advanced' are actually carrying through life an imaginative background which they acquired in childhood from (for instance) Sapper and Ian Hay. If that is so, the boys' twopenny weeklies are of the deepest importance. Here is the stuff that is read somewhere between the ages of twelve and eighteen by a very large proportion, perhaps an actual majority, of English boys, including many who will never read anything else except newspapers; and along with it they are absorbing a set of beliefs which would be regarded as hopelessly out of date in the Central Office of the Conservative Party. All the better because it is done indirectly, there is being pumped into them the conviction that the major problems of our time do not exist, that there is nothing wrong with *laissez-faire* capitalism, that foreigners are unimportant comics and that the British Empire is a sort of charity-concern which will last for ever. Considering who owns these papers, it is difficult to believe that this is unintentional. Of the twelve papers I have been discussing (*i.e.* twelve including the *Thriller* and *Detective Weekly*) seven are the property of the Amalgamated Press, which is one of the biggest press-combines in the world and controls more than a hundred different papers. The *Gem* and *Magnet*, therefore, are closely linked up with the *Daily Telegraph* and the *Financial Times*. This in itself would be enough to rouse certain suspicions, even if it were not obvious that the stories in the boys' weeklies are politically vetted. So it appears that if you feel the need of a fantasy-life in which you travel to Mars and fight lions barehanded (and what boy doesn't?), you can only have it by delivering yourself over, mentally, to people like Lord Camrose. For there is no competition. Throughout the whole of this run of papers the differences are negligible, and on this level no others exist. This raises the question, why is there no such thing as a left-wing boys' paper?

At first glance such an idea merely makes one slightly sick. It is so horribly easy to imagine what a left-wing boys' paper would be like, if it existed. I remember in 1920 or 1921 some optimistic person handing round Communist tracts among a crowd of public-school boys. The tract I received was of the question-and-answer kind:

Q. 'Can a Boy Communist be a Boy Scout, Comrade?'
A. 'No, Comrade.'
Q. 'Why, Comrade?'
A. 'Because, Comrade, a Boy Scout must salute the Union Jack, which is the symbol of tyranny and oppression.'
Etc. etc.

Now, suppose that at this moment somebody started a left-wing paper deliberately aimed at boys of twelve or fourteen. I do not suggest that the whole of its contents would be exactly like the tract I have quoted above, but does anyone doubt that they would be *something* like it? Inevitably such a paper would either consist of dreary uplift or it would be under Communist influence and given over to adulation of Soviet Russia; in either case no normal boy would ever look at it. Highbrow literature apart, the whole of the existing left-wing Press, in so far as it is at all vigorously 'left', is one long tract. The one Socialist paper in England which could live a week on its merits *as a paper* is the *Daily Herald*: and how much Socialism is there in the *Daily Herald*? At this moment, therefore, a paper with a 'left' slant and at the same time likely to have an appeal to ordinary boys in their teens is something almost beyond hoping for.

But it does not follow that it is impossible. There is no clear reason why every adventure story should necessarily be mixed up with snobbishness and gutter patriotism. For, after all, the stories in the *Hotspur* and the *Modern Boy* are not Conservative tracts; they are merely adventure stories with a Conservative bias. It is fairly easy to imagine the process being reversed. It is possible, for instance, to imagine a paper as thrilling and lively as the *Hotspur*, but with subject-matter and 'ideology' a little more up to date. It is even possible (though this raises other difficulties) to imagine a women's paper at the same literary level as the *Oracle*, dealing in approximately the same kind of story, but taking rather more account of the realities of working-class life. Such things have been done before, though not in England. In the last years of the Spanish monarchy there was a large output in Spain of left-wing novelettes, some of them evidently of Anarchist origin. Unfortunately at the time when they were appearing I did not see their social signifi-cance, and I lost the collection of them that I had, but no doubt copies would still be procurable. In get-up and style of story they were very similar to the English fourpenny novelette, except that their inspiration was 'left'. If, for instance, a story described police pursuing Anarchists through the mountains, it would be from the point of view of the Anarchists and not of the police. An example nearer to hand is the Soviet film

Chapaiev, which has been shown a number of times in London. Technically, by the standards of the time when it was made, *Chapaiev* is a first-rate film, but mentally, in spite of the unfamiliar Russian background, it is not so very remote from Hollywood. The one thing that lifts it out of the ordinary is the remarkable performance by the actor who takes the part of the White officer (the fat one) – a performance which looks very like an inspired piece of gagging. Otherwise the atmosphere is familiar. All the usual paraphernalia is there – heroic fight against odds, escape at the last moment, shots of galloping horses, love interest, comic relief. The film is in fact a fairly ordinary one, except that its tendency is 'left'. In a Hollywood film of the Russian Civil War the Whites would probably be angels and the Reds demons. In the Russian version the Reds are angels and the Whites demons. That also is a lie, but, taking the long view, it is a less pernicious lie than the other.

Here several difficult problems present themselves. Their general nature is obvious enough, and I do not want to discuss them. I am merely pointing to the fact that, in England, popular imaginative literature is a field that left-wing thought has never begun to enter. *All* fiction from the novels in the mushroom libraries downwards is censored in the interests of the ruling class. And boys' fiction above all, the blood-and-thunder stuff which nearly every boy devours at some time or other, is sodden in the worst illusions of 1910. The fact is only unimportant if one believes that what is read in childhood leaves no impression behind. Lord Camrose and his colleagues evidently believe nothing of the kind, and, after all, Lord Camrose ought to know.

Inside the Whale
11 March 1940

I

When Henry Miller's novel, *Tropic of Cancer*, appeared in 1935, it was greeted with rather cautious praise, obviously conditioned in some cases by a fear of seeming to enjoy pornography.

Among the people who praised it were T. S. Eliot, Herbert
Read, Aldous Huxley, John dos Passos, Ezra Pound – on the
whole, not the writers who are in fashion at this moment. And
in fact the subject-matter of the book, and to a certain extent
its mental atmosphere, belong to the 'twenties rather than to
the 'thirties.

Tropic of Cancer is a novel in the first person, or autobiography in the form of a novel, whichever way you like to look at
it. Miller himself insists that it is straight autobiography, but the
tempo and method of telling the story are those of a novel. It is
a story of the American Paris, but not along quite the usual
lines, because the Americans who figure in it happen to be
people without money. During the boom years, when dollars
were plentiful and the exchange-value of the franc was low,
Paris was invaded by such a swarm of artists, writers, students,
dilettanti, sight-seers, debauchees and plain idlers as the world
has probably never seen. In some quarters of the town the so-
called artists must actually have outnumbered the working
population – indeed, it has been reckoned that in the late
'twenties there were as many as 30,000 painters in Paris, most
of them impostors. The populace had grown so hardened to
artists that gruff-voiced Lesbians in corduroy breeches and
young men in Grecian or medieval costume could walk the
streets without attracting a glance, and along the Seine banks by
Notre Dame it was almost impossible to pick one's way between the sketching-stools. It was the age of dark horses and
neglected genii; the phrase on everybody's lips was '*Quand je
serai lancé*'. As it turned out, nobody was 'lancé', the slump
descended like another Ice Age, the cosmopolitan mob of
artists vanished, and the huge Montparnasse cafés which only
ten years ago were filled till the small hours by hordes of
shrieking poseurs have turned into darkened tombs in which
there are not even any ghosts. It is this world – described in,
among other novels, Wyndham Lewis's *Tarr* – that Miller is
writing about, but he is dealing only with the under side of it,
the lumpenproletarian fringe which has been able to survive
the slump because it is composed partly of genuine artists and
partly of genuine scoundrels. The neglected genii, the paranoiacs who are always 'going to' write the novel that will
knock Proust into a cocked hat, are there, but they are only

genii in the rather rare moments when they are not scouting about for the next meal. For the most part it is a story of bug-ridden rooms in workingmen's hotels, of fights, drinking bouts, cheap brothels, Russian refugees, cadging, swindling and temporary jobs. And the whole atmosphere of the poor quarters of Paris as a foreigner sees them – the cobbled alleys, the sour reek of refuse, the bistros with their greasy zinc counters and worn brick floors, the green waters of the Seine, the blue cloaks of the Republican Guard, the crumbling iron urinals, the peculiar sweetish smell of the Metro stations, the cigarettes that come to pieces, the pigeons in the Luxembourg Gardens – it is all there, or at any rate the feeling of it is there.

On the face of it no material could be less promising. When *Tropic of Cancer* was published the Italians were marching into Abyssinia and Hitler's concentration-camps were already bulging. The intellectual foci of the world were Rome, Moscow and Berlin. It did not seem to be a moment at which a novel of outstanding value was likely to be written about American dead-beats cadging drinks in the Latin Quarter. Of course a novelist is not obliged to write directly about contemporary history, but a novelist who simply disregards the major public events of the moment is generally either a footler or a plain idiot. From a mere account of the subject-matter of *Tropic of Cancer* most people would probably assume it to be no more than a bit of naughty-naughty left over from the 'twenties. Actually, nearly everyone who read it saw at once that it was nothing of the kind, but a very remarkable book. How or why remarkable? That question is never easy to answer. It is better to begin by describing the impression that *Tropic of Cancer* has left on my own mind.

When I first opened *Tropic of Cancer* and saw that it was full of unprintable words, my immediate reaction was a refusal to be impressed. Most people's would be the same, I believe. Nevertheless, after a lapse of time the atmosphere of the book, besides innumerable details, seemed to linger in my memory in a peculiar way. A year later Miller's second book, *Black Spring*, was published. By this time *Tropic of Cancer* was much more vividly present in my mind than it had been when I first read it. My first feeling about *Black Spring* was that it showed a falling-off, and it is a fact that it has not the same unity as the other book.

Yet after another year there were many passages in *Black Spring* that had also rooted themselves in my memory. Evidently these books are of the sort to leave a flavour behind them – books that 'create a world of their own', as the saying goes. The books that do this are not necessarily good books, they may be good bad books like *Raffles* or the *Sherlock Holmes* stories, or perverse and morbid books like *Wuthering Heights* or *The House with the Green Shutters*. But now and again there appears a novel which opens up a new world not by revealing what is strange, but by revealing what is familiar. The truly remarkable thing about *Ulysses*, for instance, is the commonplaceness of its material. Of course there is much more in *Ulysses* than this, because Joyce is a kind of poet and also an elephantine pedant, but his real achievement has been to get the familiar onto paper. He dared – for it is a matter of *daring* just as much as of technique – to expose the imbecilities of the inner mind, and in doing so he discovered an America which was under everybody's nose. Here is a whole world of stuff which you have lived with since childhood, stuff which you supposed to be of its nature incommunicable, and somebody has managed to communicate it. The effect is to break down, at any rate momentarily, the solitude in which the human being lives. When you read certain passages in *Ulysses* you feel that Joyce's mind and your mind are one, that he knows all about you though he has never heard your name, that there exists some world outside time and space in which you and he are together. And though he does not resemble Joyce in other ways, there is a touch of this quality in Henry Miller. Not everywhere, because his work is very uneven, and sometimes, especially in *Black Spring*, tends to slide away into mere verbiage or into the squashy universe of the surrealists. But read him for five pages, ten pages, and you feel the peculiar relief that comes not so much from understanding as from *being understood*. 'He knows all about me,' you feel; 'he wrote this specially for me.' It is as though you could hear a voice speaking to you, a friendly American voice, with no humbug in it, no moral purpose, merely an implicit assumption that we are all alike. For the moment you have got away from the lies and simplifications, the stylised, marionette-like quality of ordinary fiction, even quite good fiction, and are dealing with the recognisable experiences of human beings.

But what kind of experience? What kind of human beings? Miller is writing about the man in the street, and it is incidentally rather a pity that it should be a street full of brothels. That is the penalty of leaving your native land. It means transferring your roots into shallower soil. Exile is probably more damaging to a novelist than to a painter or even a poet, because its effect is to take him out of contact with working life and narrow down his range to the street, the café, the church, the brothel and the studio. On the whole, in Miller's books you are reading about people living the expatriate life, people drinking, talking, meditating and fornicating, not about people working, marrying and bringing up children; a pity, because he would have described the one set of activities as well as the other. In *Black Spring* there is a wonderful flashback of New York, the swarming Irish-infested New York of the O. Henry period, but the Paris scenes are the best, and, granted their utter worthlessness as social types, the drunks and dead-beats of the cafés are handled with a feeling for character and a mastery of technique that are unapproached in any at all recent novel. All of them are not only credible but completely familiar; you have the feeling that all their adventures have happened to yourself. Not that they are anything very startling in the way of adventures. Henry gets a job with a melancholy Indian student, gets another job at a dreadful French school during a cold snap when the lavatories are frozen solid, goes on drinking bouts in Le Havre with his friend Collins, the sea captain, goes to brothels where there are wonderful negresses, talks with his friend Van Norden, the novelist, who has got the great novel of the world in his head but can never bring himself to begin writing it. His friend Karl, on the verge of starvation, is picked up by a wealthy widow who wishes to marry him. There are interminable, Hamlet-like conversations in which Karl tries to decide which is worse, being hungry or sleeping with an old woman. In great detail he describes his visits to the widow, how he went to the hotel dressed in his best, how before going in he neglected to urinate, so that the whole evening was one long crescendo of torment, etc., etc. And after all, none of it is true, the widow doesn't even exist – Karl has simply invented her in order to make himself seem important. The whole book is in this vein, more or less. Why is it

that these monstrous trivialities are so engrossing? Simply because the whole atmosphere is deeply familiar, because you
have all the while the feeling that these things are happening to
you. And you have this feeling because somebody has chosen to
drop the Geneva language of the ordinary novel and drag
the *real-politik* of the inner mind into the open. In Miller's
case it is not so much a question of exploring the mechanisms
of the mind as of owning up to everyday facts and everyday
emotions. For the truth is that many ordinary people, perhaps
an actual majority, do speak and behave in just the way that is
recorded here. The callous coarseness with which the characters in *Tropic of Cancer* talk is very rare in fiction, but it is
extremely common in real life; again and again I have heard
just such conversations from people who were not even aware
that they were talking coarsely. It is worth noticing that *Tropic
of Cancer* is not a young man's book. Miller was in his forties
when it was published, and though since then he has produced
three or four others, it is obvious that this first book had been
lived with for years. It is one of those books that are slowly
matured in poverty and obscurity, by people who know
what they have got to do and therefore are able to wait. The
prose is astonishing, and in parts of *Black Spring* it is even better.
Unfortunately I cannot quote; unprintable words occur almost
everywhere. But get hold of *Tropic of Cancer*, get hold of *Black
Spring* and read especially the first hundred pages. They give
you an idea of what can still be done, even at this late date, with
English prose. In them, English is treated as a spoken language,
but spoken *without fear,* i.e., without fear of rhetoric or of
the unusual or poetical word. The adjective has come back,
after its ten years' exile. It is a flowing, swelling prose, a prose
with rhythms in it, something quite different from the
flat cautious statements and snackbar dialects that are now in
fashion.

When a book like *Tropic of Cancer* appears, it is only natural
that the first thing people notice should be its obscenity. Given
our current notions of literary decency, it is not at all easy to
approach an unprintable book with detachment. Either one
is shocked and disgusted, or one is morbidly thrilled, or one is
determined above all else not to be impressed. The last is
probably the commonest reaction, with the result that unprint-

able books often get less attention than they deserve. It is rather the fashion to say that nothing is easier than to write an obscene book, that people only do it in order to get themselves talked about and make money, etc., etc. What makes it obvious that this is *not* the case is that books which are obscene in the police-court sense are distinctly uncommon. If there were easy money to be made out of dirty words, a lot more people would be making it. But, because 'obscene' books do not appear very frequently, there is a tendency to lump them together, as a rule quite unjustifiably. *Tropic of Cancer* has been vaguely associated with two other books, *Ulysses* and *Voyage au Bout de la Nuit*, but in neither case is there much resemblance. What Miller has in common with Joyce is a willingness to mention the inane squalid facts of everyday life. Putting aside differences of technique, the funeral scene in *Ulysses*, for instance, would fit into *Tropic of Cancer*; the whole chapter is a sort of confession, an *exposé* of the frightful inner callousness of the human being. But there the resemblance ends. As a novel, *Tropic of Cancer* is far inferior to *Ulysses*. Joyce is an artist, in a sense in which Miller is not and probably would not wish to be, and in any case he is attempting much more. He is exploring different states of consciousness, dream, reverie (the 'bronze-by-gold' chapter), drunkenness, etc., and dovetailing them all into a huge complex pattern, almost like a Victorian 'plot'. Miller is simply a hard-boiled person talking about life, an ordinary American businessman with intellectual courage and a gift for words. It is perhaps significant that he *looks* exactly like everyone's idea of an American businessman. As for the comparison with *Voyage au Bout de la Nuit*, it is even further from the point. Both books use unprintable words, both are in some sense autobiographical, but that is all. *Voyage au Bout de la Nuit* is a book-with-a-purpose, and its purpose is to protest against the horror and meaninglessness of modern life – actually, indeed, of *life*. It is a cry of unbearable disgust, a voice from the cesspool. *Tropic of Cancer* is almost exactly the opposite. The thing has become so unusual as to seem almost anomalous, but it is the book of a man who is happy. So is *Black Spring*, though slightly less so, because tinged in places with nostalgia. With years of lumpen-proletarian life behind him, hunger, vagabondage, dirt, failure, nights in the open, battles with immigration officers, endless struggles for a bit of cash, Miller finds that he is enjoying himself. Exactly the aspects of life that fill Céline with horror are the ones that appeal to him. So far from protesting, he is *accepting*. And the very word 'acceptance' calls up his real affinity, another American, Walt Whitman.

But there is something rather curious in being Whitman in the nineteen-thirties. It is not certain that if Whitman himself were alive at this moment he would write anything in the least degree resembling *Leaves of Grass*. For what he is saying, after all, is 'I accept', and there is a radical difference between acceptance now and acceptance then. Whitman was writing in a time of unexampled prosperity, but more than that, he was writing in a country where freedom was something more than a word. The democracy, equality and comradeship that he is always talking about are not remote ideals, but something that existed in front of his eyes. In mid-nineteenth-century America men felt themselves free and equal, *were* free and equal, so far as that is possible outside a society of pure communism. There was poverty and there were even class-distinctions, but except for the Negroes there was no permanently submerged class. Everyone had inside him, like a kind of core, the knowledge that he could earn a decent living, and earn it without boot-licking. When you read about Mark Twain's Mississippi rafts-men and pilots, or Bret Harte's Western gold-miners, they seem more remote than the cannibals of the Stone Age. The reason is simply that they are free human beings. But it is the same even with the peaceful domesticated America of the Eastern states, the America of *Little Women*, *Helen's Babies* and 'Riding Down from Bangor'. Life has a buoyant, carefree quality that you can feel as you read, like a physical sensation in your belly. It is this that Whitman is celebrating, though actually he does it very badly, because he is one of those writers who tell you what you ought to feel instead of making you feel it. Luckily for his beliefs, perhaps, he died too early to see the deterioration in American life that came with the rise of large-scale industry and the exploiting of cheap immigrant labour.

Miller's outlook is deeply akin to that of Whitman, and nearly everyone who has read him has remarked on this. *Tropic of Cancer* ends with an especially Whitmanesque passage, in which, after the lecheries, the swindles, the fights, the drinking bouts and the imbecilities, he simply sits down and watches the Seine flowing past, in a sort of mystical acceptance of the thing-as-it-is. Only, what is he accepting? In the first place, not America, but the ancient boneheap of Europe, where every grain of soil has passed through innumerable human bodies. Secondly, not an epoch of expansion and liberty, but an epoch of fear, tyranny and regimentation. To say 'I accept' in an age like our own is to say that you accept concentration-camps, rubber truncheons, Hitler, Stalin, bombs, aeroplanes, tinned food, machine-guns, putsches, purges, slogans, Bedaux belts, gas-masks, submarines, spies, provocateurs, press-censorship, secret prisons, aspirins, Hollywood films and political murders. Not *only* those things, of course, but those things among others. And on the whole this is Henry Miller's attitude. Not quite always, because at moments he shows signs of a fairly ordinary kind of literary nostalgia. There is a long passage in the earlier part of *Black Spring*, in praise of the Middle Ages, which as prose must be one of the most remarkable pieces of writing in recent years, but which displays an attitude not very different from that of Chesterton. In *Max and the White Phagocytes* there is an attack on modern American civilisation (breakfast cereals, cellophane, etc.) from the usual angle of the literary man who hates industrialism. But in general the attitude is 'Let's swallow it whole'. And hence the seeming preoccupation with in-decency and with the dirty-handkerchief side of life. It is only seeming, for the truth is that life, ordinary everyday life, consists far more largely of horrors than writers of fiction usually care to admit. Whitman himself 'accepted' a great deal that his contemporaries found unmentionable. For he is not only writing of the prairie, he also wanders through the city and notes the shattered skull of the suicide, the 'grey sick faces of onanists', etc., etc. But unquestionably our own age, at any rate in Western Europe, is less healthy and less hopeful than the age in which Whitman was writing. Unlike Whitman, we live in a *shrinking* world. The 'democratic vistas' have ended in barbed wire. There is less feeling of creation and growth, less and less emphasis on the cradle, endlessly rocking, more and more emphasis on the teapot, endlessly stewing. To accept civilisation *as it is* practically means accepting decay. It has ceased to be a strenuous attitude and become a passive attitude – even 'decadent', if that word means anything.

But precisely because, in one sense, he is passive to experience, Miller is able to get nearer to the ordinary man than is possible to more purposive writers. For the ordinary man is also passive. Within a narrow circle (home life, and perhaps the trade union or local politics) he feels himself master of his fate, but against major events he is as helpless as against the elements. So far from endeavouring to influence the future, he simply lies down and lets things happen to him. During the past ten years literature has involved itself more and more deeply in politics, with the result that there is now less room in it for the ordinary man than at any time during the past two centuries. One can see the change in the prevailing literary attitude by comparing the books written about the Spanish Civil War with those written about the war of 1914–18. The immediately striking thing about the Spanish war books, at any rate those written in English, is their shocking dullness and badness. But what is more significant is that almost all of them, right-wing or left-wing, are written from a political angle, by cocksure partisans telling you what to think, whereas the books about the Great War were written by common soldiers or junior officers who did not even pretend to understand what the whole thing was about. Books like *All Quiet on the Western Front*, *Le Feu*, *A Farewell to Arms*, *Death of a Hero*, *Good-bye to All That*, *Memoirs of an Infantry Officer* and *A Subaltern on the Somme* were written not by propagandists but by *victims*. They are saying in effect, 'What the hell is all this about? God knows. All we can do is to endure.' And though he is not writing about war, nor, on the whole, about unhappiness, this is nearer to Miller's attitude than the omniscience which is now fashionable. The *Booster*, a short-lived periodical of which he was part-editor, used to describe itself in its advertisements as 'non-political, non-educational, non-progressive, non-co-operative, non-ethical, non-literary, non-consistent, non-contemporary', and Miller's own work could be described in nearly the same terms. It is a voice from the crowd, from the underling, from the third-class carriage, from the ordinary, non-political, non-moral, passive man.

I have been using the phrase 'ordinary man' rather loosely, and I have taken it for granted that the 'ordinary man' exists, a thing now denied by some people. I do not mean that the people Miller is writing about constitute a majority, still less that he is writing about proletarians. No English or American novelist has as yet seriously attempted that. And again, the people in *Tropic of Cancer* fall short of being ordinary to the extent that they are idle, disreputable and more or less 'artistic'. As I have said already, this is a pity, but it is the necessary result of expatriation. Miller's 'ordinary man' is neither the manual worker nor the suburban householder, but the derelict, the declassé, the adventurer, the American intellectual without roots and without money. Still, the experiences even of this type overlap fairly widely with those of more normal people. Miller has been able to get the most out of his rather limited material because he has had the courage to identify with it. The ordinary man, the 'average sensual man', has been given the power of speech, like Balaam's ass.

It will be seen that this is something out of date, or at any rate out of fashion. The average sensual man is out of fashion. The passive, non-political attitude is out of fashion. Preoccupation with sex and truthfulness about the inner life are out of fashion. American Paris is out of fashion. A book like *Tropic of Cancer*, published at such a time, must be either a tedious preciosity or something unusual, and I think a majority of the people who have read it would agree that it is not the first. It is worth trying to discover just what this escape from the current literary fashion means. But to do that one has got to see it against its background – that is, against the general development of English literature in the twenty years since the Great War.

2

When one says that a writer is fashionable one practically always means that he is admired by people under thirty. At the beginning of the period I am speaking of, the years during and immediately after the war, the writer who had the deepest hold upon the thinking young was almost certainly Housman. Among people who were adolescent in the years 1910–25, Housman had an influence which was enormous and is now not at all easy to understand. In 1920, when I was about seventeen, I probably knew the whole of *A Shropshire Lad* by heart. I wonder how much impression *A Shropshire Lad* makes at this moment on a boy of the same age and more or less the same cast of mind? No doubt he has heard of it and even glanced into it; it might strike him as rather cheaply clever – probably that would be about all. Yet these are the poems that I and my contemporaries used to recite to ourselves, over and over, in a kind of ecstasy, just as earlier generations had recited Meredith's 'Love in a Valley', Swinburne's 'Garden of Proserpine', etc., etc.

> With rue my heart is laden
> For golden friends I had,
> For many a rose-lipt maiden
> And many a lightfoot lad.
>
> By brooks too broad for leaping
> The lightfoot boys are laid;
> The rose-lipt girls are sleeping
> In fields where roses fade.

It just tinkles. But it did not seem to tinkle in 1920. Why does the bubble always burst? To answer that question one has to take account of the *external* conditions that make certain writers popular at certain times. Housman's poems had not attracted much notice when they were first published. What was there in them that appealed so deeply to a single generation, the generation born round about 1900?

In the first place, Housman is a 'country' poet. His poems are full of the charm of buried villages, the nostalgia of place-names, Clunton and Clunbury, Knighton, Ludlow, 'on Wenlock Edge', 'in summer time on Bredon', thatched roofs and the jingle of smithies, the wild jonquils in the pastures, the 'blue, remembered hills'. War poems apart, English verse of the 1910–25 period is mostly 'country'. The reason no doubt was that the rentier-professional class was ceasing once and for all to have any real relationship with the soil; but at any rate there prevailed then, far more than now, a kind of snobbism of belonging to the country and despising the town. England at that time was hardly more an agricultural country than it is now, but before the light industries began to spread themselves it was easier to think of it as one. Most middle-class boys grew up within sight of a farm, and naturally it was the picturesque side of farm life that appealed to them – the ploughing, harvesting, stack-thrashing and so forth. Unless he has to do it himself a boy is not likely to notice the horrible drudgery of hoeing turnips, milking cows with chapped teats at four o'clock in the morning, etc., etc. Just before, just after and, for that matter, during the war was the great age of the 'Nature poet', the heyday of Richard Jefferies and W. H. Hudson. Rupert Brooke's 'Grantchester', the star poem of 1913, is nothing but an enormous gush of 'country' sentiment, a sort of accumulated vomit from a stomach stuffed with place-names. Considered as a poem 'Grantchester' is something worse than worthless, but as an illustration of what the thinking middle-class young of that period *felt* it is a valuable document.

Housman, however, did not enthuse over the rambler roses in the week-ending spirit of Brooke and the others. The 'country' motif is there all the time, but mainly as a background. Most of the poems have a quasi-human subject, a kind of idealised rustic, in reality Strephon or Corydon brought up to date. This in itself had a deep appeal. Experience shows that over-civilised people enjoy reading about rustics (key-phrase, 'close to the soil') because they imagine them to be more primitive and passionate than themselves. Hence the 'dark earth' novels of Sheila Kaye-Smith, etc. And at that time a middle-class boy, with his 'country' bias, would identify with an agricultural worker as he would never have thought of doing with a town worker. Most boys had in their minds a vision of an idealised ploughman, gypsy, poacher, or gamekeeper, always pictured as a wild, free, roving blade, living a life of rabbit-snaring, cockfighting, horses, beer and women. Masefield's *Everlasting Mercy*, another valuable period-piece, immensely popular with boys round about the war years, gives you this vision in a very crude form. But Housman's Maurices and Terences could be taken seriously where Masefield's Saul Kane could not; on this side of him, Housman was Masefield with a dash of Theocritus. Moreover all his themes are adolescent – murder, suicide, unhappy love, early death. They deal with the simple, intelligible disasters that give you the feeling of being up against the 'bedrock facts' of life:

> The sun burns on the half-mown hill,
> By now the blood has dried;
> And Maurice amongst the hay lies still
> And my knife is in his side.

And again:

> They hang us now in Shrewsbury jail:
> And whistles blow forlorn,
> And trains all night groan on the rail
> To men that die at morn.

It is all more or less in the same tune. Everything comes unstuck. 'Dick lies long in the churchyard and Ned lies long in jail.' And notice also the exquisite self-pity – the 'nobody loves me' feeling:

> The diamond drops adorning
> The low mound on the lea,
> Those are the tears of morning,
> That weeps, but not for thee.

Hard cheese, old chap! Such poems might have been written expressly for adolescents. And the unvarying sexual pessimism (the girl always dies or marries somebody else) seemed like wisdom to boys who were herded together in public schools and were half-inclined to think of women as something unattainable. Whether Housman ever had the same appeal for girls I doubt. In his poems the woman's point of view is not considered, she is merely the nymph, the siren, the treacherous half-human creature who leads you a little distance and then gives you the slip.

But Housman would not have appealed so deeply to the people who were young in 1920 if it had not been for another strain in him, and that was his blasphemous, antinomian, 'cynical' strain. The fight that always occurs between the generations was exceptionally bitter at the end of the Great War; this was partly due to the war itself, and partly it was an indirect result of the Russian Revolution, but an intellectual struggle was in any case due at about that date. Owing probably to the ease and security of life in England, which even the war hardly disturbed, many people whose ideas were formed in the 'eighties or earlier had carried them quite unmodified into the nineteen-twenties. Meanwhile, so far as the younger generation was concerned, the official beliefs were dissolving like sand-castles. The slump in religious belief, for instance, was spectacular. For several years the old–young antagonism took on a quality of real hatred. What was left of the war generation had crept out of the massacre to find their elders still bellowing the slogans of 1914, and a slightly younger generation of boys were writhing under dirty-minded celibate schoolmasters. It was to these that Housman appealed, with his implied sexual revolt and his personal grievance against God. He was patriotic, it was true, but in a harmless old-fashioned way, to the tune of red coats and 'God save the Queen' rather than steel helmets and 'Hang the Kaiser'. And he was satisfyingly anti-Christian – he stood for a kind of bitter, defiant paganism, a conviction that life is short and the gods are against you, which exactly fitted the prevailing mood of the young; and all in charming fragile verse that was composed almost entirely of words of one syllable.

It will be seen that I have discussed Housman as though he were merely a propagandist, an utterer of maxims and quotable 'bits'. Obviously he was more than that. There is no need to under-rate him now because he was overrated a few years ago. Although one gets into trouble nowadays for saying so, there is a number of poems ('Into my heart an air that kills', for instance, and 'Is my team ploughing?') that are not likely to remain long out of favour. But at bottom it is always a writer's tendency, his 'purpose', his 'message', that makes him liked or disliked. The proof of this is the extreme difficulty of seeing any literary merit in a book that seriously damages your deepest beliefs. And no book is ever truly neutral. Some or other tendency is always discernible, in verse as much as in prose, even if it does no more than determine the form and the choice of imagery. But poets who attain wide popularity, like Housman, are as a rule definitely gnomic writers.

After the war, after Housman and the Nature-poets, there appears a group of writers of completely different tendency – Joyce, Eliot, Pound, Lawrence, Wyndham Lewis, Aldous Huxley, Lytton Strachey. So far as the middle and late 'twenties go, these are 'the movement', as surely as the Auden–Spender group have been 'the movement' during the past few years. It is true that not all of the gifted writers of the period can be fitted into the pattern. E. M. Forster, for instance, though he wrote his best book in 1923 or thereabouts, was essentially pre-war, and Yeats does not seem in either of his phases to belong to the 'twenties. Others who were still living, Moore, Conrad, Bennett, Wells, Norman Douglas, had shot their bolt before the war ever happened. On the other hand, a writer who should be added to the group, though in the narrowly literary sense he hardly 'belongs', is Somerset Maugham. Of course the dates do not fit exactly; most of these writers had already published books before the war, but they can be classified as post-war in the same sense that the younger men now writing are post-slump. Equally of course, you could read through most of the literary papers of the time without grasping that these people *are* 'the movement'. Even more then than at most times the big shots of literary journalism were busy pretending that the age-before-last had not come to an end. Squire ruled the *London Mercury*, Gibbs and Walpole were the gods of the lending libraries, there was a cult of cheeriness and manliness, beer and cricket, briar pipes and monogamy, and it was at all times possible to earn a few guineas by writing an article denouncing 'highbrows'. But all the same it was the despised highbrows who had captured the young. The wind was blowing from Europe, and long before 1930 it had blown the beer-and-cricket school naked, except for their knight-hoods.

But the first thing one would notice about the group of writers I have named above is that they do not look like a group. Moreover several of them would strongly object to being coupled with several of the others. Lawrence and Eliot were in reality antipathetic, Huxley worshipped Lawrence but was repelled by Joyce, most of the others would have looked down on Huxley, Strachey and Maugham, and Lewis attacked everyone in turn; indeed, his reputation as a writer rests largely on these attacks. And yet there is a certain temperamental similarity, evident enough now, though it would not have been so a dozen years ago. What it amounts to is *pessimism of outlook*. But it is necessary to make clear what is meant by pessimism.

If the keynote of the Georgian poets was 'beauty of Nature', the keynote of the post-war writers would be 'tragic sense of life'. The spirit behind Housman's poems, for instance, is not tragic, merely querulous; it is hedonism disappointed. The same is true of Hardy, though one ought to make an exception of *The Dynasts*. But the Joyce–Eliot group come later in time, puritanism is not their main adversary, they are able from the start to 'see through' most of the things that their predecessors had fought for. All of them are temperamentally hostile to the notion of 'progress'; it is felt that progress not only doesn't happen, but *ought not* to happen. Given this general similarity, there are, of course, differences of approach between the writers I have named as well as very different degrees of talent. Eliot's pessimism is partly the Christian pessimism, which implies a certain indifference to human misery, partly a lament over the decadence of Western civilisation ('We are the hollow men, we are the stuffed men,' etc., etc.), a sort of twilight-of-the-gods feeling, which finally leads him, in 'Sweeney Agonistes', for instance, to achieve the difficult feat of making modern life out to be worse than it is. With Strachey it is merely a polite eighteenth-century scepticism mixed up with a taste for debunking. With Maugham it is a kind of stoical resignation, the stiff upper lip of the pukka sahib somewhere East of Suez, carrying on with his job without believing in it, like an Antonine Emperor. Lawrence at first sight does not seem to be a pessimistic writer, because, like Dickens, he is a 'change-of-heart' man and constantly insisting that life here and now would be all right if only you looked at it a little differently. But what he is demanding is a movement away from our mechanised civilisation, which is not going to happen, and which he knows is not going to happen. Therefore his exasperation with the present turns once more into idealisation of the past, this time a safely mythical past, the Bronze Age. When Lawrence prefers the Etruscans (*his* Etruscans) to ourselves it is difficult not to agree with him, and yet, after all, it is a species of defeatism, because that is not the direction in which the world is moving. The kind of life that he is always pointing to, a life centring round the simple mysteries – sex, earth, fire, water, blood – is merely a lost cause. All he has been able to produce, therefore, is a wish that things would happen in a way in which they are manifestly not going to happen. 'A wave of generosity or a wave of death', he says, but it is obvious that there are no waves of generosity this side of the horizon. So he flees to Mexico, and then dies at forty-five, a few years before the wave of death gets going. It will be seen that once again I am speaking of these people as though they were not artists, as though they were merely propagandists putting a 'message' across. And once again it is obvious that all of them are more than that. It would be absurd, for instance, to look on *Ulysses* as *merely* a show-up of the horror of modern life, the 'dirty *Daily Mail* era', as Pound put it. Joyce actually is more of a 'pure artist' than most writers. But *Ulysses* could not have been written by someone who was merely dabbling with word-patterns; it is the product of a special vision of life, the vision of a Catholic who has lost his faith. What Joyce is saying is 'Here is life without God. Just look at it!' and his technical innovations, important though they are, are there primarily to serve this purpose.

But what is noticeable about all these writers is that what 'purpose' they have is very much up in the air. There is no attention to the urgent problems of the moment, above all no politics in the narrower sense. Our eyes are directed to Rome, to Byzantium, to Montparnasse, to Mexico, to the Etruscans, to the Subconscious, to the solar plexus – to every-where except the places where things are actually happening. When one looks back at the 'twenties, nothing is queerer than the way in which every important event in Europe escaped the notice of the English intelligentsia. The Russian Revolu-tion, for instance, all but vanishes from the English conscious-ness between the death of Lenin and the Ukraine famine – about ten years. Throughout those years Russia means Tolstoy, Dostoievski and exiled counts driving taxi-cabs. Italy means picture-galleries, ruins, churches and museums – but not Black-shirts. Germany means films, nudism and psychoanalysis – but not Hitler, of whom hardly anyone had heard till 1931. In 'cultured' circles art-for-art's-saking extended practically to a worship of the meaningless. Literature was supposed to consist solely in the manipulation of words. To judge a book by its subject-matter was the unforgivable sin, and even to be aware of its subject-matter was looked on as a lapse of taste. About 1928, in one of the three genuinely funny jokes that *Punch* has produced since the Great War, an intolerable youth is pictured informing his aunt that he intends to 'write'. 'And what are you going to write about, dear?' asks the aunt. 'My dear aunt,' says the youth crushingly, 'one doesn't write *about* anything, one just *writes*.' The best writers of the 'twenties did not subscribe to this doctrine, their 'purpose' is in most cases fairly overt, but it is usually a 'purpose' along moral-religious-cultural lines. Also, when translatable into political terms, it is in no case 'left'. In one way or another the tendency of all the writers in this group is conservative. Lewis, for instance, spent years in frenzied witch-smellings after 'Bolshevism', which he was able to detect in very unlikely places. Recently he has changed some of his views, perhaps influenced by Hitler's treatment of artists, but it is safe to bet that he will not go very far leftward. Pound seems to have plumped definitely for Fascism, at any rate the Italian variety. Eliot has remained aloof, but if forced at the pistol's point to choose between Fascism and some more democratic form of Socialism, would probably choose Fascism. Huxley starts off with the usual despair-of-life, then, under the influence of Lawrence's 'dark abdomen', tries something called Life-Worship, and finally arrives at pacifism – a tenable position, and at this moment an honourable one, but probably in the long run involving rejection of Socialism. It is also noticeable that most of the writers in this group have a certain tenderness for the Catholic Church, though not usually of a kind that an orthodox Catholic would accept.

The mental connexion between pessimism and a reactionary outlook is no doubt obvious enough. What is perhaps less obvious is just *why* the leading writers of the 'twenties were predominantly pessimistic. Why always the sense of decadence, the skulls and cactuses, the yearning after lost faith and impossible civilisations? Was it not, after all, *because* these people were writing in an exceptionally comfortable epoch? It is just in such times that 'cosmic despair' can flourish. People with empty bellies never despair of the universe, nor even think about the universe, for that matter. The whole period 1910–30 was a prosperous one, and even the war years were physically tolerable if one happened to be a non-combatant in one of the

Allied countries. As for the 'twenties, they were the golden age
of the rentier-intellectual, a period of irresponsibility such as
the world had never before seen. The war was over, the new
totalitarian states had not arisen, moral and religious tabus of all
descriptions had vanished, and the cash was rolling in. 'Disillusionment' was all the fashion. Everyone with a safe £500 a year
turned highbrow and began training himself in *taedium vitae*. It
was an age of eagles and of crumpets, facile despairs, backyard
Hamlets, cheap return tickets to the end of the night. In some
of the minor characteristic novels of the period, books like *Told
by an Idiot*, the despair-of-life reaches a Turkish-bath atmosphere of self-pity. And even the best writers of the time can be
convicted of a too Olympian attitude, a too great readiness to
wash their hands of the immediate practical problem. They see
life very comprehensively, much more so than those who
come immediately before or after them, but they see it through
the wrong end of the telescope. Not that that invalidates their
books, as books. The first test of any work of art is survival, and
it is a fact that a great deal that was written in the period 1910–
30 has survived and looks like continuing to survive. One has
only to think of *Ulysses*, *Of Human Bondage*, most of Lawrence's
early work, especially his short stories, and virtually the whole
of Eliot's poems up to about 1930, to wonder what is now
being written that will wear so well.

But quite suddenly, in the years 1930–35, something
happens. The literary climate changes. A new group of writers,
Auden and Spender and the rest of them, has made its appearance, and although technically these writers owe something
to their predecessors, their 'tendency' is entirely different.
Suddenly we have got out of the twilight of the gods into
a sort of Boy Scout atmosphere of bare knees and community singing. The typical literary man ceases to be a cultured
expatriate with a leaning towards the Church, and becomes
an eager-minded schoolboy with a leaning towards Communism. If the keynote of the writers of the 'twenties is 'tragic
sense of life', the keynote of the new writers is 'serious
purpose'.

The differences between the two schools are discussed at
some length in Mr Louis MacNeice's book *Modern Poetry*. This
book is, of course, written entirely from the angle of the

younger group and takes the superiority of their standards for granted. According to Mr MacNeice:

> The poets of *New Signatures*, unlike Yeats and Eliot, are emotionally partisan. Yeats proposed to turn his back on desire and hatred; Eliot sat back and watched other people's emotions with ennui and an ironical self-pity . . . The whole poetry, on the other hand, of Auden, Spender and Day-Lewis implies that they have desires and hatreds of their own and, further, that they think some things *ought* to be desired and others hated.

And again:

> The poets of *New Signatures* have swung back . . . to the Greek preference for information or statement. The first requirement is to have something to say, and after that you must say it as well as you can.

In other words, 'purpose' has come back, the younger writers have 'gone into politics'. As I have pointed out already, Eliot & Co. are not really so non-partisan as Mr MacNeice seems to suggest. Still, it is broadly true that in the 'twenties the literary emphasis was more on technique and less on subject-matter than it is now.

The leading figures in this group are Auden, Spender, Day-Lewis, MacNeice, and there is a long string of writers of more or less the same tendency, Isherwood, John Lehmann, Arthur Calder-Marshall, Edward Upward, Alec Brown, Philip Henderson, and many others. As before, I am lumping them together simply according to tendency. Obviously there are very great variations in talent. But when one compares these writers with the Joyce–Eliot generation, the immediately striking thing is how much easier it is to form them into a group. Technically they are closer together, politically they are almost indistinguishable, and their criticisms of one another's work have always been (to put it mildly) good natured. The outstanding writers of the 'twenties were of very varied origins, few of them had passed through the ordinary English educational mill (incidentally, the best of them, barring Lawrence, were not Englishmen), and most of them had had at some time to struggle against poverty, neglect, and even downright persecution. On the other hand, nearly all the younger writers fit easily into the public-school–university–Bloomsbury pattern. The few who are of proletarian origin are of the kind that is declassed early in life, first by means of scholarships and then by the bleaching-tub of London 'culture'. It is significant that several of the writers in this group have been not only boys but, subsequently, masters at public schools. Some years ago I described Auden as 'a sort of gutless Kipling'. As criticism this was quite unworthy, indeed it was merely a spiteful remark, but it is a fact that in Auden's work, especially his earlier work, an atmosphere of uplift – something rather like Kipling's 'If' or Newbolt's 'Play up, Play up, and Play the Game!' – never seems to be very far away. Take, for instance, a poem like 'You're leaving now, and it's up to you boys'. It is pure scoutmaster, the exact note of the ten-minutes' straight talk on the dangers of self-abuse. No doubt there is an element of parody that he intends, but there is also a deeper resemblance that he does not intend. And of course the rather priggish note that is common to most of these writers is a symptom of release. By throwing 'pure art' overboard they have freed themselves from the fear of being laughed at and vastly enlarged their scope. The prophetic side of Marxism, for example, is new material for poetry and has great possibilities:

> We are nothing.
> We have fallen
> Into the dark and shall be destroyed.
> Think though, that in this darkness
> We hold the secret hub of an idea
> Whose living sunlit wheel revolves in future years outside.
>
> (Spender, *Trial of a Judge*)

But at the same time, by being Marxised literature has moved no nearer to the masses. Even allowing for the time-lag, Auden and Spender are somewhat farther from being popular writers than Joyce and Eliot, let alone Lawrence. As before, there are many contemporary writers who are outside the current, but there is not much doubt about what *is* the current. For the middle and late 'thirties, Auden, Spender & Co. *are* 'the movement', just as Joyce, Eliot & Co. were for the 'twenties. And the movement is in the direction of some rather ill-defined thing called Communism. As early as 1934 or 1935 it was considered eccentric in literary circles not to be more or less 'left', and in another year or two there had grown up a left-wing orthodoxy that made a certain set of opinions absolutely *de rigueur* on certain subjects. The idea had begun to gain ground (vide Edward Upward and others) that a writer must either be actively 'left' or write badly. Between 1935 and 1939 the Communist Party had an almost irresistible fascination for any writer under forty. It became as normal to hear that so-and-so had 'joined' as it had been a few years earlier, when Roman Catholicism was fashionable, to hear that so-and-so had 'been received'. For about three years, in fact, the central stream of English literature was more or less directly under Communist control. How was it possible for such a thing to happen? And at the same time, what is meant by 'Communism'? It is better to answer the second question first.

The Communist movement in Western Europe began as a movement for the violent overthrow of capitalism, and degenerated within a few years into an instrument of Russian foreign policy. This was probably inevitable when the revolutionary ferment that followed the Great War had died down. So far as I know, the only comprehensive history of this subject in English is Franz Borkenau's book, *The Communist International*. What Borkenau's facts even more than his deductions make clear is that Communism could never have developed along its present lines if any real revolutionary feeling had existed in the industrialised countries. In England, for instance, it is obvious that no such feeling has existed for years past. The pathetic membership-figures of all extremist parties show this clearly. It is only natural, therefore, that the English Communist movement should be controlled by people who are mentally subservient to Russia and have no real aim except to manipulate British foreign policy in the Russian interest. Of course such an aim cannot be openly admitted, and it is this fact that gives the Communist Party its very peculiar character. The more vocal kind of Communist is in effect a Russian publicity agent posing as an international Socialist. It is a pose that is easily kept up at normal times, but becomes difficult in moments of crisis, because of the fact that the U.S.S.R. is no more scrupulous in its foreign policy than the rest of the Great Powers. Alliances, changes of front, etc., which only make sense as part of the game of power politics have to be explained and justified in terms of international Socialism. Every time Stalin swaps partners, 'Marxism' has to be hammered into a new shape. This entails sudden and violent changes of 'line', purges, denunciations, systematic destruction of party literature, etc., etc. Every Communist is in fact liable at any moment to have to alter his most fundamental convictions, or leave the party. The unquestionable dogma of Monday may become the damnable heresy of Tuesday, and so on. This has happened at least three times during the past ten years. It follows that in any Western country a Communist Party is always unstable and usually very small. Its long-term membership really consists of an inner ring of intellectuals who have identified with the Russian bureaucracy, and a slightly larger body of working-class people who feel a loyalty towards Soviet Russia without necessarily understanding its policies. Otherwise there is only a shifting membership, one lot coming and another going with each change of 'line'.

In 1930 the English Communist Party was a tiny, barely legal organisation whose main activity was libelling the Labour Party. But by 1935 the face of Europe had changed, and left-wing politics changed with it. Hitler had risen to power and begun to rearm, the Russian five-year plans had succeeded, Russia had reappeared as a great military Power. As Hitler's three targets of attack were, to all appearances, Great Britain, France and the U.S.S.R., the three countries were forced into a sort of uneasy *rapprochement*. This meant that the English or French Communist was obliged to become a good patriot and imperialist – that is, to defend the very things he had been attacking for the past fifteen years. The Comintern slogans suddenly faded from red to pink. 'World revolution' and 'Social-fascism' gave way to 'Defence of democracy' and 'Stop Hitler!' The years 1935–39 were the period of anti-Fascism and the Popular Front, the heyday of the Left Book Club, when red duchesses and 'broad-minded' deans toured the battlefields of the Spanish war and Winston Churchill was the blue-eyed boy of the *Daily Worker*. Since then, of course, there has been yet another change of 'line'. But what is important for my purpose is that it was during the 'anti-Fascist' phase that the younger English writers gravitated towards Communism.

The Fascism–democracy dogfight was no doubt an attraction in itself, but in any case their conversion was due at about that date. It was obvious that laissez-faire capitalism was finished and that there had got to be some kind of reconstruction; in the world of 1935 it was hardly possible to remain politically indifferent. But why did these young men turn towards anything so alien as Russian Communism? Why should *writers* be attracted by a form of Socialism that makes mental honesty impossible? The explanation really lies in something that had already made itself felt before the slump and before Hitler: middle-class unemployment.

Unemployment is not merely a matter of not having a job. Most people can *get* a job of sorts, even at the worst of times. The trouble was that by about 1930 there was no activity, except perhaps scientific research, the arts and left-wing politics, that a thinking person could believe in. The debunking of Western civilisation had reached its climax and 'disillusionment' was immensely widespread. Who now could take it for granted to go through life in the ordinary middle-class way, as a soldier, a clergyman, a stockbroker, an Indian Civil Servant or what-not? And how many of the values by which our grandfathers lived could now be taken seriously? Patriotism, religion, the Empire, the family, the sanctity of marriage, the Old School Tie, birth, breeding, honour, discipline – anyone of ordinary education could turn the whole lot of them inside out in three minutes. But what do you achieve, after all, by getting rid of such primal things as patriotism and religion? You have not necessarily got rid of the need for *something to believe in*. There had been a sort of false dawn a few years earlier when numbers of young intellectuals, including several quite gifted writers (Evelyn Waugh, Christopher Hollis and others), had fled into the Catholic Church. It is significant that these people went almost invariably to the Roman Church and not, for instance, to the C. of E., the Greek Church or the Protestant sects. They went, that is, to the Church with a world-wide organisation, the one with a rigid discipline, the one with power and prestige behind it. Perhaps it is even worth noticing that the only latter-day convert of really first-rate gifts, Eliot, has embraced not Romanism but Anglo-Catholicism, the ecclesiastical equivalent of Trotskyism. But I do not think one need look farther than this for the reason why the young writers of the 'thirties flocked into or towards the Communist Party. It was simply something to believe in. Here was a church, an army, an orthodoxy, a discipline. Here was a Fatherland and – at any rate since 1935 or thereabouts – a Führer. All the loyalties and superstitions that the intellect had seemingly banished could come rushing back under the thinnest of disguises. Patriotism, religion, empire, military glory – all in one word, Russia. Father, king, leader, hero, saviour – all in one word, Stalin. God – Stalin. The devil – Hitler. Heaven – Moscow. Hell – Berlin. All the gaps were filled up. So, after all, the 'Communism' of the English intellectual is something explicable enough. It is the patriotism of the deracinated.

But there is one other thing that undoubtedly contributed to the cult of Russia among the English intelligentsia during these years, and that is the softness and security of life in England itself. With all its injustices, England is still the land of habeas corpus, and the overwhelming majority of English people have no experience of violence or illegality. If you have grown up in that sort of atmosphere it is not at all easy to imagine what a despotic régime is like. Nearly all the dominant writers of the 'thirties belonged to the soft-boiled emancipated middle class and were too young to have effective memories of the Great War. To people of that kind such things as purges, secret police, summary executions, imprisonment without trial, etc., etc., are too remote to be terrifying. They can swallow totalitarianism *because* they have no experience of anything except liberalism. Look, for instance, at this extract from Mr Auden's poem *Spain* (incidentally this poem is one of the few decent things that have been written about the Spanish war):

> To-morrow for the young the poets exploding like
>   bombs,
> The walks by the lake, the weeks of perfect com-
>   munion;

> To-morrow the bicycle races
> Through the suburbs on summer evenings. But to-day
>   the struggle.
>
> To-day the deliberate increase in the chances of death,
> The conscious acceptance of guilt in the necessary
>   murder;
>   To-day the expending of powers
> On the flat ephemeral pamphlet and the boring
>   meeting.

The second stanza is intended as a sort of tabloid picture of a day in the life of a 'good party man'. In the morning a couple of political murders, a ten-minutes' interlude to stifle 'bourgeois' remorse, and then a hurried luncheon and a busy afternoon and evening chalking walls and distributing leaflets. All very edifying. But notice the phrase 'necessary murder'. It could only be written by a person to whom murder is at most a *word*. Personally I would not speak so lightly of murder. It so happens that I have seen the bodies of numbers of murdered men – I don't mean killed in battle, I mean murdered. Therefore I have some conception of what murder means – the terror, the hatred, the howling relatives, the post-mortems, the blood, the smells. To me, murder is something to be avoided. So it is to any ordinary person. The Hitlers and Stalins find murder necessary, but they don't advertise their callousness, and they don't speak of it as murder; it is 'liquidation', 'elimination' or some other soothing phrase. Mr Auden's brand of amoralism is only possible if you are the kind of person who is always somewhere else when the trigger is pulled. So much of left-wing thought is a kind of playing with fire by people who don't even know that fire is hot. The war-mongering to which the English intelligentsia gave themselves up in the period 1935–39 was largely based on a sense of personal immunity. The attitude was very different in France, where the military service is hard to dodge and even literary men know the weight of a pack.

Towards the end of Mr Cyril Connolly's recent book, *Enemies of Promise*, there occurs an interesting and revealing passage. The first part of the book is, more or less, an evaluation of present-day literature. Mr Connolly belongs exactly to the generation of the writers of 'the movement', and with not many reservations their values are his values. It is interesting to notice that among prose-writers he admires chiefly those specialising in violence – the would-be tough American school, Hemingway, etc. The latter part of the book, however, is autobiographical and consists of an account, fascinatingly accurate, of life at a preparatory school and Eton in the years 1910–20. Mr Connolly ends by remarking:

> Were I to deduce anything from my feelings on leaving Eton, it might be called *The Theory of Permanent Adolescence*. It is the theory that the experiences undergone by boys at the great public schools are so intense as to dominate their lives and to arrest their development.

When you read the second sentence in this passage, your natural impulse is to look for the misprint. Presumably there is a 'not' left out, or something. But no, not a bit of it! He means it! And what is more, he is merely speaking the truth, in an inverted fashion. 'Cultured' middle-class life has reached a depth of softness at which a public-school education – five years in a lukewarm bath of snobbery – can actually be looked back upon as an eventful period. To nearly all the writers who have counted during the 'thirties, what more has ever happened than Mr Connolly records in *Enemies of Promise*? It is the same pattern all the time; public school, university, a few trips abroad, then London. Hunger, hardship, solitude, exile, war, prison, persecution, manual labour – hardly even words. No wonder that the huge tribe known as 'the right left people' found it so easy to condone the purge-and-Ogpu side of the Russian régime and the horrors of the first Five-Year Plan. They were so gloriously incapable of understanding what it all meant.

By 1937 the whole of the intelligentsia was mentally at war. Left-wing thought had narrowed down to 'anti-Fascism', i.e., to a negative, and a torrent of hate-literature directed against Germany and the politicians supposedly friendly to Germany was pouring from the Press. The thing that, to me, was truly frightening about the war in Spain was not such violence as I witnessed, nor even the party feuds behind the lines, but the immediate reappearance in left-wing circles of the mental atmosphere of the Great War. The very people who for twenty years had sniggered over their own superiority to war hysteria were the ones who rushed straight back into the mental slum of 1915. All the familiar war-time idiocies, spy-hunting, orthodoxy-sniffing (Sniff, sniff. Are you a good anti-Fascist?), the retailing of incredible atrocity-stories, came back into vogue as though the intervening years had never happened. Before the end of the Spanish war, and even before Munich, some of the better of the left-wing writers were beginning to squirm. Neither Auden nor, on the whole, Spender wrote about the Spanish war in quite the vein that was expected of them. Since then there has been a change of feeling and much dismay and confusion, because the actual course of events has made nonsense of the left-wing orthodoxy of the last few years. But then it did not need very great acuteness to see that much of it was nonsense from the start. There is no certainty, therefore, that the next orthodoxy to emerge will be any better than the last.

On the whole the literary history of the 'thirties seems to justify the opinion that a writer does well to keep out of politics. For any writer who accepts or partially accepts the discipline of a political party is sooner or later faced with the alternative: toe the line, or shut up. It is, of course, possible to toe the line and go on writing – after a fashion. Any Marxist can demonstrate with the greatest of ease that 'bourgeois' liberty of thought is an illusion. But when he has finished his demonstration there remains the psychological *fact* that without this 'bourgeois' liberty the creative powers wither away. In the future a totalitarian literature may arise, but it will be quite different from anything we can now imagine. Literature as we know it is an individual thing, demanding mental honesty and a minimum of censorship. And this is even truer of prose than of verse. It is probably not a coincidence that the best writers of the 'thirties have been poets. The atmosphere of orthodoxy is always damaging to prose, and above all it is completely ruinous to the novel, the most anarchical of all forms of literature. How many Roman Catholics have been good novelists? Even the handful one could name have usually been bad Catholics. The novel is practically a Protestant form of art; it is a product of the free mind, of the autonomous individual. No decade in the past hundred and fifty years has been so barren of imaginative prose as the nineteen-thirties. There have been good

poems, good sociological works, brilliant pamphlets, but practically no fiction of any value at all. From 1933 onwards the
mental climate was increasingly against it. Anyone sensitive
enough to be touched by the *zeitgeist* was also involved in
politics. Not everyone, of course, was definitely *in* the political
racket, but practically everyone was on its periphery and more
or less mixed up in propaganda-campaigns and squalid controversies. Communists and near-Communists had a disproportionately large influence in the literary reviews. It was a time of
labels, slogans and evasions. At the worst moments you were
expected to lock yourself up in a constipating little cage of lies;
at the best a sort of voluntary censorship ('Ought I to say this? is
it pro-Fascist?') was at work in nearly everyone's mind. It is
almost inconceivable that good novels should be written in
such an atmosphere. Good novels are not written by ortho-
doxy-sniffers, nor by people who are conscience-stricken
about their own unorthodoxy. Good novels are written by
people who are *not frightened*. This brings me back to Henry
Miller.

3

If this were a likely moment for the launching of 'schools' of
literature, Henry Miller might be the starting-point of a new
'school'. He does at any rate mark an unexpected swing of the
pendulum. In his books one gets right away from the 'political
animal' and back to a viewpoint not only individualistic but
completely passive – the viewpoint of a man who believes the
world-process to be outside his control and who in any case
hardly wishes to control it.

I first met Miller at the end of 1936, when I was passing
through Paris on my way to Spain. What most intrigued me
about him was to find that he felt no interest in the Spanish war
whatever. He merely told me in forcible terms that to go to
Spain at that moment was the act of an idiot. He could
understand anyone going there from purely selfish motives,
out of curiosity, for instance, but to mix oneself up in such
things *from a sense of obligation* was sheer stupidity. In any case
my ideas about combating Fascism, defending democracy, etc.,
etc., were all boloney. Our civilisation was destined to be swept
away and replaced by something so different that we should

scarcely regard it as human – a prospect that did not bother him, he said. And some such outlook is implicit throughout his work. Everywhere there is the sense of the approaching cataclysm, and almost everywhere the implied belief that it doesn't matter. The only political declaration which, so far as I know, he has ever made in print is a purely negative one. A year or so ago an American magazine, the *Marxist Quarterly*, sent out a questionnaire to various American writers asking them to define their attitude on the subject of war. Miller replied in terms of extreme pacifism, but a merely personal pacifism, an individual refusal to fight, with no apparent wish to convert others to the same opinion – practically, in fact, a declaration of irresponsibility.

However, there is more than one kind of irresponsibility. As a rule, writers who do not wish to identify themselves with the historical process of the moment either ignore it or fight against it. If they can ignore it, they are probably fools. If they can understand it well enough to want to fight against it, they probably have enough vision to realise that they cannot win. Look, for instance, at a poem like 'The Scholar Gypsy', with its railing against the 'strange disease of modern life' and its magnificent defeatist simile in the final stanza. It expresses one of the normal literary attitudes, perhaps actually the prevailing attitude during the last hundred years. And on the other hand there are the 'progressives', the yea-sayers, the Shaw–Wells type, always leaping forward to embrace the ego-projections which they mistake for the future. On the whole the writers of the 'twenties took the first line and the writers of the 'thirties the second. And at any given moment, of course, there is a huge tribe of Barries and Deepings and Dells who simply don't notice what is happening. Where Miller's work is symptomatically important is in its avoidance of any of these attitudes. He is neither pushing the world-process forward nor trying to drag it back, but on the other hand he is by no means ignoring it. I should say that he believes in the impending ruin of Western civilisation much more firmly than the majority of 'revolutionary' writers; only he does not feel called upon to do anything about it. He is fiddling while Rome is burning, and, unlike the enormous majority of people who do this, fiddling with his face towards the flames.

In *Max and the White Phagocytes* there is one of those revealing passages in which a writer tells you a great deal about himself while talking about somebody else. The book includes a long essay on the diaries of Anais Nin, which I have never read, except for a few fragments, and which I believe have not been published. Miller claims that they are the only truly feminine writing that has ever appeared, whatever that may mean. But the interesting passage is one in which he compares Anais Nin – evidently a completely subjective, introverted writer – to Jonah in the whale's belly. In passing he refers to an essay that Aldous Huxley wrote some years ago about El Greco's picture, 'The Dream of Philip the Second'. Huxley remarks that the people in El Greco's pictures always look as though they were in the bellies of whales, and professes to find something peculiarly horrible in the idea of being in a 'visceral prison'. Miller retorts that, on the contrary, there are many worse things than being swallowed by whales, and the passage makes it clear that he himself finds the idea rather attractive. Here he is touching upon what is probably a very widespread fantasy. It is perhaps worth noticing that everyone, at least every English-speaking person, invariably speaks of Jonah and the *whale*. Of course the creature that swallowed Jonah was a fish, and is so described in the Bible (*Jonah* i. 17), but children naturally confuse it with a whale, and this fragment of baby-talk is habitually carried into later life – a sign, perhaps, of the hold that the Jonah myth has upon our imaginations. For the fact is that being inside a whale is a very comfortable, cosy, homelike thought. The historical Jonah, if he can be so called, was glad enough to escape, but in imagination, in day-dream, countless people have envied him. It is, of course, quite obvious why. The whale's belly is simply a womb big enough for an adult. There you are, in the dark, cushioned space that exactly fits you, with yards of blubber between yourself and reality, able to keep up an attitude of the completest indifference, no matter *what* happens. A storm that would sink all the battleships in the world would hardly reach you as an echo. Even the whale's own movements would probably be imperceptible to you. He might be wallowing among the surface waves or shooting down into the blackness of the middle seas (a mile deep, according to Herman Melville), but you would never notice the difference. Short of being dead, it is the final, unsurpassable stage of irresponsibility. And however it may be with Anais Nin, there is no question that Miller himself is inside the whale. All his best and most characteristic passages are written from the angle of Jonah, a willing Jonah. Not that he is especially introverted – quite the contrary. In his case the whale happens to be transparent. Only he feels no impulse to alter or control the process that he is undergoing. He has performed the essential Jonah act of allowing himself to be swallowed, remaining passive, *accepting*.

It will be seen what this amounts to. It is a species of quietism, implying either complete unbelief or else a degree of belief amounting to mysticism. The attitude is '*Je m'en fous*' or 'Though He slay me, yet will I trust in Him', whichever way you like to look at it; for practical purposes both are identical, the moral in either case being 'Sit on your bum'. But in a time like ours, is this a defensible attitude? Notice that it is almost impossible to refrain from asking this question. At the moment of writing we are still in a period in which it is taken for granted that books ought always to be positive, serious and 'constructive'. A dozen years ago this idea would have been greeted with titters. ('My dear aunt, one doesn't write *about* anything, one just *writes*.') Then the pendulum swung away from the frivolous notion that art is merely technique, but it swung a very long distance, to the point of asserting that a book can only be 'good' if it is founded on a 'true' vision of life. Naturally the people who believe this also believe that they are in possession of the truth themselves. Catholic critics, for instance, tend to claim that books are only 'good' when they are of Catholic tendency. Marxist critics make the same claim more boldly for Marxist books. For instance, Mr Edward Upward ('A Marxist Interpretation of Literature', in *The Mind in Chains*):

> Literary criticism which aims at being Marxist must . . . proclaim that no book written *at the present time* can be 'good' unless it is written from a Marxist or near-Marxist viewpoint.

Various other writers have made similar or comparable statements. Mr Upward italicises 'at the present time' because he realises that you cannot, for instance, dismiss *Hamlet* on the ground that Shakespeare was not a Marxist. Nevertheless his interesting essay only glances very shortly at this difficulty. Much of the literature that comes to us out of the past is permeated by and in fact founded on beliefs (the belief in the immortality of the soul, for example) which now seem to us false and in some cases contemptibly silly. Yet it is 'good' literature, if survival is any test. Mr Upward would no doubt answer that a belief which was appropriate several centuries ago might be inappropriate and therefore stultifying now. But this does not get one much farther, because it assumes that in any age there will be *one* body of belief which is the current approximation to truth, and that the best literature of the time will be more or less in harmony with it. Actually no such uniformity has ever existed. In seventeenth-century England, for instance, there was a religious and political cleavage which distinctly resembled the left–right antagonism of today. Looking back, most modern people would feel that the bourgeois-Puritan viewpoint was a better approximation to truth than the Catholic-feudal one. But it is certainly not the case that all or even a majority of the best writers of the time were Puritans. And more than this, there exist 'good' writers whose world-view would in *any* age be recognised as false and silly. Edgar Allan Poe is an example. Poe's outlook is at best a wild romanticism and at worst is not far from being insane in the literal clinical sense. Why is it, then, that stories like 'The Black Cat', 'The Tell-tale Heart', 'The Fall of the House of Usher' and so forth, which might very nearly have been written by a lunatic, do not convey a feeling of falsity? Because they are true within a certain framework, they keep the rules of their own peculiar world, like a Japanese picture. But it appears that to write successfully about such a world you have got to believe in it. One sees the difference immediately if one compares Poe's *Tales* with what is, in my opinion, an insincere attempt to work up a similar atmosphere, Julian Green's *Minuit*. The thing that immediately strikes one about *Minuit* is that there is no reason why any of the events in it should happen. Everything is completely arbitrary; there is no emotional sequence. But this is exactly what one does *not* feel with Poe's stories. Their maniacal logic, in its own setting, is quite convincing. When, for instance, the drunkard seizes the black cat and cuts its eye out with his penknife, one knows exactly *why* he did it, even to the point of feeling that one would have done the same oneself. It seems therefore that for a creative writer possession of the 'truth' is less important than emotional sincerity. Even Mr Upward would not claim that a writer needs nothing beyond a Marxist training. He also needs talent. But talent, apparently, is a matter of being able to *care*, of really *believing* in your beliefs, whether they are true or false. The difference between, for instance, Céline and Evelyn Waugh is a difference of emotional intensity. It is the difference between a genuine despair and a despair that is at least partly a pretence. And with this there goes another consideration which is perhaps less obvious: that there are occasions when an 'untrue' belief is more likely to be sincerely held than a 'true' one.

If one looks at the books of personal reminiscence written about the war of 1914–18, one notices that nearly all that have remained readable after a lapse of time are written from a passive, negative angle. They are the records of something completely meaningless, a nightmare happening in a void. That was not actually the truth about the war, but it was the truth about the individual reaction. The soldier advancing into a machine-gun barrage or standing waist-deep in a flooded trench knew only that here was an appalling experience in which he was all but helpless. He was likelier to make a good book out of his helplessness and his ignorance than out of a pretended power to see the whole thing in perspective. As for the books that were written during the war itself, the best of them were nearly all the work of people who simply turned their backs and tried not to notice that the war was happening. Mr E. M. Forster has described how in 1917 he read 'Prufrock' and others of Eliot's early poems, and how it heartened him at such a time to get hold of poems that were 'innocent of public-spiritedness':

> They sang of private disgust and diffidence, and of people who seemed genuine because they were unattractive or weak...Here was a protest, and a feeble one, and the more congenial for being feeble...He who could turn aside to complain of ladies and drawing-rooms preserved a

tiny drop of our self-respect, he carried on the human heritage.

That is very well said. Mr MacNeice, in the book I have referred to already, quotes this passage and somewhat smugly adds:

Ten years later less feeble protests were to be made by poets and the human heritage carried on rather differently... The contemplation of a world of fragments becomes boring and Eliot's successors are more interested in tidying it up.

Similar remarks are scattered throughout Mr MacNeice's book. What he wishes us to believe is that Eliot's 'successors' (meaning Mr MacNeice and his friends) have in some way 'protested' more effectively than Eliot did by publishing 'Prufrock' at the moment when the Allied armies were assaulting the Hindenburg Line. Just where these 'protests' are to be found I do not know. But in the contrast between Mr Forster's comment and Mr MacNeice's lies all the difference between a man who knows what the 1914–18 war was like and a man who barely remembers it. The truth is that in 1917 there was nothing that a thinking and sensitive person could do, except to remain human, if possible. And a gesture of helplessness, even of frivolity, might be the best way of doing that. If I had been a soldier fighting in the Great War, I would sooner have got hold of 'Prufrock' than *The First Hundred Thousand* or Horatio Bottomley's *Letters to the Boys in the Trenches*. I should have felt, like Mr Forster, that by simply standing aloof and keeping in touch with pre-war emotions, Eliot was carrying on the human heritage. What a relief it would have been at such a time, to read about the hesitations of a middle-aged highbrow with a bald spot! So different from bayonet-drill! After the bombs and the food-queues and the recruiting-posters, a human voice! What a relief!

But, after all, the war of 1914–18 was only a heightened moment in an almost continuous crisis. At this date it hardly even needs a war to bring home to us the disintegration of our society and the increasing helplessness of all decent people. It is for this reason that I think that the passive, non-cooperative attitude implied in Henry Miller's work is justified. Whether or not it is an expression of what people *ought* to feel, it probably comes somewhere near to expressing what they *do* feel. Once again it is the human voice among the bomb-explosions, a friendly American voice, 'innocent of public-spiritedness'. No sermons, merely the subjective truth. And along those lines, apparently, it is still possible for a good novel to be written. Not necessarily an edifying novel, but a novel worth reading and likely to be remembered after it is read.

While I have been writing this book another European war has broken out. It will either last several years and tear Western civilisation to pieces, or it will end inconclusively and prepare the way for yet another war which will do the job once and for all. But war is only 'peace intensified'. What is quite obviously happening, war or no war, is the break-up of laissez-faire capitalism and of the liberal-Christian culture. Until recently the full implications of this were not foreseen, because it was generally imagined that Socialism could preserve and even enlarge the atmosphere of liberalism. It is now beginning to be realised how false this idea was. Almost certainly we are moving into an age of totalitarian dictatorships – an age in which freedom of thought will be at first a deadly sin and later on a meaningless abstraction. The autonomous individual is going to be stamped out of existence. But this means that literature, in the form in which we know it, must suffer at least a temporary death. The literature of liberalism is coming to an end and the literature of totalitarianism has not yet appeared and is barely imaginable. As for the writer, he is sitting on a melting iceberg; he is merely an anachronism, a hangover from the bourgeois age, as surely doomed as the hippopotamus. Miller seems to me a man out of the common because he saw and proclaimed this fact a long while before most of his con-temporaries – at a time, indeed, when many of them were actually burbling about a renaissance of literature. Wyndham Lewis had said years earlier that the major history of the English language was finished, but he was basing this on different and rather trivial reasons. But from now onwards the all-important fact for the creative writer is going to be that this is not a writer's world. That does not mean that he cannot help to bring the new society into being, but he can take no part in the process *as a writer*. For *as a writer* he is a liberal, and what is happening is the destruction of liberalism. It seems likely, therefore, that in the remaining years of free speech any novel worth reading will follow more or less along the lines that Miller has followed – I do not mean in technique or subject-matter, but in implied outlook. The passive attitude will come back, and it will be more consciously passive than before. Progress and reaction have both turned out to be swindles. Seemingly there is nothing left but quietism – robbing reality of its terrors by simply submitting to it. Get inside the whale – or rather, admit that you are inside the whale (for you *are*, of course). Give yourself over to the world-process, stop fighting against it or pretending that you control it; simply accept it, endure it, record it. That seems to be the formula that any sensitive novelist is now likely to adopt. A novel on more positive, 'constructive' lines, and not emotionally spurious, is at present very difficult to imagine.

But do I mean by this that Miller is a 'great author', a new hope for English prose? Nothing of the kind. Miller himself would be the last to claim or want any such thing. No doubt he will go on writing – anybody who has once started always goes on writing – and associated with him there is a number of writers of approximately the same tendency, Lawrence Durrell, Michael Fraenkel and others, almost amounting to a 'school'. But he himself seems to me essentially a man of one book. Sooner or later I should expect him to descend into unintelligibility, or into charlatanism; there are signs of both in his later work. His last book, *Tropic of Capricorn*, I have not even read. This was not because I did not want to read it, but because the police and customs authorities have so far managed to prevent me from getting hold of it. But it would surprise me if it came anywhere near *Tropic of Cancer* or the opening chapters of *Black Spring*. Like certain other autobiographical novelists, he had it in him to do just one thing perfectly, and he did it. Considering what the fiction of the nineteen-thirties has been like, that is something.

Miller's books are published by the Obelisk Press in Paris. What will happen to the Obelisk Press, now that war has broken out and Jack Kahane, the publisher, is dead, I do not know, but at any rate the books are still procurable. I earnestly counsel anyone who has not done so to read at least *Tropic of Cancer*. With a little ingenuity, or by paying a little over the published price, you can get hold of it, and even if parts of it disgust you, it will stick in your memory. It is also an 'important' book, in a sense different from the sense in which that word is generally used. As a rule novels are spoken of as 'important' when they are either a 'terrible indictment' of something or other or when they introduce some technical innovation. Neither of these applies to *Tropic of Cancer*. Its importance is merely symptomatic. Here in my opinion is the only imaginative prose-writer of the slightest value who has appeared among the English-speaking races for some years past. Even if that is objected to as an overstatement, it will probably be admitted that Miller is a writer out of the ordinary, worth more than a single glance; and, after all, he is a completely negative, unconstructive, amoral writer, a mere Jonah, a passive accepter of evil, a sort of Whitman among the corpses. Symptomatically, that is more significant than the mere fact that five thousand novels are published in England every year and four thousand nine hundred of them are tripe. It is a demonstration of the *impossibility* of any major literature until the world has shaken itself into its new shape.

Review of *Mein Kampf*, by Adolf Hitler, unabridged translation
New English Weekly, 21 March 1940

It is a sign of the speed at which events are moving that Hurst and Blackett's unexpurgated edition of "Mein Kampf," published only a year ago, is edited from a pro-Hitler angle. The obvious intention of the translator's preface and notes is to tone down the book's ferocity and present Hitler in as kindly a light as possible. For at that date Hitler was still respectable. He had crushed the German labour movement, and for that the property-owning classes were willing to forgive him almost anything. Both Left and Right concurred in the very shallow notion that National Socialism was merely a version of Conservatism.

Then suddenly it turned out that Hitler was not respectable after all. As one result of this, Hurst and Blackett's edition was reissued in a new jacket explaining that all profits would be devoted to the Red Cross. Nevertheless, simply on the internal evidence of "Mein Kampf," it is difficult to believe that any real change has taken place in Hitler's aims and opinions. When one compares his utterances of a year or so ago with those made fifteen years earlier, a thing that strikes one is the rigidity of his mind, the way in which his world-view *doesn't* develop. It is the fixed vision of a monomaniac, and not likely to be much affected by the temporary manœuvres of power politics. Probably, in Hitler's own mind, the Russo-German pact represents no more than an alteration of time-table. The plan laid down in "Mein Kampf" was to smash Russia first, with the implied intention of smashing England afterwards. Now, as it has turned out, England has got to be dealt with first, because Russia was the more easily bribed of the two. But Russia's turn will come when England is out of the picture – that, no doubt, is how Hitler sees it. Whether it will turn out that way is of course a different question.

Suppose that Hitler's programme could be put into effect. What he envisages, a hundred years hence, is a continuous state of 250 million Germans with plenty of "living room" (i.e., stretching to Afghanistan or thereabouts), a horrible brainless empire in which, essentially, nothing ever happens except the training of young men for war and the endless breeding of fresh cannon-fodder. How was it that he was able to put this monstrous vision across? It is easy to say that at one stage of his career he was financed by the heavy industrialists, who saw in him the man who would smash the Socialists and Communists. They would not have backed him, however, if he had not talked a great movement into existence already. Again, the situation in Germany, with its seven million unemployed, was obviously favourable for demagogues. But Hitler could not have succeeded against his many rivals if it had not been for the attraction of his own personality, which one can feel even in the clumsy writing of "Mein Kampf," and which is no doubt overwhelming when one hears his speeches. I should like to put it on record that I have never been able to dislike Hitler. Ever since he came to power – till then, like nearly everyone,

I had been deceived into thinking that he did not matter –
I have reflected that I would certainly kill him if I could get
within reach of him, but that I could feel no personal animosity. The fact is that there is something deeply appealing about
him. One feels it again when one sees his photographs – and
I recommend especially the photograph at the beginning of
Hurst and Blackett's edition, which shows Hitler in his early
Brownshirt days. It is a pathetic, doglike face, the face of a man
suffering under intolerable wrongs. In a rather more manly way
it reproduces the expression of innumerable pictures of Christ
crucified, and there is little doubt that that is how Hitler sees
himself. The initial, personal cause of his grievance against the
universe can only be guessed at; but at any rate the grievance is
there. He is the martyr, the victim, Prometheus chained to the
rock, the self-sacrificing hero who fights single-handed against
impossible odds. If he were killing a mouse he would know
how to make it seem like a dragon. One feels, as with Napoleon, that he is fighting against destiny, that he *can't* win, and
yet that he somehow deserves to. The attraction of such a pose
is of course enormous; half the films that one sees turn upon
some such theme.

Also he has grasped the falsity of the hedonistic attitude to
life. Nearly all Western thought since the last war, certainly all
"progressive" thought, has assumed tacitly that human beings
desire nothing beyond ease, security and avoidance of pain. In
such a view of life there is no room, for instance, for patriotism
and the military virtues. The Socialist who finds his children
playing with soldiers is usually upset, but he is never able to
think of a substitute for the tin soldiers; tin pacifists somehow
won't do. Hitler, because in his own joyless mind he feels it
with exceptional strength, knows that human beings *don't* only
want comfort, safety, short working-hours, hygiene, birth-
control and, in general, common sense; they also, at least
intermittently, want struggle and self-sacrifice, not to mention
drums, flags and loyalty-parades. However they may be as
economic theories, Fascism and Nazism are psychologically
far sounder than any hedonistic conception of life. The same
is probably true of Stalin's militarised version of Socialism. All
three of the great dictators have enhanced their power by
imposing intolerable burdens on their peoples. Whereas

Socialism, and even capitalism in a more grudging way, have said to people "I offer you a good time," Hitler has said to them "I offer you struggle, danger and death," and as a result a whole nation flings itself at his feet. Perhaps later on they will get sick of it and change their minds, as at the end of the last war. After a few years of slaughter and starvation "Greatest happiness of the greatest number" is a good slogan, but at this moment "Better an end with horror than a horror without end" is a winner. Now that we are fighting against the man who coined it, we ought not to underrate its emotional appeal.

Notes on the Way
Time and Tide, 30 March and 6 April 1940

When the other day I read Dr Ley's statement that "inferior races, such as Poles and Jews" do not need so much to eat as Germans, I was suddenly reminded of the first sight I saw when I set foot on the soil of Asia – or rather, just before setting foot there.

The liner I was travelling in was docking at Colombo, and the usual swarm of coolies had come aboard to deal with the luggage. Some policemen, including a white sergeant, were superintending them. One of the coolies had got hold of a long tin uniform-case and was carrying it so clumsily as to endanger people's heads. Someone cursed at him for his carelessness. The police sergeant looked round, saw what the man was doing, and caught him a terrific kick on the bottom that sent him staggering across the deck. Several passengers, including women, murmured their approval.

Now transfer this scene to Paddington Station or Liverpool Docks. It simply could not happen. An English luggage-porter who was kicked would hit back, or at least there would be a chance of his doing so. The policeman would not kick him on such small provocation, and certainly not in front of witnesses. Above all, the onlookers would be disgusted. The most selfish millionaire in England, if he saw a fellow-Englishman kicked in that manner, would feel at least a momentary resentment. And yet here were ordinary, decent, middling people, people with incomes of about £500 a year, watching the scene with no emotion whatever except a mild approval. They were white, and the coolie was black. In other words he was sub-human, a different kind of animal.

That was nearly twenty years ago. Are things of this kind still happening in India? I should say that they probably are, but that they are happening less and less frequently. On the other hand it is tolerably certain that at this moment a German somewhere or other is kicking a Pole. It is quite certain that a German somewhere or other is kicking a Jew. And it is also certain (*vide* the German newspapers) that German farmers are being sentenced to terms of imprisonment for showing "culpable kindness" to the Polish prisoners working for them. For the sinister development of the past twenty years has been the spread of racialism to the soil of Europe itself.

Racialism is not merely an aberration of crazy professors, and it has nothing to do with nationalism. Nationalism is probably desirable, up to a point; at any rate it is unavoidable. Peoples with a well-developed national culture don't like being governed by foreigners, and the history of countries like Ireland and Poland is very largely the history of this fact. As for the theory that "the proletarian has no country", it always turns out to be nonsense in practice. We have just had another demonstration of this in Finland.

But racialism is something totally different. It is the invention not of conquered nations but of conquering nations. It is a way of pushing exploitation beyond the point that is normally possible, by pretending that the exploited *are not human beings*.

Nearly all aristocracies having real power have depended on a difference of race, Norman rules over Saxon, German over Slav, Englishman over Irishman, white man over black man, and so on and so forth. There are traces of the Norman predominance in our own language to this day. And it is much easier for the aristocrat to be ruthless if he imagines that the serf is different from himself in blood and bone. Hence the tendency to exaggerate race-differences, the current rubbish about shapes of skulls, colour of eyes, blood-counts, etc., etc. In Burma I have listened to racial theories which were less brutal than Hitler's theories about the Jews, but certainly not less idiotic.

The English in India have built up a whole mythology turning upon the supposed differences between their own bodies and those of orientals. I have often heard it asserted, for instance, that no white man can sit on his heels in the same attitude as an oriental – the attitude, incidentally, in which coal-miners sit when they eat their dinners in the pit.

People of mixed blood, even when they are completely white, are supposed to be detectable by mysterious peculiarities in their fingernails. As for the various superstitions centring round sunstroke, they ought to have been monographed long ago. And there is no question that this kind of nonsense has made it easier for us to squeeze the juice out of India. We could not, at this date, treat English industrial workers quite as Indian industrial workers are treated; not merely because they wouldn't tolerate it, but because, beyond a certain point, *we* wouldn't tolerate it. I doubt whether anyone in England now thinks it right for children of six to work in factories. But there are plenty of business-men in India who would welcome child-labour if the law allowed it.

If I thought that a victory in the present war would mean nothing beyond a new lease of life for British imperialism, I should be inclined to side with Russia and Germany. And I am aware that some of our rulers intend no more than that. They imagine that if they can win the war (or perhaps call it off and turn Germany against Russia), they will be able to enjoy another twenty years of colonial exploitation. But I believe there is a good chance that things will not work out like that. To begin with, the world-struggle is no longer between Socialism and capitalism. In so far as Socialism means no more than centralized ownership and planned production, all the industrialized countries will be "Socialist" before long. The real issue is between democratic Socialism and some form of rationalized caste-society. The former is much likelier to prevail if the western countries, where democratic ideas are deeply ingrained in the common people, are not deprived of all influence.

Socialism in the narrow economic sense has nothing to do with liberty, equality or common decency of any description. There is no reason, for instance, why a State should not be internally Socialist and externally imperialist. Technically it would be possible to "Socialize" England tomorrow and still continue to exploit India and the crown colonies for the benefit of the home population. Germany, almost without doubt, is moving rapidly towards Socialism; and yet side by side with this development there goes a perfectly clear, open determination to turn the subject peoples into a reserve of slave labour. It is quite practicable, so long as the myth of "inferior races" is believed in. Jews and Poles aren't human beings; therefore why not rob them? Hitler is only the ghost of our own past rising against us. He stands for the extension and perpetuation of our own methods, just at the moment when we are beginning to be ashamed of them.

Our real relationship with India has not altered much since the Mutiny of 1857, but our feelings about it have altered enormously in the last twenty years, and therein there is a gleam of hope. If we had to win India once again, as it was won in the eighteenth and nineteenth centuries, we should find ourselves unable to do it. Not because the military task would be harder – it would be far easier – but because the necessary supply of ruffians would not be forthcoming.

The men who conquered India for us, the Puritan adventurers with their Bibles and their swords – men who could blow hundreds of "natives" from the mouths of guns and describe the scene in their memoirs with the greatest realism and with no more compunction than one would feel for killing a chicken – they are simply a vanished race. The outlook even of ordinary Anglo-Indians has been deeply infected by Left-wing opinion at home. Gone are the days – which were only the day before yesterday – when you sent your disobedient servant along to the jail with a note saying "Please give the bearer fifteen lashes". Somehow we don't believe in our divine mission quite as we used to. When the time comes to pay our debts we shall undoubtedly wriggle, but I think there is just a chance that we shall pay up.

When war has once started there is no such thing as neutrality. All activities are war activities. Whether you want to or not, you are obliged to help either your own side or the enemy. The Pacifists, Communists, Fascists, etc., are at this moment helping Hitler. They have a perfect right to do so, provided they believe that Hitler's cause is the better and are willing to take the consequences. If I side with Britain and France, it is because I would sooner side with the older imperialisms – decadent, as Hitler quite rightly calls them – than with the new ones which are completely sure of themselves and there-fore completely merciless. Only, for Heaven's sake let us not pretend that we go into this war with clean hands. It is only while we cling to the consciousness that our hands are *not* clean that we retain the right to defend ourselves.

Reading Mr Malcolm Muggeridge's brilliant and depressing book, *The Thirties*, I thought of a rather cruel trick I once played on a wasp. He was sucking jam on my plate, and I cut him in half. He paid no attention, merely went on with his meal, while a tiny stream of jam trickled out of his severed œsophagus. Only when he tried to fly away did he grasp the dreadful thing that had happened to him. It is the same with modern man. The thing that has been cut away is his soul, and there was a period – twenty years, perhaps – during which he did not notice it.

It was absolutely necessary that the soul should be cut away. Religious belief, in the form in which we had known it, had to be abandoned. By the nineteenth century it was already in essence a lie, a semi-conscious device for keeping the rich rich and the poor poor. The poor were to be contented with their poverty, because it would all be made up to them in the world beyond the grave, usually pictured as something mid-way between Kew Gardens and a jeweller's shop. Ten thou-sand a year for me, two pounds a week for you, but we are all the children of God. And through the whole fabric of capitalist society there ran a similar lie, which it was absolutely necessary to rip out.

Consequently there was a long period during which nearly every thinking man was in some sense a rebel, and usually a quite irresponsible rebel. Literature was largely the literature of revolt or of disintegration. Gibbon, Voltaire, Rousseau, Shel-ley, Byron, Dickens, Stendhal, Samuel Butler, Ibsen, Zola, Flaubert, Shaw, Joyce – in one way or another they are all of them destroyers, wreckers, saboteurs. For two hundred years we had sawed and sawed and sawed at the branch we were sitting on. And in the end, much more suddenly than anyone had foreseen, our efforts were rewarded, and down we came. But unfortunately there had been a little mistake. The thing at the bottom was not a bed of roses after all, it was a cesspool full of barbed wire.

It is as though in the space of ten years we had slid back into the Stone Age. Human types supposedly extinct for centuries, the dancing dervish, the robber chieftain, the Grand Inquisitor, have suddenly reappeared, not as inmates of lunatic asylums, but as the masters of the world. Mechanization and a collective economy seemingly aren't enough. By themselves they lead merely to the nightmare we are now enduring; endless war and endless underfeeding for the sake of war, slave populations toiling behind barbed wire, women dragged shrieking to the block, cork-lined cellars where the executioner blows your brains out from behind. So it appears that amputation of the soul *isn't* just a simple surgical job, like having your appendix out. The wound has a tendency to go septic.

The gist of Mr Muggeridge's book is contained in two texts from *Ecclesiastes*: "Vanity of vanities, saith the preacher; all is vanity", and "Fear God, and keep His commandments: for this is the whole duty of man". It is a viewpoint that has gained a lot of ground lately, among people who would have laughed at it only a few years ago. We are living in a nightmare precisely *because* we have tried to set up an earthly paradise. We have believed in "progress", trusted to human leadership, rendered unto Caesar the things that are God's – that approximately is the line of thought.

Unfortunately Mr Muggeridge shows no sign of believing in God himself. Or at least he seems to take it for granted that this belief is vanishing from the human mind. There is not much doubt that he is right there, and if one assumes that no sanction can ever be effective except the supernatural one, it is clear what follows. There is no wisdom except in the fear of God; but nobody fears God; therefore there is no wisdom. Man's history reduces itself to the rise and fall of material civilizations, one Tower of Babel after another. In that case we can be pretty certain what is ahead of us. Wars and yet more wars, revolutions and counter-revolutions, Hitlers and super-Hitlers – and so downwards into abysses which are horrible to contemplate, though I rather suspect Mr Muggeridge of enjoying the prospect.

It must be about thirty years since Mr Hilaire Belloc, in his book *The Servile State*, foretold with astonishing accuracy the things that are happening now. But unfortunately he had no remedy to offer. He could conceive nothing between slavery and a return to small-ownership, which is obviously not going to happen and in fact cannot happen. There is the question now of averting a collectivist society. The only question is whether it is to be founded on willing co-operation or on the machine gun. The Kingdom of Heaven, old style, has definitely failed, but on the other hand "Marxist realism" has also failed, whatever it may achieve materially. Seemingly there is no alternative except the thing that Mr Muggeridge, and Mr F. A. Voigt, and the others who think like them, so earnestly warn us against: the much-derided "Kingdom of Earth", the concept of a society in which men know that they are mortal and are nevertheless willing to act as brothers.

Brotherhood implies a common father. Therefore it is often argued that men can never develop the sense of a community unless they believe in God. The answer is that in a half-conscious way most of them have developed it already. Man is not an individual, he is only a cell in an everlasting body, and he is dimly aware of it. There is no other way of explaining why it is that men will die in battle. It is nonsense to say that they only do it because they are driven. If whole armies had to be coerced, no war could ever be fought. Men die in battle – not gladly, of course, but at any rate voluntarily – because of abstractions called "honour", "duty", "patriotism" and so forth.

All that this really means is that they are aware of some organism greater than themselves, stretching into the future and the past, within which they feel themselves to be immortal. "Who dies if England live?" sounds like a piece of bombast, but if you alter "England" to whatever you prefer, you can see that it expresses one of the main motives of human conduct. People sacrifice themselves for the sake of fragmentary communities – nation, race, creed, class – and only become aware that they are not individuals in the very moment when they are facing bullets. A very slight increase of consciousness, and their sense of loyalty could be transferred to humanity itself, which is not an abstraction.

Mr Aldous Huxley's *Brave New World* was a good caricature of the hedonistic Utopia, the kind of thing that seemed possible and even imminent before Hitler appeared, but it had no relation to the actual future. What we are moving towards at this moment is something more like the Spanish Inquisition, and probably far worse, thanks to the radio and the secret police. There is very little chance of escaping it unless we can reinstate the belief in human brotherhood, without the need for a "next world" to give it meaning. It is this that leads innocent people like the Dean of Canterbury to imagine that they have discovered true Christianity in Soviet Russia. No doubt they are only the dupes of propaganda, but what makes them so willing to be deceived is their knowledge that the Kingdom of Heaven has somehow got to be brought on to the surface of the earth. We have got to be the children of God, even though the God of the Prayer Book no longer exists.

The very people who have dynamited our civilization have sometimes been aware of this. Marx's famous saying that "religion is the opium of the people" is habitually wrenched out of its context and given a meaning subtly but appreciably different from the one he gave it. Marx did not say, at any rate in that place, that religion is merely a dope handed out from above; he said that it is something the people create for themselves, to supply a need that he recognized to be a real one. "Religion is the sigh of the soul in a soulless world. Religion is the opium of the people." What is he saying except that man does *not* live by bread alone, that hatred is *not* enough, that a world worth living in cannot be founded on "realism" and machine guns? If he had foreseen how great his intellectual influence would be, perhaps he would have said it more often and more loudly.

New Words
February–April 1940?

At present the formation of new words is a slow process (I have read somewhere that English gains about six and loses about four words a year) and no new words are deliberately coined except as names for material objects. Abstract words are never coined at all, though old words (eg. "condition", "reflex" etc.) are sometimes twisted into new meanings for scientific purposes. What I am going to suggest here is that it would be quite feasible to invent a vocabulary, perhaps amounting to several thousands of words, which would deal with parts of our experience now practically unamenable to language. There are several obvious objections to the idea, and I will deal with these as they arise. The first step is to indicate the kind of purpose for which new words are needed.

Everyone who thinks at all has noticed that our language is practically useless for describing anything that goes on inside the brain. This is so generally recognized that writers of high skill (eg. Trollope and Mark Twain) will start their autobiographies by saying that they do not intend to describe their inner life, because it is of its nature indescribable. So soon as we are dealing with anything that is not concrete or visible (and even there to a great extent – look at the difficulty of describing anyone's appearance) we find that words are no liker to the reality than chessmen to living beings. To take an obvious case which will not raise side-issues, consider a dream. How do you describe a dream? Clearly you *never* describe it, because no words that convey the atmosphere of dreams exist in our language. Of course, you can give a crude approximation of some of the major facts in a dream. You can say, "I dreamed that I was walking down Regent Street with a porcupine wearing a bowler hat" etc. But this is no real description of the dream. And even if a psychologist interprets your dream in terms of "symbols", he is still going largely by guesswork; for the *real* quality of the dream, the quality that gave the porcupine its sole significance, is outside the world of words. In fact, describing a dream is like translating a poem into the language of one of Bohn's cribs; it is a paraphrase which is meaningless unless one knows the original.

I chose dreams as an instance that would not be disputed, but if it were only dreams that were indescribable, the matter might not be worth bothering about. But, as has been pointed out over and over again, the waking mind is not so different from the dreaming mind as it appears – or as we like to pretend that it appears. It is true that most of our waking thoughts are "reasonable" – that is, there exists in our minds a kind of chessboard upon which thoughts move logically and verbally; we use this part of our minds for any straightforward intellectual problem, and we get into the habit of thinking (ie. thinking in our chessboard moments) that it is the whole of the mind. But obviously it is not the whole. The disordered, unverbal world belonging to dreams is never quite absent from our minds, and if any calculation were possible I dare say it would be found that quite half the volume of our waking thoughts were of this order. Certainly the dream-thoughts take a hand even when we are trying to think verbally, they influence the verbal thoughts, and it is largely they that make our inner life valuable. Examine your thoughts at any casual moment. The main movement in it will be a stream of nameless things – so nameless that one hardly knows whether to call them thoughts, images or feelings. In the first place there are the objects you see and the sounds you hear, which are in themselves describable in words, but which as soon as they enter your mind become something quite different and totally indescribable.[4] And besides this there is the dream-life which your mind unceasingly creates for itself – and though most of this is trivial and soon forgotten, it contains things which are beautiful, funny etc. beyond anything that ever gets into words. In a way this un-verbal part of your mind is even the most important part, for it is the source of nearly all *motives*. All likes and dislikes, all aesthetic feelings, all notions of right and wrong (aesthetic and moral considerations are in any case inextricable) spring from feelings which are generally admitted to be subtler than words. When you are asked "Why do you do, or not do, so and so" you are invariably aware that your *real* reason will not go into words, even when you have no wish to conceal it; consequently you rationalise your conduct, more or less dishonestly. I don't know whether everyone would admit this, and it is a fact that some people seem unaware of being influenced by their inner life, or even of having any inner life. I notice that many people never laugh when they are alone, and I suppose that if a man does not laugh when he is alone his inner life must be relatively barren. Still, every individual man has an inner life, and is aware of the practical impossibility of understanding others or being understood – in general, of the star-like isolation in which human beings live. Nearly all literature is an attempt to escape from this isolation by roundabout means, the direct means (words in their primary meanings) being almost useless.

"Imaginative" writing is as it were a flank-attack upon positions that are impregnable from the front. A writer attempting anything that is not coldly "intellectual" can do very little with words in their primary meanings. He gets his effect if at all by using words in a tricky roundabout way, relying on their cadences and so forth, as in speech he would rely upon tone and gesture. In the case of poetry this is too well-known to be worth arguing about. No one with the smallest understanding of poetry supposes that

> "The mortal moon hath her eclipse endured,
> And the sad augurs mock their own presage"

really *means* what the words "mean" in their dictionary-sense. (The couplet is said to refer to Queen Elizabeth having got over her grand climacteric safely.) The dictionary-meaning has, as nearly always, *something* to do with the real meaning, but not more than the "anecdote" of a picture has to do with its design. And it is the same with prose, mutatis mutandis. Consider a novel, even a novel which has ostensibly nothing to do with the inner life – what is called a "straight story". Consider "Manon Lescaut". Why does the author invent this long rigmarole about an unfaithful girl and a runaway abbé? Because he has a certain feeling, vision, whatever you like to call it, and knows, possibly after experiment, that it is no use trying to convey this vision by describing it as one would describe a crayfish for a book of zoology. But by *not* describing it, by inventing something else (in this case a picaresque novel: in another age he would choose another form) he can convey it, or part of it. The art of writing is in fact largely the perversion of words, and I would even say that the less obvious this perversion is, the more thoroughly it has been done. For a writer who *seems* to twist words out of their meanings (eg. Gerard Manley Hopkins) is really, if one looks closely, making a desperate attempt to use them straightforwardly. Whereas a writer who seems to have no tricks whatever, for instance the old ballad-writers, is making an especially subtle flank-attack, though, in the case of the ballad-writers, this is no doubt unconscious. Of course one hears a lot of cant to the effect that all good art is "objective" and every true artist keeps his inner life to himself. But the people who say this do not mean it. All they mean is that they want the inner life to be expressed by an exceptionally roundabout method, as in the ballad or the "straight story".

The weakness of the roundabout method, apart from its difficulty, is that it usually fails. For anyone who is not a considerable artist (possibly for them too) the lumpishness of words results in constant falsification. Is there anyone who has ever written so much as a love letter in which he felt that he had said exactly what he intended? A writer falsifies himself both intentionally and unintentionally. Intentionally, because the accidental qualities of words constantly tempt and frighten him away from his true meaning. He gets an idea, begins trying to express it, and then, in the frightful mess of words that generally results, a pattern begins to form itself more or less accidentally. It is not by any means the pattern he wants, but it is at any rate not vulgar or disagreeable; it is "good art". He takes it, because "good art" is a more or less mysterious gift from heaven, and it seems a pity to waste it when it presents itself. Is not anyone with any degree of mental honesty conscious of telling lies all day long, both in talking and writing, simply because lies will fall into artistic shape when truth will not? Yet if words represented meanings as fully and accurately as height multiplied by base represents the area of a parallelogram, at least the *necessity* for lying would never exist. And in the mind of reader or hearer there are further falsifications, because, words not being a direct channel of thought, he constantly sees meanings which are not there. A good illustration of this is our supposed appreciation of foreign poetry. We know, from the Vie Amoureuse du Docteur Watson stuff of foreign critics, that true understanding of foreign literature is almost impossible; yet quite ignorant people profess to get, do get, vast pleasure out of poetry in foreign and even dead languages. Clearly the pleasure they derive may come from something the writer never intended, possibly from something that would make him squirm in his grave if he knew it was attributed to him. I say to myself "Vixi puellis nuper idoneus", and I repeat this over and over for five minutes for the beauty of the word "idoneus". Yet, considering the gulf of time and culture, and my ignorance of Latin, and the fact that no one even knows how Latin was pronounced, is it possible that the effect I am enjoying is the effect Horace was trying for? It is as though I were in ecstasies over the beauty of a picture, and all because of some splashes of paint which had accidentally got on to the canvas 200 years after it was painted. Notice, I am not saying that *art* would necessarily improve if words conveyed meaning more reliably. For all I know art thrives on the crudeness and vagueness of language. I am only criticizing *words* in their supposed function as vehicles of thought. And it seems to me that from the point of view of exactitude and expressiveness our language has remained in the Stone Age.

The solution I suggest is to invent new words as deliberately as we would invent new parts for a motor-car engine. Suppose that a vocabulary existed which would accurately express the life of the mind, or a great part of it. Suppose that there need be no stultifying feeling that life is inexpressible, no jiggery-pokery with artistic tricks; expressing one's meaning simply a matter of taking the right words and putting them in place, like working out an equation in algebra. I think the advantages of this would be obvious. It is less obvious, though, that to sit down and deliberately coin words is a commonsense proceeding. Before indicating a way in which satisfactory words might be coined, I had better deal with the objections which are bound to arise.

If you say to any thinking person "Let us form a society for the invention of new and subtler words", he will first of all object that it is the idea of a crank, and then probably say that our present words, properly handled, will meet all difficulties. (This last, of course, is only a theoretical objection. In practice everyone recognizes the inadequacy of language – consider such expressions as "Words fail", "It wasn't what he said, it was the way he said it" etc.) But finally he will give you an answer something like this: "Things cannot be done in that pedantic way. Languages can only grow slowly, like flowers; you can't patch them up like pieces of machinery. Any *made-up* language must be characterless and lifeless – look at Esperanto etc. The whole meaning of a word is in its slowly-acquired associations" etc.

In the first place, this argument, like most of the arguments produced when one suggests changing anything, is a long-winded way of saying that what is must be. Hitherto we have never set ourselves to the deliberate creation of words, and all living languages have grown slowly and haphazardly; *therefore* language cannot grow otherwise. At present, when we want to say anything above the level of a geometrical definition, we are obliged to do conjuring tricks with sounds, associations etc; *therefore* this necessity is inherent in the nature of words. The non sequitur is obvious. And notice that when I suggest coining abstract words I am only suggesting an extension of our present practice. For we do now coin concrete words. Aeroplanes and bicycles are invented, and we invent names for them, which is the natural thing to do. It is only a step to coining names for the now unnamed things that exist in the mind. You say to me, "Why do you dislike Mr Smith?" and I say "Because he is a liar, coward etc." and I am almost certainly giving the wrong reason. In my own mind the answer runs "Because he is a — kind of man", — standing for something which I understand, and you would understand if I could tell it you. Why not find a name for —? The only difficulty is to agree about *what* we are naming. But long before this difficulty arises, the reading, thinking type of man will have recoiled from such an idea as the invention of words. He will produce arguments like the one I indicated above, or others of a more or less sneering, question-begging kind. In reality all these arguments are humbug. The recoil comes from a deep unreasoned instinct, superstitious in origin. It is the feeling that any direct rational approach to one's difficulties, any attempt to solve the problems of life as one would solve an equation, can lead nowhere – more, is definitely *unsafe*. One can see this idea expressed everywhere in a roundabout way. All the bosh that is talked about our national genius for "muddling through", and all the squashy god-less mysticism that is urged against any hardness and soundness of intellect, mean au fond that it is *safer not to think*. This feeling starts, I am certain, in the common belief of children that the air is full of avenging demons waiting to punish presumption.[5] In adults the belief survives as a fear of too-rational thinking. I the Lord thy God am a jealous God, pride comes before a fall etc. – and the most dangerous pride is the false pride of the intellect. David was punished because he numbered the people – ie. because he used his intellect scientifically. Thus such an idea as, for instance, ectogenesis, apart from its possible effects upon the health of the race, family life etc. is felt to be *in itself* blasphemous. Similarly any attack on such a fundamental thing as language, an attack as it were on the very structure of our own minds, is blasphemy and therefore dangerous. To reform language is practically an interference with the work of God – though I don't say that anyone would put it quite in these words. This objection is important, because it would prevent most people from even considering such an idea as the reform of language. And of course the idea is useless unless undertaken by large numbers. For one man, or a clique, to try and make up a language, as I believe James Joyce is now doing, is as absurd as one man trying to play football alone. What is wanted is several thousands of gifted but normal people who would give themselves to word-invention as seriously as people now give themselves to Shakespearean research. Given these, I believe we could work wonders with language.

Now as to the means. One sees an instance of the successful invention of words, though crude and on a small scale, among the members of large families. All large families have two or three words peculiar to themselves – words which they have made up and which convey subtilized, non-dictionary meanings. They say "Mr Smith is a — kind of man", using some home-made word, and the others understand perfectly; here then, within the limits of the family, exists an adjective filling one of the many gaps left by the dictionary. What makes it possible for the family to invent these words is the basis of their common experience. Without common experience, of course, no word can mean anything. If you say to me "What does bergamot smell like?" I say "Something like verbena", and so long as you know the smell of verbena you are somewhere near understanding me. The method in inventing words, therefore, is the method of analogy based on unmistakeable common knowledge; one must have standards that can be referred to without any chance of misunderstanding, as one can refer to a physical thing like the smell of verbena. In effect it must come down to giving words a physical (probably visible) existence. Merely *talking* about definitions is futile; one can see this whenever it is attempted to define one of the words used by literary critics (eg. "sentimental",[6] "vulgar", "morbid" etc. All meaningless – or rather, having a different meaning for every one who uses them). What is needed is to *show* a meaning in some unmistakeable form, and then, when various people have identified it in their own minds and recognized it as worth naming, to give it a name. The question is simply of finding a way in which one can give thought an objective existence.

The thing that suggests itself immediately is the cinemato-graph. Everyone must have noticed the extraordinary powers that are latent in the film – the powers of distortion, of fantasy, in general of escaping the restrictions of the physical world. I suppose it is only from commercial necessity that the film has been used chiefly for silly imitations of stage-plays, instead of concentrating as it ought on things that are beyond the stage. Properly used, the film is the one possible medium for conveying mental processes. A dream, for instance, as I said above, is totally indescribable in words, but it can quite well be represented on the screen. Years ago I saw a film of Douglas Fairbanks', part of which was a representation of a dream. Most of it, of course, was silly joking about the dream where you have no clothes on in public, but for a few minutes it really was like a dream, in a manner that would have been impossible in words, or even in a picture, or, I imagine, in music. I have seen the same kind of thing by flashes in other films. For instance in "Dr Caligari" – a film, however, which was for the most part merely silly, the fantastic element being exploited for its own sake and not to convey any definite meaning. If one thinks of it, there is very little in the mind that could not *somehow* be represented by the strange distorting powers of the film. A millionaire with a private cinematograph, all the necessary props and a troupe of intelligent actors could, if he wished, make practically all of his inner life known. He could explain the real reasons of his actions instead of telling rationalized lies, point out the things that seemed to him beautiful, pathetic, funny etc. – things that an ordinary man has to keep locked up because there are no words to express them. In general, he could make other people understand him. Of course, it is not desirable that any one man, short of a genius, should make a show of his inner life. What is wanted is to discover the now nameless feelings that men have *in common*. All the powerful motives which will not go into words and which are a cause of constant lying and misunderstanding, could be tracked down, given visible form, agreed upon, and named. I am sure that the film, with its almost limitless powers of representation, could accomplish this in the hands of the right investigators; though putting thoughts into visible shape would not always be easy – in fact, at first it might be as difficult as any other art.

A note on the actual form new words ought to take. Suppose that several thousands of people with the necessary time, talents and money undertook to make additions to language; suppose that they managed to agree upon a number of new and necessary words; they would still have to guard against producing a mere Volapuk which would drop out of use as soon as it was invented. It seems to me probable that a word, even a not yet existing word, has as it were a natural form – or rather, various natural forms in various languages. If language were truly expressive there would be no need to play upon the sounds of words as we do now, but I suppose there must always be *some* correlation between the sound of a word and its meaning. An accepted (I believe) and plausible theory of the origin of language is this. Primitive man, before he had words, would naturally rely upon gesture, and like any other animal he would cry out at the moment of gesticulating, in order to attract attention. Now one instinctively makes the gesture that is appropriate to one's meaning, and all parts of the body follow suit, including the tongue. Hence certain tongue-movements – ie. certain sounds – would come to be associated with certain meanings. In poetry one can point to words which, apart from their direct meanings, regularly convey certain ideas by their sound. Thus: "Deeper than did ever *plummet* sound" (Shakespeare – more than once I think). "Past the *plunge* of *plummet*" (A. E. Housman). "The un-*plumbed*, salt, estranging sea" (Matthew Arnold) etc. Clearly, apart from direct meanings, the sound plum- or plun- has something to do with bottomless oceans. Therefore in forming new words one would have to pay attention to appropriateness of sound as well as exactitude of meaning. It would not do, as at present, to clip a new word of any real novelty by making it out of old ones, but it also would not do to make it out of a mere arbitrary collection of letters. One would have to determine the natural form of the word. Like agreeing upon the actual meanings of the words, this would need the cooperation of a large number of people.

I have written all this down hastily, and when I read through it I see that there are weak patches in my argument and much of it is commonplace. To most people in any case the whole idea of reforming language would seem either dilettantish or crankish. Yet it is worth considering what utter incomprehension exists between human beings – at least, between those who are not deeply intimate. At present, as Samuel Butler said, the best art (ie. the most perfect thought-transference) must be "lived" from one person to another. It need not be so if our language were more adequate. It is curious that when our knowledge, the complication of our lives and therefore (I think it must follow) our minds, develop so fast, language, the chief means of communication, should scarcely stir. For this reason I think that the idea of the deliberate invention of words is at least worth thinking over.

Review of *The Thirties*
by Malcolm Muggeridge

New English Weekly, 25 April 1940

Mr. Malcolm Muggeridge's "message" – for it is a message, though a negative one – has not altered since he wrote "Winter in Moscow." It boils down to a simple disbelief in the power of human beings to construct a perfect or even a tolerable society here on earth. In essence, it is the Book of Ecclesiastes with the pious interpolations left out.

No doubt everyone is familiar with this line of thought. Vanity of vanities, all is vanity. The Kingdom of Earth is forever unattainable. Every attempt to establish liberty leads directly to tyranny. One tyrant takes over from another, the captain of industry from the robber baron, the Nazi gauleiter from the captain of industry, the sword gives way to the chequebook and the chequebook to the machine-gun, the Tower of Babel perpetually rises and falls. It is the Christian pessimism, but with this important difference, that in the Christian scheme of things the Kingdom of Heaven is there to restore the balance:

> "Jerusalem, my happy home,
> Would God I were in thee!
> Would God my woes were at an end,
> Thy joys that I might see!"

And after all, even your earthly "woes" don't matter so very greatly, provided that you really "believe." Life is short and even Purgatory does not last for ever, so you are bound to be in Jerusalem before long. Mr Muggeridge, needless to say, refuses this consolation. He gives no more evidence of believing in God than of trusting in Man. Nothing is open to him, therefore, except an indiscriminate walloping of all human activities whatever. But as a social historian this does not altogether invalidate him, because the age we live in invites something of the kind. It is an age in which every *positive* attitude has turned out a failure. Creeds, parties, programmes of every description have simply flopped, one after another. The only "ism" that has justified itself is pessimism. Therefore at this moment good books can be written from the angle of Thersites, though probably not very many.

I don't think Mr Muggeridge's history of the 'thirties is strictly truthful, but I think it is nearer to essential truth than any "constructive" outlook could have made it. He is looking only on the black side, but it is doubtful whether there is any bright side to look on. What a decade! A riot of appalling folly that suddenly becomes a nightmare, a scenic railway ending in a torture-chamber. It starts off in the hangover of the "enlightened" post-war age, with Ramsay Macdonald soft-soaping into the microphone and the League of Nations flapping vague wings in the background, and it ends up with twenty thousand bombing planes darkening the sky and Himmler's masked executioner whacking women's heads off on a block borrowed from the Nuremberg museum. In between are the politics of the umbrella and the hand-grenade. The National

Government coming in to "save the pound," Macdonald fading out like the Cheshire Cat, Baldwin winning an election on the disarmament ticket in order to rearm (and then failing to rearm), the June purge, the Russian purges, the glutinous humbug of the abdication, the ideological mix-up of the Spanish war, Communists waving Union Jacks, Conservative M.Ps. cheering the news that British ships have been bombed, the Pope blessing Franco, Anglican dignitaries beaming at the wrecked churches of Barcelona, Chamberlain stepping out of his Munich aeroplane with a misquotation from Shakespeare, Lord Rothermere acclaiming Hitler as "a great gentleman," the London air-raid sirens blowing a false alarm as the first bombs drop on Warsaw. Mr Muggeridge, who is not loved in "left" circles, is often labelled "reactionary" or even "Fascist," but I don't know of any leftwing writer who has flayed Macdonald, Baldwin and Chamberlain with equal ferocity. Mixed up with the buzz of conferences and the crash of guns are the day-to-day imbecilities of the gutter press. Astrology, trunk murders, the Oxford Groupers with their "sharing" and their praying-batteries, the Rector of Stiffkey (a great favourite with Mr Muggeridge: he makes several appearances) photographed with naked female acquaintances, starving in a barrel and finally devoured by lions, James Douglas and his dog Bunch, Godfrey Winn with his yet more emetic dog and his political reflections ("God and Mr Chamberlain – for I see no blasphemy in coupling these names"), spiritualism, the Modern Girl, nudism, dog racing, Shirley Temple, B.O., halitosis, night starvation, should a doctor tell?

The book ends on a note of extreme defeatism. The peace that is not a peace slumps into a war that is not a war. The epic events that everyone had expected somehow don't happen, the all-pervading lethargy continues just as before. "Shape without form, shade without colour, paralysed force, gesture without motion." What Mr Muggeridge appears to be saying is that the English are powerless against their new adversaries because there is no longer anything that they believe in with sufficient firmness to make them willing for sacrifice. It is the struggle of people who have no faith against people who have faith in false gods. It he right, I wonder? The truth is that it is impossible to discover what the English people are really feeling and thinking, about the war or about anything else. It has been impossible all through the critical years. I don't myself believe that he is right. But one cannot be sure until something of a quite unmistakeable nature – some great disaster, probably – has brought home to the mass of the people what kind of world they are living in.

The final chapters are, to me, deeply moving, all the more because the despair and defeatism that they express is not altogether sincere. Beneath Mr Muggeridge's seeming acceptance of disaster there lies the unconfessed fact that he does after all believe in something – in England. He does not want to see England conquered by Germany, though if one judges merely by the earlier chapters one might well ask what difference it would make. I am told that some months back he left the Ministry of Information to join the army, a thing which none of the ex-warmongers of the Left has done, I believe. And I know very well what underlies these closing chapters. It is the emotion of the middle-class man, brought up in the military tradition, who finds in the moment of crisis that he is a patriot after all. It is all very well to be "advanced" and "enlightened," to snigger at Colonel Blimp and proclaim your emancipation from all traditional loyalties, but a time comes when the sand of the desert is sodden red and what have I done for thee, England, my England? As I was brought up in this tradition myself I can recognize it under strange disguises, and also sympathize with it, for even at its stupidest and most sentimental it is a comelier thing than the shallow self-righteousness of the leftwing intelligentsia.

Review of *My Life: The Autobiography of Havelock Ellis*
The Adelphi, May 1940

As the surviving writers of the nineteenth century drop away, one has the feeling that they are dying just in time. Ten years more, even five years, and they might recoil in horror from the world they have helped to create. When Havelock Ellis was born, the *Origin of Species* was a brand-new scandal; when he died, the Germans were in Prague. In between there lay eighty years of "progress" and "enlightenment", of patient, courageous effort by men like Ellis himself to chip away the bases of Christian civilisation. It had to be done, but the result was totally different from what had been intended. In every line that Havelock Ellis wrote – and for that matter even in the photograph of him that forms the frontispiece of this book – you can see what he was after: a sane, clean, friendly world, without fear and without injustice. What fun it must have been, in those hopeful days back in the 'eighties, working away for the best of all possible causes – and there were so many causes to choose from. Who could have foreseen where it would all end?

In his autobiography Havelock Ellis does not say much about his work. He is simply telling the story of his life, a studious, physically unadventurous life in which the chief landmarks were his friendship with Olive Schreiner (there is a very striking photograph of her, a wonderful vivid face, Jewish perhaps, triumphing over the hideous hairdressing of 1879) and his marriage in 1890. It was one of those queer marriages that were possible at a time when Socialism, vegetarianism, New Thought, feminism, homespun garments and the wearing of beards were all vaguely interconnected. His wife was an intellectual, idealistic woman, and deeply devoted to him, but she was not passionately attracted to him in a physical sense, nor he to her. They had not been married long when she developed homosexual tendencies, and some years later they ceased to "live together". They nevertheless continued to live together in the other sense, with the deepest affection on both sides. One day, apparently, they decided that their marital relationship must stop, and there was an end of it; otherwise their lives continued just as before. The way in which Ellis tells this extraordinary story brings one back to a consideration of his work and of the qualities that go with his defects.

He is a type now becoming extinct, the completely rational, completely civilised man. Probably it would be impossible for him to strike a blow, utter an insult, or even score a cheap repartee. With this goes his complete lack of "sense of humour", which is even more apparent in this book than in his others. In the second chapter he records some details about his mother which not one person in a thousand would consider mentionable, let alone printable. But it is exactly this deadly seriousness and inability to regard anything as absurd or indecent, that fit him for his work. Everything is there to be studied, and nothing to be laughed at. He is incapable of *being* obscene, and just for that reason he is capable of making – in I forget which of his books – a patient enquiry into the nature of obscenity. In his great book he sets out to study the phenomena of sex. This brings up the subject of abnormalities. But what is normality? – a question that would hardly trouble any commonplace mind. And this leads him to publish what must be some of the most grotesque and horrible documents ever written in the English tongue. And yet by his handling of it the whole subject is not only disinfected but, in some indefinable but unmistakable way, dignified. No one capable of "seeing" a dirty joke could have achieved such a thing.

Perhaps Ellis, dying in 1939, could look at the existing world with more satisfaction than the majority of nineteenth-century liberals. His own work holds good, at any rate for the time being. Our thoughts on sexual subjects are less hypocritical, ignorant and dirty than they were fifty years ago, and the credit is partly his. How long this state of affairs will last is a different question. But for the moment at least we have escaped from the mental atmosphere of 1898, the year in which Ellis's bookseller was prosecuted for having "sold and uttered a certain lewd wicked bawdy scandalous and obscene libel in the form of a book entitled *Studies in the Psychology of Sex: Sexual Inversion.*" Ellis repeats the story of the prosecution here, having already told it in the introduction to the book itself, which suggests that the memory was a painful one to him. Well, *Studies in the Psychology of Sex* is on the shelves of most of the County Libraries, and if the name of the judge who tried the case is still remembered, it will probably be in this connection and no other. And when Ellis died the news was on the front page of the *Daily Telegraph*; only just, but it did get there. So progress persists – or at any rate, it was persisting till recently.

To the Editor, *Time and Tide*
22 June 1940

Sir: It is almost certain that England will be invaded within the next few days or weeks, and a large-scale invasion by sea-borne troops is quite likely. At such a time our slogan should be ARM THE PEOPLE. I am not competent to deal with the wider questions of repelling the invasion, but I submit that the campaign in France and the recent civil war in Spain have made two facts clear. One is that when the civil population is unarmed, parachutists, motor cyclists and stray tanks can not only work fearful havoc but draw off large bodies of regular troops who should be opposing the main enemy. The other fact (demonstrated by the Spanish war) is that the advantages of arming the population outweigh the danger of putting weapons into the wrong hands. By-elections since the war started have shown that only a tiny minority among the common people of England are disaffected, and most of these are already marked down.

ARM THE PEOPLE is in itself a vague phrase, and I do not, of course, know what weapons are available for immediate distribution. But there are at any rate several things that can and should be done *now*, i.e. within the next three days:

1. Hand grenades. These are the only modern weapon of war that can be rapidly and easily manufactured, and they are one of the most useful. Hundreds of thousands of men in England are accustomed to using hand grenades and would be only too ready to instruct others. They are said to be useful against tanks and will be absolutely necessary if enemy parachutists with machine-guns manage to establish themselves in our big towns. I had a front-seat view of the street fighting in Barcelona in May, 1937, and it convinced me that a few hundred men with machine-guns can paralyse the life of a large city, because of the fact that a bullet will not penetrate an ordinary brick wall. They can be blasted out with artillery, but it is not always possible to bring a gun to bear. On the other hand, the early street fighting in Spain showed that armed men can be driven out of stone buildings with grenades or even sticks of dynamite if the right tactics are used.

275

2. Shotguns. There is talk of arming some of the Local Defence Volunteer contingents with shotguns. This may be necessary if all the rifles and Bren guns are needed for the regular troops. But in that case the distribution should be made *now* and all weapons should be immediately requisitioned from the gunsmiths' shops. There was talk of doing this weeks ago, but in fact many gunsmiths' windows show rows of guns which are not only useless where they are, but actually a danger, as these shops could easily be raided. The powers and limitations of the shotgun (with buckshot, lethal up to about sixty yards) should be explained to the public over the radio.

3. Blocking fields against aircraft landings. There has been much talk of this, but it has only been done sporadically. The reason is that it has been left to voluntary effort, i.e. to people who have insufficient time and no power of requisitioning materials. In a small thickly-populated country like England we could within a very few days make it impossible for an aeroplane to land anywhere except at an aerodrome. All that is needed is the labour. Local authorities should therefore have powers to conscript labour and requisition such materials as they require.

4. Painting out place-names. This has been well done as regards sign-posts, but there are everywhere shopfronts, tradesmen's vans, etc., bearing the name of their locality. Local authorities should have the power to enforce the painting-out of these immediately. This should include the brewers' names on public houses. Most of these are confined to a fairly small area, and the Germans are probably methodical enough to know this.

5. Radio sets. Every Local Defence Volunteer headquarters should be in possession of a radio receiving set, so that if necessary it can receive its orders over the air. It is fatal to rely on the telephone in a moment of emergency. As with weapons, the Government should not hesitate to requisition what it needs.

All of these are things that could be done within the space of a very few days. Meanwhile, let us go on repeating ARM THE PEOPLE, in the hope that more and more voices will take it up. For the first time in decades we have a Government with imagination, and there is at least a chance that they will listen.

Review of *English Ways* by Jack Hilton; with an Introduction by J. Middleton Murry and Photographs by J. Dixon Scott

The Adelphi, July 1940

Jack Hilton's book, which is the story of a tramp half across England and back, with his wife and himself pushing their tent and other belongings in a perambulator, has for its "title-quote" a couplet from Crabbe or some kindred author. A better one would have been:

> "For he might have been a Roos-i-an,
> A French or Turk or Proos-i-an,
> Or perhaps Eyetal-i-an:
> But in spite of all temptat-i-ons
> To belong to other nat-i-ons
> He remains an Englishman.
> He remains an Englishman!"

And how much an Englishman! Like a prize Sealyham terrier or Leghorn cock, he has all the "points" developed to the verge of caricature. Lytton Strachey, in his essay on Stendhal, remarked that people who have the national characteristics in an exaggerated form are not always approved of by their own countrymen. He instanced Shelley and Nelson, and if he had been writing a little later he would probably have added D. H. Lawrence. It is rather the same with Jack Hilton, whose vagabondish, almost anti-social attitude to life is only the native English anarchism pushed a little beyond the normal.

Once or twice in this book he refers to himself as a "lumpenproletarian". He is not actually that, but he does belong to the poorer working class, the people who make up the bulk of the English population and whom in the normal way we never hear about. Reading Jack Hilton's book, one realises how unsatisfactory these people are from the point of view of all the Nosey Parkers who are constantly trying to elevate them. They are, for instance, completely irreligious. In the Catholic ages they were probably not so, but since then the Church has lost all hold on them, except for a sort of blackmail-hold in the rural districts, and the sects never made much headway. Then again, though deeply moral, they are not puritanical. Their chosen pleasures are exactly the ones that the religious and the secular reformer unite in disapproving. Gambling, for example. Jack Hilton is evidently an inveterate gambler, in a small way. The high spot of his journey is a visit to the Derby, and Ascot week runs it a good second. He belongs to, or at least he understands, the crowds who fill the cheap seats at Lord's, line the streets at royal weddings, and swell the profits of the football pools. At the Derby he is not above waiting outside the Royal enclosure to see the King arrive, and feeling a pang of disappointment because it is only a motor car that he comes in and not a coach and six. Although with part of his mind he can see through it and despise it, he enjoys a bit of glitter and swagger, and does not object to ladies in £50 dresses and gentlemen in grey top-hats and spongebag trousers. One feels instinctively that his favourite kings would be Charles II and Edward VII.

But from the point of view of the doctrinaire socialist such a man is equally hopeless. Of course Jack Hilton is "left", as any thinking person below the £10 a week level must be, but the orthodoxy which even the mildest socialist would demand is impossible to him. He is pragmatical, a hater of theory, deeply infected with the English tradition of patching up and "making do", and, above all, he is not unhappy. Necessarily one makes men into socialists by making them discontented, and in a fairly prosperous capitalist society that is not so easy. Moreover in modern England the conditions of class war do not exist. One sees this fact everywhere in Jack Hilton's work. He is troubled by the itch of class-difference, mildly dislikes the bourgeoisie, but he would not massacre them even if he could, and looking round him in contemporary society he observes almost as much good as evil. When he sees a filthy slum he denounces it as it ought to be denounced; but on the other hand when he sees a good piece of slum-clearance (probably done by a Conservative corporation) he praises it almost as fervently. For "we must praise where there is cause as well as grouse when we find things awful" – very shocking, of course, but it probably gives one a truer idea of what the proletariat really do think than one can get from the Marxist textbooks, and it gives one a hint of what a proletarian revolution might be like, if such a thing could happen.

Our civilisation has put itself on record very elaborately in the years between the two world wars. If the British Museum library survives the bombings and heresy-hunts of the next twenty years, the people of 2000 A.D. will know us a great deal better than we know our ancestors. This book, in which life is seen mainly from the under side, is a valuable addition to contemporary history. It is more than I have indicated, because it happens to be the book of an individualist, a man who likes the country better than the town, does not object to solitude, has an eye for trees and flowers and prefers craftsmanship to mass production. But chiefly it is valuable for its glimpses of English working-class life in the late capitalist age, of the England of totes, dog-races, football pools, Woolworth's, the pictures, Gracie Fields, Wall's ice cream, potato crisps, celanese stockings, dart-boards, pin-tables, cigarettes, cups of tea, and Saturday evenings in the four ale bar. Lord knows how much of this civilisation, founded upon foreign investments and neglected agriculture, can survive, but it was a good civilisation while it lasted, and the people who grow up in it will carry some of their gentleness and decency into the iron ages that are coming.

Review of *Barbarians and Philistines: Democracy and the Public Schools* by T. C. Worsley

Time and Tide, 14 September 1940

The title of this book is not intended as a denunciation. It refers to the distinction drawn by Matthew Arnold between the "barbarian" spirit of the old landed aristocracy and the

"Philistine" spirit of the monied bourgeoisie who progressively overwhelmed them from 1830 onwards. The majority of our public schools were founded in the mid-nineteenth century, and the ones that already existed were altered out of recognition at about the same date. The new class who were coming into power naturally wanted a more civilized type of school than the Rugby described by Tom Hughes, and through the efforts of Dr Arnold and other reformers they got it. But the aristocracy had by no means disappeared, they intermarried with the bourgeoisie and deeply influenced their view of life, and the new schools were modified in consequence. The "barbarous" element persisted in the hatred of intellectuality and the worship of games, which Arnold had certainly not foreseen or intended. And the fact that the British Empire needed administrators, less adventurous and more reliable than the men who had conquered it, set the public schools to turning out the brave, stupid, fairly decent mediocrities who are still their typical products today. Indeed the system has not altered markedly since the 'eighties of the last century.

Mr Worsley, writing from the angle of a Left Wing intellectual, is naturally hostile to the public schools, but it is doubtful whether his criticisms are altogether relevant. Broadly speaking, his charge is that the public schools are "not democratic". This is unquestionably true. The atmosphere of nearly all these schools is deeply reactionary. Ninety-nine public-school boys out of a hundred, if they had votes, would vote Tory. But that is not the same as saying – and this is what Mr Worsley suggests – that the public schools produce types favourable to Fascism. On the contrary, one of the striking things about the British ruling class has been their complete failure to understand Fascism, either to combat it or to imitate it, and the old-fashioned Toryism that is absorbed in the public schools is partly responsible for this. Again, when he says that the public schools breed an undemocratic mentality, he appears to mean that they do not turn out boys who can accommodate themselves to a world of equal suffrage, free speech, intellectual tolerance and international co-operation. This would be a valid criticism if any such world lay ahead of us. But unfortunately that version of democracy is even more a lost cause than feudalism. What is ahead of us is not an age of reason but an age of bombing planes, and the sort of "democrat" that Mr Worsley seems to postulate would be even worse off in it than the average public-school boy, who has at any rate not been brought up as a pacifist or a believer in the League of Nations. The brutal side of public-school life, which intellectuals always deprecate, is not a bad training for the real world. The trouble is that in every other way these schools have remained in the nineteenth century, breeding-grounds of a privileged class which could not bring itself up to date without losing its self-confidence in the process.

Merely to make fun of the public schools, *more* Beach-comber, would hardly be worth while. It is too easy, and besides, it is flogging a dead horse, or a dying one, for all but three or four schools will be killed financially by the present war. Mr Worsley has some fun with Newbolt's celebrated *Vitäi Lampada* but he makes constructive suggestions as well. Much in the public-school system, he thinks, is well suited to boys of sixteen or under. Up to that age boys profit by an atmosphere of gang-loyalty, games-worship and homosexuality, and it is in the last two years of school that the harm is done to them. What he advocates is a system of junior universities at which the type of boy who is still teachable at sixteen can continue his education in a comparatively adult atmosphere. This war, however it ends, will leave us with big educational problems, and when the public schools have finally vanished we shall see virtues in them that are now hidden from us. But it is too early to say so, and Mr Worsley's attack on an obsolete system, if not always quite fair, will do more good than harm.

My Country Right or Left
Folios of New Writing, No. 2, Autumn 1940

Contrary to popular belief, the past was not more eventful than the present. If it seems so it is because when you look backward things that happened years apart are telescoped together, and because very few of your memories come to you genuinely virgin. It is largely because of the books, films and reminiscences that have come between that the war of 1914–18 is now supposed to have had some tremendous, epic quality that the present one lacks.

But if you were alive during that war, and if you disentangle your real memories from their later accretions, you find that it was not usually the big events that stirred you at the time. I don't believe that the battle of the Marne, for instance, had for the general public the melodramatic quality that it was afterwards given. I do not even remember hearing the phrase 'battle of the Marne' till years later. It was merely that the Germans were 22 miles from Paris – and certainly that was terrifying enough, after the Belgian atrocity stories – and then for some reason they had turned back. I was eleven when the war started. If I honestly sort out my memories and disregard what I have learned since, I must admit that nothing in the whole war moved me so deeply as the loss of the *Titanic* had done a few years earlier. This comparatively petty disaster shocked the whole world, and the shock has not quite died away even yet. I remember the terrible, detailed accounts read out at the breakfast table (in those days it was a common habit to read the newspaper aloud), and I remember that in all the long list of horrors the one that most impressed me was that at the last the *Titanic* suddenly up-ended and sank bow-foremost, so that the people clinging to the stern were lifted no less than three hundred feet into the air before they plunged into the abyss. It gave me a sinking sensation in the belly which I can still all but feel. Nothing in the war ever gave me quite that sensation.

Of the outbreak of war I have three vivid memories which, being petty and irrelevant, are uninfluenced by anything that has come later. One is of the cartoon of the 'German Emperor' (I believe the hated name 'Kaiser' was not popularized till a little later) that appeared in the last days of July. People were mildly shocked by this guying of royalty ('But he's such a handsome man, really!'), although we were on the edge of war. Another is of the time when the Army commandeered all the horses in our little country town, and a cabman burst into

tears in the market-place when his horse, which had worked
for him for years, was taken away from him. And another is of a
mob of young men at the railway station, scrambling for the
evening papers that had just arrived on the London train. And
I remember the pile of pea-green papers (some of them were
still green in those days), the high collars, the tightish trousers
and the bowler hats, far better than I can remember the names
of the terrific battles that were already raging on the French
frontier.

Of the middle years of the war, I remember chiefly the
square shoulders, bulging calves and jingling spurs of the artil-
lerymen, whose uniform I much preferred to that of the
infantry. As for the final period, if you ask me to say truthfully
what is my chief memory, I must answer simply – margarine. It
is an instance of the horrible selfishness of children that by 1917
the war had almost ceased to affect us, except through our
stomachs. In the school library a huge map of the western front
was pinned on an easel, with a red silk thread running across on
a zig-zag of drawing-pins. Occasionally the thread moved half
an inch this way or that, each movement meaning a pyramid of
corpses. I paid no attention. I was at school among boys who
were above the average level of intelligence, and yet I do not
remember that a single major event of the time appeared to us
in its true significance. The Russian Revolution, for instance,
made no impression, except on the few whose parents
happened to have money invested in Russia. Among the very
young the pacifist reaction had set in long before the war
ended. To be as slack as you dared on O.T.C. parades, and to
take no interest in the war, was considered a mark of enlightenment. The young officers who had come back, hardened by
their terrible experience and disgusted by the attitude of the
younger generation to whom this experience meant just nothing, used to lecture us for our softness. Of course they could
produce no argument that we were capable of understanding.
They could only bark at you that war was 'a good thing,' it
'made you tough,' 'kept you fit,' etc., etc. We merely sniggered
at them. Ours was the one-eyed pacifism that is peculiar to
sheltered countries with strong navies. For years after the war,
to have any knowledge of or interest in military matters,
even to know which end of a gun the bullet comes out of,

was suspect in 'enlightened' circles. 1914–18 was written off as a meaningless slaughter, and even the men who had been slaughtered were held to be in some way to blame. I have often laughed to think of that recruiting poster, 'What did you do in the Great War, daddy?' (a child is asking this question of its shame-stricken father), and of all the men who must have been lured into the army by just that poster and afterwards despised by their children for not being Conscientious Objectors.

But the dead men had their revenge after all. As the war fell back into the past, my particular generation, those who had been 'just too young,' became conscious of the vastness of the experience they had missed. You felt yourself a little less than a man, because you had missed it. I spent the years 1922–27 mostly among men a little older than myself who had been through the war. They talked about it unceasingly, with horror, of course, but also with a steadily-growing nostalgia. You can see this nostalgia perfectly clearly in the English war-books. Besides, the pacifist reaction was only a phase, and even the 'just too young' had all been trained for war. Most of the English middle class are trained for war from the cradle onwards, not technically but morally. The earliest political slogan I can remember is 'We want eight [eight dreadnoughts] and we won't wait.' At seven years old I was a member of the Navy League and wore a sailor suit with 'H.M.S. *Invincible*' on my cap. Even before my public-school O.T.C. I had been in a private-school cadet corps. On and off, I have been toting a rifle ever since I was ten, in preparation not only for war but for a particular kind of war, a war in which the guns rise to a frantic orgasm of sound, and at the appointed moment you clamber out of the trench, breaking your nails on the sandbags, and stumble across mud and wire into the machine-gun barrage. I am convinced that part of the reason for the fascination that the Spanish civil war had for people of about my age was that it was so like the Great War. At certain moments Franco was able to scrape together enough aeroplanes to raise the war to a modern level, and these were the turning-points. But for the rest it was a bad copy of 1914–18, a positional war of trenches, artillery, raids, snipers, mud, barbed wire, lice and stagnation.

In early 1937 the bit of the Aragon front that I was on must have been very like a quiet sector in France in 1915. It was only the artillery that was lacking. Even on the rare occasions when all the guns in Huesca and outside it were firing simultaneously, there were only enough of them to make a fitful unimpressive noise like the ending of a thunderstorm. The shells from Franco's six-inch guns crashed loudly enough, but there were never more than a dozen of them at a time. I know that what I felt when I first heard artillery fired 'in anger,' as they say, was at least partly disappointment. It was so different from the tremendous, unbroken roar that my senses had been waiting for for twenty years.

I don't quite know in what year I first knew for certain that the present war was coming. After 1936, of course, the thing was obvious to anyone except an idiot. For several years the coming war was a nightmare to me, and at times I even made speeches and wrote pamphlets against it. But the night before the Russo-German pact was announced I dreamed that the war had started. It was one of those dreams which, whatever Freudian inner meaning they may have, do sometimes reveal to you the real state of your feelings. It taught me two things, first, that I should be simply relieved when the long-dreaded war started, secondly, that I was patriotic at heart, would not sabotage or act against my own side, would support the war, would fight in it if possible. I came downstairs to find the newspaper announcing Ribbentrop's flight to Moscow. So war was coming, and the Government, even the Chamberlain Government, was assured of my loyalty. Needless to say this loyalty was and remains merely a gesture. As with almost everyone I know, the Government has flatly refused to employ me in any capacity whatever, even as a clerk or a private soldier. But that does not alter one's feelings. Besides, they will be forced to make use of us sooner or later.

If I had to defend my reasons for supporting the war, I believe I could do so. There is no real alternative between resisting Hitler and surrendering to him, and from a Socialist point of view I should say that it is better to resist; in any case I can see no argument for surrender that does not make nonsense of the Republican resistance in Spain, the Chinese resistance to Japan, etc., etc. But I don't pretend that that is the emotional basis of my actions. What I knew in my dream that night was that the long drilling in patriotism which the middle classes go through had done its work, and that once England was in a serious jam it would be impossible for me to sabotage. But let no one mistake the meaning of this. Patriotism has nothing to do with conservatism. It is devotion to something that is changing but is felt to be mystically the same, like the devotion of the ex-White Bolshevik to Russia. To be loyal both to Chamberlain's England and to the England of tomorrow might seem an impossibility, if one did not know it to be an everyday phenomenon. Only revolution can save England, that has been obvious for years, but now the revolution has started, and it may proceed quite quickly if only we can keep Hitler out. Within two years, maybe a year, if only we can hang on, we shall see changes that will surprise the idiots who have no foresight. I dare say the London gutters will have to run with blood. All right, let them, if it is necessary. But when the red militias are billeted in the Ritz I shall still feel that the England I was taught to love so long ago and for such different reasons is somehow persisting.

I grew up in an atmosphere tinged with militarism, and afterwards I spent five boring years within the sound of bugles. To this day it gives me a faint feeling of sacrilege not to stand to attention during 'God save the King.' That is childish, of course, but I would sooner have had that kind of upbringing than be like the left-wing intellectuals who are so 'enlightened' that they cannot understand the most ordinary emotions. It is exactly the people whose hearts have *never* leapt at the sight of a Union Jack who will flinch from revolution when the moment comes. Let anyone compare the poem John Cornford wrote not long before he was killed ('Before the Storming of Huesca') with Sir Henry Newbolt's 'There's a breathless hush in the Close tonight.' Put aside the technical differences, which are merely a matter of period, and it will be seen that the emotional content of the two poems is almost exactly the same. The young Communist who died heroically in the International Brigade was public school to the core. He had changed his allegiance but not his emotions. What does that prove? Merely the possibility of building a Socialist on the bones of a Blimp, the power of one kind of loyalty to transmute itself into another, the spiritual need for patriotism and the military virtues, for which, however little the boiled rabbits of the Left may like them, no substitute has yet been found.

1941

The Lion and the Unicorn: Socialism and the English Genius

19 February 1941

Part I: England Your England

i

As I write, highly civilized human beings are flying overhead, trying to kill me.

They do not feel any enmity against me as [an] individual, nor I against them. They are "only doing their duty", as the saying goes. Most of them, I have no doubt, are kind-hearted law-abiding men who would never dream of committing murder in private life. On the other hand, if one of them succeeds in blowing me to pieces with a well-placed bomb, he will never sleep any the worse for it. He is serving his country, which has the power to absolve him from evil.

One cannot see the modern world as it is unless one recognizes the overwhelming strength of patriotism, national loyalty. In certain circumstances it can break down, at certain levels of civilization it does not exist, but as a *positive* force there is nothing to set beside it. Christianity and international Socialism are as weak as straw in comparison with it. Hitler and Mussolini rose to power in their own countries very largely because they could grasp this fact and their opponents could not.

Also, one must admit that the divisions between nation and nation are founded on real differences of outlook. Till recently it was thought proper to pretend that all human beings are very much alike, but in fact anyone able to use his eyes knows that the average of human behaviour differs enormously from country to country. Things that could happen in one country could not happen in another. Hitler's June Purge, for instance, could not have happened in England. And, as western peoples go, the English are very highly differentiated. There is a sort of backhanded admission of this in the dislike which nearly all foreigners feel for our national way of life. Few

Europeans can endure living in England, and even Americans often feel more at home in Europe.

When you come back to England from any foreign country, you have immediately the sensation of breathing a different air. Even in the first few minutes dozens of small things conspire to give you this feeling. The beer is bitterer, the coins are heavier, the grass is greener, the advertisements are more blatant. The crowds in the big towns, with their mild knobby faces, their bad teeth and gentle manners, are different from a European crowd. Then the vastness of England swallows you up, and you lose for a while your feeling that the whole nation has a single identifiable character. Are there really such things as nations? Are we not 46 million individuals, all different? And the diversity of it, the chaos! The clatter of clogs in the Lancashire mill towns, the to-and-fro of the lorries on the Great North Road, the queues outside the Labour Exchanges, the rattle of pin-tables in the Soho pubs, the old maids biking to Holy Communion through the mists of the autumn mornings – all these are not only fragments, but *characteristic* fragments, of the English scene. How can one make a pattern out of this muddle?

But talk to foreigners, read foreign books or newspapers, and you are brought back to the same thought. Yes, there *is* something distinctive and recognizable in English civilization. It is a culture as individual as that of Spain. It is somehow bound up with solid breakfasts and gloomy Sundays, smoky towns and winding roads, green fields and red pillar-boxes. It has a flavour of its own. Moreover it is continuous, it stretches into the future and the past, there is something in it that persists, as in a living creature. What can the England of 1940 have in common with the England of 1840? But then, what have you in common with the child of five whose photograph your mother keeps on the mantelpiece? Nothing, except that you happen to be the same person.

And above all, it is *your* civilization, it is *you*. However much you hate it or laugh at it, you will never be happy away from it for any length of time. The suet puddings and the red pillar-boxes have entered into your soul. Good or evil, it is yours, you belong to it, and this side the grave you will never get away from the marks that it has given you.

Meanwhile England, together with the rest of the world, is changing. And like everything else it can change only in certain directions, which up to a point can be foreseen. That is not to say that the future is fixed, merely that certain alternatives are possible and others not. A seed may grow or not grow, but at any rate a turnip seed never grows into a parsnip. It is therefore of the deepest importance to try and determine what England *is*, before guessing what part England *can play* in the huge events that are happening.

ii

National characteristics are not easy to pin down, and when pinned down they often turn out to be trivialities or seem to have no connection with one another. Spaniards are cruel to animals, Italians can do nothing without making a deafening noise, the Chinese are addicted to gambling. Obviously such things don't matter in themselves. Nevertheless, nothing is causeless, and even the fact that Englishmen have bad teeth can tell one something about the realities of English life.

Here are a couple of generalizations about England that would be accepted by almost all observers. One is that the English are not gifted artistically. They are not as musical as the Germans or Italians, painting and sculpture have never flourished in England as they have in France. Another is that, as Europeans go, the English are not intellectual. They have a horror of abstract thought, they feel no need for any philosophy or systematic "world-view". Nor is this because they are "practical", as they are so fond of claiming for themselves. One has only to look at their methods of town-planning and water-supply, their obstinate clinging to everything that is out of date and a nuisance, a spelling system that defies analysis and a system of weights and measures that is intelligible only to the compilers of arithmetic books, to see how little they care about mere efficiency. But they have a certain power of acting without taking thought. Their world-famed hypocrisy – their double-faced attitude towards the Empire, for instance – is bound up with this. Also, in moments of supreme crisis the whole nation can suddenly draw together and act upon a species of instinct, really a code of conduct which is understood by almost everyone, though never formulated. The phrase that

GEORGE ORWELL

Hitler coined for the Germans, "a sleep-walking people", would have been better applied to the English. Not that there is anything to be proud of in being a sleep-walker.

But here it is worth noticing a minor English trait which is extremely well marked though not often commented on, and that is a love of flowers. This is one of the first things that one notices when one reaches England from abroad, especially if one is coming from southern Europe. Does it not contradict the English indifference to the arts? Not really, because it is found in people who have no aesthetic feelings whatever. What it does link up with, however, is another English characteristic which is so much a part of us that we barely notice it, and that is the addiction to hobbies and spare-time occupations, the *privateness* of English life. We are a nation of flower-lovers, but also a nation of stamp-collectors, pigeon-fanciers, amateur carpenters, coupon-snippers, darts-players, crossword-puzzle fans. All the culture that is most truly native centres round things which even when they are communal are not official – the pub, the football match, the back garden, the fireside and the "nice cup of tea". The liberty of the individual is still believed in, almost as in the nineteenth century. But this has nothing to do with economic liberty, the right to exploit others for profit. It is the liberty to have a home of your own, to do what you like in your spare time, to choose your own amusements instead of having them chosen for you from above. The most hateful of all names in an English ear is Nosey Parker. It is obvious, of course, that even this purely private liberty is a lost cause. Like all other modern peoples, the English are in process of being numbered, labelled, conscripted, "co-ordinated". But the pull of their impulses is in the other direction, and the kind of regimentation that can be imposed on them will be modified in consequence. No party rallies, no Youth Movements, no coloured shirts, no Jew-baiting or "spontaneous" demonstrations. No Gestapo either, in all probability.

But in all societies the common people must live to some extent *against* the existing order. The genuinely popular culture of England is something that goes on beneath the surface, unofficially and more or less frowned on by the authorities. One thing one notices if one looks directly at the common people, especially in the big towns, is that they are not puritan-

ESSAYS

ical. They are inveterate gamblers, drink as much beer as their wages will permit, are devoted to bawdy jokes, and use probably the foulest language in the world. They have to satisfy these tastes in the face of astonishing, hypocritical laws (licensing laws, lottery acts, etc., etc.) which are designed to interfere with everybody but in practice allow everything to happen. Also, the common people are without definite religious belief, and have been so for centuries. The Anglican Church never had a real hold on them, it was simply a preserve of the landed gentry, and the Nonconformist sects only influenced minorities. And yet they have retained a deep tinge of Christian feeling, while almost forgetting the name of Christ. The power-worship which is the new religion of Europe, and which has infected the English intelligentsia, has never touched the common people. They have never caught up with power politics. The "realism" which is preached in Japanese and Italian newspapers would horrify them. One can learn a good deal about the spirit of England from the comic coloured postcards that you see in the windows of cheap stationers' shops. These things are a sort of diary upon which the English people have unconsciously recorded themselves. Their old-fashioned outlook, their graded snobberies, their mixture of bawdiness and hypocrisy, their extreme gentleness, their deeply moral attitude to life, are all mirrored there.

The gentleness of the English civilization is perhaps its most marked characteristic. You notice it the instant you set foot on English soil. It is a land where the bus conductors are good-tempered and the policemen carry no revolvers. In no country inhabited by white men is it easier to shove people off the pavement. And with this goes something that is always written off by European observers as "decadence" or hypocrisy, the English hatred of war and militarism. It is rooted deep in history, and it is strong in the lower-middle class as well as the working class. Successive wars have shaken it but not destroyed it. Well within living memory it was common for "the redcoats" to be booed at in the street and for the landlords of respectable public-houses to refuse to allow soldiers on the premises. In peace-time, even when there are two million unemployed, it is difficult to fill the ranks of the tiny standing army, which is officered by the country gentry and a specialized

295

stratum of the middle class, and manned by farm labourers and slum proletarians. The mass of the people are without military knowledge or tradition, and their attitude towards war is invariably defensive. No politician could rise to power by promising them conquests or military "glory", no Hymn of Hate has ever made any appeal to them. In the last war the songs which the soldiers made up and sang of their own accord were not vengeful but humorous and mock-defeatist.[7] The only enemy they ever named was the sergeant-major.

In England all the boasting and flag-wagging, the "Rule Britannia" stuff, is done by small minorities. The patriotism of the common people is not vocal or even conscious. They do not retain among their historical memories the name of a single military victory. English literature, like other literatures, is full of battle-poems, but it is worth noticing that the ones that have won for themselves a kind of popularity are always a tale of disasters and retreats. There is no popular poem about Trafalgar or Waterloo, for instance. Sir John Moore's army at Corunna, fighting a desperate rear-guard action before escaping overseas (just like Dunkirk!) has more appeal than a brilliant victory. The most stirring battle-poem in English is about a brigade of cavalry which charged in the wrong direction. And of the last war, the four names which have really engraved themselves on the popular memory are Mons, Ypres, Gallipoli and Passchendaele, every time a disaster. The names of the great battles that finally broke the German armies are simply unknown to the general public.

The reason why the English anti-militarism disgusts foreign observers is that it ignores the existence of the British Empire. It looks like sheer hypocrisy. After all, the English have absorbed a quarter of the earth and held on to it by means of a huge navy. How dare they then turn round and say that war is wicked?

It is quite true that the English are hypocritical about their Empire. In the working class this hypocrisy takes the form of not knowing that the Empire exists. But their dislike of standing armies is a perfectly sound instinct. A navy employs comparatively few people, and it is an external weapon which cannot affect home politics directly. Military dictatorships exist everywhere, but there is no such thing as a naval dictatorship. What English people of nearly all classes loathe from the bottom of their hearts is the swaggering officer type, the jingle of spurs and the crash of boots. Decades before Hitler was ever heard of, the word "Prussian" had much the same significance in England as "Nazi" has to-day. So deep does this feeling go that for a hundred years past the officers of the British Army, in peace-time, have always worn civilian clothes when off duty.

One rapid but fairly sure guide to the social atmosphere of a country is the parade-step of its army. A military parade is really a kind of ritual dance, something like a ballet, expressing a certain philosophy of life. The goose-step, for instance, is one of the most horrible sights in the world, far more terrifying than a dive-bomber. It is simply an affirmation of naked power; contained in it, quite consciously and intentionally, is the vision of a boot crashing down on a face. Its ugliness is part of its essence, for what it is saying is "Yes, I *am* ugly, and you daren't laugh at me", like the bully who makes faces at his victim. Why is the goose-step not used in England? There are, heaven knows, plenty of army officers who would be only too glad to introduce some such thing. It is not used because the people in the street would laugh. Beyond a certain point, military display is only possible in countries where the common people dare not laugh at the army. The Italians adopted the goose-step at about the time when Italy passed definitely under German control, and, as one would expect, they do it less well than the Germans. The Vichy government, if it survives, is bound to introduce a stiffer parade-ground discipline into what is left of the French army. In the British army the drill is rigid and complicated, full of memories of the eighteenth century, but without definite swagger; the march is merely a formalized walk. It belongs to a society which is ruled by the sword, no doubt, but a sword which must never be taken out of the scabbard.

And yet the gentleness of English civilization is mixed up with barbarities and anachronisms. Our criminal law is as out of date as the muskets in the Tower. Over against the Nazi Storm Trooper you have got to set that typically English figure, the hanging judge, some gouty old bully with his mind rooted in the nineteenth century, handing out savage sentences. In England people are still hanged by the neck and flogged with the cat o' nine tails. Both of these punishments are obscene as well as cruel, but there has never been any genuinely popular outcry against them. People accept them (and Dartmoor, and Borstal) almost as they accept the weather. They are part of "the law", which is assumed to be unalterable.

Here one comes upon an all-important English trait: the respect for constitutionalism and legality, the belief in "the law" as something above the State and above the individual, something which is cruel and stupid, of course, but at any rate *incorruptible*.

It is not that anyone imagines the law to be just. Everyone knows that there is one law for the rich and another for the poor. But no one accepts the implications of this, everyone takes it for granted that the law, such as it is, will be respected, and feels a sense of outrage when it is not. Remarks like "They can't run me in; I haven't done anything wrong", or "They can't do that; it's against the law", are part of the atmosphere of England. The professed enemies of society have this feeling as strongly as anyone else. One sees it in prison-books like Wilfred Macartney's *Walls Have Mouths* or Jim Phelan's *Jail Journey*, in the solemn idiocies that take place at the trials of Conscientious Objectors, in letters to the papers from eminent Marxist professors, pointing out that this or that is a "miscarriage of British justice". Everyone believes in his heart that the law can be, ought to be, and, on the whole, will be impartially administered. The totalitarian idea that there is no such thing as law, there is only power, has never taken root. Even the intelligentsia have only accepted it in theory.

An illusion can become a half-truth, a mask can alter the expression of a face. The familiar arguments to the effect that democracy is "just the same as" or "just as bad as" totalitarianism never take account of this fact. All such arguments boil down to saying that half a loaf is the same as no bread. In England such concepts as justice, liberty and objective truth are still believed in. They may be illusions, but they are very powerful illusions. The belief in them influences conduct, national life is different because of them. In proof of which, look about you. Where are the rubber truncheons, where is the castor oil? The sword is still in the scabbard, and while it stays there corruption cannot go beyond a certain point. The

English electoral system, for instance, is an all-but open fraud. In a dozen obvious ways it is gerrymandered in the interest of the moneyed class. But until some deep change has occurred in the public mind, it cannot become *completely* corrupt. You do not arrive at the polling booth to find men with revolvers telling you which way to vote, nor are the votes miscounted, nor is there any direct bribery. Even hypocrisy is a powerful safeguard. The hanging judge, that evil old man in scarlet robe and horsehair wig, whom nothing short of dynamite will ever teach what century he is living in, but who will at any rate interpret the law according to the books and will in no circumstances take a money bribe, is one of the symbolic figures of England. He is a symbol of the strange mixture of reality and illusion, democracy and privilege, humbug and decency, the subtle network of compromises, by which the nation keeps itself in its familiar shape.

iii

I have spoken all the while of "the nation", "England", "Britain", as though 45 million souls could somehow be treated as a unit. But is not England notoriously two nations, the rich and the poor? Dare one pretend that there is anything in common between people with £100,000 a year and people with £1 a week? And even Welsh and Scottish readers are likely to have been offended because I have used the word "England" oftener than "Britain", as though the whole population dwelt in London and the Home Counties and neither north nor west possessed a culture of its own.

One gets a better view of this question if one considers the minor point first. It is quite true that the so-called races of Britain feel themselves to be very different from one another. A Scotsman, for instance, does not thank you if you call him an Englishman. You can see the hesitation we feel on this point by the fact that we call our islands by no less than six different names, England, Britain, Great Britain, the British Isles, the United Kingdom and, in very exalted moments, Albion. Even the differences between north and south England loom large in our own eyes. But somehow these differences fade away the moment that any two Britons are confronted by a European. It is very rare to meet a foreigner, other than an American, who can distinguish between English and Scots or even English and Irish. To a Frenchman, the Breton and the Auvergnat seem very different beings, and the accent of Marseilles is a stock joke in Paris. Yet we speak of "France" and "the French", recognizing France as an entity, a single civilization, which in fact it is. So also with ourselves. Looked at from the outside, even the cockney and the Yorkshireman have a strong family resemblance.

And even the distinction between rich and poor dwindles somewhat when one regards the nation from the outside. There is no question about the inequality of wealth in England. It is grosser than in any European country, and you have only to look down the nearest street to see it. Economically, England is certainly two nations, if not three or four. But at the same time the vast majority of the people *feel* themselves to be a single nation and are conscious of resembling one another more than they resemble foreigners. Patriotism is usually stronger than class-hatred, and always stronger than any kind of internationalism. Except for a brief moment in 1920 (the "Hands off Russia" movement) the British working class have never thought or acted internationally. For two and a half years they watched their comrades in Spain slowly strangled, and never aided them by even a single strike. But when their own country (the country of Lord Nuffield and Mr. Montagu Norman) was in danger, their attitude was very different. At the moment when it seemed likely that England might be invaded, Anthony Eden appealed over the radio for Local Defence Volunteers. He got a quarter of a million men in the first twenty-four hours, and another million in the subsequent month. One has only to compare these figures with, for instance, the number of Conscientious Objectors to see how vast is the strength of traditional loyalties compared with new ones.

In England patriotism takes different forms in different classes, but it runs like a connecting thread through nearly all of them. Only the Europeanized intelligentsia are really immune to it. As a positive emotion it is stronger in the middle class than in the upper class – the cheap public schools, for instance, are more given to patriotic demonstrations than the expensive ones – but the number of definitely treacherous rich men, the Laval-Quisling type, is probably very small. In the working class patriotism is profound, but it is unconscious. The working man's heart does not leap when he sees a Union Jack. But the famous "insularity" and "xenophobia" of the English is far stronger in the working class than in the bourgeoisie. In all countries the poor are more national than the rich, but the English working class are outstanding in their abhorrence of foreign habits. Even when they are obliged to live abroad for years they refuse either to accustom themselves to foreign food or to learn foreign languages. Nearly every Englishman of working-class origin considers it effeminate to pronounce a foreign word correctly. During the war of 1914–18 the English working class were in contact with foreigners to an extent that is rarely possible. The sole result was that they brought back a hatred of all Europeans, except the Germans, whose courage they admired. In four years on French soil they did not even acquire a liking for wine. The insularity of the English, their refusal to take foreigners seriously, is a folly that has to be paid for very heavily from time to time. But it plays its part in the English *mystique*, and the intellectuals who have tried to break it down have generally done more harm than good. At bottom it is the same quality in the English character that repels the tourist and keeps out the invader.

Here one comes back to two English characteristics that I pointed out, seemingly rather at random, at the beginning of the last chapter. One is the lack of artistic ability. This is perhaps another way of saying that the English are outside the European culture. For there is one art in which they have shown plenty of talent, namely literature. But this is also the only art that cannot cross frontiers. Literature, especially poetry, and lyric poetry most of all, is a kind of family joke, with little or no value outside its own language-group. Except for Shakespeare, the best English poets are barely known in Europe, even as names. The only poets who are widely read are Byron, who is admired for the wrong reasons, and Oscar Wilde, who is pitied as a victim of English hypocrisy. And linked up with this, though not very obviously, is the lack of philosophical faculty, the absence in nearly all Englishmen of any need for an ordered system of thought or even for the use of logic.

Up to a point, the sense of national unity is a substitute for a "world-view". Just because patriotism is all but universal and not even the rich are uninfluenced by it, there can come moments when the whole nation suddenly swings together and does the same thing, like a herd of cattle facing a wolf. There was such a moment, unmistakably, at the time of the disaster in France. After eight months of vaguely wondering what the war was about, the people suddenly knew what they had got to do: first, to get the army away from Dunkirk, and secondly to prevent invasion. It was like the awakening of a giant. Quick! Danger! The Philistines be upon thee, Samson! And then the swift unanimous action – and then, alas, the prompt relapse into sleep. In a divided nation that would have been exactly the moment for a big peace movement to arise. But does this mean that the instinct of the English will always tell them to do the right thing? Not at all, merely that it will tell them to do the same thing. In the 1931 General Election, for instance, we all did the wrong thing in perfect unison. We were as single-minded as the Gadarene swine. But I honestly doubt whether we can say that we were shoved down the slope against our will.

It follows that British democracy is less of a fraud than it sometimes appears. A foreign observer sees only the huge inequality of wealth, the unfair electoral system, the governing-class control over the Press, the radio and education, and concludes that democracy is simply a polite name for dictatorship. But this ignores the considerable agreement that does unfortunately exist between the leaders and the led. However much one may hate to admit it, it is almost certain that between 1931 and 1940 the National Government represented the will of the mass of the people. It tolerated slums, unemployment and a cowardly foreign policy. Yes, but so did public opinion. It was a stagnant period, and its natural leaders were mediocrities.

In spite of the campaigns of a few thousand left-wingers, it is fairly certain that the bulk of the English people were behind Chamberlain's foreign policy. More, it is fairly certain that the same struggle was going on in Chamberlain's mind as in the minds of ordinary people. His opponents professed to see in him a dark and wily schemer, plotting to sell England to Hitler, but it is far likelier that he was merely a stupid old man doing his best according to his very dim lights. It is difficult otherwise to explain the contradictions of his policy, his failure to grasp any of the courses that were open to him. Like the mass of the people, he did not want to pay the price either of peace or of war. And public opinion was behind him all the while, in policies that were completely incompatible with one another. It was behind him when he went to Munich, when he tried to come to an understanding with Russia, when he gave the guarantee to Poland, when he honoured it, and when he prosecuted the war half-heartedly. Only when the results of his policy became apparent did it turn against him; which is to say that it turned against its own lethargy of the past seven years. Thereupon the people picked a leader nearer to their mood, Churchill, who was at any rate able to grasp that wars are not won without fighting. Later, perhaps, they will pick another leader who can grasp that only Socialist nations can fight effectively.

Do I mean by all this that England is a genuine democracy? No, not even a reader of the *Daily Telegraph* could quite swallow that.

England is the most class-ridden country under the sun. It is a land of snobbery and privilege, ruled largely by the old and silly. But in any calculation about it one has got to take into account its emotional unity, the tendency of nearly all its inhabitants to feel alike and act together in moments of supreme crisis. It is the only great country in Europe that is not obliged to drive hundreds of thousands of its nationals into exile or the concentration camp. At this moment, after a year of war, newspapers and pamphlets abusing the Government, praising the enemy and clamouring for surrender are being sold on the streets, almost without interference. And this is less from a respect for freedom of speech than from a simple perception that these things don't matter. It is safe to let a paper like *Peace News* be sold, because it is certain that ninety-five per cent of the population will never want to read it. The nation is bound together by an invisible chain. At any normal time the ruling class will rob, mismanage, sabotage, lead us into the muck; but let popular opinion really make itself heard, let them get a tug from below that they cannot avoid feeling, and it is difficult for them not to respond. The left-wing writers who denounce the whole of the ruling class as "pro-Fascist" are

grossly over-simplifying. Even among the inner clique of politicians who brought us to our present pass, it is doubtful
whether there were any *conscious* traitors. The corruption that
happens in England is seldom of that kind. Nearly always it is
more in the nature of self-deception, of the right hand not
knowing what the left hand doeth. And being unconscious, it is
limited. One sees this at its most obvious in the English Press.
Is the English Press honest or dishonest? At normal times it is
deeply dishonest. All the papers that matter live off their
advertisements, and the advertisers exercise an indirect censorship over news. Yet I do not suppose there is one paper in
England that can be straightforwardly bribed with hard cash. In
the France of the Third Republic all but a very few of the
newspapers could notoriously be bought over the counter like
so many pounds of cheese. Public life in England has never
been *openly* scandalous. It has not reached the pitch of disintegration at which humbug can be dropped.

England is not the jewelled isle of Shakespeare's much-
quoted passage, nor is it the inferno depicted by Dr. Goebbels.
More than either it resembles a family, a rather stuffy Victorian
family, with not many black sheep in it but with all its cupboards bursting with skeletons. It has rich relations who have to
be kow-towed to and poor relations who are horribly sat upon,
and there is a deep conspiracy of silence about the source of the
family income. It is a family in which the young are generally
thwarted and most of the power is in the hands of irresponsible
uncles and bedridden aunts. Still, it is a family. It has its private
language and its common memories, and at the approach of an
enemy it closes its ranks. A family with the wrong members in
control – that, perhaps, is as near as one can come to describing
England in a phrase.

iv

Probably the battle of Waterloo *was* won on the playing-fields
of Eton, but the opening battles of all subsequent wars have
been lost there. One of the dominant facts in English life during
the past three-quarters of a century has been the decay of ability
in the ruling class.

In the years between 1920 and 1940 it was happening with
the speed of a chemical reaction. Yet at the moment of writing

it is still possible to speak of a ruling class. Like the knife which has had two new blades and three new handles, the upper fringe of English society is still almost what it was in the mid-nineteenth century. After 1832 the old landowning aristocracy steadily lost power, but instead of disappearing or becoming a fossil they simply intermarried with the merchants, manufacturers and financiers who had replaced them, and soon turned them into accurate copies of themselves. The wealthy ship-owner or cotton-miller set up for himself an alibi as a country gentleman, while his sons learned the right mannerisms at public schools which had been designed for just that purpose. England was ruled by an aristocracy constantly recruited from parvenus. And considering what energy the self-made men possessed, and considering that they were buying their way into a class which at any rate had a tradition of public service, one might have expected that able rulers could be produced in some such way.

And yet somehow the ruling class decayed, lost its ability, its daring, finally even its ruthlessness, until a time came when stuffed shirts like Eden or Halifax could stand out as men of exceptional talent. As for Baldwin, one could not even dignify him with the name of stuffed shirt. He was simply a hole in the air. The mishandling of England's domestic problems during the nineteen-twenties had been bad enough, but British foreign policy between 1931 and 1939 is one of the wonders of the world. Why? What had happened? What was it that at every decisive moment made every British statesman do the wrong thing with so unerring an instinct?

The underlying fact was that the whole position of the monied class had long ceased to be justifiable. There they sat, at the centre of a vast empire and a world-wide financial network, drawing interest and profits and spending them – on what? It was fair to say that life within the British Empire was in many ways better than life outside it. Still, the Empire was undeveloped, India slept in the Middle Ages, the Dominions lay empty, with foreigners jealously barred out, and even England was full of slums and unemployment. Only half a million people, the people in the country houses, definitely benefited from the existing system. Moreover, the tendency of small businesses to merge together into large ones robbed more and more of the monied class of their function and turned them into mere *owners*, their work being done for them by salaried managers and technicians. For long past there had been in England an entirely functionless class, living on money that was invested they hardly knew where, the "idle rich", the people whose photographs you can look at in the *Tatler* and the *Bystander*, always supposing that you want to. The existence of these people was by any standard unjustifiable. They were simply parasites, less useful to society than his fleas are to a dog.

By 1920 there were many people who were aware of all this. By 1930 millions were aware of it. But the British ruling class obviously could not admit to themselves that their usefulness was at an end. Had they done that they would have had to abdicate. For it was not possible for them to turn themselves into mere bandits, like the American millionaires, consciously clinging to unjust privileges and beating down opposition by bribery and tear-gas bombs. After all, they belonged to a class with a certain tradition, they had been to public schools where the duty of dying for your country, if necessary, is laid down as the first and greatest of the Commandments. They had to *feel* themselves true patriots, even while they plundered their countrymen. Clearly there was only one escape for them – into stupidity. They could keep society in its existing shape only by being *unable* to grasp that any improvement was possible. Difficult though this was, they achieved it, largely by fixing their eyes on the past and refusing to notice the changes that were going on round them.

There is much in England that this explains. It explains the decay of country life, due to the keeping-up of a sham feudalism which drives the more spirited workers off the land. It explains the immobility of the public schools, which have barely altered since the 'eighties of the last century. It explains the military incompetence which has again and again startled the world. Since the 'fifties every war in which England has engaged has started off with a series of disasters, after which the situation has been saved by people comparatively low in the social scale. The higher commanders, drawn from the aristocracy, could never prepare for modern war, because in order to do so they would have had to admit to themselves that the

306

world was changing. They have always clung to obsolete methods and weapons, because they inevitably saw each war as a repetition of the last. Before the Boer War they prepared for the Zulu War, before 1914 for the Boer War, and before the present war for 1914. Even at this moment hundreds of thousands of men in England are being trained with the bayonet, a weapon entirely useless except for opening tins. It is worth noticing that the navy and, latterly, the Air Force, have always been more efficient than the regular army. But the navy is only partially, and the Air Force hardly at all, within the ruling-class orbit.

It must be admitted that so long as things were peaceful the methods of the British ruling class served them well enough. Their own people manifestly tolerated them. However unjustly England might be organized, it was at any rate not torn by class warfare or haunted by secret police. The Empire was peaceful as no area of comparable size has ever been. Throughout its vast extent, nearly a quarter of the earth, there were fewer armed men than would be found necessary by a minor Balkan state. As people to live under, and looking at them merely from a liberal, *negative* standpoint, the British ruling class had their points. They were preferable to the truly modern men, the Nazis and Fascists. But it had long been obvious that they would be helpless against any serious attack from the outside.

They could not struggle against Nazism or Fascism, because they could not understand them. Neither could they have struggled against Communism, if Communism had been a serious force in western Europe. To understand Fascism they would have had to study the theory of Socialism, which would have forced them to realize that the economic system by which they lived was unjust, inefficient and out of date. But it was exactly this fact that they had trained themselves never to face. They dealt with Fascism as the cavalry generals of 1914 dealt with the machine gun – by ignoring it. After years of aggression and massacres, they had grasped only one fact, that Hitler and Mussolini were hostile to Communism. Therefore, it was argued, they *must* be friendly to the British dividend-drawer. Hence the truly frightening spectacle of Conservative M.P.s wildly cheering the news that British ships, bringing food to the Spanish Republican government, had been bombed by Italian aeroplanes. Even when they had begun to grasp that Fascism was dangerous, its essentially revolutionary nature, the huge military effort it was capable of making, the sort of tactics it would use, were quite beyond their comprehension. At the time of the Spanish civil war, anyone with as much political knowledge as can be acquired from a sixpenny pamphlet on Socialism knew that if Franco won, the result would be strategically disastrous for England; and yet generals and admirals who had given their lives to the study of war were unable to grasp this fact. This vein of political ignorance runs right through English official life, through Cabinet ministers, ambassadors, consuls, judges, magistrates, policemen. The policeman who arrests the "Red" does not understand the theories the "Red" is preaching; if he did, his own position as bodyguard of the monied class might seem less pleasant to him. There is reason to think that even military espionage is hopelessly hampered by ignorance of the new economic doctrines and the ramifications of the underground parties.

The British ruling class were not altogether wrong in thinking that Fascism was on their side. It is a fact that any rich man, unless he is a Jew, has less to fear from Fascism than from either Communism or democratic Socialism. One ought never to forget this, for nearly the whole of German and Italian propaganda is designed to cover it up. The natural instinct of men like Simon, Hoare, Chamberlain, etc., was to come to an agreement with Hitler. But – and here the peculiar feature of English life that I have spoken of, the deep sense of national solidarity, comes in – they could only do so by breaking up the Empire and selling their own people into semi-slavery. A truly corrupt class would have done this without hesitation, as in France. But things had not gone that distance in England. Politicians who would make cringing speeches about "the duty of loyalty to our conquerors" are hardly to be found in English public life. Tossed to and fro between their incomes and their principles, it was impossible that men like Chamberlain should do anything but make the worst of both worlds.

One thing that has always shown that the English ruling class are *morally* fairly sound, is that in time of war they are ready enough to get themselves killed. Several dukes, earls and what-not were killed in the recent campaign in Flanders. That could not happen if these people were the cynical scoundrels that they are sometimes declared to be. It is important not to misunderstand their motives, or one cannot predict their actions. What is to be expected of them is not treachery or physical cowardice, but stupidity, unconscious sabotage, an infallible instinct for doing the wrong thing. They are not wicked, or not altogether wicked; they are merely unteachable. Only when their money and power are gone will the younger among them begin to grasp what century they are living in.

v

The stagnation of the Empire in the between-war years affected everyone in England, but it had an especially direct effect upon two important subsections of the middle class. One was the military and imperialist middle class, generally nicknamed the Blimps, and the other the left-wing intelligentsia. These two seemingly hostile types, symbolic opposites – the halfpay colonel with his bull neck and diminutive brain, like a dinosaur, the highbrow with his domed forehead and stalk-like neck – are mentally linked together and constantly interact upon one another; in any case they are born to a considerable extent into the same families.

Thirty years ago the Blimp class was already losing its vitality. The middle-class families celebrated by Kipling, the prolific lowbrow families whose sons officered the army and navy and swarmed over all the waste places of the earth from the Yukon to the Irrawaddy, were dwindling before 1914. The thing that had killed them was the telegraph. In a narrowing world, more and more governed from Whitehall, there was every year less room for individual initiative. Men like Clive, Nelson, Nicholson, Gordon would find no place for themselves in the modern British Empire. By 1920 nearly every inch of the colonial empire was in the grip of Whitehall. Well-meaning, over-civilized men, in dark suits and black felt hats, with neatly-rolled umbrellas crooked over the left forearm, were imposing their constipated view of life on Malaya and Nigeria, Mombasa and Mandalay. The one-time empire-builders were reduced to the status of clerks, buried deeper and deeper under mounds of paper and red tape. In the early 'twenties one could see, all over the Empire, the older officials, who had known more spacious days, writhing impotently under the changes that were happening. From that time onwards it has been next door to impossible to induce young men of spirit to take any part in imperial administration. And what was true of the official world was true also of the commercial. The great monopoly companies swallowed up hosts of petty traders. Instead of going out to trade adventurously in the Indies one went to an office stool in Bombay or Singapore. And life in Bombay or Singapore was actually duller and safer than life in London. Imperialist sentiment remained strong in the middle class, chiefly owing to family tradition, but the job of administering the Empire had ceased to appeal. Few able men went east of Suez if there was any way of avoiding it.

But the general weakening of imperialism, and to some extent of the whole British morale, that took place during the nineteen-thirties, was partly the work of the left-wing intelligentsia, itself a kind of growth that had sprouted from the stagnation of the Empire.

It should be noted that there is now no intelligentsia that is not in some sense "Left". Perhaps the last right-wing intellectual was T. E. Lawrence. Since about 1930 everyone describable as an "intellectual" has lived in a state of chronic discontent with the existing order. Necessarily so, because society as it was constituted had no room for him. In an Empire that was simply stagnant, neither being developed nor falling to pieces, and in an England ruled by people whose chief asset was their stupidity, to be "clever" was to be suspect. If you had the kind of brain that could understand the poems of T. S. Eliot or the theories of Karl Marx, the higher-ups would see to it that you were kept out of any important job. The intellectuals could find a function for themselves only in the literary reviews and the left-wing political parties.

The mentality of the English left-wing intelligentsia can be studied in half a dozen weekly and monthly papers. The immediately striking thing about all these papers is their generally negative, querulous attitude, their complete lack at all times of any constructive suggestion. There is little in them except the irresponsible carping of people who have never been and never expect to be in a position of power. Another marked characteristic is the emotional shallowness of people who live in a world of ideas and have little contact with physical reality. Many intellectuals of the Left were flabbily pacifist up to 1935, shrieked for war against Germany in the years 1935–39, and then promptly cooled off when the war started. It is broadly though not precisely true that the people who were most "anti-Fascist" during the Spanish civil war are most defeatist now. And underlying this is the really important fact about so many of the English intelligentsia – their severance from the common culture of the country.

In intention, at any rate, the English intelligentsia are Europeanized. They take their cookery from Paris and their opinions from Moscow. In the general patriotism of the country they form a sort of island of dissident thought. England is perhaps the only great country whose intellectuals are ashamed of their own nationality. In left-wing circles it is always felt that there is something slightly disgraceful in being an Englishman and that it is a duty to snigger at every English institution, from horse-racing to suet puddings. It is a strange fact, but it is unquestionably true, that almost any English intellectual would feel more ashamed of standing to attention during "God Save the King" than of stealing from a poor box. All through the critical years many left-wingers were chipping away at English morale, trying to spread an outlook that was sometimes squashily pacifist, sometimes violently pro-Russian, but always anti-British. It is questionable how much effect this had, but it certainly had some. If the English people suffered for several years a real weakening of morale, so that the Fascist nations judged that they were "decadent" and that it was safe to plunge into war, the intellectual sabotage from the Left was partly responsible. Both the *New Statesman* and the *News-Chronicle* cried out against the Munich settlement, but even they had done something to make it possible. Ten years of systematic Blimp-baiting affected even the Blimps themselves and made it harder than it had been before to get intelligent young men to enter the armed forces. Given the stagnation of the Empire the military middle class must have decayed in any case, but the spread of a shallow Leftism hastened the process.

It is clear that the special position of the English intellectuals during the past ten years, as purely *negative* creatures, mere anti-Blimps, was a by-product of ruling-class stupidity. Society could not use them, and they had not got it in them to see that devotion to one's country implies "for better, for worse". Both Blimps and highbrows took for granted, as though it were a law of nature, the divorce between patriotism and intelligence. If you were a patriot you read *Blackwood's Magazine* and publicly thanked God that you were "not brainy". If you were an intellectual you sniggered at the Union Jack and regarded physical courage as barbarous. It is obvious that this preposterous convention cannot continue. The Bloomsbury highbrow, with his mechanical snigger, is as out of date as the cavalry colonel. A modern nation cannot afford either of them. Patriotism and intelligence will have to come together again. It is the fact that we are fighting a war, and a very peculiar kind of war, that may make this possible.

vi

One of the most important developments in England during the past twenty years has been the upward and downward extension of the middle class. It has happened on such a scale as to make the old classification of society into capitalists, proletarians and petit-bourgeois (small property-owners) almost obsolete.

England is a country in which property and financial power are concentrated in very few hands. Few people in modern England *own* anything at all, except clothes, furniture and possibly a house. The peasantry have long since disappeared, the independent shopkeeper is being destroyed, the small business-man is diminishing in numbers. But at the same time modern industry is so complicated that it cannot get along without great numbers of managers, salesmen, engineers, chemists and technicians of all kinds, drawing fairly large salaries. And these in turn call into being a professional class of doctors, lawyers, teachers, artists, etc., etc. The tendency of advanced capitalism has therefore been to enlarge the middle class and not to wipe it out as it once seemed likely to do.

But much more important than this is the spread of middle-class ideas and habits among the working class. The British working class are now better off in almost all ways than they were thirty years ago. This is partly due to the efforts of the Trade Unions, but partly to the mere advance of physical science. It is not always realized that within rather narrow limits the standard of life of a country can rise without a corresponding rise in real-wages. Up to a point, civilization can lift itself up by its boot-tags. However unjustly society is organized, certain technical advances are bound to benefit the whole community, because certain kinds of goods are necessarily held in common. A millionaire cannot, for example, light the streets for himself while darkening them for other people. Nearly all citizens of civilized countries now enjoy the use of good roads, germ-free water, police protection, free libraries and probably free education of a kind. Public education in England has been meanly starved of money, but it has nevertheless improved, largely owing to the devoted efforts of the teachers, and the habit of reading has become enormously more widespread. To an increasing extent the rich and the poor read the same books, and they also see the same films and listen to the same radio programmes. And the differences in their way of life have been diminished by the mass-production of cheap clothes and improvements in housing. So far as outward appearance goes, the clothes of rich and poor, especially in the case of women, differ far less then they did thirty or even fifteen years ago. As to housing, England still has slums which are a blot on civilization, but much building has been done during the past ten years, largely by the local authorities. The modern Council house, with its bathroom and electric light, is smaller than the stockbroker's villa, but it is recognizably the same kind of house, which the farm labourer's cottage is not. A person who has grown up in a Council housing estate is likely to be – indeed, visibly *is* – more middle class in outlook than a person who has grown up in a slum.

The effect of all this is a general softening of manners. It is enhanced by the fact that modern industrial methods tend always to demand less muscular effort and therefore to leave people with more energy when their day's work is done. Many workers in the light industries are less truly manual labourers than is a doctor or a grocer. In tastes, habits, manners and outlook the working class and the middle class are drawing together. The unjust distinctions remain, but the real differences diminish. The old-style "proletarian" – collarless, unshaven and with muscles warped by heavy labour – still exists, but he is constantly decreasing in numbers; he only predominates in the heavy-industry areas of the north of England.

After 1918 there began to appear something that had never existed in England before: people of indeterminate social class. In 1910 every human being in these islands could be "placed" in an instant by his clothes, manners and accent. That is no longer the case. Above all, it is not the case in the new townships that have developed as a result of cheap motor cars and the southward shift of industry. The place to look for the germs of the future England is in the light-industry areas and along the arterial roads. In Slough, Dagenham, Barnet, Letchworth, Hayes – everywhere, indeed, on the outskirts of great towns – the old pattern is gradually changing into something new. In those vast new wildernesses of glass and brick the sharp distinctions of the older kind of town, with its slums and mansions, or of the country, with its manor-houses and squalid cottages, no longer exist. There are wide gradations of income, but it is the same kind of life that is being lived at different levels, in labour-saving flats or Council houses, along the concrete roads and in the naked democracy of the swimming-pools. It is a rather restless, cultureless life, centring round tinned food, *Picture Post*, the radio and the internal combustion engine. It is a civilization in which children grow up with an intimate knowledge of magnetoes and in complete ignorance of the Bible. To that civilization belong the people who are most at home in and most definitely *of* the modern world, the technicians and the higher-paid skilled workers, the airmen and their mechanics, the radio experts, film producers, popular journalists and industrial chemists. They are the indeterminate stratum at which the older class distinctions are beginning to break down.

This war, unless we are defeated, will wipe out most of the existing class privileges. There are every day fewer people who wish them to continue. Nor need we fear that as the pattern changes life in England will lose its peculiar flavour. The new red cities of Greater London are crude enough, but these things are only the rash that accompanies a change. In whatever shape

England emerges from the war, it will be deeply tinged with the characteristics that I have spoken of earlier. The intellectuals who hope to see it Russianized or Germanized will be disappointed. The gentleness, the hypocrisy, the thoughtlessness, the reverence for law and the hatred of uniforms will remain, along with the suet puddings and the misty skies. It needs some very great disaster, such as prolonged subjugation by a foreign enemy, to destroy a national culture. The Stock Exchange will be pulled down, the horse plough will give way to the tractor, the country houses will be turned into children's holiday camps, the Eton and Harrow match will be forgotten, but England will still be England, an everlasting animal stretching into the future and the past, and, like all living things, having the power to change out of recognition and yet remain the same.

Part II: Shopkeepers at War

i

I began this book to the tune of German bombs, and I begin this second chapter in the added racket of the barrage. The yellow gun-flashes are lighting the sky, the splinters are rattling on the house-tops, and London Bridge is falling down, falling down, falling down. Anyone able to read a map knows that we are in deadly danger. I do not mean that we are beaten or need be beaten. Almost certainly the outcome depends on our own will. But at this moment we are in the soup, full fathom five, and we have been brought there by follies which we are still committing and which will drown us altogether if we do not mend our ways quickly.

What this war has demonstrated is that private capitalism – that is, an economic system in which land, factories, mines and transport are owned privately and operated solely for profit – *does not work*. It cannot deliver the goods. This fact had been known to millions of people for years past, but nothing ever came of it, because there was no real urge from below to alter the system, and those at the top had trained themselves to be impenetrably stupid on just this point. Argument and propaganda got one nowhere. The lords of property simply sat on their bottoms and proclaimed that all was for the best. Hitler's conquest of Europe, however, was a *physical* debunking of capitalism. War, for all its evil, is at any rate an unanswerable test of strength, like a try-your-grip machine. Great strength returns the penny, and there is no way of faking the result.

When the nautical screw was first invented, there was a controversy that lasted for years as to whether screw-steamers or paddle-steamers were better. The paddle-steamers, like all obsolete things, had their champions, who supported them by ingenious arguments. Finally, however, a distinguished admiral tied a screw-steamer and a paddle-steamer of equal horse-power stern to stern and set their engines running. That settled the question once and for all. And it was something similar that happened on the fields of Norway and of Flanders. Once and for all it was proved that a planned economy is stronger than a planless one. But it is necessary here to give some kind of definition to those much-abused words, Socialism and Fascism.

Socialism is usually defined as "common ownership of the means of production". Crudely: the State, representing the whole nation, owns everything, and everyone is a State employee. This does *not* mean that people are stripped of private possessions such as clothes and furniture, but it *does* mean that all productive goods, such as land, mines, ships and machinery, are the property of the State. The State is the sole large-scale producer. It is not certain that Socialism is in all ways superior to capitalism, but it is certain that, unlike capitalism, it can solve the problems of production and consumption. At normal times a capitalist economy can never consume all that it produces, so that there is always a wasted surplus (wheat burned in furnaces, herrings dumped back into the sea, etc., etc.) and always unemployment. In time of war, on the other hand, it has difficulty in producing all that it needs, because nothing is produced unless someone sees his way to making a profit out of it. In a Socialist economy these problems do not exist. The State simply calculates what goods will be needed and does its best to produce them. Production is only limited by the amount of labour and raw materials. Money, for internal purposes, ceases to be a mysterious all-powerful thing and becomes a sort of coupon or ration-ticket, issued in sufficient quantities to buy up such consumption-goods as may be available at the moment.

However, it has become clear in the last few years that "common ownership of the means of production" is not in itself a sufficient definition of Socialism. One must also add the following: approximate equality of incomes (it need be no more than approximate), political democracy, and abolition of all hereditary privilege, especially in education. These are simply the necessary safeguards against the reappearance of a class-system. Centralized ownership has very little meaning unless the mass of the people are living roughly upon an equal level, and have some kind of control over the government. "The State" may come to mean no more than a self-elected political party, and oligarchy and privilege can return, based on power rather than on money.

But what then is Fascism?

Fascism, at any rate the German version, is a form of capitalism that borrows from Socialism just such features as will make it efficient for war purposes. Internally, Germany has a good deal in common with a Socialist state. Ownership has never been abolished, there are still capitalists and workers, and – this is the important point, and the real reason why rich men all over the world tend to sympathize with Fascism – generally speaking the same people are capitalists and the same people workers as before the Nazi revolution. But at the same time the State, which is simply the Nazi Party, is in control of everything. It controls investment, raw materials, rates of interest, working hours, wages. The factory-owner still owns his factory, but he is for practical purposes reduced to the status of a manager. Everyone is in effect a State employee, though the salaries vary very greatly. The mere *efficiency* of such a system, the elimination of waste and obstruction, is obvious. In seven years it has built up the most powerful war machine the world has ever seen.

But the idea underlying Fascism is irreconcilably different from that which underlies Socialism. Socialism aims, ultimately, at a world-state of free and equal human beings. It takes the equality of human rights for granted. Nazism assumes just the opposite. The driving force behind the Nazi movement is the belief in human *inequality*, the superiority of Germans to all other races, the right of Germany to rule the world. Outside the German Reich it does not recognize any obligations. Eminent Nazi professors have "proved" over and over again that only Nordic man is fully human, have even mooted the idea that non-Nordic peoples (such as ourselves) can interbreed with gorillas! Therefore, while a species of war-Socialism exists within the German state, its attitude towards conquered nations is frankly that of an exploiter. The function of the Czechs, Poles, French, etc., is simply to produce such goods as Germany may need, and get in return just as little as will keep them from open rebellion. If we are conquered, our job will probably be to manufacture weapons for Hitler's forthcoming wars with Russia and America. The Nazis aim, in effect, at setting up a kind of caste system, with four main castes corresponding rather closely to those of the Hindu religion. At the top comes the Nazi Party, second come the mass of the German people, third come the conquered European populations. Fourth and last are to come the coloured peoples, the "semi-apes" as Hitler calls them, who are to be reduced quite openly to slavery.

However horrible this system may seem to us, *it works*. It works because it is a planned system geared to a definite purpose, world-conquest, and not allowing any private interest, either of capitalist or worker, to stand in its way. British capitalism does not work, because it is a competitive system in which private profit is and must be the main objective. It is a system in which all the forces are pulling in opposite directions and the interests of the individual are as often as not totally opposed to those of the State.

All through the critical years British capitalism, with its immense industrial plant and its unrivalled supply of skilled labour, was unequal to the strain of preparing for war. To prepare for war on the modern scale you have got to divert the greater part of your national income to armaments, which means cutting down on consumption goods. A bombing plane, for instance, is equivalent in price to fifty small motor cars, or eighty thousand pairs of silk stockings, or a million loaves of bread. Clearly you can't have *many* bombing planes without lowering the national standard of life. It is guns or butter, as

Marshal Göring remarked. But in Chamberlain's England the transition could not be made. The rich would not face the necessary taxation, and while the rich are still visibly rich it is not possible to tax the poor very heavily either. Moreover, so long as *profit* was the main object the manufacturer had no incentive to change over from consumption goods to armaments. A business-man's first duty is to his share-holders. Perhaps England needs tanks, but perhaps it pays better to manufacture motor cars. To prevent war material from reaching the enemy is common sense, but to sell in the highest market is a business duty. Right at the end of August 1939 the British dealers were tumbling over one another in their eagerness to sell Germany tin, rubber, copper and shellac – and this in the clear, certain knowledge that war was going to break out in a week or two. It was about as sensible as selling somebody a razor to cut your throat with. But it was "good business".

And now look at the results. After 1934 it was known that Germany was rearming. After 1936 everyone with eyes in his head knew that war was coming. After Munich it was merely a question of how soon the war would begin. In September 1939 war broke out. *Eight months later* it was discovered that, so far as equipment went, the British army was barely beyond the standard of 1918. We saw our soldiers fighting their way desperately to the coast, with one aeroplane against three, with rifles against tanks, with bayonets against tommy-guns. There were not even enough revolvers to supply all the officers. After a year of war the regular army was still short of 300,000 tin hats. There had even, previously, been a shortage of uniforms – this in one of the greatest woollen-producing countries in the world!

What had happened was that the whole monied class, unwilling to face a change in their way of life, had shut their eyes to the nature of Fascism and modern war. And false optimism was fed to the general public by the gutter press, which lives on its advertisements and is therefore interested in keeping trade conditions normal. Year after year the Beaverbrook press assured us in huge headlines that THERE WILL BE NO WAR, and as late as the beginning of 1939 Lord Rothermere was describing Hitler as "a great gentleman". And while

England in the moment of disaster proved to be short of every war material except ships, it is not recorded that there was any shortage of motor cars, fur coats, gramophones, lipstick, chocolates or silk stockings. And dare anyone pretend that the same tug-of-war between private profit and public necessity is not still continuing? England fights for her life, but business must fight for profits. You can hardly open a newspaper without seeing the two contradictory processes happening side by side. On the very same page you will find the government urging you to save and the seller of some useless luxury urging you to spend. Lend to Defend, but Guinness is Good for You. Buy a Spitfire, but also buy Haig and Haig, Pond's Face Cream and Black Magic Chocolates.

But one thing gives hope – the visible swing in public opinion. If we can survive this war, the defeat in Flanders will turn out to have been one of the great turning-points in English history. In that spectacular disaster the working class, the middle class and even a section of the business community could see the utter rottenness of private capitalism. Before that the case against capitalism had never been *proved*. Russia, the only definitely Socialist country, was backward and far away. All criticism broke itself against the rat-trap faces of bankers and the brassy laughter of stockbrokers. Socialism? Ha! ha! ha! Where's the money to come from? Ha! ha! ha! The lords of property were firm in their seats, and they knew it. But after the French collapse there came something that could not be laughed away, something that neither cheque-books nor policemen were any use against – the bombing. Zweee – BOOM! What's that? Oh, only a bomb on the Stock Exchange. Zweee – BOOM! Another acre of somebody's valuable slum-property gone west. Hitler will at any rate go down in history as the man who made the City of London laugh on the wrong side of its face. For the first time in their lives the comfortable were uncomfortable, the professional optimists had to admit that there was something wrong. It was a great step forward. From that time onwards the ghastly job of trying to convince artificially stupefied people that a planned economy might be better than a free-for-all in which the worst man wins – that job will never be quite so ghastly again.

ii

The difference between Socialism and capitalism is not primarily a difference of technique. One cannot simply change from one system to the other as one might install a new piece of machinery in a factory, and then carry on as before, with the same people in positions of control. Obviously there is also needed a complete shift of power. New blood, new men, new ideas – in the true sense of the word, a revolution.

I have spoken earlier of the soundness and homogeneity of England, the patriotism that runs like a connecting thread through almost all classes. After Dunkirk anyone who had eyes in his head could see this. But it is absurd to pretend that the promise of that moment has been fulfilled. Almost certainly the mass of the people are now ready for the vast changes that are necessary; but those changes have not even begun to happen.

England is a family with the wrong members in control. Almost entirely we are governed by the rich, and by people who step into positions of command by right of birth. Few if any of these people are consciously treacherous, some of them are not even fools, but as a class they are quite incapable of leading us to victory. They could not do it, even if their material interests did not constantly trip them up. As I pointed out earlier, they have been artificially stupefied. Quite apart from anything else, the rule of money sees to it that we shall be governed largely by the old – that is, by people utterly unable to grasp what age they are living in or what enemy they are fighting. Nothing was more desolating at the beginning of this war than the way in which the whole of the older generation conspired to pretend that it was the war of 1914–18 over again. All the old duds were back on the job, twenty years older, with the skull plainer in their faces. Ian Hay was cheering up the troops, Belloc was writing articles on strategy, Maurois doing broadcasts, Bairnsfather drawing cartoons. It was like a tea-party of ghosts. And that state of affairs has barely altered. The shock of disaster brought a few able men like Bevin to the front, but in general we are still commanded by people who managed to live through the years 1931–39 without even discovering that Hitler was dangerous. A generation of the unteachable is hanging upon us like a necklace of corpses.

As soon as one considers any problem of this war – and it does not matter whether it is the widest aspect of strategy or the tiniest detail of home organization – one sees that the necessary moves cannot be made while the social structure of England remains what it is. Inevitably, because of their position and upbringing, the ruling class are fighting for their own privileges, which cannot possibly be reconciled with the public interest. It is a mistake to imagine that war-aims, strategy, propaganda and industrial organization exist in watertight compartments. All are interconnected. Every strategic plan, every tactical method, even every weapon will bear the stamp of the social system that produced it. The British ruling class are fighting against Hitler, whom they have always regarded and whom some of them still regard as their protector against Bolshevism. That does not mean that they will deliberately sell out; but it does mean that at every decisive moment they are likely to falter, pull their punches, do the wrong thing.

Until the Churchill government called some sort of halt to the process, they have done the wrong thing with an unerring instinct ever since 1931. They helped Franco to overthrow the Spanish government, although anyone not an imbecile could have told them that a Fascist Spain would be hostile to England. They fed Italy with war materials all through the winter of 1939–40, although it was obvious to the whole world that the Italians were going to attack us in the spring. For the sake of a few hundred thousand dividend-drawers they are turning India from an ally into an enemy. Moreover, so long as the monied classes remain in control, we cannot develop any but a *defensive* strategy. Every victory means a change in the *status quo*. How can we drive the Italians out of Abyssinia without rousing echoes among the coloured peoples of our own Empire? How can we even smash Hitler without the risk of bringing the German Socialists and Communists into power? The left-wingers who wail that "this is a capitalist" war and that "British Imperialism" is fighting for loot have got their heads screwed on backwards. The last thing the British monied class wish for is to acquire fresh territory. It would simply be an embarrassment. Their war-aim (both unattainable and unmentionable) is simply to hang on to what they have got.

Internally, England is still the rich man's Paradise. All talk of "equality of sacrifice" is nonsense. At the same time as factory-workers are asked to put up with longer hours, advertisements for "Butler. One in family, eight in staff" are appearing in the press. The bombed-out populations of the East End go hungry and homeless while wealthier victims simply step into their cars and flee to comfortable country houses. The Home Guard swells to a million men in a few weeks, and is deliberately organized from above in such a way that only people with private incomes can hold positions of command. Even the rationing system is so arranged that it hits the poor all the time, while people with over £2000 a year are practically unaffected by it. Everywhere privilege is squandering good will. In such circumstances even propaganda becomes almost impossible. As attempts to stir up patriotic feeling, the red posters issued by the Chamberlain government at the beginning of the war broke all depth-records. Yet they could not have been much other than they were, for how could Chamberlain and his followers take the risk of rousing strong popular feeling *against Fascism*? Anyone who was genuinely hostile to Fascism must also be opposed to Chamberlain himself, and to all the others who had helped Hitler into power. So also with external propaganda. In all Lord Halifax's speeches there is not one concrete proposal for which a single inhabitant of Europe would risk the top joint of his little finger. For what war-aim can Halifax, or anyone like him, conceivably have, except to put the clock back to 1933?

It is only by revolution that the native genius of the English people can be set free. Revolution does not mean red flags and street fighting, it means a fundamental shift of power. Whether it happens with or without bloodshed is largely an accident of time and place. Nor does it mean the dictatorship of a single class. The people in England who grasp what changes are needed and are capable of carrying them through are not confined to any one class, though it is true that very few people with over £2000 a year are among them. What is wanted is a conscious open revolt by ordinary people against inefficiency, class privilege and the rule of the old. It is not primarily a question of change of government. British governments do, broadly speaking, represent the will of the people, and if we

GEORGE ORWELL

alter our structure from below we shall get the government we need. Ambassadors, generals, officials and colonial administrators who are senile or pro-Fascist are more dangerous than Cabinet ministers whose follies have to be committed in public. Right through our national life we have got to fight against privilege, against the notion that a half-witted public-schoolboy is better fitted for command than an intelligent mechanic. Although there are gifted and honest *individuals* among them, we have got to break the grip of the monied class as a whole. England has got to assume its real shape. The England that is only just beneath the surface, in the factories and the newspaper offices, in the aeroplanes and the submarines, has got to take charge of its own destiny.

In the short run, equality of sacrifice, "war communism", is even more important than radical economic changes. It is very necessary that industry should be nationalized, but it is more urgently necessary that such monstrosities as butlers and "private incomes" should disappear forthwith. Almost certainly the main reason why the Spanish Republic could keep up the fight for two and a half years against impossible odds was that there were no gross contrasts of wealth. The people suffered horribly, but they all suffered alike. When the private soldier had not a cigarette, the general had not one either. Given equality of sacrifice, the morale of a country like England would probably be unbreakable. But at present we have nothing to appeal to except traditional patriotism, which is deeper here than elsewhere, but is not necessarily bottomless. At some point or another you have got to deal with the man who says "I should be no worse off under Hitler". But what answer can you give him – that is, what answer that you can expect him to listen to – while common soldiers risk their lives for two and sixpence a day, and fat women ride about in Rolls-Royce cars, nursing Pekingeses?

It is quite likely that this war will last three years. It will mean cruel overwork, cold dull winters, uninteresting food, lack of amusements, prolonged bombing. It cannot but lower the general standard of living, because the essential act of war is to manufacture armaments instead of consumable goods. The working classes will have to suffer terrible things. And they *will* suffer them, almost indefinitely, provided that they know what they are fighting for. They are not cowards, and they are not even internationally-minded. They can stand all that the Spanish workers stood, and more. But they will want some kind of proof that a better life is ahead for themselves and their children. The one sure earnest of that is that when they are taxed and overworked they shall see that the rich are being hit even harder. And if the rich squeal audibly, so much the better.

We can bring these things about, if we really want to. It is not true that public opinion has no power in England. It never makes itself heard without achieving something; it has been responsible for most of the changes for the better during the past six months. But we have moved with glacier-like slowness, and we have learned only from disasters. It took the fall of Paris to get rid of Chamberlain and the unnecessary suffering of scores of thousands of people in the East End to get rid or partially rid of Sir John Anderson. It is not worth losing a battle in order to bury a corpse. For we are fighting against swift evil intelligences, and time presses, and

> History to the defeated
> May say Alas but cannot help or pardon.

iii

During the last six months there has been much talk of "the Fifth Column". From time to time obscure lunatics have been jailed for making speeches in favour of Hitler, and large numbers of German refugees have been interned, a thing which has almost certainly done us great harm in Europe. It is of course obvious that the idea of a large, organized army of Fifth Columnists suddenly appearing on the streets with weapons in their hands, as in Holland and Belgium, is ridiculous. Nevertheless a Fifth Column danger does exist. One can only consider it if one also considers in what way England might be defeated.

It does not seem probable that air bombing can settle a major war. England might well be invaded and conquered, but the invasion would be a dangerous gamble, and if it happened and failed it would probably leave us more united and less Blimp-ridden than before. Moreover, if England were overrun by foreign troops the English people would know that they had been beaten and would continue the struggle. It is doubtful whether they could be held down permanently, or whether Hitler wishes to keep an army of a million men stationed in these islands. A government of——, —— and —— (you can fill in the names) would suit him better. The English can probably not be bullied into surrender, but they might quite easily be bored, cajoled or cheated into it, provided that, as at Munich, they did not know that they were surrendering. It could happen most easily when the war seemed to be going well rather than badly. The threatening tone of so much of the German and Italian propaganda is a psychological mistake. It only gets home on intellectuals. With the general public the proper approach would be "Let's call it a draw". It is when a peace-offer along *those* lines is made that the pro-Fascists will raise their voices.

But who are the pro-Fascists? The idea of a Hitler victory appeals to the very rich, to the Communists, to Mosley's followers, to the pacifists, and to certain sections among the Catholics. Also, if things went badly enough on the Home front, the whole of the poorer section of the working class might swing round to a position that was defeatist though not actively pro-Hitler.

In this motley list one can see the daring of German propaganda, its willingness to offer everything to everybody. But the various pro-Fascist forces are not consciously acting together, and they operate in different ways.

The Communists must certainly be regarded as pro-Hitler, and are bound to remain so unless Russian policy changes, but they have not very much influence. Mosley's Blackshirts, though now lying very low, are a more serious danger, because of the footing they probably possess in the armed forces. Still, even in its palmiest days Mosley's following can hardly have numbered 50,000. Pacifism is a psychological curiosity rather than a political movement. Some of the extremer pacifists, starting out with a complete renunciation of violence, have ended by warmly championing Hitler and even toying with anti-semitism. This is interesting, but it is not important. "Pure" pacifism, which is a by-product of naval power, can only appeal to people in very sheltered positions. Moreover, being negative and irresponsible, it does not inspire much devotion. Of the membership of the Peace Pledge Union, less than 15 per cent even pay their annual subscriptions. None of these bodies of people, pacifists, Communists or Blackshirts, could bring a large-scale stop-the-war movement into being by their own efforts. But they might help to make things very much easier for a treacherous government negotiating surrender. Like the French Communists, they might become the half-conscious agents of millionaires.

The real danger is from above. One ought not to pay any attention to Hitler's recent line of talk about being the friend of the poor man, the enemy of plutocracy, etc., etc. Hitler's real self is in *Mein Kampf*, and in his actions. He has never persecuted the rich, except when they were Jews or when they tried actively to oppose him. He stands for a centralized economy which robs the capitalist of most of his power but leaves the structure of society much as before. The State controls industry, but there are still rich and poor, masters and men. Therefore, as against genuine Socialism, the monied class have always been on his side. This was crystal clear at the time of the Spanish civil war, and clear again at the time when France surrendered. Hitler's puppet government are not working-men, but a gang of bankers, gaga generals and corrupt right-wing politicians.

That kind of spectacular, *conscious* treachery is less likely to succeed in England, indeed is far less likely even to be tried. Nevertheless, to many payers of super-tax this war is simply an insane family squabble which ought to be stopped at all costs. One need not doubt that a "peace" movement is on foot somewhere in high places; probably a shadow Cabinet has already been formed. These people will get their chance not in the moment of defeat but in some stagnant period when boredom is reinforced by discontent. They will not talk about surrender, only about peace; and doubtless they will persuade themselves, and perhaps other people, that they are acting for the best. An army of unemployed led by millionaires quoting the Sermon on the Mount – that is our danger. But it cannot arise when we have once introduced a reasonable degree of social justice. The lady in the Rolls-Royce car is more damaging to morale than a fleet of Göring's bombing-planes.

Part III: The English Revolution

i

The English revolution started several years ago, and it began to gather momentum when the troops came back from Dunkirk. Like all else in England, it happens in a sleepy un-willing way, but it is happening. The war has speeded it up, but it has also increased, and desperately, the necessity for speed.

Progress and reaction are ceasing to have anything to do with party labels. If one wishes to name a particular moment, one can say that the old distinction between Right and Left broke down when *Picture Post* was first published. What are the politics of *Picture Post*? Or of *Cavalcade*, or Priestley's broadcasts, or the leading articles in the *Evening Standard*? None of the old classifications will fit them. They merely point to the existence of multitudes of unlabelled people who have grasped within the last year or two that something is wrong. But since a classless, ownerless society is generally spoken of as "Socialism", we can give that name to the society towards which we are now moving. The war and the revolution are inseparable. We cannot establish anything that a Western nation would regard as Socialism without defeating Hitler; on the other hand we cannot defeat Hitler while we remain economically and socially in the nineteenth century. The past is fighting the future, and we have two years, a year, possibly only a few months, to see to it that the future wins.

We cannot look to this or to any similar government to put through the necessary changes of its own accord. The initiative will have to come from below. That means that there will have to arise something that has never yet existed in England, a Socialist movement that actually has the mass of the people behind it. But one must start by recognizing why it is that English Socialism has failed.

In England there is only one Socialist party that has ever seriously mattered, the Labour Party. It has never been able to achieve any major change, because except in purely domestic matters it has never possessed a genuinely independent policy. It was and is primarily a party of the Trade Unions, devoted to raising wages and improving working conditions. This meant that all through the critical years it was directly interested in the prosperity of British capitalism. In particular it was interested in the maintenance of the British Empire, for the wealth of England was drawn largely from Asia and Africa. The standard of living of the Trade Union workers, whom the Labour Party represented, depended indirectly on the sweating of Indian coolies. At the same time the Labour Party was a Socialist party, using Socialist phraseology, thinking in terms of an old-fashioned anti-imperialism and more or less pledged to make restitution to the coloured races. It had to stand for the "independence" of India, just as it had to stand for disarmament and "progress" generally. Nevertheless everyone was aware that this was nonsense. In the age of the tank and the bombing-plane, backward agricultural countries like India and the Afri-can colonies can no more be independent than can a cat or a dog. Had any Labour Government come into office with a clear majority and then proceeded to grant India anything that could truly be called independence, India would simply have been absorbed by Japan, or divided between Japan and Russia.

To a Labour Government in power, three imperial policies would have been open. One was to continue administering the Empire exactly as before, which meant dropping all preten-sions to Socialism. Another was to set the subject peoples "free", which meant in practice handing them over to Japan, Italy and other predatory powers, and incidentally causing a catastrophic drop in the British standard of living. The third was to develop a *positive* imperial policy, and aim at transform-ing the Empire into a federation of Socialist states, like a looser and freer version of the Union of Soviet Republics. But the Labour Party's history and background made this impossible. It was a party of the Trade Unions, hopelessly parochial in out-look, with little interest in imperial affairs and no contacts among the men who actually held the Empire together. It would have had to hand over the administration of India and Africa and the whole job of imperial defence to men drawn from a different class and traditionally hostile to Socialism. Overshadowing everything was the doubt whether a Labour Government which meant business could make itself obeyed. For all the size of its following, the Labour Party had no footing

GEORGE ORWELL

in the navy, little or none in the army or Air Force, none whatever in the colonial services, and not even a sure footing in the Home civil service. In England its position was strong but not unchallengeable, and outside England all the key points were in the hands of its enemies. Once in power, the same dilemma would always have faced it: carry out your promises, and risk revolt, or continue with the same policy as the Conservatives, and stop talking about Socialism. The Labour leaders never found a solution, and from 1935 onwards it was very doubtful whether they had any wish to take office. They had degenerated into a Permanent Opposition.

Outside the Labour Party there existed several extremist parties, of whom the Communists were the strongest. The Communists had considerable influence in the Labour Party in the years 1920–26 and 1935–39. Their chief importance, and that of the whole left wing of the Labour movement, was the part they played in alienating the middle classes from Socialism.

The history of the past seven years has made it perfectly clear that Communism has no chance in Western Europe. The appeal of Fascism is enormously greater. In one country after another the Communists have been rooted out by their more up-to-date enemies, the Nazis. In the English-speaking countries they never had a serious footing. The creed they were spreading could appeal only to a rather rare type of person, found chiefly in the middle-class intelligentsia, the type who has ceased to love his own country but still feels the need of patriotism, and therefore develops patriotic sentiments towards Russia. By 1940, after working for twenty years and spending a great deal of money, the British Communists had barely 20,000 members, actually a smaller number than they had started out with in 1920. The other Marxist parties were of even less importance. They had not the Russian money and prestige behind them, and even more than the Communists they were tied to the nineteenth-century doctrine of the class war. They continued year after year to preach this out-of-date gospel, and never drew any inference from the fact that it got them no followers.

Nor did any strong native Fascist movement grow up. Material conditions were not bad enough, and no leader who could be taken seriously was forthcoming. One would have had to look a long time to find a man more barren of ideas than Sir Oswald Mosley. He was as hollow as a jug. Even the elementary fact that Fascism must not offend national sentiment had escaped him. His entire movement was imitated slavishly from abroad, the uniform and the party programme from Italy and the salute from Germany, with the Jew-baiting tacked on as an afterthought, Mosley having actually started his movement with Jews among his most prominent followers. A man of the stamp of Bottomley or Lloyd George could perhaps have brought a real British Fascist movement into existence. But such leaders only appear when the psychological need for them exists.

After twenty years of stagnation and unemployment, the entire English Socialist movement was unable to produce a version of Socialism which the mass of the people could even find desirable. The Labour Party stood for a timid reformism, the Marxists were looking at the modern world through nineteenth-century spectacles. Both ignored agriculture and imperial problems, and both antagonized the middle classes. The suffocating stupidity of left-wing propaganda had frightened away whole classes of necessary people, factory managers, airmen, naval officers, farmers, white-collar workers, shopkeepers, policemen. All of these people had been taught to think of Socialism as something which menaced their livelihood, or as something seditious, alien, "anti-British" as they would have called it. Only the intellectuals, the least useful section of the middle class, gravitated towards the movement.

A Socialist Party which genuinely wished to achieve anything would have started by facing several facts which to this day are considered unmentionable in left-wing circles. It would have recognized that England is more united than most countries, that the British workers have a great deal to lose besides their chains, and that the differences in outlook and habits between class and class are rapidly diminishing. In general, it would have recognized that the old-fashioned "proletarian revolution" is an impossibility. But all through the between-war years no Socialist programme that was both revolutionary and workable ever appeared; basically, no doubt, because no one genuinely wanted any major change to happen. The Labour leaders wanted to go on and on, drawing their salaries and periodically swapping jobs with the Conservatives. The Communists wanted to go on and on, suffering a comfortable martyrdom, meeting with endless defeats and afterwards putting the blame on other people. The left-wing intelligentsia wanted to go on and on, sniggering at the Blimps, sapping away at middle-class morale, but still keeping their favoured position as hangers-on of the dividend-drawers. Labour Party politics had become a variant of Conservatism, "revolutionary" politics had become a game of make-believe.

Now, however, the circumstances have changed, the drowsy years have ended. Being a Socialist no longer means kicking theoretically against a system which in practice you are fairly well satisfied with. This time our predicament is real. It is "the Philistines be upon thee, Samson". We have got to make our words take physical shape, or perish. We know very well that with its present social structure England cannot survive, and we have got to make other people see that fact and act upon it. We cannot win the war without introducing Socialism, nor establish Socialism without winning the war. At such a time it is possible, as it was not in the peaceful years, to be both revolutionary and realistic. A Socialist movement which can swing the mass of the people behind it, drive the pro-Fascists out of positions of control, wipe out the grosser injustices and let the working class see that they have something to fight for, win over the middle classes instead of antagonizing them, produce a workable imperial policy instead of a mixture of humbug and Utopianism, bring patriotism and intelligence into partnership – for the first time, a movement of such a kind becomes possible.

ii

The fact that we are at war has turned Socialism from a textbook word into a realizable policy.

The inefficiency of private capitalism has been proved all over Europe. Its injustice has been proved in the East End of London. Patriotism, against which the Socialists fought so long, has become a tremendous lever in their hands. People who at any other time would cling like glue to their miserable scraps of privilege, will surrender them fast enough when their country is in danger. War is the greatest of all agents of change. It speeds up all processes, wipes out minor distinctions, brings realities to the surface. Above all, war brings it home to the individual that he is *not* altogether an individual. It is only because they are aware of this that men will die on the field of battle. At this moment it is not so much a question of surrendering life as of surrendering leisure, comfort, economic liberty, social prestige. There are very few people in England who really want to see their country conquered by Germany. If it can be made clear that defeating Hitler means wiping out class privilege, the great mass of middling people, the £6 a week to £2000 a year class, will probably be on our side. These people are quite indispensable, because they include most of the technical experts. Obviously the snobbishness and political ignorance of people like airmen and naval officers will be a very great difficulty. But without those airmen, destroyer commanders, etc., etc., we could not survive for a week. The only approach to them is through their patriotism. An intelligent Socialist movement will *use* their patriotism, instead of merely insulting it, as hitherto.

But do I mean that there will be no opposition? Of course not. It would be childish to expect anything of the kind.

There will be a bitter political struggle, and there will be unconscious and half-conscious sabotage everywhere. At some point or other it may be necessary to use violence. It is easy to imagine a pro-Fascist rebellion breaking out in, for instance, India. We shall have to fight against bribery, ignorance and snobbery. The bankers and the larger business-men, the landowners and dividend-drawers, the officials with their prehensile bottoms, will obstruct for all they are worth. Even the middle classes will writhe when their accustomed way of life is menaced. But just because the English sense of national unity has never disintegrated, because patriotism is finally stronger than class-hatred, the chances are that the will of the majority will prevail. It is no use imagining that one can make fundamental changes without causing a split in the nation; but the treacherous minority will be far smaller in time of war than it would be at any other time.

The swing of opinion is visibly happening, but it cannot be counted on to happen fast enough of its own accord. This war is a race between the consolidation of Hitler's empire and the growth of democratic consciousness. Everywhere in England you can see a ding-dong battle raging to and fro – in Parliament and in the Government, in the factories and the armed forces, in the pubs and the air-raid shelters, in the newspapers and on the radio. Every day there are tiny defeats, tiny victories. Morrison for Home Security – a few yards forward. Priestley shoved off the air – a few yards back. It is a struggle between the groping and the unteachable, between the young and the old, between the living and the dead. But it is very necessary that the discontent which undoubtedly exists should take a purposeful and not merely obstructive form. It is time for *the people* to define their war-aims. What is wanted is a simple, concrete programme of action, which can be given all possible publicity, and round which public opinion can group itself.

I suggest that the following six-point programme is the kind of thing we need. The first three points deal with England's internal policy, the other three with the Empire and the world:–

I. Nationalization of land, mines, railways, banks and major industries.

II. Limitation of incomes, on such a scale that the highest tax-free income in Britain does not exceed the lowest by more than ten to one.

III. Reform of the educational system along democratic lines.

IV. Immediate Dominion status for India, with power to secede when the war is over.

V. Formation of an Imperial General Council, in which the coloured peoples are to be represented.

VI. Declaration of formal alliance with China, Abyssinia and all other victims of the Fascist powers.

The general tendency of this programme is unmistakable. It aims quite frankly at turning this war into a revolutionary war and England into a Socialist democracy. I have deliberately included in it nothing that the simplest person could not understand and see the reason for. In the form in which I have put it, it could be printed on the front page of the *Daily Mirror*. But for the purposes of this book a certain amount of amplification is needed.

I. *Nationalization*. One can "nationalize" industry by the stroke of a pen, but the actual process is slow and complicated. What is needed is that the ownership of all major industry shall be formally vested in the State, representing the common people. Once that is done it becomes possible to eliminate the class of mere *owners* who live not by virtue of anything they produce but by the possession of title-deeds and share-certificates. State ownership implies, therefore, that nobody shall live without working. How sudden a change in the conduct of industry it implies is less certain. In a country like England we cannot rip down the whole structure and build again from the bottom, least of all in time of war. Inevitably the majority of industrial concerns will continue with much the same personnel as before, the one-time owners or managing directors carrying on with their jobs as State-employees. There is reason to think that many of the smaller capitalists would actually welcome some such arrangement. The resistance will come from the big capitalists, the bankers, the landlords and the idle rich, roughly speaking the class with over £2000 a year – and even if one counts in all their dependants there are not more than half a million of these people in England. National-ization of agricultural land implies cutting out the landlord and the tithe-drawer, but not necessarily interfering with the farmer. It is difficult to imagine any reorganization of English agriculture that would not retain most of the existing farms as units, at any rate at the beginning. The farmer, when he is competent, will continue as a salaried manager. He is virtually that already, with the added disadvantage of having to make a profit and being permanently in debt to the bank. With certain kinds of petty trading, and even the small-scale ownership of land, the State will probably not interfere at all. It would be a great mistake to start by victimizing the smallholder class, for instance. These people are necessary, on the whole they are competent, and the amount of work they do depends on the feeling that they are "their own masters". But the State will certainly impose an upward limit to the ownership of land (probably fifteen acres at the very most), and will never permit any ownership of land in town areas.

From the moment that all productive goods have been declared the property of the State, the common people will feel, as they cannot feel now, that the State *is themselves*. They will be ready then to endure the sacrifices that are ahead of us, war or no war. And even if the face of England hardly seems to change, on the day that our main industries are formally nationalized the dominance of a single class will have been broken. From then onwards the emphasis will be shifted from ownership to management, from privilege to competence. It is quite possible that State-ownership will in itself bring about less social change than will be forced upon us by the common hardships of war. But it is the necessary first step without which any *real* reconstruction is impossible.

II. *Incomes*. Limitation of incomes implies the fixing of a minimum wage, which implies a managed internal currency based simply on the amount of consumption-goods available. And this again implies a stricter rationing-scheme than is now in operation. It is no use at this stage of the world's history to suggest that all human beings should have *exactly* equal incomes. It has been shown over and over again that without some kind of money reward there is no incentive to undertake certain jobs. On the other hand the money reward need not be very large. In practice it is impossible that earnings should be limited quite as rigidly as I have suggested. There will always be anomalies and evasions. But there is no reason why ten to one should not be the maximum normal variation. And within those limits some sense of equality is possible. A man with £3 a week and a man with £1 500 a year can feel themselves fellow-creatures, which the Duke of Westminster and the sleepers on the Embankment benches cannot.

III. *Education*. In wartime, educational reform must necessarily be promise rather than performance. At the moment we are not in a position to raise the school-leaving age or increase the teaching staffs of the Elementary Schools. But there are certain immediate steps that we could take towards a democratic educational system. We could start by abolishing the autonomy of the public schools and the older universities and flooding them with State-aided pupils chosen simply on grounds of ability. At present, public-school education is partly a training in class prejudice and partly a sort of tax that the middle classes pay to the upper class in return for the right to enter certain professions. It is true that the state of affairs is altering. The middle classes have begun to rebel against the expensiveness of education, and the war will bankrupt the majority of the public schools if it continues for another year or two. The evacuation is also producing certain minor changes. But there is a danger that some of the older schools, which will be able to weather the financial storm longest, will survive in some form or another as festering centres of snobbery. As for the 10,000 "private" schools that England possesses, the vast majority of them deserve nothing except suppression. They are simply commercial undertakings, and in many cases their educational level is actually lower than that of the Elementary Schools. They merely exist because of a widespread idea that there is something disgraceful in being educated by the public authorities. The State could quell this idea by declaring itself responsible for *all* education, even if at the start this were no more than a gesture. We need gestures, as well as actions. It is all too obvious that our talk of "defending democracy" is nonsense while it is a mere accident of birth that decides whether a gifted child shall or shall not get the education it deserves.

IV. *India.* What we must offer India is not "freedom", which, as I have said earlier, is impossible, but alliance, partnership – in a word, equality. But we must also tell the Indians that they are free to secede, if they want to. Without that there can be no equality of partnership, and our claim to be defending the coloured peoples against Fascism will never be believed. But it is a mistake to imagine that if the Indians were free to cut themselves adrift they would immediately do so. When a British government *offers* them unconditional independence, they will refuse it. For as soon as they have the power to secede the chief reasons for doing so will have disappeared.

A complete severance of the two countries would be a disaster for India no less than for England. Intelligent Indians know this. As things are at present, India not only cannot defend itself, it is hardly even capable of feeding itself. The whole administration of the country depends on a framework of experts (engineers, forest officers, railwaymen, soldiers, doctors) who are predominantly English and could not be replaced within five or ten years. Moreover, English is the

337

chief lingua franca and nearly the whole of the Indian intelligentsia is deeply anglicized. Any transference to foreign rule – for if the British marched out of India the Japanese and other powers would immediately march in – would mean an immense dislocation. Neither the Japanese, the Russians, the Germans nor the Italians would be capable of administering India even at the low level of efficiency that is attained by the British. They do not possess the necessary supplies of technical experts or the knowledge of languages and local conditions, and they probably could not win the confidence of indispensable go-betweens such as the Eurasians. If India were simply "liberated", i.e. deprived of British military protection, the first result would be a fresh foreign conquest, and the second a series of enormous famines which would kill millions of people within a few years.

What India needs is the power to work out its own constitution without British interference, but in some kind of partnership that ensures it military protection and technical advice. This is unthinkable until there is a Socialist government in England. For at least eighty years England has artificially prevented the development of India, partly from fear of trade competition if Indian industries were too highly developed, partly because backward peoples are more easily governed than civilized ones. It is a commonplace that the average Indian suffers far more from his own countrymen than from the British. The petty Indian capitalist exploits the town worker with the utmost ruthlessness, the peasant lives from birth to death in the grip of the moneylender. But all this is an indirect result of the British rule, which aims half-consciously at keeping India as backward as possible. The classes most loyal to Britain are the princes, the landowners and the business community – in general, the reactionary classes who are doing fairly well out of the *status quo*. The moment that England ceased to stand towards India in the relation of an exploiter, the balance of forces would be altered. No need then for the British to flatter the ridiculous Indian princes, with their gilded elephants and cardboard armies, to prevent the growth of the Indian Trade Unions, to play off Moslem against Hindu, to protect the worthless life of the moneylender, to receive the salaams of toadying minor officials, to prefer the half-barbarous Gurkha to the educated Bengali. Once check that stream of dividends that flows from the bodies of Indian coolies to the banking accounts of old ladies in Cheltenham, and the whole sahib–native nexus, with its haughty ignorance on one side and envy and servility on the other, can come to an end. Englishmen and Indians can work side by side for the development of India, and for the training of Indians in all the arts which, so far, they have been systematically prevented from learning. How many of the existing British personnel in India, commercial or official, would fall in with such an arrangement – which would mean ceasing once and for all to be "sahibs" – is a different question. But, broadly speaking, more is to be hoped from the younger men and from those officials (civil engineers, forestry and agricultural experts, doctors, educationists) who have been scientifically educated. The higher officials, the provincial governors, commissioners, judges, etc., are hopeless; but they are also the most easily replaceable.

That, roughly, is what would be meant by Dominion status if it were offered to India by a Socialist government. It is an offer of partnership on equal terms until such time as the world has ceased to be ruled by bombing-planes. But we must add to it the unconditional right to secede. It is the only way of proving that we mean what we say. And what applies to India applies, *mutatis mutandis*, to Burma, Malaya and most of our African possessions.

V and VI explain themselves. They are the necessary preliminary to any claim that we are fighting this war for the protection of peaceful peoples against Fascist aggression.

Is it impossibly hopeful to think that such a policy as this could get a following in England? A year ago, even six months ago, it would have been, but not now. Moreover – and this is the peculiar opportunity of this moment – it could be given the necessary publicity. There is now a considerable weekly press, with a circulation of millions, which would be ready to popularize – if not *exactly* the programme I have sketched above, at any rate *some* policy along those lines. There are even three or four daily papers which would be prepared to give it a sympathetic hearing. That is the distance we have travelled in the last six months.

GEORGE ORWELL

But is such a policy realizable? That depends entirely on ourselves.

Some of the points I have suggested are of the kind that could be carried out immediately, others would take years or decades and even then would not be perfectly achieved. No political programme is ever carried out in its entirety. But what matters is that that or something like it should be our declared policy. It is always the *direction* that counts. It is of course quite hopeless to expect the present government to pledge itself to any policy that implies turning this war into a revolutionary war. It is at best a government of compromise, with Churchill riding two horses like a circus acrobat. Before such measures as limitation of incomes become even thinkable, there will have to be a complete shift of power away from the old ruling class. If during this winter the war settles into another stagnant period, we ought in my opinion to agitate for a General Election, a thing which the Tory Party machine will make frantic efforts to prevent. But even without an election we can get the government we want, provided that we want it urgently enough. A real shove from below will accomplish it. As to who will be in that government when it comes, I make no guess. I only know that the right men will be there when the people really want them, for it is movements that make leaders and not leaders movements.

Within a year, perhaps even within six months, if we are still unconquered, we shall see the rise of something that has never existed before, a specifically *English* Socialist movement. Hitherto there has been only the Labour Party, which was the creation of the working class but did not aim at any fundamental change, and Marxism, which was a German theory interpreted by Russians and unsuccessfully transplanted to England. There was nothing that really touched the heart of the English people. Throughout its entire history the English Socialist movement has never produced a song with a catchy tune – nothing like *La Marseillaise* or *La Cucuracha*, for instance. When a Socialist movement native to England appears, the Marxists, like all others with a vested interest in the past, will be its bitter enemies. Inevitably they will denounce it as "Fascism". Already it is customary among the more soft-boiled intellectuals of the Left to declare that if we fight against the Nazis we shall

340

"go Nazi" ourselves. They might almost equally well say that if we fight against Negroes we shall turn black. To "go Nazi" we should have to have the history of Germany behind us. Nations do not escape from their past merely by making a revolution. An English Socialist government will transform the nation from top to bottom, but it will still bear all over it the unmistakable marks of our own civilization, the peculiar civilization which I discussed earlier in this book.

It will not be doctrinaire, nor even logical. It will abolish the House of Lords, but quite probably will not abolish the Monarchy. It will leave anachronisms and loose ends everywhere, the judge in his ridiculous horsehair wig and the lion and the unicorn on the soldier's cap-buttons. It will not set up any explicit class dictatorship. It will group itself round the old Labour Party and its mass following will be in the Trade Unions, but it will draw into it most of the middle class and many of the younger sons of the bourgeoisie. Most of its directing brains will come from the new indeterminate class of skilled workers, technical experts, airmen, scientists, architects and journalists, the people who feel at home in the radio and ferro-concrete age. But it will never lose touch with the tradition of compromise and the belief in a law that is above the State. It will shoot traitors, but it will give them a solemn trial beforehand, and occasionally it will acquit them. It will crush any open revolt promptly and cruelly, but it will interfere very little with the spoken and written word. Political parties with different names will still exist, revolutionary sects will still be publishing their newspapers and making as little impression as ever. It will disestablish the Church, but will not persecute religion. It will retain a vague reverence for the Christian moral code, and from time to time will refer to England as "a Christian country". The Catholic Church will war against it, but the Nonconformist sects and the bulk of the Anglican Church will be able to come to terms with it. It will show a power of assimilating the past which will shock foreign observers and sometimes make them doubt whether any revolution has happened.

But all the same it will have done the essential thing. It will have nationalized industry, scaled down incomes, set up a classless educational system. Its real nature will be apparent from the hatred which the surviving rich men of the world will feel for it. It will aim not at disintegrating the Empire but at turning it into a federation of Socialist states, freed not so much from the British flag as from the moneylender, the dividend-drawer and the wooden-headed British official. Its war-strategy will be totally different from that of any property-ruled state, because it will not be afraid of the revolutionary after-effects when any existing régime is brought down. It will not have the smallest scruple about attacking hostile neutrals or stirring up native rebellions in enemy colonies. It will fight in such a way that even if it is beaten its memory will be dangerous to the victor, as the memory of the French Revolution was dangerous to Metternich's Europe. The dictators will fear it as they could not fear the existing British régime, even if its military strength were ten times what it is.

But at this moment, when the drowsy life of England has barely altered, and the offensive contrast of wealth and poverty still exists everywhere, even amid the bombs, why do I dare to say that all these things "will" happen?

Because the time has come when one can predict the future in terms of an "either-or". Either we turn this war into a revolutionary war (I do not say that our policy will be *exactly* what I have indicated above – merely that it will be along those general lines) or we lose it, and much more besides. Quite soon it will be possible to say definitely that our feet are set upon one path or the other. But at any rate it is certain that with our present social structure we cannot win. Our real forces, physical, moral or intellectual, cannot be mobilized.

iii

Patriotism has nothing to do with Conservatism. It is actually the opposite of Conservatism, since it is a devotion to something that is always changing and yet is felt to be mystically the same. It is the bridge between the future and the past. No real revolutionary has ever been an inter-nationalist.

During the past twenty years the negative, *fainéant* outlook which has been fashionable among English left-wingers, the sniggering of the intellectuals at patriotism and physical cour-age, the persistent effort to chip away English morale and spread a hedonistic, what-do-I-get-out-of-it attitude to life, has done nothing but harm. It would have been harmful even if we had been living in the squashy League of Nations universe that these people imagined. In an age of Führers and bombing-planes it was a disaster. However little we may like it, toughness is the price of survival. A nation trained to think hedonistically cannot survive amid peoples who work like slaves and breed like rabbits, and whose chief national industry is war. English Socialists of nearly all colours have wanted to make a stand against Fascism, but at the same time they have aimed at making their own countrymen unwarlike. They have failed, because in England traditional loyalties are stronger than new ones. But in spite of all the "anti-Fascist" heroics of the left-wing press, what chance should we have stood when the real struggle with Fascism came, if the average Englishman had been the kind of creature that the *New Statesman*, the *Daily Worker* or even the *News-Chronicle* wished to make him?

Up to 1935 virtually all English left-wingers were vaguely pacifist. After 1935 the more vocal of them flung themselves eagerly into the Popular Front movement, which was simply an evasion of the whole problem posed by Fascism. It set out to be "anti-Fascist" in a purely negative way – "against" Fascism without being "for" any discoverable policy – and underneath it lay the flabby idea that when the time came the Russians would do our fighting for us. It is astonishing how this illusion fails to die. Every week sees its spate of letters to the press, pointing out that if we had a government with no Tories in it the Russians could hardly avoid coming round to our side. Or we are to publish high-sounding war-aims (*vide* books like *Unser Kampf*, *A Hundred Million Allies – If We Choose*, etc.), whereupon the European populations will infallibly rise on our behalf. It is the same idea all the time – look abroad for your inspiration, get someone else to do your fighting for you. Underneath it lies the frightful inferiority complex of the English intellectual, the belief that the English are no longer a martial race, no longer capable of enduring.

In truth there is no reason to think that anyone will do our fighting for us yet awhile, except the Chinese, who have been doing it for three years already.[8] The Russians may be driven to fight on our side by the fact of a direct attack, but they have made it clear enough that they will not stand up to the German army if there is any way of avoiding it. In any case they are not likely to be attracted by the spectacle of a left-wing government in England. The present Russian régime must almost certainly be hostile to any revolution in the West. The subject peoples of Europe will rebel when Hitler begins to totter, but not earlier. Our potential allies are not the Europeans but on the one hand the Americans, who will need a year to mobilize their resources even if Big Business can be brought to heel, and on the other hand the coloured peoples, who cannot be even sentimentally on our side till our own revolution has started. For a long time, a year, two years, possibly three years, England has got to be the shock-absorber of the world. We have got to face bombing, hunger, overwork, influenza, boredom and treacherous peace offers. Manifestly it is a time to stiffen morale, not to weaken it. Instead of taking the mechanically anti-British attitude which is usual on the Left, it is better to consider what the world would really be like if the English-speaking culture perished. For it is childish to suppose that the other English-speaking countries, even the U.S.A., will be unaffected if Britain is conquered.

Lord Halifax, and all his tribe, believe that when the war is over things will be exactly as they were before. Back to the crazy pavement of Versailles, back to "democracy", i.e. capitalism, back to the dole-queues and the Rolls-Royce cars, back to the grey top hats and the sponge-bag trousers, *in saecula saeculorum*. It is of course obvious that nothing of the kind is going to happen. A feeble imitation of it might just possibly happen in the case of a negotiated peace, but only for a short while. *Laissez-faire* capitalism is dead.[9] The choice lies between the kind of collective society that Hitler will set up and the kind that can arise if he is defeated.

If Hitler wins this war he will consolidate his rule over Europe, Africa and the Middle East, and if his armies have not been too greatly exhausted beforehand, he will wrench vast territories from Soviet Russia. He will set up a graded caste-society in which the German *Herrenvolk* ("master race" or "aristocratic race") will rule over Slavs and other lesser peoples whose job will be to produce low-priced agricultural products. He will reduce the coloured peoples once and for all to outright slavery. The real quarrel of the Fascist powers with British imperialism is that they know that it is disintegrating. Another twenty years along the present line of development, and India will be a peasant republic linked with England only by voluntary alliance. The "semi-apes" of whom Hitler speaks with such loathing will be flying aeroplanes and manufacturing machine guns. The Fascist dream of a slave empire will be at an end. On the other hand, if we are defeated we simply hand over our own victims to new masters who come fresh to the job and have not developed any scruples.

But more is involved than the fate of the coloured peoples. Two incompatible visions of life are fighting one another. "Between democracy and totalitarianism", says Mussolini, "there can be no compromise." The two creeds cannot even, for any length of time, live side by side. So long as democracy exists, even in its very imperfect English form, totalitarianism is in deadly danger. The whole English-speaking world is haunted by the idea of human equality, and though it would be simply a lie to say that either we or the Americans have ever acted up to our professions, still, the *idea* is there, and it is capable of one day becoming a reality. From the English-speaking culture, if it does not perish, a society of free and equal human beings will ultimately arise. But it is precisely the idea of human equality – the "Jewish" or "Judæo-Christian" idea of equality – that Hitler came into the world to destroy. He has, heaven knows, said so often enough. The thought of a world in which black men would be as good as white men and Jews treated as human brings him the same horror and despair as the thought of endless slavery brings to us.

It is important to keep in mind how irreconcilable these two viewpoints are. Some time within the next year a pro-Hitler reaction within the left-wing intelligentsia is likely enough. There are premonitory signs of it already. Hitler's positive achievement appeals to the emptiness of these people, and, in the case of those with pacifist leanings, to their masochism. One knows in advance more or less what they will say. They will start by refusing to admit that British capitalism is evolving into something different, or that the defeat of Hitler can mean any more than a victory for the British and American million-aires. And from that they will proceed to argue that, after all, democracy is "just the same as" or "just as bad as" totalitarianism. There is *not much* freedom of speech in England; therefore there is *no more* than exists in Germany. To be on the dole is a horrible experience; therefore it is *no worse* to be in the torture-chambers of the Gestapo. In general, two blacks make a white, half a loaf is the same as no bread.

But in reality, whatever may be true about democracy and totalitarianism, it is not true that they are the same. It would not be true, even if British democracy were incapable of evolving beyond its present stage. The whole conception of the militarized continental state, with its secret police, its censored literature and its conscript labour, is utterly different from that of the loose maritime democracy, with its slums and unemployment, its strikes and party politics. It is the difference between land power and sea power, between cruelty and inefficiency, between lying and self-deception, between the S.S.-man and the rent-collector. And in choosing between them one chooses not so much on the strength of what they now are as of what they are capable of becoming. But in a sense it is irrelevant whether democracy, at its highest or at its lowest, is "better" than totalitarianism. To decide that one would have to have access to absolute standards. The only question that matters is where one's real sympathies will lie when the pinch comes. The intellectuals who are so fond of balancing democracy against totalitarianism and "proving" that one is as bad as the other are simply frivolous people who have never been shoved up against realities. They show the same shallow misunderstanding of Fascism now, when they are beginning to flirt with it, as a year or two ago, when they were squealing against it. The question is not, "Can you make out a debating-society 'case' in favour of Hitler?" The question is, "Do you genuinely accept that case? Are you willing to submit to Hitler's rule? Do you want to see England conquered, or don't you?" It would be better to be sure on that point before frivolously siding with the enemy. For there is no such thing as neutrality in war; in practice one must help one side or the other.

When the pinch comes, no one bred in the Western tradition can accept the Fascist vision of life. It is important to realize that *now*, and to grasp what it entails. With all its sloth, hypocrisy and injustice, the English-speaking civilization is the only large obstacle in Hitler's path. It is a living contradiction of all the "infallible" dogmas of Fascism. That is why all Fascist writers for years past have agreed that England's power must be destroyed. England must be "exterminated", must be "annihilated", must "cease to exist". Strategically it would be possible for this war to end with Hitler in secure possession of Europe, and with the British Empire intact and British sea-power barely affected. But ideologically it is not possible; were Hitler to make an offer along those lines, it could only be treacherously, with a view to conquering England indirectly or renewing the attack at some more favourable moment. England cannot possibly be allowed to remain as a sort of funnel through which deadly ideas from beyond the Atlantic flow into the police-states of Europe. And turning it round to our own point of view, we see the vastness of the issue before us, the all-importance of preserving our democracy more or less as we have known it. But to *preserve* is always to *extend*. The choice before us is not so much between victory and defeat as between revolution and apathy. If the thing we are fighting for is altogether destroyed, it will have been destroyed partly by our own act.

It could happen that England should introduce the beginnings of Socialism, turn this war into a revolutionary war, and still be defeated. That is at any rate thinkable. But, terrible as it would be for anyone who is now adult, it would be far less deadly than the "compromise peace" which a few rich men and their hired liars are hoping for. The final ruin of England could only be accomplished by an English government acting under orders from Berlin. But that cannot happen if England has awakened beforehand. For in that case the defeat would be unmistakable, the struggle would continue, the *idea* would survive. The difference between going down fighting, and surrendering without a fight, is by no means a question of "honour" and schoolboy heroics. Hitler said once that to *accept* defeat destroys the soul of a nation. This sounds like a piece of claptrap, but it is strictly true. The defeat of 1870 did not lessen the world-influence of France. The Third Republic had more influence, intellectually, than the France of Napoleon III. But the sort of peace that Pétain, Laval & Co. have accepted can only be purchased by deliberately wiping out the national culture. The Vichy government will enjoy a spurious independence only on condition that it destroys the distinctive marks of French culture: republicanism, secularism, respect for the intellect, absence of colour prejudice. We cannot be *utterly* defeated if we have made our revolution beforehand. We may see German troops marching down Whitehall, but another process, ultimately deadly to the German power-dream, will have been started. The Spanish people were defeated, but the things they learned during those two and a half memorable years will one day come back upon the Spanish Fascists like a boomerang.

A piece of Shakespearean bombast was much quoted at the beginning of the war. Even Mr. Chamberlain quoted it once, if my memory does not deceive me:

> Come the three corners of the world in arms
> And we shall shock them. Naught shall make us rue
> If England to herself do rest but true.

It is right enough, if you interpret it rightly. But England has got to be true to herself. She is not being true to herself while the refugees who have sought our shores are penned up in concentration camps, and company directors work out subtle schemes to dodge their Excess Profits Tax. It is good-bye to the *Tatler* and the *Bystander*, and farewell to the lady in the Rolls-Royce car. The heirs of Nelson and of Cromwell are not in the House of Lords. They are in the fields and the streets, in the factories and the armed forces, in the four-ale bar and the suburban back garden; and at present they are still kept under by a generation of ghosts. Compared with the task of bringing the real England to the surface, even the winning of the war, necessary though it is, is secondary. By revolution we become more ourselves, not less. There is no question of stopping short, striking a compromise, salvaging "democracy", standing still. Nothing ever stands still. We must add to our heritage or lose it, we must grow greater or grow less, we must go forward or go backward. I believe in England, and I believe that we shall go forward.

The Frontiers of Art and Propaganda

Broadcast, 30 April 1941; *The Listener*, 29 May 1941

I am speaking on literary criticism, and in the world in which we are actually living that is almost as unpromising as speaking about peace. This is not a peaceful age, and it is not a critical age. In the Europe of the last ten years literary criticism of the older kind – criticism that is really judicious, scrupulous, fair-minded, treating a work of art as a thing of value in itself – has been next door to impossible.

If we look back at the English literature of the last ten years, not so much at the literature as at the prevailing literary atti-tude, the thing that strikes us is that it has almost ceased to be aesthetic. Literature has been swamped by propaganda. I do not mean that all the books written during that period have been bad. But the characteristic writers of the time, people like Auden and Spender and MacNeice, have been didactic, polit-ical writers, aesthetically conscious, of course, but more inter-ested in subject-matter than in technique. And the most lively criticism has nearly all of it been the work of Marxist writers, people like Christopher Caudwell and Philip Henderson and Edward Upward, who look on every book virtually as a polit-ical pamphlet and are far more interested in digging out its political and social implications than in its literary qualities in the narrow sense.

This is all the more striking because it makes a very sharp and sudden contrast with the period immediately before it. The characteristic writers of the nineteen-twenties – T. S. Eliot, for instance, Ezra Pound, Virginia Woolf – were writers who put the main emphasis on technique. They had their beliefs and prejudices, of course, but they were far more interested in technical innovations than in any moral or meaning or political implication that their work might contain. The best of them all, James Joyce, was a technician and very little else, about as near to being a 'pure' artist as a writer can be. Even D. H. Lawrence, though he was more of a 'writer with a purpose' than most of the others of his time, had not much of what we should now call social consciousness. And though I have narrowed this down to the nineteen-twenties, it had really been the same from about 1890 onwards. Throughout the whole of that period, the notion that form is more important than subject-matter, the notion of 'art for art's sake', had been taken for granted. There were writers who disagreed, of course – Bernard Shaw was one – but that was the prevailing outlook. The most important critic of the period, George Saintsbury, was a very old man in the nineteen-twenties, but he had a powerful influence up to about 1930, and Saintsbury had always firmly upheld the technical attitude to art. He claimed that he himself could and did judge any book solely on its execution, its *manner*, and was very nearly indifferent to the author's opinions.

Now, how is one to account for this very sudden change of outlook? About the end of the nineteen-twenties you get a book like Edith Sitwell's book on Pope, with a completely frivolous emphasis on technique, treating literature as a sort of embroidery, almost as though words did not have meanings; and only a few years later you get a Marxist critic like Edward Upward asserting that books can be 'good' only when they are Marxist in tendency. In a sense both Edith Sitwell and Edward Upward were representative of their period. The question is, why should their outlooks be so different?

I think one has got to look for the reason in external circumstances. Both the aesthetic and the political attitude to literature were produced, or at any rate conditioned, by the social atmosphere of a certain period. And now that another period has ended – for Hitler's attack on Poland in 1939 ended one epoch as surely as the great slump of 1931 ended another – one can look back and see more clearly than was possible a few years ago the way in which literary attitudes are affected by external events. A thing that strikes anyone who looks back over the last hundred years is that literary criticism worth bothering about, and the critical attitude towards literature, barely existed in England between roughly 1830 and 1890. It is not that good books were not produced in that period. Several of the writers of that time, Dickens, Thackeray, Trollope and others, will probably be remembered longer than any that have come after them. But there are no literary figures in Victorian England corresponding to Flaubert, Baudelaire, Gautier and a host of others. What now appears to us as aesthetic scrupulousness hardly existed. To a mid-Victorian English writer, a book was partly something that brought him money and partly a

350

vehicle for preaching sermons. England was changing very rapidly, a new moneyed class had come up on the ruins of the old aristocracy, contact with Europe had been severed, and a long artistic tradition had been broken. The mid-nineteenth-century English writers were barbarians, even when they happened to be gifted artists, like Dickens.

But in the later part of the century contact with Europe was re-established through Matthew Arnold, Pater, Oscar Wilde and various others, and the respect for form and technique in literature came back. It is from then that the notion of 'art for art's sake' – a phrase very much out of fashion, but still, I think, the best available – really dates. And the reason why it could flourish so long, and be so much taken for granted, was that the whole period between 1890 and 1930 was one of exceptional comfort and security. It was what we might call the golden afternoon of the capitalist age. Even the Great War did not really disturb it. The Great War killed ten million men, but it did not shake the world as this War will shake it and has shaken it already. Almost every European between 1890 and 1930 lived in the tacit belief that civilisation would last for ever. You might be individually fortunate or unfortunate, but you had inside you the feeling that nothing would ever fundamentally change. And in that kind of atmosphere intellectual detachment, and also dilettantism, are possible. It is that feeling of continuity, of security, that could make it possible for a critic like Saintsbury, a real old crusted Tory and High Churchman, to be scrupulously fair to books written by men whose political and moral outlook he detested.

But since 1930 that sense of security has never existed. Hitler and the slump shattered it as the Great War and even the Russian Revolution had failed to shatter it. The writers who have come up since 1930 have been living in a world in which not only one's life but one's whole scheme of values is constantly menaced. In such circumstances detachment is not possible. You cannot take a purely aesthetic interest in a disease you are dying from; you cannot feel dispassionately about a man who is about to cut your throat. In a world in which Fascism and Socialism were fighting one another, any thinking person had to take sides, and his feelings had to find their way not only into his writing but into his judgements on literature.

Literature had to become political, because anything else would have entailed mental dishonesty. One's attachments and hatreds were too near the surface of consciousness to be ignored. What books were *about* seemed so urgently important that the way they were written seemed almost insignificant.

And this period of ten years or so in which literature, even poetry, was mixed up with pamphleteering, did a great service to literary criticism, because it destroyed the illusion of pure aestheticism. It reminded us that propaganda in some form or other lurks in every book, that every work of art has a meaning and a purpose – a political, social and religious purpose – and that our aesthetic judgements are always coloured by our prejudices and beliefs. It debunked art for art's sake. But it also led for the time being into a blind alley, because it caused countless young writers to try to tie their minds to a political discipline which, if they had stuck to it, would have made mental honesty impossible. The only system of thought open to them at that time was official Marxism, which demanded a nationalistic loyalty towards Russia and forced the writer who called himself a Marxist to be mixed up in the dishonesties of power politics. And even if that was desirable, the assumptions that these writers built upon were suddenly shattered by the Russo-German pact. Just as many writers about 1930 had discovered that you cannot really be detached from contemporary events, so many writers about 1939 were discovering that you cannot really sacrifice your intellectual integrity for the sake of a political creed – or at least you cannot do so and remain a writer. Aesthetic scrupulousness is not enough, but political rectitude is not enough either. The events of the last ten years have left us rather in the air, they have left England for the time being without any discoverable literary trend, but they have helped us to define, better than was possible before, the frontiers of art and propaganda.

Tolstoy and Shakespeare

Broadcast, 7 May 1941; *The Listener*, 5 June 1941

Last week I pointed out that art and propaganda are never quite separable, and that what are supposed to be purely aesthetic judgements are always corrupted to some extent by moral or political or religious loyalties. And I added that in times of trouble, like the last ten years, in which no thinking person can ignore what is happening round him or avoid taking sides, these underlying loyalties are pushed nearer to the surface of consciousness. Criticism becomes more and more openly partisan, and even the pretence of detachment becomes very difficult. But one cannot infer from that that there is no such thing as an aesthetic judgement, that every work of art is simply and solely a political pamphlet and can be judged only as such. If we reason like that we lead our minds into a blind alley in which certain large and obvious facts become inexplicable. And in illustration of this I want to examine one of the greatest pieces of moral, non-aesthetic criticism – *anti*-aesthetic criticism, one might say – that has ever been written: Tolstoy's essay on Shakespeare.

Towards the end of his life Tolstoy wrote a terrific attack on Shakespeare purporting to show not only that Shakespeare was not the great man he was claimed to be, but that he was a writer entirely without merit, one of the worst and most contemptible writers the world has ever seen. This essay caused tremendous indignation at the time, but I doubt whether it was ever satisfactorily answered. What is more, I shall point out that in the main it was unanswerable. Part of what Tolstoy says is strictly true, and parts of it are too much a matter of personal opinion to be worth arguing about. I do not mean, of course, that there is no detail in the essay which could be answered. Tolstoy contradicts himself several times; the fact that he is dealing with a foreign language makes him misunderstand a great deal, and I think there is little doubt that his hatred and jealousy of Shakespeare make him resort to a certain amount of falsification, or at least wilful blindness. But all that is beside the point. In the main what Tolstoy says is justified after its fashion, and at the time it probably acted as a useful corrective to the silly adulation of Shakespeare that was then fashionable. The answer to it is less in anything I can say than in certain things that Tolstoy is forced to say himself.

Tolstoy's main contention is that Shakespeare is a trivial, shallow writer, with no coherent philosophy, no thoughts or ideas worth bothering about, no interest in social or religious problems, no grasp of character or probability, and, in so far as he could be said to have a definable attitude at all, with a cynical, immoral, worldly outlook on life. He accuses him of patching his plays together without caring twopence for credibility, of dealing in fantastic fables and impossible situations, of making all his characters talk in an artificial flowery language completely unlike that of real life. He also accuses him of thrusting anything and everything into his plays – soliloquies, scraps of ballads, discussions, vulgar jokes and so forth – without stopping to think whether they had anything to do with the plot, and also of taking for granted the immoral power-politics and unjust social distinctions of the times he lived in. Briefly, he accuses him of being a hasty, slovenly writer, a man of doubtful morals, and, above all, of not being a *thinker*.

Now, a good deal of this could be contradicted. It is not true, in the sense implied by Tolstoy, that Shakespeare is an immoral writer. His moral code might be different from Tolstoy's, but he very definitely *has* a moral code, which is apparent all through his work. He is much more of a moralist than, for instance, Chaucer or Boccaccio. He also is not such a fool as Tolstoy tries to make out. At moments, incidentally, one might say, he shows a vision which goes far beyond his time. In this connection I would like to draw attention to the piece of criticism which Karl Marx – who, unlike Tolstoy, admired Shakespeare – wrote on 'Timon of Athens'. But once again, what Tolstoy says is true on the whole. Shakespeare is not a thinker, and the critics who claimed that he was one of the great philosophers of the world were talking nonsense. His thoughts are simply a jumble, a rag-bag. He was like most Englishmen in having a code of conduct but no world-view, no philosophical faculty. Again, it is quite true that Shakespeare cares very little about probability and seldom bothers to make his characters coherent. As we know, he usually stole his plots from other people and hastily made them up into plays, often introducing absurdities and inconsistencies that were not present in the original. Now and again, when he happens to have got hold of a foolproof plot – 'Macbeth', for instance – his characters are reasonably consistent, but in many cases they are forced into actions which are completely incredible by any ordinary standard. Many of his plays have not even the sort of credibility that belongs to a fairy story. In any case we have no evidence that he himself took them seriously, except as a means of livelihood. In his sonnets he never even refers to his plays as part of literary achievement, and only once mentions in a rather shamefaced way that he has been an actor. So far Tolstoy is justified. The claim that Shakespeare was a profound thinker, setting forth a coherent philosophy in plays that were technically perfect and full of subtle psychological observation, is ridiculous.

Only, what has Tolstoy achieved? By this furious attack he ought to have demolished Shakespeare altogether, and he evidently believes that he has done so. From the time when Tolstoy's essay was written, or at any rate from the time when it began to be widely read, Shakespeare's reputation ought to have withered away. The lovers of Shakespeare ought to have seen that their idol had been debunked, that in fact he had no merits, and they ought to have ceased forthwith to take any pleasure in him. But that did not happen. Shakespeare is demolished, and yet somehow he remains standing. So far from his being forgotten as the result of Tolstoy's attack, it is the attack itself that has been almost forgotten. Although Tolstoy is a popular writer in England, both the translations of this essay are out of print, and I had to search all over London before running one to earth in a museum.

It appears, therefore, that though Tolstoy can explain away nearly everything about Shakespeare, there is one thing that he cannot explain away, and that is his popularity. He himself is aware of this, and greatly puzzled by it. I said earlier that the answer to Tolstoy really lies in something he himself is obliged to say. He asks himself how it is that this bad, stupid and immoral writer Shakespeare is everywhere admired, and finally he can only explain it as a sort of worldwide conspiracy to pervert the truth. Or it is a sort of collective hallucination – a hypnosis, he calls it – by which everyone except Tolstoy himself is taken in. As to how this conspiracy or delusion began, he is obliged to set it down to the machinations of certain German critics at the beginning of the nineteenth century. They started telling the wicked lie that Shakespeare is a good writer, and no one since has had the courage to contradict them. Now, one need not spend very long over a theory of this kind. It is nonsense. The enormous majority of the people who have enjoyed watching Shakespeare's plays have never been influenced by any German critics, directly or indirectly. For Shakespeare's popularity is real enough, and it is a popularity that extends to ordinary, by no means bookish people. From his lifetime onwards he has been a stage favourite in England, and he is popular not only in the English-speaking countries but in most of Europe and parts of Asia. Almost as I speak the Soviet Government are celebrating the three hundred and twenty-fifth anniversary of his death, and in Ceylon I once saw a play of his being performed in some language of which I did not know a single word. One must conclude that there is something good – something durable – in Shakespeare which millions of ordinary people can appreciate, though Tolstoy happened to be unable to do so. He can survive exposure of the fact that he is a confused thinker whose plays are full of improbabilities. He can no more be debunked by such methods than you can destroy a flower by preaching a sermon at it.

And that, I think, tells one a little more about something I referred to last week: the frontiers of art and propaganda. It shows one the limitation of any criticism that is solely a criticism of subject and of meaning. Tolstoy criticises Shakespeare not as a poet, but as a thinker and a teacher, and along those lines he has no difficulty in demolishing him. And yet all that he says is irrelevant; Shakespeare is completely unaffected. Not only his reputation but the pleasure we take in him remain just the same as before. Evidently a poet is more than a thinker and a teacher, though he has to be that as well. Every piece of writing has its propaganda aspect, and yet in any book or play or poem or what-not that is to endure there has to be a residuum of something that simply is not affected by its moral or meaning – a residuum of something we can only call art. Within certain limits, bad thought and bad morals can be good literature. If so great a man as Tolstoy could not demonstrate the contrary, I doubt whether anyone else can either.

The Meaning of a Poem

Broadcast, 14 May 1941; *The Listener*, 12 June 1941

I shall start by quoting the poem called 'Felix Randal', by Gerard Manley Hopkins, the well-known English poet – he was a Roman Catholic priest – who died in 1893.

> Felix Randal the farrier, O is he dead then? my duty all
>   ended,
> Who have watched his mould of man, big-boned and
>   hardy-handsome
> Pining, pining, till time when reason rambled in it and some
> Fatal four disorders, fleshed there, all contended?
>
> Sickness broke him. Impatient he cursed at first,
>   but mended
> Being anointed and all; though a heavenlier heart began
>   some
> Months earlier, since I had our sweet reprieve and ransom
> Tendered to him. Ah well, God rest him all road ever he
>   offended!
>
> This seeing the sick endears them to us, us too it endears.
> My tongue had taught thee comfort, touch had quenched
>   thy tears,
> Thy tears that touched my heart, child, Felix, poor Felix
>   Randal;
>
> How far from then forethought of, all thy more boisterous
>   years,
> When thou at the random grim forge, powerful amidst
>   peers,
> Didst fettle for the great grey drayhorse his bright and
>   battering sandal!

It is what people call a 'difficult' poem – I have a reason for choosing a difficult poem, which I will come back to in a moment – but no doubt the general drift of its meaning is clear enough. Felix Randal is a blacksmith – a farrier. The poet, who is also his priest, has known him in the prime of life as a big powerful man, and then he has seen him dying, worn out by

357

disease and weeping on his bed like a child. That is all there is to it, so far as the 'story' of the poem goes.

But now to come back to the reason why I deliberately chose such an obscure and one might say mannered poem. Hopkins is what people call a writer's writer. He writes in a very strange, twisted style – perhaps it is a bad style, really: at any rate, it would be a bad one to imitate – which is not at all easy to understand but which appeals to people who are pro-fessionally interested in points of technique. In criticisms of Hopkins, therefore, you will usually find all the emphasis laid on his use of language and his subject-matter very lightly touched on. And in any criticism of poetry, of course, it seems natural to judge primarily by the ear. For in verse the words – the sounds of words, their associations, and the har-monies of sound and association that two or three words together can set up – obviously matter more than they do in prose. Otherwise there would be no reason for writing in metrical form. And with Hopkins, in particular, the strangeness of his language and the astonishing beauty of some of the sound-effects he manages to bring off seem to overshadow everything else.

The best touch, one might say the especial touch, in this poem is due to a verbal coincidence. For the word that pins the whole poem together and gives it finally an air of majesty, a feeling of being tragic instead of merely pathetic, is that final word 'sandal', which no doubt only came into Hopkins' mind because it happened to rhyme with Randal. I ought perhaps to add that the word 'sandal' is more impressive to an English reader than it would be to an oriental, who sees sandals every day and perhaps wears them himself. To us a sandal is an exotic thing, chiefly associated with the ancient Greeks and Romans. When Hopkins describes the cart-horse's shoe as a sandal, he suddenly converts the cart-horse into a magnificent mythical beast, something like a heraldic animal. And he reinforces that effect by the splendid rhythm of the last line – 'Didst fettle for the great grey drayhorse his bright and battering sandal' – which is actually a hexameter, the same metre in which Homer and Vergil wrote. By a combination of sound and association he manages to lift an ordinary village death on to the plane of tragedy.

But that tragic effect cannot simply exist in the void, on the strength of a certain combination of syllables. One cannot regard a poem as simply a pattern of words on paper, like a sort of mosaic. This poem is moving because of its sound, its musical qualities, but it is also moving because of an emotional content which could not be there if Hopkins' philosophy and beliefs were different from what they were. It is the poem, first of all, of a Catholic, and secondly of a man living at a particular moment of time, the latter part of the nineteenth century, when the old English agricultural way of life – the old Saxon village community – was finally passing away. The whole feeling of the poem is Christian. It is about death, and the attitude towards death varies in the great religions of the world. The Christian attitude towards death is not that it is something to be welcomed, or that it is something to be met with stoical indifference, or that it is something to be avoided as long as possible; but that it is something profoundly tragic which has to be gone through with. A Christian, I suppose, if he were offered the chance of everlasting life on this earth would refuse it, but he would still feel that death is profoundly sad. Now this feeling conditions Hopkins' use of words. If it were not for his special relationship as priest it would not, probably, occur to him to address the dead blacksmith as 'child'. And he could not, probably, have evolved that phrase I have quoted, 'all thy more boisterous years', if he had not the special Christian vision of the necessity and the sadness of death. But, as I have said, the poem is also conditioned by the fact that Hopkins lived at the latter end of the nineteenth century. He had lived in rural communities when they were still distinctly similar to what they had been in Saxon times, but when they were just beginning to break up under the impact of the railway. Therefore he can see a type like Felix Randal, the small independent village craftsman, in perspective, as one can only see something when it is passing away. He can admire him, for instance, as an earlier writer probably could not have done. And that is why in speaking of his work he can evolve phrases like 'the random grim forge' and 'powerful amidst peers.'

But one comes back to the technical consideration that a subject of this kind is very much helped by Hopkins' own peculiar style. English is a mixture of several languages, but mainly Saxon and Norman French, and to this day, in the country districts, there is a class distinction between the two. Many agricultural labourers speak almost pure Saxon. Now, Hopkins' own language is very Saxon, he tends to string several English words together instead of using a single long Latin one, as most people do when they want to express a complicated thought, and he deliberately derived from the early English poets, the ones who come before Chaucer. In this poem, he even uses several dialect words, 'road' for way, and 'fettle' for fix. The special power he has of re-creating the atmosphere of an English village would not belong to him if it were not for the purely technical studies he had made, earlier in his life, of the old Saxon poets. It will be seen that the poem is a synthesis – but more than a synthesis, a sort of growing together – of a special vocabulary and a special religious and social outlook. The two fuse together, inseparably, and the whole is greater than the parts.

I have tried to analyse this poem as well as I can in a short period, but nothing I have said can explain, or explain away, the pleasure I take in it. That is finally inexplicable, and it is just because it *is* inexplicable that detailed criticism is worth while. Men of science can study the life-process of a flower, or they can split it up into its component elements, but any scientist will tell you that a flower does not become less wonderful, it becomes more wonderful, if you know all about it.

Literature and Totalitarianism

Broadcast, 21 May 1941; typescript

In these weekly talks I have been speaking on criticism, which, when all is said and done, is not part of the main stream of literature. A vigorous literature can exist almost without criticism and the critical spirit, as it did in nineteenth-century England. But there is a reason why, at this particular moment, the problems involved in any serious criticism cannot be ignored. I said at the beginning of my first talk that this is not a critical age. It is an age of partisanship and not of detachment, an age in which it is especially difficult to see literary merit in a book whose conclusions you disagree with. Politics – politics in the most general sense – have invaded literature to an extent that doesn't normally happen, and this has brought to the surface of our consciousness the struggle that always goes on between the individual and the community. It is when one considers the difficulty of writing honest, unbiased criticism in a time like ours that one begins to grasp the nature of the threat that hangs over the whole of literature in the coming age.

We live in an age in which the autonomous individual is ceasing to exist – or perhaps one ought to say, in which the individual is ceasing to have the illusion of being autonomous. Now, in all that we say about literature, and above all in all that we say about criticism, we instinctively take the autonomous individual for granted. The whole of modern European literature – I am speaking of the literature of the past four hundred years – is built on the concept of intellectual honesty, or, if you like to put it that way, on Shakespeare's maxim, "To thine own self be true". The first thing that we ask of a writer is that he shan't tell lies, that he shall say what he really thinks, what he really feels. The worst thing we can say about a work of art is that it is insincere. And this is even truer of criticism than of creative literature, in which a certain amount of posing and mannerism and even a certain amount of downright humbug, doesn't matter so long as the writer has a certain fundamental sincerity. Modern literature is essentially an individual thing. It is either the truthful expression of what one man thinks and feels, or it is nothing.

As I say, we take this notion for granted, and yet as soon as one puts it into words one realises how literature is menaced. For this is the age of the totalitarian state, which does not and probably cannot allow the individual any freedom whatever. When one mentions totalitarianism one thinks immediately of Germany, Russia, Italy, but I think one must face the risk that this phenomenon is going to be worldwide. It is obvious that the period of free capitalism is coming to an end and that one country after another is adopting a centralised economy that one can call Socialism or State Capitalism according as one prefers. With that the economic liberty of the individual, and to a great extent his liberty to do what he likes, to choose his own work, to move to and fro across the surface of the earth, comes to end. Now, till recently the implications of this weren't foreseen. It was never fully realised that the disappearance of economic liberty would have any effect on intellectual liberty. Socialism was usually thought of as a sort of moralised Liberalism. The state would take charge of your economic life and set you free from the fear of poverty, unemployment and so forth, but it would have no need to interfere with your private intellectual life. Art could flourish just as it had done in the liberal-capitalist age, only a little more so, because the artist would not any longer be under economic compulsions.

Now, on the existing evidence, one must admit that these ideas have been falsified. Totalitarianism has abolished freedom of thought to an extent unheard of in any previous age. And it is important to realise that its control of thought is not only negative, but positive. It not only forbids you to express – even to *think* – certain thoughts but it dictates what you *shall* think, it creates an ideology for you, it tries to govern your emotional life as well as setting up a code of conduct. And as far as possible it isolates you from the outside world, it shuts you up in an artificial universe in which you have no standards of comparison. The totalitarian state tries, at any rate, to control the thoughts and emotions of its subjects at least as completely as it controls their actions.

The question that is important for us is, can literature survive in such an atmosphere? I think one must answer shortly that it cannot. If totalitarianism becomes worldwide and permanent, what we have known as literature must come to an end. And it won't do – as may appear plausible at first – to say that what will come to an end is merely the literature of post-Renaissance Europe. I believe that literature of every kind, from the epic poem to the critical essay, is menaced by the attempt of the modern state to control the emotional life of the individual. The people who deny this usually put forward two arguments. They say, first of all, that the so-called liberty which has existed during the last few hundred years was merely a reflection of economic anarchy, and in any case largely an illusion. And they also point out that good literature, better than anything that we can produce now, was produced in past ages, when thought was hardly freer than it is in Germany or Russia at this moment. Now this is true so far as it goes. It's true, for instance, that literature could exist in medieval Europe, when thought was under rigid control – chiefly the control of the Church – and you were liable to be burnt alive for uttering a very small heresy. The dogmatic control of the Church didn't prevent, for instance, Chaucer's Canterbury Tales from being written. It's also true that medieval literature, and medieval art generally, was less an individual and more a communal thing than it is now. The English ballads, for example, probably can't be attributed to any individual at all. They were probably composed communally, as I have seen ballads being composed in Eastern countries quite recently. Evidently the anarchic liberty which has characterised the Europe of the last few hundred years, the sort of atmosphere in which there are no fixed standards whatever, isn't necessary, perhaps isn't even an advantage, to literature. Good literature can be created within a fixed framework of thought.

But there are several vital differences between totalitarianism and all the orthodoxies of the past, either in Europe or in the East. The most important is that the orthodoxies of the past *didn't change*, or at least didn't change rapidly. In medieval Europe the Church dictated what you should believe, but at least it allowed you to retain the same beliefs from birth to death. It didn't tell you to believe one thing on Monday and another on Tuesday. And the same is more or less true of any orthodox Christian, Hindu, Buddhist or Moslem today. In a sense his thoughts are circumscribed, but he passes his whole life within the same framework of thought. His emotions aren't tampered with. Now, with totalitarianism exactly the opposite is true. The peculiarity of the totalitarian state is that though it controls thought, it doesn't fix it. It sets up unquestionable dogmas, and it alters them from day to day. It needs the dogmas, because it needs absolute obedience from its subjects, but it can't avoid the changes, which are dictated by the needs of power politics. It declares itself infallible, and at the same time it attacks the very concept of objective truth. To take a crude, obvious example, every German up to September 1939 had to regard Russian Bolshevism with horror and aversion, and since September 1939 he has had to regard it with admiration and affection. If Russia and Germany go to war, as they may well do within the next few years, another equally violent change will have to take place. The German's emotional life, his loves and hatreds, are expected, when necessary, to reverse themselves overnight. I hardly need to point out the effect of this kind of thing upon literature. For writing is largely a matter of *feeling*, which can't always be controlled from outside. It is easy to pay lip-service to the orthodoxy of the moment, but writing of any consequence can only be produced when a man *feels* the truth of what he is saying; without that, the creative impulse is lacking. All the evidence we have suggests that the sudden emotional changes which totalitarianism demands of its followers are psychologically impossible. And that is the chief reason why I suggest that if totalitarianism triumphs throughout the world, literature as we have known it is at an end. And in fact, totalitarianism does seem to have had that effect so far. In Italy literature has been crippled, and in Germany it seems almost to have ceased. The most characteristic activity of the Nazis is burning books. And even in Russia the literary renaissance we once expected hasn't happened, and the most promising Russian writers show a marked tendency to commit suicide or disappear into prison.

I said earlier that liberal capitalism is obviously coming to an end, and therefore I may have seemed to suggest that freedom of thought is also inevitably doomed. But I don't believe this to be so, and I will simply say in conclusion that I believe the hope of literature's survival lies in those countries in which liberalism has struck its deepest roots, the non-military countries, Western Europe and the Americas, India and China. I believe – it may be no more than a pious hope – that though a collectivised economy is bound to come, those countries will know how to evolve a form of Socialism which is not totalitarian, in which freedom of thought can survive the disappearance of economic individualism. That, at any rate, is the only hope to which anyone who cares for literature can cling. Whoever feels the value of literature, whoever sees the central part it plays in the development of human history, must also see the life and death necessity of resisting totalitarianism, whether it is imposed on us from without or from within.

Dear Doktor Goebbels –
Your British Friends are Feeding Fine!

Daily Express, 23 July 1941

The disappearing raspberry, the invisible egg, and the onions which can be smelled but not seen, are phenomena we are all familiar with. Only because of the deadly harm they are capable of doing to morale are these stale conjuring tricks worth mentioning.

When an article is controlled in price it promptly disappears from the market. Now fruit, fish, eggs, and most vegetables cannot be kept for an indefinite time.

If they suddenly disappear it is a safe bet that they are being sold on the Q.T. at an illegal price, and, in fact, any one with moneyed acquaintances knows very well that they *are* being sold.

Eggs, for instance, are available in large quantities at 4d. each; I am informed that they always figure in the bill as "tinned peas."

Petrol, also, seems easy enough to get if you can pay about twice the proper price for it.

And apart from downright law-breaking, you have only to put your nose inside any smart hotel or restaurant to see the most obvious evasion of the spirit of the food regulations.

The "one dish" rule, for instance, is habitually broken, but the infringement does not count, because the extra dish of meat or fish is renamed hors-d'oeuvres.

In any event the fact that food eaten in restaurants is un-rationed favours the man with a large income and abundant spare time. It would be easy for anyone with more than £2,000 a year to live without ever using his ration book.

But does this kind of thing really matter? And if so, why and how does it matter?

It *doesn't* matter because of the extra material consumed. And since this fact is the favourite get-out of selfish people who buy under-the-counter raspberries and use up petrol in going to the races, it is necessary to admit it, and then put it in its place.

The actual wastage of material by the wealthy is negligible because the wealthy consist of very few people.

It is the common people, who are and must be the big consumers of all the commodities, who matter.

If you took away all the extra meat, fish and sugar that find their way into the smart hotels, and divided them among the general population, no appreciable difference would be made.

For that matter, if you taxed all large incomes out of existence, it still would not make much difference to the taxes the rest of us would have to pay.

The common people receive most of the national income, just as they eat most of the food and wear out most of the clothes, because they constitute the enormous majority.

The raspberries now disappearing down favoured throats in Harrogate and Torquay do not have much direct effect on the Battle of the Atlantic.

Therefore, it is argued, what does it matter if there is a certain amount of minor unfairness? Since the food situation as a whole is hardly affected, why shouldn't half a million fortunate people have as good a time as circumstances permit?

This argument is a complete fallacy, because it leaves out of account the effect of envy on morale, on the "we-are-all-in-it-together" feeling which is absolutely necessary in time of war.

There is no way of making war without lowering the general standard of living. The essential act of war is to divert labour from consumption goods to armaments, which means that the common people must eat less, work longer hours, put up with fewer amusements.

And why should they do so – at any rate, how can you expect them to do so – when they have before their eyes a small minority who are suffering no privations whatever?

So long as it is known that the rarer kinds of food are habitually bootlegged, how can you ask people to cut down their milk consumption and be enthusiastic about oatmeal and potatoes?

"War Socialism" can have an important moral effect even when it is of no importance statistically. The few shiploads of oranges that reached England recently are an example.

I wonder how many of those oranges got to the children in the back streets of London. If they had been shared out equally it would only have been a question of one or two oranges apiece for the whole population.

In terms of vitamins it would have made no difference whatever; but it would have given a meaning to the current talk about "equality of sacrifice."

Experience shows that human beings can put up with nearly anything so long as they feel that they are being fairly treated.

The Spanish Republicans put up with hardships which we as yet have hardly dreamed of. For the last year of the civil war the Republican Army was fighting almost without cigarettes: the soldiers put up with it because it was the same for all of them, general and private alike.

And we can do the same, if necessary.

If we are honest we must admit that, air raids apart, the civil population has not had to suffer much hardship – nothing compared with what we went through in 1918, for instance.

It is later, in the moment of crisis, when it may be necessary suddenly to impose the most drastic restrictions of every kind, that our national solidarity will be tested.

If we guard against that moment now, crack down on the Black Market, catch half a dozen food-hogs and petrol-wanglers and give them stiff enough sentences to frighten others of the same kind, prohibit the more blatant kinds of luxury, and, in general, prove that equality of sacrifice is not merely a phrase, we shall be all right.

But at present – and you can test this statement by having a look round the grill-room of any smart hotel, should you succeed in getting past the commissionaires – Dr. Goebbels's endless gibes about "British plutocracy" are hardly needed.

A few score thousand of idle and selfish people are doing his work for him unpaid.

Wells, Hitler and the World State

Horizon, August 1941

"In March or April, say the wiseacres, there is to be a stupendous knockout blow at Britain. . . . What Hitler has to do it with, I cannot imagine. His ebbing and dispersed military resources are now probably not so very much greater than the Italians' before they were put to the test in Greece and Africa."

"The German air power has been largely spent. It is behind the times and its first-rate men are mostly dead or disheartened or worn out."

"In 1914 the Hohenzollern army was the best in the world. Behind that screaming little defective in Berlin there is nothing of the sort. . . . Yet our military 'experts' discuss the waiting phantom. In their imaginations it is perfect in its equipment and invincible in discipline. Sometimes it is to strike a decisive 'blow' through Spain and North Africa and on, or march through the Balkans, march from the Danube to Ankara, to Persia, to India, or 'crush Russia', or 'pour' over the Brenner into Italy. The weeks pass and the phantom does none of these things – for one excellent reason. It does not exist to that extent. Most of such inadequate guns and munitions as it possessed must have been taken away from it and fooled away in Hitler's silly feints to invade Britain. And its raw jerry-built discipline is wilting under the creeping realisation that the Blitzkrieg is spent, and the war is coming home to roost."

These quotations are not taken from the *Cavalry Quarterly* but from a series of newspaper articles by Mr. H. G. Wells, written at the beginning of this year and now reprinted in a book entitled *Guide to the New World*. Since they were written, the German Army has overrun the Balkans and reconquered Cyrenaica, it can march through Turkey or Spain at such time as may suit it, and it has undertaken the invasion of Russia. How that campaign will turn out I do not know, but it is worth noticing that the German general staff, whose opinion is probably worth something, would not have begun it if they had not felt fairly certain of finishing it within three months. So much for the idea that the German Army is a bogey, its equipment inadequate, its morale breaking down, etc. etc.

What has Wells to set against the "screaming little defective in Berlin"? The usual rigmarole about a World State, plus the

Sankey Declaration, which is an attempted definition of fundamental human rights, of anti-totalitarian tendency. Except that he is now especially concerned with federal world control of air power, it is the same gospel as he has been preaching almost without interruption for the past forty years, always with an air of angry surprise at the human beings who can fail to grasp anything so obvious.

What is the use of saying that we need federal world control of the air? The whole question is how we are to get it. What is the use of pointing out that a World State is desirable? What matters is that not one of the five great military powers would think of submitting to such a thing. All sensible men for decades past have been substantially in agreement with what Mr. Wells says; but the sensible men have no power and, in too many cases, no disposition to sacrifice themselves. Hitler is a criminal lunatic, and Hitler has an army of millions of men, aeroplanes in thousands, tanks in tens of thousands. For his sake a great nation has been willing to overwork itself for six years and then to fight for two years more, whereas for the common-sense, essentially hedonistic world-view which Mr. Wells puts forward, hardly a human creature is willing to shed a pint of blood. Before you can even talk of world reconstruction, or even of peace, you have got to eliminate Hitler, which means bringing into being a dynamic not necessarily the same as that of the Nazis, but probably quite as unacceptable to "enlightened" and hedonistic people. What has kept England on its feet during the past year? In part, no doubt, some vague idea about a better future, but chiefly the atavistic emotion of patriotism, the ingrained feeling of the English-speaking peoples that they are superior to foreigners. For the last twenty years the main object of English left-wing intellectuals has been to break this feeling down, and if they had succeeded, we might be watching the S.S. men patrolling the London streets at this moment. Similarly, why are the Russians fighting like tigers against the German invasion? In part, perhaps, for some half-remembered ideal of Utopian Socialism, but chiefly in defence of Holy Russia (the "sacred soil of the Fatherland", etc., etc.), which Stalin has revived in an only slightly altered form. The energy that actually shapes the world springs from emotions – racial pride, leader-worship, religious belief, love of war – which liberal intellectuals mechanically write off as anachronisms, and which they have usually destroyed so completely in themselves as to have lost all power of action.

The people who say that Hitler is Antichrist, or alternatively, the Holy Ghost, are nearer an understanding of the truth than the intellectuals who for ten dreadful years have kept it up that he is merely a figure out of comic opera, not worth taking seriously. All that this idea really reflects is the sheltered conditions of English life. The Left Book Club was at bottom a product of Scotland Yard, just as the Peace Pledge Union is a product of the Navy. One development of the last ten years has been the appearance of the "political book", a sort of enlarged pamphlet combining history with political criticism, as an important literary form. But the best writers in this line – Trotsky, Rauschning, Rosenberg, Silone, Borkenau, Koestler and others – have none of them been Englishmen, and nearly all of them have been renegades from one or other extremist party, who have seen totalitarianism at close quarters and known the meaning of exile and persecution. Only in the English-speaking countries was it fashionable to believe, right up to the outbreak of war, that Hitler was an unimportant lunatic and the German tanks made of cardboard. Mr. Wells, it will be seen from the quotations I have given above, believes something of the kind still. I do not suppose that either the bombs or the German campaign in Greece have altered his opinion. A lifelong habit of thought stands between him and an understanding of Hitler's power.

Mr. Wells, like Dickens, belongs to the non-military middle class. The thunder of guns, the jingle of spurs, the catch in the throat when the old flag goes by, leave him manifestly cold. He has an invincible hatred of the fighting, hunting, swashbuckling side of life, symbolised in all his early books by a violent propaganda against horses. The principal villain of his *Outline of History* is the military adventurer, Napoleon. If one looks through nearly any book that he has written in the last forty years one finds the same idea constantly recurring: the supposed antithesis between the man of science who is working towards a planned World State and the reactionary who is trying to restore a disorderly past. In novels, Utopias, essays, films, pamphlets, the antithesis crops up, always more or less

the same. On the one side science, order, progress, internationalism, aeroplanes, steel, concrete, hygiene: on the other side
war, nationalism, religion, monarchy, peasants, Greek professors, poets, horses. History as he sees it is a series of victories
won by the scientific man over the romantic man. Now, he is
probably right in assuming that a "reasonable", planned form of
society, with scientists rather than witch-doctors in control,
will prevail sooner or later, but that is a different matter from
assuming that it is just round the corner. There survives somewhere or other an interesting controversy which took place
between Wells and Churchill at the time of the Russian Revolution. Wells accuses Churchill of not really believing his own
propaganda about the Bolsheviks being monsters dripping with
blood, etc., but of merely fearing that they were going to
introduce an era of common sense and scientific control, in
which flag-wavers like Churchill himself would have no place.
Churchill's estimate of the Bolsheviks, however, was nearer the
mark than Wells's. The early Bolsheviks may have been angels
or demons, according as one chooses to regard them, but at any
rate they were not sensible men. They were not introducing a
Wellsian Utopia but a Rule of the Saints, which, like the
English Rule of the Saints, was a military despotism enlivened
by witchcraft trials. The same misconception reappears in an
inverted form in Wells's attitude to the Nazis. Hitler is all the
war-lords and witch-doctors in history rolled into one. Therefore, argues Wells, he is an absurdity, a ghost from the past, a
creature doomed to disappear almost immediately. But unfortunately the equation of science with common sense does not
really hold good. The aeroplane, which was looked forward to
as a civilising influence but in practice has hardly been used
except for dropping bombs, is the symbol of that fact. Modern
Germany is far more scientific than England, and far more
barbarous. Much of what Wells has imagined and worked for
is physically there in Nazi Germany. The order, the planning,
the State encouragement of science, the steel, the concrete, the
aeroplanes, are all there, but all in the service of ideas appropriate to the Stone Age. Science is fighting on the side of superstition. But obviously it is impossible for Wells to accept this. It
would contradict the world-view on which his own works are
based. The war-lords and the witch-doctors *must* fail, the

common-sense World State, as seen by a nineteenth-century Liberal whose heart does not leap at the sound of bugles, *must* triumph. Treachery and defeatism apart, Hitler *cannot* be a danger. That he should finally win would be an impossible reversal of history, like a Jacobite restoration.

But is it not a sort of parricide for a person of my age (thirty-eight) to find fault with H. G. Wells? Thinking people who were born about the beginning of this century are in some sense Wells's own creation. How much influence any mere writer has, and especially a "popular" writer whose work takes effect quickly, is questionable, but I doubt whether anyone who was writing books between 1900 and 1920, at any rate in the English language, influenced the young so much. The minds of all of us, and therefore the physical world, would be perceptibly different if Wells had never existed. Only, just the singleness of mind, the one-sided imagination that made him seem like an inspired prophet in the Edwardian age, make him a shallow, inadequate thinker now. When Wells was young, the antithesis between science and reaction was not false. Society was ruled by narrow-minded, profoundly incurious people, predatory business men, dull squires, bishops, politicians who could quote Horace but had never heard of algebra. Science was faintly disreputable and religious belief obligatory. Traditionalism, stupidity, snobbishness, patriotism, superstition and love of war seemed to be all on the same side; there was need of someone who could state the opposite point of view. Back in the nineteen-hundreds it was a wonderful experience for a boy to discover H. G. Wells. There you were, in a world of pedants, clergymen and golfers, with your future employers exhorting you to "get on or get out", your parents systematically warping your sexual life, and your dull-witted schoolmasters sniggering over their Latin tags; and here was this wonderful man who could tell you about the inhabitants of the planets and the bottom of the sea, and who *knew* that the future was not going to be what respectable people imagined. A decade or so before aeroplanes were technically feasible Wells knew that within a little while men would be able to fly. He knew that because he himself *wanted* to be able to fly, and therefore felt sure that research in that direction would continue. On the other hand, even when I was a little boy, at a time when the Wright brothers had actually lifted their machine off the ground for fifty-nine seconds, the generally accepted opinion was that if God had meant us to fly He would have given us wings. Up to 1914 Wells was in the main a true prophet. In physical details his vision of the new world has been fulfilled to a surprising extent.

But because he belonged to the nineteenth century and to a non-military nation and class, he could not grasp the tremendous strength of the old world which was symbolised in his mind by fox-hunting Tories. He was, and still is, quite incapable of understanding that nationalism, religious bigotry and feudal loyalty are far more powerful forces than what he himself would describe as sanity. Creatures out of the Dark Ages have come marching into the present, and if they are ghosts they are at any rate ghosts which need a strong magic to lay them. The people who have shown the best understanding of Fascism are either those who have suffered under it or those who have a Fascist streak in themselves. A crude book like *The Iron Heel*, written nearly thirty years ago, is a truer prophecy of the future than either *Brave New World* or *The Shape of Things to Come*. If one had to choose among Wells's own contemporaries a writer who could stand towards him as a corrective, one might choose Kipling, who was not deaf to the evil voices of power and military "glory". Kipling would have understood the appeal of Hitler, or for that matter of Stalin, whatever his attitude towards them might be. Wells is too sane to understand the modern world. The succession of lower-middle-class novels which are his greatest achievement stopped short at the other war and never really began again, and since 1920 he has squandered his talents in slaying paper dragons. But how much it is, after all, to have any talents to squander.

The Art of Donald McGill

Horizon, September 1941

Who does not know the "comics" of the cheap stationers' windows, the penny or twopenny coloured post cards with their endless succession of fat women in tight bathing-dresses and their crude drawing and unbearable colours, chiefly hedge-sparrow's egg tint and Post Office red?

This question ought to be rhetorical, but it is a curious fact that many people seem to be unaware of the existence of these things, or else to have a vague notion that they are something to be found only at the seaside, like nigger minstrels or peppermint rock. Actually they are on sale everywhere – they can be bought at nearly any Woolworth's, for example – and they are evidently produced in enormous numbers, new series constantly appearing. They are not to be confused with the various other types of comic illustrated post card, such as the sentimental ones dealing with puppies and kittens or the Wendyish, sub-pornographic ones which exploit the love-affairs of children. They are a *genre* of their own, specialising in very "low" humour, the mother-in-law, baby's nappy, policemen's boots type of joke, and distinguishable from all the other kinds by having no artistic pretensions. Some half-dozen publishing houses issue them, though the people who draw them seem not to be numerous at any one time.

I have associated them especially with the name of Donald McGill because he is not only the most prolific and by far the best of contemporary post card artists, but also the most representative, the most perfect in the tradition. Who Donald McGill is, I do not know. He is apparently a trade name, for at least one series of post cards is issued simply as "The Donald McGill Comics", but he is also unquestionably a real person with a style of drawing which is recognisable at a glance. Anyone who examines his post cards in bulk will notice that many of them are not despicable even as drawings, but it would be mere dilettantism to pretend that they have any direct æsthetic value. A comic post card is simply an illustration to a joke, invariably a "low" joke, and it stands or falls by its ability to raise a laugh. Beyond that it has only "ideological" interest. McGill is a clever draughtsman with a real caricaturist's touch in the drawing of faces, but the special value of his post cards is that they are so completely typical. They represent, as it were, the norm of the comic post card. Without being in the least imitative, they are exactly what comic post cards have been any time these last forty years, and from them the meaning and purpose of the whole *genre* can be inferred.

374

Get hold of a dozen of these things, preferably McGill's – if you pick out from a pile the ones that seem to you funniest, you will probably find that most of them are McGill's – and spread them out on a table. What do you see?

Your first impression is of overpowering vulgarity. This is quite apart from the ever-present obscenity, and apart also from the hideousness of the colours. They have an utter lowness of mental atmosphere which comes out not only in the nature of the jokes but, even more, in the grotesque, staring, blatant quality of the drawings. The designs, like those of a child, are full of heavy lines and empty spaces, and all the figures in them, every gesture and attitude, are deliberately ugly, the faces grinning and vacuous, the women monstrously parodied, with bottoms like Hottentots. Your second impression, however, is of indefinable familiarity. What do these things remind you of? What are they so like? In the first place, of course, they remind you of the barely different post cards which you probably gazed at in your childhood. But more than this, what you are really looking at is something as traditional as Greek tragedy, a sort of sub-world of smacked bottoms and scrawny mothers-in-law which is a part of Western European consciousness. Not that the jokes, taken one by one, are necessarily stale. Not being debarred from smuttiness, comic post cards repeat themselves less often than the joke columns in reputable magazines, but their basic subject-matter, the *kind* of joke they are aiming at, never varies. A few are genuinely witty, in a Max Millerish style. Examples:

"I like seeing experienced girls home."
"But I'm not experienced!"
"You're not home yet!"

"I've been struggling for years to get a fur coat. How did you get yours?"
"I left off struggling."

JUDGE: "You are prevaricating, sir. Did you or did you not sleep with this woman?"
CO-RESPONDENT: "Not a wink, my lord!"

In general, however, they are not witty but humorous, and it must be said for McGill's post cards, in particular, that the drawing is often a good deal funnier than the joke beneath it. Obviously the outstanding characteristic of comic post cards is their obscenity, and I must discuss that more fully later. But I give here a rough analysis of their habitual subject-matter, with such explanatory remarks as seem to be needed:

Sex. – More than half, perhaps three-quarters, of the jokes are sex jokes, ranging from the harmless to the all but unprintable. First favourite is probably the illegitimate baby. Typical captions: "Could you exchange this lucky charm for a baby's feeding-bottle?" "She didn't ask me to the christening, so I'm not going to the wedding." Also newlyweds, old maids, nude statues and women in bathing-dresses. All of these are *ipso facto* funny, mere mention of them being enough to raise a laugh. The cuckoldry joke is very seldom exploited, and there are no references to homosexuality.

Conventions of the sex joke:

(i) Marriage only benefits the women. Every man is plotting seduction and every woman is plotting marriage. No woman ever remains unmarried voluntarily.

(ii) Sex-appeal vanishes at about the age of twenty-five. Well-preserved and good-looking people beyond their first youth are never represented. The amorous honeymooning couple reappear as the grim-visaged wife and shapeless, moustachioed, red-nosed husband, no intermediate stage being allowed for.

Home life. – Next to sex, the henpecked husband is the favourite joke. Typical caption: "Did they get an X-ray of your wife's jaw at the hospital?" – "No, they got a moving picture instead."

Conventions:

(i) There is no such thing as a happy marriage.

(ii) No man ever gets the better of a woman in argument.

Drunkenness. – Both drunkeness and teetotalism are *ipso facto* funny.

Conventions:

(i) All drunken men have optical illusions.

(ii) Drunkenness is something peculiar to middle-aged men. Drunken youths or women are never represented.

W. C. jokes. – There is not a large number of these. Chamberpots are *ipso facto* funny, and so are public lavatories. A typical post card, captioned "A Friend in Need", shows a man's hat blown off his head and disappearing down the steps of a ladies' lavatory.

Inter-working-class snobbery. – Much in these post cards suggests that they are aimed at the better-off working class and poorer middle class. There are many jokes turning on malapropisms, illiteracy, dropped aitches and the rough manners of slum-dwellers. Countless post cards show draggled hags of the stage-charwoman type exchanging "unladylike" abuse. Typical repartee: "I wish you were a statue and I was a pigeon!" A certain number produced since the war treat evacuation from the anti-evacuee angle. There are the usual jokes about tramps, beggars and criminals, and the comic maidservant appears fairly frequently. Also the comic navvy, bargee, etc.; but there are no anti Trade-Union jokes. Broadly speaking, everyone with much over or much under £5 a week is regarded as laughable. The "swell" is almost as automatically a figure of fun as the slum-dweller.

Stock figures. – Foreigners seldom or never appear. The chief locality joke is the Scotsman, who is almost inexhaustible. The lawyer is always a swindler, the clergyman always a nervous idiot who says the wrong thing. The "knut" or "masher" still appears, almost as in Edwardian days, in out-of-date-looking evening-clothes and an opera hat, or even with spats and a knobby cane. Another survival is the Suffragette, one of the big jokes of the pre-1914 period and too valuable to be relinquished. She has reappeared, unchanged in physical appearance, as the Feminist lecturer or Temperance fanatic. A feature of the last few years is the complete absence of anti-Jew post cards. The "Jew joke", always somewhat more ill-natured than the "Scotch joke", disappeared abruptly soon after the rise of Hitler.

Politics. – Any contemporary event, cult or activity which has comic possibilities (for example, "free love", feminism, A.R.P., nudism) rapidly finds it way into the picture post cards, but their general atmosphere is extremely old-fashioned.

The implied political outlook is a Radicalism appropriate to about the year 1900. At normal times they are not only not patriotic, but go in for a mild guying of patriotism, with jokes about "God save the King", the Union Jack, etc. The European situation only began to reflect itself in them at some time in 1939, and first did so through the comic aspects of A.R.P. Even at this date few post cards mention the war except in A.R.P. jokes (fat woman stuck in the mouth of Anderson shelter, Wardens neglecting their duty while young woman undresses at window she has forgotten to black out, etc. etc.). A few express anti-Hitler sentiments of a not very vindictive kind. One, not McGill's, shows Hitler, with the usual hyper-trophied backside, bending down to pick a flower. Caption: "What would *you* do, chums?" This is about as high a flight of patriotism as any post card is likely to attain. Unlike the two-penny weekly papers, comic post cards are not the product of any great monopoly company, and eventually they are not regarded as having any importance in forming public opinion. There is no sign in them of any attempt to induce an outlook acceptable to the ruling class.

Here one comes back to the outstanding, all-important feature of comic post cards – their obscenity. It is by this that everyone remembers them, and it is also central to their purpose, though not in a way that is immediately obvious.

A recurrent, almost dominant motif in comic post cards is the woman with the stuck-out behind. In perhaps half of them, or more than half, even when the point of the joke has nothing to do with sex, the same female figure appears, a plump "voluptuous" figure with the dress clinging to it as tightly as another skin and with breasts or buttocks grossly over-emphasised, according to which way it is turned. There can be no doubt that these pictures lift the lid off a very widespread repression, natural enough in a country whose women when young tend to be slim to the point of skimpiness. But at the same time the McGill post card – and this applies to all other post cards in this *genre* – is not intended as pornography but, a subtler thing, as a skit on pornography. The Hottentot figures of the women are caricatures of the Englishman's secret ideal, not portraits of it. When one examines McGill's post

378

cards more closely, one notices that his brand of humour only has meaning in relation to a fairly strict moral code. Whereas in papers like *Esquire*, for instance, or *La Vie Parisienne*, the imaginary background of the jokes is always promiscuity, the utter breakdown of all standards, the background of the McGill post card is marriage. The four leading jokes are nakedness, illegitimate babies, old maids and newly married couples, none of which would seem funny in a really dissolute or even "sophisticated" society. The post cards dealing with honeymoon couples always have the enthusiastic indecency of those village weddings where it is still considered screamingly funny to sew bells to the bridal bed. In one, for example, a young bridegroom is shown getting out of bed the morning after his wedding night. "The first morning in our own little home, darling!" he is saying; "I'll go and get the milk and paper and bring you up a cup of tea." Inset is a picture of the front doorstep; on it are four newspapers and four bottles of milk. This is obscene, if you like, but it is not immoral. Its implication – and this is just the implication [that] *Esquire* or the *New Yorker* would avoid at all costs – is that marriage is something profoundly exciting and important, the biggest event in the average human being's life. So also with jokes about nagging wives and tyrannous mothers-in-law. They do at least imply a stable society in which marriage is indissoluble and family loyalty taken for granted. And bound up with this is something I noted earlier, the fact that there are no pictures, or hardly any, of good-looking people beyond their first youth. There is the "spooning" couple and the middle-aged, cat-and-dog couple, but nothing in between. The liaison, the illicit but more or less decorous love-affair which used to be the stock joke of French comic papers, is not a post card subject. And this reflects, on a comic level, the working-class outlook which takes it as a matter of course that youth and adventure – almost, indeed, individual life – end with marriage. One of the few authentic class-differences, as opposed to class-distinctions, still existing in England is that the working classes age very much earlier. They do not live less long, provided that they survive their childhood, nor do they lose their physical activity earlier, but they do lose very early their youthful appearance. This fact is observable everywhere, but can be most easily verified by watching one of the higher age groups registering for military service; the middle- and upper-class members look, on average, ten years younger than the others. It is usual to attribute this to the harder lives that the working classes have to live, but it is doubtful whether any such difference now exists as would account for it. More probably the truth is that the working classes reach middle age earlier because they accept it earlier. For to look young after, say, thirty is largely a matter of wanting to do so. This generalisation is less true of the better-paid workers, especially those who live in council houses and labour-saving flats, but it is true enough even of them to point to a difference of outlook. And in this, as usual, they are more traditional, more in accord with the Christian past than the well-to-do women who try to stay young at forty by means of physical jerks, cosmetics and avoidance of child-bearing. The impulse to cling to youth at all costs, to attempt to preserve your sexual attraction, to see even in middle age a future for yourself and not merely for your children, is a thing of recent growth and has only precariously established itself. It will probably disappear again when our standard of living drops and our birth-rate rises. "Youth's a stuff will not endure" expresses the normal, traditional attitude. It is this ancient wisdom that McGill and his colleagues are reflecting, no doubt unconsciously, when they allow for no transition stage between the honeymoon couple and those glamourless figures, Mum and Dad.

I have said that at least half McGill's post cards are sex jokes, and a proportion, perhaps ten per cent., are far more obscene than anything else that is now printed in England. Newsagents are occasionally prosecuted for selling them, and there would be many more prosecutions if the broadest jokes were not invariably protected by double meanings. A single example will be enough to show how this is done. In one post card, captioned "They didn't believe her", a young woman is demonstrating, with her hands held apart, something about two feet long to a couple of open-mouthed acquaintances. Behind her on the wall is a stuffed fish in a glass case, and beside that is a photograph of a nearly naked athlete. Obviously it is not the fish that she is referring to, but this could never be proved. Now, it is doubtful whether there is any paper in England that would print a joke of this kind, and certainly there is no paper that does so habitually. There is an immense amount of pornography of a mild sort, countless illustrated papers cashing in on women's legs, but there is no popular literature specialising in the "vulgar", farcical aspect of sex. On the other hand, jokes exactly like McGill's are the ordinary small change of the revue and music-hall stage, and are also to be heard on the radio, at moments when the censor happens to be nodding. In England the gap between what can be said and what can be printed is rather exceptionally wide. Remarks and gestures which hardly anyone objects to on the stage would raise a public outcry if any attempt were made to reproduce them on paper. (Compare Max Miller's stage patter with his weekly column in the *Sunday Dispatch*.) The comic post cards are the only existing exception to this rule, the only medium in which really "low" humour is considered to be printable. Only in post cards and on the variety stage can the stuck-out behind, dog and lamp-post, baby's nappy type of joke be freely exploited. Remembering that, one sees what function these post cards, in their humble way, are performing.

What they are doing is to give expression to the Sancho Panza view of life, the attitude to life that Miss Rebecca West once summed up as "extracting as much fun as possible from smacking behinds in basement kitchens". The Don Quixote–Sancho Panza combination, which of course is simply the ancient dualism of body and soul in fiction form, recurs more frequently in the literature of the last four hundred years than can be explained by mere imitation. It comes up again and again, in endless variations, Bouvard and Pécuchet, Jeeves and Wooster, Bloom and Dedalus, Holmes and Watson (the Holmes–Watson variant is an exceptionally subtle one, because the usual physical characteristics of two partners have been transposed). Evidently it corresponds to something enduring in our civilisation, not in the sense that either character is to be found in a "pure" state in real life, but in the sense that the two principles, noble folly and base wisdom, exist side by side in nearly every human being. If you look into your own mind, which are you, Don Quixote or Sancho Panza? Almost certainly you are both. There is one part of you that wishes to be a hero or a saint, but another part of you is a little fat man who sees very clearly the advantages of staying alive with a whole skin. He is your unofficial self, the voice of the belly protesting against the soul. His tastes lie towards safety, soft beds, no work, pots of beer and women with "voluptuous" figures. He it is who punctures your fine attitudes and urges you to look after Number One, to be unfaithful to your wife, to bilk your debts, and so on and so forth. Whether you allow yourself to be influenced by him is a different question. But it is simply a lie to say that he is not part of you, just as it is a lie to say that Don Quixote is not part of you either, though most of what is said and written consists of one lie or the other, usually the first.

But though in varying forms he is one of the stock figures of literature, in real life, especially in the way society is ordered, his point of view never gets a fair hearing. There is a constant world-wide conspiracy to pretend that he is not there, or at least that he doesn't matter. Codes of law and morals, or religious systems, never have much room in them for a humorous view of life. Whatever is funny is subversive, every joke is ultimately a custard pie, and the reason why so large a proportion of jokes centre round obscenity is simply that all societies, as the price of survival, have to insist on a fairly high standard of sexual morality. A dirty joke is not, of course, a serious attack upon morality, but it is a sort of mental rebellion, a momentary wish that things were otherwise. So also with all other jokes, which always centre round cowardice, laziness, dishonesty or some other quality which society cannot afford to encourage. Society has always to demand a little more from human beings than it will get in practice. It has to demand faultless discipline and self-sacrifice, it must expect its subjects to work hard, pay their taxes, and be faithful to their wives, it must assume that men think it glorious to die on the battlefield and women want to wear themselves out with child-bearing. The whole of what one may call official literature is founded on such assumptions. I never read the proclamations of generals before battle, the speeches of führers and prime ministers, the solidarity songs of public schools and Left Wing political parties, national anthems, Temperance tracts, papal encyclicals and sermons against gambling and contraception, without seeming to hear in the background a chorus of raspberries from all the millions of common men to whom these high sentiments make no appeal. Nevertheless the high sentiments always win in the end, leaders who offer blood, toil, tears and sweat always get more out of their followers than those who offer safety and a good time. When it comes to the pinch, human beings are heroic. Women face childbed and the scrubbing brush, revolutionaries keep their mouths shut in the torture chamber, battleships go down with their guns still firing when their decks are awash. It is only that the other element in man, the lazy, cowardly, debt-bilking adulterer who is inside all of us, can never be suppressed altogether and needs a hearing occasionally.

The comic post cards are one expression of his point of view, a humble one, less important than the music halls, but still worthy of attention. In a society which is still basically Christian they naturally concentrate on sex jokes; in a totalitarian society, if they had any freedom of expression at all, they would probably concentrate on laziness or cowardice, but at any rate on the unheroic in one form or another. It will not do to condemn them on the ground that they are vulgar and ugly. That is exactly what they are meant to be. Their whole meaning and virtue is in their unredeemed lowness, not only in the sense of obscenity, but lowness of outlook in every direction what-ever. The slightest hint of "higher" influences would ruin them utterly. They stand for the worm's-eye view of life, for the music-hall world where marriage is a dirty joke or a comic disaster, where the rent is always behind and the clothes are always up the spout, where the lawyer is always a crook and the Scotsman always a miser, where the newlyweds make fools of themselves on the hideous beds of seaside lodging-houses and the drunken, red-nosed husbands roll home at four in the morning to meet the linen-nightgowned wives who wait for them behind the front door, poker in hand. Their existence, the fact that people want them, is symptomatically important. Like the music halls, they are a sort of saturnalia, a harmless rebellion against virtue. They express only one tendency in the human mind, but a tendency which is always there and will find its own outlet, like water. On the whole, human beings want to be good, but not too good, and not quite all the time. For:

"there is a just man that perishes in his righteousness, and there is a wicked man that prolongeth his life in his wickedness. Be not righteous over much; neither make thyself over wise; why shouldst thou destroy thyself? Be not overmuch wicked, neither be thou foolish: why shouldst thou die before thy time?"

In the past the mood of the comic post card could enter into the central stream of literature, and jokes barely different from McGill's could casually be uttered between the murders in Shakespeare's tragedies. That is no longer possible, and a whole category of humour, integral to our literature till 1800 or thereabouts, has dwindled down to these ill-drawn post cards, leading a barely legal existence in cheap stationers' windows. The corner of the human heart that they speak for might easily manifest itself in worse forms, and I for one should be sorry to see them vanish.

No, Not One

Review of *No Such Liberty* by Alex Comfort, *The Adelphi*, October 1941

Mr. Murry said years ago that the works of the best modern writers, Joyce, Eliot and the like, simply demonstrated the *impossibility* of great art in a time like the present, and since then we have moved onwards into a period in which any sort of *joy* in writing, any such notion as telling a story for the purpose of pure entertainment, has also become impossible. All writing nowadays is propaganda. If, therefore, I treat Mr. Comfort's novel as a tract, I am only doing what he himself has done already. It is a good novel as novels go at this moment, but the motive for writing it was not what Trollope or Balzac, or even Tolstoy, would have recognised as a novelist's impulse. It was written in order to put forward the "message" of pacifism, and it was to fit that "message" that the main incidents in it were devised. I think I am also justified in assuming that it is autobiographical, not in the sense that the events described in it have actually happened, but in the sense that the author identifies himself with the hero, thinks him worthy of sympathy and agrees with the sentiments that he expresses.

Here is the outline of the story. A young German doctor who has been convalescent for two years in Switzerland returns to Cologne a little before Munich to find that his wife has been helping war-resisters to escape from the country and is in imminent danger of arrest. He and she flee to Holland just in time to escape the massacre which followed on vom Rath's assassination. Partly by accident they reach England, he having been seriously wounded on the way. After his recovery he manages to get a hospital appointment, but at the outbreak of war he is brought before a tribunal and put in the B class of aliens. The reason for this is that he has declared that he will not fight against the Nazis, thinking it better to "overcome Hitler by love". Asked why he did not stay in Germany and overcome Hitler by love there, he admits that there is no answer. In the panic following on the invasion of the Low Countries he is arrested a few minutes after his wife has given birth to a baby and kept for a long time in a concentration camp where he cannot communicate with her and where the conditions of dirt, overcrowding, etc., are as bad as anything in Germany. Finally he is packed on to the "Arandora Star" (it is given another name, of course), sunk at sea, rescued, and put in another somewhat better camp. When he is at last released and makes contact with his wife, it is to find that she has been confined in another camp in which the baby has died of neglect and underfeeding. The book ends with the couple looking forward to sailing for America and hoping that the war fever will not by this time have spread there as well.

Now, before considering the implications of this story, just consider one or two facts which underlie the structure of modern society and which it is necessary to ignore if the pacifist "message" is to be accepted uncritically.

(i) Civilisation rests ultimately on coercion. What holds society together is not the policeman but the good will of common men, and yet that good will is powerless unless the policeman is there to back it up. Any government which refused to use violence in its own defence would cease almost immediately to exist, because it could be overthrown by any body of men, or even any individual, that was less scrupulous. Objectively, whoever is not on the side of the policeman is on the side of the criminal, and vice versa. In so far as it hampers the British war effort, British pacifism is on the side of the Nazis, and German pacifism, if it exists, is on the side of Britain and the U.S.S.R. Since pacifists have more freedom of action in countries where traces of democracy survive, pacifism can act more effectively against democracy than for it. Objectively the pacifist is pro-Nazi.

(ii) Since coercion can never be altogether dispensed with, the only difference is between degrees of violence. During the last twenty years there has been less violence and less militarism inside the English-speaking world than outside it, because there has been more money and more security. The hatred of war which undoubtedly characterises the English-speaking peoples is a reflection of their favoured position. Pacifism is only a considerable force in places where people feel themselves very safe, chiefly maritime states. Even in such places, turn-the-other-cheek pacifism only flourishes among the more prosperous classes, or among workers who have in some way escaped from their own class. The real working class, though they hate war and are immune to jingoism, are never really pacifist, because their life teaches them something different. To abjure violence it is necessary to have no experience of it.

If one keeps the above facts in mind one can, I think, see the events in Mr. Comfort's novel in truer perspective. It is a question of putting aside subjective feelings and trying to see whither one's actions will lead in practice and where one's motives ultimately spring from. The hero is a research worker – a pathologist. He has not been especially fortunate, he has a defective lung, thanks to the carrying-on of the British blockade into 1919, but in so far as he is a member of the middle class, doing work which he has chosen for himself, he is one of a few million favoured human beings who live ultimately on the degradation of the rest. He wants to get on with his work, wants to be out of reach of Nazi tyranny and regimentation, but he will not *act* against the Nazis in any other way than by running away from them. Arrived in England, he is in terror of being sent back to Germany, but refuses to take part in any physical effort to keep the Nazis out of England. His greatest hope is to get to America, with another three thousand miles of water between himself and the Nazis. He will only get there, you note, if British ships and planes protect him on the way, and having got there he will simply be living under the protection of American ships and planes instead of British ones. If he is lucky he will be able to continue with his work as a pathologist, at the same time keeping up his attitude of moral superiority towards the men who make his work possible. And underlying everything there will still be his position as a research-worker, a favoured person living ultimately on dividends which would cease forthwith if not extorted by the threat of violence.

I do not think this is an unfair summary of Mr. Comfort's book. And I think the relevant fact is that this story of a German doctor is written by an Englishman. The argument which is implied all the way through, and sometimes explicitly stated, that there is next to no difference between Britain and Germany, political persecution is as bad in one as in the other, those who fight against the Nazis always go Nazi themselves, would be more convincing if it came from a German. There are probably sixty thousand German refugees in this country, and there would be hundreds of thousands more if we had not meanly kept them out. Why did they come here if there is virtually no difference between the social atmosphere of the two countries? And how many of them have asked to go back? They have "voted with their feet", as Lenin put it. As I pointed out above, the comparative gentleness of the English-speaking civilisation is due to money and security, but that is not to say that no difference exists. Once let it be admitted, however, that there *is* a certain difference, that it matters quite a lot who wins, and the usual short-term case for pacifism falls to the ground. You can be explicitly pro-Nazi without claiming to be a pacifist – and there is a very strong case for the Nazis, though not many people in this country have the courage to utter it – but you can only pretend that Nazism and capitalist democracy are Tweedledum and Tweedledee if you also pretend that every horror from the June purge onwards has been cancelled by an exactly similar horror in England. In practice this has to be done by means of selection and exaggeration. Mr. Comfort is in effect claiming that a "hard case" is typical. The sufferings of this German doctor in a so-called democratic country are so terrible, he implies, as to wipe out every shred of moral justification for the struggle against Fascism. One must, however, keep a sense of proportion. Before raising a squeal because two thousand internees have only eighteen latrine buckets between them, one might as well remember what has happened these last few years in Poland, in Spain, in Czechoslovakia, etc., etc. If one clings too closely to the "those who fight against Fascism become Fascist themselves" formula, one is simply led into falsification. It is not true, for instance, as Mr. Comfort implies, that there is widespread spy-mania and that the prejudice against foreigners increases as the war gathers in momentum. The feeling against foreigners, which was one of the factors that made the internment of the refugees possible, has greatly died away, and Germans and Italians are now allowed into jobs that they would have been debarred from in peace time. It is not true, as he explicitly says, that the only difference between political persecution in England and in Germany is that in England nobody hears about it. Nor is it true that all the evil in our life is traceable to war or war-preparation. "I knew", he says, "that the English people, like the Germans, had never been happy since they put their trust in rearmament." Were they so conspicuously happy before? Is it not the truth, on the contrary, that rearmament, by reducing unemployment, made the English people somewhat happier, if anything? From my own observation I should say that, by and large, the war itself has made England happier; and this is not an argument in favour of war, but simply tells one something about the nature of so-called peace.

The fact is that the ordinary short-term case for pacifism, the claim that you can best frustrate the Nazis by not resisting them, cannot be sustained. If you don't resist the Nazis you are helping them, and ought to admit it. For then the long-term case for pacifism can be made out. You can say: "Yes, I know I am helping Hitler, and I want to help him. Let him conquer Britain, the U.S.S.R. and America. Let the Nazis rule the world; in the end they will grow into something different." That is at any rate a tenable position. It looks forward into human history, beyond the term of our own lives. What is not tenable is the idea that everything in the garden would be lovely *now* if only we stopped the wicked fighting, and that to fight back is exactly what the Nazis want us to do. Which does Hitler fear more, the P.P.U. or the R.A.F.? Which has he made greater efforts to sabotage? Is he trying to bring America into the war or to keep America out of it? Would he be deeply distressed if the Russians stopped fighting tomorrow? And after all, the history of the last ten years suggests that Hitler has a pretty shrewd idea of his own interests.

The notion that you can somehow defeat violence by submitting to it is simply a flight from fact. As I have said, it is only possible to people who have money and guns between themselves and reality. But why should they want to make this flight, in any case? Because, rightly hating violence, they do not wish to recognise that it is integral to modern society and that their own fine feelings and noble attitudes are all the fruit of injustice backed up by force. They do not want to learn where their incomes come from. Underneath this lies the hard fact, so difficult for many people to face, that individual salvation is not possible, that the choice before human beings is not, as a rule, between good and evil but between two evils. You can let the Nazis rule the world; that is evil; or you can overthrow them by war, which is also evil. There is no other choice before you, and whichever you choose you will not come out with clean hands. It seems to me that the text for our time is not "Woe to him through whom the evil cometh" but the one from which I took the title of this article, "There is not one that is righteous, no, not one". We have all touched pitch, we are all perishing by the sword. We do not have the chance, in a time like this, to say "Tomorrow we can all start being good". That is moon-shine. We only have the chance of choosing the lesser evil and of working for the establishment of a new kind of society in which common decency will again be possible. There is no such thing as neutrality in this war. The whole population of the world is involved in it, from the Esquimos to the Anda-manese, and since one must inevitably help one side or the other, it is better to know what one is doing and count the cost. Men like Darlan and Laval have at any rate had the courage to make their choice and proclaim it openly. The New Order, they say, must be established at all costs, and "il faut érabouiller l'Angleterre". Mr. Murry appears, at any rate at moments, to think likewise. The Nazis, he says, are "doing the dirty work of the Lord" (they certainly did an exceptionally dirty job when they attacked Russia), and we must be careful "lest in fighting against Hitler we are fighting against God". Those are not pacifist sentiments, since if carried to their logical conclusion they involve not only surrendering to Hitler but helping him in his various forthcoming wars, but they are at least straightforward and courageous. I do not myself see Hitler as the saviour, even the unconscious saviour, of humanity, but there is a strong case for thinking him so, far stronger than most people in England imagine. What there is no case for is to denounce Hitler and at the same time look down your nose at the people who actually keep you out of his clutches. That is simply a highbrow variant of British hypocrisy, a product of capitalism in decay, and the sort of thing for which Europeans, who at any rate understand the nature of a policeman and a dividend, justifiably despise us.

(George Orwell writes cogently and well against a kind of pacifism that was once prevalent but has almost ceased to exist. It has been sweated out of the P.P.U. by keeping up with the dour reality. The number of former pacifist stalwarts who have dropped out is legion. There remain only those who (1) believe it as a matter of religious faith that we should "resist not evil" or (2) hold it as demonstrable to the imagination that Hitlerism is "the scourge of the Lord" – the destructive dynamic of this rotten civilisation: or they hold both together. To label them simply as "helping Hitler" is a simplification to which George Orwell, of all people, should not lend himself, because he must know to what sinister uses such a label can be put. We pacifists claim that we are striving, against tremendous odds, to prepare the only kind of resistance that can ultimately prevail against Hitlerism. We do not look down our noses at the honest men who fight. They are the vanguard, but we – preposterous as it may sound – are the last reserves. We "know what we fight for and love what we know" as surely, and I believe more surely, than George Orwell of the Home Guard does. Anyway, when it comes, as it will, to the last ditch we shall be found in it together: and the streamlined men on the other side will not be all Germans.)

Editor

1942

Money and Guns

'Through Eastern Eyes,' 20 January 1942

Very often as you walk down the London streets you see side by side on a newspaper poster the news of a great battle in Russia or the Far East, and the news of a football match or a boxing contest. And maybe on a wall nearby you will see side by side a Government advertisement urging young women to join the A.T.S., and another advertisement, generally rather grimy and tattered-looking, urging the public to buy beer or whisky. And perhaps that makes you stop and ask yourself – how can a people fighting for its life find time for football matches? Isn't there something contradictory in urging people to give up their lives to their country's service, and at the same time urging them to spend their money on luxuries? But this raises the question of recreation in wartime which is not quite so simple as it looks.

A people at war – and that means, as a rule, a people that is working harder and under more trying conditions than usual – cannot get on without rest and amusement. Probably these things are more necessary in wartime than at ordinary times. And yet when you are fighting you cannot afford to waste precious material on luxury goods, because this is primarily a war of machines, and every scrap of metal used up in making gramophones, or every pound of silk used up in making stockings, means less metal for guns and aeroplanes, or less silk for parachutes and barrage balloons. We laughed at Marshal Goering when he said, some years before the war, that Germany had to choose between guns and butter, but he was only wrong in the sense that there was no need for Germany to prepare aggression against her neighbours and thus plunge the whole world into war. Once war has started, every nation has to choose between guns and butter. It is merely a question of proportion. How many guns do you need to defeat the enemy? And how much butter do you need to keep your home population healthy and contented?

393

Granted that everyone is sufficiently fed and rested, the main problem of war is to divert expenditure from consumption goods to armaments. The working population, including the armed forces when they are on leave or off duty, still need their amusements, [and] as far as possible they must make do with amusements that do not use up much material or labour-time. Also, since England is an island and shipping is very precious, they must make do as far as possible with amusements that do not waste imported materials. Beyond a certain point you cannot lower the spending capacity of the population. As a result of taxation very large incomes have almost ceased to exist, and wages have not kept up with prices, but the spending power of the mass of the people has perhaps actually increased, because there is no longer any unemployment. Boys and girls of eighteen are now earning the wages of adults, and when they have paid for their board and lodging they still have something over every week. The question is, how are they to spend it without diverting much-needed labour to the manufacture of luxury goods? In the answer to this question one can see how the war is altering the habits and even the tastes of the British people.

To make a rough division: the luxuries which have to be discarded in wartime are the more elaborate kinds of food and drink, fashionable clothes, cosmetics and scents – all of which either demand a great deal of labour or use up rare imported materials – personal service, and unnecessary journeys, which use up such precious imported things as rubber and petrol. The amusements which can be encouraged, on the other hand, are games, sports, music, the radio, dancing, literature and the arts generally. Most of these are things in which you create your amusement for yourself, rather than paying other people to create it for you. If you have two hours to spare, and if you spend it in walking, swimming, skating, or playing football, according to the time of year, you have not used up any material or made any call on the nation's labour power. On the other hand, if you use those two hours in sitting in front of the fire and eating chocolates, you are using up coal which has to be dug out of the ground and carried to you by rail, and sugar and cocoa beans which have to be transported half across the world. In the cases of a good many unnecessary luxuries, the government diverted expenditure in the right direction by simply cutting off supplies. For nearly two years no one in Britain has seen a banana, for example, sugar is not too plentiful, oranges are seen only from time to time, matches are cut down to the point at which no one ever wastes a match, travelling is much restricted, clothes are rationed fairly strictly.

At the same time, people who are working all day cannot altogether create their amusements for themselves. It is desirable, therefore, that they should concentrate on the kind of recreation that can be enjoyed communally without much wastage of labour. That brings me back to the thing I mentioned a few minutes ago – the newspaper report of a football match side by side with the report of a battle. Is it not all wrong that ten thousand citizens of a nation at war should spend two hours in watching a football match? Not really, for the only labour they are monopolising is the labour of the twenty-two players. If it is an amateur football match, as it usually is nowadays – a match between the Army and the R.A.F. for instance – those players are not even being paid. And if it is a local match, the ten thousand spectators have not even wasted any coal or petrol in getting there. They have merely had two hours' recreation, which they are probably in need of, almost without any expenditure of labour or material.

You can see from this the way in which the mere necessity of war is bringing about in the English people a more creative attitude towards their amusements. Something symptomatic of this happened during the big air raids. The people who were penned up in the Tube shelters for hours together had nothing to do, and there were no ready-made amusements available. They had to amuse themselves, so they improvised amateur concerts, which were sometimes surprisingly good and successful. But what is perhaps more significant than this is the greatly increased interest in literature that has appeared during the last two years. There has been an enormous increase in reading, partly owing to the great numbers of men who are in the army in lonely camps, where they have little or nothing to do in their spare time. Reading is one of the cheapest and least wasteful recreations in existence. An edition of tens of thousands of copies of a book does not use up as much paper or labour as a single day's issue of one newspaper, and each copy of the book may pass through hundreds of hands before it goes back to the pulping mill. But just because the habit of reading has vastly increased and people cannot read without educating themselves in the process, the average intellectual level of the books published has markedly risen. Great literature, no doubt, is not being produced, but the average book which the ordinary man reads is a better book than it would have been three years ago. One phenomenon of the war has been the enormous sale of Penguin Books, Pelican Books and other cheap editions, most of which would have been regarded by the general public as impossibly highbrow a few years back. And this in turn reacts on the newspapers, making them more serious and less sensational than they were before. It probably reacts also on the radio, and will react in time on the cinema.

Parallel with this is the revival of amateur sport and amateur theatricals in the armed forces, and of recreations, such as gardening, which are not only not wasteful, but actually productive. Though England is not primarily an agricultural country, the English people are fond of gardening, and since the war the government has done everything to encourage this. Allotments are available almost everywhere, even in the big towns, and thousands of men who might otherwise have spent their evenings playing darts in the pub, now spend them in growing vegetables for their families. Similarly, women who in peace time might have been sitting in the cinematograph are now sitting at home knitting socks and helmets for Russian soliders.

Before the war there was every incentive for the general public to be wasteful, at least so far as their means allowed. Everyone was trying to sell something to everyone else, and the successful man, so it was imagined, was the man who sold the most goods and got the most money in return. We have learned now, however, that money is valueless in itself, and only goods count. In learning it we have had to simplify our lives and fall back more and more on the resources of our own minds instead of on synthetic pleasures manufactured for us in Hollywood or by the makers of silk stockings, alcohol and chocolates. And under the pressure of that necessity we are rediscovering the simple pleasures – reading, walking, gardening, swimming, dancing, singing – which we had half forgotten in the wasteful years before the war.

Rudyard Kipling

Horizon, February 1942

It was a pity that Mr. Eliot should be so much on the defensive in the long essay with which he prefaces this selection of Kipling's poetry, but it was not to be avoided, because before one can even speak about Kipling one has to clear away a legend that has been created by two sets of people who have not read his works. Kipling is in the peculiar position of having been a by-word for fifty years. During five literary generations every enlightened person has despised him, and at the end of that time nine-tenths of those enlightened persons are forgotten and Kipling is in some sense still there. Mr. Eliot never satisfac- torily explains this fact, because in answering the shallow and familiar charge that Kipling is a "Fascist", he falls into the opposite error of defending him where he is not defensible. It is no use pretending that Kipling's view of life, as a whole, can be accepted or even forgiven by any civilised person. It is no use claiming, for instance, that when Kipling describes a British soldier beating a "nigger" with a cleaning rod in order to get money out of him, he is acting merely as a reporter and does not necessarily approve what he describes. There is not the slightest sign anywhere in Kipling's work that he disapproves of that kind of conduct – on the contrary, there is a definite strain of sadism in him, over and above the brutality which a writer of that type has to have. Kipling *is* a jingo imperialist, he *is* morally insensitive and æsthetically disgusting. It is better to start by admitting that, and then to try to find out why it is that he survives while the refined people who have sniggered at him seem to wear so badly.

And yet the "Fascist" charge has to be answered, because the first clue to any understanding of Kipling, morally or politi- cally, is the fact that he was *not* a Fascist. He was further from being one than the most humane or the most "progressive" person is able to be nowadays. An interesting instance of the way in which quotations are parroted to and fro without any attempt to look up their context or discover their meaning is the line from "Recessional", "Lesser breeds without the Law". This line is always good for a snigger in pansy-left circles. It is assumed as a matter of course that the "lesser breeds" are "natives", and a mental picture is called up of some pukka sahib in a pith helmet kicking a coolie. In its context the sense of the line is almost the exact opposite of this. The phrase "lesser breeds" refers almost certainly to the Germans, and especially the pan-German writers, who are "without the Law" in the sense of being lawless, not in the sense of being powerless. The whole poem, conventionally thought of as an orgy of boasting, is a denunciation of power politics, British as well as German. Two stanzas are worth quoting (I am quoting this as politics, not as poetry):

> "If, drunk with sight of power, we loose
> Wild tongues that have not Thee in awe,
> Such boastings as the Gentiles use,
> Or lesser breeds without the Law –
> Lord God of Hosts, be with us yet,
> Lest we forget – lest we forget!

> "For heathen heart that puts her trust
> In reeking tube and iron shard,
> All valiant dust that builds on dust,
> And guarding, calls not Thee to guard,
> For frantic boast and foolish word –
> Thy mercy on Thy People, Lord!"

Much of Kipling's phraseology is taken from the Bible, and no doubt in the second stanza he had in mind the text from Psalm cxxvii.: "Except the Lord build the house, they labour in vain that build it; except the Lord keep the city, the watchman waketh but in vain." It is not a text that makes much impression on the post-Hitler mind. No one, in our time, believes in any sanction greater than military power; no one believes that it is possible to overcome force except by greater force. There is no "law", there is only power. I am not saying that that is a true belief, merely that it is the belief which all modern men do actually hold. Those who pretend otherwise are either intellectual cowards, or power-worshippers under a thin disguise, or have simply not caught up with the age they are living in. Kipling's outlook is pre-Fascist. He still believes that pride comes before a fall and that the gods punish *hubris*. He does not foresee the tank, the bombing plane, the radio and the secret police, or their psychological results.

But in saying this, does not one unsay what I said above about Kipling's jingoism and brutality? No, one is merely saying that the nineteenth-century imperialist outlook and the modern gangster outlook are two different things. Kipling belongs very definitely to the period 1885–1902. The Great War and its aftermath embittered him, but he shows little sign of having learned anything from any event later than the Boer War. He was the prophet of British Imperialism in its expansionist phase (even more than his poems, his solitary novel, *The Light that Failed*, gives you the atmosphere of that time) and also the unofficial historian of the British Army, the old mercenary army which began to change its shape in 1914. All his confidence, his bouncing vulgar vitality, sprang out of limitations which no Fascist or near-Fascist shares.

Kipling spent the later part of his life in sulking, and no doubt it was political disappointment rather than literary vanity that accounted for this. Somehow history had not gone according to plan. After the greatest victory she had ever known, Britain was a lesser world power than before, and Kipling was quite acute enough to see this. The virtue had gone out of the classes he idealised, the young were hedonistic or disaffected, the desire to paint the map red had evaporated. He could not understand what was happening, because he had never had any grasp of the economic forces underlying imperial expansion. It is notable that Kipling does not seem to realise, any more than the average soldier or colonial administrator, that an empire is primarily a money-making concern. Imperialism as he sees it is a sort of forcible evangelising. You turn a Gatling gun on a mob of unarmed "natives", and then you establish "the Law", which includes roads, railways and a court-house. He could not foresee, therefore, that the same motives which brought the Empire into existence would end by destroying it. It was the same motive, for example, that caused the Malayan jungles to be cleared for rubber estates, and which now causes those estates to be handed over intact to the Japanese. The modern totalitarians know what they are doing, and the nineteenth-century English did not know what they were doing. Both attitudes have their advantages, but Kipling was never able to move forward from one into the other. His outlook, allowing for the fact that after all he was an artist, was that of the salaried bureaucrat who despises the "box-wallah" and often lives a lifetime without realising that the "box-wallah" calls the tune.

But because he identifies himself with the official class, he does possess one thing which "enlightened" people seldom or never possess, and that is a sense of responsibility. The middle-class Left hate him for this quite as much as for his cruelty and vulgarity. All left-wing parties in the highly industrialised countries are at bottom a sham, because they make it their business to fight against something which they do not really wish to destroy. They have internationalist aims, and at the same time they struggle to keep up a standard of life with which those aims are incompatible. We all live by robbing Asiatic coolies, and those of us who are "enlightened" all maintain that those coolies ought to be set free; but our standard of living, and hence our "enlightenment", demands that the robbery shall continue. A humanitarian is always a hypocrite, and Kipling's understanding of this is perhaps the central secret of his power to create telling phrases. It would be difficult to hit off the one-eyed pacifism of the English in fewer words than in the phrase, "making mock of uniforms that guard you while you sleep". It is true that Kipling does not understand the economic aspect of the relationship between the highbrow and the blimp. He does not see that the map is painted red chiefly in order that the coolie may be exploited. Instead of the coolie he sees the Indian Civil Servant; but even on that plane his grasp of function, of who protects whom, is very sound. He sees clearly that men can only be highly civilised while other men, inevitably less civilised, are there to guard and feed them.

How far does Kipling really identify himself with the administrators, soldiers and engineers whose praises he sings? Not so completely as is sometimes assumed. He had travelled very widely while he was still a young man, he had grown up with a brilliant mind in mainly philistine surroundings, and some streak in him that may have been partly neurotic led him to prefer the active man to the sensitive man. The nineteenth-century Anglo-Indians, to name the least sympathetic of his idols, were at any rate people who did things. It may be that all that they did was evil, but they changed the face of the earth (it is instructive to look at a map of Asia and compare the railway system of India with that of the surrounding countries), whereas they could have achieved nothing, could not have maintained themselves in power for a single week, if the normal Anglo-Indian outlook had been that of, say, E. M. Forster. Tawdry and shallow though it is, Kipling's is the only literary picture that we possess of nineteenth-century Anglo-India, and he could only make it because he was just coarse enough to be able to exist and keep his mouth shut in clubs and regimental messes. But he did not greatly resemble the people he admired. I know from several private sources that many of the Anglo-Indians who were Kipling's contemporaries did not like or approve of him. They said, no doubt truly, that he knew nothing about India, and on the other hand, he was from their point of view too much of a highbrow. While in India he tended to mix with "the wrong" people, and because of his dark complexion he was wrongly suspected of having a streak of Asiatic blood. Much in his development is traceable to his having been born in India and having left school early. With a slightly different background he might have been a good novelist or a superlative writer of music-hall songs. But how true is it that he was a vulgar flag-waver, a sort of publicity agent for Cecil Rhodes? It is true, but it is not true that he was a yes-man or a time-server. After his early days, if then, he never courted public opinion. Mr. Eliot says that what is held against him is that he expressed unpopular views in a popular style. This narrows the issue by assuming that "unpopular" means unpopular with the intelligentsia, but it is a fact that Kipling's "message" was one that the big public did not want, and, indeed, has never accepted. The mass of the people, in the 'nineties as now, were anti-militarist, bored by the Empire, and only unconsciously patriotic. Kipling's official admirers are and were the "service" middle class, the people who read *Blackwood's*. In the stupid early years of this century, the blimps, having at last discovered someone who could be called a poet and who was on their side, set Kipling on a pedestal, and some of his more sententious poems, such as "If", were given almost Biblical status. But it is doubtful whether the blimps have ever read him with attention, any more than they have read the Bible. Much of what he says they could not possibly approve. Few people who have criticised England from the inside have said bitterer things about her than this gutter patriot. As a rule it is the British working class that he is attacking, but not always. That phrase about "the flannelled fools at the wicket or the muddied oafs at the goals" sticks like an arrow to this day, and it is aimed at the Eton and Harrow match as well as the Cup-Tie Final. Some of the verses he wrote about the Boer War have a curiously modern ring, so far as their subject-matter goes. "Stellenbosch", which must have been written about 1902, sums up what every intelligent infantry officer was saying in 1918, or is saying now, for that matter.

Kipling's romantic ideas about England and the Empire might not have mattered if he could have held them without having the class-prejudices which at that time went with them. If one examines his best and most representative work, his soldier poems, especially *Barrack-Room Ballads*, one notices that what more than anything else spoils them is an underlying air of patronage. Kipling idealises the army officer, especially the junior officer, and that to an idiotic extent, but the private soldier, though lovable and romantic, has to be a comic. He is always made to speak in a sort of stylised Cockney, not very broad but with all the aitches and final "g's" carefully omitted. Very often the result is as embarrassing as the humorous recitation at a church social. And this accounts for the curious fact that one can often improve Kipling's poems, make them less facetious and less blatant, by simply going through them and translating them from Cockney into standard speech. This is especially true of his refrains, which often have a truly lyrical quality. Two examples will do (one is about a funeral and the other about a wedding):

> "So it's knock out your pipes and follow me!
> And it's finish up your swipes and follow me!
> Oh, hark to the big drum calling,
> Follow me – follow me home!"

and again:

> "Cheer for the Sergeant's wedding –
> Give them one cheer more!

> Grey gun-horses in the lando,
> And a rogue is married to a whore!"

Here I have restored the aitches, etc. Kipling ought to have known better. He ought to have seen that the two closing lines of the first of these stanzas are very beautiful lines, and that ought to have overriden his impulse to make fun of a working-man's accent. In the ancient ballads the lord and the peasant speak the same language. This is impossible to Kipling, who is looking down a distorting class-perspective, and by a piece of poetic justice one of his best lines is spoiled – for "follow me 'ome" is much uglier than "follow me home". But even where it makes no difference musically the facetiousness of his stage Cockney dialect is irritating. However, he is more often quoted aloud than read on the printed page, and most people instinctively make the necessary alterations when they quote him.

Can one imagine any private soldier, in the 'nineties or now, reading *Barrack-Room Ballads* and feeling that here was a writer who spoke for him? It is very hard to do so. Any soldier capable of reading a book of verse would notice at once that Kipling is almost unconscious of the class war that goes on in an army as much as elsewhere. It is not only that he thinks the soldier comic, but that he thinks him patriotic, feudal, a ready admirer of his officers and proud to be a soldier of the Queen. Of course that is partly true, or battles could not be fought, but "What have I done for thee, England, my England?" is essentially a middle-class query. Almost any working-man would follow it up immediately with "What has England done for me?" In so far as Kipling grasps this, he simply sets it down to "the intense selfishness of the lower classes" (his own phrase). When he is writing not of British but of "loyal" Indians he carries the "Salaam, sahib" motif to sometimes disgusting lengths. Yet it remains true that he has far more interest in the common soldier, far more anxiety that he shall get a fair deal, than most of the "liberals" of his day or our own. He sees that the soldier is neglected, meanly underpaid and hypocritically despised by the people whose incomes he safeguards. "I came to realise", he says in his posthumous memoirs, "the bare horrors of the private's life, and the unnecessary torments he endured."

He is accused of glorifying war, and perhaps he does so, but not in the usual manner, by pretending that war is a sort of football match. Like most people capable of writing battle poetry, Kipling had never been in battle, but his vision of war is realistic. He knows that bullets hurt, that under fire everyone is terrified, that the ordinary soldier never knows what the war is about or what is happening except in his own corner of the battlefield, and that British troops, like other troops, frequently run away:

"I 'eard the knives be'ind me, but I dursn't face my man,
Nor I don't know where I went to, 'cause I didn't stop to see,
Till I 'eard a beggar squealin' out for quarter as 'e ran,
An' I thought I knew the voice an' – it was me!"

Modernise the style of this, and it might have come out of one of the debunking war books of the nineteen-twenties. Or again:

"An' now the hugly bullets come peckin' through the dust,
An' no one wants to face 'em, but every beggar must;
So, like a man in irons, which isn't glad to go,
They moves 'em off by companies uncommon stiff an' slow."

Compare this with:

"Forward the Light Brigade!
Was there a man dismayed?
No! though the soldier knew
Someone had blundered."

If anything, Kipling overdoes the horrors, for the wars of his youth were hardly wars at all by our standards. Perhaps that is due to the neurotic strain in him, the hunger for cruelty. But at least he knows that men ordered to attack impossible objectives *are* dismayed, and also that fourpence a day is not a generous pension.

How complete or truthful a picture has Kipling left us of the long-service, mercenary army of the late nineteenth century? One must say of this, as of what Kipling wrote about nine-teenth-century Anglo-India, that it is not only the best but almost the only literary picture we have. He has put on record an immense amount of stuff that one could otherwise only gather from verbal tradition or from unreadable regimental histories. Perhaps his picture of army life seems fuller and more accurate than it is because any middle-class English person is likely to know enough to fill up the gaps. At any rate, reading the essay on Kipling that Mr. Edmund Wilson has just published or is just about to publish, I was struck by the number of things that are boringly familiar to us and seem to be barely intelligible to an American. But from the body of Kipling's early work there does seem to emerge a vivid and not seriously misleading picture of the old pre-machine-gun army – the sweltering barracks in Gibraltar or Lucknow, the red coats, the pipeclayed belts and the pillbox hats, the beer, the fights, the floggings, hangings and crucifixions, the bugle-calls, the smell of oats and horse-piss, the bellowing sergeants with foot-long moustaches, the bloody skirmishes, invariably mis-managed, the crowded troopships, the cholera-stricken camps, the "native" concubines, the ultimate death in the workhouse. It is a crude, vulgar picture, in which a patriotic music-hall turn seems to have got mixed up with one of Zola's gorier passages, but from it future generations will be able to gather some idea of what a long-term volunteer army was like. On about the same level they will be able to learn something of British India in the days when motorcars and refrigerators were unheard of. It is an error to imagine that we might have had better books on these subjects if, for example, George Moore, or Gissing, or Thomas Hardy, had had Kipling's opportunities. That is the kind of accident that cannot happen. It was not possible that nineteenth-century England should produce a book like *War and Peace*, or like Tolstoy's minor stories of army life, such as *Sebastopol* or *The Cossacks*, not because the talent was necessar-ily lacking but because no one with sufficient sensitiveness to write such books would ever have made the appropriate con-tacts. Tolstoy lived in a great military empire in which it seemed natural for almost any young man of family to spend a few years in the army, whereas the British Empire was and still is demilitarised to a degree which continental observers find almost incredible. Civilised men do not readily move away from the centres of civilisation, and in most languages there is a great dearth of what one might call colonial literature. It took a very improbable combination of circumstances to produce Kipling's gaudy tableau, in which Private Ortheris and Mrs. Hauksbee pose against a background of palm trees to the sound of temple bells, and one necessary circumstance was that Kipling himself was only half civilised.

Kipling is the only English writer of our time who has added phrases to the language. The phrases and neologisms which we take over and use without remembering their origin do not always come from writers we admire. It is strange, for instance, to hear the Nazi broadcasters referring to the Russian soldiers as "robots", thus unconsciously borrowing a word from a Czech democrat whom they would have killed if they could have laid hands on him. Here are half a dozen phrases coined by Kipling which one sees quoted in leaderettes in the gutter press or overhears in saloon bars from people who have barely heard his name. It will be seen that they all have a certain characteristic in common:

"East is East, and West is West.
The white man's burden.
What do they know of England who only England know?
The female of the species is more deadly than the male.
Somewhere East of Suez.
Paying the Dane-geld."

There are various others, including some that have outlived their context by many years. The phrase "killing Kruger with your mouth", for instance, was current till very recently. It is also possible that it was Kipling who first let loose the use of the word "Huns" for Germans; at any rate he began using it as soon as the guns opened fire in 1914. But what the phrases I have listed above have in common is that they are all of them phrases which one utters semi-derisively (as it might be "For I'm to be Queen o' the May, mother, I'm to be Queen o' the May"), but which one is bound to make use of sooner or later. Nothing could exceed the contempt of the *New Statesman*, for instance, for Kipling, but how many times during the Munich period did the *New Statesman* find itself quoting that phrase about paying the Dane-geld? The fact is that Kipling, apart from his snack-bar wisdom and his gift for packing much cheap picturesque-ness into a few words ("Palm and Pine" – "East of Suez" –

"The Road to Mandalay"), is generally talking about things that are of urgent interest. It does not matter, from this point of view, that thinking and decent people generally find themselves on the other side of the fence from him. "White man's burden" instantly conjures up a real problem, even if one feels that it ought to be altered to "black man's burden". One may disagree to the middle of one's bones with the political attitude implied in "The Islanders", but one cannot say that it is a frivolous attitude. Kipling deals in thoughts which are both vulgar and permanent. This raises the question of his special status as a poet, or verse-writer.

Mr. Eliot describes Kipling's metrical works as "verse" and not "poetry", but adds that it is "*great* verse", and further qualifies this by saying that a writer can only be described as a "great verse-writer" if there is some of his work "of which we cannot say whether it is verse or poetry". Apparently Kipling was a versifier who occasionally wrote poems, in which case it was a pity that Mr. Eliot did not specify these poems by name. The trouble is that whenever an æsthetic judgement on Kipling's work seems to be called for, Mr. Eliot is too much on the defensive to be able to speak plainly. What he does not say, and what I think one ought to start by saying in any discussion of Kipling, is that most of Kipling's verse is so horribly vulgar that it gives one the same sensation as one gets from watching a third-rate music-hall performer recite "The Pigtail of Wu Fang Fu" with the purple limelight on his face, *and yet* there is much of it that is capable of giving pleasure to people who know what poetry means. At his worst, and also his most vital, in poems like "Gunga Din" or "Danny Deever", Kipling is almost a shameful pleasure, like the taste for cheap sweets that some people secretly carry into middle life. But even with his best passages one has the same sense of being seduced by something spurious, and yet unquestionably seduced. Unless one is merely a snob and a liar it is impossible to say that no one who cares for poetry could get any pleasure out of such lines as:

"For the wind is in the palm-trees, and the temple-bells they say,
'Come you back, you British soldier; come you back to Mandalay!'"

and yet those lines are not poetry in the same sense as "Felix Randal" or "When icicles hang by the wall" are poetry. One can, perhaps, place Kipling more satisfactorily than by juggling with the words "verse" and "poetry", if one describes him simply as a good bad poet. He is as a poet what Harriet Beecher Stowe was as a novelist. And the mere existence of work of this kind, which is perceived by generation after generation to be vulgar and yet goes on being read, tells one something about the age we live in.

There is a great deal of good bad poetry in English, all of it, I should say, subsequent to 1790. Examples of good bad poems – I am deliberately choosing diverse ones – are "The Bridge of Sighs", "When All the World is Young, Lad", "The Charge of the Light Brigade", Bret Harte's "Dickens in Camp", "The Burial of Sir John Moore", "Jenny Kissed Me", "Keith of Ravelston", "Casabianca". All of these reek of sentimentality, and yet – not these particular poems, perhaps, but poems of this kind, are capable of giving true pleasure to people who can see clearly what is wrong with them. One could fill a fair-sized anthology with good bad poems, if it were not for the significant fact that good bad poetry is usually too well known to be worth reprinting. It is no use pretending that in an age like our own, "good" poetry can have any genuine popularity. It is, and must be, the cult of a very few people, the least tolerated of the arts. Perhaps that statement needs a certain amount of qualification. True poetry can sometimes be acceptable to the mass of the people when it disguises itself as something else. One can see an example of this in the folk-poetry that England still possesses, certain nursery rhymes and mnemonic rhymes, for instance, and the songs that soldiers make up, including the words that go to some of the bugle-calls. But in general ours is a civilisation in which the very word "poetry" evokes a hostile snigger or, at best, the sort of frozen disgust that most people feel when they hear the word "God". If you are good at playing the concertina you could probably go into the nearest public bar and get yourself an appreciative audience within five minutes. But what would be the attitude of that same audience if you suggested reading them Shakespeare's sonnets, for instance? Good bad poetry, however, can get across to the most unpromising audiences if the right atmosphere has been

worked up beforehand. Some months back Churchill produced a great effect by quoting Clough's "Endeavour" in one
of his broadcast speeches. I listened to this speech among
people who could certainly not be accused of caring for poetry,
and I am convinced that the lapse into verse impressed them
and did not embarrass them. But not even Churchill could
have got away with it if he had quoted anything much better
than this.

In so far as a writer of verse can be popular, Kipling has been
and probably still is popular. In his own lifetime some of his
poems travelled far beyond the bounds of the reading public,
beyond the world of school prize-days, Boy Scout singsongs,
limp-leather editions, pokerwork and calendars, and out into
the yet vaster world of the music halls. Nevertheless, Mr. Eliot
thinks it worth while to edit him, thus confessing to a taste
which others share but are not always honest enough to mention. The fact that such a thing as good bad poetry can exist is a
sign of the emotional overlap between the intellectual and the
ordinary man. The intellectual *is* different from the ordinary
man, but only in certain sections of his personality, and even
then not all the time. But what is the peculiarity of a good
bad poem? A good bad poem is a graceful monument to
the obvious. It records in memorable form — for verse is a
mnemonic device, among other things — some emotion
which very nearly every human being can share. The merit
of a poem like "When All the World is Young, Lad" is that,
however sentimental it may be, its sentiment is "true" sentiment in the sense that you are bound to find yourself thinking
the thought it expresses sooner or later; and then, if you happen
to know the poem, it will come back into your mind and seem
better than it did before. Such poems are a kind of rhyming
proverb, and it is a fact that definitely popular poetry is usually
gnomic or sententious. One example from Kipling will do:

> "White hands cling to the tightened rein,
> Slipping the spur from the booted heel,
> Tenderest voices cry 'Turn again,'
> Red lips tarnish the scabbarded steel,
> High hopes faint on a warm hearth-stone —
> He travels the fastest who travels alone."

There is a vulgar thought vigorously expressed. It may not be true, but at any rate it is a thought that everyone thinks. Sooner or later you will have occasion to feel that he travels the fastest who travels alone, and there the thought is, ready made and, as it were, waiting for you. So the chances are that, having once heard this line, you will remember it.

One reason for Kipling's power as a good bad poet I have already suggested – his sense of responsibility, which made it possible for him to have a world-view, even though it happened to be a false one. Although he had no direct connection with any political party, Kipling was a Conservative, a thing that does not exist nowadays. Those who now call themselves Conservatives are either Liberals, Fascists or the accomplices of Fascists. He identified himself with the ruling power and not with the opposition. In a gifted writer this seems to us strange and even disgusting, but it did have the advantage of giving Kipling a certain grip on reality. The ruling power is always faced with the question, "In such and such circumstances, what would you *do*?", whereas the opposition is not obliged to take responsibility or make any real decisions. Where it is a permanent and pensioned opposition, as in England, the quality of its thought deteriorates accordingly. Moreover, anyone who starts out with a pessimistic, reactionary view of life tends to be justified by events, for Utopia never arrives and "the gods of the copybook headings", as Kipling himself put it, always return. Kipling sold out to the British governing class, not financially but emotionally. This warped his political judgement, for the British ruling class were not what he imagined, and it led him into abysses of folly and snobbery, but he gained a corresponding advantage from having at least tried to imagine what action and responsibility are like. It is a great thing in his favour that he is not witty, not "daring", has no wish to *épater les bourgeois*. He dealt largely in platitudes, and since we live in a world of platitudes, much of what he said sticks. Even his worst follies seem less shallow and less irritating than the "enlightened" utterances of the same period, such as Wilde's epigrams or the collection of cracker-mottoes at the end of *Man and Superman*.

The Re-discovery of Europe
'Literature Between the Wars,' 1, BBC Eastern Service, 10 March 1942

When I was a small boy and was taught history – very badly, of course, as nearly everyone in England is – I used to think of history as a sort of long scroll with thick black lines ruled across it at intervals. Each of these lines marked the end of what was called a "period," and you were given to understand that what came afterwards was completely different from what had gone before. It was almost like a clock striking. For instance, in 1499 you were still in the Middle Ages, with knights in plate armour riding at one another with long lances, and then suddenly the clock struck 1500, and you were in something called the Renaissance, and everyone wore ruffs and doublets and was busy robbing treasure ships on the Spanish Main. There was another very thick black line drawn at the year 1700. After that it was the Eighteenth Century, and people suddenly stopped being Cavaliers and Roundheads and became extraordinarily elegant gentlemen in knee breeches and three-cornered hats. They all powdered their hair, took snuff and talked in exactly balanced sentences, which seemed all the more stilted because for some reason I didn't understand they pronounced most of their S's as F's. The whole of history was like that in my mind – a series of completely different periods changing abruptly at the end of a century, or at any rate at some sharply defined date.

Now in fact these abrupt transitions don't happen, either in politics, manners or literature. Each age lives on into the next – it must do so, because there are innumerable human lives spanning every gap. And yet there are such things as periods. We feel our own age to be deeply different from, for instance, the early Victorian period, and an eighteenth-century sceptic like Gibbon would have felt himself to be among savages if you had suddenly thrust him into the Middle Ages. Every now and again something happens – no doubt it's ultimately traceable to changes in industrial technique, though the connection isn't always obvious – and the whole spirit and tempo of life changes, and people acquire a new outlook which reflects itself in their political behaviour, their manners, their architecture, their literature and everything else. No one could write a poem like Gray's "Elegy in a Country Churchyard" today, for instance, and no one could have written Shakespeare's lyrics in the age of Gray. These things belong in different periods. And though, of course, those black lines across the page of history are an illusion, there are times when the transition is quite rapid, sometimes rapid enough for it to be possible to give it a fairly accurate date. One can say without grossly over-simplifying, "About such and such a year, such-and-such a style of literature began." If I were asked for the starting-point of modern literature – and the fact that we still call it "modern" shows that this particular period isn't finished yet – I should put it at 1917, the year in which T. S. Eliot published his poem "Prufrock." At any rate that date isn't more than five years out. It is certain that about the end of the last war the literary climate changed, the typical writer came to be quite a different person, and the best books of the subsequent period seemed to exist in a different world from the best books of only four or five years before.

To illustrate what I mean, I ask you to compare in your mind two poems which haven't any connection with one another, but which will do for purposes of comparison because each is entirely typical of its period. Compare, for instance, one of Eliot's characteristic earlier poems with a poem of Rupert Brooke, who was, I should say, the most admired English poet in the years before 1914. Perhaps the most representative of Brooke's poems are his patriotic ones, written in the early days of the war. A good one is the sonnet beginning "If I should die, think only this of me: That there's some corner of a foreign field That is for ever England." Now read side by side with this one of Eliot's Sweeney poems; for example, "Sweeney among the Nightingales" – you know, "The circles of the stormy moon Slide westward toward the River Plate." As I say, these poems have no connection in theme or anything else, but it's possible in a way to compare them, because each is representative of its own time and each seemed a good poem when it was written. The second still seems a good poem now.

Not only the technique but the whole spirit, the implied outlook on life, the intellectual paraphernalia of these poems are abysmally different. Between the young Englishman with a public school and university background, going out enthusiastically to die for his country with his head full of English lanes, wild roses and what not, and the rather jaded cosmopolitan American, getting glimpses of eternity in some slightly squalid restaurant in the Latin Quarter of Paris, there is a huge gulf. That might be only an individual difference, but the point is that you come upon rather the same kind of difference, a difference that raises the same comparisons, if you read side by side almost any two characteristic writers of the two periods. It's the same with the novelists as with the poets – Joyce, Lawrence, Huxley and Wyndham Lewis on the one side, and Wells, Bennett and Galsworthy on the other, for instance. The newer writers are immensely less prolific than the older ones, more scrupulous, more interested in technique, less optimistic, and, in general, less confident in their attitude to life. But more than that, you have all the time the feeling that their intellectual and æsthetic background is different, rather as you do when you compare a nineteenth-century French writer such as, say, Flaubert, with a nineteenth-century English writer like Dickens. The Frenchman seems enormously more sophisticated than the Englishman, though he isn't necessarily a better writer because of that. But let me go back a bit and consider what English literature was like in the days before 1914.

The giants of that time were Thomas Hardy – who, however, had stopped writing novels some time earlier – Shaw, Wells, Kipling, Bennett, Galsworthy and, somewhat different from the others – not an Englishman, remember, but a Pole who chose to write in English – Joseph Conrad. There were also A. E. Housman (The Shropshire Lad), and the various Georgian poets, Rupert Brooke and the others. There were also the innumerable comic writers, Sir James Barrie, W.W. Jacobs, Barry Pain and many others. If you read all those writers I've just mentioned, you would get a not misleading picture of the English mind before 1914. There were other literary tendencies at work, there were various Irish writers, for instance, and in a quite different vein, much nearer to our own time, there was the American novelist Henry James, but the main stream was the one I've indicated. But what is the common denominator between writers who are individually as far apart as Bernard Shaw and A. E. Housman, or Thomas Hardy and H. G. Wells? I think the basic fact about nearly all

413

English writers of that time is their complete unawareness of anything outside the contemporary English scene. Some are better writers than others, some are politically conscious and some aren't, but they are all alike in being untouched by any European influence. This is true even of novelists like Bennett and Galsworthy, who derived in a very superficial sense from French and perhaps Russian models. All of these writers have a background of ordinary, respectable, middle-class English life, and a half-conscious belief that this kind of life will go on for ever, getting more humane and more enlightened all the time. Some of them, like Hardy and Housman, are pessimistic in outlook, but they all at least believe that what is called progress would be desirable if it were possible. Also – a thing that generally goes with lack of æsthetic sensibility – they are all uninterested in the past, at any rate the remote past. It is very rare to find in a writer of that time anything we should now regard as a sense of history. Even Thomas Hardy, when he attempts a huge poetic drama based on the Napoleonic wars – *The Dynasts*, it's called – sees it all from the angle of a patriotic school textbook. Still more, they're all æsthetically uninterested in the past. Arnold Bennett, for instance, wrote a great deal of literary criticism, and it's clear that he is almost unable to see any merit in any book earlier than the nineteenth century, and indeed hasn't much interest in any writer other than his contemporaries. To Bernard Shaw most of the past is simply a mess which ought to be swept away in the name of progress, hygiene, efficiency and what-not. H. G. Wells, though later on he was to write a history of the world, looks at the past with the same sort of surprised disgust as a civilised man contemplating a tribe of cannibals. All of these people, whether they liked their own age or not, at least thought it was better than what had gone before, and took the literary standards of their own time for granted. The basis of all Bernard Shaw's attacks on Shakespeare is really the charge – quite true, of course – that Shakespeare wasn't an enlightened member of the Fabian Society. If any of these writers had been told that the writers immediately subsequent to them would hark back to the English poets of the sixteenth and seventeenth centuries, to the French poets of the mid-nineteenth century and to the philosophers of the Middle Ages, they would have thought it a kind of dilettantism.

But now look at the writers who begin to attract notice – some of them had begun writing rather earlier, of course – immediately after the last war: Joyce, Eliot, Pound, Huxley, Lawrence, Wyndham Lewis. Your first impression of them, compared with the others – this is true even of Lawrence – is that something has been punctured. To begin with, the notion of progress has gone by the board. They don't any longer believe that progress happens or that it ought to happen, they don't any longer believe that men are getting better and better by having lower mortality rates, more effective birth control, better plumbing, more aeroplanes and faster motorcars. Nearly all of them are homesick for the remote past, or some period of the past, from D. H. Lawrence's ancient Etruscans onwards. All of them are politically reactionary, or at best are uninterested in politics. None of them cares twopence about the various hole-and-corner reforms which had seemed important to their predecessors, such as female suffrage, temperance reform, birth control or prevention of cruelty to animals. All of them are more friendly, or at least less hostile, towards the Christian churches than the previous generation had been. And nearly all of them seem to be æsthetically alive in a way that hardly any English writer since the Romantic Revival had been.

Now, one can best illustrate what I have been saying by means of individual examples, that is, by comparing outstanding books of more or less comparable type in the two periods. As a first example, compare H. G. Wells's short stories – there's a large number of them collected together under the title of *The Country of the Blind* – with D. H. Lawrence's short stories, such as those in *England, My England* and *The Prussian Officer*.

This isn't an unfair comparison, since each of these writers was at his best, or somewhere near his best, in the short story, and each of them was expressing a new vision of life which had a great effect on the young of his generation. The ultimate subject-matter of H. G. Wells's stories is, first of all, scientific discovery, and beyond that the petty snobberies and tragicom-edies of contemporary English life, especially lower-middle-class life. His basic "message," to use an expression I don't like, is that Science can solve all the ills that humanity is heir to, but that man is at present too blind to see the possibility of his own powers. The alternation between ambitious Utopian themes, and light comedy, almost in the W. W. Jacobs vein, is very marked in Wells's work. He writes about journeys to the moon and to the bottom of the sea, and also he writes about small shopkeepers dodging bankruptcy and fighting to keep their end up in the frightful snobbery of provincial towns. The connecting link is Wells's belief in Science. He is saying all the time, if only that small shopkeeper could acquire a scientific outlook, his troubles would be ended. And of course he believes that this is going to happen, probably in the quite near future. A few more million pounds for scientific research, a few more generations scientifically educated, a few more superstitions shovelled into the dustbin, and the job is done. Now, if you turn to Lawrence's stories, you don't find this belief in Science − rather a hostility towards it, if anything − and you don't find any marked interest in the future, certainly not in a rationalised hedonistic future of the kind that Wells deals in. You don't even find the notion that the small shopkeeper, or any of the other victims of our society, would be better off if he were better educated. What you do find is a persistent implication that man has thrown away his birthright by becoming civilised. The ultimate subject-matter of nearly all Lawrence's books is the failure of contemporary men, especially in the English-speaking countries, to live their lives intensely enough. Naturally he fixes first on their sexual lives, and it is a fact that most of Lawrence's books centre round sex. But he isn't, as is sometimes supposed, demanding more of what people call sexual liberty. He is completely disillusioned about that, and he hates the so-called sophistication of Bohemian intellectuals just as much as he hates the puritanism of the middle class. What he is saying is simply that modern men aren't fully alive, whether they fail through having too narrow standards or through not having any. Granted that they can be fully alive, he doesn't much care what social or political or economic system they live under. He takes the structure of existing society, with its class distinctions and so on, almost for granted in his stories, and doesn't show any very urgent wish to change it. All he asks is that men shall live more simply, nearer to the earth, with more sense of the magic of things like vegetation, fire, water, sex, blood, than they can in a world of celluloid and concrete where the gramophones never stop playing. He imagines – quite likely he is wrong – that savages or primitive peoples live more intensely than civilised men, and he builds up a mythical figure who is not far from being the Noble Savage over again. Finally, he projects these virtues on to the Etruscans, an ancient pre-Roman people who lived in northern Italy and about whom we don't, in fact, know anything. From the point of view of H. G. Wells all this abandonment of Science and Progress, this actual wish to revert to the primitive, is simply heresy and nonsense. And yet one must admit that whether Lawrence's view of life is true or whether it is perverted, it is at least an advance on the Science-worship of H. G. Wells or the shallow Fabian progressivism of writers like Bernard Shaw. It is an advance in the sense that it results from seeing through the other attitude and not from falling short of it. Partly that was the effect of the war of 1914–18, which succeeded in debunking both Science, Progress and civilised man. Progress had finally ended in the biggest massacre in history, Science was something that created bombing planes and poison gas, civilised man, as it turned out, was ready to behave worse than any savage when the pinch came. But Lawrence's discontent with modern machine civilisation would have been the same, no doubt, if the war of 1914–18 had never happened.

Now I want to make another comparison, between James Joyce's great novel *Ulysses*, and John Galsworthy's at any rate very large novel sequence, *The Forsyte Saga*. This time it isn't a fair comparison, in effect it's a comparison between a good book and a bad one, and it also isn't quite correct chronologically, because the later parts of *The Forsyte Saga* were written in the nineteen-twenties. But the parts of it that anyone is likely to remember were written about 1910, and for my purpose the comparison is relevant, because both Joyce and Galsworthy are making efforts to cover an enormous canvas and get the spirit and social history of a whole epoch between the covers of a single book. *The Man of Property* may not seem to us *now* a very profound criticism of society, but it seemed so to its contemporaries, as you can see by what they wrote about it.

Joyce wrote *Ulysses* in the seven years between 1914 and 1921, working away all through the war, to which he probably paid little or no attention, and earning a miserable living as a teacher of languages in Italy and Switzerland. He was quite ready to work seven years in poverty and complete obscurity so as to get his great book onto paper. But what is it that it was so urgently important for him to express? Parts of *Ulysses* aren't very easily intelligible, but from the book as a whole you get two main impressions. The first is that Joyce is interested to the point of obsession with technique. This has been one of the main characteristics of modern literature, though more recently it has been a diminishing one. You get a parallel development in the plastic arts, painters, and even sculptors, being more and more interested in the material they work on, in the brush-marks of a picture, for instance, as against its design, let alone its subject-matter. Joyce is interested in mere words, the sounds and associations of words, even the pattern of words on the paper, in a way that wasn't the case with any of the preceding generation of writers, except to some extent the Polish-English writer, Joseph Conrad. With Joyce you are back to the conception of style, of fine writing, of poetic writing, perhaps even to purple passages. A writer like Bernard Shaw, on the other hand, would have said as a matter of course that the sole use of words is to express exact meanings as shortly as possible. And apart from this technical obsession, the other main theme of *Ulysses* is the squalor, even the meaninglessness of modern life after the triumph of the machine and the collapse of religious belief. Joyce – an Irishman, remember, and it's worth noting that the best English writers during the nineteen-twenties were in many cases not Englishmen – is writing as a Catholic who has lost his faith but has retained the mental framework which he acquired in his Catholic childhood and boyhood. *Ulysses*, which is a very long novel, is a description of the events of a single day, seen mostly through the eyes of an out-at-elbow Jewish commercial traveller. At the time when the book came out there was a great outcry and Joyce was accused of deliberately exploiting the sordid, but as a matter of fact, considering what everyday human life is like when you contemplate it in detail, it doesn't seem that he overdid either the squalor or the silliness of the day's events. What you do feel all through, however, is the conviction from which Joyce can't escape, that the whole of this modern world which he is describing has no meaning in it now that the teachings of the Church are no longer credible. He is yearning after the religious faith which the two or three generations preceding him had had to fight against in the name of religious liberty. But finally the main interest of the book is technical. Quite a considerable proportion of it consists of pastiche or parody – parodies of everything from the Irish legends of the Bronze Age down to contemporary newspaper reports. And one can see there that, like all the characteristic writers of his time, Joyce doesn't derive from the English nineteenth-century writers but from Europe and from the remoter past. Part of his mind is in the Bronze Age, another part in the Middle Ages, another part in the England of Elizabeth. The twentieth century, with its hygiene and its motor-cars, doesn't particularly appeal to him.

Now look again at Galsworthy's book, *The Forsyte Saga*, and you see how comparatively narrow its range is. I have said already that this isn't a fair comparison, and indeed from a strictly literary point of view it's a ridiculous one, but it will do as an illustration, in the sense that both books are intended to give a comprehensive picture of existing society. Well, the thing that strikes one about Galsworthy is that though he's trying to be iconoclastic, he has been utterly unable to move his mind outside the wealthy bourgeois society he is attacking. With only slight modifications he takes all its values for granted. All he conceives to be wrong is that human beings are a little too inhumane, a little too fond of money, and æsthetically not quite sensitive enough. When he sets out to depict what he conceives as the desirable type of human being, it turns out to be simply a cultivated, humanitarian version of the upper-middle-class rentier, the sort of person who in those days used to haunt picture galleries in Italy and subscribe heavily to the Society for the Prevention of Cruelty to Animals. And this fact – the fact that Galsworthy hasn't any really deep aversion to the social types he thinks he is attacking – gives you the clue to his weakness. It is, that he has no contact with anything outside contemporary English society. He may think he doesn't like it, but he is part of it. Its money and security, the ring of battleships that separated it from Europe, have been too much for him. At the bottom of his heart he despises foreigners, just as much as any illiterate business man in

Manchester. The feeling you have with Joyce or Eliot, or even Lawrence, that they have got the whole of human history inside their heads and can look outwards from their own place and time towards Europe and the past, isn't to be found in Galsworthy or in any characteristic English writer in the period before 1914.

Finally, one more brief comparison. Compare almost any of H. G. Wells's Utopia books, for instance *A Modern Utopia*, or *The Dream*, or *Men Like Gods*, with Aldous Huxley's *Brave New World*. Again it's rather the same contrast, the contrast between the over-confident and the deflated, between the man who believes innocently in Progress and the man who happens to have been born later and has therefore lived to see that Progress, as it was conceived in the early days of the aeroplane, is just as much of a swindle as reaction.

The obvious explanation of this sharp difference between the dominant writers before and after the war of 1914–18, is the war itself. Some such development would have happened in any case as the insufficiency of modern materialistic civilisation revealed itself, but the war speeded the process, partly by showing how very shallow the veneer of civilisation is, partly by making England less prosperous and therefore less isolated. After 1918 you couldn't live in such a narrow and padded world as you did when Britannia ruled not only the waves but also the markets. One effect of the ghastly history of the last twenty years has been to make a great deal of ancient literature seem much more modern. A lot that has happened in Germany since the rise of Hitler might have come straight out of the later volumes of Gibbon's *Decline and Fall of the Roman Empire*. Recently I saw Shakespeare's *King John* acted – the first time I had seen it, because it is a play which isn't acted very often. When I had read it as a boy it seemed to me archaic, something dug out of a history book and not having anything to do with our own time. Well, when I saw it acted, what with its intrigues and double-crossings, non-aggression pacts, quislings, people changing sides in the middle of a battle, and what-not, it seemed to me extraordinarily up to date. And it was rather the same thing that happened in the literary development between 1910 and 1920. The prevailing temper of the time gave a new reality to all sorts of themes which had seemed out of date and puerile when Bernard Shaw and his Fabians were – so they thought – turning the world into a sort of super garden city. Themes like revenge, patriotism, exile, persecution, race hatred, religious faith, loyalty, leader-worship, suddenly seemed real again. Tamerlane and Genghis Khan seem credible figures now, and Machiavelli seems a serious thinker, as they didn't in 1910. We have got out of a backwater and back into history. I haven't an unqualified admiration for the writers of the early nineteen-twenties, the writers among whom Eliot and Joyce are the chief names. Those who followed them have had to undo a great deal of what they did. Their revulsion from a shallow conception of progress drove them politically in the wrong direction, and it isn't an accident that Ezra Pound, for instance, is now shouting anti-Semitism on the Rome radio. But one must concede that their writings are more grown-up, and have a wider scope, than what went immediately before them. They broke the cultural circle in which England had existed for something like a century. They re-established contact with Europe, and they brought back the sense of history and the possibility of tragedy. On that basis all subsequent English literature that matters twopence has rested, and the development that Eliot and the others started, back in the closing years of the last war, has not yet run its course.

Review of *The Sword and the Sickle* by Mulk Raj Anand

Horizon, July 1942

In this war we have one weapon which our enemies cannot use against us, and that is the English language. Several other languages are spoken by larger numbers of people, but there is no other that has any claim to be a world-wide *lingua franca*. The Japanese administrators in the Philippines, the Chinese delegates in India, the Indian nationalists in Berlin, are all obliged to do their business in English. Therefore, although Mr. Anand's novel would still be interesting on its own merits if it had been written by an Englishman, it is impossible to read it without remembering every few pages that it is also a cultural curiosity. The growth, especially during the last few years, of an English-language Indian literature is a strange phenomenon, and it will have its effect on the post-war world, if not on the outcome of the war itself.

This novel is a sequel to *The Village* and *Across the Black Waters*. The Sikh sepoy who has fought in France and spent years as a prisoner in Germany comes home to find himself – partly because he is suspected of disaffection and partly because that is the normal fate of all soldiers in all wars – cheated out of the reward that he had imagined that he was fighting for. The rest of the story deals mostly with the peasant movement and the beginnings of the Indian Communist Party. Now, any book about India written by an Indian must at this date almost unavoidably be the story of a grievance, and I notice that Mr. Anand has already got himself into trouble by what is wrongly described as his bitterness. In reality, the book's comparative lack of bitterness is a roundabout demonstration of the English 'bad conscience' towards India. In a novel on the same subject by an English intellectual, what would you expect to find? An endless masochistic denunciation of his own race, and a series of traditional caricatures of Anglo-Indian society, with its un-bearable club life, its chota pegs, etc., etc. In the scene as the Indian sees it, however, the English hardly enter. They are merely a permanent evil, something taken almost for granted, like the climate, and though the ultimate objective is to get rid of British rule, it is almost forgotten among the weaknesses and internecine struggles of the revolutionaries themselves. European characters barely appear in the story – a reminder that in India only about one person in a thousand is technically white – and of the few that do it cannot be said that they are treated worse than the other characters. They are not treated sympa-thetically either, for on the whole the characterization is harsh and derisive (to give just one example, Mr. Gandhi's head is described as resembling 'a raw purple turnip'), and the whole book is full of the Indian melancholy and of the horribly ugly, degrading scenes which offend one's eyes all the time in the starved countries of the East. Although it ends on a compara-tively hopeful note this novel does not break the rule that books about India are depressing. Probably they must be so, quite apart from the question-mark they raise in the English conscience, because while the world remains in anything like its present shape the central problem of India, its poverty, is not soluble. How much of the special atmosphere of English-language Indian literature is due to its subject-matter is uncertain, but in reading Mr. Anand's work, or that of Ahmed Ali and several others, it is difficult not to feel that by this time another dialect, comparable perhaps to Irish-English, has grown up. One quotation will do to illustrate this:

'Conscious of his responsibility for the misadventures into which he had led them, Lalu bent down and strained to lever the dead bodies with trembling hands. A sharp odour of decomposing flesh shot up to his nostrils from Chandra's body, while his hands were smeared with blood from Nandu's neck. He sat up imagining the smell to be a whiff of the foul virulence of bacterial decay, ensuing from the vegetation of the forest through which they had come. But, as he bent down again, there was no disguising the stink of the corpse. And, in a flash, he realized that though Nandu's blood was hot now, it would soon be cold and the body would stink if it was carried all the way to Allahabad.'

There is a vaguely unEnglish flavour about this ('shot up to his nostrils', for instance, is not quite an English idiom), and yet it is obviously the work of a man who is not only at ease with the English language but thinks in it and would probably write in it by preference. This raises the question of the future, if any, of English-language Indian literature. At present English is to a great extent the official and business language of India: five million Indians are literate in it and millions more speak a debased version of it; there is a huge English-language Indian Press, and the only English magazine devoted wholly to poetry is edited by Indians. On average, too, Indians write and even pronounce English far better than any European race. Will this state of affairs continue? It is inconceivable that the present relationship between the two countries will last much longer, and when it vanishes the economic inducements for learning English will also tend to disappear. Presumably, therefore, the fate of the English language in Asia is either to fade out or to survive as a pidgin language useful for business and technical purposes. It might survive, in dialect form, as the mother-tongue of the small Eurasian community, but it is difficult to believe that it has a literary future. Mr. Anand and Ahmed Ali are much better writers than the average run of English novelists, but they are not likely to have many successors. Why, then, is it that their books have at this moment an importance that goes beyond their literary merit? Partly because they are interpreting Asia to the West, but more, I think, because they act as a Westernizing influence among their own countrymen. And at present there are reasons why the second function is more important than the first.

Anyone who has to deal in propaganda knows that a sudden change came over the Indian scene as soon as Japan entered the war. Many, perhaps most, Indian intellectuals are emotionally pro-Japanese. From their point of view Britain is the enemy, China means nothing to them, Russia is an object of lip-service only. But is it the case that the Indian anti-British intelligentsia actually wishes to see China permanently enslaved, the Soviet Union destroyed, Europe a Nazi concentration camp? No, that is not fair either: it is merely that the nationalism of defeated peoples is necessarily revengeful and short-sighted. If you discuss this question with an Indian you get an answer something like this: 'Half of me is a Socialist but the other half is a Nationalist. I know what Fascism means, I know very well that I ought to be on your side, but I hate your people so much that if we can get rid of them I hardly care what happens afterwards. I tell you that there are moments when all I want is to see China, Japan and India get together and destroy Western civilization, not only in Asia, but in Europe.' This outlook is widespread among the coloured peoples. Its emotional roots are obvious enough, the various disguises in which it is wrapped are easily seen through, but it is there, and it contains a great danger, to us and to the world. The only answer to the self-pity and race-hatred common among Indians is to point out that others besides Indians are oppressed. The only answer to nationalism is international Socialism, and the contact of Indians – to a lesser extent, of all Asiatics – with Socialist literature and Socialist thought generally is through the English language. As a general rule, Indians are reliably anti-Fascist in proportion as they are Westernized. That is why at the beginning of this review I described the English language as a weapon of war. It is a funnel for ideas deadly to the

Fascist view of life. Mr. Anand does not like us very much, and some of his colleagues hate us very bitterly; but so long as they voice their hatred in English they are in a species of alliance with us, and an ultimate decent settlement with the Indians whom we have wronged but also helped to awaken remains possible.

T. S. Eliot

Poetry (London), October–November 1942

There is very little in Eliot's later work that makes any deep impression on me. That is a confession of something lacking in myself, but it is not, as it may appear at first sight, a reason for simply shutting up and saying no more, since the change in my own reaction probably points to some external change which is worth investigating.

I know a respectable quantity of Eliot's earlier work by heart. I did not sit down and learn it, it simply stuck in my mind as any passage of verse is liable to do when it has really rung the bell. Sometimes after only one reading it is possible to remember the whole of a poem of, say, twenty or thirty lines, the act of memory being partly an act of reconstruction. But as for these three latest poems, I suppose I have read each of them two or three times since they were published, and how much do I verbally remember? 'Time and the bell have buried the day,' 'At the still point of the turning world,' 'The vast waters of the petrel and the porpoise,' and bits of the passage beginning 'O dark dark dark. They all go into the dark.' (I don't count 'In my end is my beginning,' which is a quotation.) That is about all that sticks in my head of its own accord. Now one cannot take this as proving that *Burnt Norton* and the rest are worse than the more memorable early poems, and one might even take it as proving the contrary, since it is arguable that that which lodges itself most easily in the mind is the obvious and even the vulgar. But it is clear that something has departed, some kind of current has been switched off, the later verse does not *contain* the earlier, even if it is claimed as an improvement upon it. I think one is justified in explaining this by a deterioration in Mr. Eliot's subject-matter. Before going any further, here are a couple of extracts, just near enough to one another in meaning to be comparable. The first is the conclud-ing passage of *The Dry Salvages*:

> And right action is freedom
> From past and future also.
> For most of us, this is the aim
> Never here to be realised;
> Who are only undefeated
> Because we have gone on trying;
> We, content at the last
> If our temporal reversion nourish
> (Not too far from the yew-tree)
> The life of significant soil.

Here is an extract from a much earlier poem:

> Daffodil bulbs instead of balls
> Stared from the sockets of the eyes!
> He knew that thought clings round dead limbs
> Tightening its lusts and luxuries.
>   . . .
> He knew the anguish of the marrow
> The ague of the skeleton;
> No contact possible to flesh
> Allayed the fever of the bone.

The two passages will bear comparison since they both deal with the same subject, namely death. The first of them follows upon a longer passage in which it is explained, first of all, that scientific research is all nonsense, a childish superstition on the same level as fortune-telling, and then that the only people ever likely to reach an understanding of the universe are saints, the rest of us being reduced to 'hints and guesses.' The keynote of the closing passage is, 'resignation.' There is a 'meaning' in life and also in death; unfortunately we don't know what it is, but the fact that it exists should be a comfort to us as we push up the crocuses, or whatever it is that grows under the yew trees in country churchyards. But now look at the other two stanzas I have quoted. Though fathered on to somebody else, they probably express what Mr. Eliot himself felt about death at that time, at least in certain moods. They are not voicing resignation. On the contrary, they are voicing the pagan attitude towards death, the belief in the next world as a shadowy place full of thin, squeaking ghosts, envious of the living, the belief that however bad life may be, death is worse. This conception of death seems to have been general in antiquity, and in a sense it is general now. 'The anguish of the marrow, the ague of the skeleton,' Horace's famous ode *Eheu fugaces*, and Bloom's unuttered thoughts during Paddy Dignam's funeral, are all very much of a muchness. So long as man regards himself as an individual, his attitude towards death must be one of simple resentment. And however unsatisfactory this may be, if it is intensely felt it is more likely to produce good literature than a religious faith which is not really *felt* at all, but merely accepted against the emotional grain. So far as they can be compared, the two passages I have quoted seem to me to bear this out. I do not think it is questionable that the second of them is superior as verse, and also more intense in feeling, in spite of a tinge of burlesque.

What are these three poems, *Burnt Norton* and the rest, 'about'? It is not so easy to say what they are about, but what they appear on the surface to be about is certain localities in England and America with which Mr. Eliot has ancestral connections. Mixed up with this is a rather gloomy musing upon the nature and purpose of life, with the rather indefinite conclusion I have mentioned above. Life has a 'meaning,' but it is not a meaning one feels inclined to grow lyrical about; there is faith, but not much hope, and certainly no enthusiasm. Now the subject-matter of Mr. Eliot's early poems was very different from this. They were not hopeful, but neither were they depressed or depressing. If one wants to deal in antitheses, one might say that the later poems express a melancholy faith and the earlier ones a glowing despair. They were based on the dilemma of modern man, who despairs of life and does not want to be dead, and on top of this they expressed the horror of an over-civilised intellectual confronted with the ugliness and spiritual emptiness of the machine age. Instead of 'not too far from the yew-tree' the keynote was 'weeping, weeping multitudes,' or perhaps 'the broken fingernails of dirty hands.'

Naturally these poems were denounced as 'decadent' when they first appeared, the attacks only being called off when it was perceived that Eliot's political and social tendencies were reactionary. There was, however, a sense in which the charge of 'decadence' could be justified. Clearly these poems were an end-product, the last gasp of a cultural tradition, poems which spoke only for the cultivated third-generation rentier, for people able to feel and criticise but no longer able to act. E. M. Forster praised *Prufrock* on its first appearance because 'it sang of people who were ineffectual and weak' and because it was 'innocent of public spirit' (this was during the other war, when public spirit was a good deal more rampant than it is now). The qualities by which any society which is to last longer than a generation actually has to be sustained – industry, courage, patriotism, frugality, philoprogenitiveness – obviously could not find any place in Eliot's early poems. There was only room for rentier values, the values of people too civilised to work, fight or even reproduce themselves. But that was the price that had to be paid, at any rate at that time, for writing a poem worth reading. The mood of lassitude, irony, disbelief, disgust, and not the sort of beefy enthusiasm demanded by the Squires and Herberts, was what sensitive people actually felt. It is fashionable to say that in verse only the words count and the 'meaning' is irrelevant, but in fact every poem contains a prose-meaning, and when the poem is any good it is a meaning which the poet urgently wishes to express. All art is to some extent propaganda. *Prufrock* is an expression of futility, but it is also a poem of wonderful vitality and power, culminating in a sort of rocket-burst in the closing stanzas:

> I have seen them riding seaward on the waves
> Combing the white hair of the waves blown back
> When the wind blows the water white and black.

> We have lingered in the chambers of the sea
> By sea-girls wreathed with seaweed red and brown
> Till human voices wake us, and we drown.

There is nothing like that in the later poems, although the rentier despair on which these lines are founded has been consciously dropped.

428

But the trouble is that conscious futility is something only for the young. One cannot go on 'despairing of life' into a ripe old age. One cannot go on and on being 'decadent,' since decadence means falling and one can only be said to be falling if one is going to reach the bottom reasonably soon. Sooner or later one is obliged to adopt a positive attitude towards life and society. It would be putting it too crudely to say that every poet in our time must either die young, enter the Catholic Church, or join the Communist Party, but in fact the escape from the consciousness of futility is along those general lines. There are other deaths besides physical deaths, and there are other sects and creeds besides the Catholic Church and the Communist Party, but it remains true that after a certain age one must either stop writing or dedicate oneself to some purpose not wholly aesthetic. Such a dedication necessarily means a break with the past:

> ... every attempt
> Is a wholly new start, and a different kind of failure
> Because one has only learnt to get the better of words
> For the thing one no longer has to say, or the way in which
> One is no longer disposed to say it. And so each venture
> Is a new beginning, a raid on the inarticulate
> With shabby equipment always deteriorating
> In the general mess of imprecision of feeling,
> Undisciplined squads of emotion.

Eliot's escape from individualism was into the Church, the Anglican Church as it happened. One ought not to assume that the gloomy Pétainism to which he now appears to have given himself over was the unavoidable result of his conversion. The Anglo-Catholic movement does not impose any political 'line' on its followers, and a reactionary or austrofascist tendency had always been apparent in his work, especially his prose writings. In theory it is still possible to be an orthodox religious believer without being intellectually crippled in the process; but it is far from easy, and in practice books by orthodox believers usually show the same cramped, blinkered outlook as books by orthodox Stalinists or others who are mentally unfree. The reason is that the Christian churches still demand assent to doctrines which no one seriously believes in. The most obvious case is the immortality of the soul. The various 'proofs' of personal immortality which can be advanced by Christian apologists are psychologically of no importance; what matters, psychologically, is that hardly anyone nowadays *feels* himself to be immortal. The next world may be in some sense 'believed in' but it has not anywhere near the same actuality in people's minds as it had a few centuries ago. Compare for instance the gloomy mumblings of these three poems with *Jerusalem my happy home*; the comparison is not altogether pointless. In the second case you have a man to whom the next world is as real as this one. It is true that his vision of it is incredibly vulgar – a choir practice in a jeweller's shop – but he believes in what he is saying and his belief gives vitality to his words. In the other case you have a man who does not really *feel* his faith, but merely assents to it for complex reasons. It does not in itself give him any fresh literary impulse. At a certain stage he feels the need for a 'purpose,' and he wants a 'purpose' which is reactionary and not progressive; the immediately available refuge is the Church, which demands intellectual absurdities of its members; so his work becomes a continuous nibbling round those absurdities, an attempt to make them acceptable to himself. The Church has not now any living imagery, and new vocabulary to offer:

> The rest
> Is prayer, observance, discipline, thought and action.

Perhaps what we need is prayer, observance, etc., but you do not make a line of poetry by stringing those words together. Mr. Eliot speaks also of

> the intolerable wrestle
> With words and meanings. The poetry does not matter.

I do not know, but I should imagine that the struggle with meanings would have loomed smaller, and the poetry would have seemed to matter more, if he could have found his way to some creed which did not start off by forcing one to believe the incredible.

There is no saying whether Mr. Eliot's development could have been much other than it has been. All writers who are any good develop throughout life, and the general direction of their development is determined. It is absurd to attack Eliot, as some left-wing critics have done, for being a 'reactionary' and to imagine that he might have used his gifts in the cause of democracy and Socialism. Obviously a scepticism about democracy and a disbelief in 'progress' are an integral part of him; without them he could not have written a line of his works. But it is arguable that he would have done better to go much further in the direction implied in his famous 'Anglo-Catholic and Royalist' declaration. He could not have developed into a Socialist, but he might have developed into the last apologist of aristocracy.

Neither feudalism nor indeed Fascism is necessarily deadly to poets, though both are to prose-writers. The thing that is really deadly to both is Conservatism of the half-hearted modern kind.

It is at least imaginable that if Eliot had followed wholeheartedly the anti-democratic, anti-perfectionist strain in himself he might have struck a new vein comparable to his earlier one. But the negative, Pétainism, which turns its eyes to the past, accepts defeat, writes off earthly happiness as impossible, mumbles about prayer and repentance and thinks it a spiritual advance to see life as 'a pattern of living worms in the guts of the women of Canterbury' – that, surely, is the least hopeful road a poet could take.

Looking Back on the Spanish War
[1942?]

i

First of all the physical memories, the sounds, the smells and the surfaces of things.

It is curious that more vividly than anything that came afterwards in the Spanish War I remember the week of so-called training that we received before being sent to the front – the huge cavalry barracks in Barcelona with its draughty stables and cobbled yards, the icy cold of the pump where one washed, the filthy meals made tolerable by pannikins of wine, the trousered militiawomen chopping firewood, and the roll-call in the early mornings where my prosaic English name made a sort of comic interlude among the resounding Spanish ones, Manuel Gonzalez, Pedro Aguilar, Ramon Fenellosa, Roque Ballaster, Jaime Domenech, Sebastian Viltron, Ramon Nuvo Bosch. I name those particular men because I remember the faces of all of them. Except for two who were mere riff-raff and have doubtless become good Falangists by this time, it is probable that all of them are dead. Two of them I know to be dead. The eldest would have been about twenty-five, the youngest sixteen.

One of the essential experiences of war is never to be able to escape from disgusting smells of human origin. Latrines are an overworked subject in war literature, and I would not mention them if it were not that the latrine in our barracks did its necessary bit towards puncturing my own illusions about the Spanish Civil War. The Latin type of latrine, at which you have to squat, is bad enough at its best, but these were made of some kind of polished stone so slippery that it was all you could do to keep on your feet. In addition they were always blocked. Now I have plenty of other disgusting things in my memory, but I believe it was these latrines that first brought home to me the thought, so often to recur: "Here we are, soldiers of a revolutionary army, defending Democracy against Fascism, fighting a war which is *about* something, and the detail of our lives is just as sordid and degrading as it could be in prison, let alone in a bourgeois army." Many other things reinforced this impression later; for instance, the boredom and animal hunger of trench life, the squalid intrigues over scraps of food, the mean, nagging quarrels which people exhausted by lack of sleep indulge in.

The essential horror of army life (whoever has been a soldier will know what I mean by the essential horror of army life) is barely affected by the nature of the war you happen to be fighting in. Discipline, for instance, is ultimately the same in all armies. Orders have to be obeyed and enforced by punishment if necessary, the relationship of officer and man has to be the relationship of superior and inferior. The picture of war set forth in books like *All Quiet on the Western Front* is substantially true. Bullets hurt, corpses stink, men under fire are often so frightened that they wet their trousers. It is true that the social background from which an army springs will colour its training, tactics and general efficiency, and also that the consciousness of being in the right can bolster up morale, though this affects the civilian population more than the troops. (People forget that a soldier anywhere near the front line is usually too hungry, or frightened, or cold, or, above all, too tired to bother about the political origins of the war.) But the laws of nature are not suspended for a "red" army any more than for a "white" one. A louse is a louse and a bomb is a bomb, even though the cause you are fighting for happens to be just.

Why is it worth while to point out anything so obvious? Because the bulk of the British and American intelligentsia were manifestly unaware of it then, and are now. Our memories are short nowadays, but look back a bit, dig out the files of *New Masses* or the *Daily Worker*, and just have a look at the romantic warmongering muck that our left-wingers were spilling at that time. All the stale old phrases! And the un-imaginative callousness of it! The sang-froid with which London faced the bombing of Madrid! Here I am not bothering about the counter-propagandists of the Right, the Lunns, Garvins *et hoc genus*; they go without saying. But here were the very people who for twenty years had hooted and jeered at the "glory" of war, at atrocity stories, at patriotism, even at physical courage, coming out with stuff that with the alteration of a few names would have fitted into the *Daily Mail* of 1918. If there was one thing that the British intelligentsia were committed to, it was the debunking version of war, the theory that war is all corpses and latrines and never leads to any good result. Well, the same people who in 1933 sniggered pityingly if you said that in certain circumstances you would fight for your country, in 1937 were denouncing you as a Trotsky-Fascist if you suggested that the stories in *New Masses* about freshly wounded men clamouring to get back into the fighting might be exaggerated. And the Left intelligentsia made their swing-over from "War is hell" to "War is glorious" not only with no sense of incongruity but almost without any intervening stage. Later the bulk of them were to make other transitions equally violent. There must be a quite large number of people, a sort of central core of the intelligentsia, who approved the "King and Country" declaration in 1935, shouted for a "firm line" against Germany in 1937, supported the People's Convention in 1940, and are demanding a Second Front now.

As far as the mass of the people go, the extraordinary swings of opinion which occur nowadays, the emotions which can be turned on and off like a tap, are the result of newspaper and radio hypnosis. In the intelligentsia I should say they result rather from money and mere physical safety. At a given moment they may be "pro-war" or "anti-war", but in either case they have no realistic picture of war in their minds. When they enthused over the Spanish War they knew, of course, that people were being killed and that to be killed is unpleasant, but they did feel that for a soldier in the Spanish Republican Army the experience of war was somehow not degrading. Somehow the latrines stank less, discipline was less irksome. You have only to glance at the *New Statesman* to see that they believed that; exactly similar blah is being written about the Red army at this moment. We have become too civilised to grasp the obvious. For the truth is very simple. To survive you often have to fight, and to fight you have to dirty yourself. War is evil, and it is often the lesser evil. Those who take the sword perish by the sword, and those who don't take the sword perish by smelly diseases. The fact that such a platitude is worth writing down shows what the years of *rentier* capitalism have done to us.

ii

In connection with what I have just said, a footnote on atrocities.

I have little direct evidence about the atrocities in the Spanish Civil War. I know that some were committed by the Republicans, and far more (they are still continuing) by the Fascists. But what impressed me then, and has impressed me ever since, is that atrocities are believed in or disbelieved in solely on grounds of political predilection. Everyone believes in the atrocities of the enemy and disbelieves in those of his own side, without ever bothering to examine the evidence. Recently I drew up a table of atrocities during the period between 1918 and the present; there was never a year when atrocities were not occurring somewhere or other, and there was hardly a single case when the Left and the Right believed in the same stories simultaneously. And stranger yet, at any moment the situation can suddenly reverse itself and yester-day's proved-to-the-hilt atrocity story can become a ridiculous lie, merely because the political landscape has changed.

434

In the present war we are in the curious situation that our "atrocity campaign" was done largely before the war started, and done mostly by the Left, the people who normally pride themselves on their incredulity. In the same period the Right, the atrocity-mongers of 1914–18, were gazing at Nazi Germany and flatly refusing to see any evil in it. Then as soon as war broke out it was the pro-Nazis of yesterday who were repeating horror-stories, while the anti-Nazis suddenly found themselves doubting whether the Gestapo really existed. Nor was this solely the result of the Russo-German Pact. It was partly because before the war the Left had wrongly believed that Britain and Germany would never fight and were therefore able to be anti-German and anti-British simultaneously; partly also because official war-propaganda, with its disgusting hypocrisy and self-righteousness, always tends to make thinking people sympathise with the enemy. Part of the price we paid for the systematic lying of 1914–18 was the exaggerated pro-German reaction which followed. During the years 1918–33 you were hooted at in left-wing circles if you suggested that Germany bore even a fraction of responsibility for the war. In all the denunciations of Versailles I listened to during those years I don't think I ever once heard the question, "What would have happened if Germany had won?" even mentioned, let alone discussed. So also with atrocities. The truth, it is felt, becomes untruth when your enemy utters it. Recently I noticed that the very people who swallowed any and every horror story about the Japanese in Nanking in 1937 refused to believe exactly the same stories about Hong Kong in 1942. There was even a tendency to feel that the Nanking atrocities had become, as it were, retrospectively untrue because the British Government now drew attention to them.

But unfortunately the truth about atrocities is far worse than that they are lied about and made into propaganda. The truth is that they happen. The fact often adduced as a reason for scepticism – that the same horror stories come up in war after war – merely makes it rather more likely that these stories are true. Evidently they are widespread fantasies, and war provides an opportunity of putting them into practice. Also, although it has ceased to be fashionable to say so, there is little question that what one may roughly call the "whites" commit far more and worse atrocities than the "reds". There is not the slightest doubt, for instance, about the behaviour of the Japanese in China. Nor is there much doubt about the long tale of Fascist outrages during the last ten years in Europe. The volume of testimony is enormous, and a respectable proportion of it comes from the German press and radio. These things really happened, that is the thing to keep one's eye on. They happened even though Lord Halifax said they happened. The raping and butchering in Chinese cities, the tortures in the cellars of the Gestapo, the elderly Jewish professors flung into cesspools, the machine-gunning of refugees along the Spanish roads – they all happened, and they did not happen any the less because the *Daily Telegraph* has suddenly found out about them when it is five years too late.

iii

Two memories, the first not proving anything in particular, the second, I think, giving one a certain insight into the atmosphere of a revolutionary period.

Early one morning another man and I had gone out to snipe at the Fascists in the trenches outside Huesca. Their line and ours here lay three hundred yards apart, at which range our aged rifles would not shoot accurately, but by sneaking out to a spot about a hundred yards from the Fascist trench you might, if you were lucky, get a shot at someone through a gap in the parapet. Unfortunately the ground between was a flat beetfield with no cover except a few ditches, and it was necessary to go out while it was still dark and return soon after dawn, before the light became too good. This time no Fascists appeared, and we stayed too long and were caught by the dawn. We were in a ditch, but behind us were two hundred yards of flat ground with hardly enough cover for a rabbit. We were still trying to nerve ourselves to make a dash for it when there was an uproar and a blowing of whistles in the Fascist trench. Some of our aeroplanes were coming over. At this moment a man, presumably carrying a message to an officer, jumped out of the trench and ran along the top of the parapet in full view. He was half-dressed and was holding up his trousers with both hands as he ran. I refrained from shooting at him. It is true that I am a poor shot and unlikely to hit a running man at a hundred yards, and also that I was thinking chiefly about getting back to our trench while the Fascists had their attention fixed on the aeroplanes. Still, I did not shoot partly because of that detail about the trousers. I had come here to shoot at "Fascists"; but a man who is holding up his trousers isn't a "Fascist", he is visibly a fellow creature, similar to yourself, and you don't feel like shooting at him.

What does this incident demonstrate? Nothing very much, because it is the kind of thing that happens all the time in all wars. The other is different. I don't suppose that in telling it I can make it moving to you who read it, but I ask you to believe that it is moving to me, as an incident characteristic of the moral atmosphere of a particular moment in time.

One of the recruits who joined us while I was at the barracks was a wild-looking boy from the back streets of Barcelona. He was ragged and barefooted. He was also extremely dark (Arab blood, I dare say), and made gestures you do not usually see a European make; one in particular – the arm outstretched, the palm vertical – was a gesture characteristic of Indians. One day a bundle of cigars, which you could still buy dirt cheap at that time, was stolen out of my bunk. Rather foolishly I reported this to the officer, and one of the scallywags I have already mentioned promptly came forward and said quite untruly that twenty-five pesetas had been stolen from his bunk. For some reason the officer instantly decided that the brown-faced boy must be the thief. They were very hard on stealing in the militia, and in theory people could be shot for it. The wretched boy allowed himself to be led off to the guardroom to be searched. What most struck me was that he barely attempted to protest his innocence. In the fatalism of his attitude you could see the desperate poverty in which he had been bred. The officer ordered him to take his clothes off. With a humility which was horrible to me he stripped himself naked, and his clothes were searched. Of course neither the cigars nor the money were there; in fact he had not stolen them. What was most painful of all was that he seemed no less ashamed after his innocence had been established. That night I took him to the pictures and gave him brandy and chocolate. But that too was horrible – I mean the attempt to wipe out an injury with money. For a few minutes I had half believed him to be a thief, and that could not be wiped out.

Well, a few weeks later, at the front, I had trouble with one of the men in my section. By this time I was a "*cabo*", or corporal, in command of twelve men. It was static warfare, horribly cold, and the chief job was getting sentries to stay awake and at their posts. One day a man suddenly refused to go to a certain post, which he said, quite truly, was exposed to enemy fire. He was a feeble creature, and I seized hold of him and began to drag him towards his post. This roused the feelings of the others against me, for Spaniards, I think, resent being touched more than we do. Instantly I was surrounded by a ring of shouting men: "Fascist! Fascist! Let that man go! This isn't a bourgeois army. Fascist!" etc., etc. As best I could in my bad Spanish I shouted back that orders had got to be obeyed, and the row developed into one of those enormous arguments by means of which discipline is gradually hammered out in revolutionary armies. Some said I was right, others said I was wrong. But the point is that the one who took my side the most warmly of all was the brown-faced boy. As soon as he saw what was happening he sprang into the ring and began passionately defending me. With his strange, wild, Indian gesture he kept exclaiming, "He's the best corporal we've got!" (*¡No hay cabo como el!*) Later on he applied for leave to exchange into my section.

Why is this incident touching to me? Because in any normal circumstances it would have been impossible for good feelings ever to be re-established between this boy and myself. The implied accusation of theft would not have been made any better, probably somewhat worse, by my efforts to make amends. One of the effects of safe and civilised life is an immense over-sensitiveness which makes all the primary emotions seem somewhat disgusting. Generosity is as painful as meanness, gratitude as hateful as ingratitude. But in Spain in 1936 we were not living in a normal time. It was a time when generous feelings and gestures were easier than they ordinarily are. I could relate a dozen similar incidents, not really communicable but bound up in my own mind with the special atmosphere of the time, the shabby clothes and the gay-coloured revolutionary posters, the universal use of the word "comrade", the anti-Fascist ballads printed on flimsy paper and sold for a penny, the phrases like "international proletarian solidarity", pathetically repeated by ignorant men who believed them to mean something. Could you feel friendly towards somebody, and stick up for him in a quarrel, after you had been ignominiously searched in his presence for property you were supposed to have stolen from him? No, you couldn't; but you might if you had both been through some emotionally widening experience. That is one of the by-products of revolution, though in this case it was only the beginnings of a revolution, and obviously foredoomed to failure.

iv

The struggle for power between the Spanish Republican parties is an unhappy, far-off thing which I have no wish to revive at this date. I only mention it in order to say: believe nothing, or next to nothing, of what you read about internal affairs on the Government side. It is all, from whatever source, party propaganda – that is to say, lies. The broad truth about the war is simple enough. The Spanish bourgeoisie saw their chance of crushing the labour movement, and took it, aided by the Nazis and by the forces of reaction all over the world. It is doubtful whether more than that will ever be established.

I remember saying once to Arthur Koestler, "History stopped in 1936," at which he nodded in immediate understanding. We were both thinking of totalitarianism in general, but more particularly of the Spanish Civil War. Early in life I had noticed that no event is ever correctly reported in a newspaper, but in Spain, for the first time, I saw newspaper reports which did not bear any relation to the facts, not even the relationship which is implied in an ordinary lie. I saw great battles reported where there had been no fighting, and complete silence where hundreds of men had been killed. I saw troops who had fought bravely denounced as cowards and traitors, and others who had never seen a shot fired hailed as the heroes of imaginary victories; and I saw newspapers in London retailing these lies and eager intellectuals building emotional superstructures over events that had never happened. I saw, in fact, history being written not in terms of what happened but of what ought to have happened according to various "party lines". Yet in a way, horrible as all this was, it was unimportant. It concerned secondary issues – namely, the struggle for power between the Comintern and the Spanish left-wing parties, and the efforts of the Russian Government to prevent revolution in Spain. But the broad picture of the war which the Spanish Government presented to the world was not untruthful. The main issues were what it said they were. But as for the Fascists and their backers, how could they come even as near to the truth as that? How could they possibly mention their real aims? Their version of the war was pure fantasy, and in the circumstances it could not have been otherwise.

The only propaganda line open to the Nazis and Fascists was to represent themselves as Christian patriots saving Spain from a Russian dictatorship. This involved pretending that life in Government Spain was just one long massacre (*vide* the *Catholic Herald* or the *Daily Mail* – but these were child's play compared with the continental Fascist press), and it involved immensely exaggerating the scale of Russian intervention. Out of the huge pyramid of lies which the Catholic and reactionary press all over the world built up, let me take just one point – the presence in Spain of a Russian army. Devout Franco partisans all believed in this; estimates of its strength went as high as half a million. Now, there was no Russian army in Spain. There may have been a handful of airmen and other technicians, a few hundred at the most, but an army there was not. Some thousands of foreigners who fought in Spain, not to mention millions of Spaniards, were witnesses of this. Well, their testimony made no impression at all upon the Franco propagandists, not one of whom had set foot in Government Spain. Simultaneously these people refused utterly to admit the fact of German or Italian intervention, at the same time as the German and Italian press were openly boasting about the exploits of their "legionaries". I have chosen to mention only one point, but in fact the whole of Fascist propaganda about the war was on this level.

This kind of thing is frightening to me, because it often gives me the feeling that the very concept of objective truth is fading out of the world. After all, the chances are that those lies, or at any rate similar lies, will pass into history. How will the history of the Spanish War be written? If Franco remains in power his nominees will write the history books, and (to stick to my chosen point) that Russian army which never existed will become historical fact, and schoolchildren will learn about it generations hence. But suppose Fascism is finally defeated and some kind of democratic government restored in Spain in the fairly near future; even then, how is the history of the war to be written? What kind of records will Franco have left behind him? Suppose even that the records kept on the Government side are recoverable – even so, how is a true history of the war to be written? For, as I have pointed out already, the Government also dealt extensively in lies. From the anti-Fascist angle one could write a broadly truthful history of the war, but it would be a partisan history, unreliable on every minor point. Yet, after all, *some* kind of history will be written, and after those who actually remember the war are dead, it will be universally accepted. So for all practical purposes the lie will have become truth.

I know it is the fashion to say that most of recorded history is lies anyway. I am willing to believe that history is for the most part inaccurate and biased, but what is peculiar to our own age is the abandonment of the idea that history *could* be truthfully written. In the past people deliberately lied, or they unconsciously coloured what they wrote, or they struggled after the truth, well knowing that they must make many mistakes; but in each case they believed that "the facts" existed and were more or less discoverable. And in practice there was always a considerable body of fact which would have been agreed to by almost everyone. If you look up the history of the last war in, for instance, the *Encyclopaedia Britannica*, you will find that a respectable amount of the material is drawn from German sources. A British and a German historian would disagree deeply on many things, even on fundamentals, but there would still be that body of, as it were, neutral fact on which neither would seriously challenge the other. It is just this common basis of agreement, with its implication that human beings are all one species of animal, that totalitarianism destroys. Nazi theory indeed specifically denies that such a thing as "the truth" exists. There is, for instance, no such thing as "science". There is only "German science", "Jewish science" etc. The implied objective of this line of thought is a nightmare world in which the Leader, or some ruling clique, controls not only the future but *the past*. If the Leader says of such and such an event, "It never happened" – well, it never happened. If he says that two and two are five – well, two and two are five. This prospect frightens me much more than bombs – and after our experiences of the last few years that is not a frivolous statement.

But is it perhaps childish or morbid to terrify oneself with visions of a totalitarian future? Before writing off the totalitarian world as a nightmare that can't come true, just remember that in 1925 the world of today would have seemed a nightmare that couldn't come true. Against that shifting phantasmagoric world in which black may be white tomorrow and yesterday's weather can be changed by decree, there are in reality only two safeguards. One is that however much you deny the truth, the truth goes on existing, as it were, behind your back, and you consequently can't violate it in ways that impair military efficiency. The other is that so long as some parts of the earth remain unconquered, the liberal tradition can be kept alive. Let Fascism, or possibly even a combination of several Fascisms, conquer the whole world, and those two conditions no longer exist. We in England underrate the danger of this kind of thing, because our traditions and our past security have given us a sentimental belief that it all comes right in the end and the thing you most fear never really happens. Nourished for hundreds of years on a literature in which Right invariably triumphs in the last chapter, we believe half-instinctively that evil always defeats itself in the long run. Pacifism, for instance, is founded largely on this belief. Don't resist evil, and it will somehow destroy itself. But why should it? What evidence is there that it does? And what instance is there of a modern industrialised state collapsing unless conquered from the outside by military force?

Consider for instance the re-institution of slavery. Who could have imagined twenty years ago that slavery would return to Europe? Well, slavery has been restored under our noses. The forced-labour camps all over Europe and North Africa where Poles, Russians, Jews and political prisoners of every race toil at road-making or swamp-draining for their bare rations, are simple chattel slavery. The most one can say is that the buying and selling of slaves by individuals is not yet permitted. In other ways – the breaking-up of families, for instance – the conditions are probably worse than they were on the American cotton plantations. There is no reason for thinking that this state of affairs will change while any totalitarian domination endures. We don't grasp its full implications, because in our mystical way we feel that a régime founded on slavery *must* collapse. But it is worth comparing the duration of the slave empires of antiquity with that of any modern state. Civilisations founded on slavery have lasted for such periods as four thousand years.

When I think of antiquity, the detail that frightens me is that those hundreds of millions of slaves on whose backs civilisation rested generation after generation have left behind them no record whatever. We do not even know their names. In the whole of Greek and Roman history, how many slaves' names are known to you? I can think of two, or possibly three. One is Spartacus and the other is Epictetus. Also, in the Roman room at the British Museum there is a glass jar with the maker's name inscribed on the bottom, *"Felix fecit"*. I have a vivid mental picture of poor Felix (a Gaul with red hair and a metal collar round his neck), but in fact he may not have been a slave; so there are only two slaves whose names I definitely know, and probably few people can remember more. The rest have gone down into utter silence.

v

The backbone of the resistance against Franco was the Spanish working class, especially the urban trade union members. In the long run – it is important to remember that it is only in the long run – the working class remains the most reliable enemy of Fascism, simply because the working class stands to gain most by a decent reconstruction of society. Unlike other classes or categories, it can't be permanently bribed.

To say this is not to idealise the working class. In the long struggle that has followed the Russian Revolution it is the manual workers who have been defeated, and it is impossible not to feel that it was their own fault. Time after time, in country after country, the organised working-class movements have been crushed by open, illegal violence, and their

443

comrades abroad, linked to them in theoretical solidarity, have simply looked on and done nothing; and underneath this, secret cause of many betrayals, has lain the fact that between white and coloured workers there is not even lip-service to solidarity. Who can believe in the class-conscious international proletariat after the events of the past ten years? To the British working class the massacre of their comrades in Vienna, Berlin, Madrid, or wherever it might be, seemed less interesting and less important than yesterday's football match. Yet this does not alter the fact that the working class will go on struggling against Fascism after the others have caved in. One feature of the Nazi conquest of France was the astonishing defections among the intelligentsia, including some of the left-wing political intelligentsia. The intelligentsia are the people who squeal loudest against Fascism, and yet a respectable proportion of them collapse into defeatism when the pinch comes. They are far-sighted enough to see the odds against them, and moreover they can be bribed – for it is evident that the Nazis think it worth while to bribe intellectuals. With the working class it is the other way about. Too ignorant to see through the trick that is being played on them, they easily swallow the promises of Fascism, yet sooner or later they always take up the struggle again. They must do so, because in their own bodies they always discover that the promises of Fascism cannot be fulfilled. To win over the working class permanently, the Fascists would have to raise the general standard of living, which they are unable and probably unwilling to do. The struggle of the working class is like the growth of a plant. The plant is blind and stupid, but it knows enough to keep pushing upwards towards the light, and it will do this in the face of endless discouragements. What are the workers struggling for? Simply for the decent life which they are more and more aware is now technically possible. Their consciousness of this aim ebbs and flows. In Spain, for a while, people were acting consciously, moving towards a goal which they wanted to reach and be-lieved they could reach. It accounted for the curiously buoyant feeling that life in Government Spain had during the early months of the war. The common people knew in their bones that the Republic was their friend and Franco was their enemy. They knew that they were in the right, because they were fighting for something which the world owed them and was able to give them.

One has to remember this to see the Spanish War in its true perspective. When one thinks of the cruelty, squalor, and futility of war – and in this particular case of the intrigues, the persecutions, the lies and the misunderstandings – there is always the temptation to say: "One side is as bad as the other. I am neutral." In practice, however, one cannot be neutral, and there is hardly such a thing as a war in which it makes no difference who wins. Nearly always one side stands more or less for progress, the other side more or less for reaction. The hatred which the Spanish Republic excited in millionaries, dukes, cardinals, play-boys, Blimps and what not would in itself be enough to show one how the land lay. In essence it was a class war. If it had been won, the cause of the common people everywhere would have been strengthened. It was lost, and the dividend-drawers all over the world rubbed their hands. That was the real issue; all else was froth on its surface.

vi

The outcome of the Spanish War was settled in London, Paris, Rome, Berlin – at any rate not in Spain. After the summer of 1937 those with eyes in their heads realised that the Government could not win the war unless there was some profound change in the international set-up, and in deciding to fight on Negrin and the others may have been partly influenced by the expectation that the world war which actually broke out in 1939 was coming in 1938. The much-publicised disunity on the Government side was not a main cause of defeat. The Government militias were hurriedly raised, ill-armed and unimaginative in their military outlook, but they would have been the same if complete political agreement had existed from the start. At the outbreak of war the average Spanish factory-worker did not even know how to fire a rifle (there had never been universal conscription in Spain), and the traditional pacifism of the Left was a great handicap. The thousands of foreigners who served in Spain made good infantry, but there were very few experts of any kind among them. The Trotskyist thesis that the war could have been won if the revolution had not been sabotaged was probably false. To nationalise factories, demolish churches, and issue revolutionary manifestos would not have made the armies more efficient. The Fascists won because they were the stronger; they had modern arms and the others hadn't. No political strategy could offset that.

The most baffling thing in the Spanish War was the behaviour of the great powers. The war was actually won for Franco by the Germans and Italians, whose motives were obvious enough. The motives of France and Britain are less easy to understand. In 1936 it was clear to everyone that if Britain would only help the Spanish Government, even to the extent of a few million pounds' worth of arms, Franco would collapse and German strategy would be severely dislocated. By that time one did not need to be a clairvoyant to foresee that war between Britain and Germany was coming; one could even foretell within a year or two when it would come. Yet in the most mean, cowardly, hypocritical way the British ruling class did all they could to hand Spain over to Franco and the Nazis. Why? Because they were pro-Fascist, was the obvious answer. Undoubtedly they were, and yet when it came to the final showdown they chose to stand up to Germany. It is still very uncertain what plan they acted on in backing Franco, and they may have had no clear plan at all. Whether the British ruling class are wicked or merely stupid is one of the most difficult questions of our time, and at certain moments a very important question. As to the Russians, their motives in the Spanish War are completely inscrutable. Did they, as the pinks believed, intervene in Spain in order to defend democracy and thwart the Nazis? Then why did they intervene on such a niggardly scale and finally leave Spain in the lurch? Or did they, as the Catholics maintained, intervene in order to foster revolution in Spain? Then why did they do all in their power to crush the Spanish revolutionary movements, defend private property and hand power to the middle class as against the working class? Or did they, as the Troskyists suggested, intervene simply in order to *prevent* a Spanish revolution? Then why not have backed Franco? Indeed, their actions are most easily explained if one assumes that they were acting on several contradictory motives. I believe that in the future we shall come to feel that Stalin's foreign policy, instead of being so diabolically clever as it is claimed to be, has been merely opportunistic and stupid.

But at any rate, the Spanish Civil War demonstrated that the Nazis knew what they were doing and their opponents did not. The war was fought at a low technical level and its major strategy was very simple. That side which had arms would win. The Nazis and the Italians gave arms to their Spanish Fascist friends, and the western democracies and the Russians didn't give arms to those who should have been their friends. So the Spanish Republic perished, having "gained what no republic missed".

Whether it was right, as all left-wingers in other countries undoubtedly did, to encourage the Spaniards to go on fighting when they could not win is a question hard to answer. I myself think it was right, because I believe that it is better even from the point of view of survival to fight and be conquered than to surrender without fighting. The effects on the grand strategy of the struggle against Fascism cannot be assessed yet. The ragged, weaponless armies of the Republic held out for two and a half years, which was undoubtedly longer than their enemies expected. But whether that dislocated the Fascist time-table, or whether, on the other hand, it merely postponed the major war and gave the Nazis extra time to get their war machine into trim, is still uncertain.

vii

I never think of the Spanish War without two memories coming into my mind. One is of the hospital ward at Lérida and the rather sad voices of the wounded militiamen singing some song with a refrain that ended:

Una resolucion,
Luchar hast' al fin!

Well, they fought to the end all right. For the last eighteen months of the war the Republican armies must have been fighting almost without cigarettes, and with precious little food. Even when I left Spain in the middle of 1937, meat and bread were scarce, tobacco a rarity, coffee and sugar almost unobtainable.

The other memory is of the Italian militiaman who shook my hand in the guardroom, the day I joined the militia. I wrote about this man at the beginning of my book on the Spanish War, and do not want to repeat what I said there. When I remember – oh, how vividly! – his shabby uniform and fierce, pathetic, innocent face, the complex side-issues of the war seem to fade away and I see clearly that there was at any rate no doubt as to who was in the right. In spite of power politics and journalistic lying, the central issue of the war was the attempt of people like this to win the decent life which they knew to be their birthright. It is difficult to think of this particular man's probable end without several kinds of bitterness. Since I met him in the Lenin Barracks he was probably a Trotskyist or an Anarchist, and in the peculiar conditions of our time, when people of that sort are not killed by the Gestapo they are usually killed by the GPU. But that does not affect the long-term issues. This man's face, which I saw only for a minute or two, remains with me as a sort of visual reminder of what the war was really about. He symbolises for me the flower of the European working class, harried by the police of all countries, the people who fill the mass graves of the Spanish battlefields and are now, to the tune of several millions, rotting in forced-labour camps.

When one thinks of all the people who support or have supported Fascism, one stands amazed at their diversity. What a crew! Think of a programme which at any rate for a while could bring Hitler, Pétain, Montagu Norman, Pavelitch, William Randolph Hearst, Streicher, Buchman, Ezra Pound, Juan March, Cocteau, Thyssen, Father Coughlin, the Mufti of Jerusalem, Arnold Lunn, Antonescu, Spengler, Beverley Nichols, Lady Houston, and Marinetti all into the same boat! But the clue is really very simple. They are all people with something to lose, or people who long for a hierarchical society and dread the prospect of a world of free and equal human beings. Behind all the ballyhoo that is talked about "godless" Russia and the "materialism" of the working class lies the simple intention of those with money or privileges to cling to them. Ditto, though it contains a partial truth, with all the talk about the worthlessness of social reconstruction not accompanied by a "change of heart". The pious ones, from the Pope to the yogis of California, are great on the "change of heart", much more reassuring from their point of view than a change in the economic system. Pétain attributes the fall of France to the common people's "love of pleasure". One sees this in its right perspective if one stops to wonder how much pleasure the ordinary French peasant's or workingman's life would contain compared with Pétain's own. The damned impertinence of these politicians, priests, literary men, and what not who lecture the working-class Socialist for his "materialism"! All that the workingman demands is what these others would consider the indispensable minimum without which human life cannot be lived at all. Enough to eat, freedom from the haunting terror of unemployment, the knowledge that your children will get a fair chance, a bath once a day, clean linen reasonably often, a roof that doesn't leak, and short enough working hours to leave you with a little energy when the day is done. Not one of those who preach against "materialism" would consider life livable without these things. And how easily that minimum could be attained if we chose to set our minds to it for only twenty years! To raise the standard of living of the whole world to that of Britain would not be a greater undertaking than this war we are now fighting. I don't claim, and I don't know who does, that that would solve anything in itself. It is merely that privation and brute labour have to be abolished before the real problems of humanity can be tackled. The major problem of our time is the decay of the belief in personal immortality, and it cannot be dealt with while the average human being is either drudging like an ox or shivering in fear of the secret police. How right the working classes are in their "materialism"! How right they are to realise that the real belly comes before the soul, not in the scale of values but in point of time! Understand that, and the long horror that we are enduring becomes at least intelligible. All the considerations that are likely to make one falter – the siren voices of a Pétain or of a Gandhi, the inescapable fact that in order to fight one has to degrade oneself, the equivocal moral position of Britain, with its democratic phrases and its coolie empire, the sinister development of Soviet Russia, the squalid farce of left-wing politics – all this fades away and one sees only the struggle of the gradually awakening common people against the lords of property and their hired liars and bumsuckers. The question is very simple. Shall people like that Italian soldier be allowed to live

the decent, fully human life which is now technically achievable, or shan't they? Shall the common man be pushed back
into the mud, or shall he not? I myself believe, perhaps on
insufficient grounds, that the common man will win his fight
sooner or later, but I want it to be sooner and not later – some
time within the next hundred years, say, and not some time
within the next ten thousand years. That was the real issue of
the Spanish War, and of the present war, and perhaps of other
wars yet to come.

I never saw the Italian militiaman again, nor did I ever learn
his name. It can be taken as quite certain that he is dead. Nearly
two years later, when the war was visibly lost, I wrote these
verses in his memory:

> The Italian soldier shook my hand
> Beside the guard-room table;
> The strong hand and the subtle hand
> Whose palms are only able
>
> To meet within the sound of guns,
> But oh! what peace I knew then
> In gazing on his battered face
> Purer than any woman's!
>
> For the fly-blown words that make me spew
> Still in his ears were holy,
> And he was born knowing what I had learned
> Out of books and slowly.
>
> The treacherous guns had told their tale
> And we both had bought it,
> But my gold brick was made of gold –
> Oh! who ever would have thought it?
>
> Good luck go with you, Italian soldier!
> But luck is not for the brave;
> What would the world give back to you?
> Always less than you gave.
>
> Between the shadow and the ghost,
> Between the white and the red,
> Between the bullet and the lie,
> Where would you hide your head?

For where is Manuel Gonzalez,
And where is Pedro Aguilar,
And where is Ramon Fenellosa?
The earthworms know where they are.

Your name and your deeds were forgotten
Before your bones were dry,
And the lie that slew you is buried
Under a deeper lie;

But the thing that I saw in your face
No power can disinherit:
No bomb that ever burst
Shatters the crystal spirit.

Imaginary Interview: George Orwell and Jonathan Swift
BBC African Service, 6 November 1942

ORWELL: My edition of Swift's works was printed some time between 1730 and 1740. It's in twelve small volumes, with calf covers a bit the worse for wear. It's not too easy to read, the ink is faded and the long S's are a nuisance, but I prefer it to any modern edition I've seen. When I open it and smell the dusty smell of old paper and see the woodcut illustrations and the crooked capital letters, I almost have the feeling that I can hear Swift speaking to me. I've a vivid picture of him in my mind's eye, with his knee-breeches and his three-cornered hat, and the snuff box and the spectacles he wrote about in Gulliver's Travels, though I don't believe I've ever seen a portrait of him. There's something in his way of writing that seems to tell you what his voice was like. For instance, here's one of his "Thoughts on Various Subjects": "When a true Genius appears in the world..."

SWIFT [*with contempt*]:   "When a true Genius appears in the world, you may know him by this infallible sign: that all the *Dunces* are in Confederacy against him."

ORWELL: So you *did* wear a wig, Dr. Swift. I've often wondered.

SWIFT: So you have the first collected edition of my works?

ORWELL: Yes. I bought them for five shillings at a farm-house auction.

SWIFT: I warn you to beware of all *modern* editions, even of my Travels. I have suffered from such damned dishonest editors as I believe no other writer ever had. It has been my especial misfortune to be edited usually by clergymen who thought me a disgrace to their cloth. They were tinkering with my writings long before Dr. Bowdler was ever born or thought of.

ORWELL: You see, Dr. Swift, you have put them in a difficulty. They know you are our greatest prose writer, and yet you used words and raised subjects that they couldn't approve of. In a way I don't approve of you myself.

SWIFT: I am desolated, sir.

ORWELL: I believe Gulliver's Travels has meant more to me than any other book ever written. I can't remember when I first read it, I must have been eight years old at the most, and it's lived with me ever since so that I suppose a year has never passed without my re-reading at least part of it.

SWIFT: I am vastly gratified.

ORWELL: And yet even I can't help feeling that you laid it on a bit too thick. You were too hard on humanity, and on your own country.

SWIFT: H'm!

ORWELL: For instance, here's a passage that has always stuck in my memory – also stuck in my gizzard, a little. It's at the end of Chapter VI in the second Book of Gulliver's Travels. Gulliver has just given the King of Brobdingnag a long description of life in

England. The King listens to him and then picks him up in his hand, strokes him gently and says – wait a moment, I've got the book here. But perhaps you remember the passage yourself.

SWIFT: Oh, ay. "It does not appear, from all you have said, how any one virtue is required toward the pro-curement of any one station among you; much less that men were ennobled on account of their *virtue*; [*voice up*] that priests were advanced for their *piety* or *learning*; soldiers, for their conduct or valour; judges, for their integrity; senators, for the love of their country; or counsellors for their wisdom... [*Quieter*] By what I have gathered from your own relation, and the answers I have with much pains wringed and extorted from you, I cannot but conclude the bulk of your natives to be the most pernicious race of little odious vermin that nature [*crescendo*] ever suffered to crawl upon the surface of the earth."

ORWELL: I'd allow you "pernicious" and "odious" and "vermin", Dr. Swift, but I'm inclined to cavil at "most". "The *most* pernicious". Are we in this island really worse than the *rest* of the world?

SWIFT: No. But I know you better than I know the rest of the world. When I wrote, I went upon the principle that if a lower kind of animal existed than you I could not imagine it.

ORWELL: That was 200 years ago. Surely you must admit that we have made a certain amount of progress since then?

SWIFT: Progress in quantity, yes. The buildings are taller and the vehicles move faster. Human beings are more numerous and commit greater follies. A battle kills a million where it used to kill a thou-sand. And in the matter of great men, as you still call them, I admit that your age outdoes mine. Whereas previously some petty tyrant was con-sidered to have reached the highest point of human fame if he laid waste a single province and pillaged half a dozen towns, [*with ironic*

453

pleasure] your great men nowadays can devastate whole *continents* and condemn entire races of men to *slavery*.

ORWELL: I was coming to that. One thing I feel inclined to urge in favour of my country is that we don't produce great men and don't like war. Since your day something has appeared called totalitarianism.

SWIFT: A new thing?

ORWELL: It isn't strictly new, it's merely been made practicable by modern weapons and modern methods of communication. Hobbes and other seventeenth-century writers predicted it. You yourself wrote about it with extraordinary foresight. There are passages in Part III of Gulliver's Travels that give me the feeling that I'm reading an account of the Reichstag Fire trial. But I'm thinking particularly of a passage in Part IV where the Houyhnhnm who is Gulliver's master is telling him about the habits and customs of the Yahoos. It appears that each tribe of Yahoos had a Dictator, or Fuehrer, and this Dictator liked to surround himself with yes-men. The Houyhnhnm says:

SWIFT [*quiet*]: "He had heard, indeed, some curious Houyhnhnms observe, that in most herds there was a sort of ruling Yahoo, who was always more *deformed* in body, and *mischievous* in disposition, than any of the rest. That this leader had usually a [*tenderly*] favourite, as like himself as he could get, whose employment was to lick his master's feet and [*licorously*] drive the female Yahoos to his *kennel*; for which he was now and then rewarded with a piece of ass's flesh. This favourite is hated by the whole herd, and therefore, to protect himself, keeps always near the person of his leader. He usually continues in office till a worse can be found; but the very moment he is discarded, his successor, at the head of all the Yahoos in that district, young and old, male and female, come in a body, and –"

454

ORWELL: We shall have to leave out that bit.

SWIFT: Thank you, Dr. Bowdler.

ORWELL: I remember that passage whenever I think of Goebbels or Ribbentrop, or for that matter Monsieur Laval. But looking at the world as a whole, do you find that the human being is *still* a Yahoo?

SWIFT: I had a good view of the people of London on my way here, and I assure you that I could remark very little difference. I saw round me the same hideous faces, unshapely bodies and ill-fitting clothes that could be seen in London two hundred years ago.

ORWELL: But the town had changed, even if the people had not?

SWIFT: Oh, it has grown prodigiously. Many a green field where Pope and I used to stroll after dinner on summer evenings is now a warren of bricks and mortar, for the kennelling of Yahoos.

ORWELL: But the town is a great deal safer, more orderly, than it was in your day. One can walk about nowadays without the fear of getting one's throat cut, even at night. You ought to admit some improvement there, though I suppose you won't. Besides, it's cleaner. In your day there were still lepers in London, not to mention the Plague. We have baths fairly frequently nowadays, and women don't keep their hair up for a month at a time and carry little silver goads to scratch their heads with. Do you remember writing a poem called "A Description of a Lady's Dressing Room"?

SWIFT: "Strephon, who found the room was void
And Betty otherwise employed,
Stole in, and took a strict survey
Of all the litter as it lay:
Whereof, to make the matter clear,
An inventory follows here."

ORWELL: Unfortunately I don't think the inventory is suitable for broadcasting.

SWIFT: Poor Dr. Bowdler!

ORWELL: But the point is, would you sign that poem nowadays? Tell me candidly, do we stink as we used to?

SWIFT: Certainly the smells are different. There was a new one I remarked as I came through the streets – (sniffs) –

ORWELL: It's called petrol. But don't you find that the mass of the people are more intelligent than they were, or at least better educated? How about the newspapers and the radio? Surely they have opened people's minds a little? There are very few people in England now who can't read, for instance.

SWIFT: That is why they are so easily deceived. [*Voice up*] Your ancestors two hundred years ago were full of barbarous superstitions, but they would not have been so credulous as to believe [*gentle*] your daily newspapers. As you seem to know my works, perhaps you will remember another little thing I wrote, an "Essay upon Genteel and Ingenious Conversation"?

ORWELL: Of course I remember it well. It's a description of fashionable ladies and gentlemen talking – an appalling stream of drivel which goes on and on for six hours without stopping.

SWIFT: On my way here I looked in at some of your fashionable clubs and suburban coffee shops, and listened to the conversation. I half believed that that little Essay of mine was being parodied. If there was any change, it was only that the English tongue had lost something of its earthy natural quality.

ORWELL: How about the scientific and technical achievements of the last two hundred years – railway trains, motor cars, aeroplanes and so forth? Doesn't that strike you as an advance?

SWIFT: I also passed through Cheapside on my way here. It has almost ceased to exist. Round St. Paul's there is only an acre of ruins. The Temple has been almost wiped out, and the little church outside it is only a shell. I am speaking only of the places I knew, but it is the same all over London, I believe. That is what your machines have done for you.

ORWELL: I am getting the worst of this argument, but I still feel, Dr. Swift, that there is something deeply deficient in your outlook. You remember what the king of Brobdingnag said when Gulliver described cannons and gunpowder to him?

SWIFT: "The king was struck with horror at the description I had given of those terrible engines, and the proposal I had made. He was amazed, how so *impotent* and *grovelling* an insect as I (these were his expressions) could entertain such inhuman ideas, and in so familiar a manner as to appear wholly unmoved at all the scenes of blood and desolation, which I had painted as the common effects of those destructive machines; whereof, he said, some evil genius, enemy to mankind, must have been the first contriver. As for himself, he protested, that although few things delighted him so much as new discoveries in art or in nature, yet he would rather lose half his kingdom than be privy to such a secret, which he commanded me, as I valued my life, never to mention any more."

ORWELL: I suppose the king would have spoken even more forcibly about tanks or mustard gas. But I can't help feeling that his attitude, and yours, show a certain lack of curiosity. Perhaps the most brilliant thing you ever wrote was the description of the scientific academy in Part III of Gulliver's Travels. But after all you were wrong. You thought the whole process of scientific research was absurd, because you could not believe that any tangible result would ever come out of it. But after all the results have come. Modern machine civilisation is there, for good or evil. And the poorest person nowadays is better off, so far as physical comfort goes, than a nobleman in Saxon times, or even in the reign of Queen Anne.

SWIFT: Has that added anything to true wisdom or true refinement? Let me remind you of another saying of mine: "The greatest Inventions were produced in the Times of Ignorance; as the use of the Compass, Gunpowder and Printing; and by the dullest nations, as the Germans."

ORWELL: I see now where it is that we part company, Dr. Swift. I believe that human society, and therefore human nature, can change. You don't. Do you still hold to that, after the French Revolution and the Russian Revolution?

SWIFT: You know very well what is my final word. I wrote it on the last page of Gulliver's Travels, but I will speak it again. "My reconcilement to the Yahoo kind in general might not be so difficult if they would be content with those vices and follies only, which nature has entitled them to. I am not in the least provoked at the sight of a lawyer, a pickpocket, a colonel, a fool, a lord, a gamester, a politician, a whore-master, a physician, an evidence, a suborner, an attorney, a traitor, or the like: this is all according to the due course of things: but when I behold a lump of deformity and diseases both in body and mind, smitten with *pride*, it immediately breaks all the measures of my patience; neither shall I be ever able to comprehend how such an animal . . ." [*voice fading*]

ORWELL: Ah, he's fading out! Dr. Swift! Dr. Swift! Is that your last word?

SWIFT [*voice a little stronger then finally fading out*]:   Neither shall I ever be able to comprehend how such an animal and such a vice could tally together. And therefore I here entreat those who have any tincture of this absurd vice, that they will not presume to come in my sight.

ORWELL: He's gone. I didn't get much change out of him. He was a great man, and yet he was partially blind. He could only see one thing at a time. His vision of human society is so penetrating, and yet in the last analysis it's false. He couldn't see what the simplest person sees, that life is worth living and human beings, even if they're dirty and ridiculous, are mostly decent. But after all, if he could have seen that I suppose he couldn't have written Gulliver's Travels. Ah well, let him rest in peace in Dublin, where, in the words of his epitaph, "Savage indignation can no longer lacerate his heart".

SWIFT: *Ubi saeva indignatio ulterius cor lacerare nequit.*

1943

Review of *The Development of William Butler Yeats* by V. K. Narayana Menon

Horizon, January 1943

One thing that Marxist criticism has not succeeded in doing is to trace the connection between 'tendency' and literary style. The subject-matter and imagery of a book can be explained in sociological terms, but its texture seemingly cannot. Yet some such connection there must be. One knows, for instance, that a Socialist would not write like Chesterton or a Tory imperialist like Bernard Shaw, though *how* one knows is not easy to say. In the case of Yeats, there must be some kind of connection between his wayward, even tortured style of writing and his rather sinister vision of life. Mr. Menon is chiefly concerned with the esoteric philosophy underlying Yeats's work, but the quotations which are scattered all through his interesting book serve to remind one how artificial Yeats's manner of writing was. As a rule, this artificiality is accepted as Irishism, or Yeats is even credited with simplicity because he uses short words, but in fact one seldom comes on six consecutive lines of his verse in which there is not an archaism or an affected turn of speech. To take the nearest example:

> Grant me an old man's Frenzy,
> My self must I remake
> Till I am Timon and Lear
> Or that William Blake
> Who beat upon the wall
> Till Truth obeyed his call.

The unnecessary 'that' imports a feeling of affectation, and the same tendency is present in all but Yeats's best passages. One is seldom long away from a suspicion of 'quaintness', something that links up not only with the 'nineties, the Ivory Tower and the 'calf covers of pissed-on green', but also with Rackham's drawings, Liberty art-fabrics and the *Peter Pan* never-never land, of which, after all, *The Happy Townland* is merely a more appetising example. This does not matter, because, on the whole, Yeats gets away with it, and if his straining after effect is often irritating it can also produce phrases ('the chill, footless years', 'the mackerel-crowded seas') which suddenly overwhelm one like a girl's face seen across a room. He is an exception to the rule that poets do not use poetical language:

> How many centuries spent
> The sedentary soul
> In toils of measurement
> Beyond eagle or mole,
> Beyond hearing or seeing,
> Or Archimedes' guess,
> To raise into being
> That loveliness?

Here he does not flinch from a squashy vulgar word like 'loveliness', and after all it does not seriously spoil this wonderful passage. But the same tendencies, together with a sort of raggedness which is no doubt intentional, weaken his epigrams and polemical poems. For instance (I am quoting from memory), the epigram against the critics who damned *The Playboy of the Western World*:

> Once when midnight smote the air
> Eunuchs ran through Hell and met
> On every crowded street to stare,
> Upon great Juan riding by;
> Even like these to rail and sweat,
> Staring upon his sinewy thigh.

The power which Yeats has within himself gives him the analogy ready made and produces the tremendous scorn of the last line, but even in this short poem there are six or seven unnecessary words. It would probably have been deadlier if it had been neater.

Mr. Menon's book is incidentally a short biography of Yeats, but he is above all interested in Yeats's philosophical 'system', which in his opinion supplies the subject-matter of more of Yeats's poems than is generally recognised. This system is set forth fragmentarily in various places, and at full length in

A Vision, a privately printed book which I have never read but which Mr. Menon quotes from extensively. Yeats gave conflicting accounts of its origin, and Mr. Menon hints pretty broadly that the 'documents' on which it was ostensibly founded were imaginary. Yeats's philosophical system, says Mr. Menon, 'was at the back of his intellectual life almost from the beginning. His poetry is full of it. Without it his later poetry becomes almost completely unintelligible.' As soon as we begin to read about the so-called system we are in the middle of a hocus-pocus of Great Wheels, gyres, cycles of the moon, reincarnation, disembodied spirits, astrology, and what-not. Yeats hedges as to the literalness with which he believed in all this, but he certainly dabbled in spiritualism and astrology and in earlier life had made experiments in alchemy. Although almost buried under explanations, very difficult to understand, about the phases of the moon, the central idea of his philosophical system seems to be our old friend, the cyclical universe, in which everything happens over and over again. One has not, perhaps, the right to laugh at Yeats for his mystical beliefs – for I believe it could be shown that *some* degree of belief in magic is almost universal – but neither ought one to write such things off as mere unimportant eccentricities. It is Mr. Menon's perception of this that gives his book its deepest interest. 'In the first flush of admiration and enthusiasm,' he says, 'most people dismissed the fantastical philosophy as the price we have to pay for a great and curious intellect. One did not quite realise where he was heading. And those who did, like Pound and perhaps Eliot, approved the stand that he finally took. The first reaction to this did not come, as one might have expected, from the politically minded young English poets. They were puzzled because a less rigid or artificial system than that of *A Vision* might not have produced the great poetry of Yeats's last days.' It might not, and yet Yeats's philosophy has some very sinister implications, as Mr. Menon points out.

Translated into political terms, Yeats's tendency is Fascist. Throughout most of his life, and long before Fascism was ever heard of, he had had the outlook of those who reach Fascism by the aristocratic route. He is a great hater of democracy, of the modern world, science, machinery, the concept of progress –

above all, of the idea of human equality. Much of the imagery of his work is feudal, and it is clear that he was not altogether free from ordinary snobbishness. Later these tendencies took clearer shape and led him to 'the exultant acceptance of authoritarianism as the only solution. Even violence and tyranny are not necessarily evil because the people, knowing not evil and good, would become perfectly acquiescent to tyranny. . . . Everything must come from the top. Nothing can come from the masses.' Not much interested in politics, and no doubt disgusted by his brief incursions into public life, Yeats nevertheless makes political pronouncements. He is too big a man to share the illusions of Liberalism, and as early as 1920 he foretells in a justly famous passage ('The Second Coming') the kind of world that we have actually moved into. But he appears to welcome the coming age, which is to be 'hierarchical, masculine, harsh, surgical', and he is influenced both by Ezra Pound and by various Italian Fascist writers. He describes the new civilisation which he hopes and believes will arrive: 'an aristocratic civilisation in its most completed form, every detail of life hierarchical, every great man's door crowded at dawn by petitioners, great wealth everywhere in a few men's hands, all dependent upon a few, up to the Emperor himself, who is a God dependent on a greater God, and everywhere, in Court, in the family, an inequality made law'. The innocence of this statement is as interesting as its snobbishness. To begin with, in a single phrase, 'great wealth in a few men's hands', Yeats lays bare the central reality of Fascism, which the whole of its propaganda is designed to cover up. The merely political Fascist claims always to be fighting for justice; Yeats, the poet, sees at a glance that Fascism means injustice, and acclaims it for that very reason. But at the same time he fails to see that the new authoritarian civilisation, if it arrives, will not be aristocratic, or what he means by aristocratic. It will not be ruled by noblemen with Van Dyck faces, but by anonymous millionaires, shiny-bottomed bureaucrats and murdering gangsters. Others who have made the same mistake have afterwards changed their views, and one ought not to assume that Yeats, if he had lived longer, would necessarily have followed his friend Pound, even in sympathy. But the tendency of the passage I have quoted above is obvious, and its complete throwing overboard of whatever good the past two thousand years have achieved is a disquieting symptom.

How do Yeats's political ideas link up with his leaning towards occultism? It is not clear at first glance why hatred of democracy and a tendency to believe in crystal-gazing should go together. Mr. Menon only discusses this rather shortly, but it is possible to make two guesses. To begin with, the theory that civilisation moves in recurring cycles is one way out for people who hate the concept of human equality. If it is true that 'all this', or something like it, 'has happened before', then science and the modern world are debunked at one stroke and progress becomes for ever impossible. It does not much matter if the lower orders are getting above themselves, for, after all, we shall soon be returning to an age of tyranny. Yeats is by no means alone in this outlook. If the universe is moving round on a wheel, the future must be foreseeable, perhaps even in some detail. It is merely a question of discovering the laws of its motion, as the early astronomers discovered the solar year. Believe that, and it becomes difficult not to believe in astrology or some similar system. A year before the war, examining a copy of *Gringoire*, the French Fascist weekly, much read by army officers, I found in it no less than thirty-eight advertisements of clairvoyants. Secondly, the very concept of occultism carries with it the idea that knowledge must be a secret thing, limited to a small circle of initiates. But the same idea is integral to Fascism. Those who dread the prospect of universal suffrage, popular education, freedom of thought, emancipation of women, will start off with a predilection towards secret cults. There is another link between Fascism and magic in the profound hostility of both to the Christian ethical code.

No doubt Yeats wavered in his beliefs and held at different times many different opinions, some enlightened, some not. Mr. Menon repeats for him Eliot's claim that he had the longest period of development of any poet who has ever lived. But there is one thing that seems constant, at least in all of his work that I can remember, and that is his hatred of modern Western civilisation and desire to return to the Bronze Age, or perhaps to the Middle Ages. Like all such thinkers, he tends to write in praise of ignorance. The Fool in his remarkable play, *The Hour-Glass*, is a Chestertonian figure, 'God's fool', the 'natural born innocent', who is always wiser than the wise man. The philosopher in the play dies on the knowledge that all his lifetime of thought has been wasted (I am quoting from memory again):

> The stream of the world has changed its course,
> And with the stream my thoughts have run
> Into some cloudy, thunderous spring
> That is its mountain-source:
> Ay, to a frenzy of the mind,
> That all that we have done's undone,
> Our speculation but as the wind.

Beautiful words, but by implication profoundly obscurantist and reactionary; for if it is really true that a village idiot, as such, is wiser than a philosopher, then it would be better if the alphabet had never been invented. Of course, all praise of the past is partly sentimental, because we do not live in the past. The poor do not praise poverty. Before you can despise the machine, the machine must set you free from brute labour. But that is not to say that Yeats's yearning for a more primitive and more hierarchical age was not sincere. How much of all this is traceable to mere snobbishness, product of Yeats's own position as an impoverished offshoot of the aristocracy, is a different question. And the connection between his obscurantist opinions and his tendency towards 'quaintness' of language remains to be worked out; Mr. Menon hardly touches upon it.

This is a very short book and I would greatly like to see Mr. Menon go ahead and write another book on Yeats, starting where this one leaves off. 'If the greatest poet of our times is exultantly ringing in an era of Fascism, it seems a somewhat disturbing symptom,' he says on the last page, and leaves it at that. It *is* a disturbing symptom, because it is not an isolated one. By and large the best writers of our time have been reactionary in tendency, and though Fascism does not offer any real return to the past, those who yearn for the past will accept Fascism sooner than its probable alternatives. But there are other lines of approach, as we have seen during the past two or three years. The relationship between Fascism and the literary intelligentsia badly needs investigating, and Yeats might well be the starting-point. He is best studied by someone like Mr. Menon, who can approach a poet primarily as a poet, but who also knows that a writer's political and religious beliefs are not excrescences to be laughed away, but something that will leave their mark even on the smallest detail of his work.

Not Enough Money: A Sketch of George Gissing

Tribune, 2 April 1943

All books worth reading "date," and George Gissing, perhaps the best novelist England has produced, is tied more tightly than most writers to a particular place and time. His world is the grey world of London in the 'eighties, with its gas lamps flickering in the everlasting fog, its dingy overcoats and high-crowned bowler hats, its Sunday gloom tempered by drunkenness, its unbearable "furnished apartments," and, above all, its desperate struggle against poverty by a middle class which was poor chiefly because it had remained "respectable." It is hard to think of Gissing without thinking of a hansom cab. But he did much more than preserve an atmosphere which, after all, is also preserved in the early *Sherlock Holmes* stories, and it is as a novelist that he will be remembered, even more than as an interpreter of the middle-class view of life.

When I suggest that Gissing is the best novelist we have produced I am not speaking frivolously. It is obvious that Dickens, Fielding and a dozen others are superior to him in natural talent, but Gissing is a "pure" novelist, a thing that few gifted English writers have been. Not only is he genuinely interested in character and in telling a story, but he has the great advantage of feeling no temptation to burlesque. It is a weakness of nearly all the characteristic English novelists, from Smollett to Joyce, that they want to be "like life" and at the same time want to get a laugh as often as possible. Very few English novels exist throughout on the same plane of probability. Gissing solves this problem without apparent difficulty, and it may be that his native pessimism was a help to him. For though he certainly did not lack humour, he did lack high spirits, the instinct to play the fool which made Dickens, for instance, as unable to pass a joke as some people are to pass a pub. And it is a fact that *The Odd Women*, to name only one, is more "like life" than the novels of bigger but less scrupulous writers.

At this date Gissing's best-known book is probably *The Private Papers of Henry Ryecroft*, written towards the end of his life when his worst struggles with poverty were over. But his real masterpieces are three novels, *The Odd Women*, *Demos* and *New Grub Street*, and his book on Dickens. In an article of this length I cannot even summarise the plots of the novels, but their central theme can be stated in three words – "not enough money." Gissing is the chronicler of poverty, not working-class poverty (he despises and perhaps hates the working class) but the cruel, grinding, "respectable" poverty of underfed clerks, downtrodden governesses and bankrupt tradesmen. He believed, perhaps not wrongly, that poverty causes more suffering in the middle class than in the working class. *The Odd Women*, his most perfect and also his most depressing novel, describes the fate of middle-class spinsters flung on to the world with neither money nor vocational training. *New Grub Street* records the horrors of free-lance journalism, even worse then than now. In *Demos* the money theme enters in a somewhat different way. The book is a story of the moral and intellectual corruption of a working-class Socialist who inherits a fortune. Writing as he was in the 'eighties, Gissing shows great prescience, and also a rather surprising knowledge of the inner workings of the Socialist movement. But the usual shabby-genteel motif is present in the person of the heroine, pushed into a hateful marriage by impoverished middle-class parents. Some of the social conditions Gissing describes have passed away, but the general atmosphere of his books is still horribly intelligible, so much so that I have sometimes thought that no professional writer should read *New Grub Street* and no spinster *The Odd Women*.

What is interesting is that with all his depth of understanding Gissing has no revolutionary tendency. He is frankly anti-Socialist and anti-democratic. Understanding better than almost anyone the horror of a money-ruled society, he has little wish to change it, because he does not believe that the change would make any real difference. The only worth-while objective, as he sees it, is to make a purely personal escape from the misery of poverty and then proceed to live a civilised, aesthetically decent life. He is not a snob, he does not wish for luxury or great wealth, he sees the spuriousness of the aristocracy and he despises beyond all other types the go-getting, self-made business man; but he does long for an untroubled, studious life, the kind of life that cannot be lived on less than about £400 a year. As for the working class, he regards them as savages, and says so with great frankness. However wrong he may have been in his outlook, one cannot say of him that he spoke in ignorance, for he himself came of very poor parents, and circumstances forced him to live much of his life among the poorest of the working class. His reactions are worth studying, even at this date. Here was a humane, intelligent man, of scholarly tastes, forced into intimacy with the London poor, and his conclusion was simply this: these people are savages who must on no account be allowed political power. In a more excusable form it is the ordinary reaction of the lower-middle-class man who is near enough to the working class to be afraid of them. Above all, Gissing grasped that the middle classes suffer more from economic insecurity than the working class, and are more ready to take action against it. To ignore that fact has been one of the major blunders of the Left, and from this sensitive novelist who loved Greek tragedies, hated politics and began writing long before Hitler was born, one can learn something about the origins of Fascism.

Literature and the Left

Tribune, 4 June 1943

"When a man of true Genius appears in the World, you may know him by this infallible Sign, that all the Dunces are in Conspiracy against him." So wrote Jonathan Swift, 200 years before the publication of *Ulysses*.

If you consult any sporting manual or year book you will find many pages devoted to the hunting of the fox and the hare, but not a word about the hunting of the highbrow. Yet this, more than any other, is the characteristic British sport, in season all the year round and enjoyed by rich and poor alike, with no complications from either class-feeling or political alignment.

For it should be noted that in its attitude towards "high-brows" – that is, towards any writer or artist who makes experiments in technique – the Left is no friendlier than the Right. Not only is "highbrow" almost as much a word of abuse in the *Daily Worker* as in *Punch*, but it is exactly those writers whose work shows both originality and the power to endure that Marxist doctrinaires single out for attack. I could name a long list of examples, but I am thinking especially of Joyce, Yeats, Lawrence and Eliot. Eliot, in particular, is damned in the left-wing press almost as automatically and perfunctorily as Kipling – and that by critics who only a few years back were going into raptures over the already forgotten masterpieces of the Left Book Club.

If you ask a "good party man" (and this goes for almost any party of the Left) what he objects to in Eliot, you get an answer that ultimately reduces to this. Eliot is a reactionary (he has declared himself a royalist, an Anglo-Catholic, etc.), and he is also a "bourgeois intellectual," out of touch with the common man: therefore he is a bad writer. Contained in this statement is a half-conscious confusion of ideas which vitiates nearly all politico-literary criticism.

To dislike a writer's politics is one thing. To dislike him because he forces you to think is another, not necessarily incompatible with the first. But as soon as you start talking about "good" and "bad" writers you are tacitly appealing to literary tradition and thus dragging in a totally different set of values. For what is a "good" writer? Was Shakespeare "good"? Most people would agree that he was. Yet Shakespeare is, and perhaps was even by the standards of his own time, reactionary in tendency; and he is also a difficult writer, only doubtfully accessible to the common man. What, then, becomes of the notion that Eliot is disqualified, as it were, by being an Anglo-Catholic royalist who is given to quoting Latin?

Left Wing literary criticism has not been wrong in insisting on the importance of subject-matter. It may not even have been wrong, considering the age we live in, in demanding that literature shall be first and foremost propaganda. Where it has been wrong is in making what are ostensibly literary judgements for political ends. To take a crude example, what Communist would dare to admit in public that Trotsky is a better writer than Stalin – as he is, of course? To say "X is a gifted writer, but he is a political enemy and I shall do my best to silence him" is harmless enough. Even if you end by silencing him with a tommy-gun you are not really sinning against the intellect. The deadly sin is to say "X is a political enemy: therefore he is a bad writer." And if anyone says that this kind of thing doesn't happen, I answer merely: look up the literary pages of the Left Wing press, from the *News Chronicle* to the *Labour Monthly*, and see what you find.

There is no knowing just how much the Socialist movement has lost by alienating the literary intelligentsia. But it has alienated them, partly by confusing tracts with literature, and partly by having no room in it for a humanistic culture. A writer can vote Labour as easily as anyone else, but it is very difficult for him to take part in the Socialist movement *as a writer*. Both the book-trained doctrinaire and the practical politician will despise him as a "bourgeois intellectual," and will lose no opportunity of telling him so. They will have much the same attitude towards his work as a golfing stockbroker would have. The illiteracy of politicians is a special feature of our age – as G. M. Trevelyan put it, "In the seventeenth century Members of Parliament quoted the Bible, in the eighteenth and nineteenth centuries, the classics, and in the twentieth century nothing" – and its corollary is the literary impotence of writers. In the years following the last war the best English writers were reactionary in tendency, though most of them took no direct part in politics. After them, about 1930, there came a generation of writers who tried very hard to be actively useful in the Left Wing movement. Numbers of them joined the Communist Party, and got there exactly the same reception as they would have got in the Conservative Party. That is, they were first regarded with patronage and suspicion, and then, when it was found that they would not or could not turn themselves into gramophone records, they were thrown out on their ears. Most of them retreated into individualism.

No doubt they still vote Labour but their talents are lost to the movement; and – a more sinister development – after them there comes a new generation of writers who, without being strictly non-political, are outside the Socialist movement from the start. Of the very young writers who are now beginning their careers, the most gifted are pacifists; a few may even have a leaning towards Fascism. There is hardly one to whom the mystique of the Socialist movement appears to mean anything. The ten-year-long struggle against Fascism seems to them meaningless and uninteresting, and they say so frankly. One could explain this in a number of ways, but the contemptuous attitude of the Left towards "bourgeois intellectuals" is likely to be part of the reason.

Gilbert Murray relates somewhere or other that he once lectured on Shakespeare to a Socialist debating society. At the end he called for questions in the usual way, to receive as the sole question asked: "Was Shakespeare a capitalist?" The depressing thing about this story is that it might well be true. Follow up its implications, and you perhaps get a glimpse of the reason why Céline wrote *Mea Culpa* and Auden is watching his navel in America.

Gandhi in Mayfair. Review of *Beggar My Neighbour* by Lionel Fielden

Horizon, September 1943

If you compare commercial advertising with political propaganda, one thing that strikes you is its relative intellectual honesty. The advertiser at least knows what he is aiming at – that is, money – whereas the propagandist, when he is not a lifeless hack, is often a neurotic working off some private grudge and actually desirous of the exact opposite of the thing he advocates. The ostensible purpose of Mr. Fielden's book is to further the cause of Indian independence. It will not have that effect, and I do not see much reason for thinking that he himself wishes for anything of the kind. For if someone is genuinely working for Indian independence, what is he likely to do? Obviously he will start by deciding what forces are potentially on his side, and then, as cold-bloodedly as any toothpaste advertiser, he will think out the best method of appealing to them. This is not Mr. Fielden's manner of approach. A number of motives are discernible in his book, but the immediately obvious one is a desire to work off various quarrels with the Indian Government, All-India Radio and various sections of the British Press. He does indeed marshal a number of facts about India, and towards the end he even produces a couple of pages of constructive suggestions, but for the most part his book is simply a nagging, irrelevant attack on British rule, mixed up with tourist-like gush about the superiority of Indian civilization. On the fly-leaf, just to induce that matey atmosphere which all propagandists aim at, he signs his dedicatory letter 'among the European barbarians', and then a few pages later introduces an imaginary Indian who denounces Western civilization with all the shrillness of a spinster of thirty-nine denouncing the male sex:

' . . . an Indian who is intensely proud of his own traditions, and regards Europeans as barbarians who are continually fighting, who use force to dominate other peaceful peoples, who think chiefly in terms of big business, whisky, and bridge; as people of comparatively recent growth, who, while they put an exaggerated value on plumbing, have managed to spread tuberculosis and venereal disease all over the world . . . he will say that to sit in the water in which you have washed, instead of bathing yourself in running water, is not clean, but dirty and disgusting; he will show, and I shall agree with him absolutely, that the English are a dirty and even a smelly nation compared with the Indians; he will assert, and I am not at all sure that he is wrong, that the use of half-washed forks, spoons and knives by different people for food is revoltingly barbaric when compared with the exquisite manipulation of food by Indian fingers; he will be confident that the Indian room, with its bare walls and beautiful carpets, is infinitely superior to the European clutter of uncomfortable chairs and tables', etc. etc. etc.

The whole book is written in this vein, more or less. The same nagging, hysterical note crops up every few pages, and where a comparison can be dragged in it is dragged in, the upshot always being that the East is Good and the West is Bad.

Now before stopping to inquire what service this kind of thing really does to the cause of Indian freedom, it is worth trying an experiment. Let me rewrite this passage as it might be uttered by an Englishman speaking up for his own civilization as shrilly as Mr. Fielden's Indian. It is important to notice that what he says is not more dishonest or more irrelevant than what I have quoted above:

'...an Englishman who is intensely proud of his own traditions, and regards Indians as an unmanly race who gesticulate like monkeys, are cruel to women and talk incessantly about money; as a people who take it upon themselves to despise Western science and hence are rotten with malaria and hookworm...he will say that in a hot climate washing in running water has its points, but that in cold climates all Orientals either wash as we do or as in the case of many Indian hill tribes – not at all; he will show, and I shall agree with him absolutely, that no Western European can walk through an Indian village without wishing that his smell organs had been removed beforehand; he will assert, and I am not at all sure that he is wrong, that eating with your fingers is a barbarous habit since it cannot be done without making disgusting noises; he will be confident that the English room, with its comfortable armchairs and friendly bookshelves, is infinitely superior to the bare Indian interior where the mere effort of sitting with no support to your back makes for vacuity of mind', etc. etc. etc.

Two points emerge here. To begin with, no English person would now write like that. No doubt many people think such thoughts, and even utter them behind closed doors, but to find anything of the kind in print you would have to go back ten years or so. Secondly, it is worth asking, what would be the effect of this passage on an Indian who happened to take it seriously? He would be offended, and very rightly. Well then, isn't it just possible that passages like the one I quoted from Mr. Fielden might have the same effect on a British reader? No one likes hearing his own habits and customs abused. This is not a trivial consideration, because at this moment books about India have, or could have, a special importance. There is no political solution in sight, the Indians cannot win their freedom and the British Government will not give it, and all one can for the moment do is to push public opinion in this country and America in the right direction. But that will not be done by any propaganda that is merely anti-European. A year ago, soon after the Cripps mission had failed, I saw a well-known Indian nationalist address a small meeting at which he was to explain why the Cripps offer had been refused. It was a valuable opportunity, because there were present a number of American newspaper correspondents who, if handled tactfully, might cable to America a sympathetic account of the Congress Party's case. They had come there with fairly open minds. Within about ten minutes the Indian had converted all of them into ardent supporters of the British Government, because instead of sticking to his subject he launched into an anti-British tirade quite obviously founded on spite and inferiority complex. That is just the mistake that a toothpaste advertiser would not make. But then the toothpaste advertiser is trying to sell toothpaste and not to get his own back on that Blimp who turned him out of a first-class carriage fifteen years ago.

However, Mr. Fielden's book raises wider issues than the immediate political problem. He upholds the East against the West on the ground that the East is religious, artistic and indifferent to 'progress', while the West is materialistic, scientific, vulgar and warlike. The great crime of Britain is to have forced industrialization on India. (Actually, the real crime of Britain during the last thirty years has been to do the opposite.) The West looks on work as an end in itself, but at the same time is obsessed with a 'high standard of living' (it is worth noticing that Mr. Fielden is anti-Socialist, Russophobe and somewhat contemptuous of the English working class), while India wants only to live in ancestral simplicity in a world freed from the machine. India must be independent, and at the same time must be de-industrialized. It is also suggested a number of times, though not in very clear terms, that India ought to be neutral in the present war. Needless to say, Mr. Fielden's hero is Gandhi, about whose financial background he says nothing. 'I have a notion that the legend of Gandhi may yet be a flaming inspiration to the millions of the East, and perhaps to those of the West. But it is, for the time being, the East which provides the fruitful soil, because the East has not yet fallen prone before the Golden Calf. And it may be for the East, once again,

477

to show mankind that human happiness does not depend on that particular form of worship, and that the conquest of materialism is also the conquest of war.' Gandhi makes many appearances in the book, playing rather the same part as 'Frank' in the literature of the Buchmanites.

Now, I do not know whether or not Gandhi will be a 'flaming inspiration' in years to come. When one thinks of the creatures who *are* venerated by humanity it does not seem particularly unlikely. But the statement that India 'ought' to be independent, *and* de-industrialized, *and* neutral in the present war, is an absurdity. If one forgets the details of the political struggle and looks at the strategic realities, one sees two facts which are in seeming conflict. The first is that whatever the 'ought' of the question may be, India is very unlikely ever to be independent in the sense in which Britain or Germany is now independent. The second is that India's *desire* for independence is a reality and cannot be talked out of existence.

In a world in which national sovereignty exists, India cannot be a sovereign State, because she is unable to defend herself. And the more she is the cow and spinning-wheel paradise imagined by Mr. Fielden, the more this is true. What is now called independence means the power to manufacture aeroplanes in large numbers. Already there are only five genuinely independent States in the world, and if present trends continue there will in the end be only three. On a long-term view it is clear that India has little chance in a world of power politics, while on a short-term view it is clear that the necessary first step towards Indian freedom is an Allied victory. Even that would only be a short and uncertain step, but the alternatives must lead to India's continued subjection. If we are defeated, Japan or Germany takes over India and that is the end of the story. If there is a compromise peace (Mr. Fielden seems to hint at times that this is desirable), India's chances are no better, because in such circumstances we should inevitably cling to any territories we had captured or not lost. A compromise peace is always a peace of 'grab what you can'. Mr. Fielden brings forward his imaginary Indian to suggest that if India were neutral Japan might leave her alone; I doubt whether any responsible Indian nationalist has said anything quite so stupid as that. The other idea, more popular in Left-wing circles, that India could defend herself better on her own than with our help, is a sentimentality. If the Indians were militarily superior to ourselves they would have driven us out long ago. The much-quoted example of China is very misleading here. India is a far easier country to conquer than China, if only because of its better communications, and in any case Chinese resistance depends on help from the highly-industrialized states and would collapse without it. One must conclude that for the next few years India's destiny is linked with that of Britain and the U.S.A. It might be different if the Russians could get their hands free in the West or if China were a great military power; but that again implies a complete defeat of the Axis, and points away from the neutrality which Mr. Fielden seems to think desirable. The idea put forward by Gandhi himself, that if the Japanese came they could be dealt with by sabotage and 'non-co-operation', is a delusion, nor does Gandhi show any very strong signs of believing in it. Those methods have never seriously embarrassed the British and would make no impression on the Japanese. After all, where is the Korean Gandhi?

But against this is the *fact* of Indian nationalism, which is not to be exorcized by the humbug of White Papers or by a few phrases out of Marx. And it is nationalism of an emotional, romantic, even chauvinistic kind. Phrases like 'the sacred soil of the Motherland', which now seem merely ludicrous in Britain, come naturally enough to an Indian intellectual. When the Japanese appeared to be on the point of invading India, Nehru actually used the phrase 'Who dies if India live?' So the wheel comes full circle and the Indian rebel quotes Kipling. And nationalism at this level works indirectly in favour of Fascism. Extremely few Indians are at all attracted by the idea of a federated world, the only kind of world in which India could actually be free. Even those who pay lip-service to federalism usually want only an Eastern federation, thought of as a military alliance against the West. The idea of the class struggle has little appeal anywhere in Asia, nor do Russia and China evoke much loyalty in India. As for the Nazi domination of Europe, only a handful of Indians are able to see that it affects their own destiny in any way. In some of the smaller Asiatic countries

479

the 'my country right or wrong' nationalists were exactly the ones who went over to the Japanese – a step which may not have been wholly due to ignorance.

But here there arises a point which Mr. Fielden hardly touches on, and that is: we don't know to what extent Asiatic nationalism is simply the product of our own oppression. For a century all the major Oriental nations except Japan have been more or less in subjection, and the hysteria and shortsightedness of the various nationalist movements may be the result simply of that. To realize that national sovereignty is the enemy of national freedom may be a great deal easier when you are not being ruled by foreigners. It is not certain that this is so, since the most nationalist of the Oriental nations, Japan, is also the one that has never been conquered, but at least one can say that if the solution is not along these lines, then there *is* no solution. Either power politics must yield to common decency, or the world must go spiralling down into a nightmare of which we can already catch some dim glimpses. And the necessary first step, before we can make our talk about world federation sound even credible, is that Britain shall get off India's back. This is the only large scale decent action that is possible in the world at this moment. The immediate preliminaries would be: abolish the Viceroyalty and the India Office, release the Congress prisoners, and declare India formally independent. The rest is detail.

But how are we to bring any such thing about? If it is done at this time, it can only be a voluntary act. Indian independence has no asset except public opinion in Britain and America, which is only a potential asset. Japan, Germany and the British Government are all on the other side, and India's possible friends, China and the U.S.S.R., are fighting for their lives and have little bargaining power. There remain the peoples of Britain and America, who are in a position to put pressure on their own Governments if they see a reason for doing so. At the time of the Cripps mission, for instance, it would have been quite easy for public opinion in this country to force the Government into making a proper offer, and similar opportunities may recur. Mr. Fielden, by the way, does his best to throw doubt on Cripps' personal honesty, and also lets it appear that the Congress Working Committee were unanimously against accepting the Cripps proposals, which was not the case. In fact, Cripps extorted the best terms he could get from the Government; to get better ones he would have had to have public opinion actively and intelligently behind him. There-fore the first job is – win over the ordinary people of this country. Make them see that India matters, and that India has been shamefully treated and deserves restitution. But you are not going to do that by insulting them. Indians, on the whole, grasp this better than their English apologists. After all, what is the probable effect of a book which irrelevantly abuses every English institution, rapturizes over the 'wisdom of the East' like an American schoolmarm on a conducted tour, and mixes up pleas for Indian freedom with pleas for surrender to Hitler? At best it can only convert the converted, and it may de-convert a few of those. The net effect must be to strengthen British imperialism, though its motives are probably more complex than this may seem to imply.

On the surface, Mr. Fielden's book is primarily a plea for 'spirituality' as against 'materialism'. On the one hand an un-critical reverence for everything Oriental; on the other a hatred of the West generally, and of Britain in particular, hatred of science and the machine, suspicion of Russia, contempt for the working-class conception of Socialism. The whole adds up to Parlour Anarchism – a plea for the simple life, based on divi-dends. Rejection of the machine is, of course, always founded on tacit acceptance of the machine, a fact symbolized by Gandhi as he plays with his spinning-wheel in the mansion of some cotton millionaire. But Gandhi also comes into the picture in another way. It is noticeable that both Gandhi and Mr. Fielden have an exceedingly equivocal attitude towards the present war. Although variously credited in this country with being a 'pure' pacifist and a Japanese agent, Gandhi has, in fact, made so many conflicting pronouncements on the war that it is difficult to keep track of them. At one moment his 'moral support' is with the Allies, at another it is withdrawn, at one moment he thinks it best to come to terms with the Japanese, at another he wishes to oppose them by non-violent means – at the cost, he thinks, of several million lives – at another he urges Britain to give battle in the west and leave India to be invaded, at another he 'has no wish to harm the

Allied cause' and declares that he does not want the Allied troops to leave India. Mr. Fielden's views on the war are less complicated, but equally ambiguous. In no place does he state whether or not he wishes the Axis to be defeated. Over and over again he urges that an Allied victory can lead to no possible good result, but at the same time he disclaims 'defeatism' and even argues that Indian neutrality would be useful to us in a *military* sense, i.e. that we could fight better if India were not a liability. Now, if this means anything, it means that he wants a compromise, a negotiated peace; and though he fails to say so, I do not doubt that that is what he does want. But curiously enough, this is the *imperialist* solution. The appeasers have always wanted neither defeat nor victory but a compromise with the other imperialist powers; and they too have known how to use the manifest folly of war as an argument.

For years past the more intelligent imperialists have been in favour of compromising with the Fascists, even if they had to give away a good deal in order to do so, because they have seen that only thus could imperialism be salvaged. Some of them are not afraid to hint this fairly broadly even now. If we carry the war to a destructive conclusion, the British Empire will either be lost, or democratized, or pawned to America. On the other hand it could and probably would survive in something like its present form if there were other sated imperialist powers which had an interest in preserving the existing world system. If we came to an understanding with Germany and Japan we might diminish our possessions (even that isn't certain: it is a little-noticed fact that *in territory* Britain and the U.S.A. have gained more than they have lost in this war), but we should at least be confirmed in what we had already. The world would be split up between three or four great imperial powers who, for the time being, would have no motive for quarrelling. Germany would be there to neutralize Russia, Japan would be there to prevent the development of China. Given such a world system, India could be kept in subjection almost indefinitely. And more than this, it is doubtful whether a compromise peace *could* follow any other lines. So it would seem that Parlour Anarchism is something very innocuous after all. Objectively it only demands what the worst of the appeasers want, subjectively it is of a kind to irritate the possible friends of India in this country. And does not this bear a sort of resemblance to the career of Gandhi, who has alienated the British public by his extremism and aided the British Government by his moderation? Impossibilism and reaction are usually in alliance, though not, of course, conscious alliance.

Hypocrisy is a very rare thing, true villainy is perhaps [as] difficult as virtue. We live in a lunatic world in which opposites are constantly changing into one another, in which pacifists find themselves worshipping Hitler, Socialists become nationalists, patriots become quislings, Buddhists pray for the success of the Japanese army, and the Stock Market takes an upward turn when the Russians stage an offensive. But though these people's motives are often obvious enough when seen from the outside, they are not obvious to themselves. The scenes imagined by Marxists, in which wicked rich men sit in little secret rooms and hatch schemes for robbing the workers, don't happen in real life. The robbery takes place, but it is committed by sleepwalkers. Now, one of the finest weapons that the rich have ever evolved for use against the poor is 'spirituality'. If you can induce the working-man to believe that his desire for a decent standard of living is 'materialism', you have got him where you want him. Also, if you can induce the Indian to remain 'spiritual' instead of taking up with vulgar things like trade unions, you can ensure that he will always remain a coolie. Mr. Fielden is indignant with the 'materialism' of the Western working class, whom he accuses of being even worse in this respect than the rich and of wanting not only radios but even motor-cars and fur coats. The obvious answer is that these sentiments don't come well from someone who is in a comfortable and privileged position himself. But that is only an answer, not a diagnosis, for the problem of the disaffected intelligentsia would be hardly a problem at all if ordinary dishonesty were involved.

In the last twenty years Western civilization has given the intellectual security without responsibility, and in England, in particular, it has educated him in scepticism while anchoring him almost immovably in the privileged class. He has been in the position of a young man living on an allowance from a father whom he hates. The result is a deep feeling of guilt and resentment, not combined with any genuine desire to escape. But some psychological escape, some form of self-justification there must be, and one of the most satisfactory is transferred nationalism. During the nineteen-thirties the normal transference was to Soviet Russia, but there are other alternatives, and it is noticeable that pacifism and Anarchism, rather than Stalinism, are now gaining ground among the young. These creeds have the advantage that they aim at the impossible and therefore in effect demand very little. If you throw in a touch of Oriental mysticism and Buchmanite raptures over Gandhi, you have everything that a disaffected intellectual needs. The life of an English gentleman and the moral attitude of a saint can be enjoyed simultaneously. By merely transferring your allegiance from England to India (it used to be Russia), you can indulge to the full in all the chauvinistic sentiments which would be totally impossible if you recognized them for what they were. In the name of pacifism you can compromise with Hitler, and in the name of 'spirituality' you can keep your money. It is no accident that those who wish for an inconclusive ending to the war tend to extol the East as against the West. The actual facts don't matter very much. The fact that the Eastern nations have shown themselves at least as warlike and bloodthirsty as the Western ones, that so far from rejecting industrialism, the East is adopting it as swiftly as it can – this is irrelevant, since what is wanted is the mythos of the peaceful, religious and patriarchal East to set against the greedy and materialistic West. As soon as you have 'rejected' industrialism, and hence Socialism, you are in that strange no man's land where the Fascist and the pacifist join forces. There is indeed a sort of apocalyptic truth in the statement of the German radio that the teachings of Hitler and Gandhi are the same. One realizes this when one sees Middleton Murry praising the Japanese invasion of China and Gerald Heard proposing to institute the Hindu caste system in Europe at the same time as the Hindus themselves are abandoning it. We shall be hearing a lot about the superiority of Eastern civilization in the next few years. Meanwhile this is a mischievous book, which will be acclaimed in the Left-wing Press and welcomed for quite different reasons by the more intelligent Right.

Review of *Subject India* by Henry Noel Brailsford

The Nation, 20 November 1943

If there is one point in the Indian problem that cannot be disputed – or, at any rate, is not disputed, outside the ranks of the British Conservative Party – it is that Britain ought to stop ruling India as early as possible. But this is a smaller basis of agreement than it sounds, and the answers to literally every other question are always coloured by subjective feelings. Mr. Brailsford is better equipped than the majority of writers on India in that he is not only aware of his own prejudices but possesses enough background knowledge to be unafraid of the "experts." Probably he has not been very long in India, perhaps he does not even speak any Indian language, but he differs from the vast majority of English left-wingers in having bothered to visit India at all, and in being more interested in the peasants than in the politicians.

As he rightly says, the great, central fact about India is its poverty. From birth to death, generation after generation, the peasant lives his life in the grip of the landlord or the money-lender – they are frequently the same person – tilling his tiny patch of soil with the tools and methods of the Bronze Age. Over great areas the children barely taste milk after they are weaned, and the average physique is so wretched that ninety-eight pounds is a normal weight for a full-grown man. The last detailed survey to be taken showed that the average Indian income was Rs. 62 (about £4 13s. od.) per annum: in the same period the average British income was £94. In spite of the drift to the towns that is occurring in India as elsewhere, the condition of the industrial workers is hardly better than that of the peasants. Brailsford describes them in the slums of Bombay, sleeping eight to a tiny room, with three water taps among four hundred people, and working a twelve-hour day, three hundred and sixty-five days a year, for wages of around seven and sixpence a week. These conditions will not be cured simply by the removal of British rule, but neither can they be seriously improved while the British remain, because British policy, largely unconscious, is to hamper industrialization and preserve the status quo. The worst barbarities from which Indians suffer are inflicted on them not by Europeans but by other Indians – the landlords and money-lenders, the bribe-taking minor officials, and the Indian capitalists who exploit their working people with a ruthlessness quite impossible in the West since the rise of trade unionism. But although the business community, at any rate, tends to be anti-British and is involved in the Nationalist movement, the privileged classes really depend on British arms. Only when the British have gone will what Brailsford calls the latent class war be able to develop.

Brailsford is attempting exposition rather than moral judgement, and he gives no very definite answer to the difficult question of whether, in balance, the British have done India more good than harm. As he points out, they have made possible an increase of population without making it possible for that population to be properly fed. They have saved India from war, internal and external, at the expense of destroying political liberty. Probably their greatest gift to India has been the railway. If one studies a railway map of Asia, India looks like a piece of fishing-net in the middle of a white tablecloth. And this network of communications has not only made it possible to check famines by bringing food to the afflicted areas – the famine now raging in India would hardly have been a famine at all by the standards of a hundred years ago – but to administer India as a unit, with a common system of law, internal free trade and freedom of movement, and even, for the educated minority, a lingua franca in the English language. India is potentially a nation, as Europe, with its smaller population and great racial homogeneity, is not. But since 1910 or thereabouts the British power has acted as a dead hand. Often loosely denounced as "fascist," the British régime in India is almost the exact opposite of fascism, since it has never developed the notion of positive government at all. It has remained an old-fashioned despotism, keeping the peace, collecting its taxes, and for the rest letting things slide, with hardly the faintest interest in how its subjects lived or what they thought, so long as they were outwardly obedient. As a result – to pick just one fact out of the thousands one could choose – the whole subcontinent, in this year of 1943, is incapable of manufacturing an automobile engine. In spite of all that can be said on the other side, this fact alone would justify Brailsford in his final conclusion: "Our day in India is over; we have no creative part to play."

Brailsford is justifiably bleak about the future. He sees that the handing over of power is a complicated process which cannot be achieved quickly, especially in the middle of a war, and that it will solve nothing in itself. There is still the problem of India's poverty and ignorance to be solved, and the struggle between the landlords, big business, and the labour movement to be fought out. And there is also the question of how, if at all, a backward agricultural country like India is to remain independent in a world of power politics. Brailsford gives a good account of the current political situation, in which he struggles very hard not to be engulfed by the prevailing left-wing orthodoxy. He writes judiciously about the tortuous character of Gandhi; comes nearer to being fair to Cripps than most English commentators have been – Cripps, indeed, has been the whipping-boy of the left, both British and Indian – and rightly emphasizes the importance of the Indian princes, who are often forgotten and who present a much more serious difficulty than the faked-up quarrel between Hindus and Moslems. At this moment India is such a painful subject that it is hardly possible to write a really good book about it. English books are either dishonest or irresponsible; American books are ignorant and self-righteous; Indian books are coloured by spite and an inferiority complex. Well aware of the gaps in his knowledge and the injustices he is bound to commit, Brailsford has produced not only a transparently honest but – what is much rarer in this context – a good-tempered book. Nearly all books written about the British Empire in these days have the air of being written *at* somebody – either a Blimp, or a Communist, or an American, as the case may be. Brailsford is writing primarily for the ordinary British public, the people who before all others have the power and the duty to do something about India, and whose conscience it is first necessary to move. But it is a book that the American public might find useful too. Perhaps it is worth uttering the warning that – owing to war-time conditions – there are many misprints, and as some of them have crept into the statistics these are apt to be misleading.

As I Please 1

Tribune, 3 December 1943

Scene in a tobacconist's shop. Two American soldiers sprawling across the counter, one of them just sober enough to make unwanted love to the two young women who run the shop, the other at the stage known as "fighting drunk." Enter Orwell in search of matches. The pugnacious one makes an effort and stands upright.

Soldier: "Wharrishay is, perfijious Albion. You heard that? Perfijious Albion. Never trust a Britisher. You can't trust the b——s."

Orwell: "Can't trust them with what?"

Soldier: "Wharrishay is, down with Britain. Down with the British. You wanna do anything 'bout that? Then you can ——well do it." (Sticks his face out like a tomcat on a garden wall.)

Tobacconist: "He'll knock your block off if you don't shut up."

Soldier: "Wharrishay is, down with Britain." (Subsides across the counter again. The tobacconist lifts his head delicately out of the scales.)

This kind of thing is not exceptional. Even if you steer clear of Piccadilly with its seething swarms of drunks and whores, it is difficult to go anywhere in London without having the feeling that Britain is now Occupied Territory. The general consensus of opinion seems to be that the only American soldiers with decent manners are the Negroes. On the other hand the Americans have their own justifiable complaints – in particular, they complain of the children who follow them night and day, cadging sweets.

Does this sort of thing matter? The answer is that it might matter at some moment when Anglo-American relations were in the balance, and when the still powerful forces in this country which want an understanding with Japan were able to show their faces again. At such moments popular prejudice can count for a great deal. Before the war there was no popular anti-American feeling in this country. It all dates from the arrival of the American troops, and it is made vastly worse by the tacit agreement never to discuss it in print.

Seemingly it is our fixed policy in this war not to criticise our allies, nor to answer their criticisms of us. As a result things have happened which are capable of causing the worst kind of trouble sooner or later. An example is the agreement by which American troops in this country are not liable to British courts for offences against British subjects – practically "extra-territorial rights." Not one English person in ten knows of the existence of this agreement; the newspapers barely reported it and refrained from commenting on it. Nor have people been made to realise the extent of anti-British feeling in the United States. Drawing their picture of America from films carefully edited for the British market, they have no notion of the kind of thing that Americans are brought up to believe about us. Suddenly to discover, for instance, that the average American thinks the U.S.A. had more casualties than Britain in the last war comes as a shock, and the kind of shock that can cause a violent quarrel. Even such a fundamental difficulty as the fact that an American soldier's pay is five times that of a British soldier has never been properly ventilated. No sensible person wants to whip up Anglo-American jealousy. On the contrary, it is just because one does want a good relationship between the two countries that one wants plain speaking. Our official soft-soaping policy does us no good in America, while in this country it allows dangerous resentments to fester just below the surface.

Since 1935, when pamphleteering revived, I have been a steady collector of pamphlets political, religious and what-not. To anyone who happens to come across it and has a shilling to spare I recommend *The 1946 MS.*, by Robin Maugham, published by the War Facts Press. It is a good example of that small but growing school of literature, the non-party Radical school. It purports to describe the establishment in Britain of a Fascist dictatorship, starting in 1944 and headed by a success-ful general who is (I think) drawn from a living model. I found it interesting because it gives you the average middle-class man's conception of what Fascism would be like, and more important, of the reasons why Fascism might succeed. Its appearance (along with other similar pamphlets I have in my collection) shows how far that average middle-class man has travelled since 1939, when Socialism still meant dividing the money up and what happened in Europe was none of our business.

Who wrote this?

"As we walked over the Drury Lane gratings of the cellars a most foul stench came up, and one in particular that I remember to this day. A man half dressed pushed open a broken window beneath us, just as we passed by, and there issued such a blast of corruption, made up of gases bred by filth, air breathed and rebreathed a hundred times, charged with the odours of unnameable personal uncleanness and disease, that I staggered to the gutter with a qualm which I could scarcely conquer... I did not know, till I came in actual contact with them, how far away the classes which lie at the bottom of great cities are from those above them; how completely they are inaccessible to motives which act upon ordinary human beings, and how deeply they are sunk beyond ray of sun or stars, immersed in the selfishness naturally begotten of their incessant struggle for existence and incessant warfare with society. It was an awful thought to me, ever present on those Sundays, and haunting me at other times, that men, women, and children were living in such brutish degradation, and that as they died others would take their place. Our civilisation seemed nothing but a thin film or crust lying over a volcanic pit, and I often wondered whether some day the pit would not break up through it and destroy us all."

You would know, at any rate, that this comes from some nineteenth-century writer. Actually it is from a novel, *Mark Rutherford's Deliverance*. (Mark Rutherford, whose real name was Hale White, wrote this book as a pseudo-autobiography.) Apart from the prose, you could recognise this as coming from the nineteenth century because of that description of the unendurable filth of the slums. The London slums of that day *were* like that, and all honest writers so described them. But even more characteristic is that notion of a whole block of the population being so degraded as to be beyond contact and beyond redemption.

Almost all nineteenth-century English writers are agreed upon this, even Dickens. A large part of the town working class, ruined by industrialism, are simply savages. Revolution is not a thing to be hoped for: it simply means the swamping of civilisation by the sub-human. In this novel (it is one of the best novels in English) Mark Rutherford describes the opening of a sort of mission or settlement near Drury Lane. Its object was "gradually to attract Drury Lane to come and be saved." Needless to say this was a failure. Drury Lane not only did not want to be saved in the religious sense, it didn't even want to be civilised. All that Mark Rutherford and his friend succeeded in doing, all that one could do, indeed, at that time, was to provide a sort of refuge for the few people of the neighbourhood who did not belong to their surroundings. The general masses were outside the pale.

Mark Rutherford was writing of the 'seventies, and in a footnote dated 1884 he remarks that "socialism, nationalisation of the land and other projects" have now made their appearance, and may perhaps give a gleam of hope. Nevertheless, he assumes that the condition of the working class will grow worse and not better as time goes on. It was natural to believe this (even Marx seems to have believed it), because it was hard at that time to foresee the enormous increase in the productivity of labour. Actually, such an improvement in the standard of living has taken place as Mark Rutherford and his contemporaries would have considered quite impossible.

The London slums are still bad enough, but they are nothing to those of the nineteenth century. Gone are the days when a single room used to be inhabited by four families, one in each corner, and when incest and infanticide were taken almost for granted. Above all, gone are the days when it seemed natural to write off a whole stratum of the population as irredeemable savages. The most snobbish Tory alive would not now write of the London working class as Mark Rutherford does. And Mark Rutherford – like Dickens, who shared his attitude – was a Radical! Progress does happen, hard though it may be to believe it, in this age of concentration camps and big beautiful bombs.

[*George Orwell will write this column each week.*]

491

As I Please 2
Tribune, 10 December 1943

The recently-issued special supplement to the *New Republic* entitled *The Negro: His Future in America* is worth a reading, but it raises more problems than it discusses. The facts it reveals about the present treatment of Negroes in the U.S.A. are bad enough in all conscience. In spite of the quite obvious necessities of war, Negroes are still pushed out of skilled jobs, segregated and insulted in the Army, assaulted by white policemen and discriminated against by white magistrates. In a number of the Southern States they are disenfranchised by means of a poll tax. On the other hand, those of them who have votes are so fed up with the present Administration that they are beginning to swing towards the Republican Party – that is, in effect, to give their support to Big Business. But all this is merely a single facet of the world-wide problem of colour. And what the authors of this supplement fail to point out is that that problem simply cannot be solved inside the capitalist system.

One of the big unmentionable facts of politics is the differential standard of living. An English working-man spends on cigarettes about the same sum as an Indian peasant has for his entire income. It is not easy for Socialists to admit this, or at any rate to emphasise it. If you want people to rebel against the existing system, you have got to show them that they are badly off, and it is doubtful tactics to *start* by telling an Englishman on the dole that in the eyes of an Indian coolie he would be next door to a millionaire. Almost complete silence reigns on this subject, at any rate at the European end, and it contributes to the lack of solidarity between white and coloured workers. Almost without knowing it – and perhaps without wanting to know it – the white worker exploits the coloured worker, and in revenge the coloured worker can be and is used against the white. Franco's Moors in Spain were only doing more dramatically the same thing as is done by half-starved Indians in Bombay mills or Japanese factory-girls sold into semi-slavery by their parents. As things are, Asia and Africa are simply a bottomless reserve of scab labour.

The coloured worker cannot be blamed for feeling no solidarity with his white comrades. The gap between their standard of living and his own is so vast that it makes any differences which may exist in the West seem negligible. In Asiatic eyes the European class struggle is a sham. The Socialist movement has never gained a real foothold in Asia or Africa, or even among the American Negroes: it is everywhere side-tracked by nationalism and race-hatred. Hence the spectacle of thoughtful Negroes getting ready to vote for Dewey, and Indian Congressmen preferring their own capitalists to the British Labour Party. There is no solution until the living-standards of the thousand million people who are not "white" can be forced up to the same level as our own. But as this might mean temporarily *lowering* our own standards the subject is systematically avoided by Left and Right alike.

Is there anything that one can do about this, as an individual? One can at least remember that the colour problem exists. And there is one small precaution which is not much trouble, and which can perhaps do a little to mitigate the horrors of the colour war. That is to avoid using insulting nicknames. It is an astonishing thing that few journalists, even in the Left-wing press, bother to find out which names are and which are not resented by members of other races. The word "native," which makes any Asiatic boil with rage, and which has been dropped even by British officials in India these ten years past, is flung about all over the place. "Negro" is habitually printed with a small n, a thing most Negroes resent. One's information about these matters needs to be kept up to date. I have just been carefully going through the proofs of a reprinted book of mine, cutting out the word "Chinaman" wherever it occurred and substituting "Chinese." The book was written less than a dozen years ago, but in the intervening time "Chinaman" has become a deadly insult. Even "Mahomedan" is now beginning to be resented: one should say "Moslem." These things are childish, but then nationalism is childish. And after all we ourselves do not actually like being called "Limeys" or "Britishers."

As I Please 3

Tribune, 17 December 1943

So many letters have arrived, attacking me for my remarks about the American soldiers in this country, that I must return to the subject.

Contrary to what most of my correspondents seem to think, I was not trying to make trouble between ourselves and our Allies, nor am I consumed by hatred for the United States. I am much less anti-American than most English people are at this moment. What I say, and what I repeat, is that our policy of not criticising our Allies, and not answering their criticism of us (we don't answer the Russians either, nor even the Chinese) is a mistake, and is likely to defeat its own object in the long run. And so far as Anglo-American relations go, there are three difficulties which badly need dragging into the open and which simply don't get mentioned in the British press.

1. *Anti-American feeling in Britain.* – Before the war, anti-American feeling was a middle-class, and perhaps upper-class thing, resulting from imperialist and business jealousy and disguising itself as dislike of the American accent, etc. The working class, so far from being anti-American, were becoming rapidly Americanised in speech by means of the films and jazz songs. Now, in spite of what my correspondents may say, I can hear few good words for the Americans anywhere. This obviously results from the arrival of the American troops. It has been made worse by the fact that, for various reasons, the Mediterranean campaign had to be represented as an American show while most of the casualties had to be suffered by the British. (See Philip Jordan's remarks in his *Tunis Diary*.) I am not saying that popular English prejudices are always justified: I am saying that they exist.

2. *Anti-British feeling in America.* – We ought to face the fact that large numbers of Americans are brought up to dislike and despise us. There is a large section of the press whose main accent is anti-British, and countless other papers which attack Britain in a more sporadic way. In addition there is a systematic guying of what are supposed to be British habits and manners on the stage and in comic strips and cheap magazines. The

494

typical Englishman is represented as a chinless ass with a title, a monocle and a habit of saying "Haw, haw." This legend is believed in by relatively responsible Americans, for example by the veteran novelist Theodore Dreiser, who remarks in a public speech that "the British are horse-riding aristocratic snobs." (Forty-six million horse-riding snobs!) It is a commonplace on the American stage that the Englishman is almost never allowed to play a favourable role, any more than the Negro is allowed to appear as anything more than a comic. Yet right up to Pearl Harbor the American movie industry had an agreement with the Japanese Government never to present a Japanese character in an unfavourable light!

I am not blaming the Americans for all this. The anti-British press has powerful business forces behind it, besides ancient quarrels in many of which Britain was in the wrong. As for popular anti-British feeling, we partly bring it on ourselves by exporting our worst specimens. But what I do want to emphasise is that these anti-British currents in the U.S.A. are very strong, and that the British press has consistently failed to draw attention to them. There has never been in England anything that one could call an anti-American press: and since the war there has been a steady refusal to answer criticism, and a careful censorship of the radio to cut out anything that the Americans might object to. As a result, many English people don't realise how they are regarded, and get a shock when they find out.

3. *Soldiers' Pay.* – It is now nearly two years since the first American troops reached this country, and I rarely see American and British soldiers together. Quite obviously the major cause of this is the difference of pay. You can't have really close and friendly relations with somebody whose income is five times your own. Financially, the whole American army is in the middle class. In the field this might not matter, but in the training period it makes it almost impossible for British and American soldiers to fraternise. If you don't want friendly relations between the British Army and the American Army, well and good. But if you do, you must either pay the British soldier ten shillings a day or make the American soldier bank the surplus of his pay in America. I don't profess to know which of these alternatives is the right one.

*

One way of feeling infallible is not to keep a diary. Looking back through the diary I kept in 1940 and 1941 I find that I was usually wrong when it was possible to be wrong. Yet I was not so wrong as the Military Experts. Experts of various schools were telling us in 1939 that the Maginot Line was impregnable, and that the Russo-German pact had put an end to Hitler's eastward expansion; in early 1940 they were telling us that the days of tank warfare were over; in mid-1940 they were telling us that the Germans would invade Britain forthwith; in mid-1941 that the Red Army would fold up in six weeks; in December, 1941, that Japan would collapse after 90 days; in July, 1942, that Egypt was lost – and so on, more or less indefinitely.

Where now are the men who told us those things? Still on the job, drawing fat salaries. Instead of the unsinkable battleship we have the unsinkable Military Expert.

To be politically happy these days you need to have no more memory than an animal. The people who demonstrated most loudly against Mosley's release were the leaders of the defunct People's Convention, which at the time when Mosley was interned was running a "stop the war" campaign barely distinguishable from Mosley's own. And I myself know of a ladies' knitting circle which was formed to knit comforts for the Finns, and which two years later – with no sense of incongruity – finished off various garments that had been left on its hands and sent them to the Russians. Early in 1942 a friend of mine bought some fried fish done up in a piece of newspaper of 1940. On one side was an article proving that the Red Army was no good, and on the other a write-up of that gallant sailor and well-known Anglophile, Admiral Darlan. But my favourite in this line is the *Daily Express* leader which began, a few days after the U.S.S.R. entered the war: "This paper has always worked for good relations between Britain and Soviet Russia."

Books have gone up in price like everything else, but the other day I picked up a copy of Lemprière's *Classical Dictionary*, the *Who's Who* of the ancients, for only sixpence. Opening it at random, I came upon the biography of Laïs, the famous courtesan, daughter of the mistress of Alcibiades:

"She first began to sell her favours at Corinth for 10,000 drachmas, and the immense number of princes, noblemen, philosophers, orators and plebeians who courted her, bear witness to her personal charms...Demosthenes visited Corinth for the sake of Laïs, but informed by the courtesan that admittance to her bed was to be bought at the enormous sum of about £200 English money, the orator departed, and observed that he would not buy repentance at so dear a price...She ridiculed the austerity of philosophers, and the weakness of those who pretend to have gained a superiority over their passions, by observing that sages and philosophers were not above the rest of mankind, for she found them at her door as often as the rest of the Athenians."

There is more in the same vein. However, it ends on a good moral, for "the other women, jealous of her charms, assassinated her in the temple of Venus about 340 B.C." That was 2,283 years ago. I wonder how many of the present denizens of *Who's Who* will seem worth reading about in A.D. 4226?

Review of *Collected Poems of W. H. Davies*
The Observer, 19 December 1943

Seen in bulk, W. H. Davies's work gives a somewhat different impression from that given by the handful of poems that have found their way into so many anthologies. So far as manner goes, indeed, almost any of his poems is representative. His great fault is lack of variation – a quality that one might, perhaps, call wateriness, since it gives one the feeling of drinking draught after draught of spring water, wonderfully pure and refreshing, but somehow turning one's mind in the direction of whisky after the first pint or two. On the other hand – and it is here that the anthologies have probably misrepresented him – his subject-matter is remarkably variegated. Not only did his years of vagabondage in common lodging-houses supply a large part of it, but he shows a distinct tinge of morbidity. Behind the lambs and the wildflowers there is an almost Baudelairean background of harlots, drunkenness, and corpses, and in poems like "The Rat" and "Down Underground" he does not flinch from the most horrible subjects that any writer could deal with. Yet his manner never varies, or barely varies: the clouds in the April sky and the dead girl rotting in her grave are spoken of in almost the same tone of voice.

One thing that emerges from this collection of over six hundred poems is the perfection of Davies's taste. If he lacks vitality, at least he has a sort of natural good breeding. None of his poems is perfect, there is not one in which one cannot find an unnecessary word or an annoyingly bad rhyme, and yet nothing is vulgar either. More than this, however empty he may seem, there is nothing that one can put one's finger on and say that it is silly. Like Blake, he appears to avoid silliness by not being afraid of it; and perhaps (like Blake again) this appearance is partly deceptive, and he is less artless than he seems. Davies's best qualities, as well as some of his faults, can be seen in the justly celebrated poem, "The Two Children": –

> "Ah, little boy! I see
>   You have a wooden spade.
> Into this sand you dig
>   So deep – for what?" I said.
> "There's more rich gold," said he,
>   "Down under where I stand,
> Than twenty elephants
>   Could move across the land."
>
> "Ah, little girl with wool! –
>   What are you making now?"
> "Some stockings for a bird,
>   To keep his legs from snow."
> And there those children are,
>   So happy, small, and proud:
> The boy that digs his grave.
>   The girl that knits her shroud.

How near this comes to folly and sentimentality! But the point is that it doesn't get there. Whether Davies is being deliberately cunning it would be hard to say. The almost namby-pamby language in which the poem starts may or may not be intended to give force to the two magnificent lines at the end. But at any rate, whether it is consciously or not, Davies always does avoid the silliness and vulgarity which so often seem to be in wait for him.

On the blurb of this book Sir John Squire is quoted as preferring Davies to "the fashionable poets of to-day" (at the time of writing this probably meant Mr. T. S. Eliot) and Mr. Basil de Selincourt as seeing in Davies an upholder of "our English tradition." Davies has had much praise of this kind, and has been used as a stick to beat many another contemporary, basically because he does not force anyone to think. Not to be made to think – and therefore, if possible, to prevent literature from developing – is often the aim of the academic critic. But Davies is not, as Sir John Squire and Mr. de Selincourt seem to claim, the restorer of an ancient tradition. Indeed, if there is one thing that he is not, it is traditional. He belongs in no line of descent; he does not derive from his immediate predecessors, and he has had no influence on his successors. According to his own account, he was brought up by a pious grandmother whose only books were "Paradise Lost," "The Pilgrim's Progress," Young's "Night Thoughts," and (presumably) the Bible. He read Shelley, Marlowe, and Shakespeare on the sly, as another boy might read Sexton Blake. At the age of thirty-four, when still living in a common lodging-house and never having seen even the fringes of the literary world, he began to write poems. He gives the impression of having imitated chiefly the poets of the seventeenth century; there are frequent echoes, though probably no plagiarisms. Having completed his first batch of poems, Davies attempted to sell them from door to door at threepence a copy – needless to say, without success.

Sir Osbert Sitwell contributes a pleasant and informative introduction. It is interesting to learn that when Davies was a child his grandmother once warned him, between blows, that if he did not turn over a new leaf he would end by being no better than his cousin who had "brought disgrace upon the family." This cousin was Sir Henry Irving. These poems are well edited and excellent value for the money. With its agreeable cover, good print, and – by current standards – very good paper, the book would make an attractive as well as a cheap Christmas present.

As I Please 4
Tribune, 24 December 1943

Reading Michael Roberts's book on T. E. Hulme, I was reminded once again of the dangerous mistake that the Socialist movement makes in ignoring what one might call the neo-reactionary school of writers. There is a considerable number of these writers: they are intellectually distinguished, they are influential in a quiet way, and their criticisms of the Left are much more damaging than anything that issues from the Individualist League or Conservative Central Office.

T. E. Hulme was killed in the last war and left little completed work behind him, but the ideas that he had roughly formulated had great influence, especially on the numerous writers who were grouped round the *Criterion* in the 'twenties and 'thirties. Wyndham Lewis, T. S. Eliot, Aldous Huxley, Malcolm Muggeridge, Evelyn Waugh and Graham Greene all probably owe something to him. But more important than the extent of his personal influence is the general intellectual movement to which he belonged, a movement which could fairly be described as the revival of pessimism. Perhaps its best-known living exponent is Marshal Pétain. But the new pessimism has queerer affiliations than that. It links up not only with Catholicism, Conservatism and Fascism, but also with pacifism (California brand especially) and Anarchism. It is worth noting that T. E. Hulme, the upper-middle-class English Conservative in a bowler hat, was an admirer and to some extent a follower of the Anarcho-Syndicalist, Georges Sorel.

The thing that is common to all these people, whether it is Pétain mournfully preaching "the discipline of defeat," or Sorel denouncing liberalism, or Berdyaev shaking his head over the Russian Revolution, or "Beachcomber" delivering side-kicks at Beveridge in the *Express*, or Huxley advocating non-resistance behind the guns of the American Fleet, is their refusal to believe that human society can be fundamentally improved. Man is non-perfectible, merely political changes can effect nothing, progress is an illusion. The connection between this belief and political reaction is, of course, obvious. Other-worldliness is the best alibi a rich man can have. "Men cannot be made better by act of Parliament; therefore I may as well go on drawing my dividends." No one puts it quite so coarsely as that, but the thought of all these people is along those lines: even of those who, like Michael Roberts and Hulme himself, admit that a little, just a *little*, improvement in earthly society may be thinkable.

The danger of ignoring the neo-pessimists lies in the fact that up to a point they are right. So long as one thinks in short periods it is wise not to be hopeful about the future. Plans for human betterment do normally come unstuck, and the pessimist has many more opportunities of saying "I told you so" than the optimist. By and large the prophets of doom have been righter than those who imagined that a real step forward would be achieved by universal education, female suffrage, the League of Nations, or what-not.

The real answer is to dissociate Socialism from Utopianism. Nearly all neo-pessimist apologetics consists in putting up a man of straw and knocking him down again. The man of straw is called Human Perfectibility. Socialists are accused of believing that society can be – and indeed, after the establishment of Socialism, will be – completely perfect; also that progress is *inevitable*. Debunking such beliefs is money for jam, of course.

The answer, which ought to be uttered more loudly than it usually is, is that Socialism is not perfectionist, perhaps not even hedonistic. Socialists don't claim to be able to make the world perfect: they claim to be able to make it better. And any thinking Socialist will concede to the Catholic that when economic injustice has been righted, the fundamental problem of man's place in the universe will still remain. But what the Socialist does claim is that that problem cannot be dealt with while the average human being's preoccupations are necessarily economic. It is all summed up in Marx's saying that after Socialism has arrived, human history can begin. Meanwhile the neo-pessimists are there, well entrenched in the press of every country in the world, and they have more influence and make more converts among the young than we sometimes care to admit.

From Philip Jordan's *Tunis Diary*: –
    "We discussed the future of Germany; and John [Strachey] said to an American present, 'You surely don't want a Carthaginian peace, do you?' Our American friend with great

slowness but solemnity said, 'I don't recollect we've had ever much trouble from the Carthaginians since.' Which delighted me."

It doesn't delight me. One answer to the American might have been, "No, but we've had a lot of trouble from the Romans." But there is more to it than that. What the people who talk about a Carthaginian peace don't realise is that in our day such things are simply not practicable. Having defeated your enemy you have to choose (unless you want another war within a generation) between exterminating him and treating him generously. Conceivably the first alternative is desirable, but it isn't possible. It is quite true that Carthage was utterly destroyed, its buildings levelled to the ground, its inhabitants put to the sword. Such things were happening all the time in antiquity. But the populations involved were tiny. I wonder if that American knew how many people were found within the walls of Carthage when it was finally sacked? According to the nearest authority I can lay hands on, five thousand! What is the best way of killing off 70 million Germans? Rat poison? We might keep this in mind when "Make Germany pay" becomes a battle-cry again.

Attacking me in the *Weekly Review* for attacking Douglas Reed, Mr. A. K. Chesterton remarks: " 'My country – right or wrong' is a maxim which apparently has no place in Mr. Orwell's philosophy." He also states that "all of us believe that whatever her condition Britain must win this war, or for that matter any other war in which she is engaged."

The operative phrase is *any other war*. There are plenty of us who would defend our own country, under no matter what government, if it seemed that we were in danger of actual invasion and conquest. But "any war" is a different matter. How about the Boer War, for instance? There is a neat little bit of historical irony here. Mr. A. K. Chesterton is the nephew of G. K. Chesterton, who courageously opposed the Boer War, and once remarked that "My country, right or wrong" was on the same moral level as "My mother, drunk or sober."

When you have been watching bureaucrats at play, it is some consolation to reflect that the same kind of thing is probably happening in Germany. In general one can't test this, but sometimes the wireless gives a clue. A little while back I was listening to Berlin broadcasting in English, and the speaker spent some minutes in talking about the Indian Nationalists – with whom, of course, the Nazis profess the keenest sympathy. I was interested to notice that all the Indian names were grossly mispronounced, worse even than would be done by the B.B.C. Ras Behari Bose, for instance, was rendered as Rash Beery Bose. Yet the various Indians who also broadcast from Berlin must daily go in and out of the same building as the renegade Englishman who mispronounces their names. So much for German efficiency and also, of course, for Nazi interest in Indian Nationalism.

Can Socialists be Happy?
Tribune, 24 December 1943

The thought of Christmas raises almost automatically the thought of Charles Dickens, and for two very good reasons. To begin with, Dickens is one of the few English writers who have actually written about Christmas. Christmas is the most popular of English festivals, and yet it has produced astonishingly little literature. There are the carols, mostly medieval in origin; there is a tiny handful of poems by Robert Bridges, T. S. Eliot, and some others, and there is Dickens; but there is very little else. Secondly, Dickens is remarkable, indeed almost unique, among modern writers in being able to give a convincing picture of *happiness*.

Dickens dealt successfully with Christmas twice – in a well-known chapter of *The Pickwick Papers* and in *The Christmas Carol*. The latter story was read to Lenin on his deathbed and, according to his wife, he found its "bourgeois sentimentality" completely intolerable. Now in a sense Lenin was right; but if he had been in better health he would perhaps have noticed that the story has some interesting sociological implications. To begin with, however thick Dickens may lay on the paint, however disgusting the "pathos" of Tiny Tim may be, the Cratchit family do give the impression of enjoying themselves.

They sound happy as, for instance, the citizens of William Morris's *News from Nowhere* don't sound happy. Moreover – and Dickens's understanding of this is one of the secrets of his power – their happiness derives mainly from contrast. They are in high spirits because for once in a way they have enough to eat. The wolf is at the door, but he is wagging his tail. The steam of the Christmas pudding drifts across a background of pawnshops and sweated labour, and in a double sense the ghost of Scrooge stands beside the dinner table. Bob Cratchit even wants to drink Scrooge's health, which Mrs. Cratchit rightly refuses. The Cratchits are able to enjoy their Christmas precisely because Christmas only comes once a year. Their happiness is convincing just because it is described as incomplete.

All efforts to describe *permanent* happiness, on the other hand, have been failures, from earliest history onwards. Utopias (incidentally the coined word Utopia doesn't mean "a good place," it means merely "a non-existent place") have been common in the literature of the past three or four hundred years, but the "favourable" ones are invariably unappetising, and usually lacking in vitality as well.

By far the best known modern Utopias are those of H. G. Wells. Wells's vision of the future, implicit all through his early work and partly set forth in *Anticipations* and *A Modern Utopia*, is most fully expressed in two books written in the early 'twenties, *The Dream* and *Men Like Gods*. Here you have a picture of the world as Wells would like to see it – or thinks he would like to see it. It is a world whose keynotes are enlightened hedonism and scientific curiosity. All the evils and miseries that we now suffer from have vanished. Ignorance, war, poverty, dirt, disease, frustration, hunger, fear, overwork, superstition – all vanished. So expressed, it is impossible to deny that that is the kind of world we all hope for. We all want to abolish the things that Wells wants to abolish. But is there anyone who actually wants to live in a Wellsian Utopia? On the contrary, *not* to live in a world like that, *not* to wake up in a hygienic garden suburb infested by naked schoolmarms, has actually become a conscious political motive. A book like *Brave New World* is an expression of the actual fear that modern man feels of the rationalised hedonistic society which it is within his power to create. A Catholic writer said recently

that Utopias are now technically feasible and that in consequence *how to avoid Utopia* had become a serious problem.
With the Fascist movement in front of our eyes we cannot
write this off as a merely silly remark. For one of the sources of
the Fascist movement is the desire to avoid a too-rational and
too-comfortable world.

All "favourable" Utopias seem to be alike in postulating
perfection while being unable to suggest happiness. *News from
Nowhere* is a sort of goody-goody version of the Wellsian
Utopia. Everyone is kindly and reasonable, all the upholstery
comes from Liberty's, but the impression left behind is of a
sort of watery melancholy. Lord Samuel's recent effort in the
same direction, *An Unknown Country*, is even more dismal.
The inhabitants of Bensalem (the word is borrowed from
Francis Bacon) give the impression of looking on life as simply
an evil to be got through with as little fuss as possible. All
that their wisdom has brought them is permanent low spirits.
But it is more impressive that Jonathan Swift, one of the
greatest imaginative writers who have ever lived, is no more
successful in constructing a "favourable" Utopia than the
others.

The earlier parts of *Gulliver's Travels* are probably the most
devastating attack on human society that has ever been written. Every word of them is relevant to-day; in places they
contain quite detailed prophecies of the political horrors of
our own time. Where Swift fails, however, is in trying to
describe a race of beings whom he *does* admire. In the last part,
in contrast with the disgusting Yahoos, we are shown the
noble Houyhnhnms, a race of intelligent horses who are free
from human failings. Now these horses, for all their high
character and unfailing common sense, are remarkably dreary
creatures. Like the inhabitants of various other Utopias, they
are chiefly concerned with avoiding fuss. They live unedent-
ful, subdued, "reasonable" lives, free not only from quarrels,
disorder or insecurity of any kind, but also from "passion,"
including physical love. They choose their mates on eugenic
principles, avoid excesses of affection, and appear somewhat
glad to die when their time comes. In the earlier parts of the
book Swift has shown where man's folly and scoundrelism
lead him: but take away the folly and the scoundrelism, and all

you are left with, apparently, is a tepid sort of existence, hardly worth leading.

Attempts at describing a definitely other-worldly happiness have been no more successful. Heaven is as great a flop as Utopia – though Hell, it is worth noting, occupies a respectable place in literature, and has often been described most minutely and convincingly.

It is a commonplace that the Christian Heaven, as usually portrayed, would attract nobody. Almost all Christian writers dealing with Heaven either say frankly that it is indescribable or conjure up a vague picture of gold, precious stones, and the endless singing of hymns. This has, it is true, inspired some of the best poems in the world:

> Thy walls are of chalcedony,
> Thy bulwarks diamonds square,
> Thy gates are of right orient pearl
> Exceeding rich and rare!

Or:

> Holy, holy, holy, all the saints adore Thee,
> Casting down their golden crowns about the glassy sea,
> Cherubim and seraphim falling down before Thee,
> That wast, and art, and evermore shalt be!

But what it could not do was to describe a place or condition in which the ordinary human being actively wanted to be. Many a revivalist minister, many a Jesuit priest (see, for instance, the terrific sermon in James Joyce's *Portrait of the Artist*) has frightened his congregation almost out of their skins with his word-pictures of Hell. But as soon as it comes to Heaven, there is a prompt falling-back on words like "ecstasy" and "bliss," with little attempt to say what they consist in. Perhaps the most vital bit of writing on this subject is the famous passage in which Tertullian explains that one of the chief joys of Heaven is watching the tortures of the damned.

The various pagan versions of Paradise are little better, if at all. One has the feeling that it is always twilight in the Elysian fields. Olympus, where the gods lived, with their nectar and ambrosia, and their nymphs and Hebes, the "immortal tarts" as D. H. Lawrence called them, might be a bit more homelike than the Christian Heaven, but you would not want to spend a long time there. As for the Moslem Paradise, with its seventy-seven houris per man, all presumably clamouring for attention at the same moment, it is just a nightmare. Nor are the Spiritualists, though constantly assuring us that "all is bright and beautiful," able to describe any next-world activity which a thinking person would find endurable, let alone attractive.

It is the same with attempted descriptions of perfect happiness which are neither Utopian nor other-worldly, but merely sensual. They always give an impression of emptiness or vulgarity, or both. At the beginning of *La Pucelle* Voltaire describes the life of Charles IX with his mistress, Agnes Sorel. They were "always happy," he says. And what did their happiness consist in? Apparently in an endless round of feasting, drinking, hunting and love-making. Who would not sicken of such an existence after a few weeks? Rabelais describes the fortunate spirits who have a good time in the next world to console them for having had a bad time in this one. They sing a song which can be roughly translated: "To leap, to dance, to play tricks, to drink the wine both white and red, and to do nothing all day long except count gold crowns" – how boring it sounds, after all! The emptiness of the whole notion of an everlasting "good time" is shown up in Breughel's picture "The Land of the Sluggard," where the three great lumps of fat lie asleep, head to head, with the boiled eggs and roast legs of pork coming up to be eaten of their own accord.

It would seem that human beings are not able to describe, nor perhaps to imagine, happiness except in terms of contrast. That is why the conception of Heaven or Utopia varies from age to age. In pre-industrial society Heaven was described as a place of endless rest, and as being paved with gold, because the experience of the average human being was overwork and poverty. The houris of the Moslem Paradise reflected a polygamous society where most of the women disappeared into the harems of the rich. But these pictures of "eternal bliss" always failed because as soon as the bliss became eternal (eternity being thought of as endless time), the contrast ceased to operate.

Some of the conventions which have become embedded in our literature first arose from physical conditions which have now ceased to exist. The cult of spring is an example. In the Middle Ages spring did not primarily mean swallows and wild flowers. It meant green vegetables, milk and fresh meat after several months of living on salt pork in smoky windowless huts. The spring songs were gay –

> Do nothing but eat and make good cheer,
> And thank Heaven for the merry year
> When flesh is cheap and females dear,
> And lusty lads roam here and there,
> So merrily,
> And ever among so merrily!

because there was something to be gay about. The winter was over, that was the great thing. Christmas itself, a pre-Christian festival, probably started because there had to be an occasional outburst of overeating and drinking to make a break in the unbearable northern winter.

The inability of mankind to imagine happiness except in the form of *relief*, either from effort or pain, presents Socialists with a serious problem. Dickens can describe a poverty-stricken family tucking into a roast goose, and can make them appear happy; on the other hand, the inhabitants of perfect universes seem to have no spontaneous gaiety and are usually somewhat repulsive into the bargain. But clearly we are not aiming at the kind of world Dickens described, nor, probably, at any world he was capable of imagining. The Socialist objective is not a society where everything comes right in the end, because kind old gentlemen give away turkeys. What are we aiming at, if not a society in which "charity" would be unnecessary? We want a world where Scrooge, with his dividends, and Tiny Tim, with his tuberculous leg, would both be unthinkable. But does that mean that we are aiming at some painless, effortless Utopia?

At the risk of saying something which the editors of *Tribune* may not endorse, I suggest that the real objective of Socialism is not happiness. Happiness hitherto has been a by-product, and for all we know it may always remain so. The real objective of

Socialism is human brotherhood. This is widely felt to be the case, though it is not usually said, or not said loudly enough. Men use up their lives in heart-breaking political struggles, or get themselves killed in civil wars, or tortured in the secret prisons of the Gestapo, not in order to establish some central-heated, air-conditioned, strip-lighted Paradise, but because they want a world in which human beings love one another instead of swindling and murdering one another. And they want that world as a first step. Where they go from there is not so certain, and the attempt to foresee it in detail merely confuses the issue.

Socialist thought has to deal in prediction, but only in broad terms. One often has to aim at objectives which one can only very dimly see. At this moment, for instance, the world is at war and wants peace. Yet the world has no experience of peace, and never has had, unless the Noble Savage once existed. The world wants something which it is dimly aware could exist, but which it cannot accurately define. This Christmas day, thousands of men will be bleeding to death in the Russian snows, or drowning in icy waters, or blowing one another to pieces with hand grenades on swampy islands of the Pacific; homeless children will be scrabbling for food among the wreckage of German cities. To make that kind of thing impossible is a good objective. But to say in detail what a peaceful world would be like is a different matter, and to attempt to do so is apt to lead to the horrors so enthusiastically presented by Gerald Heard.

Nearly all creators of Utopia have resembled the man who has toothache, and therefore thinks that happiness consists in not having toothache. They wanted to produce a perfect society by an endless continuation of something that had only been valuable because it was temporary. The wiser course would be to say that there are certain lines along which humanity must move, the grand strategy is mapped out, but detailed prophecy is not our business. Whoever tries to imagine perfection simply reveals his own emptiness. This is the case even with a great writer like Swift, who can flay a bishop or a politician so neatly, but who, when he tries to create a superman, merely leaves one with the impression – the very last he can have intended – that the stinking Yahoos had in them more possibility of development than the enlightened Houyhnhnms.

As I Please 5
Tribune, 31 December 1943

Reading the discussions of "war guilt" which reverberate in the correspondence columns of the newspapers, I note the surprise with which many people seem to discover that war is not crime. Hitler, it appears, has not done anything actionable. He has not raped anybody, nor carried off any pieces of loot with his own hands, nor personally flogged any prisoners, buried any wounded men alive, thrown any babies into the air and spitted them on his bayonet, dipped any nuns in petrol and touched them off with church tapers – in fact he has not done any of the things which enemy nationals are usually credited with doing in war time. He has merely precipitated a world war which will perhaps have cost twenty million lives before it ends. And there is nothing illegal in that. How could there be, when legality implies authority and there *is* no authority with the power to transcend national frontiers?

At the recent trials in Kharkov some attempt was made to fix on Hitler, Himmler and the rest the responsibility for their subordinates' crimes, but the mere fact that this had to be done shows that Hitler's guilt is not self-evident. His crime, it is implied, was not to build up an army for the purpose of aggressive war, but to instruct that army to torture its prisoners. So far as it goes, the distinction between an atrocity and an act of war is valid. An atrocity means an act of terrorism which has no genuine military purpose. One must accept such distinctions if one accepts war at all, which in practice everyone does. Nevertheless, a world in which it is wrong to murder an individual civilian and right to drop a thousand tons of high explosive on a residential area does sometimes make me wonder whether this earth of ours is not a looney-bin made use of by some other planet.

*

As the 53 bus carries me to and fro I never, at any rate when it is light enough to see, pass the little church of St. John, just across the road from Lord's, without a pang. It is a Regency church, one of the very few of the period, and when you pass that way it is well worth going inside to have a look at its friendly interior and read the resounding epitaphs of the East India Nabobs who lie buried there. But its façade, one of the most charming in London, has been utterly ruined by a hideous war memorial which stands in front of it. That seems to be a fixed rule in London – whenever you do by some chance have a decent vista, block it up with the ugliest statue you can find. And, unfortunately, we have never been sufficiently short of bronze for these things to be melted down.

If you climb to the top of the hill in Greenwich Park, you can have the mild thrill of standing exactly on longitude 0, and you can also examine the ugliest building in the world, Greenwich Observatory. Then look down the hill towards the Thames. Spread out below you are Wren's masterpiece, Greenwich Hospital (now the Naval College) and another exquisite classical building known as the Queen's House. The architects responsible for that shapeless sprawling muddle at the top of the hill had those other two buildings under their eyes while every brick was laid.

As Mr. Osbert Sitwell remarked at the time of the "Baedeker raids" – how simple-minded of the Germans to imagine that we British could be cowed by the destruction of our ancient monuments! As though any havoc of the German bombs could possibly equal the things we have done ourselves!

I see that Mr. Bernard Shaw, among others, wants to rewrite the second verse of the National Anthem. Mr. Shaw's version retains references to God and the King, but is vaguely internationalist in sentiment. This seems to me ridiculous. Not to have a national anthem would be logical. But if you do have one, its function must necessarily be to point out that we are Good and our enemies are Bad. Besides, Mr. Shaw wants to cut out the only worthwhile lines the anthem contains. All the brass instruments and big drums in the world cannot turn "God Save the King" into a good tune, but on the very rare occasions when it is sung in full it does spring to life in the two lines –

> Confound their politics,
> Frustrate their knavish tricks!

And, in fact, I had always imagined that the second verse is habitually left out because of a vague suspicion on the part of the Tories that these lines refer to themselves.

Just about two years ago, as we filed past the menu board in the canteen, I said to the next person in the queue: "A year from now you'll see 'Rat Soup' on that board, and in 1943 it will be 'Mock Rat Soup.'" Events have proved me wrong (the war at sea has turned out better than was then foreseeable), but, once again, I can claim to have been less wrong than the full-time prophets. Turning up my copy of *Old Moore's Almanac* for 1943, I find that the Germans sued for peace and were granted an armistice in June, and Japan surrendered in September. November finds us enjoying "the blessings of peace and the complete removal of lighting conditions," while "a reduction in taxation is highly appreciated." It is like this all the way through.

Old Moore repeats this performance every year, without ever losing its popularity. Nor is it hard to see why. Its psychological approach is indicated by the advert. on the cover: "Cosmo, famous Mystic, predicts VICTORY, PEACE, RECONSTRUCTION." As long as Cosmo predicts that kind of thing he is safe for a hearing.

Another ninepenny acquisition: "Chronological Tablets, exhibiting every Remarkable Occurrence from the Creation of the World down to the Present Time." Printed by J. D. Dewick, Aldersgate Street, in the year 1801.

With some interest I looked up the date of the creation of the world, and found it was in 4004 B.C., and "is supposed to have taken place in the autumn." Later in the book it is given more exactly as September, 4004.

At the end there are a number of blank sheets in which the reader can carry on the chronicle for himself. Whoever possessed this book did not carry it very far, but one of the last entries is: "Tuesday 4 May. Peace proclaimed here. General Illumination." That was the Peace of Amiens. This might warn us not to be too previous with our own illuminations when the armistice comes.

1944

As I Please 6

Tribune, 7 January 1944

Looking through the photographs in the New Year Honours List, I am struck (as usual) by the quite exceptional ugliness and vulgarity of the faces displayed there. It seems to be almost the rule that the kind of person who earns the right to call himself Lord Percy de Falcontowers should look at best like an overfed publican and at worst like a tax-collector with a duodenal ulcer. But our country is not alone in this. Anyone who is a good hand with scissors and paste could compile an excellent book entitled *Our Rulers*, and consisting simply of published photographs of the great ones of the earth. The idea first occurred to me when I saw in *Picture Post* some "stills" of Beaverbrook delivering a speech and looking more like a monkey on a stick than you would think possible for anyone who was not doing it on purpose.

When you had got together your collection of fuehrers, actual and would-be, you would notice that several qualities recur throughout the list. To begin with, they are all old. In spite of the lip-service that is paid everywhere to youth, there is no such thing as a person in a truly commanding position who is less than fifty years old. Secondly, they are nearly all under-sized. A dictator taller than five feet six inches is a very great rarity. And, thirdly, there is this almost general and sometimes quite fantastic ugliness. The collection would contain photographs of Streicher bursting a blood vessel, Japanese war lords impersonating baboons, Mussolini with his scrubby dewlap, the chinless de Gaulle, the stumpy short-armed Churchill, Gandhi with his long sly nose and huge bat's ears, Tojo displaying thirty-two teeth with gold in every one of them. And opposite each, to make a contrast, there would be a photograph of an ordinary human being from the country concerned. Opposite Hitler a young sailor from a German submarine, opposite Tojo a Japanese peasant of the old type – and so on.

But to come back to the Honours List. When you remember that nearly the whole of the rest of the world has dropped it, it does seem strange to see this flummery still continuing in England, a country in which the very notion of aristocracy perished hundreds of years ago. The race-difference on which aristocratic rule is usually founded had disappeared from England by the end of the Middle Ages, and the concept of "blue blood" as something valuable in itself, and independent of money, was vanishing in the age of Elizabeth. Since then we have been a plutocracy plain and simple. Yet we still make spasmodic efforts to dress ourselves in the colours of medieval feudalism.

Think of the Heralds' Office solemnly faking pedigrees and inventing coats of arms with mermaids and unicorns couchant, regardant and what-not, for company directors in bowler hat and striped trousers! What I like best is the careful grading by which honours are always dished out in direct proportion to the amount of mischief done – baronies for Big Business, baronetcies for fashionable surgeons, knighthoods for tame professors. But do these people imagine that by calling themselves lords, knights and so forth they somehow come to have something in common with the medieval aristocracy? Does Sir Walter Citrine, say, feel himself to be rather the same kind of person as Childe Roland (Childe Citrine to the dark tower came!), or is Lord Nuffield under the impression that we shall mistake him for a crusader in chain armour?

However, this honours-list business has one severely practical aspect, and that is that a title is a first-rate alias. Mr. X can practically cancel his past by turning himself into Lord Y. Some of the ministerial appointments that have been made during this war would hardly have been possible without some such disguise. As Tom Paine put it: "These people change their names so often that it is as hard to know them as it is to know thieves."

I write this to the tune of an electric drill. They are drilling holes in the walls of a surface shelter, removing bricks at regular intervals. Why? Because the shelter is in danger of falling down and it is necessary to give it a cement facing.

It seems doubtful whether these surface shelters were ever of much use. They would give protection against splinters and blast, but not more than the walls of an ordinary house, and the only time I saw a bomb drop anywhere near one it sliced it off the ground as neatly as if it had been done with a knife. The real point is, however, that at the time when these shelters were built it was known that they would fall down in a year or two. Innumerable people pointed this out. But nothing happened; the slovenly building continued, and somebody scooped the contract. Sure enough, a year or two later, the prophets were justified. The mortar began to fall out of the walls, and it became necessary to case the shelters in cement. Once again somebody – perhaps it was the same somebody – scooped the contract.

I do not know whether, in any part of the country, these shelters are actually used in air raids. In my part of London there has never been any question of using them; in fact, they are kept permanently locked lest they should be used for "improper purposes." There is one thing, however, that they might conceivably be useful for, and that is as block-houses in street fighting. And on the whole they have been built in the poorer streets. It would amuse me if when the time came the higher-ups were unable to crush the populace because they had thoughtlessly provided them with thousands of machine-gun nests beforehand.

On page eighteen of this number there will be found an advertisement of the *Tribune* Short Story Competition. We hope for a large number of entries, and we hope that directly and indirectly the competition may help a little towards the rehabilitation of the short story in this country.

Few people would claim that the short story has been a successful art form in England during the past twenty years. American and Irish stories are perhaps a little better, but not much. One could explain the decline of the short story on sociological grounds, but such explanations are not altogether satisfactory, because, if true, they ought to apply equally to kindred forms of literature. Contemporary novels, for instance, are on average nowhere near so bad as contemporary short stories. There must also be technical causes, and I think I can suggest two of them.

The first is something that we cannot remedy in *Tribune* – the difficulty over length. Almost certainly the short story has

GEORGE ORWELL

suffered from the dwindled size of modern magazines. Nearly all the great English short stories of the past – and the same is true of many French stories, though perhaps less true of the Russians – would be far too long for publication in any ordinary modern periodical. But I think it is also true that the short story has suffered unnecessarily from the disappearance of the Victorian "plot." About the beginning of this century the convention of the "surprise in the last chapter" fell out of fashion, and it was not sufficiently noticed that the eventless, non-dramatic kind of story is more effective when it is long than when it is short. A short story has to be a *story*. It cannot, to the same extent as the novel, depend upon "atmosphere" and character-interest, because there is not enough space to build them up. A short story which does not convey any anecdote, any dramatic change, almost invariably ends on a note of weakness and pointlessness. What innumerable stories I have read which have kept me thinking almost up to the last line – "Surely these preliminaries are leading to something? Surely something is going to happen?" – and then the invariable petering-out, to which the writer sometimes tries to give an air of profundity by means of a row of dots. I cannot help feeling that many short-story writers are inhibited by the notion that a "plot" is hopelessly old-fashioned and therefore inadmissible.

I do not suggest that this is the only thing that is wrong with the contemporary short story. But after much reading of short stories this is the impression left upon my own mind, and I offer it as a hint which may be useful to intending contributors.

As I Please 7
Tribune, 14 January 1944

The old custom of binding up magazines and periodicals in book form seems to have gone out almost entirely, which is a pity, for a year's issue of even a very stupid magazine is more readable after a lapse of time than the majority of books. I do not believe I ever had a better bargain than the dozen volumes of the *Quarterly Review*, starting in 1809, which I once picked up for two shillings at a farmhouse auction; but a good six-pennyworth was a year's issue of the *Cornhill* when either Trollope or Thackeray, I forget which, was editing it, and another good buy was some odd volumes of the *Gentleman's Magazine* of the mid-'sixties, at threepence each. I have also had some happy half-hours with Chambers's *Papers for the People*, which flourished in the 'fifties, the *Boy's Own Paper* in the days of the Boer War, the *Strand* in its great Sherlock Holmes days, and – a book I unfortunately only saw and didn't buy – a bound volume of the *Athenæum* in the early 'twenties, when Middleton Murry was editing it, and T. S. Eliot, E. M. Forster and various others were making their first impact on the big public. I do not know why no one bothers to do this nowadays, for to get a year's issue of a magazine bound costs less than buying a novel, and you can even do the job yourself if you have a spare evening and the right materials.

The great fascination of these old magazines is the completeness with which they "date." Absorbed in the affairs of the moment, they tell one about political fashions and tendencies which are hardly mentioned in the more general history books. It is interesting, for instance, to study in contemporary magazines the war scare of the early 'sixties, when it was assumed on all sides that Britain was about to be invaded, the Volunteers were formed, amateur strategists published maps showing the routes by which the French armies would converge on London, and peaceful citizens cowered in ditches while the bullets of the Rifle Clubs (the then equivalent of the Home Guard) ricocheted in all directions.

The mistake that nearly all British observers made at that time was not to notice that Germany was dangerous. The sole danger was supposed to come from France, which had shot its bolt as a military power and had in any case no reason for quarrelling with Britain. And I believe that casual readers in the future, dipping into our newspapers and magazines, will note a similar aberration in the turning-away from democracy and frank admiration for totalitarianism which overtook the British intelligentsia about 1940. Recently, turning up a back number of *Horizon*, I came upon a long article on James Burnham's *Managerial Revolution*, in which Burnham's main thesis was accepted almost without examination. It represented, many people would have claimed, the most intelligent forecast of our time. And yet – founded as it really was on a belief in the invincibility of the German army – events have already blown it to pieces.

Shortly, Burnham's thesis is this. *Laissez-faire* capitalism is finished and Socialism, at any rate in the present period of history, is impossible. What is now happening is the appearance of a new ruling class, named by Burnham the "managers." These are represented in Germany and the U.S.S.R. by the Nazis and Bolsheviks, and in the U.S.A. by the business executives. This new ruling class expropriates the capitalists, crushes the working-class movements and sets up a totalitarian society governed by the concept of efficiency. Britain is decadent and is bound to be rapidly conquered by Germany. After the conquest of Britain will come the attack on the U.S.S.R., and Russia's "military weakness" will cause her to "fall apart to east and west." You are then left with three great super-States, Germany, Japan and the U.S.A., which divide the world between them, make ceaseless war upon one another, and keep the working class in permanent subjection.

Now, there is a great deal in what Burnham says. The fact that collectivism is not inherently democratic, that you do not do away with class rule by formally abolishing private property, is becoming clearer all the time. The tendency of the world to split up into several great power blocs is also clear enough, and the fact that each of these would probably be invincible has sinister possibilities. But the test of a political theory is its power to foretell the future, and Burnham's predictions were falsified almost as soon as made. Britain was not conquered, Russia turned out not to be militarily weak, and – a much more fundamental error – Germany did attack Russia while the war against Britain was still in progress. Burnham had declared this to be impossible, on the ground that the German and Russian régimes were essentially the same and would not quarrel until the struggle against old-style capitalism was finished.

Obviously these mistakes were partly due to wish-thinking. Hating both Britain and the U.S.S.R., Burnham (and many American intellectuals of similar outlook) wanted to see both these countries conquered, and was also unable to admit that there *was* an essential difference between Russia and Germany. But the basic error of this school of thought is its contempt for the common man. A totalitarian society, it is felt, *must* be stronger than a democratic one: the expert's opinion *must* be worth more than the ordinary man's. The German army had won the first battles: therefore it must win the last one. The great strength of democracy, its power of criticism, was ignored.

It would be absurd to claim that either Britain or the U.S.A. are true democracies, but in both countries public opinion can influence policy, and while making many minor mistakes it probably avoids the biggest ones. If the German common people had had any say in the conduct of the war it is very unlikely, for instance, that they would have attacked Russia while Britain was still in the field, and still more unlikely that they would have wantonly declared war on America six months later. It takes an expert to make mistakes as big as that. When one sees how the Nazi régime has succeeded in smashing itself to pieces within a dozen years it is difficult to believe in the survival value of totalitarianism. But I would not deny that the "managerial" class *might* get control of our society, and that if they did they would lead us into some hellish places before they destroyed themselves. Where Burnham and his fellow-thinkers are wrong is in trying to spread the idea that totalitarianism is *unavoidable*, and that we must therefore do nothing to oppose it.

Review of *The Machiavellians*
by James Burnham

Manchester Evening News, 20 January 1944

It is notorious that certain sins, crimes, and vices would lack attraction if they were not forbidden. Mr. Gandhi has described the shuddering joy with which, as a child, he sneaked down to some secret haunt in the bazaar and ate a plate of beef, and our grandfathers derived acute pleasure from drinking champagne out of the satin slippers of actresses.

So also with political theories. Any theory which is obviously dishonest and immoral ("realistic" is the favourite word at this moment) will find adherents who accept it just for that reason. Whether the theory works, whether it attains the result aimed at will hardly be questioned. The mere fact that it throws ordinary decency overboard will be accepted as proof of its grown-upness and consequently of its efficacy.

Mr. Burnham, whose managerial revolution won a large if rather short-lived renown by telling American business-men what they wanted to hear, has now set forth the political doctrine which he derives from Machiavelli and Machiavelli's modern followers, Mosca, Pareto, Michels, and – though it is doubtful whether he really belongs in this school – Georges Sorel.

The world-picture which Mr. Burnham has built up from the teachings of these writers is something like this:

Progress is largely an illusion, Democracy is impossible, though useful as a myth to deceive the masses.

Society is inevitably ruled by oligarchies who hold their position by means of force and fraud, and whose sole objective is power and still more power for themselves. No revolution means more than a change of rulers.

Man, as a political animal, is moved solely by selfish motives, except so far as he is under the influence of myths.

Conscious, planned action for the good of the community is impossible, since each group is simply trying to secure its own advantage.

Politics is, and can be, nothing except a struggle for power. Human equality, human fraternity are empty phrases.

All moral codes, all "idealistic" conceptions of politics, all visions of a better society in the future are simply lies, conscious or unconscious, covering the naked struggle for power.

Having set forth this thesis Mr. Burnham contradicts it to some extent by adding that various checks on the exercise of power are desirable, in particular, freedom of speech. He also, following Pareto, points out that a ruling caste decays if it is not renewed from time to time by able recruits from the masses.

In one place he even finds himself admitting that the Anglo-Saxon version of democracy has some survival value, and that the Germans might have avoided some of their strategic mistakes if they had not crushed internal opposition.

However, the sudden outburst in favour of freedom of speech, which occupies a chapter or two, is probably only a part of Mr. Burnham's quarrel with the Roosevelt Administration. He ends by looking forward to the emergence of a new ruling class, who will rule "scientifically" by the conscious use of force and fraud, but who will to some small extent serve the common good because they will recognise that it is to their own interest to do so.

Now, when one examines a political theory of this kind, the first thing one notices is that it is no more scientific than the idealistic creeds it professes to debunk. The premise from which Mr. Burnham starts out is that a relatively decent society, a society, for instance, in which everyone has enough to eat and wars are a thing of the past, is impossible. He puts this forward as an axiom.

Why is such a thing impossible? How is it "scientific" to make this quite arbitrary assumption?

The argument implied all the way through the book is that a peaceful and prosperous society cannot exist in the future because it has never existed in the past. By the same argument one could have proved the impossibility of aeroplanes in 1900, while only a few centuries earlier one could have "proved" that civilisation is impossible except on a basis of chattel slavery.

The fact is that much of Machiavelli's teaching has been invalidated by the rise of modern technology.

When Machiavelli wrote, human equality was, if not impossible, certainly undesirable. In the general poverty of the world a privileged class was needed to keep the arts of civilisation alive. In the modern world, where there is no material reason why every human being should not enjoy a fairly high standard of living, this need disappears.

Human equality is technically possible whatever the psychological difficulties may be, and of course the philosophies of Pareto, Mr. Burnham, and the rest are simply efforts to avoid this unwelcome fact.

The scientific approach to Machiavelli's teachings would have to find out what statesmen had modelled themselves upon Machiavelli, and how successful they had been. Mr. Burnham hardly makes this test. He does remark, as an illustration of Machiavelli's prestige, that Thomas Cromwell, Henry VIII's Chancellor, always carried a copy of "The Prince" in his pocket. He does not add that Cromwell ended on the block.

In our own day, Mussolini, the conscious pupil of Machiavelli and Pareto, does not seem to have made a very brilliant success of things. And the Nazi regime, based on essentially Machiavellian principles, is being smashed to pieces by the forces which its own lack of scruple conjured up.

It would seem that the theory that there is no such thing as a "good" motive in politics, that nothing counts except force and fraud, has a hole in it somewhere, and that the Machiavellian system fails even by its own test of material success.

In the managerial revolution Mr. Burnham foretold that Britain would be swiftly conquered, that Germany would not attack Russia till the war with Britain was over, and that Russia would then be torn to pieces. These prophecies, obviously based on wish-thinking, were falsified almost as soon as made.

In the present book he has wisely refrained from foretelling anything so concrete, but assumes the same air of omniscience. It is doubtful whether he and the many others like him have done more than turn a copybook maxim on its head.

"Dishonesty is the best policy" is the sum of their wisdom. The fact that this shallow piece of naughtiness can – just because it sounds "realistic" and grown-up – be accepted without any examination does not speak well for the Anglo-American intelligentsia.

As I Please 8
Tribune, 21 January 1944

The dropping of the Forces programme and the rumours of large-scale commercial broadcasting after the war have once again set people talking about the B.B.C. and its shortcomings. We hope to publish in the not too remote future some articles on various aspects of broadcasting, but I would like to suggest here, just as something to think over, that the B.B.C. is what it is because the public is not radio-conscious. People are vaguely aware that they don't like the B.B.C. programmes, that along with some good stuff a lot of muck is broadcast, that the talks are mostly ballyhoo and that no subject of importance ever gets the honesty of discussion that it would get in even the most reactionary newspaper. But they make no effort to find out, either in general or particular terms, *why* the programmes are bad, or whether foreign programmes are any better, or what is or is not technically possible on the air.

Even quite well-informed people seem completely ignorant of what goes on inside the B.B.C. When I was working in the B.B.C. I was concerned solely with broadcasting English programmes to India. This did not save me from being constantly buttonholed by angry people who asked me whether I could not "do something about" some item on the Home Programme – which is like blaming a North Sea Coastguard for something that happens in Central Africa. A few months back there was a debate in the House of Commons in which our radio propaganda to America was criticised. Several M.P.s maintained that it was totally ineffective, which it is. But seemingly they knew this only by instinct. Not one of them was in a position to stand up and tell the House how much we spend every year in broadcasting to the U.S.A., and how many listeners this secures us – facts which they could quite easily have found out.

When the B.B.C. is attacked in the press, the attack is usually so ignorant that it is impossible to meet it. Some time ago I wrote to a well-known Irish writer, now living in England, asking him to broadcast. He sent me an indignant refusal, which incidentally revealed that he did not know (*a*) that there is a Broadcasting Corporation in India, (*b*) that Indians broadcast every day from London, and (*c*) that the B.B.C. broadcasts in Oriental languages. If people don't even know that much, of what use are their criticisms of the B.B.C. likely to be? To quite a large extent the B.B.C. is blamed for its virtues while its real faults are ignored. Everyone complains, for instance, about the Kensingtonian accent of B.B.C. newsreaders, which has been carefully selected *not* in order to cause annoyance in England, but because it is a "neutral" accent which will be intelligible wherever English is spoken. Yet how many people are aware that millions of public money are squandered in broadcasting to countries where there is virtually no audience?

Here is a little catechism for amateur radio critics.

You say you don't like the present programmes. Have you a clear idea of what kind of programmes you *would* like? If so, what steps have you taken towards securing them?

In your opinion, are the B.B.C. news bulletins truthful? Are they more or less truthful than those of other belligerent countries? Have you checked this by comparison?

Have you any ideas about the possibilities of the radio play, the short story, the feature, the discussion? If so, have you bothered to find out which of your ideas are technically feasible?

Do you think the B.B.C. would benefit by competition? Give your opinion of commercial broadcasting.

Who controls the B.B.C.? Who pays for it? Who directs its policy? How does the censorship work?

What do you know of B.B.C. propaganda to foreign countries, hostile, friendly or neutral? How much does it cost? Is it effective? How would it compare with German propaganda? Add some notes on radio propaganda in general.

I could extend this considerably, but if even a hundred thousand people in England could give definite answers to the above questions it would be a big step forward.

A correspondent reproaches me with being "negative" and "always attacking things." The fact is that we live in a time when causes for rejoicing are not numerous. But I like praising things, when there is anything to praise, and I would like here to write a few lines – they have to be retrospective, unfortunately – in praise of the Woolworth's Rose.

In the good days when nothing in Woolworth's cost over sixpence, one of their best lines was their rose bushes. They were always very young plants, but they came into bloom in their second year, and I don't think I ever had one die on me. Their chief interest was that they were never, or very seldom, what they claimed to be on their labels. One that I bought for a Dorothy Perkins turned out to be a beautiful little white rose with a yellow heart, one of the finest ramblers I have ever seen. A polyantha rose labelled yellow turned out to be deep red. Another, bought for an Albertine, was like an Albertine, but more double, and gave astonishing masses of blossom. These roses had all the interest of a surprise packet, and there was always the chance that you might happen upon a new variety which you would have the right to name John Smithii or something of that kind.

Last summer I passed the cottage where I used to live before the war. The little white rose, no bigger than a boy's catapult when I put it in, had grown into a huge vigorous bush, the Albertine or near-Albertine was smothering half the fence in a cloud of pink blossom. I had planted both of those in 1936. And I thought, "All that for sixpence!" I do not know how long a rose bush lives; I suppose ten years might be an average life. And throughout that time a rambler will be in full bloom for a month or six weeks each year, while a bush rose will be blooming, on and off, for at least four months. All that for sixpence – the price, before the war, of ten Players or a pint and a half of mild, or a week's subscription to the *Daily Mail*, or about twenty minutes of twice-breathed air in the movies!

As I Please 9
Tribune, 28 January 1944

I see that Mr. Suresh Vaidya, an Indian journalist living in England, has been arrested for refusing military service. This is not the first case of its kind, and if it is the last it will probably be because no more Indians of military age are left to be victimised.

Everyone knows without being told them the juridical aspects of Mr. Vaidya's case, and I have no wish to dwell on them. But I would like to draw attention to the commonsense aspect, which the British Government so steadily refuses to consider. Putting aside the seamen who come and go, and the handful of troops who are still here, there might perhaps be two thousand Indians in this country, of all kinds and ages. By applying conscription to them you may raise a few score extra soldiers; and by coercing the minority who "object" you may swell the British prison population by about a dozen. That is the net result from the military point of view.

But unfortunately that isn't all. By behaviour of this kind you antagonise the entire Indian community in Britain – for no Indian, whatever his views, admits that Britain had the right to declare war on India's behalf or has the right to impose compulsory service on Indians. Anything that happens in the Indian community here has prompt repercussions in India, and appreciable effects further afield. One Indian war-resister victimised does us more harm than ten thousand British ones. It seems a high price to pay for the satisfaction the Blimps probably feel at having another "Red" in their clutches. I don't expect the Blimps to see Mr. Vaidya's point of view. But they really might see, after all their experience, that making martyrs does not pay.

A correspondent has sent us a letter in defence of Ezra Pound, the American poet who transferred his allegiance to Mussolini some years before the war and has been a lively propagandist on the Rome radio. The substance of his claim is that (a) Pound did not sell himself simply for money, and (b) that when you get hold of a true poet you can afford to ignore his political opinions.

Now, of course, Pound did not sell himself solely for money. No writer ever does that. Anyone who wanted money before all else would choose some more paying profession. But I think it probable that Pound did sell himself partly for prestige, flattery and a professorship. He had a most venomous hatred for both Britain and the U.S.A., where he felt that his talents had not been fully appreciated, and obviously believed that there was a conspiracy against him throughout the English-speaking countries. Then there were several ignominious episodes in which Pound's phoney erudition was shown up, and which he no doubt found it hard to forgive. By the mid-thirties Pound was singing the praises of "the Boss" (Mussolini) in a number of English papers, including Mosley's quarterly, British Union (to which Vidkun Quisling was also a contributor). At the time of the Abyssinian war Pound was vociferously anti-Abyssinian. In 1938 or thereabouts the

Italians gave him a chair at one of their universities, and some time after war broke out he took Italian citizenship.

Whether a poet, as such, is to be forgiven his political opinions is a different question. Obviously one mustn't say "X agrees with me: therefore he is a good writer," and for the last ten years honest literary criticism has largely consisted in combating this outlook. Personally I admire several writers (Céline, for instance) who have gone over to the Fascists, and many others whose political outlook I strongly object to. But one has the right to expect ordinary decency even of a poet. I never listened to Pound's broadcasts, but I often read them in the B.B.C. Monitoring Report, and they were intellectually and morally disgusting. Anti-Semitism, for instance, is simply not the doctrine of a grown-up person. People who go in for that kind of thing must take the consequences. But I do agree with our correspondent in hoping that the American authorities do not catch Pound and shoot him, as they have threatened to do. It would establish his reputation so thoroughly that it might be a hundred years before anyone could determine dispassionately whether Pound's much-debated poems are any good or not.

The other night a barmaid informed me that if you pour beer into a damp glass it goes flat much more quickly. She added that to dip your moustache into your beer also turns it flat. I immediately accepted this without further inquiry; in fact, as soon as I got home I clipped my moustache, which I had forgotten to do for some days.

Only later did it strike me that this was probably one of those superstitions which are able to keep alive because they have the air of being scientific truths. In my notebook I have a long list of fallacies which were taught to me in my childhood, in each case not as an old wives' tale but as a scientific fact. I can't give the whole list, but here are a few hardy favourites: –

That a swan can break your leg with a blow of its wing.

That if you cut yourself between the thumb and forefinger you get lockjaw.

That powdered glass is poisonous.

That if you wash your hands in the water eggs have been boiled in (why anyone should do this is a mystery) you will get warts.

That bulls become infuriated at the sight of red.

That sulphur in a dog's drinking water acts as a tonic.

And so on and so forth. Almost everyone carries some or other of these beliefs into adult life. I have met someone of over thirty who still retained the second of the beliefs I have listed above. As for the third, it is so widespread that in India, for instance, people are constantly trying to poison one another with powdered glass, with disappointing results.

I wish now that I had read *Basic English versus the Artificial Languages* before and not after reviewing the interesting little book in which Professor Lancelot Hogben sets forth his own artificial language, Interglossa. For in that case I should have realised how comparatively chivalrous Professor Hogben had been towards the inventors of rival international languages. Controversies on serious subjects are often far from polite. Followers of the Stalinist–Trotskyist controversy will have observed that an unfriendly note tends to creep into it, and when the *Tablet* and the *Church Times* are having a go at one another the blows are not always above the belt. But for sheer dirtiness of fighting the feuds between the inventors of various of the international languages would take a lot of beating.

Tribune may before long print one or more articles on Basic English. If any language is ever adopted as a world-wide "second" language it is immensely unlikely that it will be a manufactured one, and of the existing natural ones English has much the best chance, though not necessarily in the Basic form. Public opinion is beginning to wake up to the need for an international language, though fantastic misconceptions still exist. For example, many people imagine that the advocates of an international language aim at suppressing the natural languages, a thing no one has ever seriously suggested.

At present, in spite of the growing recognition of this need, the world is growing more and not less nationalistic in language. This is partly from conscious policy (about half a dozen of the existing languages are being pushed in an imperialistic way in various parts of the world), and partly owing to the dislocation caused by the war. And the difficulties of trade, travel and intercommunication between scientists, and the time-wasting labour of learning foreign languages, still continue. In my life I have learned seven foreign languages, including two dead ones, and out of those seven I retain only one, and that not brilliantly. This would be quite a normal case. A member of a small nationality, a Dane or a Dutchman, say, has to learn three foreign languages as a matter of course, if he wants to be educated at all. Clearly this position could be bettered, and the one great difficulty is to decide which language is to be adopted as the international one. But there is going to be some ugly scrapping before that is settled, as anyone who has even glanced into this subject knows.

As I Please 10
Tribune, 4 February 1944

When Sir Walter Raleigh was imprisoned in the Tower of London, he occupied himself with writing a history of the world. He had finished the first volume and was at work on the second when there was a scuffle between some workmen beneath the window of his cell, and one of the men was killed. In spite of diligent enquiries, and in spite of the fact that he had actually seen the thing happen, Sir Walter was never able to discover what the quarrel was about: whereupon, so it is said – and if the story is not true it certainly ought to be – he burned what he had written and abandoned his project.

This story has come into my head I do not know how many times during the past ten years, but always with the reflection that Raleigh was probably wrong. Allowing for all the difficulties of research at that date, and the special difficulty of conducting research in prison, he could probably have produced a world history which had some resemblance to the real course of events. Up to a fairly recent date, the major events recorded in the history books probably happened. It is probably true that the battle of Hastings was fought in 1066, that Columbus discovered America, that Henry VIII had six wives, and so on. A certain degree of truthfulness was possible so long as it was admitted that a fact may be true even if you don't like it. Even as late as the last war it was possible for the *Encyclopædia*

Britannica, for instance, to compile its articles on the various campaigns partly from German sources. Some of the facts – the casualty figures, for instance – were regarded as neutral and in substance accepted by everybody. No such thing would be possible now. A Nazi and a non-Nazi version of the present war would have no resemblance to one another, and which of them finally gets into the history books will be decided not by evidential methods but on the battlefield.

During the Spanish Civil War I found myself feeling very strongly that a true history of this war never would or could be written. Accurate figures, objective accounts of what was happening, simply did not exist. And if I felt that even in 1937, when the Spanish Government was still in being, and the lies which the various Republican factions were telling about each other and about the enemy were relatively small ones, how does the case stand now? Even if Franco is over-thrown, what kind of records will the future historian have to go upon? And if Franco or anyone at all resembling him remains in power, the history of the war will consist quite largely of "facts" which millions of people now living know to be lies. One of these "facts," for instance, is that there was a consider-able Russian army in Spain. There exists the most abundant evidence that there was no such army. Yet if Franco remains in power, and if Fascism in general survives, that Russian army will go into the history books and future schoolchildren will believe in it. So for practical purpose the lie will have become truth.

This kind of thing is happening all the time. Out of the millions of instances which must be available, I will choose one which happens to be verifiable. During part of 1941 and 1942, when the Luftwaffe was busy in Russia, the German radio regaled its home audience with stories of devastating air-raids on London. Now, we are aware that those raids did not happen. But what use would our knowledge be if the Germans conquered Britain? For the purposes of a future historian, did those raids happen, or didn't they? The answer is: If Hitler survives, they happened, and if he falls they didn't happen. So with innumerable other events of the past ten or twenty years. Is the *Protocols of the Elders of Zion* a genuine document? Did Trotsky plot with the Nazis? How many German aero-planes were shot down in the Battle of Britain? Does Europe welcome the New Order? In no case do you get one answer which is universally accepted because it is true: in each case you get a number of totally incompatible answers, one of which is finally adopted as the result of a physical struggle. History is written by the winners.

In the last analysis our only claim to victory is that if we win the war we shall tell less lies about it than our adversaries. The really frightening thing about totalitarianism is not that it commits "atrocities" but that it attacks the concept of objective truth: it claims to control the past as well as the future. In spite of all the lying and self-righteousness that war encourages, I do not honestly think it can be said that that habit of mind is growing in Britain. Taking one thing with another, I should say that the press is slightly freer than it was before the war. I know out of my own experience that you can print things now which you couldn't print ten years ago. War-resisters have probably been less maltreated in this war than in the last one, and the expression of unpopular opinions in public is certainly safer. There is some hope, therefore, that the liberal habit of mind, which thinks of truth as something outside yourself, something to be discovered, and not as something you can make up as you go along, will survive. But I still don't envy the future historian's job. Is it not a strange commentary on our time that even the casualties in the present war cannot be estimated within several millions?

Announcing that the Board of Trade is about to remove the ban on turned-up trouser-ends, a tailor's advertisement hails this as "a first instalment of the freedom for which we are fighting."

If we were really fighting for turned-up trouser-ends, I should be inclined to be pro-Axis. Turn-ups have no function except to collect dust, and no virtue except that when you clean them out you occasionally find a sixpence there. But beneath that tailor's jubilant cry there lies another thought: that in a little while Germany will be finished, the war will be half over, rationing will be relaxed, and clothes snobbery will be in full swing again. I don't share that hope. The sooner we are able to stop food rationing the better I shall be pleased, but I would like to see clothes rationing continue till the moths have devoured the last dinner jacket and even the undertakers have shed their top hats. I would not mind seeing the whole nation in dyed battledress for five years if by that means one of the main breeding points of snobbery and envy could be eliminated. Clothes rationing was not conceived in a demo-cratic spirit, but all the same it has had a democratising effect. If the poor are not much better dressed, at least the rich are shabbier. And since no real structural change is occurring in our society, the mechanical levelling process that results from sheer scarcity is better than nothing.

A copy of *The Ingoldsby Legends* which someone gave me for Christmas, with illustrations by Cruikshank, set me wondering about the reasons for the decline in English comic draughts-manship. The decline in comic verse is easier to explain. Barham himself, Hood, Calverley, Thackeray, and other writers of the early and middle nineteenth century, could write good light verse, things in the style of

> Once, a happy child, I carolled
> On green lawns the whole day through,
> Not unpleasingly apparelled
> In a tightish suit of blue,

because on the whole, life – middle-class life – was carefree and one could go from birth to death with a boyish outlook. Except for an occasional thing like Clough's "How pleasant it is to have money," or "The Walrus and the Carpenter," English comic verse of the nineteenth century does not have any ideas in it. But with the draughtsmen it is just the other way about. The attraction of Leech, Cruikshank and a long line of them stretching back to Hogarth is in their intellectual brutality. *Punch* would not print Leech's illustrations to *Handley Cross* if they were new to-day. They are much too brutal: they even make the upper classes look as ugly as the working class! But they are funny, which *Punch* is not. How came it that we lost both our light-heartedness and our cruelty round about 1860? And why is it that now, when class-hatred is as fierce and political passion as near the surface as they were in the time of the Napoleonic wars, cartoonists who can express them are hardly to be found?

As I Please 11

Tribune, 11 February 1944

There are two journalistic activities that will always bring you a come-back. One is to attack the Catholics and the other is to defend the Jews. Recently I happened to review some books dealing with the persecution of the Jews in medieval and modern Europe. The review brought me the usual wad of anti-Semitic letters, which left me thinking for the thousandth time that this problem is being evaded even by the people whom it concerns most directly.

The disquieting thing about these letters is that they do not all come from lunatics. I don't greatly mind the person who believes in the Protocols of the Elders of Zion, nor even the discharged army officer who has been shabbily treated by the Government and is infuriated by seeing "aliens" given all the best jobs. But in addition to these types there is the small business or professional man who is firmly convinced that the Jews bring all their troubles upon themselves by underhand business methods and complete lack of public spirit. These people write reasonable, well-balanced letters, disclaim any belief in racialism, and back up everything they say with copious instances. They admit the existence of "good Jews," and usually declare (Hitler says just the same in *Mein Kampf*) that they did not start out with any anti-Jewish feeling but have been forced into it simply by observing how Jews behave.

The weakness of the Left wing attitude towards anti-Semitism is to approach it from a rationalistic angle. Obviously the charges made against Jews are not true. They cannot be true, partly because they cancel out, partly because no one people could have such a monopoly of wickedness. But simply by pointing this out one gets no further. The official Left wing view of anti-Semitism is that it is something "got up" by the ruling classes in order to divert attention away from the real evils of society. The Jews, in fact, are scapegoats. This is no doubt correct, but it is quite useless as an argument. One does not dispose of a belief by showing that it is irrational. Nor is it any use, in my experience, to talk about the persecution of the Jews in Germany. If a man has the slightest disposition towards anti-Semitism, such things bounce off his consciousness like peas off a steel helmet. The best argument of all, if rational arguments were ever of any use, would be to point out that the alleged crimes of the Jews are only possible because we live in a society which rewards crime. If all Jews are crooks, let us deal with them by so arranging our economic system that crooks cannot prosper. But what good is it to say that kind of thing to the man who believes as an article of faith that Jews dominate the Black Market, push their way to the front of queues and dodge military service?

We could do with a detailed enquiry into the causes of anti-Semitism, and it ought not to be vitiated in advance by the assumption that those causes are wholly economic. However true the "scapegoat" theory may be in general terms, it does not explain why the Jews rather than some [other] minority group are picked on, nor does it make clear what they are a scapegoat *for*. A thing like the Dreyfus Case, for instance, is not easily translated into economic terms. So far as Britain is concerned, the important things to find out are just what charges are made against the Jews, whether anti-Semitism is really on the increase (it may actually have decreased over the past thirty years), and to what extent it is aggravated by the influx of refugees since about 1938.

One not only ought not to assume that the causes of anti-Semitism are economic in a crude, direct way (unemployment, business jealousy, etc.), one also ought not to assume that "sensible" people are immune to it. It flourishes especially among literary men, for instance. Without even getting up from this table to consult a book I can think of passages in Villon, Shakespeare, Smollett, Thackeray, H. G. Wells, Aldous Huxley, T. S. Eliot and many another which would be called anti-Semitic if they had been written since Hitler came to power. Both Belloc and Chesterton flirted, or something more than flirted, with anti-Semitism, and other writers whom it is possible to respect have swallowed it more or less in its Nazi form. Clearly the neurosis lies very deep, and just what it is that people hate when they say that they hate a non-existent entity called "the Jews" is still uncertain. And it is partly the fear of finding out how widespread anti-Semitism is that prevents it from being seriously investigated.

The following lines are quoted in Anthony Trollope's *Auto-biography*: –

> "When Payne-Knight's *Taste* was issued on the town
> A few Greek verses in the text set down
> Were torn to pieces, mangled into hash,
> Hurled to the flames as execrable trash;
> In short, were butchered rather than dissected,
> And several false quantities detected;
> Till, when the smoke had risen from the cinders
> It was discovered that – the lines were Pindar's!"

Trollope does not make clear who is the author of these lines, and I should be very glad if any reader could let me know. But I also quote them for their own sake – that is, for the terrible warning to literary critics that they contain – and for the sake of drawing attention to Trollope's *Autobiography*, which is a most fascinating book, although or because it is largely concerned with money.

The dispute that has been going on in *Time and Tide* about Mr. J. F. Horrabin's *Atlas of War Geography* is a reminder that maps are tricky things, to be regarded with the same suspicion as photographs and statistics.

It is an interesting minor manifestation of nationalism that every nation colours itself red on the map. There is also a tendency to make yourself look bigger than you are, which is possible without actual forgery since every projection of the earth as a flat surface distorts some part or other. During the Empire Free Trade "crusade," there was a free distribution to schools of large coloured wall-maps which were made on a new projection and dwarfed the U.S.S.R. while exaggerating the size of India and Africa. Then there are ethnological and political maps, a most rewarding material for propaganda. During the Spanish civil war, maps were pinned up in the Spanish villages which divided the world into Socialist, Demo-cratic and Fascist States. From these you could learn that India was a democracy, while Madagascar and Indo-China (this was the period of the Popular Front Government in France) were labelled "Socialist."

The war has probably done something towards improving

our geography. People who five years ago thought the Croats rhymed with goats and drew only a very shadowy distinction between Minsk and Pinsk, could now tell you which sea the Volga flows into and indicate without much searching the whereabouts of Guadalcanal or Buthidaung. Hundreds of thousands, if not millions, of English people can nearly pronounce Dnepropetrovsk. But it takes a war to make map-reading popular. As late as the time of Wavell's Egyptian campaign I met a woman who thought that Italy was joined up with Africa, and in 1938, when I was leaving for Morocco, some of the people in my village – a very rustic village, certainly, but only 50 miles from London – asked whether it would be necessary to cross the sea to get there. If you ask any circle of people (I should particularly like to do this with the members of the House of Commons) to draw a map of Europe from memory, you get some surprising results. Any Government which genuinely cared about education would see to it that a globe map, at present an expensive rarity, was accessible to every schoolchild. Without some notion of which country is next to which, and which is the quickest route from one place to another, and where a ship can be bombed from shore, and where it can't, it is difficult to see what value the average citizen's views on foreign policy can have.

A Hundred Up [Review of *Martin Chuzzlewit* by Charles Dickens]
The Observer, 13 February 1944

It is now a hundred years since the final numbers of "MARTIN CHUZZLEWIT" were published and though it came thus early in Dickens's career (it was his fourth novel, if one counts "Pickwick" as a novel), it has more the air of being a pot-boiler than any of his books except the "Sketches." There cannot be many people living who could outline its plot from memory. Whereas books like "Oliver Twist," or "Bleak House," or "Great Expectations," have a central theme which can in some cases be reduced to a single word, the various parts of

"Martin Chuzzlewit" have not much more relationship to one another than the sounds produced by a cat walking across the piano. The best characters are "supers."

What do people remember when they think of "Martin Chuzzlewit"? The American interlude, Mrs. Gamp, and Todgers's (especially Bailey). Martin Chuzzlewit himself is a stick, Mark Tapley a tedious paradox on two legs, Pecksniff a partial failure. It is ironical that Dickens should have tried, more or less unsuccessfully, to make Pecksniff into a monumental figure of a hypocrite, and at the same time, almost incidentally, should have painted such a devasting picture of hypocrisy in the American chapters. Dickens's comic genius is dependent on his moral sense. He is funniest when he is discovering new sins. To denounce Pecksniff did not call into play his special powers, because, after all, no one supposes that hypocrisy is desirable. But to see through the pretensions of American democracy, or even, at that date, to see that Mrs. Gamp was a luxury that society might well do without, did need the eye of a Dickens. The book's lack of any real central theme can be seen in its fearful ending. It is as though Dickens were dissolving into lukewarm treacle, and – as so often when he says something that he does not really feel – whole paragraphs of the final chapter will go straight into blank verse:

> Thy life is tranquil, calm, and happy, Tom.
> In the soft strain which ever and again
> Comes stealing back upon the ear, the memory
> Of thine old love may find a voice perhaps;
> But it is a pleasant, softened, whispering memory,
> Like that in which we sometimes hold the dead,
> And does not pain or grieve thee, God be thanked!

Yet the man who could write this stuff could also record the conversations of Bailey, and could not only create Mrs. Gamp but could throw in, just for good measure, that metaphysical puzzle, Mrs. Harris.

The American chapters are a good example of Dickens's habit of telling small lies in order to emphasise what he regards as a big truth. No doubt many of the things he reports actually happened (other travellers of the time confirm him on some details) but his picture of American society as a whole cannot possibly be true: not only because no community is wholly bad, but because the chaos of real life has been deliberately left out. Every incident, every character, is simply an illustration of Dickens's thesis. Moreover, the strongest charge that he makes against the Americans, that they boast of being democratic while actually living on slave labour, is obviously unfair. It implies that American opinion as a whole acquiesced in slavery, whereas a bloody civil war was to be fought mainly on this issue only twenty years later. But Dickens says these things in order to hit at what he feels to be the real fault of the Americans, their ignorant contempt for Europe and unjustified belief in their own superiority. Perhaps there *were* a few Americans who did not edit libellous newspapers or emit sentences like "the libation of freedom must sometimes be quaffed in blood"; but to lay too much stress upon them would have been to spoil the picture. After all, the business of a caricaturist is to make his point, and these chapters have worn very much better than "American Notes."

The mental atmosphere of the American interlude is one that has since become familiar to us in the books written by British travellers to Soviet Russia. Some of these report that everything is good, others that everything is bad, but nearly all share the same propagandist outlook. A hundred years ago America, "the land of the free," had rather the same place in the European imagination that Soviet Russia has now, and "Martin Chuzzlewit" is the 1844 equivalent of André Gide's *Retour de l'URRS*. But it is a sign of the changing temper of the world that Dickens's attack, so much more violent and unfair than Gide's, could be so quickly forgiven.

"Martin Chuzzlewit" stands somewhere near the turning-point of Dickens's literary development, when he was becoming less of a picaresque writer and more of a novelist. The times were changing with the rise of the new cautious middle class, and Dickens was too much alive not to be affected by the atmosphere he lived in. "Martin Chuzzlewit" is his last completely disorderly book. In spite of its frequent flashes of genius, it is difficult to feel that by following up this vein in himself Dickens could have given us anything to compensate for the loss of "Hard Times" and "Great Expectations."

As I Please 12

Tribune, 18 February 1944

After the war there is going to be a severe housing shortage in this country, and we shall not overcome it unless we resort to prefabrication. If we stick to our traditional building methods the necessary houses will take decades to produce, and the discomfort and misery that this will lead to, the patching-up of blitzed premises and filthy slums, the rent rackets and overcrowding, are easy to foresee. So are the effects of a housing shortage on our already perilous birthrate. Meanwhile not only prefabrication, but any large, concerted effort at rehousing, has powerful vested interests working against it. The building societies, and the brick and cement trades, are directly involved, and the whole principle of private ownership in land is threatened. How could you re-build London, for instance, on a sane plan without disregarding private property rights? But the people who traffic in bugs and basements are not going to come out into the open and say clearly what they are fighting for. By far their best card is the Englishman's sentimental but partly justified yearning for a "home of his own." They will play this card over and over again, and it is up to us to counter it before it takes effect.

To begin with, prefabrication does not mean – as people are already beginning to fear that it means – that we shall all be forced to live in ugly, cramped, flimsy and unhomelike chicken houses. The thing that ought to be pointed out in this connection is that existing English houses are for the most part very badly built. They are not built to withstand either heat or cold, they are lacking in cupboards, their water pipes are so placed as to ensure that they will burst every time there is a hard frost, and they have no convenient means of rubbish-disposal. All these problems, which a speculative builder will tell you are insoluble, are easily solved in various other countries. If we tackled our rehousing problem boldly we could get rid of discomforts which have come to be accepted like the weather, but are in fact quite unnecessary. We could get rid of "blind back" houses, basements, geysers, filth-collecting gas stoves, offices where the light of day never penetrates, outdoor w.c.s, uncleanable stone sinks, and other miseries. We could put a bath in every house and install bells that actually ring, plugs that pull at the first attempt, waste-pipes that don't get blocked by a spoonful of tea-leaves. We could even, if we chose, make our rooms relatively easy to clean by streamlining them and making the corners curved instead of rectangular. But all this depends on our being able to build houses rapidly, by mass-production. Failing that, the housing shortage will be so desperate that we shall have to "make do" with every mouse-ridden ruin that remains, and encourage the speculative builder to do his worst as well.

Secondly, the dislike of flats will somehow have to be exorcised. If people are going to live in big towns they must either live in flats or put up with overcrowding: there is no way out of that. A big block of flats, covering only an acre or two of ground, will contain as many people as live in a small country town, and give them as much room-space as they would have in houses. Rebuild London in big blocks of flats, and there could be light and air for everybody, and room for green spaces, allotments, playgrounds. People could live out of the noise of the traffic, children would not grow up in a world of bricks and dustbins, and historic buildings like St. Paul's would be visible again instead of being swamped by seas of yellow brick.

Yet it is notorious that people, especially working-class people, don't like flats. They want a "home of their own." In a sense they are right, for it is true that in most blocks of working-class flats there isn't the privacy and freedom that you can get in a private house. They are not built to be noise-proof, the people who dwell in them are often burdened by nagging restrictions, and they are often quite unnecessarily uncomfortable. The first blocks built definitely as working-class flats did not even have baths. Even now they seldom have lifts, and they usually have stone stairs, which means that one lives in an endless clattering of boots. Much of this arises from the half-conscious conviction, so powerful in this country, that working-class people must not be made too comfortable. Deafening noise and irritating restrictions are not inherent in the nature of flats, and we ought to insist on that. For the feeling that four rooms are "your own" if they are on the ground, and not "your own" if they are in mid-air – and it is especially strong in women with children – is going to be a big obstacle in the way of replanning, even in areas where the Germans have already done the necessary clearance work.

A correspondent reproaches me for wanting to see clothes rationing continue until we are all equally shabby; though she adds that clothes rationing hasn't, in fact, had an equalising effect. I will quote an extract from her letter: –

"I work in a very exclusive shop just off Bond Street... When I, shivering in my 25/- utility frock, serve these elegant creatures in sables, fur caps and fur-lined boots, who regard me uncomprehendingly when I say 'Good morning, it's very cold to-day, madam' (very stupid of me – after all, how should they know?), I do not wish to see them deprived of their lovely and warm attire, but rather that such attire was available to me, and for all... We should aim not at reducing the present highest standard of living, but at raising any and everything less than the highest. It is a malicious and mean-spirited attitude that wishes to drag Etonians and Harrovians from their fortunate positions of eminence and force them down the mines. Rather, in the present reshuffling of society we should seek to make these places accessible to all."

I answer, first of all, that although clothes rationing obvi-ously bears hardest on those who don't possess large stocks of clothes already, it *has* had a certain equalising effect, because it has made people uneasy about appearing too smart. Certain garments, such as men's evening dress, have practically disap-peared; also it is now considered permissible to wear almost any clothes for almost any job. But my original point was that if clothes rationing goes on long enough even wealthy people will have worn out their extra stocks of clothes, and we shall all be somewhere near equal.

But is it not the case that we ought always to aim at levelling "up" and not levelling "down"? I answer that in some cases you can't level "up." You can't give everyone a Rolls-Royce car. You can't even give everyone a fur coat, especially in war time. As to the statement that everyone ought to go to Eton or Harrow, it is meaningless. The whole value of those places, from the point of view of the people who go there, is their exclusiveness. And since certain luxuries – high-powered cars, for instance, fur coats, yachts, country houses and what-not – obviously can't be distributed to everybody, then it is better that nobody should have them. The rich lose almost as much by their wealth as the poor lose by their poverty. Doesn't my correspondent bring that out when she speaks of those ignorant rich women who cannot even imagine what a cold morning means to a person without an overcoat?

Another correspondent writes indignantly to know what I mean by saying that *Punch* is not funny. Actually I exaggerated a little. Since 1918 I have seen three jokes in *Punch* that made me laugh. But – as I always tell puzzled foreign visitors who enquire about this – *Punch* is not meant to be funny, it is meant to be reassuring. After all, where do you most frequently see it? In club lounges and in dentists' waiting rooms. In both places it has, and is meant to have, a soothing effect. You know in advance that it will never contain anything new. The jokes you were familiar with in your childhood will still be there, just the same as ever, like a circle of old friends. The nervous curate, the apoplectic colonel, the awkward recruit, the forgetful plumber – there they all are, unchangeable as the Pyramids. Glancing through those familiar pages, the clubman knows that his dividends are all right, the patient knows that the dentist will not really break his jaw. But as to being funny, that is a different matter. Jokes that are funny usually contain that un-English thing, an idea. The *New Yorker*, though it is overrated, is quite often funny. Thus a recent number has a picture of two German soldiers leading a huge ape into the orderly room on a chain. The officer is saying to them angrily, "Can't you spell?" This seems to me funny. But it might take five seconds' thought to see the joke, and as it is an axiom of the middle class – at least the golf-playing, whisky-drinking, *Punch*-reading part of the middle class – that no decent person is capable of thought, jokes of that kind are barred from *Punch*.

As I Please 13
Tribune, 25 February 1944

A short story in the *Home Companion and Family Journal*, entitled "Hullo, Sweetheart," recounts the adventures of a young girl named Lucy Fallows who worked on the switchboard of a long-distance telephone exchange. She had "sacrificed her yearning to be in uniform" in order to take this job, but found it dull and uneventful. "So many silly people seemed to use long-distance just to blather to each other . . . She felt fed up; she felt that she was a servant to selfish people"; and there was "a cloud in her hazel eyes." However, as you will readily guess, Lucy's job soon livened up, and before long she found herself in the middle of thrilling adventures which included the sinking of a U-boat, the capture of a German sabotage crew, and a long motor-ride with a handsome naval officer who had "a crisp voice." Such is life in the Telephone Exchange.

At the end of the story there is a little note:

Any of our young readers themselves interested in the work of the Long Distance Telephone Exchange (such work as Lucy Fallows was doing) should apply to the Staff Controller, L.T.R., London, who will inform them as to the opportunities open.

I do not know whether this is an advertisement likely to have much success. I should doubt whether even girls of the age aimed at would believe that capturing U-boats enters very largely into the lives of telephone operators. But I note with interest the direct correlation between a Government recruiting advertisement and a piece of commercial fiction. Before the war the Admiralty, for instance, used to put its advertisements in the boys' adventure papers, which was a natural place to put them, but stories were not, so far as I know, written to order. Probably they are not definitely commissioned even now. It is more likely that the departments concerned keep their eye on the weekly papers (incidentally I like to think of some stripe-trousered personage in the G.P.O. reading "Hullo, Sweetheart" as part of his official duties) and push in an ad. when any story seems likely to form an attractive bait. But from that to the actual commissioning of stories to be written round the A.T.S., Women's Land Army, or any other body in need of recruits, is only a short step. One can almost hear the tired, cultured voices from the M.O.I. saying:

"Hullo! Hullo! Is that you, Tony? Oh, hullo. Look here, I've got another script for you, Tony, 'A Ticket to Paradise.' It's bus conductresses this time. They're not coming in. I believe the trousers don't fit, or something. Well, any way, Peter says make it sexy, but kind of clean – *you* know. Nothing extramarital. We want the stuff in by Tuesday. Fifteen thousand words. You can choose the hero. I rather favour the kind of outdoor man that dogs and kiddies all love – *you* know. Or very tall with a sensitive mouth. I don't mind, really. But pile on the sex, Peter says."

Something resembling this already happens with radio features and documentary films, but hitherto there has not been any very direct connection between fiction and propaganda. That half-inch ad. in the *Home Companion* seems to mark another small stage in the process of "coordination" that is gradually happening to all the arts.

Looking through Chesterton's introduction to *Hard Times* in the Everyman Edition (incidentally, Chesterton's introductions to Dickens are about the best thing he ever wrote), I note the typically sweeping statement: "There are no new ideas." Chesterton is here claiming that the ideas which animated the French Revolution were not new ones but simply a revival of doctrines which had flourished earlier and then been abandoned. But the claim that "there is nothing new under the sun" is one of the stock arguments of intelligent reactionaries. Catholic apologists, in particular, use it almost automatically. Everything that you can say or think has been said or thought before. Every political theory from Liberalism to Trotskyism can be shown to be a development of some heresy in the early Church. Every system of philosophy springs ultimately from the Greeks. Every scientific theory (if we are to believe the popular Catholic press) was anticipated by Roger Bacon and others in the thirteenth century. Some Hindu thinkers go even further and claim that not merely the scientific theories, but the products of applied science as well, aeroplanes, radio and the whole bag of tricks, were known to the ancient Hindus, who afterwards dropped them as being unworthy of their attention.

It is not very difficult to see that this idea is rooted in the fear of progress. If there is nothing new under the sun, if the past in some shape or another always returns, then the future when it comes will be something familiar. At any rate what will never come – since it has never come before – is that hated, dreaded thing, a world of free and equal human beings. Particularly comforting to reactionary thinkers is the idea of a cyclical universe, in which the same chain of events happens over and over again. In such a universe every seeming advance towards democracy simply means that the coming age of tyranny and privilege is a bit nearer. This belief, obviously superstitious though it is, is widely held nowadays, and is common among Fascists and near-Fascists.

In fact, there *are* new ideas. The idea that an advanced civilisation need not rest on slavery is a relatively new idea, for instance: it is a good deal younger than the Christian religion. But even if Chesterton's dictum were true, it would only be true in the sense that a statue is contained in every block of stone. Ideas may not change, but emphasis shifts constantly. It could be claimed, for example, that the most important part of Marx's theory is contained in the saying: "Where your treasure is, there will your heart be also." But before Marx developed it, what force had that saying had? Who had paid any attention to it? Who had inferred from it – what it certainly implies – that laws, religions and moral codes are all a super-structure built over existing property relations? It was Christ, according to the Gospel, who uttered the text, but it was Marx who brought it to life. And ever since he did so the motives of politicians, priests, judges, moralists and millionaires have been under the deepest suspicion – which, of course, is why they hate him so much.

Review of *The Edge of the Abyss* by Alfred Noyes

The Observer, 27 February 1944

Incoherent and, in places, silly though it is, this book raises a real problem and will set its readers thinking, even if their thinking only starts to be useful at about the place where Mr. Noyes leaves off. His thesis is that western civilisation is in danger of actual destruction, and that it has been brought to this pass not by economic maladjustments but by the decay of the belief in absolute good and evil. The rules of behaviour on which any stable society has to rest are dissolving:

> What promise can we trust, what firm agreement can ever be made again, in a world where millions upon millions have been educated to believe that, if it seems in their interest to violate it, no pact or pledge, however solemnly drawn up, need be regarded by "realistic" minds, or "cold statesmanship," as more than a "scrap of paper," even though its violation involve the murder by night of sleeping and innocent millions?

There is much force in this question, which Mr. Noyes repeats over and over again in various forms. In the chaos in which we are living, even the prudential reasons for common decency are being forgotten. Politics, internal or international, are probably no more immoral than they have always been, but what is new is the growing acquiescence of ordinary people in the doctrines of expediency, the callousness of public opinion in the face of the most atrocious crimes and sufferings, and the black-out memory which allows blood-stained murderers to turn into public benefactors overnight if "military necessity" demands it. Quite new, too, is the doubt cast by the various totalitarian systems on the very existence of objective truth, and the consequent large-scale falsification of history. Mr. Noyes is quite right to cry out against all this, and he probably even underemphasises the harm done to ordinary common sense by the cult of "realism," with its inherent tendency to assume that the dishonest course is always the profitable one. The loss of moral standards does, indeed, seem to undermine the sense of probability. Mr. Noyes is also within his rights in saying that the intelligentsia are more infected by totalitarian ideas than the common people, and are partly to blame for the mess we are now in. But his diagnosis of the reasons for this is very shallow, and his suggested remedies are doubtful, even from the point of view of practicability.

To begin with it will not do to suggest, as Mr. Noyes does throughout, that a decent society can only be founded on Christian principles. It amounts to saying that a good life can only be lived on the fringes of the Atlantic. About a quarter of the population of the world is nominally Christian, and the proportion is constantly diminishing. The vast block of Asia is not Christian, and without some unforeseeable miracle it never will be. Are we to say that a decent society cannot be established in Asia? If so, it cannot be established anywhere, and the whole attempt to regenerate society might as well be given up in advance. And Mr. Noyes is probably wrong in imagining that the Christian faith, as it existed in the past, can be restored even in Europe. The real problem of our time is to restore the sense of absolute right and wrong when the belief that it used to rest on – that is, the belief in personal immortality – has been destroyed. This demands faith, which is a different thing from credulity. It seems doubtful whether Mr. Noyes has fully grasped the distinction.

Then there is the question of the amount of blame attaching to "the highbrows" ("our pseudo-intellectuals" is Mr. Noyes's favourite name for them) for the breakdown of moral standards. Mr. Noyes writes on this subject in rather the same strain as the *London Mercury* of twenty years ago. "The highbrows" are gloomy, they are obscene, they attack religion, patriotism, the family, etc., etc. But they are also, it appears, in some way responsible for the rise of Hitler. Now this contradicts the facts. During the crucial years it was precisely the "pseudo-intellectuals" whom Mr. Noyes detests who cried out against the horrors of Fascism, while the Tory and clerical Press did its best to hush them up. Mr. Noyes condemns the policy of appeasement, but what was the attitude of his own Church and its Press on that subject?

On the other hand, the intellectuals whom he *does* approve of are only very doubtfully on the side of the angels. One, of course, is Carlyle, who was one of the founders of the modern worship of power and success, and who applauded the third German war of aggression as vociferously as Pound did the fifth. The other is Kipling. Kipling was not totalitarian, but his moral outlook is equivocal at best. Mr. Noyes remarks at the beginning of his book that one cannot cast out devils with the aid of Beelzebub, but he is also extremely angry because anti-British books can still be published in England and praised in British newspapers. Does it not occur to him that if we stopped doing this kind of thing the main difference between ourselves and our enemies would have disappeared?

Review of *James Joyce* by Harry Levin
Manchester Evening News, 2 March 1944

No one writing in English in our time has excited so much controversy as James Joyce, and even among his declared followers there is a division of opinion. Is *Finnegans Wake* Joyce's masterpiece, or is it simply an elephantine crossword puzzle, product of emotional sterility? On the whole Mr. Levin is a *Finnegans Wake* man. He defends not merely the obscurity but the essential frivolity of Joyce's later work, and though he will not convert anyone who does not like that kind of thing, he can at least show what Joyce was aiming at and what is the connection between *Finnegans Wake* and the relatively intelligible *Ulysses*.

Now that it begins to be possible to see it in perspective the essential process in Joyce's work appears to be the thinning out of a tragic impulse. A novelist is being gradually smothered by a lexicographer. If one compares *Dubliners*, the little book of short stories which Joyce wrote round about 1910 and published in 1914, with *Ulysses*, published in 1922, one notes an enormous increase in virtuosity in the later book, but also a relative lack of feeling.

Dubliners as well as being "slight" is often clumsy, but it is the product of someone who is intensely sorry for the people about him and indignant over their warped, miserable lives. The last story in it, *The Dead*, is one of the most touching stories in English. *Ulysses*, as Mr. Levin rightly says, is conceived primarily in a comic spirit, but even where it ought to be moving it is not. The would-be hero, Stephen Dedalus, whose problems at least seemed real in the earlier book, *Portrait of the Artist*, is by general consent completely intolerable in

Ulysses, and even Leopold Bloom, sympathetic though he is, somehow does not evoke much pity even when his situation is pitiful.

Ulysses is even now a difficult book unless one has been given certain clues beforehand, and Mr. Levin's chapters on it will be a useful guide to anyone who is reading it for the first time. They help to dispose of the merely surface difficulties, but the one great fault of *Ulysses* remains – that is, that it is impossible to be completely certain what it is aiming at. It may be first and foremost an attempt to portray life as it actually is, or an attempt to denigrate the present by comparing it with the past. Probably the second motive predominates, otherwise it is difficult to see why this tale of Dublin in 1904 should be so laboriously stretched on to the framework of the *Odyssey*.

Every episode in Odysseus's wanderings reappears in some dwindled and ridiculous form. Odysseus himself has shrunk into the out-at-elbow Jewish advertisement canvasser Leopold Bloom, the Cyclops is a dropsical Sinn Feiner, the sirens are two barmaids gossiping while Bloom tucks into liver and bacon, the chaste Penelope has turned into Mollie Bloom, with her twenty-five lovers, and so on.

If Joyce is definitely saying any one thing he appears to be saying, "Just look how we have deteriorated since the Bronze Age!" But some of the incidents are tiresome and unconvincing, and again and again the story is overwhelmed or diverted by mere literary cleverness. It is this that gives the book its fragmentary character and also its chief fascination.

If anything Mr. Levin seems rather to underrate the writing of *Ulysses*. The book is like a scrapheap littered with jewels: wonderful snatches of poetic prose ("waves, the sea-horses, champing, brightwind-bridled, steeds of Manahaan"), brilliant word pictures (for instance, of a butcher's shop: "sheepsnouts bloodypapered snivelling nosejam on sawdust"), parodies of newspaper articles and Irish Bronze Age epics, some of them uproariously funny, and experiments in the rendering of thought-processes, such as the "bronze by gold" chapter, and Bloom's silent soliloquies, which had never before been attempted in English.

But some passages, such as the elephantine conversation

about *Hamlet*, are terribly boring, and moreover Joyce, like so many English and Irish novelists, can never resist the temptation to burlesque. Nor can he ever resist turning aside to try a literary experiment: in *Ulysses* even the growling of a dog is irrelevantly turned into a poem. *Ulysses* has every merit except those that a novel ought to have. *The Dead* would still be a good story if it were told in other words, but in *Ulysses* the words are already winning as against the subject-matter.

Clearly *Ulysses* is the more original book and the more interesting to professional writers, but it would not be surprising if in the long run *Dubliners* and *Portrait of the Artist* came to be rated above it.

In *Finnegans Wake*, which starts where *Ulysses* leaves off – *Ulysses* ends with Bloom falling asleep, and the whole of *Finnegans Wake* happens in the dreaming brain of one H. C. Earwicker, a Dublin publican – the words have finally won. There is no emotional interest, and no attempt at any, and the entire book is written in a private language which Joyce has evolved by telescoping together the words of many tongues, living and dead.

Mr. Levin says that what Joyce is doing is to "escape from the nightmare of history," by which he seems to mean that H. C. Earwicker, whose initials also stand for Haveth Childers Everywhere and Here Comes Everybody, represents the entire human race. Just by having so much crammed into him, however, Earwicker loses any individual interest.

Some of Joyce's portmanteau words are expressive as well as ingenious (for instance, "umbroglio" to describe Mr. Chamberlain's foreign policy), but the book as a whole is unreadable unless one regards it as a sort of wordgame. Mr. Levin does describe it among other things as a game, and says that digging out the buried meanings is a fascinating job: which may be true, but one has the right to answer that that is not the kind of fascination one looks for in a work of art.

On *Finnegans Wake* one can suspend judgement: in fifteen years it will be either intelligible or forgotten. But now that *Ulysses* is legally purchasable again no one who is interested in contemporary literature should neglect to read it. Mr. Levin's book is an excellent introduction to it, and the fact that he also deals at length with the other books helps to put *Ulysses* in its proper perspective.

As I Please 14

Tribune, 3 March 1944

Some weeks ago a Catholic reader of *Tribune* wrote to protest against a review by Mr. Charles Hamblett. She objected to his remarks about St. Teresa, and about St. Joseph of Copertino, the saint who once flew round a cathedral carrying a bishop on his back. I answered defending Mr. Hamblett, and got a still more indignant letter in return. This letter raises a number of very important points, and at least one of them seems to me to deserve discussion. The relevance of flying saints to the Social-ist movement may not at first sight be very clear, but I think I can show that the present nebulous state of Christian doctrine has serious implications which neither Christians nor Socialists have faced.

The substance of my correspondent's letter is that it doesn't matter whether St. Teresa and the rest of them flew through the air or not: what matters is that St. Teresa's "vision of the world changed the course of history." I would concede this. Having lived in an Oriental country I have developed a certain indif-ference to miracles, and I well know that having delusions, or even being an outright lunatic, is quite compatible with what is loosely called genius. William Blake, for instance, was a lunatic in my opinion. Joan of Arc was probably a lunatic. Newton believed in astrology, Strindberg believed in magic. However, the miracles of the saints are a minor matter. It also appears from my correspondent's letter that even the most central doctrines of the Christian religion don't have to be accepted in a literal sense. It doesn't matter, for instance, whether Jesus Christ ever existed. "The figure of Christ (myth, or man, or god, it does not matter) so transcends all the rest that I only wish that everyone would look, before rejecting that version of life." Christ, therefore, may be a myth, or he may have been merely a human being, or the account given of him in the Creeds may be true. So we arrive at this position: *Tribune* must not poke fun at the Christian religion, but the existence of Christ, which innumerable people have been burnt for denying, is a matter of indifference.

Now, is this orthodox Catholic doctrine? My impression is

that it is not. I can think of passages in the writings of popular Catholic apologists such as Father Woodlock and Father Ronald Knox in which it is stated in the clearest terms that Christian doctrine means what it appears to mean, and is not to be accepted in some wishy-washy metaphorical sense. Father Knox refers specifically to the idea that it doesn't matter whether Christ actually existed, as a "horrible" idea. But what my correspondent says would be echoed by many Catholic intellectuals. If you talk to a thoughtful Christian, Catholic or Anglican, you often find yourself laughed at for being so ignorant as to suppose that anyone ever took the doctrines of the Church literally. These doctrines have, you are told, a quite other meaning which you are too crude to understand. Immortality of the soul doesn't mean that you, John Smith, will remain conscious after you are dead. Resurrection of the body doesn't mean that John Smith's body will actually be resurrected – and so on and so on. Thus the Catholic intellectual is able, for controversial purposes, to play a sort of handy-pandy game, repeating the articles of the Creed in exactly the same terms as his forefathers, while defending himself from the charge of superstition by explaining that he is speaking in parables. Substantially his claim is that though he himself doesn't believe in any very definite way in life after death, there has been no change in Christian belief, since our ancestors didn't really believe in it either. Meanwhile a vitally important fact – that one of the props of Western civilisation has been knocked away – is obscured.

I do not know whether, officially, there has been any alteration in Christian doctrine. Father Knox and my correspondent would seem to be in disagreement about this. But what I do know is that belief in survival after death – the individual survival of John Smith, still conscious of himself as John Smith – is enormously less widespread than it was. Even among professing Christians it is probably decaying; other people, as a rule, don't even entertain the possibility that it might be true. But our forefathers, so far as we know, did believe in it. Unless all that they wrote about it was intended to mislead us, they believed it in an exceedingly literal, concrete way. Life on earth, as they saw it, was simply a short period of preparation for an infinitely more important life beyond the grave. But that notion has disappeared, or is disappearing, and the consequences have not really been faced.

Western civilisation, unlike some Oriental civilisations, was founded partly on the belief in individual immortality. If one looks at the Christian religion from the outside, this belief appears far more important than the belief in God. The Western conception of good and evil is very difficult to separate from it. There is little doubt that the modern cult of power-worship is bound up with the modern man's feeling that life here and now is the only life there is. If death ends everything, it becomes much harder to believe that you can be in the right even if you are defeated. Statesmen, nations, theories, causes are judged almost inevitably by the test of material success. Supposing that one can separate the two phenomena, I would say that the decay of the belief in personal immortality has been as important as the rise of machine civilisation. Machine civilisation has terrible possibilities, as you probably reflected the other night when the ack-ack guns started up: but the other thing has terrible possibilities too, and it cannot be said that the Socialist movement has given much thought to them.

I do not want the belief in life after death to return, and in any case it is not likely to return. What I do point out is that its disappearance has left a big hole, and that we ought to take notice of that fact. Reared for thousands of years on the notion that the individual survives, man has got to make a considerable psychological effort to get used to the notion that the individual perishes. He is not likely to salvage civilisation unless he can evolve a system of good and evil which is independent of heaven and hell. Marxism, indeed, does supply this, but it has never really been popularised. Most Socialists are content to point out that once Socialism has been established we shall be happier in a material sense, and to assume that all problems lapse when one's belly is full. But the truth is the opposite: when one's belly is empty, one's only problem is an empty belly. It is when we have got away from drudgery and exploitation that we shall really start wondering about man's destiny and the reason for his existence. One cannot have any worthwhile picture of the future unless one realises how much we have lost by the decay of Christianity. Few Socialists seem to be aware of this. And the Catholic intellectuals who cling to the letter of the Creeds while reading into them meanings they were never meant to have, and who snigger at anyone simple enough to suppose that the Fathers of the Church meant what they said, are simply raising smokescreens to conceal their own disbelief from themselves.

I have very great pleasure in welcoming the reappearance of the *Cornhill Magazine* after its four years' absence. Apart from the articles – there is a good one on Mayakovsky by Maurice Bowra, and another good one by Raymond Mortimer on Brougham and Macaulay – there are some interesting notes by the editor on the earlier history of the *Cornhill*. One fact that these bring out is the size and wealth of the Victorian reading public, and the vast sums earned by literary men in those days. The first number of the *Cornhill* sold 120,000 copies. It paid Trollope £2,000 for a serial – he had demanded £3,000 – and commissioned another from George Eliot at £10,000. Except for the tiny few who managed to crash into the film world, these sums would be quite unthinkable nowadays. You would have to be a topnotcher even to get into the £2,000 class. As for £10,000, to get that for a single book you would have to be someone like Edgar Rice Burroughs. A novel nowadays is considered to have done very well if it brings its author £500 – a sum which a successful lawyer can earn in a single day. The book ramp is not so new as "Beachcomber" and other enemies of the literary race imagine.

As I Please 15
Tribune, 10 March 1944

Reading as nearly as possible simultaneously Mr. Derrick Leon's *Life* of Tolstoy, Miss Gladys Storey's book on Dickens, Harry Levin's book on James Joyce, and the autobiography (not yet published in this country) of Salvador Dali, the surrealist painter, I was struck even more forcibly than usual by the advantage that an artist derives from being born into a relatively healthy society.

When I first read *War and Peace* I must have been twenty, an age at which one is not intimidated by long novels, and my sole quarrel with his book (three stout volumes – the length of perhaps four modern novels) was that it did not go on long enough. It seemed to me that Nicholas and Natacha Rostov, Peter Besukhov, Denisov and all the rest of them, were people about whom one would gladly go on reading for ever. The fact is that the minor Russian aristocracy of that date, with their boldness and simplicity, their countrified pleasures, their stormy love affairs and enormous families, were very charming people. Such a society could not possibly be called just or progressive. It was founded on serfdom, a fact that made Tolstoy uneasy even in his boyhood, and even the "enlightened" aristocrat would have found it difficult to think of the peasant as the same species of animal as himself. Tolstoy himself did not give up beating his servants till he was well on into adult life.

The landowner exercised a sort of *droit du seigneur* over the peasants on his estate. Tolstoy had at least one bastard, and his morganatic half-brother was the family coachman. And yet one cannot feel for these simple-minded, prolific Russians the same contempt as one feels for the sophisticated cosmopolitan scum who gave Dali his livelihood. Their saving grace is that they are rustics, they have never heard of benzedrine or gilded toenails, and though Tolstoy was later to repent of the sins of his youth more vociferously than most people, he must have known that he drew his strength – his creative power as well as the strength of his vast muscles – from that rude, healthy background where one shot woodcocks on the marshes and girls thought themselves lucky if they went to three dances in a year.

One of the big gaps in Dickens is that he writes nothing, even in a burlesque spirit, about country life. Of agriculture he does not even pretend to know anything. There are some farcical descriptions of shooting in the *Pickwick Papers*, but Dickens, as a middle-class radical, would be incapable of describing such amusements sympathetically. He sees field-sports as primarily an exercise in snobbishness, which they already were in the England of that date. The enclosures, industrialism, the vast differentiation of wealth, and the cult of the pheasant and the red deer, had all combined to drive the mass of the English people off the land and make the hunting instinct, which is probably almost universal in human beings, seem merely a fetish of the aristocracy. Perhaps the best thing in *War and Peace* is the description of the wolf hunt. In the end it is the peasant's dog that outstrips those of the nobles and gets the wolf; and afterwards Natacha finds it quite natural to dance in the peasant's hut.

To see such scenes in England you would have had to go back a hundred or two hundred years, to a time when difference in status did not mean any very great difference in habits. Dickens's England was already dominated by the "Trespassers will be Prosecuted" board. When one thinks of the accepted Left Wing attitude towards hunting, shooting and the like, it is queer to reflect that Lenin, Stalin and Trotsky were all of them keen sportsmen in their day. But then they belonged to a large empty country where there was no necessary connection between sport and snobbishness, and the divorce between country and town was never complete. The society which almost any modern novelist has as his material is very much meaner, less comely and less carefree than Tolstoy's, and to grasp this has been one of the signs of talent. Joyce would have been falsifying the facts if he had made the people in *Dubliners* less disgusting than they are. But the natural advantage lay with Tolstoy: for, other things being equal, who would not rather write about Peter and Natacha than about furtive seductions in boarding-houses or drunken Catholic business-men celebrating a "retreat"?

In his book on Joyce Mr. Harry Levin gives a few biographical details, but is unable to tell us much about Joyce's last year of life. All we know is that when the Nazis entered France he escaped over the border into Switzerland, to die about a year later in his old home in Zurich. Even the whereabouts of Joyce's children is not, it seems, known for certain.

The academic critics could not resist the opportunity to kick Joyce's corpse. The *Times* gave him a mean, cagey little obituary, and then – though the *Times* has never lacked space for letters about batting averages or the first cuckoo – refused to print the letter of protest that T. S. Eliot wrote. This was in accordance with the grand old English tradition that the dead must always be flattered unless they happen to be artists. Let a politician die, and his worst enemies will stand up on the floor of the House and utter pious lies in his honour, but a writer or artist must be sniffed at, at least if he is any good. The entire British press united to insult D. H. Lawrence ("pornographer" was the usual description) as soon as he was dead. But the snooty obituaries were merely what Joyce would have expected. The collapse of France, and the need to flee from the Gestapo like a common political suspect, were a different matter, and when the war is over it will be very interesting to find out what Joyce thought about it.

Joyce was a conscious exile from Anglo-Irish philistinism. Ireland would have none of him, England and America barely tolerated him. His books were refused publication, destroyed when in type by timid publishers, banned when they came out, pirated with the tacit connivance of the authorities, and, in any case, largely ignored until the publication of *Ulysses*. He had a genuine grievance, and was extremely conscious of it. But it was also his aim to be a "pure" artist, "above the battle" and indifferent to politics. He had written *Ulysses* in Switzerland, with an Austrian passport and a British pension, during the 1914–18 war, to which he paid as nearly as possible no attention. But the present war, as Joyce found out, is not of a kind to be ignored, and I think it must have left him reflecting that a political choice *is* necessary and that even stupidity is better than totalitarianism.

One thing that Hitler and his friends have demonstrated is what a relatively good time the intellectual has had during the past hundred years. After all, how does the persecution of Joyce, Lawrence, Whitman, Baudelaire, even Oscar Wilde, compare with the kind of thing that has been happening to Liberal intellectuals all over Europe since Hitler came to power? Joyce left Ireland in disgust: he did not have to run for his life, as he did when the panzers rolled into Paris. The British Government duly banned *Ulysses* when it appeared, but it took the ban off 15 years later, and what is probably more important, it helped Joyce to stay alive while the book was written. And thereafter, thanks to the generosity of an anonymous admirer, Joyce was able to live a civilized life in Paris for nearly twenty years, working away at *Finnegans Wake* and surrounded by a circle of disciples, while industrious teams of experts translated *Ulysses* not only into various European languages but even into Japanese. Between 1900 and 1920 he had known hunger and neglect: but take it for all in all, his life would appear a pretty good one if one were viewing it from inside a German concentration camp.

What would the Nazis have done with Joyce if they could have laid hands on him? We don't know. They might even have made efforts to win him over and add him to their bag of "converted" literary men. But he must have seen that they had not only broken up the society that he was used to, but were the deadly enemies of everything that he valued. The battle which he had wanted to be "above" did, after all, concern him fairly directly, and I like to think that before the end he brought himself to utter some non-neutral comment on Hitler – and coming from Joyce it might be quite a stinger – which is lying in Zurich and will be accessible after the war.

Rejected Review of *Faith, Reason and Civilisation* by Harold J. Laski

For *Manchester Evening News*; submitted 13 March 1944   Typescript

It is about a year since Professor Laski produced his *Reflections on the Revolution of Our Time*, a larger and more elaborate book than the present one, but dealing with approximately the same subject. At that time there were unmistakable signs of uneasiness in Professor Laski's mind. There were even passages in his book which called up irresistibly the picture of a child swallowing castor oil. Now, however, Professor Laski has found out the right method of dealing with castor oil. Squirt a little lemon and brandy on top of it, hold your nose, shut your eyes, gulp the stuff down, follow it up immediately with a lump of chocolate, and really the experience becomes almost bearable.

What is this castor oil with which Professor Laski used once to have difficulties? It is the authoritarian element in Russian Socialism: more broadly, it is the extreme danger of using dictatorship as a road to democracy. Professor Laski is a Socialist, but he is also a democrat and a believer in freedom of thought. He is justly concerned about the danger of world-wide counter-revolution, and he is aware that the USSR is the real dynamo of the Socialist movement in this country and everywhere else. Therefore the USSR must be safeguarded at all costs. But this, as he sees it, means shutting one's eyes to purges, liquidations, the dictatorship of a minority, suppression of criticism and so forth. It is a painful problem, and in his last book he talked about it and about. Now, however, he has found the answer to it in an analogy – a false analogy as it happens, but evidently a comforting one for the time being.

It is, that the USSR in the modern world corresponds to the Christian Church in the period of the break-up of the Roman Empire. It is the repository of the new doctrines which can both save civilisation and make a fresh advance possible. Just as the early Christians saved the crumbling world of the ancients by giving a new meaning to life, so "the Russian idea" can revivify Western society and take the place of the religious beliefs which (Professor Laski thinks) have outlived their usefulness.

Throughout, Professor Laski uses "the Russian idea" and "Socialism" interchangeably. The Russian regime is assumed not to have altered substantially since 1917: it aims at the establishment of human brotherhood and equality just as singlemindedly as the early Church aimed at the establishment of the Kingdom of God. And it is easy to see how useful this analogy is in reconciling Professor Laski to the principle of totalitarianism. After all, anything can be forgiven to fanatics! Heresy-hunting, persecution, mental dishonesty – they were all common enough among the early Christians, who were nevertheless the founders of our civilisation. And though there were thoughtful pagans who objected to the crudity and superstition of the Christians, at bottom they were only seeking to defend their own privileges. Similarly, those in our own day who object to dictatorship are, at bottom, merely defenders of laissez-faire capitalism.

Look a little more closely at this analogy, and you can see that it is false in every particular. To begin with, Christian doctrine was formed at a time when the Church had no power. The early Christians were a hunted sect, largely consisting of slaves: the Russian government rules over a sixth of the earth. Secondly, in spite of heresies and controversies, Christian doctrine was relatively stable. Communist doctrine changes so often and so drastically that to continue believing in it is almost incompatible with mental integrity. Professor Laski ignores both of these differences. He assumes, as though it were not in dispute, that Stalin's aims are identical with Lenin's, and that the whole trend of development within the USSR has been in the direction of more democracy, more liberty and more social equality. Here and there he admits, usually in a parenthesis, that certain features of the Soviet regime are open to criticism, but always defends them on "tu quoque" lines – that is, by pointing out that similar abuses exist in Britain or the USA

Now, the problem that Professor Laski came near to meeting in his last book, but completely evades in this one, is a problem that does not necessarily involve the USSR at all, except perhaps for purposes of illustration. It is simply this: that if you set up a dictatorship, you have no way of ensuring that the dictator will do what he has promised to do. Any non-democratic version of Socialism necessarily puts all power into the hands of a small clique, and that clique has as much interest in clinging to its privileges as the capitalist class in Britain or America, or any other oligarchy. Despotism based on power instead of money is the inherent danger of Socialism, and it is vitally necessary that it should be foreseen in advance. Instead of warning his readers against it, Professor Laski has chosen to assume that it does not exist.

Why? At bottom, no doubt, because he knows that capitalism is still very strong, that after the war it is capable of making a temporary come-back, with disastrous results, and he fears that it may be demoralising to point out that Socialism also has its dangers. Therefore, don't criticise the USSR, don't insist on the all-importance of freedom of speech, don't mention doubtful subjects like the GPU and the "Soviet millionaires"; because if you speak of such things there is danger that the average man will think you are defending capitalism. That, probably, is how Professor Laski's thoughts run. And certainly the dilemma is a painful one. To work all your life for Socialism, to see at last a state definitely describable as Socialist arise and triumphantly hold its own amid a hostile world, and then to have to admit that it too has its failings – that needs courage. But we expect courage of Professor Laski, and he would write a better book if he would occasionally take the risk of giving ammunition to the reactionaries.

As I Please 16
Tribune, 17 March 1944

With no power to put my decrees into operation, but with as much authority as most of the exile "governments" now sheltering in various parts of the world, I pronounce sentence of death on the following words and expressions: –

Achilles heel, jackboot, hydra-headed, ride roughshod over, stab in the back, petty-bourgeois, stinking corpse, liquidate, iron heel, blood-stained oppressor, cynical betrayal, lackey, flunkey, mad dog, jackal, hyena, blood bath.

No doubt this list will have to be added to from time to time, but it will do to go on with. It contains a fair selection of the dead metaphors and ill-translated foreign phrases which have been current in Marxist literature for years past.

There are, of course, many other perversions of the English language besides this one. There is official English, or Stripe-trouser, the language of White Papers, Parliamentary debates (in their more decorous moments) and B.B.C. news bulletins. There are the scientists and the economists, with their instinct-ive preference for words like "contraindicate" and "deregion-alisation." There is American slang, which for all its attractiveness probably tends to impoverish the language in the long run. And there is the general slovenliness of modern English speech with its decadent vowel sounds (throughout the London area you have to use sign language to distinguish between "threepence" and "three-half-pence") and its ten-dency to make verbs and nouns interchangeable. But here I am concerned only with one kind of bad English, Marxist English, or Pamphletese, which can be studied in the *Daily Worker*, the *Labour Monthly*, *Plebs*, the *New Leader*, and similar papers.

Many of the expressions used in political literature are simply euphemisms or rhetorical tricks. "Liquidate," for instance (or "eliminate"), is a polite word for "to kill," while "realism" normally means "dishonesty." But Marxist phraseology is peculiar in that it consists largely of translations. Its characteristic vocabulary comes ultimately from German or Russian phrases which have been adopted in one country after another with no attempt to find suitable equivalents. Here, for instance, is a piece of Marxist writing – it happens to be an address delivered to the Allied armies by the citizens of Pantelleria: –

The citizens of Pantelleria "pay grateful homage to the Anglo-American forces for the promptness with which they have liberated them from the evil yoke of a megalomaniac and satanic regime which, not content with having sucked like a monstrous octopus the best energies of true Italians for twenty years, is now reducing Italy to a mass of ruins and misery for one motive only – the insane personal profit of its chiefs, who, under an ill-concealed mask of hollow, so-called patriotism, hide the basest passions, and, plotting together with the German pirates, hatch the lowest egoism and blackest treatment while all the time, with revolting cynicism, they tread on the blood of thousands of Italians."

This filthy stew of words is presumably a translation from the Italian, but the point is that one would not recognise it as such. It might be a translation from any other European language, or it might come straight out of the *Daily Worker*, so truly international is this style of writing. Its characteristic is the endless use of ready-made metaphors. In the same spirit, when Italian submarines were sinking the ships that took arms to Republican Spain, the *Daily Worker* urged the British Admiralty to "sweep the mad dogs from the seas." Clearly, people capable of using such phrases have ceased to remember that words have meanings.

A Russian friend tells me that the Russian language is richer than English in terms of abuse, so that Russian invective cannot always be accurately translated. Thus when Molotov referred to the Germans as "cannibals," he was perhaps using some word which sounded natural in Russian, but to which "cannibal" was only a rough approximation. But our local Communists have taken over, from the defunct *Inprecorr* and similar sources, a whole series of these crudely-translated phrases, and from force of habit have come to think of them as actual English expressions. The Communist vocabulary of abuse (applied to Fascists or Socialists according to the "line" of the moment) includes such terms as hyena, corpse, lackey, pirate, hangman, bloodsucker, mad dog, criminal, assassin. Whether at first, second or third hand, these are all translations, and by no means the kind of word that an English person naturally uses to express disapproval. And language of this kind is used with an astonishing indifference as to its meaning. Ask a journalist what a jackboot is, and you will find that he does not know. Yet he goes on talking about jackboots. Or what is meant by "to ride roughshod"? Very few people know that either. For that matter, in my experience, very few Socialists know the meaning of the word "proletariat."

You can see a good example of Marxist language at its worst in the words "lackey" and "flunkey." Pre-revolutionary Russia was still a feudal country in which hordes of idle menservants were part of the social set-up; in that context "lackey," as a word of abuse, had a meaning. In England, the social landscape is quite different. Except at public functions, the last time I saw a footman in livery was in 1921. And, in fact, in ordinary speech, the word "flunkey" has been obsolete since the 'nineties, and the word "lackey" for about a century. Yet they and other equally inappropriate words are dug up for pamphleteering purposes. The result is a style of writing that bears the same relation to writing real English as doing a jigsaw puzzle bears to painting a picture. It is just a question of fitting together a number of ready-made pieces. Just talk about hydra-headed jackboots riding roughshod over bloodstained hyenas, and you are all right. For confirmation of which, see almost any pamphlet issued by the Communist Party – or by any other political party, for that matter.

Review of *The Way of a Countryman* by Sir William Beach Thomas

Manchester Evening News, 23 March 1944

It is uncertain whether the general public would think of Sir William Beach Thomas primarily as a war correspondent or as a naturalist, but he is in no doubt about the matter himself. The world, as he sees it, really centres round the English village, and round the trees and hedges of that village rather than the houses and the people.

In a long life he has travelled to every corner of the earth and met everyone from George Meredith to Marshal Pétain, and from Frank Harris to Theodore Roosevelt, but a glimpse of a bittern in the East Anglian marshes, a grizzly in the Canadian rockies, a twelve-pound trout in New Zealand, means more to him than any merely human celebrity.

Even the Battle of the Somme is chiefly memorable to him because, amid the tremendous roar of the opening bombardment, he saw a grey shrike for the first time.

This book is, in some sort, an autobiography, but it is only fair to give prospective readers the warning, "If you don't like 'nature books' keep away."

Sir William's memories begin some time in the early seventies in a little village in the Shires, where his father was rector, and "four species of animal provided the bulk of our amusements . . . ponies, dogs, rabbits and foxes."

Later, he was to break records for the quarter-mile at Shrewsbury and Oxford, spend busy week-ends with Lord Northcliffe, and "cover" the Ruhr during the lamentable days of the French occupation, but none of it is so vivid to him as the memory of that village childhood.

"What a number of 'necessities of life' we did without. We had no bicycles, of course, no motor-cars, no telephones, no wireless, no gramophone, no preserved fruit – except some repulsive dried apples – no tomatoes, no bananas, no keyless watches, and few games . . . We journeyed to the nearest town, nine miles away, by pony, whose feet churned up inches of white dust."

And, needless to say, Sir William preferred it like that, including the absence of games, for though a born athlete he rightly objects to the "tyranny" of games, which was just beginning to become operative in his boyhood.

Sir William describes himself throughout as a "countryman," but for his purposes "the country" means sport, birdwatching, and botanising rather than agriculture, and his book raises certain doubts about the whole of this class of literature.

There is no question that a love of what is loosely called "nature" – a kingfisher flashing down a stream, a bullfinch's mossy nest, the caddis-flies in the ditch – is very widespread in England, cutting across age-groups and even class-distinctions, and attaining in some people an almost mystical intensity.

Whether it is a healthy symptom is another matter. It arises partly from the small size, equable climate, and varied scenery of England, but it is also probably bound up with the decay of English agriculture. Real rustics are not conscious of being picturesque, they do not construct bird sanctuaries, they are uninterested in any plant or animal that does not affect them directly.

In many languages all the smaller birds are called by the same name. Even in England a genuine farm labourer usually thinks that a frog and a toad are the same thing, and nearly always believes that all snakes are poisonous and that they sting with their tongues.

The fact is that those who really have to deal with nature have no cause to be in love with it. On the East Anglian coast the older cottages for the fishermen are built with their backs to the sea. The sea is simply an enemy from the fisherman's point of view.

Sir William's comparatively sentimental attitude towards the land is shown by the fact that he regrets the war-time destruction of the rabbit. Probably he would also regret the extermination of that even deadlier enemy of agriculture, the pheasant.

"Nature" books are a growth of the past two hundred years. The first and probably still the best of them is Gilbert White's "Natural History of Selborne."

Sir William couples with this Izaak Walton's "Compleat Angler," written a century earlier, but Walton's more limited and utilitarian book does not seem quite to belong in this category.

The most characteristic "nature writers" of all are W. H. Hudson, and Richard Jefferies. One may guess that it is on Jefferies that Sir William Beach Thomas has modelled himself. But Jefferies, for all his charm and his detailed observation, is curiously inhuman. His daydream expressed in a whole book was of an England from which the human beings had vanished and only the wild creatures remained.

The same outlook is implied in W. H. Hudson, whose only successful novel, "Green Mansions," has a heroine who is half human and half bird. Hudson also wrote a whole rapturous essay on the spectacle of a field ruined by dandelions.

Nature-worship carried to this length is inherently anti-social. The more normal attitude is expressed by Crabbe, a true countryman, who wrote at least one diatribe against wild-flowers, which in his eyes were simply weeds. Needless to say, Sir William does not much approve of Crabbe.

Sir William started his journalist career at about the same time as Shaw, Barrie, Max Beerbohm, and J. L. Garvin. That was in the bustling days when Northcliffe had just started the "Daily Mail," and the journalistic reminiscences are probably the best thing in this book.

The war of 1914–18 is hardly mentioned, though it is interesting to learn that for the first year or two the whole British Press was only allowed to send five correspondents to the front, and these were as far as possible prevented from seeing anything.

The book ends with a plea for the preservation and revival of rural England, with which everyone can agree even while suspecting that Sir William's ideal picture of rural England might contain too many rabbits and not enough tractors.

As I Please 17

Tribune, 24 March 1944

Of all the unanswered questions of our time, perhaps the most important is: "What is Fascism?"

One of the social survey organisations in America recently asked this question of a hundred different people, and got answers ranging from "pure democracy" to "pure diabolism." In this country if you ask the average thinking person to define Fascism, he usually answers by pointing to the German and Italian regimes. But this is very unsatisfactory, because even the major Fascist states differ from one another a good deal in structure and ideology.

It is not easy, for instance, to fit Germany and Japan into the same framework, and it is even harder with some of the small states which are describable as Fascist. It is usually assumed, for instance, that Fascism is inherently warlike, that it thrives in an atmosphere of war hysteria and can only solve its economic problems by means of war-preparation or foreign conquests. But clearly this is not true of, say, Portugal or the various South American dictatorships. Or again, anti-Semitism is supposed to be one of the distinguishing marks of Fascism; but some Fascist movements are not anti-Semitic. Learned controversies, reverberating for years on end in American magazines, have not even been able to determine whether or not Fascism is a form of Capitalism. But still, when we apply the term "Fascism" to Germany or Japan or Mussolini's Italy, we know broadly what we mean. It is in internal politics that this word has lost the last vestige of meaning. For if you examine the Press you will find that there is almost no set of people – certainly no political party or organised body of any kind – which has not been denounced as Fascist during the past ten years.

Here I am not speaking of the verbal use of the term "Fascist." I am speaking of what I have seen in print. I have seen the words "Fascist in sympathy," or "of Fascist tendency," or just plain "Fascist," applied in all seriousness to the following bodies of people:

Conservatives: All Conservatives, appeasers or anti-appeasers, are held to be subjectively pro-Fascist. British rule in India and the Colonies is held to be indistinguishable from Nazism. Organisations of what one might call a patriotic and traditional type are labelled crypto-Fascist or "Fascist-minded." Examples are the Boy Scouts, the Metropolitan Police, M.I.5, the British Legion. Key phrase: "The public schools are breeding-grounds of Fascism."

Socialists: Defenders of old-style capitalism (example, Sir Ernest Benn) maintain that Socialism and Fascism are the same thing. Some Catholic journalists maintain that Socialists have been the principal collaborators in the Nazi-occupied countries. The same accusation is made from a different angle by the Communist Party during its ultra-Left phases. In the period 1930–35 the *Daily Worker* habitually referred to the Labour Party as the Labour Fascists. This is echoed by other Left extremists such as Anarchists. Some Indian Nationalists consider the British trade unions to be Fascist organisations.

Communists: A considerable school of thought (examples, Rauschning, Peter Drucker, James Burnham, F. A. Voigt) refuses to recognise a difference between the Nazi and Soviet regimes, and holds that all Fascists and Communists are aiming at approximately the same thing and are even to some extent the same people. Leaders in the *Times* (pre-war) have referred to the U.S.S.R. as a "Fascist country." Again from a different angle this is echoed by Anarchists and Trotskyists.

Trotskyists: Communists charge the Trotskyists proper, i.e., Trotsky's own organisation, with being a crypto-Fascist organisation in Nazi pay. This was widely believed on the Left during the Popular Front period. In their ultra-Right phases the Communists tend to apply the same accusation to all fractions to the Left of themselves, e.g., Common Wealth or the I.L.P.

Catholics: Outside its own ranks, the Catholic Church is almost universally regarded as pro-Fascist, both objectively and subjectively.

War-resisters: Pacifists and others who are anti-war are frequently accused not only of making things easier for the Axis, but of becoming tinged with pro-Fascist feeling.

Supporters of the war: War-resisters usually base their case on the claim that British Imperialism is worse than Nazism, and tend to apply the term "Fascist" to anyone who wishes for a military victory. The supporters of the People's Convention came near to claiming that willingness to resist a Nazi invasion was a sign of Fascist sympathies. The Home Guard was denounced as a Fascist organisation as soon as it appeared. In addition, the whole of the Left tends to equate militarism with Fascism. Politically conscious private soldiers nearly always refer to their officers as "Fascist-minded" or "natural Fascists." Battle schools, spit and polish, saluting of officers are all considered conducive to Fascism. Before the war, joining the Territorials was regarded as a sign of Fascist tendencies. Conscription and a professional army are both denounced as Fascist phenomena.

ESSAYS

Nationalists: Nationalism is universally regarded as inherently Fascist, but this is held only to apply to such national movements as the speaker happens to disapprove of. Arab nationalism, Polish nationalism, Finnish nationalism, the Indian Congress Party, the Muslim League, Zionism, and the I.R.A. are all described as Fascist – but not by the same people.

It will be seen that, as used, the word "Fascism" is almost entirely meaningless. In conversation, of course, it is used even more wildly than in print. I have heard it applied to farmers, shopkeepers, Social Credit, corporal punishment, foxhunting, bullfighting, the 1922 Committee, the 1941 Committee, Kipling, Gandhi, Chiang Kai-Shek, homosexuality, Priestley's broadcasts, Youth Hostels, astrology, women, dogs and I do not know what else.

Yet underneath all this mess there does lie a kind of buried meaning. To begin with, it is clear that there are very great differences, some of them easy to point out and not easy to explain away, between the regimes called Fascist and those called democratic. Secondly, if "Fascist" means "in sympathy with Hitler," some of the accusations I have listed above are obviously very much more justified than others. Thirdly, even the people who recklessly fling the word "Fascist" in every direction attach at any rate an emotional significance to it. By "Fascism" they mean, roughly speaking, something cruel, unscrupulous, arrogant, obscurantist, anti-liberal and anti-working-class. Except for the relatively small number of Fascist sympathisers, almost any English person would accept "bully" as a synonym for "Fascist." That is about as near to a definition as this much-abused word has come.

But Fascism is also a political and economic system. Why, then, cannot we have a clear and generally accepted definition of it? Alas! we shall not get one – not yet, anyway. To say why would take too long, but basically it is because it is impossible to define Fascism satisfactorily without making admissions which neither the Fascists themselves, nor the Conservatives, nor Socialists of any colour, are willing to make. All one can do for the moment is to use the word with a certain amount of circumspection and not, as is usually done, degrade it to the level of a swearword.

Review of *Tolstoy: His Life and Work* by Derrick Leon

The Observer, 26 March 1944

Tolstoy's adult life – it starts with a brilliant, worldly, rather dissolute young aristocrat and ends with a tormented old man who had renounced every thing, or come as near renouncing it as his family would let him – is dramatic enough, but finally it is less interesting than his work, and the most valuable part of Mr. Leon's biography is the careful exposition that he gives of each of Tolstoy's books in turn, showing just how it is related to Tolstoy's spiritual development.

Tolstoy's creed, gradually developed over a period of about fifty years, could be described as Christian Anarchism. All material aims, all violence, all revolutions, in the last analysis all laws and governments, are evil: there is no happiness except in self-abnegation: man has no rights, only duties, being on earth solely to do the will of God. All this is derived from his reading of the Gospels, but before his beliefs were fully formulated he had adopted two doctrines which are only doubtfully Christian. One is a strict determinism. A man's actions, Tolstoy holds, are all predetermined, his sole freedom consisting in the knowledge of necessity. The other is a conviction of the essential misery of earthly life, and the wickedness of physical pleasures, which goes far beyond anything the churches have ever countenanced.

Mr. Leon writes as a disciple, and he does not seriously answer, though he does mention, the charge many people have made – that Tolstoy's later work is largely the projection of his own egoism. In stretching self-abnegation to mean practically a refusal of the process of life – in saying, for instance, that marriage is of its nature "misery and slavery" – it is doubtful whether he is saying much more than that he is unhappy himself and would like to make others unhappy as well. Tolstoy was, of course, extremely conscious of the dangers of egoism, indeed his life was in some sense a continuous struggle against it, but he does not seem to have seen that the form it took in himself was not a desire for money or success, but simply a taste for intellectual bullying: his essay on Shakespeare is an outstanding example of this.

Nevertheless his life-story is inspiring as well as tragic, and we should still feel him to be a remarkable man even if he had written nothing except his pamphlets. Directly, his influence on the life of our time has not been very great, because he abjured all the methods by which anything can actually be achieved. But indirectly, through individuals, it must have been enormous. No one can read Tolstoy and come away with quite the same feeling about war, violence, success, government, and "great" men – though, somewhat ironically, the special thing that he has to say is said most effectively in the novels of his middle period, "Anna Karenina" and "War and Peace," which he afterwards came to look on as almost reprehensible.

It is a pity that throughout his narrative Mr. Leon shows such an implacable hostility for the wretched Countess Tolstoy, for by assuming that in every disagreement the Countess must have been in the wrong he avoids discussion of one of the most difficult problems of a writer's life – the conflict between the literary and the private personality, or, to put it differently, between love of humanity and ordinary decency. Otherwise this is an outstanding book, and though one cannot advise people to buy books costing twenty-five shillings, at least everyone who can borrow a copy should read it.

As I Please 18

Tribune, 31 March 1944

The other day I attended a Press conference at which a newly arrived Frenchman, who was described as an "eminent jurist" – he could not give his name or other specifications because of his family in France – set forth the French point of view on the recent execution of Pucheu. I was surprised to note that he was distinctly on the defensive, and seemed to think that the shooting of Pucheu was a deed that would want a good deal of justification in British and American eyes. His main point was that Pucheu was not shot for political reasons, but for the ordinary crime of "collaborating with the enemy," which has always been punishable by death under French law.

An American correspondent asked the question: "Would collaborating with the enemy be equally a crime in the case of some petty official – an inspector of police, for example?" "Absolutely the same," answered the Frenchman. As he had just come from France he was presumably voicing French opinion, but one can assume that in practice only the most active collaborators will be put to death. Any really big-scale massacre, if it really happened, would be quite largely the punishment of the guilty by the guilty. For there is much evidence that large sections of the French population were more or less pro-German in 1940 and only changed their minds when they found out what the Germans were like.

I do not want people like Pucheu to escape, but a few very obscure quislings, including one or two Arabs, have been shot as well, and this whole business of taking vengeance on traitors and captured enemies raises questions which are strategic as well as moral. The point is that if we shoot too many of the small rats now we may have no stomach for dealing with the big ones when the time comes. It is difficult to believe that the Fascist regimes can be thoroughly crushed without the killing of the responsible individuals, to the number of some hundreds or even thousands in each country. But it could well happen that all the truly guilty people will escape in the end, simply because public opinion has been sickened beforehand by hypocritical trials and cold-blooded executions.

In effect this was what happened in the last war. Who that was alive in those years does not remember the maniacal hatred of the Kaiser that was fostered in this country? Like Hitler in this war, he was supposed to be the cause of all our ills. No one doubted that he would be executed as soon as caught and the only question was what method would be adopted. Magazine articles were written in which the rival merits of boiling in oil, drawing and quartering and breaking on the wheel were carefully examined. The Royal Academy exhibitions were full of allegorical pictures of incredible vulgarity, showing the Kaiser being thrown into Hell. And what came of it in the end? The Kaiser retired to Holland and (though he had been "dying of cancer" in 1915) lived another twenty-two years, one of the richest men in Europe.

So also with all the other "war criminals." After all the threats and promises that had been made, no war criminals were tried: to be exact, a dozen people or so were put on trial, given sentences of imprisonment and soon released. And though, of course, the failure to crush the German military caste was due to the conscious policy of the Allied leaders, who were terrified of revolution in Germany, the revulsion of feeling in ordinary people helped to make it possible. They did not want revenge when it was in their power. The Belgian atrocities, Miss Cavell, the U-boat captains who had sunk passenger ships without warning and machine-gunned the survivors – somehow it was all forgotten. Ten million innocent men had been killed and no one wanted to follow it up by killing a few thousand guilty ones.

Whether we do or don't shoot the Fascists and quislings who happen to fall into our hands is probably not very important in itself. What is important is that revenge and "punishment" should have no part in our policy or even in our day-dreams. Up to date, one of the mitigating features of this war is that in this country there has been very little hatred. There has been none of the nonsensical racialism that there was last time – no pretence that all Germans have faces like pigs, for instance. Even the word "Hun" has not really popularised itself. The Germans in this country, mostly refugees, have not been well treated, but they have not been meanly persecuted as they were last time. In the last war it would have been very unsafe, for instance, to speak German in a London street. Wretched little German bakers and hairdressers had their shops sacked by the mob. German music fell out of favour, even the breed of dachshunds almost disappeared because no one wanted to have a "German dog." And the weak British attitude in the early period of German rearmament had a direct connection with those follies of the war years.

Hatred is an impossible basis for policy, and curiously enough it can lead to over-softness as well as to over-toughness. In the war of 1914–18 the British people were whipped up into a hideous frenzy of hatred, they were fed on preposterous lies about crucified Belgian babies and German factories where corpses were made into margarine and then as soon as the war stopped they suffered the natural revulsion, which was all the stronger because the troops came home, as British troops usually do, with a warm admiration for the enemy. The result was an exaggerated pro-German reaction which set in about 1920 and lasted till Hitler was well in the saddle. Throughout those years all "enlightened" opinion (see any number of the *Daily Herald* before 1929, for instance) held it as an article of faith that Germany bore no responsibility for the war. Treitschke, Bernhardi, the Pan-Germans, the "Nordic" myth, the open boasts about "Der Tag" which the Germans had been making from 1900 onwards – all this went for nothing. The Versailles Treaty was the greatest infamy the world had ever seen: few people had even heard of Brest-Litovsk. All this was the price of that four years' orgy of lying and hatred.

Anyone who tried to awaken public opinion during the years of Fascist aggression from 1933 onwards knows what the after-effects of that hate-propaganda were like. "Atrocities" had come to be looked on as synonymous with "lies." But the stories about the German concentration camps were atrocity stories: therefore they were lies – so reasoned the average man. The left-wingers who tried to make the public see that Fascism was an unspeakable horror were fighting against their own propaganda of the past fifteen years.

That is why – though I would not save creatures like Pucheu even if I could – I am not happy when I see trials of "war criminals," especially when they are very petty criminals and when witnesses are allowed to make inflammatory political speeches. Still less am I happy to see the Left associating itself with schemes to partition Germany, enrol millions of Germans in forced labour gangs and impose reparations which will make the Versailles reparations look like a bus fare. All these vindictive day-dreams, like those of 1914–18, will simply make it harder to have a realistic post-war policy. If you think *now* in terms of "making Germany pay," you will quite likely find yourself praising Hitler in 1950. Results are what matter, and one of the results we want from this war is to be quite sure that Germany will not make war again. Whether this is best achieved by ruthlessness or generosity I am not certain: but I am quite certain that either of these will be more difficult if we allow ourselves to be influenced by hatred.

As I Please 19
Tribune, 7 April 1944

Sometimes, on top of a cupboard or at the bottom of a drawer, you come on a pre-war newspaper, and when you have got over your astonishment at its enormous size, you find yourself marvelling at its almost unbelievable stupidity. It happens that I have just come across a copy of the *Daily Mirror* of January 21st, 1936. One ought not, perhaps, to draw too many inferences from this one specimen, because the *Daily Mirror* was in those days our second silliest daily paper (the *Sketch* led, of course, as it still does), and because this particular number contains the announcement of the death of George V. It is not, therefore, entirely typical. But still, it is worth analysing, as an extreme example of the kind of stuff that was fed to us in the between-war years. If you want to know why your house has been bombed, why your son is in Italy, why the income tax is ten shillings in the pound and the butter ration is only just visible without a microscope, here is part of the reason.

The paper consists of 28 pages. Of these the first 17 are devoted in their entirety to the dead King and the rest of the Royal Family. There is a history of the King's life, articles on his activities as statesman, family man, soldier, sailor, big and small game shot, motorist, broadcaster and what-not, with, of course, photographs innumerable. Except for one advertisement and one or two letters, you would not gather from these first 17 pages that any other topic could possibly interest the *Daily Mirror*'s readers. On page 18 there appears the first item unconnected with royalty. Needless to say this is the comic strip. Pages 18 to 23 inclusive are entirely given up to amusement guides, comic articles, and so forth. On page 24 some news begins to creep in, and you read of a highway robbery, a skating contest, and the forthcoming funeral of Rudyard Kipling. There are also some details about a snake at the Zoo which is refusing its food. Then on page 26 comes the *Daily Mirror*'s sole reference to the real world, with the headline:

BOMBING PLEDGE BY DUCE
NO MORE ATTACKS ON RED CROSS.

Underneath this, to the extent of about half a column, it is explained that il Duce "deplores" the attacks on the Red Cross, which were not committed "wilfully," and it is added that the League of Nations has just turned down Abyssinia's requests for assistance and refused to investigate the charges of Italian atrocities. Turning to more congenial topics the *Daily Mirror* then follows up with a selection of murders, accidental deaths and the secret wedding of Earl Russell. The last page of the paper is headed in huge letters: LONG LIVE KING EDWARD VIII, and contains a short biography and a highly idealised photograph of the man whom the Conservative Party were to sack like a butler a year later.

Among the topics *not* mentioned in this issue of the *Daily Mirror* are the unemployed (two or three millions of them at that date), Hitler, the progress of the Abyssinian war, the disturbed political situation in France, and the trouble already obviously blowing up in Spain. And though this is an extreme instance, nearly all newspapers of those days were more or less like that. No real information about current affairs was allowed into them if it could possibly be kept out. The world – so the readers of the gutter Press were taught – was a cosy place dominated by royalty, crime, beauty-culture, sport, pornography and animals.

No one who makes the necessary comparisons can possibly doubt that our newspapers are far more intelligent than they were five years ago. Partly it is because they are so much smaller. There are only four pages or so to be filled, and the war news necessarily crowds out the rubbish. But there is also a far greater willingness to talk in a grown-up manner, to raise uncomfortable topics, to give the important news the big headlines, than there used to be, and this is bound up with the increased power of the journalist as against the advertiser. The unbearable silliness of English newspapers from about 1900 onward has had two main causes. One is that nearly the whole of the Press is in the hands of a few big capitalists who are interested in the continuance of capitalism and therefore in preventing the public from learning to think: the other is that in peacetime newspapers live off advertisements for consumption goods, building societies, cosmetics and the like, and are therefore interested in maintaining a "sunshine mentality" which will induce people to spend money. Optimism is good for trade, and more trade means more advertisements. Therefore, don't let people know the facts about the political and economic situation; divert their attention to giant pandas, channel swimmers, royal weddings and other soothing topics. The first of these causes still operates, but the other has almost lapsed. It is now so easy to make a newspaper pay, and internal trade has dwindled so greatly, that the advertiser has temporarily lost his grip. At the same time there has been an increase in censorship and official interference, but this is not nearly so crippling and not nearly so conducive to sheer silliness. It is better to be controlled by bureaucrats than by common swindlers. In proof of which, compare the *Evening Standard*, the *Daily Mirror* or even the *Daily Mail* with the things they used to be.

And yet the newspapers have not got back their prestige – on the contrary they have steadily lost prestige as against the wireless – partly because they have not yet lived down their pre-war follies, but partly also because all but a few of them retain their "stunt" make-up and their habit of pretending that there is news when there is no news. Although far more willing than they used to be to raise serious issues, most of the papers remain completely reckless about details of fact. The belief that what is "in the papers" must be true has been gradually evaporating ever since Northcliffe set out to vulgarise journalism, and the war has not yet arrested the process. Many people frankly say that they take in such and such a paper because it is lively, but that they don't believe a word of what it says.

Meanwhile the B.B.C., so far as its news goes, has gained prestige since about 1940. "I heard it on the wireless" is now almost equivalent to "I know it must be true." And throughout most of the world B.B.C. news is looked on as more reliable than that of the other belligerent nations.

How far is this justified? So far as my own experience goes, the B.B.C. is much more truthful, in a negative way, than the majority of newspapers, and has a much more responsible and dignified attitude towards news. It tells less direct lies, makes more effort to avoid mistakes, and – the thing the public probably values – keeps the news in better proportion. But none of this alters the fact that the decline in the prestige of the newspapers as against the radio is a disaster.

Radio is an inherently totalitarian thing, because it can only be operated by the Government or by an enormous corporation, and in the nature of things it cannot give the news anywhere near so exhaustively as a newspaper. In the case of the B.B.C. you have the additional fact that, though it doesn't tell deliberate lies, it simply avoids every awkward question. In even the most stupid or reactionary newspaper every subject can at least be *raised*, if only in the form of a letter. If you had nothing but the wireless to go upon, there would be some surprising gaps in your information. The Press is of its nature a more liberal, more democratic thing, and the Press lords who have dirtied its reputation, and the journalists who have more or less knowingly lent themselves to the process, have a lot to answer for.

As I Please 20
Tribune, 14 April 1944

The April issue of *Common Wealth* devotes several paragraphs to the problem of the falling British birthrate. A good deal of what it says is true, but it also lets drop the following remarks:

"The know-alls are quick to point to contraceptives, nutritional errors, infertility, selfishness, economic insecurity, etc., as basic causes of decline. But facts do not support them. In Nazi Germany, where contraceptives are illegal, the Birth Rate has reached a record low ebb, whereas in the Soviet Union, where there are no such restrictions, population is healthily on the up and up . . . Reproduction, as the Peckham experiment has helped to prove, is stimulated in an environment marked by fellowship and co-operation . . . Once meaning and purpose are restored to life, the wheels of production are kept humming, and life is again an adventure instead of just an endurance, we shall hear no more of the baby shortage."

It is not fair to the public to treat all-important subjects in this slapdash way. To begin with, you would gather from the passage quoted above that Hitler lowered the German birthrate. On the contrary, he raised it to levels unheard-of during the Weimar Republic. Before the war it was above replacement level, for the first time in many years. The catastrophic drop in the German birthrate began in 1942, and must have been partly caused by so many German males being away from home. Figures cannot be available yet, but the Russian birthrate must almost certainly have dropped over the same period.

You would also gather that the high Russian birthrate dates from the Revolution. But it was also high in Czarist times. Nor is there any mention of the countries where the birthrate is highest of all, that is, India, China, and (only a little way behind) Japan. Would it be accurate to say, for instance, that a South Indian peasant's life is "an adventure instead of just an endurance"?

The one thing that can be said with almost complete certainty on this subject is that a high birthrate goes with a low standard of living, and vice versa. There are few if any real exceptions to this. Otherwise the question is exceedingly complex. It is, all the same, vitally important to learn as much about it as we can, because there will be a calamitous drop in our own population unless the present trend is reversed within ten or, at most, twenty years. One ought not to assume, as some people do, that this is impossible, for such changes of trend have often happened before. The experts are proving now that our population will be only a few millions by the end of this century, but they were also proving in 1870 that by 1940 it would be 100 millions. To reach replacement level again, our birthrate would not have to take such a sensational upward turn as, for instance, the Turkish birthrate did after Mustapha Kemal took over. But the first necessity is to find out *why* populations rise and fall, and it is just as unscientific to assume that a high birthrate is a by-product of Socialism as to swallow everything that is said on the subject by childless Roman Catholic priests.

When I read of the goings-on in the House of Commons the week before last, I could not help being reminded of a little incident that I witnessed twenty years ago and more.

It was at a village cricket match. The captain of one side was the local squire, who, besides being exeedingly rich, was a vain, childish man to whom the winning of this match seemed extremely important. Those playing on his side were all or nearly all his own tenants.

The squire's side were batting, and he himself was out and was sitting in the pavilion. One of the batsmen accidentally hit his own wicket at about the same moment as the ball entered the wicketkeeper's hand. "That's not out," said the squire promptly, and went on talking to the person beside him. The umpire, however, gave a verdict of "out," and the batsman was half-way back to the pavilion before the squire realised what was happening. Suddenly he caught sight of the returning batsman, and his face turned several shades redder.

"What!" he cried, "he's given him out? Nonsense! Of course he's not out!" And then, standing up, he cupped his hands and shouted to the umpire: "Hi, what did you give that man out for? He wasn't out at all!"

The batsman had halted. The umpire hesitated, then recalled the batsman to the wicket and the game went on.

I was only a boy at the time, and this incident seemed to me about the most shocking thing I had ever seen. Now, so much do we coarsen with the passage of time, my reaction would merely be to inquire whether the umpire was the squire's tenant as well.

Attacking Mr. C. A. Smith and myself in the *Malvern Torch* for various remarks about the Christian religion, Mr. Sidney Dark grows very angry because I have suggested that the belief in personal immortality is decaying. "I would wager," he says, "that if a Gallup poll were taken seventy-five per cent. [of the British population] would confess to a vague belief in survival." Writing elsewhere during the same week, Mr. Dark puts it at eighty-five per cent.

Now, I find it very rare to meet anyone, of whatever background, who admits to believing in personal immortality. Still, I think it quite likely that if you asked everyone the question and put pencil and paper in his hands, a fairly large number (I am not so free with my percentages as Mr. Dark) would admit the possibility that after death there might be "something." The point Mr. Dark has missed is that the belief, such as it is, hasn't the actuality it had for our forefathers. Never, literally never in recent years, have I met anyone who gave me the impression of believing in the next world as firmly as he believed in the existence of, for instance, Australia. Belief in the next world does not influence conduct as it would if it were genuine. With that endless existence beyond death to look forward to, how trivial our lives here would seem! Most Christians profess to believe in Hell. Yet have you ever met a Christian who seemed as afraid of Hell as he was of cancer? Even very devout Christians will make jokes about Hell. They wouldn't make jokes about leprosy, or R.A.F. pilots with their faces burnt away: the subject is too painful. Here there springs into my mind a little triolet by the late G. K. Chesterton:

It's a pity that Poppa has sold his soul,
It makes him sizzle at breakfast so.
The money was useful, but still on the whole
It's a pity that Poppa has sold his soul
When he might have held on like the Baron de Coal,
And not cleared out when the price was low.
It's a pity that Poppa has sold his soul,
It makes him sizzle at breakfast so.

Chesterton, a Catholic, would presumably have said that he believed in Hell. If his next-door neighbour had been burnt to death he would not have written a comic poem about it, yet he can make jokes about somebody being fried for millions of years. I say that such belief has no reality. It is a sham currency, like the money in Samuel Butler's Musical Banks.

When anyone enters the *Tribune* office nowadays, the first thing that strikes his eyes is a huge mound of papers from beneath which a nose makes occasional and momentary appearances. This is myself dealing with the entries for the Short Story Competition. The response has been what is usually called generous. The competition closed on March 31st, but we shall not be able to announce the results for several weeks. We hope to be able to publish the winning story in our Book Number of April 28th.

Review of *Cricket Country* by Edmund Blunden

Manchester Evening News, 20 April 1944

Cricket arouses strong feelings, both "for" and "against," and during recent years it is the anti-cricket school that has been in the ascendant. Cricket has been labelled the Sport of Blimps. It has been vaguely associated with top hats, school prize days, fox-hunting, and the poems of Sir Henry Newbolt. It has been denounced by Left-wing writers, who imagine erroneously that it is played chiefly by the rich.

On the other hand, its two bitterest enemies of all are "Beachcomber" and "Timothy Shy," who see in it an English institution which they feel it their duty to belittle, along with Wordsworth, William Blake, and Parliamentary government. But there are other reasons besides spite and ignorance for the partial decline in the popularity of cricket, and some of them can be read between the lines of Mr. Blunden's apologia, eloquent though it is.

Mr Blunden is a true cricketer. The test of a true cricketer is that he shall prefer village cricket to "good" cricket. Mr. Blunden's own form, one guesses, is somewhere midway between the village green and the county ground, and he has due reverence for the famous figures of the cricketing world, whose names pepper his pages. He is old enough to have seen Ranjitsinhji play his famous leg glide, and since then he has watched first-class matches regularly enough to have seen every well-known player, English or Australian. But it is obvious that all his friendliest memories are of village cricket: and not even cricket at the country-house level, where white trousers are almost universal and a pad on each leg is *de rigueur*, but the informal village game, where everyone plays in braces, where the blacksmith is liable to be called away in mid-innings on an urgent job, and sometimes, about the time when the light begins to fail, a ball driven for four kills a rabbit on the boundary.

In his love of cricket Mr. Blunden is in good literary company. He could, he says, almost make up an eleven of poets and writers. It would include Byron (who played for Harrow), Keats, Cowper, Trollope, Francis Thompson, Gerard Manley Hopkins, Robert Bridges, and Siegfried Sassoon. Mr. Blunden might have included Blake, one of whose fragments mentions an incident all too common in village cricket, but he is perhaps wrong to number Dickens among the lovers of cricket, for Dickens's only reference to the game (in "Pickwick Papers") shows that he was ignorant of its rules. But the essential thing in this book, as in nearly everything that Mr. Blunden writes, is his nostalgia for the golden age before 1914, when the world was peaceful as it has never since been.

The well-known lines from one of his poems:

> *I have been young and now am not too old,*
> *And I have seen the righteous man forsaken,*
> *His wealth, his honour, and his quality taken:*
> *This is not what we were formerly told*

sound as though they had been written after the dictators had swallowed Europe. Actually, however, they refer to the war of 1914–18, the great turning-point of Mr. Blunden's life. The war shattered the leisurely world he had known, and, as he sadly perceives, cricket has never been quite the same since.

Several things have combined to make it less popular. To begin with, the increasing hurry and urbanisation of life are against a game which needs green fields and abundant spare time. Then there is the generally-admitted dullness of first-class cricket. Like nearly everyone else, Mr. Blunden abhors the kind of game in which 20 successive maiden overs are nothing unusual and a batsman may be in for an hour before he scores his first run. But they are the natural result of too-perfect grass and a too-solemn attitude towards batting averages. Then again cricket has been partly supplanted, at any rate among grown-up people, by golf and lawn tennis. There can be no doubt that this is a disaster for these games are not only far inferior

aesthetically to cricket but they do not have the socially binding quality that cricket, at any rate, used to have.

Contrary to what its detractors say, cricket is not an inherently snobbish game, as Mr. Blunden is careful to point out.
Since it needs about 25 people to make up a game it necessarily
leads to a good deal of social mixing. The inherently snobbish
game is golf, which causes whole stretches of countryside to be
turned into carefully-guarded class preserves.

But there is another good reason for the decline in the
popularity of cricket – a reason Mr. Blunden does not point
out, the extent to which it has been thrust down everybody's
throat. For a long period cricket was treated as though that
were a kind of religious ritual incumbent on every Englishman.
Interminable Test matches with their astronomical scores were
given large headlines in most newspapers, and every summer
tens of thousands of unwilling boys were – and still are – drilled
in a game which merely bored them. For cricket has the
peculiarity that either you like it or you don't, and either you
have a gift for it, or you have not. Unlike most games, it cannot
be learned if you have no talent to start with. In the circumstances there was bound to be a large-scale revolt against
cricket.

Even by children it is now less played than it was. It was
most truly rooted in the national life when it was voluntary and
informal – as in the Rugby of Tom Brown's schooldays, or in
the village matches on lumpy wickets, which are Mr. Blunden's most cherished memory.

Will cricket survive? Mr. Blunden believes so, in spite of the
competition from other interests that it has to face, and we may
hope that he is right. It is pleasant to find him, towards the end
of his book, still finding time for a game or two during the war,
against R.A.F. teams. This book touches on much else besides
cricket, for at the bottom of his heart it is perhaps less the game
itself than the physical surroundings that appeals to Mr. Blunden. He is the kind of cricketer who when his side is batting is
liable to stroll away from the pavilion to have a look at the
village church, and perhaps come across a quaint epitaph.

In places this book is a little over-written, because Mr.
Blunden is no more able to resist a quotation than some people
are to refuse a drink. But it is pleasant reading, and a useful

reminder that peace means something more than a temporary stoppage of the guns.

As I Please 21
Tribune, 21 April 1944

In a letter published in this week's *Tribune*, someone attacks me rather violently for saying that the B.B.C. is a better source of news than the daily papers, and is so regarded by the public. I have never, he suggests, heard ordinary working men shouting "Turn that dope off!" when the news bulletin comes on.

On the contrary, I have heard this frequently. Still more frequently I have seen the customers in a pub go straight on with their darts, music and so forth without the slightest slackening of noise when the news bulletin began. But it was not my claim that anyone likes the B.B.C., or thinks it interesting, or grown-up, or democratic, or progressive. I said only that people regard it as a relatively sound source of news. Again and again I have known people, when they see some doubtful item of news, wait to have it confirmed by the radio before they believe it. Social surveys show the same thing – i.e., that as against the radio the prestige of newspapers has declined.

And I repeat what I said before – that in my experience the B.B.C. *is* relatively truthful and, above all, has a responsible attitude towards news and does not disseminate lies simply because they are "newsy." Of course, untrue statements are constantly being broadcast and anyone can tell you of instances. But in most cases this is due to genuine error, and the B.B.C. sins much more by simply avoiding anything controversial than by direct propaganda. And after all – a point not met by our correspondent – its reputation abroad is comparatively high. Ask any refugee from Europe which of the belligerent radios is considered to be the most truthful. So also in Asia. Even in India, where the population are so hostile that they will not listen to British propaganda and will hardly listen to a British entertainment programme, they listen to B.B.C. news because they believe that it approximates to the truth.

Even if the B.B.C. passes on the British official lies, it does make some effort to sift the others. Most of the newspapers, for instance, have continued to publish without any query as to their truthfulness the American claims to have sunk the entire Japanese fleet several times over. The B.B.C., to my know-ledge, developed quite early on an attitude of suspicion towards this and certain other unreliable sources. On more than one occasion I have known a newspaper to print a piece of news – and news unfavourable to Britain – on no other authority than the German radio, because it was "newsy" and made a good "par."

If you see something obviously untruthful in a newspaper and ring up to ask "Where did you get that from?" you are usually put off with the formula: "I'm afraid Mr. So-and-So is not in the office." If you persist, you generally find that the story has no basis whatever but that it looked like a good bit of news, so in it went. Except where libel is involved, the average journalist is astonished and even contemptuous if anyone bothers about accuracy with regard to names, dates, figures and other details. And any daily journalist will tell you that one of the most important secrets of his trade is the trick of making it appear that there is news when there is no news.

Towards the end of May, 1940, newspaper posters were prohibited in order to save paper. Several newspapers, how-ever, continued to display posters for some time afterwards. On inquiry it was found that they were using old ones. Such headlines as "Panzer Divisions Hurled Back" or "French Army Standing Firm" could be used over and over again. Then came the period when the paper-sellers supplied their own posters with a slate and a bit of chalk, and in their hands the poster became a comparatively sober and truthful thing. It referred to something that was actually in the paper you were going to buy, and it usually picked out the real news and not some piece of sensational nonsense. The paper-sellers, who frequently did not know which way round a capital "S" goes, had a better idea of what is news, and more sense of responsi-bility towards the public, than their millionaire employers.

Our correspondent considers that the public and the jour-nalists rather than the proprietors are to blame for the silliness of English newspapers. You could not, he implies, make an intelligent newspaper pay because the public wants tripe. I am not certain whether this is so. For the time being most of the tripe has vanished and newspaper circulations have not declined. But I do agree – and I said so – that the journalists share the blame. In allowing their profession to be degraded they have largely acted with their eyes open, whereas, I suppose, to blame somebody like Northcliffe for making money in the quickest way is like blaming a skunk for stinking.

One mystery about the English language is why, with the biggest vocabulary in existence, it has to be constantly borrowing foreign words and phrases. Where is the sense, for instance, of saying *cul de sac* when you mean blind alley? Other totally unnecessary French phrases are *joie de vivre*, *amour propre*, *reculer pour mieux sauter*, *raison d'être*, *vis-à-vis*, *tête-à-tête*, *au pied de la lettre*, *esprit de corps*. There are dozens more of them. Other needless borrowings come from Latin (though there is a case for "i.e." and "e.g.," which are useful abbreviations), and since the war we have been much infested by German words, *Gleichschaltung*, *Lebensraum*, *Weltanschauung*, *Wehrmacht*, *Panzerdivisionen* and others being flung about with great freedom. In nearly every case an English equivalent already exists or could easily be improvised. There is also a tendency to take over American slang phrases without understanding their meaning. For example, the expression "barking up the wrong tree" is fairly widely used, but inquiry shows that most people don't know its origin nor exactly what it means.

Sometimes it is necessary to take over a foreign word, but in that case we should anglicise its pronunciation, as our ancestors used to do. If we really need the word "café" (we got on well enough with "coffee house" for two hundred years), it should either be spelled "caffay" or pronounced "cayfe." "Garage" should be pronounced "garridge." For what point is there in littering our speech with fragments of foreign pronunciation, very tiresome to anyone who does not happen to have learned that particular language?

And why is it that most of us never use a word of English origin if we can find a manufactured Greek one? One sees a good example of this in the rapid disappearance of English

GEORGE ORWELL

flower names. What until twenty years ago was universally
called a snapdragon is now called an antirrhinum, a word no
one can spell without consulting a dictionary. Forget-me-nots
are coming more and more to be called myosotis. Many other
names, Red Hot Poker, Mind Your Own Business, Love Lies
Bleeding, London Pride, are disappearing in favour of colourless Greek names out of botany textbooks. I had better not
continue too long on this subject, because last time I mentioned
flowers in this column an indignant lady wrote in to say
that flowers are bourgeois. But I don't think it a good augury
for the future of the English language that "marigold" should
be dropped in favour of "calendula," while the pleasant little
Cheddar Pink loses its name and becomes merely Dianthus
Cæsius.

As I Please 22
Tribune, 28 April 1944

On the night in 1940 when the big ack-ack barrage was fired
over London for the first time, I was in Piccadilly Circus when
the guns opened up, and I fled into the Cafe Royal to take
cover. Among the crowd inside a good-looking, well-made
youth of about twenty-five was making somewhat of a nuisance of himself with a copy of *Peace News*, which he was
forcing upon the attention of everyone at the neighbouring
tables. I got into conversation with him, and the conversation
went something like this:

The youth: "I tell you, it'll all be over by Christmas. There's
obviously going to be a compromise peace. I'm pinning my
faith to Sir Samuel Hoare. It's degrading company to be in,
I admit, but still Hoare is on our side. So long as Hoare's in
Madrid, there's always hope of a sell-out."

Orwell: "What about all these preparations that they're
making against invasion – the pillboxes that they're building
everywhere, the L.D.V.s, and so forth?"

The youth: "Oh, that merely means that they're getting
ready to crush the working class when the Germans get here.
I suppose some of them might be fools enough to try to resist,

but Churchill and the Germans between them won't take long to settle them. Don't worry, it'll soon be over."

Orwell: "Do you really want to see your children grow up Nazis?"

The youth: "Nonsense! You don't suppose the Germans are going to encourage Fascism in this country, do you? They don't want to breed up a race of warriors to fight against them. Their object will be to turn us into slaves. They'll encourage every pacifist movement they can lay hands on. That's why I'm a pacifist. They'll encourage people like me."

Orwell: "And shoot people like me?"

The youth: "That would be just too bad."

Orwell: "But why are you so anxious to remain alive?"

The youth: "So that I can get on with my work, of course."

It had come out in the conversation that the youth was a painter – whether good or bad I do not know; but, at any rate, sincerely interested in painting and quite ready to face poverty in pursuit of it. As a painter, he would probably have been somewhat better off under a German occupation than a writer or journalist would be. But still, what he said contained a very dangerous fallacy, now very widespread in the countries where totalitarianism has not actually established itself.

The fallacy is to believe that under a dictatorial government you can be free *inside*. Quite a number of people console themselves with this thought, now that totalitarianism in one form or another is visibly on the up-grade in every part of the world. Out in the street the loudspeakers bellow, the flags flutter from the rooftops, the police with their tommy-guns prowl to and fro, the face of the Leader, four feet wide, glares from every hoarding; but up in the attics the secret enemies of the regime can record their thoughts in perfect freedom – that is the idea, more or less. And many people are under the impression that this is going on now in Germany and other dictatorial countries.

Why is this idea false? I pass over the fact that modern dictatorships don't, in fact, leave the loopholes that the old-fashioned despotisms did; and also the probable weakening of the *desire* for intellectual liberty owing to totalitarian methods of education. The greatest mistake is to imagine that the human being is an autonomous individual. The secret freedom which you can supposedly enjoy under a despotic Government is nonsense, because your thoughts are never entirely your own. Philosophers, writers, artists, even scientists, not only need encouragement and an audience, they need constant stimulation from other people. It is almost impossible to think without talking. If Defoe had really lived on a desert island he could not have written *Robinson Crusoe*, nor would he have wanted to. Take away freedom of speech, and the creative faculties dry up. Had the Germans really got to England my acquaintance of the Cafe Royal would soon have found his painting deteriorating, even if the Gestapo had let him alone. And when the lid is taken off Europe, I believe one of the things that will surprise us will be to find how little worthwhile writing of any kind – even such things as diaries, for instance – have been produced in secret under the dictators.

Mr. Basil Henriques, chairman of the East London juvenile court, has just been letting himself go on the subject of the Modern Girl. English boys, he says, are "just grand," but it is a different story with girls:

> "One seldom comes across a really bad boy. The war seems to have affected girls more than boys. . . . Children now went to the pictures several times a week and saw what they imagined was the high life of America, when actually it was a great libel on that country. They also suffer from the effects of listening through the microphone to wild raucous jitterbugging noises called music. . . . Girls of 14 now dress and talk like those of 18 and 19, and put the same filth and muck on their faces."

I wonder whether Mr. Henriques knows (a) that well before the other war it was already usual to attribute juvenile crime to the evil example of the cinematograph, and (b) that the Modern Girl has been just the same for quite 2,000 years?

One of the big failures in human history has been the age-long attempt to stop women painting their faces. The philosophers of the Roman Empire denounced the frivolity of the modern woman in almost the same terms as she is denounced today. In the fifteenth century the Church denounced the damnable habit of plucking the eyebrows. The English Puritans, the Bolsheviks, and the Nazis all attempted to discourage cosmetics, without success. In Victorian England rouge was considered so disgraceful that it was usually sold under some other name, but it continued to be used.

Many styles of dress, from the Elizabethan ruff to the Edwardian hobble skirt, have been denounced from the pulpit, without effect. In the nineteen-twenties, when skirts were at their shortest, the Pope decreed that women improperly dressed were not to be admitted to Catholic churches; but somehow feminine fashions remained unaffected. Hitler's "ideal woman," an exceedingly plain specimen in a mackintosh, was exhibited all over Germany and much of the rest of the world, but inspired few imitators. I prophesy that English girls will continue to "put filth and muck on their faces" in spite of Mr. Henriques. Even in jail, it is said, the female prisoners redden their lips with the dye from the Post Office mail bags.

Just why women use cosmetics is a different question, but it seems doubtful whether sex attraction is the main object. It is very unusual to meet a man who does not think painting your fingernails scarlet is a disgusting habit, but hundreds of thousands of women go on doing it all the same. Meanwhile it might console Mr. Henriques to know that though make-up persists, it is far less elaborate than it used to be in the days when Victorian beauties had their faces "enamelled," or when it was usual to alter the contour of your cheeks by means of "plumpers," as described in Swift's poem, On a Beautiful Young Nymph Going to Bed.

As I Please 23
Tribune, 5 May 1944

For anyone who wants a good laugh I recommend a book which was published about a dozen years ago, but which I only recently succeeded in getting hold of. This is I. A. Richards's Practical Criticism.

Although mostly concerned with the general principles of literary criticism, it also describes an experiment that

Mr. Richards made with, or one should perhaps say *on*, his English students at Cambridge. Various volunteers, not actually students but presumably interested in English literature, also took part. Thirteen poems were presented to them, and they were asked to criticise them. The authorship of the poems was not revealed, and none of them was well enough known to be recognised at sight by the average reader. You are getting, therefore, specimens of literary criticism not complicated by snobbishness of the ordinary kind.

One ought not to be too superior, and there is no need to be, because the book is so arranged that you can try the experiment on yourself. The poems, unsigned, are all together at the end, and the authors' names are on a fold-over page which you need not look at till afterwards. I will say at once that I only spotted the authorship of two, one of which I knew already, and though I could date most of the others within a few decades, I made two bad bloomers, in one case attributing to Shelley a poem written in the nineteen-twenties. But still, some of the comments recorded by Dr. Richards are startling. They go to show that many people who would describe themselves as lovers of poetry have no more notion of distinguishing between a good poem and a bad one than a dog has of arithmetic.

For example, a piece of completely spurious bombast by Alfred Noyes gets quite a lot of praise. One critic compares it to Keats. A sentimental ballad from *Rough Rhymes of a Padre*, by "Woodbine Willie," also gets quite a good Press. On the other hand, a magnificent sonnet by John Donne gets a distinctly chilly reception. Dr. Richards records only three favourable criticisms and about a dozen cold or hostile ones. One writer says contemptuously that the poem "would make a good hymn," while another remarks, "I can find no other reaction except disgust." Donne was at that time at the top of his reputation and no doubt most of the people taking part in this experiment would have fallen on their faces at his name. D. H. Lawrence's poem *The Piano* gets many sneers, though it is praised by a minority. So also with a short poem by Gerard Manley Hopkins. "The worst poem I have ever read," declares one writer, while another's criticism is simply "Pish-posh!"

However, before blaming these youthful students for their bad judgement, let it be remembered that when some time ago somebody published a not very convincing fake of an eighteenth-century diary, the aged critic, Sir Edmund Gosse, librarian of the House of Lords, fell for it immediately. And there was also the case of the Parisian art critics of I forget which "school," who went into rhapsodies over a picture which was afterwards discovered to have been painted by a donkey with a paintbrush tied to its tail.

Under the heading "We Are Destroying Birds that Save Us," the *News Chronicle* notes that "beneficial birds suffer from human ignorance. There is senseless persecution of the kestrel and barn owl. No two species of birds do better work for us."

Unfortunately it isn't even from ignorance. Most of the birds of prey are killed off for the sake of that enemy of England, the pheasant. Unlike the partridge, the pheasant does not thrive in England, and apart from the neglected woodlands and the vicious game laws that it has been responsible for, all birds or animals that are suspected of eating its eggs or chicks are systematically wiped out. Before the war, near my village in Hertfordshire, I used to pass a stretch of fence where the gamekeeper kept his "larder." Dangling from the wires were the corpses of stoats, weasels, rats, hedgehogs, jays, owls, kestrels and sparrowhawks. Except for the rats and perhaps the jays, all of these creatures are beneficial to agriculture. The stoats keep down the rabbits, the weasels eat mice, and so do the kestrels and sparrowhawks, while the owls eat rats as well. It has been calculated that a barn owl destroys between 1,000 and 2,000 rats and mice in a year. Yet it has to be killed off for the sake of this useless bird which Rudyard Kipling correctly described as "lord of many a shire."

We had to postpone announcing the results of the short story competition, but we are publishing the winning story next week. The runners-up will appear, I hope, in the two subsequent weeks.

I will set forth my opinions about the English short story another week, but I will say at once that of the five or six hundred stories that were sent in, the great majority were, in my judgement, very bad. A fairly large number of competitors, more than I had expected, had a story to tell, but too many of them simply gave the bare bones of the story, making it into an anecdote, without character interest and usually written in a slovenly way. Others sent in entries which were written with more distinction, but had no interest or development in them – being, in fact, sketches and not stories. A dismayingly large number dealt with Utopias, or took place in Heaven, or brought in ghosts or magic or something of that kind. I do admit, however, that it is not easy to write a story which is about real people, and in which something happens, within the compass of 1,800 words, and I do not believe there is much hope of English short stories improving till our magazines again swell to Victorian size.

As I Please 24
Tribune, 12 May 1944

Reading recently a batch of rather shallowly optimistic "progressive" books, I was struck by the automatic way in which people go on repeating certain phrases which were fashionable before 1914. Two great favourites are "the abolition of distance" and "the disappearance of frontiers." I do not know how often I have met with the statements that "the aeroplane and the radio have abolished distance" and "all parts of the world are now interdependent."

Actually, the effect of modern inventions has been to increase nationalism, to make travel enormously more difficult, to cut down the means of communication between one country and another, and to make the various parts of the world *less*, not more dependent on one another for food and manufactured goods. This is not the result of the war. The same tendencies had been at work ever since 1918, though they were intensified after the World Depression.

Take simply the instance of travel. In the nineteenth century some parts of the world were unexplored, but there was almost no restriction on travel. Up to 1914 you did not need a passport for any country except Russia. The European emigrant, if he could scrape together a few pounds for the passage, simply set sail for America or Australia, and when he got there no questions were asked. In the eighteenth century it had been quite normal and safe to travel in a country with which your own country was at war.

In our own time, however, travel has been becoming steadily more difficult. It is worth listing the parts of the world which were already inaccessible before the war started.

First of all, the whole of central Asia. Except perhaps for a very few tried Communists, no foreigner has entered Soviet Asia for many years past. Tibet, thanks to Anglo-Russian jealousy, has been a closed country since about 1912. Sinkiang, theoretically part of China, was equally un-get-atable. Then the whole of the Japanese Empire, except Japan itself, was practically barred to foreigners. Even India has been none too accessible since 1918. Passports were often refused even to British subjects – sometimes even to Indians!

Even in Europe the limits of travel were constantly narrowing. Except for a short visit it was very difficult to enter Britain, as many a wretched anti-Fascist refugee discovered. Visas for the U.S.S.R. were issued very grudgingly from about 1935 onwards. All the Fascist countries were barred to anyone with a known anti-Fascist record. Various areas could only be crossed if you undertook not to get out of the train. And along all the frontiers were barbed wire, machine-guns and prowling sentries, frequently wearing gasmasks.

As to migration, it had practically dried up since the nineteen-twenties. All the countries of the New World did their best to keep the immigrant out unless he brought considerable sums of money with him. Japanese and Chinese immigration into the Americas had been completely stopped. Europe's Jews had to stay and be slaughtered because there was nowhere for them to go, whereas in the case of the Czarist pogroms forty years earlier they had been able to flee in all directions. How, in the face of all this, anyone can say that modern methods of travel promote intercommunication between different countries, defeats me.

Intellectual contacts have also been diminishing for a long time past. It is nonsense to say that the radio puts people in touch with foreign countries. If anything, it does the opposite. No ordinary person ever listens in to a foreign radio; but if in any country large numbers of people show signs of doing so, the government prevents it either by ferocious penalties, or by confiscating short-wave sets, or by setting up jamming stations. The result is that each national radio is a sort of totalitarian world of its own, braying propaganda night and day to people who can listen to nothing else. Meanwhile, literature grows less and less international. Most totalitarian countries bar foreign newspapers and let in only a small number of foreign books, which they subject to careful censorship and sometimes issue in garbled versions. Letters going from one country to another are habitually tampered with on the way. And in many countries, over the past dozen years, history books have been rewritten in far more nationalistic terms than before, so that children may grow up with as false a picture as possible of the world outside.

The trend towards economic self-sufficiency ("autarchy") which has been going on since about 1930 and has been intensified by the war, may or may not be reversible. The industrialisation of countries like India and South America increases their purchasing power and therefore ought, in theory, to help world trade. But what is not grasped by those who say cheerfully that "all parts of the world are interdependent," is that they don't any longer *have* to be interdependent. In an age when wool can be made out of milk and rubber out of oil, when wheat can be grown almost on the Arctic Circle, when atebrin will do instead of quinine and Vit C tablets are a tolerable substitute for fruit, imports don't matter very greatly. Any big area can seal itself off much more completely than in the days when Napoleon's Grand Army, in spite of the embargo, marched to Moscow wearing British overcoats. So long as the world tendency is towards nationalism and totalitarianism, scientific progress simply helps it along.

Here are some current prices.

Small Swiss-made alarm clock, price before the war, 5s. or 10s.: present price, £3 15s. Second-hand portable typewriter, price before the war, £12 new: present price, £30. Small, very bad-quality coconut fibre scrubbing-brush, price before the war, 3d.: present price, 1s. 9d. Gas lighter, price before the war, about 1s.: present price, 5s. 9d.

I could quote other similar prices. It is worth noticing that, for instance, the clock mentioned above must have been manufactured before the war at the old price. But, on the whole, the worst racket seems to be in second-hand goods – for instance, chairs, tables, clothes, watches, prams, bicycles and bed linen. On enquiry, I find that there is now a law against overcharging on second-hand goods. This comforts me a great deal just as it must comfort the 18 B'ers to hear about Habeas Corpus, or Indian coolies to learn that all British subjects are equal before the law.

In Hooper's *Campaign of Sedan* there is an account of the interview in which General de Wympffen tried to obtain the best possible terms for the defeated French army. "It is to your interest," he said, "from a political standpoint, to grant us honourable conditions . . . A peace based on conditions which would flatter the *amour-propre* of the Army would be durable, whereas rigorous measures would awaken bad passions, and, perhaps, bring on an endless war between France and Prussia."

Here Bismarck, the Iron Chancellor, chipped in, and his words are recorded from his memoirs:

"I said to him," he writes, "that we might build on the gratitude of a prince, but certainly not on the gratitude of a people – least of all on the gratitude of the French. That in France neither institutions nor circumstances were enduring; that governments and dynasties were constantly changing, and one need not carry out what the other had bound itself to do. . . . As things stood it would be folly if we did not make full use of our success."

The modern cult of "realism" is generally held to have started with Bismarck. That imbecile speech was considered magnificently "realistic" then, and so it would be now. Yet what Wympffen said, though he was only trying to bargain for terms, was perfectly true. If the Germans had behaved with ordinary generosity (ie. by the standards of the time) it might have been impossible to whip up the revanchiste spirit in France. What would Bismarck have said if he had been told that harsh terms now would mean a terrible defeat forty-eight years later? There is not much doubt of the answer: he would have said that the terms ought to have been harsher still. Such is "realism" – and on the same principle, when the medicine makes the patient sick, the doctor responds by doubling the dose.

As I Please 25
Tribune, 19 May 1944

Miss Vera Brittain's pamphlet, *Seed of Chaos*, is an eloquent attack on indiscriminate or "obliteration" bombing. "Owing to the R.A.F. raids," she says, "thousands of helpless and innocent people in German, Italian and German-occupied cities are being subjected to agonising forms of death and injury comparable to the worst tortures of the Middle Ages." Various well-known opponents of bombing, such as General Franco and Major-General Fuller, are brought out in support of this. Miss Brittain is not, however, taking the pacifist standpoint. She is willing and anxious to win the war, apparently. She merely wishes us to stick to "legitimate" methods of war and abandon civilian bombing, which she fears will blacken our reputation in the eyes of posterity. Her pamphlet is issued by the Bombing Restriction Committee, which has issued others with similar titles.

Now, no one in his senses regards bombing, or any other operation of war, with anything but disgust. On the other hand, no decent person cares tuppence for the opinion of posterity. And there is something very distasteful in accepting war as an instrument and at the same time wanting to dodge responsibility for its more obviously barbarous features. Pacifism is a tenable position, provided that you are willing to take the consequences. But all talk of "limiting" or "humanising" war is sheer humbug, based on the fact that the average human being never bothers to examine catchwords.

The catchwords used in this connection are "killing civilians," "massacre of women and children" and "destruction of our cultural heritage." It is tacitly assumed that air bombing does more of this kind of thing than ground warfare.

When you look a bit closer, the first question that strikes you is: Why is it worse to kill civilians than soldiers? Obviously one must not kill children if it is in any way avoidable, but it is only in propaganda pamphlets that every bomb drops on a school or an orphanage. A bomb kills a cross-section of the population; but not quite a representative selection, because the children and expectant mothers are usually the first to be evacuated, and some of the young men will be away in the army. Probably a disproportionately large number of bomb victims will be middle aged. (Up to date, German bombs have killed between six and seven thousand children in this country. This is, I believe, less than the number killed in road accidents in the same period.) On the other hand, "normal" or "legitimate" warfare picks out and slaughters all the healthiest and bravest of the young male population. Every time a German submarine goes to the bottom about fifty young men of fine physique and good nerve are suffocated. Yet people who would hold up their hands at the very words "civilian bombing" will repeat with satisfaction such phrases as "We are winning the Battle of the Atlantic." Heaven knows how many people our blitz on Germany and the occupied countries has killed and will kill, but you can be quite certain it will never come anywhere near the slaughter that has happened on the Russian front.

War is not avoidable at this stage of history, and since it has to happen it does not seem to me a bad thing that others should be killed besides young men. I wrote in 1937: "Sometimes it is a comfort to me to think that the aeroplane is altering the conditions of war. Perhaps when the next great war comes we may see that sight unprecedented in all history, a jingo with a bullet hole in him." We haven't yet seen that (it is perhaps a contradiction in terms), but at any rate the suffering of this war has been shared out more evenly than that of the last one was. The immunity of the civilian, one of the things that have made war possible, has been shattered. Unlike Miss Brittain, I don't regret that. I can't feel that war is "humanised" by being confined to the slaughter of the young and becomes "barbarous" when the old get killed as well.

As to international agreements to "limit" war, they are never kept when it pays to break them. Long before the last war the nations had agreed not to use gas, but they used it all the same. This time they have refrained, merely because gas is comparatively ineffective in a war of movement, while its use against civilian populations would be sure to provoke reprisals in kind. Against an enemy who can't hit back, e.g., the Abyssinians, it is used readily enough. War is of its nature barbarous, it is better to admit that. If we see ourselves as the savages we are, some improvement is possible, or at least thinkable.

A specimen of *Tribune*'s correspondence:

TO THE JEW-PAID EDITOR,
TRIBUNE,
LONDON.

JEWS IN THE POLISH ARMY
YOU ARE CONSTANTLY ATTACKING OUR GALLANT POLISH ALLY BE CAUSE THEY KNOW HOW TO TREAT THE JEW PEST. THEY ALSO KNOW HOW TO TREAT ALL JEW-PAID EDITORS AND COMMUNIST PAPERS. WE KNOW YOU ARE IN THE PAY OF THE YIDS AND SOVIETS.

YOU ARE A FRIEND OF THE ENEMIES OF BRITAIN. THE DAY OF RECKONING IS AT HAND. BEWARE. ALL JEW PIGS WILL BE EXTERMINATED THE HITLER WAY – THE ONLY WAY TO GET RID OF THE YIDS.

PERISH JUDAH.

Typed on a Remington typewriter (postmark S.W.), and, what is to my mind an interesting detail, this is a carbon copy.

Anyone acquainted with the type will know that no assurance, no demonstration, no proof of the most solid kind would ever convince the writer of this that *Tribune* is *not* a Communist paper and *not* in the pay of the Soviet Government. One very curious characteristic of Fascists – I am speaking of amateur Fascists: I assume that the Gestapo are cleverer – is their failure to recognise that the parties of the Left are distinct from one another and by no means aiming at the same thing. It is always assumed that they are all one gang, whatever the outward appearances may be. In the first number of Mosley's *British Union Quarterly*, which I have by me (incidentally, it contains an article by no less a person than Major Vidkun Quisling), I note that even Wyndham Lewis speaks of Stalin and Trotsky as though they were equivalent persons. Arnold Lunn, in his

Spanish Rehearsal, actually seems to suggest that Trotsky started the Fourth International on Stalin's instructions.

In just the same way, very few Communists, in my experience, will believe that the Trotskyists are not in the pay of Hitler. I have sometimes tried the experiment of pointing out that if the Trotskyists were in the pay of Hitler, or of anybody, they would occasionally have some money. But it is no use, it doesn't register. So also with the belief in the machinations of the Jews, or the belief, widespread among Indian nationalists, that all Englishmen, of whatever political colour, are in secret conspiracy with one another. The belief in the Freemasons as a revolutionary organisation is the strangest of all. In this country it would be just as reasonable to believe such a thing of the Buffaloes. Less than a generation ago, if not now, there were Catholic nuns who believed that at Masonic gatherings the Devil appeared in person, wearing full evening dress with a hole in the trousers for his tail to come through. In one form or another this kind of thing seems to attack nearly everybody, apparently answering to some obscure psychological need of our time.

Review of *'42 to '44: A Contemporary Memoir upon Human Behaviour During the Crisis of the World Revolution* by H. G. Wells

The Observer, 21 May 1944

The chief difficulty of writing a book nowadays is that pots of paste are usually sold without brushes. But if you can get hold of a brush (sometimes procurable at Woolworth's), and a pair of scissors and a good-sized blank book, you have everything you need. It is not necessary to do any actual writing. Any collection of scraps – reprinted newspaper articles, private letters, fragments of diaries, even "radio discussions" ground out by wretched hacks to be broadcast by celebrities – can be sold to the amusement-starved public. And even the paper shortage can be neutralised by – as in this case – issuing your book in a limited edition and selling it at an artificial price.

This seems to be the principle that Mr. Wells has followed. His book has gilt edges, which costs the reader an extra thirty shillings, but its contents are simply a sprawl. Quite largely it consists of a series of attacks on people who have shown insufficient enthusiasm for the document which Mr. Wells calls the "Universal Rights of Man." Other attacks (on the Catholic Church, for instance, the War Office, the Admiralty, and the Communist Party) do not seem to be occasioned by anything but bad temper. But in so far as the book has a unifying principle, it is the by now familiar idea that mankind must either develop a World State or perish.

What is very striking is that except in certain books in which he invoked a miracle, Mr. Wells has never once suggested how the World State is to be brought into being. This is to say that he has never bothered to wonder who the actual rulers of the world are, how and why they are able to hold on to power, and by what means they are to be evicted. In formulating the "Rights of Man," he does not even drop a hint as to how such a document could be disseminated in, say, Russia or China. Hitler he dismisses as simply a lunatic: that settles Hitler. He does not seriously inquire *why* millions of people are ready to lay down their lives for a lunatic, and what this probably betokens for human society. And in between his threats that *homo sapiens* must mend his ways or be destroyed he continues to repeat the slogans of 1900 as though they were self-evident truths.

For instance, it is startling to be told in 1944 that "the world is now one." One might as well say that the world is now flat. The most obvious fact about the contemporary world is that it is *not* one, and is becoming less and less of a unit every year, physically as well as psychologically.

In spite of some momentary misgivings, Mr. Wells is not ready to admit that his declaration of the "Rights of Man" is a purely Western document. Almost any Indian, for instance, would reject it at a glance. (One gathers from some angry "asides" that a number of Indians have rejected it already.) What is more serious, he is not ready to admit that even among scientists and thinkers generally the intellectual basis for world unity does not exist. He has not seen the red light of phrases like "Aryan chess" and "capitalistic astronomy."

He still talks of the need for a world encyclopaedia, ignoring the fact that there are whole branches of knowledge upon which no sort of agreement exists or is at present possible. As for the increase in human equality which Mr. Wells also considers imperatively necessary, there is no sign that that is happening either.

Intermittently, of course, Mr. Wells does realise all this, but only as a nurse notices the unaccountable naughtiness of a child. And his response is the same as the nurse's – "Now, you'll take your nice medicine or the bogey-man'll come and eat you up." *Homo sapiens* must do what he is told or he will become extinct. "Knowledge or extinction. There is no other chance for man," says Mr. Wells. It is, however, very unlikely that man will become extinct except through some unforesee-able cosmic disaster. He has about doubled his numbers in the last century and is still probably on the increase, and no com-peting species is in sight. The ants, Mr. Wells's favourites, can hardly be taken seriously. Nor is there any reason to think that man or even, in the technical sense, civilisation will be destroyed by war. Wars do a great deal of local destrution, but probably lead to a net increase in the world's industrial plant. The picture that Mr. Wells drew long ago in "The War in the Air," of the world being plunged back into the Dark Ages by a few tons of bombs, has turned out to be completely false. The machine culture thrives on bombs. The danger seemingly ahead of us is *not* extinction: it is a slave civilisation which, so far from being chaotic, might be horribly stable.

It is perhaps unnecessary to add that incoherent and – in places – annoying though it is, this book contains brilliant and imaginative passages. One expects that of Mr. Wells. More than any other writer, perhaps, he has altered the land-scape of the contemporary mind. Because of him the moon seems nearer and the Stone Age more imaginable, and for that we are immeasurably in his debt. So perhaps we can forgive a few scrappy books, even at forty-two shillings a time, from the author of "The Time Machine," "The Island of Dr. Moreau," "Love and Mr. Lewisham," and about a dozen others.

The English People

Written in early 1944 but not published until 1947

ENGLAND AT FIRST GLANCE

In peacetime, it is unusual for foreign visitors to this country to notice the existence of the English people. Even the accent referred to by Americans as "the English accent" is not in fact common to more than a quarter of the population. In cartoons in Continental papers England is personified by an aristocrat with a monocle, a sinister capitalist in a top hat, or a spinster in a Burberry. Hostile or friendly, nearly all the generalisations that are made about England base themselves on the property-owning class and ignore the other forty-five million.

But the chances of war brought to England, either as soldiers or as refugees, hundreds of thousands of foreigners who would not normally have come here, and forced them into intimate contact with ordinary people. Czechs, Poles, Germans and Frenchmen to whom "England" meant Piccadilly and the Derby found themselves quartered in sleepy East Anglian villages, in northern mining towns, or in the vast working-class areas of London whose names the world had never heard until they were blitzed. Those of them who had the gift of observation will have seen for themselves that the real England is not the England of the guide-books. Blackpool is more typical than Ascot, the top hat is a moth-eaten rarity, the language of the B.B.C. is barely intelligible to the masses. Even the prevailing physical type does not agree with the caricatures, for the tall, lanky physique which is traditionally English is almost confined to the upper classes: the working classes, as a rule, are rather small, with short limbs and brisk movements, and with a tendency among the women to grow dumpy in early middle life.

It is worth trying for a moment to put oneself in the position of a foreign observer, new to England, but unprejudiced, and able because of his work to keep in touch with ordinary, useful, unspectacular people. Some of his generalisations would be wrong, because he would not make enough allowance for the temporary dislocations resulting from war. Never having seen England in normal times, he might underrate the power of class distinctions, or think English agriculture healthier than it is, or be too much impressed by the dinginess of the London streets or the prevalence of drunkenness. But with his fresh eyes he would see a great deal that a native observer misses, and his probable impressions are worth tabulating. Almost certainly he would find the salient characteristics of the English common people to be artistic insensibility, gentleness, respect for legality, suspicion of foreigners, sentimentality about animals, hypocrisy, exaggerated class distinctions, and an obsession with sport.

As for our artistic insensibility, ever-growing stretches of beautiful countryside are ruined by planless building, the heavy industries are allowed to convert whole counties into blackened deserts, ancient monuments are wantonly pulled down or swamped by seas of yellow brick, attractive vistas are blocked by hideous statues to nonentities – and all this without any *popular* protest whatever. When England's housing problem is discussed, its æsthetic aspect simply does not enter the mind of the average man. Nor is there any widespread interest in any of the arts, except perhaps music. Poetry, the art in which above all others England has excelled, has for more than a century had no appeal whatever for the common people. It is only acceptable when – as in some popular songs and mnemonic rhymes – it is masquerading as something else. Indeed the very word "poetry" arouses either derision or embarrassment in ninety-eight people out of a hundred.

Our imaginary foreign observer would certainly be struck by our gentleness: by the orderly behaviour of English crowds, the lack of pushing and quarrelling, the willingness to form queues, the good temper of harassed, overworked people like bus conductors. The manners of the English working class are not always very graceful, but they are extremely considerate. Great care is taken in showing a stranger the way, blind people can travel across London with the certainty that they will be helped on and off every bus and across every street. In wartime a few of the policemen carried revolvers, but England has nothing corresponding to the *gendarmerie*, the semi-military police living in barracks and armed with rifles (sometimes even with tanks and aeroplanes) who are the guardians of society all the way from Calais to Tokyo. And except for certain well-defined areas in half a dozen big towns there is very little crime or violence. The average of honesty is lower in the big towns than in the country, but even in London the newsvendor can safely leave his pile of pennies on the pavement while he goes for a drink. The prevailing gentleness of manners is a recent thing, however. Well within living memory it was impossible for a smartly dressed person to walk down Ratcliff Highway without being assaulted, and an eminent jurist, asked to name a typically English crime, could answer: "Kicking your wife to death."

There is no revolutionary tradition in England, and even in extremist political parties, it is only the middle-class member-ship that thinks in revolutionary terms. The masses still more or less assume that "against the law" is a synonym for "wrong." It is known that the criminal law is harsh and full of anomalies and that litigation is so expensive as always to favour the rich against the poor: but there is a general feeling that the law, such as it is, will be scrupulously administered, that a judge or magistrate cannot be bribed, that no one will be punished without trial. An Englishman does not believe in his bones, as a Spanish or Italian peasant does, that the law is simply a racket. It is precisely this general confidence in the law that has allowed a good deal of recent tampering with Habeas Corpus to escape public notice. But it also causes some ugly situations to end peacefully. During the worst of the London blitz the authorities tried to prevent the public from using the Tube stations as shelters. The people did not reply by storming the gates, they simply bought themselves penny-halfpenny tickets: they thus had legal status as passengers, and there was no thought of turning them out again.

The traditional English xenophobia is stronger among the working class than the middle class. It was partly the resistance of the Trade Unions that prevented a really large influx of refugees from the fascist countries before the war, and when the German refugees were interned in 1940, it was not the working class that protested. The difference in habits, and especially in food and language, makes it very hard for English working people to get on with foreigners. Their diet differs a great deal from that of any European nation, and they are extremely conservative about it. As a rule they will refuse even to sample a foreign dish, they regard such things as garlic and olive oil with disgust, life is unlivable to them unless they have tea and puddings. And the peculiarities of the English language make it almost impossible for anyone who has left school at fourteen to learn a foreign language after he has grown up. In the French Foreign Legion, for instance, the British and American legionaries seldom rise out of the ranks, because they cannot learn French, whereas a German learns French in a few months. English working people, as a rule, think it effeminate even to pronounce a foreign word correctly. This is bound up with the fact that the upper classes learn foreign languages as a regular part of their education. Travelling abroad, speaking foreign tongues, enjoying foreign food, are vaguely felt to be upper-class habits, a species of snobbery, so that xenophobia is reinforced by class jealousy.

Perhaps the most horrible spectacles in England are the Dogs' Cemeteries in Kensington Gardens, at Stoke Poges (it actually adjoins the churchyard where Gray wrote his famous *Elegy*) and at various other places. But there were also the Animals' A.R.P. Centres, with miniature stretchers for cats, and in the first year of the war there was the spectacle of Animal Day being celebrated with all its usual pomp in the middle of the Dunkirk evacuation. Although its worst follies are committed by the upper-class women, the animal cult runs right through the nation and is probably bound up with the decay of agriculture and the dwindled birthrate. Several years of stringent rationing have failed to reduce the dog and cat population, and even in poor quarters of big towns the bird fanciers' shops display canary seed at prices ranging up to twenty-five shillings a pint.

Hypocrisy is so generally accepted as part of the English character that a foreign observer would be prepared to meet with it at every turn, but he would find especially ripe examples in the laws dealing with gambling, drinking, prostitution, and profanity. He would find it difficult to reconcile the anti-imperialistic sentiments which are commonly expressed in England with the size of the British Empire. If he were a continental European he would notice with ironical amusement that the English think it wicked to have a big army but see nothing wrong in having a big navy. This too he would set down as hypocrisy – not altogether fairly, for it is the fact of being an island, and therefore not needing a big army, that has allowed British democratic institutions to grow up, and the mass of the people are fairly well aware of this.

Exaggerated class distinctions have been diminishing over a period of about thirty years, and the war has probably speeded up the process, but newcomers to England are still astonished and sometimes horrified by the blatant differences between class and class. The great majority of the people can still be "placed" in an instant by their manners, clothes, and general appearance. Even the physical type differs considerably, the upper classes being on an average several inches taller than the working class. But the most striking difference of all is in language and accent. The English working class, as Mr. Wyndham Lewis has put it, are "branded on the tongue." And though class distinctions do not exactly coincide with economic distinctions, the contrast between wealth and poverty is very much more glaring, and more taken for granted, than in most countries.

The English were the inventors of several of the world's most popular games, and have spread them more widely than any other product of their culture. The word "football" is mispronounced by scores of millions who have never heard of Shakespeare or Magna Carta. The English themselves are not outstandingly good at all games, but they enjoy playing them, and to an extent that strikes foreigners as childish they enjoy reading about them and betting on them. During the between-war years the football pools did more than any other one thing to make life bearable for the unemployed. Professional footballers, boxers, jockeys, and even cricketers enjoy a popularity that no scientist or artist could hope to rival. Nevertheless sport-worship is not carried to quite such imbecile lengths as one would imagine from reading the popular press. When the brilliant lightweight boxer, Kid Lewis, stood for Parliament in his native borough, he only scored a hundred and twenty-five votes.

These traits that we have enumerated are probably the ones that would strike an intelligent foreign observer first. Out of them he might feel that he could construct a reliable picture of the English character. But then probably a thought would strike him: is there such a thing as "the English character"? Can one talk about nations as though they were individuals? And supposing that one can, is there any genuine continuity between the England of to-day and the England of the past?

As he wandered through the London streets, he would notice the old prints in the bookshop windows, and it would occur to him that if these things are representative, then England must have changed a great deal. It is not much more than a hundred years since the distinguishing mark of English life was its brutality. The common people, to judge by the prints, spent their time in an almost unending round of fighting, whoring, drunkenness, and bull-baiting. Moreover, even the physical type appears to have changed. Where are they gone, the hulking draymen and low-browed prize-fighters, the brawny sailors with their buttocks bursting out of their white trousers, and the great overblown beauties with their swelling bosoms, like the figure-heads of Nelson's ships? What had these people in common with the gentle-mannered, un-demonstrative, law-abiding English of to-day? Do such things as "national cultures" really exist?

This is one of those questions, like the freedom of the will or the identity of the individual, in which all the arguments are on one side and instinctive knowledge is on the other. It is not easy to discover the connecting thread that runs through English life from the sixteenth century onwards, but all English people who bother about such subjects feel that it exists. They feel that they understand the institutions that have come to them out of the past – Parliament, for instance, or sabbatarianism, or the subtle grading of the class system – with an inherited knowledge impossible to a foreigner. Individuals, too, are felt to conform to a national pattern. D. H. Lawrence is felt to be "very English," but so is Blake; Dr. Johnson and G. K. Chesterton are somehow the same kind of person. The belief that we resemble our ancestors – that Shakespeare, say, is more like a modern Englishman than a modern Frenchman or German – may be unreasonable, but by existing it influences conduct. Myths which are believed in tend to become true, because they set up a type, or "persona," which the average person will do his best to resemble.

During the bad period of 1940 it became clear that in Britain national solidarity is stronger than class antagonism. If it were really true that "the proletarian has no country," 1940 was the time for him to show it. It was exactly then, however, that class feeling slipped into the background, only reappearing when the immediate danger had passed. Moreover, it is probable that the stolid behaviour of the British town populations under the bombing was partly due to the existence of the national "persona" – that is, to their preconceived idea of themselves. Traditionally the Englishman is phlegmatic, unimaginative, not easily rattled: and since that is what he thinks he ought to be, that is what he tends to become. Dislike of hysteria and "fuss," admiration for stubbornness, are all but universal in England, being shared by everyone except the intelligentsia. Millions of English people willingly accept as their national emblem the bulldog, an animal noted for its obstinacy, ugliness, and impenetrable stupidity. They have a remarkable readiness to admit that foreigners are more "clever" than themselves, and yet they feel that it would be an outrage against the laws of God and Nature for England to be ruled by foreigners. Our imaginary observer would notice, perhaps, that Wordsworth's sonnets during the Napoleonic war might almost have been written during this one. He would know already that England has produced poets and scientists rather than philosophers, theologians, or pure theorists of any description. And he might end by deciding that a profound, almost unconscious patriotism and an inability to think logically are the abiding features of the English character, traceable in English literature from Shakespeare onwards.

THE MORAL OUTLOOK OF THE ENGLISH PEOPLE

For perhaps a hundred and fifty years, organised religion, or conscious religious belief of any kind, have had very little hold on the mass of the English people. Only about ten per cent of them ever go near a place of worship except to be married and buried. A vague theism and an intermittent belief in life after death are probably fairly widespread, but the main Christian doctrines have been largely forgotten. Asked what he meant by "Christianity," the average man would define it wholly in ethical terms ("unselfishness," or "loving your neighbour," would be the kind of definition he would give). This was probably much the same in the early days of the Industrial Revolution, when the old village life had been suddenly broken up and the Established Church had lost touch with its followers. But in recent times the

Nonconformist sects have also lost much of their vigour, and within the last generation the Bible-reading which used to be traditional in England has lapsed. It is quite common now to meet with young people who do not know the Bible stories even as *stories*.

But there is one sense in which the English common people have remained more Christian than the upper classes, and probably than any other European nation. This is in their non-acceptance of the modern cult of power-worship. While almost ignoring the spoken doctrines of the Church, they have held on to the one that the Church never formulated, because taking it for granted: namely, that might is not right. It is here that the gulf between the intelligentsia and the common people is widest. From Carlyle onwards, but especially in the last generation, the British intelligentsia have tended to take their ideas from Europe and have been infected by habits of thought that derive ultimately from Machiavelli. All the cults that have been fashionable in the last dozen years, communism, fascism, and pacifism, are in the last analysis forms of power-worship. It is significant that in this country, unlike most others, the Marxist version of Socialism has found its warmest adherents in the middle class. Its methods, if not its theories, obviously conflict with what is called "*bourgeois* morality" (i.e., common decency), and in moral matters it is the proletarians who are "*bourgeois.*"

One of the basic folk-tales of the English-speaking peoples is Jack the Giant-killer – the little man against the big man. Mickey Mouse, Popeye the Sailor, and Charlie Chaplin are all essentially the same figure. (Chaplin's films, it is worth noticing, were banned in Germany as soon as Hitler came to power, and Chaplin has been viciously attacked by English fascist writers.) Not merely a hatred of bullying, but a tendency to support the weaker side merely because it is weaker, are almost general in England. Hence the admiration for a "good loser" and the easy forgiveness of failures, either in sport, politics, or war. Even in very serious matters the English people do not feel that an unsuccessful action is necessarily futile. An example in the 1939–45 war was the campaign in Greece. No one expected it to succeed, but nearly everyone thought that it should be undertaken. And the popular attitude to foreign politics is nearly always coloured by the instinct to side with the under-dog.

An obvious recent instance was pro-Finnish sentiment in the Russo-Finnish war of 1940. This was genuine enough, as several by-elections fought mainly on this issue showed. Popular feeling towards the U.S.S.R. had been increasingly friendly for some time past, but Finland was a small country attacked by a big one, and that settled the issue for most people. In the American Civil War the British working classes sided with the North – the side that stood for the abolition of slavery – in spite of the fact that the Northern blockade of the cotton ports was causing great hardship in Britain. In the Franco-Prussian war, such pro-French sentiment as there was in England was among the working class. The small nationalities oppressed by the Turks found their sympathisers in the Liberal Party, at that time the party of the working class and the lower middle class. And in so far as it bothered with such issues at all, British mass sentiment was for the Abyssinians against the Italians, for the Chinese against the Japanese, and for the Spanish Republicans against Franco. It was also friendly to Germany during the period when Germany was weak and disarmed, and it is not surprising to see a similar swing of sentiment after the war.

The feeling that one ought always to side with the weaker party probably derives from the balance-of-power policy which Britain has followed from the eighteenth century onwards. A European critic would add that it is humbug, pointing in proof to the fact that Britain herself holds down subject populations in India and elsewhere. We don't, in fact, know what settlement the English common people would make with India if the decision were theirs. All political parties and all newspapers of whatever colour have conspired to prevent them from seeing the issue clearly. We do know, however, that they have sometimes championed the weak against the strong when it was obviously not to their own advantage. The best example is the Irish Civil War. The real weapon of the Irish rebels was British public opinion, which was substantially on their side and prevented the British Government from crushing the rebellion in the only way possible. Even in the Boer War there was a considerable volume of pro-Boer sentiment, though it was not strong enough to influence events.

One must conclude that in this matter the English common people have lagged behind their century. They have failed to catch up with power politics, "realism," *sacro egoismo* and the doctrine that the end justifies the means.

The general English hatred of bullying and terrorism means that any kind of violent criminal gets very little sympathy. Gangsterism on American lines could not flourish in England, and it is significant that the American gangsters have never tried to transfer their activities to this country. At need, the whole nation would combine against people who kidnap babies and fire machine-guns in the street: but even the efficiency of the English police force really depends on the fact that the police have public opinion behind them. The bad side of this is the almost universal toleration of cruel and out-of-date punishments. It is not a thing to be proud of that England should still tolerate such punishments as flogging. It continues partly because of the widespread psychological ignorance, partly because men are only flogged for crimes that forfeit nearly everyone's sympathy. There would be an outcry if it were applied to non-violent crimes, or re-instituted for military offences. Military punishments are not taken for granted in England as they are in most countries. Public opinion is almost certainly opposed to the death penalty for cowardice and desertion, though there is no strong feeling against hanging murderers. In general the English attitude to crime is ignorant and old-fashioned, and humane treatment even of child offenders is a recent thing. Still, if Al Capone were in an English jail, it would not be for evasion of income tax.

A more complex question than the English attitude to crime and violence is the survival of puritanism and the world-famed English hypocrisy.

The English people proper, the working masses who make up seventy-five per cent of the population, are not puritanical. The dismal theology of Calvinism never popularised itself in England as it did for a while in Wales and Scotland. But puritanism in the looser sense in which the word is generally used (that is, prudishness, asceticism, the "kill-joy" spirit) is something that has been unsuccessfully forced upon the working class by the class of small traders and manufacturers immediately above them. In its origin it had a clear though unconscious economic motive behind it. If you could persuade the working man that every kind of recreation was sinful, you could get more work out of him for less money. In the early nineteenth century there was even a school of thought which maintained that the working man ought not to marry. But it would be unfair to suggest that the puritan moral code was mere humbug. Its exaggerated fear of sexual immorality, which extended to a disapproval of stage plays, dancing, and even bright-coloured clothes, was partly a protest against the real corruption of the later Middle Ages: there was also the new factor of syphilis, which appeared in England about the sixteenth century and worked frightful havoc for the next century or two. A little later there was another new factor in the introduction of distilled liquors – gin, brandy, and so forth – which were very much more intoxicating than the beer and mead which the English had been accustomed to. The "temperance" movement was a well-meant reaction against the frightful drunkenness of the nineteenth century, product of slum conditions and cheap gin. But it was necessarily led by fanatics who regarded not merely drunkenness but even the moderate drinking of alcohol as sinful. During the past fifty years or so there has even been a similar drive against tobacco. A hundred years ago, or two hundred years ago, tobacco-smoking was much disapproved of, but only on the ground that it was dirty, vulgar, and injurious to health: the idea that it is a wicked self-indulgence is modern.

This line of thought has never really appealed to the English masses. At most they have been sufficiently intimidated by middle-class puritanism to take some of their pleasures rather furtively. It is universally agreed that the working classes are far more moral than the upper classes, but the idea that sexuality is wicked in itself has no popular basis. Music-hall jokes, Blackpool postcards, and the songs the soldiers make up are anything but puritanical. On the other hand, almost no one in England approves of prostitution. There are several big towns where prostitution is extremely blatant, but it is completely unattractive and has never been really tolerated. It could not be regulated and humanised as it has been in some countries, because every English person feels in his bones that it is wrong. As for the general weakening of sex morals that has happened during the past twenty or thirty years, it is probably a temporary thing, resulting from the excess of women over men in the population.

In the matter of drink, the only result of a century of "temperance" agitation has been a slight increase in hypocrisy. The practical disappearance of drunkenness as an English vice has not been due to the anti-drink fanatics, but to competing amusements, education, the improvement in industrial conditions, and the expensiveness of drink itself. The fanatics have been able to see to it that the Englishman drinks his glass of beer under difficulties and with a faint feeling of wrong-doing, but have not actually been able to prevent him from drinking it. The pub, one of the basic institutions of English life, carries on in spite of the harassing tactics of Nonconformist local authorities. So also with gambling. Most forms of gambling are illegal according to the letter of the law, but they all happen on an enormous scale. The motto of the English people might be the chorus of Marie Lloyd's song, "A little of what you fancy does you good." They are not vicious, not even lazy, but they will have their bit of fun, whatever the higher-ups may say. And they seem to be gradually winning their battle against the kill-joy minorities. Even the horrors of the English Sunday have been much mitigated during the past dozen years. Some of the laws regulating pubs – designed in every case to discourage the publican and make drinking unattractive – were relaxed during the war. And it is a very good sign that the stupid rule forbidding children to enter pubs, which tended to dehumanise the pub and turn it into a mere drinking-shop, is beginning to be disregarded in some parts of the country.

Traditionally, the Englishman's home is his castle. In an age of conscription and identity cards this cannot really be true. But the hatred of regimentation, the feeling that your spare time is your own and that a man must not be persecuted for his opinions, is deeply ingrained, and the centralising processes inevitable in wartime, and still enforced, have not destroyed it.

It is a fact that the much-boasted freedom of the British press is theoretical rather than actual. To begin with the centralised ownership of the press means in practice that unpopular opinions can only be printed in books or in newspapers with small circulations. Moreover, the English people as a whole are not

619

sufficiently interested in the printed word to be very vigilant about this aspect of their liberties, and during the last twenty years there has been much tampering with the freedom of the press, with no real popular protest. Even the demonstrations against the suppression of the *Daily Worker* were probably stage-managed by a small minority. On the other hand, freedom of speech is a reality, and respect for it is almost general. Extremely few English people are afraid to utter their political opinions in public, and there are not even very many who want to silence the opinions of others. In peacetime, when unemployment can be used as a weapon, there is a certain amount of petty persecution of "reds," but the real totalitarian atmosphere, in which the State endeavours to control people's thoughts as well as their words, is hardly imaginable.

The safeguard against it is partly the respect for integrity of conscience, and the willingness to hear both sides, which can be observed at any public meeting. But it is also partly the prevailing lack of intellectuality. The English are not sufficiently interested in intellectual matters to be intolerant about them. "Deviations" and "dangerous thoughts" do not seem very important to them. An ordinary Englishman, Conservative, Socialist, Catholic, Communist, or what not, almost never grasps the full logical implications of the creed he professes: almost always he utters heresies without noticing it. Orthodoxies, whether of the Right or the Left, flourish chiefly among the literary intelligentsia, the people who ought in theory to be the guardians of freedom of thought.

The English people are not good haters, their memory is very short, their patriotism is largely unconscious, they have no love of military glory and not much admiration for great men. They have the virtues and the vices of an old-fashioned people. To twentieth-century political theories they oppose not another theory of their own, but a moral quality which must be vaguely described as decency. On the day in 1936 when the Germans re-occupied the Rhineland I was in a northern mining town. I happened to go into a pub just after this piece of news, which quite obviously meant war, had come over the wireless, and I remarked to the others at the bar, "The German army has crossed the Rhine." With a vague air of capping a quotation someone answered, "Parley-voo." No more response than that! Nothing will ever wake these people up, I thought. But later in the evening, at the same pub, someone sang a song which had recently come out, with the chorus –

> "For you can't do that there 'ere,
> No, you can't do that there 'ere;
> Anywhere else you can do that there,
> But you can't do that there 'ere!"

And it struck me that perhaps this was the English answer to fascism. At any rate it is true that it has not happened here, in spite of fairly favourable circumstances. The amount of liberty, intellectual or other, that we enjoy in England ought not to be exaggerated, but the fact that it did not markedly diminish in nearly six years of desperate war is a hopeful symptom.

THE POLITICAL OUTLOOK OF THE ENGLISH PEOPLE

The English people are not only indifferent to fine points of doctrine, but are remarkably ignorant politically. They are only now beginning to use the political terminology which has been current for years in Continental countries. If you asked a random group of people from any stratum of the population to define capitalism, socialism, communism, anarchism, Trotskyism, fascism, you would get mostly vague answers, and some of them would be surprisingly stupid ones.

But they are also distinctly ignorant about their own political system. During recent years, for various reasons, there has been a revival of political activity, but over a longer period the interest in party politics has been dwindling. Great numbers of adult English people have never in their lives bothered to vote in an election. In big towns it is quite common for people not to know the name of their M.P or what constituency they live in. During the war years, owing to the failure to renew the registers, the young had no votes (at one time no one under twenty-nine had a vote), and did not seem much troubled by the fact. Nor does the anomalous electoral system, which usually favours the Conservative Party, though it happened to favour the Labour Party in 1945, arouse much protest. Attention focuses on policies and individuals (Chamberlain, Churchill, Cripps, Beveridge, Bevin) rather than on parties. The feeling that Parliament really controls events, and that

sensational changes are to be expected when a new government comes in, has been gradually fading ever since the first
Labour government in 1923.

In spite of many subdivisions, Britain has in effect only two
political parties, the Conservative Party and the Labour Party,
which between them broadly represent the main interests of
the nation. But during the last twenty years the tendency of
these two parties has been to resemble one another more and
more. Everyone knows in advance that any government,
whatever its political principles may be, can be relied upon
not to do certain things. Thus, no Conservative government
will ever revert to what would have been called Conservatism
in the nineteenth century. No Socialist government will massacre the propertied class, nor even expropriate them without
compensation. A good recent example of the changing temper
of politics was the reception given to the Beveridge Report.
Thirty years ago any Conservative would have denounced this
as State charity, while most Socialists would have rejected it as a
capitalist bribe. In 1944 the only discussion that arose was as to
whether it would be adopted in whole or in part. This blurring
of party distinctions is happening in almost all countries, partly
because everywhere, except, perhaps, in the U.S.A., the drift is
towards a planned economy, partly because in an age of power
politics national survival is felt to be more important than class
warfare. But Britain has certain peculiarities resulting from its
being both a small island and the centre of an Empire. To begin
with, given the present economic system, Britain's prosperity
depends partly on the Empire, while all Left parties are theoretically anti-imperialist. Politicians of the Left are therefore
aware – or have recently become aware – that once in power
they choose between abandoning some of their principles or
lowering the English standard of living. Secondly, it is impossible for Britain to go through the kind of revolutionary process
that the U.S.S.R. went through. It is too small, too highly
organised, too dependent on imported food. Civil war in
England would mean starvation or conquest by some foreign
power, or both. Thirdly and most important of all, civil war is
not *morally* possible in England. In any circumstances that we
can foresee, the proletariat of Hammersmith will not arise and
massacre the *bourgeoisie* of Kensington: they are not different

enough. Even the most drastic changes will have to happen peacefully and with a show of legality, and everyone except the "lunatic fringes" of the various political parties is aware of this.

These facts make up the background of the English political outlook. The great mass of the people want profound changes, but they do not want violence. They want to preserve their own standard of living, and at the same time they want to feel that they are not exploiting less fortunate peoples. If you issued a questionnaire to the whole nation, asking, "What do you want from politics?", the answer would be much the same in the overwhelming majority of cases. Substantially it would be: "Economic security, a foreign policy which will ensure peace, more social equality, and a settlement with India." Of these, the first is by far the most important, unemployment being an even greater nightmare than war. But few people would think it necessary to mention either capitalism or socialism. Neither word has much emotional appeal. No one's heart beats faster at the thought of nationalising the Bank of England: on the other hand, the old line of talk about sturdy individualism and the sacred rights of property is no longer swallowed by the masses. They know it is not true that "there's plenty of room at the top," and in any case most of them don't want to get to the top: they want steady jobs and a fair deal for their children.

During the last few years, owing to the social frictions arising out of the war, discontent with the obvious inefficiency of old-style capitalism, and admiration for Soviet Russia, public opinion has moved considerably to the Left, but without growing more doctrinaire or markedly bitterer. None of the political parties which call themselves revolutionary have seriously increased their following. There are about half a dozen of these parties, but their combined membership, even if one counts the remnants of Mosley's Blackshirts, would probably not amount to 150,000. The most important of them is the Communist Party, but even the Communist Party, after twenty-five years of existence, must be held to have failed. Although it has had considerable influence at moments when circumstances favoured it, it has never shown signs of growing into a mass party of the kind that exists in France or used to exist in pre-Hitler Germany.

Over a long period of years, Communist Party membership has gone up or down in response to the changes in Russian foreign policy. When the U.S.S.R. is on good terms with Britain, the British Communists follow a "moderate" line hardly distinguishable from that of the Labour Party, and their membership swells to some scores of thousands. When British and Russian policy diverge, the Communists revert to a "revolutionary" line and membership slumps again. They can, in fact, only get themselves a worthwhile following by abandoning their essential objectives. The various other Marxist parties, all of them claiming to be the true and uncorrupted successors of Lenin, are in an even more hopeless position. The average Englishman is unable to grasp their doctrines and uninterested in their grievances. And in England the conspiratorial mentality which has been developed in police-ridden European countries is a great handicap. English people in large numbers will not accept any creed whose dominant notes are hatred and illegality. The ruthless ideologies of the Continent – not merely communism and fascism, but anarchism, Trotskyism, and even ultra-montane Catholicism – are accepted in their pure form only by the intelligentsia, who constitute a sort of island of bigotry amid the general vagueness. It is significant that English revolutionary writers are obliged to use a bastard vocabulary whose key phrases are mostly translations. There are no native English words for most of the concepts they are dealing with. Even the word "proletarian," for instance, is not English and the great majority of English people do not know what it means. It is generally used, if at all, to mean simply "poor." But even so it is given a social rather than an economic slant and most people would tell you that a blacksmith or a cobbler is a proletarian and that a bank clerk is not. As for the word "*bourgeois*," it is used almost exclusively by people who are of *bourgeois* origin themselves. The only genuinely popular use of the word is as a printer's term. It is then, as one might expect, anglicised and pronounced "boorjoyce."

But there is one abstract political term which is fairly widely used and has a loose but well-understood meaning attached to it. This is the word "democracy." In a way, the English people do feel that they live in a democratic country. Not that anyone is so stupid as to take this in a literal sense. If democracy means either popular rule or social equality, it is clear that Britain is not democratic. It is, however, democratic in the secondary sense which has attached itself to that word since the rise of Hitler. To begin with, minorities have some power of making themselves heard. But more than this, public opinion cannot be disregarded when it chooses to express itself. It may have to work in indirect ways, by strikes, demonstrations and letters to the newspapers, but it can and visibly does affect government policy. A British government may be unjust, but it cannot be quite arbitrary. It cannot do the kind of thing that a totalitarian government does as a matter of course. One example out of the thousands that might be chosen is the German attack on the U.S.S.R. The significant thing is not that this was made without a declaration of war – that was natural enough – but that it was made without any propaganda build-up beforehand. The German people woke up to find themselves at war with a country that they had been ostensibly on friendly terms with on the previous evening. Our own government would not dare to do such a thing, and the English people are fairly well aware of this. English political thinking is much governed by the word "They." "They" are the higher-ups, the mysterious powers who do things to you against your will. But there is a widespread feeling that "They," though tyrannical, are not omnipotent. "They" will respond to pressure if you take the trouble to apply it: "They" are even removable. And with all their political ignorance the English people will often show surprising sensitiveness when some small incident seems to show that "They" are overstepping the mark. Hence, in the midst of seeming apathy, the sudden fuss every now and then over a rigged by-election or a too-Cromwellian handling of Parliament.

One thing that is extremely difficult to be certain about is the persistence in England of monarchist sentiment. There cannot be much doubt that at any rate in the south of England it was strong and genuine until the death of King George V. The popular response to the Silver Jubilee in 1935 took the authorities by surprise, and the celebrations had to be prolonged for an extra week. At normal times it is only the richer classes who are overtly royalist: in the West End of London, for instance, people stand to attention for "God Save the King" at the end of a picture show, whereas in the poorer quarters they walk out. But the affection shown for George V at the Silver Jubilee was obviously genuine, and it was even possible to see in it the survival, or recrudescence, of an idea almost as old as history, the idea of the King and the common people being in a sort of alliance against the upper classes; for example, some of the London slum streeets bore during the Jubilee the rather servile slogan "Poor but Loyal." Other slogans, however, coupled loyalty to the King with hostility to the landlord, such as "Long Live the King. Down with the Landlord," or more often, "No Landlords Wanted" or "Landlords Keep Away." It is too early to say whether royalist sentiment was killed outright by the Abdication, but unquestionably the Abdication dealt it a serious blow. Over the past four hundred years it has waxed or waned according to circumstances. Queen Victoria, for instance, was decidedly unpopular during part of her reign, and in the first quarter of the nineteenth century public interest in the Royal Family was not nearly as strong as it was a hundred years later. At this moment the mass of the English people are probably mildly republican. But it may well be that another long reign, similar to that of George V, would revive royalist feeling and make it – as it was between roughly 1880 and 1936 – an appreciable factor in politics.

THE ENGLISH CLASS SYSTEM

In time of war the English class system is the enemy propagandist's best argument. To Dr. Goebbels's charge that England is still "two nations," the only truthful answer would have been that she is in fact three nations. But the peculiarity of English class distinctions is not that they are unjust – for after all, wealth and poverty exist side by side in almost all countries – but that they are anachronistic. They do not exactly correspond to economic distinctions, and what is essentially an industrial and capitalist country is haunted by the ghost of a caste system.

It is usual to classify modern society under three headings: the upper class, or *bourgeoisie*, the middle class, or *petite bourgeoisie*, and the working class, or proletariat. This roughly fits the facts, but one can draw no useful inference from it unless one takes account of the subdivisions within the various classes and realises how deeply the whole English outlook is coloured by romanticism and sheer snobbishness.

England is one of the last remaining countries to cling to the outward forms of feudalism. Titles are maintained and new ones are constantly created, and the House of Lords, consisting mainly of hereditary peers, has real powers. At the same time England has no real aristocracy. The race difference on which aristocratic rule is usually founded was disappearing by the end of the Middle Ages, and the famous medieval families have almost completely vanished. The so-called old families are those that grew rich in the sixteenth, seventeenth, and eighteenth centuries. Moreover, the notion that nobility exists in its own right, that you can be a nobleman even if you are poor, was already dying out in the age of Elizabeth, a fact commented on by Shakespeare. And yet, curiously enough, the English ruling class has never developed into a *bourgeoisie* plain and simple. It has never become purely urban or frankly commercial. The ambition to be a country gentleman, to own and administer land and draw at least a part of your income from rent, has survived every change. So it comes that each new wave of parvenus, instead of simply replacing the existing ruling class, has adopted its habits, intermarried with it, and, after a generation or two, become indistinguishable from it.

The basic reason for this may perhaps be that England is very small and has an equable climate and pleasantly varied scenery. It is almost impossible in England, and not easy even in Scotland, to be more than twenty miles from a town. Rural life is less inherently boorish than it is in bigger countries with colder winters. And the comparative integrity of the British ruling class – for when all is said and done they have not behaved so contemptibly as their European opposite numbers – is probably bound up with their idea of themselves as feudal landowners. This outlook is shared by considerable sections of the middle class. Nearly everyone who can afford to do so sets up as a country gentleman, or at least makes some effort in that direction. The manor-house with its park and its walled gardens reappears in reduced form in the stockbroker's week-end cottage, in the suburban villa with its lawn and herbaceous border, perhaps even in the potted nasturtiums on the window-sill of the Bayswater flat. This widespread day-dream is undoubtedly snobbish, it has tended to stabilise class distinctions and has helped to prevent the modernisation of English agriculture: but it is mixed up with a kind of idealism, a feeling that style and tradition are more important than money.

Within the middle class there is a sharp division, cultural and not financial, between those who aim at gentility and those who do not. According to the usual classification, everyone between the capitalist and the weekly wage-earner can be lumped together as *"petite bourgeoisie."* This means that the Harley Street physician, the army officer, the grocer, the farmer, the senior civil servant, the solicitor, the clergyman, the schoolmaster, the bank manager, the speculative builder, and the fisherman who owns his own boat, are all in the same class. But no one in England feels them to belong to the same class, and the distinction between them is not a distinction of income but of accent, manners and, to some extent, outlook. Anyone who pays any attention to class differences at all would regard an army officer with £1,000 a year as socially superior to a shopkeeper with £2,000 a year. Even within the upper class a similar distinction holds good, the titled person being almost always more deferred to than an untitled person of larger income. Middle-class people are really graded according to their degree of resemblance to the aristocracy: professional men, senior officials, officers in the fighting services, university lecturers, clergymen, even the literary and scientific intelligentsia, rank higher than business men, though on the whole they earn less. It is a peculiarity of this class that their largest item of expenditure is education. Whereas a successful tradesman will send his son to the local grammar school, a clergyman with half his income will underfeed himself for years in order to send his son to a public school, although he knows that he will get no direct return for the money he spends.

There is, however, another noticeable division in the middle class. The old distinction was between the man who is "a gentleman" and the man who is "not a gentleman." In the last thirty years, however, the demands of modern industry, and the technical schools and provincial universities, have brought into being a new kind of man, middle class in income and to some extent in habits, but not much interested in his own social status. People like radio engineers and industrial chemists, whose education has not been of a kind to give them any reverence for the past, and who tend to live in blocks of flats or housing-estates where the old social pattern has broken down, are the most nearly classless beings that England possesses. They are an important section of society, because their numbers are constantly growing. The war, for instance, made necessary the formation of an enormous air force, and so you got thousands of young men of working-class origin graduating into the technical middle class by way of the R.A.F. Any serious reorganisation of industry now will have similar effects. And the characteristic outlook of the technicians is already spreading among the older strata of the middle class. One symptom of this is that intermarriage within the middle class is freer than it used to be. Another is the increasing unwillingness of people below the £2,000 a year level to bankrupt themselves in the name of education.

Another series of changes, probably dating from the Education Bill of 1871, is occurring in the working class. One cannot altogether acquit the English working class either of snobbishness or of servility. To begin with there is a fairly sharp distinction between the better-paid working class and the very poor. Even in socialist literature it is common to find contemptuous references to slum-dwellers (the German word *lumpenproletariat* is much used), and imported labourers with low standards of living, such as the Irish, are greatly looked down on. There is also, probably, more disposition to accept class distinctions as permanent, and even to accept the upper classes as natural leaders, than survives in most countries. It is significant that in the moment of disaster the man best able to unite the nation was Churchill, a Conservative of aristocratic origins. The word "Sir" is much used in England, and the man of obviously upper-class appearance can usually get more than his fair share of deference from commissionaires, ticket-collectors, policemen, and the like. It is this aspect of English life that seems most shocking to visitors from America and the Dominions. And the tendency towards servility probably did not decrease in the twenty years between the two wars: it may even have increased, owing chiefly to unemployment.

But snobbishness is never quite separable from idealism. The tendency to give the upper classes more than their due is mixed up with a respect for good manners and something vaguely describable as culture. In the South of England, at any rate, it is unquestionable that most working-class people want to re-semble the upper classes in manners and habits. The traditional attitude of looking down on the upper classes as effeminate and "la-di-dah" survives best in the heavy-industry areas. Hostile nicknames like "toff" and "swell" have almost disappeared, and even the *Daily Worker* displays advertisements for "High-class Gentleman's Tailor." Above all, throughout southern England there is almost general uneasiness about the Cockney accent. In Scotland and northern England snobbishness about the local accents does exist, but it is not nearly so strong or widespread. Many a Yorkshireman definitely prides himself on his broad U's and narrow A's, and will defend them on linguistic grounds. In London there are still people who say "fice" instead of "face," but there is probably no one who regards "fice" as superior. Even a person who claims to despise the *bourgeoisie* and all its ways will still take care that his children grow up pronouncing their aitches.

But side by side with this there has gone a considerable growth of political consciousness and an increasing impatience with class privilege. Over a period of twenty or thirty years the working class has grown politically more hostile to the upper class, culturally less hostile. There is nothing incongruous in this: both tendencies are symptoms of the levelling of manners which results from machine civilisation and which makes the English class system more and more of an anachronism.

The obvious class differences still surviving in England astonish foreign observers, but they are far less marked, and far less real, than they were thirty years ago. People of different social origins, thrown together during the war in the armed forces, or in factories or offices, or as firewatchers and Home Guards, were able to mingle more easily than they did in the 1914–18 war. It is worth listing the various influences which – mechanically, as it were – tend to make Englishmen of all classes less and less different from one another.

First of all, the improvement in industrial technique. Every year less and less people are engaged in heavy manual labour which keeps them constantly tired and, by hypertrophying certain muscles, gives them a distinctive carriage. Secondly, improvements in housing. Between the two wars rehousing was done mostly by the local authorities, who have produced a type of house (the council house, with its bathroom, garden, separate kitchen, and indoor w.c.) which is nearer to the stock-broker's villa than it is to the labourer's cottage. Thirdly, the mass production of furniture which in ordinary times can be bought on the hire-purchase system. The effect of this is that the interior of a working-class house resembles that of a middle-class house very much more than it did a generation ago. Fourthly, and perhaps most important of all, the mass production of cheap clothes. Thirty years ago the social status of nearly everyone in England could be determined from his appearance, even at two hundred yards' distance. The working classes all wore ready-made clothes, and the ready-made clothes were not only ill-fitting but usually followed the upper-class fashions of ten or fifteen years earlier. The cloth cap was practically a badge of status. It was universal among the working class, while the upper classes only wore it for golf and shooting. This state of affairs is rapidly changing. Ready-made clothes now follow the fashions closely, they are made in many different fittings to suit every kind of figure, and even when they are of very cheap cloth they are superficially not very different from expensive clothes. The result is that it grows harder every year, especially in the case of women, to determine social status at a glance.

Mass-produced literature and amusements have the same effect. Radio programmes, for instance, are necessarily the same for everybody. Films, though often extremely reactionary in their implied outlook, have to appeal to a public of millions and therefore have to avoid stirring up class antagonisms. So also with some of the big-circulation newspapers. The *Daily Express*, for instance, draws its readers from all strata of the population. So also with some of the periodicals that have appeared in the past dozen years. *Punch* is obviously a middle- and upper-class paper, but *Picture Post* is not aimed at any particular class. And lending libraries and very cheap books, such as the Penguins, popularise the habit of reading and probably have a levelling effect on literary taste. Even taste in food tends to grow more uniform owing to the multiplication of cheap but fairly smart restaurants such as those of Messrs. Lyons.

We are not justified in assuming that class distinctions are actually disappearing. The essential structure of England is still almost what it was in the nineteenth century. But real differences between man and man are obviously diminishing, and this fact is grasped and even welcomed by people who only a few years ago were clinging desperately to their social prestige.

Whatever may be the ultimate fate of the very rich, the tendency of the working class and the middle class is evidently to merge. It may happen quickly or slowly, according to circumstances. It was accelerated by the war, and another ten years of all-round rationing, utility clothes, high income tax, and compulsory national service may finish the process once and for all. The final effects of this we cannot foresee. There are observers, both native and foreign, who believe that the fairly large amount of individual freedom that is enjoyed in England depends on having a well-defined class system. Liberty, according to some, is incompatible with equality. But at least it is certain that the present drift *is* towards greater social equality, and that that is what the great mass of the English people desire.

THE ENGLISH LANGUAGE

The English language has two outstanding characteristics to which most of its minor oddities can be finally traced. These characteristics are a very large vocabulary and simplicity of grammar.

If it is not the largest in the world, the English vocabulary is certainly among the largest. English is really two languages, Anglo-Saxon and Norman-French, and during the last three centuries it has been reinforced on an enormous scale by new words deliberately created from Latin and Greek roots. But in addition the vocabulary is made much larger than it appears by the practice of turning one part of speech into another. For example, almost any noun can be used as a verb: this in effect gives an extra range of verbs, so that you have *knife* as well as *stab*, *school* as well as *teach*, *fire* as well as *burn*, and so on. Then again, certain verbs can be given as many as twenty different meanings simply by adding prepositions to them. (Examples are *get out of*, *get up*, *give out*, *take over*.) Verbs can also change into nouns with considerable freedom, and by the use of affixes such as -*y*, -*ful*, -*like*, any noun can be turned into an adjective. More freely than in most languages, verbs and adjectives can be turned into their opposites by means of the prefix *un*-. And adjectives can be made more emphatic or given a new twist by tying a noun to them: for example, *lily-white*, *sky-blue*, *coal-black*, *iron-hard*, etc.

But English is also, and to an unnecessary extent, a borrowing language. It readily takes over any foreign word that seems to fill a need, often altering the meaning in doing so. A recent example is the word *blitz*. As a verb this word did not appear in print till late in 1940, but it has already become part of the language. Other examples from the vast armoury of borrowed words are *garage*, *charabanc*, *alias*, *alibi*, *steppe*, *thug*, *role*, *menu*, *lasso*, *rendezvous*, *chemise*. It will be noticed that in most cases an English equivalent exists already, so that borrowing adds to the already large stock of synonyms.

English grammar is simple. The language is almost completely uninflected, a peculiarity which marks it off from almost all languages west of China. Any regular English verb has only three inflections, the third person singular, the present participle, and the past participle. Thus, for instance, the verb *to kill* consists of *kill*, *kills*, *killing*, *killed*, and that is all. There is, of course, a great wealth of tenses, very much subtilised in meaning, but these are made by the use of auxiliaries which themselves barely inflect. *May*, *might*, *shall*, *will*, *should*, *would* do not inflect at all, except in the obsolete second person singular. The upshot is that every person in every tense of such a verb as *to kill* can be expressed in only about thirty words including the pronouns, or about forty if one includes the second person singular. The corresponding number in, for instance, French would be somewhere near two hundred. And in English there is the added advantage that the auxiliaries which are used to make the tenses are the same in every case.

There is no such thing in English as declension of nouns, and there is no gender. Nor are there many irregular plurals or comparatives. Moreover, the tendency is always towards greater simplicity, both in grammar and syntax. Long sentences with dependent clauses grow more and more unpopular, irregular but time-saving formations such as the "American subjunctive" (*it is necessary that you go* instead of *it is necessary that you should go*) gain ground, and difficult rules, such as the difference between *shall* and *will*, or *that* and *which*, are more and more ignored. If it continues to develop along its present lines English will ultimately have more in common with the uninflected languages of East Asia than with the languages of Europe.

The greatest quality of English is its enormous range not only of meaning but of *tone*. It is capable of endless subtleties, and of everything from the most high-flown rhetoric to the most brutal coarseness. On the other hand, its lack of grammar makes it easily compressible. It is the language of lyric poetry, and also of headlines. On its lower levels it is very easy to learn, in spite of its irrational spelling. It can also for international purposes be reduced to very simple pidgin dialects, ranging from Basic to the "Bêche-de-mer" English used in the South Pacific. It is therefore well suited to be a world lingua franca, and it has in fact spread more widely than any other language.

But there are also great disadvantages, or at least great dangers, in speaking English as one's native tongue. To begin with, as was pointed out earlier in this book, the English are very poor linguists. Their own language is grammatically so simple that unless they have gone through the discipline of learning a foreign language in childhood, they are often quite unable to grasp what is meant by gender, person, and case. A completely illiterate Indian will pick up English far faster than a British soldier will pick up Hindustani. Nearly five million Indians are literate in English and millions more speak it in a debased form. There are some tens of thousands of Indians who speak English as nearly as possible perfectly; yet the number of Englishmen speaking any Indian language perfectly would not amount to more than a few scores. But the great weakness of English is its capacity for debasement. Just because it is so easy to use, it is easy to use *badly*.

To write or even to speak English is not a science but an art. There are no reliable rules: there is only the general principle that concrete words are better than abstract ones, and that the shortest way of saying anything is always the best. Mere correctness is no guarantee whatever of good writing. A sentence like "an enjoyable time was had by all present" is perfectly correct English, and so is the unintelligible mess of words on an income-tax return. Whoever writes English is involved in a struggle that never lets up even for a sentence. He is struggling against vagueness, against obscurity, against the lure of the decorative adjective, against the encroachment of Latin and Greek, and, above all, against the worn-out phrases and dead metaphors with which the language is cluttered up. In speaking, these dangers are more easily avoided, but spoken English differs from written English more sharply than is the case in most languages. In the spoken tongue every word that can be omitted is omitted, every possible abbreviation is used. Meaning is conveyed quite largely by emphasis, though curiously enough the English do not gesticulate, as one might reasonably expect them to do. A sentence like *No, I don't mean that one, I mean that one* is perfectly intelligible when spoken aloud, even without a gesture. But spoken English, when it tries to be dignified and logical, usually takes on the vices of written English, as you can see by spending half an hour either in the House of Commons or at the Marble Arch.

English is peculiarly subject to jargons. Doctors, scientists, business men, officials, sportsmen, economists, and political theorists all have their characteristic perversion of the language, which can be studied in the appropriate magazines from the *Lancet* to the *Labour Monthly*. But probably the deadliest enemy of good English is what is called "standard English." This dreary dialect, the language of leading articles, White Papers, political speeches, and B.B.C. news bulletins, is undoubtedly spreading: it is spreading downwards in the social scale, and outwards into the spoken language. Its characteristic is its reliance on ready-made phrases — *in due course, take the earliest opportunity, warm appreciation, deepest regret, explore every avenue, ring the changes, take up the cudgels, legitimate assumption, the answer is in the affirmative*, etc. etc. — which may once have been fresh and vivid, but have now become mere thought-saving devices, having the same relation to living English as a crutch has to a leg. Anyone preparing a broadcast or writing a letter to *The Times* adopts this kind of language almost instinctively, and it infects the spoken tongue as well. So much has our language been weakened that the imbecile chatter in Swift's essay on *Polite Conversation* (a satire on the upper-class talk of Swift's own day) would actually be rather a good conversation by modern standards.

This temporary decadence of the English language is due, like so much else, to our anachronistic class system. "Educated" English has grown anæmic because for long past it has not been reinvigorated from below. The people likeliest to use simple concrete language, and to think of metaphors that really call up a visual image, are those who are in contact with physical reality. A useful word like *bottleneck*, for instance, would be most likely to occur to someone used to dealing with conveyor belts: or again, the expressive military phrase *to winkle out* implies acquaintance both with winkles and with machine-gun nests. And the vitality of English depends on a steady supply of images of this kind. It follows that language, at any rate the English language, suffers when the educated classes lose touch with the manual workers. As things are at present, nearly every Englishman, whatever his origins, feels the working-class manner of speech, and even working-class idioms, to be inferior. Cockney, the most widespread dialect, is the most despised of all. Any word or usage that is supposedly Cockney is looked on as vulgar, even when, as is sometimes the case, it is merely an archaism. An example is *ain't*, which is now abandoned in favour of the much weaker form *aren't*. But *ain't* was good enough English eighty years ago, and Queen Victoria would have said *ain't*.

During the past forty years, and especially the past dozen years, English has borrowed largely from American, while America has shown no tendency to borrow from English. The reason for this is partly political. Anti-British feeling in the United States is far stronger than anti-American feeling in England, and most Americans dislike using a word or phrase which they know to be British. But American has gained a footing in England partly because of the vivid, almost poetic quality of its slang, partly because certain American usages (for instance, the formation of verbs by adding *-ise* to a noun) save time, and most of all because one can adopt an American word without crossing a class barrier. From the English point of view American words have no class label. This applies even to thieves' slang. Words like *stooge* and *stool-pigeon* are considered much less vulgar than words like *nark* and *split*. Even a very snobbish English person would probably not mind calling a policeman a *cop*, which is American, but he would object to calling him a *copper*, which is working-class English. To the working classes, on the other hand, the use of Americanisms is a way of escaping from Cockney without adopting the B.B.C. dialect, which they instinctively dislike and cannot easily master. Hence, especially in the big towns, working-class children now use American slang from the moment that they learn to talk. And there is a noticeable tendency to use American words even when they are not slang and when an English equivalent already exists: for instance, *car* for *tram*, *escalator* for *moving staircase*, *automobile* for *motor-car*.

This process will probably continue for some time. One cannot check it simply by protesting against it, and in any case many American words and expressions are well worth adopting. Some are necessary neologisms, others (for instance, *fall* for *autumn*) are old words which we ought never to have dropped. But it ought to be realised that on the whole American is a bad influence and has already had a debasing effect.

To begin with, American has some of the vices of English in an exaggerated form. The interchangeability of different parts of speech has been carried further, the distinction between transitive and intransitive verbs tends to break down, and many words are used which have no meaning whatever. For example, whereas English alters the meaning of a verb by tacking a preposition on to it, the American tendency is to burden every verb with a preposition that adds nothing to its meaning (*win out*, *lose out*, *face up to*, etc.). On the other hand, American has broken more completely than English with the past and with literary traditions. It not only produces words like *beautician*, *moronic*, and *sexualise*, but often replaces strong primary words by feeble euphemisms. For instance, many Americans seem to regard the word *death* and various words that go with it (*corpse*, *coffin*, *shroud*) as almost unmentionable. But above all, to adopt the American language wholeheartedly would probably mean a huge loss of vocabulary. For though American produces vivid and witty turns of speech, it is terribly poor in names for natural objects and localities. Even the streets in American cities are usually known by numbers instead of names. If we really intended to model our language upon American we should have, for instance, to lump the lady-bird, the daddy-long-legs, the sawfly, the water-boatman, the cockchafer, the cricket, the death-watch beetle and scores of other insects all together under the inexpressive name of *bug*. We should lose the poetic names of our wild flowers, and also, probably, our habit of giving individual names to every street, pub, field, lane, and hillock. In so far as American is adopted, that is the tendency. Those who take their language from the films, or from papers such as *Life* and *Time*, always prefer the slick time-saving word to the one with a history behind it. As to accent, it is doubtful whether the American accent has the superiority which it is now fashionable to claim for it. The "educated" English accent, a product of the last thirty years, is undoubtedly very bad and is likely to be abandoned, but the average English person probably speaks as clearly as the average American. Most English people blur their vowel sounds, but most Americans swallow their consonants. Many Americans pronounce, for instance, *water* as though it had no T in it, or even as though it had no consonant in it at all, except the w. On the whole we are justified in regarding the American language with suspicion. We ought to be ready to borrow its best words, but we ought not to let it modify the actual structure of our language.

However, there is no chance of resisting the American influence unless we can put new life into English itself. And it is difficult to do this while words and idioms are prevented from circulating freely among all sections of the population. English people of all classes now find it natural to express incredulity by the American slang phrase *sez you*. Many would even tell you in good faith that *sez you* has no English equivalent. Actually it has a whole string of them – for instance, *not half, I don't think, come off it, less of it, and then you wake up*, or simply *garn*. But most of these would be considered vulgar: you would never find an expression like *not half* in a *Times* leader, for instance. And on the other hand, many necessary abstract words, especially words of Latin origin, are rejected by the working class because they sound public-schoolish, "tony," and effeminate. Language ought to be the joint creation of poets and manual workers, and in modern England it is difficult for these two classes to meet. When they can do so again – as, in a different way, they could in the feudal past – English may show more clearly than at present its kinship with the language of Shakespeare and Defoe.

THE FUTURE OF THE ENGLISH PEOPLE

This is not a book about foreign politics, but if one is to speak of the future of the English people, one must start by considering what kind of world they will probably be living in and what special part they can play in it.

Nations do not often die out, and the English people will still be in existence a hundred years hence, whatever has happened in the meantime. But if Britain is to survive as what is called a "great" nation, playing an important and useful part in the world's affairs, one must take certain things as assured. One must assume that Britain will remain on good terms with Russia and Europe, will keep its special links with America and the Dominions, and will solve the problem of India in some amicable way. That is perhaps a great deal to assume, but without it there is not much hope for civilisation as a whole, and still less for Britain itself. If the savage international struggle of the last twenty years continues, there will only be room in the world for two or three great powers, and in the long run Britain will not be one of them. It has not either the population or the resources. In a world of power politics the English would ultimately dwindle to a satellite people, and the special thing that it is in their power to contribute might be lost.

But what is the special thing that they could contribute? The outstanding and – by contemporary standards – highly original quality of the English is their habit of *not killing one another*. Putting aside the "model" small states, which are in an exceptional position, England is the only European country where internal politics are conducted in a more or less humane and decent manner. It is – and this was true long before the rise of fascism – the only country where armed men do not prowl the streets and no one is frightened of the secret police. And the whole British Empire, with all its crying abuses, its stagnation in one place and exploitation in another, at least has the merit of being internally peaceful. It has always been able to get along with a very small number of armed men, although it contains a quarter of the population of the earth. Between the wars its total armed forces amounted to about 600,000 men, of whom a third were Indians. At the outbreak of war the entire Empire was able to mobilise about a million trained men. Almost as many could have been mobilised by, say, Rumania. The English are probably more capable than most peoples of making revolutionary changes without bloodshed. In England, if anywhere, it would be possible to abolish poverty without destroying liberty. If the English took the trouble to make their own democracy work, they would become the political leaders of western Europe, and probably of some other parts of the world as well. They would provide the much-needed alternative to Russian authoritarianism on the one hand and American materialism on the other.

But to play a leading part the English have got to know what they are doing, and they have got to retain their vitality. For this, certain developments are needed within the next decade. These are a rising birthrate, more social equality, less central-isation and more respect for the intellect.

There was a small rise in the birthrate during the war years, but that is probably of no significance, and the general curve is downwards. The position is not quite so desperate as it is sometimes said to be, but it can only be put right if the curve not only rises sharply, but does so within ten or at most twenty years. Otherwise the population will not only fall, but, what is worse, will consist predominantly of middle-aged people. If that point is reached, the decline may never be retrievable.

At bottom, the causes of the dwindled birthrate are eco-nomic. It is nonsense to say that it has happened because English people do not care for children. In the early nineteenth century they had an extremely high birthrate, and they also had an attitude towards children which now seems to us unbeliev-ably callous. With very little public disapproval, children as young as six were sold into the mines and factories, and the death of a child, the most shocking event that modern people are able to imagine, was looked on as a very minor tragedy. In a sense it is true that modern English people have small families because they are too fond of children. They feel that it is wrong to bring a child into the world unless you are completely certain of being able to provide for him, and at a level not lower than your own. For the last fifty years, to have a big family has meant that your children must wear poorer clothes than others in the same group, must have less food and less attention, and probably must go to work earlier. This held good for all classes except the very rich and the unemployed. No doubt the dearth of babies is partly due to the competing attraction of cars and radios, but its main cause is a typically English mixture of snobbishness and altruism.

The philoprogenitive instinct will probably return when fairly large families are already the rule, but the first steps towards this must be economic ones. Half-hearted family allowances will not do the trick, especially when there is a severe housing shortage, as there is now. People should be better off for having children, just as they are in a peasant community, instead of being financially crippled, as they are in ours. Any government, by a few strokes of the pen, could make childlessness as unbearable an economic burden as a big family is now: but no government has chosen to do so, because of the ignorant idea that a bigger population means more unemployed. Far more drastically than anyone has proposed hitherto, taxation will have to be graded so as to encourage child-bearing and to save women with young children from being obliged to work outside the home. And this involves readjustment of rents, better public service in the matter of nursery schools and playing grounds, and the building of bigger and more convenient houses. It also probably involves the extension and improvement of free education, so that the middle-class family shall not, as at present, be crushed out of existence by impossibly high school fees.

The economic adjustments must come first, but a change of outlook is also needed. In the England of the last thirty years it has seemed all too natural that blocks of flats should refuse tenants with children, that parks and squares should be railed off to keep the children out of them, that abortion, theoretically illegal, should be looked on as a peccadillo, and that the main aim of commercial advertising should be to popularise the idea of "having a good time" and staying young as long as possible. Even the cult of animals, fostered by the newspapers, has probably done its bit towards reducing the birthrate. Nor have the public authorities seriously interested themselves in this question till very recently. Britain to-day has a million and a half less children than in 1914, and a million and a half more dogs. Yet even now, when the government designs a prefabricated house, it produces a house with only two bedrooms – with room, that is to say, for two children at the most. When one considers the history of the years between the wars, it is perhaps surprising that the birthrate has not dropped more catastrophically than it has. But it is not likely to rise to the replacement level until those in power, as well as the ordinary people in the street, come to feel that children matter more than money.

The English are probably less irked by class distinctions, more tolerant of privilege and of absurdities like titles, than most peoples. There is nevertheless, as I have pointed out earlier, a growing wish for greater equality and a tendency, below the £2,000 a year level, for surface differences between class and class to disappear. At present this is happening only mechanically and quite largely as a result of the war. The question is how it can be speeded up. For even the change-over to a centralised economy, which, except, possibly, in the United States, is happening in all countries under one name or another, does of itself guarantee greater equality between man and man. Once civilisation has reached a fairly high technical level, class distinctions are an obvious evil. They not only lead great numbers of people to waste their lives in the pursuit of social prestige, but they also cause an immense wastage of talent. In England it is not merely the ownership of property that is concentrated in a few hands. It is also the case that all power, administrative as well as financial, belongs to a single class. Except for a handful of "self-made men" and Labour politicians, those who control our destinies are the product of about a dozen public schools and two universities. A nation is using its capacities to the full when any man can get any job that he is fit for. One has only to think of some of the people who have held vitally important jobs during the past twenty years, and to wonder what would have happened to them if they had been born into the working class, to see that this is not the case in England.

Moreover, class distinctions are a constant drain on morale, in peace as well as in war. And the more conscious, the better educated, the mass of the people become, the more this is so.

The word "They," the universal feeling that "They" hold all the power and make all the decisions, and that "They" can only be influenced in indirect and uncertain ways, is a great handicap in England. In 1940 "They" showed a marked tendency to give place to "We," and it is time that it did so permanently. Three measures are obviously necessary, and they would begin to produce their effect within a few years.

The first is a scaling-up and scaling-down of incomes. The glaring inequality of wealth that existed in England before the war must not be allowed to recur. Above a certain point – which should bear a fixed relation to the lowest current wage – all incomes should be taxed out of existence. In theory, at any rate, this has happened already, with beneficial results. The second necessary measure is greater democracy in education. A completely unified system of education is probably not desirable. Some adolescents benefit by higher education, others do not, there is need to differentiate between literary and technical education, and it is better that a few independent experimental schools should remain in existence. But it should be the rule, as it is in some countries already, for all children to attend the same schools up to the age of twelve or at least ten. After that age it becomes necessary to separate the more gifted children from the less gifted, but a uniform educational system for the early years would cut away one of the deepest roots of snobbery.

The third thing that is needed is to remove the class labels from the English language. It is not desirable that all the local accents should disappear, but there should be a manner of speaking that is definitely national and is not merely (like the accent of the B.B.C. announcers) a copy of the mannerisms of the upper classes. This national accent – a modification of Cockney, perhaps, or of one of the northern accents – should be taught as a matter of course to all children alike. After that they could, and in some parts of the country they probably would, revert to the local accent, but they should be able to speak standard English if they wished to. No one should be "branded on the tongue." It should be impossible, as it is in the United States and some European countries, to determine anyone's status from his accent.

We need, too, to be less centralised. English agriculture revived during the war, and the revival may continue, but the English people are still excessively urban in outlook. Culturally, moreover, the country is very much over-centralised. Not only is the whole of Britain in effect governed from London, but the sense of locality – of being, say, an East Anglian or a West Countryman as well as an Englishman – has been much weakened during the past century. The ambition of the farm labourer is usually to get to a town, the provincial intellectual always wants to get to London. In both Scotland and Wales there are nationalist movements, but they are founded on an economic grievance against England rather than on genuine local pride. Nor is there any important literary or artistic movement that is truly independent of London and the university towns.

It is uncertain whether this centralising tendency is completely reversible, but a good deal could be done to check it. Both Scotland and Wales could and should be a great deal more autonomous than they are at present. The provincial universities should be more generously equipped and the provincial press subsidised. (At present nearly the whole of England is "covered" by eight London newspapers. No newspaper with a large circulation, and no first-class magazine, is published outside London.) The problem of getting people, and especially young, spirited people, to stay on the land would be partly solved if farm labourers had better cottages and if country towns were more civilised and cross-country bus services more efficient. Above all, local pride should be stimulated by teaching in the elementary schools. Every child ought as a matter of course to learn something of the history and topography of its own county. People ought to be proud of their own locality, they ought to feel that its scenery, its architecture and even its cookery are the best in the world. And such feelings, which do exist in some areas of the North but have lapsed throughout the greater part of England, would strengthen national unity rather than weaken it.

It has been suggested earlier that the survival of free speech in England is partly the result of stupidity. The people are not intellectual enough to be heresy-hunters. One does not wish them to grow less tolerant, nor, having seen the results, would one want them to develop the political sophistication that prevailed in pre-Hitler Germany or pre-Pétain France. But the instincts and traditions on which the English rely served them best when they were an exceptionally fortunate people, protected by geography from major disaster. In the twentieth century the narrow interests of the average man, the rather low level of English education, the contempt for "highbrows" and the almost general deadness to æsthetic issues, are serious liabilities.

What the upper classes think about "highbrows" can be judged from the Honours Lists. The upper classes feel titles to be important: yet almost never is any major honour bestowed on anyone describable as an intellectual. With very few exceptions, scientists do not get beyond baronetcies, or literary men beyond knighthoods. But the attitude of the man in the street is no better. He is not troubled by the reflection that England spends hundreds of millions every year on beer and the football pools while scientific research languishes for lack of funds; or that we can afford greyhound tracks innumerable but not even one National Theatre. Between the wars England tolerated newspapers, films, and radio programmes of unheard-of silliness, and these produced further stupefaction in the public, blinding their eyes to vitally important problems. This silliness of the English press is partly artificial, since it arises from the fact that newspapers live off advertisements for consumption goods. During the war the papers grew very much more intelligent without losing their public, and millions of people read papers which they would have rejected as impossibly "highbrow" some years ago. There is, however, not only a low general level of taste, but a widespread unawareness that æsthetic considerations can possibly have any importance. Rehousing and town-planning, for instance, are normally discussed without even a mention of beauty or ugliness. The English are great lovers of flowers, gardening and "nature," but this is merely a part of their vague aspiration towards an agricultural life. In the main they see no objection to "ribbon development" or to the filth and chaos of the industrial towns. They see nothing wrong in scattering the woods with paper bags and filling every pool and stream with tin cans and bicycle frames. And they are all too ready to listen to any journalist who tells them to trust their instincts and despise the "highbrow."

One result of this has been to increase the isolation of the British intelligentsia. English intellectuals, especially the younger ones, are markedly hostile to their own country. Exceptions can, of course, be found, but it is broadly true that anyone who would prefer T. S. Eliot to Alfred Noyes despises England, or thinks that he ought to do so. In "enlightened" circles, to express pro-British sentiments needs considerable moral courage. On the other hand, during the past dozen years there has been a strong tendency to develop a violent nationalistic loyalty to some foreign country, usually Soviet Russia. This must probably have happened in any case, because capitalism in its later phases pushes the literary and even the scientific intellectual into a position where he has security without much responsibility. But the philistinism of the English public alienates the intelligentsia still further. The loss to society is very great. It means that the people whose vision is acutest – the people, for instance, who grasped that Hitler was dangerous ten years before this was discovered by our public men – are hardly able to make contact with the masses and grow less and less interested in English problems.

The English will never develop into a nation of philosophers. They will always prefer instinct to logic, and character to intelligence. But they must get rid of their downright contempt for "cleverness." They cannot afford it any longer. They must grow less tolerant of ugliness, and mentally more adventurous. And they must stop despising foreigners. They are Europeans and ought to be aware of it. On the other hand they have special links with the other English-speakers overseas, and special imperial responsibilities, in which they ought to take more interest than they have done during these past twenty years. The intellectual atmosphere of England is already very much livelier than it was. The war scotched if it did not kill certain kinds of folly. But there is still need for a conscious effort at national re-education. The first step towards this is an improvement in elementary education, which involves not only raising the school-leaving age but spending enough money to ensure that elementary schools are adequately staffed and equipped. And there are immense educational possibilities in the radio, the film, and – if it could be freed once and for all from commercial interests – the press.

These, then, appear to be the immediate necessities of the English people. They must breed faster, work harder, and probably live more simply, think more deeply, get rid of their snobbishness and their anachronistic class distinctions, and pay more attention to the world and less to their own backyards. Nearly all of them already love their country, but they must learn to love it intelligently. They must have a clear notion of their own destiny and not listen either to those who tell them that England is finished or to those who tell them that the England of the past can return.

If they can do that they can keep their feet in the post-war world, and if they can keep their feet they can give the example that millions of human beings are waiting for. The world is sick of chaos and it is sick of dictatorship. Of all peoples the English are likeliest to find a way of avoiding both. Except for a small minority they are fully ready for the drastic economic changes that are needed, and at the same time they have no desire either for violent revolution or for foreign conquests. They have known for forty years, perhaps, something that the Germans and the Japanese have only recently learned, and that the Russians and the Americans have yet to learn: they know that it is not possible for any one nation to rule the earth. They want above all things to live at peace, internally and externally. And the great mass of them are probably prepared for the sacrifices that peace entails.

But they will have to take their destiny into their own hands. England can only fulfil its special mission if the ordinary English in the street can somehow get their hands on power. We were told very frequently during the war years that this time, when the danger was over, there should be no lost opportunities, no recurrence of the past. No more stagnation punctuated by wars, no more Rolls-Royces gliding past dole queues, no return to the England of the Distressed Area, the endlessly stewing teapot, the empty pram, and the Giant Panda. We cannot be sure that this promise will be kept. Only we ourselves can make certain that it will come true, and if we do not, no further chance may be given to us. The past thirty years have been a long series of cheques drawn upon the accumulated good will of the English people. That reserve may not be inexhaustible. By the end of another decade it will be finally clear whether England is to survive as a great nation or not. And if the answer is to be "Yes," it is the common people who must make it so.

As I Please 26

Tribune, 26 May 1944

I was talking the other day to a young American soldier, who told me – as quite a number of others have done – that anti-British feeling is completely general in the American army. He had only recently landed in this country, and as he came off the boat he asked the Military Policeman on the dock, "How's England?"

"The girls here walk out with niggers," answered the M.P. "They call them American Indians."

That was the salient fact about England, from the M.P.'s point of view. At the same time my friend told me that anti-British feeling is not violent and there is no very clearly-defined cause of complaint. A good deal of it is probably a rationalisation of the discomfort most people feel at being away from home. But the whole subject of anti-British feeling in the United States badly needs investigation. Like anti-semitism, it is given a whole series of contradictory explanations, and again like anti-semitism, it is probably a psychological substitute for something else. *What* else is the question that needs investigating.

Meanwhile, there is one department of Anglo-American relations that seems to be going well. It was announced some months ago that no less than 20,000 English girls had already married American soldiers and sailors, and the number will have increased since. Some of these girls are being educated for their life in a new country at the "Schools for Brides of U.S. Servicemen" organised by the American Red Cross. Here they are taught practical details about American manners, customs and traditions – and also, perhaps, cured of the widespread illusion that every American owns a motor car and every American house contains a bathroom, a refrigerator and an electric washing-machine.

The May number of the *Matrimonial Post and Fashionable Marriage Advertiser* contains advertisements from 191 men seeking brides and over 200 women seeking husbands. Advertisements of this type have been running in a whole series of magazines since the 'sixties or earlier, and they are nearly always very much alike. For example:

"Bachelor, age 25, height 6 ft. 1 in., slim, fond of horticulture, animals, children, cinema, etc., would like to meet lady, age 27 to 35, with love of flowers, nature, children, must be tall, medium build, Church of Fngland."

The general run of them are just like that, though occasionally a more unusual note is struck. For instance:

"I'm 29, single, 5 ft. 10 in., English, large build, kind, quiet, varied intellectual interests, firm moral background (registered unconditionally as absolute C.O.), progressive, creative, literary inclinations. A dealer in rare stamps, income variable but quite adequate. Strong swimmer, cyclist, slight stammer occasionally. Looking for the following rarity, amiable, adaptable, educated girl, easy on eye and ear, under 30, Secretary type or similar, mentally adventurous, immune to mercenary and social incentives, bright sense of genuine humour, a reliable working partner. Capital unimportant, character vital."

The thing that is and always has been striking in these advertisements is that nearly all the applicants are remarkably eligible. It is not only that most of them are broad-minded, intelligent, home-loving, musical, loyal, sincere and affectionate, with a keen sense of humour and, in the case of women, a good figure; in the majority of cases they are financially O.K. as well. When you consider how fatally easy it is to get married, you would not imagine that a 36-year-old bachelor, "dark hair, fair complexion, slim build, height 6 ft., well educated and of considerate, jolly and intelligent disposition, income £1,000 per annum and capital," would need to find himself a bride through the columns of a newspaper. And ditto with "Adventurous young woman, Left-wing opinions, modern outlook" with "fairly full but shapely figure, medium colour curly hair, grey-blue eyes, fair skin, natural colouring, health exceptionally good, interested in music, art, literature, cinema, theatre, fond of walking, cycling, tennis, skating and rowing." Why does such a paragon have to advertise?

It should be noted that the *Matrimonial Post* is entirely above-board and checks up carefully on its advertisers.

What these things really demonstrate is the atrocious loneliness of people living in big towns. People meet for work and then scatter to widely separated homes. Anywhere in inner London it is probably exceptional to know even the names of the people who live next door.

Years ago I lodged for a while in the Portobello Road. This is hardly a fashionable quarter, but the landlady had been lady's maid to some woman of title and had a good opinion of herself. One day something went wrong with the front door and my landlady, her husband and myself were all locked out of the house. It was evident that we should have to get in by an upper window, and as there was a jobbing builder next door I suggested borrowing a ladder from him. My landlady looked somewhat uncomfortable.

"I wouldn't like to do that," she said finally. "You see we don't know him. We've been here fourteen years, and we've always taken care not to know the people on either side of us. It *wouldn't do*, not in a neighbourhood like this. If you once begin talking to them they get familiar, you see."

So we had to borrow a ladder from a relative of her husband's, and carry it nearly a mile with great labour and discomfort.

Benefit of Clergy: Some Notes on Salvador Dali
Intended for *Saturday Book*, 4, 1944

Autobiography is only to be trusted when it reveals something disgraceful. A man who gives a good account of himself is probably lying, since any life when viewed from the inside is simply a series of defeats. However, even the most flagrantly dishonest book (Frank Harris's autobiographical writings are an example) can without intending it give a true picture of its author. Dali's recently-published *Life* comes under this heading. Some of the incidents in it are flatly incredible, others have been re-arranged and romanticised, and not merely the humiliation but the persistent *ordinariness* of everyday life has been cut out. Dali is even by his own diagnosis narcissistic, and his autobiography is simply a strip-tease act conducted in pink limelight. But as a record of fantasy, of the perversion of instinct that has been made possible by the machine age, it has great value.

Here then are some of the episodes in Dali's life, from his earliest years onward. Which of them are true and which are imaginary hardly matters: the point is that this is the kind of thing that Dali would have *liked* to do.

When he is six years old there is some excitement over the appearance of Halley's comet:

'Suddenly one of my father's office clerks appeared in the drawing-room doorway and announced that the comet could be seen from the terrace. . . . While crossing the hall I caught sight of my little three-year-old sister crawling unobtrusively through a doorway. I stopped, hesitated a second, then gave her a terrible kick in the head as though it had been a ball, and continued running carried away with a "delirious joy" induced by this savage act. But my father, who was behind me, caught me and led me down into his office, where I remained as a punishment till dinner time.'

A year earlier than this Dali had 'suddenly, as most of my ideas occur' flung another little boy off a suspension bridge. Several other incidents of the same kind are recorded, including (this was when he was twenty-nine years old) knocking down and trampling on a girl 'until they had to tear her, bleeding, out of my reach.'

When he is about five he gets hold of a wounded bat which he puts into a tin pail. Next morning he finds that the bat is almost dead and is covered with ants which are devouring it. He puts it in his mouth, ants and all, and bites it almost in half.

When he is adolescent a girl falls desperately in love with him. He kisses and caresses her so as to excite her as much as possible, but refuses to go further. He resolves to keep this up for five years (he calls it his 'five year plan'), enjoying her humiliation and the sense of power it gives him. He frequently tells her that at the end of five years he will desert her, and when the time comes he does so.

Till well into adult life he keeps up the practice of masturbation, and likes to do this, apparently, in front of a looking-glass. For ordinary purposes he is impotent, it appears, till the age of thirty or so. When he first meets his future wife, Gala, he is greatly tempted to push her off a precipice. He is aware that there is something that she wants him to do to her, and after their first kiss the confession is made:

'I threw back Gala's head, pulling it by the hair, and, trembling with complete hysteria, I commanded,
'"Now tell me what you want me to do with you! But tell me slowly, looking me in the eye, with the crudest, the most ferociously erotic words that can make both of us feel the greatest shame!"
'... Then, Gala, transforming the last glimmer of her expression of pleasure into the hard light of her own tyranny, answered,
'"I want you to kill me!"'

He is somewhat disappointed by this demand, since it is merely what he wanted to do already. He contemplates throwing her off the bell-tower of the Cathedral of Toledo, but refrains from doing so.

During the Spanish civil war he astutely avoids taking sides and makes a trip to Italy. He feels himself more and more drawn towards the aristocracy, frequents smart salons, finds himself wealthy patrons, and is photographed with the plump Vicomte de Noailles, whom he describes as his 'Maecenas.' When the European war approaches he has one preoccupation only: how to find a place which has good cookery and from which he can make a quick bolt if danger comes too near. He fixes on Bordeaux, and duly flees to Spain during the Battle of France. He stays in Spain long enough to pick up a few anti-red atrocity stories, then makes for America. The story ends in a blaze of respectability. Dali, at thirty-seven, has become a devoted husband, is cured of his aberrations, or some of them, and is completely reconciled to the Catholic Church. He is also, one gathers, making a good deal of money.

However, he has by no means ceased to take pride in the pictures of his Surrealist period, with titles like *The Great Masturbator, Sodomy of a Skull with a Grand Piano*, etc. There are reproductions of these all the way through the book. Many of Dali's drawings are simply representational and have a characteristic to be noted later. But from his Surrealist paintings and photographs the two things that stand out are sexual perversity and necrophilia. Sexual objects and symbols – some of them well-known, like our old friend the high-heeled slipper, others, like the crutch and the cup of warm milk, patented by Dali himself – recur over and over again, and there is a fairly well-marked excretory motif as well. In his painting *Le Jeu Lugubre*, he says, 'the drawers bespattered with excrement were painted with such minute and realistic complacency that the whole little surrealist group was anguished by the question: Is he coprophagic or not?' Dali adds firmly that he is *not*, and that he regards this aberration as 'repulsive,' but it seems to be only at that point that his interest in excrement stops. Even when he recounts the experience of watching a woman urinate standing up, he has to add the detail that she misses her aim and dirties her shoes. It is not given to any one person to have all the vices, and Dali also boasts that he is not homosexual, but otherwise he seems to have as good an outfit of perversions as anyone could wish for.

However, his most notable characteristic is his necrophilia. He himself freely admits to this, and claims to have been cured of it. Dead faces, skulls, corpses of animals occur fairly frequently in his pictures, and the ants which devoured the dying bat make countless reappearances. One photograph shows an exhumed corpse, far gone in decomposition. Another shows the dead donkeys putrefying on top of grand pianos which formed part of the Surrealist film *Le Chien Andalou*. Dali still looks back on these donkeys with great enthusiasm:

'I "made up" the putrefaction of the donkeys with great pots of sticky glue which I poured over them. Also I emptied their eye sockets and made them larger by hacking them out with scissors. In the same way I furiously cut their mouths open to make the white rows of their teeth show to better advantage, and I added several jaws to each mouth so that it would appear that although the donkeys were already rotting they were vomiting up a little more of their own death, above those other rows of teeth formed by the keys of the black pianos.'

And finally there is the picture – apparently some kind of faked photograph – of 'Mannequin rotting in a taxicab.' Over the already somewhat bloated face and breast of the apparently dead girl, huge snails are crawling. In the caption below the picture Dali notes that these are Burgundy snails – that is, the edible kind.

Of course, in this long book of 400 quarto pages there is more than I have indicated, but I do not think that I have given an unfair account of its moral atmosphere and mental scenery. It is a book that stinks. If it were possible for a book to give a physical stink off its pages, this one would – a thought that might please Dali, who before wooing his future wife for the first time rubbed himself all over with an ointment made of goat's dung boiled up in fish glue. But against this has to be set the fact that Dali is a draughtsman of very exceptional gifts. He is also, to judge by the minuteness and the sureness of his drawings, a very hard worker. He is an exhibitionist and a careerist, but he is not a fraud. He has fifty times more talent than most of the people who would denounce his morals and jeer at his paintings. And these two sets of facts, taken together, raise a question which for lack of any basis of agreement seldom gets a real discussion.

The point is that you have here a direct, unmistakable assault on sanity and decency: and even – since some of Dali's pictures would tend to poison the imagination like a pornographic postcard – on life itself. What Dali has done and what he has imagined is debatable, but in his outlook, his character, the bedrock decency of a human being does not exist. He is as antisocial as a flea. Clearly, such people are undesirable, and a society in which they can flourish has something wrong with it.

Now, if you showed this book, with its illustrations, to Lord Elton, to Mr Alfred Noyes, to *The Times* leader-writers who exult over the 'eclipse of the highbrow,' in fact to any 'sensible' art-hating English person, it is easy to imagine what kind of response you would get. They would flatly refuse to see any merit in Dali whatever. Such people are not only unable to admit that what is morally degraded can be aesthetically right, but their real demand of every artist is that he shall pat them on the back and tell them that thought is unnecessary. And they can be especially dangerous at a time like the present, when the Ministry of Information and the British Council put power into their hands. For their impulse is not only to crush every new talent as it appears, but to castrate the past as well. Witness the renewed highbrow-baiting that is now going on in this country and America, with its outcry not only against Joyce, Proust, and Lawrence, but even against T. S. Eliot.

But if you talk to the kind of person who *can* see Dali's merits, the response that you get is not as a rule very much better. If you say that Dali, though a brilliant draughtsman, is a dirty little scoundrel, you are looked upon as a savage. If you say that you don't like rotting corpses, and that people who do like rotting corpses are mentally diseased, it is assumed that you lack the aesthetic sense. Since 'Mannequin rotting in a taxicab' is a good composition (as it undoubtedly is), it cannot be a disgusting, degrading picture: whereas Noyes, Elton, etc., would tell you that because it is disgusting it cannot be a good composition. And between these two fallacies there is no middle position: or rather, there is a middle position, but we seldom hear much about it. On the one side, *Kulturbolschevismus*: on the other (though the phrase itself is out of fashion) 'Art for Art's sake.' Obscenity is a very difficult question to discuss honestly. People are too frightened either of seeming to be shocked, or of seeming not to be shocked, to be able to define the relationship between art and morals.

It will be seen that what the defenders of Dali are claiming is a kind of *benefit of clergy*. The artist is to be exempt from the moral laws that are binding on ordinary people. Just pronounce the magic word 'Art,' and everthing is O.K. Rotting corpses with snails crawling over them are O.K.; kicking little girls on the head is O.K.; even a film like *L'Age d'Or* is O.K. It is also O.K. that Dali should batten on France for years and then scuttle off like a rat as soon as France is in danger. So long as you can paint well enough to pass the test, all shall be forgiven you.

One can see how false this is if one extends it to cover ordinary crime. In an age like our own, when the artist is an altogether exceptional person, he must be allowed a certain amount of irresponsibility, just as a pregnant woman is. Still, no one would say that a pregnant woman should be allowed to commit murder, nor would anyone make such a claim for the artist, however gifted. If Shakespeare returned to the earth tomorrow, and if it were found that his favourite recreation was raping little girls in railway carriages, we should not tell him to go ahead with it on the ground that he might write another *King Lear*. And after all, the worst crimes are not always the punishable ones. By encouraging necrophilic reveries one probably does quite as much harm as by, say, picking pockets at the races. One ought to be able to hold in one's head simultaneously the two facts that Dali is a good draughtsman and a disgusting human being. The one does not invalidate or, in a sense, affect the other. The first thing that we demand of a wall is that it shall stand up. If it stands up it is a good wall, and the question of what purpose it serves is separable from that. And yet even the best wall in the world deserves to be pulled down if it surrounds a concentration camp. In the same way it should be possible to say, 'This is a good book or a good picture, and it ought to be burned by the public hangman.' Unless one can say that, at least in imagination, one is shirking the implications of the fact that an artist is also a citizen and a human being.

Not, of course, that Dali's autobiography, or his pictures, ought to be suppressed. Short of the dirty postcards that used to be sold in Mediterranean seaport towns, it is doubtful policy to suppress anything, and Dali's fantasies probably cast useful light on the decay of capitalist civilisation. But what he clearly needs is diagnosis. The question is not so much *what* he is as *why* he is like that. It ought not to be in doubt that he is a diseased intelligence, probably not much altered by his alleged conversion, since genuine penitents, or people who have returned to sanity, do not flaunt their past vices in that complacent way. He is a symptom of the world's illness. The important thing is not to denounce him as a cad who ought to be horsewhipped, or to defend him as a genius who ought not to be questioned, but to find out *why* he exhibits that particular set of aberrations.

The answer is probably discoverable in his pictures, and those I myself am not competent to examine. But I can point to one clue which perhaps takes one part of the distance. This is the old-fashioned, over-ornate, Edwardian style of drawing to which Dali tends to return when he is not being Surrealist. Some of Dali's drawings are reminiscent of Dürer, one seems to show the influence of Beardsley, another seems to borrow something from Blake. But the most persistent strain is the Edwardian one. When I opened this book for the first time and looked at its innumerable marginal illustrations, I was haunted by a resemblance which I could not immediately pin down. I fetched up at the ornamental candlestick at the beginning of Part I. What did this thing remind me of? Finally I tracked it down. It reminded me of a large, vulgar, expensively got-up edition of Anatole France (in translation) which must have been published about 1913. That had ornamental chapter headings and tailpieces after this style. Dali's candlestick displays at one end a curly fish-like creature that looks curiously familiar (it seems to be based on the conventional dolphin), and at the other is the burning candle. This candle, which recurs in one picture after another, is a very old friend. You will find it, with the same picturesque gouts of wax arranged on its sides, in those phoney electric lights done up as candlesticks which are popular in sham-Tudor country hotels. This candle, and the design beneath it, convey at once an intense feeling of sentimentality. As though to counteract this Dali has spattered a quill-ful of ink all over the page, but without avail. The same impression keeps popping up on page after page. The design at the bottom of page 62, for instance, would nearly go into *Peter Pan*. The figure on page 224, in spite of having her cranium elongated into an immense sausage-like shape, is the witch of the fairy-tale books. The horse on page 234 and the unicorn on page 218 might be illustrations to James Branch Cabell. The rather pansified drawings of youths on pages 97, 100, and elsewhere convey the same impression. Picturesqueness keeps breaking in. Take away the skulls, ants, lobsters, telephones, and other paraphernalia, and every now and again you are back in the world of Barrie, Rackham, Dunsany and *Where the Rainbow Ends*.

Curiously enough, some of the naughty-naughty touches in Dali's autobiography tie up with the same period. When I read the passage I quoted at the beginning, about the kicking of the little sister's head, I was aware of another phantom resemblance. What was it? Of course! *Ruthless Rhymes for Heartless Homes* by Harry Graham. Such rhymes were very popular round about 1912, and one that ran:

> *Poor little Willy is crying so sore,*
> *A sad little boy is he,*
> *For he's broken his little sister's neck*
> *And he'll have no jam for tea.*

might almost have been founded on Dali's anecdote. Dali, of course, is aware of his Edwardian leanings, and makes capital out of them, more or less in a spirit of pastiche. He professes an especial affection for the year 1900, and claims that every ornamental object of 1900 is full of mystery, poetry, eroticism, madness, perversity, etc. Pastiche, however, usually implies a real affection for the thing parodied. It seems to be, if not the rule, at any rate distinctly common for an intellectual bent to be accompanied by a non-rational, even childish urge in the same direction. A sculptor, for instance, is interested in planes and curves, but he is also a person who enjoys the physical act of mucking about with clay or stone. An engineer is a person who enjoys the feel of tools, the noise of dynamos and the smell of oil. A psychiatrist usually has a leaning towards some sexual aberration himself. Darwin became a biologist partly because he was a country gentleman and fond of animals. It may be, therefore, that Dali's seemingly perverse cult of Edwardian things (for example his 'discovery of the 1900 subway entrances') is merely the symptom of a much deeper, less conscious affection. The innumerable, beautifully executed copies of textbook illustrations, solemnly labelled 'le rossignol,' 'une montre' and so on, which he scatters all over his margins, may be meant partly as a joke. The little boy in knickerbockers playing with a diabolo on page 103 is a perfect period piece. But perhaps these things are also there because Dali can't help drawing that kind of thing, because it is to that period and that style of drawing that he really belongs.

If so, his aberrations are partly explicable. Perhaps they are a way of assuring himself that he is not commonplace. The two qualities that Dali unquestionably possesses are a gift for drawing and an atrocious egoism. 'At seven,' he says in the first paragraph of his book, 'I wanted to be Napoleon. And my ambition has been growing steadily ever since.' This is worded in a deliberately startling way, but no doubt it is substantially true. Such feelings are common enough. 'I knew I was a genius,' somebody once said to me, 'long before I knew what I was going to be a genius *about*.' And suppose that you have nothing in you except your egoism and a dexterity that goes no higher than the elbow: suppose that your real gift is for a detailed, academic, representational style of drawing, your real *métier* to be an illustrator of scientific textbooks. How then do you become Napoleon?

There is always one escape: *into wickedness*. Always do the thing that will shock and wound people. At five, throw a little boy off a bridge, strike an old doctor across the face with a whip and break his spectacles – or, at any rate, dream about doing such things. Twenty years later, gouge the eyes out of dead donkeys with a pair of scissors. Along those lines you can always feel yourself original. And after all, it pays! It is much less dangerous than crime. Making all allowance for the probable suppressions in Dali's autobiography, it is clear that he has not had to suffer for his eccentricities as he would have done in an earlier age. He grew up into the corrupt world of the nineteen-twenties, when sophistication was immensely widespread and every European capital swarmed with aristocrats and rentiers who had given up sport and politics and taken to patronising the arts. If you threw dead donkeys at people they threw money back. A phobia for grasshoppers – which a few decades back would merely have provoked a snigger – was now an interesting 'complex' which could be profitably exploited. And when that particular world collapsed before the German Army, America was waiting. You could even top it all up with religious conversion, moving at one hop and without a shadow of repentance from the fashionable salons of Paris to Abraham's bosom.

That, perhaps, is the essential outline of Dali's history. But why his aberrations should be the particular ones they were, and why it should be so easy to 'sell' such horrors as rotting corpses to a sophisticated public – those are questions for the psychologist and the sociological critic. Marxist criticism has a short way with such phenomena as Surrealism. They are 'bourgeois decadence' (much play is made with the phrases 'corpse poisons' and 'decaying rentier class'), and that is that. But though this probably states a fact, it does not establish a connection. One would still like to know *why* Dali's leaning was towards necrophilia (and not, say, homosexuality), and *why* the rentiers and the aristocrats should buy his pictures instead of hunting and making love like their grandfathers. Mere moral disapproval does not get one any further. But neither ought one to pretend, in the name of 'detachment,' that such pictures as 'Mannequin rotting in a taxicab' are morally neutral. They are diseased and disgusting, and any investigation ought to start out from that fact.

Are Books Too Dear?

Manchester Evening News, 1 June 1944

The decision of Mr. H. G. Wells to publish his recent book " '42 to '44," in a limited edition at the stiff price of two guineas has set many people talking about the expensiveness of books, and whether it is necessary or justifiable. The subject is an extremely important one, but before discussing it it is perhaps worth mentioning in passing that the price of this particular book was not a financial "stunt" on Mr. Wells's part. Even if he took half the receipts he would only get about £1,000, which is not a great deal for so well-known a writer. He would have made about as much from a sale of 10,000 copies at a normal price.

In any discussion of the price of books one must take two propositions as axiomatic. One is that the more the public reads – provided that it is not reading sheer trash – the better. The other is that it is undesirable that writers should starve to death. And it is important to realise that they *would* starve, or at least would have to find other means of support, if cheap books were the rule instead of the exception.

In peace time the average book – a novel, say – is published at seven and sixpence. That is the price on the jacket, but the wholesale price is five shillings: if it is sold in a shop the bookseller takes half a crown. Out of that seven and sixpence the author's share is usually in the neighbourhood of a shilling. This means that he gets £50 (but in practice it is always less than £50, because of agents' fees and the like) on each 1,000 copies sold. Few novelists are capable of turning out more than one book a year, so that to make the very modest income of £250 a year one has to sell at least 5,000 copies of each book. And authors who are not "established" don't as a rule sell 5,000 copies: it is quite common for a writer's first book to sell only six or seven hundred.

It will be seen that from the author's point of view seven and sixpence is none too high a price. It *is* high, however, from the point of view of the public, especially as English books are on the whole none too well bound and extremely ugly to look at. And so general is the feeling that books are too expensive that many people are in the habit of proclaiming (usually with a certain air of pride) that they "never buy a book." This, however, is a delusion. Everyone who reads does buy books, indirectly, by means of library subscriptions.

If you take only one book a week out of a twopenny library you are paying for at least one new book a year, and a fraction of what you pay to the rates also goes on books for the public library. It is, in fact, the libraries and not the book-buying public that keeps the writer and publisher alive.

But while cheapness in new books is not desirable, there is an obvious need for cheap reprints. England has always been fairly well supplied with cheap reprints of "classics" (the Everyman Library, the World's Classics, etc.), but in 1935 John Lane tried, with the Penguin books, the seemingly unhopeful experiment of reprinting contemporary books at the very low price of sixpence.

Earlier attempts to do this had usually failed. The Penguin books were an instant success, partly because by 1935 the reading public had greatly expanded, partly because Lane's had the imagination to choose their books well and to produce them with legible print and an attractive cover.

The success of the Penguins has led innumerable people to say: "If they can produce a book as well as this for sixpence, why should one normally have to pay 15 times as much? Why shouldn't new books as well as old ones come out in sixpenny form?"

The answer is that this *would* be possible, but only at the price of robbing the writer of his independent status. If all books were sixpence (or, as in wartime, ninepence) each, there would never be enough of them sold to give writers a livelihood.

Books, like any other kind of merchandise, have their saturation point. If you are a person who normally spends £10 a year on books, you may, perhaps, get 30 new books for your money. If you laid it all out in Penguins you would get 400 – and after all, who wants to buy 400 books every year?

In all probability you would spend, say, £2 on books and keep the rest for gramophone records. Meanwhile the writer could not keep alive, for whereas he gets about a shilling on each copy of a seven and sixpenny book, he gets only a farthing on a Penguin. Most Penguins bring their authors only £50, and £100 is a maximum. And though it is true that some books take only a couple of months to write, between six months and a year would be an average time.

In pre-war France, as in most European countries, books were very cheap. A new book usually cost about 1s. 6d. or 2s., and as the library system was not so well developed as it is here, a book was considered to have done well if it sold 2,000 copies. The result was that only a very small number of writers could live by books alone. The others had to live off government grants and literary prizes, with all the racketeering that that implies, or by selling themselves as publicists to some political party. In totalitarian countries the writer's economic problem is solved, but only by turning him into a mouthpiece of the regime, to the destruction of his creative powers as well as his honesty.

Our literature over the past 20 years has had very grave faults, but these have not arisen from the writer's economic status. Writers have had greater freedom of expression than ever before, and at the same time they have been answerable to the general public rather than to a "patron" or the State. This can only happen so long as royalties are fairly high, and books, therefore, fairly expensive. Moreover, if books are very cheap it is impossible to produce them in great variety. A 6d. book does not pay unless it sells in scores of thousands, so that all-round cheapness in books would inevitably mean that fewer titles were produced and fewer new writers got a chance.

There is admittedly racketeering over certain books that possess snob appeal, but in general there is no case for reducing the price of *new* books. On the other hand we do deserve better selections of cheap reprints. It is a disgraceful thing that – to name only one instance – you cannot get the complete unabridged works of Swift without paying several pounds for them.

And since our books are expensive, they ought to be (and easily could be) better physical objects. They ought to be as durable as American books and as pleasant to look at as French ones.

But seven and sixpence, or in war time half a guinea, is not an unreasonable price for a book. It enables the writer to stay alive and to preserve fragments of his honesty. And after all, even with books at seven and sixpence you can take half a dozen of them out of the library for a shilling. In what other department of life will a shilling buy so much?

As I Please 27
Tribune, 2 June 1944

An extract from the Italian radio, about the middle of 1942, describing life in London:

> "Five shillings were given for one egg yesterday, and one pound sterling for a kilogram of potatoes. Rice has disappeared, even from the Black Market, and peas have become the prerogative of millionaires. There is no sugar on the market, although small quantities are still to be found at prohibitive prices."

One day there will be a big, careful, scientific enquiry into the extent to which propaganda is believed. For instance, what is the effect of an item like the one above, which is fairly typical of the Fascist radio? Any Italian who took it seriously would have to assume that Britain was due to collapse within a few weeks. When the collapse failed to happen, one would expect him to lose confidence in the authorities who had deceived him. But it is not certain that that is the reaction. For quite long periods, at any rate, people can remain undisturbed by obvious lies, either because they simply forget what is said from day to day or because they are under such a constant propaganda bombardment that they become anaesthetised to the whole business.

It seems clear that it pays to tell the truth when things are going badly, but it is by no means certain that it pays to be consistent in your propaganda. British propaganda is a good deal hampered by its efforts not to be self-contradictory. It is almost impossible, for instance, to discuss the colour question in a way that will please both the Boers and the Indians. The Germans are not troubled by a little thing like that. They just tell everyone what they think he will want to hear, assuming, probably rightly, that no one is interested in anyone else's problems. On occasion their various radio stations have even attacked one another.

One which aimed at middle-class Fascists used sometimes to warn its listeners against the pseudo-left Worker's Challenge, on the ground that the latter was "financed by Moscow."

Another thing that that enquiry, if it ever takes place, will have to deal with is the magical properties of names. Nearly all human beings feel that a thing becomes different if you call it by a different name. Thus when the Spanish civil war broke out the B.B.C. produced the name "Insurgents" for Franco's followers. This covered the fact that they were rebels while making rebellion sound respectable. During the Abyssinian war Haile Sellassie was called the Emperor by his friends and the Negus by his enemies. Catholics strongly resent being called Roman Catholics. The Trotskyists call themselves Bolshevik-Leninists but are refused this name by their opponents. Countries which have liberated themselves from a foreign conqueror or gone through a nationalist revolution almost invariably change their names, and some countries have a whole series of names, each with a different implication. Thus the U.S.S.R. is called Russia or U.S.S.R. (neutral or for short), Soviet Russia (friendly) and Soviet Union (very friendly). And it is a curious fact that of the six names by which our own country is called, the only one that does not tread on somebody or other's toes is the archaic and slightly ridiculous name "Albion."

Wading through the entries for the Short Story Competition, I was struck once again by the disability that English short stories suffer under in being all cut to a uniform length. The great short stories of the past are of all lengths from perhaps 1,500 words to 20,000. Most of Maupassant's stories, for instance, are very short, but his two masterpieces, *Boule de Suif* and *La Maison de Madame Tellier*, are decidedly long. Poe's stories vary similarly. D. H. Lawrence's *England, My England*, Joyce's *The Dead*, Conrad's *Youth*, and many stories by Henry James, would probably be considered too long for any modern English periodical. So, certainly, would a story like Mérimée's *Carmen*. This belongs to the class of "long short" stories which have almost died out in this country, because there is no place for them. They are too long for the magazines and too short to be published as books. You can, of course, publish a book containing several short stories, but this is not often done because at normal times these books never sell.

It would almost certainly help to rehabilitate the short story if we could get back to the bulky nineteenth-century magazine, which had room in it for stories of almost any length. But the trouble is that in modern England monthly and quarterly magazines of any intellectual pretensions don't pay. Even the *Criterion*, perhaps the best literary paper we have ever had, lost money for sixteen years before expiring.

Why? Because people were not willing to fork out the seven and sixpence that it cost. People won't pay that much for a mere magazine. But why then will they pay the same sum for a novel, which is no bulkier than the *Criterion*, and much less worth keeping? Because they don't pay for the novel directly. The average person never buys a new book, except perhaps a Penguin. But he does, without knowing it, buy quite a lot of books by paying twopences into lending libraries. If you could take a literary magazine out of the library just as you take a book, these magazines would become commercial propositions and would be able to enlarge their bulk as well as paying their contributors better. It is book-borrowing and not book-buying that keeps authors and publishers alive, and there seems no good reason why the lending library system should not be extended to magazines. Restore the monthly magazine – or make the weekly paper about a quarter of an inch fatter – and you might be able to restore the short story. And incidentally the book-review, which for lack of elbow room has dwindled to a perfunctory summary, might become a work of art again, as it was in the days of the *Edinburgh* and the *Quarterly*.

After reading the *Matrimonial Times* last week I looked in the Penguin *Herodotus* for a passage I vaguely remembered about the marriage customs of the Babylonians. Here it is:

> Once a year in each village the maidens of an age to marry were collected altogether into one place, while the men stood round them in a circle. Then a herald called up the damsels one by one and offered them for sale. He began with the most beautiful. When she was sold for no small sum of money, he offered for sale the one who came next to her in beauty . . . The custom was that when the herald had gone through the whole number of the beautiful damsels, he should then call up the ugliest and offer her to the men, asking who would agree to take her with the smallest marriage portion. And the man who offered to take the smallest sum had her assigned to him. The marriage portions were furnished by the money paid for the beautiful damsels, and thus the fairer maidens portioned out the uglier.

This custom seems to have worked very well and Herodotus is full of enthusiasm for it. He adds, however, that, like other good customs, it was already going out round about 450 B.C.

As I Please 28
Tribune, 9 June 1944

Arthur Koestler's recent article in *Tribune* set me wondering whether the book racket will start up again in its old vigour after the war, when paper is plentiful and there are other things to spend your money on.

Publishers have got to live, like anyone else, and you cannot blame them for advertising their wares, but the truly shameful feature of literary life before the war was the blurring of the distinction between advertisement and criticism. A number of the so-called reviewers, and especially the best known ones, were simply blurb writers. The "screaming" advertisement started some time in the nineteen-twenties, and as the competition to take up as much space and use as many superlatives as possible became fiercer, publishers' advertisements grew to be an important source of revenue to a number of papers. The literary pages of several well-known papers were practically owned by a handful of publishers, who had their quislings planted in all the important jobs. These wretches churned forth their praise – "masterpiece," "brilliant," "unforgettable" and so forth – like so many mechanical pianos. A book coming from the right publishers could be absolutely certain not only of favourable reviews, but of being placed on the "recommended" list which industrious book-borrowers would cut out and take to the library the next day.

If you published books at several different houses you soon learned how strong the pressure of advertisement was. A book coming from a big publisher, who habitually spent large sums on advertisement, might get fifty or seventy-five reviews: a book from a small publisher might get only twenty. I knew of one case where a theological publisher, for some reason, took it into his head to publish a novel. He spent a great deal of money on advertising it. It got exactly four reviews in the whole of England, and the only full-length one was in a motoring paper, which seized the opportunity to point out that the part of the country described in the novel would be a good place for a motoring tour. This man was not in the racket, his advertisements were not likely to become a regular source of revenue to the literary papers, and so they just ignored him.

Even reputable literary papers could not afford to disregard their advertisers altogether. It was quite usual to send a book to a reviewer with some such formula as, "Review this book if it seems any good. If not, send it back. We don't think it's worth while to print simply damning reviews."

Naturally, a person to whom the guinea or so that he gets for the review means next week's rent is not going to send the book back. He can be counted on to find something to praise, whatever his private opinion of the book may be.

In America even the pretence that hack-reviewers read the books they are paid to criticise has been partially abandoned. Publishers, or some publishers, send out with review copies a short synopsis telling the reviewer what to say. Once, in the case of a novel of my own, they misspelt the name of one of the characters. The same misspelling turned up in review after review. The so-called critics had not even glanced into the book – which, nevertheless, most of them were boosting to the skies.

A phrase much used in political circles in this country is "playing into the hands of." It is a sort of charm or incantation to silence uncomfortable truths. When you are told that by saying this, that or the other you are "playing into the hands of" some sinister enemy, you know that it is your duty to shut up immediately.

For example, if you say anything damaging about British imperialism, you are playing into the hands of Dr. Goebbels. If you criticise Stalin you are playing into the hands of the *Tablet* and the *Daily Telegraph*. If you criticise Chiang-Kai-Shek you are playing into the hands of Wang Ching Wei – and so on, indefinitely.

Objectively this charge is often true. It is always difficult to attack one party to a dispute without temporarily helping the other. Some of Gandhi's remarks have been very useful to the Japanese. The extreme Tories will seize on anything anti-Russian, and don't necessarily mind if it comes from Trotskyist instead of right-wing sources. The American imperialists, advancing to the attack behind a smoke-screen of novelists, are always on the look-out for any disreputable detail about the British Empire. And if you write anything truthful about the London slums, you are liable to hear it repeated on the Nazi radio a week later. But what, then, are you expected to do? Pretend there are no slums?

Everyone who has ever had anything to do with publicity or propaganda can think of occasions when he was urged to tell lies about some vitally important matter, because to tell the truth would give ammunition to the enemy. During the Spanish civil war, for instance, the dissensions on the Government side were never properly thrashed out in the left-wing Press, although they involved fundamental points of principle. To discuss the struggle between the Communists and the Anarchists, you were told, would simply give the *Daily Mail* the chance to say that the Reds were all murdering one another. The only result was that the left-wing cause as a whole was weakened. The *Daily Mail* may have missed a few horror stories because people held their tongues, but some all-important lessons were not learned, and we are suffering from the fact to this day.

As I Please 29
Tribune, 16 June 1944

Several times, by word of mouth and in writing, I have been asked why I do not make use of this column for an onslaught on the Brains Trust. "For Christ's sake take a crack at Joad," one reader put it. Now, I would not deny that the Brains Trust is a very dismal thing. I am objectively anti-Brains Trust, in the sense that I always switch off any radio from which it begins to emerge. The phoney pretence that the whole thing is spontaneous and uncensored, the steady avoidance of any serious topic and concentration on questions of the "Why do children's ears stick out" type, the muscular-curate heartiness of the question-master, the frequently irritating voices, and the thought of incompetent amateur broadcasters being paid ten or fifteen shillings a minute to say "Er – er – er," are very hard to bear. But I cannot feel the same indignation against this programme as many of my acquaintances seem to do, and it is worth explaining why.

By this time the big public is probably growing rather tired of the Brains Trust, but over a long period it was a genuinely popular programme. It was listened to not only in England, but in various other parts of the world, and its technique has been adopted by countless discussion groups in the Forces and Civil Defence. It was an idea that "took on," as the saying goes. And it is not difficult to see why. By the standards of newspaper and radio discussion prevailing in this country up to about 1940, the Brains Trust was a great step forward. It did at least make some show of aiming at free speech and at intellectual seriousness, and though latterly it has had to keep silent about "politics and religion," you could pick up from it interesting facts about birds' nest soup or the habits of porpoises, scraps of history and a smattering of philosophy. It was less obviously frivolous than the average radio programme. By and large it stood for enlight-enment, and that was why millions of listeners welcomed it, at any rate for a year or two.

It was also why the blimps loathed it, and still do. The Brains Trust is the object of endless attacks by right-wing intellectuals of the G. M. Young–A. P. Herbert type (also Mr. Douglas Reed), and when a rival brains trust under a squad of clergy-men was set up, all the blimps went about saying how much better it was than Joad and company. These people see the Brains Trust as a symbol of freedom of thought, and they realise that, however silly its programmes may be in themselves, their tendency is to start people thinking. You or I, perhaps, would not think of the B.B.C. as a dangerously subversive organisa-tion, but that is how it is regarded in some quarters, and there are perpetual attempts to interfere with its programmes. To a certain extent a man may be known by his enemies, and the dislike with which all right-thinking people have regarded the Brains Trust – and also the whole idea of discussion groups, public or private – from the very start, is a sign that there must be something good in it. That is why I feel no strong impulse to take a crack at Dr. Joad, who gets his fair share of cracks anyway. I say rather: just think what the Brains Trust would have been like if its permanent members had been (as they might so well have been) Lord Elton, Mr. Harold Nicolson and Mr. Alfred Noyes.

The squabble in the House about *Your M. P.* was perhaps less disgusting than it might have been, since after all Brendan Bracken did announce that he was not going to ban the book for export; but it was a bad symptom all the same. Mr. Beverley Baxter is not the most effective of the many guns now firing in the counter-attack of the Conservative Party – indeed he is less like a gun than a home-made mortar with a strong tendency to blow up – but it is significant that he should have the impu-dence to make the remarks he did. He wanted the book banned on the ground (a) that the author had been in prison,

(b) that it was "scurrilous," and (c) that it "might disturb our relations with Russia." Of these, (a) is a simple appeal to prejudice, while (b) and (c) boil down to saying that the book is a reminder of what the record of the Conservative Party has actually been. I have my own quarrel with books like *Your M.P.*, but at least this book is almost entirely a compilation of admitted facts, all of them easily verifiable. A great deal of it could be dug out of Hansard, which is available to anyone who can pay the sixpence a day. But, as Mr. Baxter realises, *Your M.P.* will be read by tens of thousands who would never think of looking into Hansard or even into *Who's Who*. Therefore, ban the book from export, and if possible discredit it in this country as well. It will never do to let people know who our Conservative M.P.s are, what shares they own, how they have voted on crucially important issues, and what they said about Hitler before we went to war with him. Heaven knows the Conservative Party have enough reason for wanting to keep their record dark. But a couple of years ago they did not have the nerve to say so, and there lies the difference.

Also, Brendan Bracken in his reply said that the book contained a "venomous attack" on Sir Arnold Wilson who "with the greatest gallantry gave his life for his country," the implication being that Sir Arnold Wilson's death in action made it improper to criticise him.

Sir Arnold Wilson was a brave and honourable man. When the policy he had supported came to ruin he was ready to face the consequences. In spite of his age he insisted on joining the R.A.F., and was killed in battle. I can think of plenty of other public figures who have behaved less well. But what has that to do with his pre-war record, which was mischievous in the extreme? His newspaper, the *Hitchin Mercury*, was a frankly pro-Fascist paper and buttered up the Nazi regime almost to the last. Are we supposed to believe that if a man dies well his previous actions cease to have results?

One cannot buy magazines from abroad nowadays, but I recommend anyone who has a friend in New York to try and cadge a copy of *Politics*, the new monthly magazine, edited by the Marxist literary critic, Dwight Macdonald. I don't agree with the policy of this paper, which is anti-war (not from a

pacifist angle), but I admire its combination of highbrow
political analysis with intelligent literary criticism. It is sad to
have to admit it, but we have no monthly or quarterly magazines in England to come up to the American ones – for there
are several others of rather the same stamp as *Politics*. We are still
haunted by a half-conscious idea that to have æsthetic sensibilities you must be a Tory. But of course the present superiority
of American magazines is partly due to the war. Politically,
the paper in this country most nearly corresponding to
Politics would be, I suppose, the *New Leader*. You have only
to compare the get-up, the style of writing, the range of
subjects and the intellectual level of the two papers, to see
what it means to live in a country where there are still leisure
and wood-pulp.

As I Please 30
Tribune, 23 June 1944

The week before last *Tribune* printed a centenary article on
Gerard Manley Hopkins, and it was only after this that the
chance of running across an April number of the American
Nation reminded me that 1944 is also the centenary of a much
better-known writer – Anatole France.

When Anatole France died, twenty years ago, his reputation
suffered one of those sudden slumps to which highbrow
writers who have lived long enough to become popular are
especially liable. In France, according to the charming
French custom, vicious personal attacks were made upon
him while he lay dying and when he was freshly dead. A
particularly venomous one was written by Pierre Drieu la
Rochelle, afterwards to become a collaborator of the Nazis.
In England, also, it was discovered that Anatole France was no
good. A few years later than this a young man attached to a
weekly paper (I met him afterwards in Paris and found that
he could not buy a tram ticket without assistance) solemnly
assured me that Anatole France "wrote very bad French."
France was, it seemed, a vulgar, spurious and derivative writer
whom everyone could now "see through." Round about

the same time, similar discoveries were being made about Bernard Shaw and Lytton Strachey: but curiously enough all three writers have remained very readable, while most of their detractors are forgotten.

How far the revulsion against Anatole France was genuinely literary I do not know. Certainly he had been overpraised, and one must at times get tired of a writer so mannered and so indefatigably pornographic. But it is unquestionable that he was attacked partly from political motives. He may or may not have been a great writer, but he was one of the symbolic figures in the politico-literary dogfight which has been raging for a hundred years or more. The clericals and reactionaries hated him in just the same way as they hated Zola. Anatole France had championed Dreyfus, which needed considerable courage, he had debunked Joan of Arc, he had written a comic history of France; above all, he had lost no opportunity of poking fun at the Church. He was everything that the clericals and revanchists, the people who first preached that the Boche must never be allowed to recover and afterwards sucked the blacking off Hitler's boots, most detested.

I do not know whether Anatole France's most characteristic books, for instance, *La Rôtisserie de la Reine Pédauque*, are worth re-reading at this date. Whatever is in them is really in Voltaire. But it is a different story with the four novels dealing with Monsieur Bergeret. Besides being extremely amusing these give a most valuable picture of French society in the 'nineties and the background of the Dreyfus case. There is also *Crainquebille*, one of the best short stories I have ever read, and incidentally a devastating attack on "law and order."

But though Anatole France could speak up for the working class in a story like *Crainquebille*, and though cheap editions of his works were advertised in Communist papers, one ought not really to class him as a Socialist. He was willing to work for Socialism, even to deliver lectures on it in draughty halls, and he knew that it was both necessary and inevitable, but it is doubtful whether he subjectively wanted it. The world, he once said, would get about as much relief from the coming of Socialism as a sick man gets from turning over in bed. In a crisis he was ready to identify himself with the working class, but the thought of a Utopian future depressed him, as can be seen from his book, *La Pierre Blanche*. There is an even deeper pessimism in *Les Dieux Ont Soif*, his novel about the French Revolution. Temperamentally he was not a Socialist but a Radical. At this date that is probably the rarer animal of the two, and it is his Radicalism, his passion for liberty and intellectual honesty, that give their special colour to the four novels about Monsieur Bergeret.

I have never understood why the *News-Chronicle*, whose politics are certainly a very pale pink – about the colour of shrimp paste, I should say, but still pink – allows the professional Roman Catholic "Timothy Shy" (D. B. Wyndham Lewis) to do daily sabotage in his comic column. In Lord Beaverbrook's *Express* his fellow-Catholic "Beachcomber" (J. B. Morton) is, of course, more at home.

Looking back over the twenty years or so that these two have been on the job, it would be difficult to find a reactionary cause that they have not championed. Pilsudski, Mussolini, appeasement, flogging, Franco, literary censorship – between them they have found good words for everything that any decent person instinctively objects to. They have conducted endless propaganda against Socialism, the League of Nations and scientific research. They have kept up a campaign of abuse against every writer worth reading, from Joyce onwards. They were viciously anti-German until Hitler appeared, when their anti-Germanism cooled off in a remarkable manner. At this moment, needless to say, the especial target of their hatred is Beveridge.

It is a mistake to regard these two as comics pure and simple. Every word they write is intended as Catholic propaganda, and some at least of their co-religionists think very highly of their work in this direction. Their general "line" will be familiar to anyone who has read Chesterton and kindred writers. Its essential note is denigration of England and of the Protestant countries generally. From the Catholic point of view this is necessary. A Catholic, at least an apologist, feels that he *must* claim superiority for the Catholic countries, and for the Middle Ages as against the present, just as a Communist feels that he must in all circumstances support the U.S.S.R. Hence the endless jibing of "Beachcomber" and "Timothy

Shy" at every English institution – tea, cricket, Wordsworth, Charlie Chaplin, kindness to animals, Nelson, Cromwell and what-not. Hence also "Timothy Shy's" attempts to rewrite English history and the snarls of hatred that escape him when he thinks of the defeat of the Spanish Armada. (How it sticks in his gizzard, that Spanish Armada! As though anyone cared, at this date!). Hence, even, the endless jeering at novelists, the novel being essentially a post-Reformation form of literature at which on the whole Catholics have not excelled.

From either a literary or a political point of view these two are simply the leavings on Chesterton's plate. Chesterton's vision of life was false in some ways, and he was hampered by enormous ignorance, but at least he had courage. He was ready to attack the rich and powerful, and he damaged his career by doing so. But it is the peculiarity of both "Beach-comber" and "Timothy Shy" that they take no risks with their own popularity. Their strategy is always indirect. Thus, if you want to attack the principle of freedom of speech, do it by sneering at the Brains Trust, as if it were a typical example. Dr. Joad won't retaliate! Even their deepest convictions go into cold storage when they become dangerous. Earlier in the war, when it was safe to do so, "Beachcomber" wrote viciously anti-Russian pamphlets, but no anti-Russian remarks appear in his column these days. They will again, however, if popular pro-Russian feeling dies down. I shall be interested to see whether either "Beachcomber" or "Timothy Shy" reacts to these remarks of mine. If so, it will be the first recorded instance of either of them attacking anyone likely to hit back.

As I Please 31
Tribune, 30 June 1944

I notice that apart from the widespread complaint that the German pilotless planes "seem so unnatural" (a bomb dropped by a live airman is quite natural, apparently), some journalists are denouncing them as barbarous, inhumane, and "an indis-criminate attack on civilians."

After what we have been doing to the Germans over the past two years, this seems a bit thick, but it is the normal human response to every new weapon. Poison gas, the machine-gun, the submarine, gunpowder, and even the crossbow were similarly denounced in their day. Every weapon seems unfair until you have adopted it yourself. But I would not deny that the pilotless plane, flying bomb, or whatever its correct name may be, is an exceptionally unpleasant thing, because, unlike most other projectiles, it gives you time to think. What is your first reaction when you hear that droning, zooming noise? Inevitably, it is a hope that the noise *won't stop*. You want to hear the bomb pass safely overhead and die away into the distance before the engine cuts out. In other words, you are hoping that it will fall on somebody else. So also when you dodge a shell or an ordinary bomb – but in that case you have only about five seconds to take cover and no time to speculate on the bottomless selfishness of the human being.

It cannot be altogether an accident that nationalists of the more extreme and romantic kind tend not to belong to the nation that they idealise. Leaders who base their appeal on "*la patrie*," or "the fatherland" are sometimes outright foreigners, or else come from the border-countries of great empires. Obvious examples are Hitler, an Austrian, and Napoleon, a Corsican, but there are many others. The man who may be said to have been the founder of British jingoism was Disraeli, a Spanish Jew, and it was Lord Beaverbrook, a Canadian, who tried to induce the unwilling English to describe themselves as Britons. The British Empire was largely built up by Irishmen and Scotsmen, and our most obstinate nationalists and imperialists have frequently been Ulstermen. Even Churchill, the leading exponent of romantic patriotism in our own day, is half an American. But not merely the men of action, but even the theorists of nationalism are frequently foreigners. Pan-Germanism, for instance, from which the Nazis later took many of their ideas, was largely the product of men who were not Germans: for instance, Houston Chamberlain, an Englishman, and Gobineau, a Frenchman. Rudyard Kipling was an Englishman, but of a rather doubtful kind. He came from an unusual Anglo-Indian background (his father was

curator of the Bombay Museum), he had spent his early childhood in India, and he was of small stature and very dark
complexion which caused him to be wrongly suspected of
having Asiatic blood. I have always held that if we ever have
a Hitler in this country he will be, perhaps, an Ulsterman, a
South African, a Maltese, a Eurasian, or perhaps an American –
but, at any rate, not an Englishman.

Two samples of the English language:
1. Elizabethan English:
   While the pages are at their banqueting, I keep their mules,
and to someone I cut the stirrup-leather of the mounting
side, till it hangs by a thin strap or thread, that when the great
puff-guts of the counsellor or some other hath taken his swing
to get up, he may fall flat on his side like a porker, and so furnish
the spectators with more than a hundred francs' worth of
laughter. But I laugh yet further, to think how at his home-
coming the master-page is to be swinged like green rye, which
makes me not to repent what I have bestowed in feasting
them.

(Thomas Urquhart: Translation of Rabelais.)

2. Modern American:
   The phase of detachment may be isolated from its political
context and in the division of labour become an end in itself.
Those who restrict themselves to work only such segments of
intellectual endeavour may attempt to generalise them, making
them the basis for political and personal orientation. Then the
key problem is held to arise from the fact that social science lags
behind physical science and technology, and political and social
problems are a result of this deficiency and lag. Such a position
is inadequate.

(American highbrow magazine.)

Six million books, it is said, perished in the blitz of 1940,
including a thousand irreplaceable titles. Most of them were
probably no loss, but it is dismaying to find how many standard
works are now completely out of print. Paper is forthcoming
for the most ghastly tripe, as you can see by glancing into any
bookshop window, while all the reprint editions, such as
the Everyman Library, have huge gaps in their lists. Even so

well-known a work of reference as Webster's dictionary is no longer obtainable unless you run across a copy second-hand. About a year ago I had to do a broadcast on Jack London. When I started to collect the material I found that those of his books that I most wanted had vanished so completely that even the London Library could not produce them. To get hold of them I should have had to go to the British Museum reading-room, which in these days is not at all easy of access. And this seems to me a disaster, for Jack London is one of those border-line writers whose works might be forgotten altogether unless somebody takes the trouble to revive them. Even *The Iron Heel* was distinctly a rarity for some years, and was only reprinted because Hitler's rise to power made it topical.

He is remembered chiefly by *The Iron Heel*, and – in totally different circles – by books like *White Fang* and *The Call of the Wild*, in which he exploited a typically Anglo-Saxon senti-mentality about animals. But there were also *The People of the Abyss*, his book about the London slums, *The Road*, which gives a wonderful picture of the American hoboes, and *The Jacket*, which is valuable for its prison scenes. And above all there are his short stories. When he is in a certain vein – it is chiefly when he is dealing with American city life – Jack London is one of the best short-story writers the English-speaking peoples have had. There is a story called *Just Meat*, about two burglars who get away with a big haul, and then simultaneously poison one another with strychnine, which sticks very vividly in my memory. *Love of Life*, the last story that was read to Lenin when he was dying, is another wonder-ful story, and so is *A Piece of Steak*, which describes the last battle of a worn-out prizefighter. These and other similar stories benefit by the strong streak of brutality that London had in his nature. It was this also that gave him a subjective understanding of Fascism which Socialists do not usually have, and which made *The Iron Heel* in some ways a true prophecy.

Or am I overrating those short stories? I may be, for it is many years since I have set eyes on them. Two of those I have named above were included in a book called *When God Laughs*. So far as I can discover this book has simply ceased to exist, and if anyone has a copy to sell I should be glad to hear of it.

As I Please 32
Tribune, 7 July 1944

When the Caliph Omar destroyed the libraries of Alexandria he is supposed to have kept the public baths warm for eighteen days with burning manuscripts, and great numbers of tragedies by Euripides and others are said to have perished, quite irre-coverably. I remember that when I read about this as a boy it simply filled me with enthusiastic approval. It was so many less words to look up in the dictionary – that was how I saw it. For, though I am only forty-one, I am old enough to have been educated at a time when Latin and Greek were only escapable with great difficulty, while "English" was hardly regarded as a school subject at all.

Classical education is going down the drain at last, but even now there must be far more adults who have been flogged through the entire extant works of Aeschylus, Sopho-cles, Euripides, Aristophanes, Virgil, Horace and various other Latin and Greek authors, than have read the English masterpieces of the eighteenth century. People pay lip service to Fielding and the rest of them, of course, but they don't read them, as you can discover by making a few inquiries among your friends. How many people have even read *Tom Jones*, for instance? Not so many have even read the later books of *Gulliver's Travels*. *Robinson Crusoe* has a sort of popularity in nursery versions, but the book as a whole is so little known that few people are even aware that the second part (the journey through Tartary) exists. Smollett, I imagine, is the least read of all. The central plot of Shaw's play, *Pygmalion*, is lifted straight out of *Peregrine Pickle*, and I believe that no one has ever pointed this out in print, which suggests that few people can have read the book. But what is strangest of all is that Smollett, so far as I know, has never been boosted by the Scottish Nationalists, who are so careful to claim Byron for their own. Yet Smollett, besides being one of the best novelists the English-speaking races have produced, *was* a Scotsman, and proclaimed it openly at a time when being so was anything but helpful to one's career.

Life in the civilised world.

(The family are at tea.)

Zoom–zoom–zoom!

"Is there an alert on?"

"No, it's all clear."

"I thought there was an alert on."

Zoom–zoom–zoom!

"There's another of those things coming!"

"It's all right, it's miles away."

Zoom–zoom–ZOOM!

"Look out, here it comes! Under the table, quick!"

Zoom–zoom–zoom!

"It's all right, it's getting fainter."

Zoom–zoom–ZOOM!

"It's coming back!"

"They seem to kind of circle round and come back again. They've got something on their tails that makes them do it. Like a torpedo."

ZOOM–ZOOM–ZOOM!

"Christ! It's bang overhead!"

Dead silence.

"Now get *right* underneath. Keep your head well down. What a mercy baby isn't here!"

"Look at the cat! He's frightened too."

"Of course animals *know*. They can feel the vibrations."

BOOM!

"It's all right, I told you it was miles away."

(Tea continues.)

I see that Lord Winterton, writing in the *Evening Standard*, speaks of the "remarkable reticence (by no means entirely imposed by rule or regulation) which Parliament and Press alike have displayed in this war to avoid endangering national security" and adds that it has "earned the admiration of the civilised world."

It is not only in war time that the British Press observes this voluntary reticence. One of the most extraordinary things about England is that there is almost no official censorship, and yet nothing that is acutely offensive to the governing class gets into print, at least in any place where large numbers of people are likely to read it. If it is "not done" to mention something or other, it just doesn't get mentioned. The position is summed up in the lines by (I think) Hilaire Belloc:

> You cannot hope to bribe or twist
> Thank God! the English journalist:
> But seeing what the man will do
> Unbribed, there is no reason to.

No bribes, no threats, no penalties – just a nod and a wink and the thing is done. A well-known example was the business of the Abdication. Weeks before the scandal officially broke, tens or hundreds of thousands of people had heard all about Mrs. Simpson, and yet not a word got into the Press, not even into the *Daily Worker*, although the American and European papers were having the time of their lives with the story. Yet I believe there was no definite official ban: just an official "request" and a general agreement that to break the news prematurely "would not do." And I can think of other instances of good news stories failing to see the light although there would have been no penalty for printing them.

Nowadays this kind of veiled censorship even extends to books. The M.O.I. does not, of course, dictate a party line or issue an index expurgatorius. It merely "advises." Publishers take manuscripts to the M.O.I., and the M.O.I. "suggests" that this or that is undesirable, or premature, or "would serve no good purpose." And though there is no definite prohibition, no clear statement that this or that must not be printed, official policy is never flouted. Circus dogs jump when the trainer cracks his whip, but the really well-trained dog is the one that turns his somersault when there is no whip. And that is the state we have reached in this country thanks to three hundred years of living together without a civil war.

Here is a little problem sometimes used as an intelligence test.

A man walked four miles due south from his house and shot a bear. He then walked two miles due west, then walked another four miles due north and was back at his home again. What was the colour of the bear?

The interesting point is that – so far as my own observations go – men usually see the answer to this problem and women do not.

Review of *In a Strange Land: Essays by Eric Gill*
The Observer, 9 July 1944

An uneasy awareness that medievalism is a by-product of industrialism seems to underlie much of Eric Gill's writing. With more grip on reality than Chesterton, who was saying much the same thing in a more flamboyant way, he gave the same impression of constantly nagging away at a half-truth and evading every real criticism that could be brought against him. But it must be allowed to both of them that the half-truth they got hold of was an unpopular one and therefore worthy of emphasis.

In this little book of collected essays and lectures, Gill is presenting his usual thesis: the fundamental evil of industrial society. The good life is well-nigh impossible, and the arts are mostly dead, because we live in an age in which the workman is not master of his own work. He is simply a cog in an enormous machine, performing over and over again some mechanical task of which he does not know the meaning and in which he has no interest except the wage he receives for it. His creative instincts have to be satisfied, if at all, outside his working hours, and they are constantly perverted by the mass-produced goods that capitalism forces upon him. True civilisation, Gill thinks, can only return when people choose their own work and do it in their own time, and when they are conscious of being free agents while possessing a common body of belief. This much one might accept, even though Gill makes the usual parochial claim that the common belief of humanity must be *Christian* belief, and even though his dislike of factory production is illogically mixed up with ideas about currency reform and the special wickedness of bankers.

But however much one may agree with Gill's indictment, he has no real remedy to offer. Naturally his programme is a return to peasant ownership, hand production, and, in general, to an idealised version of the Middle Ages. But there are two insuperable objections to this, neither of which he really meets. One is that the world is so manifestly not going in that direction that to wish for it is like wishing for the moon. Elsewhere in his writings, though not in this book, Gill does admit this and seems to realise that the way to a simpler life must lead through greater complexity. The other objection is that Gill and all similar thinkers have no real notion of what a non-industrial society would be like, nor, indeed, much idea of the meaning of work.

Much the best thing in this book is a diary of a trip to Ireland in 1919. As a Catholic convert, slightly Anglophobe and in love with peasant society, Gill is naturally inclined to idealise Ireland, and he does so even to the extent of claiming that the Irish country people are less ugly than the English. But whenever he encounters an Irish working man, for instance a trade union organiser, he notes with dismay that the Irishmen seem to have the same outlook as their English colleagues. That is, they think in terms of mechanisation, efficiency, shorter hours, and higher wages, and are not much interested in the sacredness of private property. "They appear," he says, "to be quite content to promote a co-operative commonwealth in which there shall be no individual ownership or responsibility – i.e., the factory system in public instead of private hands." Elsewhere in the book he explains this by saying that the working man has taken over his employer's system of values. What he does not see is that the working man's attitude is founded on hard experience. Middle-class people hardly have the right to question it.

The point is well brought out in a bit of dialogue in Shaw's "Man and Superman" between the sentimental Octavius and the chauffeur, 'Enery Straker:

Octavius: "I believe in the dignity of labour."
Straker: "That's because you never done any, Mr. Octavius."

Eric Gill, a sculptor, obviously thinks of manual labour as being of its nature creative labour, and in thinking of the past he tends to forget the lower strata of the population. The world he imagines is a world of craftsmen – owner-farmers, carpenters, handloom weavers, stonemasons, and the like – and it is also a world almost without machinery. But, of course, in a world without machinery the average person is not a craftsman but a serf, or as near it as makes no difference. The job of getting food out of the soil without machinery is so laborious that it necessarily reduces large numbers of people almost to the status of animals, and we forget this aspect of pre-industrial life precisely because the poorest classes were too worn out by drudgery to leave much record behind them. In many primitive countries to-day, the ordinary person is toiling like a slave from the age of about ten onwards, and even his seeming aesthetic superiority is probably only due to lack of opportunity. Nothing could really improve his situation except the machinery, the division of labour, and the centralised economy which Gill so much dislikes.

The book also contains an address delivered to the Peace Pledge Union, an essay on clothes, and some remarks on Ruskin and on the painter, David Jones. Gill was a pacifist, at any rate towards the end of his life, and in spite of his theories about land-ownership and cottage industries, he toyed with the idea of Socialism. But the central thing in him was his hatred of the machine. He was right, no doubt, in his denunciations of present-day society, but wrong in looking for a quick way out, and like all people who hanker for the past, he could not altogether escape affectation and pretty-prettiness. Not to be arty and crafty, not to resemble William Morris – naturally this was his claim. But one does not reject one's own age without paying the penalty, and the price Gill paid can be seen in the carvings outside Broadcasting House, in the woodcuts that adorn this book, and in his over-simplified way of writing.

As I Please 33
Tribune, 14 July 1944

I have received a number of letters, some of them quite violent ones, attacking me for my remarks on Miss Vera Brittain's anti-bombing pamphlet. There are two points that seem to need further comment.

First of all there is the charge, which is becoming quite a common one, that "we started it," i.e. that Britain was the first country to practise systematic bombing of civilians. How anyone can make this claim, with the history of the past dozen years in mind, is almost beyond me. The first act in the present war – some hours, if I remember rightly, before any declaration of war passed – was the German bombing of Warsaw. The Germans bombed and shelled the city so intensively that, according to the Poles, at one time 700 fires were raging simultaneously. They made a film of the destruction of Warsaw, which they entitled "Baptism of Fire" and sent all round the world with the object of terrorising neutrals.

Several years earlier than this the Condor Legion, sent to Spain by Hitler, had bombed one Spanish city after another. The "silent raids" on Barcelona in 1938 killed several thousand people in a couple of days. Earlier than this the Italians had bombed entirely defenceless Abyssinians and boasted of their exploits as something screamingly funny. Bruno Mussolini wrote newspaper articles in which he described bombed Abyssinians "bursting open like a rose," which, he said, was "most amusing." And the Japanese ever since 1931, and intensively since 1937, have been bombing crowded Chinese cities where there are not even any A.R.P. arrangements, let alone any A.A. guns or fighter aircraft.

I am not arguing that two blacks make a white, nor that Britain's record is a particularly good one. In a number of "little wars" from about 1920 onwards the R.A.F. has dropped its bombs on Afghans, Indians and Arabs who had little or no power of hitting back. But it is simply untruthful to say that large-scale bombing of crowded town areas, with the object of causing panic, is a British invention. It was the Fascist states who started this practice, and so long as the air war went in their favour they avowed their aims quite clearly.

The other thing that needs dealing with is the parrot cry "killing women and children." I pointed out before, but evidently it needs repeating, that it is probably somewhat better to kill a cross section of the population than to kill only the young men. If the figures published by the Germans are true, and we have really killed 1,200,000 civilians in our raids, that loss of life has probably harmed the German race somewhat less than a corresponding loss on the Russian front or in Africa and Italy.

Any nation at war will do its best to protect its children, and the number of children killed in raids probably does not correspond to their percentage of the general population. Women cannot be protected to the same extent, but the outcry against killing women, if you accept killing at all, is sheer sentimentality. Why is it worse to kill a woman than a man? The argument usually advanced is that in killing women you are killing the breeders, whereas men can be more easily spared. But this is a fallacy based on the notion that human beings can be bred like animals. The idea behind it is that since one man is capable of fertilising a very large number of women, just as a prize ram fertilises thousands of ewes, the loss of male lives is comparatively unimportant. Human beings, however, are not cattle. When the slaughter caused by a war leaves a surplus of women, the enormous majority of those women bear no children. Male lives are very nearly as important, biologically, as female ones.

In the last war the British Empire lost nearly a million men killed, of whom about three-quarters came from these islands. Most of them will have been under thirty. If all those young men had had only one child each we should now have an extra 750,000 people round about the age of 20. France, which lost much more heavily, never recovered from the slaughter of the last war, and it is doubtful whether Britain has fully recovered, either. We can't yet calculate the casualties of the present war, but the last one killed between ten and twenty million young men. Had it been conducted, as the next one will perhaps be, with flying bombs, rockets and other long-range weapons which kill old and young, healthy and unhealthy, male and female impartially, it would probably have damaged European civilisation somewhat less than it did.

Contrary to what some of my correspondents seem to think, I have no enthusiasm for air raids, either ours or the enemy's. Like a lot of other people in this country, I am growing definitely tired of bombs. But I do object to the hypocrisy of accepting force as an instrument while squealing against this or that individual weapon, or of denouncing war while wanting to preserve the kind of society that makes war inevitable.

I note in my diary for 1940 an expectation that commercial advertisements will have disappeared from the walls within a year. This seemed likely enough at the time, and a year or even two years later the disappearance seemed to be actually happening, though more slowly than I had expected. Advertisements were shrinking both in numbers and size, and the announcements of the various Ministries were more and more taking their place both on the walls and in the newspapers. Judging from this symptom alone, one would have said that commercialism was definitely on the downgrade.

In the last two years, however, the commercial ad., in all its silliness and snobbishness, has made a steady comeback. In recent years I consider that the most offensive of all British advertisements are the ones for Rose's Lime Juice, with their "young squire" motif and their P. G. Wodehouse dialogue.

"I fear you do not see me at my best this morning, Jenkins. There were jollifications last night. Your young master looked upon the wine when it was red and also upon the whisky when it was yellow. To use the vulgar phrase, I have a thick head. What do you think the doctor would prescribe, Jenkins?"

"If I might make so bold, sir, a glass of soda water with a dash of Rose's Lime Juice would probably have the desired effect."

"Go to it, Jenkins! You were always my guide, philosopher and friend," etc., etc., etc.

When you reflect that this advertisement appears, for instance in every theatre programme, so that every theatre-goer is at any rate assumed to have a secret fantasy life in which he thinks of himself as a young man of fashion with faithful old retainers, the prospect of any drastic social change recedes perceptibly.

There are also the hair-tonic adverts, which tell you how Daphne got promotion in the W.A.A.F.S. thanks to the neatness and glossiness of her hair. But these are misleading as well as whorish, for I seldom or never pass a group of officers in the W.A.A.F.S., A.T.S. or W.R.E.N.S. without having cause to reflect that, at any rate, promotion in the women's services has nothing to do with looks.

As I Please 34
Tribune, 21 July 1944

I have just found my copy of Samuel Butler's *Note-books*, the full edition of the first series, published by Jonathan Cape in 1921. It is twenty years old and none the better for having gone through several rainy seasons in Burma, but at any rate it exists, which is all to the good, for this is another of those well-known books which have now ceased to be procurable. Cape's later produced an abridged version in the *Traveller's Library*, but it is an unsatisfactory abridgement, and the second series which was published about 1934 does not contain much that is of value. It is in the first series that you will find the story of Butler's interview with a Turkish official at the Dardanelles, the description of his method of buying new-laid eggs and his endeavours to photograph a seasick bishop, and other similar trifles which in a way are worth more than his major works.

Butler's main ideas now seem either to be unimportant, or to suffer from wrong emphasis. Biologists apart, who now cares whether the Darwinian theory of evolution, or the Lamarckian version which Butler supported, is the correct one? The whole question of evolution seems less momentous than it did, because, unlike the Victorians, we do not feel that to be descended from animals is degrading to human dignity. On the other hand, Butler often makes a mere joke out of something that now seems to us vitally important. For example:

"The principal varieties and sub-varieties of the human race are not now to be looked for among the Negroes, the Circassians, the Malays or the American aborigines, but among the rich and the poor. The difference in physical organisation between these two species of man is far greater than that between the so-called types of humanity. The rich man can go from [New Zealand] to England whenever he feels inclined. The legs of the other are by an invisible fatality prevented from carrying him beyond certain narrow limits. Neither rich nor poor can yet see the philosophy of the thing, or admit that he who can tack a portion of one of the P. & O. boats on to his identity is a much more highly organised being than he who cannot."

There are innumerable similar passages in Butler's work. You could easily interpret them in a Marxist sense, but the point is that Butler himself does not do so. Finally his outlook is that of a Conservative, in spite of his successful assaults on Christian belief and the institution of a family. Poverty is degrading: therefore, take care not to be poor – that is his reaction. Hence the improbable and unsatisfying ending of *The Way of All Flesh*, which contrasts so strangely with the realism of the earlier parts.

Yet Butler's books have worn well, far better than those of more earnest contemporaries like Meredith and Carlyle, partly because he never lost the power to use his eyes and to be pleased by small things, partly because in the narrow technical sense he wrote so well. When one compares Butler's prose with the contortions of Meredith or the affectations of Stevenson, one sees what a tremendous advantage is gained simply by not trying to be clever. Butler's own ideas on the subject are worth quoting:

"I never knew a writer yet who took the smallest pains with his style and was at the same time readable. Plato's having had seventy shies at one sentence is quite enough to explain to me why I dislike him. A man may, and ought to, take a great deal of pains to write clearly, tersely and euphoniously: he will write many a sentence three or four times over – to do much more than this is worse than not rewriting at all: he will be at great pains to see that he does not repeat himself, to arrange his matter in the way that shall best enable the reader to master it, to cut out superfluous words and, even more, to eschew irrelevant matter: but in each case he will be thinking not of his own style but of his reader's convenience. . . . I should like to put it on record that I never took the smallest pains with my style, have never thought about it, and do not know or want to know whether it is a style at all or whether it is not, as I believe and hope, just common, simple, straightforwardness. I cannot conceive how any man can take thought for his style without loss to himself and his readers."

Butler adds characteristically, however, that he had made considerable efforts to improve his handwriting.

An argument that Socialists ought to be prepared to meet, since it is brought up constantly both by Christian apologists and by neo-pessimists such as James Burnham, is the alleged immutability of "human nature." Socialists are accused – I think without justification – of assuming that Man is perfectible, and it is then pointed out that human history is in fact one long tale of greed, robbery and oppression. Man, it is said, will always try to get the better of his neighbour, he will always hog as much property as possible for himself and his family. Man is of his nature sinful, and cannot be made virtuous by act of Parliament. Therefore, though economic exploitation can be controlled to some extent, the classless society is for ever impossible.

The proper answer, it seems to me, is that this argument belongs to the Stone Age. It presupposes that material goods will always be desperately scarce. The power-hunger of human beings does indeed present a serious problem, but there is no reason for thinking that the greed for mere wealth is a permanent human characteristic. We are selfish in economic matters because we all live in terror of poverty. But when a commodity is not scarce, no one tries to grab more than his fair share of it. No one tries to make a corner in air, for instance. The millionaire as well as the beggar is content with just so much air as he can breathe. Or, again, water. In this country we are not troubled by lack of water. If anything we have too much of it, especially on Bank Holidays. As a result water hardly enters into our consciousness. Yet in dried-up countries like North Africa, what jealousies, what hatreds, what appalling crimes the lack of water can cause! So also with any other kind of goods. If they were made plentiful, as they so easily might be, there is no reason to think that the supposed acquisitive instincts of the human being could not be bred out in a couple of generations. And after all, if human nature never changes, why is it that we not only don't practise cannibalism any longer, but don't even want to?

Another brain-tickler.

A business-man was in the habit of going home by a suburban train which left London at seven-thirty. One evening the night watchman, who had just come on duty, stopped him and said: –

"Excuse me, sir, but I'd advise you not to go by your usual train tonight. I dreamed last night that the train was smashed up and half the people in it were killed. Maybe you'll think I'm superstitious, but it was all so vivid that I can't help thinking it was meant as a warning."

The business-man was sufficiently impressed to wait and take a later train. When he opened the newspaper the next morning he saw that, sure enough, the train *had* been wrecked and many people killed. That evening he sent for the night watchman and said to him: –

"I want to thank you for your warning yesterday. I consider that you saved my life, and in return I should like to make you a present of thirty pounds. In addition, I have to inform you that you are sacked. Take a week's notice from today."

This was an ungrateful act, but the business-man was strictly within his rights. Why?

As I Please 35
Tribune, 28 July 1944

Some years ago, in the course of an article about boys' weekly papers, I made some passing remarks about women's papers – I mean the twopenny ones of the type of *Peg's Paper*, often called "love books." This brought me, among much other correspondence, a long letter from a woman who had contributed to and worked for the *Lucky Star*, the *Golden Star*, *Peg's Paper*, *Secrets*, the *Oracle*, and a number of kindred papers. Her main point was that I had been wrong in saying that these papers aim at creating wealth fantasy. Their stories are "in no sense Cinderella stories" and do not exploit the "she married her boss" motif. My correspondent adds:

"Unemployment is mentioned – quite frequently. . . . The dole and the trade union are certainly never mentioned. The latter may be influenced by the fact that the largest publishers of these women's magazines are a non-union house. One is never allowed to criticise the system, or to show up the class struggle for what it really is, and the word Socialist is *never* mentioned – all this is perfectly true. But it might be interesting to add that class feeling is not altogether absent. The rich are often shown as mean, and as cruel and crooked money-makers. The rich and idle beau is nearly always planning marriage without a ring, and the lass is rescued by her strong, hard-working garage hand. Men with cars are generally 'bad' and men in well-cut, expensive suits are nearly always crooks. The ideal of most of these stories is *not* an income worthy of a bank manager's wife, but a life that is 'good.' A life with an upright, kind husband, however poor, with babies and a 'little cottage.' The stories are conditioned to show that the meagre life is not so bad really, as you are at least honest and happy, and that riches bring trouble and false friends. The poor are given moral values to aspire to as something within their reach."

There are many comments I could make here, but I choose to take up the point of the moral superiority of the poor being combined with the non-mention of trade unions and Socialism. There is no doubt that this is deliberate policy. In one woman's paper I actually read a story dealing with a strike in a coal-mine, and even in that connection trade unionism was not mentioned. When the U.S.S.R. entered the war one of these papers promptly cashed in with a serial entitled "Her Soviet Lover," but we may be sure that Marxism did not enter into it very largely.

The fact is that this business about the moral superiority of the poor is one of the deadliest forms of escapism the ruling class have evolved. You may be downtrodden and swindled, but in the eyes of God you are superior to your oppressors, and by means of films and magazines you can enjoy a fantasy existence in which you constantly triumph over the people who defeat you in real life. In any form of art designed to appeal to large numbers of people, it is an almost unheard of thing for a rich man to get the better of a poor man. The rich man is usually "bad," and his machinations are invariably frustrated. "Good poor man defeats bad rich man" is an accepted formula, whereas if it were the other way about we should feel that there was something very wrong somewhere. This is as noticeable in films as in the cheap magazines, and it was perhaps most noticeable of all in the old silent films, which travelled from country to country and had to appeal to a very varied audience.

The vast majority of the people who will see a film are poor, and so it is politic to make a poor man the hero. Film magnates, Press lords and the like amass quite a lot of their wealth by pointing out that wealth is wicked.

The formula "good poor man defeats bad rich man" is simply a subtler version of "pie in the sky." It is a sublimation of the class struggle. So long as you can dream of yourself as a "strong, hard-working garage hand" giving some moneyed crook a sock on the jaw, the *real* facts can be forgotten. That is a cleverer dodge than wealth fantasy. But, curiously enough, reality does enter into these women's magazines, not through the stories but through the correspondence columns, especially in those papers that give free medical advice. Here you can read harrowing tales of "bad legs" and haemorrhoids, written by middle-aged women who give themselves such pseudonyms as "A Sufferer," "Mother of Nine," and "Always Constipated." To compare these letters with the love stories that lie cheek by jowl with them is to see how vast a part mere day-dreaming plays in modern life.

I have just been reading Arthur Koestler's novel *The Gladiators*, which describes the slave rebellion under Spartacus, about 70 B.C. It is not one of his best books, and, in any case, any novel describing a slave rebellion in antiquity suffers by having to stand comparison with *Salammbô*, Flaubert's great novel about the revolt of the Carthaginian mercenaries. But it reminded me of how tiny is the number of slaves of whom anything whatever is known. I myself know the names of just three slaves – Spartacus himself, the fabulous Æsop, who is supposed to have been a slave, and the philosopher Epictetus, who was one of those learned slaves whom the Roman pluto-crats liked to have among their retinue. All the others are not even names. We don't, for instance – or at least I don't – know the name of a single one of the myriads of human beings who built the Pyramids. Spartacus, I suppose, is much the most widely known slave there ever was. For five thousand years or more civilisation rested upon slavery. Yet when even so much as the name of a slave survives, it is because he did not obey the injunction "resist not evil," but raised violent rebellion. I think there is a moral in this for pacifists.

In spite of the appalling overcrowding of the trains (16 people in a carriage designed for 10 is fairly normal nowadays), I note that the distinction between first and third class is definitely coming back. Earlier in the war it almost lapsed for a while. If you were crowded out of the third class you went as a matter of course into the first, and no questions were asked. Now you are invariably made to pay the difference in fare – at least, if you sit down – even though it would have been quite impossible to find a place anywhere else in the train. (You can, I believe, travel in a first-class carriage with a third-class ticket if you choose to stand up the whole way.) A few years ago the railway companies would hardly have dared to enforce this distinction. By such small symptoms (another, by the way, is that evening suits are beginning to come out of their moth balls) you can judge how confident the higher-ups are and how insolent they feel it safe to be.

We published last week part of a very truculent letter about the anti-war poem entitled *The Little Apocalypse of Obadiah Hornbooke*, with the comment, "I am surprised that you publish it." Other letters and private comments took the same line.

I do not, any more than our correspondent, agree with "Obadiah Hornbooke," but that is not a sufficient reason for not publishing what he writes. Every paper has a policy, and in its political sections it will press that policy, more or less to the exclusion of all others. To do anything else would be stupid. But the literary end of a paper is another matter. Even there, of course, no paper will give space to direct attacks on the things it stands for. We wouldn't print an article in praise of anti-semitism, for instance. But granted the necessary minimum of agreement, literary merit is the only thing that matters.

Besides, if this war is about anything at all, it is a war in favour of freedom of thought. I should be the last to claim that we are morally superior to our enemies, and there is quite a strong case for saying that British imperialism is actually worse than Nazism. But there does remain the difference, not to be explained away, that in Britain you are relatively free to say and print what you like. Even in the blackest patches of the British Empire, in India, say, there is very much more freedom of expression than in a totalitarian country. I want that to remain

694

true, and by sometimes giving a hearing to unpopular opinions, I think we help it to do so.

Propaganda and Demotic Speech

Persuasion, Summer Quarter, 1944, 2, No. 2

When I was leaving England for Morocco at the end of 1938, some of the people in my village (less than fifty miles from London) wanted to know whether it would be necessary to cross the sea to get there. In 1940, during General Wavell's African campaign, I discovered that the woman from whom I bought my rations thought Cyrenaica was in Italy. A year or two ago a friend of mine, who had been giving an A.B.C.A. lecture to some A.T.s, tried the experiment of asking them a few general knowledge questions: among the answers he got were, (*a*) that there are only six Members of Parliament, and (*b*) that Singapore is the capital of India. If there were any point in doing so I could give many more instances of this kind of thing. I mention these three, simply as a preliminary reminder of the ignorance which any speech or piece of writing aimed at a large public has to take into account.

However, when you examine Government leaflets and White Papers, or leading articles in the newspapers, or the speeches and broadcasts of politicians, or the pamphlets and manifestos of any political party whatever, the thing that nearly always strikes you is their remoteness from the average man. It is not merely that they assume non-existent knowledge: often it is right and necessary to do that. It is also that clear, popular, everyday language seems to be instinctively avoided. The bloodless dialect of Government spokesmen (characteristic phrases are: in due course, no stone unturned, take the earliest opportunity, the answer is in the affirmative) is too well known to be worth dwelling on. Newspaper leaders are written either in this same dialect or in an inflated bombastic style with a tendency to fall back on archaic words (peril, valour, might, foe, succour, vengeance, dastardly, rampart, bulwark, bastion) which no normal person would ever think of using. Left-wing political parties specialise in a bastard vocabulary made up of

Russian and German phrases translated with the maximum of clumsiness. And even posters, leaflets and broadcasts which are intended to give instructions, to tell people what to do in certain circumstances, often fail in their effect. For example, during the first air raids on London, it was found that innumerable people did not know which siren meant the Alert and which the All Clear. This was after months or years of gazing at A.R.P. posters. These posters had described the Alert as a "warbling note": a phrase which made no impression, since air-raid sirens don't warble, and few people attach any definite meaning to the word.

When Sir Richard Acland, in the early months of the war, was drawing up a Manifesto to be presented to the Government, he engaged a squad of Mass Observers to find out what meaning, if any, the ordinary man attaches to the high-sounding abstract words which are flung to and fro in politics. The most fantastic misunderstandings came to light. It was found, for instance, that most people don't know that "immorality" means anything besides sexual immorality. One man thought that "movement" had something to do with constipation. And it is a nightly experience in any pub to see broadcast speeches and news bulletins make no impression on the average listener, because they are uttered in stilted bookish language and, incidentally, in an upper-class accent. At the time of Dunkirk I watched a gang of navvies eating their bread and cheese in a pub while the one o'clock news came over. Nothing registered: they just went on stolidly eating. Then, just for an instant, reporting the words of some soldier who had been hauled aboard a boat, the announcer dropped into spoken English, with the phrase, "Well, I've learned to swim this trip, anyway!" Promptly you could see ears being pricked up: it was ordinary language, and so it got across. A few weeks later, the day after Italy entered the war, Duff Cooper announced that Mussolini's rash act would "add to the ruins for which Italy has been famous." It was neat enough, and a true prophecy, but how much impression does that kind of language make on nine people out of ten? The colloquial version of it would have been: "Italy has always been famous for ruins. Well, there are going to be a damn' sight more of them now." But that is not how Cabinet Ministers speak, at any rate in public.

Examples of futile slogans, obviously incapable of stirring strong feelings or being circulated by word of mouth, are: "Deserve Victory," "Freedom is in Peril. Defend it with all your Might," "Socialism the only Solution," "Expropriate the Expropriators," "Austerity," "Evolution not Revolution," "Peace is Indivisible." Examples of slogans phrased in spoken English are: "Hands off Russia," "Make Germany Pay," "Stop Hitler," "No Stomach Taxes," "Buy a Spitfire," "Votes for Women." Examples about mid-way between these two classes are: "Go to It," "Dig for Victory," "It all depends on ME," and some of Churchill's phrases, such as "the end of the beginning," "soft underbelly," "blood, toil, tears and sweat," and "never was so much owed by so many to so few." (Significantly, in so far as this last saying has been repeated by word of mouth, the bookish phrase *in the field of human conflict* has dropped out of it.) One has to take into account the fact that nearly all English people dislike anything that sounds high-flown and boastful. Slogans like "They shall not pass," or "Better to die on your feet than live on your knees," which have thrilled continental nations, seem slightly embarrassing to an Englishman, especially a working man. But the main weakness of propagandists and popularisers is their failure to notice that spoken and written English are two different things.

When recently I protested in print against the Marxist dialect which makes use of phrases like "objectively counter-revolutionary left-deviationism" or "drastic liquidation of petty-bourgeois elements," I received indignant letters from lifelong Socialists who told me that I was "insulting the language of the proletariat." In rather the same spirit, Professor Harold Laski devotes a long passage in his last book, *Faith, Reason and Civilisation*, to an attack on Mr. T. S. Eliot, whom he accuses of "writing only for a few." Now Eliot, as it happens, is one of the few writers of our time who have tried seriously to write English as it is spoken. Lines like –

> "And nobody came, and nobody went,
> But he took in the milk and he paid the rent"

are about as near to spoken English as print can come. On the other hand, here is an entirely typical sentence from Laski's own writing:

"As a whole, our system was a compromise between democracy in the political realm – itself a very recent development in our history – and an economic power oligarchically organised which was in its turn related to a certain aristocratic vestigia still able to influence profoundly the habits of our society."

This sentence, incidentally, comes from a reprinted lecture; so one must assume that Professor Laski actually stood up on a platform and spouted it forth, parenthesis and all. It is clear that people capable of speaking or writing in such a way have simply forgotten what everyday language is like. But this is nothing to some of the other passages I could dig out of Professor Laski's writings, or better still, from Communist literature, or best of all, from Trotskyist pamphlets. Indeed, from reading the Left-wing press you get the impression that the louder people yap about the proletariat, the more they despise its language.

I have said already that spoken English and written English are two different things. This variation exists in all languages, but is probably greater in English than in most. Spoken English is full of slang, it is abbreviated wherever possible, and people of all social classes treat its grammar and syntax in a slovenly way. Extremely few English people ever button up a sentence if they are speaking extempore. Above all, the vast English vocabulary contains thousands of words which everyone uses when writing, but which have no real currency in speech: and it also contains thousands more which are really obsolete but which are dragged forth by anyone who wants to sound clever or uplifting. If one keeps this in mind, one can think of ways of ensuring that propaganda, spoken or written, shall reach the audience it is aimed at.

So far as writing goes, all one can attempt is a process of simplification. The first step – and any social survey organisation could do this for a few hundreds or thousands of pounds – is to find out which of the abstract words habitually used by politicians are really understood by large numbers of people. If phrases like "unprincipled violation of declared pledges" or "insidious threat to the basic principles of democracy" don't mean anything to the average man, then it is stupid to use them. Secondly, in writing one can keep the spoken word constantly in mind. To get genuine spoken English on to paper is a complicated matter, as I shall show in a moment. But if you habitually say to yourself, "Could I simplify this? Could I make it more like speech?" you are not likely to produce sentences like the one quoted from Professor Laski above: nor are you likely to say "eliminate" when you mean kill, or "static water" when you mean fire tank.

Spoken propaganda, however, offers greater possibilities of improvement. It is here that the problem of writing in spoken English really arises.

Speeches, broadcasts, lectures and even sermons are normally written down beforehand. The most effective orators, like Hitler or Lloyd George, usually speak extempore, but they are very great rarities. As a rule – you can test this by listening at Hyde Park Corner – the so-called extempore speaker only keeps going by endlessly tacking one cliché on to another. In any case, he is probably delivering a speech which he has delivered dozens of times before. Only a few exceptionally gifted speakers can achieve the simplicity and intelligibility which even the most tongue-tied person achieves in ordinary conversation. On the air extempore speaking is seldom even attempted. Except for a few programmes, like the Brains Trust, which in any case are carefully rehearsed beforehand, every word that comes from the B.B.C. has been written down, and is delivered exactly as written. This is not only for censorship reasons: it is also because many speakers are liable to dry up at the microphone if they have no script to follow. The result is the heavy, dull, bookish lingo which causes most radio-users to switch off as soon as a talk is announced. It might be thought that one could get nearer to colloquial speech by dictating than by writing; but actually, it is the other way about. Dictating, at any rate to a human being, is always slightly embarrassing. One's impulse is to avoid long pauses, and one necessarily does so by clutching at the ready-made phrases and the dead and stinking metaphors (ring the changes on, ride rough-shod over, cross swords with, take up the cudgels for) with which the English language is littered. A dictated script is usually less life-like than a written one. What is wanted, evidently, is some way of getting ordinary, slipshod, colloquial English on to paper.

But is this possible? I think it is, and by a quite simple method which so far as I know has never been tried. It is this: Set a fairly ready speaker down at the microphone and let him just talk, either continuously or intermittently, on any subject he chooses. Do this with a dozen different speakers, recording it every time. Vary it with a few dialogues or conversations between three or four people. Then play your recordings back and let a stenographer reduce them to writing: not in the shortened, rationalised version that stenographers usually produce, but word for word, with such punctuation as seems appropriate. You would then – for the first time, I believe – have on paper some authentic specimens of spoken English. Probably they would not be readable as a book or a newspaper article is readable, but then spoken English is not meant to be read, it is meant to be listened to. From these specimens you could, I believe, formulate the rules of spoken English and find out how it differs from the written language. And when writing in spoken English had become practicable, the average speaker or lecturer who has to write his material down beforehand could bring it far closer to his natural diction, make it more essentially speakable, than he can at present.

Of course, demotic speech is not solely a matter of being colloquial and avoiding ill-understood words. There is also the question of accent. It seems certain that in modern England the "educated" upper-class accent is deadly to any speaker who is aiming at a large audience. All effective speakers in recent times have had either cockney or provincial accents. The success of Priestley's broadcasts in 1940 was largely due to his Yorkshire accent, which he probably broadened a little for the occasion. Churchill is only a seeming exception to this rule. Too old to have acquired the modern "educated" accent, he speaks with the Edwardian upper-class twang which to the average man's ear sounds like cockney. The "educated" accent, of which the accent of the B.B.C. announcers is a sort of parody, has no asset except its intelligibility to English-speaking foreigners. In England the minority to whom it is natural don't particularly like it, while in the other three-quarters of the population it arouses an immediate class antagonism. It is also noticeable that where there is doubt about the pronunciation of a name, successful speakers will stick to the working-class pronunciation even if they know it to be wrong. Churchill, for instance, mispronounced "Nazi" and "Gestapo" as long as the common people continued to do so. Lloyd George during the last war rendered "Kaiser" as "Kayser," which was the popular version of the word.

In the early days of the war the Government had the greatest difficulty in inducing people to bother to collect their ration books. At parliamentary elections, even when there is an up-to-date register, it often happens that less than half of the electorate use their votes. Things like these are symptoms of the intellectual gulf between the rulers and the ruled. But the same gulf lies always between the intelligentsia and the common man. Journalists, as we can see by their election forecasts, never know what the public is thinking. Revolutionary propaganda is incredibly ineffective. Churches are empty all over the country. The whole idea of trying to find out what the average man thinks, instead of assuming that he thinks what he ought to think, is novel and unwelcome. Social surveys are viciously attacked from Left and Right alike. Yet some mechanism for testing public opinion is an obvious necessity of modern government, and more so in a democratic country than in a totalitarian one. Its complement is the ability to speak to the ordinary man in words that he will understand and respond to.

At present propaganda only seems to succeed when it coincides with what people are inclined to do in any case. During the present war, for instance, the Government has done extraordinarily little to preserve morale: it has merely drawn on the existing reserves of good-will. And all political parties alike have failed to interest the public in vitally important questions – in the problem of India, to name only one. But some day we may have a genuinely democratic government, a government which will want to tell people what is happening; and what must be done next, and what sacrifices are necessary, and why. It will need the mechanisms for doing so, of which the first are the right words, the right tone of voice. The fact that when you suggest finding out what the common man is like, and approaching him accordingly, you are either accused of being an intellectual snob who wants to "talk down to" the masses, or else suspected of plotting to establish an English Gestapo, shows how sluggishly nineteenth-century our notion of democracy has remained.

As I Please 36

Tribune, 4 August 1944

Apropos of saturation bombing, a correspondent who disagreed with me very strongly added that he was by no means a pacifist. He recognised, he said, that "the Hun had got to be beaten." He merely objected to the barbarous methods that we are now using.

Now, it seems to me that you do less harm by dropping bombs on people than by calling them "Huns." Obviously one does not want to inflict death and wounds if it can be avoided, but I cannot feel that mere killing is all-important. We shall all be dead in less than a hundred years, and most of us by the sordid horror known as "natural death." The truly evil thing is to act in such a way that peaceful life becomes impossible. War damages the fabric of civilisation not by the destruction it causes (the net effect of a war may even be to increase the productive capacity of the world as a whole), nor even by the slaughter of human beings, but by stimulating hatred and dishonesty. By shooting at your enemy you are not in the deepest sense wronging him. But by hating him, by inventing lies about him and bringing children up to believe them, by clamouring for unjust peace terms which make further wars inevitable, you are striking not at one perishable generation, but at humanity itself.

It is a matter of observation that the people least infected by war hysteria are the fighting soldiers. Of all people they are the least inclined to hate the enemy, to swallow lying propaganda or to demand a vindictive peace. Nearly all soldiers – and this applies even to professional soldiers in peace time – have a sane attitude towards war. They realise that it is disgusting, and that it may often be necessary. This is harder for a civilian, because the soldier's detached attitude is partly due to sheer exhaustion, to the sobering effects of danger, and to continuous friction with his own military machine. The safe and well-fed civilian has more surplus emotion, and he is apt to use it up in hating somebody or other – the enemy if he is a patriot, his own side if he is a pacifist. But the war mentality is something that can be struggled against and overcome, just as the fear of bullets can be overcome. The trouble is that neither the Peace Pledge Union nor the Never Again Society know the war mentality when they see it. Meanwhile, the fact that in this war offensive nicknames like "Hun" have not caught on with the big public seems to me a good omen.

What has always seemed to me one of the most shocking deeds of the last war was one that did not aim at killing any-one – on the contrary, it probably saved a great many lives. Before launching their big attack at Caporetto, the Germans flooded the Italian army with faked Socialist propaganda leaf-lets in which it was alleged that the German soldiers were ready to shoot their officers and fraternise with their Italian comrades, etc., etc. Numbers of Italians were taken in, came over to fraternise with the Germans, and were made prisoner – and, I believe, jeered at for their simple-mindedness. I have heard this defended as a highly intelligent and humane way of making war – which it is, if your sole aim is to save as many skins as possible. And yet a trick like that damages the very roots of human solidarity in a way that no mere act of violence could do.

I see that the railings are returning – only wooden ones, it is true, but still railings – in one London square after another. So the lawful denizens of the squares can make use of their treasured keys again, and the children of the poor can be kept out.

When the railings round the parks and squares were re-moved, the object was partly to accumulate scrap iron, but the removal was also felt to be a democratic gesture. Many more green spaces were now open to the public, and you could stay in the parks till all hours instead of being hounded out at closing time by grim-faced keepers. It was also discovered that these railings were not only unnecessary but hideously ugly. The parks were improved out of recognition by being laid open, acquiring a friendly, almost rural look that they had never had before. And had the railings vanished permanently, another improvement would probably have followed. The dreary shrubberies of laurel and privet – plants not suited to England and always dusty, at any rate in London – would probably have been grubbed up and replaced by flower beds. Like the railings, they were merely put there to keep the populace out. However, the higher-ups managed to avert this reform, like so many others, and everywhere the wooden palisades are going up, regardless of the wastage of labour and timber.

When I was in the Home Guard we used to say that the bad sign would be when flogging was introduced. That has not happened yet, I believe, but all minor social symptoms point in the same direction. The worst sign of all – and I should expect this to happen almost immediately if the Tories win the General Election – will be the reappearance in the London streets of top hats not worn by either undertakers or bank messengers.

We hope to review before long – and meanwhile I take the opportunity of drawing attention to it – an unusual book called *Branch Street*, by Marie Paneth. The author is or was a voluntary worker at a children's club, and her book reveals the almost savage conditions in which some London children still grow up. It is not quite clear, however, whether these conditions are to any extent worse as a result of the war. I should like to read – I suppose some such thing must exist somewhere, but I don't know of it – an authoritative account of the effect of the war on children. Hundreds of thousands of town children have been evacuated to country districts, many have had their schooling interrupted for months at a time, others have had terrifying experiences with bombs (earlier in the war, a little girl of eight, evacuated to a Hertfordshire village, assured me that she had been bombed out seven times), others have been sleeping in Tube shelters, sometimes for a year or so at a stretch. I would like to know to what extent the town children have adapted themselves to country life – whether they have grown interested in birds and animals, or whether they simply pine to be back among the picture-houses – and whether there has been any significant increase in juvenile crime. The children described by Mrs. Paneth sound almost like the gangs of "wild children" who were a by-product of the Russian Revolution.

*

Back in the eighteenth century, when the India muslins were one of the wonders of the world, an Indian king sent envoys to the court of Louis XV. to negotiate a trade agreement. He was aware that in Europe women wield great political influence, and the envoys brought with them a bale of costly muslins, which they had been instructed to present to Louis's mistress. Unfortunately their information was not up to date: Louis's not very stable affections had veered, and the muslins were presented to a mistress who had already been discarded. The mission was a failure, and the envoys were decapitated when they got home.

I don't know whether this story has a moral, but when I see the kind of people that our Foreign Office likes to get together with, I am often reminded of it.

As I Please 37
Tribune, 11 August 1944

A few days ago a West African wrote to inform us that a certain London dance hall had recently erected a "colour bar," presumably in order to please the American soldiers who formed an important part of its clientele. Telephone conversations with the management of the dance hall brought us the answers: (a) that the "colour bar" had been cancelled, and (b) that it had never been imposed in the first place; but I think one can take it that our informant's charge had some kind of basis. There have been other similar incidents recently. For instance, during last week a case in a magistrate's court brought out the fact that a West Indian Negro working in this country had been refused admission to a place of entertainment when he was wearing Home Guard uniform. And there have been many instances of Indians, Negroes and others being turned away from hotels on the ground that "we don't take coloured people."

It is immensely important to be vigilant against this kind of thing, and to make as much public fuss as possible whenever it happens. For this is one of those matters in which making a fuss can achieve something. There is no kind of legal disability against coloured people in this country, and, what is more, there is very little popular colour feeling. (This is not due to any inherent virtue in the British people, as our behaviour in India shows. It is due to the fact that in Britain itself there is no colour problem.)

The trouble always arises in the same way. A hotel, restaurant or what-not is frequented by people who have money to spend and who object to mixing with Indians or Negroes. They tell the proprietor that unless he imposes a colour bar they will go elsewhere. They may be a very small minority, and the proprietor may not be in agreement with them, but it is difficult for him to lose good customers; so he imposes the colour bar. This kind of thing cannot happen when public opinion is on the alert and disagreeable publicity is given to any establishment where coloured people are insulted. Anyone who knows of a provable instance of colour discrimination ought always to expose it. Otherwise the tiny percentage of colour-snobs who exist among us can make endless mischief, and the British people are given a bad name which, as a whole, they do not deserve.

In the nineteen-twenties, when American tourists were as much a part of the scenery of Paris as tobacco kiosks and tin urinals, the beginnings of a colour bar began to appear even in France. The Americans spent money like water; and restaurant proprietors and the like could not afford to disregard them. One evening, at a dance in a very well-known café, some Americans objected to the presence of a Negro who was there with an Egyptian woman. After making some feeble protests, the proprietor gave in, and the Negro was turned out.

Next morning there was a terrible hullabaloo and the cafe proprietor was hauled up before a Minister of the Government and threatened with prosecution. It had turned out that the offended Negro was the Ambassador of Haiti. People of that kind can usually get satisfaction, but most of us do not have the good fortune to be ambassadors, and the ordinary Indian, Negro or Chinese can only be protected against petty insult if other ordinary people are willing to exert themselves on his behalf.

Readers of this week's *Tribune* will notice that Mr. Reginald Reynolds, reviewing *What the German Needs*, repeats and appears to believe a story about British troops advancing to the attack behind the cover of civilian hostages. His authority for it is a casual undated reference to the *News-Chronicle*.

Now, this business of advancing behind a screen of civilian hostages is a very old favourite in the history of war propaganda. The Germans were accused of doing it in 1914, and again in 1940. But would Mr. Reynolds believe it if it were told about Germans? I very much doubt it. He would at once reject it as an "atrocity story," which it is. As it happens, his quoted authority, the *News-Chronicle*, reported last week from the Normandy front another time-honoured atrocity – dipping women in petrol and setting fire to them. (This has been a steady favourite in the wars of the last thirty years. Ideally the women should be nuns. The *News-Chronicle* made them school-mistresses, which is perhaps the next best thing.) I feel pretty certain that Mr. Reynolds would reject that one too. It is only when these tales are told about our own side that they become, from the point of view of a war-resister, true or at any rate credible; just as for a blimp they only become true when told about the enemy.

I doubt whether the war-resister's attitude is any better than the blimp's, and in essentials I don't even think it is different. During recent years many pacifists and other war-resisters have assured me that all the tales of Nazi atrocities – the concentration camps, the gas vans, the rubber truncheons, the castor oil and all the rest of it – are simply lies emanating from the British Government. Or, alternatively, they are not lies, but then we do exactly the same ourselves. All that is said about the enemy is "war propaganda," and war propaganda, as we know from the experience of 1914–18, is invariably untruthful.

God knows there was enough lying in 1914–18, but I do urge that this time there is a radical difference. For it is not the case this time that the atrocity stories have only appeared since the war started. On the contrary, there were far more of them during the period 1933–39. During that time the whole civilised world looked on in horror at the things that were done in the Fascist countries. Nor did these stories emanate from the British Government, or from any Government.

It was everywhere the Socialists and Communists who believed them and circulated them. The concentration camps, the pogroms and all the rest of it were believed in by the whole of the European Left, including the majority of pacifists. They were also believed in by the hundreds of thousands of refugees who fled from the Fascist countries. If it is true *now*, therefore, that the tales of Nazi outrages are all lies, we have to accept one of two things. Either (a) between the years 1933–39 some tens of millions of Socialists and some hundreds of thousands of refugees suffered a mass hallucination about concentration camps, or (b) atrocities happen in peace time, but stop as soon as war breaks out.

I submit that both of these are incredible, and that the case against the Nazis must be substantially true. Nazism is a quite exceptionally evil thing, and it has been responsible for outrages quite unparalleled in recent times. It is definitely worse than British Imperialism, which has plenty of crimes of its own to answer for. Not to accept this seems to me merely unrealistic.

There is a point at which incredulity becomes credulity. "The Duke of Bedford," a young pacifist writes to me, "knows – I assure you that this is so – that Hitler is a good man, and he would like to have a talk with him in order to bring out what is best in him." I suggest on the contrary that Hitler is *not* a good man, and that there is a large body of evidence to support this. I don't know, of course, whether the Duke of Bedford is correctly reported. But if he is, then I see no significant difference between his outlook and that of any fat-headed *Daily Telegraph* reader who cries out against doodle-bugs while not caring a damn for the starvation of millions of Indians.

As I Please 38
Tribune, 18 August 1944

Apropos of my remarks on the railings round London squares, a correspondent writes:

"Are the squares to which you refer public or private properties? If private, I suggest that your comments in plain language advocate nothing less than theft and should be classed as such."

If giving the land of England back to the people of England is theft, I am quite happy to call it theft. In his zeal to defend private property, my correspondent does not stop to consider how the so-called owners of the land got hold of it. They simply seized it by force, afterwards hiring lawyers to provide them with title deeds. In the case of the enclosure of the common lands, which was going on from about 1600 to 1850, the land-grabbers did not even have the excuse of being foreign conquerors; they were quite frankly taking the heritage of their own countrymen, upon no sort of pretext except that they had the power to do so.

Except for the few surviving commons, the high roads, the lands of the National Trust, a certain number of parks, and the sea shore below high-tide mark, every square inch of England is "owned" by a few thousand families. These people are just about as useful as so many tapeworms. It is desirable that people should own their own dwelling-houses, and it is probably desirable that a farmer should own as much land as he can actually farm. But the ground landlord in a town area has no function and no excuse for existence. He is merely a person who has found out a way of milking the public while giving nothing in return. He causes rents to be higher, he makes town planning more difficult, and he excludes children from green spaces: that is literally all that he does, except to draw his income. The removal of the railings in the squares was a first step against him. It was a very small step, and yet an appreciable one, as the present move to restore the railings shows. For three years or so the squares lay open, and their sacred turf was trodden by the feet of working-class children, a sight to make dividend-drawers gnash their false teeth. If that is theft, all I can say is, so much the better for theft.

I note that once again there is serious talk of trying to attract tourists to this country after the war. This, it is said, will bring in a welcome trickle of foreign currency. But it is quite safe to prophesy that the attempt will be a failure. Apart from the many other difficulties, our licensing laws, and the artificial price of drink, are quite enough to keep foreigners away. Why should people who are used to paying sixpence for a bottle of wine visit a country where a pint of beer costs a shilling? But even these prices are less dismaying to foreigners than the lunatic laws which permit you to buy a glass of beer at half-past ten while forbidding you to buy it at twenty-five past, and which have done their best to turn the pubs into mere boozing shops by excluding children from them.

How downtrodden we are in comparison with most other peoples is shown by the fact that even people who are far from being "temperance" don't seriously imagine that our licensing laws could be altered. Whenever I suggest that pubs might be allowed to open in the afternoon, or to stay open till midnight, I always get the same answer – "The first people to object would be the publicans. *They* don't want to have to stay open twelve hours a day." People assume, you see, that opening hours, whether long or short, must be regulated by the law, even for one-man businesses. In France, and in various other countries, a café proprietor opens or shuts just as it suits him. He can keep open the whole twenty-four hours if he wants to; and, on the other hand, if he feels like shutting his café and going away for a week, he can do that too. In England we have had no such liberty for about a hundred years, and people are hardly able to imagine it.

England is a country that *ought* to be able to attract tourists. It has much beautiful scenery, an equable climate, innumerable attractive villages and medieval churches, good beer, and food-stuffs of excellent natural taste. If you could walk where you chose instead of being fenced in by barbed wire and "Trespass-ers will be prosecuted" boards, if speculative builders had not been allowed to ruin every pleasant view within ten miles of a big town, if you could get a drink when you wanted it at a normal price, if an eatable meal in a country inn were a normal experience, and if Sunday were not artificially made into a day of misery, then foreign visitors might be expected to come here. But if those things were true England would no longer be England, and I fancy that we shall have to find some way of acquiring foreign currency that is more in accord with our national character.

In spite of my campaign against the jackboot – in which I am not operating single-handed – I notice that jackboots are as common as ever in the columns of the newspapers. Even in the leading articles in the *Evening Standard*, I have come upon several of them lately. But I am still without any clear information as to what a jackboot is. It is a kind of boot that you put on when you want to behave tyrannically: that is as much as anyone seems to know.

Others beside myself have noted that war, when it gets into the leading articles, is apt to be waged with remarkably old-fashioned weapons. Planes and tanks do make an occasional appearance, but as soon as an heroic attitude has to be struck, the only armaments mentioned are the sword ("We shall not sheathe the sword until," etc., etc.), the spear, the shield, the buckler, the trident, the chariot and the clarion. All of these are hopelessly out of date (the chariot, for instance, has not been in effective use since about A.D. 50), and even the purpose of some of them has been forgotten. What is a buckler, for instance? One school of thought holds that it is a small round shield, but another school believes it to be a kind of belt. A clarion, I believe, is a trumpet, but most people imagine that a "clarion call" merely means a loud noise.

One of the early Mass Observation reports, dealing with the coronation of George VI., pointed out that what are called "national occasions" always seem to cause a lapse into archaic language. The "ship of state," for instance, when it makes one of its official appearances, has a prow and a helm instead of having a bow and a wheel, like modern ships. So far as it is applied to war, the motive for using this kind of language is probably a desire for euphemism. "We will not sheathe the sword," sounds a lot more gentlemanly than "We will keep on dropping block-busters," though in effect it means the same.

One argument for Basic English is that by existing side by side with Standard English it can act as a sort of corrective to the oratory of statesmen and publicists. High-sounding phrases, when translated into Basic, are often deflated in a surprising way. For example, I presented to a Basic expert the sentence, "He little knew the fate that lay in store for him" – to be told that in Basic this would become "He was far from certain what was going to happen." It sounds decidedly less impressive, but it means the same. In Basic, I am told, you cannot make a meaningless statement without its being apparent that it is meaningless – which is quite enough to explain why so many schoolmasters, editors, politicians and literary critics object to it.

Review of *Milton: Man and Thinker* by Denis Saurat

The Observer, 20 August 1944

This book, with all its learning, does not remove the impression that Milton, considered as anything except a poet, was an uninteresting person. It cannot be said that his life was uneventful: he went blind, he was twice married, and in the period of the Commonwealth he played an important part by answering, more or less officially, the leading pamphleteers of Europe. He also had the courage to continue writing anti-Royalist pamphlets when the Restoration was obviously imminent. And yet somehow Professor Saurat's claim that Milton was a "profound thinker" as well as a "marvellous poet" does not seem to be justified. Milton is remembered by his phraseology: it is difficult to feel that he added anything to our stock of ideas.

Professor Saurat has very little to say about Milton's private life, and not a great deal about his political outlook. The main emphasis of the book is religious. Milton's creed, it seems, was a kind of Deism or pantheism, definitely heretical even by Puritan standards. He did not believe in the duality of body and soul, and therefore only doubtfully believed in individual immortality. As he saw it, the Fall and the Atonement were a struggle that took place anew in every human being, and it was a struggle between reason and passion rather than between good and evil. In this scheme of things the doctrine of the Atonement in its Christian form had no place, and Milton does not even mention the Crucifixion in "Paradise Regained." Implicit in his outlook is the belief that the Kingdom of Heaven will be finally established on this earth, as was also believed by the ancient Hebrews before the doctrine of the immortality of the soul took root.

Professor Saurat accepts Blake's dictum that Milton "was of the Devil's party without knowing it," but adds that "he was also of God's party, and, what is more important, he knew it."

"Paradise Lost" is a dramatisation of his own struggle, moral and political. The story of the Fall, which is different from the Biblical version, sets forth his own view of sexual ethics, while the relationship between Adam and Eve ("He for God only, she for God in him") emphasises the necessary subjection of Woman. There are indeed passages in "Paradise Lost" in which it is difficult not to feel that Milton is writing "at" his first wife. Professor Saurat does not say this, but he does say that Milton's subject-matter is in one way or another always himself. His political opinions sprang very directly out of his subjective feelings. Persecution made him a champion of liberty, but on the other hand he was not in favour of toleration for those he seriously disagreed with, such as the Catholics. He believed in democracy until he found that the common people were not of his way of thinking. Professor Saurat admits Milton's egotism and his tendency to base his theories on personal motives, but turns this into a virtue:

> But we may as well think ... what a powerful personality was here, a personality which, in the exercise of its normal needs, was brought up against everything that was arbitrary in the laws and customs of the time! This man was under no necessity to think in order to discover the abuses of the social order; all he had to do was to live, and he naturally came to stumble against every prejudice and to trip against every error. He was naively surprised, and wondered why everyone did not think as he did. His egotism and his pride were so deep that they acted as hardly conscious natural forces, as though human nature, trammelled, bound, and imprisoned in all other men, had held to its free course in Milton alone.

This is ingenious, but when one remembers, for instance, that Milton only became an advocate of divorce when he wanted to dissolve his own marriage, it hardly seems to hold water.

This is, of course, a book about Milton as a thinker and not as a writer, but one cannot help feeling that a little more should have been made of the fact that Milton was a poet. For his outstanding characteristic, which cannot be left out of any full account of him, is his sheer skill with words. It is fair to call it unique, not only because it has never been successfully imitated, in spite of some well-marked stylistic tricks, but because, far more than in most great poets, it is independent of meaning. Many of Milton's best verbal effects are got by monstrously irrelevant digressions, lists of names, and sheer trivialities, things like: –

> *the barren plains*
> *Of Sericana, where Chineses drive*
> *With sails and wind their cany wagons light.*

If Milton did a service to the human intellect, it was not by writing pamphlets against Salmasius but by weaving noble words round comparatively simple thoughts. For instance: –

> *I did but prompt the age to quit their clogs,*
> *By the known rules of ancient liberty,*
> *When straight a barbarous noise environs me*
> *Of owls and cuckoos, asses, apes and dogs.*

Over a period of 300 years, how many defenders of free speech must have drawn strength from that line, "By the known rules of ancient liberty"! However, perhaps Professor Saurat will write another book about Milton, considered this time as a poet.

As I Please 39
Tribune, 25 August 1944

A certain amount of material dealing with Burma and the Burma campaign has been passed on to me by the India-Burma Association, which is an unofficial body representing the European communities in those countries, and standing for a "moderate" policy based on the Cripps proposals.

The India-Burma Association complains with justice that Burma has been extraordinarily ill-served in the way of publicity. Not only has the general public no interest in Burma, in spite of its obvious importance from many points of view, but the authorities have not even succeeded in producing an attractive booklet which would tell people what the problems of

Burma are and how they are related to our own. Newspaper reports of the fighting in Burma, from 1942 onwards, have been consistently uninformative, especially from a political point of view. As soon as the Japanese attack began the newspapers and the B.B.C. adopted the practice of referring to all the inhabitants of Burma as "Burmans," even applying this name to the quite distinct and semi-savage peoples of the far north. This is not only about as accurate as calling a Swede an Italian, but masks the fact that the Japanese find their support mostly among the Burmese proper, the minorities being largely pro-British. In the present campaign, when prisoners are taken, the newspaper reports never state whether they are Japanese or whether they are Burmese and Indian partisans – a point of very great importance.

Almost all the books that have been published about the campaign of 1942 are misleading. I know what I am talking about, because I have had most of them to review. They have either been written by American journalists with no background knowledge and a considerable anti-British bias, or by British officials who are on the defensive and anxious to cover up everything discreditable. Actually, the British officials and military men have been blamed for much that was not their fault, and the view of the Burma campaign held by left wingers in this country was almost as distorted as that held by the blimps. But this trouble arises because there is no official effort to publicise the truth. For to my knowledge manuscripts do exist which give valuable information, but which, for commercial reasons, cannot find publishers.

I can give three examples. In 1942 a young Burman who had been a member of the Thakin (extreme Nationalist) party and had intrigued with the Japanese fled to India, having changed his mind about the Japanese when he saw what their rule was like. He wrote a short book which was published in India under the title of *What Happened in Burma* and which was obviously authentic in the main. The Indian Government in its negligent way sent exactly two copies to England. I tried to induce various publishers to re-issue it, but failed every time: they all gave the same reason – it was not worth wasting paper on a subject which the big public was not interested in. Later a Major Enriquez, who has published various travel books dealing with Burma, brought to England a diary covering the Burma campaign and the retreat into India. It was an extremely revealing – in places a disgracefully revealing – document, but it suffered the same fate as the other book. At the moment I am reading another manuscript which gives valuable background material about Burma's history, its economic conditions, its system of land tenure, and so forth. But I would bet a small sum that it won't be published either, at any rate until the paper shortage lets up.

If paper and money are not forthcoming for books of this kind – books which may spill a lot of beans but do help to counteract the lies put about by Axis sympathisers – then the Government must not be surprised if the public knows nothing about Burma and cares less. And what applies to Burma applies to scores of other important but neglected subjects.

Meanwhile here is a suggestion. Whenever a document appears which is not commercially saleable but which is likely to be useful to future historians, it should be submitted to a committee set up by, for instance, the British Museum. If they consider it historically valuable they should have the power to print off a few copies and store them for the use of scholars. At present a manuscript rejected by the commercial publishers almost always ends up in the dustbin. How many possible correctives to accepted lies must have perished in this way!

At a time when muck floods the bookshops while good books go out of print, I was rather glad to see recently that one or two of Leonard Merrick's novels have been re-issued in a cheap edition.

Leonard Merrick is a writer who seems to me never to have quite had his due. He was not trying to be anything but a popular writer, he has many of the characteristic faults of the pre-1914 period, and he takes almost for granted the middle-class values of that time. But his books are not only sincere, they have the fascination that belongs to all books which deal with the diffi-culty of earning a living. The most characteristic of them are about struggling artists, usually actors, but Art with a big A hardly enters: everything centres round the ghastly effort to pay the rent and remain "respectable" at the same time. Ever since reading Leonard Merrick, the horrors of a travelling actor's life – the Sunday journeys and draughty ill-lit theatres, the catcalling audiences, the theatrical lodgings presided over by "Ma," the white china chamberpot and the permanent smell of fried fish, the sordid rivalries and love affairs, the swindling manager who disappears with all the takings in the middle of the tour – have had their own special corner in my mind.

To anyone who wants to try Leonard Merrick, I would say: lay off the Paris books, which are William J. Locke-ish and tiresome, and read either *The Man Who was Good*, *The House of Lynch* or *The Position of Peggy Harper*. In a different vein, but also worth reading, is *The Worldlings*.

I wish some botanist among my readers would give me a clear ruling about the name of the weed with a pink flower which grows so profusely on blitzed sites.

I was brought up to call this plant Willowherb. Another similar but distinct plant, which grows in marshy places, I was taught to call Rosebay or French Willow. But I notice that Sir William Beach Thomas, writing in the *Observer*, calls the plant on the blitzed sites Rosebay Willowherb, thus combining the two names. The only wildflower book I have consulted gives no help. Other people who have referred to the plant seem to use all three names interchangeably. I should like the point cleared up, if only for the satisfaction of knowing whether a Nature Correspondent of fifty years' standing can be wrong.

Raffles and Miss Blandish

28 August 1944; *Horizon*, October 1944; *Politics*, November 1944

Nearly half a century after his first appearance, Raffles, "the amateur cracksman," is still one of the best-known characters in English fiction. Very few people would need telling that he played cricket for England, had bachelor chambers in the Albany and burgled the Mayfair houses which he also entered as a guest. Just for that reason he and his exploits make a suitable background against which to examine a more modern crime story such as *No Orchids for Miss Blandish*. Any such choice is necessarily arbitrary – I might equally well have chosen *Arsène*

Lupin, for instance – but at any rate *No Orchids* and the Raffles books[10] have the common quality of being crime stories which play the limelight on the criminal rather than the policeman. For sociological purposes they can be compared. *No Orchids* is the 1939 version of glamourised crime, *Raffles* the 1900 version. What I am concerned with here is the immense difference in moral atmosphere between the two books, and the change in the popular attitude that this probably implies.

At this date, the charm of *Raffles* is partly in the period atmosphere, and partly in the technical excellence of the stories. Hornung was a very conscientious and, on his level, a very able writer. Anyone who cares for sheer efficiency must admire his work. However, the truly dramatic thing about Raffles, the thing that makes him a sort of by-word even to this day (only a few weeks ago, in a burglary case, a magistrate referred to the prisoner as "a Raffles in real life"), is the fact that he is *a gentleman*. Raffles is presented to us – and this is rubbed home in countless scraps of dialogue and casual remarks – not as an honest man who has gone astray, but as a public-school man who has gone astray. His remorse, when he feels any, is almost purely social: he has disgraced "the old school," he has lost his right to enter "decent society," he has forfeited his amateur status and become a cad. Neither Raffles nor Bunny appears to feel at all strongly that stealing is wrong in itself, though Raffles does once justify himself by the casual remark that "the distribution of property is all wrong anyway." They think of themselves not as sinners but as renegades, or simply as outcasts. And the moral code of most of us is still so close to Raffles's own that we do feel his situation to be an especially ironical one. A West End clubman who is really a burglar! That is almost a story in itself, is it not? But how if it were a plumber or a greengrocer who was really a burglar? Would there be anything inherently dramatic in that? No – although the theme of the "double life," of respectability covering crime, is still there. Even Charles Peace in his clergyman's dog-collar seems somewhat less of a hypocrite than Raffles in his Zingari blazer.

Raffles, of course, is good at all games, but it is peculiarly fitting that his chosen game should be cricket. This allows not only of endless analogies between his cunning as a slow bowler and his cunning as a burglar, but also helps to define the exact nature of his crime. Cricket is not in reality a very popular game in England – it is nowhere near so popular as football, for instance – but it gives expression to a well-marked trait in the English character, the tendency to value "form" or "style" more highly than success. In the eyes of any true cricket-lover it is possible for an innings of ten runs to be "better" (i.e. more elegant) than an innings of a hundred runs: cricket is also one of the very few games in which the amateur can excel the professional. It is a game full of forlorn hopes and sudden dramatic changes of fortune, and its rules are so ill-defined that their interpretation is partly an ethical business. When Larwood, for instance, practised body-line bowling in Australia he was not actually breaking any rule: he was merely doing something that was "not cricket." Since cricket takes up a lot of time and is rather expensive to play, it is predominantly an upper-class game, but for the whole nation it is bound up with such concepts as "good form," "playing the game," etc., and it has declined in popularity just as the tradition of "don't hit a man when he's down" has declined. It is not a twentieth-century game, and nearly all modern-minded people dislike it. The Nazis, for instance, were at pains to discourage cricket, which had gained a certain footing in Germany before and after the last war. In making Raffles a cricketer as well as a burglar Hornung was not merely providing him with a plausible disguise; he was also drawing the sharpest moral contrast that he was able to imagine.

Raffles, no less than *Great Expectations* or *Le Rouge et le Noir*, is a story of snobbery, and it gains a great deal from the precariousness of Raffles's social position. A cruder writer would have made the "gentleman burglar" a member of the peerage, or at least a baronet. Raffles, however, is of upper-middle-class origin and is only accepted by the aristocracy because of his personal charm. "We were in Society but not of it," he says to Bunny towards the end of the book; and "I was asked about for my cricket." Both he and Bunny accept the values of "Society" unquestioningly, and would settle down in it for good if only they could get away with a big enough haul. The ruin that constantly threatens them is all the blacker because they only doubtfully "belong." A duke who has served a prison sentence is still a duke, whereas a mere man-about

GEORGE ORWELL

town if once disgraced, ceases to be "about town" for ever-more. The closing chapters of the book, when Raffles has been exposed and is living under an assumed name, have a twilight-of-the-gods feeling, a mental atmosphere rather similar to that of Kipling's poem, *Gentleman Rankers*:

> A trooper of the forces –
> I, who kept my own six horses! etc.

Raffles now belongs irrevocably to the "cohorts of the damned." He can still commit successful burglaries, but there is no way back into Paradise, which means Piccadilly and the M.C.C. According to the public-school code there is only one means of rehabilitation: death in battle. Raffles dies fighting against the Boers (a practised reader would foresee this from the start), and in the eyes of both Bunny and his creator this cancels his crimes.

Both Raffles and Bunny, of course, are devoid of religious belief, and they have no real ethical code, merely certain rules of behaviour which they observe semi-instinctively. But it is just here that the deep moral difference between *Raffles* and *No Orchids* becomes apparent. Raffles and Bunny, after all, are gentlemen, and such standards as they do have are not to be violated. Certain things are "not done," and the idea of doing them hardly arises. Raffles will not, for example, abuse hospi-tality. He will commit a burglary in a house where he is staying as a guest, but the victim must be a fellow-guest and not the host. He will not commit murder,[11] and he avoids violence wherever possible and prefers to carry out his robberies unarmed. He regards friendship as sacred, and is chivalrous though not moral in his relations with women. He will take extra risks in the name of "sportsmanship," and sometimes even for aesthetic reasons. And above all he is intensely patri-otic. He celebrates the Diamond Jubilee ("For sixty years, Bunny, we've been ruled over by absolutely the finest sover-eign the world has ever seen") by despatching to the Queen, through the post, an antique gold cup which he has stolen from the British Museum. He steals, from partly political motives, a pearl which the German Emperor is sending to one of the enemies of Britain, and when the Boer War begins to go badly his one thought is to find his way into the fighting line. At the front he unmasks a spy at the cost of revealing his own identity, and then dies gloriously by a Boer bullet. In this combination of crime and patriotism he resembles his near-contemporary Arsène Lupin, who also scores off the German Emperor and wipes out his very dirty past by enlisting in the Foreign Legion.

It is important to note that by modern standards Raffles's crimes are very petty ones. Four hundred pounds' worth of jewellery seems to him an excellent haul. And though the stories are convincing in their physical detail, they contain very little sensationalism – very few corpses, hardly any blood, no sex crimes, no sadism, no perversions of any kind. It seems to be the case that the crime story, at any rate on its higher levels, has greatly increased in bloodthirstiness during the past twenty years. Some of the early detective stories do not even contain a murder. The Sherlock Holmes stories, for instance, are not all murders, and some of them do not even deal with an indictable crime. So also with the John Thorndyke stories, while of the Max Carrados stories only a minority are murders. Since 1918, however, a detective story not containing a murder has been a great rarity, and the most disgusting details of dismemberment and exhumation are commonly exploited. Some of the Peter Wimsey stories, for instance, seem to point to definite necrophilia. The Raffles stories, written from the angle of the criminal, are much less anti-social than many modern stories written from the angle of the detective. The main impression that they leave behind is of boyishness. They belong to a time when people had standards, though they happened to be foolish standards. Their key phrase is "not done." The line that they draw between good and evil is as senseless as a Polynesian taboo, but at least, like the taboo, it has the advantage that everyone accepts it.

So much for *Raffles*. Now for a header into the cesspool. *No Orchids for Miss Blandish*, by James Hadley Chase, was published in 1939 but seems to have enjoyed its greatest popularity in 1940, during the Battle of Britain and the blitz. In its main outlines its story is this:

Miss Blandish, the daughter of a millionaire, is kidnapped by some gangsters who are almost immediately surprised and killed off by a larger and better organised gang. They hold her to ransom and extract half a million dollars from her father.

Their original plan had been to kill her as soon as the ransom-money was received, but a chance keeps her alive. One of the gang is a young man named Slim whose sole pleasure in life consists in driving knives into other people's bellies. In childhood he has graduated by cutting up living animals with a pair of rusty scissors. Slim is sexually impotent, but takes a kind of fancy to Miss Blandish. Slim's mother, who is the real brains of the gang, sees in this the chance of curing Slim's impotence, and decides to keep Miss Blandish in custody till Slim shall have succeeded in raping her. After many efforts and much persuasion, including the flogging of Miss Blandish with a length of rubber hosepipe, the rape is achieved. Meanwhile Miss Blandish's father has hired a private detective, and by means of bribery and torture the detective and the police manage to round up and exterminate the whole gang. Slim escapes with Miss Blandish and is killed after a final rape, and the detective prepares to restore Miss Blandish to her family. By this time, however, she has developed such a taste for Slim's caresses[12] that she feels unable to live without him, and she jumps out of the window of a skyscraper.

Several other points need noticing before one can grasp the full implications of this book. To begin with its central story is an impudent plagiarism of William Faulkner's novel, *Sanctuary*. Secondly it is not, as one might expect, the product of an illiterate hack, but a brilliant piece of writing, with hardly a wasted word or a jarring note anywhere. Thirdly, the whole book, récit as well as dialogue, is written in the American language: the author, an Englishman who has (I believe) never been in the United States, seems to have made a complete mental transference to the American underworld. Fourthly, the book sold, according to its publishers, no less than half a million copies.

I have already outlined the plot, but the subject-matter is much more sordid and brutal than this suggests. The book contains eight full-dress murders, an unassessable number of casual killings and woundings, an exhumation (with a careful reminder of the stench), the flogging of Miss Blandish, the torture of another woman with redhot cigarette ends, a strip-tease act, a third-degree scene of unheard-of cruelty, and much else of the same kind. It assumes great sexual sophistication in its readers (there is a scene, for instance, in which a gangster, presumably of masochistic tendency, has an orgasm in the moment of being knifed), and it takes for granted the most complete corruption and self-seeking as the norm of human behaviour. The detective, for instance, is almost as great a rogue as the gangsters, and actuated by nearly the same motives. Like them, he is in pursuit of "five hundred grand." It is necessary to the machinery of the story that Mr. Blandish should be anxious to get his daughter back, but apart from this such things as affection, friendship, good-nature or even ordinary politeness simply do not enter. Nor, to any great extent, does normal sexuality. Ultimately only one motive is at work throughout the whole story: the pursuit of power.

It should be noticed that the book is not in the ordinary sense pornography. Unlike most books that deal in sexual sadism, it lays the emphasis on the cruelty and not on the pleasure. Slim, the ravisher of Miss Blandish, has "wet, slobbering lips": this is disgusting, and it is meant to be disgusting. But the scenes describing cruelty to women are comparatively perfunctory. The real high-spots of the book are cruelties committed by men upon other men: above all the third-degreeing of the gangster, Eddie Schultz, who is lashed into a chair and flogged on the windpipe with truncheons, his arms broken by fresh blows as he breaks loose. In another of Mr. Chase's books, *He Won't Need It Now*, the hero, who is intended to be a sympathetic and perhaps even noble character, is described as stamping on somebody's face, and then, having crushed the man's mouth in, grinding his heel round and round in it. Even when physical incidents of this kind are not occurring, the mental atmosphere of these books is always the same. Their whole theme is the struggle for power and the triumph of the strong over the weak. The big gangsters wipe out the little ones as mercilessly as a pike gobbling up the little fish in a pond; the police kill off the criminals as cruelly as the angler kills the pike. If ultimately one sides with the police against the gangsters it is merely because they are better organised and more powerful, because, in fact, the law is a bigger racket than crime. Might is right: vae victis.

As I have mentioned already, *No Orchids* enjoyed its greatest vogue in 1940, though it was successfully running as a play till

723

some time later. It was, in fact, one of the things that helped to console people for the boredom of being bombed. Early in the war the *New Yorker* had a picture of a little man approaching a news-stall littered with papers with such headlines as GREAT TANK BATTLES IN NORTHERN FRANCE, BIG NAVAL BATTLE IN THE NORTH SEA, HUGE AIR BATTLES OVER THE CHANNEL, etc. etc. The little man is saying, "*Action Stories*, please." That little man stood for all the drugged millions to whom the world of the gangsters and the prize-ring is more "real," more "tough" than such things as wars, revolutions, earthquakes, famines and pestilences. From the point of view of a reader of *Action Stories*, a description of the London blitz, or of the struggles of the European underground parties, would be "sissy stuff." On the other hand some puny gun-battle in Chicago, resulting in perhaps half a dozen deaths, would seem genuinely "tough." This habit of mind is now extremely widespread. A soldier sprawls in a muddy trench, with the machine-gun bullets crackling a foot or two overhead and whiles away his intolerable boredom by reading an American gangster story. And what is it that makes that story so exciting? Precisely the fact that people are shooting at each other with machine-guns! Neither the soldier nor anyone else sees anything curious in this. It is taken for granted that an imaginary bullet is more thrilling than a real one.

The obvious explanation is that in real life one is usually a passive victim, whereas in the adventure story one can think of oneself as being at the centre of events. But there is more to it than that. Here it is necessary to refer again to the curious fact of *No Orchids* being written – with technical errors, perhaps, but certainly with considerable skill – in the American language.

There exists in America an enormous literature of more or less the same stamp as *No Orchids*. Quite apart from books, there is the huge array of "pulp magazines," graded so as to cater for different kinds of fantasy but nearly all having much the same mental atmosphere. A few of them go in for straight pornography but the great majority are quite plainly aimed at sadists and masochists. Sold at threepence a copy under the title of Yank Mags,[13] these things used to enjoy considerable popularity in England, but when the supply dried up owing to the war, no satisfactory substitute was forthcoming. English imitations of the "pulp magazine" do now exist, but they are poor things compared with the original. English crook films, again, never approach the American crook film in brutality. And yet the career of Mr. Chase shows how deep the American influence has already gone. Not only is he himself living a continuous fantasy-life in the Chicago underworld, but he can count on hundreds of thousands of readers who know what is meant by a "clipshop" or the "hotsquat," do not have to do mental arithmetic when confronted by "fifty grand," and understand at sight a sentence like "Johnnie was a rummy and only two jumps ahead of the nut-factory." Evidently there are great numbers of English people who are partly Americanised in language and, one ought to add, in moral outlook. For there was no popular protest against *No Orchids*. In the end it was withdrawn, but only retrospectively, when a later work, *Miss Callaghan comes to Grief* brought Mr. Chase's books to the attention of the authorities. Judging by casual conversations at the time, ordinary readers got a mild thrill out of the obscenities in *No Orchids*, but saw nothing undesirable in the book as a whole. Many people, incidentally, were under the impression that it was an American book re-issued in England.

The thing that the ordinary reader *ought* to have objected to – almost certainly would have objected to, a few decades earlier – was the equivocal attitude towards crime. It is implied throughout *No Orchids* that being a criminal is only reprehensible in the sense that it does not pay. Being a policeman pays better, but there is no moral difference, since the police use essentially criminal methods. In a book like *He Won't Need It Now* the distinction between crime and crime-prevention practically disappears. This is a new departure for English sensational fiction, in which till recently there has always been a sharp distinction between right and wrong and a general agreement that virtue must triumph in the last chapter. English books glorifying crime (modern crime, that is – pirates and highwaymen are different) are very rare. Even a book like *Raffles*, as I have pointed out, is governed by powerful taboos, and it is clearly understood that Raffles's crimes must be expiated sooner or later. In America, both in life and fiction, the tendency to tolerate crime, even to admire the criminal so long as he is successful, is very much more marked. It is, indeed, ultimately this attitude that has made it possible for crime to flourish upon so huge a scale. Books have been written about Al Capone that are hardly different in tone from the books written about Henry Ford, Stalin, Lord Northcliffe and all the rest of the "log cabin to White House" brigade. And switching back eighty years, one finds Mark Twain adopting much the same attitude towards the disgusting bandit Slade, hero of twenty-eight murders, and towards the Western desperadoes generally. They were successful, they "made good," therefore he admired them.

In a book like *No Orchids* one is not, as in the old-style crime story, simply escaping from dull reality into an imaginary world of action. One's escape is essentially into cruelty and sexual perversion. *No Orchids* is aimed at the power-instinct which *Raffles* or the Sherlock Holmes stories are not. At the same time the English attitude towards crime is not so superior to the American as I may have seemed to imply. It too is mixed up with power-worship, and has become more noticeably so in the last twenty years. A writer who is worth examining is Edgar Wallace, especially in such typical books as *The Orator* and the Mr. J. G. Reeder stories. Wallace was one of the first crime-story writers to break away from the old tradition of the private detective and make his central figure a Scotland Yard official. Sherlock Holmes is an amateur, solving his problems without the help and even, in the earlier stories, against the opposition of the police. Moreover, like Dupin, he is essentially an intellectual, even a scientist. He reasons logically from observed fact, and his intellectuality is constantly contrasted with the routine methods of the police. Wallace objected strongly to this slur, as he considered it, on Scotland Yard, and in several newspaper articles he went out of his way to denounce Holmes by name. His own ideal was the detective-inspector who catches criminals not because he is intellectually brilliant but because he is part of an all-powerful organisation. Hence the curious fact that in Wallace's most characteristic stories the "clue" and the "deduction" play no part. The criminal is always defeated either by an incredible coincidence, or because in some unexplained manner the police know all about the crime beforehand. The tone of the stories makes it quite clear that Wallace's admiration for the police is pure bully-worship. A Scotland Yard detective is the most powerful kind of being that he can imagine, while the criminal figures in his mind as an outlaw against whom anything is permissible, like the condemned slaves in the Roman arena. His policemen behave much more brutally than British policemen do in real life – they hit people without provocation, fire revolvers past their ears to terrify them, and so on – and some of the stories exhibit a fearful intellectual sadism. (For instance, Wallace likes to arrange things so that the villain is hanged on the same day as the heroine is married.) But it is sadism after the English fashion: that is to say it is unconscious, there is not overtly any sex in it, and it keeps within the bounds of the law. The British public tolerates a harsh criminal law and gets a kick out of monstrously unfair murder trials: but still that is better, on any count, than tolerating or admiring crime. If one must worship a bully, it is better that he should be a policeman than a gangster. Wallace is still governed to some extent by the concept of "not done." In *No Orchids* anything is "done" so long as it leads on to power. All the barriers are down, all the motives are out in the open. Chase is a worse symptom than Wallace, to the extent that all-in wrestling is worse than boxing, or Fascism is worse than capitalist democracy.

In borrowing from William Faulkner's *Sanctuary*, Chase only took the plot; the mental atmosphere of the two books is not similar. Chase really derives from other sources, and this particular bit of borrowing is only symbolic. What it symbolises is the vulgarisation of ideas which is constantly happening, and which probably happens faster in an age of print. Chase has been described as "Faulkner for the masses," but it would be more accurate to describe him as Carlyle for the masses. He is a popular writer – there are many such in America, but they are still rarities in England – who has caught up with what it is now fashionable to call "realism," meaning the doctrine that might is right. The growth of "realism" has been the great feature of the intellectual history of our own age. Why this should be so is a complicated question. The interconnection between sadism, masochism, success-worship, power-worship, nationalism and totalitarianism is a huge subject whose edges have barely been scratched, and even to mention it is considered somewhat indelicate. To take merely the first example that comes to mind, I believe no one has ever pointed out the sadistic and masochistic element in Bernard Shaw's work, still less suggested that this probably has some connection with Shaw's admiration for dictators.

Fascism is often loosely equated with sadism, but nearly always by people who see nothing wrong in the most slavish worship of Stalin. The truth is, of course, that the countless English intellectuals who kiss the arse of Stalin are not different from the minority who give their allegiance to Hitler or Mussolini, nor from the efficiency experts who preached "punch," "drive," "personality" and "learn to be a Tiger Man" in the nineteen-twenties, nor from the older generation of intellectuals, Carlyle, Creasey and the rest of them, who bowed down before German militarism. All of them are worshipping power and successful cruelty. It is important to notice that the cult of power tends to be mixed up with a love of cruelty and wickedness *for their own sakes*. A tyrant is all the more admired if he happens to be a bloodstained crook as well, and "the end justifies the means" often becomes, in effect, "the means justify themselves provided they are dirty enough." This idea colours the outlook of all sympathisers with totalitarianism, and accounts, for instance, for the positive delight with which many English intellectuals greeted the Nazi-Soviet pact. It was a step only doubtfully useful to the USSR, but it was entirely unmoral, and for that reason to be admired: the explanations of it, which were numerous and self-contradictory, could come afterwards.

Until recently the characteristic adventure stories of the English-speaking peoples have been stories in which the hero fights *against odds*. This is true all the way from Robin Hood to Popeye the Sailor. Perhaps the basic myth of the Western world is Jack the Giant Killer. But to be brought up to date this should be renamed Jack the Dwarf Killer, and there already exists a considerable literature which teaches, either overtly or implicitly, that one should side with the big man against the little man. Most of what is now written about foreign policy is simply an embroidery on this theme, and for several decades such phrases as "play the game," "don't hit a man when he's down" and "it's not cricket" have never failed to draw a snigger

728

from anyone of intellectual pretensions. What is comparatively new is to find the accepted pattern according to which (a) right is right and wrong is wrong, whoever wins, and (b) weakness must be respected, disappearing from popular literature as well. When I first read D. H. Lawrence's novels, at the age of about twenty, I was puzzled by the fact that there did not seem to be any classification of the characters into "good" and "bad." Lawrence seemed to sympathise with all of them about equally, and this was so unusual as to give me the feeling of having lost my bearings. Today no one would think of looking for heroes and villains in a serious novel, but in lowbrow fiction one still expects to find a sharp distinction between right and wrong and between legality and illegality. The common people, on the whole, are still living in the world of absolute good and evil from which the intellectuals have long since escaped. But the popularity of *No Orchids* and the American books and magazines to which it is akin shows how rapidly the doctrine of "realism" is gaining ground.

Several people, after reading *No Orchids*, have remarked to me, "It's pure Fascism." This is a correct description, although the book has not the smallest connection with politics and very little with social or economic problems. It has merely the same relation to Fascism as, say, Trollope's novels have to nineteenth-century capitalism. It is a daydream appropriate to a totalitarian age. In his imagined world of gangsters Chase is presenting, as it were, a distilled version of the modern political scene, in which such things as mass bombing of civilians, the use of hostages, torture to obtain confessions, secret prisons, execution without trial, floggings with rubber truncheons, drownings in cesspools, systematic falsification of records and statistics, treachery, bribery and quislingism are normal and morally neutral, even admirable when they are done in a large and bold way. The average man is not directly interested in politics, and when he reads he wants the current struggles of the world to be translated into a simple story about individuals. He can take an interest in Slim and Fenner as he could not in the GPU and the Gestapo. People worship power in the form in which they are able to understand it. A twelve-year-old boy worships Jack Dempsey. An adolescent in a Glasgow slum worships Al Capone. An aspiring pupil at a business college worships Lord Nuffield. A *New Statesman* reader worships Stalin. There is a difference in intellectual maturity, but none in moral outlook. Thirty years ago the heroes of popular fiction had nothing in common with Mr. Chase's gangsters and detectives, and the idols of the English liberal intelligentsia were also comparatively sympathetic figures. Between Holmes and Fenner on the one hand, and between Abraham Lincoln and Stalin on the other, there is a similar gulf.

One ought not to infer too much from the success of Mr. Chase's books. It is possible that it is an isolated phenomenon, brought about by the mingled boredom and brutality of war. But if such books should definitely acclimatise themselves in England, instead of being merely a half-understood import from America, there would be good grounds for dismay. In choosing *Raffles* as a background for *No Orchids*, I deliberately chose a book which by the standards of its time was morally equivocal. Raffles, as I have pointed out, has no real moral code, no religion, certainly no social consciousness. All he has is a set of reflexes – the nervous system, as it were, of a gentleman. Give him a sharp tap on this reflex or that (they are called "sport," "pal," "woman," "king and country" and so forth), and you get a predictable reaction. In Mr. Chase's book there are no gentlemen, and no taboos. Emancipation is complete, Freud and Machiavelli have reached the outer suburbs. Comparing the schoolboy atmosphere of the one book with the cruelty and corruption of the other, one is driven to feel that snobbishness, like hypocrisy, is a check upon behaviour whose value from a social point of view has been underrated.

As I Please 40
Tribune, 1 September 1944

It is not my primary job to discuss the details of contemporary politics, but this week there is something that cries out to be said. Since, it seems, nobody else will do so, I want to protest against the mean and cowardly attitude adopted by the British press towards the recent rising in Warsaw.

As soon as the news of the rising broke, the *News-Chronicle* and kindred papers adopted a markedly disapproving attitude. One was left with the general impression that the Poles deserved to have their bottoms smacked for doing what all the Allied wirelesses had been urging them to do for years past, and that they would not be given and did not deserve to be given any help from outside. A few papers tentatively suggested that arms and supplies might be dropped by the Anglo-Americans, a thousand miles away: no one, so far as I know, suggested that this might be done by the Russians, perhaps twenty miles away. The *New Statesman*, in its issue of August 18, even went so far as to doubt whether appreciable help could be given from the air in such circumstances. All or nearly all the papers of the Left were full of blame for the "*émigré*" London Government which had "prematurely" ordered its followers to rise when the Red Army was at the gates. This line of thought is adequately set forth in a letter to last week's *Tribune* from Mr. G. Barraclough. He makes the following specific charges: –

(1) The Warsaw rising was "not a spontaneous popular rising," but was "begun on orders from the soi-disant Polish Government in London."

(2) The order to rise was given "without consultation with either the British or Soviet Governments," and "no attempt was made to co-ordinate the rising with Allied action."

(3) The Polish resistance movement is no more united round the London Government than the Greek resistance movement is united round King George of the Hellenes. (This is further emphasised by frequent use of the words "*émigré*," "soi-disant," etc., applied to the London Government.)

(4) The London Government precipitated the rising in order to be in possession of Warsaw when the Russians arrived, because in that case "the bargaining position of the *émigré* Government would be improved." The London Government, we are told, "is ready to betray the Polish people's cause to bolster up its own tenure of precarious office," with much more to the same effect.

No shadow of proof is offered for any of these charges, though (1) and (2) are of a kind that could be verified and may well be true. My own guess is that (2) is true and (1) partly true. The third charge makes nonsense of the first two. If the London Government is not accepted by the mass of the people in Warsaw, why should they raise a desperate insurrection on its orders? By blaming Sosnokowski and the rest for the rising, you are automatically assuming that it is to them that the Polish people looks for guidance. This obvious contradiction has been repeated in paper after paper, without, so far as I know, a single person having the honesty to point it out. As for the use of such expressions as "*émigré*," it is simply a rhetorical trick. If the London Poles are *émigrés*, so are the Polish National Committee of Liberation, besides the "free" Governments of all the occupied countries. Why does one become an *émigré* by emigrating to London and not by emigrating to Moscow?

Charge No. (4) is morally on a par with the *Osservatore Romano*'s suggestion that the Russians held up their attack on Warsaw in order to get as many Polish resisters as possible killed off. It is the unproved and unprovable assertion of a mere propagandist who has no wish to establish the truth, but is simply out to do as much dirt on his opponent as possible. And all that I have read about this matter in the press – except for some very obscure papers and some remarks in *Tribune*, the *Economist* and the *Evening Standard* – is on the same level as Mr. Barraclough's letter.

Now, I know nothing of Polish affairs and even if I had the power to do so I would not intervene in the struggle between the London Polish Government and the Moscow National Committee of Liberation. What I am concerned with is the attitude of the British intelligentsia, who cannot raise between them one single voice to question what they believe to be Russian policy, no matter what turn it takes, and in this case have had the unheard-of meanness to hint that our bombers ought not to be sent to the aid of our comrades fighting in Warsaw. The enormous majority of Left-wingers who swallow the policy put out by the *News-Chronicle*, etc., know no more about Poland than I do. All they know is that the Russians object to the London Government and have set up a rival organisation, and so far as they are concerned that settles the matter. If tomorrow Stalin were to drop the Committee of Liberation and recognise the London Government, the whole British intelligentsia would flock after him like a troop of parrots. Their attitude towards Russian foreign policy is not "Is this policy right or wrong?" but "This is Russian policy: how can we make it appear right?" And this attitude is defended, if at all, solely on grounds of power. The Russians are powerful in Eastern Europe, we are not: therefore we must not oppose them. This involves the principle, of its nature alien to Socialism, that you must not protest against an evil which you cannot prevent.

I cannot discuss here why it is that the British intelligentsia, with few exceptions, have developed a nationalistic loyalty towards the U.S.S.R. and are dishonestly uncritical of its policies. In any case, I have discussed it elsewhere. But I would like to close with two considerations which are worth thinking over.

First of all, a message to English Left-wing journalists and intellectuals generally. "Do remember that dishonesty and cowardice always have to be paid for. Don't imagine that for years on end you can make yourself the boot-licking propagandist of the Soviet regime, or any other regime, and then suddenly return to mental decency. Once a whore, always a whore."

Secondly, a wider consideration. Nothing is more important in the world today than Anglo-Russian friendship and co-operation, and that will not be attained without plain speaking. The best way to come to an agreement with a foreign nation is *not* to refrain from criticising its policies, even to the extent of leaving your own people in the dark about them. At present, so slavish is the attitude of nearly the whole British press that ordinary people have very little idea of what is happening, and may well be committed to policies which they will repudiate in five years' time. In a shadowy sort of way we have been told that the Russian peace terms are a super-Versailles, with partition of Germany, astronomical reparations, and forced labour on a huge scale. These proposals go practically uncriticised, while in much of the Left-wing press hack-writers are even hired to extol them. The result is that the average man has no notion of the enormity of what is proposed. I don't know whether, when the time comes, the Russians will really want to put such terms into operation. My guess is that they won't. But what I do know is that if any such thing were done, the British and probably the American public would never support it when the passion of war had died down. Any flagrantly unjust peace settlement will simply have the result, as it did last time, of making the British people unreasonably sympathetic with the victims. Anglo-Russian friendship depends upon there being a policy which both countries can agree upon, and this is impossible without free discussion and genuine criticism *now*. There can be no real alliance on the basis of "Stalin is always right." The first step towards a real alliance is the dropping of illusions.

Finally, a word to the people who will write me letters about this. May I once again draw attention to the title of this column and remind everyone that the Editors of *Tribune* are not necessarily in agreement with all that I say, but are putting into practice their belief in freedom of speech?

As I Please 41
Tribune, 8 September 1944

For a book of 32 pages, Sir Osbert Sitwell's *A Letter to My Son* contains a quite astonishing quantity of invective. I imagine that it is the invective, or rather the eminence of the people it is directed against, that has led Sir Osbert to change his publisher. But in among passages that are sometimes unfair and occasionally frivolous, he manages to say some penetrating things about the position of the artist in a modern centralised society. Here, for instance, are some excerpts: –

"The true artist has always had to fight, but it is, and will be, a more ferocious struggle for you, and the artists of your generation, than ever before. The working man, this time, will be better looked after, he will be flattered by the press and bribed with Beveridge schemes, because he possesses a plurality of votes. But who will care for you or your fate, who will trouble to defend the cause of the young writer, painter, sculptor, musician? And what inspiration will you be offered when theatre, ballet, concert-hall lie in ruins, and, owing to the break in training, there are no great executant artists for several decades? Above all, do not underestimate the amount and intensity of genuine ill-will that people will feel for you; not the working man, for though not highly educated he has a mild respect for the arts and no preconceived notions, not the few remaining patricians, but the vast army between them, the fat middle classes and the little men. And here I must make special mention of the civil servant as enemy.... At the best, you will be ground down between the small but powerful authoritarian minority of art directors, museum rack-eteers, the chic, giggling modistes who write on art and litera-ture, publishers, journalists and dons (who will, to do them justice, try to help you, if you will write as they tell you) – and the enormous remainder, who would not mind, who would indeed be pleased, if they saw you starve. For we English are unique in that, albeit an art-producing nation, we are not an art-loving one. In the past the arts depended on a small number of very rich patrons. The enclave they formed has never been re-established. The very name 'art-lover' stinks.... The privi-leges you hold to-day, then, as an artist, are those of Ishmael, the hand of every man is against you. Remember, therefore, that outcasts must never be afraid."

These are not my views. They are the views of an intelligent Conservative who underrates the virtues of democracy and attributes to feudalism certain advantages which really belong to capitalism. It is a mistake, for instance, to yearn after an aristocratic patron. The patron could be just as hard a master as the B.B.C., and he did not pay your salary so regularly. François Villon had, I suppose, as rough a time as any poet in our own day, and the literary man starving in a garret was one of the characteristic figures of the eighteenth century. At best, in an age of patronage you had to waste time and talent on revolting flatteries, as Shakespeare did. Indeed, if one thinks of the artist as an Ishmael, an autonomous individual who owes nothing to society, then the golden age of the artist was the age of capitalism. He had then escaped from the patron and not yet been captured by the bureaucrat. He could – at any rate a writer, a musician, an actor and perhaps even a painter could – make his living off the big public, who were uncertain of what they wanted and would to a great extent take what they were given. Indeed, for about a hundred years it was possible to make your livelihood by openly insulting the public, as the careers of, say, Flaubert, Tolstoy, D.H. Lawrence, and even Dickens show.

But all the same there is much in what Sir Osbert Sitwell says. Laissez-faire capitalism is passing away, and the independent status of the artist must necessarily disappear with it. He must become either a spare-time amateur or an official. When you see what has happened to the arts in the totalitarian countries, and when you see the same thing happening here in a more veiled way through the M.O.I., the B.B.C. and the film companies – organisations which not only buy up promising young writers and geld them and set them to work like cab-horses, but manage to rob literary creation of its individual character and turn it into a sort of conveyor-belt process – the prospects are not encouraging. Yet it remains true that capitalism, which in many ways was kind to the artist and the intellectual generally, is doomed and is not worth saving any way. So you arrive at these two antithetical facts: (1) Society cannot be arranged for the benefit of artists; (2) without artists civilisation perishes. I have never yet seen this dilemma solved (there must be a solution), and it is not often that it is honestly discussed.

I have before me an exceptionally disgusting photograph, from the *Star* of August 29, of two partially undressed women, with shaven heads and with swastikas painted on their faces, being led through the streets of Paris amid grinning onlookers. The *Star* – not that I am picking on the *Star*, for most of the press has behaved likewise – reproduces this photograph with seeming approval.

I don't blame the French for doing this kind of thing. They have had four years of suffering, and I can partially imagine how they feel towards the collaborators. But it is a different matter when newspapers in this country try to persuade their readers that shaving women's heads is a nice thing to do. As soon as I saw this *Star* photograph, I thought, "Where have I seen something like this before?" Then I remembered. Just about ten years ago, when the Nazi regime was beginning to get into its stride, very similar pictures of humiliated Jews being led through the streets of German cities were exhibited in the

British press – but with this difference, that on that occasion we were not expected to approve.

Recently another newspaper published photographs of the dangling corpses of Germans hanged by the Russians in Kharkov, and carefully informed its readers that these executions had been filmed and that the public would shortly be able to witness them at the news theatres. (Were children admitted, I wonder?)

There is a saying of Nietzsche which I have quoted before (not in this column, I think), but which is worth quoting again: –

He who fights too long against dragons becomes a dragon himself: and if thou gaze too long into the abyss, the abyss will gaze into thee.

"Too long," in this context, should perhaps be taken as meaning "after the dragon is beaten."

The correspondents who wrote in answer to my query about the weed which grows on blitzed sites are too numerous to thank individually, but I would like to thank them collectively. The upshot is that Sir William Beach Thomas was right. The plant *is* called Rosebay Willowherb. The name of the other plant I referred to is not completely certain, but as there are, it seems, nine kinds of willowherb, this must be one of them. As a piece of information which may be useful at a time when whisky costs twenty-seven shillings a bottle, I pass on the statement of one of my correspondents that "an infusion of the whole plant is extremely intoxicating." If anyone is brave enough to try this, I shall be interested to learn the results.

Arthur Koestler
11 September 1944 Typescript

One striking fact about English literature during the present century is the extent to which it has been dominated by foreigners – for example, Conrad, Henry James, Shaw, Joyce,

Yeats, Pound and Eliot. Still, if you chose to make this a matter of national prestige and examine our achievement in the various branches of literature, you would find that England made a fairly good showing until you came to what may be roughly described as political writing, or pamphleteering. I mean by this the special class of literature that has arisen out of the European political struggle since the rise of Fascism. Under this heading novels, autobiographies, books of "reportage," sociological treatises and plain pamphlets can all be lumped together, all of them having a common origin and to a great extent the same emotional atmosphere.

Some of the outstanding figures in this school of writers are Silone, Malraux, Salvemini, Borkenau, Victor Serge and Koestler himself. Some of these are imaginative writers, some not, but they are all alike in that they are trying to write contemporary history, but *unofficial* history, the kind that is ignored in the textbooks and lied about in the newspapers. Also they are all alike in being continental Europeans. It may be an exaggeration, but it cannot be a very great one, to say that whenever a book dealing with totalitarianism appears in this country, and still seems worth reading six months after publication, it is a book translated from some foreign language. English writers, over the past dozen years, have poured forth an enormous spate of political literature, but they have produced almost nothing of aesthetic value, and very little of historical value either. The Left Book Club, for instance, has been running ever since 1936. How many of its chosen volumes can you even remember the names of? Nazi Germany, Soviet Russia, Spain, Abyssinia, Austria, Czechoslovakia – all that these and kindred subjects have produced, in England, are slick books of reportage, dishonest pamphlets in which propaganda is swallowed whole and then spewed up again, half digested, and a very few reliable guidebooks and textbooks. There has been nothing resembling, for instance, *Fontamara* or *Darkness at Noon*, because there is almost no English writer to whom it has happened to see totalitarianism from the inside. In Europe, during the past decade and more, things have been happening to middle-class people which in England do not even happen to the working class. Most of the European writers I mentioned above, and scores of others like them, have been obliged to break the law in order to engage in politics at all: some of them have thrown bombs and fought in street battles, many have been in prison or the concentration camp, or fled across frontiers with false names and forged passports. One cannot imagine, say, Professor Laski indulging in activities of that kind. England is lacking, therefore, in what one might call concentration-camp literature. The special world created by secret police forces, censorship of opinion, torture and frame-up trials is, of course, known about and to some extent disapproved of, but it has made very little emotional impact. One result of this is that there exists in England almost no literature of disillusionment about the Soviet Union. There is the attitude of ignorant disapproval, and there is the attitude of uncritical admiration, but very little in between. Opinion on the Moscow sabotage trials, for instance, was divided, but divided chiefly on the question of whether the accused were guilty. Few people were able to see that whether justified or not the trials were an unspeakable horror. And English disapproval of the Nazi outrages has also been an unreal thing, turned on and off like a tap according to political expediency. To understand such things one has to be able to imagine oneself as the victim, and for an Englishman to write *Darkness at Noon* would be as unlikely an accident as for a slave-trader to write *Uncle Tom's Cabin*.

Koestler's published work really centres about the Moscow trials. His main theme is the decadence of revolutions owing to the corrupting effects of power, but the special nature of the Stalin dictatorship has driven him back into a position not far removed from pessimistic Conservativism. I do not know how many books he has written in all. He is a Hungarian whose earlier books were written in German, and five books have been published in England: *Spanish Testament*, *The Gladiators*, *Darkness at Noon*, *Scum of the Earth*, and *Arrival and Departure*. The subject matter of all of them is similar, and none of them ever escapes for more than a few pages from the atmosphere of nightmare. Of the five books, the action of three takes place entirely or almost entirely in prison.

In the opening months of the Spanish civil war Koestler was the *News-Chronicle's* correspondent in Spain, and early in 1937 he was taken prisoner when the Fascists captured Malaga. He was nearly shot out of hand, then spent some months imprisoned in a fortress, listening every night to the roar of rifle fire, as batch after batch of Republicans was executed, and being most of the time in acute danger of execution himself. This was not a chance adventure which "might have happened to anybody," but was in accordance with Koestler's life style. A politically indifferent person would not have been in Spain at that date, a more cautious observer would have got out of Malaga before the Fascists arrived, and a British or American newspaperman would have been treated with more consideration. The book that Koestler wrote about this, *Spanish Testament*, has remarkable passages, but apart from the scrappiness that is usual in a book of reportage, it is definitely false in places. In the prison scenes Koestler successfully establishes the nightmare atmosphere which is, so to speak, his patent, but the rest of the book is too much coloured by the Popular Front orthodoxy of the time. One or two passages even look as though they had been doctored for the purposes of the Left Book Club. At that time Koestler still was, or recently had been, a member of the Communist Party, and the complex politics of the civil war made it impossible for any Communist to write quite honestly about the internal struggle on the Government side. The sin of nearly all leftwingers from 1933 onwards is that they have wanted to be anti-Fascist without being anti-totalitarian. In 1937 Koestler already knew this, but did not feel free to say so. He came much nearer to saying it – indeed, he did say it, though he put on a mask to do so – in his next book, *The Gladiators*, which was published about a year before the war and for some reason attracted very little attention.

The Gladiators is in some ways an unsatisfactory book. It is about Spartacus, the Thracian gladiator who raised a slaves' rebellion in Italy round about 65 B.C., and any book on such a subject is handicapped by challenging comparison with *Salammbô*. In our own age it would not be possible to write a book like *Salammbô* even if one had the talent. The great thing about *Salammbô*, even more important than its physical detail, is its utter mercilessness. Flaubert could think himself into the stony cruelty of antiquity, because in the mid-nineteenth century one still had peace of mind. One had time to travel in the past.

Nowadays the present and the future are too terrifying to be escaped from, and if one bothers with history it is in order to find modern meanings there. Koestler makes Spartacus into an allegorical figure, a primitive version of the proletarian dictator. Whereas Flaubert has been able, by a prolonged effort of the imagination, to make his mercenaries truly pre-Christian, Spartacus is a modern man dressed up. But this might not matter if Koestler were fully aware of what his allegory means. Revolutions always go wrong – that is the main theme. It is on the question of *why* they go wrong that he falters, and his uncertainty enters into the story and makes the central figures enigmatic and unreal.

For several years the rebellious slaves are uniformly successful. Their numbers swell to a hundred thousand, they overrun great areas of southern Italy, they defeat one punitive expedition after another, they ally themselves with the pirates who at that time were the masters of the Mediterranean, and finally they set to work to build a city of their own, to be named the City of the Sun. In this city human beings are to be free and equal, and above all they are to be happy: no slavery, no hunger, no injustice, no floggings, no executions. It is the dream of a just society which seems to haunt the human imagination ineradicably and in all ages, whether it is called the Kingdom of Heaven or the classless society, or whether it is thought of as a Golden Age which once existed in the past and from which we have degenerated. Needless to say the slaves fail to achieve it. No sooner have they formed themselves into a community than their way of life turns out to be as unjust, laborious and fear-ridden as any other. Even the cross, symbol of slavery, has to be revived for the punishment of malefactors. The turning point comes when Spartacus finds himself obliged to crucify twenty of his oldest and most faithful followers. After that the City of the Sun is doomed, the slaves split up and are defeated in detail, the last fifteen thousand of them being captured and crucified in one batch.

The serious weakness of this story is that the motives of Spartacus himself are never made clear. The Roman lawyer Fulvius, who joins the rebellion and acts as its chronicler, sets forth the familiar dilemma of ends and means. You can achieve nothing unless you are willing to use force and cunning, but in using them you pervert your original aims. Spartacus, however, is not represented as power-hungry, nor on the other hand as a visionary. He is driven onwards by some obscure force which he does not understand, and he is frequently in two minds as to whether it would not be better to throw up the whole adventure and flee to Alexandria while the going is good. The slaves' republic is in any case wrecked rather by hedonism than by the struggle for power. The slaves are discontented with their liberty because they still have to work, and the final break-up happens because the more turbulent and less civilized slaves, chiefly Gauls and Germans, continue to behave like bandits after the republic has been established. This may be a true account of events – naturally we know very little about the slave rebellions of antiquity – but by allowing the Sun City to be destroyed because Crixus the Gaul cannot be prevented from looting and raping, Koestler has faltered between allegory and history. If Spartacus is the prototype of the modern revolutionary – and obviously he is intended as that – he should have gone astray because of the impossibility of combining power with righteousness. As it is, he is an almost passive figure, acted upon rather than acting, and at times not convincing. The story partly fails because the central problem of revolution has been avoided, or at least has not been solved.

It is again avoided in a subtler way in the next book, Koestler's masterpiece, *Darkness at Noon*. Here however the story is not spoiled, because it deals with individuals and its interest is psychological. It is an episode picked out from a background that does not have to be questioned. *Darkness at Noon* describes the imprisonment and death of an Old Bolshevik, Rubashov, who first denies and ultimately confesses to crimes which he is well aware he has not committed. The grown-upness, the lack of surprise or denunciation, the pity and irony with which the story is told show the advantage, when one is handling a theme of this kind, of being a European. The book reaches the stature of tragedy, whereas an English or American writer could at most have made it into a polemical tract. Koestler has digested his material and can treat it on the aesthetic level. At the same time his handling of it has a political implication, not important in this case but likely to be damaging in later books.

Naturally the whole book centres round one question: Why did Rubashov confess? He is not guilty – that is, not guilty of anything except the essential crime of disliking the Stalin regime. The concrete acts of treason in which he is supposed to have engaged are all imaginary. He has not even been tortured, or not very severely. He is worn down by solitude, toothache, lack of tobacco, bright lights glaring in his eyes, and continuous questioning, but these in themselves would not be enough to overcome a hardened revolutionary. The Nazis have previously done worse to him without breaking his spirit. The confessions obtained in the Russian state trials are capable of three explanations: –

(1) That the accused were guilty.

(2) That they were tortured, and perhaps blackmailed by threats to relatives and friends.

(3) That they were actuated by despair, mental bankruptcy and the habit of loyalty to the Party.

For Koestler's purpose in *Darkness at Noon* (1) is ruled out, and though this is not the place to discuss the Russian purges, I must add that what little verifiable evidence there is suggests that the trials of the Old Bolsheviks were frame-ups. If one assumes that the accused were not guilty – at any rate, not guilty of the particular things they confessed to – then (2) is the commonsense explanation. Koestler, however, plumps for (3), which is also accepted by the Trotskyist Boris Souvarine, in his pamphlet *Cauchemar en URSS*. Rubashov ultimately confesses because he cannot find in his own mind any reason for not doing so. Justice and objective truth have long ceased to have any meaning for him. For decades he has been simply the creature of the Party, and what the Party now demands is that he shall confess to non-existent crimes. In the end, though he has had to be bullied and weakened first, he is somewhat proud of his decision to confess. He feels superior to the poor Czarist officer who inhabits the next cell and who talks to Rubashov by tapping on the wall. The Czarist officer is shocked when he learns that Rubashov intends to capitulate. As he sees it from his "bourgeois" angle, everyone ought to stick to his guns, even a Bolshevik. Honour, he says, consists in doing what you think right. "Honour is to be useful without fuss," Rubashov taps back; and he reflects with a certain satisfaction that he is tapping with his pince-nez while the other, the relic of the past, is tapping with a monocle.

Like Bukharin, Rubashov is "looking out upon black darkness." What is there, what code, what loyalty, what notion of good and evil, for the sake of which he can defy the Party and endure further torment? He is not only alone, he is also hollow. He has himself committed worse crimes than the one that is now being perpetrated against him. For example, as a secret envoy of the Party in Nazi Germany, he has got rid of disobedient followers by betraying them to the Gestapo. Curiously enough, if he has any inner strength to draw upon, it is the memories of his boyhood when he was the son of a landowner. The last thing he remembers, when he is shot from behind, is the leaves of the poplar trees on his father's estate. Rubashov belongs to the older generation of Bolsheviks that was largely wiped out in the purges. He is aware of art and literature, and of the world outside Russia. He contrasts sharply with Gletkin, the young GPU man who conducts his interrogation, and who is the typical "good party man," completely without scruples or curiosity, a thinking gramophone. Rubashov, unlike Gletkin, does not have the Revolution as his starting point. His mind was not a blank sheet when the party got hold of it. His superiority to the other is finally traceable to his bourgeois origin.

One cannot, I think, argue that *Darkness at Noon* is simply a story dealing with the adventures of an imaginary individual. Clearly it is a political book, founded on history and offering an interpretation of disputed events. Rubashov might be Trotsky, Bukharin, Rakovsky or some other relatively civilized figure among the Old Bolsheviks. If one writes about the Moscow trials one must answer the question, "Why did the accused confess?", and which answer one makes is a political decision. Koestler answers, in effect, "Because these people had been rotted by the Revolution which they served," and in doing so he comes near to claiming that revolutions are of their nature bad. If one assumes that the accused in the Moscow trials were made to confess by means of some kind of terrorism, one is only saying that one particular set of revolutionary leaders has gone astray. Individuals, and not the situation, are to blame.

The implication of Koestler's book, however, is that Rubashov in power would be no better than Gletkin: or rather, only better in that his outlook is still partly pre-revolutionary. Revolution, Koestler seems to say, is a corrupting process. Really enter into the Revolution and you must end up as either Rubashov or Gletkin. It is not merely that "power corrupts": so also do the ways of attaining power. Therefore, all efforts to regenerate society *by violent means* lead to the cellars of the Ogpu. Lenin leads to Stalin, and would have come to resemble Stalin if he had happened to survive.

Of course, Koestler does not say this quite explicitly, and perhaps is not altogether conscious of it. He is writing about darkness, but it is darkness at what ought to be noon. Part of the time he feels that things might have turned out differently. The notion that so-and-so has "betrayed," that things have only gone wrong because of individual wickedness, is ever-present in leftwing thought. Later, in *Arrival and Departure*, Koestler swings over much further towards the anti-revolutionary position, but in between these two books there is another, *Scum of the Earth*, which is straight autobiography and has only an indirect bearing upon the problems raised by *Darkness at Noon*. True to his life style, Koestler was caught in France by the outbreak of war, and, as a foreigner and a known anti-fascist, was promptly arrested and interned by the Daladier Government. He spent the first nine months of war mostly in a prison camp, then, during the collapse of France, escaped and travelled by devious routes to England, where he was once again thrown into prison as an enemy alien. This time he was soon released, however. The book is a valuable piece of reportage, and together with a few other scraps of honest writing that happened to be produced at the time of the debacle, it is a reminder of the depths that bourgeois democracy can descend to. At this moment, with France newly liberated and the witch-hunt after collaborators in full swing, we are apt to forget that in 1940 various observers on the spot considered that about 40 per cent of the French population was either actively pro-German or completely apathetic. Truthful war books are never acceptable to non-combatants, and Koestler's book did not have a very good reception. Nobody came well out of it – neither the bourgeois politicians, whose idea of conducting an anti-fascist war was to jail every leftwinger they could lay hands on, nor the French Communists, who were effectively pro-Nazi and did their best to sabotage the French war effort, nor the common people, who were just as likely to follow mountebanks like Doriot as responsible leaders. Koestler records some fantastic conversations with fellow-victims in the concentration camp, and adds that till then, like most middle-class Socialists and Communists, he had never made contact with real proletarians, only with the educated minority. He draws the pessimistic conclusion: "Without education of the masses, no social progress; without social progress, no education of the masses." In *Scum of the Earth* Koestler ceases to idealise the common people. He has abandoned Stalinism, but he is not a Trotskyist either. This is the book's real link with *Arrival and Departure*, in which what is normally called a revolutionary outlook is dropped, perhaps for good.

Arrival and Departure is not a satisfactory book. The pretence that it is a novel is very thin; in effect it is a tract purporting to show that revolutionary creeds are rationalisations of neurotic impulses. With all too neat a symmetry, the book begins and ends with the same action – a leap into a foreign country. A young ex-Communist who has made his escape from Hungary jumps ashore in Portugal, where he hopes to enter the service of Britain, at that time the only power fighting against Germany. His enthusiasm is somewhat cooled by the fact that the British consulate is uninterested in him and almost ignores him for a period of several months, during which his money runs out and other astuter refugees escape to America. He is successively tempted by the World in the form of a Nazi propagandist, the Flesh in the form of a French girl, and – after a nervous breakdown – the Devil in the form of a psycho-analyst. The psycho-analyst drags out of him the fact that his revolutionary enthusiasm is not founded on any real belief in historical necessity, but on a morbid guilt complex arising from an attempt in early childhood to blind his baby brother. By the time that he gets an opportunity of serving the Allies he has lost all reason for wanting to do so, and he is on the point of leaving for America when his irrational impulses seize hold of him again. In practice he cannot abandon the struggle. When the book ends he is floating down in a parachute over the dark landscape of his native country, where he will be employed as a secret agent of Britain.

As a political statement (and the book is not much more), this is insufficient. Of course it is true in many cases, and it may be true in all cases, that revolutionary activity is the result of personal maladjustment. Those who struggle against society are, on the whole, those who have reason to dislike it, and normal healthy people are no more attracted by violence and illegality than they are by war. The young Nazi in *Arrival and Departure* makes the penetrating remark that one can see what is wrong with the leftwing movement by the ugliness of its women. But after all, this does not invalidate the Socialist case. Actions have results, irrespective of their motives. Marx's ultimate motives may well have been envy and spite, but this does not prove that his conclusions were false. In making the hero of *Arrival and Departure* take his final decision from a mere instinct not to shirk action and danger, Koestler is making him suffer a sudden loss of intelligence. With such a history as he has behind him, he would be able to see that certain things have to be done, whether our reasons for doing them are "good" or "bad." History has to move in a certain direction, even if it has to be pushed that way by neurotics. In *Arrival and Departure* Peter's idols are overthrown one after the other. The Russian Revolution has degenerated, Britain, symbolised by the aged consul with gouty fingers, is no better, the international class-conscious proletariat is a myth. But the conclusion (since, after all, Koestler and his hero "support" the war) ought to be that getting rid of Hitler is still a worthwhile objective, a necessary bit of scavenging in which motives are almost irrelevant.

To take a rational political decision one must have a picture of the future. At present Koestler seems to have none, or rather to have two which cancel out. As an ultimate objective he believes in the Earthly Paradise, the Sun State which the gladiators set out to establish, and which has haunted the imagination of Socialists, Anarchists and religious heretics for hundreds of years. But his intelligence tells him that the Earthly Paradise is receding into the far distance and that what is actually ahead of us is bloodshed, tyranny and privation. Recently he described himself as a "short-term pessimist." Every kind of horror is blowing up over the horizon, but somehow it will all come right in the end. This outlook is probably gaining ground among thinking people: it results from the very great difficulty, once one has abandoned orthodox religious belief, of accepting life on earth as inherently miserable, and on the other hand from the realization that to make life livable is a much bigger problem than it recently seemed. Since about 1930 the world has given no reason for optimism whatever. Nothing is in sight except a welter of lies, hatred, cruelty and ignorance, and beyond our present troubles loom vaster ones which are only now entering into the European consciousness. It is quite possible that man's major problems will *never* be solved. But it is also unthinkable! Who is there who dares to look at the world of today and say to himself, "It will always be like this: even in a million years it cannot get appreciably better?" So you get the quasi-mystical belief that for the present there is no remedy, all political action is useless, but that somehow, somewhere in space and time, human life will cease to be the miserable brutish thing it now is.

The only easy way out is that of the religious believer, who regards this life merely as a preparation for the next. But few thinking people now believe in life after death, and the number of those who do is probably diminishing. The Christian churches would probably not survive on their own merits if their economic basis were destroyed. The real problem is how to restore the religious attitude while accepting death as final. Men can only be happy when they do not assume that the object of life is happiness. It is most unlikely, however, that Koestler would accept this. There is a well-marked hedonistic strain in his writings, and his failure to find a political position after breaking with Stalinism is a result of this.

The Russian Revolution, the central event in Koestler's life, started out with high hopes. We forget these things now, but a quarter of a century ago it was confidently expected that the Russian Revolution would lead to Utopia. Obviously this has not happened. Koestler is too acute not to see this, and too sensitive not to remember the original objective. Moreover, from his European angle he can see such things as purges and mass deportations for what they are: he is not, like Shaw or Laski, looking at them through the wrong end of the telescope. Therefore he draws the conclusion: This is what revolutions lead to. There is nothing for it except to be a "short-term pessimist," ie. to keep out of politics, make a sort of oasis within which you and your friends can remain sane, and hope that somehow things will be better in a hundred years. At the basis of this lies his hedonism, which leads him to think of the Earthly Paradise as desirable. Perhaps, however, whether desirable or not, it isn't possible. Perhaps some degree of suffering is ineradicable from human life, perhaps the choice before Man is always a choice of evils, perhaps even the aim of Socialism is not to make the world perfect but to make it better. All revolutions are failures, but they are not all the same failure. It is his unwillingness to admit this that has led Koestler's mind temporarily into a blind alley and that makes *Arrival and Departure* seem shallow compared with the earlier books.

As I Please 42
Tribune, 15 September 1944

About the end of 1936, as I was passing through Paris on the way to Spain, I had to visit somebody at an address I did not know, and I thought that the quickest way of getting there would probably be to take a taxi. The taxi-driver did not know the address either. However, we drove up the street and asked the nearest policeman, whereupon it turned out that the address I was looking for was only about a hundred yards away. So I had taken the taxi-driver off the rank for a fare which in English money was about threepence.

The taxi-driver was furiously angry. He began accusing me, in a roaring voice and with the maximum of offensiveness, of having "done it on purpose." I protested that I had not known where the place was, and that I obviously would not have taken a taxi if I had known. "You knew very well!" he yelled back at me. He was an old, grey, thick-set man, with ragged grey moustaches and a face of quite unusual malignity. In the end I lost my temper, and, my command of French coming back to me in my rage, I shouted at him, "You think you're too old for me to smash your face in. Don't be too sure!" He backed up against the taxi, snarling and full of fight, in spite of his sixty years.

Then the moment came to pay. I had taken out a ten-franc note. "I've no change!" he yelled as soon as he saw the money. "Go and change it for yourself!"

"Where can I get change?"

"How should I know? That's your business."

So I had to cross the street, find a tobacconist's shop and get change. When I came back I gave the taxi-driver the exact fare, telling him that after his behaviour I saw no reason for giving him anything extra; and after exchanging a few more insults we parted.

This sordid squabble left me at the moment violently angry, and a little later saddened and disgusted. "Why do people have to behave like that?" I thought.

But that night I left for Spain. The train, a slow one, was packed with Czechs, Germans, Frenchmen, all bound on the same mission. Up and down the train you could hear one phrase repeated over and over again, in the accents of all the languages of Europe – *là-bas* (down there). My third-class carriage was full of very young, fair-haired, underfed Germans in suits of incredible shoddiness – the first *ersatz* cloth I had seen – who rushed out at every stopping-place to buy bottles of cheap wine and later fell asleep in a sort of pyramid on the floor of the carriage. About halfway down France the ordinary passengers dropped off. There might still be a few nondescript journalists like myself, but the train was practically a troop train, and the countryside knew it. In the morning, as we crawled across southern France, every peasant working in the fields turned round, stood solemnly upright and gave the anti-Fascist salute. They were like a guard of honour, greeting the train mile after mile.

As I watched this, the behaviour of the old taxi-driver gradually fell into perspective. I saw now what had made him so unnecessarily offensive. This was 1936, the year of the great strikes, and the Blum government was still in office. The wave of revolutionary feeling which had swept across France had affected people like taxi-drivers as well as factory workers. With my English accent I had appeared to him as a symbol of the idle, patronising foreign tourists who had done their best to turn France into something midway between a museum and a brothel. In his eyes an English tourist meant a bourgeois. He was getting a bit of his own back on the parasites who were normally his employers. And it struck me that the motives of the polyglot army that filled the train, and of the peasants with raised fists out there in the fields, and my own motive in going to Spain, and the motive of the old taxi-driver in insulting me, were at bottom all the same.

The official statement on the doodle-bug, even taken together with Churchill's earlier statement, is not very revealing, because no clear figures have been given of the number of people affected. All we are told is that on average something under thirty bombs have hit London daily. My own estimate, based simply on such "incidents" as I have witnessed, is that on average every doodle-bug hitting London makes thirty houses uninhabitable, and that anything up to five thousand people have been rendered homeless daily. At that rate between a quarter and half a million people will have been blitzed out of their homes in the last three months.

It is said that good billiard-players chalk their cues before making a stroke, and bad players afterwards. In the same way, we should have got on splendidly in this war if we had prepared for each type of blitz before and not after it happened. Shortly before the outbreak of war an official, returning from some conference with other officials in London, told me that the authorities were prepared for air-raid casualties of the order of 200,000 in the first week. Enormous supplies of collapsible cardboard coffins had been laid in, and mass graves were being dug. There were also special preparations for a great increase in mental disorders. As it turned out the casualties were comparatively few, while mental disorders, I believe, actually declined. On the other hand, the authorities had failed to foresee that blitzed people would be homeless and would need food, clothes, shelter and money. They had also, while foreseeing the incendiary bomb, failed to realise that you would need an alternative water supply if the mains were burst by bombs.

By 1942 we were all set for the blitz of 1940. Shelter facilities had been increased, and London was dotted with water tanks which would have saved its historic buildings if only they had been in existence when the fires were happening. And then along came the doodle-bug, which, instead of blowing three or four houses out of existence, makes a large number uninhabitable, while leaving their interiors more or less intact. Hence another unforeseen headache – storage of furniture. The furniture from a doodle-bugged house is nearly always salvaged, but finding places to put it in, and labour to move it, has been almost too much for the local authorities. In general it has to be dumped in derelict and unguarded houses, where such of it as is not looted is ruined by damp.

The most significant figures in Duncan Sandys's speech were those dealing with the Allied counter-measures. He stated, for instance, that whereas the Germans shot off 8,000 doodle-bugs, or something under 8,000 tons of high explosive, we dropped 100,000 tons of bombs on the bases, besides losing 450 aeroplanes and shooting off hundreds of thousands or millions of A.A. shells. One can only make rough calculations at this date, but it looks as though the doodle-bug may have a big future before it in forthcoming wars. Before writing it off as a flop, it is worth remembering that artillery scored only a partial success at the battle of Crécy.

Tobias Smollett: Scotland's Best Novelist
Tribune, 22 September 1944

"Realism," a much abused word, has at least four current meanings, but when applied to novels it normally means a photographic imitation of everyday life. A "realistic" novel is one in which the dialogue is colloquial and physical objects are described in such a way that you can visualise them. In this sense almost all modern novels are more "realistic" than those of the past, because the describing of everyday scenes and the construction of natural-sounding dialogue are largely a matter of technical tricks which are passed on from one generation to another, gradually improving in the process. But there is another sense in which the stilted, artificial novelists of the eighteenth century are more "realistic" than almost any of their successors, and that is in their attitude towards human motives. They may be weak at describing scenery, but they are extraordinarily good at describing scoundrelism. This is true even of Fielding, who in *Tom Jones* and *Amelia* already shows the moralising tendency which was to mark English novels for a hundred and fifty years. But it is much truer of Smollett, whose outstanding intellectual honesty may have been connected with the fact that he was not an Englishman.

Smollett is a picaresque novelist, a writer of long, formless tales full of farcical and improbable adventures. He derives to some extent from Cervantes, whom he translated into English and whom he also plagiarised in *Sir Lancelot Greaves*. Inevitably a great deal that he wrote is no longer worth reading, even including, perhaps, his most-praised book, *Humphrey Clinker*, which is written in the form of letters and was considered comparatively respectable in the nineteenth century, because most of its obscenities are hidden under puns. But Smollett's real masterpieces are *Roderick Random* and *Peregrine Pickle*, which are frankly pornographic in a harmless way and which contain some of the best passages of sheer farce in the English language.

Dickens, in *David Copperfield*, names these two books among his childhood favourites, but the resemblance some-times claimed as existing between Smollett and Dickens is very superficial. In *Pickwick Papers*, and in several others of Dickens's early books, you have the picaresque form, the endless travel-ling to and fro, the fantastic adventures, the willingness to sacrifice no matter what amount of probability for the sake of a joke; but the moral atmosphere has greatly altered. Between Smollett's day and Dickens's there had happened not only the French Revolution, but the rise of a new industrial middle class, Low Church in its theology and puritanical in its outlook. Smollett writes of the middle class, but the mer-cantile and professional middle class, the kind of people who are cousins to a landowner and take their manners from the aristocracy.

Duelling, gambling and fornication seem almost morally neutral to him. It so happens that in private life he was a better man than the majority of writers. He was a faithful husband who shortened his life by overworking for the sake of his family, a sturdy republican who hated France as the country of the Grand Monarchy, and a patriotic Scotsman at a time when – the 1745 rebellion being a fairly recent memory – it was far from fashionable to be a Scotsman. But he has very little sense of sin. His heroes do things, and do them on almost every page, which in any nineteenth-century English novel would instantly call forth vengeance from the skies. He accepts as a law of nature the viciousness, the nepotism and the disorder of eighteenth-century society, and therein lies his charm. Many of his best passages would be ruined by any intrusion of the moral sense.

Both *Peregine Pickle* and *Roderick Random* follow roughly the same course. Both heroes go through great vicissitudes of fortune, travel widely, seduce numerous women, suffer imprisonment for debt, and end up prosperous and happily married. Of the two, Peregrine is somewhat the greater blackguard, because he has no profession – Roderick is a naval surgeon, as Smollett himself had been for a while – and can consequently devote more time to seductions and practical jokes. But neither is ever shown acting from an unselfish motive, nor is it admitted that such things as religious belief, political conviction or even ordinary honesty are serious factors in human affairs.

In the world of Smollett's novels there are only three virtues. One is feudal loyalty (Roderick and Peregrine each have a retainer who is faithful through thick and thin), another is masculine "honour," i.e., willingness to fight on any provocation, and another is female "chastity," which is inextricably mixed up with the idea of capturing a husband. Otherwise anything goes. It is nothing out of the way to cheat at cards, for instance. It seems quite natural to Roderick, when he has got hold of £1,000 from somewhere, to buy himself a smart outfit of clothes and go to Bath posing as a rich man, in hopes of entrapping an heiress. When he is in France and out of a job, he decides to join the army, and as the French army happens to be the nearest one, he joins that, and fights against the British at the battle of Dettingen: he is nevertheless ready soon afterwards to fight a duel with a Frenchman who has insulted Britain.

Peregrine devotes himself for months at a time to the elaborate and horribly cruel practical jokes in which the eighteenth century delighted. When, for instance, an unfortunate English painter is thrown into the Bastille for some trifling offence and is about to be released, Peregrine and his friends, playing on his ignorance of the language, let him think that he has been sentenced to be broken on a wheel. A little later they tell him that this punishment has been commuted to castration, and then extract a last bit of fun out of his terrors by letting him think that he is escaping in disguise when he is merely being released from the prison in the normal way.

Why are these petty rogueries worth reading about? In the first place because they are funny. In the Continental writers from whom Smollett derived there may be better things than the description of Peregrine Pickle's adventures on the Grand Tour, but there is nothing better of that particular kind in English. Secondly, by simply ruling out "good" motives and showing no respect whatever for human dignity, Smollett often attains a truthfulness that more serious novelists have missed. He is willing to mention things which do happen in real life but are almost invariably kept out of fiction. Roderick Random, for instance, at one stage of his career, catches a venereal disease – the only English novel-hero, I believe, to whom this has happened. And the fact that Smollett, in spite of his fairly enlightened views, takes patronage, official jobbery and general corruption for granted gives great historical interest to certain passages in his books.

Smollett had been for a while in the Navy, and in *Roderick Random* we are given not only an unvarnished account of the Cartagena expedition, but an extraordinarily vivid and disgusting description of the inside of a warship, in those days a sort of floating compendium of disease, discomfort, tyranny and incompetence. The command of Roderick's ship is for a while given to a young man of family, a scented homosexual fop who has hardly seen a ship in his life, and who spends the whole voyage in his cabin to avoid contact with the vulgar sailormen, almost fainting when he smells tobacco. The scenes in the debtors' prison are even better. In the prisons of those days, a debtor who had no resources might actually starve to death unless he could keep alive by begging from more fortunate prisoners. One of Roderick's fellow-prisoners is so reduced that he has no clothes at all, and preserves decency as best he can by wearing a very long beard. Some of the prisoners, needless to say, are poets, and the book includes a self-contained story, "Mr. Melopoyn's

Tragedy," which should make anyone who thinks aristocratic patronage a good basis for literature think twice.

Smollett's influence on subsequent English writers has not been as great as that of his contemporary, Fielding. Fielding deals in the same kind of boisterous adventure, but his sense of sin never quite leaves him. It is interesting, in *Joseph Andrews*, to watch Fielding start out with the intention of writing a pure farce, and then, in spite of himself as it were, begin punishing vice and rewarding virtue in the way that was to be customary in English novels until almost yesterday. Tom Jones would fit into a novel by Meredith, or for that matter by Ian Hay, whereas Peregrine Pickle seems to belong to a more European background. The writers nearest to Smollett are perhaps Surtees and Marryat, but when sexual frankness ceased to be possible, picaresque literature was robbed of perhaps half of its subject matter. The eighteenth-century inn where it was almost abnormal to go into the right bedroom was a lost dominion.

In our own day various English writers – Evelyn Waugh, for instance, and Aldous Huxley in his early novels – drawing on other sources, have tried to revive the picaresque tradition. One has only to watch their eager efforts to be shocking, and their readiness to be shocked themselves – whereas Smollett was merely trying to be funny in what seemed to him the natural way – to see what an accumulation of pity, decency and public spirit lies between that age and ours.

As I Please 43
Tribune, 6 October 1944

By permission of a correspondent, I quote passages from a letter of instruction which she recently received from a well-known school of journalism. I should explain that when she undertook her "course" the instructor asked her to supply the necessary minimum of information about her background and experience, and then told her to write a couple of specimen essays on some subject interesting to her. Being a miner's wife, she chose to write about coal-mining. Here is the reply she got from someone calling himself the "Assistant Director of Studies." I shall have to quote from it at some length:

"I have read your two exercises with care and interest. You should have a good deal to write about. But do be careful of getting a bee in your bonnet. Miners are not the only men who have a hard time. How about young naval officers, earning less than a skilled miner – who must spend three or four years from home and family, in ice or the tropics? How about the many retired folks on a tiny pension or allowance, whose previous £2 or £3 have been reduced by *half* by the income tax? We all make sacrifices in this war – and the so-called upper classes are being hard hit indeed.

"Instead of writing propaganda for Socialist newspapers you will do better to describe – for the housewives – what life is like in a mining village. Do not go out of your way to be hostile to owners and managers – who are ordinary fellow-creatures – but, if you must air a grievance, do so tolerantly, and fit it in with your plot or theme.

"Many of your readers will be people who are not in the least inclined to regard employers as slave drivers and capitalist villains of society. . . . Write simply and naturally, without any attempt at long words or sentences. Remember that your task is to *entertain*. No reader will bother after a hard day's work to read a list of somebody else's woes. Keep a strict eye on your inclination to write about the 'wrongs' of mining. There are *millions* of people who will not forget that miners did strike while our sons and husbands were fighting the Germans. Where would the miners be if the troops had refused to fight? I mention this to help you keep a sense of perspective. I advise you against writing very controversial things. They are hard to sell. A plain account of mining life will stand a far better chance. . . . the average reader is willing to read facts about other ways of life – but unless he is a fool or knave, he will not listen to *one-sided* propaganda. So forget your grievances, and tell us something of how *you* manage in a typical mining village. One of the women's magazines will, I'm sure, consider a housewife's article on that subject."

My correspondent, who, it seems, had agreed in advance to pay £11 for this course, sent the letter on to me with the query: Did I think that her instructor was trying to influence her to give her writings an acceptable political slant? Was an attempt being made to talk her out of writing like a Socialist?

I do think so, of course, but the implications of this letter are worse than that. This is not a subtle capitalist plot to dope the workers. The writer of that slovenly letter is not a sinister plotter but simply an ass (a female ass, I should say by the style) upon whom years of bombing and privation have made no impression. What it demonstrates is the unconquerable, weed-like vitality of pre-war habits of mind. The writer assumes, it will be seen, that the only purpose of journalism is to tickle money out of the pockets of tired business men, and that the best way of doing this is to avoid telling unpleasant truths about present-day society. The reading public, so he (or she) reasons, don't like being made to think: therefore don't make them think. You are after the big dough, and no other consideration enters.

Anyone who has had anything to do with "courses" in free-lance journalism, or has even come as near to them as studying the now-defunct *Writer* and the *Writer's and Artist's Yearbook*, will recognise the tone of that letter. "Remember that your task is to *entertain*." "No reader will bother after a hard day's work to read a list of somebody else's woes," and "I advise you against writing very controversial things. They are hard to sell." I pass over the fact that even from a commercial point of view such advice is misleading. What is significant is the assumption that nothing ever changes, that the public always will be and always must be the same mob of nitwits wanting only to be doped, and that no sane person would sit down behind a typewriter with any other object than to produce saleable drivel.

When I started writing, about fifteen years ago, various people – who, however, didn't succeed in getting £11 out of me in return – gave me advice almost identical with what I have quoted above. Then too, it seemed, the public did not want to hear about "unpleasant" things like unemployment, and articles on "controversial" subjects were "hard to sell." The dreary sub-world of the free-lance journalist, the world of furnished bed-sitting rooms, hired typewriters and self-addressed envelopes, was entirely dominated by the theory that "your task is to entertain." But at that time there was some excuse. To begin with, there was widespread unemployment, and every newspaper and magazine was besieged by hordes of amateurs struggling frantically to earn odd guineas; and in addition the Press was incomparably sillier than it is now, and there was some truth in the claim that editors would not print "gloomy" contributions. If you looked on writing as simply and solely a way of making money, then cheer-up stuff was probably the best line. What is depressing is to see that for the —— school of journalism the world has stood still. The bombs have achieved nothing. And, indeed, when I read that letter I had the same feeling that the pre-war world is back upon us as I had a little while ago when, through the window of some chambers in the Temple, I watched somebody – with great care and evident pleasure in the process – polishing a top hat.

It is superfluous to say that long railway journeys are not pleasant in these days, and for a good deal of the discomfort that people have to suffer, the railway companies are not to blame. It is not their fault that there is an enormous to-and-fro of civilian traffic at a time when the Armed Forces are monopolising most of the rolling stock, nor that an English railway carriage is built with the seeming object of wasting as much space as possible. But journeys which often entail standing for six or eight hours in a crowded corridor could be made less intolerable by a few reforms.

To begin with, the First Class nonsense should be scrapped once and for all. Secondly, any woman carrying a baby should have a priority right to a seat. Thirdly, waiting rooms should be left open all night. Fourthly, if timetables cannot be adhered to, porters and other officials should be in possession of correct information, and not, as at present, tell you that you will have to change when you won't, and vice versa. Also – a thing that is bad enough in peace time but is even worse at this moment – why is it that there is no cheap way of moving luggage across a big town? What do you do if you have to move a heavy trunk from Paddington to Camden Town? You take a taxi. And suppose you can't afford a taxi, what do you do then? Presumably you borrow a handcart, or balance the trunk on a perambulator. Why are there not cheap luggage-vans, just as there are buses for human passengers? Or why not make it possible to carry luggage on the Underground?

This evening, as King's Cross discharged another horde of returned evacuees, I saw a man and woman, obviously worn out by a long journey, trying to board a bus. The woman carried a squalling baby and clutched a child of about six by the other hand; the man was carrying a broken suitcase tied with rope and the elder child's cot. They were refused by one bus after another. Of course, no bus could take a cot on board. How could it be expected to? But, on the other hand, how were those people to get home? It ended by the woman boarding a bus with the two children, while the man trailed off carrying the cot. For all I know he had a five-mile walk ahead of him.

In war time one must expect this kind of thing. But the point is that if those people had made the same journey, similarly loaded, in peace time, their predicament would have been just the same. For

> The rain it raineth every day
> Upon the just and unjust feller,
> But more upon the just because
> The unjust has the just's umbrella.

Our society is not only so arranged that if you have money you can buy luxuries with it. After all, that is what money is for. It is also so arranged that if you don't have money you pay for it at every hour of the day with petty humiliations and totally unnecessary discomforts – such as, for instance, walking home with a suitcase cutting your fingers off when a mere half-crown would get you there in five minutes.

As I Please 44
Tribune, 13 October 1944

Sir Osbert Sitwell's little book, and my remarks on it, brought in an unusually large amount of correspondence, and some of the points that were raised seem to need further comment.

One correspondent solved the whole problem by asserting that society can get along perfectly well without artists. It can also get along without scientists, engineers, doctors, bricklayers or road-menders – for the time being. It can even get along without sowing next year's harvest, provided it is understood that everyone is going to starve to death in about twelve months' time.

This notion, which is fairly widespread and has been encouraged by people who should know better, simply restates the problem in a new form. What the artist does is not immediately and obviously necessary in the same way as what the milkman or the coalminer does. Except in the ideal society which has not yet arrived, or in very chaotic and prosperous ages like the one that is just ending, this means in practice that the artist must have some kind of patron – a ruling class, the Church, the State, or a political party. And the question "Which is best?" normally means "Which interferes least?"

Several correspondents pointed out that one solution is for the artist to have an alternative means of livelihood. "It is quite feasible," says Mr. P. Philips Price, "to write and devote oneself to Socialism whilst accepting the patronage of the B.B.C., M.O.I., Rank or C.E.M.A.... the only way out is some minor form of prostitution, part time." The difficulty here is that the practice of writing or any other art takes up a lot of time and energy. Moreover, the kind of job that a writer gets in wartime, if he is not in the Forces (or even if he is – for there is always P.R.), usually has something to do with propaganda. But this is itself a kind of writing. To compose a propaganda pamphlet or a radio feature needs just as much work as to write something you believe in, with the difference that the finished product is worthless. I could give a whole list of writers of promise or performance who are now being squeezed dry like oranges in some official job or other. It is true that in most cases it is voluntary. They want the war to be won, and they know that everyone must sacrifice something. But still the result is the same. They will come out of the war with nothing to show for their labours and with not even the stored-up experience that the soldier gets in return for his physical suffering.

If a writer is to have an alternative profession, it is much better that it should have nothing to do with writing. A particularly successful holder of two jobs was Trollope, who produced two thousand words between seven and nine o'clock every morning before leaving for his work at the Post Office.

But Trollope was an exceptional man, and as he also hunted three days a week and was usually playing whist till midnight, I suspect that he did not overwork himself in his official duties.

Other correspondents pointed out that in a genuinely Socialist society the distinction between the artist and the ordinary man would vanish. Very likely, but then no such society yet exists. Others rightly claimed that State patronage is a better guarantee against starvation than private patronage, but seemed to me too ready to disregard the censorship that this implies. The usual line was that it is better for the artist to be a responsible member of a community than an anarchic individualist. The issue, however, is not between irresponsible "self-expression" and discipline; it is between truth and lies.

Artists don't so much object to *æsthetic* discipline. Architects will design theatres or churches equally readily, writers will switch from the three-volume novel to the one-volume, or from the play to the film, according to the demand. But the point is that this is a political age. A writer inevitably writes – and less directly this applies to all the arts – about contemporary events, and his impulse is to tell what he believes to be the truth. But no government, no big organisation, will pay for the truth. To take a crude example: can you imagine the British Government commissioning E. M. Forster to write *A Passage to India*? He could only write it because he was *not* dependent on State aid. Multiply that instance by a million, and you see the danger that is involved – not, indeed, in a centralised economy as such, but in our going forward into a collectivist age without remembering that the price of liberty is eternal vigilance.

Recently I was told the following story, and I have every reason to believe that it is true.

Among the German prisoners captured in France there are a certain number of Russians. Some time back two were captured who did not speak Russian or any other language that was known either to their captors or their fellow-prisoners. They could, in fact, only converse with one another. A professor of Slavonic languages, brought down from Oxford, could make nothing of what they were saying. Then it happened that a sergeant who had served on the frontiers of India overheard them talking and recognised their language, which he was able to speak a little. It was Tibetan! After some questioning, he managed to get their story out of them.

Some years earlier they had strayed over the frontier into the Soviet Union and been conscripted into a labour battalion, afterwards being sent to western Russia when the war with Germany broke out. They were taken prisoner by the Germans and sent to North Africa; later they were sent to France, then exchanged into a fighting unit when the Second Front opened, and taken prisoner by the British. All this time they had been able to speak to nobody but one another, and had no notion of what was happening or who was fighting whom.

It would round the story off neatly if they were now conscripted into the British Army and sent to fight the Japanese, ending up somewhere in Central Asia, quite close to their native village, but still very much puzzled as to what it is all about.

An Indian journalist sends me a cutting of an interview he had with Bernard Shaw. Shaw says one or two sensible things and does state that the Congress leaders ought not to have been arrested, but on the whole it is a disgusting exhibition. Here are some samples: –

Q. – Supposing you were a National leader of India. How would you have dealt with the British? What would have been your methods to achieve Indian independence?

A. – Please do not suppose a situation that can never happen. The achievement of Indian independence is not my business.

Q. – What do you think is the most effective way of getting the British out of India? What should the Indian people do?

A. – Make them superfluous by doing their work better. Or assimilate them by cross-fertilisation. British babies do not thrive in India.

What kind of answers are those to give to people who are labouring under a huge and justified grievance? Shaw also refuses to send birthday greetings to Gandhi, on the ground that this is a practice he never follows, and advises the Indian people not to bother if Britain repudiates the huge credit balance which India has piled up in this country during the war. I wonder what impression this interview would give to some young Indian student who has been a couple of years in jail and has dimly heard of Bernard Shaw as one of Britain's leading "progressive" thinkers? Is it surprising if even very level-headed Indians are liable to a recurrent suspicion that "all Englishmen are the same"?

As I Please 45
Tribune, 20 October 1944

Reading recently a book on Brigadier-General Wingate, who was killed early this year in Burma, I was interested to note that Wingate's "Chindits," who marched across Upper Burma in 1943, were wearing not the usual clumsy and conspicuous pith helmets, but slouch hats like those worn in the Gurkha regiments. This sounds a very small point, but it is of considerable social significance, and twenty or even ten years ago it would have been impossible. Nearly everyone, including nearly any doctor, would have predicted that large numbers of these men would perish of sunstroke.

Till recently the Europeans in India had an essentially superstitious attitude towards heat apoplexy, or sunstroke as it is usually called. It was supposed to be something dangerous to Europeans but not to Asiatics. When I was in Burma I was assured that the Indian sun, even at its coolest, had a peculiar deadliness which could only be warded off by wearing a helmet of cork or pith. "Natives," their skulls being thicker, had no need of these helmets, but for a European even a double felt hat was not a reliable protection.

But why should the sun in Burma, even on a positively chilly day, be deadlier than in England? Because we were nearer to the equator and the rays of the sun were more perpendicular. This astonished me, for obviously the rays of the sun are only perpendicular round about noon. How about the early morning, when the sun is creeping over the horizon and the rays are parallel with the earth? It is exactly then, I was told, that they are at their most dangerous. But how about the rainy season, when one frequently does not see the sun for days at a time? Then of all times, the old-stagers told me, you should cling to your topi. (The pith helmet is called a "topi," which is Hindustani for "hat.") The deadly rays filter through the envelope of cloud just the same, and on a dull day you are in danger of forgetting it. Take your topi off in the open for one moment, even for one moment, and you may be a dead man. Some people, not content with cork and pith, believed in the mysterious virtues of red flannel and had little patches of it sewn into their shirts over the top vertebra. The Eurasian community, anxious to emphasise their white ancestry, used at that time to wear topis even larger and thicker than those of the British.

My own disbelief in all this dated from the day when my topi was blown off my head and carried away down a stream, leaving me to march bareheaded all day without ill-effects. But I soon noticed other facts that conflicted with the prevailing belief. To begin with some Europeans (for instance sailors working in the rigging of ships) did habitually go bareheaded in the sun. Again, when cases of sunstroke occurred (for they do occur), they did not seem to be traceable to any occasion when the victim had taken his hat off. They happened to Asiatics as well as to Europeans, and were said to be commonest among stokers on coal-burning ships, who were subjected to fierce heat but not to sunshine. The final blow was the discovery that the topi, supposedly the only protection against the Indian sun, is quite a recent invention. The early Europeans in India knew nothing of it. In short, the whole thing was bunkum.

But why should the British in India have built up this superstition about sunstroke? Because an endless emphasis on the differences between the "natives" and yourself is one of the necessary props of imperialism. You can only rule over a subject race, especially when you are in a small minority, if you honestly believe yourself to be racially superior, and it helps towards this if you can believe that the subject race is *biologically* different. There were quite a number of ways in which Europeans in India used to believe, without any evidence, that Asiatic bodies differed from their own. Even quite considerable anatomical differences were supposed to exist. But this nonsense about Europeans being subject to sunstroke, and Orientals not, was the most cherished superstition of all.

The thin skull was the mark of racial superiority, and the pith topi was a sort of emblem of imperialism.

That is why it seems to me a sign of the changing times that Wingate's men, British, Indians and Burmese alike, set forth in ordinary felt hats. They suffered from dysentery, malaria, leeches, lice, snakes and Japanese, but I do not think any cases of sunstroke were recorded. And above all, there seems to have been no official protest and no feeling that the abandonment of the topi was a subtle blow at white prestige.

In Mr. Stanley Unwin's recent pamphlet, *Publishing in Peace and War*, some interesting facts are given about the quantities of paper allotted by the Government for various purposes. Here are the present figures: –

Newspapers	250,000 tons
H.M. Stationery Office	100,000 ,,
Periodicals (nearly)	50,000 ,,
Books	22,000 ,,

A particularly interesting detail is that out of the 100,000 tons allotted to the Stationery Office, the War Office gets no less than 25,000 tons, or more than the whole book trade put together.

I haven't personally witnessed, but I can imagine, the kind of wastage of paper that goes on in the War Office and the various ministries. I know what happens in the B.B.C. Would you credit, for instance, that of every radio programme that goes out on the air, even the inconceivable rubbish of cross-talk comedians, at least six copies are typed – sometimes as many as fifteen copies? For years past all this trash has been filed somewhere or other in enormous archives. At the same time paper for books is so short that even the most hackneyed "classic" is liable to be out of print, many schools are short of textbooks, new writers get no chance to start and even established writers have to expect a gap of a year or two years between finishing a book and seeing it published. And incidentally the export trade in English books has been largely swallowed up by America.

This part of Mr. Unwin's pamphlet is a depressing story. He writes with justified anger of the contemptuous attitude towards books shown by one Government department after another. But in fact the English as a whole, though some-what better in this respect than the Americans, have not much reverence for books. It is in the small countries, such as Finland and Holland, that the book-consumption per head is largest. Is it not rather humiliating to be told that a few years before the war a remote town like Reykjavik had a better display of *British* books than any English town of comparable size?

As I Please 46
Tribune, 27 October 1944

Reading, a week or two ago, Mr. C. S. Lewis's recently-published book, *Beyond Personality* (it is a series of reprinted broadcasts on theology), I learned from the blurb on the dust jacket that a critic who should, and indeed does, know better had likened an earlier book, *The Screwtape Letters*, to *The Pilgrim's Progress*. "I do not hesitate to compare Mr. Lewis's achievement with *Pilgrim's Progress*" were his quoted words. Here is a sample, entirely representative, from the later book: —

> "Well, even on the human level, you know, there are two kinds of pretending. There's a bad kind, where the pretence is *instead of* the real thing, as when a man pretends he's going to help you instead of really helping you. But there's also a good kind, where the pretence *leads up to* the real thing. When you're not feeling particularly friendly but know you ought to be, the best thing you can do, very often, is to put on a friendly manner and behave as if you were a much nicer chap than you actually are. And in a few minutes, as we've all noticed, you will be *really* feeling friendlier than you were. Very often the only way to get a quality is to start behaving as if you had it already. That's why children's games are so important. They're always pretending to be grown-ups – playing soldiers, playing shop. But all the time they are hardening their muscles and sharpening their wits, so that the pretence of being grown-ups helps them in earnest."

The book is like this all the way through, and I think most of us would hesitate a long time before equating Mr. Lewis with Bunyan. One must make some allowance for the fact that these essays are reprinted broadcasts, but even on the air it is not really necessary to insult your hearers with homey little asides like "you know" and "mind you," or Edwardian slang like "awfully," "jolly well," "specially" for "especially," "awful cheek," and so forth. The idea, of course, is to persuade the suspicious reader, or listener, that one can be a Christian and a "jolly good chap" at the same time. I don't imagine that the attempt would have much success, and in any case the cotton wool with which the B.B.C. stuffs its speakers' mouths makes any real discussion of theological problems impossible, even from an orthodox angle. But Mr. Lewis's vogue at this moment, the time allowed to him on the air and the exaggerated praise he has received, are bad symptoms and worth noticing.

Students of popular religious apologetics will notice early in the book a side-kick at "all these people who turn up every few years with some patent simplified religion of their own," and various hints that unbelief is "out of date," "old-fashioned," and so forth. And they will remember Ronald Knox saying much the same thing fifteen years ago, and R.H. Benson twenty or thirty years before that, and they will know in which pigeonhole Mr. Lewis should be placed.

A kind of book that has been endemic in England for quite sixty years is the silly-clever religious book, which goes on the principle not of threatening the unbeliever with Hell, but of showing him up as an illogical ass, incapable of clear thought and unaware that everything he says has been said and refuted before. This school of literature started, I think, with W. H. Mallock's *New Republic*, which must have been written about 1880, and it has had a long line of practitioners – R. H. Benson, Chesterton, Father Knox, "Beachcomber" and others, most of them Catholics, but some, like Dr. Cyril Alington and (I suspect) Mr. Lewis himself, Anglicans. The line of attack is always the same. Every heresy has been uttered before (with the implication that it has also been refuted before); and theology is only understood by theologians (with the implication that you should leave your thinking to the priests). Along these lines one can, of course, have a lot of clean fun by "correcting loose thinking" and pointing out that so-and-so is only saying what Pelagius said in A.D. 400 (or whenever it was), and has in any case used the word transubstantiation in the wrong sense. The special targets of these people have been T. H. Huxley, H. G. Wells, Bertrand Russell, Professor Joad, and others who are associated in the popular mind with Science and Rationalism. They have never had much difficulty in demolishing them – though I notice that most of the demolished ones are still there, while some of the Christian apologists themselves begin to look rather faded.

One reason for the extravagant boosting that these people always get in the Press is that their political affiliations are invariably reactionary. Some of them were frank admirers of Fascism as long as it was safe to be so. That is why I draw attention to Mr. C. S. Lewis and his chummy little wireless talks, of which no doubt there will be more. They are not really so unpolitical as they are meant to look. Indeed they are an outflanking movement in the big counter-attack against the Left which Lord Elton, A. P. Herbert, G. M. Young, Alfred Noyes and various others have been conducting for two years past.

I notice that in his new book, *Adam and Eve*, Mr. Middleton Murry instances the agitation against Mosley's release from internment as a sign of the growth of totalitarianism, or the totalitarian habit of mind, in this country. The common people, he says, still detest totalitarianism: but he adds in a later footnote that the Mosley business has shaken this opinion somewhat. I wonder whether he is right.

On the face of it, the demonstrations against Mosley's release were a very bad sign. In effect people were agitating against Habeas Corpus. In 1940 it was a perfectly proper action to intern Mosley, and in my opinion it would have been quite proper to shoot him if the Germans had set foot in Britain. When it is a question of national existence, no government can stand on the letter of the law: otherwise a potential quisling has only to avoid committing any indictable offence, and he can remain at liberty, ready to go over to the enemy and act as their gauleiter as soon as they arrive. But by 1943 the situation was totally different. The chance of a serious German invasion had passed, and Mosley (though possibly he may make a comeback at some future date – I won't prophesy about that) was merely a ridiculous failed politician with varicose veins. To continue imprisoning him without trial was an infringement of every principle we are supposedly fighting for.

But there was also strong popular feeling against Mosley's release, and not, I think, for reasons so sinister as Mr. Murry implies. The comment one most frequently heard was "They've only done it because he's a rich man," which was a simplified way of saying "Class privilege is on the up-grade again." It is a commonplace that the political advance we seemed to make in 1940 has been gradually filched away from us again. But though the ordinary man sees this happening, he is curiously unable to combat it: there seems to be nowhere to take hold. In a way, politics has stopped. There has been no general election, the elector is conscious of being unable to influence his M.P., Parliament has no control over the Government. You may not like the way things are going, but what exactly can you do about it? There is no concrete act against which you can plausibly protest.

But now and again something happens which is obviously symptomatic of the general trend – something round which existing discontents can crystallise. "Lock up Mosley" was a good rallying cry. Mosley, in fact, was a symbol, as Beveridge still is and as Cripps was in 1942. I don't believe Mr. Murry need bother about the implications of this incident. In spite of all that has happened, the failure of any genuinely totalitarian outlook to gain ground among the ordinary people of this country is one of the most surprising and encouraging phenomena of the war.

As I Please 47
Tribune, 3 November 1944

Penguin Books have now started publishing books in French, very nicely got up, at half-a-crown each. Among those to appear shortly is the latest instalment of André Gide's Journal, which covers a year of the German occupation. As I glanced through an old favourite, Anatole France's *Les Dieux Ont Soif* (it is a novel about the Reign of Terror during the French Revolution), the thought occurred to me: what a remarkable anthology one could make of pieces of writing describing executions! There must be hundreds of them scattered through literature, and – for a reason I think I can guess – they must be far better written on average than battle pieces.

Among the examples I remember at the moment are Thackeray's description of the hanging of Courvoisier, the crucifixion of the gladiators in *Salammbô*, the final scene of *A Tale of Two Cities*, a piece from a letter or diary of Byron's, describing a guillotining, and the beheading of two Scottish noblemen after the 1745 rebellion, described by, I think, Horace Walpole. There is a very fine chapter describing a guillotining in Arnold Bennett's *Old Wives' Tale*, and a horrible one in one of Zola's novels (the one about the Sacré Cœur). Then there is Jack London's short story, *The Chinago*, Plato's account of the death of Socrates – but one could extend the list indefinitely. There must also be a great number of specimens in verse, for instance the old hanging ballads, to which Kipling's *Danny Deever* probably owes something.

The thing that I think very striking is that no one, or no one I can remember, ever writes of an execution *with approval*. The dominant note is always horror. Society, apparently, cannot get along without capital punishment – for there are some people whom it is simply not safe to leave alive – and yet there is no one, when the pinch comes, who feels it right to kill another human being in cold blood. I watched a man hanged once. There was no question that everybody concerned knew this to be a dreadful, unnatural action. I believe it is always the same – the whole jail, warders and prisoners alike, is upset when there is an execution. It is probably the fact that capital punishment is accepted as necessary, and yet instinctively felt to be wrong, that gives so many descriptions of executions their tragic atmosphere. They are mostly written by people who have actually watched an execution and feel it to be a terrible and only partly comprehensible experience which they want to record; whereas battle literature is largely written by people who have never heard a gun go off and think of a battle as a sort of football match in which nobody gets hurt.

Perhaps it was a bit previous to say that no one writes of an execution with approval, when one thinks of the way our newspapers have been smacking their chops over the bumping-off of wretched quislings in France and elsewhere. I recall, in one paper, a whole series of photos showing the execution of Caruso, the ex-chief of the Rome police. You saw the huge, fat body being straddled across a chair with his back to the firing squad, then the cloud of smoke issuing from the rifle barrels and the body slumping sideways. The editor who saw fit to publish this thought it a pleasant titbit, I suppose, but then he had not had to watch the actual deed. I think I can imagine the feelings of the man who took the photographs, and of the firing squad.

To the lovers of useless knowledge (and I know there are a lot of them, from the number of letters I always get when I raise any question of this kind) I present a curious little problem arising out of the recent Pelican, *Shakespeare's England*. A writer named Fynes Morrison, touring England in 1607, describes melons as growing freely. Andrew Marvell, in a very well-known poem written about fifty years later, also refers to melons. Both references make it appear that the melons grew in the open, and indeed they must have done so if they grew at all. The hotbed was a recent invention in 1600, and glasshouses, if they existed, must have been a very great rarity. I imagine it would be quite impossible to grow a melon in the open in England nowadays. They are hard enough to grow under glass, whence their price. Fynes Morrison also speaks of grapes growing in large enough quantities to make wine. Is it possible that our climate has changed radically in the last three hundred years? Or was the so-called melon actually a pumpkin?

As from November 10th, *Tribune* intends to replan its book reviews. The present policy of trying to give every book a review of about a column is felt to be unsatisfactory, because with the small space at our disposal we cannot keep up to date, and the more important books frequently do not get the detailed treatment they deserve. The best solution seems to be to make some reviews shorter and others longer.

Daniel George's novel reviews will not be affected, but for the rest we intend to have about nine very short notices – a sort of guide to the current books – and one very long one, probably of about 1,500 words. This will allow us to cover rather more books than at present and keep more nearly up to date, but it will have the added advantage that serious books can be seriously treated. In every week there is at least *one* book that deserves a full-length review, even if its importance is only indirect.

From years of experience as a book reviewer I should say that the rock-bottom minimum in which you can both summarise and criticise a book is 800 words. But a book review is seldom of much value *as a piece of writing* if it is under 1,000 words. The generally higher standard of criticism in monthly and quarterly magazines is partly due to the fact that the reviewers are less pinched for space. In the old days of the *Edinburgh* and the *Quarterly*, a hundred years ago, a reviewer often had fifteen pages to play with!

If this policy does not work out well we shall scrap it, but we shall give it several months' trial. Our aim is to produce leading reviews which thoroughly criticise the chosen book and at the same time are worth-while articles in themselves. Apart from people who already write fairly frequently for *Tribune*, we have collected a first-rate team of reviewers, including Herbert Read, Stephen Spender, Franz Borkenau, Hugh Kingsmill, Michael Roberts, Mulk Raj Anand, Arturo Barea, Arthur Koestler and several others.

As I Please 48

Tribune, 17 November 1944

Some weeks ago, in the course of some remarks on schools of journalism, I carelessly described the magazine the *Writer* as being "defunct." As a result I have received a severe letter from its proprietors, who enclose a copy of the November issue of the *Writer* and call on me to withdraw my statement.

I withdraw it readily. The *Writer* is still alive and seems to be much the same as ever, though it has changed its format since

GEORGE ORWELL

I knew it. And I think this specimen copy is worth examining for the light it throws on schools of journalism and the whole business of extracting fees from struggling free-lance journalists.

The articles are of the usual type – "Plotting Technique (fifteenth instalment)" by William A. Bagley, etc. – but I am more interested in the advertisements, which take up more than a quarter of the space. The majority of them are from people who profess to be able to teach you how to make money out of writing. A surprising number undertake to supply you with ready-made plots. Here are a few specimens:

"Plotting without tears. Learn my way. The simplest method ever. Money returned if dissatisfied. 5/- post free."

"Inexhaustible plotting method for women's Press, 5/3d. Gives real mastery. Ten days' approval."

"PLOTS. Our plots are set out in sequence all ready for write-up, with lengths for each sequence. No remoulding necessary – just the requisite clothing of words. All types supplied."

"PLOTS: in vivid scenes. With striking opening lines for actual use in story. Specimen conversation, including authentic dialect. . . . Short-short, 5/-. Short story, 6/6d. Long-complete (with tense, breathless 'curtains') 8/6d. Radio plays, 10/6d. Serial, novel, novelette (chapter by chapter, appropriate prefix, prose or poetical quotations if desired), 15/6d. – 1 gn."

There are many others. Somebody called Mr. Martin Walter claims to have reduced story-construction to an exact science and "eventually evolved the Plot Formula according to which his own stories and those of his students throughout the world are constructed. . . . Whether you aspire to write the 'literary' story or the popular story, or to produce stories for any existing market, remember that Mr. Walter's Formula *alone* tells you just what a 'plot' is and how to produce one." The Formula only costs you a guinea, it appears. Then there are the "Fleet Street journalists" who are prepared to revise your manuscripts for you at 2/6 per thousand words. Nor are the poets forgotten:

774

"GREETINGS.

"Are you poets neglecting the great post-war demand for sentiments?

"Do you specialise and do you know what is needed?

"Aida Reuben's famous Greeting Card Course is available to approved students willing to work hard. Her book 'Sentiment and Greeting Card Publishers,' published at 3/6d., may be obtained from," etc., etc.

I do not wish to say anything offensive, but to anyone who is inclined to respond to the sort of advertisement quoted above, I offer this consideration. If these people really know how to make money out of writing, why aren't they just doing it instead of peddling their secret at 5/- a time? Apart from any other consideration, they would be raising up hordes of competitors for themselves. This number of the *Writer* contains about 30 advertisements of this stamp, and the *Writer* itself, besides giving advice in its articles, also runs its own Literary Bureau in which manuscripts are "criticised by acknowledged experts" at so much a thousand words. If each of these various teachers had even ten successful pupils a week, they would between them be letting loose on to the market some fifteen thousand successful writers per annum!

Also, isn't it rather curious that the "Fleet Street journalists," "established authors" and "well-known novelists" who either run these courses or write the testimonials for them are not named – or, when named, are seldom or never people whose published work you have seen anywhere? If Bernard Shaw or J. B. Priestley offered to teach you how to make money out of writing, you might feel that there was something in it. But who would buy a bottle of hair restorer from a bald man?

If the *Writer* wants some more free publicity it shall have it, but I dare say this will do to go on with.

One favourite way of falsifying history nowadays is to alter dates. Maurice Thorez, the French Communist, has just been amnestied by the French Government (he was under sentence for deserting from the army). Apropos of this, one London newspaper remarks that Thorez "will now be able to return from Moscow, where he has been living in exile for the last six years."

On the contrary, he has been in Moscow for at most five years, as the editor of this newspaper is well aware. Thorez, who for several years past has been proclaiming his anxiety to defend France against the Germans, was called up at the outbreak of war in 1939, and failed to make an appearance. Some time later he turned up in Moscow.

But why the alteration of date? In order to make it appear that Thorez deserted, if he did desert, a year *before* the war and not after the fighting had started. This is merely one act in the general effort to whitewash the behaviour of the French and other Communists during the period of the Russo-German pact. I could name other similar falsifications in recent years. Sometimes you can give an event a quite different colour by switching its date only a few weeks. But it doesn't much matter so long as we all keep our eyes open and see to it that the lies do not creep out of the newspapers and into the history books.

A correspondent who lacks the collecting instinct has sent a copy of *Principles or Prejudices*, a sixpenny pamphlet by Kenneth Pickthorn, the Conservative M.P., with the advice (underlined in red ink): "Burn when read."

I wouldn't think of burning it. It has gone straight into my archives. But I agree that it is a disgusting piece of work, and that this whole series of pamphlets (the *Signpost Booklets*, by such authors as G. M. Young, Douglas Woodruff and Captain L. D. Gammans) is a bad symptom. Mr. Pickthorn is one of the more intelligent of the younger Tory M.P.s ("younger" in political circles means under sixty), and in this pamphlet he is trying to present Toryism in a homely and democratic light while casting misleading little snacks at the Left. Look at this, for instance, for a misrepresentation of the theory of Marxism:

"Not one of the persons who say that economic factors govern the world believes it about himself. If Karl Marx had been more economically than politically interested he could have done better for himself than by accepting the kindnesses of the capitalist Engels and occasionally selling articles to American newspapers."

Aimed at ignorant people, this is meant to imply that Marxism regards *individual* acquisitiveness as the motive force in history. Marx not only did not say this, he said almost the opposite of it. Much of the pamphlet is an attack on the notion of internationalism, and is backed up by such remarks as: "No British statesman should feel himself authorised to spend British blood for the promotion of something superior to British interests." Fortunately, Mr. Pickthorn writes too badly to have a very wide appeal, but some of the other pamphleteers in this series are cleverer. The Tory Party used always to be known as "the stupid party." But the publicists of this group have a fair selection of brains among them, and when Tories grow intelligent it is time to feel for your watch and count your small change.

As I Please 49
Tribune, 24 November 1944

There have been innumerable complaints lately about the rudeness of shopkeepers. People say, I think with truth, that shopkeepers appear to take a sadistic pleasure in telling you that they don't stock the thing you ask for. To go in search of some really rare object, such as a comb or a tin of boot polish, is a miserable experience. It means trailing from shop to shop and getting a series of curt or actually hostile negatives. But even the routine business of buying the rations and the bread is made as difficult as possible for busy people. How is a woman to do her household shopping if she is working till six every day while most of the shops shut at five? She can only do it by fighting round crowded counters during her lunch hour. But it is the snubs that they get when they ask for some article which is in short supply that people dread most. Many shopkeepers seem to regard the customer as a kind of mendicant and to feel that they are conferring a favour on him by selling him anything. And there are other justified grievances – for instance, the shameless overcharging on uncontrolled goods such as secondhand furniture, and the irritating trick, now very common, of displaying in the window goods which are not on sale.

But before blaming the shopkeeper for all this, there are several things one ought to remember. To begin with, irritability and bad manners are on the increase everywhere. You have only to observe the behaviour of normally longsuffering people like 'bus conductors to realise this. It is a neurosis produced by the war. But, in addition, many small independent shopkeepers (in my experience you are treated far more politely in big shops) are people with a well-founded grievance against society. Some of them are in effect the ill-paid employees of wholesale firms, others are being slowly crushed by the competition of the chain stores, and they are often treated with the greatest inconsiderateness by the local authorities. Sometimes a rehousing scheme will rob a shopkeeper of half his customers at one swoop. In war time this may happen even more drastically owing to bombing and the call-up. And war has other special irritations for the shopkeeper. Rationing puts a great deal of extra work on to grocers, butchers, etc., and it is very exasperating to be asked all day long for articles which you have not got.

But after all, the main fact is that at normal times both the shop assistant and the independent shopkeeper are downtrodden. They live to the tune of "the customer is always right." In peace time, in capitalist society, everyone is trying to sell goods which there is never enough money to buy, whereas in war time money is plentiful and goods scarce. Matches, razor blades, torch batteries, alarm clocks and teats for babies' feeding bottles are precious rarities, and the man who possesses them is a powerful being, to be approached cap in hand. I don't think one can blame the shopkeeper for getting a bit of his own back, when the situation is temporarily reversed. But I do agree that the behaviour of some of them is disgusting, and that when one is treated with more than normal haughtiness it is a duty to the rest of the public not to go to that shop again.

Examining recently a copy of *Old Moore's Almanac*, I was reminded of the fun I used to extract in my boyhood from answering advertisements. Increase your height, earn five pounds a week in your spare time, drink habit conquered in three days, electric belts, bust developers and cures for obesity, insomnia, bunions, backache, red noses, stammering, blushing, piles, bad legs, flat feet and baldness – all the old favourites were there, or nearly all. Some of these advertisements have remained totally unchanged for at least thirty years.

You cannot, I imagine, get much benefit from any of these nostrums, but you can have a lot of fun by answering the advertisements and then, when you have drawn them out and made them waste a lot of stamps in sending successive wads of testimonials, suddenly leaving them cold. Many years ago I answered an advertisement from Winifred Grace Hartland (the advertisement used to carry a photograph of her – a radiant woman with a sylphlike figure), who undertook to cure obesity. In replying to my letter she assumed that I was a woman – this surprised me at the time, though I realise now that the dupes of these advertisements are almost all female. She urged me to come and see her at once. "Do come," she wrote, "before ordering your summer frocks, as after taking my course your figure will have altered out of recognition." She was particularly insistent that I should make a personal visit, and gave an address somewhere in London Docks. This went on for a long time, during which the fee gradually sank from two guineas to half a crown, and then I brought the matter to an end by writing to say that I had been cured of my obesity by a rival agency.

Years later I came across a copy of the cautionary list which *Truth* used to issue from time to time in order to warn the public against swindlers. It revealed that there was no such person as Winifred Grace Hartland, this swindle being run by two American crooks named Harry Sweet and Dave Little. It is curious that they should have been so anxious for a personal visit, and indeed I have since wondered whether Harry Sweet and Dave Little were actually engaged in shipping consignments of fat women to the harems of Istanbul.

Everyone has a list of books which he is "always meaning to read," and now and again one gets round to reading one of them. One that I recently crossed off my list was George Bourne's *Memoirs of a Surrey Labourer*. I was slightly disappointed with it, because, though it is a true story, Bettesworth, the man it is about, was not quite an ordinary labourer. He had been a farm worker, but had become a jobbing gardener, and his relation with George Bourne was that of servant and master. Nevertheless there is some remarkable detail in it, and it gives a true picture of the cruel, sordid end with which a lifetime of heavy work on the land is often rewarded. The book was written more than thirty years ago, but things have not changed fundamentally. Immediately before the war, in my own village in Hertfordshire, two old men were ending their days in much the same bare misery as George Bourne describes.

Another book I recently read, or rather re-read, was *The Follies and Frauds of Spiritualism*, issued about twenty years ago by the Rationalist Press Association. This is probably not an easy book to get hold of, but I can equally recommend Mr. Bechhofer Roberts's book on the same subject. An interesting fact that these and similar books bring out is the number of scientists who have been taken in by spiritualism. The list includes Sir William Crookes, Wallace the biologist, Lombroso, Flammarion the astronomer (he afterwards changed his mind, however), Sir Oliver Lodge, and a whole string of German and Italian professors. These people are not, perhaps, the topnotchers of the scientific world, but you do not find, for instance, poets in comparable numbers falling a prey to the mediums. Elizabeth Barrett Browning is supposed to have been taken in by the famous medium Home, but Browning himself saw through him at a glance and wrote a scarifying poem about him (*Sludge the Medium*). Significantly, the people who are *never* converted to spiritualism are conjurors.

Funny, But Not Vulgar

1 December 1944; *Leader Magazine*, 28 July 1945

The great age of English humorous writing – not witty and not satirical, but simply humorous – was the first three-quarters of the nineteenth century.

Within that period lie Dickens's enormous output of comic writings, Thackeray's brilliant burlesques and short stories, such as *The Fatal Boots* and *A Little Dinner at Timmins's*, Surtees's *Handley Cross*, Lewis Carroll's *Alice in Wonderland*, Douglas Jerrold's *Mrs. Caudle's Curtain Lectures*, and a considerable body of humorous verse by Thomas Barham, Thomas Hood, Edward Lear, Arthur Hugh Clough, Charles Stuart Calverley, and others. Two other comic masterpieces, F. Anstey's *Vice Versa* and the two Grossmiths' *Diary of a Nobody*, lie only just outside the period

I have named. And, at any rate until 1860 or thereabouts, there was still such a thing as comic draughtsmanship, witness Cruikshank's illustrations to Dickens, Leech's illustrations to Surtees, and even Thackeray's illustrations of his own work.

I do not want to exaggerate by suggesting that, within our own century, England has produced no humorous writing of any value. There have been, for instance, Barry Pain, W. W. Jacobs, Stephen Leacock, P. G. Wodehouse, H. G. Wells in his lighter moments, Evelyn Waugh, and – a satirist rather than a humorist – Hilaire Belloc. Still, we have not only produced no laugh-getter of anything like the stature of *Pickwick Papers*, but, what is probably more significant, there is not and has not been for decades past, any such thing as a first-rate humorous periodical. The usual charge against *Punch*, that it "isn't what it was," is perhaps unjustified at this moment, since *Punch* is somewhat funnier than it was ten years ago: but it is also very much *less* funny than it was ninety years ago.

And comic verse has lost all its vitality – there has been no English light verse of any value within this century, except Mr. Belloc's, and a poem or two by Chesterton – while a drawing that is funny in its own right, and not merely because of the joke it illustrates, is a great rarity.

All this is generally admitted. If you want a laugh you are likelier to go to a music-hall or a Disney film, or switch on Tommy Handley, or buy a few of Donald McGill's postcards, than to resort to a book or a periodical. It is generally recognised, too, that American comic writers and illustrators are superior to our own. At present we have nobody to set against either James Thurber or Damon Runyan.

We do not know with certainty how laughter originated or what biological purpose it serves, but we do know, in broad terms, what causes laughter.

A thing is funny when – in some way that is not actually offensive or frightening – it upsets the established order. Every joke is a tiny revolution. If you had to define humour in a single phrase, you might define it as dignity sitting on a tintack. Whatever destroys dignity, and brings down the mighty from their seats, preferably with a bump, is funny. And the bigger the fall, the bigger the joke. It would be better fun to throw a custard pie at a bishop than at a curate. With this general principle in mind, one can, I think, begin to see what has been wrong with English comic writing during the present century.

Nearly all English humorists to-day are too genteel, too kind-hearted and too consciously lowbrow. P. G. Wodehouse's novels, or A. P. Herbert's verses, seem always to be aimed at prosperous stockbrokers whiling away an odd half hour in the lounge of some suburban golf course. They and all their kind are dominated by an anxiety not to stir up mud, either moral, religious, political or intellectual. It is no accident that most of the best comic writers of our time – Belloc, Chesterton, "Timothy Shy" and the recent "Beachcomber" – have been Catholic apologists; that is, people with a serious purpose and a noticeable willingness to hit below the belt. The silly-ass tradition in modern English humour, the avoidance of brutality and horror of intelligence, is summed up in the phrase *funny without being vulgar.* "Vulgar" in this context usually means "obscene," and it can be admitted at once that the best jokes are not necessarily dirty ones. Edward Lear and Lewis Carroll, for instance, never made jokes of that description, and Dickens and Thackeray very rarely.

On the whole, the early-Victorian writers avoided sex jokes, though a few, for instance Surtees, Marryat and Barham, retained traces of eighteenth-century coarseness. But the point is that the modern emphasis on what is called "clean fun" is really the symptom of a general unwillingness to touch upon any serious or controversial subject. Obscenity is, after all, a kind of subversiveness. Chaucer's "Miller's Tale" is a rebellion in the moral sphere, as *Gulliver's Travels* is a rebellion in the political sphere. The truth is that you cannot be memorably funny without *at some point* raising topics which the rich, the powerful and the complacent would prefer to see left alone.

I named above some of the best comic writers of the nineteenth century, but the case becomes much stronger if one draws in the English humorists of earlier ages – for instance, Chaucer, Shakespeare, Swift and the picaresque novelists, Smollett, Fielding and Sterne. It becomes stronger, again, if one considers foreign writers, both ancient and modern: for example, Aristophanes, Voltaire, Rabelais, Boccaccio and

Cervantes. All of these writers are remarkable for their brutality and coarseness. People are tossed in blankets, they fall through cucumber frames, they are hidden in washing baskets, they rob, lie, swindle, and are caught out in every conceivable humiliating situation. And all great humorous writers show a willingness to attack the beliefs and the virtues on which society necessarily rests. Boccaccio treats Hell and Purgatory as a ridiculous fable, Swift jeers at the very conception of human dignity, Shakespeare makes Falstaff deliver a speech in favour of cowardice in the middle of a battle. As for the sanctity of marriage, it was the principal subject of humour in Christian society for the better part of a thousand years.

All this is not to say that humour is, of its nature, immoral or anti-social. A joke is at most a temporary rebellion against virtue, and its aim is not to degrade the human being but to remind him that he is already degraded. A willingness to make extremely obscene jokes can co-exist with very strict moral standards, as in Shakespeare. Some comic writers, like Dickens, have a direct political purpose, others, like Chaucer or Rabelais, accept the corruption of society as something inevitable; but no comic writer of any stature has ever suggested that society is *good*.

Humour is the debunking of humanity, and nothing is funny except in relation to human beings. Animals, for instance, are only funny because they are caricatures of ourselves. A lump of stone could not of itself be funny; but it can become funny if it hits a human being in the eye, or if it is carved into human likeness.

However, there are subtler methods of debunking than throwing custard pies. There is also the humour of pure fantasy, which assaults man's notion of himself as not only a dignified but a rational being. Lewis Carroll's humour consists essentially in making fun of logic, and Edward Lear's in a sort of poltergeist interference with common sense. When the Red Queen remarks, "*I've* seen hills compared with which you'd call that one a valley," she is in her way attacking the bases of society as violently as Swift or Voltaire. Comic verse, as in Lear's poem *The Courtship of the Yonghy-Bonghy-Bò*, often depends on building up a fantastic universe which is just similar enough to the real universe to rob it of its dignity. But more often it depends on anti-climax – that is, on starting out with high-flown language and then suddenly coming down with a bump. For instance, Calverley's lines:

> Once, a happy child, I carolled
> On green lawns the whole day through,
> Not unpleasingly apparelled
> In a tightish suit of blue,

in which the first two lines would give the impression that this is going to be a sentimental poem about the beauties of childhood. Or Mr. Belloc's various invocations to Africa in *The Modern Traveller*:

> O Africa, mysterious land,
> Surrounded by a lot of sand,
> And full of grass and trees . . .
> Far land of Ophir, mined for gold
> By lordly Solomon of old,
> Who, sailing northward to Perim,
> Took all the gold away with him
> And left a lot of holes, etc.

Bret Harte's sequel to *Maud Muller*, with such couplets as –

> But the very day that they were mated
> Maud's brother Bob was intoxicated

plays essentially the same trick, and so in a different way do Voltaire's mock epic, *La Pucelle*, and many passages in Byron.

English light verse in the present century – witness the work of Owen Seaman, Harry Graham, A. P. Herbert, A. A. Milne and others – has mostly been poor stuff, lacking not only in fancifulness but in intellectuality. Its authors are too anxious not to be highbrows – even, though they are writing in verse, not to be poets. Early-Victorian light verse is generally haunted by the ghost of poetry; it is often extremely skilful as verse, and it is sometimes allusive and "difficult." When Barham wrote –

> Your Callipyge's injured behind,
> Bloudie Jack,

> Your de Medici's injured before,
> And your Anadyomene's injured in so many
> Places, I think there's a score,
> If not more,
> Of her fingers and toes on the floor

he was performing a feat of sheer virtuosity which the most serious poet would respect. Or, to quote Calverley again, in his *Ode to Tobacco*:

> Thou, who when fears attack,
> Bidst them avaunt, and Black
> Care, at the horseman's back
> Perching, unseatest;
> Sweet when the morn is grey,
> Sweet when they've cleared away
> Lunch, and at close of day
> Possibly sweetest!

Calverley is not afraid, it will be seen, to put a tax on his reader's attention and to drag in a recondite Latin allusion. He is not writing for lowbrows, and – particularly in his *Ode to Beer* – he can achieve magnificent anti-climaxes because he is willing to sail close to true poetry and to assume considerable knowledge in his readers.

It would seem that you *cannot* be funny without being vulgar – that is, vulgar by the standards of the people at whom English humorous writing in our own day seems mostly to be aimed. For it is not only sex that is "vulgar." So are death, childbirth and poverty, the other three subjects upon which the best music-hall humour turns. And respect for the intellect and strong political feeling, if not actually vulgar, are looked upon as being in doubtful taste. You cannot be really funny if your main aim is to flatter the comfortable classes: it means leaving out too much. To be funny, indeed, you have got to be serious. *Punch*, for at least forty years past, has given the impression of trying not so much to amuse as to reassure. Its implied message is that all is for the best and nothing will ever really change.

It was by no means with that creed that it started out.

As I Please 50

Tribune, 1 December 1944

V2 (I am told that you can now mention it in print so long as you just call it V2 and don't describe it too minutely) supplies another instance of the contrariness of human nature. People are complaining of the sudden unexpected wallop with which these things go off. "It wouldn't be so bad if you got a bit of warning," is the usual formula. There is even a tendency to talk nostalgically of the days of V1. The good old doodle-bug did at least give you time to get under the table, etc., etc. Whereas, in fact, when the doodle-bugs were actually dropping, the usual subject of complaint was the uncomfortable waiting period before they went off. Some people are never satisfied. Personally, I am no lover of V2, especially at this moment when the house still seems to be rocking from a recent explosion, but what most depresses me about these things is the way they set people talking about the next war. Every time one goes off I hear gloomy references to "next time," and the reflection: "I suppose they'll be able to shoot them across the Atlantic by that time." But if you ask who will be fighting whom when this universally expected war breaks out, you get no clear answer. It is just war in the abstract – the notion that human beings could ever behave sanely having apparently faded out of many people's memories.

Maurice Baring, in his book on Russian literature, which was published in 1907 and must have been the means of introducing many people in this country to the great Russian novelists, remarks that English books were always popular in Russia. Among other favourites he mentions *The Diary of a Nobody* (which, by the way, is reprinted by the Everyman Library, if you can run across a copy).

I have always wondered what on earth *The Diary of a Nobody* could be like in a Russian translation, and indeed I have faintly suspected that the Russians may have enjoyed it because when translated it was just like Chekhov. But in a way it would be a very good book to read if you wanted to get a picture of English life, even though it was written in the 'eighties and has an intensely strong smell of that period. Charles Pooter is a true Englishman both in native gentleness and his impenetrable stupidity. The interesting thing, however, is to follow this book up to its origins. What does it ultimately derive from? Almost certainly, I think, from *Don Quixote*, of which, indeed, it is a sort of modern anglicised version. Pooter is a high-minded, even adventurous man, constantly suffering disasters brought upon him by his own folly, and surrounded by a whole tribe of Sancho Panzas. But apart from the comparative mildness of the things that befall him, one can see in the endings of the two books the enormous difference between the age of Cervantes and our own.

In the end the Grossmiths have to take pity on poor Pooter. Everything, or nearly everything, comes right, and at the last there is a tinge of sentimentality which does not quite fit in with the rest of the book. The fact is that, in spite of the way we actually behave, we cannot any longer feel that the infliction of pain is merely funny. Nietzsche remarks somewhere that the pathos of *Don Quixote* may well be a modern discovery. Quite likely Cervantes didn't mean Don Quixote to seem pathetic – perhaps he just meant him to be funny and intended it as a screaming joke when the poor old man has half his teeth knocked out by a sling-stone. However this may be with Don Quixote, I am fairly certain that it is true of Falstaff. Except possibly for the final scene in *Henry V*, there is nothing to show that Shakespeare sees Falstaff as a pathetic as well as a comic figure. He is just a punching-bag for fortune, a sort of Billy Bunter with a gift for language. The thing that seems saddest to us is Falstaff's helpless dependence on his odious patron, Prince Harry, whom Sir John Masefield aptly described as a "disgusting beefy brute." There is no sign, or, at any rate, no clear sign, that Shakespeare sees anything pathetic or degrading in such a relationship.

Say what you like, things *do* change. A few years ago I was walking across Hungerford Bridge with a lady aged about sixty or perhaps less. The tide was out, and as we looked down at the beds of filthy, almost liquid mud, she remarked:

"When I was a little girl we used to throw pennies to the mudlarks down there."

I was intrigued and asked what mudlarks were. She explained that in those days professional beggars, known as mudlarks, used to sit under the bridge waiting for people to throw them pennies. The pennies would bury themselves deep in the mud, and the mudlarks would plunge in head first and recover them. This was considered a most amusing spectacle.

Is there anyone who would degrade himself in that way nowadays? And how many people are there who would get a kick out of watching it?

Shortly before his assassination, Trotsky had completed a *Life* of Stalin. One may assume that it was not an altogether unbiased book, but obviously a biography of Stalin by Trotsky – or, for that matter, a biography of Trotsky by Stalin – would be a winner from a selling point of view. A very well-known American firm of publishers were to issue it. The book had been printed and – this is the point that I have been waiting to verify before mentioning this matter in my notes – the review copies had been sent out when the U.S.A. entered the war. The book was immediately withdrawn, and the reviewers were asked to co-operate in "avoiding any comment whatever regarding the biography and its postponement."

They have co-operated remarkably well. This affair has gone almost unmentioned in the American Press and, as far as I know, entirely unmentioned in the British Press, although the facts were well known and obviously worth a paragraph or two.

Since the American entry into the war made the U.S.A. and the U.S.S.R. allies, I think that to withdraw the book was an understandable if not particularly admirable deed. What is disgusting is the general willingness to suppress all mention of it. A little while back I attended a meeting of the P.E.N. Club, which was held to celebrate the tercentenary of *Areopagitica*, Milton's famous tract on the freedom of the Press. There were countless speeches emphasising the importance of preserving intellectual liberty, even in wartime. If I remember rightly, Milton's phrase about the special sin of "murdering" a book was printed on the P.E.N. leaflet for the occasion. But I heard no references to this particular murder, the facts of which were no doubt known to plenty of people there.

Here is another little brain-tickler. The following often-quoted passage comes from Act V of Shakespeare's tragedy, *Timon of Athens*:

> Come not to me again: but say to Athens
> Timon hath made his everlasting mansion
> Upon the beachèd verge of the salt flood:
> Who once a day with his embossed froth
> The turbulent surge shall cover.

This passage contains three errors. What are they?

As I Please 51
Tribune, 8 December 1944

For years past I have been an industrious collector of pamphlets, and a fairly steady reader of political literature of all kinds. The thing that strikes me more and more – and it strikes a lot of other people, too – is the extraordinary viciousness and dishonesty of political controversy in our time. I don't mean merely that controversies are acrimonious. They ought to be that when they are on serious subjects. I mean that almost nobody seems to feel that an opponent deserves a fair hearing or that the objective truth matters so long as you can score a neat debating point. When I look through my collection of pamphlets – Conservative, Communist, Catholic, Trotskyist, Pacifist, Anarchist or what-have-you – it seems to me that almost all of them have the same mental atmosphere, though the points of emphasis vary. Nobody is searching for the truth, everybody is putting forward a "case" with complete disregard for fairness or accuracy, and the most plainly obvious facts can be ignored by those who don't want to see them. The same propaganda tricks are to be found almost everywhere. It would take many pages of this paper merely to classify them, but here I draw attention to one very widespread controversial habit – disregard of an opponent's motives. The key-word here is "objectively."

We are told that it is only people's objective actions that matter, and their subjective feelings are of no importance. Thus, pacifists, by obstructing the war effort, are "objectively" aiding the Nazis: and therefore the fact that they may be personally hostile to Fascism is irrelevant. I have been guilty of saying this myself more than once. The same argument is applied to Trotskyists. Trotskyists are often credited, at any rate by Communists, with being active and conscious agents of Hitler; but when you point out the many and obvious reasons why this is unlikely to be true, the "objectively" line of talk is brought forward again. To criticise the Soviet Union helps Hitler: therefore "Trotskyism is Fascism." And when this has been established, the accusation of conscious treachery is usually repeated.

This is not only dishonest; it also carries a severe penalty with it. If you disregard people's motives, it becomes much harder to foresee their actions. For there are occasions when even the most misguided person can see the results of what he is doing. Here is a crude but quite possible illustration. A pacifist is working in some job which gives him access to important military information, and is approached by a German secret agent. In those circumstances his subjective feelings *do* make a difference. If he is subjectively pro-Nazi he will sell his country, and if he isn't, he won't. And situations essentially similar though less dramatic are constantly arising.

In my opinion a few pacifists are inwardly pro-Nazi, and extremist Left-wing parties will inevitably contain Fascist spies. The important thing is to discover *which* individuals are honest and which are not, and the usual blanket accusation merely makes this more difficult. The atmosphere of hatred in which controversy is conducted blinds people to considerations of this kind. To admit that an opponent might be both honest and intelligent is felt to be intolerable. It is more immediately satisfying to shout that he is a fool or a scoundrel, or both, than to find out what he is really like. It is this habit of mind, among other things, that has made political prediction in our time so remarkably unsuccessful.

The following leaflet (printed) was passed to an acquaintance of mine in a pub:

"LONG LIVE THE IRISH!

"The first American soldier to kill a Jap was Mike Murphy.

"The first American pilot to sink a Jap battleship was Colin Kelly.

"The first American family to lose five sons in one action and have a naval vessel named after them were the Sullivans.

"The first American to shoot a Jap plane was Dutch O'Hara.

"The first coastguardsman to spot a German spy was John Conlan.

"The first American soldier to be decorated by the President was Pat Powers.

"The first American admiral to be killed leading his ship into battle was Dan Callahan.

"The first American son-of-a-bitch to get four new tyres from the Ration Board was Abie Goldstein."

The origin of this thing might just possibly be Irish, but it is much likelier to be American. There is nothing to indicate where it was printed, but it probably comes from the printing-shop of some American organisation in this country. If any further manifestos of the same kind turn up, I shall be interested to hear of them.

This number of *Tribune* includes a long letter from Mr. Martin Walter, Controller of the British Institute of Fiction-writing Science, Ltd., in which he complains that I have traduced him. He says (a) that he did not claim to have reduced fiction-writing to an exact science, (b) that numbers of successful writers *have* been produced by his teaching methods, and (c) he asks whether *Tribune* accepts advertisements that it believes to be fraudulent.

With regard to (a). "It is claimed by this Institute that these problems (of fiction-writing) have been solved by Martin Walter, who, convinced of the truth of the hypothesis that *every art is a science at heart*, analysed over 5,000 stories and eventually evolved the Plot Formula according to which all his own stories and those of his students throughout the world are constructed." "I had established that the nature of the 'plot' is strictly scientific." Statements of this type are scattered throughout Mr. Walter's booklets and advertisements. If this is not a claim to have reduced fiction-writing to an exact science, what the devil is it?

With regard to (b). Who are these successful writers whom Mr. Walter has launched upon the world? Let us hear their names, and the names of their published works, and then we shall know where we are.

With regard to (c). A periodical ought not to accept advertisements which have the appearance of being fraudulent, but it cannot sift everything beforehand. What is to be done, for instance, about publishers' advertisements, in which it is invariably claimed that every single book named is of the highest possible value? What is most important in this connection is that a periodical should not let its editorial columns be influenced by its advertisements. *Tribune* has been very careful not to do that – it has not done it in the case of Mr. Walter himself, for instance.

It may interest Mr. Walter to know that I should never have referred to him, if he had not accompanied the advertisement he inserted some time ago with some free copies of his booklets (including the Plot Formula), and the suggestion that I might like to mention them in my column. It was this that drew my attention to him. Now I have given him his mention, and he does not seem to like it.

Answer to last week's problem. The three errors are:

(a) The "who" should be "whom."

(b) Timon was buried below the high-tide mark. The sea would cover him twice a day, not once, as there are always two high tides within the twenty-four hours.

(c) It wouldn't cover him at all, as there is no perceptible tide in the Mediterranean.

Oysters and Brown Stout
Tribune, 22 December 1944

G. K. Chesterton said once that every novelist writes one book whose title seems to be a summing-up of his attitude to life. He instanced, for Dickens, *Great Expectations*, and for Scott, *Tales of a Grandfather.*

What title would one choose as especially representative of Thackeray? The obvious one is *Vanity Fair*, but I believe that if one looked more closely one would choose either *Christmas Books*, *Burlesques*, or *A Book of Snobs* – at any rate, one would choose the title of one of the collections of scraps which Thackeray had previously contributed to *Punch* and other magazines. Not only was he by nature a burlesque writer, but he was primarily a journalist, a writer of fragments, and his most characteristic work is not fully separable from the illustrations. Some of the best of these are by Cruikshank, but Thackeray was also a brilliant comic draughtsman himself, and in some of his very short sketches the picture and the letterpress belong organically together. All that is best in his full-length novels seems to have grown out of his contributions to *Punch*, and even *Vanity Fair* has a fragmentary quality that makes it possible to begin reading in it at almost any place, without looking back to see what has happened earlier.

At this date some of his major works – for instance, *Esmond* or *The Virginians* – are barely readable, and only once, in a rather short book, *A Shabby Genteel Story*, did he write what we should now regard as a serious novel. Thackeray's two main themes are snobbishness and extravagance, but he is at his best when he handles them in the comic vein, because – unlike Dickens, for instance – he has very little social insight and not even a very clear moral code. *Vanity Fair*, it is true, is a valuable social document as well as being an extremely readable and amusing book. It records, with remarkable fidelity so far as physical detail goes, the ghastly social competition of the early nineteenth century, when an aristocracy which could no longer pay its way was still the arbiter of fashion and of behaviour. In *Vanity Fair*, and indeed throughout Thackeray's writings, it is almost exceptional to find anyone living inside his income.

To live in a house which is too big for you, to engage servants whom you cannot pay, to ruin yourself by giving pretentious dinner parties with hired footmen, to bilk your tradesmen, to overdraw your banking account, to live permanently in the clutches of moneylenders – this is almost the norm of human behaviour. It is taken for granted that anyone who is not halfway to being a saint will ape the aristocracy if possible.

The desire for expensive clothes, gilded carriages and hordes of liveried servants is assumed to be a natural instinct, like the desire for food and drink. And the people Thackeray is best able to describe are those who are living the fashionable life upon no income whatever – people like Becky Sharp and Rawdon Crawley in *Vanity Fair*, or the innumerable seedy adventurers, Major Loder, Captain Rook, Captain Costigan, Mr. Deuceace, whose life is an endless to-and-fro between the card-table and the sponging-house.

So far as it goes, Thackeray's picture of society is probably true. The types he depicts, the mortgage-ridden aristocrats, the brandy-drinking army officers, the elderly bucks with their stays and their dyed whiskers, the matchmaking mothers, the vulgar City magnates, did exist. But he is observing chiefly externals. In spite of endless musings on the French Revolution, a subject that fascinated him, he does not see that the structure of society is altering: he sees the nation-wide phenomenon of snobbery and extravagance, without seeing its deeper causes. Moreover, unlike Dickens, he does not see that the social struggle is three-sided: his sympathies hardly extend to the working class, whom he is conscious of chiefly as servants. Nor is he ever certain where he himself stands. He cannot make up his mind whether the raffish upper class or the money-grubbing middle class is more objectionable. Not having any definite social, political or, probably, religious convictions, he can hardly imagine any virtues except simplicity, courage and, in the case of women, "purity." (Thackeray's "good" women, incidentally, are completely intolerable.) The implied moral of both *Vanity Fair* and *Pendennis* is the rather empty one: "Don't be selfish, don't be worldly, don't live outside your income." And *A Shabby Genteel Story* says the same thing in a more delicate way.

But Thackeray's narrow intellectual range is actually an advantage to him when he abandons the attempt to portray real human beings. A thing that is very striking is the vitality of his *minor* writings, even of things that he himself must have thought of as purely ephemeral. If you dip almost anywhere in his collected works – even in his book reviews, for instance – you come upon the characteristic flavour. Partly it is the atmosphere of surfeit which belongs to the early nineteenth century, an atmosphere compounded of oysters, brown stout, brandy and water, turtle soup, roast sirloin, haunch of venison, Madeira and cigar smoke, which Thackeray is well able to convey because he has a good grip on physical detail and is extremely interested in food.

He writes about food perhaps more often even than Dickens, and more accurately. His account of his dinners in Paris – not expensive dinners, either – in *Memorials of Gormandising* is fascinating reading. *The Ballad of the Bouillabaisse* is one of the best poems of that kind in English. But the characteristic flavour of Thackeray is the flavour of burlesque, of a world where no one is good and nothing is serious. It pervades all the best passages in his novels, and it reaches its perfection in short sketches and stories like *Dr. Birch and His Young Friends*, *The Rose and the Ring*, *The Fatal Boots* and *A Little Dinner at Timmins's*.

The Rose and the Ring is a sort of charade, similar in spirit to the *Ingoldsby Legends*; *A Little Dinner at Timmins's* is a relatively naturalistic story, and *The Fatal Boots* is about midway between the two. But in all these and similar pieces Thackeray has got away from the difficulty that besets most novelists and has never been solved by any characteristically English novelist – the difficulty of combining characters who are meant to be real and exist "in the round" with mere figures of fun.

English writers from Chaucer onwards have found it very difficult to resist burlesque, but as soon as burlesque enters the reality of the story suffers. Fielding, Dickens, Trollope, Wells, even Joyce, have all stumbled over this problem. Thackeray, in the best of his short pieces, solves it by making *all* his characters into caricatures. There is no question of the hero of *The Fatal Boots* existing "in the round." He is as flat as an ikon. In *A Little Dinner at Timmins's* – one of the best comic short stories ever written, though it is seldom reprinted – Thackeray is really doing the same thing as he did in *Vanity Fair*, but without the complicating factor of having to simulate real life and introduce disinterested motives. It is a simple little story, exquisitely told and rising gradually to a sort of crescendo which stops at exactly the right moment. A lawyer who has received an unusually large fee decides to celebrate it by giving a dinner party. He is at once led into much greater expense than he can afford, and there follows a series of disasters which leave him heavily in debt, with his friends alienated and his mother-in-law permanently installed in his home. From start to finish no one has had anything from the dinner party except misery. And when, at the end, Thackeray remarks, "Why, in fact, did the Timminses give that party at all?" one feels that the folly of social ambition has been more conclusively demonstrated than it is by *Vanity Fair*. This is the kind of thing that Thackeray could do perfectly, and it is the recurrence of farcical incidents like this, rather than their central story, that makes the longer novels worth reading.

Review of *An Interlude in Spain* by Charles d'Ydewalle, translated by Eric Sutton
The Observer, 24 December 1944

Unwilling witnesses are generally accounted the most reliable, and Mr. Charles d'Ydewalle is at least partly an unwilling witness against Franco's Spain. He is a Belgian journalist (evidently a devout Catholic), and during the Spanish civil war he was a warm partisan of General Franco, in whose territory he appears to have spent some months. When his own country was subjugated by the Germans and he set out on the round-about journey to England, he was quite confident that Nationalist Spain, whose "crusade" he had supported as best he could, would offer no obstacle. It was therefore with some surprise that he found himself arrested and flung into jail almost as soon as he had set foot on Spanish soil.

This was towards the end of 1941. He was not released until eight months later, and at no time did he discover what offence, if any, he was charged with. Presumably he had been arrested because his flight to England indicated Allied sympathies. He was incarcerated first of all in the Model Prison in Barcelona, which had been built to hold 700 prisoners and at this time was holding 8,000. Later he was placed in a concentration camp among refugees of many different nationalities. Here the conditions were comparatively sympathetic; it was possible to buy small luxuries; one could choose one's hut mates, and there was international rivalry in the matter of digging tunnels under the barbed wire. It was the Model Prison that opened or partially opened Mr. d'Ydewalle's eyes to the nature of the regime.

At the end of 1941, nearly three years after the ending of the civil war, people were still being shot, in this prison alone, at the rate of five or six a week. In addition there was torture, presumably for the purpose of extracting confessions, and on occasion the torturer "went too far." Political prisoners and ordinary criminals were more or less mixed up together, but the majority of the prisoners were left-overs from the civil war, usually serving sentences of thirty years. In many cases, Mr. d'Ydewalle noted, this would take them to the ripe age of ninety-five or so. The shootings were carried out with the maximum of cruelty. No one knew, until the actual morning of execution, whether he was to be shot or not.

Early every morning there would be a trampling of boots and a clanking of bayonets along the corridor, and suddenly this door or that would be thrown open and a name called out. Later in the day the dead man's mattress would be seen lying outside the cell door. Sometimes a man was reprieved and then shot a day or two later for some different offence. But there were no shootings on Sundays or holidays. The display of religiosity with which the life of the prison was conducted stuck in Mr. d'Ydewalle's gizzard almost more than the cruelty.

Mr. d'Ydewalle spent only a day or two in Spain as a free man, but in the concentration camp he noted that the wretched Spanish soldiers who guarded them were glad to beg scraps of food from the better-off internees. He does not record things like this with any satisfaction, and is reluctant to draw their full moral. To the end, indeed, he seems to have remained convinced that in the civil war Franco was in the right, and that it was only afterwards that things went wrong. In prison he sometimes comforted himself with the thought that the wretched victims round about him had been doing the same thing to Nationalist sympathisers only a few years before. He reiterates his belief in "red atrocities," and shows more than a trace of anti-Semitism.

The main impression that the book conveys is one of bewilderment. Why had he been locked up? How could the "glorious crusade" have led to this kind of thing? He even expresses astonishment that a regime calling itself Catholic could lend its support to Hitler and Mussolini: which does seem to be carrying simplicity rather far, since General Franco can hardly be accused of having concealed his political affiliations.

Naturally it is not easy for someone who in good faith supported the Nationalist cause at the time of the civil war to admit that the horrors of the Model Prison were implicit in the Nationalist regime from the beginning. But Mr. d'Ydewalle also had the handicap of coming from a comparatively orderly and well-governed country and therefore not having any preliminary understanding of totalitarianism.

The essential fact about a totalitarian regime is that it has no laws. People are not punished for specific offences, but because they are considered to be politically or intellectually undesirable. What they have done or not done is irrelevant. It took Mr. d'Ydewalle some time to get used to this idea, and, as he observed, there were other Western European prisoners who had difficulty in grasping it as well. When he had been several months in jail some British soldiers, escaped from France, came to join him. He told them about the shootings. At the beginning they flatly disbelieved him, and only gradually, as mattress after mattress appeared outside this cell or that, came to realise that what he said was true: whereupon they commented, not inaptly, "Well, give me England every time."

This book is a useful footnote to history. The author's simplicity of outlook is an advantage to him as a narrator. But, if one may make a guess, the next variant of General Franco who appears will not have Mr. d'Ydewalle's support.

As I Please 52
Tribune, 29 December 1944

I am indebted to an article by Mr. Dwight Macdonald in the September number of *Politics*, the New York monthly, for some extracts from a book entitled *Kill – or Get Killed: a Manual of Hand-to-Hand Fighting* by Major Rex Applegate.

This book, a semi-official American publication, not only gives extensive information about knifing, strangling, and the various horrors that come under the heading of "unarmed combat," but describes the battle schools in which soldiers are trained for house-to-house fighting. Here are some sample directions:

" . . . Before entering the tunnel, the coach exposes dummy A and the student uses the knife on it. While the student is proceeding from target No. 1 to target No.4, the 'Gestapo Torture Scene' or the 'Italian Cursing' sequence is played over the loudspeaker . . . Target No. 9 is in darkness, and as the student enters this compartment the 'Jap Rape' sequence is used . . . While the coach is reloading the student's pistol, the 'Get that American son-of-a-bitch' sequence is used. As the coach and student pass through the curtain into the next compartment, they are confronted by a dummy which has a knife stuck in its back, and represents a dead body. This dummy is illuminated by a green light and is not to be fired at by the student, although practically all of them do."

Mr. Macdonald comments: "There is one rather interesting problem in operating the course. Although the writer never states so directly, it would seem there is danger that the student's inhibitions will be broken down so thoroughly that he will shoot or stab the coach who accompanies him . . . The coach is advised to keep himself in a position to grab the student's gun arm 'at any instant'; after the three dummies along the course have been stabbed, 'the knife is taken away from the student to prevent accident'; and finally: 'There is no place on the course where total darkness prevails while instructor is near student.'"

I believe the similar battle courses in the British army have now been discontinued or toned down, but it is worth remembering that *something like* this is inevitable if one wants military efficiency. No ideology, no consciousness of having "something to fight for," is fully a substitute for it. This deliberate brutalising of millions of human beings is part of the price of society in its present form. The Japanese, incidentally, have been experts at this kind of thing for hundreds of years. In the old days the sons of aristocrats used to be taken at a very early age to witness executions, and if any boy showed the slightest sign of nausea he was promptly made to swallow large quantities of rice stained the colour of blood.

The English common people are not great lovers of military glory, and I have pointed out elsewhere that when a battle poem wins really wide popularity, it usually deals with a disaster and not a victory. But the other day, when I repeated this in some connection, there came into my head the once popular song – it might be popular again if one of the gramophone companies would bother to record it – "Admiral Benbow." This rather jingoistic ballad seems to contradict my theory, but I believe it may have owed some of its popularity to the fact that it had a class war angle which was understood at the time.

Admiral Benbow, when going into action against the French, was suddenly deserted by his subordinate captains and left to fight against heavy odds. As the ballad puts it:

> "Said Kirby unto Wade, 'We will run, we will run,'
> Said Kirby unto Wade, 'We will run;
> For I value no disgrace
> Nor the losing of my place,
> But the enemy I won't face,
> Nor his guns, nor his guns.'"

So Benbow was left to fight single-handed and, though victorious, he himself was killed. There is a gory but possibly authentic description of his death:

> "Brave Benbow lost his legs, by chain shot,
>   by chain shot,
> Brave Benbow lost his legs, by chain shot:
> Brave Benbow lost his legs
> And all on his stumps he begs,
> 'Fight on, my English lads,
> 'Tis our lot, 'tis our lot.'
>
> The surgeon dressed his wounds, Benbow cries,
>   Benbow cries,
> The surgeon dressed his wounds, Benbow cries;
> 'Let a cradle now in haste
> On the quarter-deck be placed,

That the enemy I may face
Till I die, till I die.'"

The point is that Benbow was an ordinary seaman who had risen from the ranks. He had started off as a cabin boy. And his captains are supposed to have fled from the action because they did not want to see so plebeian a commander win a victory. I wonder whether it was this tradition that made Benbow into a popular hero and caused his name to be commemorated not only in the ballad but on the signs of innumerable public-houses?

I believe no recording of this song exists, but – as I discovered when I was broadcasting and wanted to use similar pieces as five-minute fill-ups – it is only one of a long list of old popular songs and folk songs which have not been recorded. Until recently, at any rate, I believe there was not even a record of "Tom Bowling" or of "Greensleeves," i.e., the words as well as the music. Others that I failed to get hold of were "A cottage well thatched with Straw," "Green grow the rushes, O," "Blow away the morning dew," and "Come lasses and lads." Other well-known songs are recorded in mutilated versions, and usually sung by professional singers with such a stale perfunctoriness that you seem to smell the whisky and cigarette smoke coming off the record. The collection of recorded carols is also very poor. You can't, I believe, get hold of "Minstrels and Maids," "Like silver lamps in a distant shrine," or "Dives and Lazarus," or other old favourites. On the other hand, if you want a record of "Roll out the barrel," "Boomps-a-daisy," etc., you would find quite a number of different renderings to choose from.

A correspondent in *Tribune* of December 15 expressed his "horror and disgust" at hearing that Indian troops had been used against the Greeks, and compared this to the action of Franco in using Moorish troops against the Spanish Republic.

It seems to me important that this ancient red herring should not be dragged across the trail. To begin with, the Indian troops are not strictly comparable to Franco's Moors. The reactionary Moorish chieftains, bearing rather the same relationship to Franco as the Indian Princes do to the British Conservative

Party, sent their men to Spain with the conscious aim of crushing democracy. The Indian troops are mercenaries, serving the British from family tradition or for the sake of a job, though latterly a proportion of them have probably begun to think of themselves as an *Indian* army, nucleus of the armed forces of a future independent India. It is not likely that their presence in Athens had any political significance. Probably it was merely that they happened to be the nearest troops available.

But in addition, it is of the highest importance that Socialists should have no truck with colour prejudice. On a number of occasions – the Ruhr occupation of 1923 and the Spanish civil war, for instance – the cry "using coloured troops" has been raised, as though it were somehow worse to be shot up by Indians or Negroes than by Europeans. Our crime in Greece is to have interfered in Greek internal affairs at all: the colour of the troops who carry out the orders is irrelevant. In the case of the Ruhr occupation, it was perhaps justifiable to protest against the use of Senegalese troops, because the Germans probably felt this as an added humiliation, and the French may have used black troops for that very reason. But such feelings are not universal in Europe, and I doubt whether there is anywhere any prejudice against Indian troops, who are conspicuously well-behaved.

Our correspondent might have made the point that in an affair of this kind it is particularly mean to make use of politically ignorant colonial troops who don't understand in what a dirty job they are being mixed up. But at least don't let us insult the Indians by suggesting that their presence in Athens is somehow more offensive than that of the British.

1945

Review of *Der Führer* by Conrad Heiden

Manchester Evening News, 4 January 1945

About eight years ago, from the same publishing house as has just produced "Der Führer," there appeared another fat and imposing book about Hitler, entitled, significantly, "Hitler, the Pawn." Its thesis, then a widely accepted one, was that Hitler was a nonentity, a mere puppet of German big business.

Later events have made that incredible, and Mr. Heiden's long, detailed but very readable book is an attempt to disentangle the extremely complex causes – causes which are intellectual and religious as well as economic and political – that have allowed a semi-lunatic to gain control of a great nation and cause the death of some tens of millions of human beings.

Mr. Heiden ends his story with the June purge of 1934 – which, as he points out, is not altogether an arbitrary stopping-point, because with that atrocious deed there began a new historical phase which has not yet ended.

The story starts some time before Hitler's birth. It starts, to be precise, in 1864, with an illegal and now forgotten pamphlet attacking Napoleon III.

Somewhat later the Czarist secret police were to get hold of this pamphlet and concoct out of it that celebrated forgery, "The Protocols of the Elders of Zion." Their object was to frighten the Czar with tales of a Jewish conspiracy and thus provoke him into violent measures against the Russian Revolutionaries.

Rosenberg, the racial theorist, a Baltic Russian, and at the time of the revolution a student in Moscow, brought a copy of the protocols with him when he fled to Germany: and it was from this source that Hitler derived the anti-Semitism that was to be both a cherished delusion and a cunning political device.

Mr. Heiden follows up Hitler's early history with great minuteness, plugging the gaps in "Mein Kampf" with the statements of a painter named Hanisch, who shared Hitler's poverty for several years in Vienna.

It appears from Mr. Heiden's researches that the autobiographical part of "Mein Kampf" is reasonably truthful. Even on his own showing, Hitler was a complete failure, even a ne'er-do-well, until the outbreak of war in 1914. His main characteristics were laziness, an inability to make friends, a hatred of the society which had failed to give him a decent livelihood, and a vague leaning towards painting.

(Many dictators, it is worth noticing, are failed artists – Henry VIII and Frederick the Great both wrote bad verse, and Napoleon and Mussolini wrote plays which nobody would produce.)

The war was Hitler's great opportunity. He loved every moment of it, and it appears to be true, though it has often been denied, that he served with distinction and was decorated for bravery. He says himself that he wept when the war stopped, and from then onwards to restore the atmosphere of war was his main aim.

In the chaotic Germany of 1918 it was natural for a man of Hitler's temperament to plunge into conspiratorial politics. He joined the German Workers' party – later to become the National Socialist party – which at that date consisted of six members and had as its entire equipment a single briefcase and a cigar-box which was used as a cash-box.

The disbanded Reichswehr officers, who were already planning to rebuild the German Army in defiance of the Versailles Treaty, were on the look-out for a political party which could act as a cover for their aims, and the German Workers' party, with its sham-Socialist programme, seemed to them to have possibilities.

Hitler, therefore, had a measure of support almost from the start, but it was not until some time later, when he was already a political force to be counted with, that the industrialists began to finance him in a big way.

As a politician he had three great assets. One was his complete lack of pity, affection, or human ties of any kind. Another was his bottomless belief in himself and contempt for everybody else. And the third was his powerful and impressive voice, which within a few minutes could make any audience forget his Charlie Chaplin-like appearance.

Within a few years he had talked a formidable movement into existence, pouring out on platform after platform a message – anti-Jewish, anti-Capitalist, anti-Bolshevik, and anti-French – which appealed equally to the unemployed workers, the ruined middle-class, and the officers who were pining for another war.

However, to win supreme power was another matter, and for years the history of the National Socialist party was one of ups and downs. Broadly speaking, when things went badly, Hitler's star rose; when they went well, it sank. In the prosperous period of the middle twenties, the period of the Dawes Plan, the economic recovery in Britain and the U.S.A. and the N.E.P. in Russia the National Socialist party seemed likely to disappear.

Then came the great depression, and Hitler rose again like a rocket. We shall never know whether even at that late date he might have been defeated, but at any rate it is a fact that his only real enemies inside Germany, the Communists and the Social Democrats, persisted in fighting one another instead of combining against the common enemy.

Having made use of their dissensions, Hitler destroyed both of them, and finally made quite sure of his position by massacring the Left Wing of his own party. The rest of the story is only too well known.

This book gives useful background information about others besides Hitler – in particular, Hess, Goering, Roehm, and Houston Chamberlain the strange renegade Englishman who was one of the founders of the Pan-German Movement. It is a valuable book because it neither underrates Hitler nor overrates him. It does not, that is to say, explain him away in narrow economic terms, nor does it pretend that the major problems of the world will be solved by his disappearance. To quote Mr. Heiden's own words: –

"Hitler was able to enslave his own people because he was able to give them something that even the traditional religions could no longer provide – the belief in a meaning to existence beyond the narrowest self-interest. The real degradation began when people realised that they were in league with the devil, but felt that even the devil was preferable to the emptiness of an existence which lacked a larger significance.

"The problem to-day is to give that larger significance and dignity to a life that has been dwarfed by the world of material things. Until that problem is solved, the annihilation of Nazism will be no more than the removal of one symptom of the world's unrest."

As I Please 53
Tribune, 5 January 1945

I have just been looking through a bound volume of the *Quarterly Review* for the year 1810, which was, I think, the second year of the *Quarterly Review*'s existence.

1810 was not quite the blackest period, from the British point of view, of the Napoleonic war, but it was nearly the blackest. It perhaps corresponded to 1941 in the present war. Britain was completely isolated, its commerce barred from every European port by the Berlin decrees. Italy, Spain, Prussia, Denmark, Switzerland and the Low Countries had all been subjugated. Austria was in alliance with France. Russia was also in an uneasy agreement with France, but it was known that Napoleon intended to invade Russia shortly. The United States, though not yet in the war, was openly hostile to Britain. There was no visible cause for hope, except the revolt in Spain, which had once again given Britain a foothold on the Continent and opened the South American countries to British trade. It is therefore interesting to observe the tone of voice in which the *Quarterly Review* – a Conservative paper which emphatically supported the war – speaks about France and about Napoleon at this desperate moment.

Here is the *Quarterly* on the alleged war-making propensities of the French people. It is reviewing a pamphlet by a Mr. Walsh, an American who had just returned from France.

"We doubt the continued action of those military propensities which Mr. Walsh ascribes to the French people. Without at all questioning the lively picture which he has drawn of the exultation excited amongst the squalid and famished inhabitants of Paris at the intelligence of every fresh triumph of their armies, we may venture to observe that such exultation

808

is, everywhere, the usual concomitant of such events; that the gratification of national vanity is something, and that the festivities which victory brings with it may afford a pleasing dissipation to wretches who are perfectly free from any feelings of ambition. Our belief indeed is, that those feelings are, at present, nearly confined to the breast of the great conqueror; and that amongst his subjects, we may almost say among his officers and armies, the universal wish is for PEACE."

Compare this with the utterances of Lord Vansittart, or, indeed, of the greater part of the Press. The same article contains several tributes to the military genius of Napoleon. But the thing I find most impressive is that this year's issue of the *Quarterly* contains numerous reviews of recently-published French books – and they are careful, serious reviews, not different in tone from the rest of its articles. There is, for instance, an article of about 9,000 words on the publication of the French scientific body known as the Société d'Arcueil. The French scientists, Gay-Lussac, Laplace and the rest of them, are treated with the utmost respect, and given their "Monsieur" every time. From reading this article it would be impossible to discover that there was a war on.

Can you imagine current German books being reviewed in the British Press during the present war? No, I don't think you can. I do not, indeed, remember hearing the name of a single book published in Germany throughout the war. And if a contemporary German book did get mentioned in the Press, it would almost certainly be misrepresented in some way. Looking through the reviews of French books in the *Quarterly*, I note that only when they are on directly political subjects does any propaganda creep in, and even then it is extremely mild by our standards. As for art, literature and science, their international character is taken for granted. And yet, I suppose, Britain was fighting for existence in the Napoleonic war just as surely as in this one, and relative to the populations involved the war was not much less bloody or exhausting. . . .

When Burma comes into the centre of the news again, somebody could do a useful job by evolving a sensible method of spelling Burmese place names. What is the average newspaper-reader to make of names like Taungdwingyi, Myaungmya and Nyaungbinzeik?

When the Japs invaded Burma at the beginning of 1942, efforts were made to get correct pronunciation of Burmese names on the radio. The B.B.C. announcers took no notice and went merrily ahead, mispronouncing every name that could be mispronounced. Since then the newspapers have made matters a little worse by supplying their own pronunciations, which are generally wrong.

At present, Burmese names are spelt by transliterating the Burmese characters as nearly as possible. This is a very bad system unless one knows the Burmese alphabet. How is the average person to know that in a Burmese name e spells ay, ai spells eye, gy spells j, ky spells ch, and so on? It should be quite easy to evolve a better system, and the British public, which can now make quite a good stab at pronouncing Dniepropetrovsk, could also learn to pronounce Kyaukse and Kungyangon if it were taught how.

I have been re-reading with some interest *The Fairchild Family*, which was written in 1813 and was for fifty years or more a standard book for children. Unfortunately I only possess the first volume, but even that, in its unexpurgated state – for various pretty-pretty versions, with all the real meat cut out, have been issued in recent years – is enough of a curiosity.

The tone of the book is sufficiently indicated by the sentence: "Papa," said Lucy (Lucy was aged nine, by the way), "may we say some verses about mankind having bad hearts?" And, of course, Papa is only too willing, and out come the verses, all correctly memorised. Or here is Mrs. Fairchild, telling the children how when she herself was a child she disobeyed orders by picking cherries in company with the servant girl:

"Nanny was given up to her mother to be flogged; and I was shut up in the dark room, where I was to be kept several days upon bread and water. At the end of three days my aunts sent for me, and talked to me for a long time.

"'You broke the Fourth Commandment,' said my Aunt Penelope, 'which is, *Remember the Sabbath day to keep it holy*: and you broke the Fifth, which is, *Honour your parents.*... You broke the Eighth too, which is, *Thou shalt not steal*. Besides,' said my Aunt Grace, 'the shame and disgrace of climbing trees in such low company, after all the care and pains we have taken with you, and the delicate manner in which we have reared you.'"

The whole book is in this vein, with a long prayer at the end of every chapter, and innumerable hymns and verses from the Bible interspersed through the text. But its chief feature is the fearful visitations from Heaven which fall upon the children whenever they misbehave themselves. If they swing in the swing without leave, they fall out and break several teeth; if they forget to say their prayers they fall into the trough of pig-swill; the theft of a few damsons is punished by an attack of pneumonia and a narrow escape from death. On one occasion Mr. Fairchild catches his children quarrelling. After the usual flogging, he takes them for a long walk to see the rotting body of a murderer hanging on a gibbet – the result, as he points out, of a quarrel between two brothers.

A curious and interesting feature of the book is that the Fairchild children, reared upon these stern principles, seem to be rather exceptionally untrustworthy. As soon as their parents' backs are turned they invariably misbehave them-selves, which suggests that flogging and bread and water are not a very satisfactory treatment after all. It is worth recording, by the way, that the author, Mrs. Sherwood, brought up several children, and at any rate they did not actually die under her ministrations.

As I Please 54
Tribune, 12 January 1945

Some time back a correspondent wrote to ask whether I had seen the exhibition of waxworks, showing German atrocities, which has been on show in London for a year or more. It is advertised outside with such captions as: HORRORS OF THE CONCENTRATION CAMP. COME INSIDE AND SEE REAL NAZI TORTURES. FLOGGING, CRUCIFIXION, GAS CHAMBERS, ETC. CHILDREN'S AMUSEMENT SECTION NO EXTRA CHARGE.

I did go and see this exhibition a long time ago, and I would like to warn prospective visitors that it is most disappointing. To begin with many of the figures are not life-size, and I suspect that some of them are not even real waxworks, but merely dressmakers' dummies with new heads attached. And secondly, the tortures are not nearly so fearful as you are led to expect by the posters outside. The whole exhibition is grubby, unlifelike and depressing. But the exhibitors are, I suppose, doing their best, and the captions are interesting in the complete frankness of their appeal to sadism and masochism. Before the war, if you were a devotee of all-in wrestling, or wrote letters to your M.P. to protest against the abolition of flogging, or haunted second-hand bookshops in search of such books as *The Pleasures of the Torture Chamber*, you laid yourself open to very unpleasant suspicions. Moreover, you were probably aware of your own motives and somewhat ashamed of them. Now, however, you can wallow in the most disgusting descriptions of torture and massacre, not only without any sensation of guilt, but with the feeling that you are performing a praiseworthy political action.

I am not suggesting that the stories about Nazi atrocities are untrue. To a great extent I think they are true. These horrors certainly happened in German concentration camps before the war, and there is no reason why they should have stopped since. But they are played up largely because they give the newspapers a pretext for pornography. This morning's papers are splashing the official British Army Report on Nazi atrocities. They are careful to inform you that naked women were flogged, some-times spotlighting this detail by means of a headline. The journalists responsible know very well what they are doing. They know that innumerable people get a sadistic kick out of thinking about torture, especially the torture of women, and they are cashing in on this widespread neurosis. No qualms need be felt, because these deeds are committed by the enemy, and the enjoyment that one gets out of them can be disguised as disapproval. And one can get a very similar kick out of barbar-ous actions committed by one's own side so long as they are thought of as the just punishment of evil-doers.

We have not actually got to the point of Roman gladiatorial shows yet, but we could do so if the necessary pretext were supplied. If, for instance, it were announced that the leading war criminals were to be eaten by lions or trampled to death by elephants in the Wembley Stadium, I fancy that the spectacle would be quite well attended.

I invite attention to an article entitled "The Truth about Mihailovich?" (the author of it also writes for *Tribune*, by the way) in the current *World Review*. It deals with the campaign in the British Press and the B.B.C. to brand Mihailovich as a German agent.

Jugoslav politics are very complicated and I make no pretence of being an expert on them. For all I know it was entirely right on the part of Britain as well as the U.S.S.R. to drop Mihailovich and support Tito. But what interests me is the readiness, once this decision had been taken, of reputable British newspapers to connive at what amounted to forgery in order to discredit the man whom they had been backing a few months earlier. There is no doubt that this happened. The author of the article gives details of one out of a number of instances in which material facts were suppressed in the most impudent way. Presented with very strong evidence to show that Mihailovich was *not* a German agent, the majority of our newspapers simply refused to print it, while repeating the charges of treachery just as before.

Very similar things happened during the Spanish civil war. Then, Anarchists, Trotskyists and others who opposed Franco, but also opposed the official political line of the Spanish Republican Government, were accused of being traitors in Fascist pay. Various British newspapers sympathetic to the Republic took up this charge and repeated it with picturesque exaggerations of their own, at the same time refusing to print any kind of reply, even in letter form. They had the excuse that the Spanish Republic was fighting for its life and that to discuss its internecine troubles too frankly was to give a handle to the pro-Fascist Press in this country. Still, they did confuse the issues and make entirely unfounded accusations against innocent people. And, then as now, if you protested you got the answer, first, that the charges were true, and secondly, that perhaps they weren't true but that these people were politically undesirable and deserved what they got.

I recognise the force of this argument. In fighting against Fascism you cannot always be bound by the Marquess of Queensberry rules, and sometimes a lie is almost unavoidable. There are always unscrupulous opponents on the look-out for damaging admissions, and on some questions the truth is so complex that a plain statement of the facts simply misleads the general public. Still, I think it could be shown from the history of the past twenty years that totalitarian methods of controversy – falsification of history, personal libel, refusal of a fair hearing to opponents, and so forth – have on the whole worked against the interests of the Left.

A lie is a boomerang, and sometimes it comes back surprisingly soon. During the Spanish civil war one Left-wing paper employed a certain journalist to "write up" the charges against the Spanish Trotskyists, which he did with considerable unscrupulousness. It was impossible to answer him, at any rate in the columns of this particular paper. Less than three years later this man was being hired by another paper to do the worst kind of "anti-Red" propaganda during the Russian war against Finland. And I suppose that the anti-Russian lies which he told in 1940 carried all the more weight because the pro-Russian lies which he was telling in 1937 had not been exposed.

In the same number of *World Review* I note that Mr. Edward Hulton remarks rather disapprovingly that "the small city of Athens possesses far more daily newspapers than London." All I can say is, good luck to Athens! It is only when there are large numbers of newspapers, expressing all tendencies, that there is some chance of getting at the truth. Counting evenings, London has only twelve daily papers, and they cover the whole of the South of England and penetrate as far north as Glasgow. When they all decide to tell the same lie, there is no minority Press to act as a check. In pre-war France the Press was largely venal and scurrilous, but you could dig more news out of it than out of the British Press, because every political faction had its paper and every viewpoint got a hearing. I shall be surprised if Athens keeps its multiplicity of newspapers under the kind of government that we apparently intend to impose.

Review of *The Unquiet Grave: A World Cycle* by Palinurus

The Observer, 14 January 1945

"Palinurus" is the easily penetrable pseudonym of a well-known literary critic, but even without knowing his identity one could infer that the writer of this book is about 40, is inclined to stoutness, has lived much in Continental Europe, and has never done any real work. His book is a kind of diary, or rather journal, interspersed with quotations from Pascal, Lao-Tze, La Rochefoucauld, and others, and having as its dominant note a refined, rather pessimistic, hedonism. In his previous incarnations, the author says, he was "a melon, a lobster, a lemur, a bottle of wine, Aristippus," and the periods in which he lived were the Augustan age in Rome and "then in Paris and London from 1660 to 1740, and lastly from 1770 to 1850. . . . Afternoons at Holland House, dinners chez Magny."

With his background of classical culture, religious scepticism, travel, leisure, country houses, and civilised meals, "Palinurus" naturally contemplates the modern world without enthusiasm and even, at moments, with sheer aristocratic disdain: but also – and this is the peculiar mark of our age – with self-accusation and the consciousness of being an end-product, a mere ghost, like the cultivated pagans of A.D. 400. On almost every page this book exhibits that queer product of capitalist democracy, an inferiority complex resulting from a private income. The author wants his comforts and privileges, and is ashamed of wanting them: he feels that he has a right to them, and yet feels certain that they are doomed to disappear. Before very long the mob will rise and destroy its exploiters, but in doing so it will also destroy civilisation:

> The English masses are lovable: they are kind, decent, tolerant, practical, and not stupid. The tragedy is that there are too many of them, and that they are aimless, having outgrown the servile functions for which they were encouraged to multiply. One day these huge crowds will have to seize power because there will be nothing else for them to do, and yet they neither demand power nor are ready to make use of it: they will only learn to be bored in a new way. Sooner or

later the population of England will turn Communist, and then it will take over. Some form of Communism is the only effective religion for the working class; its coming is therefore as inevitable as was that of Christianity. The Liberal Die-hard then comes to occupy historically the same position as the "good pagan": he is doomed to extinction.

Throughout the book this is repeated over and over again, in varying forms. The Beehive State is upon us, the individual will be stamped out of existence, the future is with the holiday camp, the doodle-bug, and the secret police. "Palinurus," however, differs from most of his similarly placed contemporaries in not acquiescing in the process. He refuses to desert the sinking ship of individualism. To the statement that man "will find fulfilment only through participation in the communal life of an organised group", he answers "No" seven times over. Yet he sees no escape from the Beehive future. He sees, or thinks he sees, ways in which order and liberty, reason and myth, might be combined, but he does not believe that is the turn civilisation will take. Finally, he has no resource except a sort of lonely defiance, as of the last mammoth, or, like Faustus, trying to forget damnation in the embraces of Helen.

This outlook, product of totalitarianism and the perversion of science, is probably gaining ground, and if only for that reason this rather fragmentary book is a valuable document. It is a cry of despair from the rentier who feels that he has no right to exist, but also feels that he is a finer animal than the proletarian. Its error lies in assuming that a collectivist society would destroy human individuality. The ordinary English Communist or "fellow-traveller" makes the same assumption, and yields up his intellectual integrity in a frenzy of masochism. "Palinurus" refuses to yield, but just as blindly as the other he takes "Communism" at its own valuation.

The mechanism is the same in both cases. They are *told* that the aim of Socialism or Communism is to make men resemble insects: they are conscious that they are privileged people, and that if they resist Socialism their motives must be doubtful: therefore, they look no deeper. It does not occur to them that the so-called collectivist systems now existing only try to wipe out the individual because they are *not* really collectivist and certainly not egalitarian – because, in fact, they are a sham covering a new form of class privilege. If one can see this, one can defy the insect-men with a good conscience. But certainly it is a lot harder to see it, or at any rate to say it aloud, if one is carrying the burden of an unearned income.

As I Please 55
Tribune, 19 January 1945

Last week Henri Béraud, the French journalist, was sentenced to death – later commuted to life imprisonment – for collaboration with the Germans. Béraud used to contribute to the Fascist weekly paper *Gringoire*, which in its later years had become the most disgusting rag it is possible to imagine. I have seldom been so angered by anything in the Press as by its cartoon when the wretched Spanish refugees streamed into France with Italian aeroplanes machine-gunning them all the way. The Spaniards were pictured as a procession of villainous-looking men, each pushing a handcart piled with jewellery and bags of gold. *Gringoire* kept up an almost continuous outcry for the suppression of the French Communist Party, but it was equally fierce against even the mildest politicians of the Left. One can get an idea of the moral level at which it conducted political controversy from the fact that it once published a cartoon showing Léon Blum in bed with his own sister. Its advertisement columns were full of ads. for clairvoyants and books of pornography. This piece of rubbish was said to have a circulation of 500,000.

At the time of the Abyssinian war Béraud wrote a violent pro-Italian article in which he proclaimed "I hate England," and gave his reasons for doing so. It is significant that it was mostly people of this type, who had made no secret of their Fascist sympathies for years beforehand, that the Germans had to make use of for Press propaganda in France. A year or two ago Mr. Raymond Mortimer published an article on the activity of French writers during the war, and there have been several similar articles in American magazines. When one pieces these together, it becomes clear that the French literary intelligentsia has behaved extremely well under the German occupation. I wish I could feel certain that the English literary intelligentsia as a whole would have behaved equally well if we had had the Nazis here. But it is true that if Britain had also been overrun, the situation would have been hopeless and the temptation to accept the New Order very much stronger.

I think I owe a small apology to the twentieth century. Apropos of my remarks about the *Quarterly Review* for 1810 – in which I pointed out that French books could get favourable reviews in England at the height of the war with France – two correspondents have written to tell me that during the present war German scientific publications have had fair treatment in the scientific Press in this country. So perhaps we aren't such barbarians after all.

But I still feel that our ancestors were better at remaining sane in war time than we are. If you ever have to walk from Fleet Street to the Embankment, it is worth going into the office of the *Observer* and having a look at something that is preserved in the waiting-room. It is a framed page from the *Observer* (which is one of our oldest newspapers) for a certain day in June, 1815. In appearance it is very like a modern newspaper, though slightly worse printed, and with only five columns on the page. The largest letters used are not much more than a quarter of an inch high. The first column is given up to "Court and Society," then follow several columns of advertisements, mostly of rooms to let. Halfway down the last column is a headline SANGUINARY BATTLE IN FLANDERS. COMPLETE DEFEAT OF THE CORSICAN USURPER. This is the first news of Waterloo!

"To-day there are only eighty people in the United Kingdom with net incomes of over six thousand pounds a year." (Mr. Quintin Hogg, M.P., in his pamphlet *The Times We Live In*.)

There are also about eighty ways in the English and American languages of expressing incredulity – for example, *garn, come off it, you bet, sez you, oh yeah, not half, I don't think, less of it* or *and the pudding!* But I think *and then you wake up* is the exactly suitable answer to a remark like the one quoted above.

Recently I read the biography of Edgar Wallace which was written by Margaret Lane some years ago. It is a real "log cabin to White House" story, and by implication a frightful commentary on our age. Starting off with every possible disadvantage – an illegitimate child, brought up by very poor foster parents in a slum street – Wallace worked his way up by sheer ability, enterprise and hard work. His output was enormous. In his later years he was turning out eight books a year, besides plays, radio scripts and much journalism. He thought nothing of composing a full-length book in less than a week. He took no exercise, worked behind a glass screen in a super-heated room, smoked incessantly and drank vast quantities of sweetened tea. He died of diabetes at the age of 57.

It is clear from some of his more ambitious books that Wallace did in some sense take his work seriously, but his main aim was to make money, and he made it. Towards the end of his life he was earning round about £50,000 a year. But it was all fairy gold. Besides losing money by financing theatres and keeping strings of racehorses which seldom won, Wallace spent fantastic sums on his various houses, where he kept a staff of twenty servants. When he died very suddenly in Hollywood, it was found that his debts amounted to £140,000, while his liquid assets were practically nil. However, the sales of his books were so vast that his royalties amounted to £26,000 in the two years following his death.

The curious thing is that this utterly wasted life – a life of sitting almost continuously in a stuffy room and covering acres of paper with slightly pernicious nonsense – is what is called, or would have been called a few years ago, "an inspiring story." Wallace did what all the "get on or get out" books, from Smiles's *Self Help* onwards, have told you to do. And the world gave him the kind of rewards he would have asked for, after his death as well as in life. When his body was brought home –

"He was carried on board the *Berengaria* . . . They laid a Union Jack over him, and covered him with flowers. He lay alone in the empty saloon under his burden of wreaths, and no journey that he had ever taken had been made in such quiet dignity and state. When the ship crept into Southampton Water her flag was flying at half-mast, and the flags of Southampton slipped gently down to salute him. The bells of Fleet Street tolled, and Wyndham's was dark."

All that and £50,000 a year as well! They also gave Wallace a plaque on the wall at Ludgate Circus. It is queer to think that London could commemorate Wallace in Fleet Street and Barrie in Kensington Gardens, but has never yet got round to giving Blake a monument in Lambeth.

As I Please 56
Tribune, 26 January 1945

The other night I attended a mass meeting of an organisation called the League for European Freedom. Although officially an all-party organisation – there was one Labour M.P. on the platform – it is, I think it is safe to say, dominated by the anti-Russian wing of the Tory Party.

I am all in favour of European freedom, but I feel happier when it is coupled with freedom elsewhere – in India, for example. The people on the platform were concerned with the Russian actions in Poland, the Baltic countries, etc., and the scrapping of the principles of the Atlantic Charter that those actions imply. More than half of what they said was justified, but curiously enough they were almost as anxious to defend our own coercion of Greece as to condemn the Russian coercion of Poland. Victor Raikes, the Tory M.P., who is an able and outspoken reactionary, made a speech which I should have considered a good one if it had referred only to Poland and Yugoslavia. But after dealing with those two countries he went on to speak about Greece, and then suddenly black became white, and white black. There was no booing, no interjections from the quite large audience – no one there, apparently, who could see that the forcing of quisling governments upon unwilling peoples is equally undesirable whoever does it.

It is very hard to believe that people like this are really interested in political liberty as such. They are merely concerned because Britain did not get a big enough cut in the sordid bargain that appears to have been driven at Teheran. After the meeting I talked with a journalist whose contacts among influential people are much more extensive than mine. He said he thought it probable that British policy will shortly take a violent anti-Russian swing, and that it would be quite easy to manipulate public opinion in that direction if necessary. For a number of reasons I don't believe he was right, but if he does turn out to be right, then ultimately it is *our* fault and not that of our adversaries.

No one expects the Tory Party and its press to spread enlightenment. The trouble is that for years past it has been impossible to extract a grown-up picture of foreign politics from the Left-wing press either. When it comes to such issues as Poland, the Baltic countries, Yugoslavia or Greece, what difference is there between the Russophile press and the extreme Tory press? The one is simply the other standing on its head. The *News Chronicle* gives the big headlines to the fighting in Greece but tucks away the news that "force has had to be used" against the Polish Home Army in small print at the bottom of a column. The *Daily Worker* disapproves of dictatorship in Athens, the *Catholic Herald* disapproves of dictatorship in Belgrade. There is no one who is able to say – at least, no one who has the chance to say in a newspaper of big circulation – that this whole dirty game of spheres of influence, quislings, purges, deportations, one-party elections and hundred per cent. plebiscites is morally the same whether it is done by ourselves, the Russians or the Nazis. Even in the case of such frank returns to barbarism as the use of hostages, disapproval is only felt when it happens to be the enemy and not ourselves who is doing it.

And with what result? Well, one result is that it becomes much easier to mislead public opinion. The Tories are able to precipitate scandals when they want to, partly because on certain subjects the Left refuses to talk in a grown-up manner. An example was the Russo-Finnish war of 1940. I do not defend the Russian action in Finland, but it was not especially wicked. It was merely the same kind of thing as we ourselves did when we seized Madagascar. The public could be shocked by it, and indeed worked up into a dangerous fury about it, because for years they had been falsely taught that Russian foreign policy was morally different from that of other countries. And it struck me as I listened to Mr. Raikes the other night that if the Tories do choose to start spilling the beans about the Lublin Committee, Marshal Tito and kindred subjects, there will be – thanks to prolonged self-censorship on the Left – plenty of beans for them to spill.

But political dishonesty has its comic side. Presiding over that meeting of the League for European Freedom was no less a person than the Duchess of Atholl. It is only about seven years since the Duchess – "the red duchess" as she was affectionately nicknamed – was the pet of the *Daily Worker* and lent the considerable weight of her authority to every lie that the Communists happened to be uttering at the moment. Now she is fighting against the monster that she helped to create. I am sure that neither she nor her Communist ex-friends see any moral in this.

I want to correct an error that I made in this column last week. It seems that there *is* a plaque to William Blake, and that it is somewhere near St. George's church in Lambeth. I had looked for one in that area and had failed to find it. My apologies to the L.C.C.

If one cares about the preservation of the English language, a point one often has to decide is whether it is worth putting up a struggle when a word changes its meaning.

Some words are beyond redemption. One could not, I imagine, restore "impertinent" to its original meaning, or "journal," or "decimate." But how about the use of "infer" for "imply" ("He didn't actually say I was a liar, but he inferred it"), which has been gaining ground for some years? Ought one to protest against it? And ought one to acquiesce when certain words have their meanings arbitrarily narrowed? Examples are "immoral" (nearly always taken as meaning sexually immoral), and "criticise" (always taken as meaning criticise unfavourably). It is astonishing what numbers of words have come to have a purely sexual significance, partly owing to the need of the newspapers for euphemisms. Constant use of such phrases as "intimacy took place twice" has practically killed the original meaning of "intimacy," and quite a dozen other words have been perverted in the same way.

Obviously this kind of thing ought to be prevented if possible, but it is uncertain whether one can achieve anything by struggling against the current usage. The coming and going of words is a mysterious process whose rules we do not understand. In 1940 the word "wallop," meaning mild beer, suddenly became current all over London. I had never heard it until that date, but it seems that it was not a new word, but had been peculiar to one quarter of London. Then it suddenly spread all over the place, and now it appears to have died out again. Words can also revive, for no very clear reason, after lying dormant for hundreds of years: for example the word "car," which had never had any currency in England except in high-flown classical poetry, but was resurrected about 1900 to describe the newly invented automobile.

Possibly, therefore, the degradation which is certainly happening to our language is a process which one cannot arrest by conscious action. But I would like to see the attempt made. And as a start I would like to see a few dozen journalists declare war on some obviously bad usage – for example, the disgusting verb "to contact," or the American habit of tying an unnecessary preposition on to every verb – and see whether they could kill it by their concerted efforts.

As I Please 57
Tribune, 2 February 1945

I have just been re-reading, with great interest, an old favourite of my boyhood, *The Green Curve*, by "Ole Luk-Oie." "Ole Luk-Oie" was the pseudonym of Major Swinton (afterwards General Swinton), who was, I believe, one of the rather numerous people credited with the invention of the tank. The stories in this book, written about 1908, are the forecasts of an intelligent professional soldier who had learned the lessons of the Boer War and the Russo-Japanese War, and it is interesting to compare them with what actually happened a few years later.

One story, written as early as 1907 (at which date no aeroplane had actually risen off the ground for more than a few seconds), describes an air raid. The aeroplanes carry eight-pounder bombs! Another story, written in the same year, deals with a German invasion of England, and I was particularly interested to notice that in this story the Germans are already nicknamed "Huns." I had been inclined to attribute the use of the word "Hun," for German, to Kipling, who certainly used it in the poem that he published during the first week of the last war.

In spite of the efforts of several newspapers, "Hun" has never caught on in this war, but we have plenty of other offensive nicknames. Someone could write a valuable monograph on the use of question-begging names and epithets, and their effect in obscuring political controversies. It would bring out the curious fact that if you simply accept and apply to yourself a name intended as an insult, it may end by losing its insulting character. This appears to be happening to "Trotskyist," which is already dangerously close to being a compliment. So also with "Conchy" during the last war. Another example is "Britisher." This word was used for years as a term of opprobrium in the Anglophobe American Press. Later on, Northcliffe and others, looking round for some substitute for "Englishman" which should have an Imperialistic and jingoistic flavour, found "Brit-isher" ready to hand, and took it over. Since then the word has had an aura of gutter patriotism, and the kind of person who tells you that "what these natives need is a firm hand," also tells you that he is "proud to be a Britisher" – which is about equivalent to a Chinese Nationalist describing himself as a "Chink."

A leaflet recently received from the Friends' Peace Committee states that if the current scheme to remove all Poles from the areas to be taken over by the U.S.S.R., and, in compensation, all Germans from the portions of Germany to be taken over by Poland, is put into operation, "this will involve the transfer of not less than seven million people."

Some estimates, I believe, put it higher than this, but let us assume it to be seven millions. This is equivalent to uprooting and transplanting the entire population of Australia, or the combined populations of Scotland and Ireland. I am no expert on transport or housing, and I would like to hear from somebody better qualified a rough estimate (a) of how many wagons and locomotives, running for how long, would be involved in transporting those seven million people, plus their livestock, farm machinery and household goods; or, alternatively, (b) of how many of them are going to die of starvation and exposure if they are simply shipped off without their livestock, etc.

I fancy the answer to (a) would show that this enormous crime cannot actually be carried through, though it might be started, with confusion, suffering and the sowing of irreconcilable hatreds as the result. Meanwhile, the British people should be made to understand, with as much concrete detail as possible, what kind of policies their statesman are committing them to.

A not-too-distant explosion shakes the house, the windows rattle in their sockets, and in the next room the 1964 class wakes up and lets out a yell or two. Each time this happens I find myself thinking, "Is it possible that human beings can continue with this lunacy very much longer?" You know the answer, of course. Indeed, the difficulty nowadays is to find anyone who thinks that there will *not* be another war in the fairly near future.

Germany, I suppose, will be defeated this year, and when Germany is out of the way Japan will not be able to stand up to the combined power of Britain and the U.S.A. Then there will be a peace of exhaustion, with only minor and unofficial wars raging all over the place, and perhaps this so-called peace may last for decades. But after that, by the way the world is actually shaping, it may well be that war will *become permanent*. Already, quite visibly and more or less with the acquiescence of all of us, the world is splitting up into the two or three huge super-states forecast in James Burnham's *Managerial Revolution*. One cannot draw their exact boundaries as yet, but one can see more or less what areas they will comprise. And if the world does settle down into this pattern, it is likely that these vast states will be permanently at war with one another, though it will not necessarily be a very intensive or bloody kind of war. Their problems, both economic and psychological, will be a lot simpler if the doodle-bugs are more or less constantly whizzing to and fro.

If these two or three super-states do establish themselves, not only will each of them be too big to be conquered, but they will be under no necessity to trade with one another, and in a position to prevent all contact between their nationals. Already, for a dozen years or so, large areas of the earth have been cut off from one another, although technically at peace.

Some months ago, in this column, I pointed out that modern scientific inventions have tended to prevent rather than increase international communication. This brought me several angry letters from readers, but none of them were able to show that what I had said was false. They merely retorted that if we had Socialism, the aeroplane, the radio, etc., would not be perverted to wrong uses. Very true, but then we haven't Socialism. As it is, the aeroplane is primarily a thing for dropping bombs and the radio primarily a thing for whipping up nationalism. Even before the war there was enormously less contact between the peoples of the earth than there had been thirty years earlier, and education was perverted, history rewritten and freedom of thought suppressed to an extent undreamed of in earlier ages. And there is no sign whatever of these tendencies being reversed.

Maybe I am pessimistic. But, at any rate those are the thoughts that cross my mind (and a lot of other people's too, I believe) every time the explosion of a V bomb booms through the mist.

A little story I came upon in a book.

Someone receives an invitation to go out lion hunting. "But," he exclaims, "I haven't lost any lions!"

As I Please 58
Tribune, 9 February 1945

Every time I wash up a batch of crockery I marvel at the unimaginativeness of human beings who can travel under the sea and fly through the clouds, and yet have not known how to eliminate this sordid time-wasting drudgery from their daily lives. If you go into the Bronze Age room in the British

Museum (when it is open again) you will notice that some of our domestic appliances have barely altered in three thousand years. A saucepan, say, or a comb, is very much the same thing as it was when the Greeks were besieging Troy. In the same period we have advanced from the leaky galley to the 50,000 ton liner, and from the ox cart to the aeroplane.

It is true that in the modern labour-saving house in which a tiny percentage of human beings live, a job like washing-up takes rather less time than it used to. With soap-flakes, abundant hot water, plate racks, a well-lighted kitchen, and – what very few houses in England have – an easy method of rubbish-disposal, you can make it more tolerable than it used to be when copper dishes had to be scoured with sand in porous stone sinks by the light of a candle. But certain jobs (for instance, cleaning out a frying-pan which has had fish in it) are inherently disgusting, and this whole business of messing about with dish mops and basins of hot water is incredibly primitive. At this moment the block of flats I live in is partly uninhabitable: not because of enemy action, but because accumulations of snow have caused water to pour through the roof and bring down the plaster from the ceilings. It is taken for granted that this calamity will happen every time there is an exceptionally heavy fall of snow. For three days there was no water in the taps because the pipes were frozen: that, too, is a normal, almost yearly, experience. And the newspapers have just announced that the number of burst pipes is so enormous that the job of repairing them will not be completed till the end of 1945 – when, I suppose, there will be another big frost and they will all burst again. If our methods of making war had kept pace with our methods of keeping house, we should be just about on the verge of discovering gunpowder.

To come back to washing-up. Like sweeping, scrubbing and dusting, it is of its nature an uncreative and life-wasting job. You cannot make an art out of it as you can out of cooking or gardening. What, then, is to be done about it? Well, this whole problem of housework has three possible solutions. One is to simplify our way of living very greatly; another is to assume, as our ancestors did, that life on earth is inherently miserable, and that it is entirely natural for the average woman to be a broken-down drudge at the age of thirty; and the other is to devote as much intelligence to rationalising the interiors of our houses as we have devoted to transport and communications.

I fancy we shall choose the third alternative. If one thinks simply in terms of saving trouble and plans one's home as ruthlessly as one would plan a machine, it is possible to imagine houses and flats which would be comfortable and would entail very little work. Central heating, rubbish chutes, proper consumption of smoke, cornerless rooms, electrically-warmed beds and elimination of carpets would make a lot of difference. But as for washing-up, I see no solution except to do it communally, like laundry. Every morning the municipal van will stop at your door and carry off a box of dirty crocks, handing you a box of clean ones (marked with your initial, of course) in return. This would be hardly more difficult to organise than the daily diaper service which was operating before the war. And though it would mean that some people would have to be full-time washers-up, as some people are now full-time laundry-workers, the all-over saving in labour and fuel would be enormous. The alternatives are to continue fumbling about with greasy dish mops, or to eat out of paper containers.

A sidelight on the habits of book reviewers.

Some time ago I was commissioned to write an essay for an annual scrapbook which shall be nameless. At the very last minute (and when I had had the money, I am glad to say) the publishers decided that my essay must be suppressed. By this time the book was actually in process of being bound. The essay was cut out of every copy, but for technical reasons it was impossible to remove my name from the list of contributors on the title page.

Since then I have received a number of press cuttings referring to this book. In each case I am mentioned as being "among the contributors," and not one reviewer has yet spotted that the contribution attributed to me is not actually there.

Now that "explore every avenue" and "leave no stone unturned" have been more or less laughed out of existence, I think it is time to start a campaign against some more of the worn-out and useless metaphors with which our language is littered.

Three that we could well do without are "cross swords with," "ring the changes on," and "take up the cudgels for." How lifeless these and similar expressions have become you can see from the fact that in many cases people do not even remember their original meaning. What is meant by "ringing the changes," for instance? Probably it once had something to do with church bells, but one could not be sure without consulting a dictionary. "Take up the cudgels for" possibly derives from the almost obsolete game of singlestick. When an expression has moved as far from its original meaning as this, its value as a metaphor – that is, its power of providing a concrete illustration – has vanished. There is no sense whatever in writing "X took up the cudgels for Y." One should either say "X defended Y" or think of a new metaphor which genuinely makes one's meaning more vivid.

In some cases these overworked expressions have actually been severed from their original meaning by means of a misspelling. An example is "plain sailing" (plane sailing). And the expression "toe the line" is now coming to be spelled quite frequently "tow the line." People who are capable of this kind of thing evidently don't attach any definite meaning to the words they use.

I wonder whether people read Bret Harte nowadays. I do not know why, but for an hour past some stanzas from *The Society upon the Stanislaus* have been running in my head. It describes a meeting of an archæological society which ended in disorder:

Then Abner Dean of Angel's raised a point of order, when
A chunk of old red sandstone took him in the abdomen:
And he smiled a kind of sickly smile, and curled up on the
    floor,
And the subsequent proceedings interested him no more.

It has perhaps been unfortunate for Bret Harte's modern reputation that of his two funniest poems, one turns on colour prejudice and the other on class snobbery. But there are a number that are worth re-reading, including one or two serious ones: especially *Dickens in Camp*, the now almost forgotten poem which Bret Harte wrote after Dickens's death and which was about the finest tribute Dickens ever had.

As I Please 59
Tribune, 16 February 1945

Last week I received a copy of a statement on the future of Burma, issued by the Burma Association, an organisation which includes most of the Burmese resident in this country. How representative this organisation is I am not certain, but probably it voices the wishes of a majority of politically-conscious Burmese. For reasons I shall try to make clear presently, the statement just issued is an important document. Summarised as shortly as possible, it makes the following demands: –

(i) An amnesty for Burmese who have collaborated with the Japs during the occupation. (ii) Statement by the British Government of a definite date at which Burma shall attain Dominion status. The period, if possible, to be less than six years. The Burmese people to summon a Constituent Assembly in the meantime. (iii) No interim of "direct rule." (iv) The Burmese people to have a greater share in the economic development of their own country. (v) The British Government to make an immediate unequivocal statement of its intentions towards Burma.

The striking thing about these demands is how moderate they are. No political party with any tinge of nationalism, or any hope of getting a mass following, could possibly ask for less. But why do these people pitch their claims so low? Well, I think one can guess at two reasons. To begin with, the experience of Japanese occupation has probably made Dominion status seem a more tempting goal than it seemed three years ago. But – much more important – if they demand so little it is probably because they expect to be offered even less. And I should guess that they expect right. Indeed, of the very modest suggestions listed above, only the first is likely to be carried out.

The Government has never made any clear statement about the future of Burma, but there have been persistent rumours that when the Japs are driven out there is to be a return to "direct rule," which is a polite name for military dictatorship.

And what is happening, politically, in Burma at this moment? We simply don't know: nowhere have I seen in any newspaper one word about the way in which the reconquered territories are being administered. To grasp the significance of this one has to look at the map of Burma. A year ago Burma proper was in Japanese hands and the Allies were fighting in wild territories thinly populated by rather primitive tribes who have never been much interfered with and are traditionally pro-British. Now they are penetrating into the heart of Burma, and some fairly important towns, centres of administration, have fallen into their hands. Several million Burmese must be once again under the British flag. Yet we are told nothing whatever about the form of administration that is being set up. Is it surprising if every thinking Burmese fears the worst?

It is vitally important to interest the British public in this matter, if possible. Our eyes are fixed on Europe, we forget that at the other end of the world there is a whole string of countries awaiting liberation and in nearly every case hoping for something better than a mere change of conquerors. Burma will probably be the first British territory to be reconquered, and it will be a test case: a more important test than Greece or Belgium, not only because more people are involved, but because it will be almost wholly a British responsibility. It will be a fearful disaster if through apathy and ignorance we let Churchill, Amery and Co. put across some reactionary settlement which will lose us the friendship of the Burmese people for good.

For a year or two after the Japanese have gone, Burma will be in a receptive mood and more pro-British than it has been for a dozen years past. Then is the moment to make a generous gesture. I don't know whether Dominion status is the best possible solution. But if the politically conscious section of the Burmese ask for Dominion status, it would be monstrous to let the Tories refuse it in a hopeless effort to bring back the past. And there must be a date attached to it, a not too distant date. Whether these people remain inside the British Commonwealth or outside it, what matters in the long run is that we should have their friendship – and we *can* have it if we do not play them false at the moment of crisis. When the moment comes for Burma's future to be settled, thinking Burmese will not turn their eyes towards Churchill. They will be looking at *us*, the Labour movement, to see whether our talk about democracy, self-determination, racial equality and what-not has any truth in it. I do not know whether it will be in our power to force a decent settlement upon the Government; but I do know that we shall harm ourselves irreparably if we do not make at least as much row about it as we did in the case of Greece.

When asked, "Which is the wisest of the animals?" a Japanese sage replied, "The one that man has not yet discovered."

I have just seen in a book the statement that the grey seals, the kind that are found round the coasts of Britain, number only ten thousand. Presumably there are so few of them because they have been killed off, like many another over-trustful animal. Seals are quite tame, and appear to be very inquisitive. They will follow a boat for miles, and sometimes they will even follow you when you are walking round the shore. There is no good reason for killing them. Their coats are no use for fur, and except for eating a certain amount of fish they do no harm.

They breed mostly on uninhabited islands. Let us hope that some of the islands remain uninhabited, so that these unfortunate brutes may escape being exterminated entirely. However, we are not quite such persistent slaughterers of rare animals as we used to be. Two species of birds, the bittern and the spoonbill, extinct for many years, have recently succeeded in re-establishing themselves in Britain. They have even been encouraged to breed in some places. Thirty years ago, any bittern that dared to show its beak in this country would have been shot and stuffed immediately.

The Gestapo is said to have teams of literary critics whose job is to determine, by means of stylistic comparison, the authorship of anonymous pamphlets. I have always thought that, if only it were in a better cause, this is exactly the job I would like to have.

To any of our readers whose tastes lie in the same direction, I present this problem: Who is now writing "Beachcomber's" column in the *Daily Express*? It is certainly not Mr. J. B. Morton, who was "Beachcomber" until recently. I have heard that it is Mr. Osbert Lancaster, the cartoonist, but that was merely a piece of gossip, and I have not made any careful examination. But I would bet five shillings that the present "Beachcomber," unlike Mr. Morton, is not a Catholic.

In Defence of P. G. Wodehouse
The Windmill, No. 2, [July] 1945

When the Germans made their rapid advance through Belgium in the early summer of 1940, they captured, among other things, Mr. P. G. Wodehouse, who had been living through-out the early part of the war in his villa at Le Touquet, and seems not to have realised until the last moment that he was in any danger. As he was led away into captivity, he is said to have remarked, "Perhaps after this I shall write a serious book." He was placed for the time being under house arrest, and from his subsequent statements it appears that he was treated in a fairly friendly way, German officers in the neighbourhood fre-quently "dropping in for a bath or a party".

Over a year later, on 25th June 1941, the news came that Wodehouse had been released from internment and was living at the Adlon Hotel in Berlin. On the following day the public was astonished to learn that he had agreed to do some broad-casts of a "non-political" nature over the German radio. The full texts of these broadcasts are not easy to obtain at this date, but Wodehouse seems to have done five of them between 26th June and 2nd July, when the Germans took him off the air again. The first broadcast, on 26th June, was not made on the Nazi radio but took the form of an interview with Harry Flannery, the representative of the Columbia Broadcast-ing System, which still had its correspondents in Berlin. Wodehouse also published in the *Saturday Evening Post* an article which he had written while still in the internment camp.

The article and the broadcasts dealt mainly with Wodehouse's experiences in internment, but they did include a very few comments on the war. The following are fair samples:

"I never was interested in politics. I'm quite unable to work up any kind of belligerent feeling. Just as I'm about to feel belligerent about some country I meet a decent sort of chap. We go out together and lose any fighting thoughts or feelings."

"A short time ago they had a look at me on parade and got the right idea; at least they sent us to the local lunatic asylum. And I have been there forty-two weeks. There is a good deal to be said for internment. It keeps you out of the saloon and helps you to keep up with your reading. The chief trouble is that it means you are away from home for a long time. When I join my wife I had better take along a letter of introduction to be on the safe side."

"In the days before the war I had always been modestly proud of being an Englishman, but now that I have been some months resident in this bin or repository of Englishmen I am not so sure. . . . The only concession I want from Germany is that she gives me a loaf of bread, tells the gentlemen with muskets at the main gate to look the other way, and leaves the rest to me. In return I am prepared to hand over India, an autographed set of my books, and to reveal the secret process of cooking sliced potatoes on a radiator. This offer holds good till Wednesday week."

The first extract quoted above caused great offence. Wodehouse was also censured for using (in the interview with Flannery) the phrase "whether Britain wins the war or not", and he did not make things better by describing in another broadcast the filthy habits of some Belgian prisoners among whom he was interned. The Germans recorded this broadcast and repeated it a number of times. They seem to have supervised his talks very lightly, and they allowed him not only to be funny about the discomforts of internment but to remark that "the internees at Trost camp all fervently believe that Britain will eventually win". The general upshot of the talks, however, was that he had not been ill treated and bore no malice.

These broadcasts caused an immediate uproar in England. There were questions in Parliament, angry editorial comments in the press, and a stream of letters from fellow-authors, nearly all of them disapproving, though one or two suggested that it would be better to suspend judgement, and several pleaded that Wodehouse probably did not realise what he was doing. On 15th July, the Home Service of the B.B.C. carried an extremely violent Postscript by "Cassandra" of the *Daily Mirror*, accusing Wodehouse of "selling his country". This postscript made free use of such expressions as "Quisling" and "worshipping the Führer". The main charge was that Wodehouse had agreed to do German propaganda as a way of buying himself out of the internment camp.

"Cassandra's" Postscript caused a certain amount of protest, but on the whole it seems to have intensified popular feeling against Wodehouse. One result of it was that numerous lending libraries withdrew Wodehouse's books from circulation. Here is a typical news item:

> "Within twenty-four hours of listening to the broadcast of Cassandra, the *Daily Mirror* columnist, Portadown (North Ireland) Urban District Council banned P. G. Wodehouse's books from their public library. Mr. Edward McCann said that Cassandra's broadcast had clinched the matter. Wodehouse was funny no longer." (*Daily Mirror*.)

In addition the B.B.C. banned Wodehouse's lyrics from the air and was still doing so a couple of years later. As late as December 1944 there were demands in Parliament that Wodehouse should be put on trial as a traitor.

There is an old saying that if you throw enough mud some of it will stick, and the mud has stuck to Wodehouse in a rather peculiar way. An impression has been left behind that Wodehouse's talks (not that anyone remembers what he said in them) showed him up not merely as a traitor but as an ideological sympathiser with Fascism. Even at the time several letters to the press claimed that "Fascist tendencies" could be detected in his books, and the charge has been repeated since. I shall try to analyse the mental atmosphere of those books in a moment, but it is important to realise that the events of 1941 do not convict Wodehouse of anything worse than stupidity. The really interesting question is how and why he could be so stupid. When Flannery met Wodehouse (released, but still under guard) at the Adlon Hotel in June 1941, he saw at once that he was dealing with a political innocent, and when preparing him

GEORGE ORWELL

for their broadcast interview he had to warn him against making some exceedingly unfortunate remarks, one of which was by implication slightly anti-Russian. As it was, the phrase "whether England wins or not" did get through. Soon after the interview Wodehouse told him that he was also going to broadcast on the Nazi radio, apparently not realising that this action had any special significance. Flannery comments:[14]

> "By this time the Wodehouse plot was evident. It was one of the best Nazi publicity stunts of the war, the first with a human angle.... Plack (Goebbels's assistant) had gone to the camp near Gleiwitz to see Wodehouse, found that the author was completely without political sense, and had an idea. He suggested to Wodehouse that in return for being released from the prison camp he write a series of broadcasts about his experiences; there would be no censorship and he would put them on the air himself. In making that proposal Plack showed that he knew his man. He knew that Wodehouse made fun of the English in all his stories and that he seldom wrote in any other way, that he was still living in the period about which he wrote and had no conception of Nazism and all it meant. Wodehouse was his own Bertie Wooster."

The striking of an actual bargain between Wodehouse and Plack seems to be merely Flannery's own interpretation. The arrangement may have been of a much less definite kind, and to judge from the broadcasts themselves, Wodehouse's main idea in making them was to keep in touch with his public and – the comedian's ruling passion – to get a laugh. Obviously they are not the utterances of a Quisling of the type of Ezra Pound or John Amery, nor, probably, of a person capable of understanding the nature of Quislingism. Flannery seems to have warned Wodehouse that it would be unwise to broadcast, but not very forcibly. He adds that Wodehouse (though in one broadcast he refers to himself as an Englishman) seemed to regard himself as an American citizen. He had contemplated naturalisation, but had never filled in the necessary papers. He even used, to Flannery, the phrase, "We're not at war with Germany".

836

I have before me a bibliography of P. G. Wodehouse's works. It names round about fifty books, but is certainly incomplete. It is as well to be honest, and I ought to start by admitting that there are many books by Wodehouse – perhaps a quarter or a third of the total – which I have not read. It is not, indeed, easy to read the whole output of a popular writer who is normally published in cheap editions. But I have followed his work fairly closely since 1911, when I was eight years old, and am well acquainted with its peculiar mental atmosphere – an atmosphere which has not, of course, remained completely unchanged, but shows little alteration since about 1925. In the passage from Flannery's book which I quoted above there are two remarks which would immediately strike any attentive reader of Wodehouse. One is to the effect that Wodehouse "was still living in the period about which he wrote", and the other that the Nazi Propaganda Ministry made use of him because he "made fun of the English". The second statement is based on a misconception to which I will return presently. But Flannery's other comment is quite true and contains in it part of the clue to Wodehouse's behaviour.

A thing that people often forget about P. G. Wodehouse's novels is how long ago the better-known of them were written. We think of him as in some sense typifying the silliness of the nineteen-twenties and nineteen-thirties, but in fact the scenes and characters by which he is best remembered had all made their appearance before 1925. Psmith first appeared in 1909, having been foreshadowed by other characters in earlier school-stories. Blandings Castle, with Baxter and the Earl of Emsworth both in residence, was introduced in 1915. The Jeeves–Wooster cycle began in 1919, both Jeeves and Wooster having made brief appearances earlier. Ukridge appeared in 1924. When one looks through the list of Wodehouse's books from 1902 onwards, one can observe three fairly well-marked periods. The first is the school-story period. It includes such books as *The Gold Bat*, *The Pothunters*, etc., and has its high-spot in *Mike* (1909). *Psmith in the City*, published in the following year, belongs in this category, though it is not directly concerned with school life. The next is the American period. Wodehouse seems to have lived in the United States from about 1913 to 1920, and for a while showed signs of becoming

Americanised in idiom and outlook. Some of the stories in *The Man with Two Left Feet* (1917) appear to have been influenced by O. Henry, and other books written about this time contain Americanisms (*e.g.* "highball" for "whisky and soda") which an Englishman would not normally use *in propria persona*. Nevertheless, almost all the books of this period – *Psmith, Journalist*; *The Little Nugget*; *The Indiscretions of Archie*; *Piccadilly Jim* and various others – depend for their effect on the *contrast* between English and American manners. English characters appear in an American setting, or *vice versa*: there is a certain number of purely English stories, but hardly any purely American ones. The third period might fitly be called the country-house period. By the early nineteen-twenties Wodehouse must have been making a very large income, and the social status of his characters moved upwards accordingly, though the Ukridge stories form a partial exception. The typical setting is now a country mansion, a luxurious bachelor flat or an expensive golf club. The school-boy athleticism of the earlier books fades out, cricket and football giving way to golf, and the element of farce and burlesque becomes more marked. No doubt many of the later books, such as *Summer Lightning*, are light comedy rather than pure farce, but the occasional attempts at moral earnestness which can be found in *Psmith, Journalist*; *The Little Nugget*; *The Coming of Bill*; *The Man with Two Left Feet* and some of the school stories, no longer appear. Mike Jackson has turned into Bertie Wooster. That, however, is not a very startling metamorphosis, and one of the most noticeable things about Wodehouse is his *lack* of development. Books like *The Gold Bat* and *Tales of St. Austin's*, written in the opening years of this century, already have the familiar atmosphere. How much of a formula the writing of his later books had become one can see from the fact that he continued to write stories of English life although throughout the sixteen years before his internment he was living at Hollywood and Le Touquet.

Mike, which is now a difficult book to obtain in an un-abridged form, must be one of the best "light" school stories in English. But though its incidents are largely farcical, it is by no means a satire on the public-school system, and *The Gold Bat*, *The Pothunters*, etc., are even less so. Wodehouse was educated at Dulwich, and then worked in a bank and graduated into

838

novel-writing by way of very cheap journalism. It is clear that for many years he remained "fixated" on his old school and loathed the unromantic job and the lower-middle-class surroundings in which he found himself. In the early stories the "glamour" of public-school life (house matches, fagging, teas round the study fire, etc.) is laid on fairly thick, and the "play the game" code of morals is accepted with not many reservations. Wrykyn, Wodehouse's imaginary public school, is a school of a more fashionable type than Dulwich, and one gets the impression that between *The Gold Bat* (1904) and *Mike* (1909) Wrykyn itself has become more expensive and moved farther from London. Psychologically the most revealing book of Wodehouse's early period is *Psmith in the City*. Mike Jackson's father has suddenly lost his money, and Mike, like Wodehouse himself, is thrust at the age of about eighteen into an ill-paid subordinate job in a bank. Psmith is similarly employed, though not from financial necessity. Both this book and *Psmith, Journalist* (1915) are unusual in that they display a certain amount of political consciousness. Psmith at this stage chooses to call himself a Socialist – in his mind, and no doubt in Wodehouse's, this means no more than ignoring class distinctions – and on one occasion the two boys attend an open-air meeting on Clapham Common and go home to tea with an elderly Socialist orator, whose shabby-genteel home is described with some accuracy. But the most striking feature of the book is Mike's inability to wean himself from the atmosphere of school. He enters upon his job without any pretence of enthusiasm, and his main desire is not, as one might expect, to find a more interesting and useful job, but simply to be playing cricket. When he has to find himself lodgings he chooses to settle at Dulwich, because there he will be near a school and will be able to hear the agreeable sound of the ball striking against the bat. The climax of the book comes when Mike gets the chance to play in a county match and simply walks out of his job in order to do so. The point is that Wodehouse here sympathises with Mike: indeed he identifies himself with him, for it is clear enough that Mike bears the same relation to Wodehouse as Julien Sorel to Stendhal. But he created many other heroes essentially similar. Through the books of this and the next period there passes a whole series of young men to whom playing games and "keeping fit" are a sufficient life-work. Wodehouse is almost incapable of imagining a desirable job. The great thing is to have money of your own, or, failing that, to find a sinecure. The hero of *Something Fresh* (1915) escapes from low-class journalism by becoming physical-training instructor to a dyspeptic millionaire: this is regarded as a step up, morally as well as financially.

In the books of the third period there is no narcissism and no serious interludes, but the implied moral and social background has changed much less than might appear at first sight. If one compares Bertie Wooster with Mike, or even with the rugger-playing prefects of the earliest school stories, one sees that the only real difference between them is that Bertie is richer and lazier. His ideals would be almost the same as theirs, but he fails to live up to them. Archie Moffam, in *The Indiscretions of Archie* (1921), is a type intermediate between Bertie and the earlier heroes: he is an ass, but he is also honest, kind-hearted, athletic and courageous. From first to last Wodehouse takes the public-school code of behaviour for granted, with the difference that in his later, more sophisticated period he prefers to show his characters violating it or living up to it against their will:

"Bertie! You wouldn't let down a pal?"

"Yes, I would."

"But we were at school together, Bertie."

"I don't care."

"The old school, Bertie, the old school!"

"Oh, well – dash it!"

Bertie, a sluggish Don Quixote, has no wish to tilt at windmills, but he would hardly think of refusing to do so when honour calls. Most of the people whom Wodehouse intends as sympathetic characters are parasites, and some of them are plain imbeciles, but very few of them could be described as immoral. Even Ukridge is a visionary rather than a plain crook. The most immoral, or rather un-moral, of Wodehouse's characters is Jeeves, who acts as a foil to Bertie Wooster's comparative high-mindedness and perhaps symbolises the widespread English belief that intelligence and unscrupulousness are much the same thing. How closely Wodehouse sticks to conventional morality can be seen from the fact that nowhere in his books is there anything in the nature of a sex joke. This is an enormous sacrifice for a farcical writer to make. Not only are there no dirty jokes, but there are hardly any compromising situations: the horns-on-the-forehead motif is almost completely avoided. Most of the full-length books, of course, contain a "love interest", but it is always at the light-comedy level: the love affair, with its complications and its idyllic scenes, goes on and on, but, as the saying goes, "nothing happens". It is significant that Wodehouse, by nature a writer of farces, was able to collaborate more than once with Ian Hay, a serio-comic writer and an exponent (vide *Pip*, etc.) of the "clean-living Englishman" tradition at its silliest.

In *Something Fresh* Wodehouse had discovered the comic possibilities of the English aristocracy, and a succession of ridiculous but, save in a very few instances, not actually contemptible barons, earls and what-not followed accordingly. This had the rather curious effect of causing Wodehouse to be regarded, outside England, as a penetrating satirist of English society. Hence Flannery's statement that Wodehouse "made fun of the English", which is the impression he would probably make on a German or even an American reader. Some time after the broadcasts from Berlin I was discussing them with a young Indian Nationalist who defended Wodehouse warmly. He took it for granted that Wodehouse *had* gone over to the enemy, which from his own point of view was the right thing to do. But what interested me was to find that he regarded Wodehouse as an anti-British writer who had done useful work by showing up the British aristocracy in their true colours. This is a mistake that it would be very difficult for an English person to make, and is a good instance of the way in which books, especially humorous books, lose their finer nuances when they reach a foreign audience. For it is clear enough that Wodehouse is *not* anti-British, and not anti-upper class either. On the contrary, a harmless old-fashioned snobbishness is perceptible all through his work. Just as an intelligent Catholic is able to see that the blasphemies of Baudelaire or James Joyce are not seriously damaging to the Catholic faith, so an English reader can see that in creating such characters as Hildebrand Spencer Poyns de Burgh John Han-neyside Coombe-Crombie, 12th Earl of Dreever, Wodehouse is not really attacking the social hierarchy. Indeed, no one who genuinely despised titles would write of them so much. Wodehouse's attitude towards the English social system is the same as his attitude towards the public-school moral code – a mild facetiousness covering an unthinking acceptance. The Earl of Emsworth is funny because an earl ought to have more dignity, and Bertie Wooster's helpless dependence on Jeeves is funny partly because the servant ought not to be superior to the master. An American reader can mistake these two, and others like them, for hostile caricatures, because he is inclined to be Anglophobe already and they correspond to his preconceived ideas about a decadent aristocracy. Bertie Wooster, with his spats and his cane, is the traditional stage Englishman. But, as any English reader would see, Wodehouse intends him as a sympathetic figure, and Wodehouse's real sin has been to present the English upper classes as much nicer people than they are. All through his books certain problems are consistently avoided. Almost without exception his moneyed young men are unassuming, good mixers, not avaricious: their tone is set for them by Psmith, who retains his own upper-class exterior but bridges the social gap by addressing everyone as "Comrade".

But there is another important point about Bertie Wooster: his out-of-dateness. Conceived in 1917 or thereabouts, Bertie really belongs to an epoch earlier than that. He is the "knut" of the pre-1914 period, celebrated in such songs as "Gilbert the Filbert" or "Reckless Reggie of the Regent's Palace". The kind of life that Wodehouse writes about by preference, the life of the "clubman" or "man about town", the elegant young man who lounges all the morning in Piccadilly with a cane under his arm and a carnation in his buttonhole, barely survived into the nineteen-twenties. It is significant that Wodehouse could publish in 1936 a book entitled *Young Men in Spats*. For who was wearing spats at that date? They had gone out of fashion quite ten years earlier. But the traditional "knut", the "Piccadilly Johnny", *ought* to wear spats, just as the pantomime Chinese ought to wear a pigtail. A humorous writer is not obliged to keep up to date, and having struck one or two good veins, Wodehouse continued to exploit them with a regularity that was no doubt all the easier because he did not set foot in

England during the sixteen years that preceded his internment. His picture of English society had been formed before 1914, and it was a naïve, traditional and, at bottom, admiring picture. Nor did he ever become genuinely Americanised. As I have pointed out, spontaneous Americanisms do occur in the books of the middle period, but Wodehouse remained English enough to find American slang an amusing and slightly shocking novelty. He loves to thrust a slang phrase or a crude fact in among Wardour Street English ("With a hollow groan Ukridge borrowed five shillings from me and went out into the night"), and expressions like "a piece of cheese" or "bust him on the noggin" lend themselves to this purpose. But the trick had been developed before he made any American contacts, and his use of garbled quotations is a common device of English writers running back to Fielding. As Mr. John Hayward has pointed out,[15] Wodehouse owes a good deal to his knowledge of English literature and especially of Shakespeare. His books are aimed, not, obviously, at a highbrow audience, but at an audience educated along traditional lines. When, for instance, he describes somebody as heaving "the kind of sigh that Prometheus might have heaved when the vulture dropped in for its lunch", he is assuming that his readers will know something of Greek mythology. In his early days the writers he admired were probably Barry Pain, Jerome K. Jerome, W. W. Jacobs, Kipling and F. Anstey, and he has remained closer to them than to the quick-moving American comic writers such as Ring Lardner or Damon Runyan. In his radio interview with Flannery, Wodehouse wondered whether "the kind of people and the kind of England I write about will live after the war", not realising that they were ghosts already. "He was still living in the period about which he wrote," says Flannery, meaning, probably, the nineteen-twenties. But the period was really the Edwardian age, and Bertie Wooster, if he ever existed, was killed round about 1915.

If my analysis of Wodehouse's mentality is accepted, the idea that in 1941 he consciously aided the Nazi propaganda machine becomes untenable and even ridiculous. He *may* have been induced to broadcast by the promise of an earlier release (he was due for release a few months later, on reaching his sixtieth birthday), but he cannot have realised that what he did would be damaging to British interests. As I have tried to show, his moral outlook has remained that of a public-school boy, and according to the public-school code, treachery in time of war is the most unforgivable of all the sins. But how could he fail to grasp that what he did would be a big propaganda score for the Germans and would bring down a torrent of disapproval on his own head? To answer this one must take two things into consideration. First, Wodehouse's complete lack – so far as one can judge from his printed works – of political awareness. It is nonsense to talk of "Fascist tendencies" in his books. There are no post-1918 tendencies at all. Throughout his work there is a certain uneasy awareness of the problem of class distinctions, and scattered through it at various dates there are ignorant though not unfriendly references to Socialism. In *The Heart of a Goof* (1926) there is a rather silly story about a Russian novelist, which seems to have been inspired by the factional struggle then raging in the U.S.S.R. But the references in it to the Soviet system are entirely frivolous and, considering the date, not markedly hostile. That is about the extent of Wodehouse's political consciousness, so far as it is discoverable from his writings. Nowhere, so far as I know, does he so much as use the word "Fascism" or "Nazism". In left-wing circles, indeed in "enlightened" circles of any kind, to broadcast on the Nazi radio, to have any truck with the Nazis whatever, would have seemed just as shocking an action before the war as during it. But that is a habit of mind that had been developed during nearly a decade of ideological struggle against Fascism. The bulk of the British people, one ought to remember, remained anæsthetic to that struggle until late into 1940. Abyssinia, Spain, China, Austria, Czechoslovakia – the long series of crimes and aggressions had simply slid past their consciousness or were dimly noted as quarrels occurring among foreigners and "not our business". One can gauge the general ignorance from the fact that the ordinary Englishman thought of "Fascism" as an exclusively Italian thing and was bewildered when the same word was applied to Germany. And there is nothing in Wodehouse's writings to suggest that he was better informed, or more interested in politics, than the general run of his readers.

The other thing one must remember is that Wodehouse happened to be taken prisoner at just the moment when the war reached its desperate phase. We forget these things now, but until that time feelings about the war had been noticeably tepid. There was hardly any fighting, the Chamberlain government was unpopular, eminent publicists like Lloyd George and Bernard Shaw were hinting that we should make a compromise peace as quickly as possible, trade union and Labour Party branches all over the country were passing anti-war resolutions. Afterwards, of course, things changed. The Army was with difficulty extricated from Dunkirk, France collapsed, Britain was alone, the bombs rained on London, Goebbels announced that Britain was to be "reduced to degradation and poverty". By the middle of 1941 the British people knew what they were up against and feelings against the enemy were far fiercer than before. But Wodehouse had spent the intervening year in internment, and his captors seem to have treated him reasonably well. He had missed the turning-point of the war, and in 1941 he was still reacting in terms of 1939. He was not alone in this. On several occasions about this time the Germans brought captured British soldiers to the microphone, and some of them made remarks at least as tactless as Wodehouse's. They attracted no attention, however. And even an outright Quisling like John Amery was afterwards to arouse much less indignation than Wodehouse had done.

But why? Why should a few rather silly but harmless remarks by an elderly novelist have provoked such an outcry? One has to look for the probable answer amid the dirty requirements of propaganda warfare.

There is one point about the Wodehouse broadcasts that is almost certainly significant – the date. Wodehouse was released two or three days before the invasion of the U.S.S.R., and at a time when the higher ranks of the Nazi party must have known that the invasion was imminent. It was vitally necessary to keep America out of the war as long as possible, and in fact, about this time, the German attitude towards the U.S.A. did become more conciliatory than it had been before. The Germans could hardly hope to defeat Russia, Britain and the U.S.A. in combination, but if they could polish off Russia quickly – and presumably they expected to do so – the Americans might never intervene. The release of Wodehouse was only a minor move, but it was not a bad sop to throw to the American isolationists. He was well known in the United States, and he was – or so the Germans calculated – popular with the Anglophobe public as a caricaturist who made fun of the silly-ass Englishman with his spats and his monocle. At the microphone he could be trusted to damage British prestige in one way or another, while his release would demonstrate that the Germans were good fellows and knew how to treat their enemies chivalrously. That presumably was the calculation, though the fact that Wodehouse was only broadcasting for about a week suggests that he did not come up to expectations.

But on the British side similar though opposite calculations were at work. For the two years following Dunkirk, British morale depended largely upon the feeling that this was not only a war for democracy but a war which the common people had to win by their own efforts. The upper classes were discredited by their appeasement policy and by the disasters of 1940, and a social levelling process appeared to be taking place. Patriotism and left-wing sentiments were associated in the popular mind, and numerous able journalists were at work to tie the association tighter. Priestley's 1940 broadcasts, and "Cassandra's" articles in the *Daily Mirror*, were good examples of the demagogic propaganda flourishing at that time. In this atmosphere, Wodehouse made an ideal whipping-boy. For it was generally felt that the rich were treacherous, and Wodehouse – as "Cassandra" vigorously pointed out in his broadcast – was a rich man. But he was the kind of rich man who could be attacked with impunity and without risking any damage to the structure of society. To denounce Wodehouse was not like denouncing, say, Beaverbrook. A mere novelist, however large his earnings may happen to be, is not *of* the possessing class. Even if his income touches £50,000 a year he has only the outward semblance of a millionaire. He is a lucky outsider who has fluked into a fortune – usually a very temporary fortune – like the winner of the Calcutta Derby Sweep. Consequently, Wodehouse's indiscretion gave a good propaganda opening. It was a chance to "expose" a wealthy parasite without drawing attention to any of the parasites who really mattered.

In the desperate circumstances of the time, it was excusable to be angry at what Wodehouse did, but to go on denouncing him three or four years later – and more, to let an impression remain that he acted with conscious treachery – is not excusable. Few things in this war have been more morally disgusting than the present hunt after traitors and Quislings. At best it is largely the punishment of the guilty by the guilty. In France, all kinds of petty rats – police officials, penny-a-lining journalists, women who have slept with German soldiers – are hunted down while almost without exception the big rats escape. In England the fiercest tirades against Quislings are uttered by Conservatives who were practising appeasement in 1938 and Communists who were advocating it in 1940. I have striven to show how the wretched Wodehouse – just because success and expatriation had allowed him to remain mentally in the Edwardian age – became the *corpus vile* in a propaganda experiment, and I suggest that it is now time to regard the incident as closed. If Ezra Pound is caught and shot by the American authorities, it will have the effect of establishing his reputation as a poet for hundreds of years; and even in the case of Wodehouse, if we drive him to retire to the United States and renounce his British citizenship, we shall end by being horribly ashamed of ourselves. Meanwhile, if we really want to punish the people who weakened national morale at critical moments, there are other culprits who are nearer home and better worth chasing.

Anti-Semitism in Britain
Contemporary Jewish Record, April 1945

There are about 400,000 known Jews in Britain, and in addition some thousands or, at most, scores of thousands of Jewish refugees who have entered the country from 1934 onwards. The Jewish population is almost entirely concentrated in half a dozen big towns and is mostly employed in the food, clothing and furniture trades. A few of the big monopolies, such as the I.C.I., one or two leading newspapers and at least one big chain of department stores are Jewish-owned or partly Jewish-owned, but it would be very far from the truth to say that

British business life is dominated by Jews. The Jews seem, on the contrary, to have failed to keep up with the modern tendency towards big amalgamations and to have remained fixed in those trades which are necessarily carried out on a small scale and by old-fashioned methods.

I start off with these background facts, which are already known to any well-informed person, in order to emphasize that there is no real Jewish "problem" in England. The Jews are not numerous or powerful enough, and it is only in what are loosely called "intellectual circles" that they have any noticeable influence. Yet it is generally admitted that anti-Semitism is on the increase, that it has been greatly exacerbated by the war, and that humane and enlightened people are not immune to it. It does not take violent forms (English people are almost invariably gentle and law-abiding), but it is ill-natured enough, and in favourable circumstances it could have political results. Here are some samples of anti-Semitic remarks that have been made to me during the past year or two:

Middle-aged office employee: "I generally come to work by bus. It takes longer, but I don't care about using the Underground from Golders Green nowadays. There's too many of the Chosen Race travelling on that line."

Tobacconist (woman): "No, I've got no matches for you. I should try the lady down the street. *She's* always got matches. One of the Chosen Race, you see."

Young intellectual, Communist or near-Communist: "No, I do *not* like Jews. I've never made any secret of that. I can't stick them. Mind you, I'm not anti-Semitic, of course."

Middle-class woman: "Well, no one could call me anti-Semitic, but I do think the way these Jews behave is too absolutely stinking. The way they push their way to the head of queues, and so on. They're so abominably selfish. I think they're responsible for a lot of what happens to them."

Milk roundsman: "A Jew don't do no work, not the same as what an Englishman does. 'E's too clever. We work with this 'ere" (flexes his bicep). "They work with that there" (taps his forehead).

Chartered accountant, intelligent, left-wing in an undirected way: "These bloody Yids are all pro-German. They'd change sides tomorrow if the Nazis got here. I see a lot of them

848

in my business. They admire Hitler at the bottom of their hearts. They'll always suck up to anyone who kicks them."

Intelligent woman, on being offered a book dealing with anti-Semitism and German atrocities: 'Don't show it me, *please* don't show it to me. It'll only make me hate the Jews more than ever."

I could fill pages with similar remarks, but these will do to go on with. Two facts emerge from them. One – which is very important and which I must return to in a moment – is that above a certain intellectual level people are ashamed of being anti-Semitic and are careful to draw a distinction between "anti-Semitism" and "disliking Jews." The other is that anti-Semitism is an irrational thing. The Jews are accused of specific offences (for instance, bad behaviour in food queues) which the person speaking feels strongly about, but it is obvious that these accusations merely rationalize some deep-rooted prejudice. To attempt to counter them with facts and statistics is useless, and may sometimes be worse than useless. As the last of the above-quoted remarks shows, people can remain anti-Semitic, or at least anti-Jewish, while being fully aware that their outlook is indefensible. If you dislike somebody, you dislike him and there is an end of it: your feelings are not made any better by a recital of his virtues.

It so happens that the war has encouraged the growth of anti-Semitism and even, in the eyes of many ordinary people, given some justification for it. To begin with, the Jews are one people of whom it can be said with complete certainty that they will benefit by an Allied victory. Consequently the theory that "this is a Jewish war" has a certain plausibility, all the more so because the Jewish war effort seldom gets its fair share of recognition. The British Empire is a huge heterogeneous organization held together largely by mutual consent, and it is often necessary to flatter the less reliable elements at the expense of the more loyal ones. To publicize the exploits of Jewish soldiers, or even to admit the existence of a considerable Jewish army in the Middle East, rouses hostility in South Africa, the Arab countries and elsewhere: it is easier to ignore the whole subject and allow the man in the street to go on thinking that Jews are exceptionally clever at dodging military service. Then again, Jews are to be found in exactly those trades which are bound to incur unpopularity with the civilian public in war time. Jews are mostly concerned with selling food, clothes, furniture and tobacco – exactly the commodities of which there is a chronic shortage, with consequent over-charging, black-marketing and favouritism. And again, the common charge that Jews behave in an exceptionally cowardly way during air raids was given a certain amount of colour by the big raids of 1940. As it happened, the Jewish quarter of Whitechapel was one of the first areas to be heavily blitzed, with the natural result that swarms of Jewish refugees distrib-uted themselves all over London. If one judged merely from these war-time phenomena, it would be easy to imagine that anti-Semitism is a quasi-rational thing, founded on mistaken premises. And naturally the anti-Semite thinks of himself as a reasonable being. Whenever I have touched on this subject in a newspaper article, I have always had a considerable "come-back," and invariably some of the letters are from well-balanced, middling people – doctors, for example – with no apparent economic grievance. These people always say (as Hitler says in *Mein Kampf*) that they started out with no anti-Jewish prejudice but were driven into their present position by mere observation of the facts. Yet one of the marks of anti-Semitism is an ability to believe stories that could not possibly be true. One could see a good example of this in the strange accident that occurred in London in 1942, when a crowd, frightened by a bomb-burst nearby, fled into the mouth of an Underground station, with the result that something over a hundred people were crushed to death. The very same day it was repeated all over London that "the Jews were responsible." Clearly, if people will believe this kind of thing, one will not get much further by arguing with them. The only useful approach is to discover *why* they can swallow absurdities on one particular subject while remaining sane on others.

But now let me come back to that point I mentioned earlier – that there is widespread awareness of the prevalence of anti-Semitic feeling, and unwillingness to admit sharing it. Among educated people, anti-Semitism is held to be an unforgivable sin and in a quite different category from other kinds of racial prejudice. People will go to remarkable lengths to demonstrate that they are *not* anti-Semitic. Thus, in 1943 an intercession service on behalf of the Polish Jews was held in a synagogue in St. John's Wood. The local authorities declared themselves anxious to participate in it, and the service was attended by the mayor of the borough in his robes and chain, by representatives of all the churches, and by detachments of RAF, Home Guards, nurses, Boy Scouts and what-not. On the surface it was a touching demonstration of solidarity with the suffering Jews. But it was essentially a *conscious* effort to behave decently by people whose subjective feelings must in many cases have been very different. That quarter of London is partly Jewish, anti-Semitism is rife there, and, as I well knew, some of the men sitting round me in the synagogue were tinged by it. Indeed, the commander of my own platoon of Home Guards, who had been especially keen beforehand that we should "make a good show" at the intercession service, was an ex-member of Mosley's Blackshirts. While this division of feeling exists, tolerance of mass violence against Jews, or, what is more important, anti-Semitic legislation, are not possible in England. It is not at present possible, indeed, that anti-Semitism should *become respectable*. But this is less of an advantage than it might appear.

One effect of the persecutions in Germany has been to prevent anti-Semitism from being seriously studied. In England a brief inadequate survey was made by Mass Observation a year or two ago, but if there has been any other investigation of the subject, then its findings have been kept strictly secret. At the same time there has been conscious suppression, by all thoughtful people, of anything likely to wound Jewish susceptibilities. After 1934 the "Jew joke" disappeared as though by magic from postcards, periodicals and the music-hall stage, and to put an unsympathetic Jewish character into a novel or short story came to be regarded as anti-Semitism. On the Palestine issue, too, it was *de rigueur* among enlightened people to accept the Jewish case as proved and avoid examining the claims of the Arabs – a decision which might be correct on its own merits, but which was adopted primarily because the Jews were in trouble and it was felt that one must not criticize them. Thanks to Hitler, therefore, you had a situation in which the press was in effect censored in favour of the Jews while in private anti-Semitism was on the up-grade, even, to some extent, among sensitive and intelligent people. This was particularly noticeable in 1940 at the time of the internment of the refugees. Naturally, every thinking person felt that it was his duty to protest against the wholesale locking-up of unfortunate foreigners who for the most part were only in England because they were opponents of Hitler. Privately, however, one heard very different sentiments expressed. A minority of the refugees behaved in an exceedingly tactless way, and the feeling against them necessarily had an anti-Semitic under-current, since they were largely Jews. A very eminent figure in the Labour Party – I won't name him, but he is one of the most respected people in England – said to me quite violently: "We never asked these people to come to this country. If they choose to come here, let them take the consequences." Yet this man would as a matter of course have associated himself with any kind of petition or manifesto against the internment of aliens. This feeling that anti-Semitism is something sinful and disgraceful, something that a civilized person does not suffer from, is unfavourable to a scientific approach, and indeed many people will admit that they are frightened of probing too deeply into the subject. They are frightened, that is to say, of discovering not only that anti-Semitism is spreading, but that they themselves are infected by it.

To see this in perspective one must look back a few decades, to the days when Hitler was an out-of-work house-painter whom nobody had heard of. One would then find that though anti-Semitism is sufficiently in evidence now, it is probably *less* prevalent in England than it was thirty years ago. It is true that anti-Semitism as a fully thought-out racial or religious doctrine has never flourished in England. There has never been much feeling against intermarriage, or against Jews taking a prominent part in public life. Nevertheless, thirty years ago it was accepted more or less as a law of nature that a Jew was a figure of fun and – though superior in intelligence – slightly deficient in "character." In theory a Jew suffered from no legal disabilities, but in effect he was debarred from certain professions. He would probably not have been accepted as an officer in the Navy, for instance, nor in what is called a "smart" regiment in the Army. A Jewish boy at a public school almost invariably had a bad time. He could, of course, live down his Jewishness if he was exceptionally charming or athletic, but it was an initial disability comparable to a stammer or a birthmark. Wealthy Jews tended to disguise themselves under aristocratic English or Scottish names, and to the average person it seemed quite natural that they should do this, just as it seems natural for a criminal to change his identity if possible. About twenty years ago, in Rangoon, I was getting into a taxi with a friend when a small ragged boy of fair complexion rushed up to us and began a complicated story about having arrived from Colombo on a ship and wanting money to get back. His manner and appearance were difficult to "place," and I said to him:

"You speak very good English. What nationality are you?"

He answered eagerly in his chi-chi accent: "I am a *Joo*, sir!"

And I remember turning to my companion and saying, only partly in joke, "He admits it openly." All the Jews I had known till then were people who were ashamed of being Jews, or at any rate preferred not to talk about their ancestry, and if forced to do so tended to use the word "Hebrew."

The working-class attitude was no better. The Jew who grew up in Whitechapel took it for granted that he would be assaulted, or at least hooted at, if he ventured into one of the Christian slums nearby, and the "Jew joke" of the music halls and the comic papers was almost consistently ill-natured. There was also literary Jew-baiting, which in the hands of Belloc, Chesterton and their followers reached almost a Continental level of scurrility. Non-Catholic writers were sometimes guilty of the same thing in a milder form. There has been a perceptible anti-Semitic strain in English literature from Chaucer onwards, and without even getting up from this table to consult a book I can think of passages which *if written now* would be stigmatized as anti-Semitism, in the works of Shakespeare, Smollett, Thackeray, Bernard Shaw, H. G. Wells, T. S. Eliot, Aldous Huxley and various others. Offhand, the only English writers I can think of who, before the days of Hitler, made a definite effort to stick up for Jews are Dickens and Charles Reade. And however little the average intellectual may have agreed with the opinions of Belloc and Chesterton, he did not acutely disapprove of them. Chesterton's endless tirades against Jews, which he thrust into stories and essays upon the flimsiest pretexts, never got him into trouble – indeed Chesterton was one of the most generally respected figures in English literary life. Anyone who wrote in that strain *now* would bring down a storm of abuse upon himself, or more probably would find it impossible to get his writings published.

If, as I suggest, prejudice against Jews has always been pretty widespread in England, there is no reason to think that Hitler has genuinely diminished it. He has merely caused a sharp division between the politically conscious person who realizes that this is not a time to throw stones at the Jews, and the unconscious person whose native anti-Semitism is increased by the nervous strain of the war. One can assume, therefore, that many people who would perish rather than admit to anti-Semitic feelings are secretly prone to them. I have already indicated that I believe anti-Semitism to be essentially a neurosis, but of course it has its rationalizations, which are sincerely believed in and are partly true. The rationalization put forward by the common man is that the Jew is an exploiter. The partial justification for this is that the Jew, in England, is generally a small business man – that is to say a person whose depredations are more obvious and intelligible than those of, say, a bank or an insurance company. Higher up the intellectual scale, anti-Semitism is rationalized by saying that the Jew is a person who spreads disaffection and weakens national morale. Again there is some superficial justification for this. During the past twenty-five years the activities of what are called "intellectuals" have been largely mischievous. I do not think it an exaggeration to say that if the "intellectuals" had done their work a little more thoroughly, Britain would have surrendered in 1940. But the disaffected intelligentsia inevitably included a large number of Jews. With some plausibility it can be said that the Jews are the enemies of our native culture and our national morale. Carefully examined, the claim is seen to be nonsense, but there are always a few prominent individuals who can be cited in support of it. During the past few years there has been what amounts to a counterattack against the rather shallow Leftism which was fashionable in the previous decade and which was exemplified by such organizations as the Left Book Club. This counterattack (see for instance such books as Arnold Lunn's *The Good Gorilla* or Evelyn Waugh's *Put Out More Flags*) has an anti-Semitic strain, and it would probably be more marked if the subject were not so obviously dangerous. It so happens that for some decades past Britain has had no nationalist intelligentsia worth bothering about. But British nationalism, i.e. nationalism of an intellectual kind, may revive, and probably will revive if Britain comes out of the present war greatly weakened. The young intellectuals of 1950 may be as naively patriotic as those of 1914. In that case the kind of anti-Semitism which flourished among the anti-Dreyfusards in France, and which Chesterton and Belloc tried to import into this country, might get a foothold.

I have no hard-and-fast theory about the origins of anti-Semitism. The two current explanations that it is due to economic causes, or on the other hand that it is a legacy from the Middle Ages – seem to me unsatisfactory, though I admit that if one combines them they can be made to cover the facts. All I would say with confidence is that anti-Semitism is part of the larger problem of nationalism, which has not yet been seriously examined, and that the Jew is evidently a scapegoat, though *for what* he is a scapegoat we do not yet know. In this essay I have relied almost entirely on my own limited experience, and perhaps every one of my conclusions would be negatived by other observers. The fact is that there are almost no data on this subject. But for what they are worth I will summarize my opinions. Boiled down, they amount to this:

There is more anti-Semitism in England than we care to admit, and the war has accentuated it, but it is not certain that it is on the increase if one thinks in terms of decades rather than years.

It does not at present lead to open persecution, but it has the effect of making people callous to the sufferings of Jews in other countries.

It is at bottom quite irrational and will not yield to argument.

The persecutions in Germany have caused much concealment of anti-Semitic feeling and thus obscured the whole picture.

The subject needs serious investigation.

Only the last point is worth expanding. To study any subject scientifically one needs a detached attitude, which is obviously harder when one's own interests or emotions are involved. Plenty of people who are quite capable of being objective about sea urchins, say, or the square root of 2, become schizo-phrenic if they have to think about the sources of their own income. What vitiates nearly all that is written about anti-Semitism is the assumption in the writer's mind that *he himself* is immune to it. "Since I know that anti-Semitism is irrational," he argues, "it follows that I do not share it." He thus fails to start his investigation in the one place where he could get hold of some reliable evidence – that is, in his own mind.

It seems to me a safe assumption that the disease loosely called nationalism is now almost universal. Anti-Semitism is only one manifestation of nationalism, and not everyone will have the disease in that particular form. A Jew, for example, would not be anti-Semitic: but then many Zionist Jews seem to me to be merely anti-Semites turned upside-down, just as many Indians and Negroes display the normal colour preju-dices in an inverted form. The point is that something, some psychological vitamin, is lacking in modern civilization, and as a result we are all more or less subject to this lunacy of believing that whole races or nations are mysteriously good or mysteri-ously evil. I defy any modern intellectual to look closely and honestly into his own mind without coming upon nationalistic loyalties and hatreds of one kind or another. It is the fact that he can feel the emotional tug of such things, and yet see them dispassionately for what they are, that gives him his status as an intellectual. It will be seen, therefore, that the starting point for any investigation of anti-Semitism should not be, "Why does this obviously irrational belief appeal to other people?" but "Why does anti-Semitism appeal to *me*? What is there about it that I feel to be true?" If one asks this question one at least discovers one's own rationalizations, and it may be possible to find out what lies beneath them. Anti-Semitism should be investigated – I will not say by anti-Semites, but at any rate by people who know that they are not immune to that kind of emotion. When Hitler has disappeared a real inquiry into this subject will be possible, and it would probably be best to start not by debunking anti-Semitism, but by marshalling all the justifications for it that can be found, in one's own mind or anybody else's. In that way one might get some clues that would lead to its psychological roots. But that anti-Semitism will be definitively *cured*, without curing the larger disease of nationalism, I do not believe.

Poetry and the Microphone
Written Summer 1943?; *The New Saxon Pamphlet*, No. 3, March 1945

About a year ago I and a number of others were engaged in broadcasting literary programmes to India, and among other things we broadcast a good deal of verse by contemporary and near-contemporary English writers – for example, Eliot, Herbert Read, Auden, Spender, Dylan Thomas, Henry Treece, Alex Comfort, Robert Bridges, Edmund Blunden, D. H. Lawrence. Whenever it was possible we had poems broadcast by the people who wrote them. Just why these particular programmes (a small and remote outflanking movement in the radio war) were instituted there is no need to explain here, but I should add that the fact we were broadcasting to an Indian audience dictated our technique to some extent. The essential point was that our literary broadcasts were aimed at the Indian university students, a small and hostile audience, unapproachable by anything that could be described as British propaganda. It was known in advance that we could not hope for more than a few thousand listeners at the most, and this gave us an excuse to be more "highbrow" than is generally possible on the air.

If you are broadcasting poetry to people who know your language but don't share your cultural background, a certain amount of comment and explanation is unavoidable, and the formula we usually followed was to broadcast what purported to be a monthly literary magazine. The editorial staff were supposedly sitting in their office, discussing what to put into the next number. Somebody suggested one poem, someone else suggested another, there was a short discussion and then came the poem itself, read in a different voice, preferably the author's own. This poem naturally called up another, and so the programme continued, usually with at least half a minute of discussion between any two items. For a half-hour programme, six voices seemed to be the best number. A programme of this sort was necessarily somewhat shapeless, but it could be given a certain appearance of unity by making it revolve round a single central theme. For example, one number of our imaginary magazine was devoted to the subject of war. It included two poems by Edmund Blunden, Auden's *September, 1941*, extracts from a long poem by G. S. Fraser (*A Letter to Anne Ridler*), Byron's *Isles of Greece* and an extract from T. E. Lawrence's *Revolt in the Desert*. These half-dozen items, with the arguments that preceded and followed them, covered reasonably well the possible attitudes towards war. The poems and the prose extract took about twenty minutes to broadcast, the arguments about eight minutes.

This formula may seem slightly ridiculous and also rather patronising, but its advantage is that the element of mere instruction, the textbook motif, which is quite unavoidable if one is going to broadcast serious and sometimes "difficult" verse, becomes a lot less forbidding when it appears as an informal discussion. The various speakers can ostensibly say to one another what they are in reality saying to the audience. Also, by such an approach you at least give a poem a context, which is just what poetry lacks from the average man's point of view. But of course there are other methods. One which we frequently used was to set a poem in music. It is announced that in a few minutes' time such and such a poem will be broadcast; then the music plays for perhaps a minute, then fades out into the poem, which follows without any title or announcement, then the music is faded in again and plays up for another minute or two – the whole thing taking perhaps five minutes. It is necessary to choose appropriate music, but needless to say, the real purpose of the music is to insulate the poem from the rest of the programme. By this method you can have, say, a Shakespeare sonnet within three minutes of a news bulletin without, at any rate to my ear, any gross incongruity.

These programmes that I have been speaking of were of no great value in themselves, but I have mentioned them because of the ideas they aroused in myself and some others about the possibilities of the radio as a means of popularising poetry. I was early struck by the fact that the broadcasting of a poem by the person who wrote it does not merely produce an effect upon the audience, if any, but also on the poet himself. One must remember that extremely little in the way of broadcasting poetry has been done in England, and that many people who write verse have never even considered the idea of reading it aloud. By being set down at a microphone, especially if this happens at all regularly, the poet is brought into a new relationship with his work, not otherwise attainable in our time and country. It is a commonplace that in modern times – the last two hundred years, say – poetry has come to have less and less connection either with music or with the spoken word. It needs print in order to exist at all, and it is no more expected that a poet, as such, will know how to sing or even to declaim than it is expected that an architect will know how to plaster a ceiling. Lyrical and rhetorical poetry have almost ceased to be written, and a hostility towards poetry on the part of the common man has come to be taken for granted in any country where everyone can read. And where such a breach exists it is always inclined to widen, because the concept of poetry as primarily something printed, and something intelligible only to a minority, encourages obscurity and "cleverness." How many people do not feel quasi-instinctively that there must be something wrong with any poem whose meaning can be taken in at a single glance? It seems unlikely that these tendencies will be checked unless it again becomes normal to read verse aloud, and it is difficult to see how this can be brought about except by using the radio as a medium. But the special advantage of the radio, its power to select the right audience, and to do away with stage-fright and embarrassment, ought here to be noticed.

In broadcasting your audience is conjectural, but it is an audience of *one*. Millions may be listening, but each is listening alone, or as a member of a small group, and each has (or ought to have) the feeling that you are speaking to him individually. More than this it is reasonable to assume that your audience is sympathetic, or at least interested, for anyone who is bored can promptly switch you off by turning a knob. But though presumably sympathetic, the audience *has no power over you*. It is just here that a broadcast differs from a speech or a lecture. On the platform, as anyone used to public speaking knows, it is almost impossible not to take your tone from the audience. It is always obvious within a few minutes what they will respond to and what they will not, and in practice you are almost compelled to speak for the benefit of what you estimate as the stupidest person present, and also to ingratiate yourself by means of the ballyhoo known as "personality." If you don't do so, the result is always an atmosphere of frigid embarrassment. That grisly thing, a "poetry reading," is what it is because there will always be some among the audience who are bored or all-but frankly hostile and who can't remove themselves by the simple act of turning a knob. And it is at bottom the same difficulty – the fact that a theatre audience is not a selected one – that makes it impossible to get a decent performance of Shakespeare in England. On the air these conditions do not exist. The poet *feels* that he is addressing people to whom poetry means something, and it is a fact that poets who are used to broadcasting can read into the microphone with a virtuosity they would not equal if they had a visible audience in front of them. The element of make-believe that enters here does not greatly matter. The point is that in the only way now possible the poet has been brought into a situation in which reading verse aloud seems a natural unembarrassing thing, a normal exchange between man and man: also he has been led to think of his work as *sound* rather than as a pattern on paper. By that much the reconciliation between poetry and the common man is nearer. It already exists at the poet's end of the aether-waves, whatever may be happening at the other end.

However, what is happening at the other end cannot be disregarded. It will be seen that I have been speaking as though the whole subject of poetry were embarrassing, almost indecent, as though popularising poetry were essentially a strategic manoeuvre, like getting a dose of medicine down a child's throat or establishing tolerance for a persecuted sect. But unfortunately that or something like it is the case. There can be no doubt that in our civilisation poetry is by far the most discredited of the arts, the only art, indeed, in which the average man refuses to discern *any* value. Arnold Bennett was hardly exaggerating when he said that in the English-speaking countries the word "poetry" would disperse a crowd quicker than a fire hose. And as I have pointed out, a breach of this kind tends to widen simply because of its existence, the common man becoming more and more anti-poetry, the poet more and more arrogant and unintelligible, until the divorce between poetry and popular culture is accepted as a sort of law of nature, although in fact it belongs only to our own time and to a comparatively small area of the earth. We live in an age in which the average human being in the highly-civilised countries is aesthetically inferior to the lowest savage. This state of affairs is generally looked upon as being incurable by any *conscious* act, and on the other hand is expected to right itself of its own accord as soon as society takes a comelier shape. With slight variations the Marxist, the anarchist and the religious believer will all tell you this, and in broad terms it is undoubtedly true. The ugliness amid which we live has spiritual and economic causes and is not to be explained by the mere going-astray of tradition at some point or other. But it does not follow that no improvement is possible within our present framework, nor that an aesthetic improvement is not a necessary part of the general redemption of society. It is worth stopping to wonder, therefore, whether it would not be possible even now to rescue poetry from its special position as the most-hated of the arts and win for it at least the same degree of toleration as exists for music. But one has to start by asking, in what way and to what extent is poetry unpopular?

On the face of it, the unpopularity of poetry is as complete as it could be. But on second thoughts, this has to be qualified in a rather peculiar way. To begin with, there is still an appreciable amount of folk poetry (nursery rhymes, etc.) which is universally known and quoted and forms part of the background of everyone's mind. There is also a handful of ancient songs and ballads which have never gone out of favour. In addition there is the popularity, or at least the toleration, of "good bad" poetry, generally of a patriotic or sentimental kind. This might seem beside the point if it were not that "good bad" poetry has all the characteristics which, ostensibly, make the average man dislike true poetry. It is in verse, it rhymes, it deals in lofty sentiments and unusual language – all this to a very marked degree, for it is almost axiomatic that bad poetry is more "poetical" than good poetry. Yet if not actively liked it is at least tolerated. For example, just before writing this I have been listening to a couple of B.B.C. comedians doing their usual turn before the 9 o'clock news. In the last three minutes one of the two comedians suddenly announces that he "wants to be serious for a moment" and proceeds to recite a piece of patriotic balderdash entitled *A Fine Old English Gentleman*, in praise of His Majesty the King. Now, what is the reaction of the audience to the sudden lapse into the worst sort of rhyming heroics? It cannot be very violently negative, or there would be a sufficient volume of indignant letters to stop the B.B.C. doing this kind of thing. One must conclude that though the big public is hostile to *poetry*, it is not strongly hostile to *verse*. After all, if rhyme and metre were disliked for their own sakes, neither songs nor dirty limericks could be popular. Poetry is disliked because it is associated with unintelligibility, intellectual pretentiousness and a general feeling of Sunday-on-a-weekday. Its name creates in advance the same sort of bad impression as the word "God," or a parson's dog-collar. To a certain extent, popularising poetry is a question of breaking down an acquired inhibition. It is a question of getting people to listen instead of uttering a mechanical raspberry. If true poetry could be introduced to the big public in such a way as to make it seem *normal*, as that piece of rubbish I have just listened to presumably seemed normal, then part of the prejudice against it might be overcome.

It is difficult to believe that poetry can ever be popularised again without some deliberate effort at the education of public taste, involving strategy and perhaps even subterfuge. T. S. Eliot once suggested that poetry, particularly dramatic poetry, might be brought back into the consciousness of or-dinary people through the medium of the music hall; he might have added the pantomine, whose vast possibilities do not seem ever to have been completely explored. *Sweeney Agonistes* was perhaps written with some such idea in mind, and it would in fact be conceivable as a music-hall turn, or at least as a scene in a revue. I have suggested the radio as a more hopeful medium, and I have pointed out its technical advantages, particularly from the point of view of the poet. The reason why such a suggestion sounds hopeless at first hearing is that few people are able to imagine the radio being used for the dissemination of anything except tripe. People listen to the stuff that does actually dribble from the loudspeakers of the world, and con-clude that it is for that and nothing else that the wireless exists. Indeed the very word "wireless" calls up a picture either of roaring dictators or of genteel throaty voices announcing that three of our aircraft have failed to return. Poetry on the air sounds like the Muses in striped trousers. Nevertheless one ought not to confuse the capabilities of an instrument with the use it is actually put to. Broadcasting is what it is, not because there is something inherently vulgar, silly and dishonest about the whole apparatus of microphone and transmitter, but because all the broadcasting that now happens all over the world is under the control of governments or great monopoly companies which are actively interested in maintaining the status quo and therefore in preventing the common man from becoming too intelligent. Something of the same kind has happened to the cinema, which, like the radio, made its appearance during the monopoly stage of capitalism and is fantastically expensive to operate. In all the arts the tendency is similar. More and more the channels of production are under the control of bureaucrats, whose aim is to destroy the artist or at least to castrate him. This would be a bleak outlook if it were not that the totalitarianisation which is now going on, and must undoubtedly continue to go on, in every country of the world, is mitigated by another process which it was not easy to foresee even as short a time as five years ago.

This is, that the huge bureaucratic machines of which we are all part are beginning to work creakily because of their mere size and their constant growth. The tendency of the modern state is to wipe out the freedom of the intellect, and yet at the same time every state, especially under the pressure of war, finds itself more and more in need of an intelligentsia to do its publicity for it. The modern state needs, for example, pamphlet-writers, poster artists, illustrators, broadcasters, lecturers, film producers, actors, song-composers, even painters and sculptors, not to mention psychologists, sociologists, biochemists, mathematicians and what-not. The British Government started the present war with the more or less openly declared intention of keeping the literary intelligentsia out of it; yet after three years of war almost every writer, however undesirable his political history or opinions, has been sucked into the various Ministries or the B.B.C., and even those who enter the armed forces tend to find themselves after a while in Public Relations or some other essentially literary job. The Government has absorbed these people, unwillingly enough, because it found itself unable to get on without them. The ideal, from the official point of view, would have been to put all publicity into the hands of "safe" people like A. P. Herbert or Ian Hay: but since not enough of these were available, the existing intelligentsia had to be utilised, and the tone and even to some extent the content of official propaganda have been modified accordingly. No one acquainted with the Government pamphlets, A.B.C.A. lectures, documentary films and broadcasts to occupied countries which have been issued during the past two years imagines that our rulers would sponsor this kind of thing if they could help it. Only, the bigger the machine of government becomes, the more loose ends and forgotten corners there are in it. This is perhaps a small consolation, but it is not a despicable one. It means that in countries where there is already a strong liberal tradition, bureaucratic tyranny can perhaps never be complete. The striped-trousered ones will rule, but so long as they are forced to maintain an intelligentsia, the intelligentsia will have a certain amount of autonomy. If the Government needs, for example, documentary films, it must employ people specially interested in the technique of the film, and it must allow them the necessary minimum of freedom; consequently, films that are all wrong from the bureaucratic point of view will always have a tendency to appear. So also with painting, photography, script-writing, reportage, lecturing and all the other arts and half-arts of which a complex modern state has need.

The application of this to the radio is obvious. At present the loudspeaker is the enemy of the creative writer, but this may not necessarily remain true when the volume and scope of broadcasting increase. As things are, although the B.B.C. does keep up a feeble show of interest in contemporary literature, it is harder to capture five minutes on the air in which to broadcast a poem than twelve hours in which to disseminate lying propaganda, tinned music, stale jokes, faked "discussions" or what-have-you. But that state of affairs may alter in the way I have indicated, and when that time comes serious experiment in the broadcasting of verse, with complete disregard for the various hostile influences which prevent any such thing at present, would become possible. I don't claim it as certain that such an experiment would have very great results. The

864

radio was bureaucratised so early in its career that the relationship between broadcasting and literature has never been thought out. It is not certain that the microphone is the instrument by which poetry could be brought back to the common people and it is not even certain that poetry would gain by being more of a spoken and less of a written thing. But I do urge that these possibilities exist, and that those who care for literature might turn their minds more often to this much-despised medium, whose powers for good have perhaps been obscured by the voices of Professor Joad and Doctor Goebbels.

Notes on Nationalism
Polemic: A Magazine of Philosophy, Psychology & Aesthetics, No. 1
[October] 1945

Somewhere or other Byron makes use of the French word *longueur*, and remarks in passing that though in England we happen not to have the *word*, we have the *thing* in considerable profusion. In the same way, there is a habit of mind which is now so widespread that it affects our thinking on nearly every subject, but which has not yet been given a name. As the nearest existing equivalent I have chosen the word "nationalism," but it will be seen in a moment that I am not using it in quite the ordinary sense, if only because the emotion I am speaking about does not always attach itself to what is called a nation – that is, a single race or a geographical area. It can attach itself to a church or a class, or it may work in a merely negative sense, *against* something or other and without the need for any positive object of loyalty.

By "nationalism" I mean first of all the habit of assuming that human beings can be classified like insects and that whole blocks of millions or tens of millions of people can be confidently labelled "good" or "bad".[16] But secondly – and this is much more important – I mean the habit of identifying oneself with a single nation or other unit, placing it beyond good and evil and recognizing no other duty than that of advancing its interests. Nationalism is not to be confused with patriotism.

Both words are normally used in so vague a way that any definition is liable to be challenged, but one must draw a distinction between them, since two different and even opposing ideas are involved. By "patriotism" I mean devotion to a particular place and a particular way of life, which one believes to be the best in the world but has no wish to force upon other people. Patriotism is of its nature defensive, both militarily and culturally. Nationalism, on the other hand, is inseparable from the desire for power. The abiding purpose of every nationalist is to secure more power and more prestige, *not* for himself but for the nation or other unit in which he has chosen to sink his own individuality.

So long as it is applied merely to the more notorious and identifiable nationalist movements in Germany, Japan and other countries, all this is obvious enough. Confronted with a phenomenon like Nazism, which we can observe from the outside, nearly all of us would say much the same things about it. But here I must repeat what I said above, that I am only using the word "nationalism" for lack of a better. Nationalism, in the extended sense in which I am using the word, includes such movements and tendencies as Communism, political Catholicism, Zionism, anti-Semitism, Trotskyism and Pacifism. It does not necessarily mean loyalty to a government or a country, still less to *one's own* country, and it is not even strictly necessary that the units in which it deals should actually exist. To name a few obvious examples, Jewry, Islam, Christendom, the Proletariat and the White Race are all of them the objects of passionate nationalistic feeling: but their existence can be seriously questioned, and there is no definition of any one of them that would be universally accepted.

It is also worth emphasizing once again that nationalist feeling can be purely negative. There are, for example, Trotskyists who have become simply the enemies of the U.S.S.R. without developing a corresponding loyalty to any other unit. When one grasps the implications of this, the nature of what I mean by nationalism becomes a good deal clearer. A nationalist is one who thinks solely, or mainly, in terms of competitive prestige. He may be a positive or a negative nationalist – that is, he may use his mental energy either in boosting or in denigrating – but at any rate his thoughts always turn on victories, defeats, triumphs and humiliations. He sees history, especially contemporary history, as the endless rise and decline of great power units, and every event that happens seems to him a demonstration that his own side is on the up grade and some hated rival on the down grade. But finally, it is important not to confuse nationalism with mere worship of success. The nationalist does not go on the principle of simply ganging up with the strongest side. On the contrary, having picked his side, he persuades himself that it *is* the strongest, and is able to stick to his belief even when the facts are overwhelmingly against him. Nationalism is power-hunger tempered by self-deception. Every nationalist is capable of the most flagrant dishonesty, but he is also – since he is conscious of serving something bigger than himself – unshakeably certain of being in the right.

Now that I have given this lengthy definition, I think it will be admitted that the habit of mind I am talking about is widespread among the English intelligentsia, and more widespread there than among the mass of the people. For those who feel deeply about contemporary politics, certain topics have become so infected by considerations of prestige that a genuinely rational approach to them is almost impossible. Out of the hundreds of examples that one might choose, take this question: Which of the three great allies, the U.S.S.R., Britain and the U.S.A., has contributed most to the defeat of Germany? In theory it should be possible to give a reasoned and perhaps even a conclusive answer to this question. In practice, however, the necessary calculations cannot be made, because anyone likely to bother his head about such a question would inevitably see it in terms of competitive prestige. He would therefore *start* by deciding in favour of Russia, Britain or America as the case might be, and only *after* this would begin searching for arguments that seemed to support his case. And there are whole strings of kindred questions to which you can only get an honest answer from someone who is indifferent to the whole subject involved, and whose opinion on it is probably worthless in any case. Hence, partly, the remarkable failure in our time of political and military prediction. It is curious to reflect that out of all the "experts" of all the schools, there was not a single one who was able to foresee so likely an event as the Russo-German Pact of 1939.[17] And when the news of the Pact broke, the most wildly divergent explanations of it were given, and predictions were made which were falsified almost immediately, being based in nearly every case not on a study of probabilities but on a desire to make the U.S.S.R. seem good or bad, strong or weak. Political or military commentators, like astrologers, can survive almost any mistake, because their more devoted followers do not look to them for an appraisal of the facts but for the stimulation of nationalistic loyalties.[18] And æsthetic judgements, especially literary judgements, are often corrupted in the same way as political ones. It would be difficult for an Indian Nationalist to enjoy reading Kipling or for a Conservative to see merit in Mayakovsky, and there is always a temptation to claim that any book whose tendency one disagrees with must be a bad book from a *literary* point of view. People of strongly nationalistic outlook often perform this sleight of hand without being conscious of dishonesty.

In England, if one simply considers the number of people involved, it is probable that the dominant form of nationalism is old-fashioned British jingoism. It is certain that this is still widespread, and much more so that most observers would have believed a dozen years ago. However, in this essay I am concerned chiefly with the reactions of the intelligentsia, among whom jingoism and even patriotism of the old kind are almost dead, though they now seem to be reviving among a minority. Among the intelligentsia, it hardly needs saying that the dominant form of nationalism is Communism – using this word in a very loose sense, to include not merely Communist Party members but "fellow travellers" and Russophiles generally. A Communist, for my purpose here, is one who looks upon the U.S.S.R. as his Fatherland and feels it his duty to justify Russian policy and advance Russian interests at all costs. Obviously such people abound in England to-day, and their direct and indirect influence is very great. But many other forms of nationalism also flourish, and it is by noticing the points of resemblance between different and even seemingly opposed currents of thought that one can best get the matter into perspective.

Ten or twenty years ago, the form of nationalism most closely corresponding to Communism today was political Catholicism. Its most outstanding exponent – though he was perhaps an extreme case rather than a typical one – was G. K. Chesterton. Chesterton was a writer of considerable talent who chose to suppress both his sensibilities and his intellectual honesty in the cause of Roman Catholic propaganda. During the last twenty years or so of his life, his entire output was in reality an endless repetition of the same thing, under its laboured cleverness as simple and boring as "Great is Diana of the Ephesians." Every book that he wrote, every paragraph, every sentence, every incident in every story, every scrap of dialogue, had to demonstrate beyond possibility of mistake the superiority of the Catholic over the Protestant or the pagan. But Chesterton was not content to think of this superiority as merely intellectual or spiritual: it had to be translated into terms of national prestige and military power, which entailed an ignorant idealization of the Latin countries, especially France. Chesterton had not lived long in France, and his picture of it – as a land of Catholic peasants incessantly singing the *Marseillaise* over glasses of red wine – had about as much relation to reality as *Chu Chin Chow* has to every-day life in Baghdad. And with this went not only an enormous over-estimation of French military power (both before and after 1914–18 he maintained that France, by itself, was stronger than Germany), but a silly and vulgar glorification of the actual process of war. Chesterton's battle poems, such as *Lepanto* or *The Ballad of Saint Barbara*, make *The Charge of the Light Brigade* read like a pacifist tract: they are perhaps the most tawdry bits of bombast to be found in our language. The interesting thing is that had the romantic rubbish which he habitually wrote about France and the French army been written by somebody else about Britain and the British army, he would have been the first to jeer. In home politics he was a Little Englander, a true hater of jingoism and imperialism, and according to his lights a true friend of democracy. Yet when he looked outwards into the international field, he could forsake his principles without even noticing that he was doing so. Thus, his almost mystical belief in the virtues of democracy did not prevent him from admiring Mussolini. Mussolini had destroyed the representative government and the freedom of the press for which Chesterton had struggled so hard at home, but Mussolini was an Italian and had made Italy strong, and that settled the matter. Nor did

Chesterton ever find a word to say against imperialism and the conquest of coloured races when they were practised by Italians or Frenchmen. His hold on reality, his literary taste, and even to some extent his moral sense, were dislocated as soon as his nationalistic loyalties were involved.

Obviously there are considerable resemblances between political Catholicism as exemplified by Chesterton, and Communism. So there are between either of these and, for instance, Scottish Nationalism, Zionism, anti-Semitism or Trotskyism. It would be an over-simplification to say that all forms of nationalism are the same, even in their mental atmosphere, but there are certain rules that hold good in all cases. The following are the principal characteristics of nationalist thought: –

OBSESSION. As nearly as possible, no nationalist ever thinks, talks or writes about anything except the superiority of his own power unit. It is difficult if not impossible for any nationalist to conceal his allegiance. The smallest slur upon his own unit, or any implied praise of a rival organization, fills him with uneasiness which he can only relieve by making some sharp retort. If the chosen unit is an actual country, such as Ireland or India, he will generally claim superiority for it not only in military power and political virtue, but in art, literature, sport, the structure of the language, the physical beauty of the inhabitants, and perhaps even in climate, scenery and cooking. He will show great sensitiveness about such things as the correct display of flags, relative size of headlines and the order in which different countries are named.[19] Nomenclature plays a very important part in nationalist thought. Countries which have won their independence or gone through a nationalist revolution usually change their names, and any country or other unit round which strong feelings revolve is likely to have several names, each of them carrying a different implication. The two sides in the Spanish civil war had between them nine or ten names expressing different degrees of love and hatred. Some of these names (*e.g.* "Patriots" for Franco-supporters, or "Loyalists" for Government-supporters) were frankly question-begging, and there was no single one of them which the two rival factions could have agreed to use. All nationalists consider it a duty to spread their own language to the detriment of rival languages, and among English-speakers this struggle reappears in subtler form as a struggle between dialects. Anglophobe Americans will refuse to use a slang phrase if they know it to be of British origin, and the conflict between Latinizers and Germanizers often has nationalist motives behind it. Scottish nationalists insist on the superiority of Lowland Scots, and Socialists whose nationalism takes the form of class hatred tirade against the B.B.C. accent and even the broad A. One could multiply instances. Nationalist thought often gives the impression of being tinged by belief in sympathetic magic – a belief which probably comes out in the widespread custom of burning political enemies in effigy, or using pictures of them as targets in shooting galleries.

INSTABILITY. The intensity with which they are held does not prevent nationalist loyalties from being transferable. To begin with, as I have pointed out already, they can be and often are fastened upon some foreign country. One quite commonly finds that great national leaders, or the founders of nationalist movements, do not even belong to the country they have glorified. Sometimes they are outright foreigners, or more often they come from peripheral areas where nationality is doubtful. Examples are Stalin, Hitler, Napoleon, de Valera, Disraeli, Poincaré, Beaverbrook. The Pan-German movement was in part the creation of an Englishman, Houston Chamberlain. For the past fifty or a hundred years, transferred nationalism has been a common phenomenon among literary intellectuals. With Lafcadio Hearne the transference was to Japan, with Carlyle and many others of his time to Germany, and in our own age it is usually Russia. But the peculiarly interesting fact is that re-transference is also possible. A country or other unit which has been worshipped for years may suddenly become detestable, and some other object of affection may take its place with almost no interval. In the first version of H. G. Wells's *Outline of History*, and others of his writings about that time, one finds the United States praised almost as extravagantly as Russia is praised by Communists today: yet within a few years this uncritical admiration had turned into hostility. The bigoted Communist who changes in a space of weeks, or even days, into an equally bigoted Trotskyist is a common spectacle. In continental Europe Fascist movements were largely recruited from among Communists, and the opposite process may well happen within the next few years. What remains constant in the nationalist is his own state of mind: the object of his feelings is changeable, and may be imaginary.

But for an intellectual, transference has an important function which I have already mentioned shortly in connection with Chesterton. It makes it possible for him to be much *more* nationalistic – more vulgar, more silly, more malignant, more dishonest – than he could ever be on behalf of his native country, or any unit of which he had real knowledge. When one sees the slavish or boastful rubbish that is written about Stalin, the Red Army, etc. by fairly intelligent and sensitive people, one realizes that this is only possible because some kind of dislocation has taken place. In societies such as ours, it is unusual for anyone describable as an intellectual to feel a very deep attachment to his own country. Public opinion – that is, the section of public opinion of which he as an intellectual is aware – will not allow him to do so. Most of the people surrounding him are sceptical and disaffected, and he may adopt the same attitude from imitativeness or sheer cowardice: in that case he will have abandoned the form of nationalism that lies nearest to hand without getting any closer to a genuinely internationalist outlook. He still feels the need for a Fatherland, and it is natural to look for one somewhere abroad. Having found it, he can wallow unrestrainedly in exactly those emotions from which he believes that he has emancipated himself. God, the King, the Empire, the Union Jack – all the overthrown idols can reappear under different names, and because they are not recognized for what they are they can be worshipped with a good conscience. Transferred nationalism, like the use of scapegoats, is a way of attaining salvation without altering one's conduct.

INDIFFERENCE TO REALITY. All nationalists have the power of not seeing resemblances between similar sets of facts. A British Tory will defend self-determination in Europe and oppose it in India with no feeling of inconsistency. Actions are held to be good or bad, not on their own merits but according to who does them, and there is almost no kind of outrage – torture, the use of hostages, forced labour, mass deportations, imprisonment without trial, forgery, assassination, the bombing of civilians – which does not change its moral colour when it is committed by "our" side. The Liberal *News Chronicle* published, as an example of shocking barbarity, photographs of Russians hanged by the Germans, and then a year or two later published with warm approval almost exactly similar photographs of Germans hanged by the Russians.[20] It is the same with historical events. History is thought of largely in nationalist terms, and such things as the Inquisition, the tortures of the Star Chamber, the exploits of the English buccaneers (Sir Francis Drake, for instance, who was given to sinking Spanish prisoners alive), the Reign of Terror, the heroes of the Mutiny blowing hundreds of Indians from the guns, or Cromwell's soldiers slashing Irishwomen's faces with razors, become morally neutral or even meritorious when it is felt that they were done in "the right" cause. If one looks back over the past quarter of a century, one finds that there was hardly a single year when atrocity stories were not being reported from some part of the world: and yet in not one single case were these atrocities – in Spain, Russia, China, Hungary, Mexico, Amritsar, Smyrna – believed in and disapproved of by the English intelligentsia as a whole. Whether such deeds were reprehensible, or even whether they happened, was always decided according to political predilection.

The nationalist not only does not disapprove of atrocities committed by his own side, but has a remarkable capacity for not even hearing about them. For quite six years the English admirers of Hitler contrived not to learn of the existence of Dachau and Buchenwald. And those who are loudest in denouncing the German concentration camps are often quite unaware, or only very dimly aware, that there are also concentration camps in Russia. Huge events like the Ukraine famine of 1933, involving the deaths of millions of people, have actually escaped the attention of the majority of English Russophiles. Many English people have heard almost nothing about the extermination of German and Polish Jews during the present war. Their own anti-Semitism has caused this vast crime to bounce off their consciousness. In nationalist thought there are facts which are both true and untrue, known and unknown. A known fact may be so unbearable that it is habitually pushed aside and not allowed to enter into logical processes, or on the other hand it may enter into every calculation and yet never be admitted as a fact, even in one's own mind.

Every nationalist is haunted by the belief that the past can be altered. He spends part of his time in a fantasy world in which things happen as they should – in which, for example, the Spanish Armada was a success or the Russian Revolution was crushed in 1918 – and he will transfer fragments of this world to the history books whenever possible. Much of the propagandist writing of our time amounts to plain forgery. Material facts are suppressed, dates altered, quotations removed from their context and doctored so as to change their meaning. Events which, it is felt, ought not to have happened are left unmentioned and ultimately denied.[21] In 1927 Chiang Kai-Shek boiled hundreds of Communists alive, and yet within ten years he had become one of the heroes of the Left. The realignment of world politics had brought him into the anti-Fascist camp, and so it was felt that the boiling of the Communists "didn't count", or perhaps had not happened. The primary aim of propaganda is, of course, to influence contemporary opinion, but those who rewrite history do probably believe with part of their minds that they are actually thrusting facts into the past. When one considers the elaborate forgeries that have been committed in order to show that Trotsky did not play a valuable part in the Russian civil war, it is difficult to feel that the people responsible are merely lying. More probably they feel that their own version *was* what happened in the sight of God, and that one is justified in rearranging the records accordingly.

Indifference to objective truth is encouraged by the sealing-off of one part of the world from another, which makes it harder and harder to discover what is actually happening. There can often be a genuine doubt about the most enormous events. For example, it is impossible to calculate within millions, perhaps even tens of millions, the number of deaths caused by the present war. The calamities that are constantly being reported – battles, massacres, famines, revolutions – tend to inspire in the average person a feeling of unreality. One has no way of verifying the facts, one is not even fully certain that they have happened, and one is always presented with totally different interpretations from different sources. What were the rights and wrongs of the Warsaw rising of August 1944? Is it true about the German gas ovens in Poland? Who was really to blame for the Bengal famine? Probably the truth is discoverable, but the facts will be so dishonestly set forth in almost any newspaper that the ordinary reader can be forgiven either for swallowing lies or for failing to form an opinion. The general uncertainty as to what is really happening makes it easier to cling to lunatic beliefs. Since nothing is ever quite proved or disproved, the most unmistakeable fact can be impudently denied. Moreover, although endlessly brooding on power, victory, defeat, revenge, the nationalist is often somewhat uninterested in what happens in the real world. What he wants is to *feel* that his own unit is getting the better of some other unit, and he can more easily do this by scoring off an adversary than by examining the facts to see whether they support him. All nationalist controversy is at the debating-society level. It is always entirely inconclusive, since each contestant invariably believes himself to have won the victory. Some nationalists are not far from schizophrenia, living quite happily amid dreams of power and conquest which have no connection with the physical world.

I have examined as best I can the mental habits which are common to all forms of nationalism. The next thing is to classify those forms, but obviously this cannot be done comprehensively. Nationalism is an enormous subject. The world is tormented by innumerable delusions and hatreds which cut across one another in an extremely complex way, and some of the most sinister of them have not yet even impinged on the European consciousness. In this essay I am concerned with nationalism as it occurs among the English intelligentsia. In them, much more often than in ordinary English people, it is unmixed with patriotism and can therefore be studied pure. Below are listed the varieties of nationalism now flourishing among English intellectuals, with such comments as seem to be needed. It is convenient to use three headings, Positive, Transferred and Negative, though some varieties will fit into more than one category: –

POSITIVE NATIONALISM

(i.) NEO-TORYISM. Exemplified by such people as Lord Elton, A. P. Herbert, G. M. Young, Professor Pickthorne, by the literature of the Tory Reform Committee, and by such magazines as the *New English Review* and the *Nineteenth Century and After*. The real motive force of Neo-Toryism, giving it its nationalistic character and differentiating it from ordinary Conservatism, is the desire not to recognize that British power and influence have declined. Even those who are realistic enough to see that Britain's military position is not what it was, tend to claim that "English ideas" (usually left undefined) must dominate the world. All Neo-Tories are anti-Russian, but sometimes the main emphasis is anti-American. The significant thing is that this school of thought seems to be gaining ground among youngish intellectuals, sometimes ex-Communists, who have passed through the usual process of disillusionment and become disillusioned with that. The Anglophobe who suddenly becomes violently pro-British is a fairly common figure. Writers who illustrate this tendency are F. A. Voigt, Malcolm Muggeridge, Evelyn Waugh, Hugh Kingsmill, and a psychologically similar development can be observed in T. S. Eliot, Wyndham Lewis and various of their followers.

(ii.) CELTIC NATIONALISM. Welsh, Irish and Scottish nationalism have points of difference but are alike in their anti-English orientation. Members of all three movements have opposed the war while continuing to describe themselves as pro-Russian, and the lunatic fringe has even contrived to be simultaneously pro-Russian and pro-Nazi. But Celtic nationalism is not the same thing as Anglophobia. Its motive force is a belief in the past and future greatness of the Celtic peoples, and it has a strong tinge of racialism. The Celt is supposed to be spiritually superior to the Saxon – simpler, more creative, less vulgar, less snobbish, etc. – but the usual power-hunger is there under the surface. One symptom of it is the delusion that Eire, Scotland or even Wales could preserve its independence unaided and owes nothing to British protection. Among writers, good examples of this school of thought are Hugh MacDiarmid and Sean O'Casey. No modern Irish writer, even of the stature of Yeats or Joyce, is completely free from traces of nationalism.

(iii.) ZIONISM. This has the usual characteristics of a nation-alist movement, but the American variant of it seems to be more violent and malignant than the British. I classify it under Direct and not Transferred nationalism because it flourishes almost exclusively among the Jews themselves. In England, for several rather incongruous reasons, the intelligentsia are mostly pro-Jew on the Palestine issue, but they do not feel strongly about it. All English people of good will are also pro-Jew in the sense of disapproving of Nazi persecution. But any actual nationalistic loyalty, or belief in the innate superiority of Jews, is hardly to be found among Gentiles.

TRANSFERRED NATIONALISM

(i.) COMMUNISM.

(ii.) POLITICAL CATHOLICISM.

(iii.) COLOUR FEELING. The old-style contemptuous atti-tude towards "natives" has been much weakened in England, and various pseudo-scientific theories emphasizing the super-iority of the white race have been abandoned.[22] Among the intelligentsia, colour feeling only occurs in the transposed form, that is, as a belief in the innate superiority of the coloured races. This is now increasingly common among English intellectuals, probably resulting more often from masochism and sexual frustration than from contact with the Oriental and Negro nationalist movements. Even among those who do not feel strongly on the colour question, snobbery and imitation have a powerful influence. Almost any English intellectual would be scandalized by the claim that the white races are superior to the coloured, whereas the opposite claim would seem to him unexceptional even if he disagreed with it. Nationalistic attach-ment to the coloured races is usually mixed up with the belief that their sex lives are superior, and there is a large underground mythology about the sexual prowess of Negroes.

(iv.) CLASS FEELING. Among upper-class and middle-class intellectuals, only in the transposed form – i.e. as a belief in the superiority of the proletariat. Here again, inside the intelli-gentsia, the pressure of public opinion is overwhelming. Nationalistic loyalty towards the proletariat, and most vicious theoretical hatred of the bourgeoisie, can and often do co-exist with ordinary snobbishness in every-day life.

(v.) PACIFISM. The majority of pacifists either belong to obscure religious sects or are simply humanitarians who object to taking life and prefer not to follow their thoughts beyond that point. But there is a minority of intellectual pacifists whose real though unadmitted motive appears to be hatred of western democracy and admiration for totalitarianism. Pacifist propaganda usually boils down to saying that one side is as bad as the other, but if one looks closely at the writings of the younger intellectual pacifists, one finds that they do not by any means express impartial disapproval but are directed almost entirely against Britain and the United States. Moreover they do not as a rule condemn violence as such, but only violence used in defence of the western countries. The Russians, unlike the British, are not blamed for defending themselves by warlike means, and indeed all pacifist propaganda of this type avoids mention of Russia or China. It is not claimed, again, that the Indians should abjure violence in their struggle against the British. Pacifist literature abounds with equivocal remarks which, if they mean anything, appear to mean that statesmen of the type of Hitler are preferable to those of the type of Churchill, and that violence is perhaps excusable if it is violent enough. After the fall of France, the French pacifists, faced by a real choice which their English colleagues have not had to make, mostly went over to the Nazis, and in England there appears to have been some small overlap of membership between the Peace Pledge Union and the Blackshirts. Pacifist writers have written in praise of Carlyle, one of the intellectual fathers of Fascism. All in all it is difficult not to feel that pacifism, as it appears among a section of the intelligentsia, is secretly inspired by an admiration for power and successful cruelty. The mistake was made of pinning this emotion to Hitler, but it could easily be retransferred.

NEGATIVE NATIONALISM

(i.) ANGLOPHOBIA. Within the intelligentsia, a derisive and mildly hostile attitude towards Britain is more or less compulsory, but it is an unfaked emotion in many cases. During the war it was manifested in the defeatism of the intelligentsia, which persisted long after it had become clear that the Axis powers could not win. Many people were undisguisedly pleased when Singapore fell or when the British were driven out of Greece, and there was a remarkable unwillingness to believe in good news, *e.g.* el Alamein, or the number of German planes shot down in the Battle of Britain. English left-wing intellectuals did not, of course, actually want the Germans or Japanese to win the war, but many of them could not help getting a certain kick out of seeing their own country humiliated, and wanted to feel that the final victory would be due to Russia, or perhaps America, and not to Britain. In foreign politics many intellectuals follow the principle that any faction backed by Britain must be in the wrong. As a result, "enlightened" opinion is quite largely a mirror-image of Conservative policy. Anglophobia is always liable to reversal, hence that fairly common spectacle, the pacifist of one war who is a bellicist in the next.

(ii.) ANTI-SEMITISM. There is little evidence about this at present, because the Nazi persecutions have made it necessary for any thinking person to side with the Jews against their oppressors. Anyone educated enough to have heard the word "anti-Semitism" claims as a matter of course to be free of it, and anti-Jewish remarks are carefully eliminated from all classes of literature. Actually anti-Semitism appears to be widespread, even among intellectuals, and the general conspiracy of silence probably helps to exacerbate it. People of Left opinions are not immune to it, and their attitude is sometimes affected by the fact that Trotskyists and Anarchists tend to be Jews. But anti-Semitism comes more naturally to people of Conservative tendency, who suspect the Jews of weakening national morale and diluting the national culture. Neo-Tories and political Catholics are always liable to succumb to anti-Semitism, at least intermittently.

(iii.) TROTSKYISM. This word is used so loosely as to include Anarchists, democratic Socialists and even Liberals. I use it here to mean a doctrinaire Marxist whose main motive is hostility to the Stalin regime. Trotskyism can be better studied in obscure pamphlets or in papers like the *Socialist Appeal* than in the works of Trotsky himself, who was by no means a man of one idea. Although in some places, for instance in the United States, Trotskyism is able to attract a fairly large number of adherents and develop into an organized movement with a petty fuehrer of its own, its inspiration is essentially negative. The Trotskyist is *against* Stalin just as the Communist is *for* him, and, like the majority of Communists, he wants not so much to alter the external world as to feel that the battle for prestige is going in his own favour. In each case there is the same obsessive fixation on a single subject, the same inability to form a genuinely rational opinion based on probabilities. The fact that Trotskyists are everywhere a persecuted minority, and that the accusation usually made against them, *i.e.* of collaborating with the Fascists, is obviously false, creates an impression that Trotskyism is intellectually and morally superior to Communism; but it is doubtful whether there is much difference. The most typical Trotskyists, in any case, are ex-Communists, and no one arrives at Trotskyism except *via* one of the left-wing movements. No Communist, unless tethered to his party by years of habit, is secure against a sudden lapse into Trotskyism. The opposite process does not seem to happen equally often, though there is no clear reason why it should not.

In the classification I have attempted above, it will seem that I have often exaggerated, oversimplified, made unwarranted assumptions and left out of account the existence of ordinarily decent motives. This was inevitable, because in this essay I am trying to isolate and identify tendencies which exist in all our minds and pervert our thinking, without necessarily occurring in a pure state or operating continuously. It is important at this point to correct the oversimplified picture which I have been obliged to make. To begin with, one has no right to assume that *everyone*, or even every intellectual, is infected by nationalism; secondly, nationalism can be intermittent and limited. An intelligent man may half-succumb to a belief which attracts him but which he knows to be absurd, and he may keep it out of his mind for long periods, only reverting to it in moments of anger or sentimentality, or when he is certain that no important issue is involved. Thirdly, a nationalistic creed may be adopted in good faith from non-nationalist motives. Fourthly, several kinds of nationalism, even kinds that cancel out, can co-exist in the same person.

All the way through I have said "the nationalist does this" or "the nationalist does that", using for purposes of illustration the extreme, barely sane type of nationalist who has no neutral areas in his mind and no interest in anything except the struggle for power. Actually such people are fairly common, but they are not worth powder and shot. In real life Lord Elton, D. N. Pritt, Lady Houston, Ezra Pound, Lord Vansittart, Father Coughlin and all the rest of their dreary tribe have to be fought against, but their intellectual deficiencies hardly need pointing out. Monomania is not interesting, and the fact that no nationalist of the more bigoted kind can write a book which still seems worth reading after a lapse of years has a certain deodorizing effect. But when one has admitted that nationalism has not triumphed everywhere, that there are still people whose judgements are not at the mercy of their desires, the fact does remain that the nationalistic habit of thought is widespread, so much so that various large and pressing problems – India, Poland, Palestine, the Spanish civil war, the Moscow trials, the American Negroes, the Russo-German pact or what-have-you – cannot be, or at least never are, discussed upon a reasonable level. The Eltons and Pritts and Coughlins, each of them simply an enormous mouth bellowing the same lie over and over again, are obviously extreme cases, but we deceive ourselves if we do not realize that we can all resemble them in unguarded moments. Let a certain note be struck, let this or that corn be trodden on – and it may be a corn whose very existence has been unsuspected hitherto – and the most fair-minded and sweet-tempered person may suddenly be transformed into a vicious partisan, anxious only to "score" over his adversary and indifferent as to how many lies he tells or how many logical errors he commits in doing so. When Lloyd George, who was an opponent of the Boer War, announced in the House of Commons that the British communiqués, if one added them together, claimed the killing of more Boers than the whole Boer nation contained, it is recorded that Arthur Balfour rose to his feet and shouted "Cad!" Very few people are proof against lapses of this type. The Negro snubbed by a white woman, the Englishman who hears England ignorantly criticized by an American, the Catholic apologist reminded of the Spanish Armada, will all react in much the same way. One prod to the nerve of nationalism, and the intellectual decencies can vanish, the past can be altered, and the plainest facts can be denied.

If one harbours anywhere in one's mind a nationalistic loyalty or hatred, certain facts, although in a sense known to be true, are inadmissible. Here are just a few examples. I list below five types of nationalist, and against each I append a fact which it is impossible for that type of nationalist to accept, even in his secret thoughts: –

BRITISH TORY. Britain will come out of this war with reduced power and prestige.

COMMUNIST. If she had not been aided by Britain and America, Russia would have been defeated by Germany.

IRISH NATIONALIST. Eire can only remain independent because of British protection.

TROTSKYIST. The Stalin regime is accepted by the Russian masses.

PACIFIST. Those who "abjure" violence can only do so because others are committing violence on their behalf.

All of these facts are grossly obvious if one's emotions do not happen to be involved: but to the kind of person named in each case they are also *intolerable*, and so they have to be denied, and false theories constructed upon their denial. I come back to the astonishing failure of military prediction in the present war. It is, I think, true to say that the intelligentsia have been more wrong about the progress of the war than the common people, and that they were wrong precisely because they were more swayed by partisan feelings. The average intellectual of the Left believed, for instance, that the war was lost in 1940, that the Germans were bound to overrun Egypt in 1942, that the Japanese would never be driven out of the lands they had conquered, and that the Anglo-American bombing offensive was making no impression on Germany. He could believe these things because his hatred of the British ruling class forbade him to admit that British plans could succeed. There is no limit to the follies that can be swallowed if one is under the influence of feelings of this kind. I have heard it confidently stated, for instance, that the American troops had been brought to Europe not to fight the Germans but to crush an English revolution. One has to belong to the intelligentsia to believe things like that: no ordinary man could be such a fool. When Hitler invaded Russia, the officials of the M.O.I. issued "as background" a warning that Russia might be expected to collapse in six weeks. On the other hand the Communists regarded every phase of the war as a Russian victory, even when the Russians were driven back almost to the Caspian sea and had lost several million prisoners. There is no need to multiply instances. The point is that as soon as fear, hatred, jealousy and power-worship are involved, the sense of reality becomes unhinged. And, as I have pointed out already, the sense of right and wrong becomes unhinged also. There is no crime, absolutely none, that cannot be condoned when "our" side commits it. Even if one does not deny that the crime has happened, even if one knows that it is exactly the same crime as one has condemned in some other case, even if one admits in an intellectual sense that it is unjustified – still one cannot *feel* that it is wrong. Loyalty is involved, and so pity ceases to function.

The reason for the rise and spread of nationalism is far too big a question to be raised here. It is enough to say that, in the forms in which it appears among English intellectuals, it is a distorted reflection of the frightful battles actually happening in the external world, and that its worst follies have been made possible by the break-down of patriotism and religious belief. If one follows up this train of thought, one is in danger of being led into a species of Conservatism, or into political quietism. It can be plausibly argued, for instance – it is even probably true – that patriotism is an inoculation against nationalism, that monarchy is a guard against dictatorship, and that organized religion is a guard against superstition. Or again it can be argued that *no* unbiased outlook is possible, that *all* creeds and causes involve the same lies, follies and barbarities; and this is often advanced as a reason for keeping out of politics altogether. I do not accept this argument, if only because in the modern world no one describable as an intellectual *can* keep out of politics in the sense of not caring about them. I think one must engage in politics – using the word in a wide sense – and that one must have preferences: that is, one must recognize that some causes are objectively better than others, even if they are advanced by equally bad means. As for the nationalistic loves and hatreds that I have spoken of, they are part of the make-up of most of us, whether we like it or not. Whether it is possible to get rid of them I do not know, but I do believe that it is possible to struggle against them, and that this is essentially a *moral* effort. It is a question first of all of discovering

883

what one really is, what one's own feelings really are, and then of making allowance for the inevitable bias. If you hate and fear Russia, if you are jealous of the wealth and power of America, if you despise Jews, if you have a sentiment of inferiority towards the British ruling class, you cannot get rid of those feelings simply by taking thought. But you can at least recognize that you have them, and prevent them from contaminating your mental processes. The emotional urges which are inescapable, and are perhaps even necessary to political action, should be able to exist side by side with an acceptance of reality. But this, I repeat, needs a *moral* effort, and contemporary English literature, so far as it is alive at all to the major issues of our time, shows how few of us are prepared to make it.

Personal Notes on Scientifiction

Leader Magazine, 21 July 1945

Recently a friend in America sent me a batch of ten-cent illustrated papers of the kind which are known generically as "comics" and consist entirely of coloured strip cartoons. Although bearing such titles as *Marvel Comics* or *Famous Funnies*, they are, in fact, mainly given over to "scientifiction" – that is, steel robots, invisible men, prehistoric monsters, death rays, invasions from Mars, and such-like.

Seen in the mass these things are very disquieting. Quite obviously they tend to stimulate fantasies of power, and in the last resort their subject matter boils down to magic and sadism. You can hardly look at a page without seeing somebody flying through the air (a surprising number of the characters are able to fly), or somebody socking somebody else on the jaw, or an under-clad young woman fighting for her honour – and her ravisher is just as likely to be a steel robot or a fifty-foot dinosaur as a human being. The whole thing is just a riot of nonsensical sensationalism, with none of the genuine scientific interest of the H.G. Wells stories from which this class of fiction originally sprang.

Who reads these papers is uncertain. Evidently they are intended primarily for children, but the advertisements and the ever-present sex appeal suggest that they are read by adults as well.

What is strange, when one looks at this poisonous rubbish, is to remember that several generations of English children were brought up largely on American children's books, because on the whole those were the best. At the top of the list came *Uncle Tom's Cabin*, *Uncle Remus*, and *Tom Sawyer* and *Huckleberry Finn*: then, more in the nature of girls' books, there were Louisa M. Alcott's *Little Women*, *Good Wives* and *Little Men* (the last-named one was a bit *too* high-minded, however), and James Habberton's *Helen's Babies*: and also – these were definitely girls' books, but still not to be despised – *Rebecca of Sunnybrook Farm* and Susan Coolidge's "Katy" books. Later in time there were Booth Tarkington's "Penrod" stories, Ernest Thompson Seton's *Wild Animals I Have Known* and other similar books, and Jack London's *White Fang* and *Call of the Wild*: not to mention the Buffalo Bill stories and the Buster Brown comic supplements.

From these and kindred sources the English child acquired quite a detailed picture of the American scene. He knew a lot about woodchucks, gophers, chipmunks, raccoon hunting, buggy riding, keeping the woodpile full, prairie dogs, whip-poor-wills, coyotes, covered wagons and the mortgage on the old homestead. The peculiarity of the American books, and especially those written prior to about 1880, was their whole-some, high-spirited atmosphere, and the decent simple civil-isation that they implied. The basis of nearly all of them was home life and the Bible. And though a book like *Little Women* may now seem over-civilised as well as faintly ridiculous, it is still a pleasant patch for one's memory to linger on.

It is queer that, after so short an interval of time, the typical juvenile literature of America should be stuff that many English parents would actually hesitate to put into a child's hands.

Everyone has at least one story about the imbecilities of war-time censorship. My own favourite instance is a War Office pamphlet which I happen to possess, entitled *German Infantry Weapons* and giving a short account of the rifles, machine guns, etc. in use in the German army. It is marked on the cover: "Not to fall into enemy hands."

Now that the war, or at least a good part of it, is over, would it not be possible to let up on some of the sillier kinds of restrictions – for example, censorship of letters passing between allied countries? Letters from the United States usually reach me plastered with censor's stamps, and I know from the time they take to get there my outgoing letters are suffering the same fate.

Throughout the war I have been writing periodical articles for American magazines. All of them, of course, have been opened en route, and not only have a number been tampered with in the most pettifogging way, but in some cases the censors have actually cut passages without letting the recipient know that any deletion has been made.

War is war, and I do not mind this kind of thing very much, but I do mind the delay which trans-Atlantic censorship is still causing. Quite recently, airmail letters from London to New York were liable to take as much as six weeks. They could do the journey quicker than that in a sailing ship.

Another peacetime pleasure I am looking forward to is being able to buy decent maps again. The panic legislation of 1940 forbade the selling of maps larger in scale than one inch to the mile, and at that time even Home Guards trying to buy maps of their own areas had every kind of difficulty put in their way. Possibly the ban has now been lifted, but maps on even the smallest scale are still difficult to get. I wonder when it will again be possible to walk into a stationer's shop and buy the excellent 25 inch to the mile Ordnance maps, which show every cowshed and almost every tree and on which you can easily mark down a good blackberry bush or a root of sweetbriar with sufficient accuracy to be sure of finding it again the following year?

However, one cannot leave the subject of censorship without remarking that, in England, official censorship is not the only or the worst kind. It is wonderful what a number of good stories fail to get into the newspapers, *not* because of any official ban, but because they happen to conflict with the orthodoxy of the moment and there is consequently an all-round tacit agreement that it "wouldn't do" to print them.

For example, I am told that the last speech made to his ministers by Mr. Arciszewsky, the premier of the outgoing London Polish Government, began:

"In the words of a man whom we once trusted, I have nothing to offer you except blood, toil, tears and sweat . . . " but I believe none of the papers had the guts to mention it.

As I passed the church door I paused for a moment to listen to the hymn that was being sung inside. The words that floated out to me – not the words as they would have appeared on paper, but as they were actually pronounced and as I transliterated them a few minutes later – were something like this:

> *Er*bide with me farce – falls the *ye*ventide –
> *Ther* darkness deeperns – Lord with me erbide –
> When *nuther* helpers – fail ern comforts flee –
> Help *pov* the helpless *so er* – bide with me!

And it struck me, not for the first time, that something really ought to be done about modern South-English pronunciation. It is a good general rule that one accent is not intrinsically better or worse than another, but something is clearly wrong when people's manner of speaking leads to misunderstanding, or when the sounds they make cannot be rendered by the existing methods of spelling.

Most of us now speak in so slovenly a way that if you ask for a threepenny bus ticket you are as often as not given a three-halfpenny one, or vice versa. And how exactly would one write down the mystic formula which any two Londoners invariably utter after concluding a transaction? The nearest you could come to it would be "nkew," or perhaps simply "N.Q." Or take the current pronunciation of such words as "passionate," "deliberate," "vegetable," "actual" or "average." The closest possible renderings would, I should say, be: "pashnit," "delibrit," "vejtbl," "ackchl," "avridge."

In countless words ending in -ion, -ate, -ial and so forth, the vowel sounds have simply slipped out and been replaced by sounds for which there is no equivalent in our alphabet. What is the final vowel sound in "elephant," for instance? There just isn't one, the current pronunciation of the word being something like "elefnt": or at any rate it is certainly nearer to "ele*phunt*" than "elephant."

All of which suggests that if we are ever to have that rational spelling about which there is talk and controversy from time to time, more will be involved than a good system of phonetics and foolproof rules. The Oxford dictionary can give you an accurate phonetic rendering of a word like "culture," but it still spells it as though there were a "t" in it and ignores the fact that the current pronunciation is "culcher."

The spelling reformers will have to make up their minds whether to reform our pronunciation as well, or whether to accept spoken English as past praying for and adjust the written language accordingly.

The Freedom of the Press (*Animal Farm*)
London, 17 August 1945; New York, 26 August 1946

This book was first thought of, so far as the central idea goes, in 1937, but was not written down until about the end of 1943. By the time when it came to be written it was obvious that there would be great difficulty in getting it published (in spite of the present book shortage which ensures that anything describable as a book will 'sell'), and in the event it was refused by four publishers. Only one of these had any ideological motive. Two had been publishing anti-Russian books for years, and the other had no noticeable political colour. One publisher actually started by accepting the book, but after making the preliminary arrangements he decided to consult the Ministry of Information, who appear to have warned him, or at any rate strongly advised him, against publishing it. Here is an extract from his letter:

> I mentioned the reaction I had had from an important official in the Ministry of Information with regard to *Animal Farm*. I must confess that this expression of opinion has given me seriously to think. . . . I can see now that it might be regarded as something which it was highly ill-advised to publish at the present time. If the fable were addressed generally to dictators and dictatorships at large then publication would be all right, but the fable does follow, as I see now, so completely the progress of the Russian Soviets and their two dictators, that it can apply only to Russia, to the exclusion of the other

dictatorships. Another thing: it would be less offensive if the predominant caste in the fable were not pigs. I think the choice of pigs as the ruling caste will no doubt give offence to many people, and particularly to anyone who is a bit touchy, as undoubtedly the Russians are.

This kind of thing is not a good symptom. Obviously it is not desirable that a government department should have any power of censorship (except security censorship, which no one objects to in war time) over books which are not officially sponsored. But the chief danger to freedom of thought and speech at this moment is not the direct interference of the MOI or any official body. If publishers and editors exert themselves to keep certain topics out of print, it is not because they are frightened of prosecution but because they are frightened of public opinion. In this country intellectual cowardice is the worst enemy a writer or journalist has to face, and that fact does not seem to me to have had the discussion it deserves.

Any fairminded person with journalistic experience will admit that during this war *official* censorship has not been particularly irksome. We have not been subjected to the kind of totalitarian 'co-ordination' that it might have been reason-able to expect. The press has some justified grievances, but on the whole the Government has behaved well and has been surprisingly tolerant of minority opinions. The sinister fact about literary censorship in England is that it is largely volun-tary. Unpopular ideas can be silenced, and inconvenient facts kept dark, without the need for any official ban. Anyone who has lived long in a foreign country will know of instances of sensational items of news – things which on their own merits would get the big headlines – being kept right out of the British press, not because the Government intervened but because of a general tacit agreement that 'it wouldn't do' to mention that particular fact. So far as the daily newspapers go, this is easy to understand. The British press is extremely centralised, and most of it is owned by wealthy men who have every motive to be dishonest on certain important topics. But the same kind of veiled censorship also operates in books and periodicals, as well as in plays, films and radio. At any given moment there is an orthodoxy, a body of ideas which it is assumed that all right-thinking people will accept without question. It is not exactly forbidden to say this, that or the other, but it is 'not done' to say it, just as in mid-Victorian times it was 'not done' to mention trousers in the presence of a lady. Anyone who challenges the prevailing orthodoxy finds himself silenced with surprising effectiveness. A genuinely unfashionable opinion is almost never given a fair hearing, either in the popular press or in the highbrow periodicals.

At this moment what is demanded by the prevailing orthodoxy is an uncritical admiration of Soviet Russia. Everyone knows this, nearly everyone acts on it. Any serious criticism of the Soviet régime, any disclosure of facts which the Soviet government would prefer to keep hidden, is next door to unprintable. And this nation-wide conspiracy to flatter our ally takes place, curiously enough, against a background of genuine intellectual tolerance. For though you are not allowed to criticise the Soviet government, at least you are reasonably free to criticise our own. Hardly anyone will print an attack on Stalin, but it is quite safe to attack Churchill, at any rate in books and periodicals. And throughout five years of war, during two or three of which we were fighting for national survival, countless books, pamphlets and articles advocating a compromise peace have been published without interference. More, they have been published without exciting much disapproval. So long as the prestige of the USSR is not involved, the principle of free speech has been reasonably well upheld. There are other forbidden topics, and I shall mention some of them presently, but the prevailing attitude towards the USSR is much the most serious symptom. It is, as it were, spontaneous, and is not due to the action of any pressure group.

The servility with which the greater part of the English intelligentsia have swallowed and repeated Russian propaganda from 1941 onwards would be quite astounding if it were not that they have behaved similarly on several earlier occasions. On one controversial issue after another the Russian viewpoint has been accepted without examination and then publicised with complete disregard to historical truth or intellectual decency. To name only one instance, the BBC celebrated the twenty-fifth anniversary of the Red Army without mentioning Trotsky. This was about as accurate as commemorating the battle of Trafalgar without mentioning Nelson, but it evoked no protest from the English intelligentsia. In the internal struggles in the various occupied countries, the British press has in almost all cases sided with the faction favoured by the Russians and libelled the opposing faction, sometimes suppressing material evidence in order to do so. A particularly glaring case was that of Colonel Mihailovich, the Jugoslav Chetnik leader. The Russians, who had their own Jugoslav protégé in Marshal Tito, accused Mihailovich of collaborating with the Germans. This accusation was promptly taken up by the British press: Mihailovich's supporters were given no chance of answering it, and facts contradicting it were simply kept out of print. In July of 1943 the Germans offered a reward of 100,000 gold crowns for the capture of Tito, and a similar reward for the capture of Mihailovich. The British press 'splashed' the reward for Tito, but only one paper mentioned (in small print) the reward for Mihailovich; and the charges of collaborating with the Germans continued. Very similar things happened during the Spanish civil war. Then, too, the factions on the Republican side which the Russians were determined to crush were recklessly libelled in the English leftwing press, and any statement in their defence, even in letter form, was refused publication. At present, not only is serious criticism of the USSR considered reprehensible, but even the fact of the existence of such criticism is kept secret in some cases. For example, shortly before his death Trotsky had written a biography of Stalin. One may assume that it was not an altogether unbiased book, but obviously it was saleable. An American publisher had arranged to issue it and the book was in print – I believe the review copies had been sent out – when the USSR entered the war. The book was immediately withdrawn. Not a word about this has ever appeared in the British press, though clearly the existence of such a book, and its suppression, was a news item worth a few paragraphs.

It is important to distinguish between the kind of censorship that the English literary intelligentsia voluntarily impose upon themselves, and the censorship that can sometimes be enforced by pressure groups. Notoriously, certain topics cannot be discussed because of 'vested interests'. The best-known case is the patent medicine racket. Again, the Catholic Church has considerable influence in the press and can silence criticism of itself to some extent. A scandal involving a Catholic priest is almost never given publicity, whereas an Anglican priest who gets into trouble (e.g. the Rector of Stiffkey) is headline news. It is very rare for anything of an anti-Catholic tendency to appear on the stage or in a film. Any actor can tell you that a play or film which attacks or makes fun of the Catholic Church is liable to be boycotted in the press and will probably be a failure. But this kind of thing is harmless, or at least it is understandable. Any large organisation will look after its own interests as best it can, and overt propaganda is not a thing to object to. One would no more expect the *Daily Worker* to publicise unfavourable facts about the USSR than one would expect the *Catholic Herald* to denounce the Pope. But then every thinking person knows the *Daily Worker* and the *Catholic Herald* for what they are. What is disquieting is that where the USSR and its policies are concerned one cannot expect intelligent criticism or even, in many cases, plain honesty from Liberal writers and journalists who are under no direct pressure to falsify their opinions. Stalin is sacrosanct and certain aspects of his policy must not be seriously discussed. This rule has been almost universally observed since 1941, but it had operated, to a greater extent than is sometimes realised, for ten years earlier than that. Throughout that time, criticism of the Soviet régime *from the left* could only obtain a hearing with difficulty. There was a huge output of anti-Russian literature, but nearly all of it was from the Conservative angle and manifestly dishonest, out of date and actuated by sordid motives. On the other side there was an equally huge and almost equally dishonest stream of pro-Russian propaganda, and what amounted to a boycott on anyone who tried to discuss all-important questions in a grown-up manner. You could, indeed, publish anti-Russian books, but to do so was to make sure of being ignored or misrepresented by nearly the whole of the highbrow press. Both publicly and privately you were warned that it was 'not done'. What you said might possibly be true, but it was 'inopportune' and 'played into the hands of' this or that reactionary interest. This attitude was usually defended on the ground that the international situation, and the urgent need for an Anglo-Russian alliance, demanded it; but it was clear that this was a rationalisation. The English intelligentsia, or a great part of it, had developed a nationalistic loyalty towards the USSR, and in their hearts they felt that to cast any doubt on the wisdom of Stalin was a kind of blasphemy. Events in Russia and events elsewhere were to be judged by different standards. The endless executions in the purges of 1936–38 were applauded by life-long opponents of capital punishment, and it was considered equally proper to publicise famines when they happened in India and to conceal them when they happened in the Ukraine. And if this was true before the war, the intellectual atmosphere is certainly no better now.

But now to come back to this book of mine. The reaction towards it of most English intellectuals will be quite simple: 'It oughtn't to have been published.' Naturally, those reviewers who understand the art of denigration will not attack it on political grounds but on literary ones. They will say that it is a dull, silly book and a disgraceful waste of paper. This may well be true, but it is obviously not the whole of the story. One does not say that a book 'ought not to have been published' merely because it is a bad book. After all, acres of rubbish are printed daily and no one bothers. The English intelligentsia, or most of them, will object to this book because it traduces their Leader and (as they see it) does harm to the cause of progress. If it did the opposite they would have nothing to say against it, even if its literary faults were ten times as glaring as they are. The success of, for instance, the Left Book Club over a period of four or five years shows how willing they are to tolerate both scurrility and slip-shod writing, provided that it tells them what they want to hear.

The issue involved here is quite a simple one: Is every opinion, however unpopular – however foolish, even – entitled to a hearing? Put it in that form and nearly any English intellec-tual will feel that he ought to say 'Yes'. But give it a concrete shape, and ask, 'How about an attack on Stalin? Is *that* entitled to a hearing?', and the answer more often than not will be 'No'. In that case the current orthodoxy happens to be challenged, and so the principle of free speech lapses. Now, when one demands liberty of speech and of the press, one is not demanding absolute liberty. There always must be, or at any rate there always will be, some degree of censorship, so long as organised societies endure. But freedom, as Rosa Luxemburg said, is 'freedom for the other fellow'. The same principle is contained

893

in the famous words of Voltaire: 'I detest what you say; I will defend to the death your right to say it.' If the intellectual liberty which without a doubt has been one of the distinguishing marks of western civilisation means anything at all, it means that everyone shall have the right to say and to print what he believes to be the truth, provided only that it does not harm the rest of the community in some quite unmistakable way. Both capitalist democracy and the western versions of Socialism have till recently taken that principle for granted. Our Government, as I have already pointed out, still makes some show of respecting it. The ordinary people in the street – partly, perhaps, because they are not sufficiently interested in ideas to be intolerant about them – still vaguely hold that 'I suppose everyone's got a right to their own opinion.' It is only, or at any rate it is chiefly, the literary and scientific intelligentsia, the very people who ought to be the guardians of liberty, who are beginning to despise it, in theory as well as in practice.

One of the peculiar phenomena of our time is the renegade Liberal. Over and above the familiar Marxist claim that 'bourgeois liberty' is an illusion, there is now a widespread tendency to argue that one can only defend democracy by totalitarian methods. If one loves democracy, the argument runs, one must crush its enemies by no matter what means. And who are its enemies? It always appears that they are not only those who attack it openly and consciously, but those who 'objectively' endanger it by spreading mistaken doctrines. In other words, defending democracy involves destroying all independence of thought. This argument was used, for instance, to justify the Russian purges. The most ardent Russophile hardly believed that all of the victims were guilty of all the things they were accused of: but by holding heretical opinions they 'objectively' harmed the régime, and therefore it was quite right not only to massacre them but to discredit them by false accusations. The same argument was used to justify the quite conscious lying that went on in the leftwing press about the Trotskyists and other Republican minorities in the Spanish civil war. And it was used again as a reason for yelping against *habeas corpus* when Mosley was released in 1943.

These people don't see that if you encourage totalitarian methods, the time may come when they will be used against

894

you instead of for you. Make a habit of imprisoning Fascists without trial, and perhaps the process won't stop at Fascists. Soon after the suppressed *Daily Worker* had been reinstated, I was lecturing to a workingmen's college in South London. The audience were working-class and lower-middle-class intellectuals – the same sort of audience that one used to meet at Left Book Club branches. The lecture had touched on the freedom of the press, and at the end, to my astonishment, several questioners stood up and asked me: Did I not think that the lifting of the ban on the *Daily Worker* was a great mistake? When asked why, they said that it was a paper of doubtful loyalty and ought not to be tolerated in war time. I found myself defending the *Daily Worker*, which has gone out of its way to libel me more than once. But where had these people learned this essentially totalitarian outlook? Pretty certainly they had learned it from the Communists themselves! Tolerance and decency are deeply rooted in England, but they are not indestructible, and they have to be kept alive partly by conscious effort. The result of preaching totalitarian doctrines is to weaken the instinct by means of which free peoples know what is or is not dangerous. The case of Mosley illustrates this. In 1940 it was perfectly right to intern Mosley, whether or not he had committed any technical crime. We were fighting for our lives and could not allow a possible quisling to go free. To keep him shut up, without trial, in 1943 was an outrage. The general failure to see this was a bad symptom, though it is true that the agitation against Mosley's release was partly factitious and partly a rationalisation of other discontents. But how much of the present slide towards Fascist ways of thought is traceable to the 'anti-Fascism' of the past ten years and the unscrupulousness it has entailed?

It is important to realise that the current Russomania is only a symptom of the general weakening of the western liberal tradition. Had the MOI chipped in and definitely vetoed the publication of this book, the bulk of the English intelligentsia would have seen nothing disquieting in this. Uncritical loyalty to the USSR happens to be the current orthodoxy, and where the supposed interests of the USSR are involved they are willing to tolerate not only censorship but the deliberate falsification of history. To name one instance. At the death of John Reed, the author of *Ten Days that*

Shook the World – a first-hand account of the early days of the Russian Revolution – the copyright of the book passed into the hands of the British Communist Party, to whom I believe Reed had bequeathed it. Some years later the British Communists, having destroyed the original edition of the book as completely as they could, issued a garbled version from which they had eliminated mentions of Trotsky and also omitted the introduction written by Lenin. If a radical intelligentsia had still existed in Britain, this act of forgery would have been exposed and denounced in every literary paper in the country. As it was there was little or no protest. To many English intellectuals it seemed quite a natural thing to do. And this tolerance of plain dishonesty means much more than that admiration of Russia happens to be fashionable at this moment. Quite possibly that particular fashion will not last. For all I know, by the time this book is published my view of the Soviet régime may be the generally-accepted one. But what use would that be in itself? To exchange one orthodoxy for another is not necessarily an advance. The enemy is the gramophone mind, whether or not one agrees with the record that is being played at the moment.

I am well acquainted with all the arguments against freedom of thought and speech – the arguments which claim that it cannot exist, and the arguments which claim that it ought not to. I answer simply that they don't convince me and that our civilisation over a period of four hundred years has been founded on the opposite notion. For quite a decade past I have believed that the existing Russian régime is a mainly evil thing, and I claim the right to say so, in spite of the fact that we are allies with the USSR in a war which I want to see won. If I had to choose a text to justify myself, I should choose the line from Milton:

> By the known rules of ancient liberty.

The word *ancient* emphasises the fact that intellectual freedom is a deep-rooted tradition without which our characteristic western culture could only doubtfully exist. From that tradition many of our intellectuals are visibly turning away. They have accepted the principle that a book should be published or suppressed, praised or damned, not on its merits but according to political expediency. And others who do not actually hold this view assent to it from sheer cowardice. An example of this is the failure of the numerous and vocal English pacifists to raise their voices against the prevalent worship of Russian militarism. According to those pacifists, all violence is evil, and they have urged us at every stage of the war to give in or at least to make a compromise peace. But how many of them have ever suggested that war is also evil when it is waged by the Red Army? Apparently the Russians have a right to defend themselves, whereas for us to do so is a deadly sin. One can only explain this contradiction in one way: that is by a cowardly desire to keep in with the bulk of the intelligentsia, whose patriotism is directed towards the USSR rather than towards Britain. I know that the English intelligentsia have plenty of reason for their timidity and dishonesty, indeed I know by heart the arguments by which they justify themselves. But at least let us have no more nonsense about defending liberty against Fascism. If liberty means anything at all it means the right to tell people what they do not want to hear. The common people still vaguely subscribe to that doctrine and act on it. In our country – it is not the same in all countries: it was not so in republican France, and it is not so in the USA today – it is the liberals who fear liberty and the intellectuals who want to do dirt on the intellect: it is to draw attention to that fact that I have written this preface.

Review of *The Brothers Karamazov* and *Crime and Punishment* by Fyodor Dostoevsky; translated by Constance Garnett

The Observer, 7 October 1945

Constance Garnett's translations, now to be re-issued, were the first full translations of Dostoevsky to be made direct from Russian into English, and they appeared in the years immediately preceding the last war. At that date it must have been a wonderful experience to read Dostoevsky. It must have given many readers the feeling that an earlier generation had had from Flaubert and a later one was to get from Joyce – the feeling that here was a country of the mind which one had always known to exist, but which one had never thought of as lying within the scope of fiction. More than almost any novelist, Dostoevsky is able to give his reader the feeling: "He knows my secret thoughts; he is writing about *me*." It is hard to think of anything in English fiction to compare, for instance, with the scene near the beginning of CRIME AND PUNISHMENT, in which the drunken official Marmeladov describes how his daughter Sonia has been driven on to the streets to support the rest of the starving family.

In the eyes of an English reader Dostoevsky gained something by his foreignness – Marmeladov's remark that he got drunk in order to repent afterwards was, as people used to say, "very Russian" – but his basic quality was his enormous capacity for pity. He was sympathetic towards all his characters, even the respectable ones. The breakdown of the hero–villain antithesis, combined with a strict moral code, was something new, and it is not surprising that for a while he seemed a great thinker as well as a great novelist.

At this date, especially when one has just waded through the 800 pages of THE BROTHERS KARAMOZOV, one can see faults which were less apparent thirty years ago. The impression one often gets from Dostoevsky is of looking at a series of pictures which are incredibly lifelike except that they are all in monochrome. In a way, all his characters are the same kind of person, there are no exceptional people, or perhaps it would be truer to say there are no ordinary people. Priests, peasants, criminals, policemen, prostitutes, business men, ladies of fashion, soldiers, all seem to mingle easily in the same world: above all, everybody tells everybody else about the state of his soul. It is worth comparing the conversations that take place in "Crime and Punishment" between Raskolnikov and the police official, Porfiry Petrovitch, with the kind of conversation that might actually take place, in England, between a neurotic university student and an inspector of police. One enormous hurdle which every novelist has to face – the problem of bringing the man of thought and the man of action into the same picture – has been simply by-passed.

Apart from the famous chapter, entitled "The Grand Inquisitor," "The Brothers Karamazov" is heavy going. Its theme does not seem to justify its vast bulk, about a third of which consists of introductory matter, and passages in it make it easy to believe that Dostoevsky habitually wrote on a corner of the kitchen table and corrected nothing. "Crime and Punishment" is quite another matter. It is an illustration of the extraordinary psychological insight of this book that one takes Raskolnikov's actions entirely for granted although, before the murder is committed, no sufficient motive for it is indicated. It seems quite credible that an intelligent and sensitive young man should suddenly commit a disgusting and almost purposeless crime: and the reason for this must be that Dostoevsky knew exactly what it feels like to be a murderer. A more conscious piece of artistry, forming a wonderful enclave in the book, is the dream of the dying horse by which Raskolnikov's crime is foreshadowed.

Messrs. Heinemann intend to re-issue the whole series of Constance Garnett's translations, and at eight and sixpence a volume they are good value. One volume to look out for – it is one of the less well known of Dostoevsky's books and not easy to obtain during recent years – is "The House of the Dead": this describes, under a thin disguise of fiction, Dostoevsky's own experiences as a prisoner in Siberia, and contains the never-to-be-forgotten short story, "The Husband of Akulka."

Revenge Is Sour
Tribune, 9 November 1945

Whenever I read phrases like "war guilt trials," "punishment of war criminals," and so forth, there comes back into my mind the memory of something I saw in a prisoner-of-war camp in South Germany, earlier this year.

Another correspondent and myself were being shown round the camp by a little Viennese Jew who had been enlisted in the branch of the American army which deals with the interrogation of prisoners. He was an alert, fair-haired, rather good-looking youth of about twenty-five, and politically so much more knowledgeable than the average American officer that it was a pleasure to be with him. The camp was on an airfield, and, after we had been round the cages, our guide led us to a hangar where various prisoners who were in a different category from the others were being "screened."

Up at one end of the hangar about a dozen men were lying in a row on the concrete floor. These, it was explained, were S.S. officers who had been segregated from the other prisoners. Among them was a man in dingy civilian clothes who was lying with his arm across his face and apparently asleep. He had strangely and horribly deformed feet. The two of them were quite symmetrical, but they were clubbed out into an extraordinary globular shape which made them more like a horse's hoof than anything human. As we approached the group the little Jew seemed to be working himself up into a state of excitement.

"That's the real swine!" he said, and suddenly he lashed out with his heavy army boot and caught the prostrate man a fearful kick right on the bulge of one of his deformed feet.

"Get up, you swine!" he shouted as the man started out of sleep, and then repeated something of the kind in German. The prisoner scrambled to his feet and stood clumsily to attention. With the same air of working himself up into a fury – indeed he was almost dancing up and down as he spoke – the Jew told us the prisoner's history. He was a "real" Nazi: his party number indicated that he had been a member since the very early days, and he had held a post corresponding to a general in the political branch of the S.S. It could be taken as quite certain that he had had charge of concentration camps and had presided over tortures and hangings. In short, he represented everything that we had been fighting against during the past five years.

Meanwhile, I was studying his appearance. Quite apart from the scrubby, unfed, unshaven look that a newly captured man generally has, he was a disgusting specimen. But he did not look brutal or in any way frightening: merely neurotic and, in a low way, intellectual. His pale, shifty eyes were deformed by powerful spectacles. He could have been an unfrocked clergyman, an actor ruined by drink, or a spiritualist medium. I have seen very similar people in London common lodging-houses, and also in the Reading Room of the British Museum. Quite obviously he was mentally unbalanced – indeed, only doubtfully sane, though at this moment sufficiently in his right mind to be frightened of getting another kick. And yet everything that the Jew was telling me of his history could have been true, and probably was true! So the Nazi torturer of one's imagination, the monstrous figure against whom one had struggled for so many years, dwindled to this pitiful wretch, whose obvious need was not for punishment, but for some kind of psychological treatment.

Later, there were further humiliations. Another S.S. officer, a large brawny man, was ordered to strip to the waist and show the blood-group number tattooed on his under-arm; another was forced to explain to us how he had lied about being a member of the S.S. and attempted to pass himself off as an ordinary soldier of the Wehrmacht. I wondered whether the Jew was getting any real kick out of this new-found power that he was exercising. I concluded that he wasn't really enjoying it, and that he was merely – like a man in a brothel, or a boy smoking his first cigar, or a tourist traipsing round a picture gallery – *telling* himself that he was enjoying it, and behaving as he had planned to behave in the days when he was helpless.

It is absurd to blame any German or Austrian Jew for getting his own back on the Nazis. Heaven knows what scores this particular man may have had to wipe out: very likely his whole family had been murdered; and, after all, even a wanton kick to a prisoner is a very tiny thing compared with the outrages committed by the Hitler regime. But what this scene, and much else that I saw in Germany, brought home to me was that the whole idea of revenge and punishment is a childish daydream. Properly speaking, there is no such thing as revenge. Revenge is an act which you want to commit when you are powerless and because you are powerless: as soon as the sense of impotence is removed, the desire evaporates also.

Who would not have jumped for joy, in 1940, at the thought of seeing S.S. officers kicked and humiliated? But when the thing becomes possible, it is merely pathetic and disgusting. It is said that when Mussolini's corpse was exhibited in public, an old woman drew a revolver and fired five shots into it, exclaiming, "Those are for my five sons!" It is the kind of story that the newspapers make up, but it might be true. I wonder how much satisfaction she got out of those five shots, which, doubtless, she had dreamed years earlier of firing. The condition of her being able to get near enough to Mussolini to shoot at him was that he should be a corpse.

In so far as the big public in this country is responsible for the monstrous peace settlement now being forced on Germany, it is because of a failure to see in advance that punishing an enemy brings no satisfaction. We acquiesced in crimes like the expulsion of all Germans from East Prussia – crimes which in some cases we could not prevent but might at least have protested against – because the Germans had angered and frightened us, and therefore we were certain that when they were down we should feel no pity for them. We persist in these policies, or let others persist in them on our behalf, because of a vague feeling that, having set out to punish Germany, we ought to go ahead and do it. Actually there is little acute hatred of Germany left in this country, and even less, I should expect to find, in the army of occupation. Only the minority of sadists, who must have their "atrocities" from one source or another, take a keen interest in the hunting-down of war criminals and quislings. If you ask the average man what crime Goering, Ribbentrop and the rest are to be charged with at their trial, he cannot tell you. Somehow the punishment of these monsters ceases to seem attractive when it becomes possible: indeed, once under lock and key, they almost cease to be monsters.

Unfortunately, there is often need of some concrete incident before one can discover the real state of one's feelings. Here is another memory from Germany. A few hours after Stuttgart was captured by the French army, a Belgian journalist and myself entered the town, which was still in some disorder. The Belgian had been broadcasting throughout the war for the European Service of the B.B.C., and, like nearly all Frenchmen or Belgians, he had a very much tougher attitude towards "the Boche" than an Englishman or an American would have. All the main bridges into the town had been blown up, and we had to enter by a small footbridge which the Germans had evidently made efforts to defend. A dead German soldier was lying supine at the foot of the steps. His face was a waxy yellow. On his breast someone had laid a bunch of the lilac which was blossoming everywhere.

The Belgian averted his face as we went past. When we were well over the bridge he confided to me that this was the first time he had seen a dead man. I suppose he was thirty-five years old, and for four years he had been doing war propaganda over the radio. For several days after this, his attitude was quite different from what it had been earlier. He looked with disgust at the bomb-wrecked town and the humiliations the Germans were undergoing, and even on one occasion intervened to prevent a particularly bad bit of looting. When we left, he gave the residue of the coffee we had brought with us to the Germans on whom we were billeted. A week earlier he would probably have been scandalised at the idea of giving coffee to a "Boche." But his feelings, he told me, had undergone a change at the sight of "*ce pauvre mort*" beside the bridge: it had suddenly brought home to him the meaning of war. And yet, if we had happened to enter the town by another route, he might have been spared the experience of seeing even one corpse out of the – perhaps – twenty million that the war has produced.

You and the Atom Bomb
Tribune, 19 October 1945

Considering how likely we all are to be blown to pieces by it within the next five years, the atomic bomb has not roused so much discussion as might have been expected. The newspapers have published numerous diagrams, not very helpful to the average man, of protons and neutrons doing their stuff, and there has been much reiteration of the useless statement that the bomb "ought to be put under international control." But curiously little has been said, at any rate in print, about the question that is of most urgent interest to all of us, namely: "How difficult are these things to manufacture?"

Such information as we – that is, the big public – possess on this subject has come to us in a rather indirect way, apropos of President Truman's decision not to hand over certain secrets to the U.S.S.R. Some months ago, when the bomb was still only a rumour, there was a widespread belief that splitting the atom was merely a problem for the physicists, and that when they had solved it a new and devastating weapon would be within reach of almost everybody. (At any moment, so the rumour went, some lonely lunatic in a laboratory might blow civilisation to smithereens, as easily as touching off a firework.)

Had that been true, the whole trend of history would have been abruptly altered. The distinction between great States and small States would have been wiped out, and the power of the State over the individual would have been greatly weakened. However, it appears from President Truman's remarks, and various comments that have been made on them, that the bomb is fantastically expensive and that its manufacture demands an enormous industrial effort, such as only three or four countries in the world are capable of making. This point is of cardinal importance, because it may mean that the discovery of the atomic bomb, so far from reversing history, will simply intensify the trends which have been apparent for a dozen years past.

It is a commonplace that the history of civilisation is largely the history of weapons. In particular, the connection between the discovery of gunpowder and the overthrow of feudalism by the bourgeoisie has been pointed out over and over again. And though I have no doubt exceptions can be brought forward, I think the following rule would be found generally true: that ages in which the dominant weapon is expensive or difficult to make will tend to be ages of despotism, whereas when the dominant weapon is cheap and simple, the common people have a chance. Thus, for example, tanks, battleships and bombing planes are inherently tyrannical weapons, while rifles, muskets, longbows and hand grenades are inherently democratic weapons. A complex weapon makes the strong stronger, while a simple weapon – so long as there is no answer to it – gives claws to the weak.

The great age of democracy and of national self-determination was the age of the musket and the rifle. After the invention of the flint-lock, and before the invention of the percussion cap, the musket was a fairly efficient weapon, and at the same time so simple that it could be produced almost anywhere. Its combination of qualities made possible the success of the American and French revolutions, and made a popular insurrection a more serious business than it could be in our own day. After the musket came the breech-loading rifle. This was a comparatively complex thing, but it could still be produced in scores of countries, and it was cheap, easily smuggled and economical of ammunition. Even the most backward nation could always get hold of rifles from one source or another, so that Boers, Bulgars, Abyssinians, Moroccans – even Tibetans – could put up a fight for their independence, sometimes with success. But thereafter every development in military technique has favoured the State as against the individual, and the industrialised country as against the backward one. There are fewer and fewer foci of power. Already, in 1939, there were only five States capable of waging war on the grand scale, and now there are only three – ultimately, perhaps, only two. This trend has been obvious for years, and was pointed out by a few observers even before 1914. The one thing that might reverse it is the discovery of a weapon – or, to put it more broadly, of a method of fighting – not dependent on huge concentrations of industrial plant.

From various symptoms one can infer that the Russians do not yet possess the secret of making the atomic bomb; on the other hand, the consensus of opinion seems to be that they will possess it within a few years. So we have before us the prospect of two or three monstrous super-States, each possessed of a weapon by which millions of people can be wiped out in a few seconds, dividing the world between them. It has been rather hastily assumed that this means bigger and bloodier wars, and perhaps an actual end to the machine civilisation. But suppose – and really this is the likeliest development – that the surviving great nations make a tacit agreement never to use the atomic bomb against one another? Suppose they only use it, or the threat of it, against people who are unable to retaliate? In that case we are back where we were before, the only difference being that power is concentrated in still fewer hands and that the outlook for subject peoples and oppressed classes is still more hopeless.

When James Burnham wrote *The Managerial Revolution* it seemed probable to many Americans that the Germans would win the European end of the war, and it was therefore natural to assume that Germany and not Russia would dominate the Eurasian land mass, while Japan would remain master of East Asia. This was a miscalculation, but it does not affect the main argument. For Burnham's geographical picture of the new world has turned out to be correct. More and more obviously the surface of the earth is being parcelled off into three great empires, each self-contained and cut off from contact with the outer world, and each ruled, under one disguise or another, by a self-elected oligarchy. The haggling as to where the frontiers are to be drawn is still going on, and will continue for some years, and the third of the three super-States – East Asia, dominated by China – is still potential rather than actual. But the general drift is unmistakable, and every scientific discovery of recent years has accelerated it.

We were once told that the aeroplane had "abolished frontiers"; actually it is only since the aeroplane became a serious weapon that frontiers have become definitely impassable. The radio was once expected to promote international understanding and co-operation; it has turned out to be a means of insulating one nation from another. The atomic bomb may complete the process by robbing the exploited classes and peoples of all power to revolt, and at the same time putting the possessors of the bomb on a basis of military equality. Unable to conquer one another, they are likely to continue ruling the world between them, and it is difficult to see how the balance can be upset except by slow and unpredictable demographic changes.

For forty or fifty years past, Messrs. H. G. Wells and others have been warning us that man is in danger of destroying himself with his own weapons, leaving the ants or some other gregarious species to take over. Anyone who has seen the ruined cities of Germany will find this notion at least thinkable. Nevertheless, looking at the world as a whole, the drift for many decades has been not towards anarchy but towards the reimposition of slavery. We may be heading not for general breakdown but for an epoch as horribly stable as the slave empires of antiquity. James Burnham's theory has been much discussed, but few people have yet considered its ideological implications – that is, the kind of world-view, the kind of beliefs, and the social structure that would probably prevail in a State which was at once *unconquerable* and in a permanent state of "cold war" with its neighbours.

Had the atomic bomb turned out to be something as cheap and easily manufactured as a bicycle or an alarm clock, it might well have plunged us back into barbarism, but it might, on the other hand, have meant the end of national sovereignty and of the highly-centralised police State. If, as seems to be the case, it is a rare and costly object as difficult to produce as a battleship, it is likelier to put an end to large-scale wars at the cost of prolonging indefinitely a "peace that is no peace."

What is Science?
Tribune, 26 October 1945

In last week's *Tribune*, there was an interesting letter from Mr. J. Stewart Cook, in which he suggested that the best way of avoiding the danger of a "scientific hierarchy" would be to see to it that every member of the general public was, as far as possible, scientifically educated. At the same time, scientists should be brought out of their isolation and encouraged to take a greater part in politics and administration.

As a general statement, I think most of us would agree with this, but I notice that, as usual, Mr. Cook does not define Science, and merely implies in passing that it means certain exact sciences whose experiments can be made under laboratory conditions. Thus, adult education tends "to neglect scientific studies in favour of literary, economic and social subjects," economics and sociology not being regarded as branches of Science, apparently. This point is of great importance. For the word Science is at present used in at least two meanings, and the whole question of scientific education is obscured by the current tendency to dodge from one meaning to the other.

Science is generally taken as meaning either (a) the exact sciences, such as chemistry, physics, &c., or (b) a method of thought which obtains verifiable results by reasoning logically from observed fact.

If you ask any scientist, or indeed almost any educated person, "What is Science?" you are likely to get an answer approximating to (b). In everyday life, however, both in speaking and in writing, when people say "Science" they mean (a). Science means something that happens in a laboratory: the very word calls up a picture of graphs, test tubes, balances, Bunsen burners, microscopes. A biologist, an astronomer, perhaps a psychologist or a mathematician, is described as a "man of science": no one would think of applying this term to a statesman, a poet, a journalist or even a philosopher. And those who tell us that the young must be scientifically educated mean, almost invariably, that they should be taught more about radioactivity, or the stars, or the physiology of their own bodies, rather than that they should be taught to think more exactly.

This confusion of meaning, which is partly deliberate, has in it a great danger. Implied in the demand for more scientific education is the claim that if one has been scientifically trained one's approach to *all* subjects will be more intelligent than if one had had no such training. A scientist's political opinions, it is assumed, his opinions on sociological questions, on morals, on philosophy, perhaps even on the arts, will be more valuable than those of a layman. The world, in other words, would be a better place if the scientists were in control of it. But a "scientist," as we have just seen, means in practice a specialist in one of the exact sciences. It follows that a chemist or a physicist, as such, is politically more intelligent than a poet or a lawyer, as such. And, in fact, there are already millions of people who do believe this.

But is it really true that a "scientist," in this narrower sense, is any likelier than other people to approach non-scientific problems in an objective way? There is not much reason for thinking so. Take one simple test – the ability to withstand nationalism. It is often loosely said that "Science is international," but in practice the scientific workers of all countries line up behind their own governments with fewer scruples than are felt by the writers and the artists. The German scientific community, as a whole, made no resistance to Hitler. Hitler may have ruined the long-term prospects of German Science, but there were still plenty of gifted men to do the necessary research on such things as synthetic oil, jet planes, rocket projectiles and the atomic bomb. Without them the German war machine could never have been built up.

On the other hand, what happened to German literature when the Nazis came to power? I believe no exhaustive lists have been published, but I imagine that the number of German scientists – Jews apart – who voluntarily exiled themselves or were persecuted by the regime was much smaller than the number of writers and journalists. More sinister than this, a number of German scientists swallowed the monstrosity of "racial Science." You can find some of the statements to which they set their names in Professor Brady's *The Spirit and Structure of German Fascism*.

But, in slightly different forms, it is the same picture everywhere. In England, a large proportion of our leading scientists accept the structure of capitalist society, as can be seen from the comparative freedom with which they are given knighthoods, baronetcies and even peerages. Since Tennyson, no English writer worth reading – one might, perhaps make an exception of Sir Max Beerbohm – has been given a title. And those English scientists who do not simply accept the *status quo* are frequently Communists, which means that, however intellectually scrupulous they may be in their own line of work, they are ready to be uncritical and even dishonest on certain subjects. The fact is that a mere training in one or more of the exact sciences, even combined with very high gifts, is no guarantee of a humane or sceptical outlook. The physicists of half a dozen great nations, all feverishly and secretly working away at the atomic bomb, are a demonstration of this.

But does all this mean that the general public should *not* be more scientifically educated? On the contrary! All it means is that scientific education for the masses will do little good, and probably a lot of harm, if it simply boils down to more physics, more chemistry, more biology, etc., to the detriment of literature and history. Its probable effect on the average human being would be to narrow the range of his thoughts and make him more than ever contemptuous of such knowledge as he did not possess: and his political reactions would probably be somewhat less intelligent than those of an illiterate peasant who retained a few historical memories and a fairly sound æsthetic sense.

Clearly, scientific education ought to mean the implanting of a rational, sceptical, experimental habit of mind. It ought to mean acquiring a *method* – a method that can be used on any problem that one meets – and not simply piling up a lot of facts. Put it in those words, and the apologist of scientific education will usually agree. Press him further, ask him to particularise, and somehow it always turns out that scientific education means more attention to the exact sciences, in other words – more *facts*. The idea that Science means a way of looking at the world, and not simply a body of knowledge, is in practice strongly resisted. I think sheer professional jealousy is part of the reason for this. For if Science is simply a method or an attitude, so that anyone whose thought-processes are sufficiently rational can in some sense be described as a scientist – what then becomes of the enormous prestige now enjoyed by the chemist, the physicist, etc., and his claim to be somehow wiser than the rest of us?

A hundred years ago, Charles Kingsley described Science as "making nasty smells in a laboratory." A year or two ago a young industrial chemist informed me, smugly, that he "could not see what was the use of poetry." So the pendulum swings to and fro, but it does not seem to me that one attitude is any better than the other. At the moment, Science is on the up-grade, and so we hear, quite rightly, the claim that the masses should be scientifically educated: we do not hear, as we ought, the counter claim that the scientists themselves would benefit by a little education. Just before writing this, I saw in an American magazine the statement that a number of British and American physicists refused from the start to do research on the atomic bomb, well knowing what use would be made of it. Here you have a group of sane men in the middle of a world of lunatics. And though no names were published, I think it would be a safe guess that all of them were people with some kind of general cultural background, some acquaintance with history or literature or the arts – in short, people whose interests were not, in the current sense of the word, purely scientific.

Review of *Drums under the Windows* by Sean O'Casey

The Observer, 28 October 1945

W. B. Yeats said once that a dog does not praise its fleas, but this is somewhat contradicted by the special status enjoyed in this country by Irish nationalist writers. Considering what the history of Anglo-Irish relations has been, it is not surprising that there should be Irishmen whose life-work is abusing England:

what does call for remark is that they should be able to look to the English public for support and in some cases should even, like Mr. O'Casey himself, prefer to live in the country which is the object of their hatred.

This is the third volume of Mr. O'Casey's autobiography, and it seems to cover roughly the period 1910 to 1916. In so far as one can dig it out from masses of pretentious writing, the subject matter is valuable and interesting. Mr. O'Casey, younger son of a poverty-stricken Protestant family, worked for years as a navvy, and was at the same time deeply involved in the nationalist movement and the various cultural movements that were mixed up with it. Several of his brothers and sisters died in circumstances of gaunt poverty which would excuse a good deal of bitterness against the English occupation. He was the associate of Larkin, Connolly, the Countess Markievicz, and other leading political figures, and he had a front-seat view of the Easter Rebellion in 1916. But the cloudy manner in which the book is written makes it difficult to pin down facts or chronology. It is all in the third person ("Sean did this" and "Sean did that"), which gives an unbearable effect of narcissism, and large portions of it are written in a simplified imitation of the style of "Finnegans Wake," a sort of Basic Joyce, which is sometimes effective in a humorous aside, but is hopeless for narrative purposes.

However, Mr. O'Casey's outstanding characteristic is the romantic nationalism which he manages to combine with Communism. This book contains literally no reference to England which is not hostile or contemptuous. On the other hand, there is hardly a page which does not contain some such passage as this:

Cathleen ni Houlihan, in her bare feet, is singing, for her pride that had almost gone is come back again. In tattered gown, and hair uncombed, she sings, shaking the ashes from her hair, and smoothing out the bigger creases in her dress; she is
> Singing of men that in battle array
> Ready in heart and ready in hand,

GEORGE ORWELL

> *March with banner and bugle and fife*
> *To the death, for their native land.*

Or again:

> Cathleen, the daughter of Houlihan, walks firm now, a flush on her haughty cheek. She hears the murmur in the people's hearts. Her lovers are gathering round her, for things are changed, changed utterly: "A terrible beauty is born."

If one substitutes "Britannia" for "Cathleen ni Houlihan" in these and similar passages (Cathleen ni Houlihan, incidentally, makes her appearance several times in every chapter), they can be seen at a glance for the bombast that they are. But why is it that the worst extremes of jingoism and racialism have to be tolerated when they come from an Irishman? Why is a statement like "My country right or wrong" reprehensible if applied to England and worthy of respect if applied to Ireland (or for that matter to India)? For there is no doubt that some such convention exists and that "enlightened" opinion in England can swallow even the most blatant nationalism so long as it is not British nationalism. Poems like "Rule, Britannia!" or "Ye Mariners of England" would be taken seriously if one inserted at the right places the name of some foreign country, as one can see by the respect accorded to various French and Russian war poets to-day.

So far as Ireland goes, the basic reason is probably England's bad conscience. It is difficult to object to Irish nationalism without seeming to condone centuries of English tyranny and exploitation. In particular, the incident with which Mr. O'Casey's book ends, the summary execution of some twenty or thirty rebels who ought to have been treated as prisoners of war, was a crime and a mistake. Therefore anything that is said about it has to pass unchallenged, and Yeats's poem on the subject, which makes a sort of theme song for Mr. O'Casey's book, has to be accepted uncriticised as a great poem. Actually it is not one of Yeats's better poems. But how can an Englishman, conscious that his country was in the wrong on that and many other occasions, say anything of the kind? So literary judgement is perverted by political sympathy, and

Mr. O'Casey and others like him are able to remain almost immune from criticism. It seems time to revise our attitude, for there is no real reason why Cromwell's massacres should cause us to mistake a bad or indifferent book for a good one.

Introduction to *Love of Life and Other Stories* by Jack London
October or November 1945

In her little book, *Memories of Lenin*, Nadezhda Krupskaya relates that when Lenin was in his last illness she used to read aloud to him in the evenings:

> Two days before his death I read to him in the evening a tale by Jack London, *Love of Life* – it is still lying on the table in his room. It was a very fine story. In a wilderness of ice, where no human being had set foot, a sick man, dying of hunger, is making for the harbour of a big river. His strength is giving out, he cannot walk but keeps slipping, and beside him there slides a wolf – also dying of hunger. There is a fight between them: the man wins. Half dead, half demented, he reaches his goal. That tale greatly pleased Ilyich [Lenin]. Next day he asked me to read him more Jack London.

However, Krupskaya goes on, the next tale turned out to be "saturated with bourgeois morals," and "Ilyich smiled and dismissed it with a wave of his hand." These two pieces by Jack London were the last things that she read to him.

The story, *Love of Life*, is even grimmer than Krupskaya suggests in her short summary of it, for it actually ends with the man eating the wolf, or at any rate biting into its throat hard enough to draw blood. That is the sort of theme towards which Jack London was irresistibly drawn, and this episode of Lenin's deathbed readings is of itself not a bad criticism of London's work. He was a writer who excelled in describing cruelty, whose main theme, indeed, was the cruelty of Nature, or at any rate of contemporary life; he was also an extremely variable

913

writer, much of whose work was produced hurriedly and at low pressure; and he had in him a strain of feeling which Krupskaya is probably right in calling "bourgeois" – at any rate, a strain which did not accord with his democratic and Socialist convictions.

During the last twenty years Jack London's short stories have been rather unaccountably forgotten – how thoroughly forgotten, one could gauge by the completeness with which they were out of print. So far as the big public went, he was remembered by various animal books, particularly *White Fang* and *The Call of the Wild* – books which appealed to the Anglo-Saxon sentimentality about animals – and after 1933 his reputation took an upward bound because of *The Iron Heel*, which had been written in 1907, and is in some sense a prophecy of Fascism. *The Iron Heel* is not a good book, and on the whole its predictions have not been borne out. Its dates and its geography are ridiculous, and London makes the mistake, which was usual at that time, of assuming that revolution would break out first in the highly industrialised countries. But on several points London was right where nearly all other prophets were wrong, and he was right because of just that strain in his nature that made him a good short-story writer and a doubtfully reliable Socialist.

London imagines a proletarian revolution breaking out in the United States and being crushed, or partially crushed, by a counter-offensive of the capitalist class; and, following on this, a long period during which society is ruled over by a small group of tyrants known as the Oligarchs, who are served by a kind of S.S. known as the Mercenaries. An underground struggle against dictatorship was the kind of thing that London could imagine, and he foresaw certain of the details with surprising accuracy: he foresaw, for instance, that peculiar horror of totali-tarian society, the way in which suspected enemies of the régime *simply disappear*. But the book is chiefly notable for maintaining that capitalist society would not perish of its "contradictions," but that the possessing class would be able to form itself into a vast corporation and even evolve a sort of perverted Socialism, sacrificing many of its privileges in order to preserve its superior status. The passages in which London analyses the mentality of the Oligarchs are of great interest:

They, as a class [writes the imaginary author of the book], believed that they alone maintained civilisation. It was their belief that, if they ever weakened, the great beast would engulf them and everything of beauty and joy and wonder and good in its cavernous and slime-dripping maw. Without them, anarchy would reign and humanity would drop backward into the primitive night out of which it had so painfully emerged ... In short, they alone, by their unremitting toil and self-sacrifice, stood between weak humanity and the all-devouring beast: and they believed it, firmly believed it.

I cannot lay too great stress upon this high ethical righteousness of the whole Oligarch class. This has been the strength of the Iron Heel, and too many of the comrades have been slow or loath to realise it. Many of them have ascribed the strength of the Iron Heel to its system of reward and punishment. This is a mistake. Heaven and hell may be the prime factors of zeal in the religion of a fanatic; but for the great majority of the religious, heaven and hell are incidental to right and wrong. Love of the right, desire for the right, unhappiness with anything less than the right – in short, right conduct, is the prime factor of religion. And so with the Oligarchy ... The great driving force of the Oligarchs is the belief that they are doing right.

From these and similar passages it can be seen that London's understanding of the nature of a ruling class – that is, the characteristics which a ruling class must have if it is to survive – went very deep. According to the conventional left-wing view, the "capitalist" is simply a cynical scoundrel, without honour or courage, and intent only on filling his own pockets. London knew that that view is false. But why, one might justly ask, should this hurried, sensational, in some ways childish writer have understood that particular thing so much better than the majority of his fellow Socialists?

The answer is surely that London could foresee Fascism because he had a Fascist streak in himself: or at any rate a marked strain of brutality and an almost unconquerable preference for the strong man as against the weak man. He knew instinctively that the American business-men would fight when their possessions were menaced, because in their place he would have fought himself. He was an adventurer and a man of action as few writers have ever been. Born into dire poverty, he had already escaped from it at sixteen, thanks to his commanding character and powerful physique: his early years were spent among oyster pirates, gold prospectors, tramps and prizefighters, and he was ready to admire toughness wherever he found it. On the other hand he never forgot the sordid miseries of his childhood, and he never faltered in his loyalty to the exploited classes. Much of his time was spent in working and lecturing for the Socialist movement, and when he was already a successful and famous man he could explore the worst depths of poverty in the London slums, passing himself off as an American sailor, and compile a book (*The People of the Abyss*) which still has sociological value. His outlook was democratic in the sense that he hated exploitation and hereditary privilege, and that he felt most at home in the company of people who worked with their hands: but his instinct lay towards acceptance of a "natural aristocracy" of strength, beauty and talent. Intellectually he knew, as one can see from various remarks in *The Iron Heel*, that Socialism ought to mean the meek inheriting the earth, but that was not what his temperament demanded. In much of his work one strain in his character simply kills the other off: he is at his best where they interact, as they do in certain of his short stories.

Jack London's great theme is the cruelty of Nature. Life is a savage struggle, and victory has nothing to do with justice. In the best of his short stories there is a startling lack of comment, a suspension of judgement, arising out of the fact that he both delights in the struggle and perceives its cruelty. Perhaps the best thing he ever wrote is *Just Meat*. Two burglars have got away with a big haul of jewellery: each is intent on swindling the other out of his share, and they poison one another simultaneously with strychnine, the story ending with the two men dead on the floor. There is almost no comment, and certainly no "moral." As Jack London sees it, it is simply a fragment of life, the kind of thing that happens in the present-day world: nevertheless it is doubtful whether such a plot would occur to any writer who was not fascinated by cruelty. Or take a story like *The "Francis Spaight."* The starving crew of a waterlogged ship has decided to resort to cannibalism, and have just nerved themselves to begin when another ship heaves in sight. It is characteristic of Jack London that the second ship should appear after and not before the cabin boy's throat has been cut. A still more typical story is *A Piece of Steak*. London's love of boxing and admiration for sheer physical strength, his perception of the meanness and cruelty of a competitive society, and at the same time his instinctive tendency to accept *vae victis* as a law of Nature, are all expressed here. An old prizefighter is fighting his last battle: his opponent is a beginner, young and full of vigour, but without experience. The old man nearly wins, but in the end his ring-craft is no match for the youthful resilience of the other. Even when he has him at his mercy he is unable to strike the blow that would finish him, because he has been underfed for weeks before the fight and his muscles cannot make the necessary effort. He is left bitterly reflecting that if only he had had a good piece of steak on the day of the fight he would have won.

The old man's thoughts all run upon the theme: "Youth will be served." First you are young and strong, and you knock out older men and make money which you squander: then your strength wanes and in turn you are knocked out by younger men, and then you sink into poverty. This does in fact tell the story of the average boxer's life, and it would be a gross exaggeration to say that Jack London *approves* of the way in which men are used up like gladiators by a society which cannot even bother to feed them. The detail of the piece of steak – not strictly necessary, since the main point of the story is that the younger man is bound to win by virtue of his youth – rubs in the economic implication. And yet there is something in London that takes a kind of pleasure in the whole cruel process. It is not so much an approval of the harshness of Nature, as a mystical belief that Nature *is* like that. Nature is "red in tooth and claw." Perhaps fierceness is bad, but fierceness is the price of survival. The young slay the old, the strong slay the weak, by an inexorable law. Man fights against the elements or against his fellow man, and there is nothing except his own toughness to help him through. London would have said that he was merely describing life as it is actually lived, and in his best stories he does so: still, the constant recurrence of the same theme – struggle, toughness, survival – shows which way his inclinations pointed.

London had been deeply influenced by the theory of the Survival of the Fittest. His book, *Before Adam* – an inaccurate but very readable story of pre-history, in which ape-men and early and late Palæolithic men are all shown as existing simultaneously – is an attempt to popularise Darwin. Although Darwin's main thesis has not been shaken, there has been, during the past twenty or thirty years, a change in the interpretation put upon it by the average thinking man. In the late nineteenth century Darwinism was used as a justification for laissez-faire capitalism, for power politics and for the exploiting of subject peoples. Life was a free-for-all in which the fact of survival was proof of fitness to survive: this was a comforting thought for successful business men, and it also led naturally, though not very logically, to the notion of "superior" and "inferior" races. In our day we are less willing to apply biology to politics, partly because we have watched the Nazis do just that thing, with great thoroughness and with horrible results. But when London was writing, a crude version of Darwinism was widespread and must have been difficult to escape. He himself was even capable at times of succumbing to racial mysticism. He toyed for a while with a race theory similar to that of the Nazis, and throughout his work the cult of the "Nordic" is fairly well marked. It ties up on the one hand with his admiration for prizefighters, and on the other with his anthropomorphic view of animals: for there seems to be good reason for thinking that an exaggerated love of animals generally goes with a rather brutal attitude towards human beings. London was a Socialist with the instincts of a buccaneer and the education of a nineteenth-century materialist. In general the background of his stories is not industrial, nor even civilised. Most of them take place – and much of his own life was lived – on ranches or South Sea islands, in ships, in prison or in the wastes of the Arctic: places where a man is either alone and dependent on his own strength and cunning, or where life is naturally patriarchal.

Nevertheless, London did write from time to time about contemporary industrial society, and on the whole he was at his best when he did so. Apart from his short stories, there are *The*

People of the Abyss, *The Road* (a brilliant little book describing London's youthful experiences as a tramp), and certain passages in *The Valley of the Moon*, which have the tumultuous history of American trade unionism as their background. Although the tug of his impulses was away from civilisation, London had read deeply in the literature of the Socialist movement, and his early life had taught him all he needed to know about urban poverty. He himself was working in a factory at the age of eleven, and without that experience behind him he could hardly have written such a story as *The Apostate*. In this story, as in all his best work, London does not comment, but he does unquestionably aim at rousing pity and indignation. It is generally when he writes of more primitive scenes that his moral attitude becomes equivocal. Take, for instance, a story like *Make Westing*. With whom do London's sympathies lie – with Captain Cullen or with George Dorety? One has the impression that if he were forced to make a choice he would side with the Captain, who commits two murders but does succeed in getting his ship round Cape Horn. On the other hand, in a story like *The Chinago*, although it is told in the usual pitiless style, the "moral" is plain enough for anyone who wants to find it. London's better angel is his Socialist convictions, which come into play when he deals with such subjects as coloured exploitation, child labour or the treatment of criminals, but are hardly involved when he is writing about explorers or animals. It is probably for this reason that a high proportion of his better writings deal with urban life. In stories like *The Apostate*, *Just Meat*, *A Piece of Steak* and *Semper Idem*, however cruel and sordid they may seem, something is keeping him on the rails and checking his natural urge towards the glorification of brutality. That "something" is his knowledge, theoretical as well as practical, of what industrial capitalism means in terms of human suffering.

Jack London is a very uneven writer. In his short and restless life he poured forth an immense quantity of work, setting himself to produce 1,000 words every day and generally achieving it. Even his best stories have the curious quality of being well told and yet not well written: they are told with admirable economy, with just the right incidents in just the right place, but the texture of the writing is poor, the phrases

are worn and obvious, and the dialogue is erratic. His reputation has had its ups and downs, and for a long period he seems
to have been much more admired in France and Germany than
in the English-speaking countries. Even before the triumph of
Hitler, which brought *The Iron Heel* out of its obscurity, he had
a certain renown as a left-wing and "proletarian" writer –
rather the same kind of renown as attaches to Robert Tressell,
W. B. Traven or Upton Sinclair. He has also been attacked by
Marxist writers for his "Fascist tendencies." These tendencies
unquestionably existed in him, so much so that if one imagines
him as living on into our own day, instead of dying in 1915, it is
very hard to be sure where his political allegiance would have
lain. One can imagine him in the Communist Party, one can
imagine him falling a victim to Nazi racial theory, and one
can imagine him the quixotic champion of some Trotskyist or
Anarchist sect. But, as I have tried to make clear, if he had been
a politically reliable person he would probably have left behind
nothing of interest. Meanwhile his reputation rests mainly on
The Iron Heel, and the excellence of his short stories has been
almost forgotten. A dozen of the best of them are collected in
this volume, and a few more are worth rescuing from the
museum shelves and the second-hand boxes. It is to be
hoped, too, that new editions of *The Road*, *The Jacket*, *Before
Adam* and *The Valley of the Moon* will appear when paper
becomes more plentiful. Much of Jack London's work is
scamped and unconvincing, but he produced at least six
volumes which deserve to stay in print, and that is not a bad
achievement from a life of only forty-one years.

Review of *Mind at the End of Its Tether* by H. G. Wells

Manchester Evening News, 8 November 1945

Mr. Wells explains in his preface that his new book "Mind at
the End of Its Tether" is intended to supersede "'42 to '44," a
book of essays which was published last year and which had
been flung together rather hurriedly, because at that time he
did not expect to live much longer.

The present book (it is only 34 pages) brings to a conclusive end the series of essays, memoranda, pamphlets through which the writer has experimented, challenged discussion, and assembled material bearing upon the fundamental nature of life and time. So far as fundamentals go, he has nothing more and never will have anything more to say.

It is, indeed, hard to see how Mr. Wells could add much to his present message, since that message is to the effect that – if his reasoning is correct – life on this planet is now due to come to an end.

"This world," he says, "is at the end of its tether; and the end of everything we call life is close at hand and cannot be evaded." It is not completely clear whether this means all life or merely human life, but, at any rate, homo sapiens is doomed.

A series of events has forced upon the intelligent observer the realisation that the human story has already come to an end, and that homo sapiens, as he has been pleased to call himself, is, in his present form, played out. The stars in their courses have turned against him and he has to give place to some other animal better adapted to face the fate that closes in more and more swiftly upon mankind.

One could hardly have anything more final than that. A little later, however, Mr. Wells seems to suggest that the inheriting species may belong to the hominidæ.[23] A small minority of adaptable human beings may survive if they are capable of turning into something else: the new animal may be an entirely alien strain, or it may arise as a new modification of the hominidæ, and even as a direct continuation of the human phylum,[24] but it will certainly not be human. There is no way out for man but steeply up or steeply down. Adapt or perish, now as ever, is nature's inexorable imperative.

In other words, the price of survival is an evolutionary leap so abrupt that the product of it will not be a human being. However, in the last sentence of the book it is once again stated that life itself is coming to an "inevitable end," so that it hardly seems to matter whether or not a few transformed hominidæ are present at the final death-agony.

The fact is that this is an incoherent book, and, in spite of its shortness, probably unfinished. And yet the issues it raises are interesting. This is not a moment at which one can simply disregard the statement that humanity is doomed. It quite well may be doomed. Mr. Wells does not give his reasons for thinking that life itself is coming to an end, but so far as mankind is concerned he is presumably thinking of the power of modern weapons and our complete failure to produce a social and political organisation capable of controlling them.

It is interesting to learn that he wrote this book before the arrival of the atomic bomb – which, however, he himself prophesied years ago in "The World Set Free."

It is certainly true that man must either alter his habits quickly or see civilisation blown to pieces – and it may be true, as Mr. Wells suggests, that the great mass of mankind is simply unteachable and the necessary change can only happen through an evolutionary change in a chosen minority.

But one is obliged to ask – where is this minority to come from? We ourselves are the only hominidæ on this planet, and there are no great differences between the various races of man – and as for an evolutionary change so drastic that the resulting creature would be definitely "not human," it is hardly likely to happen in a few generations. So it would seem that the necessary new species is not in sight, in which case life is finished. And yet a faint doubt, not due entirely to wish-thinking, keeps intruding itself.

Are we really done for? If the worst came to the worst and a shower of atom bombs descended on every great city in the world, would that necessarily be the end? The end of machine civilisation – yes, but probably not of human life. It is worth remembering how numerous the human race has become in recent centuries. The population of Europe is probably ten times what it was in Roman times, and that of North America a hundred times what it was in the days of Columbus. One could kill off 95 per cent of humanity, and the world would still be more populous than it was in the Stone Age. The survivors would revert to savagery, but they would probably retain knowledge of the use of metals – and at any rate it would be a long time before they had another chance of monkeying with atomic bombs.

It would be simply dishonest to pretend that this is one of Mr. Wells's better books.

Indeed, it is hardly a book at all, merely a series of short, disjointed essays which have probably been written with considerable effort between bouts of illness. And yet it has the power that Mr. Wells's writings have always had – the power of arresting the reader's attention and forcing him to think and argue. The thesis that it puts forward may be far-fetched, it may even be slightly absurd, but it has a sort of grandeur.

It calls up that world of cooling stars and battling dinosaurs which Mr. Wells has made so peculiarly his own. Mr. Wells is 79 and may not, he thinks, live very much longer. Nevertheless, while writing this book he has been contemplating another, to be entitled "Decline and Fall of Monarchy and Competitive Imperialisms." Let us hope that he writes it. Meanwhile, in spite of its incoherence, the present book is well worth the hour or so that it takes to read it.

Catastrophic Gradualism
C.W. Review, November 1945

There is a theory which has not yet been accurately formulated or given a name, but which is very widely accepted and is brought forward whenever it is necessary to justify some action which conflicts with the sense of decency of the average human being. It might be called, until some better name is found, the Theory of Catastrophic Gradualism. According to this theory, nothing is ever achieved without bloodshed, lies, tyranny and injustice, but on the other hand no considerable change for the better is to be expected as the result of even the greatest upheaval. History necessarily proceeds by calamities, but each succeeding age will be as bad, or nearly as bad, as the last. One must not protest against purges, deportations, secret police forces and so forth, because these are the price that has to be paid for progress: but on the other hand "human nature" will always see to it that progress is slow or even imperceptible. If you object to dictatorship you are a reactionary, but if you expect dictatorship to produce good results you are a sentimentalist.

At present this theory is most often used to justify the Stalin régime in the USSR, but it obviously could be – and, given appropriate circumstances, would be – used to justify other forms of totalitarianism. It has gained ground as a result of the failure of the Russian Revolution – failure, that is, in the sense that the Revolution has not fulfilled the hopes that it aroused twenty-five years ago. In the name of Socialism the Russian régime has committed almost every crime that can be imagined, but at the same time its evolution is *away* from Socialism, unless one re-defines that word in terms that no Socialist of 1917 would have accepted. To those who admit these facts, only two courses are open. One is simply to repudiate the whole theory of totalitarianism, which few English intellectuals have the courage to do: the other is to fall back on Catastrophic Gradualism. The formula usually employed is "You can't make an omelette without breaking eggs." And if one replies, "Yes, but where is the omelette?", the answer is likely to be: "Oh well, you can't expect everything to happen all in a moment."

Naturally this argument is pushed backward into history, the design being to show that every advance was achieved at the cost of atrocious crimes, and could not have been achieved otherwise. The instance generally used is the overthrow of feudalism by the bourgeoisie, which is supposed to foreshadow the overthrow of Capitalism by Socialism in our own age. Capitalism, it is argued, was once a progressive force, and therefore its crimes were justified, or at least were unimportant. Thus, in a recent number of the *New Statesman*, Mr. Kingsley Martin, reproaching Arthur Koestler for not possessing a true "historical perspective," compared Stalin with Henry VIII. Stalin, he admitted, had done terrible things, but on balance he had served the cause of progress, and a few million "liquidations" must not be allowed to obscure this fact. Similarly, Henry VIII's character left much to be desired, but after all he had made possible the rise of Capitalism, and therefore on balance could be regarded as a friend of humanity.

Now, Henry VIII has not a very close resemblance to Stalin; Cromwell would provide a better analogy; but, granting Henry VIII the importance given to him by Mr. Martin, where does this argument lead? Henry VIII made possible the rise of Capitalism, which led to the horrors of the Industrial Revolution and thence to a cycle of enormous wars, the next of which may well destroy civilization altogether. So, telescoping the process, we can put it like this: "Everything is to be forgiven to Henry VIII, because it was ultimately he who enabled us to blow ourselves to pieces with atomic bombs." You are led into similar absurdities if you make Stalin responsible for our present condition and the future which appears to lie before us, and at the same time insist that his policies must be supported. The motives of those English intellectuals who support the Russian dictatorship are, I think, different from what they publicly admit, but it is logical to condone tyranny and massacre if one assumes that progress is inevitable. If each epoch is as a matter of course better than the last, then any crime or any folly that pushes the historical process forward can be justified. Between, roughly, 1750 and 1930 one could be forgiven for imagining that progress of a solid measurable kind was taking place. Latterly, this has become more and more difficult, whence the theory of Catastrophic Gradualism. Crime follows crime, one ruling class replaces another, the Tower of Babel rises and falls, but one mustn't resist the process – indeed, one must be ready to applaud any piece of scoundrelism that comes off – because in some mystical way, in the sight of God, or perhaps in the sight of Marx, this is Progress. The alternative would be to stop and consider (a) to what extent is history pre-determined? and (b) what is meant by progress? At this point one has to call in the Yogi to correct the Commissar.

In his much-discussed essay, Koestler is generally assumed to have come down heavily on the side of the Yogi. Actually, if one assumes the Yogi and the Commissar to be at opposite points of the scale, Koestler is somewhat nearer to the Commissar's end. He believes in action, in violence where necessary, in government, and consequently in the shifts and compromises that are inseparable from government. He supported the war, and the Popular Front before it. Since the appearance of Fascism he has struggled against it to the best of his ability, and for many years he was a member of the Communist Party. The long chapter in his book in which he criticizes the USSR is even vitiated by a lingering loyalty to his old party and by a resulting tendency to make all bad developments date from the rise of Stalin: whereas one ought, I believe, to admit that all the seeds of evil were there from the start and that things would not have been substantially different if Lenin or Trotsky had remained in control. No one is less likely than Koestler to claim that we can put everything right by watching our navels in California. Nor is he claiming, as religious thinkers usually do, that a "change of heart" must come *before* any genuine political improvement. To quote his own words:

> Neither the saint nor the revolutionary can save us; only the synthesis of the two. Whether we are capable of achieving it I do not know. But if the answer is in the negative, there seems to be no reasonable hope of preventing the destruction of European civilization, either by total war's successor Absolute War, or by Byzantine conquest – within the next few decades.

That is to say, the "change of heart" must happen, but it is not really happening unless at each step it issues in action. On the other hand, no change in the structure of society can by itself effect a real improvement. Socialism used to be defined as "common ownership of the means of production," but it is now seen that if common ownership means no more than centralized control, it merely paves the way for a new form of oligarchy. Centralized control is a necessary pre-condition of Socialism, but it no more produces Socialism than my typewriter would of itself produce this article I am writing. Throughout history, one revolution after another – although usually producing a temporary relief, such as a sick man gets by turning over in bed – has simply led to a change of masters, because no serious effort has been made to eliminate the power instinct: or if such an effort has been made, it has been made only by the saint, the Yogi, the man who saves his own soul at the expense of ignoring the community. In the minds of active revolutionaries, at any rate the ones who "got there," the longing for a just society has always been fatally mixed up with the intention to secure power for themselves.

Koestler says that we must learn once again the technique of contemplation, which "remains the only source of guidance in ethical dilemmas where the rule-of-thumb criteria of social utility fail." By "contemplation" he means "the will not to will," the conquest of the desire for power. The practical men have led us to the edge of the abyss, and the intellectuals in whom acceptance of power politics has killed first the moral sense, and then the sense of reality, are urging us to march rapidly forward without changing direction. Koestler maintains that history is not at all moments predetermined, but that there are turning-points at which humanity is free to choose the better or the worse road. One such turning-point (which had not appeared when he wrote the book) is the Atomic Bomb. Either we renounce it, or it destroys us. But renouncing it is both a moral effort and a political effort. Koestler calls for "a new fraternity in a new spiritual climate, whose leaders are tied by a vow of poverty to share the life of the masses, and debarred by the laws of the fraternity from attaining unchecked power"; he adds, "if this seems utopian, then Socialism is a utopia." It may not even be a utopia – its very name may in a couple of generations have ceased to be a memory – unless we can escape from the folly of "realism." But that will not happen without a change in the individual heart. To that extent, though no further, the Yogi is right as against the Commissar.

Good Bad Books
Tribune, 2 November 1945

Not long ago a publisher commissioned me to write an introduction for a reprint of a novel by Leonard Merrick. This publishing house, it appears, is going to re-issue a long series of minor and partly-forgotten novels of the twentieth century. It is a valuable service in these bookless days, and I rather envy the person whose job it will be to scout round the three-penny boxes, hunting down copies of his boyhood favourites.

A type of book which we hardly seem to produce in these days, but which flowered with great richness in the late nineteenth and early twentieth centuries, is what Chesterton called the "good bad book": that is, the kind of book that has no literary pretensions but which remains readable when more serious productions have perished. Obviously outstanding books in this line are *Raffles* and the Sherlock Holmes stories, which have kept their place when innumerable "problem novels," "human documents" and "terrible indictments" of this or that have fallen into deserved oblivion. (Who has worn better, Conan Doyle or Meredith?) Almost in the same class as these I put R. Austin Freeman's earlier stories – *The Singing Bone*, *The Eye of Osiris* and others – Ernest Bramah's *Max Carrados*, and, dropping the standard a bit, Guy Boothby's Tibetan thriller, *Dr. Nikola*, a sort of schoolboy version of Huc's *Travels in Tartary*, which would probably make a real visit to Central Asia seem a dismal anti-climax.

But apart from thrillers, there were the minor humorous writers of the period. For example, Pett Ridge – but I admit his full-length books no longer seem readable – E. Nesbit (*The Treasure Seekers*), George Birmingham, who was good so long as he kept off politics, the pornographic Binstead ("Pitcher" of the *Pink 'Un*), and, if American books can be included, Booth Tarkington's Penrod stories. A cut above most of these was Barrie Pain. Some of Pain's humorous writings are, I suppose, still in print, but to anyone who comes across it I recommend what must now be a very rare book – *The Octave of Claudius*, a brilliant exercise in the macabre. Somewhat later in time there was Peter Blundell, who wrote in the W. W. Jacobs vein about Far Eastern seaport towns, and who seems to be rather unaccountably forgotten, in spite of having been praised in print by H. G. Wells.

However, all the books I have been speaking of are frankly "escape" literature. They form pleasant patches in one's memory, quiet corners where the mind can browse at odd moments, but they hardly pretend to have anything to do with real life. There is another kind of good bad book which is more seriously intended, and which tells us, I think, something about the nature of the novel and the reasons for its present decadence. During the last fifty years there has been a whole series of writers – some of them are still writing – whom it is quite impossible to call "good" by any strictly literary standard, but who are natural novelists and who seem to attain sincerity partly because they are not inhibited by good taste. In this class I put Leonard Merrick himself, W. L. George, J. D. Beresford, Ernest Raymond, May Sinclair, and – at a lower level than the others but still essentially similar – A. S. M. Hutchinson.

Most of these have been prolific writers, and their output has naturally varied in quality. I am thinking in each case of one or two outstanding books: for example. Merrick's *Cynthia*,

J. D. Beresford's *A Candidate for Truth*, W. L. George's *Caliban*, May Sinclair's *The Combined Maze*, and Ernest Raymond's *We, the Accused*. In each of these books the author has been able to identify himself with his imagined characters, to feel with them and invite sympathy on their behalf, with a kind of abandonment that cleverer people would find it difficult to achieve. They bring out the fact that intellectual refinement can be a disadvantage to a story-teller, as it would be to a music-hall comedian.

Take, for example, Ernest Raymond's *We, the Accused* – a peculiarly sordid and convincing murder story, probably based on the Crippen case. I think it gains a great deal from the fact that the author only partly grasps the pathetic vulgarity of the people he is writing about, and therefore does not despise them. Perhaps it even – like Theodore Dreiser's *An American Tragedy* – gains something from the clumsy, long-winded manner in which it is written; detail is piled on detail, with almost no attempt at selection, and in the process an effect of terrible, grinding cruelty is slowly built up. So also with *A Candidate for Truth*. Here there is not the same clumsiness, but there is the same ability to take seriously the problems of commonplace people. So also with *Cynthia* and at any rate the earlier part of *Caliban*. The greater part of what W. L. George wrote was shoddy rubbish, but in this particular book, based on the career of Northcliffe, he achieved some memorable and truthful pictures of lower-middle-class London life. Parts of this book are probably autobiographical, and one of the advantages of good bad writers is their lack of shame in writing autobiography. Exhibition and self-pity are the bane of the novelist, and yet if he is too frightened of them his creative gift may suffer.

The existence of good bad literature – the fact that one can be amused or excited or even moved by a book that one's intellect simply refuses to take seriously – is a reminder that art is not the same thing as cerebration. I imagine that by any test that could be devised, Carlyle would be found to be a more intelligent man than Trollope. Yet Trollope has remained readable and Carlyle has not: with all his cleverness he had not even the wit to write in plain straightforward English. In novelists, almost as much as in poets, the connection between intelligence and creative power is hard to establish. A good novelist may be a prodigy of self-discipline like Flaubert, or he may be an intellectual sprawl like Dickens. Enough talent to set up dozens of ordinary writers has been poured into Wyndham Lewis's so-called novels, such as *Tarr* or *Snooty Baronet*. Yet it would be a very heavy labour to read one of these books right through. Some indefinable quality, a sort of literary vitamin, which exists even in a book like *If Winter Comes*, is absent from them.

Perhaps the supreme example of the "good bad" book is *Uncle Tom's Cabin*. It is an unintentionally ludicrous book, full of preposterous melodramatic incidents; it is also deeply moving and essentially true; it is hard to say which quality outweighs the other. But *Uncle Tom's Cabin*, after all, is trying to be serious and to deal with the real world. How about the frankly escapist writers, the purveyors of thrills and "light" humour? How about *Sherlock Holmes*, *Vice Versa*, *Dracula*, *Helen's Babies* or *King Solomon's Mines*? All of these are definitely absurd books, books which one is more inclined to laugh *at* than *with*, and which were hardly taken seriously even by their authors; yet they have survived, and will probably continue to do so. All one can say is that, while civilisation remains such that one needs distraction from time to time, "light" literature has its appointed place; also that there is such a thing as sheer skill, or native grace, which may have more survival value than erudition or intellectual power. There are music-hall songs which are better poems than three-quarters of the stuff that gets into the anthologies:

> Come where the booze is cheaper,
> Come where the pots hold more,
> Come where the boss is a bit of a sport,
> Come to the pub next door!

Or again:

> Two lovely black eyes –
> Oh, what a surprise!
> Only for calling another man wrong,
> Two lovely black eyes!

I would far rather have written either of those than, say, *The Blessed Damozel* or *Love in the Valley*. And by the same token I would back *Uncle Tom's Cabin* to outlive the complete works of

Virginia Woolf or George Moore, though I know of no strictly literary test which would show where the superiority lies.

The Prevention of Literature

Polemic, January 1946; *The Atlantic Monthly*, March 1947

About a year ago I attended a meeting of the P.E.N. Club, the occasion being the tercentenary of Milton's *Areopagitica* – a pamphlet, it may be remembered, in defence of freedom of the Press. Milton's famous phrase about the sin of "killing" a book was printed on the leaflets advertising the meeting which had been circulated beforehand.

There were four speakers on the platform. One of them delivered a speech which did deal with the freedom of the Press, but only in relation to India; another said, hesitantly, and in very general terms, that liberty was a good thing; a third delivered an attack on the laws relating to obscenity in literature. The fourth devoted most of his speech to a defence of the Russian purges. Of the speeches from the body of the hall, some reverted to the question of obscenity and the laws that deal with it, others were simply eulogies of Soviet Russia. Moral liberty – the liberty to discuss sex questions frankly in print – seemed to be generally approved, but political liberty was not mentioned. Out of this concourse of several hundred people, perhaps half of whom were directly connected with the writing trade, there was not a single one who could point out that freedom of the Press, if it means anything at all, means the freedom to criticise and oppose. Significantly, no speaker quoted from the pamphlet which was ostensibly being commemorated. Nor was there any mention of the various books that have been "killed" in this country and the United States during the war. In its net effect the meeting was a demonstration in favour of censorship.[25]

There was nothing particularly surprising in this. In our age, the idea of intellectual liberty is under attack from two directions. On the one side are its theoretical enemies, the apologists of totalitarianism, and on the other its immediate, practical enemies, monopoly and bureaucracy. Any writer or journalist who wants to retain his integrity finds himself thwarted by the general drift of society rather than by active persecution. The sort of things that are working against him are the concentration of the Press in the hands of a few rich men, the grip of monopoly on radio and the films, the unwillingness of the public to spend money on books, making it necessary for nearly every writer to earn part of his living by hackwork, the encroachment of official bodies like the M.O.I. and the British Council, which help the writer to keep alive but also waste his time and dictate his opinions, and the continuous war atmosphere of the past ten years, whose distorting effects no one has been able to escape. Everything in our age conspires to turn the writer, and every other kind of artist as well, into a minor official, working on themes handed to him from above and never telling what seems to him the whole of the truth. But in struggling against this fate he gets no help from his own side: that is, there is no large body of opinion which will assure him that he is in the right. In the past, at any rate throughout the Protestant centuries, the idea of rebellion and the idea of intellectual integrity were mixed up. A heretic – political, moral, religious, or æsthetic – was one who refused to outrage his own conscience. His outlook was summed up in the words of the Revivalist hymn:

> Dare to be a Daniel,
> Dare to stand alone;
> Dare to have a purpose firm,
> Dare to make it known.

To bring this hymn up to date one would have to add a "Don't" at the beginning of each line. For it is the peculiarity of our age that the rebels against the existing order, at any rate the most numerous and characteristic of them, are also rebelling against the idea of individual integrity. "Daring to stand alone" is ideologically criminal as well as practically dangerous. The independence of the writer and the artist is eaten away by vague economic forces, and at the same time it is undermined by those who should be its defenders. It is with the second process that I am concerned here.

Freedom of speech and of the Press are usually attacked by arguments which are not worth bothering about. Anyone who has experience in lecturing and debating knows them backwards. Here I am not trying to deal with the familiar claim that freedom is an illusion, or with the claim that there is more freedom in totalitarian countries than in democratic ones, but with the much more tenable and dangerous proposition that freedom is undesirable and that intellectual honesty is a form of anti-social selfishness. Although other aspects of the question are usually in the foreground, the controversy over freedom of speech and of the Press is at bottom a controversy over the desirability, or otherwise, of telling lies. What is really at issue is the right to report contemporary events truthfully, or as truthfully as is consistent with the ignorance, bias and self-deception from which every observer necessarily suffers. In saying this I may seem to be saying that straightforward "reportage" is the only branch of literature that matters: but I will try to show later that at every literary level, and probably in every one of the arts, the same issue arises in more or less subtilised forms. Meanwhile, it is necessary to strip away the irrelevancies in which this controversy is usually wrapped up.

The enemies of intellectual liberty always try to present their case as a plea for discipline versus individualism. The issue truth-versus-untruth is as far as possible kept in the background. Although the point of emphasis may vary, the writer who refuses to sell his opinions is always branded as a mere egoist. He is accused, that is, either of wanting to shut himself up in an ivory tower, or of making an exhibitionist display of his own personality, or of resisting the inevitable current of history in an attempt to cling to unjustified privileges. The Catholic and the Communist are alike in assuming that an opponent cannot be both honest and intelligent. Each of them tacitly claims that "the truth" has already been revealed, and that the heretic, if he is not simply a fool, is secretly aware of "the truth" and merely resists it out of selfish motives. In Communist literature the attack on intellectual liberty is usually masked by oratory about "petty-bourgeois individualism", "the illusions of nineteenth-century liberalism", etc., and backed up by words of abuse such as "romantic" and "sentimental", which, since they do not have any agreed meaning, are difficult to answer. In this way the controversy is manœuvred away from its real issue. One can accept, and most enlightened people would accept, the Communist thesis that pure freedom will only exist in a classless society, and that one is most nearly free when one is working to bring about such a society. But slipped in with this is the quite unfounded claim that the Communist party is itself aiming at the establishment of the classless society, and that in the U.S.S.R. this aim is actually on the way to being realised. If the first claim is allowed to entail the second, there is almost no assault on common sense and common decency that cannot be justified. But meanwhile, the real point has been dodged. Freedom of the intellect means the freedom to report what one has seen, heard, and felt, and not to be obliged to fabricate imaginary facts and feelings. The familiar tirades against "escapism", "individualism", "romanticism" and so forth, are merely a forensic device, the aim of which is to make the perversion of history seem respectable.

Fifteen years ago, when one defended the freedom of the intellect, one had to defend it against Conservatives, against Catholics, and to some extent – for in England they were not of great importance – against Fascists. To-day one has to defend it against Communists and "fellow travellers". One ought not to exaggerate the direct influence of the small English Communist party, but there can be no question about the poisonous effect of the Russian *mythos* on English intellectual life. Because of it, known facts are suppressed and distorted to such an extent as to make it doubtful whether a true history of our times can ever be written. Let me give just one instance out of the hundreds that could be cited. When Germany collapsed, it was found that very large numbers of Soviet Russians – mostly, no doubt, from non-political motives – had changed sides and were fighting for the Germans. Also, a small but not negligible proportion of the Russian prisoners and Displaced Persons refused to go back to the U.S.S.R., and some of them, at least, were repatriated against their will. These facts, known to many journalists on the spot, went almost unmentioned in the British Press, while at the same time Russophile publicists in England continued to justify the purges and deportations of 1936–38 by claiming that the U.S.S.R. "had no quislings". The fog of lies and misinformation that surrounds such subjects as the Ukraine famine, the Spanish civil war, Russian policy in Poland, and so forth, is not due entirely to conscious dishonesty, but any writer or journalist who is fully sympathetic to the U.S.S.R. – sympathetic, that is, in the way the Russians themselves would want him to be – does have to acquiesce in deliberate falsification on important issues. I have before me what must be a very rare pamphlet, written by Maxim Litvinoff in 1918 and outlining the recent events in the Russian Revolution. It makes no mention of Stalin, but gives high praise to Trotsky, and also to Zinoviev, Kamenev, and others. What could be the attitude of even the most intellectually scrupulous Communist towards such a pamphlet? At best, he would take the obscurantist attitude that it is an undesirable document and better suppressed. And if for some reason it should be decided to issue a garbled version of the pamphlet, denigrating Trotsky and inserting references to Stalin, no Communist who remained faithful to his party could protest. Forgeries almost as gross as this have been committed in recent years. But the significant thing is not that they happen, but that even when they are known, they provoke no reaction from the Left-wing intelligentsia as a whole. The argument that to tell the truth would be "inopportune" or would "play into the hands of" somebody or other is felt to be unanswerable, and few people are bothered by the prospect that the lies which they condone will get out of the newspapers and into the history books.

The organised lying practised by totalitarian states is not, as is sometimes claimed, a temporary expedient of the same nature as military deception. It is something integral to totalitarianism, something that would still continue even if concentration camps and secret police forces had ceased to be necessary. Among intelligent Communists there is an underground legend to the effect that although the Russian government is obliged now to deal in lying propaganda, frame-up trials, and so forth, it is secretly recording the facts and will publish them at some future time. We can, I believe, be quite certain that this is not the case, because the mentality implied by such an action is that of a liberal historian who believes that the past cannot be altered and that a correct knowledge of history is valuable as a matter of course. From the totalitarian point of view history is something to be created rather than learned. A totalitarian state is in effect a theocracy, and its ruling caste, in order to keep its position, has to be thought of as infallible. But since, in practice, no one is infallible, it is frequently necessary to rearrange past events in order to show that this or that mistake was not made, or that this or that imaginary triumph actually happened. Then, again, every major change in policy demands a corresponding change of doctrine and a revaluation of prominent historical figures. This kind of thing happens everywhere, but clearly it is likelier to lead to outright falsification in societies where only one opinion is permissible at any given moment. Totalitarianism demands, in fact, the continuous alteration of the past, and in the long run probably demands a disbelief in the very existence of objective truth. The friends of totalitarianism in this country usually tend to argue that since absolute truth is not attainable, a big lie is no worse than a little lie. It is pointed out that all historical records are biased and inaccurate, or, on the other hand, that modern physics has proved that what seems to us the real world is an illusion, so that to believe in the evidence of one's senses is simply vulgar philistinism. A totalitarian society which succeeded in perpetuating itself would probably set up a schizophrenic system of thought, in which the laws of common sense held good in everyday life and in certain exact sciences, but could be disregarded by the politician, the historian, and the sociologist. Already there are countless people who would think it scandalous to falsify a scientific textbook, but would see nothing wrong in falsifying a historical fact. It is at the point where literature and politics cross that totalitarianism exerts its greatest pressure on the intellectual. The exact sciences are not, at this date, menaced to anything like the same extent. This difference partly accounts for the fact that in all countries it is easier for the scientists than for the writers to line up behind their respective governments.

To keep the matter in perspective, let me repeat what I said at the beginning of this essay: that in England the immediate enemies of truthfulness, and hence of freedom of thought, are the Press lords, the film magnates, and the bureaucrats, but that on a long view the weakening of the desire for liberty among the intellectuals themselves is the most serious symptom of all. It may seem that all this time I have been talking about the effects of censorship, not on literature as a whole, but merely on one department of political journalism. Granted that Soviet

Russia constitutes a sort of forbidden area in the British Press, granted that issues like Poland, the Spanish civil war, the Russo-German pact, and so forth, are debarred from serious discussion, and that if you possess information that conflicts with the prevailing orthodoxy you are expected either to distort it or to keep quiet about it – granted all this, why should literature in the wider sense be affected? Is every writer a politician, and is every book necessarily a work of straightforward "reportage"? Even under the tightest dictatorship, cannot the individual writer remain free inside his own mind and distil or disguise his unorthodox ideas in such a way that the authorities will be too stupid to recognise them? And if the writer himself is in agreement with the prevailing orthodoxy, why should it have a cramping effect on him? Is not literature, or any of the arts, likeliest to flourish in societies in which there are no major conflicts of opinion and no sharp distinctions between the artist and his audience? Does one have to assume that every writer is a rebel, or even that a writer as such is an exceptional person?

Whenever one attempts to defend intellectual liberty against the claims of totalitarianism, one meets with these arguments in one form or another. They are based on a complete misunderstanding of what literature is, and how – one should perhaps rather say *why* – it comes into being. They assume that a writer is either a mere entertainer or else a venal hack who can switch from one line of propaganda to another as easily as an organ grinder changes tunes. But after all, how is it that books ever come to be written? Above a quite low level, literature is an attempt to influence the views of one's contemporaries by recording experience. And so far as freedom of expression is concerned, there is not much difference between a mere journalist and the most "unpolitical" imaginative writer. The journalist is unfree, and is conscious of unfreedom, when he is forced to write lies or suppress what seems to him important news: the imaginative writer is unfree when he has to falsify his subjective feelings, which from his point of view are facts. He may distort and caricature reality in order to make his meaning clearer, but he cannot misrepresent the scenery of his own mind: he cannot say with any conviction that he likes what he dislikes, or believes what he disbelieves. If he is forced to do so, the only result is that his creative faculties dry up. Nor can the imaginative writer solve the problem by keeping away from controversial topics. There is no such thing as genuinely non-political literature, and least of all in an age like our own, when fears, hatreds, and loyalties of a directly political kind are near to the surface of everyone's consciousness. Even a single tabu can have an all-round crippling effect upon the mind, because there is always the danger that any thought which is freely followed up may lead to the forbidden thought. It follows that the atmosphere of totalitarianism is deadly to any kind of prose writer, though a poet, at any rate a lyric poet, might possibly find it breathable. And in any totalitarian society that survives for more than a couple of generations, it is probable that prose literature, of the kind that has existed during the past four hundred years, must actually *come to an end*.

Literature has sometimes flourished under despotic regimes, but, as has often been pointed out, the despotisms of the past were not totalitarian. Their repressive apparatus was always inefficient, their ruling classes were usually either corrupt or apathetic or half-liberal in outlook, and the prevailing religious doctrines usually worked against perfectionism and the notion of human infallibility. Even so it is broadly true that prose literature has reached its highest levels in periods of democracy and free speculation. What is new in totalitarianism is that its doctrines are not only unchallengeable but also unstable. They have to be accepted on pain of damnation, but on the other hand they are always liable to be altered at a moment's notice. Consider, for example, the various attitudes, completely incompatible with one another, which an English Communist or "fellow traveller" has had to adopt towards the war between Britain and Germany. For years before September 1939 he was expected to be in a continuous stew about "the horrors of Nazism" and to twist everything he wrote into a denunciation of Hitler; after September 1939, for twenty months, he had to believe that Germany was more sinned against than sinning, and the word "Nazi", at least so far as print went, had to drop right out of his vocabulary. Immediately after hearing the 8 o'clock news bulletin on the morning of June 22, 1941, he had to start believing once again that Nazism was the most hideous evil the world had ever seen. Now, it is easy for a politician to make such changes: for a writer the case is somewhat different. If he is to switch his allegiance at exactly the right moment, he must either tell lies about his subjective feelings, or else suppress them altogether. In either case he has destroyed his dynamo. Not only will ideas refuse to come to him, but the very words he uses will seem to stiffen under his touch. Political writing in our time consists almost entirely of prefabricated phrases bolted together like the pieces of a child's Meccano set. It is the unavoidable result of self-censorship. To write in plain, vigorous language one has to think fearlessly, and if one thinks fearlessly one cannot be politically orthodox. It might be otherwise in an "age of faith", when the prevailing orthodoxy has been long established and is not taken too seriously. In that case it would be possible, or might be possible, for large areas of one's mind to remain unaffected by what one officially believed. Even so, it is worth noticing that prose literature almost disappeared during the only age of faith that Europe has ever enjoyed. Throughout the whole of the Middle Ages there was almost no imaginative prose literature and very little in the way of historical writing: and the intellectual leaders of society expressed their most serious thoughts in a dead language which barely altered during a thousand years.

Totalitarianism, however, does not so much promise an age of faith as an age of schizophrenia. A society becomes totalitarian when its structure becomes flagrantly artificial: that is, when its ruling class has lost its function but succeeds in clinging to power by force or fraud. Such a society, no matter how long it persists, can never afford to become either tolerant or intellectually stable. It can never permit either the truthful recording of facts, or the emotional sincerity, that literary creation demands. But to be corrupted by totalitarianism one does not have to live in a totalitarian country. The mere prevalence of certain ideas can spread a poison that makes one subject after another impossible for literary purposes. Wherever there is an enforced orthodoxy – or even two orthodoxies, as often happens – good writing stops. This was well illustrated by the Spanish civil war. To many English intellectuals the war was a deeply moving experience, but not an experience about which they could write sincerely. There were only two things that you were allowed to say, and both of them were palpable lies: as a result,

939

GEORGE ORWELL

the war produced acres of print but almost nothing worth reading.

It is not certain whether the effects of totalitarianism upon verse need be so deadly as its effects on prose. There is a whole series of converging reasons why it is somewhat easier for a poet than for a prose writer to feel at home in an authoritarian society. To begin with, bureaucrats and other "practical" men usually despise the poet too deeply to be much interested in what he is saying. Secondly, what the poet is saying – that is, what his poem "means" if translated into prose – is relatively unimportant even to himself. The thought contained in a poem is always simple, and is no more the primary purpose of the poem than the anecdote is the primary purpose of a picture. A poem is an arrangement of sounds and associations, as a painting is an arrangement of brush-marks. For short snatches, indeed, as in the refrain of a song, poetry can even dispense with meaning altogether. It is therefore fairly easy for a poet to keep away from dangerous subjects and avoid uttering heresies: and even when he does utter them, they may escape notice. But above all, good verse, unlike good prose, is not necessarily an individual product. Certain kinds of poems, such as ballads, or, on the other hand, very artificial verse forms, can be composed co-operatively by groups of people. Whether the ancient English and Scottish ballads were originally produced by individuals, or by the people at large, is disputed; but at any rate they are non-individual in the sense that they constantly change in passing from mouth to mouth. Even in print no two versions of a ballad are ever quite the same. Many primitive peoples compose verse communally. Someone begins to improvise, probably accompanying himself on a musical instrument, somebody else chips in with a line or a rhyme when the first singer breaks down, and so the process continues until there exists a whole song or ballad which has no identifiable author.

In prose, this kind of intimate collaboration is quite impossible. Serious prose, in any case, has to be composed in solitude, whereas the excitement of being part of a group is actually an aid to certain kinds of versification. Verse – and perhaps good verse of its kind, though it would not be the highest kind – might survive under even the most inquisitorial regime.

Even in a society where liberty and individuality had been extinguished, there would still be need either for patriotic songs and heroic ballads celebrating victories, or for elaborate exercises in flattery: and these are the kinds of poetry that can be written to order, or composed communally, without necessarily lacking artistic value. Prose is a different matter, since the prose writer cannot narrow the range of his thoughts without killing his inventiveness. But the history of totalitarian societies, or of groups of people who have adopted the totalitarian outlook, suggests that loss of liberty is inimical to *all* forms of literature. German literature almost disappeared during the Hitler regime, and the case was not much better in Italy. Russian literature, so far as one can judge by translations, has deteriorated markedly since the early days of the Revolution, though some of the verse appears to be better than the prose. Few if any Russian novels that it is possible to take seriously have been translated for about fifteen years. In western Europe and America large sections of the literary intelligentsia have either passed through the Communist party or been warmly sympathetic to it, but this whole leftward movement has produced extraordinarily few books worth reading. Orthodox Catholicism, again, seems to have a crushing effect upon certain literary forms, especially the novel. During a period of three hundred years, how many people have been at once good novelists and good Catholics? The fact is that certain themes cannot be celebrated in words, and tyranny is one of them. No one ever wrote a good book in praise of the Inquisition. Poetry *might* survive in a totalitarian age, and certain arts or half-arts, such as architecture, might even find tyranny beneficial, but the prose writer would have no choice between silence and death. Prose literature as we know it is the product of rationalism, of the Protestant centuries, of the autonomous individual. And the destruction of intellectual liberty cripples the journalist, the sociological writer, the historian, the novelist, the critic, and the poet, in that order. In the future it is possible that a new kind of literature, not involving individual feeling or truthful observation, may arise, but no such thing is at present imaginable. It seems much likelier that if the liberal culture that we have lived in since the Renaissance actually comes to an end, the literary art will perish with it.

Of course, print will continue to be used, and it is interesting to speculate what kinds of reading matter would survive in a rigidly totalitarian society. Newspapers will presumably continue until television technique reaches a higher level, but apart from newspapers it is doubtful even now whether the great mass of people in the industrialised countries feel the need for any kind of literature. They are unwilling, at any rate, to spend anywhere near as much on reading matter as they spend on several other recreations. Probably novels and stories will be completely superseded by film and radio productions. Or perhaps some kind of low-grade sensational fiction will survive, produced by a sort of conveyor-belt process that reduces human initiative to the minimum.

It would probably not be beyond human ingenuity to write books by machinery. But a sort of mechanising process can already be seen at work in the film and radio, in publicity and propaganda, and in the lower reaches of journalism. The Disney films, for instance, are produced by what is essentially a factory process, the work being done partly mechanically and partly by teams of artists who have to subordinate their individual style. Radio features are commonly written by tired hacks to whom the subject and the manner of treatment are dictated beforehand: even so, what they write is merely a kind of raw material to be chopped into shape by producers and censors. So also with the innumerable books and pamphlets commissioned by government departments. Even more machine-like is the production of short stories, serials, and poems for the very cheap magazines. Papers such as the *Writer* abound with advertisements of Literary Schools, all of them offering you ready-made plots at a few shillings a time. Some, together with the plot, supply the opening and closing sentences of each chapter. Others furnish you with a sort of algebraical formula by the use of which you can construct your plots for yourself. Others offer packs of cards marked with characters and situations, which have only to be shuffled and dealt in order to produce ingenious stories automatically. It is probably in some such way that the literature of a totalitarian society would be produced, if literature were still felt to be necessary. Imagination – even consciousness, so far as possible – would be eliminated from the process of writing. Books would be planned in their broad lines by bureaucrats, and would pass through so many hands that when finished they would be no more an individual product than a Ford car at the end of the assembly line. It goes without saying that anything so produced would be rubbish; but anything that was not rubbish would endanger the structure of the state. As for the surviving literature of the past, it would have to be suppressed or at least elaborately rewritten.

Meanwhile totalitarianism has not fully triumphed anywhere. Our own society is still, broadly speaking, liberal. To exercise your right of free speech you have to fight against economic pressure and against strong sections of public opinion, but not, as yet, against a secret police force. You can say or print almost anything so long as you are willing to do it in a hole-and-corner way. But what is sinister, as I said at the beginning of this essay, is that the conscious enemies of liberty are those to whom liberty ought to mean most. The public do not care about the matter one way or the other. They are not in favour of persecuting the heretic, and they will not exert themselves to defend him. They are at once too sane and too stupid to acquire the totalitarian outlook. The direct, conscious attack on intellectual decency comes from the intellectuals themselves.

It is possible that the Russophile intelligentsia, if they had not succumbed to that particular myth, would have succumbed to another of much the same kind. But at any rate the Russian myth is there, and the corruption it causes stinks. When one sees highly educated men looking on indifferently at oppression and persecution, one wonders which to despise more, their cynicism or their short-sightedness. Many scientists, for example, are uncritical admirers of the U.S.S.R. They appear to think that the destruction of liberty is of no importance so long as their own line of work is for the moment unaffected. The U.S.S.R. is a large, rapidly developing country which has acute need of scientific workers and, consequently, treats them generously. Provided that they steer clear of dangerous subjects such as psychology, scientists are privileged persons. Writers, on the other hand, are viciously persecuted. It is true that literary prostitutes like Ilya Ehrenburg or Alexei Tolstoy are paid huge sums of money, but the only thing which is of any value to the writer as such – his freedom of expression – is taken away from him. Some, at least, of the English scientists who speak so enthusiastically of the opportunities enjoyed by scientists in Russia are capable of understanding this. But their reflection appears to be: "Writers are persecuted in Russia. So what? I am not a writer." They do not see that *any* attack on intellectual liberty, and on the concept of objective truth, threatens in the long run every department of thought.

For the moment the totalitarian state tolerates the scientist because it needs him. Even in Nazi Germany, scientists, other than Jews, were relatively well treated, and the German scientific community, as a whole, offered no resistance to Hitler. At this stage of history, even the most autocratic ruler is forced to take account of physical reality, partly because of the lingering-on of liberal habits of thought, partly because of the need to prepare for war. So long as physical reality cannot be altogether ignored, so long as two and two have to make four when you are, for example, drawing the blueprint of an aeroplane, the scientist has his function, and can even be allowed a measure of liberty. His awakening will come later, when the totalitarian state is firmly established. Meanwhile, if he wants to safeguard the integrity of science, it is his job to develop some kind of solidarity with his literary colleagues and not regard it as a matter of indifference when writers are silenced or driven to suicide, and newspapers systematically falsified.

But however it may be with the physical sciences, or with music, painting, and architecture, it is – as I have tried to show – certain that literature is doomed if liberty of thought perishes. Not only is it doomed in any country which retains a totalitarian structure; but any writer who adopts the totalitarian outlook, who finds excuses for persecution and the falsification of reality, thereby destroys himself as a writer. There is no way out of this. No tirades against "individualism" and "the ivory tower", no pious platitudes to the effect that "true individuality is only attained through identification with the community", can get over the fact that a bought mind is a spoiled mind. Unless spontaneity enters at some point or another, literary creation is impossible, and language itself becomes ossified. At some time in the future, if the human mind becomes something totally different from what it now is, we may learn to separate literary creation from intellectual honesty. At present we know only that the imagination, like certain wild animals, will not breed in captivity. Any writer or journalist who denies that fact – and nearly all the current praise of the Soviet Union contains or implies such a denial – is, in effect, demanding his own destruction.

Review of *The Prussian Officer* by D. H. Lawrence
Tribune, 16 November 1945

Reviews ought not to consist of personal reminiscences, but perhaps it is worth recording how I first became acquainted with D. H. Lawrence's work, because it happened that I read him before I had heard of him, and the qualities which then impressed me were probably the essential ones.

In 1919 I went into my schoolmaster's study for some purpose, and, not finding him there, picked up a magazine with a blue cover which was on the table. I was then sixteen and wallowing in Georgian poetry. My idea of a good poem would have been Rupert Brooke's *Grantchester*. As soon as I opened the magazine I was completely overwhelmed by a poem which describes a woman standing in the kitchen and watching her husband approaching across the fields. On the way he takes a rabbit out of a snare and kills it. Then he comes in, throws the dead rabbit on the table, and, his hands still stinking of rabbit's fur, takes the woman in his arms. In a sense she hates him, but she is utterly swallowed up in him. More than the sexual encounter, the "beauty of Nature" which Lawrence deeply felt, but which he was also able to turn on and off like a tap, impressed me; especially the lines (referring to a flower):

> Then her bright breast she will uncover
> And yield her honeydrop to her lover.

But I failed to notice the name of the author, or even of the magazine, which must have been the *English Review*.

Four or five years later, still not having heard of Lawrence, I got hold of the volume of short stories now reprinted as a

Penguin. Both "The Prussian Officer" and "The Thorn in the Flesh" impressed me deeply. What struck me was not so much Lawrence's horror and hatred of military discipline, as his understanding of its nature. Something told me that he had never been a soldier, and yet he could project himself into the atmosphere of an army, and the German army at that. He had built all this up, I reflected, from watching a few German soldiers walking about in some garrison town. From another story, "The White Stocking" (also in this collection, though I think I read it later), I deduced the moral that women behave better if they get a sock on the jaw occasionally.

Clearly there is more in Lawrence than this, but I think these first impacts left me with a broadly true picture of him. He was in essence a lyric poet, and an undisciplined enthusiasm for "Nature," i.e., the surface of the earth, was one of his principal qualities, though it has been much less noticed than his preoccupation with sex. And on top of this he had the power of understanding, or seeming to understand, people totally different from himself, such as farmers, gamekeepers, clergymen and soldiers – one might add coalminers, for though Lawrence himself had worked in the pit at the age of thirteen, clearly he was not a typical miner. His stories are a kind of lyric poem, produced by just looking at some alien, inscrutable human being and suddenly experiencing an intense imaginative vision of his inner life.

How true these visions were is debatable. Like some Russian writers of the nineteenth century, Lawrence often seems to by-pass the novelist's problem by making all his characters equally sensitive. All the people in his stories, even those to whom he is hostile, seem to experience the same kind of emotions, everyone can make contact with everyone else, and class barriers, in the form in which we know them, are almost obliterated. Yet he does often seem to have an extraordinary power of knowing imaginatively something that he could not have known by observation. Somewhere in one of his books he remarks that when you shoot at a wild animal, the action is not the same as shooting at a target. You do not look along the sights: you aim by an instinctive movement of the whole body, and it is as though your will were driving the bullet forward. This is quite true, and yet I do not suppose

Lawrence had ever shot at a wild animal. Or consider the death scene at the end of "England My England" (which is not in the present collection, unfortunately). Lawrence had never been in circumstances remotely similar to those he was describing. He had merely had a private vision of the feelings of a soldier under fire. Perhaps it is true to experience, perhaps not: but at least it is emotionally true, and therefore convincing.

With few exceptions Lawrence's full-length novels are, it is generally admitted, difficult to get through. In the short stories his faults do not matter so much, because a short story can be purely lyrical, whereas a novel has to take account of probability and has to be cold-bloodedly constructed. In *The Prussian Officer* there is an extraordinarily good, longish story called "Daughters of the Vicar." An Anglican clergyman of the ordinary middle-class type is marooned in a mining village where he and his family are half-starved on a tiny stipend, and where he has no function, the mining folk having no need of him and no sympathy with him. It is the typical impoverished middle-class family in which the children grow up with a false consciousness of social superiority dragging upon them like a ball and fetter. The usual problem arises: how are the daughters to get married? The elder daughter gets the chance to marry a comparatively well-to-do clergyman. He happens to be a dwarf, suffering from some internal disease, and an utterly inhuman creature, more like a precocious and disagreeable child than a man. By the standards of most of the family she has done the right thing: she has married a gentleman. The younger daughter, whose vitality is not to be defeated by snobbishness, throws family prestige overboard and marries a healthy young coalminer.

It will be seen that this story has a close resemblance to *Lady Chatterley's Lover*. But in my opinion it is much better and more convincing than the novel, because the single imaginative impulse is strong enough to sustain it. Probably Lawrence had watched, somewhere or other, the underfed, downtrodden, organ-playing daughter of a clergyman wearing out her youth, and had a sudden vision of her escaping into the warmer world of the working class, where husbands are plentiful. It is a fit subject for a short story, but when drawn out to novel length it raises difficulties to which Lawrence was unequal. In another story in this book, "The Shades of Spring," there is a game-keeper who is presented as a wild natural creature, the opposite of the over-conscious intellectual. Such figures appear again and again in Lawrence's books, and I think it is true to say that they are more convincing in the short stories, where we do not have to know too much about them, than in the novels (for example, *Lady Chatterley's Lover* or *The Woman Who Rode Away*), where, in order to be set into action, they have to be credited with complex thoughts which destroy their status as unspoiled animals. Another story, "Odour of Chrysanthemums," deals with the death of a miner in a pit accident. He is a drunkard, and up to the moment of his death his wife has wanted nothing so much as to be rid of him. Only when she is washing his dead body does she perceive, as though for the first time, how beautiful he is. That is the kind of thing Lawrence could do, and in the first paragraph of the story there is a wonderful example of his power of visual description. But one could not make a full-length novel out of such an episode, nor, without other more prosaic ingredients, out of a series of such episodes.

This is not quite the best volume of Lawrence's short stories, and it is to be hoped that the Penguin Library will follow it up by reprinting *England My England*. That contains, apart from the name story, "Fannie and Annie," "The Horse-dealer's Daughter," and, above all, "The Fox." This last story is perhaps the best thing Lawrence ever did, but it has the unusual quality of centring round an idea that might have occurred to anybody, so that one can enjoy the mental exercise of imagining the same story as it might have been told by Tolstoy, Maupassant, Henry James or Edgar Wallace. But the present volume contains at least six stories of the first rank, and only one ("A Fragment of Stained Glass") that is definitely a failure.

Bare Christmas for the Children
Evening Standard, 1 December 1945

The toyshops are not quite so empty as they were this time last year, but that is about the most one can say.

Among the classes of toys that still seem to be completely "out" are rubber and celluloid articles of every kind – no balloons, no swans or goldfish to float in your bath – wax dolls, Meccano sets, and of course, the ingenious clockwork toys that once used to come to us from Germany.

Toy tricycles, if they still exist, are second-hand rarities, though scooters are fairly numerous, and also dolls' prams of very poor quality. Bows and arrows may still be procurable, but I have not seen any, and even pocket knives are hard to come by.

The rag dolls and the wooden toys – carts, tommy guns and the like – are as badly made and expensive as ever. Rag books seem to have vanished years ago. On the other hand, lead soldiers are fairly common again. They are lead soldiers of the inferior kind, flat and gilded all over, but perhaps they seem thrilling enough to the seven-year-old child who has never seen those realistic models, complete with gasmask and blancoed gaiters, that were on sale before the war.

Fretsaws are also procurable, though spare blades are not easy to get. And you can buy Plasticine once again, and other kinds of modelling wax, and kaleidoscopes; also paint-boxes and brushes of not absolutely bad quality. But good drawing paper is not so easy to find, and it still seems impossible to get hold of a BB pencil.

Here and there you can find those agreeable little grocer's shops with scales, tin canisters and a wooden counter; and a very welcome feature is the reappearance of chemistry outfits, one of the most absorbing of all toys for an intelligent boy of about twelve.

In one London shop I saw quite elaborate sets with test tubes, flasks and spirit lamps – though I admit that when I learned the price I felt as though I had been hit over the head with a rubber club.

It will once again be rather a bare Christmas from the child's point of view, but one ought to remember that the importance of manufactured toys is exaggerated. Very young children hardly need toys.

It is absurd, for instance, to give a doll to a baby, as people habitually do. To the baby a doll is merely a soft object, in no way superior to a knotted towel, and even at the toddling age it is generally happier with the fire tongs, or a stone inside a tin can, than with anything that comes out of a shop.

Certain toys you can make for yourself if you have the tools. A wooden truck, or even the simpler kind of hobby-horse, is stronger as well as cheaper if you make it yourself, and you can buy the wheels at any wood shop.

Beyond a quite low age children often seem to get their greatest enjoyment out of things that cannot strictly be called toys: for instance, carpentering tools, sewing materials, beads, linoleum for making lino-cuts, china-clay and plaster of paris. It is curious that though carpentering and fretwork have been adapted for play purposes, tin-smithing and black-smithing have not.

From the age of about eight onwards a bright child wants to be either making something or breaking something. A boy of twelve gets almost inexhaustible pleasure out of a catapult, which he makes for himself at the cost of about sixpence.

It was because of this universal passion that the Belisha beacons had to be made out of metal instead of glass.

For children who live in the country, one of the most fascinating toys, during about two-thirds of the year, is a pond-water aquarium, for which one uses a small accumulator jar or a 7lb. pickle jar. The creatures that live in it – tadpoles, caddis flies and water fleas – need little attention, and the aquarium is a more interesting object in the middle of the dinner table than a bowl of flowers.

When the toy trade becomes normal again, I hope that several old favourites which had already vanished before the war will come back again. Whip tops are still in fashion, but peg tops seem to have dropped out in recent years. There were two kinds: a coloured one which you threw over your shoulder, and a white one, much harder to handle, which you threw underhand.

One of the greatest joys of my own childhood were those little brass cannons on wooden gun-carriages which are now hardly to be found outside an antique shop. The smallest had barrels the size of your little finger, the largest were six or eight inches long, cost ten shillings and went off with a noise like the Day of Judgment.

To fire them you needed gunpowder, which the shops sometimes refused to sell you, but a resourceful boy could make gunpowder for himself if he took the precaution of buying the ingredients from three different chemists.

One of the advantages of being a child thirty years ago was the lighter-hearted attitude that then prevailed towards fire-arms. Up till not long before the other war you could walk into any bicycle shop and buy a revolver, and even when the authorities began to take an interest in revolvers, you could still buy for 7s. 6d. a fairly lethal weapon known as a Saloon Rifle. I bought my first Saloon Rifle at the age of ten, with no questions asked.

Normal healthy children enjoy explosions. I think I have heard more explosions – though not such large ones, certainly – since VE Day than I heard in the six years preceding it.

Meanwhile you would have difficulty even in buying an airgun, and such as exist are mostly poor things.

Let us hope that this time next year it will be different, and all the rare or unprocurable toys will be back in the shops again; not only airguns, but motorcars with pedals and a chain drive, clockwork mice to frighten your aunt, locomotives with real boilers in them, dolls' sewing machines, wooden bricks square enough to stand on one another, ninepins whose balls are round instead of being egg-shaped, and – not strictly toys, but no child's upbringing is complete without them – new editions of Struwwelpeter and the Beatrix Potter books, now only obtainable by much searching through the shelves of second-hand book-shops.

The Case for the Open Fire
Evening Standard, 8 December 1945

Before long the period of hurriedly constructed prefabs will be over, and Britain will be tackling on a big scale the job of building permanent houses.

It will then be necessary to decide what kind of heating we want our houses to have, and one can be sure in advance that a small but noisy minority will want to do away with the old-fashioned coal fire.

These people – they are also the people who admire gaspipe chairs and glass-topped tables, and regard labour-saving as an end in itself – will argue that the coal fire is wasteful, dirty and inefficient. They will urge that dragging buckets of coal upstairs is a nuisance and that raking out the cinders in the morning is a grisly job, and they will add that the fogs of our cities are made thicker by the smoking of thousands of chimneys.

All of which is perfectly true, and yet comparatively unimportant if one thinks in terms of living and not merely of saving trouble.

I am not arguing that coal fires should be the sole form of heating, merely that every house or flat should have at least one open fire round which the family can sit. In our climate anything that keeps you warm is to be welcomed, and under ideal conditions every form of heating apparatus would be installed in every house.

For any kind of workroom central heating is the best arrangement. It needs no attention, and, since it warms all parts of the room evenly, one can group the furniture according to the needs of work.

For bedrooms, gas or electric fires are best. Even the humble oilstove throws out a lot of heat, and has the virtue of being portable. It is a great comfort to carry an oilstove with you into the bathroom on a winter morning. But for a room that is to be lived in, only a coal fire will do.

The first great virtue of a coal fire is that, just because it only warms one end of the room, it forces people to group themselves in a sociable way. This evening, while I write, the same pattern is being reproduced in hundreds of thousands of British homes.

To one side of the fireplace sits Dad, reading the evening paper. To the other side sits Mum, doing her knitting. On the hearthrug sit the children, playing snakes and ladders. Up against the fender, roasting himself, lies the dog. It is a comely pattern, a good background to one's memories, and the survival of the family as an institution may be more dependent on it than we realise.

Then there is the fascination, inexhaustible to a child, of the fire itself. A fire is never the same for two minutes together, you can look into the red heart of the coals and see caverns or faces or salamanders, according to your imagination: you can even, if your parents will let you, amuse yourself by heating the poker red-hot and bending it between the bars, or sprinkling salt on the flames to turn them green.

A gas or electric fire, or even an anthracite stove, is a dreary thing by comparison. The most dismal objects of all are those phoney electric fires which are so constructed as to look like coal fires. Is not the mere fact of imitation an admission that the real thing is superior?

If, as I maintain, an open fire makes for sociability and has an æsthetic appeal which is particularly important to young children, it is well worth the trouble that it entails.

It is quite true that it is wasteful, messy and the cause of avoidable work: all the same things could be said with equal truth of a baby. The point is that household appliances should be judged not simply by their efficiency but by the pleasure and comfort that one gets out of them.

A vacuum cleaner is good because it saves much dreary labour with brush and pan. Gaspipe furniture is bad because it destroys the friendly look of a room without appreciably adding to one's comfort.

Our civilisation is haunted by the notion that the quickest way of doing anything is invariably the best. The agreeable warming-pan, which warms the whole bed as hot as toast before you jump into it, went out in favour of the clammy, unsatisfying hot-water bottle simply because the warming-pan is a nuisance to carry upstairs and has to be polished daily.

Some people, obsessed by "functionalism," would make every room in the house as bare, clean and labour-saving as a prison cell. They do not reflect that houses are meant to be lived in and that you therefore need different qualities in different rooms. In the kitchen, efficiency; in the bedrooms, warmth; in the living-room, a friendly atmosphere – which in this country demands a good, prodigal coal fire for about seven months of the year.

I am not denying that coal fires have their drawbacks, especially in these days of dwindled newspapers. Many a devout Communist has been forced against all his principles to take in a capitalist paper merely because the Daily Worker is not large enough to light the fire with.

Also there is the slowness with which a fire gets under way in the morning. It would be a good idea, when the new houses are built, if every open fireplace were provided with what used to be called a "blower" – that is, a removable sheet of metal which can be used to create a draught. This works far better than a pair of bellows.

But even the worst fire, even a fire which smokes in your face and has to be constantly poked, is better than none.

In proof of which, imagine the dreariness of spending Christmas evening in sitting – like the family of Arnold Bennett's super-efficient hero in his novel The Card – round a gilded radiator!

Politics and the English Language

Payments Book, 11 December 1945; *Horizon*, April 1946

Most people who bother with the matter at all would admit that the English language is in a bad way, but it is generally assumed that we cannot by conscious action do anything about it. Our civilization is decadent, and our language – so the argument runs – must inevitably share in the general collapse. It follows that any struggle against the abuse of language is a sentimental archaism, like preferring candles to electric light or hansom cabs to aeroplanes. Underneath this lies the half-conscious belief that language is a natural growth and not an instrument which we shape for our own purposes.

Now, it is clear that the decline of a language must ultimately have political and economic causes: it is not due simply to the bad influence of this or that individual writer. But an effect can become a cause, reinforcing the original cause and producing the same effect in an intensified form, and so on indefinitely. A man may take to drink because he feels himself to be a failure, and then fail all the more completely because he drinks. It is rather the same thing that is happening to the English language. It becomes ugly and inaccurate because our thoughts are foolish, but the slovenliness of our language makes it easier for us to have foolish thoughts. The point is that the process is reversible. Modern English, especially written English, is full of bad habits which spread by imitation and which can be avoided if one is willing to take the necessary trouble. If one gets rid of these habits one can think more clearly, and to think clearly is a necessary first step towards political regeneration: so that the fight against bad English is not frivolous and is not the exclusive concern of professional writers. I will come back to this presently, and I hope that by that time the meaning of what I have said here will have become clearer. Meanwhile, here are five specimens of the English language as it is now habitually written.

These five passages have not been picked out because they are especially bad – I could have quoted far worse if I had chosen – but because they illustrate various of the mental vices from which we now suffer. They are a little below the average, but are fairly representative samples. I number them so that I can refer back to them when necessary:

(1) 'I am not, indeed, sure whether it is not true to say that the Milton who once seemed not unlike a seventeenth-century Shelley had not become, out of an experience ever more bitter in each year, more alien [sic] to the founder of that Jesuit sect which nothing could induce him to tolerate.'

Professor Harold Laski (Essay in *Freedom of Expression*).

(2) 'Above all, we cannot play ducks and drakes with a native battery of idioms which prescribes such egregious collocations of vocables as the Basic *put up with* for *tolerate* or *put at a loss* for *bewilder*.'

Professor Lancelot Hogben (*Interglossa*).

(3) 'On the one side we have the free personality: by definition it is not neurotic, for it has neither conflict nor dream. Its desires, such as they are, are transparent, for they are just what institutional approval keeps in the forefront of consciousness; another institutional pattern would alter their number and intensity; there is little in them that is natural, irreducible, or culturally dangerous. But *on the other side*, the social bond itself is nothing but the mutual reflection of these self-secure integrities. Recall the definition of love. Is not this the very picture of a small academic? Where is there a place in this hall of mirrors for either personality or fraternity?'

Essay on psychology in *Politics* (New York).

(4) 'All the "best people" from the gentlemen's clubs, and all the frantic fascist captains, united in common hatred of Socialism and bestial horror of the rising tide of the mass revolutionary movement, have turned to acts of provocation, to foul incendiarism, to medieval legends of poisoned wells, to legalize their own destruction of proletarian organizations, and rouse the agitated petty-bourgeoisie to chauvinistic fervour on behalf of the fight against the revolutionary way out of the crisis.'

Communist pamphlet.

(5) 'If a new spirit *is* to be infused into this old country, there is one thorny and contentious reform which must be tackled, and that is the humanization and galvanization of the B.B.C. Timidity here will bespeak canker and atrophy of the soul. The heart of Britain may be sound and of strong beat, for instance, but the British lion's roar at present is like that of Bottom in Shakespeare's *Midsummer Night's Dream* – as gentle as any sucking dove. A virile new Britain cannot continue indefinitely to be traduced in the eyes, or rather ears, of the world by the effete languors of Langham Place, brazenly masquerading as "standard English". When the Voice of Britain is heard at nine o'clock, better far and infinitely less ludicrous to hear aitches honestly dropped than the present priggish, inflated, inhibited, school-ma'amish arch braying of blameless bashful mewing maidens!'

Letter in *Tribune*.

Each of these passages has faults of its own, but, quite apart from avoidable ugliness, two qualities are common to all of them. The first is staleness of imagery: the other is lack of precision. The writer either has a meaning and cannot express it, or he inadvertently says something else, or he is almost indifferent as to whether his words mean anything or not. This mixture of vagueness and sheer incompetence is the most marked characteristic of modern English prose, and especially of any kind of political writing. As soon as certain topics are raised, the concrete melts into the abstract and no one seems able to think of turns of speech that are not hackneyed: prose consists less and less of *words* chosen for the sake of their meaning, and more and more of *phrases* tacked together like the sections of a prefabricated hen-house. I list below, with notes and examples, various of the tricks by means of which the work of prose-construction is habitually dodged:

Dying metaphors. A newly invented metaphor assists thought by evoking a visual image, while on the other hand a metaphor which is technically 'dead' (e.g. *iron resolution*) has in effect reverted to being an ordinary word and can generally be used without loss of vividness. But in between these two classes there is a huge dump of worn-out metaphors which have lost all evocative power and are merely used because they save people the trouble of inventing phrases for themselves. Examples are: *Ring the changes on, take up the cudgels for, toe the line, ride roughshod over, stand shoulder to shoulder with, play into the hands of, no axe to grind, grist to the mill, fishing in troubled waters, rift within the lute, on the order of the day, Achilles' heel, swan song, hotbed.* Many of these are used without knowledge of their meaning (what is a 'rift', for instance?), and incompatible metaphors are frequently mixed, a sure sign that the writer is not interested in what he is saying. Some metaphors now current have been twisted out of their original meaning without those who use them even being aware of the fact. For example, *toe the line* is sometimes written *tow the line*. Another example is *the hammer and the anvil*, now always used with the implication that the anvil gets the worst of it. In real life it is always the anvil that breaks the hammer, never the other way about: a writer who stopped to think what he was saying would be aware of this, and would avoid perverting the original phrase.

Operators, or *verbal false limbs.* These save the trouble of picking out appropriate verbs and nouns, and at the same time pad each sentence with extra syllables which give it an appearance of symmetry. Characteristic phrases are: *render inoperative, militate against, prove unacceptable, make contact with, be subjected to, give rise to, give grounds for, have the effect of, play a leading part (role) in, make itself felt, take effect, exhibit a tendency to, serve the purpose of,* etc., etc. The keynote is the elimination of simple verbs. Instead of being a single word, such as *break, stop, spoil, mend, kill,* a verb becomes a *phrase,* made up of a noun or adjective tacked on to some general-purposes verb such as

prove, serve, form, play, render. In addition, the passive voice is
wherever possible used in preference to the active, and noun
constructions are used instead of gerunds (*by examination of*
instead of *by examining*). The range of verbs is further cut
down by means of the *-ize* and *de-* formations, and banal
statements are given an appearance of profundity by means of
the *not un-* formation. Simple conjunctions and prepositions
are replaced by such phrases as *with respect to, having regard to, the
fact that, by dint of, in view of, in the interests of, on the hypothesis
that*; and the ends of sentences are saved from anticlimax by
such resounding commonplaces as *greatly to be desired, cannot be
left out of account, a development to be expected in the near future,
deserving of serious consideration, brought to a satisfactory conclusion*,
and so on and so forth.

Pretentious diction. Words like *phenomenon, element, individual
(as noun), objective, categorical, effective, virtual, basic, primary, promote, constitute, exhibit, exploit, utilize, eliminate, liquidate*, are
used to dress up simple statements and give an air of scientific
impartiality to biased judgements. Adjectives like *epoch-making,
epic, historic, unforgettable, triumphant, age-old, inevitable, inexorable, veritable*, are used to dignify the sordid processes of international politics, while writing that aims at glorifying war
usually takes on an archaic colour, its characteristic words
being: *realm, throne, chariot, mailed fist, trident, sword, shield,
buckler, banner, jackboot, clarion.* Foreign words and expressions
such as *cul de sac, ancien régime, deus ex machina, mutatis mutandis,
status quo, gleichschaltung, weltanschauung*, are used to give an air
of culture and elegance. Except for the useful abbreviations *i.e.,
e.g.*, and *etc.*, there is no real need for any of the hundreds of
foreign phrases now current in English. Bad writers, and especially scientific, political and sociological writers, are nearly
always haunted by the notion that Latin or Greek words are
grander than Saxon ones, and unnecessary words like *expedite,
ameliorate, predict, extraneous, deracinated, clandestine, subaqueous*
and hundreds of others constantly gain ground from their
Anglo-Saxon opposite numbers.[26] The jargon peculiar to
Marxist writing (*hyena, hangman, cannibal, petty bourgeois, these
gentry, lacquey, flunkey, mad dog, White Guard*, etc.) consists
largely of words and phrases translated from Russian, German

or French; but the normal way of coining a new word is to use a Latin or Greek root with the appropriate affix and, where necessary, the -ize formation. It is often easier to make up words of this kind (*deregionalize, impermissible, extramarital, non-fragmentary* and so forth) than to think up the English words that will cover one's meaning. The result, in general, is an increase in slovenliness and vagueness.

Meaningless words. In certain kinds of writing, particularly in art criticism and literary criticism, it is normal to come across long passages which are almost completely lacking in meaning.[27] Words like *romantic, plastic, values, human, dead, sentimental, natural, vitality,* as used in art criticism, are strictly meaningless, in the sense that they not only do not point to any discoverable object, but are hardly even expected to do so by the reader. When one critic writes, 'The outstanding feature of Mr. X's work is its living quality', while another writes, 'The immediately striking thing about Mr. X's work is its peculiar deadness', the reader accepts this as a simple difference of opinion. If words like *black* and *white* were involved, instead of the jargon words *dead* and *living*, he would see at once that language was being used in an improper way. Many political words are similarly abused. The word *Fascism* has now no meaning except in so far as it signifies 'something not desirable'. The words *democracy, socialism, freedom, patriotic, realistic, justice,* have each of them several different meanings which cannot be reconciled with one another. In the case of a word like *democracy*, not only is there no agreed definition, but the attempt to make one is resisted from all sides. It is almost universally felt that when we call a country democratic we are praising it: consequently the defenders of every kind of régime claim that it is a democracy, and fear that they might have to stop using the word if it were tied down to any one meaning. Words of this kind are often used in a consciously dishonest way. That is, the person who uses them has his own private definition, but allows his hearer to think he means something quite different. Statements like *Marshal Pétain was a true patriot, The Soviet Press is the freest in the world, The Catholic Church is opposed to persecution,* are almost always made with intent to deceive. Other words used in variable meanings, in most cases more or less dishonestly, are: *class, totalitarian, science, progressive, reactionary, bourgeois, equality.*

Now that I have made this catalogue of swindles and perversions, let me give another example of the kind of writing that they lead to. This time it must of its nature be an imaginary one. I am going to translate a passage of good English into modern English of the worst sort. Here is a well-known verse from *Ecclesiastes*:

'I returned, and saw under the sun, that the race is not to the swift, nor the battle to the strong, neither yet bread to the wise, nor yet riches to men of understanding, nor yet favour to men of skill; but time and chance happeneth to them all.'

Here it is in modern English:

'Objective consideration of contemporary phenomena compels the conclusion that success or failure in competitive activities exhibits no tendency to be commensurate with innate capacity, but that a considerable element of the unpredictable must invariably be taken into account.'

This is a parody, but not a very gross one. Exhibit (3), above, for instance, contains several patches of the same kind of English. It will be seen that I have not made a full translation. The beginning and ending of the sentence follow the original meaning fairly closely, but in the middle the concrete illustrations – race, battle, bread – dissolve into the vague phrase 'success or failure in competitive activities'. This had to be so, because no modern writer of the kind I am discussing – no one capable of using phrases like 'objective consideration of contemporary phenomena' – would ever tabulate his thoughts in that precise and detailed way. The whole tendency of modern prose is away from concreteness. Now analyse these two sentences a little more closely. The first contains 49 words but only 60 syllables, and all its words are those of everyday life. The second contains 38 words of 90 syllables: 18 of its words are from Latin roots, and one from Greek. The first sentence contains six vivid images, and only one phrase ('time and chance') that could be called vague. The second contains not a single fresh, arresting phrase, and in spite of its 90 syllables it gives only a shortened version of the meaning contained in the first. Yet without a doubt it is the second kind of sentence that is gaining ground in modern English. I do not want to exaggerate. This kind of writing is not yet universal, and outcrops of simplicity will occur here and there in the worst-written page. Still, if you or I were told to write a few lines on the uncertainty of human fortunes, we should probably come much nearer to my imaginary sentence than to the one from *Ecclesiastes*.

As I have tried to show, modern writing at its worst does not consist in picking out words for the sake of their meaning and inventing images in order to make the meaning clearer. It consists in gumming together long strips of words which have already been set in order by someone else, and making the results presentable by sheer humbug. The attraction of this way of writing is that it is easy. It is easier – even quicker, once you have the habit – to say *In my opinion it is a not unjustifiable assumption that* than to say *I think*. If you use ready-made phrases, you not only don't have to hunt about for words; you also don't have to bother with the rhythms of your sentences, since these phrases are generally so arranged as to be more or less euphonious. When you are composing in a hurry – when you are dictating to a stenographer, for instance, or making a public speech – it is natural to fall into a pretentious, Latinized style. Tags like *a consideration which we should do well to bear in mind* or *a conclusion to which all of us would readily assent* will save many a sentence from coming down with a bump. By using stale metaphors, similes and idioms, you save much mental effort, at the cost of leaving your meaning vague, not only for your reader but for yourself. This is the significance of mixed metaphors. The sole aim of a metaphor is to call up a visual image. When these images clash – as in *The Fascist octopus has sung its swan song, the jackboot is thrown into the melting pot* – it can be taken as certain that the writer is not seeing a mental image of the objects he is naming; in other words he is not really thinking. Look again at the examples I gave at the beginning of this essay. Professor Laski (1) uses five negatives in 53 words. One of these is superfluous, making nonsense of the whole passage, and in addition there is the slip *alien* for akin, making further nonsense, and several avoidable pieces of clumsiness which increase the general vagueness. Professor Hogben (2) plays ducks and drakes with a battery which is able to write prescriptions, and, while disapproving of the everyday phrase *put up with*, is unwilling to look *egregious* up in the dictionary and see what it means. (3), if one takes an uncharitable attitude towards it, is simply meaningless: probably one could work out its intended meaning by reading the whole of the article in which it occurs. In (4), the writer knows more or less what he wants to say, but an accumulation of stale phrases chokes him like tea leaves blocking a sink. In (5), words and meaning have almost parted company. People who write in this manner usually have a general emotional meaning – they dislike one thing and want to express solidarity with another – but they are not interested in the detail of what they are saying. A scrupulous writer, in every sentence that he writes, will ask himself at least four questions, thus: What am I trying to say? What words will express it? What image or idiom will make it clearer? Is this image fresh enough to have an effect? And he will probably ask himself two more: Could I put it more shortly? Have I said anything that is avoidably ugly? But you are not obliged to go to all this trouble. You can shirk it by simply throwing your mind open and letting the ready-made phrases come crowding in. They will construct your sentences for you – even think your thoughts for you, to a certain extent – and at need they will perform the important service of partially concealing your meaning even from yourself. It is at this point that the special connection between politics and the debasement of language becomes clear.

In our time it is broadly true that political writing is bad writing. Where it is not true, it will generally be found that the writer is some kind of rebel, expressing his private opinions and not a 'party line'. Orthodoxy, of whatever colour, seems to demand a lifeless, imitative style. The political dialects to be found in pamphlets, leading articles, manifestos, White Papers and the speeches of under-secretaries do, of course, vary from party to party, but they are all alike in that one almost never finds in them a fresh, vivid, home-made turn of speech. When one watches some tired hack on the platform mechanically repeating the familiar phrases – *bestial atrocities, iron heel, blood-stained tyranny, free peoples of the world, stand shoulder to shoulder* – one often has a curious feeling that one is not watching a live human being but some kind of dummy: a feeling which suddenly becomes stronger at moments when the light catches the speaker's spectacles and turns them into blank discs which seem to have no eyes behind them. And this is not altogether fanciful. A speaker who uses that kind of phraseology has gone some distance towards turning himself into a machine. The appropriate noises are coming out of his larynx, but his brain is not involved as it would be if he were choosing his words for himself. If the speech he is making is one that he is accustomed to make over and over again, he may be almost unconscious of what he is saying, as one is when one utters the responses in church. And this reduced state of consciousness, if not indispensable, is at any rate favourable to political conformity.

In our time, political speech and writing are largely the defence of the indefensible. Things like the continuance of British rule in India, the Russian purges and deportations, the dropping of the atom bombs on Japan, can indeed be defended, but only by arguments which are too brutal for most people to face, and which do not square with the professed aims of political parties. Thus political language has to consist largely of euphemism, question-begging and sheer cloudy vagueness. Defenceless villages are bombarded from the air, the inhabitants driven out into the countryside, the cattle machine-gunned, the huts set on fire with incendiary bullets: this is called *pacification*. Millions of peasants are robbed of their farms and sent trudging along the roads with no more than they can carry: this is called *transfer of population* or *rectification of frontiers*. People are imprisoned for years without trial, or shot in the back of the neck or sent to die of scurvy in Arctic lumber camps: this is called *elimination of unreliable elements*. Such phraseology is needed if one wants to name things without calling up mental pictures of them. Consider for instance some comfortable English professor defending Russian totalitarianism. He cannot say outright, 'I believe in killing off your opponents when you can get good results by doing so'. Probably, therefore, he will say something like this:

'While freely conceding that the Soviet régime exhibits certain features which the humanitarian may be inclined to deplore, we must, I think, agree that a certain curtailment of the right to political opposition is an unavoidable concomitant of transitional periods, and that the rigours which the Russian people have been called upon to undergo have been amply justified in the sphere of concrete achievement.'

The inflated style is itself a kind of euphemism. A mass of Latin words falls upon the facts like soft snow, blurring the outlines and covering up all the details. The great enemy of clear language is insincerity. When there is a gap between one's real and one's declared aims, one turns as it were instinctively to long words and exhausted idioms, like a cuttlefish squirting out ink. In our age there is no such thing as 'keeping out of politics'. All issues are political issues, and politics itself is a mass of lies, evasions, folly, hatred and schizophrenia. When the general atmosphere is bad, language must suffer. I should expect to find – this is a guess which I have not sufficient knowledge to verify – that the German, Russian and Italian languages have all deteriorated in the last ten or fifteen years, as a result of dictatorship.

But if thought corrupts language, language can also corrupt thought. A bad usage can spread by tradition and imitation, even among people who should and do know better. The debased language that I have been discussing is in some ways very convenient. Phrases like *a not unjustifiable assumption*, *leaves much to be desired*, *would serve no good purpose*, *a consideration which we should do well to bear in mind*, are a continuous temptation, a packet of aspirins always at one's elbow. Look back through this essay, and for certain you will find that I have again and again committed the very faults I am protesting against. By this morning's post I have received a pamphlet dealing with conditions in Germany. The author tells me that he 'felt impelled' to write it. I open it at random, and here is almost the first sentence that I see: '(The Allies) have an opportunity not only of achieving a radical transformation of Germany's social and political structure in such a way as to avoid a nationalistic reaction in Germany itself, but at the same time of laying the foundations of a co-operative and unified Europe.' You see, he 'feels impelled' to write – feels, presumably, that he has something new to say – and yet his words, like cavalry horses answering the bugle, group themselves automatically into the familiar dreary pattern. This invasion of one's mind by ready-made phrases (*lay the foundations*, *achieve a radical transformation*) can only be prevented if one is constantly on guard against them, and every such phrase anaesthetizes a portion of one's brain.

I said earlier that the decadence of our language is probably curable. Those who deny this would argue, if they produced an argument at all, that language merely reflects existing social conditions, and that we cannot influence its development by any direct tinkering with words and constructions. So far as the general tone or spirit of a language goes, this may be true, but it is not true in detail. Silly words and expressions have often disappeared, not through any evolutionary process but owing to the conscious action of a minority. Two recent examples were *explore every avenue* and *leave no stone unturned*, which were killed by the jeers of a few journalists. There is a long list of flyblown metaphors which could similarly be got rid of if enough people would interest themselves in the job; and it should also be possible to laugh the *not un-* formation out of existence,[28] to reduce the amount of Latin and Greek in the average sentence, to drive out foreign phrases and strayed scientific words, and, in general, to make pretentiousness unfashionable. But all these are minor points. The defence of the English language implies more than this, and perhaps it is best to start by saying what it does *not* imply.

To begin with, it has nothing to do with archaism, with the salvaging of obsolete words and turns of speech, or with the setting-up of a 'standard English' which must never be departed from. On the contrary, it is especially concerned with the scrapping of every word or idiom which has outworn its usefulness. It has nothing to do with correct grammar and syntax, which are of no importance so long as one makes one's meaning clear, or with the avoidance of Americanisms, or with having what is called a 'good prose style'. On the other hand it is not concerned with fake simplicity and the attempt to make written English colloquial. Nor does it even imply in every case preferring the Saxon word to the Latin one, though it does imply using the fewest and shortest words that will cover one's meaning. What is above all needed is to let the meaning choose the word, and not the other way about. In prose, the worst thing one can do with words is to surrender to them. When you think of a concrete object, you think wordlessly, and then, if you want to describe the thing you have been visualizing, you probably hunt about till you find the exact words that seem to fit it. When you think of something abstract you are more inclined to use words from the start, and unless you make a conscious effort to prevent it, the existing dialect will come rushing in and do the job for you, at the expense of blurring or even changing your meaning. Probably it is better to put off using words as long as possible and get one's meaning as clear as one can through pictures or sensations. Afterwards one can choose – not simply *accept* – the phrases that will best cover the meaning, and then switch round and decide what impression one's words are likely to make on another person. This last effort of the mind cuts out all stale or mixed images, all prefabricated phrases, needless repetitions, and humbug and vagueness generally. But one can often be in doubt about the effect of a word or a phrase, and one needs rules that one can rely on when instinct fails. I think the following rules will cover most cases:

(i) Never use a metaphor, simile or other figure of speech which you are used to seeing in print.

(ii) Never use a long word where a short one will do.

(iii) If it is possible to cut a word out, always cut it out.

(iv) Never use the passive where you can use the active.

(v) Never use a foreign phrase, a scientific word or a jargon word if you can think of an everyday English equivalent.

(vi) Break any of these rules sooner than say anything outright barbarous. These rules sound elementary, and so they are, but they demand a deep change of attitude in anyone who has grown used to writing in the style now fashionable. One could keep all of them and still write bad English, but one could not write the kind of stuff that I quoted in those five specimens at the beginning of this article.

I have not here been considering the literary use of language, but merely language as an instrument for expressing and not for concealing or preventing thought. Stuart Chase and others have come near to claiming that all abstract words are meaningless, and have used this as a pretext for advocating a kind of political quietism. Since you don't know what Fascism is, how can you struggle against Fascism? One need not swallow such absurdities as this, but one ought to recognize that the present political chaos is connected with the decay of language, and that one can probably bring about some improvement by starting at the verbal end. If you simplify your English, you are freed from the worst follies of orthodoxy. You cannot speak any of the necessary dialects, and when you make a stupid remark its stupidity will be obvious, even to yourself. Political language – and with variations this is true of all political parties, from Conservatives to Anarchists – is designed to make lies sound truthful and murder respectable, and to give an appearance of solidity to pure wind. One cannot change this all in a moment, but one can at least change one's own habits, and from time to time one can even, if one jeers loudly enough, send some worn-out and useless phrase – some *jackboot*, *Achilles' heel*, *hotbed*, *melting pot*, *acid test*, *veritable inferno* or other lump of verbal refuse – into the dustbin where it belongs.

The Sporting Spirit

Tribune, 14 December 1945

Now that the brief visit of the Dynamo football team has come to an end, it is possible to say publicly what many thinking people were saying privately before the Dynamos ever arrived. That is, that sport is an unfailing cause of ill-will, and that if such a visit as this had any effect at all on Anglo-Soviet relations, it could only be to make them slightly worse than before.

Even the newspapers have been unable to conceal the fact that at least two of the four matches played led to much bad feeling. At the Arsenal match, I am told by someone who was there, a British and a Russian player came to blows and the crowd booed the referee. The Glasgow match, someone else informs me, was simply a free-for-all from the start. And then there was the controversy, typical of our nationalistic age, about the composition of the Arsenal team. Was it really an all-England team, as claimed by the Russians, or merely a league team, as claimed by the British? And did the Dynamos end their tour abruptly in order to avoid playing an all-England team? As usual, everyone answers these questions according to his political predilections. Not quite everyone, however. I noted with interest, as an instance of the vicious passions that football provokes, that the sporting correspondent of the Russophile *News Chronicle* took the anti-Russian line and maintained that Arsenal was *not* an all-England team. No doubt the controversy will continue to echo for years in the footnotes of history books. Meanwhile the result of the Dynamos' tour, in so far as it has had any result, will have been to create fresh animosity on both sides.

And how could it be otherwise? I am always amazed when I hear people saying that sport creates goodwill between the nations, and that if only the common peoples of the world could meet one another at football or cricket, they would have no inclination to meet on the battlefield. Even if one didn't know from concrete examples (the 1936 Olympic Games, for instance) that international sporting contests lead to orgies of hatred, one could deduce it from general principles.

Nearly all the sports practised nowadays are competitive. You play to win, and the game has little meaning unless you do your utmost to win. On the village green, where you pick up sides and no feeling of local patriotism is involved, it is possible to play simply for the fun and the exercise: but as soon as the question of prestige arises, as soon as you feel that you and some larger unit will be disgraced if you lose, the most savage combative instincts are aroused. Anyone who has played even in a school football match knows this. At the international level sport is frankly mimic warfare. But the significant thing is not the behaviour of the players but the attitude of the spectators: and, behind the spectators, of the nations who work themselves into furies over these absurd contests, and seriously believe – at any rate for short periods – that running, jumping and kicking a ball are tests of national virtue.

Even a leisurely game like cricket, demanding grace rather than strength, can cause much ill-will, as we saw in the controversy over body-line bowling and over the rough tactics of the Australian team that visited England in 1921. Football, a game in which everyone gets hurt and every nation has its own style of play which seems unfair to foreigners, is far worse. Worst of all is boxing. One of the most horrible sights in the world is a fight between white and coloured boxers before a mixed audience. But a boxing audience is always disgusting, and the behaviour of the women, in particular, is such that the Army, I believe, does not allow them to attend its contests. At any rate, two or three years ago, when Home Guards and regular troops were holding a boxing tournament, I was placed on guard at the door of the hall, with orders to keep the women out.

In England, the obsession with sport is bad enough, but even fiercer passions are aroused in young countries where games-playing and nationalism are both recent developments. In countries like India or Burma, it is necessary at football matches to have strong cordons of police to keep the crowd from invading the field. In Burma, I have seen the supporters of one side break through the police and disable the goalkeeper of the opposing side at a critical moment. The first big football match that was played in Spain, about fifteen years ago, led to an uncontrollable riot. As soon as strong feelings of rivalry are aroused, the notion of playing the game according to the rules always vanishes. People want to see one side on top and the other side humiliated, and they forget that victory gained through cheating or through the intervention of the crowd is meaningless. Even when the spectators don't intervene phys-ically, they try to influence the game by cheering their own side and "rattling" opposing players with boos and insults. Serious sport has nothing to do with fair play. It is bound up with hatred, jealousy, boastfulness, disregard of all rules and sadistic pleasure in witnessing violence: in other words it is war minus the shooting.

Instead of blah-blahing about the clean, healthy rivalry of the football field and the great part played by the Olympic Games in bringing the nations together, it is more useful to inquire how and why this modern cult of sport arose. Most of the games we now play are of ancient origin, but sport does not seem to have been taken very seriously between Roman times and the nineteenth century. Even in the English public schools the games cult did not start till the later part of the last century. Dr. Arnold, generally regarded as the founder of the modern public school, looked on games as simply a waste of time. Then, chiefly in England and the United States, games were built up into a heavily-financed activity, capable of attracting vast crowds and rousing savage passions, and the infection spread from country to country. It is the most violently com-bative sports, football and boxing, that have spread the widest.

There cannot be much doubt that the whole thing is bound up with the rise of nationalism – that is, with the lunatic modern habit of identifying oneself with large power units and seeing everything in terms of competitive prestige. Also, organised games are more likely to flourish in urban communities where the average human being lives a sedentary or at least a confined life, and does not get much opportunity for creative labour. In a rustic community a boy or young man works off a good deal of his surplus energy by walking, swimming, snowballing, climbing trees, riding horses, and by various sports involving cruelty to animals, such as fishing, cock-fighting and ferreting for rats. In a big town one must indulge in group activities if one wants an outlet for one's physical strength or for one's sadistic impulses. Games are taken seriously in London and New York, and they were taken seriously in Rome and Byzantium: in the Middle Ages they were played, and probably played with much physical brutality, but they were not mixed up with politics nor a cause of group hatreds.

If you wanted to add to the vast fund of ill-will existing in the world at this moment, you could hardly do it better than by a series of football matches between Jews and Arabs, Germans and Czechs, Indians and British, Russians and Poles, and Italians and Jugoslavs, each match to be watched by a mixed audience of 100,000 spectators. I do not, of course, suggest that sport is one of the main causes of international rivalry; big-scale sport is itself, I think, merely another effect of the causes that have produced nationalism. Still, you do make things worse by sending forth a team of eleven men, labelled as national champions, to do battle against some rival team, and allowing it to be felt on all sides that whichever nation is defeated will "lose face".

I hope, therefore, that we shan't follow up the visit of the Dynamos by sending a British team to the U.S.S.R. If we must do so, then let us send a second-rate team which is sure to be beaten and cannot be claimed to represent Britain as a whole. There are quite enough real causes of trouble already, and we need not add to them by encouraging young men to kick each other on the shins amid the roars of infuriated spectators.

In Defence of English Cooking

Evening Standard, 15 December 1945

We have heard a good deal of talk in recent years about the desirability of attracting foreign tourists to this country. It is well known that England's two worst faults, from a foreign visitor's point of view, are the gloom of our Sundays and the difficulty of buying a drink.

Both of those are due to fanatical minorities who will need a lot of quelling, including extensive legislation. But there is one point on which public opinion could bring about a rapid change for the better: I mean cooking.

It is commonly said, even by the English themselves, that English cooking is the worst in the world. It is supposed to be not merely incompetent, but also imitative, and I even read quite recently, in a book by a French writer, the remark: "The best English cooking is, of course, simply French cooking."

Now that is simply not true. As anyone who has lived long abroad will know, there is a whole host of delicacies which it is quite impossible to obtain outside the English–speaking countries. No doubt the list could be added to, but here are some of the things that I myself have sought for in foreign countries and failed to find.

First of all, kippers, Yorkshire pudding, Devonshire cream, muffins and crumpets. Then a list of puddings that would be interminable if I gave it in full: I will pick out for special mention Christmas pudding, treacle tart and apple dumplings. Then an almost equally long list of cakes: for instance, dark plum cake (such as you used to get at Buszard's before the war), shortbread and saffron buns. Also innumerable kinds of biscuit, which exist, of course, elsewhere, but are generally admitted to be better and crisper in England.

Then there are the various ways of cooking potatoes that are peculiar to our own country. Where else do you see potatoes roasted under the joint, which is far and away the best way of cooking them? Or the delicious potato cakes that you get in the north of England? And it is far better to cook new potatoes in the English way – that is, boiled with mint then served with a little melted butter or margarine – than to fry them, as is done in most countries.

Then there are the various sauces peculiar to England. For instance, bread sauce, horseradish sauce, mint sauce, and apple sauce, not to mention red currant jelly, which is excellent with mutton as well as with hare, and various kinds of sweet pickle, which we seem to have in greater profusion than most countries.

What else? Outside these islands I have never seen a haggis, except one that came out of a tin, nor Dublin prawns, nor Oxford marmalade, nor several other kinds of jam (marrow jam and bramble jelly, for instance), nor sausages of quite the same kind as ours.

Then there are the English cheeses. There are not many of them, but I fancy that Stilton is the best cheese of its type in the world, with Wensleydale not far behind. English apples are also outstandingly good, particularly the Cox's Orange Pippin.

And finally, I would like to put in a word for English bread. All bread is good, from the enormous Jewish loaves flavoured with caraway seeds to the Russian rye bread which is the colour of black treacle. Still, if there is anything quite as good as the soft part of the crust from an English cottage loaf (how soon shall we be seeing cottage loaves again?), I do not know of it.

No doubt some of the things I have named above *could* be obtained in continental Europe, just as it is *possible* in London to obtain vodka or bird's nest soup. But they are all native to our shores, and over huge areas they are literally unheard of.

South of, say, Brussels, I do not imagine that you would succeed in getting hold of a suet pudding. In French there is not even a word that exactly translates "suet." The French, also, never use mint in cookery, and do not use black currants except as the basis of a drink.

It will be seen that we have no cause to be ashamed of our cookery, so far as originality goes, or so far as the ingredients go. And yet, it must be admitted that there is a serious snag from the foreign visitor's point of view. This is, that you practically don't find good English cooking outside a private house. If you want, say, a good, rich slice of Yorkshire pudding, you are more likely to get it in the poorest English home than in a restaurant, which is where the visitor necessarily eats most of his meals.

It is a fact that restaurants which are distinctively English, and which also sell good food, are very hard to find. Pubs, as a rule, sell no food at all, other than potato crisps and tasteless sandwiches. The expensive restaurants and hotels almost all imitate French cookery and write their menus in French, while if you want a good cheap meal you gravitate naturally towards a Greek, Italian or Chinese restaurant.

We are not likely to succeed in attracting tourists while England is thought of as a country of bad food and unintelligible by-laws. At present one cannot do much about it, but sooner or later rationing will come to an end, and then will be the moment for our cookery to revive. It is not a law of nature that every restaurant in England should be either foreign or bad, and the first step towards an improvement will be a less long-suffering attitude in the British public itself.

Nonsense Poetry: *The Lear Omnibus* edited by R. L. Megroz

Tribune, 21 December 1945

In many languages, it is said, there is no nonsense poetry, and there is not a great deal of it even in English. The bulk of it is in nursery rhymes and scraps of folk poetry, some of which may not have been strictly nonsensical at the start, but have become so because their original application has been forgotten. For example, the rhyme about Margery Daw:

> See-saw, Margery Daw,
> Dobbin shall have a new master
> He shall have but a penny a day
> Because he can't go any faster.

Or the other version that I learned in Oxfordshire as a little boy:

> See-saw, Margery Daw,
> Sold her bed and lay upon straw.
> Wasn't she a silly slut
> To sell her bed and lie upon dirt?

It may be that there was once a real person called Margery Daw, and perhaps there was even a Dobbin who somehow came into the story. When Shakespeare makes Edgar in *King Lear* quote "Pillicock sat on Pillicock hill," and similar fragments, he is uttering nonsense, but no doubt these fragments come from forgotten ballads in which they once had a meaning. The typical scrap of folk poetry which one quotes almost unconsciously is not exactly nonsense but a sort of musical comment on some recurring event, such as "One a penny, two a penny, Hot-Cross buns," or "Polly put the kettle on, we'll all have tea." Some of these seemingly frivolous rhymes actually express a deeply pessimistic view of life, the churchyard wisdom of the peasant. For instance:

> Solomon Grundy,
> Born on Monday,
> Christened on Tuesday,
> Married on Wednesday,
> Took ill on Thursday,
> Worse on Friday,
> Died on Saturday.
> Buried on Sunday,
> And that was the end of Solomon Grundy

which is a gloomy story, but remarkably similar to yours or mine.

Until Surrealism made a deliberate raid on the Unconscious, poetry that aimed at being nonsense, apart from the meaningless refrains of songs, does not seem to have been common. This gives a special position to Edward Lear, whose nonsense rhymes have just been edited by Mr. R. L. Megroz, who was also responsible for the Penguin edition a year or two before the war. Lear was one of the first writers to deal in pure fantasy, with imaginary countries and made-up words, without any satirical purpose. His poems are not all of them equally nonsensical; some of them get their effect by a perversion of logic, but they are all alike in that their underlying feeling is sad and not bitter. They express a kind of amiable lunacy, a natural sympathy with whatever is weak and absurd. Lear could fairly be called the originator of the Limerick, though verses in almost the same metrical form are to be found in earlier writers, and what is sometimes considered a weakness in his Limericks – that is, the fact that the rhyme is the same in the first and last lines – is part of their charm. The very slight change increases the impression of ineffectuality, which might be spoiled if there were some striking surprise. For example:

> There was a young lady of Portugal,
> Whose ideas were excessively nautical;
> She climbed up a tree
> To examine the sea,
> But declared she would never leave Portugal.

It is significant that almost no Limericks since Lear's have been both printable and funny enough to seem worth quoting. But he is really seen at his best in certain longer poems, such as "The Owl and the Pussy-cat" or "The Courtship of the Yonghy-Bonghy-Bo":

> On the Coast of Coromandel,
> Where the early pumpkins blow,
> In the middle of the woods
> Lived the Yonghy-Bonghy-Bo.
> Two old chairs, and half a candle –
> One old jug without a handle –
> These were all his worldly goods:
> In the middle of the woods,
> These were all the worldly goods,
> Of the Yonghy-Bonghy-Bo,
> Of the Yonghy-Bonghy-Bo.

Later there appears a lady with some white Dorking hens, and an inconclusive love affair follows. Mr. Megroz thinks, plausibly enough, that this may refer to some incident in Lear's own life. He never married, and it is easy to guess that there was something seriously wrong in his sex life. A psychiatrist could no doubt find all kinds of significances in his drawings and in the recurrence of certain made-up words such as "runcible." His health was bad, and as he was the youngest of twenty-one children in a poor family, he must have known anxiety and hardship in very early life. It is clear that he was unhappy and by nature solitary, in spite of having good friends.

Aldous Huxley, in praising Lear's fantasies as a sort of assertion of freedom, has pointed out that the "They" of the Limericks represents commonsense, legality and the duller virtues generally. "They" are the realists, the practical men, the sober citizens in bowler hats who are always anxious to stop you doing anything worth doing. For instance:

> There was an Old Man of Whitehaven,
> Who danced a quadrille with a raven:
> But they said, "It's absurd
> To encourage this bird!"
> So they smashed that Old Man of Whitehaven.

To smash somebody just for dancing a quadrille with a raven is exactly the kind of thing that "They" would do. Herbert Read has also praised Lear, and is inclined to prefer his verse to that of Lewis Carroll, as being purer fantasy. For myself, I must say that I find Lear funniest when he is least arbitrary and when a touch of burlesque or perverted logic makes its appearance. When he gives his fancy free play, as in his imaginary names, or in things like "Three Receipts for Domestic Cookery," he can be silly and tiresome. "The Pobble who has no Toes" is haunted by the ghost of logic, and I think it is the element of sense in it that makes it funny. The Pobble, it may be remembered, went fishing in the Bristol Channel –

> And all the sailors and Admirals cried,
> When they saw him nearing the further side –
> "He has gone to fish, for his Aunt Jobiska's
> Runcible Cat with crimson whiskers!"

The thing that is funny here is the burlesque touch, the Admirals. What is arbitrary – the word "runcible," and the cat's crimson whiskers – is merely rather embarrassing. While the Pobble was in the water some unidentified creatures came and ate his toes off, and when he got home his aunt remarked –

> "It's a fact the whole world knows,
> That Pobbles are happier without their toes,"

which once again is funny because it has a meaning, and one might even say a political significance. For the whole theory of authoritarian government is summed up in the statement that

Pobbles were happier without their toes. So also with the well-known Limerick:

> There was an Old Person of Basing,
> Whose presence of mind was amazing;
> He purchased a steed,
> Which he rode at full speed,
> And escaped from the people of Basing.

It is not quite arbitrary. The funniness is in the gentle implied criticism of the people of Basing, who once again are "They," the respectable ones, the right-thinking, art-hating majority.

The writer closest to Lear among his contemporaries was Lewis Carroll, who, however, was less essentially fantastic – and, in my opinion, funnier. Since then, as Mr. Megroz points out in his Introduction, Lear's influence has been considerable, but it is hard to believe that it has been altogether good. The silly whimsiness of present-day children's books could perhaps be partly traced back to him. At any rate, the idea of deliberately setting out to write nonsense, though it came off in Lear's case, is a doubtful one. Probably the best nonsense poetry is produced gradually and accidentally, by communities rather than by individuals. As a comic draughtsman, on the other hand, Lear's influence must have been beneficial. James Thurber, for instance, must surely owe something to Lear, directly or indirectly. With large numbers of Lear's own illustrations, and an informative Introduction, this book should make a first-rate Christmas present.

Banish This Uniform
Evening Standard, 22 December 1945

A few weeks ago I received a dinner invitation (it was for some kind of public function) marked with the words "Informal Dress."

At a time like the present, when "informal" would be a very polite term for such clothes as most of us have left, these words might seem superfluous; but what they really meant, of course, was, "You don't have to wear a dinner jacket."

Already, therefore, there are people who need to be told this – even, perhaps, people who would actually welcome the chance of buckling themselves into boiled shirts again. It is easy to foresee that I shall soon get another invitation marked "Evening Dress Optional," and then it will only be a short step before the dreary black-and-white uniform will be just as compulsory at theatres, dances and expensive restaurants as it was seven years ago.

At this moment no one – no man, that is to say – would buy himself a complete evening outfit. Without bootleg clothing coupons, it would be impossible to do so. But not all the pre-war "dress" suits have been devoured by moths or cut down into two-piece suits for ladies, and some of them are beginning to emerge from their obscurity again.

This is the moment, therefore, to decide once and for all whether evening dress for men is to revive, and if so, in what form.

In principle, evening clothes are a civilised institution. To change into special garments before going to a friend's house, or to some kind of recreation, freshens you up and cuts the evening off from the working part of the day.

But evening clothes, as they existed before the war, were only satisfactory from the feminine point of view. A woman chooses an evening dress with the object of beautifying herself, and, if possible, of being different from other women. She can do this with comparative cheapness, so that for many years past female evening dress extended to nearly every social level.

For men, on the other hand, evening clothes have always been a nuisance and even their devotees have valued them chiefly for snobbish reasons.

To begin with, men's evening clothes are fantastically expensive. To buy yourself the complete outfit – tails, dinner jacket, black overcoat, patent-leather shoes and all – would have cost £50 at the least, even at pre-war prices.

And because these clothes were expensive, and were also supposedly uniform, they were hedged round with all kinds of petty conventions, which you could only disregard at the price of being made to feel uncomfortable. To wear a white waistcoat with a dinner jacket or a soft shirt with tails, to have two studs in your shirt-front when other people were wearing only one, even to have too broad or too narrow a stripe of braid down your trouser-leg was enough to make you into an outcast.

Even the correct tying of an evening tie needed years of practice before one could master it. The whole thing was a snobbish ritual which terrified the inexperienced and repelled anyone of democratic outlook.

Secondly, men's evening clothes are far from comfortable. A boiled shirt is a misery, and for dancing one could hardly have a less suitable neckwear than a high, stiff collar which becomes a sodden rag half-way through the evening.

And lastly, these clothes are quite unnecessarily ugly. They are all in black and white, a colour scheme which only suits an ash blond or an exceptionally dark negro. But it must be admitted that the green or purple dinner jackets in which a few bold spirits sometimes made their appearance were not much better. The change of colour could not do away with the ugly lines which are common to most of the clothes worn by modern men.

Our clothes are ugly, and have been so for nearly a hundred years, because they are a mere arrangement of cylinders and do not either follow the lines of the body or make use of the flow of draperies. The least ugly clothes are usually those that are functionally designed, such as a boiler suit or a reasonably well-fitting battledress.

Could we not, then, evolve a style of evening dress which it would be a pleasure to put on, and which at the same time would have no snobbish implications?

It is no use saying "Let everyone wear what he chooses." Men in order to feel comfortable have to feel that they are not strikingly different from other men. Our imaginary evening dress would have to be truly national, like battledress, which is practically the same for all ranks from general to private. Secondly, it would have to be cheap. Thirdly, it would have to be comfortable – that is to say, definitely more comfortable, more suited to relaxation, than the clothes worn in the daytime.

And finally it would have to be decorative, which is not in the least incompatible with cheapness, as one can see in any

Eastern country, where the poorest peasant is a pleasanter object to look at, so far as his clothes go, than the most expensively-dressed European.

If we are ever to escape by conscious effort from the ugliness of modern masculine attire, now – when existing stocks are near rock bottom – is surely the time to do it. But if we can't design a new and agreeable form of evening dress at least let us see to it that the old one, with its vulgarity, its expensiveness and its attendant misery of hunting for lost collar studs under the chest of drawers, does not come back.

1946

Just Junk – But Who Could Resist It?

Saturday Essay, *Evening Standard*, 5 January 1946

Which is the most attractive junk shop in London is a matter of taste, or for debate: but I could lead you to some first-rate ones in the dingier areas of Greenwich, in Islington near the Angel, in Holloway, in Paddington, and in the hinterland of the Edgware Road. Except for a couple near Lord's – and even those are in a section of street that happens to have fallen into decay – I have never seen a junk shop worth a second glance in what is called a "good" neighbourhood.

A junk shop is not to be confused with an antique shop. An antique shop is clean, its goods are attractively set out and priced at about double their value and once inside the shop you are usually bullied into buying something.

A junk shop has a fine film of dust over the window, its stock may include literally anything that is not perishable, and its proprietor, who is usually asleep in a small room at the back, displays no eagerness to make a sale.

Also, its finest treasures are never discoverable at first glimpse; they have to be sorted out from among a medley of bamboo cake-stands, Britannia-ware dish-covers, turnip watches, dog-eared books, ostrich eggs, typewriters of extinct makes, spectacles without lenses, decanters without stoppers, stuffed birds, wire fire guards, bunches of keys, boxes of nuts and bolts, conch shells from the Indian Ocean, boot trees, Chinese ginger jars and pictures of Highland cattle.

Some of the things to look out for in the junk shop are Victorian brooches and lockets of agate or other semi-precious stones.

Perhaps five out of six of these things are hideously ugly, but there are also very beautiful objects among them. They are set in silver, or more often in pinchbeck, a charming alloy which for some reason is no longer made.

Other things worth looking for are papier mâché snuffboxes with pictures painted on the lid, lustre-ware jugs, muzzle-loading pistols made round about 1830, and ships in bottles.

These are still made, but the old ones are always the best, because of the elegant shape of the Victorian bottles and the delicate green of the glass.

Or, again, musical boxes, horse brasses, copper powder-horns, Jubilee mugs (for some reason the 1887 Jubilee produced much pleasanter keepsakes than the Diamond Jubilee ten years later), and glass paper-weights with pictures at the bottom.

There are others that have a piece of coral enclosed in the glass, but these are always fantastically expensive. Or you may come across a scrap book full of Victorian fashion-plates and pressed flowers or even, if you are exceptionally lucky, the scrap book's big brother, a scrap screen.

Scrap screens – all too rare nowadays – are simply ordinary wooden or canvas screens with coloured scraps cut out and pasted all over them in such a way as to make more or less coherent pictures. The best were made round about 1880, but if you buy one at a junk shop it is sure to be defective, and the great charm of owning such a screen lies in patching it up yourself.

You can use coloured reproductions from art magazines, Christmas cards, postcards, advertisements, book jackets, even cigarette cards. There is always room for one more scrap, and with careful placing anything can be made to look congruous.

Thus, merely in one corner of my own scrap screen, Cézanne's card-players with a black bottle between them are impinging on a street scene in medieval Florence, while on the other side of the street one of Gauguin's South Sea islanders is sitting beside an English lake where a lady in leg-of-mutton sleeves is paddling a canoe. They all look perfectly at home together.

All these things are curiosities, but one does find useful things in the junk shop as well.

In a shop in Kentish Town, since blitzed, I once bought an old French sword-bayonet, price sixpence, which did four years' service as a fire-poker. And during the last few years the junk shop has been the only place where you could buy certain carpentering tools – a jack plane for instance – or such useful objects as corkscrews, clock keys, skates, wine glasses, copper saucepans, and spare pram wheels.

In some shops you can find keys to fit almost any lock, others specialise in pictures and are therefore useful when you need a frame. Indeed, I have often found that the cheapest way of buying a frame is to buy a picture and then throw away the picture.

But the attraction of the junk shop does not lie solely in the bargains you pick up, nor even in the aesthetic value which – at a generous estimate – 5 per cent of its contents may possess. Its appeal is to the jackdaw inside all of us, the instinct that makes a child hoard copper nails, clock springs, and the glass marbles out of lemonade bottles. To get pleasure out of a junk shop you are not obliged to buy anything, nor even to want to buy anything.

I know a shop in Tottenham Court Road where I have never, over a period of many years, seen anything that was not offensively ugly and another, not far from Baker Street, where there is nearly always something tempting. The first appeals to me almost as strongly as the second.

Another shop, in the Chalk Farm area, sells nothing but rubbishy fragments of old metal. For as long as I can remember the same worn-out tools and lengths of lead piping have been lying in the trays, the same gas stoves have been mouldering in the doorway. I have never bought anything there, never even seen anything that I contemplated buying. Yet it would be all but impossible for me to pass that way without crossing the street to have a good look.

Pleasure Spots
Tribune, 11 January 1946

Some months ago I cut out of a shiny magazine some paragraphs written by a female journalist and describing the pleasure resort of the future. She had recently been spending some time at Honolulu, where the rigours of war do not seem to have been very noticeable. However, "a transport pilot . . .

told me that with all the inventiveness packed into this war, it was a pity someone hadn't found out how a tired and life-hungry man could relax, rest, play poker, drink, and make love, all at once, and round the clock, and come out of it feeling good and fresh and ready for the job again." This reminded her of an entrepreneur she had met recently who was planning a "pleasure spot which he thinks will catch on tomorrow as dog-racing and dance halls did yesterday." The entrepreneur's dream is described in some detail: –

His blue-prints pictured a space covering several acres, under a series of sliding roofs – for the British weather is unreliable – and with a central space spread over with an immense dance floor made of translucent plastic which can be illuminated from beneath. Around it are grouped other functional spaces, at different levels. Balcony bars and restaurants commanding high views of the city roofs, and ground-level replicas. A battery of skittle alleys. Two blue lagoons: one, periodically agitated by waves, for strong swimmers, and another, a smooth and summery pool, for playtime bathers. Sunlight lamps over the pools to simulate high summer on days when the roofs don't slide back to disclose a hot sun in a cloudless sky. Rows of bunks on which people wearing sun-glasses and slips can lie and start a tan or deepen an existing one under a sunray lamp.

Music seeping through hundreds of grills connected with a central distributing stage, where dance or symphonic orchestras play or the radio programme can be caught, amplified, and disseminated. Outside, two 1,000-car parks. One, free. The other, an open-air cinema drive-in, cars queueing to move through turnstiles, and the film thrown on a giant screen facing a row of assembled cars. Uniformed male attendants check the cars, provide free air and water, sell petrol and oil. Girls in white satin slacks take orders for buffet dishes and drinks, and bring them on trays.

Whenever one hears such phrases as "pleasure spot," "pleasure resort," "pleasure city," it is difficult not to remember the often-quoted opening of Coleridge's *Kubla Khan*: –

In Xanadu did Kubla Khan
A stately pleasure-dome decree:

Where Alph, the sacred river, ran
Through caverns measureless to man
Down to a sunless sea.
So twice five miles of fertile ground
With walls and towers were girdled round:
And there were gardens bright with sinuous rills
Where blossomed many an incense-bearing tree;
And here were forests ancient as the hills,
Enfolding sunny spots of greenery.

But it will be seen that Coleridge has got it all wrong. He strikes a false note straight off with that talk about "sacred" rivers and "measureless" caverns. In the hands of the above-mentioned entrepreneur, Kubla Khan's project would have become something quite different. The caverns, air-conditioned, discreetly lighted and with their original rocky interior buried under layers of tastefully-coloured plastics, would be turned into a series of tea-grottos in the Moorish, Caucasian or Hawaiian styles. Alph, the sacred river, would be dammed up to make an artificially-warmed bathing pool, while the sunless sea would be illuminated from below with pink electric lights, and one would cruise over it in real Venetian gondolas each equipped with its own radio set. The forests and "spots of greenery" referred to by Coleridge would be cleaned up to make way for glass-covered tennis courts, a bandstand, a roller-skating rink and perhaps a nine-hole golf course. In short, there would be everything that a "life-hungry" man could desire.

I have no doubt that, all over the world, hundreds of pleasure resorts similar to the one described above are now being planned, and perhaps are even being built. It is unlikely that they will be finished – world events will see to that – but they represent faithfully enough the modern civilised man's idea of pleasure. Something of the kind is already partially attained in the more magnificent dance halls, movie palaces, hotels, restaurants and luxury liners. On a pleasure cruise or in a Lyons Corner House one already gets something more than a glimpse of this future paradise. Analysed, its main characteristics are these: –

(a) One is never alone.
(b) One never does anything for oneself.

(c) One is never within sight of wild vegetation or natural objects of any kind.

(d) Light and temperature are always artificially regulated.

(e) One is never out of the sound of music.

The music – and if possible it should be the same music for everybody – is the most important ingredient. Its function is to prevent thought and conversation, and to shut out any natural sound, such as the song of birds or the whistling of the wind, that might otherwise intrude. The radio is already consciously used for this purpose by innumerable people. In very many English homes the radio is literally never turned off, though it is manipulated from time to time so as to make sure that only light music will come out of it. I know people who will keep the radio playing all through a meal and at the same time continue talking just loudly enough for the voices and the music to cancel out. This is done with a definite purpose. The music prevents the conversation from becoming serious or even coherent, while the chatter of voices stops one from listening attentively to the music and thus prevents the onset of that dreaded thing, thought. For

> The lights must never go out.
> The music must always play,
> Lest we should see where we are,
> Lost in a haunted wood,
> Children afraid of the dark
> Who have never been happy or good.

It is difficult not to feel that the unconscious aim in the most typical modern pleasure resorts is a return to the womb. For there, too, one was never alone, one never saw daylight, the temperature was always regulated, one did not have to worry about work or food, and one's thoughts, if any, were drowned by a continuous rhythmic throbbing.

When one looks at Coleridge's very different conception of a "pleasure dome," ones see that it revolves partly round gardens and partly round caverns, rivers, forests and mountains with "deep romantic chasms" – in short, round what is called Nature. But the whole notion of admiring Nature, and feeling a sort of religious awe in the presence of glaciers, deserts or waterfalls, is bound up with the sense of man's littleness and weakness against the power of the universe. The moon is beautiful partly because we cannot reach it, the sea is impressive because one can never be sure of crossing it safely. Even the pleasure one takes in a flower – and this is true even of a botanist who knows all there is to be known about the flower – is dependent partly on the sense of mystery. But meanwhile man's power over Nature is steadily increasing. With the aid of the atomic bomb we could literally move mountains: we could even, so it is said, alter the climate of the earth by melting the polar ice-caps and irrigating the Sahara. Isn't there, therefore, something sentimental and obscurantist in preferring bird-song to swing music and in wanting to leave a few patches of wildness here and there instead of covering the whole surface of the earth with a network of *Autobahnen* flooded by artificial sunlight?

The question only arises because in exploring the physical universe man had made no attempt to explore himself. Much of what goes by the name of pleasure is simply an effort to destroy consciousness. If one started by asking, What is man? What are his needs? How can he best express himself? one would discover that merely having the power to avoid work and live one's life from birth to death in electric light and to the tune of tinned music is not a reason for doing so. Man needs warmth, society, leisure, comfort and security: he also needs solitude, creative work and the sense of wonder. If he recognised this he could use the products of science and industrialism eclectically, applying always the same test: does this make me more human or less human? He would then learn that the highest happiness does *not* lie in relaxing, resting, playing poker, drinking and making love simultaneously. And the instinctive horror which all sensitive people feel at the progressive mechanisation of life would be seen not to be a mere sentimental archaism, but to be fully justified. For man only stays human by preserving large patches of simplicity in his life, while the tendency of many modern inventions – in particular the film, the radio and the aeroplane – is to weaken his consciousness, dull his curiosity, and, in general, drive him nearer to the animals.

GEORGE ORWELL

A Nice Cup of Tea
Saturday Essay, *Evening Standard*, 12 January 1946

If you look up "tea" in the first cookery book that comes to hand you will probably find that it is unmentioned; or at most you will find a few lines of sketchy instructions which give no ruling on several of the most important points.

This is curious, not only because tea is one of the mainstays of civilisation in this country, as well as in Eire, Australia and New Zealand, but because the best manner of making it is the subject of violent disputes.

When I look through my own recipe for the perfect cup of tea, I find no fewer than 11 outstanding points. On perhaps two of them there would be pretty general agreement, but at least four others are acutely controversial. Here are my own 11 rules, every one of which I regard as golden:

First of all, one should use Indian or Ceylonese tea. China tea has virtues which are not to be despised nowadays – it is economical, and one can drink it without milk – but there is not much stimulation in it. One does not feel wiser, braver or more optimistic after drinking it. Anyone who uses that comforting phrase, "a nice cup of tea," invariably means Indian tea.

Secondly, tea should be made in small quantities – that is, in a teapot. Tea out of an urn is always tasteless, while Army tea, made in a cauldron, tastes of grease and whitewash. The teapot should be made of china or earthenware. Silver or Britannia-ware pots produce inferior tea and enamel pots are worse: though curiously enough a pewter teapot (a rarity nowadays) is not so bad.

Thirdly, the pot should be warmed beforehand. This is better done by placing it on the hob than by the usual method of swilling it out with hot water.

Fourthly, the tea should be strong. For a pot holding a quart, if you are going to fill it nearly to the brim, six heaped teaspoons would be about right. In a time of rationing this is not an ideal that can be realised on every day of the week, but I maintain that one strong cup of tea is better than 20 weak ones. All true tea-lovers not only like their tea strong, but like it a little stronger with each year that passes – a fact which is recognised in the extra ration issued to old age pensioners.

Fifthly, the tea should be put straight into the pot. No strainers, muslin bags or other devices to imprison the tea. In some countries teapots are fitted with little dangling baskets under the spout, to catch the stray leaves, which are supposed to be harmful. Actually one can swallow tea-leaves in considerable quantities without ill effect, and if the tea is not loose in the pot it never infuses properly.

Sixthly, one should take the teapot to the kettle, and not the other way about. The water should be actually boiling at the moment of impact, which means that one should keep it on the flame while one pours. Some people add that one should only use water that has been freshly brought to the boil, but I have never noticed that this makes any difference.

Seventhly, after making the tea, one should stir it or, better, give the pot a good shake, afterwards allowing the leaves to settle.

Eighthly, one should drink out of a breakfast cup – that is, the cylindrical type of cup, not the flat, shallow type. The breakfast cup holds more, and with the other kind one's tea is always half cold before one has well started on it.

Ninthly, one should pour the cream off the milk before using it for tea. Milk that is too creamy always gives tea a sickly taste.

Tenthly, one should pour tea into the cup first. This is one of the most controversial points of all; indeed in every family in Britain there are probably two schools of thought on the subject.

The milk-first school can bring forward some fairly strong arguments, but I maintain that my own argument is unanswerable. This is that, by putting the tea in first and then stirring as one pours, one can exactly regulate the amount of milk, whereas one is liable to put in too much milk if one does it the other way round.

Lastly, tea – unless one is drinking it in the Russian style – should be drunk *without sugar*. I know very well that I am in a minority here. But still, how can you call yourself a true tea-lover if you destroy the flavour of your tea by putting sugar in it? It would be equally reasonable to put in pepper or salt.

Tea is meant to be bitter, just as beer is meant to be bitter. If you sweeten it, you are no longer tasting the tea, you are merely tasting the sugar: you could make a very similar drink by dissolving sugar in plain hot water.

Some people would answer that they don't like tea in itself, that they only drink it in order to be warmed and stimulated, and they need sugar to take the taste away. To those misguided people I would say: Try drinking tea without sugar for, say, a fortnight, and it is very unlikely that you will ever want to ruin your tea by sweetening it again.

These are not the only controversial points that arise in connection with tea-drinking, but they are sufficient to show how subtilised the whole business has become.

There is also the mysterious social etiquette surrounding the teapot (why is it considered vulgar to drink out of your saucer, for instance?) and much might be written about the subsidiary uses of tea leaves, such as telling fortunes, predicting the arrival of visitors, feeding rabbits, healing burns and sweeping the carpet.

It is worth paying attention to such details as warming the pot and using water that is really boiling, so as to make quite sure of wringing out of one's ration the 20 good, strong cups that two ounces, properly handled, ought to represent.

The Politics of Starvation
Tribune, 18 January 1946

A few days ago I received a wad of literature from the "Save Europe Now" committee, which has been attempting – without much encouragement from the Government or help from the Press – to increase the supply of food from this country to Europe. They quote a series of statements from authoritative sources, which I will come back to in a moment, and which go to show that whereas we are reasonably well off and the United States is enjoying an orgy of over-eating, a good part of Europe is lapsing into brute starvation.

In the *Observer* of January 13, however, I have just read a signed article by Air Chief Marshal Sir Philip Joubert, expressing the contrary opinion: –

> To one returning from overseas in this seventh winter of war (writes Sir Philip), the appearance of the British people is tragic. They seem morose, lacking in spring; and laughter

comes with difficulty. The children look pallid and suety – fat but not fit. They compare very ill with the rosy-cheeked youngsters of Denmark, who have all the meat and fat they need, with plenty of fruit in season.

His main thesis is that we need more meat, fats and eggs – i.e. more of the rationed foods – and less starch. The official figures showing that, in fact, we are healthier than we were before the war convey a false impression: first – this is a quite extraordinary argument – because health and nutrition were admittedly in a bad way before the war, so that the present improvement is nothing to write home about; secondly because the drop in the death-rate merely means a "greater expectation of existence" and one must not "confuse existence with life." Unless we can attain "liveliness, vitality, vigour," for which meat, fat, fruit and cane sugar are required, we cannot make the effort needed for the task of reconstruction. Sir Philip ends his article: –

> As for those who would cut our present ration further so as to give more to the Germans, there must be many who would reply to their demands, "I would sooner that my children, brought up in freedom and good-will towards men, should enjoy full vigour than the Germans, who may be using their strength to make war on the world again in another generation."

It will be seen that he is assuming (a) that any further export of food means a cut in rations here, and (b) that it is only proposed to send food to Germany. And in fact that is the form in which the big public has heard of this project, although those responsible have emphasised from the start that they were only proposing a *voluntary* surrender of certain foodstuffs, by those sections of the population to whom it would do no harm, and were *not* proposing it for the sole benefit of Germany.

Now here are a few facts from the latest bulletin of the "Save Europe Now" Committee. In Budapest, in November, the chemists were closing down for lack of supplies, the hospitals had neither windows, fuel nor anæsthetics, and it was calculated that the town contained 30,000 stray children, some of whom had formed themselves into criminal bands. In December, "independent observers" considered that unless fresh food

GEORGE ORWELL

supplies were brought quickly, a million people would die of starvation in Hungary this winter. In Vienna (November) "the food for hospital surgeons consists of unsweetened coffee, a very thin soup and bread. Less than 500 calories in all," while the Austrian Secretary of State, in December, described the thickly populated areas of eastern Austria as being menaced by "boundless misery, epidemics, crime, physical and moral decline." In Czechoslovakia, in November, the Foreign Minister appealed to Britain and the U.S.A. to send fats and meat to save 700,000 "very badly fed children, of whom 50 per cent. already have tuberculosis." In Germany, the Saar children are "slowly starving." In the British zone, Field-Marshal Montgomery said that he was "entirely dependent on imports of wheat if he was to maintain the present ration scales for the German people, ranging from 1,200 to 1,500 calories." This was in November. About the same time General Eisenhower, speaking of the French zone, said that "the normal ration of 1,100 calories a day for the average consumer was consistently not met." And so on. Meanwhile it appears that our own average consumption is about 2,800 or 2,900 calories a day, while the most recent figures of deaths from tuberculosis, and of deaths of mothers in childbirth and of children of all ages up to five, are the lowest ever recorded. As for the U.S.A., consumption of butter has just risen largely and meat rationing has come to an end. The Secretary of Agriculture estimates that "the lifting of rationing will make meat available for civilians at the rate of 165 lb. annually – the prewar supply was in the neighbourhood of 125 lb."

Even if the above figures do not convey much impression, who has not seen the photographs of skeleton-like children in Greece and other places – children to whom no one would think of applying Sir Philip Joubert's term, "suety"? Yet there has undoubtedly been considerable resistance to the idea that we should send more food to Europe. The "Save Europe Now" Committee, though they are now pursuing more limited aims, started off with the suggestion that those who felt inclined should sacrifice their points, or some of their points, and that the Government should forward the food so saved to the famine-stricken areas. The scheme was discouraged officially, but it also had a cold reception from many

994

private persons. People who would have been in a position to give it good publicity were frankly frightened of it, and the general public was allowed to imagine that what was proposed was to take food from British housewives in order to give it to German war criminals. Indeed, the whole manner in which this business has been discussed illustrates the curious dishonesty that infects every political issue nowadays.

There are two things that make what one might call the official Left, Labour or Communist, nervous of any scheme which might mean sending extra food to Germany. One is fear of the working-class reaction. The working classes, so it is said, would resent even a voluntary arrangement which meant, in effect, that people in the higher income groups, who buy unrationed foods and eat some of their meals in restaurants, should give up their surplus. The average woman in the fish queue, it is feared, would answer: "If there's really any food to spare, let *us* have it. Or why not give it to the coal miners?" I don't know whether this would really be the reaction, if the issues were fully explained. I suspect that some of the people who argue thus have in mind the sordid consideration that if we are to sacrifice food in sufficient quantities to make any difference, it would mean not merely giving up points but curtailing restaurant feeding. In practice, whatever it may be in intention, our rationing system is thoroughly undemocratic, and an all-round row on the subject of the export of food might draw attention to this fact. That is part of the reason, I think, why this question has not been fully discussed in print.

But another consideration, even less mentionable, also enters. Food is a political weapon, or is thought of as a political weapon. The hungriest areas are either in the Russian zone or in the parts of Europe that are divided between the U.S.S.R. and the Western Allies. Many people calculate that if we send more food to, say, Hungary, British or American influence in Hungary will increase: whereas if we let the Hungarians starve and the Russians feed them, they are more likely to look towards the U.S.S.R. All those who are strongly Russophile are therefore against sending extra food to Europe, while some people are probably in favour of sending food merely because they see it as a way of weakening Russian prestige. No one has been honest enough to avow such motives, but you have only

GEORGE ORWELL

to look through the lists of those who have – and of those who haven't – supported the "Save Europe Now" campaign to see how the land lies.

The folly of all such calculations lies in supposing that you can ever get good results from starvation. Whatever the ultimate political settlement in Europe may be, it can only be worse if it has been preceded by years of hunger, misery, banditry and ignorance. Air Marshal Joubert advises us to feed ourselves rather than feed German children who will be fighting against us a generation hence. This is the "realistic" view. In 1918 the "realistic" ones were also in favour of keeping up the blockade after the Armistice. We did keep up the blockade, and the children we starved then were the young men who were bombing us in 1940. No one, perhaps, could have foreseen just that result, but people of good will could and did foresee that the results of wantonly starving Germany, and of making a vindictive peace, would be evil. So also with raising our own rations, as we shall perhaps be doing before long, while famine descends on Europe. But if we do decide to do this, at least let the issues be plainly discussed, and let the photographs of starving children be well publicised in the press, so that the people of this country may realise just what they are doing.

Songs We Used to Sing
Saturday Essay, *Evening Standard*, 19 January 1946

A fascinating game, which can be played equally well in one's bath or on top of a bus, is to sort out and range in their right order all the popular songs one can remember.

Usually one can date the prime favourites within a year or two, and it is interesting to notice that they fall into a sort of pattern, more or less corresponding to the history of our times.

The earliest song I can remember, which must have been in 1907 or 1908, was "Rhoda had a pagoda." It was an inconceivably silly song, but it was certainly popular. After that, until the arrival of ragtime, there comes a vague period of about four years during which I cannot tie the prevailing songs down to a definite date.

Some of them were, "Every nice girl loves a sailor," "My little grey home in the West," "Oh, stop your tickling, Jock," "Jones of the Lancers" (or was that a Victorian song revived?) and "Pop goes the weasel."

I also think that –

"Oh, lucky Jim!

"'Ow I envy 'im!"

– that favourite of ventriloquists' dummies – must belong to that time. About 1912 came the American ragtime songs. There was about a year during which one was never out of the sound of –

"Everybody's doing it, doing it, doing it:

"Everybody's doing it. Doing what? Turkey trot."

and others at about the same mental level. On the whole the songs of that overfed, restless period before 1914, the period of the hobble skirt and the women's suffrage agitation, were exceptionally silly.

In 1913 or 1914 there came a spate of Irish songs. One of them was "Tipperary," which was to be sung all over the world in a thousand different accents because the first British troops to land in France happened to be singing it, just as in other years they might have happened to be singing "Daisy, Daisy" or "Roll out the barrel." To 1914 also belongs "Gilbert the filbert, the knut with the 'K'"; and, I think, "Good-bye, little girl, goodbye."

The earlier World War One songs were patriotic. Besides the recruiting song, "We don't want to lose you," there were "Pack up your troubles in your old kit-bag," "When we've wound up the watch on the Rhine," and "Keep the home fires burning."

Later, about 1917, came more nostalgic ones: "If you were the only girl in the world" and various songs from "Chu Chin Chow." The war songs petered out with "K-k-k-Katie," "The wild, wild women," and, a sort of rock bottom of silliness:

"I don't wanna get well,

"I don't wanna get well,

"I'm in love, with a bee-yoo-tiful nurse!"

After the war the songs looked up, and in 1920, or 1921, there came the lively "Where do the flies go in the winter time?" and "Coal black mammy."

To that time, also, belongs "I'm forever blowing bubbles."

I think the best popular songs of our time belong to the middle twenties. I cannot give exact dates to "Ma, he's kissing me," "Why did I kiss that girl?" and "Maggie! Yes, Ma? Come right upstairs!" but they all belong round about 1925.

But the three great smash-hits were: "Yes, we have no bananas" (1923), "'Tain't gonna rain no more" (1924) and "Show me the way to go home" (1925). The first two of these, at any rate, went round the world like an influenza epidemic and were sung even by primitive tribes in the remotest forests of Asia and South America.

A bit later, and almost equally popular, were: "When it's night-time in Italy," "Chick, chick, chick, chick, chicken" and "I'm gonna take a water-melon to my girl to-night."

"Yes, sir, that's my baby" and "I want to *be* happy" must, I think, be earlier – perhaps about 1924. All of these songs were American, and in their gaiety and their rather charming silliness they were a perfect expression of a period when war was far away.

Between these songs and 1930 I remember nothing except "Bye-bye, blackbird" (1927).

In 1930 and 1931, more or less coinciding with the slump, there was a run of mournful, nostalgic songs: "Dannie boy," "I'm dancing with tears in my eyes," "The bells are ringing for Sally, but not for Sally and me."

"River stay away from my door" also belongs to 1930.

Since about 1930 there has been no real smash-hit – no song that all the nations were singing simultaneously. In this country, I should say, the most popular were "Wheezy-Anna" (1932), "Roll out the barrel" (1939), and "Boomps-a-Daisy" (1940).

During the last two years of war the greatest favourite among the soldiers, British and American as well as German, was probably the sentimental "Lili Marlene." With the doubtful exception of "There'll always be an England," there has been no English war song that was both overtly patriotic and genuinely popular.

But there have been several songs in recent years whose words seemed to be a reflection of the existing political situation. "You can't do that there 'ere" (1935) was perhaps a half-conscious response to Hitler, and "Wishing will make it so" (1938) expressed only too well the mood of a large part of the population at that time.

1. The Intellectual Revolt

Manchester Evening News, 24 January 1946

During recent years it has become more and more obvious that old-style, laissez-faire capitalism is finished.

Far back in the nineteenth century this fact had been grasped by various clear-sighted individuals, and it was later made apparent to millions by the disaster of the 1914–18 war, by the success of the Russian revolution, and by the rise of the Fascist regimes, which were not strictly capitalist and could solve problems before which the old democracies, such as Britain or the United States, remained helpless.

The events of the last six years have merely underlined the lesson. Unmistakably, the drift everywhere is towards planned economies and away from an individualistic society in which property rights are absolute and money-making is the chief incentive.

However, simultaneously with this development there has happened an intellectual revolt which is not simply the uneasiness of property-owners who see their privileges menaced. If not a majority, at any rate a large proportion of the best minds of our time are dismayed by the turn of events and doubtful whether mere economic security is a worthwhile objective.

There is a widespread disappointment with the Russian form of Socialism, and, lying deeper than this, a mistrust of the whole machine of civilisation and its implied aims. Naturally, this intellectual revolt takes almost as many forms as there are individual thinkers, but there are certain main tendencies, which can be grouped as follows: –

1. The Pessimists. – Those who deny that a planned society can lead either to happiness or to true progress.

2. The Left-wing Socialists. – Those who accept the principle of planning, but are chiefly concerned to combine it with individual liberty.

3. The Christian Reformers. – Those who wish to combine revolutionary social change with adherence to Christian doctrine.

4. The Pacifists. – Those who wish to get away from the centralised State and from the whole principle of government by coercion.

Of course, there is an overlap between these different schools of thought, and some of them also overlap with ordinary Conservatism on the one side or with orthodox Socialism on the other.

Still, a large number of distinguished and representative thinkers can be accurately grouped under these headings. In the first of these four essays I deal with those I have labelled "Pessimists."

Perhaps the best expression of the pessimistic viewpoint, at any rate in English and in recent years, is F. A. Voigt's "Unto Cæsar," which was published about 1938. This heavily documented book is in the main an examination of Communism and Nazism, written round the thesis that societies which set out to establish the "earthly paradise" always end in tyranny.

Voigt assumes throughout his book that Russian Communism and German Fascism are for practical purposes the same thing and have almost the same objective. This is certainly an over-simplification and is unable to explain all the known facts. Nevertheless Voigt makes out a very strong case for narrowing down the scope of politics and not expecting too much from political action.

His basic argument is quite simple. A statesman who aims at perfection, and thinks that he knows how to reach it, will stop at nothing to drive others along the same road, and his political ideals will be inextricably mixed up with his desire to remain in power. Perfection, in practice, is never attained, and the terrorism used in pursuit of it simply breeds the need for fresh terrorism. Consequently the attempt to establish liberty and equality always ends in the police state: whereas more limited aims, based on the realisation that man's nature is full of evil, may lead to a fairly decent society.

Approximately the same line is taken by the American writer, Peter Drucker, author of "The End of Economic Man" and "The Future of Industrial Man." Drucker was one of the very small handful of publicists who foretold the Russo-German Pact of 1939. Particularly in the second of the above-named books, he argues the need for what he calls a "Conservative revolution" meaning not a return of capitalism, but the revival of the idea of a "mixed society" in which there is a system of checks and balances which make it impossible for any one section of the community to become all-powerful.

This, Drucker argues, was the real aim of the eighteenth-century leaders of the American revolution. Other writers who have advanced rather similar arguments against perfectionism are Michael Roberts (in his book on T. E. Hulme), Malcolm Muggeridge ("The Thirties") and Hugh Kingsmill in "The Poisoned Crown." The last-named book consists of four studies of Queen Elizabeth, Cromwell, Napoleon, and Abraham Lincoln – it is perhaps a somewhat perverse book, but it contains some penetrating remarks on dictatorship.

The whole problem of Utopian aims, and their tendency to end in tyranny, is discussed by Bertrand Russell in a number of books, particularly "The Scientific Outlook," "Freedom and Organisation," and "Power: a New Analysis." Russell has held very different political views at different periods of his life, but his vision of the future has been almost uniformly pessimistic, and he is inclined to think that liberty and efficiency are of their nature incompatible.

The planned, centralised State has also been attacked on the ground that, even in terms of its own objectives, it does not work. Perhaps the ablest exposition of this viewpoint is Professor Hayek's "The Road to Serfdom," which was published in 1944 and raised a great deal of discussion, especially in the United States.

Hayek argues that centralism and detailed planning not only destroy liberty but are incapable of affording as high a standard of living as laissez-faire capitalism. He claims that before Hitler came to power his essential work had been done for him by the German Social-Democrats and Communists, who had succeeded in breaking down the average German's desire for liberty and independence.

His main argument is that a centralised economy necessarily gives great power to the bureaucrats at the centre, and that people who want power for its own sake will gravitate towards the key positions. A rather similar line is taken in "Contempt of Freedom," by Professor Michael Polanyi of Manchester

University, who studied conditions in the U.S.S.R. over a number of years and subjected the Webbs' famous book, "Soviet Communism – a New Civilisation?" to some searching criticism. The biologist James Baker has also argued ("Science and the Planned State") that scientific research cannot flourish under the rule of a bureaucracy.

Finally, one can number among the "pessimists" James Burnham, whose book "The Managerial Revolution" made such a stir when it was published five years ago. More particularly in his next published book, "The Machiavellians," Burnham argues that neither Socialism nor full democracy are attainable aims, and that the most we can do is to establish safeguards – for example, autonomous trade unions and a free press – against the abuse of power.

He goes much further than the other writers I have named, in that he denies even the possibility of decent political behaviour and merely advocates that we should use political trickery for limited ends instead of extravagant ones; but at many points his world-view coincides with that of the others.

The term "pessimist" fits all of these writers in so much that they refuse to believe in the possibility of an earthly Utopia, while most of them also do not believe in a "next world" in which this one will be put right. Except perhaps for Drucker and Burnham, who wish to guide the existing trend rather than oppose it, the weakness of all of them is that they are not advocating any policy likely to get a large following.

Hayek's able defence of capitalism, for instance, is wasted labour, since hardly anyone wishes for the return of old-style capitalism. Faced with the choice between serfdom and economic insecurity the masses everywhere would probably choose outright serfdom, at least if it were called by some other name. Most of the others are putting forward what is in essence a religious view of life without the consolations of orthodox religion.

If one were obliged to give the writers of this school a political label one would have to call them Conservatives – but in most cases theirs is a romantic Conservatism, which fights against irreversible facts. But that is not to deny that they and other writers of kindred tendency have uttered much useful criticism of the folly and wickedness of the Totalitarian age.

2. What Is Socialism?
Manchester Evening News, 31 January 1946

Until the twentieth century, and indeed until the nineteen-thirties, all Socialist thought was in some sense Utopian. Socialism had nowhere been tested in the physical world, and in the mind of almost everyone, including its enemies, it was bound up with the idea of liberty and equality.

Only let economic injustice be brought to an end and all other forms of tyranny would vanish also. The age of human brotherhood would begin, and war, crime, disease, poverty, and overwork would be things of the past. There were some who disliked this objective, and many who assumed that it would never be reached, but that at least was the objective.

Thinkers as far apart as Karl Marx and William Morris, Anatole France and Jack London, all had a roughly similar picture of the Socialist future, though they might differ violently as to the best way of getting there.

After 1930 an ideological split began to appear in the Socialist movement. By this time "Socialism" was no longer a mere word evoking a dream. A huge and powerful country, Soviet Russia, had adopted a Socialist economy and was rapidly reconstructing its national life, and in nearly all countries there was an unmistakable swing towards public ownership and large-scale planning. At the same time for the word "Socialism" there grew up in Germany the monstrosity of Nazism, which called itself Socialism and did have certain quasi-Socialist features, but embodied them in one of the most cruel and cynical regimes the world has ever seen. Evidently it was time for the word "Socialism" to be re-defined.

What is Socialism? Can you have Socialism without liberty, without equality, and without internationalism? Are we still aiming at universal human brotherhood, or must we be satisfied with a new kind of caste society in which we surrender our individual rights in return for economic security?

Among recent books, perhaps the best discussion of these questions is to be found in Arthur Koestler's book "The Yogi and the Commissar," published about a year ago.

According to Koestler, what is now needed is, "a synthesis of the saint and the revolutionary." To put it in different words – revolutions have to happen, there can be no moral progress without drastic economic changes, and yet the revolutionary wastes his labour if he loses touch with ordinary human decency. Somehow the dilemma of ends and means must be resolved. We must be able to act, even to use violence, and yet not be corrupted by action. In specific political terms, this means rejection of Russian Communism on the one hand and of Fabian gradualism on the other.

Like most writers of similar tendency, Koestler is an ex-Communist, and inevitably his sharpest reaction is against the developments that have appeared in Soviet policy since about 1930. His best book is a novel, "Darkness at Noon," dealing with the Moscow sabotage trials.

Other writers who can be placed roughly in the same category are Ignazio Silone, André Malraux, and the Americans John Dos Passos and James Farrell.

One might add André Gide, who only arrived at Communism, or indeed at political consciousness, late in life, but, having done so, passed almost at once into the ranks of the rebels. One can also add the French Trotskyist, Victor Serge, and the Italian, Gaetano Salvemini, the historian of Fascism. Salvemini is a Liberal rather than a Socialist, but he resembles the others in that his main emphasis is anti-totalitarian, and he has been deeply involved in the internal struggles of the Left.

In spite of the superficial resemblance that appears at certain moments, there is no real affinity between dissident Socialists like Koestler or Silone, and enlightened Conservatives like Voigt or Drucker. Silone's book of political dialogues, "The School for Dictators," may seem on the surface as pessimistic, and as critical of the existing Left Wing parties as "Unto Cæsar," but the underlying world-view is very different.

The point is that a Socialist or Communist, as such – and perhaps this applies most of all to the one who breaks with his own party on a point of doctrine – is a person who believes the "earthly paradise" to be possible. Socialism is in the last analysis an optimistic creed and not easy to square with the doctrine of original sin.

A Socialist is not obliged to believe that human society can actually be made perfect, but almost any Socialist does believe that it could be a great deal better than it is at present, and that most of the evil that men do results from the warping effects of injustice and inequality. The basis of Socialism is humanism. It can co-exist with religious belief, but not with the belief that man is a limited creature who will always misbehave himself if he gets half a chance.

The emotion behind books like "Darkness at Noon," or Gide's "Return from the U.S.S.R.," or Eugene Lyons's "Assignment in Utopia," or others of similar tendency, is not simply disappointment because the expected paradise has not arrived quickly enough. It is also a fear that the original aims of the Socialist movement are becoming blurred.

It is certainly true that orthodox Socialist thought, either reformist or revolutionary, has lost some of the messianic quality that it had 30 years ago. This results from the growing complexity of industrial life, from the day-to-day needs of the struggle against Fascism, and from the example of Soviet Russia. In order to survive the Russian Communists were forced to abandon, at any rate temporarily, some of the dreams with which they had started out.

Strict economic equality was found to be impracticable; freedom of speech, in a backward country which had passed through civil war, was too dangerous; internationalism was killed by the hostility of the capitalist powers.

From about 1925 onwards Russian policies, internal and external, grew harsher and less idealistic, and the new spirit was carried abroad by the Communist parties of the various countries. The history of these Communist parties can be conveniently studied in Franz Borkenau's book "The Communist International."

In spite of much courage and devotion the main effect of Communism in Western Europe has been to undermine the belief in democracy and tinge the whole Socialist movement with Machiavellianism. It is not only the writers I have named who are in revolt against these tendencies. There is a whole host of others, great and small, who have gone through a similar development. To name only a few: Freda Utley, Max Eastman, Ralph Bates, Stephen Spender, Philip Toynbee, Louis Fischer.

Except, perhaps, for Max Eastman none of these writers could be said to have reverted towards Conservatism. They are all aware of the need for planned societies and for a high level of industrial development. But they want the older conception of Socialism, which laid its stress on liberty and equality and drew its inspiration from the belief in human brotherhood, to be kept alive.

The viewpoint that they are expressing exists in the Left Wing of the Socialist movement everywhere, or at least in the more advanced countries, where a high standard of living is taken for granted. In more primitive countries political extremism is more likely to take the form of anarchism. Among those who believe in the possibility of human progress a three-cornered struggle is always going on between Machiavellianism, bureaucracy, and Utopianism.

At this moment it is difficult for Utopianism to take shape in a definite political movement. The masses everywhere want security much more than they want equality, and do not generally realise that freedom of speech and of the Press are of urgent importance to themselves. But the desire for earthly perfection has a very long history behind it.

If one studied the genealogy of the ideas for which writers like Koestler and Silone stand, one would find it leading back through Utopian dreamers like William Morris and mystical democrats like Walt Whitman, through Rousseau, through the English diggers and levellers, through the peasant revolts of the Middle Ages, and back to the early Christians and the slave rebellions of antiquity.

The pamphlets of Gerrard Winstanley, the digger from Wigan, whose experiment in primitive Communism was crushed by Cromwell, are in some ways strangely close to modern Left Wing literature.

The "earthly paradise" has never been realised, but as an idea it never seems to perish in spite of the ease with which it can be debunked by practical politicians of all colours.

Underneath it lies the belief that human nature is fairly decent to start with and is capable of indefinite development. This belief has been the main driving force of the Socialist movement, including the underground sects who prepared the way for the Russian revolution, and it could be claimed that the Utopians, at present a scattered minority, are the true upholders of Socialist tradition.

Freda Utley, "The Dream We Lost." Max Eastman, "Since Lenin Died," "Artists in Uniform." Louis Fischer, "Men and Politics." Arthur Koestler, "The Gladiators," "Scum of the Earth." Ignazio Silone, "Fontamara," "Bread and Wine," "The Seed Beneath the Snow." André Malraux, "Storm Over Shanghai," "Days of Hope." Gaetano Salvemini, "Under the Axe of Fascism." Gerrard Winstanley, "Selections."

3. The Christian Reformers
Manchester Evening News, 7 February 1946

The belief in life after death and the desire for earthly happiness are not irreconcilable, but they pull in opposite directions. If there is a life beyond the grave our chief purpose must be to prepare for that life, and the necessary spiritual discipline may lie in pain, sorrow, poverty, and all the other things that the social reformer wants to get rid of.

In any case, the idea of submission to the will of God, and the idea of increasing human control over nature, are felt to be inimical. On the whole, therefore, the Christian churches – and especially the Catholic, Orthodox, Anglican, and Lutheran churches, each of them bound up with a well-established social order – have been hostile to the idea of progress and have resisted any political theory tending to weaken the institution of private property.

However, one cannot equate Christian belief with Conservatism. Even in the Middle Ages there were already heretical sects which preached revolutionary political doctrines, and after the Reformation there was a close connection between Radicalism and Protestantism. The roots of the English Socialist movement lie partly in Nonconformity.

In our own time, however, there has has been a more far-reaching development in the attempt to reconcile orthodox, other-worldly, Christian belief with revolutionary Socialism. Catholic Socialist parties have appeared all over the Continent.

The Russian Orthodox Church, or an important part of it, has made its peace with the Soviet Government, and corresponding currents of thought have shown themselves in the Church of England.

There is more than one reason for this development, but it would not have happened if individual Christians, both priests and laymen, had not become more and more convinced of the inherent wickedness of capitalist society. It would not do, as in the past, to preach that God made rich and poor and that what mattered was the saving of souls.

As Pastor Niemöller put it, the conditions of poverty in a great city were such as to make a Christian life impossible. Perhaps the teachings of Christ pointed the way to pure Communism. At any rate, they evidently demanded a radical redistribution of property.

During the last 20 years the most distinguished religious thinkers have not been political reactionaries in the ordinary sense: that is, they have not been defenders of *laissez-faire* capitalism. There are many gradations of opinion among them, but it is possible to sort out three main tendencies.

First, there are those who simply identify Christianity with Communism and lay their main emphasis on the political and economic implications of the Gospel. Some, of whom the Dean of Canterbury is the best known, consider Soviet Russia to be the nearest existing approach to a truly Christian Society.

Professor John Macmurray ("The Clue to History") goes almost as far along this road as the Dean of Canterbury, and holds that the anti-religious bias of the Soviet regime is simply an error which can and should be rectified. Professor Macmurray, however, rejects the doctrine of personal immortality, so that he can hardly be considered an orthodox believer.

Another Anglican writer who has made utterances more or less in the same sense, though with much more emphasis on the sanctity of the individual, is Sydney Dark ("I Sit and I Think and I Wonder"), the one-time editor of the "Church Times." In spite of some recent efforts in France, there has never been any sign of a real reconciliation between Russian Communism and the Catholic Church. Within the Church of England, however, Left Wing sympathies seem to be strongest among the Anglo-Catholics who are doctrinally nearest to Rome.

Secondly, there are those who accept Socialism as the inevitable and even the desirable next step in human history, but are chiefly concerned to Christianise the new Socialist society and prevent it from cutting its spiritual links with the past. The two most distinguished writers in this school are the French Bergsonian writer, Jacques Maritain, and the Russian émigré writer, Nicolai Berdyaev.

Maritain, whose "Christianity and Democracy" was published in this country last year, is a very subtle thinker and deeply respected in the Catholic world, and he has done great service to the cause of Socialism by managing to reconcile the idea of social progress with strict Catholic orthodoxy. During the war he used all the weight of his intellectual authority against the Pétain regime, and during the Spanish Civil War he refused to be stampeded into acclaiming Franco as the champion of Christendom.

The Catholic novelist Georges Bernanos ("The Diary of a Country Priest" and "A Diary of My Times") took a similar stand, but in a more vehement way. As a thinker, however, Bernanos should probably be placed in the third of these groups I am considering. The nearest English equivalent to Maritain is the Catholic historian Christopher Dawson. Berdyaev's case is different from that of the others in that he started as a Marxian Socialist and only later became a religious believer.

He left Russia at the time of the Revolution, but, though extremely hostile to Bolshevism, he has written of it with more understanding and respect than most of its opponents, and his remarks on the connection between the primitive faith of the Russian peasant and the violence of the Revolution are of great interest.

All the writers in this group would admit that if the Church has lost the support of the masses it is largely by tolerating social injustice. The political expression of this new viewpoint is Christian Socialism, which has already reached impressive proportions in France.

Finally – and in a way this is the most interesting group – there are those who admit the injustice of present-day society and are ready for drastic changes but reject Socialism and, by implication, industrialism. As long ago as 1911 Hilaire Belloc wrote his very prescient book "The Servile State," in which he foretold that capitalist society would soon degenerate into something resembling what afterwards came to be called Fascism.

Belloc's remedy was the splitting-up of large property and a return to a peasant proprietorship. Belloc's friend, G. K. Chesterton, made this idea the basis of a political movement which he called Distributism. Chesterton, a convert to Catholicism, had the mental background of a nineteenth-century radical, and his desire for a simpler form of society was combined with an almost mystical belief in democracy and the virtues of the common man.

His movement never gained a large following, and after his death a few of his disciples drifted into the British Union of Fascists, while others looked for a remedy in currency reform. Nevertheless, his doctrines reappear, essentially unchanged, in T. S. Eliot's idea of a Christian society. The significance of Chesterton is that he expresses in a simplified – indeed, a caricatured – form, certain tendencies that exist in every Christian reformer.

The specifically Christian virtues are likeliest to flourish in small communities, where life is simple and the family is a natural unit. Therefore the tug of Christian thought, even in those who admit the necessity for planning and centralised ownership, is always away from a highly complex, luxurious society, and towards the mediæval village. Even a writer like Professor Macmurray, who can accept Russian Communism almost without reservations, wants people to live in what he calls "a workaday world," where life will not be too easy.

Mediævalism, as it is presented by Chesterton, or even by Eliot, is not serious politics. It is merely a symptom of the malaise which any sensitive person feels before the spectacle of machine civilisation.

But Christian thinkers who are more realistic than Chesterton still have to face an unsolved problem. They claim, rightly, that if our civilisation does not regenerate itself morally it is likely to perish – and they may be right in adding that, at least in Europe, its moral code must be based on Christian principles. But the Christian religion includes, as an integral part of itself, doctrines which large numbers of people can no longer be brought to accept.

The belief in personal immortality, for instance, is almost certainly dwindling. If the Church clings to such doctrines it cannot attract the great mass of the people – but if it abandons them it will have lost its *raison d'être* and may well disappear.

This is merely to say over again, in different words, that Christianity is of its nature "other-wordly," while Socialism is of its nature "this worldly." Nearly all religious discussion, in our time, revolves round this problem, but no satisfying answer has been found.

Meanwhile, the fact that writers and thinkers of the stature of Maritain, Eliot, Reinhold Niebuhr, and Christopher Dawson have been forced not only to take an interest in contemporary politics but to come down on what is loosely called the "progressive" side, helps to counteract the too-easy optimism and the ill-thought-out materialism which are among the weaknesses of the left-wing movement.

Dean of Canterbury, "Marxism and the Individual" (pamphlet). Jacques Maritain, "True Humanism," "Science and Wisdom," "The Rights of Man." Nicolas Berdyaev, "Christianity and Class War," "Russian Religious Psychology and Communist Atheism." E. Lampert, "Nicolas Berdyaev and the New Middle Ages." Christopher Dawson, "Beyond Politics," "The Judgment of the Nations." Reinhold Niebuhr, "Moral Man and Immoral Society."

4. Pacifism and Progress
Manchester Evening News, 14 February 1946

"Pacifism" is a vague word, since it is usually taken as expressing a mere negative, that is, a refusal to perform military service or rejection of war as an instrument of policy.

This does not of itself carry any definite political implication, nor is there any general agreement as to what activities a war-resister ought to accept or refuse.

The majority of conscientious objectors are merely unwilling to take life and are ready to do some kind of alternative job, such as agricultural work, in which their contribution to the war effort is indirect instead of direct.

On the other hand, the really uncompromising war-resisters, who refuse every form of national service and are ready to face persecution for their beliefs, are often people who have no theoretical objection to violence, but are merely opponents of the Government which happens to be waging the war.

Hence there were many Socialists who opposed the war of 1914–18 and supported that of 1939–45, and, granting their premises, there was no inconsistency in this.

The whole theory of pacifism, if one assumes it to mean outright renunciation of violence, is open to very serious objections. It is obvious that any Government that is unwilling to use force must be at the mercy of any other Government, or even of any individual, that is less scrupulous – so that the refusal to use force simply tends to make civilised life impossible.

However, there are people describable as pacifists who are quite intelligent enough to see and admit this and who still have an answer. And though, of course, there are differences of opinion among them, their answer is something like this:

Of course, civilisation now rests upon force. It rests not only on guns and bombing planes, but on prisons, concentration camps, and the policeman's truncheon. And it is quite true that if peaceful people refuse to defend themselves, the immediate effect is to give more power to gangsters like Hitler and Mussolini. But it is also true that the use of force makes real progress impossible. The good society is one in which human beings are equal and in which they co-operate with one another willingly and not because of fear or economic compulsion.

This is what Socialists, Communists and Anarchists, in their different ways, are all aiming at. Obviously it cannot be reached in a moment, but to accept war as an instrument is to take a step away from it.

The waging of war, and the preparation for war, make necessary the centralised modern state, which destroys liberty and perpetuates inequalities. Moreover, every war breeds fresh wars. Even if human life is not wiped out altogether – and this is quite a likely development, considering the destructiveness of present-day weapons – there can be no genuine advance while the process continues.

Probably there will be actual degeneration, because the tendency is for each war to be more brutal and degrading than the last. At some point or another the cycle must be broken. Even at the cost of accepting defeat and foreign domination, we must begin to act pacifically and refuse to return evil for evil.

The seeming result of this, at the start, will be to make evil stronger but that is the price we have to pay for the barbarous history of the past 400 years. Even if it is still necessary to struggle against oppression we must struggle against it by non-violent means. The first step towards sanity is to break the cycle of violence.

Among the writers who can be roughly grouped as pacifists, and who would probably accept what I have said above as a preliminary statement of their views, are Aldous Huxley, John Middleton Murry, the late Max Plowman, the anarchist, poet, and critic, Herbert Read, and a number of very young writers such as Alex Comfort and D. S. Savage.

The two thinkers to whom all of these writers are in some degree indebted are Tolstoi and Gandhi. But one can distinguish among them at least two schools of thought – the real point at issue is the acceptance or non-acceptance of the State and of mechanical civilisation.

In his earlier pacifist writings, such as "Ends and Means," Huxley stressed chiefly the destructive folly of war, and rather overplayed the argument that one cannot bring about a good result by using evil methods. More recently he seems to have arrived at the conclusion that political action is inherently evil, and that, strictly speaking, it is not possible for society to be saved – only individuals can be saved, and then only by means of religious exercises which the ordinary person is hardly in a position to undertake.

In effect this is to despair of human institutions and counsel disobedience to the State, though Huxley has never made any definite political pronouncement. Middleton Murry arrived at pacifism by way of Socialism, and his attitude to the State is somewhat different. He does not demand that it should be simply abolished, and he realises that machine civilisation cannot be scrapped, or at any rate is not going to be scrapped.

In a recent book, "Adam and Eve," he makes the interesting though disputable point that, if we are to retain the machine, full employment is an objective that should not be aimed at. A highly developed industry, if it is working full time, will produce an unusable surplus of goods, and hence lead to the scramble for markets, and the competition in armaments, whose natural end is war.

What is to be aimed at is a decentralised society, agricultural rather than industrial, and prizing leisure more highly than luxury. Such a society, Murry thinks, would be inherently peaceful, and would not invite attack, even from aggressive neighbours.

Herbert Read, curiously enough, although as an anarchist he regards the State as something to be repudiated utterly, is not hostile to the machine. A high level of industrial development would, he thinks, be compatible with the complete absence of central controls. Some of the younger pacifist writers, such as Comfort and Savage, do not offer any programme for society as a whole, but lay their emphasis on the need to preserve one's own individuality against the encroachment either of the State or of political parties.

It will be seen that the real problem is whether pacifism is compatible with the struggle for material comfort. On the whole, the direction of pacifist thought is towards a kind of primitivism. If you want a high standard of living you must have a complex industrial society – but that implies planning, organisation, and coercion – in other words, it implies the State, with its prisons, its police forces, and its inevitable wars. The more extreme pacifists would say that the very existence of the State is incompatible with true peace.

It is clear that if one thinks along these lines it is almost impossible to imagine any complete and rapid regeneration of society. The pacifist and anarchist ideal can only be realised piecemeal, if at all. Hence the idea, which has haunted anarchist thought for 100 years past, of self-contained agricultural communities, within which the classless, non-violent society can exist, as it were, in small patches.

At different times such communities have actually existed in various parts of the world – in nineteenth-century Russia and America, in France and Germany during the between-war years, and in Spain for a brief period during the Civil War.

In Britain, also, small groups of conscientious objectors have attempted something of the kind in recent years. The idea is not simply to escape from society – it is rather to create spiritual oases like the monasteries of the dark ages, from which a new attitude towards life can gradually diffuse itself.

The trouble with such communities is that they are never genuinely independent of the outside world, and that they can only exist so long as the State, which they regard as their enemy, chooses to tolerate them. In a wider sense the same criticism applies to the pacifist movement as a whole.

It can only survive where there is some degree of democracy, and in many parts of the world it has never been able to exist at all. There was no pacifist movement in Nazi Germany, for instance.

The tendency of pacifism, therefore, is always to weaken those Governments and social systems that are most favourable to it. During the ten years before the war there is little doubt that the prevalence of pacifist ideas in Britain, France, and the U.S.A. encouraged Fascist aggression. And even in their subjective feelings, English and American pacifists often seem to be more hostile to capitalist democracy than to totalitarianism. But in a negative sense their criticism has been useful.

They have rightly insisted that present-day society, even when the guns do not happen to be firing, is not peaceful, and they have kept alive the idea – somewhat neglected since the Russian Revolution – that the aim of progress is to abolish the authority of the State and not to strengthen it.

Aldous Huxley, "Grey Eminence," "What are You Going to Do About It?" I and II (pamphlets); Max Plowman, "Bridge into the Future" (letters); Herbert Read, "Poetry and Anarchism"; Alex Comfort, "No Such Liberty"; D. S. Savage, "The Personal Principle"; Leo Tolstoi, "What, Then, Must We Do?"; Wilfred Wellock, "A Mechanistic or a Human Society?" (pamphlet); Roy Walker, "The Wisdom of Gandhi" (pamphlet).

But Are We Really Ruder? No

Saturday Essay, *Evening Standard*, 26 January 1946

The news that the Mayor of Hendon, Middlesex, is despatching 15,500 letters to children in his borough, urging them to be more courteous, raises once again the question of whether English manners have deteriorated since the war.

The Mayor thinks they have, and attributes the present day lack of courtesy to imitation of the "tough-guy training of soldiers." He is anxious that children should give up their seats to elderly people in buses, make themselves useful in the home by cleaning shoes and running errands, and enrol themselves in a "Guild of Courtesy" for which 15,000 membership buttons are being prepared.

The first criticism anyone might make is that it seems rather unfair to put the blame on the Army. Soldiers, no doubt, have to be trained in toughness, but when it is not fighting the British Army is the best-mannered in the world.

It has been impossible to travel in Europe recently without being greeted with almost embarrassing compliments on the "correct" bearing of the British troops. They have, indeed, been more successful ambassadors for their country than other people who are more highly paid for the job.

And when one considers the way in which it was customary for British soldiers to behave not so very long ago, in India, for instance, or even as near home as Malta or Gibraltar, it is difficult not to feel that we have grown rapidly more civilised in the years before the wars.

I do not think I have ever been in a country where a blind man or a foreigner asking the way gets more attention than he does in England, or where fewer quarters of big towns are unsafe at night, or where people are less inclined to shove you off the pavement or grab your place on a bus or train.

Even in the present overcrowded state of the railways, you can leave your overcoat on the seat and come back ten minutes later to find your place still empty. The other passengers will have respected your prior right to it, even though by this time the corridor is jammed with people. As for queueing-up, during the past five or ten years it has become what the psychologists call a conditioned reflex. If you put a dozen English people together, they form themselves into a queue almost instinctively.

At the end of the other war, when the transport shortage was about as bad as it is now, there was no queueing for buses. It was every man for himself, and the person with the sharpest elbows and the fewest scruples got on board first.

It is quite true that a certain number of children, generally suffering from the effects of evacuation, have run wild and turned into little savages, and that in everyone the accumulating discomforts of war have produced a nervous tension which occasionally shows itself in meaningless outbursts of temper.

When I recall the breaches of manners which I have met with – or committed, for that matter – during the war years, I find that it is nearly always the same picture: a sudden explosion of rage against some total stranger who has not in fact committed any real offence.

The rudest people of all are shopkeepers, especially fishmongers and tobacconists. But most shopkeepers are harassed and overworked, and it is only natural that they should want to get their own back after years of enforced servility.

My own fishmonger conducts himself like an oriental monarch of the old school. He only opens his shop for three hours a day, frequently arriving half an hour late, and the few kippers that he distributes seem like largesse except that you don't get them free.

Many of his customers address him as "Sir." But after all, between 1919 and 1939 he was probably calling other people "Sir," and who shall blame him if he makes the most of his brief moment of power?

If one considers, not simply the war years, but the last two or three decades, there is not the slightest doubt that there has been an all-round softening of manners, as well as a considerable evening-out of class distinctions. Many things have contributed to it – films, radio, slum clearance, the mass production of cheap clothes, and the improvement in elementary education.

In a strictly æsthetic sense, no doubt, our manners have not improved. A certain vulgarity is inherent in industrial civilisation, and when it comes to such things as gestures, movements and the wearing of clothes, any European, from a professor of philosophy to a costermonger, is inferior to an Indian or Chinese peasant.

But the general development of our age, with more and more people every year living in houses with bathrooms, getting used to eating in public, learning to speak the dialect of the B.B.C. and modelling their appearance on film stars, has been away from uncouthness. And together with the surface improvement I should say that there has been an increase in true civility and considerateness.

Much of the effort of the war, especially the smooth running of such things as rationing and fire-watching, would have been impossible without it.

Meanwhile, if our manners sometimes seem to lack polish, I do not think the Mayor of Hendon need worry.

To wait 20 minutes for a bus in leaky shoes, and then come home to find that the gas fire is not working, does not make for urbanity. More fuel, more transport, warmer clothes, better-lighted streets and a less monotonous diet – these things will be found to have a greater civilising influence than wearing the badge of the Guild of Courtesy in your button-hole.

Bad Climates are Best
Evening Standard, 2 February 1946

The time was when I used to say that what the English climate needed was a minor operation, comparable to the removal of tonsils in a human being.

Just cut out January and February, and we should have nothing to complain about.

Now, however, I feel that I would not remove even those two months, supposing that I had the power.

This is not entirely an academic question, for, if our popular scientific writers are to be believed, we are within sight of being able to control the climate. By the use of atomic energy, it seems, we could melt the polar ice caps, irrigate the Sahara, divert the Gulf Stream, move chains of mountains from one place to another, and, in short, alter the planet out of recognition.

And if the day ever comes when Britain has to decide what kind of climate it is to have (it will be done by plebiscite,

I suppose, or on the basis of a Gallup Poll), I hope we opt for what is called a "bad" climate and not what is miscalled a "perfect" one.

The great thing about the English climate is its variation. It is not merely that you never know what the weather is going to do to-morrow, but that each season of the year, and indeed each month, has its own clear-cut personality, like an old friend – or, in the case of two or three months, an old enemy.

In very many parts of the world this is not so. In most Eastern lands there are only three seasons, the hot weather, the cold weather and the rains, and in each of those three periods one day is just like another day.

In very hot climates there is not even anything corresponding to spring or autumn; there are always flowers in bloom, the trees are evergreen, the birds are nesting all the year round. Down near the Equator even the length of the day barely alters, so that you never have the pleasure of a long summer evening or of breakfasting by artificial light.

I am going to try the experiment of running through the months of the year and seeing what associations they automatically call up.

They will not all be pleasant ones, but I think it will be found that they are sharply differentiated from one another. I will start off with March.

March. – Wallflowers (especially the old-fashioned brown ones). Icy winds sweeping round street corners and blowing grit into your eyes. Hares having boxing matches in the young corn.

April. – The smell of the earth after a shower. The pleasure of hearing the cuckoo punctually on the fourteenth; also of seeing the first swallow – which, in fact, is usually a sand-martin.

May. – Stewed rhubarb. The pleasure of not wearing underclothes.

June. – Cloud-bursts. The smell of hay. Going for walks after supper. The back-breaking labour of earthing up potatoes.

July. – Going to the office in shirt sleeves. The endless pop-pop-pop of cherry stones as one treads the London pavements.

August. – Midges. Plums. Sea bathing. Beds of geraniums, painful to look at. The dusty smell of water-carts.

September. – Blackberries. The first leaves turning. Heavy dew in the early mornings. The pleasure of seeing a fire in the grate again.

October. – Utterly windless days. Yellow elm trees looming up out of the mist, with all their leaves dead and none fallen.

November. – Raging gales. The smell of rubbish fires.

December. – Owls hooting. Cat ice on the puddles. Roast chestnuts. The sun hanging over the roof-tops like a crimson ball which one can study with the naked eye.

Those are merely my own associations. Anyone else's, I suppose, would be different, but they would probably be just as varied.

I cannot believe that in, say, California or New Zealand, or in the pleasure resorts of the Riviera, the months have so individual a flavour.

But how about **January** and **February**? February, I admit, is a particularly detestable month, with no virtue except its shortness. But in fairness to our climate one ought to remember that if we did not have this period of damp and cold, the rest of the year would be quite different.

The flavour of our fruits and vegetables depends on the rain-sodden soil and the slow coming of the spring. With the doubtful exception of the banana and the pineapple, no fruit worth eating grows in a hot country. Even the orange and the lemon come from fairly temperate lands like Spain or Palestine, and the characteristic tropical fruits – mangoes, paw-paws, custard apples – are watery, tasteless things.

Fruits like apples and strawberries all need a period of frost and heavy rain, and never attain their best flavour in countries where the summer is really hot. The most attractive flowers also need a cold winter. In the plains of India, for instance, it is easy enough to grow zinnias or petunias, but the most skilful gardener alive could not grow a primrose or a wallflower or a daffodil.

If we want to make January and February less unpleasant than they are, we might start by building our houses more intelligently.

For instance, it would not be a bad idea to arrange the water pipes so that they do not burst every time there is a hard frost.

But that is a different question. What we shall have to decide, if this notion of changing the climate ever becomes practicable, is whether we want a dead level of continuous sunshine, or a few exquisite days paid for with fog, mud and sleet. When Shakespeare, describing this time of year, wrote:

> When all aloud the wind doth blow
> And coughing drowns the parson's saw.
> And birds sit brooding in the snow
> And Marian's nose looks red and raw

he was describing rather disagreeable phenomena, and yet there is a kind of affection in the lines, a perception that everything has its place.

There is a time to sit in the garden in a deck chair, and there is a time to have chilblains and a dripping nose. Perhaps five days out of seven our climate gives us cause to curse it, but there are also days, especially in spring and autumn, when even the streets of London take on a beauty that is not to be found in sunnier lands.

Books *v.* Cigarettes
Tribune, 8 February 1946

A couple of years ago a friend of mine, a newspaper editor, was fire-watching with some factory workers. They fell to talking about this newspaper, which most of them read and approved of, but when he asked them what they thought of the literary section, the answer he got was: "You don't suppose we read that stuff, do you? Why, half the time you're talking about books that cost twelve and sixpence! Chaps like us couldn't spend twelve and sixpence on a book." These, he said, were men who thought nothing of spending several pounds on a day trip to Blackpool.

This idea that the buying, or even the reading, of books is an expensive hobby and beyond the reach of the average person is so widespread that it deserves some detailed examination. Exactly what reading costs, reckoned in terms of pence per hour, is difficult to estimate, but I have made a start by inventorying my own books and adding up their total price. After allowing for various other expenses, I can make a fairly good guess at my expenditure over the last fifteen years.

The books that I have counted and priced are the ones I have here, in my flat. I have about an equal number stored in another place, so that I shall double the final figure in order to arrive at the complete amount. I have not counted oddments such as proof copies, defaced volumes, cheap paper-covered editions, pamphlets, or magazines, unless bound up into book form. Nor have I counted the kind of junky books – old school textbooks and so forth – that accumulate in the bottoms of cupboards. I have counted only those books which I have acquired voluntarily, or else would have acquired voluntarily, and which I intend to keep. In this category I find that I have 442 books, acquired in the following ways: –

Bought (mostly secondhand) 251
Given to me or bought with book tokens 33
Review copies and complimentary copies 143
Borrowed and not returned 10
Temporarily on loan 5

TOTAL 442

Now as to the method of pricing. Those books that I have bought, I have listed at their full price, as closely as I can determine it. I have also listed at their full price the books that have been given to me, and those that I have temporarily borrowed, or borrowed and kept. This is because book-giving, book-borrowing and book-stealing more or less even out. I possess books that do not strictly speaking belong to me, but many other people also have books of mine: so that the books I have not paid for can be taken as balancing others which I have paid for but no longer possess. On the other hand I have listed the review and complimentary copies at half price. That is about what I would have paid for them secondhand, and they are mostly books that I would only have bought secondhand, if at all. For the prices I have sometimes had to rely on guesswork, but my figures will not be far out. The costs were as follows: –

	£	s.	d.
Bought	36	9	0
Gifts	10	10	6
Review copies, etc.	25	11	9
Borrowed and not returned	4	16	9
On loan	3	10	6
Shelves	2	0	0
TOTAL	82	17	6

Adding the other batch of books that I have elsewhere, it seems that I possess, altogether, nearly 900 books, at a cost of £165 15s. This is the accumulation of about fifteen years – actually more, since some of these books date from my childhood: but call it fifteen years. This works out at £11 1s. a year, but there are other charges that must be added in order to estimate my full reading expenses. The biggest will be for newspapers and periodicals, and for this I think £8 a year would be a reasonable figure. Eight pounds a year covers the cost of two daily papers, one evening paper, two Sunday papers, one weekly review and one or two monthly magazines. This brings the figure up to £19 1s., but to arrive at the grand total one has to make a guess. Obviously one often spends money on books without afterwards having anything to show for it. There are library subscriptions, and there are also the books, chiefly Penguins and other cheap editions, which one buys and then loses or throws away. However, on the basis of my other figures, it looks as though £6 a year would be quite enough to add for expenditure of this kind. So my total reading expenses over the past fifteen years have been in the neighbourhood of £25 a year.

Twenty-five pounds a year sounds quite a lot until you begin to measure it against other kinds of expenditure. It is nearly 9s. 9d. a week, and at present 9s. 9d. is the equivalent of about 83 cigarettes (Players): even before the war it would have bought you less than 200 cigarettes. With prices as they now are, I am spending far more on tobacco than I do on books. I smoke six ounces a week, at half-a-crown an ounce, making nearly £40 a year. Even before the war, when the same tobacco cost 8d. an ounce, I was spending over £10 a year on it: and if I also averaged a pint of beer a day, at sixpence, these two items together will have cost me close on £20 a year. This was probably not much above the national average. In 1938 the people of this country spent nearly £10 per head per annum on alcohol and tobacco: however, 20 per cent. of the population were children under 15 and another 40 per cent. were women, so that the average smoker and drinker must have been spending much more than £10. In 1944, the annual expenditure per head on these items was no less than £23. Allow for the women and children as before, and £40 is a reasonable individual figure. Forty pounds a year would just about pay for a packet of Woodbines every day and half a pint of mild six days a week – not a magnificent allowance. Of course, all prices are now inflated, including the price of books: still, it looks as though the cost of reading, even if you buy books instead of borrowing them and take in a fairly large number of periodicals, does not amount to more than the combined cost of smoking and drinking.

It is difficult to establish any relationship between the price of books and the value one gets out of them. "Books" includes novels, poetry, textbooks, works of reference, sociological treatises and much else, and length and price do not correspond to one another, especially if one habitually buys books secondhand. You may spend ten shillings on a poem of 500 lines, and you may spend sixpence on a dictionary which you consult at odd moments over a period of twenty years. There are books that one reads over and over again, books that become part of the furniture of one's mind and alter one's whole attitude to life, books that one dips into but never reads through, books that one reads at a single sitting and forgets a week later: and the cost, in terms of money, may be the same in each case. But if one regards reading simply as a recreation, like going to the pictures, then it is possible to make a rough estimate of what it costs. If you read nothing but novels and "light" literature, and bought every book that you read, you would be spending – allowing eight shillings as the price of a book, and four hours as the time spent in reading it – two shillings an hour. This is about what it costs to sit in one of the more expensive seats in the cinema. If you concentrated on more serious books, and still bought everything that you read, your expenses would be about the same. The books would cost more, but they would take longer to read. In either case you would still possess the books after you had read them, and they would be saleable at about a third of their purchase price. If you bought only secondhand books, your reading expenses would, of course, be much less: perhaps sixpence an hour would be a fair estimate. And on the other hand if you don't buy books, but merely borrow them from the lending library, reading costs you round about a halfpenny an hour: if you borrow them from the public library, it costs you next door to nothing.

I have said enough to show that reading is one of the cheaper recreations: after listening to the radio, probably *the* cheapest. Meanwhile, what is the actual amount that the British public spends on books? I cannot discover any figures, though no doubt they exist. But I do know that before the war this country was publishing annually about 15,000 books, which included reprints and schoolbooks. If as many as ten thousand copies of each book were sold – and even allowing for the schoolbooks, this is probably a high estimate – the average person was only buying, directly or indirectly, about three books a year. These three books taken together might cost £1, or probably less.

These figures are guesswork, and I should be interested if someone would correct them for me. But if my estimate is anywhere near right, it is not a proud record for a country which is nearly 100 per cent. literate and where the ordinary man spends more on cigarettes than an Indian peasant has for his whole livelihood. And if our book-consumption remains as low as it has been, at least let us admit that it is because reading is a less exciting pastime than going to the dogs, the pictures or the pub, and not because books, whether bought or borrowed, are too expensive.

The Moon Under Water

Saturday Essay, *Evening Standard*, 9 February 1946

My favourite public-house, the Moon Under Water, is only two minutes from a bus stop, but it is on a side-street, and drunks and rowdies never seem to find their way there, even on Saturday nights.

Its clientele, though fairly large, consists mostly of "regulars" who occupy the same chair every evening and go there for conversation as much as for the beer.

If you are asked why you favour a particular public-house, it would seem natural to put the beer first, but the thing that most appeals to me about the Moon Under Water is what people call its "atmosphere."

To begin with, its whole architecture and fittings are un-compromisingly Victorian. It has no glass-topped tables or other modern miseries, and, on the other hand, no sham roof-beams, ingle-nooks or plastic panels masquerading as oak. The grained woodwork, the ornamental mirrors behind the bar, the cast-iron fireplaces, the florid ceiling stained dark yellow by tobacco-smoke, the stuffed bull's head over the mantelpiece – everything has the solid, comfortable ugliness of the nineteenth century.

In winter there is generally a good fire burning in at least two of the bars, and the Victorian lay-out of the place gives one plenty of elbow-room. There are a public bar, a saloon bar, a ladies' bar, a bottle-and-jug for those who are too bashful to buy their supper beer publicly, and, upstairs, a dining-room.

Games are only played in the public, so that in the other bars you can walk about without constantly ducking to avoid flying darts.

In the Moon Under Water it is always quiet enough to talk. The house possesses neither a radio nor a piano, and even on Christmas Eve and such occasions the singing that happens is of a decorous kind.

The barmaids know most of their customers by name, and take a personal interest in everyone. They are all middle-aged women – two of them have their hair dyed in quite surprising shades – and they call everyone "dear," irrespective of age or sex. ("Dear," not "Ducky": pubs where the barmaid calls you "ducky" always have a disagreeable raffish atmosphere.)

Unlike most pubs, the Moon Under Water sells tobacco as well as cigarettes, and it also sells aspirins and stamps, and is obliging about letting you use the telephone.

You cannot get dinner at the Moon Under Water, but there is always the snack counter where you can get liver-sausage sandwiches, mussels (a speciality of the house), cheese, pickles and those large biscuits with caraway seeds in them which only seem to exist in public-houses.

Upstairs, six days a week, you can get a good, solid lunch – for example, a cut off the joint, two vegetables and boiled jam roll – for about three shillings.

The special pleasure of this lunch is that you can have draught stout with it. I doubt whether as many as 10 per cent of London pubs serve draught stout, but the Moon Under Water is one of them. It is a soft, creamy sort of stout, and it goes better in a pewter pot.

They are particular about their drinking vessels at the Moon Under Water, and never, for example, make the mistake of serving a pint of beer in a handleless glass. Apart from glass and pewter mugs, they have some of those pleasant strawberry-pink china ones which are now seldom seen in London. China mugs went out about 30 years ago, because most people like their drink to be transparent, but in my opinion beer tastes better out of china.

The great surprise of the Moon Under Water is its garden. You go through a narrow passage leading out of the saloon, and find yourself in a fairly large garden with plane trees, under which there are little green tables with iron chairs round them. Up at one end of the garden there are swings and a chute for the children.

On summer evenings there are family parties, and you sit under the plane trees having beer or draught cider to the tune of delighted squeals from children going down the chute. The prams with the younger children are parked near the gate.

Many as are the virtues of the Moon Under Water, I think that the garden is its best feature, because it allows whole families to go there instead of Mum having to stay at home and mind the baby while Dad goes out alone.

And though, strictly speaking, they are only allowed in the garden, the children tend to seep into the pub and even to fetch drinks for their parents. This, I believe, is against the law, but it is a law that deserves to be broken, for it is the puritanical nonsense of excluding children – and therefore, to some extent, women – from pubs that has turned these places into mere boozing-shops instead of the family gathering-places that they ought to be.

The Moon Under Water is my ideal of what a pub should be – at any rate, in the London area. (The qualities one expects of a country pub are slightly different.)

But now is the time to reveal something which the discerning and disillusioned reader will probably have guessed already. There is no such place as the Moon Under Water.

That is to say, there may well be a pub of that name, but I don't know of it, nor do I know any pub with just that combination of qualities.

I know pubs where the beer is good but you can't get meals, others where you can get meals but which are noisy and crowded, and others which are quiet but where the beer is generally sour. As for gardens, offhand I can only think of three London pubs that possess them.

But, to be fair, I do know of a few pubs that almost come up to the Moon Under Water. I have mentioned above ten qualities that the perfect pub should have and I know one pub that has eight of them. Even there, however, there is no draught stout, and no china mugs.

And if anyone knows of a pub that has draught stout, open fires, cheap meals, a garden, motherly barmaids and no radio, I should be glad to hear of it, even though its name were something as prosaic as the Red Lion or the Railway Arms.

Decline of the English Murder
Tribune, 15 February 1946

It is Sunday afternoon, preferably before the war. The wife is already asleep in the armchair, and the children have been sent out for a nice long walk. You put your feet up on the sofa, settle your spectacles on your nose, and open the *News of the World*. Roast beef and Yorkshire, or roast pork and applesauce, followed up by suet pudding and driven home, as it were, by a cup of mahogany-brown tea, have put you in just the right mood. Your pipe is drawing sweetly, the sofa cushions are soft underneath you, the fire is well alight, the air is warm and stagnant. In these blissful circumstances, what is it that you want to read about?

Naturally, about a murder. But what kind of murder? If one examines the murders which have given the greatest amount of pleasure to the British public, the murders whose story is known in its general outline to almost everyone and which have been made into novels and re-hashed over and over again by the Sunday papers, one finds a fairly strong family resemblance running through the greater number of them. Our great period in murder, our Elizabethan period, so to speak, seems to have been between roughly 1850 and 1925, and the murderers whose reputation has stood the test of time are the following: Dr. Palmer of Rugely, Jack the Ripper, Neill Cream, Mrs. Maybrick, Dr. Crippen, Seddon, Joseph Smith, Armstrong, and Bywaters and Thompson. In addition, in 1919 or thereabouts, there was another very celebrated case which fits into the general pattern but which I had better not mention by name, because the accused man was acquitted.

Of the above-mentioned nine cases, at least four have had successful novels based on them, one has been made into a popular melodrama, and the amount of literature surrounding them, in the form of newspaper write-ups, criminological treatises and reminiscences by lawyers and police officers, would make a considerable library. It is difficult to believe that any recent English crime will be remembered so long and so intimately, and not only because the violence of external events has made murder seem unimportant, but because the prevalent type of crime seems to be changing. The principal *cause célèbre* of the war years was the so-called Cleft Chin Murder, which has now been written up in a popular booklet; the verbatim account of the trial was published some time last year by Messrs. Jarrolds with an introduction by Mr. Bechhofer Roberts. Before returning to this pitiful and sordid case, which is only interesting from a sociological and perhaps a legal point of view, let me try to define what it is that the readers of Sunday papers mean when they say fretfully that "you never seem to get a good murder nowadays."

In considering the nine murders I named above, one can start by excluding the Jack the Ripper case, which is in a class by itself. Of the other eight, six were poisoning cases, and eight of the ten criminals belonged to the middle class. In one way or another, sex was a powerful motif in all but two cases, and in at least four cases respectability – the desire to gain a secure position in life, or not to forfeit one's social position by some scandal such as a divorce – was one of the main reasons for committing murder. In more than half the cases, the object was to get hold of a certain known sum of money such as a legacy or an insurance policy, but the amount involved was nearly always small. In most of the cases the crime only came to light slowly, as the result of careful investigations which started off with the suspicions of neighbours or relatives; and in nearly every case there was some dramatic coincidence, in which the finger of Providence could be clearly seen, or one of those episodes that no novelist would dare to make up, such as Crippen's flight across the Atlantic with his mistress dressed as a boy, or Joseph Smith playing "Nearer, my God, to Thee" on the harmonium while one of his wives was drowning in the next room. The background of all these crimes, except Neill Cream's, was essentially domestic; of twelve victims, seven were either wife or husband of the murderer.

With all this in mind one can construct what would be, from a *News of the World* reader's point of view, the "perfect" murder. The murderer should be a little man of the professional class – a dentist or a solicitor, say – living an intensely respectable life somewhere in the suburbs, and preferably in a semi-detached house, which will allow the neighbours to hear suspicious sounds through the wall. He should be either chairman of the local Conservative Party branch, or a leading Nonconformist and strong Temperance advocate. He should go astray through cherishing a guilty passion for his secretary or the wife of a rival professional man, and should only bring himself to the point of murder after long and terrible wrestles with his conscience. Having decided on murder, he should plan it all with the utmost cunning, and only slip up over some tiny, unforeseeable detail. The means chosen should, of course, be poison. In the last analysis he should commit murder because this seems to him less disgraceful, and less damaging to his career, than being detected in adultery. With this kind of background, a crime can have dramatic and even tragic qualities which make it memorable and excite pity for both victim and murderer. Most of the crimes mentioned above have a touch of this atmosphere, and in three cases, including the one I referred to but did not name, the story approximates to the one I have outlined.

Now compare the Cleft Chin Murder. There is no depth of feeling in it. It was almost chance that the two people concerned committed that particular murder, and it was only by good luck that they did not commit several others. The background was not domesticity, but the anonymous life of the dance-halls and the false values of the American film. The two culprits were an eighteen-year-old ex-waitress named Elizabeth Jones, and an American army deserter, posing as an officer, named Karl Hulten. They were only together for six days, and it seems doubtful whether, until they were arrested, they even learned one another's true names. They met casually in a tea-shop, and that night went out for a ride in a stolen army truck. Jones described herself as a strip-tease artist, which was not strictly true (she had given one unsuccessful performance in this line), and declared that she wanted to do something dangerous, "like being a gun-moll." Hulten described himself as a big-time Chicago gangster, which was also untrue. They met a girl bicycling along the road, and to show how tough he was Hulten ran over her with his truck, after which the pair robbed her of the few shillings that were on her. On another occasion they knocked out a girl to whom they had offered a lift, took her coat and handbag and threw her into a river. Finally, in the most wanton way, they murdered a taxi-driver who happened to have £8 in his pocket. Soon afterwards they parted. Hulten was caught because he had foolishly kept the dead man's car, and Jones made spontaneous confessions to the police. In court each prisoner incriminated the other. In between crimes, both of them seem to have behaved with the utmost callousness: they spent the dead taxi-driver's £8 at the dog races.

Judging from her letters, the girl's case has a certain amount of psychological interest, but this murder probably captured the headlines because it provided distraction amid the doodle-bugs and the anxieties of the Battle of France. Jones and Hulten committed their murder to the tune of V1, and were convicted to the tune of V2. There was also considerable excitement because – as has become usual in England – the man was sentenced to death and the girl to imprisonment. According to Mr. Raymond, the reprieving of Jones caused widespread indignation and streams of telegrams to the Home Secretary: in her native town, "She should hang" was chalked on the walls beside pictures of a figure dangling from a gallows. Considering that only ten women have been hanged in Britain in this century, and that the practice has gone out largely because of popular feeling against it, it is difficult not to feel that this clamour to hang an eighteen-year-old girl was due partly to the brutalising effects of war. Indeed, the whole meaningless story, with its atmosphere of dance-halls, movie-palaces, cheap perfume, false names and stolen cars, belongs essentially to a war period.

Perhaps it is significant that the most talked-of English murder of recent years should have been committed by an American and an English girl who had become partly Ameri-canised. But it is difficult to believe that this case will be so long remembered as the old domestic poisoning dramas, product of a stable society where the all-prevailing hypocrisy did at least ensure that crimes as serious as murder should have strong emotions behind them.

Words and Henry Miller
Tribune, 22 February 1946

It is a pity that some publisher cannot take his courage in his hands and re-issue *Tropic of Cancer*. About a year later he could recoup his losses by publishing a book entitled *What I Saw in Prison*, or words to that effect, and meanwhile a few copies of the forbidden text would have reached the public before the entire edition was burned by the public hangman, or whoever it is that has the job of burning banned books in this country. As it is, *Tropic of Cancer* must be one of the rarest of contemporary books – though it is said that a pirated edition was circulating in America two or three years ago – and even *Black Spring* is not easily procurable. Fragments of Henry Miller's writings are printed all over the place, while the parts that are worth anything remain inaccessible. In criticising him one has to rely on memory, and since the person who reads the criticism may never get a chance to read the books, the whole process is rather like taking a blind man to see a firework display.

The present selection includes the short story – it is perhaps rather a sketch than a story – "Max," the excellent autobiographical sketch "Via Dieppe–Newhaven," three chapters, heavily blue-pencilled, from *Black Spring*, a scenario for a surrealist film, and a number of critical essays and fragments. The book closes with a biographical note which is probably truthful in its main outlines, and which ends like this:–

> "I want to be read by less and less people; I have no interest in the life of the masses, nor in the intentions of the existing governments of the world. I hope and believe that the whole civilised world will be wiped out in the next hundred years or so. I believe that man can exist, and in an infinitely better, larger way, without 'civilisation.'"

To compare "Via Newhaven–Dieppe" with, for instance, the fragment from *Hamlet*, the enormous book of letters which Miller wrote in collaboration with Michael Fraenkel, is to get a good idea of what Miller can and cannot do. "Via Newhaven–Dieppe" is a truthful and even moving piece of writing. It records an unsuccessful attempt by Miller to pay a short visit to England in 1935. The immigration officials nosed out the fact that he had very little money in his pockets, and he was promptly clapped into a police-court cell and sent back across the Channel on the following day, the whole thing being done with the maximum of stupidity and offensiveness. The only person who showed a spark of decency in the whole affair was the simple police constable who had to guard Miller through the night. The book in which this sketch occurs was published in 1938, and I remember reading it just after Munich and reflecting that, though the Munich settlement was not a thing to be proud of, this little episode made me feel more ashamed of my country. Not that the British officials at Newhaven behaved much worse than that kind of person behaves everywhere. But somehow the whole thing was saddening. A couple of bureaucrats had got an artist at their mercy, and the mixture of spite, cunning and stupidity with which they handled him made one wonder what is the use of all this talk about democracy, freedom of the press, and what-not.

"Via Newhaven–Dieppe" is in the same vein as *Tropic of Cancer*. For forty years or more Miller had led an insecure, disreputable kind of life, and he had two outstanding gifts, both of which could perhaps be traced back to a common origin. One was a complete lack of ordinary shame, and the other was an ability to write a bold, florid, rhythmical prose of a kind that had hardly been seen in English for twenty years past. On the other hand he had no power of self-discipline, no sense of responsibility, and perhaps not much imagination, as opposed to fancy. He was therefore best equipped as an autobiographical writer, and liable to dry up when the material drawn from his past life came to an end.

After *Black Spring* it was to be expected that Miller would descend into charlatanism of one kind or another, and in fact a great deal of his later writing is simply a banging on the big drum – noise proceeding from emptiness. Let anyone read the two essays in this book, "The Universe of Death" (a criticism of Proust and Joyce) and "An Open Letter to Surrealists Everywhere." In nearly 70 pages, it is astonishing how little he says, and how impressively he says it. The arresting but in fact almost meaningless phrase "universe of death" strikes a characteristic note. One of Miller's tricks is to be constantly using apocalyptic language, to sprinkle every page with phrases like "cosmological flux," "lunar attraction" and "interstellar spaces" or with sentences like "The orbit over which I am travelling leads me farther and farther away from the dead sun which gave me birth." The second sentence in the essay on Proust and Joyce is: "Whatever has happened in literature since Dostoievski has happened on the other side of death." What rubbish it is, when you think it out! The key words in this kind of writing are "death," "life," "birth," "sun," "moon," "womb," "cosmic" and "catastrophe," and by free use of them the most banal statement can be made to sound picturesque, while what is outright meaningless can be given an air of mystery and profundity. Even the title of this book, *The Cosmological Eye*, doesn't actually mean anything, but it sounds as though it *ought* to mean something.

When one digs them out from beneath the flamboyant language, Miller's opinions are mostly commonplace, and often reactionary. They boil down to a sort of nihilistic quietism. He disclaims interest in politics – at the beginning of this book he announces that he has "become God" and is "absolutely indifferent to the fate of the world" – but in fact he is constantly making political pronouncements, including flimsy racial generalisations about the "French soul," the "German soul," etc. He is an extreme pacifist and on the other hand has a yearning for violence, provided that it is happening somewhere else, thinks life wonderful but hopes and expects to see everything blown to pieces before long, and talks a good deal about "great men" and "aristocrats of the spirit." He refuses to bother about the difference between Fascism and Communism, because "society is made up of individuals." This has come to be a familiar attitude nowadays, and it would be a respectable one if it were carried to its logical conclusion, which would mean remaining passive in the face of war, revolution, Fascism or anything else. Actually, those who talk in the same vein as Miller always take care to stay inside bourgeois–democratic society, making use of its protection while disclaiming responsibility for it: on the other hand, when a real choice has to be made, the quietist attitude never seems to survive. At bottom, Miller's outlook is that of a simple individualist who recognises no obligations to anyone else – at any rate, no obligations to society as a whole – and does not even feel the need to be consistent in his opinions. Much of his later work is merely a statement of this fact in more resounding words.

As long as Miller was simply an outcast and vagabond, having unpleasant experiences with policemen, landladies, wives, duns, whores, editors and such-like, his irresponsible attitude did no harm – indeed, as a basis for a book like *Tropic of Cancer*, it was the best attitude. The great thing about *Tropic of Cancer* was that it had no moral. But if you are going to utter judgements on God, the universe, war, revolution, Hitler,

Marxism and "the Jews," then Miller's particular brand of intellectual honesty is not enough. Either one must genuinely keep out of politics, or one must recognise that politics is the science of the possible. Here and there in Miller's later writing there is a slab of unpretentious autobiography – "Via New-haven–Dieppe" is one example, and there are comparable passages even in the unreadable Hamlet book – and then once again the old magic reappears. Miller's real gift is his power of describing the under side of life, but probably he needs misfortune to prod him into using it. However, it seems that his life in California during the past five or six years has not been all jam, and perhaps one of these days he will stop writing empty sentences about death and the universe and revert to the thing that he is really fitted to do. But he must give up "being God," because the only good book that God ever wrote was the Old Testament.

Meanwhile this selection will give new readers a not too misleading impression of Miller's work. But as it was found possible to print three chapters of *Black Spring*, with asterisks here and there, it was a pity not to do the same with *Tropic of Cancer*, parts of which are not markedly obscene and could easily be made presentable with an occasional row of dots in the right places.

Classics Reviewed: *The Martyrdom of Man*
Tribune, 15 March 1946

If one were obliged to write a history of the world, would it be better to record the true facts, so far as one could discover them, or would it be better simply to make the whole thing up? The answer is not so self-evident as it appears. The purpose of anyone who writes the history of any large epoch must necessarily be to impose a pattern on events, or at least to discover a pattern, and for that purpose a sound general theory, or even an instinctive grasp of probability, might be more useful than a mountain of learning. A history constructed imaginatively would never be right about any single event, but it might come nearer to essential truth than a mere compilation of names and dates in which no one statement was demonstrably untrue.

One feels this strongly with that queer, unhonoured masterpiece, Winwood Reade's *The Martyrdom of Man*. Not, of course, that Reade was simply making his history up. In a way, indeed, he was reasserting the value of empirical knowledge as against tradition and authority, since his main aim was to attack current religious beliefs, and his method of doing so was to insist on the known facts, including New Testament texts which orthodox believers prefer to forget about. Again, he was ready to take over large blocks of information from specialists in various fields, and in his preface to the book he indicates some of his sources, stating plainly that "there is scarcely anything in this work which I can claim as my own. I have taken not only facts and ideas, but phrases and even paragraphs, from other writers." And yet his book is essentially a work of imagination and not merely a record of events. He did not, perhaps, start out with a preconceived idea of the pattern of history, but by his reading and his travels he believes that he has found the pattern, and once it is found the details drop into place. The book is a kind of vision, or epic, inspired by the conception of progress. Man is Prometheus: he has stolen the fire and been terribly punished for it, but in the end he will turn the gods out of heaven and the reign of reason will begin.

In spite of its clear and powerful writing, *The Martyrdom of Man* is not a well-arranged book. It is somewhat uncouthly divided into four main parts, headed War, Religion, Liberty and Intellect, which are supposed to summarise the main stages of human development, and the fourth section partly recapitulates what has been said earlier. And of course it is inclined to be lopsided, as any attempt at universal history probably always must be. For a European it is almost impossible not to think of "the world" as meaning the fringes of the Mediterranean and the Atlantic, and neither India nor China enters much into Reade's scheme of things. Neither do England, Russia or South America. The centre of the world, as he sees it, is Egypt and the countries of the Middle East, and he is at his best in dealing with the slave empires of antiquity and the rise of the Semitic religions. Take this typical passage:

"Rome lived upon its principal till ruin stared it in the face. Industry is the only true source of wealth, and there was no industry in Rome. By day the Ostia road was crowded with carts and muleteers, carrying to the great city the silks and spices of the East, the marble of Asia Minor, the timber of the Atlas, the grain of Africa and Egypt; and the carts brought out nothing but loads of dung. That was their return cargo."

In the mingled qualities of this passage – its irony, its air of assured knowledge, its insistence on the importance of economic processes, and alongside with this its retention of picturesqueness – one can see, I think, the reason for Reade's popular appeal. People felt that for once they were getting history from someone who knew all the facts and yet was not a professor – not a hanger-on of the upper classes and the Established Church. Reade has no resemblance to the dry-as-dust "economic historian." The romantic, pageant-like side of history, the swelling sails of the Phoenician galleys, the brass shields of the Roman soldiers, the knights, the castles, the tournaments, and the resounding names – Caesar, Alexander, Hannibal, Nebuchadnezzar, Charlemagne – it is all present in his work, but somehow with a new slant, as though he were saying all the while: "Just look at it like this, and it all falls into place." An outstanding quality of the book is its masterly handling of time. History is made to flow: great epochs are summarised in a paragraph, Egyptians merge into Persians, Persians into Greeks, Greeks into Romans, barbarism fades into feudalism, feudalism into capitalism, in such a way that one seems to see it streaming past like a panorama, with its essential principles laid bare and yet with its colour and much of its detail retained.

In the introduction to the *Thinker's Library* edition (Watts, 2/6) Mr. J. M. Robertson points out that *The Martyrdom of Man* is remarkable

"at once for its continuous impact on two generations of readers and for its steady success in the face of a bitterly or contemptuously hostile literary and newspaper press. Without a word of respectable literary approval, without an advertisement by the publishers, it made its way from the year of publication, and it has gone on selling for more than sixty years, edition following edition up to the present."

The book is, as it were, unofficial history. Reade was aiming at the emancipated, at people not frightened of the truth, but his book was essentially a popular one, repudiating almost from its first pages the values of bourgeois society. One may guess that its deepest appeal, as well as the reason for the hostility of the Press, lay in its humanist interpretation of Christianity. In 1872, when the book was published, it needed courage to take this line, but it still seemed a revolutionary book forty or fifty years later. I well remember its effect on me when I first read it at the age of about seventeen. When I came upon Reade's description of the typical Hebrew prophet, and saw the words "As soon as he received his mission he ceased to wash," I felt profoundly, "This man is on my side." Then I went on and read Reade's examination of the character of Jesus. It was a curiously liberating experience. Here was somebody who neither accepted Jesus as the Son of God, nor, as was the fashion at that time, as a Great Moral Teacher, but simply presented him as a fallible human being like any other – a noble character on the whole, but with serious faults, and, in any case, only one of a long line of very similar Jewish fanatics. Not till a century after his death, said Reade, did various pagan legends belonging to Osiris and Apollo become attached to him.

Was this a true explanation? I did not know then, and do not know now. One would have to be a specialist to give an opinion. But at least Reade's account of the life of Jesus *could* be a true one, whereas the version that was thrust upon me by my schoolmasters outraged common sense. Reade was an emancipating writer because he seemed to speak as man to man, to resolve history into an intelligible pattern in which there was no need for miracles. Even if he was wrong, he was grown-up.

Although it is inspired by the concept of progress, and although it has influenced the Left-Wing movement over two generations, one ought not to regard *The Martyrdom of Man* as a Socialist book. Reade had been much influenced by the Darwinian theory of the struggle for survival, and in some ways his outlook is distinctly reactionary. He explicitly declares his disbelief in Socialism, is convinced of the valuable effects of commercial competition, thinks that imperialism should be encouraged, and seems to regard orientals as natural inferiors. He also toys with the dangerous idea that there are different orders of truth and that a false belief should sometimes not be exploded if it is socially valuable. But he says some very prescient things – he says, for instance, that Communism, if established, might harden into a caste system, which was a penetrating remark to make in 1871 – and he sees clearly that human equality cannot be realised except at a high level of mechanical civilisation. His objectives are such as most Social- ists would accept, although his attitude towards existing society is not. He is a sort of irregular ally of the Socialist movement, fighting chiefly on the religious front. Many thousands of working-class readers must have disagreed with some of his conclusions and yet felt that they had a good friend in this scholar who had turned against the priests, and so could make the past not only intelligible but also alive.

In Front of Your Nose
Tribune, 22 March 1946

Many recent statements in the press have declared that it is almost, if not quite, impossible for us to mine as much coal as we need for home and export purposes, because of the impossi- bility of inducing a sufficient number of miners to remain in the pits. One set of figures which I saw last week estimated the annual "wastage" of mineworkers at 60,000 and the annual intake of new workers at 10,000. Simultaneously with this – and sometimes in the same column of the same paper – there have been statements that it would be undesirable to make use of Poles or Germans because this might lead to unemployment in the coal industry. The two utterances do not always come from the same sources but there must certainly be many people who are capable of holding these totally contradictory ideas in their heads at a single moment.

This is merely one example of a habit of mind which is extremely widespread, and perhaps always has been. Bernard

Shaw, in the preface to *Androcles and the Lion*, cites as another example the first chapter of the Gospel of Matthew, which starts off by establishing the descent of Joseph, father of Jesus, from Abraham. In the first verse, Jesus is described as "the son of David, the son of Abraham," and the genealogy is then followed up through fifteen verses: then, in the next verse but one, it is explained that as a matter of fact Jesus was *not* descended from Abraham, since he was not the son of Joseph. This, says Shaw, presents no difficulty to a religious believer, and he names as a parallel case the rioting in the East End of London by the partisans of the Tichborne Claimant, who declared that a British working-man was being done out of his rights.

Medically, I believe, this manner of thinking is called schizophrenia: at any rate, it is the power of holding simultaneously two beliefs which cancel out. Closely allied to it is the power of ignoring facts which are obvious and unalterable, and which will have to be faced sooner or later. It is especially in our political thinking that these vices flourish. Let me take a few sample subjects out of the hat. They have no organic connection with each other: they are merely cases, taken almost at random, of plain, unmistakable facts being shirked by people who in another part of their mind are aware of those facts.

Hong Kong. For years before the war everyone with knowledge of Far Eastern conditions knew that our position in Hong Kong was untenable and that we should lose it as soon as a major war started. This knowledge, however, was intolerable, and government after government continued to cling to Hong Kong instead of giving it back to the Chinese. Fresh troops were even pushed into it, with the certainty that they would be uselessly taken prisoner, a few weeks before the Japanese attack began. Then war came, and Hong Kong promptly fell – as everyone had known all along that it would do.

Conscription. For years before the war, nearly all enlightened people were in favour of standing up to Germany: the majority of them were also against having enough armaments to make such a stand effective. I know very well the arguments that are put forward in defence of this attitude; some of them are justified, but in the main they are simply forensic excuses.

As late as 1939, the Labour Party voted against conscription, a step which probably played its part in bringing about the Russo-German pact and certainly had a disastrous effect on morale in France. Then came 1940, and we nearly perished for lack of a large, efficient army, which we could only have had if we had introduced conscription at least three years earlier.

The Birth Rate. Twenty or twenty-five years ago, contraception and enlightenment were held to be almost synonymous. To this day, the majority of people argue – the argument is variously expressed, but always boils down to more or less the same thing – that large families are impossible for economic reasons. At the same time, it is widely known that the birth-rate is highest among the low-standard nations, and, in our own population, highest among the worst-paid groups. It is also argued that a smaller population would mean less unemployment and more comfort for everybody, while on the other hand it is well established that a dwindling and ageing population is faced with calamitous and perhaps insoluble economic problems. Necessarily the figures are uncertain, but it is quite possible that in only 70 years our population will amount to about eleven millions, over half of whom will be Old Age Pensioners. Since, for complex reasons, most people don't want large families, the frightening facts can exist somewhere or other in their consciousness, simultaneously known and not known.

U.N.O. In order to have any efficacy whatever, a world organisation must be able to override big States as well as small ones. It must have power to inspect and limit armaments, which means that its officials must have access to every square inch of every country. It must also have at its disposal an armed force bigger than any other armed force and responsible only to the organisation itself. The two or three great States that really matter have never even pretended to agree to any of these conditions, and they have so arranged the constitution of U.N.O. that their own actions cannot even be discussed. In other words, U.N.O.'s usefulness as an instrument of world peace is nil. This was just as obvious before it began functioning as it is now. Yet only a few months ago millions of well-informed people believed that it was going to be a success.

There is no use in multiplying examples. The point is that we are all capable of believing things which we *know* to be untrue, and then, when we are finally proved wrong, impudently twisting the facts so as to show that we were right. Intellectually, it is possible to carry on this process for an indefinite time: the only check on it is that sooner or later a false belief bumps up against solid reality, usually on a battlefield.

When one looks at the all-prevailing schizophrenia of democratic societies, the lies that have to be told for vote-catching purposes, the silence about major issues, the distortions of the press, it is tempting to believe that in totalitarian countries there is less humbug, more facing of the facts. There, at least, the ruling groups are not dependent on popular favour and can utter the truth crudely and brutally. Goering could say "Guns before butter," while his democratic opposite numbers had to wrap the same sentiment up in hundreds of hypocritical words.

Actually, however, the avoidance of reality is much the same everywhere, and has much the same consequences. The Russian people were taught for years that they were better off than everybody else, and propaganda posters showed Russian families sitting down to abundant meals while the proletariat of other countries starved in the gutter. Meanwhile the workers in the western countries were so much better off than those of the U.S.S.R. that non-contact between Soviet citizens and outsiders had to be a guiding principle of policy. Then, as a result of the war, millions of ordinary Russians penetrated far into Europe, and when they return home the original avoidance of reality will inevitably be paid for in frictions of various kinds. The Germans and the Japanese lost the war quite largely because their rulers were unable to see facts which were plain to any dispassionate eye.

To see what is in front of one's nose needs a constant struggle. One thing that helps towards it is to keep a diary, or, at any rate, to keep some kind of record of one's opinions about important events. Otherwise, when some particularly absurd belief is exploded by events, one may simply forget that one ever held it. Political predictions are usually wrong, but even when one makes a correct one, to discover *why* one was right can be very illuminating. In general, one is only right when either wish or fear coincides with reality. If one recognises this, one cannot, of course, get rid of one's subjective feelings, but one can to some extent insulate them from one's thinking and make predictions cold-bloodedly, by the book of arithmetic. In private life most people are fairly realistic. When one is making out one's weekly budget, two and two invariably make four. Politics, on the other hand, is a sort of subatomic or non-Euclidean world where it is quite easy for the part to be greater than the whole or for two objects to be in the same place simultaneously. Hence the contradictions and absurdities I have chronicled above, all finally traceable to a secret belief that one's political opinions, unlike the weekly budget, will not have to be tested against solid reality.

Some Thoughts on the Common Toad
Tribune, 12 April 1946

Before the swallow, before the daffodil, and not much later than the snowdrop, the common toad salutes the coming of spring after his own fashion, which is to emerge from a hole in the ground, where he has lain buried since the previous autumn, and crawl as rapidly as possible towards the nearest suitable patch of water. Something – some kind of shudder in the earth, or perhaps merely a rise of a few degrees in the temperature – has told him that it is time to wake up: though a few toads appear to sleep the clock round and miss out a year from time to time – at any rate, I have more than once dug them up, alive and apparently well, in the middle of the summer.

At this period, after his long fast, the toad has a very spiritual look, like a strict Anglo-Catholic towards the end of Lent. His movements are languid but purposeful, his body is shrunken, and by contrast his eyes look abnormally large. This allows one to notice, what one might not at another time, that a toad has about the most beautiful eye of any living creature. It is like gold, or more exactly it is like the gold-coloured semi-precious stone which one sometimes sees in signet rings, and which I think is called a chrysoberyl.

For a few days after getting into the water the toad concentrates on building up his strength by eating small insects. Presently he has swollen to his normal size again, and then he goes through a phase of intense sexiness. All he knows, at least if he is a male toad, is that he wants to get his arms round something, and if you offer him a stick, or even your finger, he will cling to it with surprising strength and take a long time to discover that it is not a female toad. Frequently one comes upon shapeless masses of ten or twenty toads rolling over and over in the water, one clinging to another without distinction of sex. By degrees, however, they sort themselves out into couples, with the male duly sitting on the female's back. You can now distinguish males from females, because the male is smaller, darker and sits on top, with his arms tightly clasped round the female's neck. After a day or two the spawn is laid in long strings which wind themselves in and out of the reeds and soon become invisible. A few more weeks, and the water is alive with masses of tiny tadpoles which rapidly grow larger, sprout hind-legs, then fore-legs, then shed their tails: and finally, about the middle of the summer, the new generation of toads, smaller than one's thumb-nail but perfect in every particular, crawl out of the water to begin the game anew.

I mention the spawning of the toads because it is one of the phenomena of Spring which most deeply appeal to me, and because the toad, unlike the skylark and the primrose, has never had much of a boost from the poets. But I am aware that many people do not like reptiles or amphibians, and I am not suggesting that in order to enjoy the Spring you have to take an interest in toads. There are also the crocus, the missel thrush, the cuckoo, the blackthorn, etc. The point is that the pleasures of Spring are available to everybody, and cost nothing. Even in the most sordid street the coming of Spring will register itself by some sign or other, if it is only a brighter blue between the chimney pots or the vivid green of an elder sprouting on a blitzed site. Indeed it is remarkable how Nature goes on existing unofficially, as it were, in the very heart of London. I have seen a kestrel flying over the Deptford gasworks, and I have heard a first-rate performance by a blackbird in the Euston Road. There must be some hundreds of thousands, if not millions, of birds living inside the four-mile radius, and it is rather a pleasing thought that none of them pays a halfpenny of rent.

As for Spring, not even the narrow and gloomy streets round the Bank of England are quite able to exclude it. It comes seeping in everywhere, like one of those new poison gases which pass through all filters. The Spring is commonly referred to as "a miracle," and during the past five or six years this worn-out figure of speech has taken on a new lease of life. After the sort of winters we have had to endure recently, the Spring does seem miraculous, because it has become gradually harder and harder to believe that it is actually going to happen. Every February since 1940 I have found myself thinking that this time Winter is going to be permanent. But Persephone, like the toads, always rises from the dead at about the same moment. Suddenly, towards the end of March, the miracle happens and the decaying slum in which I live is transfigured. Down in the square the sooty privets have turned bright green, the leaves are thickening on the chestnut trees, the daffodils are out, the wallflowers are budding, the policeman's tunic looks positively a pleasant shade of blue, the fishmonger greets his customers with a smile, and even the sparrows are quite a different colour, having felt the balminess of the air and nerved themselves to take a bath, their first since last September.

Is it wicked to take a pleasure in Spring and other seasonal changes? To put it more precisely, is it politically reprehensible, while we are all groaning, or at any rate ought to be groaning, under the shackles of the capitalist system, to point out that life is frequently more worth living because of a blackbird's song, a yellow elm tree in October, or some other natural phenom-enon which does not cost money and does not have what the editors of Left-wing newspapers call a class angle? There is no doubt that many people think so. I know by experience that a favourable reference to "Nature" in one of my articles is liable to bring me abusive letters, and though the key-word in these letters is usually "sentimental," two ideas seem to be mixed up in them. One is that any pleasure in the actual process of life encourages a sort of political quietism. People, so the thought runs, ought to be discontented, and it is our job to multiply our wants and not simply to increase our enjoyment of the things we have already. The other idea is that this is the age of machines and that to dislike the machine, or even to want to limit its domination, is backward-looking, reactionary and slightly ridiculous. This is often backed up by the statement that a love of Nature is a foible of urbanised people who have no notion what Nature is really like. Those who really have to deal with the soil, so it is argued, do not love the soil, and do not take the faintest interest in birds or flowers, except from a strictly utilitarian point of view. To love the country one must live in the town, merely taking an occasional week-end ramble at the warmer times of year.

This last idea is demonstrably false. Medieval literature, for instance, including the popular ballads, is full of an almost Georgian enthusiasm for Nature, and the art of agricultural peoples such as the Chinese and Japanese centres always round trees, birds, flowers, rivers, mountains. The other idea seems to me to be wrong in a subtler way. Certainly we ought to be discontented, we ought not simply to find out ways of making the best of a bad job, and yet if we kill all pleasure in the actual process of life, what sort of future are we preparing for ourselves? If a man cannot enjoy the return of Spring, why should he be happy in a labour-saving Utopia? What will he do with the leisure that the machine will give him? I have always suspected that if our economic and political problems are ever really solved, life will become simpler instead of more complex, and that the sort of pleasure one gets from finding the first primrose will loom larger than the sort of pleasure one gets from eating an ice to the tune of a Wurlitzer. I think that by retaining one's childhood love of such things as trees, fishes, butterflies and – to return to my first instance – toads, one makes a peaceful and decent future a little more probable, and that by preaching the doctrine that nothing is to be admired except steel and concrete, one merely makes it a little surer that human beings will have no outlet for their surplus energy except in hatred and leader-worship.

At any rate, Spring is here, even in London N.1, and they can't stop you enjoying it. This is a satisfying reflection. How many a time have I stood watching the toads mating, or a pair of hares having a boxing match in the young corn, and thought of all the important persons who would stop me enjoying this if they could. But luckily they can't. So long as you are not actually ill, hungry, frightened or immured in a prison or a holiday camp, Spring is still Spring. The atom bombs are piling up in the factories, the police are prowling through the cities, the lies are streaming from the loudspeakers, but the earth is still going round the sun, and neither the dictators nor the bureaucrats, deeply as they disapprove of the process, are able to prevent it.

A Good Word for the Vicar of Bray
Tribune, 26 April 1946

Some years ago a friend took me to the little Berkshire church of which the celebrated Vicar of Bray was once the incumbent. (Actually it is a few miles from Bray, but perhaps at that time the two livings were one.) In the churchyard, there stands a magnificent yew tree which, according to a notice at its foot, was planted by no less a person than the Vicar of Bray himself. And it struck me at the time as curious that such a man should have left such a relic behind him.

The Vicar of Bray, though he was well equipped to be a leader-writer on the *Times*, could hardly be described as an admirable character. Yet, after this lapse of time, all that is left of him is a comic song and a beautiful tree, which has rested the eyes of generation after generation and must surely have outweighed any bad effects which he produced by his political quislingism.

Thibaw, the last King of Burma, was also far from being a good man. He was a drunkard, he had five hundred wives – he seems to have kept them chiefly for show, however – and when he came to the throne his first act was to decapitate seventy or eighty of his brothers. Yet he did posterity a good turn by planting the dusty streets of Mandalay with tamarind trees which cast a pleasant shade until the Japanese incendiary bombs burned them down in 1942.

The poet, James Shirley, seems to have generalised too freely when he said that "Only the actions of the just Smell sweet and blossom in their dust." Sometimes the actions of the unjust make quite a good showing after the appropriate lapse of time. When I saw the Vicar of Bray's yew tree it reminded me of something, and afterwards I got hold of a book of selections from the writings of John Aubrey and re-read a pastoral poem which must have been written some time in the first half of the seventeenth century, and which was inspired by a certain Mrs. Overall.

Mrs. Overall was the wife of a Dean and was extensively unfaithful to him. According to Aubrey she "could scarcely denie any one," and she had "the loveliest Eies that were ever seen, but wondrous wanton." The poem (the "shepherd swaine" seems to have been somebody called Sir John Selby) starts off:

> Downe lay the Shepherd Swaine
> So sober and demure
> Wishing for his wench againe
> So bonny and so pure
> With his head on hillock lowe
> And his arms akimboe
> And all was for the losse of his
> Hye nonny nonny noe. . . .
>
> Sweet she was, as kind a love
> As ever fetter'd Swaine;
> Never such a daynty one
> Shall man enjoy again.
> Sett a thousand on a rowe
> I forbid that any showe
> Ever the like of her
> Hye nonny nonny noe.

As the poem proceeds through another five verses, the refrain "hye nonny nonny noe" takes on an unmistakably obscene meaning, but it ends with the exquisite stanza:

> But gone she is the prettiest lasse
> That ever trod on plaine.
> What ever hath betide of her
> Blame not the Shepherd Swaine.
> For why? She was her owne Foe.
> And gave herself the overthrowe

By being so franke of her
Hye nonny nonny noe.

Mrs. Overall was no more an exemplary character than the Vicar of Bray, though a more attractive one. Yet in the end all that remains of her is a poem which still gives pleasure to many people, though for some reason it never gets into the anthologies. The suffering which she presumably caused, and the misery and futility in which her own life must have ended, have been transformed into a sort of lingering fragrance like the smell of tobacco-plants on a summer evening.

But to come back to trees. The planting of a tree, especially one of the long-living hardwood trees, is a gift which you can make to posterity at almost no cost and with almost no trouble, and if the tree takes root it will far outlive the visible effect of any of your other actions, good or evil. A year or two ago I wrote a few paragraphs in *Tribune* about some sixpenny rambler roses from Woolworth's which I had planted before the war. This brought me an indignant letter from a reader who said that roses are bourgeois, but I still think that my sixpence was better spent than if it had gone on cigarettes or even on one of the excellent Fabian Research Pamphlets.

Recently, I spent a day at the cottage where I used to live, and noted with a pleased surprise – to be exact, it was a feeling of having done good unconsciously – the progress of the things I had planted nearly ten years ago. I think it is worth recording what some of them cost, just to show what you can do with a few shillings if you invest them in something that grows.

First of all there were the two ramblers from Woolworth's, and three polyantha roses, all at sixpence each. Then there were two bush roses which were part of a job lot from a nursery garden. This job lot consisted of six fruit trees, three rose bushes and two gooseberry bushes, all for ten shillings. One of the fruit trees and one of the rose bushes died, but the rest are all flourishing. The sum total is five fruit trees, seven roses and two gooseberry bushes, all for twelve and sixpence. These plants have not entailed much work, and have had nothing spent on them beyond the original amount. They never even received any manure, except what I occasionally collected in a bucket when one of the farm horses happened to have halted outside the gate.

Between them, in nine years, those seven rose bushes will have given what would add up to a hundred or a hundred and fifty months of bloom. The fruit trees, which were mere saplings when I put them in, are now just about getting in their stride. Last week one of them, a plum, was a mass of blossom, and the apples looked as if they were going to do fairly well. What had originally been the weakling of the family, a Cox's Orange Pippin – it would hardly have been included in the job lot if it had been a good plant – had grown into a sturdy tree with plenty of fruit spurs on it. I maintain that it was a public-spirited action to plant that Cox, for these trees do not fruit quickly and I did not expect to stay there long. I never had an apple off it myself, but it looks as if somebody else will have quite a lot. By their fruits ye shall know them, and the Cox's Orange Pippin is a good fruit to be known by. Yet I did not plant it with the conscious intention of doing anybody a good turn. I just saw the job lot going cheap and stuck the things into the ground without much preparation.

A thing which I regret, and which I will try to remedy some time, is that I have never in my life planted a walnut. Nobody does plant them nowadays – when you see a walnut it is almost invariably an old tree. If you plant a walnut you are planting it for your grandchildren, and who cares a damn for his grandchildren? Nor does anybody plant a quince, a mulberry or a medlar. But these are garden trees which you can only be expected to plant if you have a patch of ground of your own. On the other hand, in any hedge or in any piece of waste ground you happen to be walking through, you can do something to remedy the appalling massacre of trees, especially oaks, ashes, elms and beeches, which has happened during the war years.

Even an apple tree is liable to live for about 100 years, so that the Cox I planted in 1936 may still be bearing fruit well into the twenty-first century. An oak or a beech may live for hundreds of years and be a pleasure to thousands or tens of thousands of people before it is finally sawn up into timber. I am not suggesting that one can discharge all one's obligations towards society by means of a private re-afforestation scheme. Still, it might not be a bad idea, every time you commit an anti-social act, to make a note of it in your diary, and then, at the appropriate season, push an acorn into the ground.

And, if even one in twenty of them came to maturity, you might do quite a lot of harm in your lifetime, and still, like the Vicar of Bray, end up as a public benefactor after all.

James Burnham and the Managerial Revolution

Polemic 3, 1 May 1946

James Burnham's book, *The Managerial Revolution*, made a considerable stir both in the United States and in this country at the time when it was published, and its main thesis has been so much discussed that a detailed exposition of it is hardly necessary. As shortly as I can summarise it, the thesis is this: —

Capitalism is disappearing, but Socialism is not replacing it. What is now arising is a new kind of planned, centralised society which will be neither capitalist nor, in any accepted sense of the word, democratic. The rulers of this new society will be the people who effectively control the means of production: that is, business executives, technicians, bureaucrats, and soldiers, lumped together by Burnham under the name of "managers." These people will eliminate the old capitalist class, crush the working class, and so organise society that all power and economic privilege remain in their own hands. Private property rights will be abolished, but common ownership will not be established. The new "managerial" societies will not consist of a patchwork of small, independent states, but of great super-states grouped round the main industrial centres in Europe, Asia, and America. These super-states will fight among themselves for possession of the remaining uncaptured portions of the earth, but will probably be unable to conquer one another completely. Internally, each society will be hierarchical, with an aristocracy of talent at the top and a mass of semi-slaves at the bottom.

In his next published book, *The Machiavellians*, Burnham elaborates and also modifies his original statement. The greater part of the book is an exposition of the theories of Machiavelli and of his modern disciples, Mosca, Michels, and Pareto: with doubtful justification, Burnham adds to these the syndicalist writer, Georges Sorel. What Burnham is mainly concerned to show is that a democratic society has never existed and, so far as we can see, never will exist. Society is of its nature oligarchical, and the power of the oligarchy always rests upon force and fraud. Burnham does not deny that "good" motives may operate in private life, but he maintains that politics consists of the struggle for power, and nothing else. All historical changes finally boil down to the replacement of one ruling class by another. All talk about democracy, liberty, equality, fraternity, all revolutionary movements, all visions of Utopia, or "the classless society," or "the Kingdom of Heaven on earth," are humbug (not necessarily conscious humbug) covering the ambitions of some new class which is elbowing its way into power. The English Puritans, the Jacobins, the Bolsheviks, were in each case simply power-seekers using the hopes of the masses in order to win a privileged position for themselves. Power can sometimes be won or maintained without violence, but never without fraud, because it is necessary to make use of the masses, and the masses would not co-operate if they knew that they were simply serving the purposes of a minority. In each great revolutionary struggle the masses are led on by vague dreams of human brotherhood, and then, when the new ruling class is well established in power, they are thrust back into servitude. This is practically the whole of political history, as Burnham sees it.

Where the second book departs from the earlier one is in asserting that the whole process could be somewhat moralised if the facts were faced more honestly. *The Machiavellians* is subtitled *Defenders of Freedom*. Machiavelli and his followers taught that in politics decency simply does not exist, and, by doing so, Burnham claims, made it possible to conduct political affairs more intelligently and less oppressively. A ruling class which recognised that its real aim was to stay in power would also recognise that it would be more likely to succeed if it served the common good, and might avoid stiffening into a hereditary aristocracy. Burnham lays much stress on Pareto's theory of the "circulation of the élites." If it is to stay in power a ruling class must constantly admit suitable recruits from below, so that the ablest men may always be at the top and a new class of power-hungry malcontents cannot come into being. This is likeliest to happen, Burnham considers, in a society which retains democratic habits – that is, where opposition is permitted and certain bodies such as the press and the trade unions can keep their autonomy. Here Burnham undoubtedly contradicts his earlier opinion. In *The Managerial Revolution*, which was written in 1940, it is taken as a matter of course that "managerial" Germany is in all ways more efficient than a capitalist democracy such as France or Britain. In the second book, written in 1942, Burnham admits that the Germans might have avoided some of their more serious strategic errors if they had permitted freedom of speech. However, the main thesis is not abandoned. Capitalism is doomed, and Socialism is a dream. If we grasp what is at issue we may guide the course of the managerial revolution to some extent, but the revolution is *happening*, whether we like it or not. In both books, but especially the earlier one, there is a note of unmistakable relish over the cruelty and wickedness of the processes that are being discussed. Although he reiterates that he is merely setting forth the facts and not stating his own preferences, it is clear that Burnham is fascinated by the spectacle of power, and that his sympathies were with Germany so long as Germany appeared to be winning the war. A more recent essay, *Lenin's Heir*, published in the *Partisan Review* about the beginning of 1945, suggests that this sympathy has since been transferred to the USSR. *Lenin's Heir*, which provoked violent controversy in the American left-wing press, has not yet been reprinted in England, and I must return to it later.

It will be seen that Burnham's theory is not, strictly speaking, a new one. Many earlier writers have foreseen the emergence of a new kind of society, neither capitalist nor Socialist, and probably based upon slavery: though most of them have differed from Burnham in not assuming this development to be *inevitable*. A good example is Hilaire Belloc's book, *The Servile State*, published in 1911. *The Servile State* is written in a tiresome style, and the remedy it suggests (a return to small-scale peasant ownership) is for many reasons impossible: still, it does foretell with remarkable insight the kind of things that have been happening from about 1930 onwards. Chesterton, in a less methodical way, predicted the disappearance of democracy and private property, and the rise of a slave society which might be called either capitalist or Communist. Jack London, in *The Iron Heel* (1909), foretold some of the essential features of Fascism, and such books as Wells's *The Sleeper Awakes* (1900), Zamyatin's *We* (1923), and Aldous Huxley's *Brave New World* (1930), all described imaginary worlds in which the special problems of capitalism had been solved without bringing liberty, equality, or true happiness any nearer. More recently, writers like Peter Drucker and F. A. Voigt have argued that Fascism and Communism are substantially the same thing. And indeed, it has always been obvious that a planned and centralised society is liable to develop into an oligarchy or a dictatorship. Orthodox Conservatives were unable to see this, because it comforted them to assume that Socialism "wouldn't work," and that the disappearance of capitalism would mean chaos and anarchy. Orthodox Socialists could not see it, because they wished to think that they themselves would soon be in power, and therefore assumed that when capitalism disappears, Socialism takes its place. As a result they were unable to foresee the rise of Fascism, or to make correct predictions about it after it had appeared. Later, the need to justify the Russian dictatorship and to explain away the obvious resemblances between Communism and Nazism clouded the issue still more. But the notion that industrialism must end in monopoly, and that monopoly must imply tyranny, is not a startling one.

Where Burnham differs from most other thinkers is in trying to plot the course of the "managerial revolution" accurately on a world scale, and in assuming that the drift towards totalitarianism is irresistible and must not be fought against, though it may be guided. According to Burnham, writing in 1940, "managerialism" has reached its fullest development in the USSR, but is almost equally well developed in Germany, and has made its appearance in the United States. He describes the New Deal as "primitive managerialism." But the trend is the same everywhere, or almost everywhere. Always *laissez-faire* capitalism gives way to planning and State interference, the mere *owner* loses power as against the technician and the bureaucrat, but Socialism – that is to say, what used to be called Socialism – shows no sign of emerging:

Some apologists try to excuse Marxism by saying that it has "never had a chance." This is far from the truth. Marxism and the Marxist parties have had dozens of chances. In Russia a Marxist party took power. Within a short time it abandoned Socialism; if not in words, at any rate in the effect of its actions. In most European nations there were during the last months of the first world war and the years immediately thereafter, social crises which left a wide-open door for the Marxist parties: without exception they proved unable to take and hold power. In a large number of countries – Germany, Denmark, Norway, Sweden, Austria, England, Australia, New Zealand, Spain, France, the reformist Marxist parties have administered the governments, and have uniformly failed to introduce Socialism or make any genuine step towards Socialism. . . . These parties have, in practice, at every historical test – and there have been many – either failed Socialism or abandoned it. This is the fact which neither the bitterest foe nor the most ardent friend of Socialism can erase. This fact does not, as some think, prove anything about the moral quality of the Socialist ideal. But it does constitute unblinkable evidence that, whatever its moral quality, Socialism is not going to come.

Burnham does not, of course, deny that the new "managerial" regimes, like the regimes of Russia and Nazi Germany, may be *called* Socialist. He means merely that they will not *be* Socialist in any sense of the word which would have been accepted by Marx, or Lenin, or Keir Hardie, or William Morris, or indeed, by any representative Socialist prior to about 1930. Socialism, until recently, was supposed to connote political democracy, social equality, and internationalism. There is not the smallest sign that any of these things is in a way to being established anywhere, and the one great country in which something described as a proletarian revolution once happened, *i.e.*, the USSR, has moved steadily away from the old concept of a free and equal society aiming at universal human brotherhood. In an almost unbroken progress since the early days of the Revolution, liberty has been chipped away and representative institutions smothered, while inequalities have increased and nationalism and militarism have grown stronger. But at the same time, Burnham insists, there has been no tendency to return to capitalism. What is happening is simply the growth of "managerialism," which, according to Burnham, is in progress everywhere, though the manner in which it comes about may vary from country to country.

Now, as an interpretation of what *is happening*, Burnham's theory is extremely plausible, to put it at the lowest. The events of, at any rate, the last fifteen years in the USSR can be far more easily explained by this theory than by any other. Evidently the USSR is not Socialist, and can only be called Socialist if one gives the word a meaning different from what it would have in any other context. On the other hand, prophecies that the Russian regime would revert to capitalism have always been falsified, and now seem further than ever from being fulfilled. In claiming that the process had gone almost equally far in Nazi Germany, Burnham probably exaggerates, but it seems certain that the drift was away from old-style capitalism and towards a planned economy with an adoptive oligarchy in control. In Russia the capitalists were destroyed first and the workers were crushed later. In Germany the workers were crushed first, but the elimination of the capitalists had at any rate begun, and calculations based on the assumption that Nazism was "simply capitalism," were always contradicted by events. Where Burnham seems to go most astray is in believing "managerialism" to be on the up-grade in the United States, the one great country where free capitalism is still vigorous. But if one considers the world-movement as a whole, his conclusions are difficult to resist; and even in the United States the all-prevailing faith in *laissez-faire* may not survive the next great economic crisis. It has been urged against Burnham that he assigns far too much importance to the "managers," in the narrow sense of the word – that is, factory bosses, planners, and technicians – and seems to assume that even in Soviet Russia it is these people, and not the Communist Party chiefs, who are the real holders of power. However, this is a secondary error, and it is partially corrected in *The Machiavellians*. The real question is not whether the people who wipe their boots on us during the next fifty years are to be called managers, bureaucrats, or politicians: the question is whether capitalism, now obviously doomed, is to give way to oligarchy or to true democracy.

But curiously enough, when one examines the predictions which Burnham has based on his general theory, one finds that in so far as they are verifiable, they have been falsified. Numbers of people have pointed this out already. However, it is worth following up Burnham's predictions in detail, because they form a sort of pattern which is related to contemporary events, and which reveals, I believe, a very important weakness in present-day political thought.

To begin with, writing in 1940, Burnham takes a German victory more or less for granted. Britain is described as "dissolving," and as displaying "all the characteristics which have distinguished decadent cultures in past historical transitions," while the conquest and integration of Europe which Germany achieved in 1940 is described as "irreversible." "England," writes Burnham, "no matter with what non-European allies, cannot conceivably hope to conquer the European continent." Even if Germany should somehow manage to lose the war, she could not be dismembered or reduced to the status of the Weimar Republic, but is bound to remain as the nucleus of a unified Europe. The future map of the world, with its three great super-states is, in any case, already settled in its main outlines: and "the nuclei of these three super-states are, whatever may be their future names, the previously existing nations, Japan, Germany, and the United States."

Burnham also commits himself to the opinion that Germany will not attack the USSR until after Britain has been defeated. In a condensation of his book published in the *Partisan Review* of May–June 1941, and presumably written later than the book itself, he says:

> As in the case of Russia, so with Germany, the third part of the managerial problem – the contest for dominance with other sections of managerial society – remains for the future. First had to come the death blow that assured the toppling of the capitalist world order, which meant above all the destruction of the foundations of the British Empire (the keystone of the capitalist world order) both directly and through the smashing of the European political structure, which was a necessary prop of the Empire. This is the basic explanation of the Nazi-Soviet Pact, which is not intelligible on other grounds. The future conflict between Germany and Russia will be a managerial conflict proper; prior to the great world-managerial battles, the end of the capitalist order must be assured.

> *The belief that Nazism is "decadent capitalism" . . . makes it impossible to explain reasonably the Nazi-Soviet Pact. From this belief followed the always-expected war between Germany and Russia, not the actual war to the death between Germany and the British Empire. The war between Germany and Russia is one of the managerial wars of the future, not of the anti-capitalist wars of yesterday and to-day.*

However, the attack on Russia will come later, and Russia is certain, or almost certain, to be defeated. "There is every reason to believe . . . that Russia will split apart, with the western half gravitating towards the European base and the eastern towards the Asiatic." This quotation comes from *The Managerial Revolution*. In the above-quoted article, written probably about six months later, it is put more forcibly: "the Russian weaknesses indicate that Russia will not be able to endure, that it will crack apart, and fall towards east and west." And in a supplementary note which was added to the English (Pelican) edition, and which appears to have been written at the end of 1941, Burnham speaks as though the "cracking apart" process were already happening. The war, he says, "is part of the means whereby the western half of Russia is being integrated into the European super-state."

Sorting these various statements out, we have the following prophecies:

1. Germany is bound to win the war.

2. Germany and Japan are bound to survive as great states, and to remain the nuclei of power in their respective areas.

3. Germany will not attack the USSR until after the defeat of Britain.

4. The USSR is bound to be defeated.

However, Burnham has made other predictions besides these. In a short article in the *Partisan Review*, in the summer of 1944, he gives his opinion that the USSR will gang up with Japan in order to prevent the total defeat of the latter, while the American Communists will be set to work to sabotage the eastern end of the war. And finally, in an article in the same magazine in the winter of 1944–45, he claims that Russia, destined so short a while ago to "crack apart," is within sight of conquering the whole of Eurasia. This article, which was the cause of violent controversies among the American intelligent-sia, has not been reprinted in England. I must give some account of it here, because its manner of approach and its emotional tone are of a peculiar kind, and by studying them one can get nearer to the real roots of Burnham's theory.

The article is entitled *Lenin's Heir*, and it sets out to show that Stalin is the true and legitimate guardian of the Russian Revolution, which he has not in any sense "betrayed" but has merely carried forward on lines that were implicit in it from the start. In itself, this is an easier opinion to swallow than the usual Trotskyist claim that Stalin is a mere crook who has perverted the Revolution to his own ends, and that things would some-how have been different if Lenin had lived or Trotsky had remained in power. Actually there is no strong reason for thinking that the main lines of development would have been very different. Well before 1923 the seeds of a totalitarian society were quite plainly there. Lenin, indeed, is one of those politicians who win an undeserved reputation by dying pre-maturely.[29] Had he lived, it is probable that he would either have been thrown out, like Trotsky, or would have kept himself in power by methods as barbarous, or nearly as barbar-ous, as those of Stalin. The *title* of Burnham's essay, therefore, sets forth a reasonable thesis, and one would expect him to support it by an appeal to the facts.

However, the essay barely touches upon its ostensible sub-ject-matter. It is obvious that anyone genuinely concerned to show that there has been continuity of policy as between Lenin and Stalin, would start by outlining Lenin's policy and then explain in what way Stalin's has resembled it. Burnham does not do this. Except for one or two cursory sentences he says nothing about Lenin's policy, and Lenin's name only occurs five times in an essay of twelve pages: in the first seven pages, apart from the title, it does not occur at all. The real aim of the essay is to present Stalin as a towering, superhuman figure, indeed a species of demigod, and Bolshevism as an irresistible force which is flowing over the earth and cannot be halted until it reaches the outermost borders of Eurasia. In so far as he makes any attempt to prove his case, Burnham does so by repeating over and over again that Stalin is "a great man" – which is probably true, but is almost completely irrelevant. Moreover, though he does advance some solid arguments for believing in Stalin's genius, it is clear that in his mind the idea of "greatness" is inextricably mixed up with the idea of cruelty and dishonesty. There are curious passages in which it seems to be suggested that Stalin is to be admired *because of* the limitless suffering that he has caused:

Stalin proves himself a "great man," in the grand style. The accounts of the banquets, staged in Moscow for the visiting dignitaries, set the symbolic tone. With their enormous menus of sturgeon, and roasts, and fowl, and sweets; their streams of liquor; the scores of toasts with which they end; the silent, unmoving secret police behind each guest; all against the winter background of the starving multitudes of besieged Leningrad; the dying millions at the front; the jammed concentration camps; the city crowds kept by their minute rations just at the edge of life; there is little trace of dull mediocrity or the hand of Babbitt. We recognise, rather, the tradition of the most spectacular of the Tsars, of the Great Kings of the Medes and Persians, of the Khanate of the Golden Horde, of the banquet we assign to the gods of the Heroic Ages in tribute to the insight that insolence, and indifference, and brutality on such a scale remove beings from the human level. . . . Stalin's political techniques show a freedom from conventional restrictions that is incompatible with mediocrity: the mediocre man is custom-bound. Often it is the scale of his operations that sets them apart. It is usual, for example, for men active in practical life to engineer an occasional frame-up. But to carry out a frame-up against tens of thousands of persons, important percentages of whole strata of society, including most of one's own comrades, is so far out of the ordinary that the long-run mass conclusion is either that the frame-up must be true — at least "have some truth in it" — or that power so immense must be submitted to — is a "historical necessity," as intellectuals put it. . . . There is nothing unexpected in letting a few individuals starve for reasons of state; but to starve by deliberate decision, several millions, is a type of action attributed ordinarily only to gods.

In these and other similar passages there may be a tinge of irony, but it is difficult not to feel that there is also a sort of fascinated admiration. Towards the end of the essay Burnham compares Stalin with those semi-mythical heroes, like Moses or Asoka, who embody in themselves a whole epoch, and can justly be credited with feats that they did not actually perform. In writing of Soviet foreign policy and its supposed objectives, he touches an even more mystical note:

> *Starting from the magnetic core of the Eurasian heartland, the Soviet power, like the reality of the One of Neo-Platonism overflowing in the descending series of the emanative progression, flows outward, west into Europe, south into the Near East, east into China, already lapping the shores of the Atlantic, the Yellow and China Seas, the Mediterranean, and the Persian Gulf. As the undifferentiated One, in its progression, descends through the stages of Mind, Soul, and Matter, and then through its fatal Return back to itself; so does the Soviet power, emanating from the integrally totalitarian centre, proceed outwards by Absorption (the Baltics, Bessarabia, Bukovina, East Poland), Domination (Finland, the Balkans, Mongolia, North China and, to-morrow, Germany), Orienting Influence (Italy, France, Turkey, Iran, Central and south China . . .), until it is dissipated in MH ON, the outer material sphere, beyond the Eurasian boundaries, of momentary Appeasement and Infiltration (England, the United States).*

I do not think it is fanciful to suggest that the unnecessary capital letters with which this passage is loaded are intended to have a hypnotic effect on the reader. Burnham is trying to build up a picture of terrifying, irresistible power, and to turn a normal political manœuvre like infiltration into Infiltration adds to the general portentousness. The essay should be read in full. Although it is not the kind of tribute that the average Russophile would consider acceptable, and although Burnham himself would probably claim that he is being strictly objective, he is in effect performing an act of homage, and even of self-abasement. Meanwhile, this essay gives us another prophecy to add to the list: *i.e.*, that the USSR will conquer the whole of Eurasia, and probably a great deal more. And one must remember that Burnham's basic theory contains, in itself, a prediction which still has to be tested – that is, that whatever else happens, the "managerial" form of society is bound to prevail.

Burnham's earlier prophecy, of a German victory in the war and the integration of Europe round the German nucleus, was falsified, not only in its main outlines, but in some important details. Burnham insists all the way through that

"managerialism" is not only more efficient than capitalist democracy or Marxian Socialism, but also more acceptable to the
masses. The slogans of democracy and national self-determination, he says, no longer have any mass appeal: "managerialism," on the other hand, can rouse enthusiasm, produce
intelligible war aims, establish fifth columns everywhere, and
inspire its soldiers with a fanatical morale. The "fanaticism" of
the Germans, as against the "apathy" or "indifference" of the
British, French, etc. is much emphasised, and Nazism is represented as a revolutionary force sweeping across Europe and
spreading its philosophy "by contagion." The Nazi fifth
columns "cannot be wiped out," and the democratic nations
are quite incapable of projecting any settlement which the
German or other European masses would prefer to the New
Order. In any case, the democracies can only defeat Germany if
they go "still further along the managerial road than Germany
has yet gone."

The germ of truth in all this is that the smaller European
states, demoralised by the chaos and stagnation of the pre-war
years, collapsed rather more quickly than they need have done,
and might conceivably have accepted the New Order if the
Germans had kept some of their promises. But the actual
experience of German rule aroused almost at once such a fury
of hatred and vindictiveness as the world has seldom seen. After
about the beginning of 1941 there was hardly any need of a
positive war aim, since getting rid of the Germans was a
sufficient objective. The question of morale, and its relation
to national solidarity, is a nebulous one, and the evidence can
be so manipulated as to prove almost anything. But if one goes
by the proportion of prisoners to other casualties, and the
amount of quislingism, the totalitarian states come out of the
comparison worse than the democracies. Hundreds of thousands of Russians appear to have gone over to the Germans
during the course of the war, while comparable numbers of
Germans and Italians had gone over to the Allies before the war
started: the corresponding number of American or British
renegades would have amounted to a few scores. As an
example of the inability of "capitalist ideologies" to enlist
support, Burnham cites "the complete failure of voluntary
military recruiting in England (as well as the entire British

GEORGE ORWELL

Empire) and in the United States." One would gather from this that the armies of the totalitarian states were manned by volunteers. Actually, no totalitarian state has ever so much as considered voluntary recruitment for any purpose, nor, throughout history, has a large army ever been raised by voluntary means.[30] It is not worth listing the many similar arguments that Burnham puts forward. The point is that he assumes that the Germans must win the propaganda war as well as the military one, and that, at any rate in Europe, this estimate was not borne out by events.

It will be seen that Burnham's predictions have not merely, when they were verifiable, turned out to be wrong, but that they have sometimes contradicted one another in a sensational way. It is this last fact that is significant. Political predictions are usually wrong, because they are usually based on wishthinking, but they can have symptomatic value, especially when they change abruptly. Often the revealing factor is the date at which they are made. Dating Burnham's various writings as accurately as can be done from internal evidence, and then noting what events they coincided with, we find the following relationships: –

In *The Managerial Revolution* Burnham prophesies a German victory, postponement of the Russo-German war until after Britain is defeated, and, subsequently, the defeat of Russia. The book, or much of it, was written in the second half of 1940 – *i.e.*, at a time when the Germans had overrun Western Europe and were bombing Britain, and the Russians were collaborating with them fairly closely, and in what appeared, at any rate, to be a spirit of appeasement.

In the supplementary note added to the English edition of the book, Burnham appears to assume that the USSR is already beaten and the splitting-up process is about to begin. This was published in the spring of 1942 and presumably written at the end of 1941; *i.e.*, when the Germans were in the suburbs of Moscow.

The prediction that Russia would gang up with Japan against the USA was written early in 1944, soon after the conclusion of a new Russo-Japanese treaty.

The prophecy of Russian world-conquest was written in the winter of 1944, when the Russians were advancing rapidly in Eastern Europe while the Western Allies were still held up in Italy and northern France.

It will be seen that at each point Burnham is predicting *a continuation of the thing that is happening*. Now the tendency to do this is not simply a bad habit, like inaccuracy or exaggeration, which one can correct by taking thought. It is a major mental disease, and its roots lie partly in cowardice and partly in the worship of power, which is not fully separable from cowardice.

Suppose in 1940 you had taken a Gallup Poll, in England, on the question "Will Germany win the war?" You would have found, curiously enough, that the group answering "Yes" contained a far higher percentage of intelligent people – people with I.Q. of over 120, shall we say – than the group answering "No." The same would have held good in the middle of 1942. In this case the figures would not have been so striking, but if you had made the question "Will the Germans capture Alexandria?" or "Will the Japanese be able to hold on to the territories they have captured?", then once again there would have been a very marked tendency for intelligence to concentrate in the "Yes" group. In every case the less-gifted person would have been likelier to give a right answer.

If one went simply by these instances, one might assume that high intelligence and bad military judgement always go together. However, it is not so simple as that. The English intelligentsia, on the whole, were more defeatist than the mass of the people – and some of them went on being defeatist at a time when the war was quite plainly won – partly because they were better able to visualise the dreary years of warfare that lay ahead. Their morale was worse because their imaginations were stronger. The quickest way of ending a war is to lose it, and if one finds the prospect of a long war intolerable, it is natural to disbelieve in the possibility of victory. But there was more to it than that. There was also the disaffection of large numbers of intellectuals, which made it difficult for them not to side with any country hostile to Britain. And deepest of all, there was admiration – though only in a very few cases conscious admiration – for the power, energy, and cruelty of the Nazi regime. It would be a useful though tedious labour to go through the left-wing press and enumerate all the hostile references to

Nazism during the years 1935–45. One would find, I have little doubt, that they reached their high-water mark in 1937–38 and 1944–45, and dropped off noticeably in the years 1939–42 – that is, during the period when Germany seemed to be winning. One would find, also, the same people advocating a compromise peace in 1940 and approving the dismemberment of Germany in 1945. And if one studied the reactions of the English intelligentsia towards the USSR, there, too, one would find genuinely progressive impulses mixed up with admiration for power and cruelty. It would be grossly unfair to suggest that power-worship is the only motive for Russophile feeling, but it is one motive, and among intellectuals it is probably the strongest one.

Power-worship blurs political judgement because it leads, almost unavoidably, to the belief that present trends will continue. Whoever is winning at the moment will always seem to be invincible. If the Japanese have conquered South Asia, then they will keep South Asia for ever; if the Germans have captured Tobruk, they will infallibly capture Cairo; if the Russians are in Berlin, it will not be long before they are in London: and so on. This habit of mind leads also to the belief that things will happen more quickly, completely, and catastrophically than they ever do in practice. The rise and fall of empires, the disappearance of cultures and religions, are expected to happen with earthquake suddenness, and processes which have barely started are talked about as though they were already at an end. Burnham's writings are full of apocalyptic visions. Nations, governments, classes, and social systems are constantly described as expanding, contracting, decaying, dissolving, toppling, crashing, crumbling, crystallising, and, in general, behaving in an unstable and melodramatic way. The slowness of historical change, the fact that any epoch always contains a great deal of the last epoch, is never sufficiently allowed for. Such a manner of thinking is bound to lead to mistaken prophecies, because, even when it gauges the direction of events rightly, it will miscalculate their tempo. Within the space of five years Burnham foretold the domination of Russia by Germany and of Germany by Russia. In each case he was obeying the same instinct: the instinct to bow down before the conqueror of the moment, to accept the existing trend as irreversible. With this in mind one can criticise his theory in a broader way.

The mistakes I have pointed out do not disprove Burnham's theory, but they do cast light on his probable reasons for holding it. In this connection one cannot leave out of account the fact that Burnham is an American. Every political theory has a certain regional tinge about it, and every nation, every culture, has its own characteristic prejudices and patches of ignorance. There are certain problems that must almost inevitably be seen in a different perspective according to the geographical situation from which one is looking at them. Now, the attitude that Burnham adopts, of classifying Communism and Fascism as much the same thing, and at the same time accepting both of them – or, at any rate, not assuming that either must be violently struggled against – is essentially an American attitude, and would be almost impossible for an Englishman or any other western European. English writers who consider Communism and Fascism to be *the same thing*, invariably hold that both are monstrous evils which must be fought to the death: on the other hand, any Englishman who believes Communism and Fascism to be opposites will feel that he ought to side with one or the other.[31] The reason for this difference of outlook is simple enough and, as usual, is bound up with wish-thinking. If totalitarianism triumphs and the dreams of the geopoliticians come true, Britain will disappear as a world power and the whole of western Europe will be swallowed by some single great state. This is not a prospect that it is easy for an Englishman to contemplate with detachment. Either he does not want Britain to disappear – in which case he will tend to construct theories proving the thing that he wants – or, like a minority of intellectuals, he will decide that his country is finished and transfer his allegiance to some foreign power. An American does not have to make the same choice. Whatever happens, the United States will survive as a great power, and from the American point of view it does not make much difference whether Europe is dominated by Russia or by Germany. Most Americans who think of the matter at all would prefer to see the world divided between two or three monster states which had reached their natural boundaries and could bargain with one another on economic issues without being troubled by ideological differences. Such a world-picture

fits in with the American tendency to admire size for its own sake
and to feel that success constitutes justification, and it fits in with
the all-prevailing anti-British sentiment. In practice, Britain and
the United States have twice been forced into alliance against
Germany, and will probably, before long, be forced into alliance
against Russia: but, subjectively, a majority of Americans would
prefer either Russia or Germany to Britain, and, as between
Russia and Germany, would prefer whichever seemed stronger
at the moment.[32] It is, therefore, not surprising that Burnham's
world-view should often be noticeably close to that of the
American imperialists on the one side, or to that of the isolationists on the other. It is a "tough" or "realistic" world-view which
fits in with the American form of wish-thinking. The almost
open admiration for Nazi methods which Burnham shows in the
earlier of his two books, and which would seem shocking to
almost any English reader, depends ultimately on the fact that the
Atlantic is wider than the Channel.

As I have said earlier, Burnham has probably been more
right than wrong about the present and the immediate past. For
quite fifty years past the general drift has almost certainly been
towards oligarchy. The ever-increasing concentration of industrial and financial power; the diminishing importance of the
individual capitalist or shareholder, and the growth of the new
"managerial" class of scientists, technicians, and bureaucrats;
the weakness of the proletariat against the centralised state; the
increasing helplessness of small countries against big ones; the
decay of representative institutions and the appearance of one-
party regimes based on police terrorism, faked plebiscites, etc.:
all these things seem to point in the same direction. Burnham
sees the trend and assumes that it is irresistible, rather as a rabbit
fascinated by a boa constrictor might assume that a boa constrictor is the strongest thing in the world. When one looks a
little deeper, one sees that all his ideas rest upon two axioms
which are taken for granted in the earlier book and made partly
explicit in the second one. They are:

(a) Politics is essentially the same in all ages.

(b) Political behaviour is different from other kinds of
behaviour.

To take the second point first. In *The Machiavellians*, Burnham
insists that politics is simply the struggle for power. Every great

social movement, every war, every revolution, every political programme, however edifying and Utopian, really has behind it the ambitions of some sectional group which is out to grab power for itself. Power can never be restrained by any ethical or religious code, but only by other power. The nearest possible approach to altruistic behaviour is the perception by a ruling group that it will probably stay in power longer if it behaves decently. But curiously enough, these generalisations only apply to political behaviour, not to any other kind of behaviour. In everyday life, as Burnham sees and admits, one cannot explain every human action by applying the principle of *cui bono?* Obviously, human beings have impulses which are not selfish. Man, therefore, is an animal that can act morally when he acts as an individual, but becomes unmoral when he acts collectively. But even this generalisation only holds good for the higher groups. The masses, it seems, have vague aspirations towards liberty and human brotherhood, which are easily played upon by power-hungry individuals or minorities. So that history consists of a series of swindles, in which the masses are first lured into revolt by the promise of Utopia, and then, when they have done their job, enslaved over again by new masters.

Political activity, therefore, is a special kind of behaviour, characterised by its complete unscrupulousness, and occurring only among small groups of the population, especially among dissatisfied groups whose talents do not get free play under the existing form of society. The great mass of the people – and this is where (b) ties up with (a) – will always be unpolitical. In effect, therefore, humanity is divided into two classes: the self-seeking, hypocritical minority, and the brainless mob whose destiny is always to be led or driven, as one gets a pig back to the sty by kicking it on the bottom or by rattling a stick inside a swill-bucket, according to the needs of the moment. And this beautiful pattern is to continue for ever. Individuals may pass from one category to another, whole classes may destroy other classes and rise to the dominant position, but the division of humanity into rulers and ruled is unalterable. In their capabilities, as in their desires and needs, men are not equal. There is an "iron law of oligarchy," which would operate even if democracy were not impossible for mechanical reasons.

It is curious that in all his talk about the struggle for power, Burnham never stops to ask *why* people want power. He seems to assume that power-hunger, although only dominant in comparatively few people, is a natural instinct that does not have to be explained, like the desire for food. He also assumes that the division of society into classes serves the same purpose in all ages. This is practically to ignore the history of hundreds of years. When Burnham's master, Machiavelli, was writing, class divisions were not only unavoidable, but desirable. So long as methods of production were primitive, the great mass of the people were necessarily tied down to dreary, exhausting manual labour: and a few people had to be set free from such labour, otherwise civilisation could not maintain itself, let alone make any progress. But since the arrival of the machine the whole pattern has altered. The justification for class distinctions, if there is a justification, is no longer the same, because there is no mechanical reason why the average human being should continue to be a drudge. True, drudgery persists; class distinctions are probably re-establishing themselves in a new form, and individual liberty is on the downgrade: but as these developments are now technically avoidable, they must have some psychological cause which Burnham makes no attempt to discover. The question that he ought to ask, and never does ask, is: why does the lust for naked power become a major human motive exactly *now*, when the dominion of man over man is ceasing to be necessary? As for the claim that "human nature," or "inexorable laws" of this and that, make Socialism impossible, it is simply a projection of the past into the future. In effect, Burnham argues that because a society of free and equal human beings has never existed, it never can exist. By the same argument one could have demonstrated the impossibility of aeroplanes in 1900, or of motor cars in 1850.

The notion that the machine has altered human relationships, and that in consequence Machiavelli is out of date, is a very obvious one. If Burnham fails to deal with it, it can, I think, only be because his own power-instinct leads him to brush aside any suggestion that the Machiavellian world of force, fraud, and tyranny may somehow come to an end. It is important to bear in mind what I said above: that Burnham's theory is only a variant – an American variant, and interesting because of its comprehensiveness – of the power-worship now so prevalent among intellectuals. A more normal variant, at any rate in England, is Communism. If one examines the people who, having some idea of what the Russian regime is like, are strongly Russophile, one finds that, on the whole, they belong to the "managerial" class of which Burnham writes. That is, they are not managers in the narrow sense, but scientists, technicians, teachers, journalists, broadcasters, bureaucrats, professional politicians: in general, middling people who feel themselves cramped by a system that is still partly aristocratic, and are hungry for more power and more prestige. These people look towards the USSR and see in it, or think they see, a system which eliminates the upper class, keeps the working class in its place, and hands unlimited power to people very similar to themselves. It was only *after* the Soviet regime became unmistakably totalitarian that English intellectuals, in large numbers, began to show an interest in it. Burnham, although the English Russophile intelligentsia would repudiate him, is really voicing their secret wish: the wish to destroy the old, equalitarian version of Socialism and usher in a hierarchical society where the intellectual can at last get his hands on the whip. Burnham at least has the honesty to say that Socialism isn't coming; the others merely say that Socialism *is* coming, and then give the word "Socialism" a new meaning which makes nonsense of the old one. But his theory, for all its appearance of objectivity, is the rationalisation of a wish. There is no strong reason for thinking that it tells us anything about the future, except perhaps the immediate future. It merely tells us what kind of world the "managerial" class themselves, or at least the more conscious and ambitious members of the class, would like to live in.

Fortunately the "managers" are not so invincible as Burnham believes. It is curious how persistently, in *The Managerial Revolution*, he ignores the advantages, military as well as social, enjoyed by a democratic country. At every point the evidence is squeezed in order to show the strength, vitality, and durability of Hitler's crazy regime. Germany is expanding rapidly, and "rapid territorial expansion has always been a sign, not of decadence . . . but of renewal." Germany makes war successfully, and "the ability to make war well is never a sign of

decadence but of its opposite." Germany also "inspires in
millions of persons a fanatical loyalty. This, too, never accompanies decadence." Even the cruelty and dishonesty of the Nazi
regime are cited in its favour, since "the young, new, rising
social order is, as against the old, more likely to resort on a large
scale to lies, terror, persecution." Yet, within only five years
this young, new, rising social order had smashed itself to pieces
and become, in Burnham's usage of the word, decadent. And
this had happened quite largely because of the "managerial"
(*i.e.*, undemocratic) structure which Burnham admires. The
immediate cause of the German defeat was the unheard-of folly
of attacking the USSR while Britain was still undefeated and
America was manifestly getting ready to fight. Mistakes of this
magnitude can only be made, or at any rate they are most likely
to be made, in countries where public opinion has no power.
So long as the common man can get a hearing, such elementary
rules as not fighting all your enemies simultaneously are less
likely to be violated.

But, in any case, one should have been able to see from the
start that such a movement as Nazism could not produce any
good or stable result. Actually, so long as they were winning,
Burnham seems to have seen nothing wrong with the methods
of the Nazis. Such methods, he says, only appear wicked
because they are new:

> There is no historical law that polite manners and "justice" shall
> conquer. In history there is always the question of whose manners
> and whose justice. A rising social class and a new order of society
> have got to break through the old moral codes just as they must break
> through the old economic and political institutions. Naturally, from
> the point of view of the old, they are monsters. If they win, they take
> care in due time of manners and morals.

This implies that literally anything can become right or
wrong if the dominant class of the moment so wills it. It ignores
the fact that certain rules of conduct have to be observed if
human society is to hold together at all. Burnham, therefore,
was unable to see that the crimes and follies of the Nazi regime
must lead by one route or another to disaster. So also with his
newfound admiration for Stalinism. It is too early to say in just
what way the Russian regime will destroy itself. If I had to

make a prophecy, I should say that a continuation of the Russian policies of the last fifteen years – and internal and external policy, of course, are merely two facets of the same thing – can only lead to a war conducted with atomic bombs, which will make Hitler's invasion look like a tea-party. But at any rate, the Russian regime will either democratise itself, or it will perish. The huge, invincible, everlasting slave empire of which Burnham appears to dream will not be established, or, if established, will not endure, because slavery is no longer a stable basis for human society.

One cannot always make positive prophecies, but there are times when one ought to be able to make negative ones. No one could have been expected to foresee the exact results of the Treaty of Versailles, but millions of thinking people could and did foresee that those results would be bad. Plenty of people, though not so many in this case, can foresee that the results of the settlement now being forced on Europe will also be bad. And to refrain from admiring Hitler or Stalin – that, too, should not require an enormous intellectual effort. But it is partly a moral effort. That a man of Burnham's gifts should have been able for a while to think of Nazism as something rather admirable, something that could and probably would build up a workable and durable social order, shows what damage is done to the sense of reality by the cultivation of what is now called "realism."

Confessions of a Book Reviewer
Tribune, 3 May 1946

In a cold but stuffy bed-sitting room littered with cigarette ends and half-empty cups of tea, a man in a moth-eaten dressing gown sits at a rickety table, trying to find room for his type-writer among the piles of dusty papers that surround it. He cannot throw the papers away because the wastepaper basket is already overflowing, and besides, somewhere among the unanswered letters and unpaid bills it is possible that there is a cheque for two guineas which he is nearly certain he forgot to pay into the bank. There are also letters with addresses which ought to be entered in his address book. He has lost his address book, and the thought of looking for it, or indeed of looking for anything, afflicts him with acute suicidal impulses.

He is a man of 35, but looks 50. He is bald, has varicose veins and wears spectacles, or would wear them if his only pair were not chronically lost. If things are normal with him he will be suffering from malnutrition, but if he has recently had a lucky streak he will be suffering from a hangover. At present it is half past eleven in the morning, and according to his schedule he should have started work two hours ago; but even if he had made any serious effort to start he would have been frustrated by the almost continuous ringing of the telephone bell, the yells of the baby, the rattle of an electric drill out in the street, and the heavy boots of his creditors clumping up and down the stairs. The most recent interruption was the arrival of the second post, which brought him two circulars and an income tax demand printed in red.

Needless to say this person is a writer. He might be a poet, a novelist, or a writer of film scripts or radio features, for all literary people are very much alike, but let us say that he is a book reviewer. Half hidden among the pile of papers is a bulky parcel containing five volumes which his editor has sent with a note suggesting that they "ought to go well together." They arrived four days ago, but for 48 hours the reviewer was prevented by moral paralysis from opening the parcel. Yesterday in a resolute moment he ripped the string off it and found the five volumes to be *Palestine at the Cross Roads*, *Scientific Dairy Farming*, *A Short History of European Democracy* (this one is 680 pages and weighs four pounds), *Tribal Customs in Portuguese East Africa*, and a novel, *It's Nicer Lying Down*, probably included by mistake. His review – 800 words, say – has got to be "in" by mid-day tomorrow.

Three of these books deal with subjects of which he is so ignorant that he will have to read at least 50 pages if he is to avoid making some howler which will betray him not merely to the author (who of course knows all about the habits of book reviewers), but even to the general reader. By four in the afternoon he will have taken the books out of their wrapping paper but will still be suffering from a nervous inability to open them. The prospect of having to read them, and even the smell of the paper, affects him like the prospect of eating cold ground-rice pudding flavoured with castor oil. And yet curiously enough his copy will get to the office in time. Somehow it always does get there in time. At about nine p.m. his mind will grow relatively clear, and until the small hours he will sit in a room which grows colder and colder, while the cigarette smoke grows thicker and thicker, skipping expertly through one book after another and laying each down with the final comment, "God, what tripe!" In the morning, blear-eyed, surly and unshaven, he will gaze for an hour or two at a blank sheet of paper until the menacing finger of the clock frightens him into action. Then suddenly he will snap into it. All the stale old phrases – "a book that no one should miss," "something memorable on every page," "of special value are the chapters dealing with, etc., etc." – will jump into their places like iron filings obeying the magnet, and the review will end up at exactly the right length and with just about three minutes to go. Meanwhile another wad of ill-assorted, unappetising books will have arrived by post. So it goes on. And yet with what high hopes this down-trodden, nerve-racked creature started his career, only a few years ago.

Do I seem to exaggerate? I ask any regular reviewer – anyone who reviews, say, a minimum of 100 books a year – whether he can deny in honesty that his habits and character are such as I have described. Every writer, in any case, is rather that kind of person, but the prolonged, indiscriminate reviewing of books is a quite exceptionally thankless, irritating and exhausting job. It not only involves praising trash – though it does involve that, as I will show in a moment – but constantly *inventing* reactions towards books about which one has no spontaneous feelings whatever. The reviewer, jaded though he may be, is professionally interested in books, and out of the thousands that appear annually, there are probably fifty or a hundred that he would enjoy writing about. If he is a top-notcher in his profession he may get hold of ten or twenty of them: more probably he gets hold of two or three. The rest of his work, however conscientious he may be in praising or damning, is in essence humbug. He is pouring his immortal spirit down the drain, half a pint at a time.

The great majority of reviewers give an inadequate or misleading account of the book that is dealt with. Since the war publishers have been less able than before to twist the tails of literary editors and evoke a paean of praise for every book that they produce, but on the other hand the standard of reviewing has gone down owing to lack of space and other inconveniences. Seeing the results, people sometimes suggest that the solution lies in getting book-reviewing out of the hands of hacks. Books on specialized subjects ought to be dealt with by experts, and on the other hand a good deal of reviewing, especially of novels, might well be done by amateurs. Nearly every book is capable of arousing passionate feeling, if it is only a passionate dislike, in some or other reader, whose ideas about it would surely be worth more than those of a bored professional. But, unfortunately, as every editor knows, that kind of thing is very difficult to organize. In practice the editor always finds himself reverting to his team of hacks – his "regulars," as he calls them.

None of this is remediable so long as it is taken for granted that every book deserves to be reviewed. It is almost impossible to mention books in bulk without grossly over-praising the great majority of them. Until one has some kind of professional relationship with books one does not discover how bad the majority of them are. In much more than nine cases out of ten the only objectively truthful criticism would be, "This book is worthless," while the truth about the reviewer's own reaction would probably be: "This book does not interest me in any way, and I would not write about it unless I were paid to." But the public will not pay to read that kind of thing. Why should they? They want some kind of guide to the books they are asked to read, and they want some kind of evaluation. But as soon as values are mentioned, standards collapse. For if one says – and nearly every reviewer says this kind of thing at least once a week – that "King Lear" is a good play and *The Four Just Men* is a good thriller, what meaning is there in the word "good"?

The best practice, it has always seemed to me, would be simply to ignore the great majority of books and to give very long reviews – 1,000 words is a bare minimum – to the few that seem to matter. Short notes of a line or two on forthcoming books can be useful, but the usual middle-length review of about 600 words is bound to be worthless even if the reviewer genuinely wants to write it. Normally he doesn't want to write it, and the week-in, week-out production of snippets soon reduces him to the crushed figure in a dressing gown whom I described at the beginning of this article. However, everyone in this world has someone else whom he can look down on, and I must say, from experience of both trades, that the book reviewer is better off than the film critic, who cannot even do his work at home, but has to attend trade shows at eleven in the morning and, with one or two notable exceptions, is expected to sell his honour for a glass of inferior sherry.

Review of *Of Ants and Men* by Caryl P. Haskins

The Observer, 5 May 1946

Physically, ants are about as unlike men as they could well be, but in their behaviour they present a sort of parody of human activities, and their social organisation is so much more efficient than our own that it can be used not merely for purposes of analogy but as an object-lesson by means of which we can criticise our own institutions. Dr. Haskins's book does in passing supply a great deal of information about the habits of ants, but his main aim is to decide whether any real parallel exists between ants and human beings. Can we profitably "go to the ant," as Solomon advised? Does the physical and social evolution of the ant cast any light on the probable direction of our own development?

His book is full of strange and – from the point of view of the ordinary, insect-hating person – rather horrible things. Some of the facts which he casually mentions are stranger than anything in human society – stranger in the sense that the institutions of ants are so much more various and more fully developed. For example, whereas man has domesticated perhaps fifty species of birds and animals, ants have domesticated some three thousand species of insects. Then, again, there is the extraordinary differentiation of function in ants, showing itself not only in the division into sexed and sexless types, but most sensationally of all in the variation in size. Sometimes, in the same nest, the queen or soldier may be several hundred times the bulk of the ordinary worker. These creatures, having the same size-relation to one another as a dog and a mouse, co-operate in apparent amity, each being perfectly specialised for its own job. Thus, the famous "parasol" ants live by cultivating a species of fungus which they grow in a compost of chewed leaves. The cutting and carrying of the leaves is done by relatively large ants, but the gardens are attended to by tiny "minims."

There are grain-storing ants, whose hoards have sometimes been so large as to become the subject of human litigation, carnivorous ants, slave-making ants – these have perhaps the most astonishing habits of all – and there are also exceptionally adaptable ants which appear to have changed their way of life in a quite short space of time and replaced more conservative species over large areas of the earth. But there are strange gaps in the horrible efficiency of the ants, and one of these is their toleration of parasites. Apart from the many kinds of aphid which the ants keep as "cows," there are other insects which manage to live a robber existence inside their nests, and others which are apparently kept as pets possibly because they give off a pleasant smell. Sometimes these become so numerous that the whole economy of the nest is upset and the ants die off together with their guests.

Dr. Haskins comes to no definite conclusions as to whether we can or cannot anticipate our own development by observing that of the ants; but he is inclined to consider that, so far as ants go, totalitarianism represents an advance on democracy. The more primitive, less successful ants are comparatively democratic in their social structure, whereas the wonderfully organised communities of the more highly-developed species have much in common with both Fascism and Communism. But it remains true, as he admits throughout, that ants are individually so different from ourselves as to make any comparison only doubtfully valid. Ants live in a different world from ourselves, and it is questionable whether they are conscious, as we understand consciousness. Each ant comes out of its cocoon knowing what it needs to know, and then, without any attempt at independent activity, repeats a pattern which in some cases has been repeated for millions of years. Sometimes the stupidity revealed is almost unbelievable. Take the habits of the parasitic ant, *Bothriomyrmex decapitans*: —

> Shortly after having gained entry into populous formicaries of the host colony, the queens of this species seek out the brood mothers of the communities, considerably larger than themselves. Mounting the backs of the rightful owners, the *Bothriomyrmex* females spend the next several days in sawing off, from the top, the heads of these brood queens. As soon as the heads drop, the impostors are adopted by their foster-workers.

Similar manoeuvres are attempted in human politics, but they are not tolerated so easily, and it is difficult not to feel that we have more control over our own destiny than even the most gifted kinds of ant. Still, when one considers their boldness, their fecundity, their power of living in almost any climate and on almost any kind of food, and above all their unquestioning loyalty to their own kind, one is left thinking that it is a good job that ants are not larger.

Why I Write
Gangrel, [No. 4, Summer] 1946

From a very early age, perhaps the age of five or six, I knew that when I grew up I should be a writer. Between the ages of about seventeen and twenty-four I tried to abandon this idea, but I did so with the consciousness that I was outraging my true nature and that sooner or later I should have to settle down and write books.

I was the middle child of three, but there was a gap of five years on either side, and I barely saw my father before I was eight. For this and other reasons I was somewhat lonely, and I soon developed disagreeable mannerisms which made me unpopular throughout my schooldays. I had the lonely child's habit of making up stories and holding conversations with imaginary persons, and I think from the very start my literary ambitions were mixed up with the feeling of being isolated and undervalued. I knew that I had a facility with words and a power of facing unpleasant facts, and I felt that this created a sort of private world in which I could get my own back for my failure in everyday life. Nevertheless the volume of serious – i.e. seriously intended – writing which I produced all through my childhood and boyhood would not amount to half a dozen pages. I wrote my first poem at the age of four or five, my mother taking it down to dictation. I cannot remember anything about it except that it was about a tiger and the tiger had 'chair-like teeth' – a good enough phrase, but I fancy the poem was a plagiarism of Blake's 'Tiger, Tiger'. At eleven, when the war of 1914–18 broke out, I wrote a patriotic poem which was printed in the local newspaper, as was another, two years later, on the death of Kitchener. From time to time, when I was bit older, I wrote bad and usually unfinished 'nature poems' in the Georgian style. I also, about twice, attempted a short story which was a ghastly failure. That was the total of the would-be serious work that I actually set down on paper during all those years.

However, throughout this time I did in a sense engage in literary activities. To begin with there was the made-to-order stuff which I produced quickly, easily and without much pleasure to myself. Apart from school work, I wrote *vers d'occasion*, semi-comic poems which I could turn out at what now seems to me astonishing speed – at fourteen I wrote a whole rhyming play, in imitation of Aristophanes, in about a week – and helped to edit school magazines, both printed and in manuscript. These magazines were the most pitiful burlesque stuff that you could imagine, and I took far less trouble with them than I now would with the cheapest journalism. But side by side with all this, for fifteen years or more, I was carrying out a literary exercise of a quite different kind: this was the making up of a continuous 'story' about myself, a sort of diary existing only in the mind. I believe this is a common habit of children and adolescents. As a very small child I used to imagine that I was, say, Robin Hood and picture myself as the hero of thrilling adventures, but quite soon my 'story' ceased to be narcissistic in a crude way and became more and more a mere description of what I was doing and the things I saw. For minutes at a time this kind of thing would be running through my head: 'He pushed the door open and entered the room. A yellow beam of sunlight, filtering through the muslin curtains, slanted on to the table, where a matchbox, half open, lay beside the inkpot. With his right hand in his pocket he moved across to the window. Down in the street a tortoiseshell cat was chasing a dead leaf,' etc., etc. This habit continued till I was about twenty-five, right through my non-literary years. Although I had to search, and did search, for the right words, I seemed to be making this descriptive effort almost against my will, under a kind of compulsion from outside. The 'story' must, I suppose, have reflected the styles of the various writers I admired at different ages, but so far as I remember it always had the same meticulous descriptive quality.

When I was about sixteen I suddenly discovered the joy of mere words, i.e. the sounds and associations of words. The lines from *Paradise Lost* –

> *So hee with difficulty and labour hard*
> *Moved on: with difficulty and labour hee,*

which do not now seem to me so very wonderful, sent shivers down my backbone; and the spelling 'hee' for 'he' was an added pleasure. As for the need to describe things, I knew all about it already. So it is clear what kind of books I wanted to write, in so far as I could be said to want to write books at that time. I wanted to write enormous naturalistic novels with unhappy endings, full of detailed descriptions and arresting similes, and also full of purple passages in which words were used partly for the sake of their sound. And in fact my first completed novel, *Burmese Days*, which I wrote when I was thirty but projected much earlier, is rather that kind of book.

I give all this background information because I do not think one can assess a writer's motives without knowing something of his early development. His subject-matter will be determined by the age he lives in – at least this is true in tumultuous, revolutionary ages like our own – but before he ever begins to write he will have acquired an emotional attitude from which he will never completely escape. It is his job, no doubt, to discipline his temperament and avoid getting stuck at some immature stage, or in some perverse mood: but if he escapes from his early influences altogether, he will have killed his impulse to write. Putting aside the need to earn a living, I think there are four great motives for writing, at any rate for writing prose. They exist in different degrees in every writer, and in any one writer the proportions will vary from time to time, according to the atmosphere in which he is living. They are:

(i) Sheer egoism. Desire to seem clever, to be talked about, to be remembered after death, to get your own back on grown-ups who snubbed you in childhood, etc., etc. It is humbug to pretend that this is not a motive, and a strong one. Writers share this characteristic with scientists, artists, politicians, lawyers, soldiers, successful business men – in short, with the whole top crust of humanity. The great mass of human beings are not acutely selfish. After the age of about thirty they abandon individual ambition – in many cases, indeed, they almost abandon the sense of being individuals at all – and live chiefly for others, or are simply smothered under drudgery. But there is also the minority of gifted, wilful people who are determined to live their own lives to the end, and writers belong in this class. Serious writers, I should say, are on the whole more vain and self-centred than journalists, though less interested in money.

(ii) Aesthetic enthusiasm. Perception of beauty in the external world, or, on the other hand, in words and their right arrangement. Pleasure in the impact of one sound on another, in the firmness of good prose or the rhythm of a good story. Desire to share an experience which one feels is valuable and ought not to be missed. The aesthetic motive is very feeble in a lot of writers, but even a pamphleteer or a writer of textbooks will have pet words and phrases which appeal to him for non-utilitarian reasons; or he may feel strongly about typography, width of margins, etc. Above the level of a railway guide, no book is quite free from æsthetic considerations.

(iii) Historical impulse. Desire to see things as they are, to find out true facts and store them up for the use of posterity.

(iv) Political purpose – using the word 'political' in the widest possible sense. Desire to push the world in a certain direction, to alter other people's idea of the kind of society that they should strive after. Once again, no book is genuinely free from political bias. The opinion that art should have nothing to do with politics is itself a political attitude.

It can be seen how these various impulses must war against one another, and how they must fluctuate from person to person and from time to time. By nature – taking your 'nature' to be the state you have attained when you are first adult – I am a person in whom the first three motives would outweigh the fourth. In a peaceful age I might have written ornate or merely descriptive books, and might have remained almost unaware of my political loyalties. As it is I have been forced into becoming a sort of pamphleteer. First I spent five years in an unsuitable profession (the Indian Imperial Police, in Burma), and then I underwent poverty and the sense of failure. This increased my natural hatred of authority and made me for the first time fully aware of the existence of the working classes, and the job in Burma had given me some understanding of the nature of imperialism: but these experiences were not enough to give me an accurate political orientation. Then came Hitler, the Spanish civil war, etc. By the end of 1935 I had still failed to reach a firm decision. I remember the last three stanzas of a little poem that I wrote at that date, expressing my dilemma:

> I am the worm who never turned,
> The eunuch without a harem;
> Between the priest and the commissar
> I walk like Eugene Aram;

> And the commissar is telling my fortune
> While the radio plays,
> But the priest has promised an Austin Seven,
> For Duggie always pays.

> I dreamed I dwelt in marble halls,
> And woke to find it true;
> I wasn't born for an age like this;
> Was Smith? Was Jones? Were you?

The Spanish war and other events in 1936–37 turned the scale and thereafter I knew where I stood. Every line of serious work that I have written since 1936 has been written, directly or indirectly, *against* totalitarianism and *for* democratic Socialism, as I understand it. It seems to me nonsense, in a period like our own, to think that one can avoid writing of such subjects. Everyone writes of them in one guise or another. It is simply a question of which side one takes and what approach one follows. And the more one is conscious of one's political bias, the more chance one has of acting politically without sacrificing one's aesthetic and intellectual integrity.

What I have most wanted to do throughout the past ten years is to make political writing into an art. My starting point is always a feeling of partisanship, a sense of injustice. When I sit down to write a book, I do not say to myself, 'I am going to produce a work of art'. I write it because there is some lie that I want to expose, some fact to which I want to draw attention, and my initial concern is to get a hearing. But I could not do the work of writing a book, or even a long magazine article, if it were not also an aesthetic experience. Anyone who cares to examine my work will see that even when it is downright propaganda it contains much that a full-time politician would consider irrelevant. I am not able, and I do not want, completely to abandon the world-view that I acquired in childhood. So long as I remain alive and well I shall continue to feel strongly about prose style, to love the surface of the earth, and to take a pleasure in solid objects and scraps of useless information. It is no use trying to suppress that side of myself. The job is to reconcile my ingrained likes and dislikes with the essentially public, non-individual activities that this age forces on all of us.

It is not easy. It raises problems of construction and of language, and it raises in a new way the problem of truthfulness. Let me give just one example of the cruder kind of difficulty that arises. My book about the Spanish civil war, *Homage to Catalonia*, is, of course, a frankly political book, but in the main it is written with a certain detachment and regard for form. I did try very hard in it to tell the whole truth without violating my literary instincts. But among other things it contains a long chapter, full of newspaper quotations and the like, defending the Trotskyists who were accused of plotting with Franco. Clearly such a chapter, which after a year or two would lose its interest for any ordinary reader, must ruin the book. A critic whom I respect read me a lecture about it. 'Why did you put in all that stuff?' he said. 'You've turned what might have been a good book into journalism.' What he said was true, but I could not have done otherwise. I happened to know, what very few people in England had been allowed to know, that innocent men were being falsely accused. If I had not been angry about that I should never have written the book.

In one form or another this problem comes up again. The problem of language is subtler and would take too long to discuss. I will only say that of late years I have tried to write less picturesquely and more exactly. In any case I find that by the time you have perfected any style of writing, you have always outgrown it. *Animal Farm* was the first book in which I tried, with full consciousness of what I was doing, to fuse political purpose and artistic purpose into one whole. I have not written a novel for seven years, but I hope to write another fairly soon. It is bound to be a failure, every book is a failure, but I do know with some clarity what kind of book I want to write.

Looking back through the last page or two, I see that I have made it appear as though my motives in writing were wholly public-spirited. I don't want to leave that as the final impression. All writers are vain, selfish and lazy, and at the very bottom of their motives there lies a mystery. Writing a book is a horrible, exhausting struggle, like a long bout of some painful illness. One would never undertake such a thing if one were not driven on by some demon whom one can neither resist or understand. For all one knows that demon is simply the same instinct that makes a baby squall for attention. And yet it is also true that one can write nothing readable unless one constantly struggles to efface one's own personality. Good prose is like a window pane. I cannot say with certainty which of my motives are the strongest, but I know which of them deserve to be followed. And looking back through my work, I see that it is invariably where I lacked a *political* purpose that I wrote lifeless books and was betrayed into purple passages, sentences without meaning, decorative adjectives and humbug generally.

GEORGE ORWELL

The Cost of Letters
Horizon, September 1946

George Orwell's answers to a questionnaire on "The Cost of Letters" in *Horizon*, September 1946, in which several writers were asked:

1. How much do you think a writer needs to live on?
2. Do you think a serious writer can earn this sum by his writing, and if so, how?
3. If not, what do you think is the most suitable second occupation for him?
4. Do you think literature suffers from the diversion of a writer's energy into other employments or is enriched by it?
5. Do you think the State or any other institution should do more for writers?
6. Are you satisfied with your own solution of the problem and have you any specific advice to give to young people who wish to earn their living by writing?

1. At the present purchasing value of money, I think £10 a week after payment of income tax is a minimum for a married man, and perhaps £6 a week for an unmarried man. The *best* income for a writer, I should say – again at the present value of money – is about £1,000 a year. With that he can live in reasonable comfort, free from duns and the necessity to do hackwork, without having the feeling that he has definitely moved into the privileged class. I do not think one can with justice expect a writer to do his best on a working-class income. His first necessity, just as indispensable to him as are tools to a carpenter, is a comfortable, well-warmed room where he can be sure of not being interrupted; and, although this does not sound much, if one works out what it means in terms of domestic arrangements, it implies fairly large earnings. A writer's work is done at home, and if he lets it happen he will be subjected to almost constant interruption. To be protected against interruption always costs money, directly or indirectly. Then again, writers need books and periodicals in great numbers, they need space and furniture for filing papers, they spend a great deal on correspondence, they need at any rate part-time secretarial help, and most of them probably benefit by travelling, by living in what they consider sympa-

thetic surroundings, and by eating and drinking the things they like best and by being able to take their friends out to meals or have them to stay. It all costs money. Ideally I would like to see every human being have the same income, provided that it were a fairly high income: but so long as there is to be differentiation, I think the writer's place is in the middle bracket, which means, at present standards, round about £1,000 a year.

2. No. I am told that at most a few hundred people in Great Britain earn their living solely by writing books, and most of those are probably writers of detective stories, etc. In a way it is easier for people like Ethel M. Dell to avoid prostitution than it is for a serious writer.

3. If it can be so arranged as not to take up the whole of his time, I think a writer's second occupation should be something non-literary. I suppose it would be better if it were also something congenial. But I can just imagine, for instance, a bank clerk or an insurance agent going home and doing serious work in his evenings; whereas the effort is too much to make if one has already squandered one's energies on semi-creative work such as teaching, broadcasting or composing propaganda for bodies such as the British Council.

4. Provided one's whole time and energies are not used up, I think it benefits. After all, one must make some sort of contact with the ordinary world. Otherwise, what is one to write about?

5. The only thing the State could usefully do is to divert more of the public money into buying books for the public libraries. If we are to have full Socialism, then clearly the writer must be State-supported, and ought to be placed among the better-paid groups. But so long as we have an economy like the present one, in which there is a great deal of State enterprise but also large areas of private capitalism, then the less truck a writer has with the State, or any other organized body, the better for him and his work. There are invariably strings tied to any kind of organized patronage. On the other hand, the old kind of private patronage, in which the writer is in effect the dependant of some individual rich man, is obviously undesirable. By far the best and least exacting patron is the big public. Unfortunately the British public won't at present spend money

on books, although it reads more and more and its average of taste, I should say, has risen greatly in the last twenty years. At present, I believe, the average British citizen spends round about £1 a year on books, whereas he spends getting on for £25 on tobacco and alcohol combined. Via the rates and taxes he could easily be made to spend more without even knowing it – as, during the war years, he spent far more than usual on radio, owing to the subsidizing of the B.B.C. by the Treasury. If the Government could be induced simply to earmark larger sums for the purchase of books, without in the process taking over the whole book trade and turning it into a propaganda machine, I think the writer's position would be eased and literature might also benefit.

6. Personally I am satisfied, i.e. in a financial sense, because I have been lucky, at any rate during the last few years. I had to struggle desperately at the beginning, and if I had listened to what people said to me I would never have been a writer. Even until quite recently, whenever I have written anything which I took seriously, there have been strenuous efforts, sometimes by quite influential people, to keep it out of print. To a young writer who is conscious of having something in him, the only advice I can give is not to take advice. Financially, of course, there are tips I could give, but even those are of no use unless one has some kind of talent. If one simply wants to make a living by putting words on paper, then the B.B.C., the film companies, and the like are reasonably helpful. But if one wants to be primarily a *writer*, then, in our society, one is an animal that is tolerated but not encouraged – something rather like a house sparrow – and one gets on better if one realizes one's position from the start.

Politics vs. Literature: An Examination of *Gulliver's Travels*

Polemic 5, September–October 1946

In *Gulliver's Travels* humanity is attacked, or criticised, from at least three different angles, and the implied character of Gulliver himself necessarily changes somewhat in the process.

In Part I he is the typical eighteenth-century voyager, bold, practical and unromantic, his homely outlook skilfully impressed on the reader by the biographical details at the beginning, by his age (he is a man of forty, with two children, when his adventures start), and by the inventory of the things in his pockets, especially his spectacles, which make several appearances. In Part II he has in general the same character, but at moments when the story demands it he has a tendency to develop into an imbecile who is capable of boasting of 'our noble Country, the Mistress of Arts and Arms, the Scourge of France', etc., etc., and at the same time of betraying every available scandalous fact about the country which he professes to love. In Part III he is much as he was in Part I, though, as he is consorting chiefly with courtiers and men of learning, one has the impression that he has risen in the social scale. In Part IV he conceives a horror of the human race which is not apparent, or only intermittently apparent, in the earlier books, and changes into a sort of unreligious anchorite whose one desire is to live in some desolate spot where he can devote himself to meditating on the goodness of the Houyhnhnms. However, these inconsistencies are forced upon Swift by the fact that Gulliver is there chiefly to provide a contrast. It is necessary, for instance, that he should appear sensible in Part I and at least intermittently silly in Part II, because in both books the essential manoeuvre is the same, i.e. to make the human being look ridiculous by imagining him as a creature six inches high. Whenever Gulliver is not acting as a stooge there is a sort of continuity in his character, which comes out especially in his resourcefulness and his observation of physical detail. He is much the same kind of person, with the same prose style, when he bears off the warships of Blefuscu, when he rips open the belly of the monstrous rat, and when he sails away upon the ocean in his frail coracle made from the skins of Yahoos. Moreover, it is difficult not to feel that in his shrewder moments Gulliver is simply Swift himself, and there is at least one incident in which Swift seems to be venting his private grievance against contemporary Society. It will be remembered that when the Emperor of Lilliput's palace catches fire, Gulliver puts it out by urinating on it. Instead of being congratulated on his presence of mind, he finds that he has committed a capital offence by making water in the precincts of the palace, and

> I was privately assured, that the Empress, conceiving the greatest Abhorrence of what I had done, removed to the most distant Side of the Court, firmly resolved that those buildings should never be repaired for her Use; and, in the Presence of her chief Confidents, could not forbear vowing Revenge.

According to Professor G. M. Trevelyan (*England under Queen Anne*), part of the reason for Swift's failure to get preferment was that the Queen was scandalised by the *Tale of a Tub* – a pamphlet in which Swift probably felt that he had done a great service to the English Crown, since it scarifies the Dissenters and still more the Catholics while leaving the Established Church alone. In any case no one would deny that *Gulliver's Travels* is a rancorous as well as a pessimistic book, and that especially in Parts I and III it often descends into political partisanship of a narrow kind. Pettiness and magnanimity, republicanism and authoritarianism, love of reason and lack of curiosity, are all mixed up in it. The hatred of the human body with which Swift is especially associated is only dominant in Part IV, but somehow this new preoccupation does not come as a surprise. One feels that all these adventures, and all these changes of mood, could have happened to the same person, and the inter-connection between Swift's political loyalties and his ultimate despair is one of the most interesting features of the book.

Politically, Swift was one of those people who are driven into a sort of perverse Toryism by the follies of the progressive party of the moment. Part I of *Gulliver's Travels*, ostensibly a satire on human greatness, can be seen, if one looks a little deeper, to be simply an attack on England, on the dominant Whig party, and on the war with France, which – however bad the motives of the Allies may have been – did save Europe from being tyrannised over by a single reactionary power. Swift was not a Jacobite nor strictly speaking a Tory, and his declared aim in the war was merely a moderate peace treaty and not the outright defeat of England. Nevertheless there is a tinge of quislingism in his attitude, which comes out in the ending of Part I and slightly interferes with the allegory. When Gulliver flees from Lilliput (England) to Blefuscu (France) the assumption that a human being six inches high is inherently contemptible seems to be dropped. Whereas the people of Lilliput have behaved towards Gulliver with the utmost treachery and meanness, those of Blefuscu behave generously and straightforwardly, and indeed this section of the book ends on a different note from the all-round disillusionment of the earlier chapters. Evidently Swift's animus is, in the first place, against *England*. It is 'your Natives' (i.e. Gulliver's fellow-countrymen) whom the King of Brobdingnag considers to be 'the most pernicious Race of little odious Vermin that Nature ever suffered to crawl upon the surface of the Earth', and the long passage at the end, denouncing colonisation and foreign conquest, is plainly aimed at England, although the contrary is elaborately stated. The Dutch, England's allies and target of one of Swift's most famous pamphlets, are also more or less wantonly attacked in Part III. There is even what sounds like a personal note in the passage in which Gulliver records his satisfaction that the various countries he has discovered cannot be made colonies of the British Crown:

> The *Houyhnhnms*, indeed, appear not to be so well prepared for War, a Science to which they are perfect Strangers, and especially against missive Weapons. However, supposing myself to be a Minister of State, I could never give my advice for invading them. . . . Imagine twenty thousand of them breaking into the midst of an *European* army, confounding the Ranks, overturning the Carriages, battering the Warriors' Faces into Mummy, by terrible Yerks from their hinder Hoofs . . .

Considering that Swift does not waste words, that phrase, 'battering the warriors' faces into mummy', probably indicates a secret wish to see the invincible armies of the Duke of Marlborough treated in a like manner. There are similar touches elsewhere. Even the country mentioned in Part III, where 'the Bulk of the People consist, in a Manner, wholly of Discoverers, Witnesses, Informers, Accusers, Prosecutors, Evidences, Swearers, together with their several subservient and

GEORGE ORWELL

subaltern Instruments, all under the Colours, the Conduct, and
Pay of Ministers of State', is called Langdon, which is within
one letter of being an anagram of England. (As the early
editions of the book contain misprints, it may perhaps have
been intended as a complete anagram.) Swift's *physical* repulsion from humanity is certainly real enough, but one has the
feeling that his debunking of human grandeur, his diatribes
against lords, politicians, court favourites, etc., has mainly a
local application and springs from the fact that he belonged to
the unsuccessful party. He denounces injustice and oppression,
but he gives no evidence of liking democracy. In spite of his
enormously greater powers, his implied position is very similar
to that of the innumerable silly-clever Conservatives of our
own day – people like Sir Alan Herbert, Professor G. M.
Young, Lord Elton, the Tory Reform Committee or the
long line of Catholic apologists from W. H. Mallock onwards:
people who specialise in cracking neat jokes at the expense of
whatever is 'modern' and 'progressive', and whose opinions
are often all the more extreme because they know that they
cannot influence the actual drift of events. After all, such a
pamphlet as *An Argument to prove that the Abolishing of Christianity*, etc. is very like 'Timothy Shy' having a bit of clean fun with
the Brains Trust, or Father Ronald Knox exposing the errors of
Bertrand Russell. And the ease with which Swift has been
forgiven – and forgiven, sometimes, by devout believers – for
the blasphemies of *A Tale of a Tub* demonstrates clearly enough
the feebleness of religious sentiments as compared with political ones.

However, the reactionary cast of Swift's mind does not
show itself chiefly in his political affiliations. The important
thing is his attitude towards Science, and, more broadly, towards intellectual curiosity. The famous Academy of Lagado,
described in Part III of *Gulliver's Travels*, is no doubt a justified
satire on most of the so-called scientists of Swift's own day.
Significantly, the people at work in it are described as 'Projectors', that is, people not engaged in disinterested research but
merely on the look-out for gadgets which will save labour and
bring in money. But there is no sign – indeed, all through the
book there are many signs to the contrary – that 'pure' science
would have struck Swift as a worth-while activity. The more

serious kind of scientist has already had a kick in the pants in Part II, when the 'Scholars' patronised by the King of Brobdingnag try to account for Gulliver's small stature:

> After much Debate, they concluded unanimously that I was only *Relplum Scalcath*, which is interpreted literally, *Lusus Naturae*; a Determination exactly agreeable to the modern philosophy of *Europe*, whose Professors, disdaining the old Evasion of *occult Causes*, whereby the followers of *Aristotle* endeavoured in vain to disguise their Ignorance, have invented this wonderful Solution of all Difficulties, to the unspeakable Advancement of human Knowledge.

If this stood by itself one might assume that Swift is merely the enemy of *sham* science. In a number of places, however, he goes out of his way to proclaim the uselessness of all learning or speculation not directed towards some practical end:

> The Learning of (the Brobdingnagians) is very defective, consisting only in Morality, History, Poetry, and Mathematics, wherein they must be allowed to excel. But, the last of these is wholly applied to what may be useful in Life, to the Improvement of Agriculture, and all mechanical Arts; so that among us it would be little esteemed. And as to Ideas, Entities, Abstractions, and Transcendentals, I could never drive the least Conception into their Heads.

The Houyhnhnms, Swift's ideal beings, are backward even in a mechanical sense. They are unacquainted with metals, have never heard of boats, do not, properly speaking, practise agriculture (we are told that the oats which they live upon 'grow naturally'), and appear not to have invented wheels.[33] They have no alphabet, and evidently have not much curiosity about the physical world. They do not believe that any inhabited country exists beside their own, and though they understand the motions of the sun and moon, and the nature of eclipses, 'this is the utmost Progress of their *Astronomy*'. By contrast, the philosophers of the flying island of Laputa are so continuously absorbed in mathematical speculations that before speaking to them one has to attract their attention by flapping them on the ear with a bladder. They have catalogued ten thousand fixed stars, have settled the periods of ninety-three comets, and have discovered, in advance of the astronomers of Europe, that Mars has two moons – all of which information Swift evidently regards as ridiculous, useless and uninteresting. As one might expect, he believes that the scientist's place, if he has a place, is in the laboratory and that scientific knowledge has no bearing on political matters:

> What I . . . thought altogether unaccountable, was the strong Disposition I observed in them towards News and Politics, perpetually enquiring into Public Affairs, giving their judgments in Matters of State, and passionately disputing every Inch of a Party Opinion. I have, indeed, observed the same Disposition among most of the Mathematicians I have known in *Europe*, though I could never discover the least Analogy between the two Sciences; unless those People suppose, that, because the smallest Circle hath as many Degrees as the largest, therefore the Regulation and Management of the World require no more Abilities, than the Handling and Turning of a Globe.

Is there not something familiar in that phrase 'I could never discover the least analogy between the two sciences'? It has precisely the note of the popular Catholic apologists who profess to be astonished when a scientist utters an opinion on such questions as the existence of God or the immortality of the soul. The scientist, we are told, is an expert only in one restricted field: why should his opinions be of value in any other? The implication is that theology is just as much an exact science as, for instance, chemistry, and that the priest is also an expert whose conclusions on certain subjects must be accepted. Swift in effect makes the same claim for the politician, but he goes one better in that he will not allow the scientist – either the 'pure' scientist or the *ad-hoc* investigator – to be a useful person in his own line. Even if he had not written Part III of *Gulliver's Travels*, one could infer from the rest of the book that, like Tolstoy and like Blake, he hates the very idea of studying the processes of Nature. The 'Reason' which he so admires in the Houyhnhnms does not primarily mean the power of drawing logical inferences from observed facts. Although he never defines it, it appears in most contexts to mean either common sense – i.e. acceptance of the obvious and contempt for quibbles and abstractions – or absence of passion and superstition. In general he assumes that we know all that we need to know already, and merely use our knowledge incorrectly. Medicine, for instance, is a useless science, because if we lived in a more natural way, there would be no diseases. Swift, however, is not a simple-lifer or an admirer of the Noble Savage. He is in favour of civilisation and the arts of civilisation. Not only does he see the value of good manners, good conversation, and even learning of a literary and historical kind, he also sees that agriculture, navigation and architecture need to be studied and could with advantage be improved. But his implied aim is a static, incurious civilisation – the world of his own day, a little cleaner, a little saner, with no radical change and no poking into the unknowable. More than one would expect in any-one so free from accepted fallacies, he reveres the past, especially classical antiquity, and believes that modern man has degenerated sharply during the past hundred years.[34] In the island of sorcerers, where the spirits of the dead can be called up at will:

> I desired that the Senate of *Rome* might appear before me in one large Chamber, and a modern Representative in Counterview, in another. The first seemed to be an Assembly of Heroes and Demy-Gods, the other a Knot of Pedlars, Pickpockets, Highwaymen, and Bullies.

Although Swift uses this section of Part III to attack the truthfulness of recorded history, his critical spirit deserts him as soon as he is dealing with Greeks and Romans. He remarks, of course, upon the corruption of imperial Rome, but he has an almost unreasoning admiration for some of the leading figures of the ancient world:

> I was struck with profound Veneration at the Sight of *Brutus*, and could easily discover the most consummate Virtue, the greatest Intrepidity and Firmness of Mind, the truest Love of his Country, and general Benevolence for mankind, in every Lineament of his Countenance. . . . I had the Honour to have much Conversation with *Brutus*, and was told, that his Ancestor *Junius*, *Socrates*, *Epaminondas*, *Cato* the younger,

Sir Thomas More, and himself, were perpetually together: a *Sextumvirate*, to which all the Ages of the World cannot add a seventh.

It will be noticed that of these six people, only one is a Christian. This is an important point. If one adds together Swift's pessimism, his reverence for the past, his incuriosity and his horror of the human body, one arrives at an attitude common among religious reactionaries – that is, people who defend an unjust order of Society by claiming that this world cannot be substantially improved and only the 'next world' matters. However, Swift shows no sign of having any religious beliefs, at least in any ordinary sense of the words. He does not appear to believe seriously in life after death, and his idea of goodness is bound up with republicanism, love of liberty, courage, 'benevolence' (meaning in effect public spirit), 'reason' and other pagan qualities. This reminds one that there is another strain in Swift, not quite congruous with his disbelief in progress and his general hatred of humanity.

To begin with, he has moments when he is 'constructive' and even 'advanced'. To be occasionally inconsistent is almost a mark of vitality in Utopia books, and Swift sometimes inserts a word of praise into a passage that ought to be purely satirical. Thus, his ideas about the education of the young are fathered on to the Lilliputians, who have much the same views on this subject as the Houyhnhnms. The Lilliputians also have various social and legal institutions (for instance, there are old age pensions, and people are rewarded for keeping the law as well as punished for breaking it) which Swift would have liked to see prevailing in his own country. In the middle of this passage Swift remembers his satirical intention and adds, 'In relating these and the following Laws, I would only be understood to mean the original Institutions, and not the most scandalous Corruptions into which these people are fallen by the degenerate Nature of Man': but as Lilliput is supposed to represent England, and the laws he is speaking of have never had their parallel in England, it is clear that the impulse to make constructive suggestions has been too much for him. But Swift's greatest contribution to political thought, in the narrower sense of the words, is his attack, especially in Part III, on what would now be called totalitarianism. He has an extraordinarily clear prevision of the spy-haunted 'police State', with its endless heresy-hunts and treason trials, all really designed to neutralise popular discontent by changing it into war hysteria. And one must remember that Swift is here inferring the whole from a quite small part, for the feeble governments of his own day did not give him illustrations ready-made. For example, there is the professor at the School of Political Projectors who 'shewed me a large Paper of Instructions for discovering Plots and Conspiracies', and who claimed that one can find people's secret thoughts by examining their excrement:

> Because Men are never so serious, thoughtful, and intent, as when they are at Stool, which he found by frequent Experiment: for in such Conjunctures, when he used meerly as a Trial to consider what was the best Way of murdering the King, his Ordure would have a Tincture of Green; but quite different when he thought only of raising an Insurrection, or burning the Metropolis.

The professor and his theory are said to have been suggested to Swift by the – from our point of view – not particularly astonishing or disgusting fact that in a recent State trial some letters found in somebody's privy had been put in evidence. Later in the same chapter we seem to be positively in the middle of the Russian purges:

> In the Kingdom of Tribnia, by the Natives called Langdon . . . the Bulk of the People consist, in a Manner, wholly of Discoverers, Witnesses, Informers, Accusers, Prosecutors, Evidences, Swearers. . . . It is first agreed, and settled among them, what suspected Persons shall be accused of a Plot: Then, effectual Care is taken to secure all their Letters and Papers, and put the Owners in Chains. These papers are delivered to a Sett of Artists, very dexterous in finding out the mysterious Meanings of Words, Syllables, and Letters. . . . Where this Method fails, they have two others more effectual, which the Learned among them call *Acrostics* and *Anagrams*. *First*, they can decypher all initial Letters into political Meanings: Thus, N shall signify a Plot, B a

Regiment of Horse, L a Fleet at Sea: Or, *Secondly*, by transposing the Letters of the Alphabet in any suspected Paper, they can lay open the deepest Designs of a discontented Party. So, for Example, if I should say in a Letter to a Friend, *Our Brother Tom has just got the Piles*, a skilful Decypherer would discover that the same Letters, which compose that Sentence, may be analysed in the following Words: *Resist – a Plot is brought Home – The Tour*. And this is the anagrammatic Method.

Other professors at the same school invent simplified languages, write books by machinery, educate their pupils by inscribing the lesson on a wafer and causing them to swallow it, or propose to abolish individuality altogether by cutting off part of the brain of one man and grafting it on to the head of another. There is something queerly familiar in the atmosphere of these chapters, because, mixed up with much fooling, there is a perception that one of the aims of totalitarianism is not merely to make sure that people will think the right thoughts, but actually to make them *less conscious*. Then, again, Swift's account of the Leader who is usually to be found ruling over a tribe of Yahoos, and of the 'favourite' who acts first as a dirtyworker and later as a scapegoat, fits remarkably well into the pattern of our own times. But are we to infer from all this that Swift was first and foremost an enemy of tyranny and a champion of the free intelligence? No: his own views, so far as one can discern them, are not markedly liberal. No doubt he hates lords, kings, bishops, generals, ladies of fashion, orders, titles and flummery generally, but he does not seem to think better of the common people than of their rulers, or to be in favour of increased social equality, or to be enthusiastic about representative institutions. The Houyhnhnms are organised upon a sort of caste system which is racial in character, the horses which do the menial work being of different colours from their masters and not interbreeding with them. The educational system which Swift admires in the Lilliputians takes hereditary class distinctions for granted, and the children of the poorest class do not go to school, because 'their Business being only to till and cultivate the Earth...therefore their Education is of little Consequence to the Public'. Nor does he seem to have been strongly in favour of freedom of speech and the Press, in spite of the toleration which his own writings enjoyed. The King of Brobdingnag is astonished at the multiplicity of religious and political sects in England, and considers that those who hold 'opinions prejudicial to the public' (in the context this seems to mean simply heretical opinions), though they need not be obliged to change them, ought to be obliged to conceal them: for 'as it was Tyranny in any Government to require the first, so it was Weakness not to enforce the second'. There is a subtler indication of Swift's own attitude in the manner in which Gulliver leaves the land of the Houyhnhnms. Intermittently, at least, Swift was a kind of anarchist, and Part IV of *Gulliver's Travels* is a picture of an anarchistic Society, not governed by law in the ordinary sense, but by the dictates of 'Reason', which are voluntarily accepted by everyone. The General Assembly of the Houyhnhnms 'exhorts' Gulliver's master to get rid of him, and his neighbours put pressure on him to make him comply. Two reasons are given. One is that the presence of this unusual Yahoo may unsettle the rest of the tribe, and the other is that a friendly relationship between a Houyhnhnm and a Yahoo is 'not agreeable to Reason or Nature, or a Thing ever heard of before among them'. Gulliver's master is somewhat unwilling to obey, but the 'exhortation' (a Houyhnhnm, we are told, is never *compelled* to do anything, he is merely 'exhorted' or 'advised') cannot be disregarded. This illustrates very well the totalitarian tendency which is implicit in the anarchist or pacifist vision of Society. In a Society in which there is no law, and in theory no compulsion, the only arbiter of behaviour is public opinion. But public opinion, because of the tremendous urge to conformity in gregarious animals, is less tolerant than any system of law. When human beings are governed by 'thou shalt not', the individual can practise a certain amount of eccentricity: when they are supposedly governed by 'love' or 'reason', he is under continuous pressure to make him behave and think in exactly the same way as everyone else. The Houyhnhnms, we are told, were unanimous on almost all subjects. The only question they ever *discussed* was how to deal with the Yahoos. Otherwise there was no room for disagreement among them, because the truth is always either self-evident, or else it is undiscoverable and unimportant. They had apparently no word for 'opinion' in their language, and in their conversations there was no 'difference of sentiments'. They had reached, in fact, the highest stage of totalitarian organisation, the stage when conformity has become so general that there is no need for a police force. Swift approves of this kind of thing because among his many gifts neither curiosity nor good-nature was included. Disagreement would always seem to him sheer perversity. 'Reason,' among the Houyhnhnms, he says, 'is not a Point Problematical, as with us, where men can argue with Plausibility on both Sides of a Question; but strikes you with immediate Conviction; as it must needs do, where it is not mingled, obscured, or discoloured by Passion and Interest.' In other words, we know everything already, so why should dissident opinions be tolerated? The totalitarian Society of the Houyhnhnms, where there can be no freedom and no development, follows naturally from this.

We are right to think of Swift as a rebel and iconoclast, but except in certain secondary matters, such as his insistence that women should receive the same education as men, he cannot be labelled 'Left'. He is a Tory anarchist, despising authority while disbelieving in liberty, and preserving the aristocratic outlook while seeing clearly that the existing aristocracy is degenerate and contemptible. When Swift utters one of his characteristic diatribes against the rich and powerful, one must probably, as I said earlier, write off something for the fact that he himself belonged to the less successful party, and was personally disappointed. The 'outs', for obvious reasons, are always more radical than the 'ins'.[35] But the most essential thing in Swift is his inability to believe that life – ordinary life on the solid earth, and not some rationalised, deodorised version of it – could be made worth living. Of course, no honest person claims that happiness is *now* a normal condition among adult human beings; but perhaps it *could* be made normal, and it is upon this question that all serious political controversy really turns. Swift has much in common – more, I believe, than has been noticed – with Tolstoy, another disbeliever in the possibility of happiness. In both men you have the same anarchistic outlook covering an authoritarian cast of mind; in both a similar hostility to Science, the same impatience with opponents, the same inability to see the importance of any question not interesting to themselves; and in both cases a sort of horror of the actual process of life, though in Tolstoy's case it was arrived at later and in a different way. The sexual unhappiness of the two men was not of the same kind, but there was this in common, that in both of them a sincere loathing was mixed up with a morbid fascination. Tolstoy was a reformed rake who ended by preaching complete celibacy, while continuing to practise the opposite into extreme old age. Swift was presumably impotent, and had an exaggerated horror of human dung: he also thought about it incessantly, as is evident throughout his works. Such people are not likely to enjoy even the small amount of happiness that falls to most human beings, and, from obvious motives, are not likely to admit that earthly life is capable of much improvement. Their incuriosity, and hence their intolerance, spring from the same root.

Swift's disgust, rancour and pessimism would make sense against the background of a 'next world' to which this one is the prelude. As he does not appear to believe seriously in any such thing, it becomes necessary to construct a paradise supposedly existing on the surface of the earth, but something quite different from anything we know, with all that he disapproves of – lies, folly, change, enthusiasm, pleasure, love and dirt – eliminated from it. As his ideal being he chooses the horse, an animal whose excrement is not offensive. The Houyhnhnms are dreary beasts – this is so generally admitted that the point is not worth labouring. Swift's genius can make them credible, but there can have been very few readers in whom they have excited any feeling beyond dislike. And this is not from wounded vanity at seeing animals preferred to men; for, of the two, the Houyhnhnms are much liker to human beings than are the Yahoos, and Gulliver's horror of the Yahoos, together with his recognition that they are the same kind of creature as himself, contains a logical absurdity. This horror comes upon him at his very first sight of them. 'I never beheld,' he says, 'in all my Travels, so disagreeable an Animal, nor one against which I naturally conceived so strong an Antipathy.' But in comparison with what are the Yahoos disgusting? Not with the Houyhnhnms, because at this time Gulliver has not seen a Houyhnhnm. It can only be in comparison with himself, i.e. with a human being. Later, however, we are to be told that the Yahoos *are* human beings, and human society becomes insupportable to Gulliver because all men are Yahoos. In that case why did he not conceive his disgust of humanity earlier? In effect we are told that the Yahoos are fantastically different from men, and yet are the same. Swift has over-reached himself in his fury, and is shouting at his fellow-creatures: 'You are filthier than you are!' However, it is impossible to feel much sympathy with the Yahoos, and it is not because they oppress the Yahoos that the Houyhnhnms are unattractive. They are unattractive because the 'Reason' by which they are governed is really a desire for death. They are exempt from love, friendship, curiosity, fear, sorrow and – except in their feelings towards the Yahoos, who occupy rather the same place in their community as the Jews in Nazi Germany – anger and hatred. 'They have no Fondness for their Colts or Foles, but the Care they take, in educating them, proceeds entirely from the Dictates of *Reason*.' They lay store by 'Friendship' and 'Benevolence', but 'these are not confined to particular Objects, but universal to the whole Race'. They also value conversation, but in their conversations there are no differences of opinion, and 'nothing passed but what was useful, expressed in the fewest and most significant Words'. They practise strict birth control, each couple producing two offspring and thereafter abstaining from sexual intercourse. Their marriages are arranged for them by their elders, on eugenic principles, and their language contains no word for 'love', in the sexual sense. When somebody dies they carry on exactly as before, without feeling any grief. It will be seen that their aim is to be as like a corpse as is possible while retaining physical life. One or two of their characteristics, it is true, do not seem to be strictly 'reasonable' in their own usage of the word. Thus, they place a great value not only on physical hardihood but on athleticism, and they are devoted to poetry. But these exceptions may be less arbitrary than they seem. Swift probably emphasises the physical strength of the Houyhnhnms in order to make clear that they could never be conquered by the hated human race, while a taste for poetry may figure among their qualities because poetry appeared to Swift as the antithesis of Science, from his point of view the most useless of all pursuits. In Part III he names 'Imagination, Fancy, and Invention' as desirable faculties in which the Laputan mathematicians (in spite of their love of music) were wholly lacking. One must remember that although Swift was an admirable writer of comic verse, the kind of poetry he thought valuable would probably be didactic poetry. The poetry of the Houyhnhnms, he says –

> must be allowed to excel (that of) all other Mortals; wherein the Justness of their Similes, and the Minuteness, as well as exactness, of their Descriptions, are, indeed, inimitable. Their Verses abound very much in both of these; and usually contain either some exalted Notions of Friendship and Benevolence, or the Praises of those who were Victors in Races, and other bodily Exercises.

Alas, not even the genius of Swift was equal to producing a specimen by which we could judge the poetry of the Houyhnhnms. But it sounds as though it were chilly stuff (in heroic couplets, presumably), and not seriously in conflict with the principles of 'Reason'.

Happiness is notoriously difficult to describe, and pictures of a just and well-ordered Society are seldom either attractive or convincing. Most creators of 'favourable' Utopias, however, are concerned to show what life could be like if it were lived more fully. Swift advocates a simple refusal of life, justifying this by the claim that 'Reason' consists in thwarting your instincts. The Houyhnhnms, creatures without a history, continue for generation after generation to live prudently, maintaining their population at exactly the same level, avoiding all passion, suffering from no diseases, meeting death indifferently, training up their young in the same principles – and all for what? In order that the same process may continue indefinitely. The notions that life here and now is worth living, or that it could be made worth living, or that it must be sacrificed for some future good, are all absent. The dreary world of the Houyhnhnms was about as good a Utopia as Swift could construct, granting that he neither believed in a 'next world' nor could get any pleasure out of certain normal activities. But it is not really set up as something desirable in itself, but as the justification for another attack on humanity. The aim, as usual, is to humiliate Man by reminding him that he is weak and ridiculous, and above all that he stinks; and the ultimate motive, probably, is a kind of envy, the envy of the ghost for the living, of the man who knows he cannot be happy for the others who – so he fears – may be a little happier than himself. The political expression of such an outlook must be either reactionary or nihilistic, because the person who holds it will want to prevent Society from developing in some direction in which his pessimism may be cheated. One can do this either by blowing everything to pieces, or by averting social change. Swift ultimately blew everything to pieces in the only way that was feasible before the atomic bomb – that is, he went mad – but, as I have tried to show, his political aims were on the whole reactionary ones.

From what I have written it may have seemed that I am *against* Swift, and that my object is to refute him and even to belittle him. In a political and moral sense I am against him, so far as I understand him. Yet curiously enough he is one of the writers I admire with least reserve, and *Gulliver's Travels*, in particular, is a book which it seems impossible for me to grow tired of. I read it first when I was eight – one day short of eight, to be exact, for I stole and furtively read the copy which was to be given me next day on my eighth birthday – and I have certainly not read it less than half a dozen times since. Its fascination seems inexhaustible. If I had to make a list of six books which were to be preserved when all others were destroyed, I would certainly put *Gulliver's Travels* among them. This raises the question: what is the relationship between agreement with a writer's opinions, and enjoyment of his work?

If one is capable of intellectual detachment, one can *perceive* merit in a writer whom one deeply disagrees with, but *enjoyment* is a different matter. Supposing that there is such a thing as good or bad art, then the goodness or badness must reside in the work of art itself – not independently of the observer, indeed, but independently of the mood of the observer. In one sense, therefore, it cannot be true that a poem is good on Monday and bad on Tuesday. But if one judges the poem by the appreciation it arouses, then it can certainly be true, because appreciation, or enjoyment, is a subjective condition which cannot be commanded. For a great deal of his waking life, even the most cultivated person has no aesthetic feelings whatever, and the power to have aesthetic feelings is very easily destroyed. When you are frightened, or hungry, or are suffering from toothache or sea-sickness, *King Lear* is no better from your point of view than *Peter Pan*. You may know in an intellectual sense that it is better, but that is simply a fact which you remember: you will not *feel* the merit of *King Lear* until you are normal again. And aesthetic judgement can be upset just as disastrously – more disastrously, because the cause is less readily recognised – by political or moral disagreement. If a book angers, wounds or alarms you, then you will not enjoy it, whatever its merits may be. If it seems to you a really pernicious book, likely to influence other people in some undesirable way, then you will probably construct an aesthetic theory to show that it *has* no merits. Current literary criticism consists quite largely of this kind of dodging to and fro between two sets of standards. And yet the opposite process can also happen: enjoyment can overwhelm disapproval, even though one clearly recognises that one is enjoying something inimical. Swift, whose world-view is so peculiarly unacceptable, but who is nevertheless an extremely popular writer, is a good instance of this. Why is it that we don't mind being called Yahoos, although firmly convinced that we are *not* Yahoos?

It is not enough to make the usual answer that of course Swift was wrong, in fact he was insane, but he was 'a good writer'. It is true that the literary quality of a book is to some small extent separable from its subject-matter. Some people have a native gift for using words, as some people have a naturally 'good eye' at games. It is largely a question of timing and of instinctively knowing how much emphasis to use. As an example near at hand, look back at the passage I quoted earlier, starting 'In the Kingdom of Tribnia, by the Natives called Langdon'. It derives much of its force from the final sentence: 'And this is the anagrammatic Method.' Strictly speaking this sentence is unnecessary, for we have already seen the anagram deciphered, but the mock-solemn repetition, in which one seems to hear Swift's own voice uttering the words, drives home the idiocy of the activities described, like a final tap to a nail. But not all the power and simplicity of Swift's prose, nor the imaginative effort that has been able to make not one but a whole series of impossible worlds more credible than the majority of history books – none of this would enable us to enjoy Swift if his world-view were truly wounding or shocking. Millions of people, in many countries, must have enjoyed *Gulliver's Travels* while more or less seeing its anti-human implications: and even the child who accepts Parts I and II as a simple story gets a sense of absurdity from thinking of human beings six inches high. The explanation must be that Swift's world-view is felt to be *not* altogether false – or it would probably be more accurate to say, not false all the time. Swift is a diseased writer. He remains permanently in a depressed mood which in most people is only intermittent, rather as though someone suffering from jaundice or the after-effects of influenza should have the energy to write books. But we all know that mood, and something in us responds to the expression of it. Take, for instance, one of his most characteristic works, *The Lady's Dressing Room*: one might add the kindred poem, *Upon a Beautiful Young Nymph Going to Bed*. Which is truer, the viewpoint expressed in these poems, or the viewpoint implied in Blake's phrase, 'The naked female human form divine'? No doubt Blake is nearer the truth, and yet who can fail to feel a sort of pleasure in seeing that fraud, feminine delicacy, exploded for once? Swift falsifies his picture of the world by refusing to see anything in human life except dirt, folly and wickedness, but the part which he abstracts from the whole does exist, and it is something which we all know about while shrinking from mentioning it. Part of our minds – in any normal person it is the dominant part – believes that man is a noble animal and life is worth living: but there is also a sort of inner self which at least intermittently stands aghast at the horror of existence. In the queerest way, pleasure and disgust are linked together. The human body is beautiful: it is also repulsive and ridiculous, a fact which can be verified at any swimming pool. The sexual organs are objects of desire and also of loathing, so much so that in many languages, if not in all languages, their names are used as words of abuse. Meat is delicious, but a butcher's shop makes one feel sick: and indeed all our food springs ultimately from dung and dead bodies, the two things which of all others seem to us the most horrible. A child, when it is past the infantile stage but still looking at the world with fresh eyes, is moved by horror almost as often as by wonder – horror of snot and spittle, of the dogs' excrement on the pavement, the dying toad full of maggots, the sweaty smell of grown-ups, the hideousness of old men, with their bald heads and bulbous noses. In his endless harping on disease, dirt and deformity, Swift is not actually inventing anything, he is merely leaving something out. Human behaviour, too, especially in politics, is as he describes it, although it contains other more important factors which he refuses to admit. So far as we can see, both horror and pain are necessary to the continuance of life on this planet, and it is therefore open to pessimists like Swift to say: 'If horror and pain must always be with us, how can life be significantly improved?' His attitude is in effect the Christian attitude, minus the bribe of a 'next world' – which, however, probably has less hold upon the minds of believers than the conviction that this world is a vale of tears and the grave is a place of rest. It is, I am certain, a wrong attitude, and one which could have harmful effects upon behaviour; but something in us responds to it, as it responds to the gloomy words of the burial service and the sweetish smell of corpses in a country church.

It is often argued, at least by people who admit the importance of subject-matter, that a book cannot be 'good' if it expresses a palpably false view of life. We are told that in our own age, for instance, any book that has genuine literary merit will also be more or less 'progressive' in tendency. This ignores the fact that throughout history a similar struggle between progress and reaction has been raging, and that the best books of any one age have always been written from several different viewpoints, some of them palpably more false than others. In so far as a writer is a propagandist, the most one can ask of him is that he shall genuinely believe in what he is saying, and that it shall not be something blazingly silly. Today, for example, one can imagine a good book being written by a Catholic, a Communist, a Fascist, a pacifist, an anarchist, perhaps by an old-style Liberal or an ordinary Conservative: one cannot imagine a good book being written by a spiritualist, a Buchmanite or a member of the Ku Klux Klan. The views that a writer holds must be compatible with sanity, in the medical sense, and with the power of continuous thought: beyond that what we ask of him is talent, which is probably another name for conviction. Swift did not possess ordinary wisdom, but he did possess a terrible intensity of vision, capable of picking out a single hidden truth and then magnifying it and distorting it. The durability of *Gulliver's Travels* goes to show that, if the force of belief is behind it, a world-view which only just passes the test of sanity is sufficient to produce a great work of art.

How the Poor Die
Now [n.s.] No. 6 [November 1946]

In the year 1929 I spent several weeks in the Hopital X, in the fifteenth Arrondissement of Paris. The clerks put me through the usual third-degree at the reception desk, and indeed I was kept answering questions for some twenty minutes before they would let me in. If you have ever had to fill up forms in a Latin country you will know the kind of questions I mean. For some days past I had been unequal to translating Reaumur into Fahrenheit, but I know that my temperature was round about 103, and by the end of the interview I had some difficulty in standing on my feet. At my back a resigned little knot of patients, carrying bundles done up in coloured handkerchiefs, waited their turn to be questioned.

After the questioning came the bath – a compulsory routine for all newcomers, apparently, just as in prison or the workhouse. My clothes were taken away from me, and after I had sat shivering for some minutes in five inches of warm water I was given a linen nightshirt and a short blue flannel dressing-gown – no slippers, they had none big enough for me, they said – and led out into the open air. This was a night in February and I was suffering from pneumonia. The ward we were going to was 200 yards away and it seemed that to get to it you had to cross the hospital grounds. Someone stumbled in front of me with a lantern. The gravel path was frosty underfoot, and the wind whipped the nightshirt round my bare calves. When we got into the ward I was aware of a strange feeling of familiarity whose origin I did not succeed in pinning down till later in the night. It was a long, rather low, ill-lit room, full of murmuring voices and with three rows of beds surprisingly close together. There was a foul smell, faecal and yet sweetish. As I lay down I saw on a bed nearly opposite me a small, round-shouldered, sandy-haired man sitting half naked while a doctor and a student performed some strange operation on him. First the doctor produced from his black bag a dozen small glasses like wine glasses, then the student burned a match inside each glass to exhaust the air, then the glass was popped on to the man's back or chest and the vacuum drew up a huge yellow blister. Only after some moments did I realise what they were doing to him. It was something called cupping, a treatment which you can read about in old medical textbooks but which till then I had vaguely thought of as one of those things they do to horses.

The cold air outside had probably lowered my temperature, and I watched this barbarous remedy with detachment and even a certain amount of amusement. The next moment, however, the doctor and the student came across to my bed, hoisted me upright and without a word began applying the same set of glasses, which had not been sterilised in any way. A few feeble protests that I uttered got no more response than if I had been an animal. I was very much impressed by the impersonal way in which the two men started on me. I had never been in the public ward of a hospital before, and it was my first experience of doctors who handle you without speaking to you, or, in a human sense, taking any notice of you. They only put on six glasses in my case, but after doing so they scarified the blisters and applied the glasses again. Each glass now drew out about a dessert-spoonful of dark-coloured blood. As I lay down again, humiliated, disgusted and frightened by the thing that had been done to me, I reflected that now at least they would leave me alone. But no, not a bit of it. There was another treatment coming, the mustard poultice, seemingly a matter of routine like the hot bath. Two slatternly nurses had already got the poultice ready, and they lashed it round my chest as tight as a strait jacket while some men who were wandering about the ward in shirt and trousers began to collect round my bed with half-sympathetic grins. I learned later that watching a patient have a mustard poultice was a favourite pastime in the ward. These things are normally applied for a quarter of an hour and certainly they are funny enough if you don't happen to be the person inside. For the first five minutes the pain is severe, but you believe you can bear it. During the second five minutes this belief evaporates, but the poultice is buckled at the back and you can't get it off. This is the period the onlookers most enjoy. During the last five minutes, I noted, a sort of numbness supervenes. After the poultice had been removed a waterproof pillow packed with ice was thrust beneath my head and I was left alone. I did not sleep, and to the best of my knowledge this was the only night of my life – I mean the only night spent in bed – in which I have not slept at all, not even a minute.

During my first hour in the Hopital X I had had a whole series of different and contradictory treatments, but this was misleading, for in general you got very little treatment at all, either good or bad, unless you were ill in some interesting and instructive way. At five in the morning the nurses came round, woke the patients and took their temperatures, but did not wash them. If you were well enough you washed yourself, otherwise you depended on the kindness of some walking patient. It was generally patients, too, who carried the bed-bottles and the grim bedpan, nicknamed *la casserole*. At eight breakfast arrived, called army-fashion *la soupe*. It was soup, too, a thin vegetable soup with slimy hunks of bread floating about in it. Later in the day the tall, solemn, black-bearded doctor made his rounds, with an interne and a troop of students following at his heels, but there were about sixty of us in the ward and it was evident that he had other wards to attend to as well. There were many beds past which he walked day after day, sometimes followed by imploring cries. On the other hand if you had some disease with which the students wanted to familiarise themselves you got plenty of attention of a kind. I myself, with an exceptionally fine specimen of a bronchial rattle, sometimes had as many as a dozen students queuing up to listen to my chest. It was a very queer feeling – queer, I mean, because of their intense interest in learning their job, together with a seeming lack of any perception that the patients were human beings. It is strange to relate, but sometimes as some young student stepped forward to take his turn at manipulating you he would be actually tremulous with excitement, like a boy who has at last got his hands on some expensive piece of machinery. And then ear after ear – ears of young men, of girls, of negroes – pressed against your back, relays of fingers solemnly but clumsily tapping, and not from any one of them did you get a word of conversation or a look direct in your face. As a non-paying patient, in the uniform nightshirt, you were primarily *a specimen*, a thing I did not resent but could never quite get used to.

After some days I grew well enough to sit up and study the surrounding patients. The stuffy room, with its narrow beds so close together that you could easily touch your neighbour's hand, had every sort of disease in it except, I suppose, acutely infectious cases. My right-hand neighbour was a little red-haired cobbler with one leg shorter than the other, who used to announce the death of any other patient (this happened a number of times, and my neighbour was always the first to hear of it) by whistling to me, exclaiming "Numero 43!" (or whatever it was) and flinging his arms above his head. This man had not much wrong with him, but in most of the other beds within my angle of vision some squalid tragedy or some plain horror was being enacted. In the bed that was foot to foot with mine there lay, until he died (I didn't see him die – they moved him to another bed), a little weazened man who was suffering from I do not know what disease, but something that made his whole body so intensely sensitive that any movement from side to side, sometimes even the weight of the bedclothes, would make him shout out with pain. His worst suffering was when he urinated, which he did with the greatest difficulty. A nurse would bring him the bedbottle and then for a long time stand beside his bed, whistling, as grooms are said to do with horses, until at last with an agonised shriek of "*Je pisse!*" he would get started. In the bed next to him the sandy-haired man whom I had seen being cupped used to cough up blood-streaked mucus at all hours. My left-hand neighbour was a tall, flaccid-looking young man who used periodically to have a tube inserted into his back and astonishing quantities of frothy liquid drawn off from some part of his body. In the bed beyond that a veteran of the war of 1870 was dying, a handsome old man with a white imperial, round whose bed, at all hours when visiting was allowed, four elderly female relatives dressed all in black sat exactly like crows, obviously scheming for some pitiful legacy.

In the bed opposite me in the further row was an old bald-headed man with drooping moustaches and greatly swollen face and body, who was suffering from some disease that made him urinate almost incessantly. A huge glass receptacle stood always beside his bed. One day his wife and daughter came to visit him. At sight of them the old man's bloated face lit up with a smile of surprising sweetness, and as his daughter, a pretty girl of about twenty, approached the bed I saw that his hand was slowly working its way from under the bedclothes. I seemed to see in advance the gesture that was coming – the girl kneeling beside the bed, the old man's hand laid on her head in his dying blessing. But no, he merely handed her the bedbottle, which she promptly took from him and emptied into the receptacle.

About a dozen beds away from me was Numero 57 – I think that was his number – a cirrhosis of the liver case. Everyone in the ward knew him by sight because he was sometimes the subject of a medical lecture. On two afternoons a week the tall, grave doctor would lecture in the ward to a party of students, and on more than one occasion old Numero 57 was wheeled on a sort of trolley into the middle of the ward, where the doctor would roll back his nightshirt, dilate with his fingers a huge flabby protuberance on the man's belly – the diseased liver, I suppose – and explain solemnly that this was a disease attributable to alcoholism, commoner in the wine-drinking countries. As usual he neither spoke to his patient nor gave him a smile, a nod or any kind of recognition. While he talked, very grave and upright, he would hold the wasted body beneath his two hands, sometimes giving it a gentle roll to and fro, in just the attitude of a woman handling a rolling-pin. Not that Numero 57 minded this kind of thing. Obviously he was an old hospital inmate, a regular exhibit at lectures, his liver long since marked down for a bottle in some pathological museum. Utterly uninterested in what was said about him, he would lie with his colourless eyes gazing at nothing, while the doctor showed him off like a piece of antique china. He was a man of about sixty, astonishingly shrunken. His face, pale as vellum, had shrunken away till it seemed no bigger than a doll's.

One morning my cobbler neighbour woke me by plucking at my pillow before the nurses arrived. "Numero 57!" – he flung his arms above his head. There was a light in the ward, enough to see by. I could see old Numero 57 lying crumpled up on his side, his face sticking out over the side of the bed, and towards me. He had died some time during the night, nobody knew when. When the nurses came they received the news of his death indifferently and went about their work. After a long time, an hour or more, two other nurses marched in abreast like soldiers, with a great clumping of sabots, and knotted the corpse up in the sheets, but it was not removed till some time later. Meanwhile, in the better light, I had had time for a good look at Numero 57. Indeed I lay on my side to look at him. Curiously enough he was the first dead European I had seen. I had seen dead men before, but always Asiatics and usually people who had died violent deaths. Numero 57's eyes were still open, his mouth also open, his small face contorted into an expression of agony. What most impressed me however was the whiteness of his face. It had been pale before, but now it was little darker than the sheets. As I gazed at the tiny, screwed-up face it struck me that this disgusting piece of refuse, waiting to be carted away and dumped on a slab in the dissecting-room, was an example of "natural" death, one of the things you pray for in the Litany. There you are, then, I thought, that's what is waiting for you, twenty, thirty, forty years hence: that is how the lucky ones die, the ones who live to be old. One wants to live, of course, indeed one only stays alive by virtue of the fear of death, but I think now, as I thought then, that it's better to die violently and not too old. People talk about the horrors of war, but what weapon has man invented that even approaches in cruelty some of the commoner diseases? "Natural" death, almost by definition, means something slow, smelly and painful. Even at that, it makes a difference if you can achieve it in your own home and not in a public institution. This poor old wretch who had just flickered out like a candle-end was not even important enough to have anyone watching by his deathbed. He was merely a number, then a "subject" for the students' scalpels. And the sordid publicity of dying in such a place! In the Hopital X the beds were very close together and there were no screens. Fancy, for instance, dying like the little man whose bed was for a while foot to foot with mine, the one who cried out when the bedclothes touched him! I dare say "Je pisse!" were his last recorded words. Perhaps the dying don't bother about such things – that at least would be the standard answer: nevertheless dying people are often more or less normal in their minds till within a day or so of the end.

In the public wards of a hospital you see horrors that you don't seem to meet with among people who manage to die in their own homes, as though certain diseases only attacked people at the lower income levels. But it is a fact that you would not in any English hospitals see some of the things I saw in the Hopital X. This business of people just dying like animals, for instance, with nobody standing by, nobody inter-ested, the death not even noticed till the morning – this happened more than once. You certainly would not see that in England, and still less would you see a corpse left exposed to the view of the other patients. I remember that once in a cottage hospital in England a man died while we were at tea, and though there were only six of us in the ward the nurses managed things so adroitly that the man was dead and his body removed without our even hearing about it till tea was over. A thing we perhaps underrate in England is the advantage we enjoy in having large numbers of well-trained and rigidly-disciplined nurses. No doubt English nurses are dumb enough, they may tell fortunes with tea-leaves, wear Union Jack badges and keep photographs of the Queen on their mantelpieces, but at least they don't let you lie unwashed and constipated on an unmade bed, out of sheer laziness. The nurses at the Hopital X still had a tinge of Mrs. Gamp about them, and later, in the military hospitals of Republican Spain, I was to see nurses almost too ignorant to take a temperature. You wouldn't, either, see in England such dirt as existed in the Hopital X. Later on, when I was well enough to wash myself in the bathroom, I found that there was kept there a huge packing case into which the scraps of food and dirty dressings from the ward were flung, and the wainscotings were infested by crickets.

When I had got back my clothes and grown strong on my legs I fled from the Hopital X, before my time was up and without waiting for a medical discharge. It was not the only hospital I have fled from, but its gloom and bareness, its sickly smell and, above all, something in its mental atmosphere stand out in my memory as exceptional. I had been taken

there because it was the hospital belonging to my arrondissement, and I did not learn till after I was in it that it bore a
bad reputation. A year or two later the celebrated Swindler,
Madame Hanaud, who was ill while on remand, was taken to
the Hopital X, and after a few days of it she managed to elude
her guards, took a taxi and drove back to the prison, explaining
that she was more comfortable there. I have no doubt that the
Hopital X was quite untypical of French hospitals even at that
date. But the patients, nearly all of them working-men, were
surprisingly resigned. Some of them seemed to find the conditions almost comfortable, for at least two were destitute
malingerers who found this a good way of getting through
the winter. The nurses connived because the malingerers
made themselves useful by doing odd jobs. But the attitude of
the majority was: of course this is a lousy place, but what else do
you expect? It did not seem strange to them that you should be
woken at five and then wait three hours before starting the day
on watery soup, or that people should die with no one at their
bedside, or even that your chance of getting medical attention
should depend on catching the doctor's eye as he went past.
According to their traditions that was what hospitals were like.
If you are seriously ill, and if you are too poor to be treated in
your own home, then you must go into hospital, and once there
you must put up with harshness and discomfort, just as you
would in the army. But on top of this I was interested to find a
lingering belief in the old stories that have now almost faded
from memory in England – stories, for instance, about doctors
cutting you open out of sheer curiosity or thinking it funny to
start operating before you were properly "under". There were
dark tales about a little operating-room said to be situated just
beyond the bathroom. Dreadful screams were said to issue from
this room. I saw nothing to confirm these stories and no doubt
they were all nonsense, though I did see two students kill a
sixteen-year-old boy, or nearly kill him (he appeared to be
dying when I left the hospital, but he may have recovered
later) by a mischievous experiment which they probably
could not have tried on a paying patient. Well within living
memory it used to be believed in London that in some of the big
hospitals patients were killed off to get dissection subjects. I
didn't hear this tale repeated at the Hopital X, but I should think

some of the men there would have found it credible. For it was a hospital in which not the methods, perhaps, but something of the atmosphere of the nineteenth century had managed to survive, and therein lay its peculiar interest.

During the past fifty years or so there has been a great change in the relationship between doctor and patient. If you look at almost any literature before the later part of the nineteenth century, you find that a hospital is popularly regarded as much the same thing as a prison, and an old-fashioned, dungeon-like prison at that. A hospital is a place of filth, torture and death, a sort of antechamber to the tomb. No one who was not more or less destitute would have thought of going into such a place for treatment. And especially in the early part of the last century, when medical science had grown bolder than before without being any more successful, the whole business of doctoring was looked on with horror and dread by ordinary people. Surgery, in particular, was believed to be no more than a peculiarly grue-some form of sadism, and dissection, possible only with the aid of bodysnatchers, was even confused with necromancy. From the nineteenth century you could collect a large horror-literature connected with doctors and hospitals. Think of poor old George III, in his dotage, shrieking for mercy as he sees his surgeons approaching to "bleed him till he faints"! Think of the conver-sations of Bob Sawyer and Benjamin Allen, which no doubt are hardly parodies, or the field hospitals in *La Debâcle* and *War and Peace*, or that shocking description of an amputation in Melville's *Whitejacket*! Even the names given to doctors in nineteenth-century English fiction, Slasher, Carver, Sawyer, Fillgrave and so on, and the generic nickname "sawbones", are about as grim as they are comic. The anti-surgery tradition is perhaps best expressed in Tennyson's poem, *The Children's Hospital*, which is essentially a pre-chloroform document though it seems to have been written as late as 1880. Moreover, the outlook which Tennyson records in this poem had a lot to be said for it. When you consider what an operation without anæsthetics must have been like, what it notoriously *was* like, it is difficult not to suspect the motives of people who would undertake such things. For these bloody horrors which the students so eagerly looked forward to ("A magnificent sight if Slasher does it!") were admittedly more or less useless: the patient who did not die of shock usually died of gangrene, a result which was taken for granted. Even now doctors can be found whose motives are questionable. Anyone who has had much illness, or who has listened to medical students talking, will know what I mean. But anæsthetics were a turning point, and disinfectants were another. Nowhere in the world, probably, would you now see the kind of scene described by Axel Munthe in *The Story of San Michele*, when the sinister surgeon in top hat and frock coat, his starched shirtfront spattered with blood and pus, carves up patient after patient with the same knife and flings the severed limbs into a pile beside the table. Moreover, national health insurance has partly done away with the idea that a working-class patient is a pauper who deserves little consideration. Well into this century it was usual for "free" patients at the big hospitals to have their teeth extracted with no anæsthetic. They didn't pay, so why should they have an anæsthetic – that was the attitude. That too has changed.

And yet every institution will always bear upon it some lingering memory of its past. A barrack-room is still haunted by the ghost of Kipling, and it is difficult to enter a workhouse without being reminded of *Oliver Twist*. Hospitals began as a kind of casual ward for lepers and the like to die in, and they continued as places where medical students learned their art on the bodies of the poor. You can still catch a faint suggestion of their history in their characteristically gloomy architecture. I would be far from complaining about the treatment I have received in any English hospital, but I do know that it is a sound instinct that warns people to keep out of hospitals if possible, and especially out of the public wards. Whatever the legal position may be, it is unquestionable that you have far less control over your own treatment, far less certainty that frivolous experiments will not be tried on you, when it is a case of "accept the discipline or get out". And it is a great thing to die in your own bed, though it is better still to die in your boots. However great the kindness and the efficiency, in every hospital death there will be some cruel, squalid detail, some thing perhaps too small to be told but leaving terribly painful memories behind, arising out of the haste, the crowding, the impersonality of a place where every day people are dying among strangers.

The dread of hospitals probably still survives among the very poor, and in all of us it has only recently disappeared. It is a dark patch not far beneath the surface of our minds. I have said earlier that when I entered the ward at the Hopital X I was conscious of a strange feeling of familiarity. What the scene reminded me of, of course, was the reeking, pain-filled hospitals of the nineteenth century, which I had never seen but of which I had a traditional knowledge. And something, perhaps the black-clad doctor with his frowsy black bag, or perhaps only the sickly smell, played the queer trick of unearthing from my memory that poem of Tennyson's, *The Children's Hospital*, which I had not thought of for twenty years. It happened that as a child I had had it read aloud to me by a sick-nurse whose own working life might have stretched back to the time when Tennyson wrote the poem. The horrors and sufferings of the old-style hospitals were a vivid memory to her. We had shuddered over the poem together, and then seemingly I had forgotten it. Even its name would probably have recalled nothing to me. But the first glimpse of the ill-lit, murmurous room, with the beds so close together, suddenly roused the train of thought to which it belonged, and in the night that followed I found myself remembering the whole story and atmosphere of the poem, with many of its lines complete.

As I Please 60
Tribune, 8 November 1946

Someone has just sent me a copy of an American fashion magazine which shall be nameless. It consists of 325 large quarto pages, of which no fewer than 15 are given up to articles on world politics, literature, etc. The rest consists entirely of pictures with a little letterpress creeping round their edges: pictures of ball dresses, mink coats, step-ins, panties, brassieres, silk stockings, slippers, perfumes, lipsticks, nail varnish – and, of course, of the women, unrelievedly beautiful, who wear them or make use of them. I do not know just how many drawings or photographs of women occur throughout the whole volume, but as there are 45 of them, all beautiful, in the first 50 pages, one can work it out roughly.

One striking thing when one looks at these pictures is the overbred, exhausted, even decadent style of beauty that now seems to be striven after. Nearly all of these women are immensely elongated. A thin-boned, ancient-Egyptian type of face seems to predominate: narrow hips are general, and slender non-prehensile hands like those of a lizard are everywhere. Evidently it is a real physical type, for it occurs as much in the photographs as in the drawings. Another striking thing is the prose style of the advertisements, an extraordinary mixture of sheer lushness with clipped and sometimes very expressive technical jargon. Words like suave-mannered, custom-finished, contour-conforming, mitt-back, innersole, backdip, midriff, swoosh, swash, curvaceous, slenderize and pet-smooth are flung about with evident full expectation that the reader will understand them at a glance. Here are a few sample sentences taken at random:

"A new Shimmer Sheen colour that sets your hands and his head in a whirl." "Bared and beautifully bosomy." "Feathery-light Milliken Fleece to keep her kitten-snug!" "Others see you through a veil of sheer beauty, *and they wonder why*!" "Gentle discipline for curves in lacy lastex pantie-girdle." "An exclamation point of a dress that depends on fluid fabric for much of its drama." "Suddenly your figure lilts . . . lovely in the litheness of a Foundette pantie-girdle." "Lovely to look at, lovelier to wear is this original Lady Duff gown with its shirred cap sleeves and accentuated midriff." "Supple and tissue-light, yet wonderfully curve-holding." "The miracle of figure flattery!" "Moulds your bosom into proud feminine lines." "Isn't it wonderful to know that Corsees wash and wear and whittle you down . . . even though they weigh only four ounces!" "The distilled witchery of one woman who was forever desirable . . . forever beloved . . . Forever Amber." And so on and so on and so on.

A fairly diligent search through the magazine reveals two discreet allusions to grey hair, but if there is anywhere a direct mention of fatness or middle-age I have not found it. Birth and death are not mentioned either: nor is work, except that a few recipes for breakfast dishes are given. The male sex enters directly or indirectly into perhaps one advertisement in twenty, and photographs of dogs or kittens appear here and there. In only two pictures, out of about three hundred, is a child represented.

On the front cover there is a coloured photograph of the usual elegant female standing on a chair while a grey-haired, spectacled, crushed-looking man in shirt-sleeves kneels at her feet, doing something to the edge of her skirt. If one looks closely one finds that actually he is about to take a measurement with a yard-measure. But to a casual glance he looks as though he were kissing the hem of the woman's garment – not a bad symbolical picture of American civilisation, or at least of one important side of it.

One interesting example of our unwillingness to face facts and our consequent readiness to make gestures which are known in advance to be useless, is the present campaign to Keep Death off the Roads.

The newspapers have just announced that road deaths for September dropped by nearly 80 as compared with the previous September. This is very well so far as it goes, but the improvement will probably not be kept – at any rate, it will not be progressive – and meanwhile everyone knows that you *can't* solve the problem while our traffic system remains what it is. Accidents happen because on narrow, inadequate roads, full of blind corners and surrounded by dwelling houses, vehicles and pedestrians are moving in all directions at all speeds from three miles an hour to sixty or seventy. If you really want to keep death off the roads, you would have to replan the whole road system in such a way as to make collisions impossible. Think out what this means (it would involve, for example, pulling down and rebuilding the whole of London), and you can see that it is quite beyond the power of any nation at this moment. Short of that you can only take palliative measures, which ultimately boil down to making people more careful.

But the only palliative measure that would make a real difference is a drastic reduction in speed. Cut down the speed limit to twelve miles an hour in all built-up areas, and you would cut out the vast majority of accidents. But this, everyone will assure you, is "impossible." Why is it impossible? Well, it would be unbearably irksome. It would mean that every road journey took twice or three times as long as it takes at present. Besides, you could never get people to observe such a speed limit. What driver is going to crawl along at twelve miles an hour when he knows that his engine would do fifty? It is not even easy to keep a modern car down to twelve miles an hour and remain in high gear – and so on and so forth, all adding up to the statement that slow travel is of its nature intolerable.

In other words we value speed more highly than we value human life. Then why not say so, instead of every few years having one of these hypocritical campaigns (at present it is "Keep Death off the Roads" – a few years back it was "Learn the Kerb Step"), in the full knowledge that while our roads remain as they are, and present speeds are kept up, the slaughter must continue?

A sidelight on bread rationing. My neighbour in Scotland this summer was a crofter engaged on the enormous labour of reclaiming a farm which has been derelict for several years. He has no helper except a sister, he has only one horse, and he possesses only the most primitive machinery, which does not even include a reaper. Throughout this summer he certainly did not work less than fourteen hours a day, six days a week. When bread rationing started he put in for the extra ration, only to find that, though he could, indeed, get more bread than a sedentary worker, he was not entitled to the full agricultural labourer's ration. The reason? That within the meaning of the act he is not an agricultural labourer! Since he is "on his own" he ranks as a farmer, and it is assumed that he eats less bread than he would do if he were working for wages for somebody else.

When I was talking to some friends the other night, a question came up which we could none of us answer and which I should like someone to elucidate for me. The question is: on what principle are jurymen chosen? The theory is, I believe, that they are chosen at random from the whole population. At any rate, that is what trial "by your peers" ought to mean in a democracy. But I have a strong impression – and my friends thought the same – that no one strictly describable as a working-man normally finds his way on to a jury. The people summoned as jurors always seem to be small business or professional men. Is there perhaps some property qualification which is not mentioned but is merely applied? I should like to know, because if the facts are what I think they are – that is, that juries are drawn from the middle class while the accused in criminal cases often belong to the working class – they deserve more publicity than I have ever seen them get.

As I Please 61
Tribune, 15 November 1946

As the clouds, most of them much larger and dirtier than a man's hand, come blowing up over the political horizon, there is one fact that obtrudes itself over and over again. This is that the Government's troubles, present and future, arise quite largely from its failure to publicise itself properly.

People are not told with sufficient clarity what is happening, and why, and what may be expected to happen in the near future. As a result, every calamity, great or small, takes the mass of the public by surprise, and the Government incurs unpopularity by doing things which any government, of whatever colour, would have to do in the same circumstances.

Take one question which has been much in the news lately but has never been properly thrashed out: the immigration of foreign labour into this country. Recently we have seen a tremendous outcry at the T.U.C. conference against allowing Poles to work in the two places where labour is most urgently needed – in the mines and on the land.

It will not do to write this off as something "got up" by Communist sympathisers, nor on the other hand to justify it by saying that the Polish refugees are all Fascists who "strut about" wearing monocles and carrying brief-cases.

The question is, would the attitude of the British trade unions be any friendlier if it were a question, not of alleged Fascists but of the admitted victims of Fascism?

For example, hundreds of thousands of homeless Jews are now trying desperately to get to Palestine. No doubt many of them will ultimately succeed, but others will fail. How about inviting, say, 100,000 Jewish refugees to settle in this country?

Or what about the Displaced Persons, numbering nearly a million, who are dotted in camps all over Germany, with no future and no place to go, the United States and the British Dominions having already refused to admit them in significant numbers? Why not solve their problem by offering them British citizenship?

It is easy to imagine what the average Briton's answer would be. Even before the war, with the Nazi persecutions in full swing, there was no popular support for the idea of allowing large numbers of Jewish refugees into this country: nor was there any strong move to admit the hundreds of thousands of Spaniards who had fled from Franco to be penned up behind barbed wire in France.

For that matter, there was very little protest against the internment of the wretched German refugees in 1940. The comments I most often overheard at the time were "What did they want to come here for?" and "They're only after our jobs."

The fact is that there is strong popular feeling in this country against foreign immigration. It arises partly from simple xenophobia, partly from fear of undercutting in wages, but above all from the out-of-date notion that Britain is overpopulated and that more population means more unemployment.

Actually, so far from having more workers than jobs, we have a serious labour shortage which will be accentuated by the continuance of conscription, and which will grow worse, not better, because of the ageing of the population.

Meanwhile our birth-rate is still frighteningly low, and several hundred thousand women of marriageable age have no chance of getting husbands. But how widely are these facts known or understood?

In the end it is doubtful whether we can solve our problems without encouraging immigration from Europe. In a tentative way the Government has already tried to do this, only to be met by ignorant hostility, because the public has not been told the relevant facts beforehand. So also with countless other unpopular things that will have to be done from time to time.

But the most necessary step is not to prepare public opinion for particular emergencies, but to raise the general level of political understanding: above all, to drive home the fact, which has never been properly grasped, that British prosperity depends largely on factors outside Britain.

This business of publicising and explaining itself is not easy for a Labour Government, faced by a press which at bottom is mostly hostile. Nevertheless, there are other ways of communicating with the public, and Mr. Attlee and his colleagues might well pay more attention to the radio, a medium which very few politicians in this country have ever taken seriously.

There is one question which at first sight looks both petty and disgusting but which I should like to see answered. It is this. In the innumerable hangings of war criminals which have taken place all over Europe during the past few years, which method has been followed – the old method of strangulation, or the modern, comparatively humane method which is supposed to break the victim's neck at one snap?

A hundred years ago or more, people were hanged by simply hauling them up and letting them kick and struggle until they died, which might take a quarter of an hour or so. Later the drop was introduced, theoretically making death instantaneous, though it does not always work very well.

In recent years, however, there seems to have been a tendency to revert to strangulation. I did not see the news-film of the hanging of the German war criminals at Kharkov, but the descriptions in the British press appeared to show that the older method was used. So also with various executions in the Balkan countries.

The newspaper accounts of the Nuremberg hangings were ambiguous. There was talk of a drop, but there was also talk of the condemned men taking ten or twenty minutes to die. Perhaps, by a typically Anglo-Saxon piece of compromise, it was decided to use a drop but to make it too short to be effective.

It is not a good symptom that hanging should still be the accepted form of capital punishment in this country. Hanging is a barbarous, inefficient way of killing anybody, and at least one fact about it – quite widely known, I believe – is so obscene as to be almost unprintable.

Still, until recently we did feel rather uneasy on the subject, and we did have our hangings in private. Indeed, before the war public execution was a thing of the past in nearly every civilised country. Now it seems to be returning, at least for political crimes, and though we ourselves have not actually reintroduced it as yet, we participate at second hand by watching the news films.

It is queer to look back and think that only a dozen years ago the abolition of the death penalty was one of those things that every enlightened person advocated as a matter of course, like divorce reform or the independence of India. Now, on the other hand, it is a mark of enlightenment not merely to approve of executions but to raise an outcry because there are not more of them.

Therefore it seems to me of some importance to know whether strangulation is now coming to be the normal practice. For if people are being taught to gloat not only over death but over a peculiarly horrible form of torture, it marks another turn on the downward spiral that we have been following ever since 1933.

Quotation wanted.

A character in one of Chekhov's stories, I forget which, remarks: "As Shakespeare says, 'Happy is he who in his youth is young.'" I have never been able to find this line, nor does it sound like Shakespeare. Possibly the translator re-translated it from the Russian instead of looking up the original. Can anybody tell me where it occurs?

As I Please 62
Tribune, 22 November 1946

The query I raised two weeks ago, about the methods used in selecting jurymen, is answered authoritatively by a contributor in this week's issue. It also brought in a considerable stream of letters, nearly all of them enclosing a copy of a recently issued Government form which has to be filled in by anyone claiming exemption from jury service. I had received a copy of this myself through the usual channels, and had immediately flung it into the wastepaper basket, but actually it contains most of the information that I wanted. Reading it through, I note with interest the qualifications needed by "special jurors," whatever "special jurors" may be. They have to be read to be believed:

> The following jurors are qualified to be special jurors: Persons legally entitled to be called an "Esquire" and persons of higher degree; bankers and merchants; occupiers of private dwelling-houses the net annual value of which is not less than £100 in towns containing, according to the last census, 20,000 inhabitants and upwards or £50 elsewhere; occupiers of premises other than a farm the net annual value of which is not less than £100; occupiers of farms the net annual value of which is not less than £300.

Study this paragraph in detail, and you will see that it has been worded, and very carefully worded, so as to exclude everyone who does not belong socially as well as financially to the Upper Crust. This form is being circulated after a Labour Government with a crushing majority has been in office for fifteen months.

Several of the people who wrote to me stated that, so far as their own knowledge goes, manual workers are not in practice excluded from jury service, or are not always excluded. One correspondent, chairman of a Labour Party branch, adds that the trouble is not that manual workers are actually debarred from jury service, but that they dodge it whenever they can, for financial reasons. Jurors are not paid, so that serving on a jury means losing a day or two's wages. Incidentally, the fact that they are not paid gives them a strong motive for getting the job done as hurriedly as possible, and must have been responsible for many a wrong verdict.

How easy it would be to put this right by paying every juryman a reasonable fee – £1 a day, say – to compensate him for loss of time.

I notice that among the various categories of people exempted from jury service are "Apothecaries certificated by the Court of Examiners of the Apothecaries Company," and pharmaceutical chemists generally. There seems to be an echo from *Pickwick Papers* here. At the hearing of Mrs. Bardell's breach of promise case, it will be remembered, a chemist who is being sworn in for service on the jury remarks that "there'll be murder before this trial's over," adding after he has taken the oath: "I've left nobody but an errand boy in my shop.

He's a very nice boy, my Lord, but he is not much acquainted with drugs; and I know that the prevailing impression on his mind is, that Epsom salts means oxalic acid; and syrup of senna, laudanum. That's all, my Lord." Could it be, I wonder, that chemists earned their exemption as a result of some imaginative official happening to read this passage?

I wonder whether the Ministry concerned has ever turned its thoughts towards peat as a source of domestic fuel. At this moment my coal cellar is empty, and judging by experiences last winter it will remain empty for a long time, but I am writing this beside a peat fire which warms the room comfortably enough. In London peat is fantastically expensive, but that is merely a racket which can be practised because the price is not controlled and because people will pay anything sooner than freeze. I imagine that the natural price of peat would be somewhat less than that of coal, weight for weight.

There are enormous quantities of peat in Scotland, and it occurs in Wales and in a few parts of England. In Scotland it is dug in a very primitive way. The people scoop it out in small blocks with a kind of spade, and lay the blocks out on the grass to dry. When they are dry on one side they are placed upright in threes, then a little later they are built up into small piles, then into larger piles, and finally are carted home about two months after they are dug. All this has to be done in the spring and early summer, because at other times of year there is either too much rain, or the grass is too long, for the peat to get dry. I believe it used to be reckoned that if a family used no other fuel, it would mean a month's work, including drying and carting, to get a year's supply.

Of course, if peat were being dug in a big way, there would be no need to use these crude methods or to depend on fine weather for drying. People who are not accustomed to peat are sometimes put against it because they do not know the right way to light it, or do not realise that it must be stored in a dry place, but with a few simple instructions it should be easy to popularise it as a domestic fuel. It gives out less heat than coal, but it is cleaner and easier to handle, and, unlike wood, it is suitable for small fireplaces. A few million tons of it a year would make a lot of difference if, as seems likely, we are never going to have quite enough coal again.

In current discussions of the Royal Commission that is to inquire into the Press, the talk is always of the debasing influence exerted by owners and advertisers. It is not said often enough that a nation gets the newspapers it deserves. Admittedly, this is not the whole of the truth. When the bulk of the Press is owned by a handful of people, one has not much choice, and the fact that during the war the newspapers temporarily became more intelligent, without losing circulation, suggests that the public taste is not quite so bad as it seems. Still, our newspapers are not all alike; some of them are more intelligent than others, and some are more popular than others. And when you study the relationship between intelligence and popularity, what do you find?

Below I list in two columns our nine leading national daily papers. In the first column these are ranged in order of intelligence, so far as I am able to judge it: in the other they are ranged in order of popularity, as measured by circulation. By intelligence I do not mean agreement with my own opinions. I mean a readiness to present news objectively, to give prominence to the things that really matter, to discuss serious questions even when they are dull, and to advocate policies which are at least coherent and intelligible. As to the circulation, I may have misplaced one or two papers, as I have no recent figures, but my list will not be far out. Here are the two lists: —

INTELLIGENCE	POPULARITY
1. *Manchester Guardian.*	1. *Express.*
2. *Times.*	2. *Herald.*
3. *News-Chronicle.*	3. *Mirror.*
4. *Telegraph.*	4. *News-Chronicle.*
5. *Herald.*	5. *Mail.*
6. *Mail.*	6. *Graphic.*
7. *Mirror.*	7. *Telegraph.*
8. *Express.*	8. *Times.*
9. *Graphic.*	9. *Manchester Guardian.*

It will be seen that the second list is very nearly – not quite, for life is never so neat as that – the first turned upside down. And even if I have not ranged these papers in quite the right order, the general relationship holds good. The paper that has the best reputation for truthfulness, the *Manchester Guardian*, is the one that is not read even by those who admire it. People complain that it is "so dull." On the other hand countless people read the *Daily* — while saying frankly that they "don't believe a word of it."

In these circumstances it is difficult to foresee a radical change, even if the special kind of pressure exerted by owners and advertisers is removed. What matters is that in England we do possess juridical liberty of the Press, which makes it possible to utter one's true opinions fearlessly in papers of comparatively small circulation. It is vitally important to hang on to that. But no Royal Commission can make the big-circulation Press much better than it is, however much it manipulates the methods of control. We shall have a serious and truthful popular Press when public opinion actively demands it. Till then, if the news is not distorted by business-men it will be distorted by bureaucrats, who are only one degree better.

Riding Down from Bangor

Tribune, 22 November 1946

The reappearance of *Helen's Babies*, in its day one of the most popular books in the world – within the British Empire alone it was pirated by twenty different publishing firms, the author receiving a total profit of £40 from a sale of some hundreds of thousands or millions of copies – will ring a bell in any literate person over 35. Not that the present edition is an altogether satisfactory one. It is a cheap little book with rather unsuitable illustrations, various American dialect words appear to have been cut out of it, and the sequel, *Other People's Children*, which was often bound up with it in earlier editions, is missing. Still, it is pleasant to see *Helen's Babies* in print again. It had become almost a rarity in recent years, and it is one of the best of the little library of American books on which people born at about the turn of the century were brought up.

The books one reads in childhood, and perhaps most of all the bad and good-bad books, create in one's mind a sort of false map of the world, a series of fabulous countries into which one can retreat at odd moments throughout the rest of life, and which in some cases can even survive a visit to the real countries which they are supposed to represent. The pampas, the Amazon, the coral islands of the Pacific, Russia, land of birch-tree and samovar, Transylvania with its boyars and vampires, the China of Guy Boothby, the Paris of du Maurier – one could continue the list for a long time. But one other imaginary country that I acquired early in life was called America. If I pause on the word "America," and, deliberately putting aside the existing reality, call up my childhood vision of it, I see two pictures – composite pictures, of course, from which I am omitting a good deal of the detail.

One is of a boy sitting in a whitewashed stone schoolroom. He wears braces and has patches on his shirt, and if it is summer he is barefooted. In the corner of the schoolroom there is a bucket of drinking water with a dipper. The boy lives in a farmhouse, also of stone and also whitewashed, which has a mortgage on it. He aspires to be President, and is expected to keep the woodpile full. Somewhere in the background of the picture, but completely dominating it, is a huge black Bible. The other picture is of a tall, angular man, with a shapeless hat pulled down over his eyes, leaning against a wooden paling and whittling at a stick. His lower jaw moves slowly but ceaselessly. At very long intervals he emits some piece of wisdom such as "A woman is the orneriest critter there is, 'ceptin' a mule," or "When you don't know a thing to do, don't do a thing"; but more often it is merely a jet of tobacco juice that issues from the gap in his front teeth. Between them those two pictures summed up my earliest impression of America. And of the two, the first – which, I suppose, represented New England, the other representing the South – had the stronger hold upon me.

The books from which these pictures were derived included, of course, books which it is still possible to take seriously, such as *Tom Sawyer* and *Uncle Tom's Cabin*, but the most richly American flavour was to be found in minor works which are now almost forgotten. I wonder, for instance, if anyone still reads *Rebecca of Sunnybrook Farm*, which remained a popular favourite long enough to be filmed with Mary Pickford in the leading part. Or how about the "Katy" books by Susan Coolidge (*What Katy Did at School*, etc.), which, although girls' books and therefore "soppy," had the fascination of foreignness? Louisa M. Alcott's *Little Women* and *Good Wives* are, I suppose, still flickeringly in print, and certainly they still have their devotees. As a child I loved both of them, though I was less pleased by the third of the trilogy, *Little Men*. That model school where the worst punishment was to have to whack the schoolmaster, on "this hurts me more than it hurts you" principles, was rather difficult to swallow.

Helen's Babies belonged in much the same world as *Little Women*, and must have been published round about the same date. Then there were Artemus Ward, Bret Harte, and various songs, hymns and ballads, besides poems dealing with the Civil War, such as *Barbara Frietchie* (" 'Shoot if you must this old grey head, But spare your country's flag,' she said") and *Little Gifford of Tennessee*. There were other books so obscure that it hardly seems worth mentioning them, and magazine stories of which I remember nothing except that the old homestead always seemed to have a mortgage on it. There was also *Beautiful Joe*, the American reply to *Black Beauty*, of which you might just possibly pick up a copy in a sixpenny box. All the books I have mentioned were written well before 1900, but something of the special American flavour lingered on into this century in, for instance, the Buster Brown coloured supplements, and even in Booth Tarkington's "Penrod" stories, which will have been written round about 1910. Perhaps there was even a tinge of it in Ernest Thompson Seton's animal books (*Wild Animals I Have Known*, etc.), which have now fallen from favour but which drew tears from the pre-1914 child as surely as *Misunderstood* had done from the children of a generation earlier.

Somewhat later my picture of nineteenth-century America was given greater precision by a song which is still fairly well known and which can be found (I think) in the *Scottish Students' Song Book*. As usual in these bookless days I cannot get hold of a copy, and I must quote fragments from memory. It begins:

> Riding down from Bangor
> On an Eastern train,
> Bronzed with weeks of hunting
> In the woods of Maine –
> Quite extensive whiskers,
> Beard, moustache as well –
> Sat a student fellow,
> Tall and slim and swell.

Presently an aged couple and a "village maiden," described as "beautiful, petite," get into the carriage. Quantities of cinders are flying about, and before long the student fellow gets one in his eye: the village maiden extracts it for him, to the scandal of the aged couple. Soon after this the train shoots into a long tunnel, "black as Egypt's night." When it emerges into the daylight again the maiden is covered with blushes, and the cause of her confusion is revealed when –

> There suddenly appeared
> A tiny little ear-ring
> In that horrid student's beard!

I do not know the date of the song, but the primitiveness of the train (no lights in the carriage, and a cinder in one's eye a normal accident) suggests that it belongs well back in the nineteenth century.

What connects this song with books like *Helen's Babies* is first of all a sort of sweet innocence – the climax, the thing you are supposed to be slightly shocked at, is an episode with which any modern piece of naughty-naughty would *start* – and, secondly, a faint vulgarity of language mixed up with a certain cultural pretentiousness. *Helen's Babies* is intended as a humorous, even a farcical book, but it is haunted all the way through by words like "tasteful" and "ladylike," and it is funny chiefly because its tiny disasters happen against a background of conscious gentility. "Handsome, intelligent, composed, taste-fully dressed, without a suspicion of the flirt or the languid woman of fashion about her, she awakened to the utmost my every admiring sentiment" – thus is the heroine described,

1132

figuring elsewhere as "erect, fresh, neat, composed, bright-eyed, fair-faced, smiling and observant." One gets beautiful glimpses of a now-vanished world in such remarks as: "I believe you arranged the floral decorations at St. Zephaniah's Fair last winter, Mr. Burton? 'Twas the most tasteful display of the season." But in spite of the occasional use of "'twas," and other archaisms – "parlour" for sitting-room, "chamber" for bedroom, "real" as an adverb, and so forth – the book does not "date" very markedly, and many of its admirers imagine it to have been written round about 1900. Actually it was written in 1875, a fact which one might infer from internal evidence, since the hero, aged twenty-eight, is a veteran of the Civil War.

The book is very short, and the story is a simple one. A young bachelor is prevailed on by his sister to look after her house and her two sons, aged five and three, while she and her husband go on a fortnight's holiday. The children drive him almost mad by an endless succession of such acts as falling into ponds, swallowing poison, throwing keys down wells, cutting themselves with razors, and the like, but also facilitate his engagement to "a charming girl, whom, for about a year, I had been adoring from afar." These events take place in an outer suburb of New York, in a society which now seems astonishingly sedate, formal, domesticated and, according to current conceptions, un-American. Every action is governed by etiquette. To pass a carriage full of ladies when your hat is crooked is an ordeal; to recognise an acquaintance in church is ill-bred; to become engaged after a ten-days' courtship is a severe social lapse. We are accustomed to thinking of American society as more crude, adventurous and, in a cultural sense, democratic than our own, and from writers like Mark Twain, Whitman and Bret Harte, not to mention the cowboy and Red Indian stories of the weekly papers, one draws a picture of a wild anarchic world peopled by eccentrics and desperadoes who have no traditions and no attachment to one place. That aspect of nineteenth-century America did of course exist, but in the more populous eastern states a society similar to Jane Austen's seems to have survived longer than it did in England. And it is hard not to feel that it was a better kind of society than that which arose from the sudden industrialisation of the later part of the century. The people in *Helen's Babies* or *Little Women* may be mildly ridiculous, but they are uncorrupted. They have something that is perhaps best described as integrity, or good morale, founded partly on an unthinking piety. It is a matter of course that everyone attends church on Sunday morning and says grace before meals and prayers at bedtime: to amuse the children one tells them Bible stories, and if they ask for a song it is probably "Glory, glory Hallelujah." Perhaps it is also a sign of spiritual health in the light literature of this period that death is mentioned freely. "Baby Phil," the brother of Budge and Toddie, has died shortly before *Helen's Babies* opens, and there are various tear-jerking references to his "tiny coffin." A modern writer attempting a story of this kind would have kept coffins out of it.

English children are still Americanised by way of the films, but it would no longer be generally claimed that American books are the best ones for children. Who, without misgivings, would bring up a child on the coloured "comics" in which sinister professors manufacture atomic bombs in underground laboratories while Superman whizzes through the clouds, the machine-gun bullets bouncing off his chest like peas, and platinum blondes are raped, or very nearly, by steel robots and fifty-foot dinosaurs? It is a far cry from Superman to the Bible and the woodpile. The earlier children's books, or books readable by children, had not only innocence but a sort of native gaiety, a buoyant, carefree feeling, which was the product, presumably, of the unheard-of freedom and security which nineteenth-century America enjoyed. That is the connecting link between books so seemingly far apart as *Little Women* and *Life on the Mississippi*. The society described in the one is subdued, bookish and home-loving, while the other tells of a crazy world of bandits, gold mines, duels, drunkenness and gambling hells: but in both one can detect an underlying confidence in the future, a sense of freedom and opportunity.

Nineteenth-century America was a rich, empty country which lay outside the main stream of world events, and in which the twin nightmares that beset nearly every modern man, the nightmare of unemployment and the nightmare of State interference, had hardly come into being. There were social distinctions, more marked than those of today, and there was poverty (in *Little Women*, it will be remembered, the family is at one time so hard up that one of the girls sells her hair to the barber), but there was not, as there is now, an all-prevailing sense of helplessness. There was room for everybody, and if you worked hard you could be certain of a living – could even be certain of growing rich: this was generally believed, and for the greater part of the population it was even broadly true. In other words, the civilisation of nineteenth-century America was capitalist civilisation at its best. Soon after the Civil War the inevitable deterioration started. But for some decades, at least, life in America was much better fun than life in Europe – there was more happening, more colour, more variety, more opportunity – and the books and songs of that period had a sort of bloom, a childlike quality. Hence, I think, the popularity of *Helen's Babies* and other "light" literature, which made it normal for the English child of thirty or forty years ago to grow up with a theoretical knowledge of raccoons, woodchucks, chipmunks, gophers, hickory trees, water-melons and other unfamiliar fragments of the American scene.

As I Please 63
Tribune, 29 November 1946

Here is an analysis of the front page of my morning newspaper, on an ordinary, uneventful day in November, 1946.

The big headline goes to the U.N. conference, at which the U.S.S.R. is putting forward demands for an inquiry into the strength of Anglo-American forces in ex-enemy or allied countries. This is obviously intended to forestall a demand for inspection of forces inside the U.S.S.R., and it is plain to see that the resulting discussion will lead to nothing except recriminations and a prestige victory for this side or that, with no advance, and no attempt at any advance, towards genuine international agreement.

The fighting in Greece is growing more serious. The constitutional opposition is swinging more and more towards support of the rebels, while the Government is alleging that the so-called rebels are in fact guerillas operating from across the frontier.

There is further delay in calling the Indian Constituent Assembly (this column has a footnote: "Blood-bath in India: Page Two"), and Mr. Gandhi has starved himself into a condition which is causing anxiety.

The American coal strike is continuing, and is likely to "have disastrous effects on world grain supplies." Owing to other recent strikes, the United States has cancelled delivery of two million tons of steel to Britain, which will further complicate the British housing problem. There is also an unofficial "go slow" movement on the Great Western Railway.

Another bomb has gone off in Jerusalem, with a number of casualties. There is also news of various minor unavoidable calamities, such as a plane crash, the likelihood of floods all over England, and a collision of ships in the Mersey, with the apparent loss of 100 head of cattle, which I suppose would represent one week's meat ration for about 40,000 people.

There is no definitely good news at all on the front page. There are items, such as a rise in British exports during October, which look as if they might be good, but which might turn out to be bad if one had sufficient knowledge to interpret them. There is also a short statement to the effect that the occupying powers in Germany "may" shortly reach a better agreement. But this is hardly more than the expression of a pious wish, unsupported by evidence.

I repeat that this pageful of disasters is merely the record of an average day, when nothing much is happening: and incidentally it occurs in a newspaper which, rather more than most, tries to put a good face on things.

When one considers how things have gone since 1930 or thereabouts, it is not easy to believe in the survival of civilisation. I do not argue from this that the only thing to do is to abjure practical politics, retire to some remote place and concentrate either on individual salvation or on building up self-supporting communities against the day when the atom bombs have done their work. I think one must continue the political struggle, just as a doctor must try to save the life of a patient who is probably going to die. But I do suggest that we shall get nowhere unless we start by recognising that political behaviour is largely non-rational, that the world is suffering from some kind of mental disease which must be diagnosed before it can be cured. The significant point is that nearly all the calamities that happen to us are quite unnecessary. It is commonly assumed that what human beings want is to be comfortable. Well, we now have it in our power to be comfortable, as our ancestors had not. Nature may occasionally hit back with an earthquake or a cyclone, but by and large she is beaten. And yet exactly at the moment when there is, or could be, plenty of everything for everybody, nearly our whole energies have to be taken up in trying to grab territories, markets and raw materials from one another. Exactly at the moment when wealth might be so generally diffused that no government need fear serious opposition, polit- ical liberty is declared to be impossible and half the world is ruled by secret police forces. Exactly at the moment when superstition crumbles and a rational attitude towards the universe becomes feasible, the right to think one's own thoughts is denied as never before. The fact is that human beings only started fighting one another in earnest when there was no longer anything to fight about.

It is not easy to find a direct economic explanation of the behaviour of the people who now rule the world. The desire for pure power seems to be much more dominant than the desire for wealth. This has often been pointed out, but curiously enough the desire for power seems to be taken for granted as a natural instinct, equally prevalent in all ages, like the desire for food. Actually it is no more natural, in the sense of being biologically necessary, than drunkenness or gambling. And if it has reached new levels of lunacy in our own age, as I think it has, then the question becomes: what is the special quality in modern life that makes a major human motive out of the impulse to bully others? If we could answer that question – seldom asked, never followed up – there might occasionally be a bit of good news on the front page of your morning paper.

However, it is always possible, in spite of appearances, that the age we live in is *not* worse than the other ages that have preceded it, nor perhaps even greatly different. At least this possibility occurs to me when I think of an Indian proverb which a friend of mine once translated: –

In April was the jackal born,
In June the rain-fed rivers swelled:

> "Never in all my life," said he,
> "Have I so great a flood beheld."

I suppose the shortage of clocks and watches is nobody's fault, but is it necessary to let their prices rocket as they have done in the last year or two?

Early this year I saw ex-Army watches exhibited in a show-case at a little under £4 each. A week or two later I succeeded in buying one of them for £5. Recently their price seems to have risen to £8. A year or two ago, alarm clocks, which at that time could not be bought without a permit, were on sale at 16 shillings each. This was the controlled price, and presumably it did not represent an actual loss to the manufacturer. The other day I saw precisely similar clocks at 45 shillings – a jump of 180 per cent. Is it really conceivable that the cost price has increased correspondingly?

Incidentally, for 45 shillings you can, if you are on the phone, arrange for the telephone operator to call you every morning for nearly 18 months, which is a lot longer than the life of the average alarm clock.

Under the heading, "The Return of the Jews to Palestine," Samuel Butler records in his *Note-Books*:

A man called on me last week and proposed gravely that I should write a book upon an idea which had occurred to a friend of his, a Jew living in New Bond Street. . . . If only I would help, the return of the Jews to Palestine would be rendered certain and easy. There was no trouble about the poor Jews, he knew how he could get them back at any time; the difficulty lay with the Rothschilds, the Oppenheims and such; with my assistance, however, the thing could be done.

I am afraid I was rude enough to decline to go into the scheme on the ground that I did not care twopence whether the Rothschilds and Oppenheims went back to Palestine or not. This was felt to be an obstacle; but then he began to try and make me care, whereupon, of course, I had to get rid of him.

This was written in 1883. And who would have foreseen that only about sixty years later nearly all the Jews in Europe would be trying to get back to Palestine of their own accord, while nearly everybody else would be trying to stop them?

As I Please 64

Tribune, 6 December 1946

With great enjoyment I have just been re-reading *Trilby*, George du Maurier's justly popular novel, one of the finest specimens of that "good bad" literature which the English-speaking peoples seem to have lost the secret of producing. *Trilby* is an imitation of Thackeray, a very good imitation and immensely readable – Bernard Shaw, if I remember rightly, considered it to be *better* than Thackeray in many ways – but to me the most interesting thing about it is the different impressions one derives from reading it first before and then after the career of Hitler.

The thing that now hits one in the eye in reading *Trilby* is its anti-semitism. I suppose, although few people actually read the book now, its central story is fairly widely known, the name of Svengali having become a by-word, like that of Sherlock Holmes. A Jewish musician – not a composer, but a brilliant pianist and music-teacher – gets into his power an orphaned Irish girl, a painter's model, who has a magnificent voice but happens to be tone deaf. Having hypnotised her one day to cure an attack of neuralgia, he discovers that when she is in the hypnotic trance she can be taught to sing in tune.

Thereafter, for about two years, the pair of them travel from one European capital to another, the girl singing every night to enormous and ecstatic audiences, and never even knowing, in her waking life, that she is a singer. The end comes when Svengali dies suddenly in the middle of a concert and Trilby breaks down and is booed off the stage. That is the main story, though of course there is much else, including an unhappy love affair and three clean-living English painters who make a foil for Svengali's villainy.

There is no question that the book is anti-semitic. Apart from the fact that Svengali's vanity, treacherousness, selfishness, personal uncleanliness and so forth are constantly connected with the fact that he is a Jew, there are the illustrations. Du Maurier, better known for his drawings in *Punch* than for his writings, illustrated his own book, and he made Svengali into a sinister caricature of the traditional type. But what is most interesting is the divergence of the anti-semitism of that date – 1895, the period of the Dreyfus case – and that of today.

To begin with, du Maurier evidently holds that there are two kinds of Jew, good ones and bad ones, and that there is a racial difference between them. There enters briefly into the story another Jew, Glorioli, who possesses all the virtues and qualities that Svengali lacks. Glorioli is "one of the Sephardim" – of Spanish extraction, that is – whereas Svengali, who comes from German Poland, is "an Oriental Israelite Hebrew Jew." Secondly, du Maurier considers that to have a dash of Jewish blood is an advantage. We are told that the hero, Little Billee, may have had some Jewish blood, of which there was a suggestion in his features, and "fortunately for the world, and especially for ourselves, most of us have in our veins at least a minim of that precious fluid." Clearly, this is not the Nazi form of anti-semitism.

And yet the tone of all the references to Svengali is almost unconsciously contemptuous, and the fact that du Maurier chose a Jew to play such a part is significant. Svengali, who cannot sing himself and has to sing, as it were, through Trilby's lungs, represents that well-known type, the clever underling who acts as the brains of some more impressive person.

It is queer how freely du Maurier admits that Svengali is more gifted than the three Englishmen, even than Little Billee, who is represented, unconvincingly, as a brilliant painter. Svengali has "genius," but the others have "character," and "character" is what matters. It is the attitude of the rugger-playing prefect towards the spectacled "swot," and it was probably the normal attitude towards Jews at that time. They were natural inferiors, but of course they were cleverer, more sensitive and more artistic than ourselves, because such qualities are of secondary importance. Nowadays the English are less sure of themselves, less confident that stupidity always wins in the end, and the prevailing form of anti-semitism has changed, not altogether for the better.

In last week's *Tribune* Mr. Julian Symons remarked – rightly, I think – that Aldous Huxley's later novels are much inferior to his earlier ones. But he might have added that this kind of falling-off is usual in imaginative writers, and that it only goes unnoticed when a writer is, so to speak, carried forward by the momentum of his earlier books. We value H. G. Wells, for example, for *Tono-Bungay, Mr. Polly, The Time Machine*, etc. If he had stopped writing in 1920 his reputation would stand quite as high as it does: if we knew him only by the books he wrote after that date, we should have rather a low opinion of him. A novelist does not, any more than a boxer or a ballet dancer, last for ever. He has an initial impulse which is good for three or four books, perhaps even for a dozen, but which must exhaust itself sooner or later. Obviously one cannot lay down any rigid rule, but in many cases the creative impulse seems to last for about 15 years: in a prose writer these 15 years would probably be between the ages of 30 and 45, or thereabouts. A few writers, it is true, have a much longer lease of life, and can go on developing when they are middle-aged or even old. But these are usually writers (examples: Yeats, Eliot, Hardy, Tolstoy) who make a sudden, almost violent change in their style, or their subject-matter, or both, and who may even tend to repudiate their earlier work.

Many writers, perhaps most, ought simply to stop writing when they reach middle age. Unfortunately our society will not let them stop. Most of them know no other way of earning a living, and writing, with all that goes with it – quarrels, rivalries, flattery, the sense of being a semi-public figure – is habit-forming. In a reasonable world a writer who had said his say would simply take up some other profession. In a competitive society he feels, just as a politician does, that retirement is death. So he continues long after his impulse is spent, and, as a rule, the less conscious he is of imitating himself, the more grossly he does it.

Early this year I met an American publisher who told me that his firm had just had a nine-months lawsuit from which it had emerged partially victorious, though out of pocket. It concerned the printing of a four-letter word which most of us use every day, generally in the present participle.

The United States is usually a few years ahead of Britain in these matters. You could print "b——" in full in American books at a time when it had to appear in English ones as B dash. Recently it has become possible in England to print the word in full in a book, but in periodicals it still has to be B dash. Only five or six years ago it was printed in a well-known monthly magazine, but the last-minute panic was so great that a weary staff had to black the word out by hand.

As to the other word, the four-letter one, it is still unprintable in periodicals in this country, but in books it can be represented by its first letter and a dash. In the United States this point was reached at least a dozen years ago. Last year the publishing firm in question tried the experiment of printing the word in full. The book was suppressed, and after nine months of litigation the suppression was upheld. But in the process an important step forward was made. It was ruled that you may now print the first and last letters of the word with two asterisks in between, clearly indicating that it had four letters. This makes it reasonably sure that within a few years the word will be printable in full.

So does progress continue – and it is genuine progress, in my opinion, for if only our half-dozen "bad" words could be got off the lavatory wall and on to the printed page, they would soon lose their magical quality, and the habit of swearing, degrading to our thoughts and weakening to our language, might become less common.

As I Please 65
Tribune, 13 December 1946

A correspondent writes:

"I would be so pleased if you could draw attention to the problem which seems to be in danger of becoming completely neglected. Do M.P.s, or any other people in authority, realise the immense amount of time, energy and nervous force that many citizens have to lose through the appalling insufficiency of laundries?"

I do not know whether M.P.s, as such, are aware of the present state of our laundry service, but anyone who has to fetch his washing for himself, at any rate in my district of London, will agree with every word that my correspondent says. Merely to get yourself "taken on" by a laundry is a difficult feat, not to be achieved until you have lived several months in the district and practised a good deal of intrigue and flattery into the bargain. Then there are the slowness and irregularity of deliveries, the dreary waiting in queues on rainy winter mornings, the lost articles, the inefficient checking system, the smashed buttons, the handkerchiefs which come back hardly whiter than they went. And worst of all, perhaps, the difficulty of getting your own washing back when you are sent somebody else's by mistake, because it is always due to some shortcoming "down at the works," and the bored young woman behind the counter knows nothing about it.

All this is only too true. But my correspondent goes on:

"If M.P.s considered the people, would not one of their first tasks be to nationalise the laundries? The laundry should be as smooth-running as the postal service. Is it fantastic to suggest that everything which makes for the easier running of the home should be a prime concern of a people's government?"

Unfortunately, nationalisation would not of itself make the laundries more efficient, any more than nationalising my typewriter would make it easier to write this article. Nationalisation is a long-term measure which in most cases does not effect an improvement but merely prepares the way for an improvement. Nationalising the coal mines, for instance, makes possible the heavy expenditure and the centralised control which are necessary before the mines can be brought up to date. But it will not for several years produce any more coal or make the lot of the miner any more bearable.

If the laundries were nationalised tomorrow they would have to carry straight on with the same personnel and equipment, and their efficiency would not greatly increase while the present shortages continue. The laundries are in a bad way because they lack soap, fuel, machinery, transport and, above all, labour. If they were given priority in any of these things, some other public utility would have to suffer. Everything leads back to the shortage of labour, which is made worse, in our present exhausted state, by the absence of any incentive to work long hours. We have entered on an uncomfortable reconstruction period which may last for years, and I wish the spokesmen of the Government would say so more boldly. Otherwise great numbers of people may lose all enthusiasm for nationalisation, having looked forward to it as a sort of panacea, and then found that it makes no immediate difference.

But I do agree that when life becomes livable again, the laundry system needs thorough reorganisation. It is a disgrace, for instance, that there has never really been a way of getting babies' clothes washed outside the house. Before the war there existed – it may recently have started up again – a diaper service which delivered twelve clean "nappies" daily. Only a few people could afford this luxury, and babies' clothes other than "nappies"always had to be washed at home, because no laundry was cheap or rapid enough to deal with the vast quantity of pants, cot sheets and so forth that the average baby works its way through. What must have been the effect on our birth-rate of that endless struggle with piles of dirty baby-linen in draughty stone-floored sculleries or in the tiny bathrooms of flats?

Recently I received a copy of Sir Stanley Unwin's interesting and useful book, *The Truth about Publishing*, which has appeared in a number of editions from 1926 onwards, and has recently been expanded and brought up to date. I particularly value it because it assembles certain figures which one might have difficulty in finding elsewhere. A year or so ago, writing in *Tribune* on the cost of reading matter, I made a guess at the average yearly expenditure on books in this country, and put it at £1 a head. It seems that I was pitching it too high. Here are some figures of national expenditure in 1945: –

Alcoholic beverages .... £685 millions
Tobacco .... £548 millions
Books.............................. £ 23 millions

In other words the average British citizen spends about 2d. a week on books, whereas he spends nearly 10 shillings on drink and tobacco. I suppose this noble figure of 2d. would include the amount spent on school textbooks and other books which are bought, so to speak, involuntarily. Is it any wonder that when recently a questionnaire was sent out by *Horizon*, asking twenty-one poets and novelists how they thought a writer could best earn his living, not one of them said plainly that he might earn it by writing books?

When one reads the reports of Uno conferences, or international negotiations of any kind, it is difficult not to be reminded of *L'Attaque* and similar war games that children used to play, with cardboard pieces representing battleships, aeroplanes and so forth, each of which had a fixed value and could be countered in some recognised way. In fact, one might almost invent a new game called Uno, to be played in enlightened homes where the parents do not want their children to grow up with a militaristic outlook.

The pieces in this game are called the proposal, the *démarche*, the formula, the stumbling block, the stalemate, the deadlock, the bottleneck and the vicious circle. The object of the game is to arrive at a formula, and though details vary, the general outline of play is always much the same. First the players assemble, and somebody leads off with the proposal. This is countered by the stumbling block, without which the game could not develop. The stumbling block then changes into a bottleneck, or more often into a deadlock or a vicious circle. A deadlock and a vicious circle occurring simultaneously produce a stalemate, which may last for weeks. Then suddenly someone plays the *démarche*. The *démarche* makes it possible to produce a formula, and once the formula has been found the players can go home, leaving everything as it was at the beginning.

At the moment of writing, the front page of my morning paper has broken out into a pink rash of optimism. It seems that everything is going to be all right after all. The Russians will agree to inspection of armaments, and the Americans will internationalise the atomic bomb. On another page of the same paper are reports of events in Greece which amount to a state of war between the two groups of powers who are being so chummy in New York.

But while the game of deadlocks and bottlenecks goes on, another more serious game is also being played. It is governed by two axioms. One is that there can be no peace without a general surrender of sovereignty: the other is that no country capable of defending its sovereignty ever surrenders it. If one keeps these axioms in mind one can generally see the relevant facts in international affairs through the smoke-screen with which the newspapers surround them. At the moment the main facts are: —

(i) The Russians, whatever they may say, will not agree to genuine inspection of their territories by foreign observers.

(ii) The Americans, whatever they may say, will not let slip the technological lead in armaments.

(iii) No country is now in a condition to fight an all-out major war.

These, although they may be superseded later, are at present the real counters in the real game, and one gets nearer the truth by constantly remembering them than by alternately rejoicing and despairing over the day-to-day humbug of conferences.

As I Please 66
Tribune, 20 December 1946

An advertisement in my Sunday paper sets forth in the form of a picture the four things that are needed for a successful Christmas. At the top of the picture is a roast turkey; below that, a Christmas pudding; below that, a dish of mince pies; and below that, a tin of —'s Liver Salt.

It is a simple recipe for happiness. First the meal, then the antidote, then another meal. The ancient Romans were the great masters of this technique. However, having just looked up the word *vomitorium* in the Latin dictionary, I find that after all it does *not* mean a place where you went to be sick after dinner. So perhaps this was not a normal feature of every Roman home, as is commonly believed.

Implied in the above-mentioned advertisement is the notion that a good meal means a meal at which you over-eat yourself. In principle I agree. I only add in passing that when we gorge ourselves this Christmas, if we do get the chance to gorge ourselves, it is worth giving a thought to the thousand million human beings, or thereabouts, who will be doing no such thing. For in the long run our Christmas dinners would be safer if we could make sure that everyone else had a Christmas dinner as well. But I will come back to that presently.

The only reasonable motive for not over-eating at Christmas would be that somebody else needs the food more than you do. A deliberately austere Christmas would be an absurdity. The whole point of Christmas is that it is a debauch – as it was probably long before the birth of Christ was arbitrarily fixed at that date. Children know this very well. From their point of view Christmas is not a day of temperate enjoyment, but of fierce pleasures which they are quite willing to pay for with a certain amount of pain. The awakening at about 4 a.m. to inspect your stocking; the quarrels over toys all through the morning, and the exciting whiffs of mincemeat and sage-and-onions escaping from the kitchen door; the battle with enormous platefuls of turkey, and the pulling of the wishbone; the darkening of the windows and the entry of the flaming plum-pudding; the hurry to make sure that everyone has a piece on his plate while the brandy is still alight; the momentary panic when it is rumoured that Baby has swallowed the three-penny bit; the stupor all through the afternoon; the Christmas cake with almond icing an inch thick; the peevishness next morning and the castor oil on December 27th – it is an up and-down business, by no means all pleasant, but well worth while for the sake of its more dramatic moments.

Teetotallers and vegetarians are always scandalised by this attitude. As they see it, the only rational objective is to avoid pain and to stay alive as long as possible. If you refrain from drinking alcohol, or eating meat, or whatever it is, you may expect to live an extra five years, while if you over-eat or over-drink you will pay for it in acute physical pain on the following day. Surely it follows that all excesses, even a once-a-year outbreak such as Christmas, should be avoided as a matter of course?

Actually it doesn't follow at all. One may decide, with full knowledge of what one is doing, that an occasional good time is worth the damage it inflicts on one's liver. For health is not the only thing that matters: friendship, hospitality, and the heightened spirits and change of outlook that one gets by eating and drinking in good company are also valuable. I doubt whether, on balance, even outright drunkenness does harm, provided it is infrequent – twice a year, say. The whole experience, including the repentance afterwards, makes a sort of break in one's mental routine, comparable to a weekend in a foreign country, which is probably beneficial.

In all ages men have realised this. There is a wide consensus of opinion, stretching back to the days before the alphabet, that whereas habitual soaking is bad, conviviality is good, even if one does sometimes feel sorry for it next morning. How enormous is the literature of eating and drinking, especially drinking, and how little that is worth while has been said on the other side! Offhand I can't remember a single poem in praise of water, i.e. water regarded as a drink. It is hard to imagine what one could say about it. It quenches thirst: that is the end of the story. As for poems in praise of wine, on the other hand, even the surviving ones would fill a shelf of books. The poets started turning them out on the very day when the fermentation of the grape was first discovered. Whisky, brandy and other distilled liquors have been less eloquently praised, partly because they came later in time. But beer has had quite a good press, starting well back in the Middle Ages, long before anyone had learned to put hops in it. Curiously enough, I can't remember a poem in praise of stout, not even draught stout, which is better than the bottled variety, in my opinion. There is an extremely disgusting description in *Ulysses* of the stout-vats in Dublin. But there is a sort of back-handed tribute to stout in the fact that this description, though widely known, has not done much towards putting the Irish off their favourite drink.

The literature of eating is also large, though mostly in prose. But in all the writers who have enjoyed describing food, from Rabelais to Dickens and from Petronius to Mrs. Beeton, I cannot remember a single passage which puts dietetic consider-ations first. Always food is felt to be an end in itself. No one has written memorable prose about vitamins, or the dangers of an excess of proteins, or the importance of masticating everything thirty-two times. All in all, there seems to be a heavy weight of testimony on the side of over-eating and over-drinking, pro-vided always that they take place on recognised occasions, and not too frequently.

But ought we to over-eat and over-drink this Christmas? We ought not to, nor will most of us get the opportunity. I am writing in praise of Christmas, but in praise of Christmas 1947, or perhaps 1948. The world as a whole is not exactly in a condition for festivities this year. Between the Rhine and the Pacific there cannot be very many people who are in need of —'s Liver Salt. In India there are, and always have been, about 100 million people who only get one square meal a day. In China, conditions are no doubt much the same. In Germany, Austria, Greece and elsewhere, scores of millions of people are existing on a diet which keeps breath in the body but leaves no strength for work. All over the war-wrecked areas from Brussels to Stalingrad, other uncounted millions are living in the cellars of bombed houses, in hide-outs in the forests, or in squalid huts behind barbed wire. It is not so pleasant to read almost simultaneously that a large proportion of our Christmas turkeys will come from Hungary, and that the Hungarian writers and journalists – presumably not the worse-paid section of the community – are in such desperate straits that they would be glad to receive presents of saccharine and cast-off clothing from English sympathisers. In such circum-stances we could hardly have a "proper" Christmas, even if the materials for it existed.

But we will have one sooner or later, in 1947, or 1948, or maybe even in 1949. And when we do, there may be no gloomy voices of vegetarians or teetotallers to lecture us about the things that we are doing to the linings of our stomachs. One celebrates a feast for its own sake, and not for any supposed benefit to the lining of one's stomach. Meanwhile Christmas is here, or nearly. Santa Claus is rounding up his reindeer, the postman staggers from door to door beneath his bulging sack of Christmas cards, the black markets are humming, and Britain has imported over 7,000 crates of mistletoe from France. So I wish everyone an old-fashioned Christmas in 1947, and meanwhile, half a turkey, three tangerines, and a bottle of whisky at not more than double the legal price.

As I Please 67
Tribune, 27 December 1946

Somewhere or other – I think it is in the preface to *Saint Joan* – Bernard Shaw remarks that we are more gullible and superstitious today than we were in the Middle Ages, and as an example of modern credulity he cites the widespread belief that the earth is round. The average man, says Shaw, can advance not a single reason for thinking that the earth is round. He merely swallows this theory because there is something about it that appeals to the twentieth-century mentality.

Now, Shaw is exaggerating, but there is something in what he says, and the question is worth following up, for the sake of the light it throws on modern knowledge. Just why *do* we believe that the earth is round? I am not speaking of the few thousand astronomers, geographers and so forth who could give ocular proof, or have a theoretical knowledge of the proof, but of the ordinary newspaper-reading citizen, such as you or me.

As for the Flat Earth theory, I believe I could refute it. If you stand by the seashore on a clear day, you can see the masts and funnels of invisible ships passing along the horizon. This phenomenon can only be explained by assuming that the earth's surface is curved. But it does not follow that the earth is spherical. Imagine another theory called the Oval Earth theory, which claims that the earth is shaped like an egg. What can I say against it?

Against the Oval Earth man, the first card I can play is the analogy of the sun and moon. The Oval Earth man promptly answers that I don't know, by my own observation, that those bodies are spherical. I only know that they are round, and they may perfectly well be flat discs. I have no answer to that one. Besides, he goes on, what reason have I for thinking that the earth must be the same shape as the sun and moon? I can't answer that one either.

My second card is the earth's shadow: when cast on the moon during eclipses, it appears to be the shadow of a round object. But how do I know, demands the Oval Earth man, that eclipses of the moon are caused by the shadow of the earth? The answer is that I don't know, but have taken this piece of information blindly from newspaper articles and science booklets.

Defeated in the minor exchanges, I now play my queen of trumps: the opinion of the experts. The Astronomer Royal, who ought to know, tells me that the earth is round. The Oval Earth man covers the queen with his king. Have I tested the Astronomer Royal's statement, and would I even know a way of testing it? Here I bring out my ace. Yes, I do know one test. The astronomers can foretell eclipses, and this suggests that their opinions about the solar system are pretty sound. I am therefore justified in accepting their say-so about the shape of the earth.

If the Oval Earth man answers – what I believe is true – that the ancient Egyptians, who thought the sun goes round the earth, could also predict eclipses, then bang goes my ace. I have only one card left: navigation. People can sail ships round the world, and reach the places they aim at, by calculations which assume that the earth is spherical. I believe that finishes the Oval Earth man, though even then he may possibly have some kind of counter.

It will be seen that my reasons for thinking that the earth is round are rather precarious ones. Yet this is an exceptionally elementary piece of information. On most other questions I should have to fall back on the expert much earlier, and would be less able to test his pronouncements. And much the greater part of our knowledge is at this level. It does not rest on reasoning or on experiment, but on authority. And how can it be otherwise, when the range of knowledge is so vast that the expert himself is an ignoramus as soon as he strays away from his own speciality? Most people, if asked to prove that the earth is round, would not even bother to produce the rather weak arguments I have outlined above. They would start off by saying that "everyone knows" the earth to be round, and if pressed further, would become angry. In a way Shaw is right. This *is* a credulous age, and the burden of knowledge which we now have to carry is partly responsible.

Opinions may differ about the verdict in Professor Laski's libel case. But even if one feels that the verdict was technically justified, I think it should be remembered that Professor Laski took this action – in effect – on behalf of the Labour Party. It was an incident in the General Election – a reply, felt at the time to be necessary, to the anti-red propaganda of part of the Conservative Press. It will therefore be extremely unfair if he is left to pay the very heavy costs unaided. May I remind everyone again that contributions should be sent to Morgan Phillips, Secretary, Labour Party, Transport House.

The Laski case will presumably lead to further discussions about the composition of juries, particularly Special Juries, but I wish it would have the incidental effect of drawing people's attention once again to the present state of the law of libel.

I believe the libel trade, like some other trades, went through a slack period during the war, but a few years before that the bringing of frivolous libel actions was a major racket and a nightmare to editors, publishers, authors and journalists alike. Some people used to declare that it would be better if the libel laws were abolished altogether, or at any rate greatly relaxed, so that newspapers had as much latitude as they used to have, for instance, in pre-war France. I cannot agree with this. Innocent people have a right to protection against slander. The racket arose not so much because the law is unduly strict as because it is possible to obtain damages for a libel from which one has not suffered any pecuniary loss.

The sufferers are not so much the big newspapers, which have fleets of retained lawyers and can afford to pay damages, as publishers and small periodicals. I do not know the exact provisions of the law, but from interviews with terrified solicitors which I have sometimes had before a book went to press, I gather that it is almost impossible to invent a fictitious character which might not be held to be a portrait of a real person. As a result, a blackmailing libel action is an easy way of picking up money. Publishing houses and periodicals are often insured against libel up to a certain sum, which means that they will pay a smallish claim sooner than fight an action. In one case I have even heard of collusion being practised. A arranged to libel B, B threatened an action, and the pair of them split the proceeds.

It seems to me that the way to put this right is to make sure that a libel action cannot be profitable. Except where it can be shown that actual loss has been suffered, let no damages be paid. On the other hand, where a libel is proved, the guilty party should make a retraction in print, which at present does not usually happen. Big newspapers would be much more frightened of that than of paying out £10,000 damages, while, if no money payments were made, the motive for blackmailing actions would have disappeared.

A correspondent has sent me a copy of one of the disgusting American "comics" which I referred to a few weeks ago. The two main stories in it are about a beautiful creature called the Hangman, who has a green face, and, like so many characters in American strips, can fly. On the front page there is a picture of what is either an ape-like lunatic, or an actual ape dressed up as a man, strangling a woman so realistically that her tongue is sticking four inches out of her mouth. Another item is a python looping itself round a man's neck and then hanging him by suspending itself over a balustrade. Another is a man jumping out of a skyscraper window and hitting the pavement with a splash. There is much else of the same kind.

My correspondent asks me whether I think this is the kind of thing that should be put into the hands of children, and also whether we could not find something better on which to spend our dwindling dollars.

Certainly I would keep these things out of children's hands if possible. But I would not be in favour of actually prohibiting their sale. The precedent is too dangerous. But meanwhile, *are* we actually using dollars to pay for this pernicious rubbish? The point is not completely unimportant, and I should like to see it cleared up.

1947

As I Please 68

Tribune, 3 January 1947

Nearly a quarter of a century ago I was travelling on a liner to Burma. Though not a big ship, it was a comfortable and even a luxurious one, and when one was not asleep or playing deck games one usually seemed to be eating. The meals were of that stupendous kind that steamship companies used to vie with one another in producing, and in between times there were snacks such as apples, ices, biscuits and cups of soup, lest anyone should find himself fainting from hunger. Moreover, the bars opened at ten in the morning, and, since we were at sea, alcohol was relatively cheap.

The ships of this line were mostly manned by Indians, but apart from the officers and the stewards they carried four European quartermasters whose job was to take the wheel. One of these quartermasters, though I suppose he was only aged forty or so, was one of those old sailors on whose back you almost expect to see barnacles growing. He was a short, powerful, rather ape-like man, with enormous forearms covered by a mat of golden hair. A blond moustache which might have belonged to Charlemagne completely hid his mouth. I was only twenty years old and very conscious of my parasitic status as a mere passenger, and I looked up to the quartermasters, especially the fair-haired one, as godlike beings on a par with the officers. It would not have occurred to me to speak to one of them without being spoken to first.

One day, for some reason, I came up from lunch early. The deck was empty except for the fair-haired quartermaster, who was scurrying like a rat along the side of the deck-houses, with something partially concealed between his monstrous hands. I had just time to see what it was before he shot past me and vanished into a doorway. It was a pie dish containing a half-eaten baked custard pudding.

At one glance I took in the situation – indeed, the man's air of guilt made it unmistakable. The pudding was a left-over from one of the passengers' tables. It had been illicitly given to him by a steward, and he was carrying it off to the seamen's quarters to devour it at leisure. Across more than twenty years I can still faintly feel the shock of astonishment that I felt at that moment. It took me some time to see the incident in all its bearings: but do I seem to exaggerate when I say that this sudden revelation of the gap between function and reward – the revelation that a highly-skilled craftsman, who might literally hold all our lives in his hands, was glad to steal scraps of food from our table – taught me more than I could have learned from half a dozen Socialist pamphlets?

A news item to the effect that Yugoslavia is now engaged on a purge of writers and artists led me to look once again at the reports of the recent literary purge in the U.S.S.R., when Zoschenko, Akhmatova and others were expelled from the Writers' Union.

In England this kind of thing is not happening to us as yet, so that we can view it with a certain detachment, and, curiously enough, as I look again at the accounts of what happened, I feel somewhat more sorry for the persecutors than for their victims. Chief among the persecutors is Andrei Zhdanov, considered by some to be Stalin's probable successor. Zhdanov, though he has conducted literary purges before, is a full-time politician with – to judge from his speeches – about as much knowledge of literature as I have of aerodynamics. He does not give the impression of being, according to his own lights, a wicked or dishonest man. He is truly shocked by the defection of certain Soviet writers, which appears to him as an incomprehensible piece of treachery, like a military mutiny in the middle of a battle. The purpose of literature is to glorify the Soviet Union; surely that must be obvious to everyone? But instead of carrying out their plain duty, these misguided writers keep straying away from the paths of propaganda, producing non-political works, and even, in the case of Zoschenko, allowing a satirical note to creep into their writings. It is all very painful and bewildering. It is as though you set a man to work in an excellent, up-to-date, air-conditioned factory, gave him high wages, short hours, good canteens and playing-grounds, a comfortable flat, a nursery-school for his children, all-round social insurance and music while you work – only to find the ungrateful fellow throwing spanners into the machinery on his very first day.

What makes the whole thing somewhat pathetic is the general admission – an honest admission, seeing that Soviet publicists are not in the habit of decrying their own country – that Russian literature as a whole is not what it ought to be. Since the U.S.S.R. represents the highest existing form of civilisation, it is obvious that it ought to lead the world in literature as in everything else. "Surely," says Zhdanov, "our new Socialist system, embodying all that is best in the history of human civilisation and culture, is capable of creating the most advanced literature, which will leave far behind the best creations of olden times." *Izvestia* (as quoted by the New York paper, *Politics*), goes further: "Our culture stands on an immeasurably higher level than bourgeois culture. . . . Is it not clear that our culture has the right not to act as pupil and imitator but, on the contrary, to teach others the general human morals?" And yet somehow the expected thing never happens. Directives are issued, resolutions are passed unanimously, recalcitrant writers are silenced: and yet for some reason a vigorous and original literature, unmistakably superior to that of capitalist countries, fails to emerge.

All this has happened before, and more than once. Freedom of expression has had its ups and downs in the U.S.S.R., but the general tendency has been towards tighter censorship. The thing that politicians are seemingly unable to understand is that you cannot produce a vigorous literature by terrorising everyone into conformity. A writer's inventive faculties will not work unless he is allowed to say approximately what he feels. You can destroy spontaneity and produce a literature which is orthodox but feeble, or you can let people say what they choose and take the risk that some of them will utter heresies. There is no way out of that dilemma so long as books have to be written by individuals.

That is why, in a way, I feel sorrier for the persecutors than for the victims. It is probable that Zoschenko and the others at least have the satisfaction of understanding what is happening to them: the politicians who harry them are merely attempting the impossible. For Zhdanov and his kind to say, "The Soviet Union can exist without literature," would be reasonable. But that is just what they can't say. They don't know what literature is, but they know that it is important, that it has prestige value, and that it is necessary for propaganda purposes, and they would like to encourage it, if only they knew how. So they continue with their purges and directives, like a fish bashing its nose against the wall of an aquarium again and again, too dim-witted to realise that glass and water are not the same thing.

From *The Thoughts of the Emperor Marcus Aurelius*:

> In the morning when thou risest unwillingly, let this thought be present – I am rising to the work of a human being. Why then am I dissatisfied if I am going to do the things for which I exist and for which I was brought into the world? Or have I been made for this, to lie in the bed-clothes and keep myself warm? – But this is more pleasant – Dost thou exist then to take thy pleasure, and not at all for action or exertion? Dost thou not see the little plants, the little birds, the ants, the spiders, the bees working together to put in order their several parts of the universe? And art thou unwilling to do the work of a human being, and dost thou not make haste to do that which is according to thy nature?

It is a good plan to print this well-known exhortation in large letters and hang it on the wall opposite your bed. And if that fails, as I am told it sometimes does, another good plan is to buy the loudest alarm clock you can get and place it in such a position that you have to get out of bed and go round several pieces of furniture in order to silence it.

As I Please 69
Tribune, 17 January 1947

The *Daily Herald* for January 1, 1947, has a headline MEN WHO SPOKE FOR HITLER HERE, and underneath this a photograph of two Indians who are declared to be Brijlal Mukerjee and Anjit Singh, and are described as having come "from Berlin." The news column below the photograph goes on to say that "four Indians who might have been shot as traitors" are staying at a London hotel, and further describes the group of Indians who broadcast over the German radio during the war as "collaborators." It is worth looking a bit more closely at these various statements.

To begin with, there are at least two errors of fact, one of them a very serious one. Anjit Singh did not broadcast on the Nazi radio, but only from Italian stations, while the man described as "Brijlal Mukerjee" is an Indian who has been in England throughout the war and is well known to myself and many other people in London. But these inaccuracies are really the symptom of an attitude of mind which comes out more clearly in the phraseology of the report.

What right have we to describe the Indians who broadcast on the German radio as "collaborators"? They were citizens of an occupied country, hitting back at the occupying power in the way that seemed to them best. I am not suggesting that the way they chose was the right one. Even from the narrow point of view which would assume that Indian independence is the only cause that matters, I think they were gravely wrong, because if the Axis had won the war – and their efforts must have aided the Axis to some extent – India would merely have had a new and worse master. But the line they took was one that could perfectly well be taken in good faith, and cannot with fairness or even with accuracy be termed "collaboration." The word "collaboration" is associated with people like Quisling and Laval. It implies, first of all, treachery to one's own country, secondly, full co-operation with the conqueror, and thirdly, ideological agreement, or at least partial agreement. But how does this apply to the Indians who sided with the Axis? They were not being traitors to their own country – on the contrary, they were working for its independence, as they believed – and they recognised no obligation to Britain. Nor did they co-operate in the same manner as Quisling, etc. The Germans allowed them a separate broadcasting unit on which they said what they liked and followed, in many cases, a political line quite different from the Axis one. In my opinion they were mistaken and mischievous, but in moral attitude, and probably in the effects of what they did, they were quite different from ordinary renegades.

Meanwhile one has to consider the effect of this kind of thing in India. Rightly or wrongly, these men will be welcomed as heroes when they get home, and the fact that British newspapers insult them will not go unnoticed. Nor will the slovenly handling of the photographs. The caption "Brijlal Mukerjee" appears under the face of a totally different person. No doubt the photograph was taken at the reception which the repatriated Indians were given by their fellow-countrymen in London, and the photographer snapped the wrong man by mistake. But suppose the person in question had been William Joyce. In that case, don't you think the *Daily Herald* would have taken good care that it *was* photographing William Joyce and not somebody else? But since it's only an Indian, a mistake of this kind doesn't matter – so runs the unspoken thought. And this happens not in the *Daily Graphic*, but in Britain's sole Labour newspaper.

I hope everyone who can get access to a copy will take at least a glance at Victor Gollancz's recently published book, *In Darkest Germany* (Gollancz, 8/6). It is not a literary book, but a piece of brilliant journalism intended to shock the public of this country into some kind of consciousness of the hunger, disease, chaos and lunatic mismanagement prevailing in the British zone. This business of making people *conscious* of what is happening outside their own small circle is one of the major problems of our time, and a new literary technique will have to be evolved to meet it. Considering that the people of this country are not having a very comfortable time, you can't, perhaps, blame them for being somewhat callous about suffering elsewhere, but the remarkable thing is the extent to which they manage to remain unaware of it. Tales of starvation, ruined cities, concentration camps, mass deportations, homeless refugees, persecuted Jews – all this is received with a sort of incurious surprise, as though such things had never been heard of before but at the same time were not particularly interesting. The now-familiar photographs of skeleton-like children make very little impression. As time goes on and the horrors pile up, the mind seems to secrete a sort of self-protecting ignorance which needs a harder and harder shock to pierce it, just as the body will become immunised to a drug and require bigger and bigger doses.

Half of Victor Gollancz's book consists of photographs, and he has taken the wise precaution of including himself in a good many of them. This at least proves that the photographs are genuine and cuts out the routine charge that they have been obtained from an agency and are "all propaganda." But I think the best device in the book, after innumerable descriptions of people living on "biscuit soup," potatoes and cabbage, skim milk and ersatz coffee, was to include some menus of dinners in the messes provided for the Control Commission. Mr. Gollancz says that he slipped a menu card into his pocket whenever he could do so unobserved, and he prints half a dozen of them. Here is the first on the list:

Consommé in cups

———

Fried Soles in Butter
Fresh potatoes

———

Dutch Steak
Mashed Potatoes
Cauliflower

———

Raspberry Cream

———

Cheese

———

Coffee.

These accounts of starvation in Europe seem to link up with a paragraph, headed "This Week's Hint for Dog-lovers," which I cut out of the *Evening Standard* just before Christmas:

Your dog may also have that "after Christmas hangover" feeling if you have been indulging him with too many titbits. Many owners like to give their pets "a taste of everything," regardless of the fact that many of the items of Christmas fare are unsuitable for dogs.

No permanent harm may be done, but if the dog seems dull, the tongue loses colour and the breath becomes offensive, a dose of castor oil is indicated.

Twelve hours rest from food, followed by a light diet for a few days, usually effects a speedy cure – and from eight to twelve grains of carbonate of bismuth may be given three times a day. The dog should be encouraged to drink barley water rather than plain water.

Signed by a Fellow of the Zoological Society.

Looking through what I have written above, I notice that I have used the phrase "a totally different person." For the first time it occurs to me what a stupid expression this is. As though there could be such a thing as a partially different person! I shall try to cut this phrase (and also "a very different person" and "a different person altogether") out of my vocabulary from now onwards.

But there are other words and phrases which obviously deserve to go on the scrapheap, but which continue to be used because there seems to be no convenient substitute. An example is the word "certain." We say, for instance, "After a certain age one's hair turns grey," or "There will probably be a certain amount of snow in February." In all such sentences, "certain" means *uncertain*. Why do we have to use this word in two opposite meanings? And yet, unless one pedantically says "after an uncertain age," etc., there appears to be no other word which will exactly cover the required meaning.

As I Please 70
Tribune, 24 January 1947

Recently I was listening to a conversation between two small business-men in a Scottish hotel. One of them, an alert-looking, well-dressed man of about forty-five, was something to do with the Federation of Master Builders. The other, a good deal older, with white hair and a broad Scottish accent, was some kind of wholesale tradesman. He said grace before his meals, a thing I had not seen anyone do for many a year. They belonged, I should say, in the £2,000-a-year and the £1,000-a-year income groups respectively.

We were sitting round a rather inadequate peat fire, and the conversation started off with the coal shortage. There was no coal, it appeared, because the British miners refused to dig it out, but on the other hand it was important not to let Poles work in the pits because this would lead to unemployment. There was severe unemployment in Scotland already. The older man then remarked with quiet satisfaction that he was very glad – "varra glad indeed" – that Labour had won the general election. Any government that had to clean up after the war was in for a bad time, and as a result of five years of rationing, housing shortage, unofficial strikes and so forth, the general public would see through the promises of the Socialists and vote Conservative next time.

They began talking about the housing problem, and almost immediately they were back to the congenial subject of the Poles. The younger man had just sold his flat in Edinburgh at a good profit and was trying to buy a house. He was willing to pay £2,700. The other was trying to sell his house for £1,500 and buy a smaller one. But it seemed that it was impossible to buy houses or flats nowadays. The Poles were buying them all up, and "where they get the money from is a mystery." The Poles were also invading the medical profession. They even had their own medical school in Edinburgh or Glasgow (I forget which) and were turning out doctors in great numbers while "our lads" found it impossible to buy practices. Didn't everyone know that Britain had more doctors than it could use? Let the Poles go back to their own country. There were too many people in this country already. What was needed was emigration.

The younger man remarked that he belonged to several business and civic associations, and that on all of them he made a point of putting forward resolutions that the Poles should be sent back to their own country. The older one added that the Poles were "very degraded in their morals." They were responsible for much of the immorality that was prevalent nowadays. "Their ways are not our ways," he concluded piously. It was not mentioned that the Poles pushed their way to the head of queues, wore bright-coloured clothes and displayed cowardice during air raids, but if I had put forward a suggestion to this effect I am sure it would have been accepted.

One cannot, of course, do very much about this kind of thing. It is the contemporary equivalent of anti-semitism. By

1947, people of the kind I am describing would have caught up with the fact that anti-semitism is discreditable, and so the scapegoat is sought elsewhere. But the race hatred and mass delusions which are part of the pattern of our time might be somewhat less bad in their effects if they were not reinforced by ignorance. If in the years before the war, for instance, the facts about the persecution of Jews in Germany had been better known, the subjective popular feeling against Jews would probably not have been less, but the actual treatment of Jewish refugees might have been better. The refusal to allow refugees in significant numbers into this country would have been branded as disgraceful. The average man would still have felt a grudge against the refugees, but in practice more lives would have been saved.

So also with the Poles. The thing that most depressed me in the above-mentioned conversation was the recurrent phrase, "let them go back to their own country." If I had said to those two business-men, "Most of these people have no country to go back to," they would have gaped. Not one of the relevant facts would have been known to them. They would never have heard of the various things that have happened to Poland since 1939, any more than they would have known that the over-population of Britain is a fallacy or that local unemployment can co-exist with a general shortage of labour. I think it is a mistake to give such people the excuse of ignorance. You can't actually change their feelings, but you can make them understand what they are saying when they demand that homeless refugees shall be driven from our shores, and the knowledge may make them a little less actively malignant.

The other week, in the *Spectator*, Mr. Harold Nicolson was consoling himself as best he could for having reached the age of sixty. As he perceived, the only positive satisfaction in growing older is that after a certain point you can begin boasting of having seen things that no one will ever have the chance to see again. It set me wondering what boasts I could make myself, at forty-four, or nearly. Mr. Nicolson had seen the Czar, surrounded by his bodyguard of enormous Cossacks, blessing the Neva. I never saw that, but I did see Marie Lloyd, already almost a legendary figure, and I saw Little Tich – who, I think, did not die till about 1928, but who must have retired at about the same time as Marie Lloyd – and I have seen a whole string of crowned heads and other celebrities from Edward VII onwards. But on only two occasions did I feel, at the time, that I was seeing something significant, and on one of those occasions it was the circumstances and not the person concerned that made me feel this.

One of these celebrities was Pétain. It was at Foch's funeral in 1929. Pétain's personal prestige in France was very great. He was honoured as the defender of Verdun, and the phrase "They shall not pass" was popularly supposed to have been coined by him. He was given a place to himself in the procession, with a gap of several yards in front of and behind him. As he stalked past – a tall, lean, very erect figure, though he must have been seventy years old or thereabouts, with great sweeping white moustaches like the wings of a gull – a whisper of "*Voilà Pétain!*" went rippling through the vast crowd. His appearance impressed me so much that I dimly felt, in spite of his considerable age, that he might still have some kind of distinguished future ahead of him.

The other celebrity was Queen Mary. One day I was walking past Windsor Castle when a sort of electric shock seemed to go through the street. People were taking their hats off, soldiers springing to attention. And then, clattering over the cobbles, there came a huge, plum-coloured open carriage drawn by four horses with postillions. I believe it was the first and last time in my life that I have seen a postillion. On the rear seat, with his back to the carriage, another groom sat stiffly upright, with his arms folded. The groom who sat at the back used to be called the tiger. I hardly noticed the Queen, my eyes were fixed on that strange, archaic figure at the back, immobile as a waxwork, with his white breeches that looked as though he had been poured into them, and the cockade on his top hat. Even at that date (1920 or thereabouts) it gave me a wonderful feeling of looking backwards through a window into the nineteenth century.

Some scraps of literary intelligence: –

A few weeks ago I quoted an Indian proverb in this column, and erroneously said that it had been translated by a friend of mine. Actually the verse I quoted comes from Kipling. This illustrates something I have pointed out elsewhere – that Kipling is one of those writers whom one quotes unconsciously.

The *Partisan Review*, one of the best of the American high-brow magazines – rather like a synthesis of *Horizon* and *Polemic* – is to be published in London from February onwards.

Zamyatin's novel *We*, about which I wrote an article in *Tribune* a year or so ago, is to be reissued in this country. A fresh translation is being made from the Russian. Look out for this book.

As I Pleased 71
Tribune, 31 January 1947

One's relations with a newspaper or a magazine are more variable and intermittent than they can be with a human being. From time to time a human being may dye his hair or become converted to Roman Catholicism, but he cannot change himself fundamentally, whereas a periodical will go through a whole series of different existences under the same name. *Tribune* in its short life has been two distinct papers, if not three, and my own contacts with it have varied sharply, starting off, if I remember rightly, with a rap on the knuckles.

I did not learn of the existence of *Tribune* till some time in 1939. It had started early in 1937, but of the thirty months that intervened before the outbreak of war I spent five in hospital and thirteen abroad. What first drew my attention to it, I believe, was a none too friendly review of a novel of mine. During the period 1939–42 I produced three or four books and reprints, and I think it is true that I never had what is called a "good" review in *Tribune* until after I became a member of the staff. (The two events were unconnected, needless to say.) Somewhat later, in the cold winter of 1939, I started writing for *Tribune*, though at first, curiously enough, without seeing it regularly or getting a clear idea of what kind of paper it was.

Raymond Postgate, who was then editor, had asked me to do the novel reviews from time to time. I was not paid (until recently it was unusual for contributors to left-wing papers to be paid), and I only saw the paper on the somewhat rare occasions when I went up to London and visited Postgate in a bare and dusty office near London Wall. *Tribune* (until a good deal later everyone called it "the" *Tribune*) was at that time in difficulties. It was still a threepenny paper aimed primarily at the industrial workers and following more or less the Popular Front line which had been associated with the Left Book Club and the Socialist League. With the outbreak of war its circulation had taken a severe knock, because the Communists and near-Communists who had been among its warmest supporters now refused to help in distributing it. Some of them went on writing for it, however, and the futile controversy between "supporters" and "opposers" of the war continued to rumble in its columns while the German armies gathered for the spring offensives.

Early in 1940 there was a large meeting in a public hall, the purpose of which was to discuss both the future of *Tribune* and the policy of the left wing of the Labour Party. As is usual on such occasions nothing very definite was said, and what I chiefly remember is a political tip which I received from an inside source. The Norway campaign was ending in disaster, and I had walked to the hall past gloomy posters. Two M.P.s, whom I will not name, had just arrived from the House.

"What chance is there," I asked them, "of this business getting rid of Chamberlain?"

"Not a hope," they both said. "He's solid."

I don't remember dates, but I think it can only have been a week or two before Chamberlain was out of the Premiership.

After that *Tribune* passed out of my consciousness for nearly two years. I was very busy trying to earn a living and write a book amid the bombs and the general disorganisation, and any spare time I had was taken up by the Home Guard, which was still an amateur force and demanded an immense amount of work from its members. When I became aware of *Tribune* again I was working in the Eastern Service of the B.B.C. It was now an almost completely different paper. It had a different make-up, cost sixpence, was orientated chiefly towards foreign policy, and was rapidly acquiring a new public which mostly belonged, I should say, to the out-at-elbow middle class. Its prestige among the B.B.C. personnel was very striking. In the libraries where commentators went to prime themselves it was one of the most sought-after periodicals, not only because it was largely written by people who knew something at first hand about Europe, but because it was then the only paper of any standing which criticised the Government. Perhaps "criticised" is an over-mild word. Sir Stafford Cripps had gone into the Government, and the fiery personality of Aneurin Bevan gave the paper its tone. On one occasion there were some surprisingly violent attacks on Churchill by someone who called himself Thomas Rainsboro'. This was obviously a pseudonym, and I spent a whole afternoon trying to determine the authorship by stylistic evidence, as the literary critics employed by the Gestapo were said to do with anonymous pamphlets. Finally I decided that "Thomas Rainsboro'" was a certain W—. A day or two later I met Victor Gollancz, who said to me:

"Do you know who wrote those Thomas Rainsboro' articles in *Tribune?* I've just heard. It was W—."

This made me feel very acute, but a day or two later I heard that we were both wrong.

During this period I occasionally wrote articles for *Tribune*, but only at long intervals, because I had little time or energy. However, towards the end of 1943 I decided to give up my job in the B.B.C., and I was asked to take over the literary editorship of *Tribune*, in place of John Atkins, who was expecting call-up. I went on being literary editor, as well as writing the "As I Please" column, until the beginning of 1945. It was interesting, but it is not a period that I look back on with pride. The fact is that I am no good at editing. I hate planning ahead, and I have a psychical or even physical inability to answer letters. My most essential memory of that time is of pulling out a drawer here and a drawer there, finding it in each case to be stuffed with letters and manuscripts which ought to have been dealt with weeks earlier, and hurriedly shutting it up again. Also, I have a fatal tendency to accept manuscripts which I know very well are too bad to be printed. It is questionable whether anyone who has had long experience as a freelance journalist ought to become an editor. It is too like taking a convict out of his cell and making him governor of the prison. Still, it was "all experience," as they say, and I have friendly memories of my cramped little office looking out on a back yard, and the three of us who shared it huddling in the corner as the doodle-bugs came zooming over, and the peaceful click-click of the typewriters starting up again as soon as the bomb had crashed.

Early in 1945 I went to Paris as correspondent for the *Observer*. In Paris *Tribune* had a prestige which was somewhat astonishing and which dated from before the liberation. It was impossible to buy it, and the ten copies which the British Embassy received weekly did not, I believe, get outside the walls of the building. Yet all the French journalists I met seemed to have heard of it and to know that it was the one paper in England which had neither supported the Government uncritically, nor opposed the war, nor swallowed the Russian myth. At that time there was – I should like to be sure that it still exists – a weekly paper named *Libertés*, which was roughly speaking the opposite number of *Tribune* and which during the occupation had been clandestinely produced on the same machines as printed the *Pariser Zeitung*.

Libertés, which was opposed to the Gaullists on one side and the Communists on the other, had almost no money and was distributed by groups of volunteers on bicycles. On some weeks it was mangled out of recognition by the censorship; often nothing would be left of an article except some such title as "The Truth About Indo-China" and a completely blank column beneath it. A day or two after I reached Paris I was taken to a semi-public meeting of the supporters of *Libertés*, and was amazed to find that about half of them knew all about me and about *Tribune*. A large working-man in black corduroy breeches came up to me, exclaimed "Ah, vous êtes Georges Orrvell!" and crushed the bones of my hand almost to pulp. He had heard of me because *Libertés* made a practice of translating extracts from *Tribune*. I believe one of the editors used to go to the British Embassy every week and demand to see a copy. It seemed to me somehow touching that one could have acquired, without knowing it, a public among people like this: whereas among the huge tribe of American journalists at the Hotel Scribe, with their glittering uniforms and their stupendous salaries, I never encountered one who had heard of *Tribune*.

For six months during the summer of 1946 I gave up being a writer in *Tribune* and became merely a reader, and no doubt from time to time I shall do the same again; but I hope that my association with it may long continue, and I hope that in 1957 I shall be writing another anniversary article. I do not even hope that by that time *Tribune* will have slaughtered all its rivals. It takes all sorts to make a world, and if one could work these things out one might discover that even the — serves a useful purpose. Nor is *Tribune* itself perfect, as I should know, having seen it from the inside. But I do think that it is the only existing weekly paper that makes a genuine effort to be both progressive and humane – that is, to combine a radical Socialist policy with a respect for freedom of speech and a civilised attitude towards literature and the arts: and I think that its relative popularity, and even its survival in its present form for five years or more, is a hopeful symptom.

As I Please 72

Tribune, 7 February 1947

Recently I have been looking through Mr. Peter Hunot's *Man About the House*, published a month or two back by the Pilot Press. Books telling you how to do household repairs are fairly numerous, but I think this is about the best I have seen. The author gathered his experience the hard way, by taking over a nearly derelict house and making it habitable with his own hands. He thus concentrates on the sort of difficulties that do actually arise in real life, and does not, like the author of another book in my possession, tell you how to mend Venetian blinds while ignoring electrical fittings. I looked up all the domestic calamities that I have had to deal with during the past year, and found all of them mentioned, except mice, which perhaps hardly come under the heading of decorations and repairs. The book is also simply written and well illustrated, and takes account of the difficulty nowadays of getting hold of tools and materials.

But I still think that there is room for a very large, comprehensive book of this type, a sort of dictionary or encyclopedia with every conceivable household job tabulated under alphabetical headings. You would then be able to look up *Tap, how to stop a dripping*, or *Floorboards, causes of squeaking in*, with the same certainty of getting the right answer as when you look up madeira cake or Welsh rarebit in Mrs. Beeton's cookery book. The time was when the amateur handyman, with his tack hammer and his pocketful of rawl-plugs, was looked on as a mere eccentric, a joke to his friends and a nuisance to his women-folk. Nowadays, however, you either do your repairs yourself or they don't get done, and most of us are still remarkably helpless. How many people even know how to replace a broken sash cord, for instance?

As Mr. Hunot points out, much of the tinkering that now goes on would be unnecessary, or would be much easier, if our houses were sensibly built. Even so simple a precaution as putting fuse boxes in get-at-able places would save a lot of nuisance, and the miserable business of putting up shelves could be greatly simplified without any extra materials or radical change in methods. I hear rumours that the new houses now being built will have the pipes so placed that they will not freeze, but surely this cannot be true. There will be a snag somewhere, and the annual freeze-up will happen as usual. Burst water-pipes are a part of the English winter, no less than muffins or roasted chestnuts, and doubt-less Shakespeare would have mentioned them in the song at the end of *Love's Labour's Lost*, if there had been water-pipes in those days.

It is too early to cheer, but I must say that up to date the phenomena of the freeze-up have been less unpleasant than those of 1940. On that occasion the village where I lived was not only so completely snowed up that for a week or more it was impossible to get out of it, or for any food vans to get in, but every tap and pump in the village froze so hard that for several days we had no water except melted snow. The dis-agreeable thing about this is that snow is always dirty, except just after it has fallen. I have noticed this even in the high peaks of the Atlas mountains, miles from human habitation. The everlasting snow which looks so virginal, is in fact distinctly grimy when you get close to it.

About the time when Sir Stafford Cripps came back from India, I heard it remarked that the Cripps offer had not been extended to Burma because the Burmese would have accepted it. I don't know whether any such calculation really entered into the minds of Churchill and the rest. It is perfectly possible: at any rate, I think that responsible Burmese politicians would have accepted such an offer, although at that moment Burma was in process of being overrun by the Japanese. I also believe that an offer of Dominion Status would have been gladly accepted if we had made it in 1944 and had named a definite date. As it is, the suspicions of the Burmese have been well roused, and it will probably end by our simply getting out of Burma on the terms least advantageous to both countries.

If that happens, I should like to think that the position of the racial minorities could be safeguarded by something better than promises. They number ten to twenty per cent. of the population, and they present several different kinds of problem. The biggest group, the Karens, are a racial enclave living largely within Burma proper. The Kachins and other frontier tribes are a good deal more backward and more different from the Burmese in customs and appearance. They have never been under Burmese rule – indeed, their territories were only very sketchily occupied even by the British. In the past they were well able to maintain their independence, but probably would not be able to do so in the face of modern weapons. The other big group, the Shans, who are racially akin to the Siamese, enjoyed some faint traces of autonomy under British rule. The minority who are in the most difficult position of all are the Indians. There were over a million of them in Burma before the war. Two hundred thousand of them fled to India at the time of the Japanese invasion – an act which demonstrated better than any words could have done their real position in the country.

I remember twenty years ago a Karen remarking to me, "I hope the British will stay in Burma for two hundred years." – "Why?" – "Because we do not wish to be ruled by Burmese." Even at the time it struck me that sooner or later this would become a problem. The fact is that the question of minorities is literally insoluble so long as nationalism remains a real force. The desire of some of the peoples of Burma for autonomy is genuine, but it cannot be satisfied in any secure way unless the sovereignty of Burma as a whole is interfered with. The same problem comes up in a hundred other places. Ought the Sudan to be independent of Egypt? Ought Ulster to be independent of Eire? Ought Eire to be independent of Britain? And so on. Whenever A is oppressing B, it is clear to people of good will that B ought to be independent, but then it always turns out that there is another group, C, which is anxious to be independent of B. The question is always *how large* must a minority be before it deserves autonomy. At best, each case can only be treated on its merits in a rough and ready way: in practice, no one is consistent in his thinking on this subject, and the minorities which win the most sympathy are those that have the best means of publicity. Who is there who champions equally the Jews, the Balts, the Indonesians, the expelled Germans, the Sudanese, the Indian Untouchables and the South African Kaffirs? Sympathy for one group almost invariably entails callousness towards another.

When H. G. Wells's *The Island of Doctor Moreau* was reprinted in the Penguin Library, I looked to see whether the slips and misprints which I remembered in earlier editions had been repeated in it. Sure enough, they were still there. One of them is a particularly stupid misprint, of a kind to make most writers squirm. In 1941 I pointed this out to H. G. Wells, and asked him why he did not remove it. It had persisted through edition after edition ever since 1896. Rather to my surprise, he said that he remembered the misprint, but could not be bothered to do anything about it. He no longer took the faintest interest in his early books: they had been written so long ago that he no longer felt them to be part of himself. I have never been quite sure whether to admire this attitude or not. It is magnificent to be so free from literary vanity. And yet, what writer of Wells's gifts, if he had had any power of self-criticism or regard for his own reputation, would have poured out in fifty years a total of ninety-five books, quite two-thirds of which have already ceased to be readable?

GEORGE ORWELL

As I Please 73
Tribune, 14 February 1947

Here are some excerpts from a letter from a Scottish Nationalist. I have cut out anything likely to reveal the writer's identity.
The frequent references to Poland are there because the letter
is primarily concerned with the presence of exiled Poles in
Scotland:

> The Polish forces have now discovered how untrue it is to say
> "An Englishman's word is his bond." We could have told you
> so hundreds of years ago. The invasion of Poland was only an
> excuse for these brigands in bowler hats to beat up their rivals
> the Germans and the Japs, with the help of Americans, Poles,
> Scots, Frenchmen, etc., etc. Surely no Pole believes any
> longer in English promises. Now that the war is over you
> are to be cast aside and dumped in Scotland. If this leads to
> friction between the Poles and Scots so much the better. Let
> them slit each other's throats and two problems would be
> thereupon "solved." Dear, kind little England! It is time for
> all Poles to shed any ideas they may have about England as a
> champion of freedom. Look at her record in Scotland, for
> instance. And please don't refer to us as "Britons." There is
> *no* such race. We are Scots and that's good enough for us. The
> English changed their name to British; but even if a criminal
> changes his name he can be known by his fingerprints. . . .
> Please disregard any anti-Polish statement in the John
> O'Groat Journal. It is a boot-licking pro-English (pro-
> Moscow you would call it) rag. Scotland experienced
> her Yalta in 1707 when English gold achieved what English
> guns could not do. But we will never accept defeat. After
> more than two hundred years we are still fighting for
> our country and will never acknowledge defeat whatever
> the odds.

There is a good deal more in the letter, but this should be
enough. It will be noted that the writer is not attacking England from what is called a "left" standpoint, but on the ground
that Scotland and England are enemies *as nations*. I don't know
whether it would be fair to read race-theory into this letter, but

1176

certainly the writer hates us as bitterly as a devout Nazi would hate a Jew. It is not a hatred of the capitalist class, or anything like that, but *of England*. And though the fact is not sufficiently realised, there is an appreciable amount of this kind of thing knocking about. I have seen almost equally violent statements in print.

Up to date the Scottish Nationalist movement seems to have gone almost unnoticed in England. To take the nearest example to hand, I don't remember having seen it mentioned in *Tribune*, except occasionally in book reviews. It is true that it is a small movement, but it could grow, because there is a basis for it. In this country I don't think it is enough realised − I myself had no idea of it until a few years ago − that Scotland has a case against England. On economic grounds it may not be a very strong case. In the past, certainly, we have plundered Scotland shamefully, but whether it is *now* true that England as a whole exploits Scotland as a whole, and that Scotland would be better off if fully autonomous, is another question. The point is that many Scottish people, often quite moderate in outlook, are beginning to think about autonomy and to feel that they are pushed into an inferior position. They have a good deal of reason. In some areas, at any rate, Scotland is almost an occupied country. You have an English or Anglicised upper-class, and a Scottish working-class which speaks with a markedly different accent, or even, part of the time, in a different language. This is a more dangerous kind of class division than any now existing in England. Given favourable circumstances it might develop in an ugly way, and the fact that there was a progressive Labour Government in London might not make much difference.

No doubt Scotland's major ills will have to be cured along with those of England. But meanwhile there are things that could be done to ease the cultural situation. One small but not negligible point is the language. In the Gaelic-speaking areas, Gaelic is not taught in the schools. I am speaking from limited experience, but I should say that this is beginning to cause resentment. Also, the B.B.C. only broadcasts two or three half-hour Gaelic programmes a week, and they give the impression of being rather amateurish programmes. Even so they are eagerly listened to. How easy it would be to buy a little goodwill by putting on a Gaelic programme at least once daily.

At one time I would have said that it is absurd to keep alive an archaic language like Gaelic, spoken by only a few hundred thousand people. Now I am not so sure. To begin with, if people feel that they have a special culture which ought to be preserved, and that the language is part of it, difficulties should not be put in their way when they want their children to learn it properly. Secondly, it is probable that the effort of being bi-lingual is a valuable education in itself. The Scottish Gaelic-speaking peasants speak beautiful English, partly, I think, because English is an almost foreign language which they sometimes do not use for days together. Probably they benefit intellectually by having to be aware of dictionaries and grammatical rules, as their English opposite numbers would not be.

At any rate, I think we should pay more attention to the small but violent separatist movements which exist within our own island. They may look very unimportant now, but, after all, the Communist Manifesto was once a very obscure document, and the Nazi Party only had six members when Hitler joined it.

To change the subject a bit, here is an excerpt from another letter. It is from a whisky distiller:

> We regret we are reluctantly compelled to return your cheque as owing to Mr. Strachey's failure to fulfil his promise to release barley for distilling in Scotland we dare not take on any new business.... When you have difficulty in obtaining a drink it will be some consolation to you to know that Mr. Strachey has sent 35,000 tons of barley to NEUTRAL Eire for brewing purposes.

People must be feeling very warmed-up when they put that kind of thing into a business letter which, by the look of it, is almost a circular letter. It doesn't matter very much, because whisky distillers and even their customers don't add up to many votes. But I wish I could feel sure that the people who make remarks like the one I overheard in the greengrocer's queue yesterday – "Government! They couldn't govern a sausage-shop, this lot couldn't!" – were equally few in numbers.

Skelton is not an easy poet to get hold of, and I have never yet possessed a complete edition of his works. Recently, in a selection I had picked up, I looked for and failed to find a poem which I remember reading years ago. It was what is called a macaronic poem – part English, part Latin – and was an elegy on the death of somebody or other. The only passage I can recall runs:

> Sepultus est among the weeds,
> God forgive him his misdeeds,
> With hey ho, rumbelo,
> Rumpopulorum,
> Per omnia saecula,
> Saecula saeculorum.

It has stuck in my mind because it expresses an outlook totally impossible in our own age. Today there is literally no one who could write of death in that light-hearted manner. Since the decay of the belief in personal immortality, death has never seemed funny, and it will be a long time before it does so again. Hence the disappearance of the facetious epitaph, once a common feature of country churchyards. I should be astonished to see a comic epitaph dated later than 1850. There is one in Kew, if I remember rightly, which might be about that date. About half the tombstone is covered with a long panegyric on his dead wife by a bereaved husband: at the bottom of the stone is a later inscription which reads, "Now he's gone, too."

One of the best epitaphs in English is Landor's epitaph on "Dirce," a pseudonym for I do not know whom. It is not exactly comic, but it is essentially profane. If I were a woman it would be my favourite epitaph – that is to say, it would be the one I should like to have for myself. It runs:

> Stand close around, ye Stygian set,
> With Dirce in the boat conveyed,
> Lest Charon, seeing her, forget
> That he is old and she a shade.

It would almost be worth being dead to have that written about you.

As I Please 74
Manchester Evening News, for *Tribune*, 21 February 1947

The news that, for the second time in the last few months, a play banned from the stage is to be broadcast by the B.B.C. (which will probably enable it to reach a much bigger public than it would if it were acted) brings out once again the absurdity of the rules governing literary censorship in Britain.

It is only stage plays and films that have to be submitted for censorship before they appear. So far as books go you can print what you like and take the risk of prosecution. Thus, banned plays like Granville Barker's "Waste" and Bernard Shaw's "Mrs. Warren's Profession" could immediately appear in book form with no danger of prosecution, and no doubt sell all the better for the scandal that had happened beforehand. It is fair to say that, if they are any good, banned plays usually see the light sooner or later. Even "Waste," which brought in politics as well as sex, was finally allowed to appear thirty years after it was written, when the topicality which gave it a good deal of its force had vanished.

The trouble with the Lord Chamberlain's censorship of plays is not that it happens, but that it is barbarous and stupid – being, apparently, done by bureaucrats with no literary training. If there is to be censorship, it is better that it should happen beforehand, so that the author may know where he stands. Books are only very rarely banned in Britain, but the bannings that do happen are usually quite arbitrary. "The Well of Loneliness," for example, was suppressed, while other books on the same theme, appearing round about the same time, went unnoticed.

The book that gets dropped on is the one that happens to have been brought to the attention of some illiterate official. Perhaps half the novels now published might suffer this fate if they happened to get into the right hands. Indeed – though the dead are always respectable – I doubt whether Petronius, or Chaucer, or Rabelais, or Shakespeare would remain unbowdlerised if our magistrates and police were greater readers.

As I Please 75A
Daily Herald for *Tribune*, 27 February 1947

Recently I was looking through a child's illustrated alphabet, published this year. It is what is called a "travel alphabet." Here are the rhymes accompanying three of the letters, J, N and U:

> J for the Junk which the Chinaman finds
> Is useful for carrying goods of all kinds.

> N for the Native from Africa's land.
> He looks very fierce with his spear in his hand.

> U for the Union Jacks Pam and John carry
> While out for a hike with their nice Uncle Harry.

The "native" in the picture is a Zulu dressed only in some bracelets and a fragment of leopard skin. As for the Junk, the detail of the picture is very small, but the "Chinamen" portrayed in it appear to be wearing pigtails.

Perhaps there is not much to object to in the presence of the Union Jack. This is an age of competing nationalisms, and who shall blame us if we flourish our own emblems along with all the rest? But is it really necessary, in 1947, to teach children to use expressions like "native" and "Chinaman"?

The last-named word has been regarded as offensive by the Chinese for at least a dozen years. As for "native," it was being officially discountenanced even in India as long as twenty years ago.

It is no use answering that it is childish for an Indian or an African to feel insulted when he is called a "native." We all have these feelings in one form or another. If a Chinese wants to be called a Chinese and not a Chinaman, if a Scotsman objects to being called a Scotchman, or if a Negro demands his capital N, it is only the most ordinary politeness to do what is asked of one.

The sad thing about this alphabet-book is that the writer obviously has no intention of insulting the "lower" races. He is merely not quite aware that they are human beings like ourselves. A "native" is a comic black man with very few clothes on; a "Chinaman" wears a pigtail and travels in a junk – which is about as true as saying that an Englishman wears a top hat and travels in a hansom cab.

This unconsciously patronising attitude is learned in childhood and then, as here, passed on to a new generation of children. And sometimes it pops up in quite enlightened people, with disconcerting results; as for instance at the end of 1941, when China officially became our Ally, and at the first important anniversary the B.B.C. celebrated the occasion by flying the Chinese flag over Broadcasting House, and flying it upside-down.

As I Please 75B
Manchester Evening News for *Tribune*, 28 February 1947

One thing one notices in these days when typewriters have become so scarce is the astonishing badness of nearly everyone's handwriting.

A handwriting which is both pleasant to look at and easy to read is now a very rare thing. To bring about an improvement we should probably have to evolve a generally accepted "style" of writing such as we possessed in the past and have now lost.

For several centuries in the Middle Ages the professional scribes wrote an exquisite script, or rather a series of scripts, which no one now living could equal. Then handwriting declined, reviving in the nineteenth century after the invention of the steel pen. The style then favoured was "copperplate." It was neat and legible, but it was full of unnecessary lines and did not fit in with the modern tendency to get rid of ornament wherever possible. Then it became the fashion to teach children script, usually with disastrous results. To write script with real neatness one practically has to learn to draw, and it is impossible to write it as rapidly as a cursive hand. Many young or youngish people now make use of an uneasy compromise between script and copperplate, and indeed there are many adult and fully literate people whose handwriting has never properly "formed."

It would be interesting to know whether there is any connection between neat handwriting and literary ability. I must say that the modern examples I am able to think of do not seem to prove much. Miss Rebecca West has an exquisite handwriting, and so has Mr. Middleton Murry. Sir Osbert Sitwell, Mr. Stephen Spender, and Mr. Evelyn Waugh all have handwritings which, to put it as politely as possible, are not good. Professor Laski writes a hand which is attractive to look at but difficult to read. Arnold Bennett wrote a beautiful tiny hand over which he took immense pains. H. G. Wells had an attractive but untidy writing. Carlyle's writing was so bad that one compositor is said to have left Edinburgh in order to get away from the job of setting it up. Mr. Bernard Shaw writes a small, clear but not very elegant hand. And as for the most famous and respected of living English novelists, his writing is such that when I was at the B.B.C. and had the honour of putting him on the air once a month there was only one secretary in the whole department who could decipher his manuscripts.

Lear, Tolstoy and the Fool
Polemic, 7; March 1947

Tolstoy's pamphlets are the least-known part of his work, and his attack on Shakespeare[36] is not even an easy document to get hold of, at any rate in an English translation. Perhaps, therefore, it will be useful if I give a summary of the pamphlet before trying to discuss it.

Tolstoy begins by saying that throughout life Shakespeare has aroused in him 'an irresistible repulsion and tedium'. Conscious that the opinion of the civilized world is against him, he has made one attempt after another on Shakespeare's works, reading and re-reading them in Russian, English and German; but 'I invariably underwent the same feelings; repulsion, weariness and bewilderment'. Now, at the age of seventy-five, he has once again re-read the entire works of Shakespeare, including the historical plays, and

I have felt with even greater force, the same feelings – this time, however, not of bewilderment, but of firm, indubitable conviction that the unquestionable glory of a great genius which Shakespeare enjoys, and which compels writers of our time to imitate him and readers and spectators to discover in him non-existent merits – thereby distorting their aesthetic and ethical understanding – is a great evil, as is every untruth.

Shakespeare, Tolstoy adds, is not merely no genius, but is not even 'an average author', and in order to demonstrate this fact he will examine *King Lear*, which, as he is able to show by quotations from Hazlitt, Brandes and others, has been extravagantly praised and can be taken as an example of Shakespeare's best work.

Tolstoy then makes a sort of exposition of the plot of *King Lear*, finding it at every step to be stupid, verbose, unnatural, unintelligible, bombastic, vulgar, tedious and full of incredible events, 'wild ravings', 'mirthless jokes', anachronisms, irrelevancies, obscenities, worn-out stage conventions and other faults both moral and aesthetic. *Lear* is, in any case, a plagiarism of an earlier and much better play, *King Leir*, by an unknown author, which Shakespeare stole and then ruined. It is worth quoting a specimen paragraph to illustrate the manner in which Tolstoy goes to work. Act III, Scene 2 (in which Lear, Kent and the Fool are together in the storm) is summarized thus:

> Lear walks about the heath and says words which are meant to express his despair: he desires that the winds should blow so hard that they (the winds) should crack their cheeks and that the rain should flood everything, that lightning should singe his white head, and the thunder flatten the world and destroy all germs 'that make ungrateful man'! The fool keeps uttering still more senseless words. Enter Kent: Lear says that for some reason during this storm all criminals shall be found out and convicted. Kent, still unrecognized by Lear, endeavours to persuade him to take refuge in a hovel. At this point the fool utters a prophecy in no wise related to the situation and they all depart.

Tolstoy's final verdict on *Lear* is that no unhypnotized observer, if such an observer existed, could read it to the end with any feeling except 'aversion and weariness'. And exactly the same is true of 'all the other extolled dramas of Shakespeare, not to mention the senseless dramatized tales, *Pericles*, *Twelfth Night*, *The Tempest*, *Cymbeline*, *Troilus and Cressida*'.

Having dealt with *Lear* Tolstoy draws up a more general indictment against Shakespeare. He finds that Shakespeare has a certain technical skill which is partly traceable to his having been an actor, but otherwise no merits whatever. He has no power of delineating character or of making words and actions spring naturally out of situations, his language is uniformly exaggerated and ridiculous, he constantly thrusts his own random thoughts into the mouth of any character who happens to be handy, he displays a 'complete absence of aesthetic feeling', and his words 'have nothing whatever in common with art and poetry'. 'Shakespeare might have been whatever you like,' Tolstoy concludes, 'but he was not an artist.' Moreover, his opinions are not original or interesting, and his tendency is 'of the lowest and most immoral'. Curiously enough, Tolstoy does not base this last judgement on Shakespeare's own utterances, but on the statements of two critics, Gervinus and Brandes. According to Gervinus (or at any rate Tolstoy's reading of Gervinus) 'Shakespeare taught . . . that one *may be too good*', while according to Brandes 'Shakespeare's fundamental principle . . . is that *the end justifies the means*'. Tolstoy adds on his own account that Shakespeare was a jingo patriot of the worst type, but apart from this he considers that Gervinus and Brandes have given a true and adequate description of Shakespeare's view of life.

Tolstoy then recapitulates in a few paragraphs the theory of art which he had expressed at greater length elsewhere. Put still more shortly, it amounts to a demand for dignity of subject matter, sincerity, and good craftsmanship. A great work of art must deal with some subject which is 'important to the life of mankind', it must express something which the author genuinely feels, and it must use such technical methods as will produce the desired effect. As Shakespeare is debased in outlook, slipshod in execution and incapable of being sincere even for a moment, he obviously stands condemned.

But here there arises a difficult question. If Shakespeare is all that Tolstoy has shown him to be, how did he ever come to be so generally admired? Evidently the answer can only lie in a sort of mass hypnosis, or 'epidemic suggestion'. The whole civilized world has somehow been deluded into thinking Shakespeare a good writer, and even the plainest demonstration to the contrary makes no impression, because one is not dealing with a reasoned opinion but with something akin to religious faith. Throughout history, says Tolstoy, there has been an endless series of these 'epidemic suggestions' – for example, the Crusades, the search for the Philosopher's Stone, the craze for tulip-growing which once swept over Holland, and so on and so forth. As a contemporary instance he cites, rather significantly, the Dreyfus case, over which the whole world grew violently excited for no sufficient reason. There are also sudden shortlived crazes for new political and philosophical theories, or for this or that writer, artist or scientist – for example, Darwin, who (in 1903) is 'beginning to be forgotten'. And in some cases a quite worthless popular idol may remain in favour for centuries, for 'it also happens that such crazes, having arisen in consequence of special reasons accidentally favouring their establishment, correspond in such a degree to the views of life spread in society, and especially in literary circles, that they are maintained for a long time'. Shakespeare's plays have continued to be admired over a long period because 'they corresponded to the irreligious and immoral frame of mind of the upper classes of his time and ours'.

As to the manner in which Shakespeare's fame *started*, Tolstoy explains it as having been 'got up' by German professors towards the end of the eighteenth century. His reputation 'originated in Germany, and thence was transferred to England'. The Germans chose to elevate Shakespeare because, at a time when there was no German drama worth speaking about and French classical literature was beginning to seem frigid and artificial, they were captivated by Shakespeare's 'clever development of scenes' and also found in him a good expression of their own attitude towards life. Goethe pronounced Shakespeare a great poet, whereupon all the other critics flocked after him like a troop of parrots, and the general infatuation has lasted ever since. The result has been a further debasement of the drama – Tolstoy is careful to include his own plays when condemning the contemporary stage – and a further corruption of the prevailing moral outlook. It follows that 'the false glorification of

Shakespeare' is an important evil which Tolstoy feels it his duty to combat.

This, then, is the substance of Tolstoy's pamphlet. One's first feeling is that in describing Shakespeare as a bad writer he is saying something demonstrably untrue. But this is not the case. In reality there is no kind of evidence or argument by which one can show that Shakespeare, or any other writer, is 'good'. Nor is there any way of definitely proving that — for instance — Warwick Deeping is 'bad'. Ultimately there is no test of literary merit except survival, which is itself merely an index to majority opinion. Artistic theories such as Tolstoy's are quite worthless, because they not only start out with arbitrary assumptions, but depend on vague terms ('sincere', 'important' and so forth) which can be interpreted in any way one chooses. Properly speaking one cannot *answer* Tolstoy's attack. The interesting question is: why did he make it? But it should be noticed in passing that he uses many weak or dishonest arguments. Some of these are worth pointing out, not because they invalidate his main charge but because they are, so to speak, evidence of malice.

To begin with, his examination of *King Lear* is not 'impartial', as he twice claims. On the contrary, it is a prolonged exercise in misrepresentation. It is obvious that when you are summarizing *King Lear* for the benefit of someone who has not read it, you are not really being impartial if you introduce an important speech (Lear's speech when Cordelia is dead in his arms) in this manner: 'Again begin Lear's awful ravings, at which one feels ashamed, as at unsuccessful jokes.' And in a long series of instances Tolstoy slightly alters or colours the passages he is criticizing, always in such a way as to make the plot appear a little more complicated and improbable, or the language a little more exaggerated. For example, we are told that Lear 'has no necessity or motive for his abdication', although his reason for abdicating (that he is old and wishes to retire from the cares of State) has been clearly indicated in the first scene. It will be seen that even in the passage which I quoted earlier, Tolstoy has wilfully misunderstood one phrase and slightly changed the meaning of another, making nonsense of a remark which is reasonable enough in its context. None of these mis-readings is very gross in itself, but their cumulative effect is to exaggerate the psychological incoherence of the play. Again, Tolstoy is not able to explain why Shakespeare's plays were still in print, and still on the stage, two hundred years after his death (*before* the 'epidemic suggestion' started, that is); and his whole account of Shakespeare's rise to fame is guess-work punctuated by outright mis-statements. And again, various of his accusations contradict one another: for example, Shakespeare is a mere entertainer and 'not in earnest', but on the other hand he is constantly putting his own thoughts into the mouths of his characters. On the whole it is difficult to feel that Tolstoy's criticisms are uttered in good faith. In any case it is impossible that he should fully have believed in his main thesis – believed, that is to say, that for a century or more the entire civilized world had been taken in by a huge and palpable lie which he alone was able to see through. Certainly his dislike of Shakespeare is real enough, but the reasons for it may be different, or partly different, from what he avows; and therein lies the interest of his pamphlet.

At this point one is obliged to start guessing. However, there is one possible clue, or at least there is a question which may point the way to a clue. It is: why did Tolstoy, with thirty or more plays to choose from, pick out *King Lear* as his especial target? True, *Lear* is so well known and has been so much praised that it could justly be taken as representative of Shake-speare's best work; still, for the purpose of a hostile analysis Tolstoy would probably choose the play he disliked most. Is it not possible that he bore an especial enmity towards this particular play because he was aware, consciously or uncon-sciously, of the resemblance between Lear's story and his own? But it is better to approach this clue from the opposite direction – that is, by examining *Lear* itself, and the qualities in it that Tolstoy fails to mention.

One of the first things an English reader would notice in Tolstoy's pamphlet is that it hardly deals with Shakespeare as a poet. Shakespeare is treated as a dramatist, and in so far as his popularity is not spurious, it is held to be due to tricks of stagecraft which give good opportunities to clever actors. Now, so far as the English-speaking countries go, this is not true. Several of the plays which are most valued by lovers of Shakespeare (for instance, *Timon of Athens*) are seldom or never acted, while some of the most actable, such as *A Midsummer Night's Dream*, are the least admired. Those who care most for Shakespeare value him in the first place for his use of language, the 'verbal music' which even Bernard Shaw, another hostile critic, admits to be 'irresistible'. Tolstoy ignores this, and does not seem to realize that a poem may have a special value for those who speak the language in which it was written. However, even if one puts oneself in Tolstoy's place and tries to think of Shakespeare as a foreign poet it is still clear that there is something that Tolstoy has left out. Poetry, it seems, is *not* solely a matter of sound and association, and valueless outside its own language-group: otherwise, how is it that some poems, including poems written in dead languages, succeed in crossing frontiers? Clearly a lyric like 'Tomorrow is Saint Valentine's Day' could not be satisfactorily translated, but in Shakespeare's major work there is something describable as poetry that can be separated from the words. Tolstoy is right in saying that *Lear* is not a very good play, as a play. It is too drawn-out and has too many characters and sub-plots. One wicked daughter would have been quite enough, and Edgar is a superfluous character: indeed it would probably be a better play if Gloucester and both his sons were eliminated. Nevertheless, something, a kind of pattern, or perhaps only an atmosphere, survives the complications and the *longueurs*. *Lear* can be imagined as a puppet show, a mime, a ballet, a series of pictures. Part of its poetry, perhaps the most essential part, is inherent in the story and is dependent neither on any particular set of words, nor on flesh-and-blood presentation.

Shut your eyes and think of *King Lear*, if possible without calling to mind any of the dialogue. What do you see? Here at any rate is what I see: a majestic old man in a long black robe, with flowing white hair and beard, a figure out of Blake's drawings (but also, curiously enough, rather like Tolstoy), wandering through a storm and cursing the heavens, in company with a Fool and a lunatic. Presently the scene shifts, and the old man, still cursing, still understanding nothing, is holding a dead girl in his arms while the Fool dangles on a gallows somewhere in the background. This is the bare skeleton of the play, and even here Tolstoy wants to cut out most of what is essential. He objects to the storm, as being unnecessary, to the

Fool, who in his eyes is simply a tedious nuisance and an excuse for making bad jokes, and to the death of Cordelia, which, as he sees it, robs the play of its moral. According to Tolstoy, the earlier play, *King Leir*, which Shakespeare adapted

> terminates more naturally and more in accordance with the moral demands of the spectator than does Shakespeare's: namely, by the King of the Gauls conquering the husbands of the elder sisters, and by Cordelia, instead of being killed, restoring Leir to his former position.

In other words the tragedy ought to have been a comedy, or perhaps a melodrama. It is doubtful whether the sense of tragedy is compatible with belief in God: at any rate, it is not compatible with disbelief in human dignity and with the kind of 'moral demand' which feels cheated when virtue fails to triumph. A tragic situation exists precisely when virtue does *not* triumph but when it is still felt that man is nobler than the forces which destroy him. It is perhaps more significant that Tolstoy sees no justification for the presence of the Fool. The Fool is integral to the play. He acts not only as a sort of chorus, making the central situation clearer by commenting on it more intelligently than the other characters, but as a foil to Lear's frenzies. His jokes, riddles and scraps of rhyme, and his endless digs at Lear's high-minded folly, ranging from mere derision to a sort of melancholy poetry ('All thy other titles thou hast given away; that thou wast born with'), are like a trickle of sanity running through the play, a reminder that somewhere or other, in spite of the injustices, cruelties, intrigues, deceptions and misunderstandings that are being enacted here, life if going on much as usual. In Tolstoy's impatience with the Fool one gets a glimpse of his deeper quarrel with Shakespeare. He objects, with some justification, to the raggedness of Shakespeare's plays, the irrelevancies, the incredible plots, the exaggerated language: but what at bottom he probably most dislikes is a sort of exuberance, a tendency to take – not so much a pleasure, as simply an interest in the actual process of life. It is a mistake to write Tolstoy off as a moralist attacking an artist. He never said that art, as such, is wicked or meaningless, nor did he even say that technical virtuosity is unimportant. But his main aim, in

his later years, was to narrow the range of human consciousness. One's interests, one's points of attachment to the physical
world and the day-to-day struggle, must be as few and not as
many as possible. Literature must consist of parables, stripped of
detail and almost independent of language. The parables – this
is where Tolstoy differs from the average vulgar puritan – must
themselves be works of art, but pleasure and curiosity must be
excluded from them. Science, also, must be divorced from
curiosity. The business of science, he says, is not to discover
what happens, but to teach men how they ought to live. So also
with history and politics. Many problems (for example, the
Dreyfus case) are simply not worth solving, and he is willing to
leave them as loose ends. Indeed his whole theory of 'crazes' or
'epidemic suggestions', in which he lumps together such things
as the Crusades and the Dutch passion of tulip-growing, shows
a willingness to regard many human activities as mere ant-like
rushings to and fro, inexplicable and uninteresting. Clearly he
could have no patience with a chaotic, detailed, discursive
writer like Shakespeare. His reaction is that of an irritable old
man who is being pestered by a noisy child. 'Why do you keep
jumping up and down like that? Why can't you sit still like
I do?' In a way the old man is in the right, but the trouble is that
the child has a feeling in its limbs which the old man has lost.
And if the old man knows of the existence of this feeling, the
effect is merely to increase his irritation: he would make
children senile, if he could. Tolstoy does not know, perhaps,
just *what* he misses in Shakespeare, but he is aware that he
misses something, and he is determined that others shall be
deprived of it as well. By nature he was imperious as well as
egotistical. Well after he was grown up he would still occasionally strike his servant in moments of anger, and somewhat later,
according to his English biographer, Derrick Leon, he felt 'a
frequent desire upon the slenderest provocation to slap the
faces of those with whom he disagreed'. One does not necessarily get rid of that kind of temperament by undergoing
religious conversion, and indeed it is obvious that the illusion
of having been reborn may allow one's native vices to flourish
more freely than ever, though perhaps in subtler forms. Tolstoy
was capable of abjuring physical violence and of seeing what
this implies, but he was not capable of tolerance or humility,

and even if one knew nothing of his other writings, one could deduce his tendency towards spiritual bullying from this single pamphlet.

However, Tolstoy is not simply trying to rob others of a pleasure he does not share. He is doing that, but his quarrel with Shakespeare goes further. It is the quarrel between the religious and the humanist attitudes towards life. Here one comes back to the central theme of *King Lear*, which Tolstoy does not mention, although he sets forth the plot in some detail.

Lear is one of the minority of Shakespeare's plays that are unmistakably *about* something. As Tolstoy justly complains, much rubbish has been written about Shakespeare as a philosopher, as a psychologist, as a 'great moral teacher', and what-not. Shakespeare was not a systematic thinker, his most serious thoughts are uttered irrelevantly or indirectly, and we do not know to what extent he wrote with a 'purpose' or even how much of the work attributed to him was actually written by him. In the Sonnets he never even refers to the plays as part of his achievement, though he does make what seems to be a half-ashamed allusion to his career as an actor. It is perfectly possible that he looked on at least half of his plays as mere pot-boilers and hardly bothered about purpose or probability so long as he could patch up something, usually from stolen material, which would more or less hang together on the stage. However, that is not the whole story. To begin with, as Tolstoy himself points out, Shakespeare has a habit of thrusting uncalled-for general reflections into the mouths of his characters. This is a serious fault in a dramatist, but it does not fit in with Tolstoy's picture of Shakespeare as a vulgar hack who has no opinions of his own and merely wishes to produce the greatest effect with the least trouble. And more than this, about a dozen of his plays, written for the most part later than 1600, do unquestionably have a meaning and even a moral. They revolve round a central subject which in some cases can be reduced to a single word. For example, *Macbeth* is about ambition, *Othello* is about jealousy, and *Timon of Athens* is about money. The subject of *Lear* is renunciation, and it is only by being wilfully blind that one can fail to understand what Shakespeare is saying.

Lear renounces his throne but expects everyone to continue treating him as a king. He does not see that if he surrenders power, other people will take advantage of his weakness: also that those who flatter him the most grossly, i.e. Regan and Goneril, are exactly the ones who will turn against him. The moment he finds that he can no longer make people obey him as he did before, he falls into a rage which Tolstoy describes as 'strange and unnatural', but which in fact is perfectly in character. In his madness and despair, he passes through two moods which again are natural enough in his circumstances, though in one of them it is probable that he is being used partly as a mouthpiece for Shakespeare's own opinions. One is the mood of disgust in which Lear repents, as it were, for having been a king, and grasps for the first time the rottenness of formal justice and vulgar morality. The other is a mood of impotent fury in which he wreaks imaginary revenges upon those who have wronged him. 'To have a thousand with red burning spits Come hissing in upon 'em!', and:

> 'It were a delicate stratagem to shoe
> A troop of horse with felt: I'll put't in proof;
> And when I have stol'n upon these sons-in-law,
> Then kill, kill, kill, kill, kill!'

Only at the end does he realize, as a sane man, that power, revenge and victory are not worth while:

> 'No, no, no, no! Come, let's away to prison...
> ... and we'll wear out
> In a wall'd prison, packs and sects of great ones
> That ebb and flow by the moon.'

But by the time he makes this discovery it is too late, for his death and Cordelia's are already decided on. That is the story, and, allowing for some clumsiness in the telling, it is a very good story.

But is it not also curiously similar to the history of Tolstoy himself? There is a general resemblance which one can hardly avoid seeing, because the most impressive event in Tolstoy's life, as in Lear's, was a huge gratuitous act of renunciation. In his old age he renounced his estate, his title and his copyrights, and made an attempt – a sincere attempt, though it was not successful – to escape from his privileged position and live the life of a peasant. But the deeper resemblance lies in the fact that

1193

Tolstoy, like Lear, acted on mistaken motives and failed to get the results he had hoped for. According to Tolstoy, the aim of every human being is happiness, and happiness can only be attained by doing the will of God. But doing the will of God means casting off all earthly pleasures and ambitions, and living only for others. Ultimately, therefore, Tolstoy renounced the world under the expectation that this would make him happier. But if there is one thing certain about his later years, it is that he was *not* happy. On the contrary, he was driven almost to the edge of madness by the behaviour of the people about him, who persecuted him precisely *because* of his renunciation. Like Lear, Tolstoy was not humble and not a good judge of character. He was inclined at moments to revert to the attitudes of an aristocrat, in spite of his peasant's blouse, and he even had two children whom he had believed in and who ultimately turned against him – though, of course, in a less sensational manner than Regan and Goneril. His exaggerated revulsion from sexuality was also distinctly similar to Lear's. Tolstoy's remark that marriage is 'slavery, satiety, repulsion' and means putting up with the proximity of 'ugliness, dirtiness, smell, sores', is matched by Lear's well-known outburst:

> 'But to the girdle do the gods inherit,
> Beneath is all the fiends';
> There's hell, there's darkness, there's the sulphurous pit,
> Burning, scalding, stench, consumption', etc., etc.

And though Tolstoy could not foresee it when he wrote his essay on Shakespeare, even the ending of his life – the sudden unplanned flight across country, accompanied only by a faithful daughter, the death in a cottage in a strange village – seems to have in it a sort of phantom reminiscence of *Lear*.

Of course, one cannot assume that Tolstoy was aware of this resemblance, or would have admitted it if it had been pointed out to him. But his attitude towards the play must have been influenced by its theme. Renouncing power, giving away your lands, was a subject on which he had reason to feel deeply. Probably, therefore, he would be more angered and disturbed by the moral that Shakespeare draws than he would be in the case of some other play – *Macbeth*, for example – which did not touch so closely on his own life. But what exactly *is* the moral of *Lear*? Evidently there are two morals, one explicit, the other implied in the story.

Shakespeare starts by assuming that to make yourself powerless is to invite an attack. This does not mean that *everyone* will turn against you (Kent and the Fool stand by Lear from first to last), but in all probability *someone* will. If you throw away your weapons, some less scrupulous person will pick them up. If you turn the other cheek, you will get a harder blow on it than you got on the first one. This does not always happen, but it is to be expected, and you ought not to complain if it does happen. The second blow is, so to speak, part of the act of turning the other cheek. First of all, therefore, there is the vulgar, commonsense moral drawn by the Fool: 'Don't relinquish power, don't give away your lands.' But there is also another moral. Shakespeare never utters it in so many words, and it does not very much matter whether he was fully aware of it. It is contained in the story, which, after all, he made up, or altered to suit his purposes. It is: 'Give away your lands if you want to, but don't expect to gain happiness by doing so. Probably you won't gain happiness. If you live for others, you must live *for others*, and not as a roundabout way of getting an advantage for yourself.'

Obviously neither of these conclusions could have been pleasing to Tolstoy. The first of them expresses the ordinary, belly-to-earth selfishness from which he was genuinely trying to escape. The other conflicts with his desire to eat his cake and have it – that is, to destroy his own egoism and by so doing to gain eternal life. Of course, *Lear* is not a sermon in favour of altruism. It merely points out the results of practising self-denial for selfish reasons. Shakespeare had a considerable streak of worldliness in him, and if he had been forced to take sides in his own play, his sympathies would probably have lain with the Fool. But at least he could see the whole issue and treat it at the level of tragedy. Vice is punished, but virtue is not rewarded. The morality of Shakespeare's later tragedies is not religious in the ordinary sense, and certainly is not Christian. Only two of them, *Hamlet* and *Othello*, are supposedly occurring inside the Christian era, and even in those, apart from the antics of the ghost in *Hamlet*, there is no indication of a 'next world' where everything is to be put right. All of these tragedies start out with the humanist assumption that life, although full of sorrow, is worth living, and that Man is a noble animal – a belief which Tolstoy in his old age did not share.

Tolstoy was not a saint, but he tried very hard to make himself into a saint, and the standards he applied to literature were other-worldly ones. It is important to realize that the difference between a saint and an ordinary human being is a difference of kind and not of degree. That is, the one is not to be regarded as an imperfect form of the other. The saint, at any rate Tolstoy's kind of saint, is not trying to work an improvement in earthly life: he is trying to bring it to an end and put something different in its place. One obvious expression of this is the claim that celibacy is 'higher' than marriage. If only, Tolstoy says in effect, we would stop breeding, fighting, struggling and enjoying, if we could get rid not only of our sins but of everything else that binds us to the surface of the earth – including love, in the ordinary sense of caring more for one human being than another – then the whole painful process would be over and the Kingdom of Heaven would arrive. But a normal human being does not want the Kingdom of Heaven: he wants life on earth to continue. This is not solely because he is 'weak', 'sinful' and anxious for a 'good time'. Most people get a fair amount of fun out of their lives, but on balance life is suffering, and only the very young or the very foolish imagine otherwise. Ultimately it is the Christian attitude which is self-interested and hedonistic, since the aim is always to get away from the painful struggle of earthly life and find eternal peace in some kind of Heaven or Nirvana. The humanist attitude is that the struggle must continue and that death is the price of life. 'Men must endure Their going hence, even as their coming hither: Ripeness is all' – which is an un-Christian sentiment. Often there is a seeming truce between the humanist and the religious believer, but in fact their attitudes cannot be reconciled: one must choose between this world and the next. And the enormous majority of human beings, if they understood the issue, would choose this world. They do make that choice when they continue working, breeding and dying instead of crippling their faculties in the hope of obtaining a new lease of existence elsewhere.

We do not know a great deal about Shakespeare's religious beliefs, and from the evidence of his writings it would be difficult to prove that he had any. But at any rate he was not a saint or a would-be saint: he was a human being, and in some ways not a very good one. It is clear, for instance, that he liked to stand well with the rich and powerful, and was capable of flattering them in the most servile way. He is also noticeably cautious, not to say cowardly, in his manner of uttering unpopular opinions. Almost never does he put a subversive or sceptical remark into the mouth of a character likely to be identified with himself. Throughout his plays the acute social critics, the people who are not taken in by accepted fallacies, are buffoons, villains, lunatics or persons who are shamming insanity or are in a state of violent hysteria. *Lear* is a play in which this tendency is particularly well-marked. It contains a great deal of veiled social criticism – a point Tolstoy misses – but it is all uttered either by the Fool, by Edgar when he is pretending to be mad, or by Lear during his bouts of madness. In his sane moments Lear hardly ever makes an intelligent remark. And yet the very fact that Shakespeare had to use these subterfuges shows how widely his thoughts ranged. He could not restrain himself from commenting on almost everything, although he put on a series of masks in order to do so. If one has once read Shakespeare with attention, it is not easy to go a day without quoting him, because there are not many subjects of major importance that he does not discuss or at least mention somewhere or other, in his unsystematic but illuminating way. Even the irrelevancies that litter every one of his plays – the puns and riddles, the lists of names, the scraps of *reportage* like the conversation of the carriers in *Henry IV*, the bawdy jokes, the rescued fragments of forgotten ballads – are merely the products of excessive vitality. Shakespeare was not a philosopher or a scientist, but he did have curiosity: he loved the surface of the earth and the process of life – which, it should be repeated, is *not* the same thing as wanting to have a good time and stay alive as long as possible. Of course, it is not because of the quality of his thought that Shakespeare has survived, and he might not even be remembered as a dramatist if he had not also been a poet. His main hold on us is through language. How deeply Shakespeare himself was fascinated by the music of words can probably be inferred from the speeches of Pistol. What Pistol says is largely meaningless, but if one considers his lines singly they are magnificent rhetorical verse. Evidently, pieces of resounding nonsense ('Let floods o'erswell, and fiends for food howl on', etc.) were constantly appearing in Shakespeare's mind of their own accord, and a half-lunatic character had to be invented to use them up. Tolstoy's native tongue was not English, and one cannot blame him for being unmoved by Shakespeare's verse, nor even, perhaps, for refusing to believe that Shakespeare's skill with words was something out of the ordinary. But he would also have rejected the whole notion of valuing poetry for its texture – valuing it, that is to say, as a kind of music. If it could somehow have been proved to him that his whole explanation of Shakespeare's rise to fame is mistaken, that inside the English-speaking world, at any rate, Shakespeare's popularity is genuine, that his mere skill in placing one syllable beside another has given acute pleasure to generation after generation of English-speaking people – all this would not have been counted as a merit to Shakespeare, but rather the contrary. It would simply have been one more proof of the irreligious, earthbound nature of Shakespeare and his admirers. Tolstoy would have said that poetry is to be judged by its meaning, and that seductive sounds merely cause false meanings to go unnoticed. At every level it is the same issue – this world against the next: and certainly the music of words is something that belongs to this world.

A sort of doubt has always hung round the character of Tolstoy, as round the character of Gandhi. He was not a vulgar hypocrite, as some people declared him to be, and he would probably have imposed even greater sacrifices on himself than he did, if he had not been interfered with at every step by the people surrounding him, especially his wife. But on the other hand it is dangerous to take such men as Tolstoy at their disciples' valuation. There is always the possibility – the prob-ability, indeed – that they have done no more than exchange one form of egoism for another. Tolstoy renounced wealth, fame and privilege; he abjured violence in all its forms and was ready to suffer for doing so; but it is not so easy to believe that he abjured the principle of coercion, or at least the *desire* to coerce others. There are families in which the father will say to his child, 'You'll get a thick ear if you do that again,' while the mother, her eyes brimming over with tears, will take the child in her arms and murmur lovingly, 'Now, darling, *is* it kind to Mummy to do that?' And who would maintain that the second method is less tyrannous than the first? The distinction that really matters is not between violence and non-violence, but between having and not having the appetite for power. There are people who are convinced of the wickedness both of armies and of police forces, but who are nevertheless much more intolerant and inquisitorial in outlook than the normal person who believes that it is necessary to use violence in certain circumstances. They will not say to somebody else, 'Do this, that and the other or you will go to prison,' but they will, if they can, get inside his brain and dictate his thoughts for him in the minutest particulars. Creeds like pacifism and anarchism, which seem on the surface to imply a complete renunciation of power, rather encourage this habit of mind. For if you have embraced a creed which appears to be free from the ordinary dirtiness of politics – a creed from which you yourself cannot expect to draw any material advantage – surely that proves that you are in the right? And the more you are in the right, the more natural that everyone else should be bullied into thinking likewise.

If we are to believe what he says in his pamphlet, Tolstoy had never been able to see any merit in Shakespeare, and was always astonished to find that his fellow-writers, Turgenev, Fet and others, thought differently. We may be sure that in his unregenerate days Tolstoy's conclusion would have been: 'You like Shakespeare – I don't. Let's leave it at that.' Later, when his perception that it takes all sorts to make a world had deserted him, he came to think of Shakespeare's writings as something dangerous to himself. The more pleasure people took in Shakespeare, the less they would listen to Tolstoy. Therefore nobody must be *allowed* to enjoy Shakespeare, just as nobody must be allowed to drink alcohol or smoke tobacco. True, Tolstoy would not prevent them by force. He is not demanding that the police shall impound every copy of Shakespeare's works. But he will do dirt on Shakespeare, if he can. He will try to get inside the mind of every lover of Shakespeare and kill his enjoyment by every trick he can think of, including – as I

1GEORGE ORWELL

have shown in my summary of his pamphlet – arguments which are self-contradictory or even doubtfully honest.

But finally the most striking thing is how little difference it all makes. As I said earlier, one cannot *answer* Tolstoy's pamphlet, at least on its main counts. There is no argument by which one can defend a poem. It defends itself by surviving, or it is indefensible. And if this test is valid, I think the verdict in Shakespeare's case must be 'not guilty'. Like every other writer, Shakespeare will be forgotten sooner or later, but it is unlikely that a heavier indictment will ever be brought against him. Tolstoy was perhaps the most admired literary man of his age, and he was certainly not its least able pamphleteer. He turned all his powers of denunciation against Shakespeare, like all the guns of a battleship roaring simultaneously. And with what result? Forty years later, Shakespeare is still there, completely unaffected, and of the attempt to demolish him nothing remains except the yellowing pages of a pamphlet which hardly anyone has read, and which would be forgotten altogether if Tolstoy had not also been the author of *War and Peace* and *Anna Karenina*.

As I Please 76

Tribune, 7 March 1947

One of the great faults of the present Government is its failure to tell the people what is happening and why. That is so generally agreed that in itself it is hardly worth saying over again. However, with the wartime machinery of propaganda largely scrapped, and the Press under control of private owners, some of whom are none too friendly, it is not easy for the Government to publicise itself. Posters – at any rate, posters like the present ones – will not achieve much, films are expensive, pamphlets and White Papers are not read by the big public. The most obvious means of publicity is the radio, and we are up against the difficulty that politicians in this country are seldom radio-conscious.

During the recent crisis, people were to be heard remarking that the Minister of this or that ought to "come to the micro-

1200

phone" more frequently. But it is not much use coming to the microphone unless what you say is listened to. When I worked in the B.B.C., and frequently had to put eminent people on the air, I was struck by the fact that few professional politicians seemed to realise that broadcasting is an art that has to be learned, and that it is quite different from platform speaking. A first-rate performer in one medium may be hopeless in the other, unless re-trained. Ernest Bevin, for instance, is a good platform speaker but a poor broadcaster. Attlee is better, so far as his voice goes, but does not seem to have a gift for the telling phrase. Churchill's wartime broadcasts were good of their Corinthian kind, but Churchill, unlike most of the others, gives the impression of having studied microphone technique.

When a speaker is invisible, he not only cannot make use of his personal charm, if any, he also cannot make gestures to emphasise his points. He cannot act with his body, and therefore has to act much more elaborately with his larynx. A good exercise for anyone trying to improve his microphone delivery is to have one of his speeches recorded, and then listen to it. This is an astonishing and even shocking experience. Not only does one's voice, heard externally, sound completely different from what it sounds like inside one's skull, but it always sounds much less emphatic. To sound natural on the air one has to have the impression, internally, that one is overacting. If one speaks as one would in everyday life, or on a platform, one always sounds bored. That, indeed, is the impression that the majority of untrained broadcasters do give, especially when they speak from scripts: and when the speaker sounds bored, the audience is apt to follow suit.

Some time ago a foreign visitor asked me if I could recommend a good, representative anthology of English verse. When I thought it over I found that I could not name a single one that seemed to me satisfactory. Of course there are innumerable period anthologies, but nothing, so far as I know, that attempts to cover the whole of English literature except Palgrave's *Golden Treasury* and, more comprehensive and more up-to-date, the *Oxford Book of English Verse*.

Now, I do not deny that the *Oxford Book* is useful, that there is a great deal of good stuff in it, and that every schoolchild ought to have a copy, in default of something better. Still, when you look at the last 50 pages, you think twice about recommending such a book to a foreigner who may imagine that it is really representative of English verse. Indeed, the whole of this part of the book is a lamentable illustration of what happens to professors of literature when they have to exercise independent judgement. Up to 1850, or thereabouts, one could not go very wrong in compiling an anthology, because, after all, it is on the whole the best poems that have survived. But as soon as Sir Arthur Quiller-Couch reached his contemporaries, all semblance of taste deserted him.

The *Oxford Book* stops at 1900, and it is true that the last decades of the nineteenth century were a poor period for verse. Still, there were poets even in the 'nineties. There was Ernest Dowson – *Cynara* is not my idea of a good poem, but I would sooner have it than Henley's "England, My England" – there was Hardy, who published his first poems in 1898, and there was Housman, who published *A Shropshire Lad* in 1896. There was also Hopkins, who was not in print or barely in print, but whom Sir Arthur Quiller-Couch must have known about. None of these appears in the *Oxford Book*. Yeats, who had already published a great deal at that date, does appear shortly, but he is not represented by his best poems: neither is Kipling, who, I think, did write one or two poems (for instance, "How far is St. Helena") which deserve to be included in a serious anthology. And on the other hand, just look at the stuff that *has* been included! Sir Henry Newbolt's Old Cliftonian keeping a stiff upper lip on the North-West Frontier; other patriotic pieces by Henley and Kipling; and page after page of weak, sickly, imitative verse by Andrew Lang, Sir William Watson, A. C. Benson, Alice Meynell and others now forgotten. What is one to think of an anthologist who puts Newbolt and Edmund Gosse in the same volume with Shakespeare, Wordsworth and Blake?

Perhaps I am just being ignorant and there does already exist a comprehensive anthology running all the way from Chaucer to Dylan Thomas and including no tripe. But if not, I think it is time to compile one, or at least to bring the *Oxford Book* up to date by making a completely new selection of poets from Tennyson onwards.

*

Looking through what I have written above, I see that I have spoken rather snootily of Dowson's *Cynara*. I know it is a bad poem, but it is bad in a good way, or good in a bad way, and I do not wish to pretend that I never admired it. Indeed, it was one of the favourites of my boyhood. I am quoting from memory:

> I have forgot much, Cynara, gone with the wind,
> Flung roses, roses riotously with the throng
> Dancing, to put thy pale lost lilies out of mind;
> But I was desolate and sick of an old passion –
> Yea, all the time, because the dance was long –
> I have been faithful to thee, Cynara, in my fashion.

Surely those lines possess, if not actual merit, at least the same kind of charm as belongs to a pink geranium or a soft-centre chocolate.

As I Please 77

Tribune, 14 March 1947

I have not yet read more than a newspaper paragraph about Nu Speling, in connection with which somebody is introducing a Bill in Parliament, but if it is like most other schemes for rationalising our spelling, I am against it in advance, as I imagine most people will be.

Probably the strongest reason for resisting rationalised spelling is laziness. We have all learned to read and write already, and we don't want to have to do it over again. But there are other more respectable objections. To begin with, unless the scheme were rigidly enforced, the resulting chaos, with some newspapers and publishing houses accepting it, others refusing it, and others adopting it in patches, would be fearful. Then again, anyone who had learned only the new system would find it very difficult to read books printed in the old one, so that the huge labour of re-spelling the entire literature of the past would have to be undertaken. And again, you can only fully rationalise spelling if you give a fixed value to each letter. But this means standardising pronunciation, which could not be done in this country without an unholy row. What do you do, for instance, about words like "butter" or "glass," which are pronounced in different ways in London and Newcastle? Other words, such as "were," are pronounced in two different ways according to individual inclination, or according to context.

However, I do not want to pre-judge the inventors of Nu Speling. Perhaps they have already thought of a way round these difficulties. And certainly our existing spelling system is preposterous and must be a torment to foreign students. This is a pity, because English is well fitted to be the universal second language, if there ever is such a thing. It has a large start over any natural language and an enormous start over any manufactured one, and apart from the spelling it is very easy to learn. Would it not be possible to rationalise it by little and little, a few words every year? Already some of the more ridiculous spellings do tend to get killed off unofficially. For instance, how many people now spell "hiccup" as "hiccough"?

Another thing I am against in advance – for it is bound to be suggested sooner or later – is the complete scrapping of our present system of weights and measures.

Obviously you have got to have the metric system for certain purposes. For scientific work it has long been in use, and it is also needed for tools and machinery, especially if you want to export them. But there is a strong case for keeping on the old measurements for use in everyday life. One reason is that the metric system does not possess, or has not succeeded in establishing, a large number of units that can be visualised. There is, for instance, effectively no unit between the metre, which is more than a yard, and the centimetre, which is less than half an inch. In English you can describe someone as being five feet three inches high, or five feet nine inches, or six feet one inch, and your hearer will know fairly accurately what you mean. But I have never heard a Frenchman say, "He is a hundred and forty-two centimetres high"; it would not convey any visual image. So also with the various other measurements. Rods and acres, pints, quarts and gallons, pounds, stones and hundredweights, are all of them units with which we are intimately familiar, and we should be slightly poorer without

ESSAYS

them. Actually, in countries where the metric system is in force a few of the old measurements tend to linger on for everyday purposes, although officially discouraged.

There is also the literary consideration, which cannot be left quite out of account. The names of the units in the old system are short homely words which lend themselves to vigorous speech. Putting a quart into a pint pot is a good image, which could hardly be expressed in the metric system. Also, the literature of the past deals only in the old measurements, and many passages would become an irritation if one had to do a sum in arithmetic when one read them, as one does with those tiresome versts in a Russian novel.

> The emmet's inch and eagle's mile
> Make lame philosophy to smile:

fancy having to turn that into millimetres!

I have just been reading about a party of German teachers, journalists, trade union delegates and others who have been on a visit to this country. It appears that while here they were given food parcels by trade unions and other organisations, only to have them taken away again by the Customs officials at Harwich. They were not even allowed to take out of the country the 15 lb. of food which is permitted to a returning prisoner of war. The newspaper reporting this adds without apparent irony that the Germans in question had been here "on a six weeks' course in democracy."

I wonder whether it would be possible, before the next bout of cold weather comes along, to do something about the racket in firewood? Last week I paid fifteen shillings for a hundred logs. They were very small logs, weighing I should say a pound to a pound and a half each, so that weight for weight they will have been twice or three times as expensive as coal. A day or two later I heard of logs being sold at a pound or thirty shillings a hundred. In any case, much of the wood that is hawked round the streets in cold weather is full of sap and almost unburnable.

Incidentally, does not the weather we have just been through reinforce my earlier plea for better use of our peat resources? At the time various people said to me: "Ah, but you see, English people aren't used to peat. You'd never get them to use it." During the last two weeks, most of the people known to me have used anything, not despising the furniture as a last resort. I kept going for a day myself on a blitzed bedstead, and wrote an article by its grateful warmth.

The other day I had occasion to write something about the teaching of history in private schools, and the following scene, which was only rather loosely connected with what I was writing, floated into my memory. It was less than fifteen years ago that I witnessed it.

"Jones!"

"Yessir!"

"Causes of the French Revolution."

"Please, sir, the French Revolution was due to three causes, the teachings of Voltaire and Rousseau, the oppression of the nobles by the people and –"

At this moment a faint chill, like the first premonitory symptom of an illness, falls upon Jones. Is it possible that he has gone wrong somewhere? The master's face is inscrutable. Swiftly Jones casts his mind back to the unappetising little book, with the gritty brown cover, a page of which is memorised daily. He could have sworn he had the whole thing right. But at this moment Jones discovers for the first time the deceptiveness of visual memory. The whole page is clear in his mind, the shape of every paragraph accurately recorded, but the trouble is that there is no saying which way round the words go. He had made sure it was the oppression of the nobles by the people; but then it might have been the oppression of the people by the nobles. It is a toss-up. Desperately he takes his decision – better to stick to his first version. He gabbles on:

"The oppression of the nobles by the people and –"

"JONES!"

Is that kind of thing still going on, I wonder?

To forestall a flood of letters: –

As I have found out since writing my column last week, there are already several inclusive anthologies which deal with modern verse more satisfactorily than the *Oxford Book*.

As I Please 78
Tribune, 21 March 1947

The atomic bomb is frightening, but to anyone who wants to counteract it by a different kind of fright I recommend Mr. Mark Abrams's book, *The Population of Great Britain*, published in 1945. This can be read in conjunction with the Mass Observation survey, *Britain and Her Birth-rate*, published about the same time, and other recent books on the same subject. They all tell more or less the same story, and it has very unpleasant implications for anyone who expects to be alive in 1970.

At present, as Mr. Abrams's figures show, the age composition of our population is favourable, if one thinks in terms of labour units. We still have the benefit of the relatively high birth-rate just before and just after the 1914–18 war, so that well over half our population is of working age. But the trouble is that we can't freeze the figures at this point. The working population grows older all the time, and sufficient children are not being born. In 1881, when our total population was only about two-thirds of what it is now, the number of babies (under four) was actually larger by about half a million, while the number of old people (over 65) was less by something over three millions. In 1881 more than a third of the population was under 14: today the corresponding figure is less than a quarter. If there had been an Old Age Pension in 1881, less than 5 per cent. of the population would have been eligible for it: today more than 10 per cent. are eligible for it. To see the full significance of this one has to look forward a bit.

By 1970, Mr. Abrams calculates, the number of people over 55 may well be 14 millions – this in a population which may be smaller than the present one. That is to say that about one person in three will be almost past work: or, to put it differently, that every two able-bodied people will be supporting one old person between them! When Mr. Abrams produced his book, the birth-rate had been rising during the later war years, and I believe it has again risen during 1946, but not to anywhere near replacement level: in any case the sudden jump in births may have happened merely because, owing to the war, people have been marrying earlier. The downward trend has been happening for more than half a century, and some of its effects cannot be escaped from, but the worst would be avoided if the birth-rate reached and stayed at the point where the average family was four children, and not, as at present, a little over two. But this must happen within the next decade; otherwise there will not be enough women of child-bearing age to restore the situation.

It is curious how little dismay the dropping birth-rate caused until very recently. Even now, as the Mass Observation report brings out, most people merely think that it means a smaller population and do not realise that it also means an ageing population. Thirty years ago, even ten or fifteen years ago, to advocate smaller families was a mark of enlightenment. The key phrases were "surplus population" and "the multiplication of the unfit." Even now there is strong social pressure against large families, not to mention the crude economic consideration. All writers on this subject seem to agree that the causes of the decline are complex and that it may not be possible to reverse the trend merely by family allowances, day nurseries, etc. But clearly there must be *some* financial inducement, because, in an industrialised society which is also socially competitive, a large family is an unbearable economic burden. At the best it means making sure that your children will start off with a poorer chance in life than you had yourself.

Over the past twenty-five years, what innumerable people must have kept their families down from directly economic motives! It is a queer kind of prudence if you consider the community and not the individual. In another twenty-five years the parents of today will be past work, and the children they have not had will not be there to support them. I wonder if the Old Age Pension will stay at the equivalent of £1 a week when one person in three is in receipt of it?

I wonder if there exists – indeed I am sure something of the kind must exist – a short and simple textbook from which the ordinary citizen can get a working knowledge of the laws he lives under? Recently I had occasion to refer in this column to the rules governing the selection of juries. No doubt it was very ignorant on my part not to know that juries are picked out on a system that tends to exclude the working class; but evidently thousands of other people did not know it either, and the discovery came as a shock. Every now and again this kind of thing happens. By some chance or other – for instance, by reading the reports of a murder case – one finds out how the law stands on a certain subject, and it is frequently so stupid or so unfair that one would not have believed it if one had not seen it in black and white.

For instance, I have just been reading the Government White Paper dealing with the confession made by David Ware in the Manchester murder case. Walter Rowland, since hanged, had been convicted of the murder, and Ware afterwards made a confession which Rowland's counsel attempted to use as evidence at the appeal. After reading the White Paper I have not the slightest doubt that the confession was spurious and that it was right to disregard it. But that is not the point. It came out in the appeal proceedings that the judges had no power to hear evidence of that kind. True or false, the confession could not be admitted as evidence. An innocent man might be convicted, the real criminal might make an unmistakeably genuine confession, and the innocent man might still be hanged, unless the Home Secretary chose to intervene. Did you know that that is how the law stands? I certainly didn't, and the incident shows how rash it is to try to infer what the law would be on any given subject, using common sense as a starting-point.

Here is another instance, but in this case my ignorance is probably less excusable. In a recent *cause célèbre*, in which the accused was acquitted, it came out that the very heavy costs of the defence were paid by a Sunday paper. I confess that I had not realised until then that when you are found not guilty on a criminal charge, you still have to pay your own costs. I had vaguely imagined that when the Crown is discovered to be in the wrong, it pays up, like the unsuccessful claimant in a civil suit. However, it seems that if you are actually indigent, the Crown will provide you with counsel, but it takes care not to be seriously out of pocket by doing so. In this case, it is stated, the leading counsel briefed by the Sunday paper received about £500, whereas if briefed by the Crown he would have received less than £20. Apply that to an ordinary burglary or embezzlement case, where there is not much notoriety to be won, and see what it means to an indigent person's chance of getting the best possible defence.

What an outcry there has been over the suspension of the weekly papers! Even the *Smallholder* protested, and there was a very sharp editorial comment in *Practical Engineering*. The *Universe*, if I remember rightly, said that this was the prelude to the imposition of Press censorship. And in general the idea seems to have seeped round that there was some kind of political motive for the suspension – the motive, presumably, being to prevent comment on the Government's mistakes.

A well-known writer said to me that the banning of weekly papers was much the same kind of thing as the "co-ordination" of the Press in totalitarian countries. This seems to me the point at which suspicion turns into folly. Obviously there was no idea of silencing criticism, since the daily papers were left alone. The Beaverbrook Press, for instance, is far more hostile to the Government than any weekly paper of standing, besides having an enormously larger circulation. How much ignorant abuse Shinwell might have escaped, if during the crisis he had made even one public appearance to explain what he was doing!

Preface to the Ukrainian Edition of
Animal Farm
[March 1947]

I have been asked to write a preface to the Ukrainian translation of *Animal Farm*. I am aware that I write for readers about whom I know nothing, but also that they too have probably never had the slightest opportunity to know anything about me.

In this preface they will most likely expect me to say something of how *Animal Farm* originated but first I would like to say something about myself and the experiences by which I arrived at my political position.

I was born in India in 1903. My father was an official in the English administration there, and my family was one of those ordinary middle-class families of soldiers, clergymen, government officials, teachers, lawyers, doctors, etc. I was educated at Eton, the most costly and snobbish of the English Public Schools.[37] But I had only got in there by means of a scholarship; otherwise my father could not have afforded to send me to a school of this type.

Shortly after I left school (I wasn't quite twenty years old then) I went to Burma and joined the Indian Imperial Police. This was an armed police, a sort of *gendarmerie* very similar to the Spanish *Guardia Civil* or the *Garde Mobile* in France. I stayed five years in the service. It did not suit me and made me hate imperialism, although at that time nationalist feelings in Burma were not very marked, and relations between the English and the Burmese were not particularly unfriendly. When on leave in England in 1927, I resigned from the service and decided to become a writer: at first without any especial success. In 1928–29 I lived in Paris and wrote short stories and novels that nobody would print (I have since destroyed them all). In the following years I lived mostly from hand to mouth, and went hungry on several occasions. It was only from 1934 onwards that I was able to live on what I earned from my writing. In the meantime I sometimes lived for months on end amongst the poor and half-criminal elements who inhabit the worst parts of the poorer quarters, or take to the streets, begging and stealing. At that time I associated with them through lack of money, but later their way of life interested me very much for its own sake. I spent many months (more systematically this time) studying the conditions of the miners in the north of England. Up to 1930 I did not on the whole look upon myself as a Socialist. In fact I had as yet no clearly defined political views. I became pro-Socialist more out of disgust with the way the poorer section of the industrial workers were oppressed and neglected than out of any theoretical admiration for a planned society.

In 1936 I got married. In almost the same week the civil war broke out in Spain. My wife and I both wanted to go to Spain and fight for the Spanish Government. We were ready in six months, as soon as I had finished the book I was writing. In

Spain I spent almost six months on the Aragon front until, at Huesca, a Fascist sniper shot me through the throat.

In the early stages of the war foreigners were on the whole unaware of the inner struggles between the various political parties supporting the Government. Through a series of accidents I joined not the International Brigade like the majority of foreigners, but the POUM militia – i.e. the Spanish Trotskyists.

So in the middle of 1937, when the Communists gained control (or partial control) of the Spanish Government and began to hunt down the Trotskyists, we both found ourselves amongst the victims. We were very lucky to get out of Spain alive, and not even to have been arrested once. Many of our friends were shot, and others spent a long time in prison or simply disappeared.

These man-hunts in Spain went on at the same time as the great purges in the USSR and were a sort of supplement to them. In Spain as well as in Russia the nature of the accusations (namely, conspiracy with the Fascists) was the same and as far as Spain was concerned I had every reason to believe that the accusations were false. To experience all this was a valuable object lesson: it taught me how easily totalitarian propaganda can control the opinion of enlightened people in democratic countries.

My wife and I both saw innocent people being thrown into prison merely because they were suspected of unorthodoxy. Yet on our return to England we found numerous sensible and well-informed observers believing the most fantastic accounts of conspiracy, treachery and sabotage which the press reported from the Moscow trials.

And so I understood, more clearly than ever, the negative influence of the Soviet myth upon the western Socialist movement.

And here I must pause to describe my attitude to the Soviet régime.

I have never visited Russia and my knowledge of it consists only of what can be learned by reading books and newspapers. Even if I had the power, I would not wish to interfere in Soviet domestic affairs: I would not condemn Stalin and his associates merely for their barbaric and undemocratic methods.

It is quite possible that, even with the best intentions, they could not have acted otherwise under the conditions prevailing there.

But on the other hand it was of the utmost importance to me that people in western Europe should see the Soviet régime for what it really was. Since 1930 I had seen little evidence that the USSR was progressing towards anything that one could truly call Socialism. On the contrary, I was struck by clear signs of its transformation into a hierarchical society, in which the rulers have no more reason to give up their power than any other ruling class. Moreover, the workers and intelligentsia in a country like England cannot understand that the USSR of today is altogether different from what it was in 1917. It is partly that they do not want to understand (i.e. they want to believe that, somewhere, a really Socialist country does actually exist), and partly that, being accustomed to comparative freedom and moderation in public life, totalitarianism is completely incomprehensible to them.

Yet one must remember that England is not completely democratic. It is also a capitalist country with great class privileges and (even now, after a war that has tended to equalise everybody) with great differences in wealth. But nevertheless it is a country in which people have lived together for several hundred years without major conflict, in which the laws are relatively just and official news and statistics can almost invariably be believed, and, last but not least, in which to hold and to voice minority views does not involve any mortal danger. In such an atmosphere the man in the street has no real understanding of things like concentration camps, mass deportations, arrests without trial, press censorship, etc. Everything he reads about a country like the USSR is automatically translated into English terms, and he quite innocently accepts the lies of totalitarian propaganda. Up to 1939, and even later, the majority of English people were incapable of assessing the true nature of the Nazi régime in Germany, and now, with the Soviet régime, they are still to a large extent under the same sort of illusion.

This has caused great harm to the Socialist movement in England, and had serious consequences for English foreign policy. Indeed, in my opinion, nothing has contributed so much to the corruption of the original idea of Socialism as the belief that Russia is a Socialist country and that every act of its rulers must be excused, if not imitated.

And so for the past ten years I have been convinced that the destruction of the Soviet myth was essential if we wanted a revival of the Socialist movement.

On my return from Spain I thought of exposing the Soviet myth in a story that could be easily understood by almost anyone and which could be easily translated into other languages. However, the actual details of the story did not come to me for some time until one day (I was then living in a small village) I saw a little boy, perhaps ten years old, driving a huge cart-horse along a narrow path, whipping it whenever it tried to turn. It struck me that if only such animals became aware of their strength we should have no power over them, and that men exploit animals in much the same way as the rich exploit the proletariat.

I proceeded to analyse Marx's theory from the animals' point of view. To them it was clear that the concept of a class struggle between humans was pure illusion, since whenever it was necessary to exploit animals, all humans united against them: the true struggle is between animals and humans. From this point of departure, it was not difficult to elaborate the story. I did not write it out till 1943, for I was always engaged on other work which gave me no time; and in the end I included some events, for example the Teheran Conference, which were taking place while I was writing. Thus the main outlines of the story were in my mind over a period of six years before it was actually written.

I do not wish to comment on the work; if it does not speak for itself, it is a failure. But I should like to emphasise two points: first, that although the various episodes are taken from the actual history of the Russian Revolution, they are dealt with schematically and their chronological order is changed; this was necessary for the symmetry of the story. The second point has been missed by most critics, possibly because I did not emphasise it sufficiently. A number of readers may finish the book with the impression that it ends in the complete reconciliation of the pigs and the humans. That was not my intention; on the contrary I meant it to end on a loud note of discord, for I wrote it immediately after the Teheran Conference which everybody thought had established the best possible relations between the USSR and the West. I personally did not believe that such good relations would last long; and as events have shown, I wasn't far wrong.

I don't know what more I need add. If anyone is interested in personal details, I should add that I am a widower with a son almost three years old, that by profession I am a writer, and that since the beginning of the war I have worked mainly as a journalist.

The periodical to which I contribute most regularly is *Tribune*, a socio-political weekly which represents, generally speaking, the left wing of the Labour Party. The following of my books might most interest the ordinary reader (should any reader of this translation find copies of them): *Burmese Days* (a story about Burma), *Homage to Catalonia* (arising from my experiences in the Spanish Civil War), and *Critical Essays* (essays mainly about contemporary popular English literature and instructive more from the sociological than from the literary point of view).

As I Please 79
Tribune, 28 March 1947

I have been reading with interest the February–March bulletin of Mass-Observation, which appears just ten years after this organisation first came into being. It is curious to remember with what hostility it was greeted at the beginning. It was violently attacked in the *New Statesman*, for instance, where Mr. Stonier declared that the typical Mass-Observer would have "elephant ears, a loping walk and a permanent sore eye from looking through keyholes," or words to that effect. Another attacker was Mr. Stephen Spender. But on the whole the opposition to this or any other kind of social survey comes from people of Conservative opinions, who often seem to be genuinely indignant at the idea of finding out what the big public is thinking.

If asked why, they generally answer that what is discovered is of no interest, and that in any case any intelligent person always knows already what are the main trends of public opinion. Another argument is that social surveys are an interference with individual liberty and a first step towards totalitarianism. The *Daily Express* ran this line for several years and tried to laugh the small social survey unit instituted by the Ministry of Information out of existence by nicknaming it Cooper's Snoopers. Of course, behind much of this opposition there lies a well-justified fear of finding that mass sentiment on many subjects is not Conservative.

But some people do seem sincerely to feel that it is a bad thing for the Government to know too much about what people are thinking, just as others feel that it is a kind of presumption when the Government tries to educate public opinion. Actually you can't have democracy unless both processes are at work. Democracy is only possible when the law-makers and administrators know what the masses want, and what they can be counted on to understand. If the present Government paid more attention to this last point, they would word some of their publicity differently. Mass-Observation issued a report last week on the White Paper on the economic situation. They found, as usual, that the abstract words and phrases which are flung to and fro in official announcements mean nothing to countless ordinary citizens. Many people are even flummoxed by the word "assets," which is thought to have something to do with "assist"!

The Mass-Observation bulletin gives some account of the methods its investigators use, but does not touch on a very important point, and that is the manner in which social surveys are financed. Mass-Observation itself appears to keep going in a hand-to-mouth way by publishing books and by undertaking specific jobs for the Government or for commercial organisations. Some of its best surveys, such as that dealing with the birth-rate, were carried out for the Advertising Service Guild. The trouble with this method is that a subject only gets investigated if some large, wealthy organisation happens to be interested in it. An obvious example is anti-semitism, which I believe has never been looked into, or only in a very sketchy way. But anti-semitism is only one variant of the great modern disease of nationalism. We know very little about the real causes of nationalism, and we might conceivably be on the way towards curing it if we knew more. But who is sufficiently interested to put up the thousands of pounds that an exhaustive survey would cost?

For some weeks there has been correspondence in the *Observer* about the persistence of "spit and polish" in the Armed Forces. The last issue had a good letter from someone who signed himself "Conscript," describing how he and his comrades were forced to waste their time in polishing brass, blacking the rubber hoses on stirrup pumps with boot polish, scraping broom handles with razor blades, and so on. But "Conscript" then goes on to say:

> When an officer (a major) carried out routine reading of King's Regulations regarding venereal disease, he did not hesitate to add: "There is nothing to be ashamed of if you have the disease – it is quite natural. But make sure that you report for treatment at once."

I must say that it seems to me strange, amid the other idiocies mentioned, to object to one of the few sensible things in the army system, i.e., its straightforward attitude towards venereal disease. We shall never be able to stamp out syphilis and gonorrhoea until the stigma of sinfulness is removed from them. When full conscription was introduced in the 1914–1918 war it was discovered, if I remember rightly, that nearly half the population suffered or had suffered from some form of venereal disease, and this frightened the authorities into taking a few precautions. During the inter-war years the struggle against venereal disease languished, so far as the civilian population went. There was provision for treatment of those already infected, but the proposal to set up "early treatment centres," as in the Army, was quelled by the puritans. Then came another war, with the increase in venereal disease that war necessarily causes, and another attempt to deal with the problem. The Ministry of Health posters are timid enough, but even these would have provoked an outcry from the pious ones if military necessity had not called them into being.

You can't deal with these diseases so long as they are thought of as visitations of God, in a totally different category from all other diseases. The inevitable result of that is concealment and quack remedies. And it is humbug to say that "clean living is the only real remedy." You are bound to have promiscuity and prostitution in a society like ours, where people mature sexually at about fifteen and are discouraged from marrying till they are in their twenties, where conscription and the need for mobility of labour break up family life, and where young people living in big towns have no regular way of forming acquaintanceships. It is impossible to solve the problem by making people more moral, because they won't, within any foreseeable time, become as moral as all that. Besides, many of the victims of venereal disease are husbands or wives who have not themselves committed any so-called immoral act. The only sensible course is to recognise that syphilis and gonorrhoea are merely *diseases*, more preventable if not more curable than most, and that to suffer from them is not disgraceful. No doubt the pious ones would squeal. But in doing so they might avow their real motives, and then we should be a little nearer to wiping out this evil.

For the last five minutes I have been gazing out of the window into the square, keeping a sharp look-out for signs of spring. There is a thinnish patch in the clouds with a faint hint of blue behind it, and on a sycamore tree there are some things that look as if they might be buds. Otherwise it is still winter. But don't worry! Two days ago, after a careful search in Hyde Park, I came on a hawthorn bush that was definitely in bud, and some birds, though not actually singing, were making noises like an orchestra tuning up. Spring is coming after all, and recent rumours that this was the beginning of another Ice Age were unfounded. In only three weeks' time we shall be listening to the cuckoo, which usually gives tongue about the fourteenth of April. Another three weeks after that, and we shall be basking under blue skies, eating ices off barrows and neglecting to lay up fuel for next winter.

How appropriate the ancient poems in praise of spring have seemed these last few years! They have a meaning that they did not have in the days when there was no fuel shortage and you could get almost anything at any time of year. Of all passages celebrating spring, I think I like best those two stanzas from the beginning of one of the Robin Hood ballads. I modernise the spelling:

> When shaws be sheen and swards full fair,
> And leaves both large and long,
> It is merry walking in the fair forest
> To hear the small birds' song.
>
> The woodwele sang and would not cease,
> Sitting upon the spray,
> So loud he wakened Robin Hood
> In the greenwood where he lay.

But what exactly was the woodwele? The Oxford Dictionary seems to suggest that it was the woodpecker, which is not a notable songster, and I should be interested to know whether it can be identified with some more probable bird.

Burnham's View of the Contemporary World Struggle

The New Leader (New York), 29 March 1947

One fallacy left over from the nineteenth century and still influencing our thoughts is the notion that two major wars cannot happen within a few years of one another. The American Civil War and the Franco-Prussian War, it is true, occurred almost simultaneously, but they were fought in different continents and by different people. Otherwise the rule seemed to hold good that you can only get people to fight when everyone who remembers what the last war was like is beyond military age. Even the gap between the two World Wars – twenty-one years – was large enough to ensure that very few men took part in both of them as common soldiers. Hence the widespread vague belief, or hope, that a third world war could not break out before about 1970, by which time, it is hopefully argued, "all sorts of things may have happened."

As James Burnham points out,[38] the atomic bomb has altered all that. His book is, in effect, a product of atomic weapons: it is a revision, almost an abandonment of his earlier world-picture, in the light of the fact that great nations are now in a position actually to annihilate one another. When weapons have reached this level of deadliness, one cannot take the risk of letting the enemy get his blow in first, so that as soon as two hostile nations possess atomic bombs, the explosion will follow almost immediately. In Burnham's opinion, we have perhaps ten years, but more probably only five, before the third world war, which has been raging unofficially ever since 1944, enters its open phase.

No doubt it is not necessary to say what powers this war will be between. Burnham's main aim in writing his book is to urge the United States to seize the initiative and establish what amounts to a world empire now, before Communism swallows the whole of Eurasia. The actual continuity of civilization, he says, is threatened by the existence of atomic weapons, and there is no safeguard except to make sure that only one nation possesses them. Ideally, atomic energy would be controlled by an international authority, but no such thing exists or is likely to exist for a long time to come, and meanwhile the only serious competitors for world power are the United States and the USSR. However, the struggle is not merely between Western democracy and Communism. Burnham's definition of Communism is central to the book, and it is worth stopping to examine it.

He does not accept the now widely-spread belief that Communism is simply Russian imperialism. In its way, it is a genuinely international movement, and the USSR is merely the base, or nucleus, from which it expands, sucking one territory after another into its system. Even if the system covered the whole earth, the real centre of power and government would no doubt continue to be the Eurasian "heartland"; but world Communism does not so much mean conquest by Russia as conquest by a special form of social organization. Communism is not in the ordinary sense a political movement: it is a world-wide conspiratorial movement for the capture of power. Its aim is to establish everywhere a system similar to that which prevails in Soviet Russia – that is, a system which is technically collectivist, but which concentrates all power in a very few hands, is based on forced labour, and eliminates all real or imaginary opponents by means of terrorism. It can expand even outside the striking range of the Red Army, because in every country there are a few people who are its devoted adherents, others, more numerous, who are in some degree deceived, and yet others who will more or less accept Communism so long as it seems to be winning and they are offered no alternative. In every country which they are unable to dominate, the Communists act as a Fifth Column, working through cover organizations of every kind, playing on working-class aspirations and the ignorance of well-meaning liberals, always with the object of sowing demoralization against the day when war breaks out. All Communist activities are really directed towards this war. Unless Communism can be forced back upon the defensive, there is no chance of the war being averted, since the inevitability of a "final struggle" is part of the Leninist mythology and is believed in as an article of faith.

After discussing the nature of Communism and of Soviet foreign policy, Burnham examines the strategic situation. "Communism" – that is to say, the USSR with its satellite nations and Fifth Columns – has enormous advantages in manpower, in natural resources, in the inaccessibility of the Eurasian "heartland," in the quasi-religious appeal of the Communist myth, and above all, perhaps, in the quality of its leadership. The supreme commanders of the Communist movement are men who have no aim in life except to capture power and who are not troubled by scruples nor obliged to take much account of public opinion. They are both experts and fanatics, whereas their opponents are bungling, half-hearted amateurs. On the other hand, "Communism" is technologically backward and suffers from the disadvantage that its mythology is most easily swallowed by people who have not seen Russian rule at close quarters. The United States is relatively weak in manpower and its geographical position is none too strong, but in industrial output and technique it is far ahead of all rivals, and it has potential allies all over the world, especially in western Europe. The greatest handicap of the United States, therefore, is the lack of any definite world-view: if the American people understood their own strength, and also the danger that threatens them, the situation would be retrievable.

Burnham discusses what ought to be done, what could be done, and what probably will be done. He writes off pacifism as a practical remedy. In principle it could solve the world's ills, but since significant numbers of people cannot be induced to adopt it, it can only provide salvation for scattered individuals, not for societies. The real alternatives before the world are domination by Communism and domination by the United States. Obviously the latter is preferable, and the United States must act swiftly and make its purpose unmistakably clear. It must start off by proposing a union – not an alliance, but a complete fusion – with Britain and the British Dominions, and strive to draw the whole of Western Europe into its orbit. It must ruthlessly extirpate Communism within its own borders. It must frankly set itself up as the world's champion against Communism, and conduct unremitting propaganda to the people of the Russian-occupied countries, and still more to the Russian people themselves, making clear to them that not they but their rulers are regarded as the enemy. It must take up the firmest possible attitude towards the USSR, always understanding that a threat or gesture not backed by military force is useless. It must stick by its friends and not make gifts of food and machinery to its enemies. And above all, the United States must have a clear policy. Unless it has a definite, intelligible plan for world organization it cannot seize the initiative from Communism. It is on this point that Burnham is most pessimistic. At present, the American people as a whole have no grasp of the world situation, and American foreign policy is weak, unstable and contradictory. It must be so, because – quite apart from the sabotage of "fellow-travellers" and the intrusion of home politics – there is no general, over-riding purpose. In outlining a policy for the United States, Burnham says, he is only pointing out what *could* be done. What probably *will* happen is yet more confusion and vacillation, leading in five or ten years to a war which the United States will enter at grave disadvantage.

That is the general outline of Burnham's argument, though I have slightly re-arranged the order in which he presents it. It will be seen that he is demanding, or all but demanding, an immediate preventive war against Russia. True, he does not *want* the war to happen, and he thinks that it may possibly be prevented if sufficient firmness is shown. Still, the main point of his plan is that only one country should be allowed to possess the atomic bombs: and the Russians, unless crippled in war, are bound to get hold of them sooner or later. It will also be seen that Burnham is largely scrapping his earlier world-picture, and not merely the geographical aspect of it. In *The Managerial Revolution*, Burnham foretold the rise of three super-states which would be unable to conquer one another and would divide the world between them. Now the super-states have dwindled to two, and, thanks to atomic weapons, neither of them is invincible. But more has changed than that. In *The Managerial Revolution* it was implied that all three super-states would be very much alike. They would all be totalitarian in structure: that is, they would be collectivist but not democratic, and would be ruled over by a caste of managers, scientists and bureaucrats who would destroy old-style capitalism and keep the working class permanently in subjection. In other words, something rather like "Communism" would prevail everywhere. In *The Machiavellians*, Burnham somewhat toned down his theory, but continued to insist that politics is only the struggle for power, and that government has to be based on force and fraud. Democracy is unworkable, and in any case the masses do not want it and will not make sacrifices in defence of it. In his present book, however, Burnham is in effect the champion of old-style democracy. There is, he now decides, a great deal in Western society that is worth preserving. Managerialism, with its forced labour, deportation, massacres and frame-up trials, is not really the unavoidable next stage in human development, and we must all get together and quell it before it is too late. All the available forces must rally immediately under the banner of anti-Communism. It is essentially a conservative programme, making its appeal to the love of liberty and ordinary decency, but not to international sentiment.

Before criticizing Burnham's thesis, there is one thing that must be said. This is that Burnham has intellectual courage, and writes about real issues. He is certain to be denounced as a warmonger for writing this book. Yet if the danger is as acute as he believes, the course he suggests would probably be the right one: and more than this, he avoids the usual hypocritical attitude of "condemning" Russian policy while denying that it could be right in any circumstances to go to war. In international politics, as he realizes, you must either be ready to practise appeasement indefinitely, or at some point you must be ready to fight. He also sees that appeasement is an unreal policy, since a great nation, conscious of its own strength, never really carries it through. All that happens is that sooner or later some demand is felt to be intolerable, and one flounders into a war that might have been avoided by taking a firm attitude earlier. It is not fashionable to say such things nowadays, and Burnham deserves credit for saying them. However, it does not follow that he is right in his main argument. The important thing is the time factor. How much time have we got before the moment of crisis? Burnham, as usual, sees everything in the darkest colours and allows us only five years, or at most ten. If that were right, an American world empire would probably be the only hope. On the other hand, if we have twenty years in which to manoeuvre, there are other and better possibilities which ought not to be abandoned.

Unless the signs are very deceiving, the USSR is preparing for war against the Western democracies. Indeed, as Burnham rightly says, the war is already happening in a desultory way. How soon it could break out into full-scale conflict is a difficult question, bringing in all kinds of military, economic and scientific problems on which the ordinary journalist or political observer has no data. But there is one point, very important to Burnham's argument, which can be profitably discussed, and that is the position of the Communist parties and the "fellow-travellers" and the reliance placed on them by Russian strategy.

Burnham lays great stress on the Communist tactic of "infiltration." The Communists and their associates, open and secret, and the liberals who play their game unknowingly, are everywhere. They are in the trade unions, in the armed forces, in the State Department, in the press, in the churches, in cultural organizations, in every kind of league or union or committee with ostensibly progressive aims, seeping into everything like a filter-passing virus. For the moment they spread confusion and disaffection, and presently, when the crisis comes, they will hit out with all their strength. Moreover, a Communist is psychologically quite different from an ordinary human being. According to Burnham:

> The true Communist . . . is a "dedicated man." He has no life apart from his organization and his rigidly systematic set of ideas. Everything that he does, everything that he has, family, job, money, belief, friends, talents, life, everything is subordinated to his Communism. He is not a Communist just on election day or at Party headquarters. He is a Communist always. He eats, reads, makes love, thinks, goes to parties, changes residence, laughs, insults, always as a Communist. For him, the world is divided into just two classes of human beings: the Communists, and all the rest.

And again:

> The Moscow Show Trials revealed what has always been true of the Communist morality: that it is not merely the material possessions or the life of the individual which must be subordinated, but his reputation, his conscience, his honor, his dignity. He must lie and grovel, cheat and inform and betray, for Communism, as well as die. There is no restraint, no limit.

There are many similar passages. They all sound true enough until one begins applying them to the Communists whom one actually knows. No doubt, Burnham's description of the "true Communist" holds good for a few hundred thousand or a few million fanatical, dehumanized people, mostly inside the USSR, who are the nucleus of the movement. It holds good for Stalin, Molotov, Zhdanov, etc., and the more faithful of their agents abroad. But if there is one well-attested fact about the Communist parties of almost all countries, it is the rapid turnover in membership. People drift in, sometimes by scores of thousands at a time, and presently drift out again. In a country like the United States or Britain, a Communist Party consists essentially of an inner ring of completely subservient long-term members, some of whom have salaried jobs; a larger group of industrial workers who are faithful to the party but do not necessarily grasp its real aims; and a shifting mass of people who are full of zeal to start with, but rapidly cool off. Certainly every effort is made to induce in Communist Party members the totalitarian mentality that Burnham describes. In a few cases this succeeds permanently, in many others temporarily: still, it is possible to meet thinking people who have remained Communists for as much as ten years before resigning or being expelled, and who have not been intellectually crippled by the experience. In principle, the Communist parties all over the world are Quisling organizations, existing for the purpose of espionage and disruption, but they are not necessarily so efficient and dangerous as Burnham makes out. One ought not to think of the Soviet Government as controlling in every country a huge secret army of fanatical warriors, completely devoid of fear or scruples and having no thought except to live and die for the Workers' Fatherland. Indeed, if Stalin really disposed of such a weapon as that, one would be wasting one's time in trying to resist him.

Also, it is not altogether an advantage to a political party to sail under false colours. There is always the danger that its followers may desert it at some moment of crisis when its actions are plainly against the general interest. Let me take an example near at hand. The British Communist Party appears to have given up, at any rate for the time being, the attempt to become a mass party, and to have concentrated instead on capturing key positions, especially in the trade unions. So long as they are not obviously acting as a sectional group, this gives the Communists an influence out of proportion to their numbers. Thus, owing to having won the leadership to several important unions, a handful of Communist delegates can swing several million votes at a Labour Party conference. But this results from the undemocratic inner working of the Labour Party, which allows a delegate to speak on behalf of millions of people who have barely heard of him and may be in complete disagreement with him. In a parliamentary election, where the individual votes on his own behalf, a Communist candidate can as a rule get almost no support. In the 1945 general election, the Communist Party won only 100,000 votes in the country as a whole, although in theory it controls several million votes merely inside the trade unions. When public opinion is dormant, a great deal can be achieved by groups of wire-pullers, but in moments of emergency, a political party must have a mass following as well. An obvious illustration of this was the failure of the British Communist Party, in spite of much trying, to disrupt the war effort during the period 1939–41. Certainly the Communists are everywhere a serious force, above all in Asia, where they have, or can plausibly present themselves as having, something to offer to the colonial populations. But one should not assume, as Burnham seems to do, that they can draw their followers after them, whatever policy they choose to adopt.

There is also the question of the "fellow-travellers," "cryptos" and sympathizers of various shades who further the aims of the Communists without having any official connection with them. Burnham does not claim that these people are all crooks or conscious traitors, but he does seem to believe that they will always continue in the same strain, even if the world situation deteriorates into open warfare. But after all, the disillusioned "fellow-traveller" is a common figure, like the disillusioned Communist. The important thing to do with these people – and it is extremely difficult since one has only inferential evidence – is to sort them out and determine which of them is honest and which is not. There is, for instance, a whole group of MPs in the British Parliament (Pritt, Zilliacus, etc.) who are commonly nicknamed "the cryptos." They have undoubtedly done a great deal of mischief, especially in confusing public opinion about the nature of the puppet regimes in Eastern Europe; but one ought not hurriedly to assume that they are all equally dishonest or even that they all hold the same opinions. Probably some of them are actuated by nothing worse than stupidity. After all, such things have happened before.

There was also the pro-Fascist bias of British Tories and corresponding strata in the United States in the years before 1939. When one saw British Conservative MPs cheering the news that British ships had been bombed by Italian aeroplanes in the service of Franco, it was tempting to believe that these people were actually treacherous to their own country. But when the pinch came, it was found that they were subjectively quite as patriotic as anyone else. They had merely based their opinions on a syllogism which lacked a middle term: Fascism is opposed to Communism; therefore it is on our side. In left-wing circles there is the corresponding syllogism: Communism is opposed to capitalism; therefore it is progressive and demo-cratic. This is stupid, but it can be accepted in good faith by people who will be capable of seeing through it sooner or later. The question is not whether the "cryptos" and "fellow-travellers" advance the interests of the USSR against those of the democracies. Obviously they do so. The real question is, how many of them would continue on the same lines if war were really imminent? For a major war – unless it is a war waged by a few specialists, a Pearl Harbor with atomic bombs – is not possible until the issues have become fairly clear.

I have dwelt on this question of the Communist fifth columns inside the democratic countries, because it is more nearly verifiable than the other questions raised by Burnham's book. About the USSR itself we are reduced to guesswork. We do not know how strong the Russians are, how badly they have been crippled by the war, to what extent their recovery will depend on American aid, how much internal disaffection they have to contend with, or how soon they will get hold of atomic weapons. All we know with certainty is that at present no great country except the United States is physically able to make war, and the United States is not psychologically pre-pared to do so. At the one point where some kind of evidence is available, Burnham seems to me to overstate his case. After all, that is his besetting sin. He is too fond of apocalyptic visions, too ready to believe that the muddled processes of history will happen suddenly and logically. But suppose he is wrong. Suppose the ship is not sinking, only leaking. Suppose that Communism is not yet strong enough to swallow the world and that the danger of war can be staved off for twenty years or more: then we don't have to accept Burnham's remedy – or, at least, we don't have to accept it immediately and without question.

Burnham's thesis, if accepted, demands certain immediate actions. One thing that it *appears* to demand is a preventive war in the very near future, while the Americans have atomic bombs and the Russians have not. Even if this inference is unjustified, there can be no doubt about the reactionary nature of other points in Burnham's programme. For instance, writing in 1946, Burnham considers that, for strategic reasons, full independence ought not to be granted to India. This is the kind of decision that sometimes has to be taken under pressure of military necessity, but which is indefensible in any normal circumstances. And again, Burnham is in favour of suppressing the American Communist Party, and of doing the job thoroughly, which would probably mean using the same methods as the Communists, when in power, use against *their* opponents. Now, there are times when it is justifiable to suppress a political party. If you are fighting for your life, and if there is some organization which is plainly acting on behalf of the enemy, and is strong enough to do harm, then you have got to crush it. But to suppress the Communist Party *now*, or at any time when it did not unmistakably endanger national survival, would be calamitous. One has only to think of the people who would approve! Burnham claims, perhaps rightly, that when once the American empire had been established, it might be possible to pass on to some more satisfactory kind of world organization. But the first appeal of his programme must be to conservatives, and if such an empire came into being, the strongest intellectual influence in it would probably be that of the Catholic Church.

Meanwhile there is one other solution which is at any rate thinkable, and which Burnham dismisses almost unmentioned. That is, somewhere or other – not in Norway or New Zealand, but over a large area – to make democratic Socialism work. If one could somewhere present the spectacle of economic security without concentration camps, the pretext for the Russian dictatorship would disappear and Communism would lose much of its appeal. But the only feasible area is Western Europe plus Africa. The idea of forming this vast territory into a Socialist United States has as yet hardly gained any ground, and the practical and psychological difficulties in the way are enormous. Still, it is a *possible* project if people really wanted it, and if there were ten or twenty years of assured peace in which to bring it about. And since the initiative would have to come in the first place from Britain, the important thing is that this idea should take root among British Socialists. At present, so far as the idea of a unified Europe has any currency at all, it is associated with Churchill. Here one

comes back to one of the main points in Burnham's programme – the fusion of Britain with the United States.

Burnham assumes that the main difficulty in the way of this
would be national pride, since Britain would be very much
the junior partner. Actually there is not much pride of that
kind left, and has not been for many years past. On the whole,
anti-American feeling is strongest among those who are also
anti-imperialist and anti-military. This is true not only of
Communists and "fellow-travellers" who are anxious to
make mischief, but of people of good will who see that to be
tied to America probably means preserving capitalism in Britain. I have several times overheard or taken part in conversations something like this:

"How I hate the Americans! Sometimes they make me feel
almost pro-Russian."

"Yes, but they're not actually our enemies. They helped us
in 1940, when the Russians were selling oil to the Germans.
We can't stand on our own feet much longer, and in the end
we may have to choose between knuckling under to Russia or
going in with America."

"I refuse to choose. They're just a pair of gangsters."

"Yes, but supposing you *had* to choose. Suppose there was
no other way out, and you had to live under one system or the
other. Which would you choose, Russia or America?"

"Oh, well, of course, if one *had* to choose, there's no
question about it – America."

Fusion with the United States is widely realized to be one
way out of our difficulties. Indeed, we have been almost a
dependency of the United States ever since 1940, and our
desperate economic plight drives us in this direction all the
faster. The union desired by Burnham may happen almost of its
own accord, without formal arrangement and with no plan or
idea behind it. A noisy but, I believe, very small minority
would like Britain to be integrated into the Soviet system.
The mass of the British people would never accept this, but
the thinking ones among them do not regard the probable
alternative – absorption by America – with enthusiasm. Most
English left-wingers at present favour a niggling policy of
"getting along with Russia" by being strong enough to prevent
an attack and weak enough to disarm suspicion. Under this lies

the hope that when the Russians become more prosperous, they may become more friendly. The other way out for Britain, the Socialist United States of Europe, has not as yet much magnetism. And the more the pessimistic world-view of Burnham and others like him prevails, the harder it is for such ideas to take hold.

Burnham offers a plan which would probably work, but which is a *pis aller* and should not be accepted willingly. In the end, the European peoples may have to accept American domination as a way of avoiding domination by Russia, but they ought to realize, while there is yet time, that there are other possibilities. In rather the same way, English Socialists of almost all colours accepted the leadership of Churchill during the war. Granted that they did not want Britain to be defeated, they could hardly help themselves, because effectively there was no one else, and Churchill was preferable to Hitler. But the situation might have been different if the European peoples could have grasped the nature of Fascism about five years earlier. In that case the war, if it happened at all, might have been a different kind of war, fought under different leaders for different ends.

The tendency of writers like Burnham, whose key concept is "realism," is to overrate the part played in human affairs by sheer force. I do not say that he is wrong all the time. He is quite right to insist that gratitude is not a factor in international politics; that even the most high-minded policy is no use unless you can show a practical way of putting it into effect, and that in the affairs of nations and societies, as opposed to individuals, one cannot hope for more than temporary and imperfect solutions. And he is probably right in arguing from this that one cannot apply to politics the same moral code that one practises or tries to practise in private life. But somehow his picture of the world is always slightly distorted. *The Managerial Revolution*, for instance, seemed to me a good description of what is actually happening in various parts of the world, i.e., the growth of societies neither capitalist nor socialist, and organized more or less on the lines of a caste system. But Burnham went on to argue that because this *was* happening, nothing else *could* happen, and the new, tightly-knit totalitarian state *must* be stronger than the chaotic democracies. Therefore, among other things, Germany had to win the war. Yet in the event Germany collapsed at least partly because of her totalitarian structure. A more democratic, less efficient country would not have made such errors in politics and strategy, nor would it have aroused such a volume of hatred throughout the world.

Of course, there is more in Burnham's book than the mere proposal for the setting-up of an American empire, and in detail there is much with which one can agree. I think he is mainly right in his account of the way in which Communist propaganda works, and the difficulty of countering it, and he is certainly right in saying that one of the most important problems at this moment is to find a way of speaking to the Russian people over the heads of their rulers. But the central subject of this book, as of almost everything that Burnham writes, is power. Burnham is always fascinated by power, whether he is for it or against it, and he always sees it a little larger than life. First it was Germany that was to swallow the world, then Russia, now perhaps America. When *The Managerial Revolution* was published, I for one derived the impression that Burnham's sympathies were on the whole with Germany, and at any rate that he was anxious that the United States should not throw good money after bad by coming to the rescue of Britain. The much-discussed essay, *Lenin's Heir*, which was a dissertation – a rhapsody, rather – on the strength, cunning and cruelty of Stalin, could be interpreted as expressing either approval or disapproval. I myself took it to be an expression of approval, though of a rather horrified kind.

It now appears that this was wrong. Burnham is not in favour of Stalin or Stalinism, and he has begun to find virtues in the capitalist democracy which he once considered moribund. But the note of fascination is still there. Communism may be wicked, but at any rate it is *big*: it is a terrible, all-devouring monster which one fights against but which one cannot help admiring. Burnham thinks always in terms of monsters and cataclysms. Hence he does not even mention, or barely mentions, two possibilities which should at least have been discussed in a book of this scope. One is that the Russian regime may become more liberal and less dangerous a generation hence, if war has not broken out in the meantime. Of course, this would not happen with the consent of the ruling clique, but it is thinkable that the mechanics of the situation may bring it about. The other possibility is that the great powers will be simply too frightened of the effects of atomic weapons ever to make use of them. But that would be much too dull for Burnham. Everything must happen suddenly and completely, and the choice must be all or nothing, glory or bust:

> It may be that the darkness of great tragedy will bring to a quick end the short, bright history of the United States – for there is enough truth in the dream of the New World to make the action tragic. The United States is called before the rehearsals are completed. Its strength and promise have not been matured by the wisdom of time and suffering. And the summons is for nothing less than the leadership of the world, for that or nothing. If it is reasonable to expect failure, that is only a measure of how great the triumph could be.

It may be that modern weapons have speeded things up to the point at which Burnham would be right. But if one can judge from the past, even from such huge calamities as the fall of the Roman Empire, history never happens quite so melo-dramatically as that.

As I Please 80
Tribune, 4 April 1947

The Royal Commission on the Press is now getting to work, after mysterious delays. Presumably it will be a long time before it reaches any definite conclusions, and still longer before its findings are acted upon. Nevertheless, it seems to me that now is the time to start discussing the problem of preserving a free Press in a socialised economy. Because, unless we become aware of the difficulties before they are actually upon us, the ultimate condition of the Press in this country will be worse than it need be.

During the fuel crisis I remarked to several people on the badness of Government publicity, to be met each time with the answer that the present Government has hardly any organs of expression under its control. That, of course, is true. I then said, "Why not take over the *Daily* — and run it as a Government organ?" This suggestion was always greeted with horror. Apparently to nationalise the Press would be "Fascism," while "freedom of the Press" consists in allowing a few millionaires to coerce hundreds of journalists into falsifying their opinions. But I pass over the question of how free the British Press is at present. The point is, what will finally happen if the present trend towards nationalisation continues?

Sooner or later, it seems to me, the Press is certain to be nationalised, so far as its major organs go. It could hardly continue to exist as a huge patch of private enterprise, like a sort of game reserve, in the middle of a collectivised economy. But does that mean that *all* channels of expression will ultimately be under the control of bureaucrats? Some such thing could quite easily happen if the people most concerned are indifferent to their fate. One can quite well imagine newspapers, periodicals, magazines, books, films, radio, music and the drama all being lumped together and "co-ordinated" under the guidance of some enormous Ministry of Fine Arts (or whatever its name might be). It is not a pleasant prospect, but I believe it can be averted if the danger is realised in advance.

What is meant by freedom of the Press? The Press is free, I should say, when it is easy and not illegal to get minority opinions into print and distribute them to the public. Britain is luckier in this respect than most countries, and it is fair to say that this is partly due to the variations that exist in the big commercial Press. The leading daily papers, few though they are, contain more shades of difference than a Government-controlled Press would be likely to do. Still, the main guardians of minority opinion are the small independent weekly and monthly papers, and the book-publishing houses. It is only through those channels that you can make sure of getting a hearing for *any* opinion that does not express a libel or an incitement to violence. Therefore, if the big Press is certain to be nationalised anyway, could not this principle be laid down in advance: that nationalisation shall only apply to so much of the Press as comes under the heading of "big business," while small concerns will be left alone?

Obviously the proprietor of a chain of a hundred newspapers is a capitalist. So is a small publisher or the owner-editor of a monthly magazine, strictly speaking. But you are not obliged to treat them both alike, just as in abolishing large-scale ownership of land you are not obliged to rob the smallholder or market gardener of his few acres. So long as a minority Press can exist, and count on continued existence, even in a hole and corner way, the essential freedom will be safeguarded. But the first step is to realise that nationalisation is inevitable, and lay our plans accordingly. Otherwise the people specially concerned, the journalists, artists, actors, etc., may have no bargaining power when the time comes, and that unappetising Ministry of Fine Arts may engulf the whole lot of them.

Recently I was talking to the editor of a newspaper with a very large circulation, who told me that it was now quite easy for his paper to live on its sales alone. This would probably continue to be true, he said, until the paper situation improved, which would mean reverting to pre-war bulk, at enormously greater expense. Until then, advertisements would be of only secondary importance as a source of revenue.

If that is so – and I believe many papers could now exist without advertisements – is not this just the moment for an all-out drive against patent medicines? Before the war it was never possible to attack patent medicines in a big way, because the Press, which would have had to make the exposure, lived partly off advertisements for them. As a start, some enterprising publisher might track down and reprint the two volumes of that rare and very entertaining book, *Secret Remedies*. This was issued, if I remember rightly, by the British Medical Association – at any rate, by some association of doctors – the first volume appearing about 1912 and the second during the nineteen-twenties. It consisted simply of a list of existing proprietary medicines, with a statement of their claims, an analysis of their contents, and an estimate of their cost. There was very little comment, which in most cases was hardly necessary. I distinctly remember that one "consumption cure" sold to the public at thirty-five shillings a bottle was estimated to cost a halfpenny.

Neither volume made much impact on the public. The Press, for reasons indicated above, practically ignored both issues, and they are now so rare that I have not seen a copy for years. (Incidentally, if any reader has a copy I would gladly buy it – especially the second volume, which I think is the rarer.) If reissued, the book would need bringing up to date, for the claim to cure certain diseases is now forbidden by law, while many new kinds of rubbish have come on to the market. But many of the old ones are still there – that is the significant point. Is it not possible that the consumption of patent medicines might decrease if people were given a clearer idea of the nature and the real cost of the stuff they are pouring down their throats?

A few weeks back a correspondent in *Tribune* asked why we are not allowed to grow and cure tobacco for our own use. In practice, I think, you can do so. There is a law against it, but it is not strictly enforced – at any rate, I have certainly known people who grew their own tobacco, and even prepared it in cakes like the commercial article. I tried some once, and thought it the perfect tobacco for a non-smoker. The trouble with English tobacco is that it is so mild that you can hardly taste it. This is not, I believe, due to the lack of sun but to some deficiency in the soil. However, any tobacco is better than none, and a few thousand acres laid down to it in the south of England might help us through the cigarette shortage which is likely to happen this year, without using up any dollars or robbing the State of any revenue.

I have just been reading about the pidgin English (or "bêche-la-mer") used in the Solomon and New Hebrides Islands in the South Pacific. It is the lingua franca between many islands whose inhabitants speak different languages or dialects. As it has only a tiny vocabulary and is lacking in many necessary parts of speech, it has to make use of astonishing circumlocutions. An aeroplane, for instance, is called "lanich (launch) belong fly allsame pigeon." A violin is described thus: "One small bokkis (box) belong whiteman all he scratch him belly belong him sing out good fella." Here is a passage in what seems, judging by the other extracts given, to be very high-class pidgin. It announces the Coronation of King George VI:

King George, he dead. Number one son, Edward, he no want him clothes. Number two son he like. Bishop he make plenty talk along new King. He say: "You look out good along all the people?" King he talk: "Yes." Then bishop and plenty Government official and storekeeper and soldier and bank manager and policeman, all he stand up and sing and blow him trumpet. Finish.

There are similar pidgins, most of them not quite so bad, in other parts of the world. In some cases the people who first formed them were probably influenced by the feeling that a subject race ought to talk comically. But there are areas where a lingua franca of some kind is indispensable, and the perversions actually in use make one see what a lot there is to be said for Basic.

Review of *Lady Gregory's Journals*, edited by Lennox Robinson

The New Yorker, 19 April 1947

Lady Gregory is one of the central figures in the Irish literary revival. It would be difficult to think of her without also thinking of Yeats and the Abbey Theatre, just as one could hardly hear the phrase "the nineties" without having at least a fleeting vision of Beardsley and the *Yellow Book*. But the associations that her name calls up are not all of them pleasant ones. She is also the subject of a memorable sneer, in "Ulysses," which is worth quoting because, cruel and probably unfair though it is, it does help to bring this unfortunate, good-hearted old woman into truer perspective. In "Ulysses," Joyce has Buck Mulligan say, "Longworth is awfully sick ... after what you wrote about that old hake Gregory. O you inquisitional drunken jew jesuit! She gets you a job on the paper and then you go and slate her drivel to Jaysus. Couldn't you do the Yeats touch?"

Was that really how Yeats and the rest of them thought of her? Was she simply an old fool to be blarneyed and made use of ? Evidently, it was not so crude as that; besides, in her old age – always at her wits' end for rent and taxes, riding to and fro in buses, lunching off tea and bread and butter — she was hardly worth sponging on. But Joyce's words are perhaps true at the level of caricature. Something of that kind is always partly true of the enlightened aristocrat, the person who wants to be an artist as well as a patron, especially when, as in this case, there is a difference of race and religion and culture on top of the simple class distinction.

Augusta Gregory (her maiden name was Persse) was born into the landed gentry of Ireland — the people who lived in tumbledown mansions with hordes of servants, streamed across the countryside in pink coats, and, partly because of poverty and remoteness, kept up a claret-drinking, Horace-quoting eighteenth-century refinement that their English counterparts had lost. They called themselves Irish, and politically they were often the worst enemies that England had, but they were generally Protestants and, as their names show, largely English in extraction. "Lady Gregory's Journals," which has been edited by Lennox Robinson and published by Macmillan, covers the fourteen years from 1916 to 1930, and rambles across a multitude of subjects, some of them very trivial ones. Mr. Robinson has rearranged the journals by what is probably the best system; that is, he has taken half a dozen dominant themes and grouped the entries around them, so one passes the same dates over and over again. The most important of these themes are Coole Park (the country place, celebrated by Yeats, that Lady Gregory inherited from her husband), the Abbey Theatre, the Terror and the Civil War, and the long, complicated battle over Sir Hugh Lane's collection of pictures. In most of these contexts, Lady Gregory was fighting against the British government, but in all of them, in a less direct, less conscious way, she was fighting against the native Irish, whom she loved and championed but by no means resembled.

The ambiguity of Lady Gregory's position comes out particularly in the period of the "troubles." She was in sympathy with the agrarian revolution, she planned to sell her land to the government and remain in Coole Park only as a tenant, and in any case she and her husband had had a good record as landlords, but none of this stopped the peasants from constantly prowling around her dwindled demesne, cutting down the young trees in the plantations, stealing the fruit that she was always ready to give away, and making blackmailing demands for "subscriptions." She was on their side, but they were not altogether on hers, and it is queer to watch her torn one way politically and the other way emotionally, approving the breakup of the great estates and yet yearning to keep the beloved house and gardens for her grandchildren. Even her horror of the Black and Tans, the banditti let loose by the British government in 1919, was coloured by class feeling. On hearing that fifteen officers of the Guards had volunteered to join this force, Lady Gregory remarked, "I say... it would be an improvement to have at least gentlemen." She wrote articles in the British press denouncing the Black and Tans, but – once again with an eye on her grandchildren – left the articles unsigned, because she wanted to preserve Coole unburned.

Lady Gregory's son, Robert, had been killed in Italy in the first World War, fighting for the British government. Even after the Easter Rising, it still seemed natural to her to send her grandson to Harrow and to defend the English public-school system against Bernard Shaw. Politically, she was always for Ireland against England – even, to some extent, for the Republicans against the Free State government – but instinct and training pulled her in the other direction. So far as the Abbey Theatre went, it was chiefly the puritanism and hypocrisy of the Catholic Irish that had to be fought against. When O'Casey's "The Plough and the Stars" was first performed, the audience stormed the stage because members of the Citizen Army were shown carrying their flag into a public house. There were also objections to the inclusion of a prostitute among the characters, on the ground that there were no prostitutes in Dublin. How ready Lady Gregory was to put her own feelings aside, and how close her ties were with the fashionable English world, is revealed in the struggle over the Lane pictures. Her nephew, Sir Hugh Lane, had amassed an extremely valuable collection of paintings, which he left in his will to the National Gallery, in London. Later, shortly before being drowned in the sinking of the Lusitania, he added a codicil leaving them to the city of Dublin instead. It was evident that he meant them to go to Dublin, but the codicil, not having been witnessed, was not legal, and the incident ended with the British government's keeping the pictures, or most of them. Intermittently for years, right through every kind of public and private disaster, Lady Gregory was pulling wires in London – a shabby old figure with dripping umbrella, but able because of her family connections to get the ear of a surprising variety of influential people. She did not care what their political colour might be if there was any chance that they would help her to recover the Lane pictures. She even contemplated trying the Royal Family, and was told that "the King would be no use . . . the Queen might possibly do something." Oddly enough, the British politician who backed her up most strongly was the vicious reactionary and Unionist Sir Edward Carson, who had armed the Ulster Volunteers in 1912 and prosecuted Casement in 1916.

There was almost no English or Irish literary man of her day, nor were there many people distinguished in other fields, whom Lady Gregory did not know or at least meet, and her diaries contain a considerable amount of informative gossip about Shaw, Yeats, Kipling, Cosgrave, De Valera, Michael Collins, and many another. She herself almost never makes a witty or illuminating remark, but she gives the impression of being a good observer and a truthful reporter, and her account, for instance, of John Dillon's comments on the Easter Rising probably has real historical value. These diaries cover only the fag end of her enormous life. She was born in 1852 and married in 1880 a man much older than herself. At the date when the diaries start, her husband had been dead a quarter of a century, her son had only two years to live, the hardest part of the struggle for the Abbey Theatre was over, and the chance of a decent settlement between England and Ireland had passed away. It was certainly a heroic life, and probably it was a useful one. Without her, Yeats might have written less, and it is conceivable that O'Casey would never have been heard of. In 1930, aged seventy-eight, with cancer of the breast and with not much money, she could be on the whole contented: "I used long ago to say I should like, I thought, to live until Richard's 21st birthday. And it comes tomorrow. . . . It is a contrast to Robert's coming-of-age, with the gathering of cousins and the big feast and dance for the tenants – Coole no longer ours. But the days of landed property have passed. It is better so. Yet I wish someone of our blood would after my death care enough for what has been a home so long, to keep it open."

However, no one could keep Coole open, for it was demolished after Lady Gregory's death. Roxboro', the house where she was born, had been burned down years earlier, during the "troubles." Since then, the Anglo-Irish gentry have vanished or turned into fossils, the priests have tightened their grip, and the Irish literary movement has not lived up to its promise. The tensions that produced it have been resolved and the special type represented by Lady Gregory – the conqueror who identifies himself with the subject race – has no longer much function.

Toward European Unity

Partisan Review, July–August 1947

A socialist today is in the position of a doctor treating an all but hopeless case. As a doctor, it is his duty to keep the patient alive, and therefore to assume that the patient has at least a chance of recovery. As a scientist, it is his duty to face the facts, and therefore to admit that the patient will probably die. Our activities as socialists only have meaning if we assume that socialism *can* be established, but if we stop to consider what probably *will* happen, then we must admit, I think, that the chances are against us. If I were a bookmaker, simply calculating the probabilities and leaving my own wishes out of account, I would give odds against the survival of civilization within the next few hundred years. As far as I can see, there are three possibilities ahead of us:

1. That the Americans will decide to use the atomic bomb while they have it and the Russians haven't. This would solve nothing. It would do away with the particular danger that is now presented by the USSR, but would lead to the rise of new empires, fresh rivalries, more wars, more atomic bombs, etc. In any case this is, I think, the least likely outcome of the three, because a preventive war is a crime not easily committed by a country that retains any traces of democracy.

2. That the present "cold war" will continue until the USSR, and several other countries, have atomic bombs as well. Then there will only be a short breathing-space before whizz! go the rockets, wallop! go the bombs, and the industrial centres of the world are wiped out, probably beyond repair. Even if any one state, or group of states, emerges from such a war as technical victor, it will probably be unable to build up the machine civilization anew. The world, therefore, will once again be inhabited by a few million, or a few hundred million human beings living by subsistence agriculture, and probably, after a couple of generations, retaining no more of the culture of the past than a knowledge of how to smelt metals. Conceivably this is a desirable outcome, but obviously it has nothing to do with socialism.

3. That the fear inspired by the atomic bomb and other weapons yet to come will be so great that everyone will refrain from using them. This seems to me the worst possibility of all. It would mean the division of the world among two or three vast superstates, unable to conquer one another and unable to be overthrown by any internal rebellion. In all probability their structure would be hierarchic, with a semi-divine caste at the top and outright slavery at the bottom, and the crushing out of liberty would exceed anything that the world has yet seen. Within each state the necessary psychological atmosphere would be kept up by complete severance from the outer world, and by a continuous phony war against rival states. Civilizations of this type might remain static for thousands of years.

Most of the dangers that I have outlined existed and were foreseeable long before the atomic bomb was invented. The only way of avoiding them that I can imagine is to present somewhere or other, on a large scale, the spectacle of a community where people are relatively free and happy and where the main motive in life is not the pursuit of money or power. In other words, democratic socialism must be made to work throughout some large area. But the only area in which it could conceivably be made to work, in any near future, is western Europe. Apart from Australia and New Zealand, the tradition of democratic socialism can only be said to exist – and even there it only exists precariously – in Scandinavia,

Germany, Austria, Czecho-Slovakia, Switzerland, the Low Countries, France, Britain, Spain, and Italy. Only in those countries are there still large numbers of people to whom the word "socialism" has some appeal and for whom it is bound up with liberty, equality, and internationalism. Elsewhere it either has no foothold or it means something different. In North America the masses are contented with capitalism, and one cannot tell what turn they will take when capitalism begins to collapse. In the USSR there prevails a sort of oligarchical collectivism which could only develop into democratic social-ism against the will of the ruling minority. Into Asia even the word "socialism" has barely penetrated. The Asiatic nationalist movements are either fascist in character, or look toward Moscow, or manage to combine both attitudes: and at present all movements among the coloured peoples are tinged by racial mysticism. In most of South America the position is essentially similar, so is it in Africa and the Middle East. Socialism does not exist anywhere, but even as an idea it is at present valid only in Europe. Of course, socialism cannot properly be said to be established until it is world-wide, but the process must begin somewhere, and I cannot imagine it beginning except through the federation of the western European states, transformed into socialist republics without colonial dependencies. Therefore a socialist United States of Europe seems to me the only worth-while political objective today. Such a federation would con-tain about 250 million people, including perhaps half the skilled industrial workers of the world. I do not need to be told that the difficulties of bringing any such thing into being are enor-mous and terrifying, and I will list some of them in a moment. But we ought not to feel that it is of its nature impossible, or that countries so different from one another would not volun-tarily unite. A western European union is in itself a less im-probable concatenation than the Soviet Union or the British Empire.

Now as to the difficulties. The greatest difficulty of all is the apathy and conservatism of people everywhere, their unaware-ness of danger, their inability to imagine anything new – in general, as Bertrand Russell put it recently, the unwillingness of the human race to acquiesce in its own survival. But there are also active malignant forces working against European unity, and there are existing economic relationships on which the European peoples depend for their standard of life and which are not compatible with true socialism. I list what seem to me to be the four main obstacles, explaining each of them as shortly as I can manage:

1. Russian hostility. The Russians cannot but be hostile to any European union not under their own control. The reasons, both the pretended and the real ones, are obvious. One has to count, therefore, with the danger of a preventive war, with the systematic terrorizing of the smaller nations, and with the sabotage of the Communist parties everywhere. Above all there is the danger that the European masses will continue to believe in the Russian myth. As long as they believe it, the idea of a socialist Europe will not be sufficiently magnetic to call forth the necessary effort.

2. American hostility. If the United States remains capitalist, and especially if it needs markets for exports, it cannot regard a socialist Europe with a friendly eye. No doubt it is less likely than the USSR to intervene with brute force, but American pressure is an important factor because it can be exerted most easily on Britain, the one country in Europe which is outside the Russian orbit. Since 1940 Britain has kept its feet against the European dictators at the expense of becoming almost a dependency of the USA. Indeed, Britain can only get free of America by dropping the attempt to be an extra-European power. The English-speaking Dominions, the colonial dependencies, except perhaps in Africa, and even Britain's supplies of oil, are all hostages in American hands. Therefore there is always the danger that the United States will break up any European coalition by drawing Britain out of it.

3. Imperialism. The European peoples, and especially the British, have long owed their high standard of life to direct or indirect exploitation of the coloured peoples. This relationship has never been made clear by official socialist propaganda, and the British worker, instead of being told that, by world standards, he is living above his income, has been taught to think of himself as an overworked, down-trodden slave. To the masses everywhere "socialism" means, or at least is associated with, higher wages, shorter hours, better houses, all-round social insurance, etc., etc. But it is by no means certain that

we can afford these things if we throw away the advantages we derive from colonial exploitation. However evenly the national income is divided up, if the income as a whole falls, the working-class standard of living must fall with it. At best there is liable to be a long and uncomfortable reconstruction period for which public opinion has nowhere been prepared. But at the same time the European nations *must* stop being exploiters abroad if they are to build true socialism at home. The first step toward a European socialist federation is for the British to get out of India. But this entails something else. If the United States of Europe is to be self-sufficient and able to hold its own against Russia and America, it must include Africa and the Middle East. But that means that the position of the indigenous peoples in those countries must be changed out of recognition – that Morocco or Nigeria or Abyssinia must cease to be colonies or semi-colonies and become autonomous republics on a complete equality with the European peoples. This entails a vast change of outlook and a bitter, complex struggle which is not likely to be settled without bloodshed. When the pinch comes the forces of imperialism will turn out to be extremely strong, and the British worker, if he has been taught to think of socialism in materialistic terms, may ultimately decide that it is better to remain an imperial power at the expense of playing second fiddle to America. In varying degrees all the European peoples, at any rate those who are to form part of the proposed union, will be faced with the same choice.

4. The Catholic Church. As the struggle between East and West becomes more naked, there is danger that democratic socialists and mere reactionaries will be driven into combining in a sort of Popular Front. The Church is the likeliest bridge between them. In any case the Church will make every effort to capture and sterilize any movement aiming at European unity. The dangerous thing about the Church is that it is *not* reactionary in the ordinary sense. It is not tied to laissez-faire capitalism or to the existing class system, and will not necessarily perish with them. It is perfectly capable of coming to terms with socialism, or appearing to do so, provided that its own position is safeguarded. But if it is allowed to survive as a powerful organization, it will make the establishment of true socialism impossible, because its influence is and always must

be against freedom of thought and speech, against human equality, and against any form of society tending to promote earthly happiness.

When I think of these and other difficulties, when I think of the enormous mental readjustment that would have to be made, the appearance of a socialist United States of Europe seems to me a very unlikely event. I don't mean that the bulk of the people are not prepared for it, in a passive way. I mean that I see no person or group of persons with the slightest chance of attaining power and at the same time with the imaginative grasp to see what is needed and to demand the necessary sacrifices from their followers. But I also can't at present see any other hopeful objective. At one time I believed that it might be possible to form the British Empire into a federation of socialist republics, but if that chance ever existed, we lost it by failing to liberate India, and by our attitude toward the coloured peoples generally. It may be that Europe is finished and that in the long run some better form of society will arise in India or China. But I believe that it is only in Europe, if anywhere, that democratic socialism could be made a reality in short enough time to prevent the dropping of the atom bombs.

Of course, there are reasons, if not for optimism, at least for suspending judgement on certain points. One thing in our favour is that a major war is not likely to happen immediately. We could, I suppose, have the kind of war that consists in shooting rockets, but not a war involving the mobilization of tens of millions of men. At present any large army would simply melt away, and that may remain true for ten or even twenty years. Within that time some unexpected things might happen. For example, a powerful socialist movement might for the first time arise in the United States. In England it is now the fashion to talk of the United States as "capitalistic," with the implication that this is something unalterable, a sort of racial characteristic like the colour of eyes or hair. But in fact it cannot be unalterable, since capitalism itself has manifestly no future, and we cannot be sure in advance that the next change in the United States will not be a change for the better.

Then, again, we do not know what changes will take place in the USSR if war can be staved off for the next generation or so. In a society of that type, a radical change of outlook always

seems unlikely, not only because there can be no open opposition but because the regime, with its complete hold over
education, news, etc., deliberately aims at preventing the pendulum swing between generations which seems to occur naturally in liberal societies. But for all we know the tendency of
one generation to reject the ideas of the last is an abiding
human characteristic which even the NKVD will be unable
to eradicate. In that case there may by 1960 be millions of
young Russians who are bored by dictatorship and loyalty
parades, eager for more freedom, and friendly in their attitude
toward the West.

Or again, it is even possible that if the world falls apart into
three unconquerable superstates, the liberal tradition will be
strong enough within the Anglo-American section of the
world to make life tolerable and even offer some hope of
progress. But all this is speculation. The actual outlook, so far
as I can calculate the probabilities, is very dark, and any serious
thought should start out from that fact.

In Defence of Comrade Zilliacus

August–September? 1947; intended for *Tribune* but not published

George Orwell
Barnhill
Isle of Jura, Argyll

Some weeks ago Mr K. Zilliacus addressed a long and, as usual,
abusive letter to *Tribune*, in which he accused it of having no
definite and viable foreign policy, but of being in effect an anti-
Russian paper while keeping up a show of hostility to Ernest
Bevin. Bevin, he said, was far more realistic than *Tribune*, since
he grasped that to oppose Russia it was necessary to rely on
America and "bolster up Fascism," while *Tribune* was merely
sitting on the fence, uttering contradictory slogans and getting
nowhere.

I am not often in agreement with Mr Zilliacus, and it is
therefore all the more of a pleasure to record my agreement
with him on this occasion. Granting him his own special

terminology, I think his accusation is fully justified. One must remember, of course, that in the mouths of Mr Zilliacus and his associates, words like democracy, Fascism or totalitarianism do not bear quite their normal meanings. In general they tend to turn into their opposites, Fascism meaning unfaked elections, democracy meaning minority rule, and so on. But this does not alter the fact that he is dwelling on real issues – issues on which *Tribune* has consistently, over a period of years, failed to make its position clear. He knows that the only big political questions in the world today are: for Russia–against Russia, for America–against America, for democracy–against democracy. And though he may describe his own activities in different words from what most of us would use, at least we can see at a glance where he stands.

But where does *Tribune* stand? I know, or think I know, what foreign policy *Tribune* favours, but I know it by inference and from private contacts. Casual readers can, and to my knowledge do, draw very different impressions. If one had to sum up *Tribune*'s *apparent* policy in a single word, the name one would have to coin for it would be anti-Bevinism. The first rule of this "ism" is that when Bevin says or does something, a way must be found of showing that it is wrong, even if it happens to be what *Tribune* was advocating in the previous week. The second rule is that though Russian policy may be criticised, extenuating circumstances must always be found. The third rule is that when the United States can be insulted, it must be insulted. The effect of framing a policy on these principles is that one cannot even find out what solution *Tribune* offers for the specific problems it most discusses. To take some examples. Is *Tribune* in favour of clearing out of Greece unconditionally? Does *Tribune* think the USSR should have the Dardanelles? Is *Tribune* in favour of unrestricted Jewish immigration into Palestine? Does *Tribune* think Egypt should be allowed to annex the Sudan? In some cases I know the answers, but I think it would be very difficult to discover them simply by reading the paper.

Part of the trouble, I believe, is that after building Bevin up into Public Enemy Number One, *Tribune* has found out that it is not genuinely in disagreement with him. Certainly there are real differences over Palestine, Spain and perhaps Greece, but broadly, I think, he and *Tribune* stand for the same kind of policy. There are, it is generally agreed, only three possible foreign policies for Great Britain. One is to do as Mr Zilliacus would have us do, ie., to become part of the Russian system, with a government perhaps less servile than that of Poland or Czechoslovakia, but essentially similar. Another is to move definitely into the orbit of the United States. And another is to become part of a federation of western European Socialist republics, including if possible Africa, and again if possible (though this is less likely) the British dominions. *Tribune*, I infer – for it has never been clearly stated – favours the third policy, and so I believe does Bevin, that is to say, the Government. But *Tribune* is not only involved in its personal feud with Bevin; it is also unwilling to face two facts – very unpopular facts at the moment – which must be faced if one is to discuss a Western union seriously. One is that such a union could hardly succeed without a friendly America behind it, and the other is that however peaceful its intentions might be, it would be bound to incur Russian hostility. It is exactly here that *Tribune* has failed as an organ of opinion. All its other equivocations, I believe, spring from a dread of flouting fashionable opinion on the subject of Russia and America.

One very noticeable thing in *Tribune* is the pretence that Bevin's policy is exclusively his own. Apparently he is a sort of runaway horse dragging an unwilling Cabinet behind him, and our policy would have been quite different – above all, our relations with the USSR would have been better – if only we had had a more enlightened foreign secretary. Now it is obvious that this cannot be so. A minister who is really thwarting the will of the rest of the government does not stay in office for two years. Why then the attempt to put all the blame on one person? Was it not because otherwise it would have been necessary to say a very unpopular thing: namely that a Labour Government, as such, is almost bound to be on bad terms with the government of the USSR? With a government headed by Pritt and Zilliacus we could no doubt have excellent relations, of a kind, with Russia, and with a government headed by Churchill and Beaverbrook we could probably patch up some kind of arrangement: but any government genuinely representative of the Labour movement *must* be regarded with hostility. From the point of view of the Russians and the Communists, Social Democracy is a deadly enemy, and to do them justice they have frequently admitted it. Even such controversial questions as the formation of a Western union are irrelevant here. Even if we had no influence in Europe and made no attempt to interfere there, it would still be to the interest of the Russian government to bring about the failure of the British Labour Government, if possible. The reason is clear enough. Social Democracy, unlike capitalism, offers an alternative to Communism, and if somewhere or other it can be made to work on a big scale – if it turns out that after all it *is* possible to introduce Socialism without secret police forces, mass deportations and so forth – then the excuse for dictatorship vanishes. With a Labour Government in office, relations with Russia, bad already, were bound to deteriorate. Various observers pointed this out at the time of the General Election, but I do not remember *Tribune* doing so, then or since. Was it not because it was easier, more popular, to encourage the widespread delusion that "a government of the Left can get on better with Russia" and that Communism is much the same thing as Socialism, only more so – and then, when things didn't turn out that way, to register pained surprise and look round for a scapegoat?

And what, I wonder, is behind *Tribune*'s persistent anti-Americanism? In *Tribune* over the past year I can recall three polite references to America (one of those was a reference to Henry Wallace) and a whole string of petty insults. I have just received a letter from some students at an American university. They ask me if I can explain why *Tribune* thinks it necessary to boo at America. What am I to say to these people? I shall tell them what I believe to be the truth – namely that *Tribune*'s anti-Americanism is not sincere but is an attempt to keep in with fashionable opinion. To be anti-American nowadays is to shout with the mob. Of course it is only a minor mob, but it is a vocal one. Although there was probably some growth of ill-feeling as a result of the presence of the American troops, I do not believe the mass of the people in this country are anti-American politically, and certainly they are not so culturally. But politico-literary intellectuals are not usually frightened of mass opinion. What they are frightened of is the prevailing opinion within their own group. At any given moment there is always an orthodoxy, a parrot cry which must be repeated, and in the more active section of the Left the orthodoxy of the moment is anti-Americanism. I believe part of the reason (I am thinking of some remarks in Mr G. D. H. Cole's last 1143-page compilation) is the idea that if we can cut our links with the United States we might succeed in staying neutral in the case of Russia and America going to war. How anyone can believe this, after looking at the map and remembering what happened to neutrals in the late war, I do not know. There is also the rather mean consideration that the Americans are *not* really our enemies, that they are unlikely to start dropping atomic bombs on us or even to let us starve to death, and therefore that we can safely take liberties with them if it pays to do so. But at any rate the orthodoxy is there. To speak favourably of America, to recall that the Americans helped us in 1940 when the Russians were supplying the Germans with oil and setting on their Communist parties to sabotage the war effort, is to be branded as a "reactionary." And I suspect that when *Tribune* joins in the chorus it is more from fear of this label than from genuine conviction.

Surely, if one is going to write about foreign policy at all, there is one question that should be answered plainly. It is: "If you *had* to choose between Russia and America, which would you choose?" It will not do to give the usual quibbling answer, "I refuse to choose." In the end the choice may be forced upon us. We are no longer strong enough to stand alone, and if we fail to bring a western European union into being, we shall be obliged, in the long run, to subordinate our policy to that of one Great Power or the other. And in spite of all the fashionable chatter of the moment, everyone knows in his heart that we should choose America. The great mass of people in this country would, I believe, make this choice almost instinctively. Certainly there is a small minority that would choose the other way. Mr Zilliacus, for instance, is one of them. I think he is wrong, but at least he makes his position clear. I also know perfectly well what *Tribune*'s position is. But has *Tribune* ever made it clear?

How subject we are in this country to the intellectual tyranny of minorities can be seen from the composition of the press. A foreign observer who judged Britain solely by its press would assume that the Conservative party was out and away the strongest party, with the Liberals second, the Communists third and the Labour party nowhere. The one genuine mass party has no daily paper that is undisputedly its own, and among the political weeklies it has no reliable supporter. Suppose *Tribune* came out with a plain statement of the principles that are implicit in some of its individual decisions – in its support of conscription, for instance. Would it be going against the main body of Labour party opinion? I doubt it. But it would be going against the fashionable minority who can make things unpleasant for a political journalist. These people have a regular technique of smears and ridicule – a whole specialised vocabulary designed to show that anyone who will not repeat the accepted catchwords is a rather laughable kind of lunatic. Mr Zilliacus, for instance, accuses *Tribune* of being "rabidly anti-Russian" (or "rabidly anti-Communist" – it was one or the other). The key-word here is rabid. Other words used in this context are insensate, demented, "sick with hatred" (the *New Republic*'s phrase) and maniacal. The upshot is that if from time to time you express a mild distaste for slave-labour camps or one-candidate elections, you are either insane or actuated by the worst motives. In the same way, when Henry Wallace is asked by a newspaper interviewer why he issues falsified versions of his speeches to the press, he replies: "So you are one of these people who are clamouring for war with Russia?" It doesn't answer the question, but it would frighten most people into silence. Or there is the milder kind of ridicule that consists in pretending that a reasoned opinion is indistinguishable from an absurd out-of-date prejudice. If you do not like Communism you are a red-baiter, a believer in Bolshevik atrocities, the nationalisation of women, Moscow Gold, and so on. Similarly, when Catholicism was almost as fashionable among the English intelligentsia as Communism is now, anyone who said that the Catholic Church was a sinister organisation and no friend to democracy, was promptly accused of swallowing the worst follies of the No-Popery organisations, of looking under his bed lest Jesuits should be concealed there, of believing stories about babies' skeletons dug up from the floors of nunneries, and all the rest of it. But a few people stuck to their opinion, and I think it is safe to say that the Catholic Church is less fashionable now than it was then.

After all, what does it matter to be laughed at? The big public, in any case, usually doesn't see the joke, and if you state your principles clearly and stick to them, it is wonderful how people come round to you in the end. There is no doubt about whom *Tribune* is frightened of. It is frightened of the Communists, the fellow-travellers and the fellow-travellers of fellow-travellers. Hence its endless equivocations: a paragraph of protest when this of our friends is shot – silence when that one is shot, denunciation of this one faked election – qualified approval of that one, and so on. The result is that in American papers I have more than once seen the phrase "the Foot-Zilliacus group" (or words to that effect). Of course Foot and Zilliacus are not allies, but they can appear so from the outside. Meanwhile, does this kind of thing even conciliate the people it is aimed at? Does it conciliate Mr Zilliacus, for instance? He has been treated with remarkable tenderness by *Tribune*. He has been allowed to infest its correspondence columns like a perennial weed, and when a little while ago *Tribune* reviewed a book of his, I looked in vain in that review for any plain statement of what he is or whose interests he is serving. Instead there was only a mild disagreement, a suggestion that he was perhaps a little over-zealous, a little given to special pleading – all this balanced by praise wherever possible, and headed by the friendly title, "The Fighting Propagandist." But is Mr Zilliacus grateful? On the contrary, only a few weeks later he turns round and without any provocation delivers a good hard boot on the shins.

It is hard to blame him, since he knows very well that *Tribune* is not on his side and does not really like him. But whereas he is willing to make this clear, *Tribune*, in spite of occasional side-thrusts, is not. I do not claim for Mr Zilliacus that he is honest, but at least he is sincere. We know where he stands, and he prefers to hit his enemies rather than his friends. Of course it is true that he is saying what is safe and fashionable at this moment, but I imagine he would stick to his opinions if the tide turned.

1948

Marx and Russia

The Observer, 15 February 1948

The word "Communism," unlike "Fascism," has never degenerated into a meaningless term of abuse. Nevertheless, a
certain ambiguity does cling to it, and at the least it means two
different things, only rather tenuously connected: a political
theory, and a political movement which is not in any noticeable way putting the theory into practice. On the face of it, the
deeds of the Cominform might seem more important than the
prophecies of Marx, but, as Mr. John Plamenatz reminds us in
his recently-published booklet, the original vision of Communism must never be forgotten, since it is still the dynamo
which supplies millions of adherents with faith and hence with
the power to act.

Originally, "Communism" meant a free and just society
based on the principle of "to each according to his needs."
Marx gave this vision probability by making it part of a seemingly inevitable historical process. Society was to dwindle
down to a tiny class of possessors and an enormous class of
dispossessed, and one day, almost automatically, the dispossessed were to take over. Only a few decades after Marx's
death the Russian Revolution broke out, and the men who
guided its course proclaimed themselves, and believed themselves, to be Marx's most faithful disciples. But their success
really depended on throwing a good deal of their master's
teaching overboard.

Marx had foretold that revolution would happen first in the
highly industrialised countries. It is now clear that this was an
error, but he was right in this sense, that the kind of revolution
that he foresaw could not happen in a backward country like
Russia, where the industrial workers were a minority. Marx
had envisaged an overwhelmingly powerful proletariat sweeping aside a small group of opponents, and then governing
democratically, through elected representatives. What actually
happened, in Russia, was the seizure of power by a small body

of classless professional revolutionaries, who claimed to represent the common people but were not chosen by them nor genuinely answerable to them.

From Lenin's point of view this was unavoidable. He and his group had to stay in power, since they alone were the true inheritors of the Marxist doctrine, and it was obvious that they could not stay in power democratically. The "dictatorship of the proletariat" had to mean the dictatorship of a handful of intellectuals, ruling through terrorism. The Revolution was saved, but from then onwards the Russian Communist party developed in a direction of which Lenin would probably have disapproved if he had lived longer.

Placed as they were, the Russian Communists necessarily developed into a permanent ruling caste, or oligarchy, recruited not by birth but by adoption. Since they could not risk the growth of opposition they could not permit genuine criticism, and since they silenced criticism they often made avoidable mistakes: then, because they could not admit that the mistakes were their own they had to find scapegoats, sometimes on an enormous scale.

The upshot is that the dictatorship has grown tighter as the regime has grown more secure, and that Russia is perhaps farther from egalitarian Socialism to-day than she was 30 years ago. But, as Mr. Plamenatz rightly warns us, never for one moment should we imagine that the original fervour has faded. The Communists may have perverted their aims, but they have not lost their mystique. The belief that they and they alone are the saviours of humanity is as unquestioning as ever. In the years 1935–39 and 1941–44 it was easy to believe that the U.S.S.R. had abandoned the idea of world revolution, but it is now clear that this was not the case. The idea has never been dropped: it has merely been modified, "revolution" tending more and more to mean "conquest."

No doubt unavoidably in so short a book, Mr. Plamenatz confines himself to one facet of his subject, and says very little about the role and character of the Communist parties outside the U.S.S.R. He also barely touches on the question of whether the Russian regime will, or indeed can, grow more liberal of its own accord. This last question is all-important, but for lack of precedents one can only guess at the answer.

Meanwhile, we are faced with a world-wide political movement which threatens the very existence of Western civilisation, and which has lost none of its vigour because it has become in a sense corrupt. Mr. Plamenatz concludes bleakly that though the U.S.S.R. will not necessarily precipitate an aggressive war against the West, its rulers regard a struggle to the death as inevitable, and will never come to any real agreement with those whom they regard as their natural enemies. Evidently, as Commander Stephen King-Hall says in his Introduction, if we want to combat Communism we must start by understanding it. But beyond understanding there lies the yet more difficult task of being understood, and – a problem that few people seem to have seriously considered as yet – of finding some way of making our point of view known to the Russian people.

Review of *The Atlantic Islands* by Kenneth Williamson

The Observer, 29 February 1948

The Faeroe Islands, to judge by Mr. Kenneth Williamson's photographs, are almost completely treeless. They are volcanic islands rising in perpendicular cliffs out of cloudy, stormy seas, with their cultivable soil distributed in such narrow pockets that the farmer cannot even use a plough, but has to do everything with a clumsy handleless spade. They have no natural wealth except their fisheries. Nevertheless, whereas most of the island groups fringing Britain are being rapidly depopulated, these others, even poorer and barer, have quadrupled their population in the last hundred years.

Perhaps this is partly because the Faeroese have succeeded in remaining owner-peasants, with no landlord class and no very great differences of wealth. Most of the land is cultivated on the primitive strip system, and the grazing grounds are owned communally. Mr. Williamson, who was stationed in the Faeroes for several years during the war, found the Faeroese a tough, simple, rustic people, but by no means uncultivated, for the local schools are fairly good and a proportion of the children are sent to Denmark to finish their education. They are of pure Viking stock and still speak their ancient Norwegian dialect, only rather unwillingly using Danish for official purposes. Except perhaps in the folk-lore (there is a story of a seal-wife which seems to have an Irish sound) the original Celtic inhabitants have left hardly any traces.

How essentially poor the islands are can be seen from the local diet, which consists quite largely of whale meat and sea birds. With scanty soil and rather chilly summers it is not worth growing grain, and the chief crops are hay and potatoes, which means that not many sheep or cattle can be kept through the winter. Apart from mutton dried in the wind like biltong, the people's animal food has to come out of the sea. The annual massacre of the whales – schools of them are driven into the harbour of Thorshavn, the capital, and there slaughtered with bill-hooks, turning the sea crimson in their death-struggles – is an important event; the hunting of the sea birds is even more so. The Faeroese eat not only gannets, which are eaten in some other places, but guillemots, gulls, cormorants, and above all, puffins. Mr. Williamson is an enthusiast for Faeroese cookery, but most of the dishes he describes are slightly horrible to read about. Their key-note seems to be the combination of fishy and greasy meat with sweet sauces.

The Faeroese are exceedingly hospitable. Any stranger arriving at a farmhouse, Mr. Williamson says, is assumed to be dying of starvation, and has to act accordingly. It must be a little difficult to respond when one is offered boiled puffins with strawberry jam.

Nationalism is not yet strong in the Faeroes, and only a very few of the inhabitants objected to the islands being occupied by Britain during the war. Moreover, the Faeroes were our most reliable source of fish throughout the war, and at one time were responsible for three-quarters of the British supply. All through the dark days of 1940 and 1941, when the Iceland boats refused to sail without air escorts which Britain could not provide, the tiny Faeroese boats plied to and fro, their sole armament one Bren gun each. They were bombed, machine-gunned, blown up by mines and even torpedoed. But they also made a good deal of money, which has been employed in bringing the fishing fleet up to date, on the assumption that the trade with Britain will continue. One would like to learn for certain, from some authoritative source, that this hope is not being disappointed.

Writers and Leviathan
Politics and Letters, Summer 1948

The position of the writer in an age of State control is a subject that has already been fairly largely discussed, although most of the evidence that might be relevant is not yet available. In this place I do not want to express an opinion either for or against State patronage of the arts, but merely to point out that *what kind* of State rules over us must depend partly on the prevailing intellectual atmosphere: meaning, in this context, partly on the attitude of writers and artists themselves, and on their willing-ness or otherwise to keep the spirit of Liberalism alive. If we find ourselves in ten years' time cringing before somebody like Zhdanov, it will probably be because that is what we have deserved. Obviously there are strong tendencies towards totalitarianism at work within the English literary intelligentsia already. But here I am not concerned with any organised and conscious movement such as Communism, but merely with the effect, on people of good will, of political thinking and the need to take sides politically.

This is a political age. War, Fascism, concentration camps, rubber truncheons, atomic bombs, etc., are what we daily think about, and therefore to a great extent what we write about, even when we do not name them openly. We cannot help this. When you are on a sinking ship, your thoughts will be about sinking ships. But not only is our subject-matter narrowed, but our whole attitude towards literature is coloured by loyalties which we at least intermittently realise to be non-literary. I often have the feeling that even at the best of times literary criticism is fraudulent, since in the absence of any accepted standards whatever – any *external* reference which can give meaning to the statement that such and such a book is 'good' or 'bad' – every literary judgement consists in trumping up a set of rules to justify an instinctive preference. One's real reaction to a book, when one has a reaction at all, is usually 'I like this book' or 'I don't like it', and what follows is a rationalisation. But 'I like this book' is not, I think, a non-literary reaction; the non-literary reaction is 'This book is on my side, and therefore I must discover merits in it'. Of course, when one praises a book for political reasons one may be emotionally sincere, in the sense that one does feel strong approval of it, but also it often happens that party solidarity demands a plain lie. Anyone used to reviewing books for political periodicals is well aware of this. In general, if you are writing for a paper that you are in agreement with, you sin by commission, and if for a paper of the opposite stamp, by omission. At any rate, innumerable controversial books – books for or against Soviet Russia, for or against Zionism, for or against the Catholic Church, etc. – are judged before they are read, and in effect before they are written. One knows in advance what reception they will get in what papers. And yet, with a dishonesty that sometimes is not even quarter-conscious, the pretence is kept up that genuinely literary standards are being applied.

Of course, the invasion of literature by politics was bound to happen. It must have happened, even if the special problem of totalitarianism had never arisen, because we have developed a sort of compunction which our grandparents did not have, an awareness of the enormous injustice and misery of the world, and a guilt-stricken feeling that one ought to be doing something about it, which makes a purely aesthetic attitude towards life impossible. No one, now, could devote himself to literature as single-mindedly as Joyce or Henry James. But unfortunately, to accept political responsibility now means yielding oneself over to orthodoxies and 'party lines', with all the timidity and dishonesty that that implies. As against the Victorian writers, we have the disadvantage of living among clear-cut political ideologies and of usually knowing at a glance what thoughts are heretical. A modern literary intellectual lives and writes in constant dread – not, indeed, of public opinion in the wider sense, but of public opinion within his own group. As a rule, luckily, there is more than one group, but also at any given moment there is a dominant orthodoxy, to offend against which needs a thick skin and sometimes means cutting one's income in half for years on end. Obviously, for about fifteen years past, the dominant orthodoxy, especially among the young, has been 'left'. The key words are 'progressive', 'democratic' and 'revolutionary', while the labels which you must at all costs avoid having gummed upon you are 'bourgeois', 'reactionary' and 'Fascist'. Almost everyone nowadays, even the majority of Catholics and Conservatives, is 'progressive', or at least wishes to be thought so. No one, so far as I know, ever describes himself as a 'bourgeois', just as no one literate enough to have heard the word ever admits to being guilty of anti-semitism. We are all of us good democrats, anti-Fascist, anti-imperialist, contemptuous of class distinctions, impervious to colour prejudice, and so on and so forth. Nor is there much doubt that the present-day 'left' orthodoxy is better than the rather snobbish, pietistic Conservative orthodoxy which prevailed twenty years ago, when the *Criterion* and (on a lower level) the *London Mercury* were the dominant literary magazines. For at the least its implied objective is a viable form of society which large numbers of people actually want. But it also has its own falsities which, because they cannot be admitted, make it impossible for certain questions to be seriously discussed.

The whole left-wing ideology, scientific and utopian, was evolved by people who had no immediate prospect of attaining power. It was, therefore, an extremist ideology, utterly contemptuous of kings, governments, laws, prisons, police forces, armies, flags, frontiers, patriotism, religion, conventional morality, and, in fact, the whole existing scheme of things. Until well within living memory the forces of the left in all countries were fighting against a tyranny which appeared to be invincible, and it was easy to assume that if only *that* particular tyranny – capitalism – could be overthrown, Socialism would follow. Moreover, the left had inherited from Liberalism certain distinctly questionable beliefs, such as the belief that the truth will prevail and persecution defeats itself, or that man is naturally good and is only corrupted by his environment. This perfectionist ideology has persisted in nearly all of us, and it is in the name of it that we protest when (for instance) a Labour government votes huge incomes to the King's daughters or shows hesitation about nationalising steel. But we have also

accumulated in our minds a whole series of unadmitted contradictions, as a result of successive bumps against reality.

The first big bump was the Russian Revolution. For somewhat complex reasons, nearly the whole of the English left has
been driven to accept the Russian régime as 'Socialist', while
silently recognising that its spirit and practice are quite alien to
anything that is meant by 'Socialism' in this country. Hence
there has arisen a sort of schizophrenic manner of thinking, in
which words like 'democracy' can bear two irreconcilable
meanings, and such things as concentration camps and mass
deportations can be right and wrong simultaneously. The next
blow to the left-wing ideology was the rise of Fascism, which
shook the pacifism and internationalism of the left without
bringing about a definite restatement of doctrine. The experience of German occupation taught the European peoples
something that the colonial peoples knew already, namely,
that class antagonisms are not all-important and that there is
such a thing as national interest. After Hitler it was difficult to
maintain seriously that 'the enemy is in your own country' and
that national independence is of no value. But though we all
know this and act upon it when necessary, we still feel that to
say it aloud would be a kind of treachery. And finally, the
greatest difficulty of all, there is the fact that the left is now in
power and is obliged to take responsibility and make genuine
decisions.

Left governments almost invariably disappoint their supporters because, even when the prosperity which they have
promised is achievable, there is always need of an uncomfortable transition period about which little has been said beforehand. At this moment we see our own government, in its
desperate economic straits, fighting in effect against its own
past propaganda. The crisis that we are now in is not a sudden
unexpected calamity, like an earthquake, and it was not caused
by the war, but merely hastened by it. Decades ago it could be
foreseen that something of this kind was going to happen. Ever
since the nineteenth century our national income, dependent
partly on interest from foreign investments, and on assured
markets and cheap raw materials in colonial countries, had
been extremely precarious. It was certain that, sooner or later,
something would go wrong and we should be forced to make

our exports balance our imports: and when that happened the British standard of living, including the working-class standard, was bound to fall, at least temporarily. Yet the left-wing parties, even when they were vociferously anti-imperialist, never made these facts clear. On occasion they were ready to admit that the British workers had benefited, to some extent, by the looting of Asia and Africa, but they always allowed it to appear that we could give up our loot and yet in some way contrive to remain prosperous. Quite largely, indeed, the workers were won over to Socialism by being told that they were exploited, whereas the brute truth was that, in world terms, they were exploiters. Now, to all appearances, the point has been reached when the working-class living-standard *cannot* be maintained, let alone raised. Even if we squeeze the rich out of existence, the mass of the people must either consume less or produce more. Or am I exaggerating the mess we are in? I may be, and I should be glad to find myself mistaken. But the point I wish to make is that this question, among people who are faithful to the left ideology, cannot be genuinely discussed. The lowering of wages and raising of working hours are felt to be inherently anti-Socialist measures, and must therefore be dismissed in advance, whatever the economic situation may be. To suggest that they may be unavoidable is merely to risk being plastered with those labels that we are all terrified of. It is far safer to evade the issue and pretend that we can put everything right by redistributing the existing national income.

To accept an orthodoxy is always to inherit unresolved contradictions. Take for instance the fact, which came out in Mr. Winkler's essay in this series, that all sensitive people are revolted by industrialism and its products, and yet are aware that the conquest of poverty and the emancipation of the working class demand not less industrialisation, but more and more. Or take the fact that certain jobs are absolutely necessary and yet are never done except under some kind of coercion. Or take the fact that it is impossible to have a positive foreign policy without having powerful armed forces. One could multiply examples. In every such case there is a conclusion which is perfectly plain but which can only be drawn if one is privately disloyal to the official ideology. The normal response is to push the question, unanswered, into a corner of one's mind, and then continue repeating contradictory catchwords. One does not have to search far through the reviews and magazines to discover the effects of this kind of thinking.

I am not, of course, suggesting that mental dishonesty is peculiar to Socialists and left-wingers generally, or is commonest among them. It is merely that acceptance of *any* political discipline seems to be incompatible with literary integrity. This applies equally to movements like Pacifism and Personalism, which claim to be outside the ordinary political struggle. Indeed, the mere sound of words ending in -ism seems to bring with it the smell of propaganda. Group loyalties are necessary, and yet they are poisonous to literature, so long as literature is the product of individuals. As soon as they are allowed to have any influence, even a negative one, on creative writing, the result is not only falsification, but often the actual drying-up of the inventive faculties.

Well, then, what? Do we have to conclude that it is the duty of every writer to 'keep out of politics'? Certainly not! In any case, as I have said already, no thinking person can or does genuinely keep out of politics, in an age like the present one. I only suggest that we should draw a sharper distinction than we do at present between our political and our literary loyalties, and should recognise that a willingness to *do* certain distasteful but necessary things does not carry with it any obligation to swallow the beliefs that usually go with them. When a writer engages in politics he should do so as a citizen, as a human being, but not *as a writer*. I do not think that he has the right, merely on the score of his sensibilities, to shirk the ordinary dirty work of politics. Just as much as anyone else, he should be prepared to deliver lectures in draughty halls, to chalk pavements, to canvass voters, to distribute leaflets, even to fight in civil wars if it seems necessary. But whatever else he does in the service of his party, he should never write for it. He should make it clear that his writing is a thing apart. And he should be able to act co-operatively while, if he chooses, completely rejecting the official ideology. He should never turn back from a train of thought because it may lead to a heresy, and he should not mind very much if his unorthodoxy is smelt out, as it probably will be. Perhaps it is even a bad sign in a writer if he is not suspected of reactionary tendencies to-day, just as it was a bad sign if he was not suspected of Communist sympathies twenty years ago.

But does all this mean that a writer should not only refuse to be dictated to by political bosses, but also that he should refrain from writing *about* politics? Once again, certainly not! There is no reason why he should not write in the most crudely political way, if he wishes to. Only he should do so as an individual, an outsider, at the most an unwelcome guerrilla on the flank of a regular army. This attitude is quite compatible with ordinary political usefulness. It is reasonable, for example, to be willing to fight in a war because one thinks the war ought to be won, and at the same time to refuse to write war propaganda. Sometimes, if a writer is honest, his writings and his political activities may actually contradict one another. There are occasions when that is plainly undesirable: but then the remedy is not to falsify one's impulses, but to remain silent.

To suggest that a creative writer, in a time of conflict, must split his life into two compartments, may seem defeatist or frivolous: yet in practice I do not see what else he can do. To lock yourself up in the ivory tower is impossible and undesirable. To yield subjectively, not merely to a party machine, but even to a group ideology, is to destroy yourself as writer. We feel this dilemma to be a painful one, because we see the need of engaging in politics while also seeing what a dirty, degrading business it is. And most of us still have a lingering belief that every choice, even every political choice, is between good and evil, and that if a thing is necessary it is also right. We should, I think, get rid of this belief, which belongs to the nursery. In politics one can never do more than decide which of two evils is the less, and there are some situations from which one can only escape by acting like a devil or a lunatic. War, for example, may be necessary, but it is certainly not right or sane. Even a general election is not exactly a pleasant or edifying spectacle. If you have to take part in such things – and I think you do have to, unless you are armoured by old age or stupidity or hypocrisy – then you also have to keep part of yourself inviolate. For most people the problem does not arise in the same form, because their lives are split already. They are truly alive only in their leisure hours, and there is no emotional connection between their work and their political activities. Nor are they generally

GEORGE ORWELL

asked, in the name of political loyalty, to debase themselves as
workers. The artist, and especially the writer, is asked just that –
in fact, it is the only thing that politicians ever ask of him. If he
refuses, that does not mean that he is condemned to inactivity.
One half of him, which in a sense is the whole of him, can act as
resolutely, even as violently if need be, as anyone else. But his
writings, in so far as they have any value, will always be the
product of the saner self that stands aside, records the things that
are done and admits their necessity, but refuses to be deceived
as to their true nature.

Britain's Left-Wing Press
Progressive (Madison, Wisconsin), June 1948

The outstanding peculiarity of the British press as a whole is its
extreme concentration; there are relatively few papers, and the
bulk of them is owned by a small ring of people. This is partly
due to the small size of the country, which makes it possible for
the London daily papers to be on sale in the early morning as far
north as Glasgow.

A few first-class provincial papers, such as the Manchester
Guardian, do indeed exist, but none of them has a large circulation, and in effect the whole country up to and beyond the
Scottish border is covered by eight London dailies. As for
weekly reviews and monthly magazines, nothing of any importance is published outside London.

This special structure of the British press has existed for 30
years. Thus by the time an independent left-wing press became
politically possible, it was already financially impossible. To
start a new paper that could compete with the existing ones
would need a capital of several million pounds, and no new
daily or evening paper, apart from the tiny *Daily Worker*, has
been launched in London since 1918. The following figures,
which are necessarily approximate, will give some idea of how
readership is distributed in a country which has recently been
voting predominantly Labour.

If one considers only papers with a definite political orientation, and leaves the provincial press out of account, the total

weekly circulation of the British press is something over 100 millions. Of this, about 23 millions are accounted for by papers that could be described as "Left." But this includes the Liberal *News-Chronicle*, which is certainly "enlightened," or "progressive," but would not in all circumstances be a reliable supporter of a Labour Government. If one counts only papers having a definite affiliation with a left-wing party, then the figure is about 14 millions, or less than one-seventh of the total. At present there are in Britain only six left-wing papers of any consequence. These six papers are:

THE DAILY HERALD. Circulation over two millions, the third highest among British daily papers. *The Herald* can be regarded as the official Labour Party paper, but it represents essentially the trade-union (and more conservative) end of the party. It was founded in 1914, and for the next 15 years, with a policy and attitude very much more radical than it displays today, it floundered along under a series of editors, always on the verge of bankruptcy. Even when its circulation touched 400,000 it could not be made to pay its way, because at that time commercial advertisers were unwilling to patronize a left-wing paper.

In 1929 *The Herald* was re-organized, its stock divided half-and-half between the Trade Union Congress and Odham's, a big publishing firm which owns several low-class weeklies. In the process *The Herald* was transformed into an ordinary popular paper, so far as tone and make-up go, but it was agreed that Odham's should have no control over its political policy, which should be directed by the Labour Party.

This agreement has been kept. Although it sometimes has good foreign correspondents, *The Herald* is a very dull paper, much inferior as reading matter to several other papers of the same stamp. It has, nevertheless, kept a steady circulation of two millions for more than a dozen years, partly, no doubt, because it gives full information on trade-union affairs. Its public is almost entirely working-class.

REYNOLD'S NEWS. Sunday paper, circulation about 700,000. (This is a small circulation as British Sunday papers go. One of them claims seven millions!) *Reynold's* is sometimes referred to in the American press as "a fellow travellers' paper," but this is not strictly true. Officially it is the paper of the Cooperative Party, which is the political organ of the cooperative movement and is now more or less completely merged with the Labour Party. There is, however, a strong Communist influence in *Reynold's*, affecting even its book reviews. It sometimes gives the impression of being three papers in one – partly Cooperative, partly Communist, and in part an ordinary Sunday paper devoted to sports, crime, and the Royal Family. *Reynold's* sometimes has intelligent articles, but on the whole it is an unsatisfactory paper, combining a sectarian atmosphere with the faults of the gutter press.

THE NEW STATESMAN AND NATION. Weekly review, circulation about 80,000. *The New Statesman* was founded in 1913, and since then has "incorporated" three rival papers of similar stamp: it is now by far the most influential of British political weeklies. Once again, it is usual to describe *The New Statesman* as "fellow-travelling," and once again this is not strictly true, though in this case I should say that it is substantially true.

On occasion *The New Statesman* has turned definitely against the Communist line, as for instance during the Russo-German pact, and it may perhaps do so again if Russian aggression in Europe goes much further. But over a period of about 20 years *The New Statesman* has probably done more than any one thing – certainly more than any one periodical – to spread an uncritically Russophile attitude among the British intelligentsia, all the more so because it has no connection with the Communist Party and preserves an ostensibly detached attitude towards the U.S.S.R.

Apart from H. Kingsley Martin, its editor, many well-known left-wing publicists are or have at some time been associated with it: Leonard Woolf, H. N. Brailsford, John Strachey, Harold Laski, J. B. Priestley, R. H. S. Crossman, and others.

On technical grounds *The New Statesman* deserves its pre-eminence. Over many years it has remained at a high journalistic level and has preserved, if not a completely consistent policy, at any rate a distinctive attitude. The whole of the "enlightened" pinkish middle class reads it as a matter of habit. Its position corresponds fairly closely to that of *The New Republic* in America, but it is, I should say, a somewhat more adult paper.

   TRIBUNE. Weekly review, circulation uncertain, but probably about 20,000. *Tribune* was founded a year or two before the war, and was at that time a rather vociferous paper costing threepence (five cents), with a mainly working-class circulation. It was controlled by Sir Stafford Cripps, who had recently been disciplined by the Labour Party for forming a fractional organization, the Socialist League. The Communists, who were then in their Popular Front phase, regarded *Tribune* with approval and helped to distribute it.

   After the Russo-German pact and the outbreak of war this support fell away, and *Tribune*'s circulation, which had never been large, dropped to 2,000. In 1941, when Cripps had joined the Government and had therefore been obliged to sever his connection with the paper, it was taken over by Aneurin Bevan, the present Minister of Health.

   Bevan reorganized it as a sixpenny paper of roughly the same stamp as *The New Statesman*, and during the remainder of the war it was probably the best, and certainly by far the most independent, of left-wing periodicals. It was, indeed, the only English paper which, while maintaining a responsible attitude and supporting the war effort, was radically critical of the Churchill Government. It was also the only paper on the Left which made any effort to counter Soviet Russian propaganda.

   After the 1945 general election Bevan joined the Government, and *Tribune* became the organ of a group of young Labour MPs of whom Michael Foot is probably the best known. This group (not to be confused with the crypto-Communists) supports the Government's programme in the main but is critical of its foreign policy, especially in regard to Greece and Palestine.

   Unavoidably, *Tribune* has lost some of its vigour since Labour took office. It suffers from the embarrassment that always besets rebels when their own side has won, and in addition, its attacks on Ernest Bevin's foreign policy have been somewhat unreal, since on the all-important issue of standing up to Russia it is not genuinely in opposition. A few Communists and fellow-travellers occasionally write for *Tribune*, but all of those who have anything to do with determining its policy are extremely anti-Communist. In spite of surface appearances, it is much the most reliable supporter that the present Government has among weekly papers. Its public, most of which it gained during the war, is probably middle-class in the main, since it is generally accepted that the British working class will not pay more than threepence for a weekly paper.

FORWARD. Weekly review of essentially working-class type, published in Glasgow. *Forward* could hardly be called an influential paper, and its circulation is probably small, but it is interesting as an expression of the old-style, rebellious, maximalist version of socialism which still flourishes on the banks of the Clyde. It is almost always in disagreement with the Government, but its policy is extremely erratic: it is pro-Russian wherever possible, but on the other hand it is anti-Communist and is a strong defender of the freedom of speech and press. *Forward* is directed by Emrys Hughes, a rather turbulent back-bench Labour MP. Well-known writers such as Bernard Shaw, Bertrand Russell, and Sean O'Casey write for it occasionally.

THE DAILY WORKER. Circulation uncertain, but probably reaches 100,000 at times. *The Daily Worker* was founded in 1929 and was suppressed for about two years during the war for defeatist activities. Since its early days it has improved considerably, and sometimes has good scientific articles and book reviews, but it has remained a propaganda sheet rather than a newspaper. On the other hand, compared with the continental or even the American Communist press, *The Daily Worker* is not a very scurrilous paper. It is kept going partly by voluntary subscriptions from sympathizers. Recent attempts to finance it by selling shares to the general public were only partially successful.

These six papers that I have enumerated are all that Britain possesses – that is, all that is of the slightest importance – in the way of a left-wing press. Beyond this there are only obscure sheets dealing with trade-union intelligence or purely local affairs, and thin little magazines which hardly pretend to be aimed at the big public, and one or two periodicals devoted to direct Soviet propaganda and not having much bearing on British politics.

Of the small sectarian magazines, the Communist *Labour Monthly* probably has the widest circulation. Considering the smallness of their resources, the Communists are a great deal more enterprising than the Labour Party. They issue innumerable pamphlets, and they even own or control a chain of bookshops in which, naturally, their own publications are to the fore. They also, for some years before and during the war, exercised considerable influence on the Liberal *News-Chronicle* (circulation about one and a half millions).

But of course it is not Communist competition that is really important from the Labour Party's point of view. The essential fact is that the Government which undoubtedly represents the mass of the people is daily attacked and misrepresented by a huge and on the whole efficient Tory press, while not having any asset of its own except a single daily paper. As for the British Broadcasting Company, which is an independent corporation, it is neither a friend nor an enemy. Its foreign services are under government supervision, but in home politics it could fairly be described as neutral.

For more than a year a commission appointed by the Government has been inquiring – rather gingerly, and in the face of some opposition – into the state of the British press. Whatever its findings, they are not likely to lead to any very drastic changes, since the press is not one of the industries marked down for nationalization in the near future. But it is probable that something will be done to limit the multiple ownership of newspapers. At present it can happen – does happen in one or two cases – that a single press lord owns or controls as many as 100 periodicals of one kind or another, and dictates the policy of all of them.

It is also probable that a new London evening paper will be launched in conjunction with *The Daily Herald*. The Left obviously needs better publicity, but in a still mainly capitalist country, with a public that has been used for decades to reading the same papers, it is not easy for a left-wing press to grow up unless it is heavily subsidized.

The whole question has been much discussed during the past two years, without any very definite conclusion being reached. On the one hand, the majority of British journalists would be delighted to see the press lords overthrown: on the other hand, all journalists of whatever colour are alarmed at the prospect of a state-controlled or party-controlled press. The Labour Party, with its huge membership and steady flow of funds, could certainly afford to publicize itself a great deal better than it does at present. But whether any political party, having subsidized a press of its own, would then have the imagination to conduct it in a non-totalitarian manner, remains to be seen.

Review of *Spearhead: Ten Years' Experimental Writing in America*, edited by James Laughlin
Times Literary Supplement, 17 April 1948

The exchange of literary intelligence between country and country is still far from brisk, even where there is no political obstruction. Only the other day a critic in a French weekly review could remark that, so far as he was aware, the United States had not produced any new writers since 1939. We ourselves, not being dependent on translations, are able to be a little better informed, but even so it is a fact that most of the younger American writers are only known to this country because of stray contributions to magazines. Few of them have yet appeared here in book form. *Spearhead*, Mr. James Laughlin's anthology of recent American prose and verse, is therefore useful, although, as he admits himself, it is not fully representative.

An anthology of this kind is not, of course, intended to give a picture of the American literary scene as a whole. Mr. Laughlin has explicitly confined himself to experimental and "non-commercial" writing, and most of the contents are drawn from such magazines as the *Kenyon Review* and the *Partisan Review*, or from his own annual miscellany, *New Directions*. Even so, the selection is less interesting than it might have been, since it consists almost entirely of "creative" writing – that is, poems and stories – while much of the best and liveliest American writing of the past ten years has been done by literary critics and political essayists. An anthology based mainly on the "little reviews" ought not to leave out Lionel Trilling, Dwight Macdonald, Clement Greenberg and Nicola Chiaramonte: one might also have expected to find Edmund Wilson, Mary McCarthy and Saul Bellow. However, this book does introduce to the English reader a number of young writers who are less known here than they deserve to be – for example, Paul Goodman, Karl Shapiro, Delmore Schwarz and Randall Jarrell. There are also, of course, contributions from various "established" writers (William Carlos Williams, E. E. Cummings, Henry Miller and others), and even from such veterans as Ezra Pound and Gertrude Stein.

One fact this book brings out is that American literary intellectuals are still very much on the defensive. There is evidently much more feeling that the writer is a hunted heretic and that "*avant garde*" literature, as it is rather solemnly called, is totally different from popular literature, than exists in England. But one cannot help noticing, while reading Mr. Laughlin's introduction and then the items that follow it, that this feeling of isolation is largely unjustified. To begin with, the "*avant garde*" and the "commercial" obviously overlap, and are even difficult to distinguish from one another. A number of the stories in this book, notably those of Jack Jones, Robert Lowry and Tennessee Williams, would fit easily into dozens of big-circulation magazines. But in addition, it is doubtful whether American literature has had during the past ten or fifteen years the "experimental" character that Mr. Laughlin claims for it. During that period literature has extended its subject-matter, no doubt, but there has been little or no technical innovation. There has also been surprisingly little interest in prose as such, and an all-round tolerance of ugly and slovenly writing. Even in verse it could probably be shown that there has been no real innovator since Auden, or even since Eliot, to whom Auden and his associates admittedly owed a great deal.

No English prose-writer in the immediate past has played with words as Joyce did, nor on the other hand has anyone made a deliberate attempt to simplify language as Hemingway did. As for the sort of cadenced "poetic" prose that used to be written by, for instance, Conrad, Lawrence or Forster, no one nowadays attempts anything of the kind. The most recent writer of intentionally rhythmical prose is Henry Miller, whose first book was published in 1935, when he was already not a young man. A striking thing about the prose-writers in Mr. Laughlin's collection is how like one another they all are in manner, except when they drop into dialect. The Anarchist Paul Goodman, for instance, certainly has unusual subject-matter for his stories, but his manner of approach is conservative enough. So also with the stories – again, unusual in theme – by H. J. Kaplan and John Berryman. No one to-day could produce a book of parodies corresponding to Max Beerbohm's *A Christmas Garland*: the differences between one writer and another, at any rate the surface differences, are not great enough. It is true, however, that the contemporary lack of interest in the technique of prose has its good side, in that a writer who is not expected to have a "style" is not tempted to practise affectations. This reflection is forced on one by the most noticeably mannered writer in the collection, Djuna Barnes, who seems to have been disastrously influenced by Rabelais, or possibly by Joyce.

The verse in this anthology is very uneven, and a better selection would have been possible. Randall Jarrell, for instance, is represented by five poems, including the excellent "Camp in the Prussian Forest"; but his tiny masterpiece, "The Ball Turret Gunner," which ends with the memorable line, "When I died they washed me out of the turret with a hose," is not there. Perhaps the best poem in the book is by E. E. Cummings. He is an irritating writer, partly because of his largely meaningless typographical tricks, partly because his restless bad temper soon provokes a counter-reaction in the reader, but he has a gift for telling phrases (for instance, his often-quoted description of Soviet Russia – "Vicariously childlike kingdom of slogan"), and, at his best, for neat, rapidly moving verse. In this collection he is at the top of his form in a short poem in praise of Olaf, a conscientious objector, which has slightly the air of being a pastiche of *Struwwelpeter*. Olaf's barely printable punishments at the hands of the military are first described, and then: –

Our president, being of which
assertions duly notified
threw the yellowsonofabitch
into a dungeon, where he died

Christ (of His mercy infinite)
i pray to see; and Olaf, too
preponderatingly because
unless statistics lie he was
more brave than me; more blond than you.

Throughout this anthology the best poems, almost without exception, are the ones that rhyme and scan in a more or less regular manner. Much of the "free" verse is simply prose arranged in lines of arbitrary length, or sometimes in highly elaborate patterns, with the initial word moving this way and that across the page, apparently on the theory that a visual effect is the same thing as a musical rhythm. If one takes passages of this so-called verse and rearranges them as prose, it becomes actually indistinguishable from prose, except, in some cases, by its sub-ject-matter. A couple of examples will be enough:

It was an icy day. We buried the cat, then took her box and set match to it in the back yard. Those fleas that escaped earth and fire died by the cold. (William Carlos Williams.)

The old guy put down his beer. Son, he said (and a girl came over to the table where we were: asked us by Jack Christ to buy her a drink). Son, I am going to tell you something the like of which nobody ever was told. (Ken-neth Patchen.)

Kenneth Rexroth's long poem, "The Phoenix and the Tortoise," which again looks like prose if rearranged as prose, is perhaps in a different category. Such a passage as this, for instance: —

The institution is a device
For providing molecular
Process with delusive credentials.
"Value is the reflection
Of satisfied appetite,

> The formal aspect of the tension
> Generated by resolution
> Of fact." Over-specialization,
> Proliferation, gigantism.

is not verse in the ordinary sense, but this is probably due not to sheer slovenliness but to the notion, perhaps derived from Ezra Pound or from translations of Chinese poems, that poetry can consist of lapidary statements without any rhythmical quality. The weakness of this method of writing is that it sacrifices not only the musical appeal of verse but also its mnemonic function. It is precisely the fact of having recognizable rhythms, and usually rhyme as well, that makes it possible for verse, unlike prose, to exist apart from the printed page. An enormous amount of "free" verse has been produced during the past thirty or forty years, but only so much of it has survived, in the sense of being remembered by heart, as contained cadences of a kind impossible in prose. The chief reason, at any rate in England and America, for breaking away from conventional verse-forms was that the English language is exceptionally poor in rhymes; a deficiency already obvious to the poet of the nineties who wrote: –

> From Austin back to Chaucer,
> My wearied eyes I shove,
> But never came across a
> New word to rhyme with love.

This shortcoming naturally had a cumulative effect, and by the Georgian period it had led to an unbearable staleness and artificiality. The way out was through the total or partial abandonment of rhyme, or through double rhymes and the use of colloquial words which would previously have been considered undignified, but which allowed the stock of available rhymes to be extended. This, however, did not do away with the need for rhythm but, if anything, increased it. Indeed, successful rhymeless poems – for example, Auden's *Spain*, or many passages in Eliot's work – tend to be written in strongly accented, non-iambic metres. Recently, as one can see even in this anthology, there has been a tendency to return to traditional stanza forms, usually with a touch of raggedness

ESSAYS

that is a legacy from "free" verse. Karl Shapiro, for instance, is
very successful in handling what is really an adaptation of the
popular ballad, as in his poem "Fireworks": –

> In the garden of pleistocene flowers we wander like Alice
> Where seed sends a stalk in the heavens and pops from a pod
> A Blue blossom that hangs in the distance and opens its
>   chalice
> And falls in the dust of itself and goes out with a nod.
> How the hairy tarantulas crawl in the soft of the ether
> Where showers of lilies explode in the jungle of creepers;
> How the rockets of sperm hurtle up to the moon and
>   beneath her
> Deploy for the eggs of the astral and sorrowful sleepers!

Of the short stories in this anthology perhaps the best is John
Berryman's "The Imaginary Jew"; it describes a young man
who goes to a political meeting, full of generous sentiments and
disgusted by anti-semitism, and then suddenly gains a much
deeper insight into the Jewish problem through the accident of
being mistaken for a Jew himself. Paul Goodman's story, "A
Ceremonial," which supposedly takes place "not long after the
establishment among us of reasonable institutions" – that is,
after the Anarchist revolution – is a spirited attempt to describe
happiness, a feat which no writer has ever quite accomplished.
H. J. Kaplan's longish story, "The Mohammedans," is the kind
of which one feels inclined to say that it shows great talent but
one is not certain what it is about. Georg Mann's satire on
Communism, "Azef Wischmeier, the Bolshevik Bureaucrat,"
would have been funny if it had been a dozen pages long
instead of nearly fifty. There is a long extract from Henry
Miller's *Tropic of Capricorn*. Like all of its author's earlier
writings, it contains some fine passages, but it would have
been better to pick a chapter from the less *exagéré Tropic of
Cancer*, which remains Miller's masterpiece, and which is still a
very rare book, so successfully has it been hunted down by the
police of all countries.

Apart from the written pieces, the anthology includes two
sets of fairly good but not outstanding photographs. One set,
taken by Walker Evans, accompanies a piece of "reportage" on
the southern cotton farmers by James Agee. The other set, by

Wright Morris, consists of photographs of buildings, mostly ruinous, each accompanied by a long caption in the form of a sort of prose poem. These captions are nothing very much in themselves, but the idea is a good one and might be profitably followed up. The other chief curiosity of the book is a collection, compiled by Mr. Laughlin, of the poems of Samuel Greenberg, a Jewish youth, son of very poor parents, who died about 1918, aged less than twenty. They are queer poems, full of misspellings and neologisms, and sometimes more like growing embryos than completed writings, but they show considerable power. Mr. Laughlin demonstrates by parallel quotations that Hart Crane lifted numerous lines from Greenberg without acknowledgement.

All in all, this book is useful, in that it introduces about forty American writers, of whom more than half are unknown or barely known in England; but it would have been a good deal better if it had been compiled expressly for an English audience. Actually it is a book designed for America, evidently imported into this country in sheets (Henry Miller's favourite verb has been laboriously blacked out by hand, over a stretch of fifty pages), and it is likely to give English readers a somewhat lopsided impression. It should be repeated that where American writing particularly excels at this moment is in literary criticism and in political and sociological essays. This, no doubt, is largely because in the United States there is more money, more paper and more spare time. The magazines are fatter, the "angels" are richer, and, above all, the intelligentsia, in spite of its sense of grievance, is numerous enough to constitute a public in itself. Long, serious controversies, of a kind extinct in England, can still happen; and, for instance, the battles that raged round the question of "supporting" the late war, or round the ideas of James Burnham or Van Wyck Brooks, produced material that would have been better worth reprinting, and more representative, than much of the contents of *Spearhead*. Moreover, the book suffers from the fact that it is neither uncompromisingly "highbrow," nor, on the other hand, is it a cross-section of current American literature. It leaves out several of the best living American writers on the ground that they are not *avant garde*, while at the same time it includes Kay Boyle and William Saroyan. It also – but perhaps this is unavoidable in any bulky anthology compiled from contemporary work – includes one or two pieces of sheer rubbish. The editors of the Falcon Press are to be congratulated for their enterprise, but another time they would do better to choose their material for themselves and to cast the net more widely.

Review of *The Soul of Man under Socialism* by Oscar Wilde

The Observer, 9 May 1948

Oscar Wilde's work is being much revived now on stage and screen, and it is well to be reminded that Salome and Lady Windermere were not his only creations. Wilde's "The Soul of Man under Socialism," for example, first published nearly 60 years ago, has worn remarkably well. Its author was not in any active sense a Socialist himself, but he was a sympathetic and intelligent observer; although his prophecies have not been fulfilled, they have not been made simply irrelevant by the passage of time.

Wilde's vision of Socialism, which at that date was probably shared by many people less articulate than himself, is Utopian and anarchistic. The abolition of private property, he says, will make possible the full development of the individual and set us free from "the sordid necessity of living for others." In the Socialist future there will not only be no want and no insecurity, there will also be no drudgery, no disease, no ugliness, no wastage of the human spirit in futile enmities and rivalries.

Pain will cease to be important: indeed, for the first time in his history, Man will be able to realise his personality through joy instead of through suffering. Crime will disappear, since there will be no economic reason for it. The State will cease to govern and will survive merely as an agency for the distribution of necessary commodities. All the disagreeable jobs will be done by machinery, and everyone will be completely free to choose his own work and his own manner of life. In effect, the world will be populated by artists, each striving after perfection in the way that seems best to him.

To-day, these optimistic forecasts make rather painful reading. Wilde realised, of course, that there were authoritarian tendencies in the Socialist movement, but he did not believe they would prevail, and with a sort of prophetic irony he wrote: "I hardly think that any Socialist, nowadays, would seriously propose that an inspector should call every morning at each house to see that each citizen rose up and did manual labour for eight hours" – which, unfortunately, is just the kind of thing that countless modern Socialists would propose. Evidently something has gone wrong. Socialism, in the sense of economic collectivism, is conquering the earth at a speed that would hardly have seemed possible 60 years ago, and yet Utopia, at any rate Wilde's Utopia, is no nearer. Where, then, does the fallacy lie?

If one looks more closely one sees that Wilde makes two common but unjustified assumptions. One is that the world is immensely rich and is suffering chiefly from maldistribution. Even things out between the millionaire and the crossing-sweeper, he seems to say, and there will be plenty of everything for everybody. Until the Russian Revolution, this belief was very widely held – "starving in the midst of plenty" was a favourite phrase – but it was quite false, and it survived only because Socialists thought always of the highly developed Western countries and ignored the fearful poverty of Asia and Africa. Actually, the problem for the world as a whole is not how to distribute such wealth as exists but how to increase production, without which economic equality merely means common misery.

Secondly, Wilde assumes that it is a simple matter to arrange that all the unpleasant kinds of work shall be done by machinery. The machines, he says, are our new race of slaves: a tempting metaphor, but a misleading one, since there is a vast range of jobs – roughly speaking, any job needing great flexibility – that no machine is able to do. In practice, even in the most highly-mechanised countries, an enormous amount of dull and exhausting work has to be done by unwilling human muscles. But this at once implies direction of labour, fixed working hours, differential wage rates, and all the regimentation that Wilde abhors. Wilde's version of Socialism could only be realised in a world not only far richer but also technically far more advanced than the present one. The abolition of private property does not of itself put food into anyone's mouth. It is merely the first step in a transitional period that is bound to be laborious, uncomfortable, and long.

But that is not to say that Wilde is altogether wrong. The trouble with transitional periods is that the harsh outlook which they generate tends to become permanent. To all appearances this is what has happened in Soviet Russia. A dictatorship supposedly established for a limited purpose has dug itself in, and Socialism comes to be thought of as meaning concentration camps and secret police forces. Wilde's pamphlet and other kindred writings – "News from Nowhere," for instance – consequently have their value. They may demand the impossible, and they may – since a Utopia necessarily reflects the aesthetic ideas of its own period – sometimes seem "dated" and ridiculous; but they do at least look beyond the era of food queues and party squabbles, and remind the Socialist movement of its original, half-forgotten objective of human brotherhood.

George Gissing
May–June 1948?

In the shadow of the atomic bomb it is not easy to talk confidently about progress. However, if it can be assumed that we are *not* going to be blown to pieces in about ten years' time, there are many reasons, and George Gissing's novels are among them, for thinking that the present age is a good deal better than the last one. If Gissing were still alive he would be younger than Bernard Shaw, and yet already the London of which he wrote seems almost as distant as that of Dickens. It is the fog-bound, gas-lit London of the 'eighties, a city of drunken puritans, where clothes, architecture and furniture had reached their rock-bottom of ugliness, and where it was almost normal for a working-class family of ten persons to inhabit a single room. On the whole Gissing does not write of the worst depths of poverty, but one can hardly read his descriptions of lower-middle-class life, so obviously truthful in their dreariness, without feeling that we have improved perceptibly on that black-coated, money-ruled world of only sixty years ago.

Everything of Gissing's – except perhaps one or two books written towards the end of his life – contains memorable passages, and anyone who is making his acquaintance for the first time might do worse than start with *In the Year of the Jubilee*. It was rather a pity, however, to use up paper in reprinting two of his minor works when the books by which he ought to be remembered are and have been for years completely unprocurable. *The Odd Women*, for instance, is about as thoroughly out of print as a book can be. I possess a copy myself, in one of those nasty little red-covered cheap editions that flourished before the 1914 war, but that is the only copy I have ever seen or heard of. *New Grub Street*, Gissing's masterpiece, I have never succeeded in buying. When I have read it, it has been in soup-stained copies borrowed from public lending libraries: so also with *Demos*, *The Nether World* and one or two others. So far as I know, only *The Private Papers of Henry Ryecroft*, the book on Dickens, and *A Life's Morning*, have been in print at all recently. However, the two now reprinted are well worth reading, especially *In the Year of the Jubilee*, which is the more sordid and therefore the more characteristic.

In his introduction Mr William Plomer remarks that "generally speaking, Gissing's novels are about money and women," and Miss Myfanwy Evans says something very similar in introducing *The Whirlpool*. One might, I think, widen the definition and say that Gissing's novels are a protest against the form of self-torture that goes by the name of respectability. Gissing was a bookish, perhaps over-civilized man, in love with classical antiquity, who found himself trapped in a cold, smoky, Protestant country where it was impossible to be comfortable without a thick padding of money between yourself and the outer world. Behind his rage and querulousness there lay a perception that the horrors of life in late-Victorian England were largely unnecessary. The grime, the stupidity, the ugliness, the sex-starvation, the furtive debauchery, the vulgarity, the bad manners, the censoriousness – these things were unnecessary, since the puritanism of which they were a relic no longer upheld the structure of society. People who might, without becoming less efficient, have been reasonably happy chose instead to be miserable, inventing senseless tabus with which to terrify themselves. Money was a nuisance not merely because without it you starved; what was more important was that unless you had quite a lot of it – £300 a year, say – society would not allow you to live gracefully or even peacefully. Women were a nuisance because even more than men they were the believers in tabus, still enslaved to respectability even when they had offended against it. Money and women were therefore the two instruments through which society avenged itself on the courageous and the intelligent. Gissing would have liked a little more money for himself and some others, but he was not much interested in what we should now call social justice. He did not admire the working class as such, and he did not believe in democracy. He wanted to speak not for the multitude, but for the exceptional man, the sensitive man, isolated among barbarians.

In *The Odd Women* there is not a single major character whose life is not ruined either by having too little money, or by getting it too late in life, or by the pressure of social conventions which are obviously absurd but which cannot be questioned. An elderly spinster crowns a useless life by taking to drink; a young pretty girl marries a man old enough to be her father; a struggling schoolmaster puts off marrying his sweetheart until both of them are middle-aged and withered; a good-natured man is nagged to death by his wife; an exceptionally intelligent, spirited man misses his chance to make an adventurous marriage and relapses into futility: in each case the ultimate reason for the disaster lies in obeying the accepted social code, or in not having enough money to circumvent it. In *A Life's Morning* an honest and gifted man meets with ruin and death because it is impossible to walk about a big town with no hat on. His hat is blown out of the window when he is travelling in the train, and as he has not enough money to buy another, he misappropriates some money belonging to his employer, which sets going a series of disasters. This is an interesting example of the changes in outlook that can suddenly make an all-powerful tabu seem ridiculous. Today, if you had somehow contrived to lose your trousers, you would probably embezzle money rather than walk about in your under-pants. In the 'eighties the necessity would have seemed equally strong in the case of a hat. Even thirty or forty years ago, indeed, bareheaded men were booed at in the street. Then, for no very clear reason, hatlessness became respectable, and today the particular tragedy described by Gissing – entirely plausible in its context – would be quite impossible.

The most impressive of Gissing's books is *New Grub Street*. To a professional writer it is also an upsetting and demoralizing book, because it deals among other things with that much-dreaded occupational disease, sterility. No doubt the number of writers who suddenly lose the power to write is not large, but it is a calamity that *might* happen to anybody at any moment, like sexual impotence. Gissing, of course, links it up with his habitual themes – money, the pressure of the social code, and the stupidity of women.

Edwin Reardon, a young novelist – he has just deserted a clerkship after having a fluky success with a single novel – marries a charming and apparently intelligent young woman, with a small income of her own. Here, and in one or two other places, Gissing makes what now seems the curious remark that it is difficult for an educated man who is not rich to get married. Reardon brings it off, but his less successful friend, who lives in an attic and supports himself by ill-paid tutoring jobs, has to accept celibacy as a matter of course. If he did succeed in finding himself a wife, we are told, it could only be an unedu-cated girl from the slums. Women of refinement and sensibility will not face poverty. And here one notices again the deep difference between that day and our own. Doubtless Gissing is right in implying all through his books that intelligent women are very rare animals; and if one wants to marry a woman who is intelligent *and* pretty, then the choice is still further restricted, according to a well-known arithmetical rule. It is like being allowed to choose only among albinos, and left-handed albinos at that. But what comes out in Gissing's treatment of his odious heroine, and of certain others among his women, is that at that date the idea of delicacy, refinement, even intelligence, in the case of a woman, was hardly separable from the idea of superior social status and expensive physical surroundings. The sort of woman whom a writer would want to marry was also the sort of woman who would shrink from living in an attic. When Gissing wrote *New Grub Street* that was probably true, and it could, I think, be justly claimed that it is not true today.

Almost as soon as Reardon is married it becomes apparent that his wife is merely a silly snob, the kind of woman in whom "artistic tastes" are no more than a cover for social competitiveness. In marrying a novelist she has thought to marry someone who will rapidly become famous and shed reflected glory upon herself. Reardon is a studious, retiring, ineffectual man, a typical Gissing hero. He has been caught up into an expensive, pretentious world in which he knows he will never be able to maintain himself, and his nerve fails almost immediately. His wife, of course, has not the faintest understanding of what is meant by literary creation. There is a terrible passage – terrible, at least, to anyone who earns his living by writing – in which she calculates the number of pages that it would be possible to write in a day, and hence the number of novels that her husband may be expected to produce in a year – with the reflection that really it is not a very laborious profession. Meanwhile Reardon has been stricken dumb. Day after day he sits at his desk: nothing happens, nothing comes! Finally, in panic, he manufactures a piece of rubbish; his publisher, because Reardon's previous book had been successful, dubiously accepts it. Thereafter he is unable to produce anything that even looks as if it might be printable. He is finished.

The desolating thing is that if only he could get back to his clerkship and his bachelorhood, he would be all right. The hardboiled journalist who finally marries Reardon's widow sums him up accurately by saying that he is the kind of man who, if left to himself, would write a fairly good book every two years. But, of course, he is not left to himself. He cannot revert to his old profession, and he cannot simply settle down to live on his wife's money: public opinion, operating through his wife, harries him into impotence and finally into the grave. Most of the other literary characters in the book are not much more fortunate, and the troubles that beset them are still very much the same today. But at least it is unlikely that the book's central disaster would now happen in quite that way or for quite those reasons. The chances are that Reardon's wife would be less of a fool, and that he would have fewer scruples about walking out on her if she made life intolerable for him. A woman of rather similar type turns up in *The Whirlpool* in the person of Alma Frothingham. By contrast there are the three Miss Frenches in *In the Year of the Jubilee*, who represent the emerging lower-middle class – a class which, according to

Gissing, was getting hold of money and power which it was not fitted to use – and who are quite surprisingly coarse, rowdy, shrewish and unmoral. At first sight Gissing's "ladylike" and "unladylike" women seem to be very different and even opposite kinds of animal, and this seems to invalidate his implied condemnation of the female sex in general. The connecting link between them, however, is that all of them are miserably limited in outlook. Even the clever and spirited ones, like Rhoda in *The Odd Women* (an interesting early specimen of the New Woman), cannot think in terms of generalities, and cannot get away from ready-made standards. In his heart Gissing seems to feel that women are natural inferiors. He wants them to be better educated, but, on the other hand, he does not want them to have freedom, which they are certain to misuse. On the whole the best women in his books are the self-effacing, home-keeping ones.

It is very much to be hoped that a complete edition of Gissing's works will be published when paper becomes more plentiful. There are several of his books that I have never read, because I have never been able to get hold of them, and these unfortunately include *Born in Exile*, which is said by some people to be his best book. But merely on the strength of *New Grub Street*, *Demos* and *The Odd Women* I am ready to maintain that England has produced very few better novelists. This perhaps sounds like a rash statement until one stops to consider what is meant by a novel. The word "novel" is commonly used to cover almost any kind of story – *The Golden Asse*, *Anna Karenina*, *Don Quixote*, *The Improvisatore*, *Madame Bovary*, *King Solomon's Mines* or anything else you like – but it also has a narrower sense in which it means something hardly existing before the nineteenth century and flourishing chiefly in Russia and France. A novel, in this sense, is a story which attempts to describe credible human beings, and – without necessarily using the technique of naturalism – to show them acting on everyday motives and not merely undergoing strings of improbable adventures. A true novel, sticking to this definition, will also contain at least two characters, probably more, who are described from the inside and on the same level of probability – which, in effect, rules out novels written in the first person. If one accepts this definition, it becomes apparent that the novel is not an art-form in which England has excelled. The writers commonly paraded as "great English novelists" have a way of turning out either to be not true novelists, or not to be Englishmen. Gissing was not a writer of picaresque tales, or burlesques, or comedies, or political tracts: he was interested in individual human beings, and the fact that he can deal sympathetically with several different sets of motives, and make a credible story out of the collision between them, makes him exceptional among English writers.

Certainly there is not much of what is usually called beauty, not much lyricism, in the situations and characters that he chooses to imagine, and still less in the texture of his writing. His prose, indeed, is often disgusting. Here are a couple of samples:

> Not with impunity could her thought accustom itself to stray in regions forbidden, how firm soever her resolve to hold bodily aloof. (*The Whirlpool*).

> The ineptitude of uneducated English women in all that relates to their attire is a fact that it boots not to enlarge upon. (*In the Year of the Jubilee.*)

However, he does not commit the faults that really matter. It is always clear what he means, he never "writes for effect," he knows how to keep the balance between récit and dialogue and how to make dialogue sound probable while not contrasting too sharply with the prose that surrounds it. A much more serious fault than his inelegant manner of writing is the smallness of his range of experience. He is only acquainted with a few strata of society, and, in spite of his vivid understanding of the pressure of circumstance on character, does not seem to have much grasp of political or economic forces. In a mild way his outlook is reactionary, from lack of foresight rather than from ill-will. Having been obliged to live among them, he regarded the working class as savages, and in saying so he was merely being intellectually honest; he did not see that they were capable of becoming civilized if given slightly better opportunities. But, after all, what one demands from a novelist is not prophecy, and part of the charm of Gissing is that he belongs so unmistakeably to his own time, although his time treated him badly.

The English writer nearest to Gissing always seems to me to be his contemporary, or near-contemporary, Mark Rutherford. If one simply tabulates their outstanding qualities, the two men appear to be very different. Mark Rutherford was a less prolific writer than Gissing, he was less definitely a novelist, he wrote much better prose, his books belong less recognizably to any particular time, and he was in outlook a social reformer and, above all, a puritan. Yet there is a sort of haunting resemblance, probably explained by the fact that both men lack that curse of English writers, a "sense of humour." A certain low-spiritedness, an air of loneliness, is common to both of them. There are, of course, funny passages in Gissing's books, but he is not chiefly concerned with getting a laugh – above all, he has no impulse towards burlesque. He treats all his major characters more or less seriously, and with at least an attempt at sympathy. Any novel will inevitably contain minor characters who are mere grotesques or who are observed in a purely hostile spirit, but there is such a thing as impartiality, and Gissing is more capable of it than the great majority of English writers. It is a point in his favour that he had no very strong moral purpose. He had, of course, a deep loathing of the ugliness, emptiness and cruelty of the society he lived in, but he was concerned to describe it rather than to change it. There is usually no one in his books who can be pointed to as the villain, and even when there is a villain he is not punished. In his treatment of sexual matters Gissing is surprisingly frank, considering the time at which he was writing. It is not that he writes pornography or expresses approval of sexual promiscuity, but simply that he is willing to face the facts. The unwritten law of English fiction, the law that the hero as well as the heroine of a novel should be virgin when married, is disregarded in his books, almost for the first time since Fielding.

Like most English writers subsequent to the mid-nineteenth century, Gissing could not imagine any desirable destiny other than being a writer or a gentleman of leisure. The dichotomy between the intellectual and the lowbrow already existed, and a person capable of writing a serious novel could no longer picture himself as fully satisfied with the life of a businessman, or a soldier, or a politician, or what-not. Gissing did not, at least consciously, even want to be the kind of writer that he was. His ideal, a rather melancholy one, was to have a moderate private income and live in a small comfortable house in the country, preferably unmarried, where he could wallow in books, especially the Greek and Latin classics. He might perhaps have realized this ideal if he had not managed to get himself into prison immediately after winning an Oxford scholarship: as it was he spent his life in what appeared to him to be hackwork, and when he had at last reached the point where he could stop writing against the clock, he died almost immediately, aged only about forty-five. His death, described by H. G. Wells in his *Experiment in Autobiography*, was of a piece with his life. The twenty novels, or thereabouts, that he produced between 1880 and 1900 were, so to speak, sweated out of him during his struggle towards a leisure which he never enjoyed and which he might not have used to good advantage if he had had it: for it is difficult to believe that his temperament really fitted him for a life of scholarly research. Perhaps the natural pull of his gifts would in any case have drawn him towards novel-writing sooner or later. If not, we must be thankful for the piece of youthful folly which turned him aside from a comfortable middle-class career and forced him to become the chronicler of vulgarity, squalor and failure.

Such, Such Were the Joys
1939?–June 1948?

Soon after I arrived at St Cyprian's (not immediately, but after a week or two, just when I seemed to be settling into the routine of school life) I began wetting my bed. I was now aged eight, so that this was a reversion to a habit which I must have grown out of at least four years earlier.

Nowadays, I believe, bed-wetting in such circumstances is taken for granted. It is a normal reaction in children who have been removed from their homes to a strange place. In those days, however, it was looked on as a disgusting crime which the child committed on purpose and for which the proper cure was a beating. For my part I did not need to be told it was a crime. Night after night I prayed, with a fervour never previously attained in my prayers, "Please God, do not let me wet my bed! Oh, please God, do not let me wet my bed!", but it made remarkably little difference. Some nights the thing happened, others not. There was no volition about it, no consciousness. You did not properly speaking *do* the deed: you merely woke up in the morning and found that the sheets were wringing wet.

After the second or third offence I was warned that I should be beaten next time, but I received the warning in a curiously roundabout way. One afternoon, as we were filing out from tea, Mrs Wilkes, the headmaster's wife, was sitting at the head of one of the tables, chatting with a lady of whom I know nothing, except that she was on an afternoon's visit to the school. She was an intimidating, masculine-looking person wearing a riding habit, or something that I took to be a riding habit. I was just leaving the room when Mrs Wilkes called me back, as though to introduce me to the visitor.

Mrs Wilkes was nicknamed Flip, and I shall call her by that name, for I seldom think of her by any other. (Officially, however, she was addressed as Mum, probably a corruption of the "Ma'am" used by public schoolboys to their housemasters' wives.) She was a stocky square-built woman with hard red cheeks, a flat top to her head, prominent brows and deepset, suspicious eyes. Although a great deal of the time she was full of false heartiness, jollying one along with mannish slang ("*Buck* up, old chap!" and so forth), and even using one's Christian name, her eyes never lost their anxious, accusing look. It was very difficult to look her in the face without feeling guilty, even at moments when one was not guilty of anything in particular.

"Here is a little boy," said Flip, indicating me to the strange lady, "who wets his bed every night. Do you know what I am going to do if you wet your bed again?" she added, turning to me. "I am going to get the Sixth Form to beat you."

The strange lady put on an air of being inexpressibly shocked, and exclaimed "I-should-*think*-so!" And here there occurred one of those wild, almost lunatic misunderstandings which are part of the daily experience of childhood. The Sixth Form was a group of older boys who were selected as having "character" and were empowered to beat smaller boys. I had not yet learned of their existence, and I mis-heard the phrase "the Sixth Form" as "Mrs Form". I took it as referring to the strange lady – I thought, that is, that her name was Mrs Form. It was an improbable name, but a child has no judgement in such matters. I imagined, therefore, that it was *she* who was to be deputed to beat me. It did not strike me as strange that this job should be turned over to a casual visitor in no way connected with the school. I merely assumed that "Mrs Form" was a stern disciplinarian who enjoyed beating people (somehow her appearance seemed to bear this out) and I had an immediate terrifying vision of her arriving for the occasion in full riding kit and armed with a hunting whip. To this day I can feel myself almost swooning with shame as I stood, a very small, round-faced boy in short corduroy knickers, before the two women. I could not speak. I felt that I should die if "Mrs Form" were to beat me. But my dominant feeling was not fear or even resentment: it was simply shame because one more person, and that a woman, had been told of my disgusting offence.

A little later, I forget how, I learned that it was not after all "Mrs Form" who would do the beating. I cannot remember whether it was that very night that I wetted my bed again, but at any rate I did wet it again quite soon, Oh, the despair, the feeling of cruel injustice, after all my prayers and resolutions, at once again waking between the clammy sheets! There was no chance of hiding what I had done. The grim statuesque matron, Margaret by name, arrived in the dormitory specially to inspect my bed. She pulled back the clothes, then drew herself up, and the dreaded words seemed to come rolling out of her like a peal of thunder:

"REPORT YOURSELF TO the headmaster after breakfast!"

I put REPORT YOURSELF in capitals because that was how it appeared in my mind. I do not know how many times I heard that phrase during my early years at St Cyprian's. It was only very rarely that it did not mean a beating. The words always had a portentous sound in my ears, like muffled drums or the words of the death sentence.

When I arrived to report myself, Flip was doing something or other at the long shiny table in the ante-room to the study. Her uneasy eyes searched me as I went past. In the study Mr Wilkes, nicknamed Sambo, was waiting. Sambo was a round-shouldered, curiously oafish-looking man, not large but shambling in gait, with a chubby face which was like that of an overgrown baby, and which was capable of good-humour. He knew, of course, why I had been sent to him, and had already taken a bone-handled riding crop out of the cupboard, but it was part of the punishment of reporting yourself that you had to proclaim your offence with your own lips. When I had said my say, he read me a short but pompous lecture, then seized me by the scruff of the neck, twisted me over and began beating me with the riding crop. He had a habit of continuing his lecture while he flogged you, and I remember the words "you dir-ty lit-tle boy" keeping time with the blows. The beating did not hurt (perhaps, as it was the first time, he was not hitting me very hard), and I walked out feeling very much better. The fact that the beating had not hurt was a sort of victory and partially wiped out the shame of the bed-wetting. Perhaps I was even incautious enough to wear a grin on my face. Some small boys were hanging about in the passage outside the door of the ante-room.

"D'you get the cane?"

"It didn't hurt," I said proudly.

Flip had heard everything. Instantly her voice came screaming after me:

"Come here! Come here this instant! What was that you said?'

"I said it didn't hurt," I faltered out.

"How dare you say a thing like that? Do you think that is a proper thing to say? Go in and REPORT YOURSELF AGAIN!"

This time Sambo laid on in real earnest. He continued for a length of time that frightened and astonished me – about five minutes, it seemed – ending up by breaking the riding crop. The bone handle went flying across the room.

"Look what you've made me do!" he said furiously, holding up the broken crop.

I had fallen into a chair, weakly snivelling. I remember that this was the only time throughout my boyhood when a beating actually reduced me to tears, and curiously enough I was not even now crying because of the pain. The second beating had not hurt very much either. Fright and shame seemed to have anaesthetised me. I was crying partly because I felt that this was expected of me, partly from genuine repentance, but partly also because of a deeper grief which is peculiar to childhood and not easy to convey: a sense of desolate loneliness and helplessness, of being locked up not only in a hostile world but in a world of good and evil where the rules were such that it was actually not possible for me to keep them.

I knew that the bed-wetting was (a) wicked and (b) outside my control. The second fact I was personally aware of, and the first I did not question. It was possible, therefore, to commit a sin without knowing that you committed it, without wanting to commit it, and without being able to avoid it. Sin was not necessarily something that you did: it might be something that happened to you. I do not want to claim that this idea flashed into my mind as a complete novelty at this very moment, under the blows of Sambo's cane: I must have had glimpses of it even before I left home, for my early childhood had not been altogether happy. But at any rate this was the great, abiding lesson of my boyhood: that I was in a world where it was *not possible* for me to be good. And the double beating was a turning-point, for it brought home to me for the first time the harshness of the environment into which I had been flung. Life was more terrible, and I was more wicked, than I had imagined. At any rate, as I sat snivelling on the edge of a chair in Sambo's study, with not even the self-possession to stand up while he stormed at me, I had a conviction of sin and folly and weakness, such as I do not remember to have felt before.

In general, one's memories of any period must necessarily weaken as one moves away from it. One is constantly learning new facts, and old ones have to drop out to make way for them. At twenty I could have written the history of my schooldays with an accuracy which would be quite impossible now. But it can also happen that one's memories grow sharper after a long lapse of time, because one is looking at the past with fresh eyes and can isolate and, as it were, notice facts which previously existed undifferentiated among a mass of others. Here are two things which in a sense I remembered, but which did not strike me as strange or interesting until quite recently. One is that the second beating seemed to me a just and reasonable punishment. To get one beating, and then to get another and far fiercer one on top of it, for being so unwise as to show that the first had not hurt – that was quite natural. The gods are jealous, and when you have good fortune you should conceal it. The other is that I accepted the broken riding crop as my own crime. I can still recall my feeling as I saw the handle lying on the carpet – the feeling of having done an ill-bred clumsy thing, and ruined an expensive object. *I* had broken it: so Sambo told me, and so I believed. This acceptance of guilt lay unnoticed in my memory for twenty or thirty years.

So much for the episode of the bed-wetting. But there is one more thing to be remarked. This is that I did not wet my bed again – at least, I did wet it once again, and received another beating, after which the trouble stopped. So perhaps this barbarous remedy does work, though at a heavy price, I have no doubt.

ii.

St Cyprian's was an expensive and snobbish school which was in process of becoming more snobbish, and, I imagine, more expensive. The public school with which it had special connections was Harrow, but during my time an increasing proportion of the boys went on to Eton. Most of them were the children of rich parents, but on the whole they were the unaristocratic rich, the sort of people who live in huge shrubberied houses in Bournemouth or Richmond, and who have cars and butlers but not country estates. There were a few exotics among them – some South American boys, sons of Argentine beef barons, one or two Russians, and even a Siamese prince, or someone who was described as a prince.

Sambo had two great ambitions. One was to attract titled boys to the school, and the other was to train up pupils to win scholarships at public schools, above all at Eton. He did, towards the end of my time, succeed in getting hold of two boys with real English titles. One of them, I remember, was a wretched, drivelling little creature, almost an albino, peering upwards out of weak eyes, with a long nose at the end of which a dewdrop always seemed to be trembling. Sambo always gave these boys their titles when mentioning them to a third person, and for their first few days he actually addressed them to their faces as "Lord So-and-so". Needless to say he found ways of drawing attention to them when any visitor was being shown round the school. Once, I remember, the little fair-haired boy had a choking fit at dinner, and a stream of snot ran out of his nose on to his plate in a way horrible to see. Any lesser person would have been called a dirty little beast and ordered out of the room instantly: but Sambo and Flip laughed it off in a "boys will be boys" spirit.

All the very rich boys were more or less undisguisedly favoured. The school still had a faint suggestion of the Victorian "private academy" with its "parlour boarders", and when I later read about that kind of school in Thackeray I immediately saw the resemblance. The rich boys had milk and biscuits in the middle of the morning, they were given riding lessons once or twice a week, Flip mothered them and called them by their Christian names, and above all they were never caned. Apart from the South Americans, whose parents were safely distant, I doubt whether Sambo ever caned any boy whose father's income was much above £2,000 a year. But he was sometimes willing to sacrifice financial profit to scholastic prestige. Occasionally, by special arrangement, he would take at greatly reduced fees some boy who seemed likely to win scholarships and thus bring credit on the school. It was on these terms that I was at St Cyprian's myself: otherwise my parents could not have afforded to send me to so expensive a school.

I did not at first understand that I was being taken at reduced fees; it was only when I was about eleven that Flip and Sambo began throwing the fact in my teeth. For my first two or three years I went through the ordinary educational mill: then, soon after I had started Greek (one started Latin at eight, Greek at ten), I moved into the scholarship class, which was taught, so far as classics went, largely by Sambo himself. Over a period of two or three years the scholarship boys were crammed with learning as cynically as a goose is crammed for Christmas. And with what learning! This business of making a gifted boy's career depend on a competitive examination, taken when he is only twelve or thirteen, is an evil thing at best, but there do appear to be preparatory schools which send scholars to Eton, Winchester, etc. without teaching them to see everything in terms of marks. At St Cyprian's the whole process was frankly a preparation for a sort of confidence trick. Your job was to learn exactly those things that would give an examiner the impression that you knew more than you did know, and as far as possible to avoid burdening your brain with anything else. Subjects which lacked examination-value, such as geography, were almost completely neglected, mathematics was also neglected if you were a "classical", science was not taught in any form – indeed it was so despised that even an interest in natural history was discouraged – and even the books you were encouraged to read in your spare time were chosen with one eye on the "English paper". Latin and Greek, the main scholarship subjects, were what counted, but even these were deliberately taught in a flashy, unsound way. We never, for example, read right through even a single book of a Greek or Latin author: we merely read short passages which were picked out because they were the kind of thing likely to be set as an "unseen translation". During the last year or so before we went up for our scholarships, most of our time was spent in simply working our way through the scholarship papers of previous years. Sambo had sheaves of these in his possession from every one of the major public schools. But the greatest outrage of all was the teaching of history.

There was in those days a piece of nonsense called the Harrow History Prize, an annual competition for which many preparatory schools entered. It was a tradition for St Cyprian's to win it every year, as well we might, for we had mugged up every paper that had been set since the competition started, and the supply of possible questions was not inexhaustible. They were the kind of stupid question that is answered by rapping out a name or a quotation. Who plundered the Begums? Who was beheaded in an open boat? Who caught the Whigs bathing and ran away with their clothes? Almost all our historical teaching was on this level. History was a series of unrelated, unintelligible but — in some way that was never explained to us — important facts with resounding phrases tied to them. Disraeli brought peace with honour. Hastings was astonished at his moderation. Pitt called in the New World to redress the balance of the Old. And the dates, and the mnemonic devices! (Did you know, for example, that the initial letters of "A black Negress was my aunt: there's her house behind the barn" are also the initial letters of the battles in the Wars of the Roses?) Flip, who "took" the higher forms in history, revelled in this kind of thing. I recall positive orgies of dates, with the keener boys leaping up and down in their places in their eagerness to shout out the right answers, and at the same time not feeling the faintest interest in the meaning of the mysterious events they were naming.

"1587?"

"Massacre of St Bartholomew!"

"1707?"

"Death of Aurangzeeb!"

"1713?"

"Treaty of Utrecht!"

"1773?"

"Boston Tea Party!"

"1520?"

"Oo, Mum, please, Mum –"

"Please, Mum, please, Mum! Let me tell him, Mum!"

"Well! 1520?"

"Field of the Cloth of Gold!"

And so on.

But history and such secondary subjects were not bad fun. It was in "classics" that the real strain came. Looking back, I realise that I then worked harder than I have ever done since, and yet at the time it never seemed possible to make quite the effort that was demanded of one. We would sit round the long shiny table, made of some very pale-coloured, hard wood, with Sambo goading, threatening, exhorting, sometimes joking, very occasionally praising, but always prodding, prodding away at one's mind to keep it up to the right pitch of concentration, as one might keep a sleepy person awake by sticking pins into him.

"Go on, you little slacker! Go on, you idle, worthless little boy! The whole trouble with you is that you're bone and horn idle. You eat too much, that's why. You wolf down enormous meals, and then when you come here you're half asleep. Go on, now, put your back into it. You're not *thinking*. Your brain doesn't sweat."

He would tap away at one's skull with his silver pencil, which, in my memory, seems to have been about the size of a banana, and which certainly was heavy enough to raise a bump: or he would pull the short hairs round one's ears, or, occasionally, reach out under the table and kick one's shin. On some days nothing seemed to go right, and then it would be: "All right, then, I know what you want. You've been asking for it the whole morning. Come along, you useless little slacker. Come into the study." And then whack, whack, whack, whack, and back one would come, red-wealed and smarting – in later years Sambo had abandoned his riding crop in favour of a thin rattan cane which hurt very much more – to settle down to work again. This did not happen very often, but I do remember, more than once, being led out of the room in the middle of a Latin sentence, receiving a beating and then going straight ahead with the same sentence, just like that. It is a mistake to think such methods do not work. They work very well for their special purpose. Indeed, I doubt whether classical education ever has been or can be successfully carried on without corporal punishment. The boys themselves believed in its efficacy. There was a boy named Hardcastle, with no brains to speak of, but evidently in acute need of a scholarship. Sambo was flogging him towards the goal as one might do with a foundered horse. He went up for a scholarship at Uppingham, came back with a consciousness of having done badly, and a day or two later received a severe beating for idleness. "I wish I'd had that caning before I went up for the exam," he said sadly – a remark which I felt to be contemptible, but which I perfectly well understood.

The boys of the scholarship class were not all treated alike. If a boy were the son of rich parents to whom the saving of fees was not all-important, Sambo would goad him along in a comparatively fatherly way, with jokes and digs in the ribs and perhaps an occasional tap with the pencil, but no hair-pulling and no caning. It was the poor but "clever" boys who suffered. Our brains were a gold-mine in which he had sunk money, and the dividends must be squeezed out of us. Long before I had grasped the nature of my financial relationship with Sambo, I had been made to understand that I was not on the same footing as most of the other boys. In effect there were three castes in the school. There was the minority with an aristocratic or millionaire background, there were the children of the ordinary suburban rich, who made up the bulk of the school, and there were a few underlings like myself, the sons of clergymen, Indian civil servants, struggling widows and the like. These poorer ones were discouraged from going in for "extras" such as shooting and carpentery, and were humiliated over clothes and petty possessions. I never, for instance, succeeded in getting a cricket bat of my own, because "Your parents wouldn't be able to afford it." This phrase pursued me throughout my schooldays. At St Cyprian's we were not allowed to keep the money we brought back with us, but had to "give it in" on the first day of term, and then from time to time were allowed to spend it under supervision. I and similarly-placed boys were always choked off from buying expensive toys like model aeroplanes, even if the necessary money stood to our credit. Flip, in particular, seemed to aim consciously at inculcating a humble outlook in the poorer boys. "Do you think that's the sort of thing a boy like you should buy?" I remember her saying to somebody – and she said this in front of the whole school; "You know you're not going to grow up with money, don't you? Your people aren't rich. You must learn to be sensible. Don't get above yourself!" There was also the weekly pocket-money, which we took out in sweets, dispersed by Flip from a large table. The millionaires had sixpence a week, but the normal sum was threepence. I and one or two others were only allowed twopence. My parents had not given instructions to this effect, and the saving of a penny a week could not conceivably have made any difference to them: it was a mark of status. Worse yet was the detail of the birthday cakes. It was usual for each boy, on his birthday, to have a large iced cake with candles, which was shared out at tea between the whole school. It was provided as a matter of routine and went on his parents' bill. I never had such a cake, though my parents would have paid for it readily enough. Year after year, never daring to ask, I would miserably hope that this year a cake would appear. Once or twice I even rashly pretended to my companions that this time I *was* going to have a cake. Then came teatime, and no cake, which did not make me more popular.

Very early it was impressed upon me that I had no chance of a decent future unless I won a scholarship at a public school. Either I won my scholarship, or I must leave school at fourteen and become, in Sambo's favourite phrase "a little office boy at forty pounds a year". In my circumstances it was natural that I should believe this. Indeed, it was universally taken for granted at St Cyprian's that unless you went to a "good" public school (and only about fifteen schools came under this heading) you were ruined for life. It is not easy to convey to a grown-up person the sense of strain, of nerving oneself for some terrible, all-deciding combat, as the date of the examination crept nearer – eleven years old, twelve years old, then thirteen, the fatal year itself! Over a period of about two years, I do not think there was ever a day when "the exam", as I called it, was quite out of my waking thoughts. In my prayers it figured invariably: and whenever I got the bigger portion of a wishbone, or picked up a horse-shoe, or bowed seven times to the new moon, or succeeded in passing through a wishing-gate without touching the sides, then the wish I earned by doing so went on "the exam" as a matter of course. And yet curiously enough I was also tormented by an almost irresistible impulse *not* to work. There were days when my heart sickened at the labours ahead of me, and I stood stupid as an animal before the most elementary difficulties. In the holidays, also, I could not work. Some of the scholarship boys received extra tuition from a certain Mr Knowles, a likeable, very hairy man who wore shaggy suits and lived in a typical bachelor's "den" – booklined walls, over-whelming stench of tobacco – somewhere in the town. During the holidays Mr Knowles used to send us extracts from Latin authors to translate, and we were supposed to send back a wad of work once a week. Somehow I could not do it. The empty paper and the black Latin dictionary lying on the table, the consciousness of a plain duty shirked, poisoned my leisure, but somehow I could not start, and by the end of the holidays I would only have sent Mr Knowles fifty or a hundred lines. Undoubtedly part of the reason was that Sambo and his cane were far away. But in term-time, also, I would go through periods of idleness and stupidity when I would sink deeper and deeper into disgrace and even achieve a sort of feeble, snivelling defiance, fully conscious of my guilt and yet unable or unwilling – I could not be sure which – to do any better. Then Sambo or Flip would send for me, and this time it would not even be a caning.

Flip would search me with her baleful eyes. (What colour were those eyes, I wonder? I remember them as green, but actually no human being has green eyes. Perhaps they were hazel.) She would start off in her peculiar, wheedling, bullying style, which never failed to get right through one's guard and score a hit on one's better nature.

"I don't think it's awfully decent of you to behave like this, is it? Do you think it's quite playing the game by your mother and father to go on idling your time away, week after week, month after month? Do you *want* to throw all your chances away? You know your people aren't rich, don't you? You know they can't afford the same things as other boys' parents. How are they to send you to a public school if you don't win a scholarship? I know how proud your mother is of you. Do you *want* to let her down?"

"I don't think he wants to go to a public school any longer," Sambo would say, addressing himself to Flip with a pretence that I was not there. "I think he's given up that idea. He wants to be a little office boy at forty pounds a year."

The horrible sensation of tears – a swelling in the breast, a tickling behind the nose – would already have assailed me. Flip would bring out her ace of trumps:

"And do you think it's quite fair to *us*, the way you're behaving? After all we've done for you? You *do* know what we've done for you, don't you?" Her eyes would pierce deep into me, and though she never said it straight out, I did know. "We've had you here all these years – we even had you here for a week in the holidays so that Mr Knowles could coach you. We don't *want* to have to send you away, you know, but we can't keep a boy here just to eat up our food, term after term. *I* don't think it's very straight, the way you're behaving. Do you?'

I never had any answer except a miserable "No, Mum," or "Yes, Mum," as the case might be. Evidently it was *not* straight, the way I was behaving. And at some point or other the unwanted tear would always force its way out of the corner of my eye, roll down my nose, and splash.

Flip never said in plain words that I was a non-paying pupil, no doubt because vague phrases like "all we've done for you" had a deeper emotional appeal. Sambo, who did not aspire to be loved by his pupils, put it more brutally, though, as was usual with him, in pompous language. "You are living on my bounty" was his favourite phrase in this context. At least once I listened to these words between blows of the cane. I must say that these scenes were not frequent, and except on one occasion they did not take place in the presence of other boys. In public I was reminded that I was poor and that my parents "wouldn't be able to afford" this or that, but I was not actually reminded of my dependent position. It was a final unanswerable argument, to be brought forth like an instrument of torture when my work became exceptionally bad.

To grasp the effect of this kind of thing on a child of ten or twelve, one has to remember that the child has little sense of proportion or probability. A child may be a mass of egoism and rebelliousness, but it has no accumulated experience to give it confidence in its own judgements. On the whole it will accept what it is told, and it will believe in the most fantastic way in the knowledge and powers of the adults surrounding it. Here is an example.

I have said that at St Cyprian's we were not allowed to keep our own money. However, it was possible to hold back a shilling or two, and sometimes I used furtively to buy sweets which I kept hidden in the loose ivy on the playing-field wall. One day when I had been sent on an errand I went into a sweetshop a mile or more from the school and bought some chocolates. As I came out of the shop I saw on the opposite pavement a small sharp-faced man who seemed to be staring very hard at my school cap. Instantly a horrible fear went through me. There could be no doubt as to who the man was. He was a spy placed there by Sambo! I turned away unconcernedly, and then, as though my legs were doing it of their own accord, broke into a clumsy run. But when I got round the next corner I forced myself to walk again, for to run was a sign of guilt, and obviously there would be other spies posted here and there about the town. All that day and the next I waited for the summons to the study, and was surprised when it did not come. It did not seem to me strange that the headmaster of a private school should dispose of an army of informers, and I did not even imagine that he would have to pay them. I assumed that any adult, inside the school or outside, would collaborate voluntarily in preventing us from breaking the rules. Sambo was all-powerful, and it was natural that his agents should be everywhere. When this episode happened I do not think I can have been less than twelve years old.

I hated Sambo and Flip, with a sort of shamefaced, remorseful hatred, but it did not occur to me to doubt their judgement. When they told me that I must either win a public-school scholarship or become an office boy at fourteen, I believed that those were the unavoidable alternatives before me. And above all, I believed Sambo and Flip when they told me they were my benefactors. I see now, of course, that from Sambo's point of view I was a good speculation. He sank money in me, and he looked to get it back in the form of prestige. If I had "gone off", as promising boys sometimes do, I imagine that he would have got rid of me swiftly. As it was I won him two scholarships when the time came, and no doubt he made full use of them in his prospectuses. But it is difficult for a child to realise that a school is primarily a commercial venture. A child believes that the school exists to educate and that the schoolmaster disciplines him either for his own good, or from a love of bullying. Flip and Sambo had chosen to befriend me, and their friendship included canings, reproaches and humiliations, which were good for me and saved me from an office stool. That was their version, and I believed in it. It was therefore clear that I owed them a vast debt of gratitude. But I was *not* grateful, as I very well knew. On the contrary, I hated both of them. I could not control my subjective feelings, and I could not conceal them from myself. But it is wicked, is it not, to hate your benefactors? So I was taught, and so I believed. A child accepts the codes of behaviour that are presented to it, even when it breaks them. From the age of eight, or even earlier, the consciousness of sin was never far away from me. If I contrived to seem callous and defiant, it was only a thin cover over a mass of shame and dismay. All through my boyhood I had a profound conviction that I was no good, that I was wasting my time, wrecking my talents, behaving with monstrous folly and wickedness and ingratitude – and all this, it seemed, was inescapable, because I lived among laws which were absolute, like the law of gravity, but which it was not possible for me to keep.

iii.

No one can look back on his schooldays and say with truth that they were altogether unhappy.

I have good memories of St Cyprian's, among a horde of bad ones. Sometimes on summer afternoons there were wonderful expeditions across the Downs to a village called Birling Gap, or to Beachy Head, where one bathed dangerously among the chalk boulders and came home covered with cuts. And there were still more wonderful midsummer evenings when, as a special treat, we were not driven off to bed as usual but allowed to wander about the grounds in the long twilight, ending up with a plunge into the swimming bath at about nine o'clock. There was the joy of waking early on summer mornings and getting in an hour's undisturbed reading (Ian Hay, Thackeray, Kipling and H. G. Wells were the favourite authors of my boyhood) in the sunlit, sleeping dormitory. There was also cricket, which I was no good at but with which I conducted a sort of hopeless love affair up to the age of about eighteen. And there was the pleasure of keeping caterpillars – the silky green and purple puss-moth, the ghostly green poplar-hawk, the privet hawk, large as one's third finger, specimens of which could be illicitly purchased for sixpence at a shop in the town – and, when one could escape long enough from the master who was "taking the walk", there was the excitement of dredging the dew-ponds on the Downs for enormous newts with orange-coloured bellies. This business of being out for a walk, coming across something of fascinating interest and then being dragged away from it by a yell from the master, like a dog jerked onwards by the leash, is an important feature of school life, and helps to build up the conviction, so strong in many children, that the things you most want to do are always unattainable.

Very occasionally, perhaps once during each summer, it was possible to escape altogether from the barrack-like atmosphere of school, when Siller, the second master, was permitted to take one or two boys for an afternoon of butterfly hunting on a common a few miles away. Siller was a man with white hair and a red face like a strawberry, who was good at natural history, making models and plaster casts, operating magic lanterns, and things of that kind. He and Mr Knowles were the only adults in any way connected with the school whom I did not either dislike or fear. Once he took me into his room and showed me in confidence a plated, pearl-handled revolver – his "six-shooter", he called it – which he kept in a box under his bed. And oh, the joy of those occasional expeditions! The ride of two or three miles on a lonely little branch line, the afternoon of charging to and fro with large green nets, the beauty of the enormous dragon flies which hovered over the tops of the grasses, the sinister killing-bottle with its sickly smell, and then tea in the parlour of a pub with large slices of pale-coloured cake! The essence of it was in the railway journey, which seemed to put magic distances between yourself and school.

Flip, characteristically, disapproved of these expeditions, though not actually forbidding them. "And have you been catching *little butterflies*?" she would say with a vicious sneer when one got back, making her voice as babyish as possible. From her point of view, natural history ("bug-hunting" she would probably have called it) was a babyish pursuit which a boy should be laughed out of as early as possible. Moreover it was somehow faintly plebeian, it was traditionally associated with boys who wore spectacles and were no good at games, it did not help you to pass exams, and above all it smelt of science and therefore seemed to menace classical education. It needed a considerable moral effort to accept Siller's invitation. How I dreaded that sneer of *little butterflies*! Siller, however, who had been at the school since its early days, had built up a certain independence for himself: he seemed able to handle Sambo, and ignored Flip a good deal. If it ever happened that both of them were away, Siller acted as deputy headmaster, and on those occasions, instead of reading the appointed lesson for the day at morning chapel, he would read us stories from the Apocrypha.

Most of the good memories of my childhood, and up to the age of about twenty, are in some way connected with animals. So far as St Cyprian's goes, it also seems, when I look back, that all my good memories are of summer. In winter your nose ran continually, your fingers were too numb to button your shirt (this was an especial misery on Sundays, when we wore Eton collars), and there was the daily nightmare of football – the cold, the mud, the hideous greasy ball that came whizzing at one's face, the gouging knees and trampling boots of the bigger boys. Part of the trouble was that in winter, after the age of about ten, I was seldom in good health, at any rate during term time. I had defective bronchial tubes and a lesion in one lung which was not discovered till many years later. Hence I not only had a chronic cough, but running was a torment to me. In those days however, "wheeziness", or "chestiness", as it was called, was either diagnosed as imagination or was looked on as essentially a moral disorder, caused by over-eating. "You wheeze like a concertina," Sambo would say disapprovingly as he stood behind my chair; "You're perpetually stuffing yourself with food, that's why." My cough was referred to as a "stomach cough", which made it sound both disgusting and reprehensible. The cure for it was hard running, which, if you kept it up long enough, ultimately "cleared your chest".

It is curious, the degree – I will not say of actual hardship, but of squalor and neglect, that was taken for granted in upper-class schools of that period. Almost as in the days of Thackeray, it seemed natural that a little boy of eight or ten should be a miserable, snotty-nosed creature, his face almost permanently dirty, his hands chapped, his nails bitten, his handkerchief a sodden horror, his bottom frequently blue with bruises. It was partly the prospect of actual physical discomfort that made the thought of going back to school lie in one's breast like a lump of lead during the last few days of the holidays.

A characteristic memory of St Cyprian's is the astonishing hardness of one's bed on the first night of term. Since this was an expensive school, I took a social step upwards by attending it, and yet the standard of comfort was in every way far lower than in my own home, or, indeed, than it would have been in a prosperous working-class home. One only had a hot bath once a week, for instance. The food was not only bad, it was also insufficient. Never before or since have I seen butter or jam scraped on bread so thinly. I do not think I can be imagining the fact that we were under-fed, when I remember the lengths we would go in order to steal food. On a number of occasions I remember creeping down at two or three o'clock in the morning through what seemed like miles of pitch-dark stair-ways and passages – barefooted, stopping to listen after each step, paralysed with about equal fear of Sambo, ghosts and burglars – to steal stale bread from the pantry. The assistant masters had their meals with us, but they had somewhat better food, and if one got half a chance it was usual to steal left-over scraps of bacon rind or fried potato when their plates were removed.

As usual, I did not see the sound commercial reason for this under-feeding. On the whole I accepted Sambo's view that a boy's appetite is a sort of morbid growth which should be kept in check as much as possible. A maxim often repeated to us at St Cyprian's was that it is healthy to get up from a meal feeling as hungry as when you sat down. Only a generation earlier than this it had been common for school dinners to start off with a slab of unsweetened suet pudding, which, it was frankly said, "broke the boys' appetites". But the under-feeding was probably less flagrant at preparatory schools, where a boy was wholly dependent on the official diet, than at public schools, where he was allowed – indeed, expected – to buy extra food for himself. At some schools, he would literally not have had enough to eat unless he had bought regular supplies of eggs, sausages, sardines, etc.; and his parents had to allow him money for this purpose. At Eton, for instance, at any rate in College, a boy was given no solid meal after mid-day dinner. For his afternon tea he was given only tea and bread and butter, and at eight o'clock he was given a miserable supper of soup or fried fish, or more often bread and cheese, with water to drink. Sambo went down to see his eldest son at Eton and came back in snobbish ecstasies over the luxury in which the boys lived. "They give them fried fish for supper!" he exclaimed, beaming all over his chubby face. "There's no school like it in the world." Fried fish! The habitual supper of the poorest of the working class! At very cheap boarding-schools it was no doubt worse. A very early memory of mine is of seeing the boarders at a grammar school – the sons, probably, of farmers and shopkeepers – being fed on boiled lights.

Whoever writes about his childhood must beware of exaggeration and self-pity. I do not want to claim that I was a martyr or that St Cyprian's was a sort of Dotheboys Hall. But I should be falsifying my own memories if I did not record that they are largely memories of disgust. The overcrowded, under-fed, under-washed life that we led *was* disgusting, as I recall it. If I shut my eyes and say "school", it is of course the physical surroundings that first come back to me: the flat playing-field with its cricket pavilion and the little shed by the rifle range, the draughty dormitories, the dusty splintery passages, the square of asphalt in front of the gymnasium, the raw-looking pinewood chapel at the back. And at almost every point some filthy detail obtrudes itself. For example, there were the pewter bowls out of which we had our porridge. They had overhanging rims, and under the rims there were accumulations of sour porridge, which could be flaked off in long strips. The porridge itself, too, contained more lumps, hair and unexplained black things than one would have thought possible, unless someone were putting them there on purpose. It was never safe to start on that porridge without investigating it first. And there was the slimy water of the plunge bath – it was twelve or fifteen feet long, the whole school was supposed to go into it every morning, and I doubt whether the water was changed at all frequently – and the always-damp towels with their cheesy smell; and, on occasional visits in the winter, the murky sea-water of the Devonshire Baths, which came straight in from the beach and on which I once saw floating a human turd. And the sweaty smell of the changing-room with its greasy basins, and, giving on this, the row of filthy, dilapidated lavatories, which had no fastenings of any kind on the doors, so that whenever you were sitting there someone was sure to come crashing in. It is not easy for me to think of my schooldays without seeming to breathe in a whiff of something cold and evil-smelling – a sort of compound of sweaty stockings, dirty towels, faecal smells blowing along corridors, forks with old food between the prongs, neck-of-mutton stew, and the banging doors of the lavatories and the echoing chamberpots in the dormitories.

It is true that I am by nature not gregarious, and the W.C. and dirty-handkerchief side of life is necessarily more obtrusive when great numbers of human beings are crushed together in a small space. It is just as bad in an army, and worse, no doubt, in a prison. Besides, boyhood is the age of disgust. After one has learned to differentiate, and before one has become hardened – between seven and eighteen, say – one seems always to be walking the tightrope over a cesspool. Yet I do not think I exaggerate the squalor of school life, when I remember how health and cleanliness were neglected, in spite of the hoo-ha about fresh air and cold water and keeping in hard training. It was common to remain constipated for days together. Indeed, one was hardly encouraged to keep one's bowels open, since the only aperients tolerated were Castor Oil or another almost equally horrible drink called Liquorice Powder. One was supposed to go into the plunge bath every morning, but some boys shirked it for days on end, simply making themselves scarce when the bell sounded, or else slipping along the edge of the bath among the crowd, and then wetting their hair with a little dirty water off the floor. A little boy of eight or nine will not necessarily keep himself clean unless there is someone to see that he does it. There was a new boy named Bachelor, a pretty, mother's darling of a boy, who came a little while before I left. The first thing I noticed about him was the beautiful pearly whiteness of his teeth. By the end of that term his teeth were an extraordinary shade of green. During all that time, apparently, no one had taken sufficient interest in him to see that he brushed them.

But of course the differences between home and school were more than physical. That bump on the hard mattress, on the first night of term, used to give me a feeling of abrupt awakening, a feeling of: "This is reality, this is what you are up against." Your home might be far from perfect, but at least it was a place ruled by love rather than by fear, where you did not have to be perpetually on your guard against the people surrounding you. At eight years old you were suddenly taken out of this warm nest and flung into a world of force and fraud and secrecy, like a goldfish into a tank full of pike. Against no matter what degree of bullying you had no redress. You could only have defended yourself by sneaking, which, except in a few rigidly defined circumstances, was the unforgivable sin. To write home and ask your parents to take you away would have been even less thinkable, since to do so would have been to admit yourself unhappy and unpopular, which a boy will never do. Boys are Erewhonians: they think that misfortune is disgraceful and must be concealed at all costs. It might perhaps have been considered permissible to complain to your parents about bad food, or an unjustified caning, or some other ill-treatment inflicted by masters and not by boys. The fact that Sambo never beat the richer boys suggests that such complaints were made occasionally. But in my own peculiar circumstances I could never have asked my parents to intervene on my behalf. Even before I understood about the reduced fees, I grasped that they were in some way under an obligation to Sambo, and therefore could not protect me against him. I have mentioned already that throughout my time at St Cyprian's I never had a cricket bat of my own. I had been told this was because "your parents couldn't afford it". One day in the holidays, by some casual remark, it came out that they had provided ten shillings to buy me one: yet no cricket bat appeared. I did not protest to my parents, let alone raise the subject with Sambo. How could I? I was dependent on him, and the ten shillings was merely a fragment of what I owed him. I realise now of course, that it is immensely unlikely that Sambo had simply stuck to the money. No doubt the matter had slipped his memory. But the point is that I assumed that he had stuck to it, and that he had a right to do so if he chose.

How difficult it is for a child to have any real independence of attitude could be seen in our behaviour towards Flip. I think it would be true to say that every boy in the school hated and feared her. Yet we all fawned on her in the most abject way, and the top layer of our feelings towards her was a sort of guilt-stricken loyalty. Flip, although the discipline of the school depended more on her than on Sambo, hardly pretended to dispense strict justice. She was frankly capricious. An act which might get you a caning one day, might next day be laughed off as a boyish prank, or even commended because it "showed you had guts". There were days when everyone cowered before those deepset, accusing eyes, and there were days when she was like a flirtatious queen surrounded by courtier-lovers, laughing and joking, scattering largesse, or the promise of largesse ("And if you win the Harrow History Prize I'll give you a new case for your camera!"), and occasionally even packing three or four favoured boys into her Ford car and carrying them off to a teashop in town, where they were allowed to buy coffee and cakes. Flip was inextricably mixed up in my mind with Queen Elizabeth, whose relations with Leicester and Essex and Raleigh were intelligible to me from a very early age. A word we all constantly used in speaking of Flip was "favour". "I'm in good favour", we would say, or "I'm in bad favour". Except for the handful of wealthy or titled boys, no one was permanently in good favour, but on the other hand even the outcasts had patches of it from time to time. Thus, although my memories of Flip are mostly hostile, I also remember considerable periods when I basked under her smiles, when she called me "old chap" and used my Christian name, and allowed me to frequent her private library, where I first made acquaintance with "Vanity Fair". The high-water mark of good favour was to be invited to serve at table on Sunday nights when Flip and Sambo had guests to dinner. In clearing away, of course, one had a chance to finish off the scraps, but one also got a servile pleasure from standing behind the seated guests and darting deferentially forward when something was wanted. Whenever one had the chance to suck up, one did suck up, and at the first smile one's hatred turned into a sort of cringing love. I was always tremendously proud when I succeeded in making Flip laugh. I have even, at her command, written vers d'occasion, comic verses to celebrate memorable events in the life of the school.

I am anxious to make it clear that I was not a rebel, except by force of circumstances. I accepted the codes that I found in being. Once, towards the end of my time, I even sneaked to Siller about a suspected case of homosexuality. I did not know very well what homosexuality was, but I knew that it happened and was bad, and that this was one of the contexts in which it was proper to sneak. Siller told me I was "a good fellow", which made me feel horribly ashamed. Before Flip one seemed as helpless as a snake before the snake-charmer. She had a hardly-varying vocabulary of praise and abuse, a whole series of set phrases, each of which promptly called forth the appropriate response. There was "*Buck* up, old chap!", which inspired one to paroxysms of energy; there was "Don't *be* such a fool!" (or, "It's pathetic, isn't it?"), which made one feel a born idiot; and there was "It isn't very straight of you, is it?", which always brought one to the brink of tears. And yet all the while, at the middle of one's heart, there seemed to stand an incorruptible inner self who knew that whatever one did – whether one laughed or snivelled or went into frenzies of gratitude for small favours – one's only true feeling was hatred.

iv.

I had learned early in my career that one can do wrong against one's will, and before long I also learned that one can do wrong without ever discovering what one has done or why it was wrong. There were sins that were too subtle to be explained, and there were others that were too terrible to be clearly mentioned. For example, there was sex, which was always smouldering just under the surface and which suddenly blew up into a tremendous row when I was about twelve.

At some preparatory schools homosexuality is not a problem, but I think that St Cyprian's may have acquired a "bad tone" thanks to the presence of the South American boys, who would perhaps mature a year or two earlier than an English boy. At that age I was not interested, so I do not actually know what went on, but I imagine it was group masturbation. At any rate, one day the storm suddenly burst over our heads. There were summonses, interrogations, confessions, floggings, repentances, solemn lectures of which one understood nothing except that some irredeemable sin known as "swinishness" or "beastliness" had been committed. One of the ringleaders, a boy named Cross, was flogged, according to eyewitnesses, for a quarter of an hour continuously before being expelled. His yells rang through the house. But we were all implicated, more or less, or felt ourselves to be implicated. Guilt seemed to hang in the air like a pall of smoke. A solemn, black-haired imbecile of an assistant master, who was later to be a Member of Parliament, took the older boys to a secluded room and delivered a talk on the Temple of the Body.

"Don't you realise what a wonderful thing your body is?" he said gravely. "You talk of your motor-car engines, your Rolls-Royces and Daimlers and so on. Don't you understand that no engine ever made is fit to be compared with your body? And then you go and wreck it, ruin it – for life!"

He turned his cavernous black eyes on me and added sadly:

"And you, whom I'd always believed to be quite a decent person after your fashion – you, I hear, are one of the very worst".

A feeling of doom descended upon me. So I was guilty too. I too had done the dreadful thing, whatever it was, that wrecked you for life, body and soul, and ended in suicide or the lunatic asylum. Till then I had hoped that I was innocent, and the conviction of sin which now took possession of me was perhaps all the stronger because I did not know what I had done. I was not among those who were interrogated and flogged, and it was not until after the row was well over that I even learned about the trivial accident which had connected my name with it. Even then I understood nothing. It was not till about two years later that I fully grasped what that lecture on the Temple of the Body had referred to.

At this time I was in an almost sexless state, which is normal, or at any rate common, in boys of that age; I was therefore in the position of simultaneously knowing and not knowing what used to be called the Facts of Life. At five or six, like many children, I had passed through a phase of sexuality. My friends were the plumber's children up the road, and we used sometimes to play games of a vaguely erotic kind. One was called "playing at doctors", and I remember getting a faint but definitely pleasant thrill from holding a toy trumpet, which was supposed to be a stethoscope, against a little girl's belly. About the same time I fell deeply in love, a far more worshipping kind of love than I have ever felt for anyone since, with a girl named Elsie at the convent school which I attended. She seemed to me grown up, so I suppose she must have been fifteen. After that, as so often happens, all sexual feeling seemed to go out of me for many years. At twelve I knew more than I had known as a young child, but I understood less, because I no longer knew the essential fact that there is something pleasant in sexual activity. Between roughly seven and fourteen, the whole subject seemed to me uninteresting and, when for some reason I was forced to think of it, disgusting. My knowledge of the so-called Facts of Life was derived from animals, and was therefore distorted, and in any case was only intermittent. I knew that animals copulated and that human beings had bodies resembling those of animals: but that human beings also copulated I only knew, as it were, reluctantly, when something, a phrase in the Bible, perhaps, compelled me to remember it. Not having desire, I had no curiosity, and was willing to leave many questions unanswered. Thus, I knew in principle how the baby gets into the woman, but I did not know how it gets out again, because I had never followed the subject up. I knew all the dirty words, and in my bad moments I would repeat them to myself, but I did not know what the worst of them meant, nor want to know. They were abstractly wicked, a sort of verbal charm. While I remained in this state, it was easy for me to remain ignorant of any sexual misdeeds that went on about me, and to be hardly wiser even when the row broke. At most, through the veiled and terrible warnings of Flip, Sambo and all the rest of them, I grasped that the crime of which we were all guilty was somehow connected with the sexual organs. I had noticed, without feeling much interest, that one's penis sometimes stands up of its own accord (this starts happening to a boy long before he has any conscious sexual desires), and I was inclined to believe, or half-believe, that *that* must be the crime. At any rate, it was something to do with the penis – so much I understood. Many other boys, I have no doubt, were equally in the dark.

After the talk on the Temple of the Body (days later, it seems in retrospect: the row seemed to continue for days), a dozen of us were seated at the long shiny table which Sambo used for the scholarship class, under Flip's lowering eye. A long, desolate wail rang out from a room somewhere above. A very small boy named Duncan, aged no more than about ten, who was implicated in some way, was being flogged, or was recovering from a flogging. At the sound, Flip's eyes searched our faces, and settled upon me.

"*You see*", she said.

I will not swear that she said, "You see what you have done", but that was the sense of it. We were all bowed down with shame. It was *our* fault. Somehow or other we had led poor Duncan astray: *we* were responsible for his agony and his ruin. Then Flip turned upon another boy named Clapham. It is thirty years ago, and I cannot remember for certain whether she merely quoted a verse from the Bible, or whether she actually brought out a Bible and made Clapham read it; but at any rate the text indicated was:

"Whoso shall offend one of these little ones that believe in me, it were better for him that a millstone were hanged about his neck, and that he were drowned in the depth of the sea".

That, too, was terrible. Duncan was one of these little ones; we had offended him; it were better that a millstone were hanged about our necks and that we were drowned in the depth of the sea.

"Have you thought about that, Clapham – have you thought what it means?" Flip said. And Clapham broke down into snivelling tears.

Another boy, Hardcastle, whom I have mentioned already, was similarly overwhelmed with shame by the accusation that he "had black rings round his eyes".

"Have you looked in the glass lately, Hardcastle?" said Flip. "Aren't you ashamed to go about with a face like that? Do you think everyone doesn't know what it means when a boy has black rings round his eyes?"

Once again the load of guilt and fear seemed to settle down upon me. Had *I* got black rings round my eyes? A couple of years later I realised that these were supposed to be a symptom by which masturbators could be detected. But already, without knowing this, I accepted the black rings as a sure sign of depravity, *some* kind of depravity. And many times, even before I grasped the supposed meaning, I have gazed anxiously into the glass, looking for the first hint of that dreaded stigma, the confession which the secret sinner writes upon his own face.

These terrors wore off, or became merely intermittent, without affecting what one might call my official beliefs. It was still true about the madhouse and the suicide's grave, but it was no longer acutely frightening. Some months later it happened that I once again saw Cross, the ringleader who had been flogged and expelled. Cross was one of the outcasts, the son of poor middle-class parents, which was no doubt part of the reason why Sambo had handled him so roughly. The term after his expulsion he went on to Eastbourne College, the small local public school, which was hideously despised at St Cyprian's and looked on as "not really" a public school at all. Only a very few boys from St Cyprian's went there, and Sambo always spoke of them with a sort of contemptuous pity. You had no chance if you went to a school like that: at the best your destiny would be a clerkship. I thought of Cross as a person who at thirteen had already forfeited all hope of any decent future. Physically, morally and socially he was finished. Moreover I assumed that his parents had only sent him to Eastbourne College because after his disgrace no "good" school would have him.

During the following term, when we were out for a walk, we passed Cross in the street. He looked completely normal. He was a strongly-built, rather good-looking boy with black hair. I immediately noticed that he looked better than when I had last seen him – his complexion, previously rather pale, was pinker – and that he did not seem embarrassed at meeting us. Apparently he was not ashamed either of having been expelled, or of being at Eastbourne College. If one could gather anything from the way he looked at us as we filed past, it was that he was glad to have escaped from St Cyprian's. But the encounter made very little impression on me. I drew no inference from the fact that Cross, ruined in body and soul, appeared to be happy and in good health. I still believed in the sexual mythology that had been taught me by Sambo and Flip. The mysterious, terrible dangers were still there. Any morning the black rings might appear round your eyes and you would know that you too were among the lost ones. Only it no longer seemed to matter very much. These contradictions can exist easily in the mind of a child, because of its own vitality. It accepts – how can it do otherwise? – the nonsense that its elders tell it, but its youthful body, and the sweetness of the physical world, tell it another story. It was the same with Hell, which up to the age of about fourteen I officially believed in. Almost certainly Hell existed, and there were occasions when a vivid sermon could scare you into fits. But somehow it never lasted. The fire that waited for you was real fire, it would hurt in the same way as when you burnt your finger, and *for ever*, but most of the time you could contemplate it without bothering.

v.

The various codes which were presented to you at St Cyprian's – religious, moral, social and intellectual – contradicted one another if you worked out their implications. The essential conflict was between the tradition of nineteenth-century as-ceticism and the actually existing luxury and snobbery of the pre-1914 age. On the one side were low-church Bible Chris-tianity, sex puritanism, insistence on hard work, respect for academic distinction, disapproval of self-indulgence: on the other, contempt for "braininess" and worship of games, con-tempt for foreigners and the working class, an almost neurotic dread of poverty, and, above all, the assumption not only that money and privilege are the things that matter, but that it is better to inherit them than to have to work for them. Broadly, you were bidden to be at once a Christian and a social success, which is impossible. At the time I did not perceive that the various ideals which were set before us cancelled out. I merely saw that they were all, or nearly all, unattainable, so far as I was concerned, since they all depended not only on what you did but on what you *were*.

Very early, at the age of only ten or eleven, I reached the conclusion – no one told me this, but on the other hand I did not simply make it up out of my own head: somehow it was in the air I breathed – that you were no good unless you had £100,000. I had perhaps fixed on this particular sum as a result of reading Thackeray. The interest on £100,000 would be £4,000 a year (I was in favour of a safe 4 per cent), and this seemed to me the minimum income that you must possess if you were to belong to the real top crust, the people in the country houses. But it was clear that I could never find my way into that paradise, to which you did not really belong unless you were born into it. You could only *make* money, if at all, by a mysterious operation called "going into the City", and when you came out of the City, having won your £100,000, you were fat and old. But the truly enviable thing about the top-notchers was that they were rich while young. For people like me, the ambitious middle-class, the examination passers, only a bleak, laborious kind of success was possible. You clambered upwards on a ladder of scholarships into the Home Civil Service or the Indian Civil Service, or possibly you became a barrister. And if at any point you "slacked" or "went off" and missed one of the rungs in the ladder, you became "a little office boy at forty pounds a year". But even if you climbed to the highest niche that was open to you, you could still only be an underling, a hanger-on of the people who really counted.

Even if I had not learned this from Sambo and Flip, I would have learned it from the other boys. Looking back, it is aston-ishing how intimately, intelligently snobbish we all were, how knowledgeable about names and addresses, how swift to detect small differences in accents and manners and the cut of clothes. There were some boys who seemed to drip money from their pores even in the bleak misery of the middle of a winter term. At the beginning and end of the term, especially, there was naively snobbish chatter about Switzerland, and Scotland with its ghillies and grouse moors, and "my uncle's yacht", and "our place in the country", and "my pony" and "my pater's touring car". There never was, I suppose, in the history of the world a time when the sheer vulgar fatness of wealth, without any kind of aristocratic elegance to redeem it, was so obtrusive as in those years before 1914. It was the age when crazy millionaires in curly top hats and lavender waistcoats gave champagne parties in rococo houseboats on the Thames, the age of diabolo and hobble skirts, the age of the "knut" in his grey bowler and cutaway coat, the age of *The Merry Widow*, Saki's novels, *Peter Pan* and *Where the Rainbow Ends*, the age when people talked about chocs and cigs and ripping and topping and heavenly, when they went for divvy weekends at Brighton and had scrumptious teas at the Troc. From the whole decade before 1914 there seems to breathe forth a smell of the more vulgar, un-grown-up kinds of luxury, a smell of brilliantine and creme de menthe and soft-centre chocolates, – an atmosphere, as it were, of eating everlasting strawberry ices on green lawns to the tune of the Eton Boating Song. The extraordinary thing was the way in which everyone took it for granted that this oozing, bulging wealth of the English upper and upper-middle classes would last for ever, and was part of the order of things. After 1918 it was never quite the same again. Snobbishness and expensive habits came back, certainly, but they were self-conscious and on the defensive. Before the war the worship of money was entirely unreflecting and untroubled by any pang of conscience. The goodness of money was as unmistakeable as the goodness of health or beauty, and a glittering car, a title or a horde of servants was mixed up in people's minds with the idea of actual moral virtue.

At St Cyprian's, in term time, the general bareness of life enforced a certain democracy, but any mention of the holidays, and the consequent competitive swanking about cars and butlers and country houses, promptly called class distinctions into being. The school was pervaded by a curious cult of Scotland, which brought out the fundamental contradiction in our standard of values. Flip claimed Scottish ancestry, and she favoured the Scottish boys, encouraging them to wear kilts in their ancestral tartan instead of the school uniform, and even christened her youngest child by a Gaelic name. Ostensibly we were supposed to admire the Scots because they were "grim" and "dour" ("stern" was perhaps the key word), and irresistible on the field of battle. In the big schoolroom there was a steel engraving of the charge of the Scots Greys at Waterloo, all looking as though they enjoyed every moment of it. Our picture of Scotland was made up of burns, braes, kilts, sporrans, claymores, bagpipes and the like, all somehow mixed up with the invigorating effects of porridge, Protestantism and a cold climate. But underlying this was something quite different. The real reason for the cult of Scotland was that only very rich people could spend their summers there. And the pretended belief in Scottish superiority was a cover for the bad conscience of the occupying English, who had pushed the Highland peasantry off their farms to make way for the deer forests, and then compensated them by turning them into servants. Flip's face always beamed with innocent snobbishness when she spoke of Scotland. Occasionally she even attempted a trace of Scottish accent. Scotland was a private paradise which a few initiates could talk about and make outsiders feel small.

"You going to Scotland this hols?"

"Rather! We go every year".

"My pater's got three miles of river".

"My pater's giving me a new gun for the twelfth. There's jolly good black game where we go. Get out, Smith! What are you listening for? You've never been in Scotland. I bet you don't know what a black-cock looks like".

Following on this, imitations of the cry of a black-cock, of the roaring of a stag, of the accent of "our ghillies", etc., etc.

And the questionings that new boys of doubtful social origin were sometimes put through – questionings quite surprising in their mean-minded particularity, when one reflects that the inquisitors were only twelve or thirteen!

"How much a year has your pater got? What part of London do you live in? Is that Knightsbridge or Kensington? How many bathrooms has your house got? How many servants do your people keep? Have you got a butler? Well, then, have you got a cook? Where do you get your clothes made? How many shows did you go to in the hols? How much money did you bring back with you?" etc., etc.

I have seen a little new boy, hardly older than eight, desperately lying his way through such a catechism:

"Have your people got a car?"

"Yes".

"What sort of car?"

"Daimler".

"How many horse-power?"

(Pause, and leap in the dark.) "Fifteen".

"What kind of lights?"

The little boy is bewildered.

"What kind of lights? Electric or acetylene?"

(A longer pause, and another leap in the dark.) "Acetylene".

"Coo! He says his pater's car's got acetylene lamps. They went out years ago. It must be as old as the hills".

"Rot! He's making it up. He hasn't got a car. He's just a navvy. Your pater's a navvy".

And so on.

By the social standards that prevailed about me, I was no good, and could not be any good. But all the different kinds of virtue seemed to be mysteriously interconnected and to belong to much the same people. It was not only money that mattered: there were also strength, beauty, charm, athleticism and some-thing called "guts" or "character", which in reality meant the power to impose your will on others. I did not possess any of these qualities. At games, for instance, I was hopeless. I was a fairly good swimmer and not altogether contemptible at cricket, but these had no prestige value, because boys only attach importance to a game if it requires strength and courage. What counted was football, at which I was a funk. I loathed the game, and since I could see no pleasure or usefulness in it, it was very difficult for me to show courage at it. Football, it seemed to me, is not really played for the pleasure of kicking a ball about, but is a species of fighting. The lovers of football are large, boisterous, nobbly boys who are good at knocking down and trampling on slightly smaller boys. That was the pattern of school life – a continuous triumph of the strong over the weak. Virtue consisted in winning: it consisted in being bigger, stronger, handsomer, richer, more popular, more elegant, more unscrupulous than other people – in dominating them, bullying them, making them suffer pain, making them look foolish, getting the better of them in every way. Life was hierarchical and whatever happened was right. There were the strong, who deserved to win and always did win, and there were the weak, who deserved to lose and always did lose, everlastingly.

I did not question the prevailing standards, because so far as I could see there were no others. How could the rich, the strong, the elegant, the fashionable, the powerful, be in the wrong? It was their world, and the rules they made for it must be the right ones. And yet from a very early age I was aware of the impossibility of any *subjective* conformity. Always at the centre of my heart the inner self seemed to be awake, pointing out the difference between the moral obligation and the psychological *fact*. It was the same in all matters, worldly or other-worldly. Take religion, for instance. You were supposed to love God and I did not question this. Till the age of about fourteen I believed in God, and believed that the accounts given of him were true. But I was well aware that I did not love him. On the contrary, I hated him, just as I hated Jesus and the Hebrew patriarchs. If I had sympathetic feelings towards any character in the Old Testament, it was towards such people as Cain, Jezebel, Haman, Agag, Sisera: in the New Testament my friends, if any, were Ananias, Caiaphas, Judas and Pontius Pilate. But the whole business of religion seemed to be strewn with psychological impossibilities. The Prayer Book told you, for example, to love God and fear him: but how could you love someone whom you feared? With your private affections it was the same. What you *ought* to feel was usually clear enough, but the appropriate emotion could not be commanded. Obviously it was my duty to feel grateful towards Flip and Sambo; but I was not grateful. It was equally clear that one ought to love one's father, but I knew very well that I merely disliked my own father, whom I had barely seen before I was eight and who appeared to me simply as a gruff-voiced elderly man forever saying "Don't". It was not that one did not want to possess the right qualities or feel the correct emotions, but that one could not. The good and the possible never seemed to coincide.

There was a line of verse that I came across not actually while I was at St Cyprian's, but a year or two later, and which seemed to strike a sort of leaden echo in my heart. It was: "The armies of unalterable law". I understood to perfection what it meant to be Lucifer, defeated and justly defeated, with no possibility of revenge. The schoolmasters with their canes, the millionaires with their Scottish castles, the athletes with their curly hair – these were the armies of the unalterable law. It was not easy, at that date, to realise that in fact it *was* alterable. And according to that law I was damned. I had no money, I was weak, I was ugly, I was unpopular, I had a chronic cough, I was cowardly, I smelt. This picture, I should add, was not altogether fanciful. I was an unattractive boy. St Cyprian's soon made me so, even if I had not been so before. But a child's belief in its own shortcomings is not much influenced by facts. I believed, for example, that I "smelt", but this was based simply on general probability. It was notorious that disagreeable people smelt, and therefore presumably I did so too. Again, until after I had left school for good I continued to believe that I was preternaturally ugly. It was what my school-fellows had told me, and I had no other authority to refer to. The conviction that it was *not possible* for me to be a success went deep enough to influence my actions till far into adult life. Until I was about thirty I always planned my life on the assumption not only that any major undertaking was bound to fail, but that I could only expect to live a few years longer.

But this sense of guilt and inevitable failure was balanced by something else: that is, the instinct to survive. Even a creature that is weak, ugly, cowardly, smelly and in no way justifiable still wants to stay alive and be happy after its own fashion. I could not invert the existing scale of values, or turn myself into a success, but I could accept my failure and make the best of it. I could resign myself to being what I was, and then endeavour to survive on those terms.

To survive, or at least to preserve any kind of independence, was essentially criminal, since it meant breaking rules which you yourself recognised. There was a boy named Cliffy Burton who for some months oppressed me horribly. He was a big, powerful, coarsely handsome boy with a very red face and curly black hair, who was forever twisting somebody's arm, wringing somebody's ear, flogging somebody with a riding crop (he was a member of Sixth Form), or performing prod-igies of activity on the football field. Flip loved him (hence the fact that he was habitually called by his Christian name), and Sambo commended him as a boy who "had character" and "could keep order". He was followed about by a group of toadies who nicknamed him Strong Man.

One day, when we were taking off our overcoats in the changing-room, Burton picked on me for some reason. I "answered him back", whereupon he gripped my wrist, twisted it round and bent my forearm back upon itself in a hideously painful way. I remember his handsome, jeering red face bearing down upon mine. He was, I think, older than I, besides being enormously stronger. As he let go of me a terrible, wicked resolve formed itself in my heart. I would get back on him by hitting him when he did not expect it. It was a strategic moment, for the master who had been "taking" the walk would be coming back almost immediately, and then there could be no fight. I let perhaps a minute go by, walked up to Burton with the most harmless air I could assume, and then, getting the weight of my body behind it, smashed my fist into his face. He was flung backwards by the blow, and some blood ran out of his mouth. His always sanguine face turned almost black with rage. Then he turned away to rinse his mouth at the washing-basins.

"*All right!*" he said to me between his teeth as the master led us away.

For days after this he followed me about, challenging me to fight. Although terrified out of my wits, I steadily refused to fight. I said that the blow in the face had served him right, and there was an end of it. Curiously enough he did not simply fall upon me there and then, which public opinion would probably have supported him in doing. So gradually the matter tailed off, and there was no fight.

Now, I had behaved wrongly, by my own code no less than his. To hit him unawares was wrong. But to refuse afterwards to fight, knowing that if we fought he would beat me – that was far worse: it was cowardly. If I had refused because I disapproved of fighting, or because I genuinely felt the matter to be closed, it would have been all right; but I had refused merely because I was afraid. Even my revenge was made empty by that fact. I had struck the blow in a moment of mindless violence, deliberately not looking far ahead and merely determined to get my own back for once and damn the consequences. I had had time to realise that what I did was wrong, but it was the kind of crime from which you could get some satisfaction. Now all was nullified. There had been a sort of courage in the first act, but my subsequent cowardice had wiped it out.

The fact I hardly noticed was that though Burton formally challenged me to fight, he did not actually attack me. Indeed, after receiving that one blow he never oppressed me again. It was perhaps twenty years before I saw the significance of this. At the time I could not see beyond the moral dilemma that is presented to the weak in a world governed by the strong: Break the rules, or perish. I did not see that in that case the weak have the right to make a different set of rules for themselves; because, even if such an idea had occurred to me, there was no one in my environment who could have confirmed me in it. I lived in a world of boys, gregarious animals, questioning nothing, accepting the law of the stronger and avenging their own humiliations by passing them down to someone smaller. My situation was that of countless other boys, and if potentially I was more of a rebel than most, it was only because, by boyish standards, I was a poorer specimen. But I never did rebel intellectually, only emotionally. I had nothing to help me except my dumb selfishness, my inability – not, indeed, to despise myself, but to *dislike* myself – my instinct to survive.

It was about a year after I hit Cliffy Burton in the face that I left St Cyprian's for ever. It was the end of a winter term. With a sense of coming out from darkness into sunlight I put on my Old Boy's tie as we dressed for the journey. I well remember the feeling of that brand-new silk tie round my neck, a feeling of emancipation, as though the tie had been at once a badge of manhood and an amulet against Flip's voice and Sambo's cane. I was escaping from bondage. It was not that I expected, or even intended, to be any more successful at a public school than I had been at St Cyprian's. But still, I was escaping. I knew that at a public school there would be more privacy, more neglect, more chance to be idle and self-indulgent and degenerate. For years past I had been resolved – unconsciously at first, but consciously later on – that when once my scholarship was won I would "slack off" and cram no longer. This resolve, by the way, was so fully carried out that between the ages of thirteen and twenty-two or -three I hardly ever did a stroke of avoidable work.

Flip shook hands to say good-bye. She even gave me my Christian name for the occasion. But there was a sort of patronage, almost a sneer, in her face and in her voice. The tone in which she said good-bye was nearly the tone in which she had been used to say *little butterflies*. I had won two scholarships, but I was a failure, because success was measured not by what you did but by what you *were*. I was "not a good type of boy" and could bring no credit on the school. I did not possess character or courage or health or strength or money, or even good manners, the power to look like a gentleman.

"Good-bye", Flip's parting smile seemed to say; "it's not worth quarrelling now. You haven't made much of a success of your time at St Cyprian's, have you? And I don't suppose you'll get on awfully well at a public school either. We made a mistake, really, in wasting our time and money on you. This kind of education hasn't much to offer to a boy with your background and your outlook. Oh, don't think we don't understand you! We know all about those ideas you have at the back of your head, we know you disbelieve in everything we've taught you, and we know you aren't in the least grateful for all we've done for you. But there's no use in bringing it all up now. We aren't responsible for you any longer, and we shan't be seeing you again. Let's just admit that you're one of our failures and part without ill-feeling. And so, good-bye".

That at least was what I read into her face. And yet how happy I was, that winter morning, as the train bore me away with the gleaming new silk tie (dark green, pale blue and black, if I remember rightly) round my neck! The world was opening before me, just a little, like a grey sky which exhibits a narrow crack of blue. A public school would be better fun than St Cyprian's, but at bottom equally alien. In a world where the prime necessities were money, titled relatives, athleticism, tailor-made clothes, neatly-brushed hair, a charming smile, I was no good. All I had gained was a breathing-space. A little quietude, a little self-indulgence, a little respite from cramming – and then, ruin. What kind of ruin I did not know: perhaps the colonies or an office stool, perhaps prison or an early death. But first a year or two in which one could "slack off" and get the benefit of one's sins, like Doctor Faustus. I believed firmly in my evil destiny, and yet I was acutely happy. It is the advantage of being thirteen that you can not only live in the moment, but do so with full consciousness, foreseeing the future and yet not caring about it. Next term I was going to Wellington. I had also won a scholarship at Eton, but it was uncertain whether there would be a vacancy, and I was going to Wellington first. At Eton you had a room to yourself – a room which might even have a fire in it. At Wellington you had your own cubicle, and could make yourself cocoa in the evenings. The privacy of it, the grown-upness! And there would be libraries to hang about in, and summer afternoons when you could shirk games and mooch about the countryside alone, with no master driving you along. Meanwhile there were the holidays. There was the .22 rifle that I had bought the previous holidays (the Crackshot, it was called, costing twenty-two and sixpence), and Christmas was coming next week. There were also the pleasures of over-eating. I thought of some particularly voluptuous cream buns with could be bought for twopence each at a shop in our town. (This was 1916, and food-rationing had not yet started.) Even the detail that my journey-money had been slightly miscalculated, leaving about a shilling over – enough for an unforeseen cup of coffee and a cake or two somewhere on the way – was enough to fill me with bliss. There was time for a bit of happiness before the future closed in upon me. But I did know that the future was dark. Failure, failure, failure – failure behind me, failure ahead of me – that was by far the deepest conviction that I carried away.

vi.

All this was thirty years ago and more. The question is: Does a child at school go through the same kind of experiences nowadays?

The only honest answer, I believe, is that we do not with certainty know. Of course it is obvious that the present-day *attitude* towards education is enormously more humane and sensible than that of the past. The snobbishness that was an integral part of my own education would be almost unthinkable today, because the society that nourished it is dead. I recall a conversation that must have taken place about a year before I left St Cyprian's. A Russian boy, large and fair-haired, a year older than myself, was questioning me.

"How much a year has your father got?"

I told him what I thought it was, adding a few hundreds to make it sound better. The Russian boy, neat in his habits, produced a pencil and a small notebook and made a calculation.

"My father has over two hundred times as much money as yours", he announced with a sort of amused contempt.

The was in 1915. What happened to that money a couple of years later, I wonder? And still more I wonder, do conversations of that kind happen at preparatory schools now?

Clearly there has been a vast change of outlook, a general growth of "enlightenment", even among ordinary, unthinking middle-class people. Religious belief, for instance, has largely vanished, dragging other kinds of nonsense after it. I imagine that very few people nowadays would tell a child that if it masturbates it will end in the lunatic asylum. Beating, too, has become discredited, and has even been abandoned at many schools. Nor is the under-feeding of children looked on as a normal, almost meritorious act. No one now would openly set out to give his pupils as little food as they could do with, or tell them that it is healthy to get up from a meal as hungry as you sat down. The whole status of children has improved, partly because they have grown relatively less numerous. And the diffusion of even a little psychological knowledge has made it harder for parents and schoolteachers to indulge their aberrations in the name of discipline. Here is a case, not known to me personally, but known to someone I can vouch for, and happening within my own lifetime. A small girl, daughter of a clergyman, continued wetting her bed at an age when she should have grown out of it. In order to punish her for this dreadful deed, her father took her to a large garden party and there introduced her to the whole company as a little girl who wetted her bed: and to underline her wickedness he had previously painted her face black. I do not suggest that Flip and Sambo would actually have done a thing like this, but I doubt whether it would have much surprised them. After all, things do change. And yet —!

The question is not whether boys are still buckled into Eton collars on Sunday, or told that babies are dug up under gooseberry bushes. That kind of thing is at an end, admittedly. The real question is whether it is still normal for a schoolchild to live for years amid irrational terrors and lunatic misunderstandings.

And here one is up against the very great difficulty of knowing what a child really feels and thinks. A child which appears reasonably happy may actually be suffering horrors which it cannot or will not reveal. It lives in a sort of alien under-water world which we can only penetrate by memory or divination. Our chief clue is the fact that we were once children ourselves, and many people appear to forget the atmosphere of their own childhood almost entirely. Think for instance of the unnecessary torments that people will inflict by sending a child back to school with clothes of the wrong pattern, and refusing to see that this matters! Over things of this kind a child will sometimes utter a protest, but a great deal of the time its attitude is one of simple concealment. Not to expose your true feelings to an adult seems to be instinctive from the age of seven or eight onwards. Even the affection that one feels for a child, the desire to protect and cherish it, is a cause of misunderstandings. One can love a child, perhaps, more deeply than one can love another adult, but it is rash to assume that the child feels any love in return. Looking back on my childhood, after the infant years were over, I do not believe that I ever felt love for any mature person except my mother, and even her I did not trust, in the sense that shyness made me conceal most of my real feelings from her. Love, the spontaneous, unqualified emotion of love, was something I could only feel for people who were young. Towards people who were old – and remember that "old" to a child means over thirty, or even over twenty-five – I could feel reverence, respect, admiration or compunction, but I seemed cut off from them by a veil of fear and shyness mixed up with physical distaste. People are too ready to forget the child's *physical* shrinking from the adult. The enormous size of grown-ups, their ungainly, rigid bodies, their coarse, wrinkled skins, their great relaxed eyelids, their yellow teeth, and the whiffs of musty clothes and beer and sweat and tobacco that disengage from them at every movement! Part of the reason for the ugliness of adults, in a child's eyes, is that the child is usually looking upwards, and few faces are at their best when seen from below. Besides, being fresh and unmarked itself, the child has impossibly high standards in the matter of skin and teeth and complexion. But the greatest barrier of all is the child's misconception about age. A child can hardly envisage life beyond thirty, and in judging people's ages it will make fantastic mistakes. It will think that a person of twenty-five is forty, that a person of forty is sixty-five, and so on. Thus, when I fell in love with Elsie I took her to be grown-up. I met her again, when I was thirteen and she, I think, must have been twenty-three; she now seemed to me a middle-aged woman, somewhat past her best. And the child thinks of growing old as an almost obscene calamity, which for some mysterious reason will never happen to itself. All who have passed the age of thirty are joyless grotesques, endlessly fussing about things of no importance and staying alive without, so far as the child can see, having anything to live for. Only child life is real life. The schoolmaster who imagines that he is loved and trusted by his boys is in fact mimicked and laughed at behind his back. An adult who does not seem dangerous nearly always seems ridiculous.

I base these generalisations on what I can recall of my own childhood outlook. Treacherous though memory is, it seems to me the chief means we have of discovering how a child's mind works. Only by resurrecting our own memories can we realise how incredibly distorted is the child's vision of the world. Consider this, for example. How would St Cyprian's appear to me now, if I could go back, at my present age, and see it as it was in 1915? What should I think of Sambo and Flip, those terrible, all-powerful monsters? I should see them as a couple of silly, shallow, ineffectual people, eagerly clambering up a social ladder which any thinking person could see to be on the point of collapse. I would no more be frightened of them than I would be frightened of a dormouse. Moreover, in those days they seemed to me fantastically old, whereas – though of this I am not certain – I imagine they must have been somewhat younger than I am now. And how would Cliffy Burton appear, with his blacksmith's arms and his red, jeering face? Merely a scruffy little boy, barely distinguishable from hundreds of other scruffy little boys. The two sets of facts can lie side by side in my mind, because those happen to be my own memories. But it would be very difficult for me to see with the eyes of any other child, except by an effort of the imagination which might lead me completely astray. The child and the adult live in different worlds. If that is so, we cannot be certain that school, at any rate boarding-school, is not still for many children as dreadful an experience as it used to be. Take away God, Latin, the cane, class distinctions and sexual taboos, and the fear, the hatred, the snobbery and the misunderstanding might still all be there. It will have been seen that my own main trouble was an utter lack of any sense of proportion or probability. This led me to accept outrages and believe absurdities, and to suffer torments over things which were in fact of no importance. It is not enough to say that I was "silly" and "ought to have known better". Look back into your own childhood and think of the nonsense you used to believe and the trivialities which could make you suffer. Of course my own case had its individual variations, but essentially it was that of countless other boys. The weakness of the child is that it starts with a blank sheet. It neither understands nor questions the society in which it lives, and because of its credulity other people can work upon it, infecting it with the sense of inferiority and the dread of offending against mysterious, terrible laws. It may be that everything that happened to me at St Cyprian's could happen in the most "enlightened" school, though perhaps in subtler forms. Of one thing, however, I do feel fairly sure, and that is that boarding-schools are worse than day schools. A child has a better chance with the sanctuary of its home near at hand. And I think the characteristic faults of the English upper and middle classes may be partly due to the practice, general until recently, of sending children away from home as young as nine, eight or even seven.

I have never been back to St Cyprian's. Reunions, old boys' dinners and such-like leave me something more than cold, even when my memories are friendly. I have never even been down to Eton, where I was relatively happy, though I did once pass through it in 1933 and noted with interest that nothing seemed to have changed, except that the shops now sold radios. As for St Cyprian's, for years I loathed its very name so deeply that I could not view it with enough detachment to see the significance of the things that happened to me there. In a way, it is only within the last decade that I have really thought over my schooldays, vividly though their memory has always haunted me. Nowadays, I believe, it would make very little impression on me to see the place again, if it still exists. (I remember hearing a rumour some years ago that it had been burnt down.) If I had to pass through Eastbourne I would not make a detour to avoid the school: and if I happened to pass the school itself I might even stop for a moment by the low brick wall, with the steep bank running down from it, and look across the flat playing-field at the ugly building with the square of asphalt in front of it. And if I went inside and smelt again the inky, dusty smell of the big schoolroom, the rosiny smell of the chapel, the stagnant smell of the swimming bath and the cold reek of the lavatories, I think I should only feel what one invariably feels in revisiting any scene of childhood: How small everything has grown, and how terrible is the deterioration in myself! But it is a fact that for many years I could hardly have borne to look at it again. Except upon dire necessity I would not have set foot in Eastbourne. I even conceived a prejudice against Sussex, as the county that contained St Cyprian's, and as an adult I have only once been in Sussex, on a short visit. Now, however, the place is out of my system for good. Its magic works no longer, and I have not even enough animosity left to make me hope that Flip and Sambo are dead or that the story of the school being burnt down was true.

Review of *Great Morning* by Osbert Sitwell

The Adelphi, July–September 1948

As the successive wars, like ranges of hills, rear their bulk between ourselves and the past, autobiography becomes a sort of antiquarianism. One need only be a little over forty to remember things that are as remote from the present age as chain armour or girdles of chastity. Many people have remarked nostalgically on the fact that before 1914 you could travel to any country in the world, except perhaps Russia, without a passport. But what strikes me in retrospect as even more startling is that in those days you could walk into a bicycle shop – an ordinary bicycle shop, not even a gunsmith's – and buy a revolver and cartridges, with no questions asked. Clearly, that is not the kind of social atmosphere that we shall ever see again, and when Sir Osbert Sitwell writes of "before 1914" with open regret, his emotion can hardly be called reactionary. Reaction implies an effort to restore the past, and though the world might conceivably be pushed back to the pattern of 1938, there can be no more question of restoring the Edwardian age than of reviving Albigensianism.

Not that Sir Osbert's early years were altogether carefree, as readers of the first two volumes of his autobiography will have noticed. His father, Sir George Sitwell, was a trying man to have any dealings with: an architectural genius gone astray, who squandered fantastic sums in megalomaniac building schemes, which extended even to altering the landscape and constructing artificial lakes whose water seeped into the coalmines below and caused endless lawsuits – all this while considering a shilling a week sufficient pocket-money for a boy of nineteen, and even refusing to rescue his wife from the clutches of a money-lender. Architecture apart, his main purpose in life – not, perhaps, from downright malice but as a sort of prolonged practical joke – was to force everyone connected with him into doing whatever he or she most disliked. Osbert, whose antipathy to horses was well known, was driven into a cavalry regiment, then escaped into the Grenadier Guards, then, when he seemed too happy in the Guards, was found a job in the Town Clerk's office in Scarborough, after receiving lessons in pot-hooks (to improve his handwriting) at the age of twenty. The war rescued him from this, but his brother and sister were similarly treated. Nevertheless the last few years before the war were happy ones, and, making all allowance for his abnormal position as a rich man's son, he is probably right in feeling that English life then had a gaiety that has never been recovered.

Life in the Guards was pleasant because it meant being stationed in London, which in its turn meant theatres, music and picture galleries. Osbert's brother officers were civilized and tolerant, and his colonel even excused him for sitting in a café with Jacob Epstein, who was in private's uniform. It was the age of Chaliapin and the Russian Ballet, and of the revival in England of a serious interest in music and painting. It was also the age of ragtime and the tango, of the knuts in their grey top hats, of house-boats and hobble skirts, and of a splashing to and fro of wealth such as the world had not seen since the early Roman empire. The Victorian puritanism had at last broken down, money was pouring in from all directions, and the sense of guilt which is now inseparable from a privileged position had not yet developed. Barney Barnato and Sir William Whiteley were held up as models to emulate, and it was meritorious not merely to be rich, but to look rich. Life in London was a ceaseless round of entertainment, on a scale unheard-of before and barely imaginable now:

> One band in a house was no longer enough, there must be two, even three. Electric fans whirled on the top of enormous blocks of ice, buried in banks of hydrangeas, like the shores from which the barque departs for Cythera. Never had there been such displays of flowers.... Never had Europe seen such mounds of peaches, figs, nectarines and strawberries at all seasons, brought from their steamy tents of glass. Champagne bottles stood stacked on the sideboards. ... As guests, only the poor of every race were barred. Even foreigners could enter, if they were rich.

There was also the life of the country houses, with their platoons of servants. Osbert, inimical to horses, was no hunting man, but he enjoyed his shooting expeditions in spite of, or perhaps because of the fact that he never succeeded in killing anything, and his talks with the crabbed old gamekeeper, a type of man now extinct – the type that accepts a position of vassalage, and within that framework is able to enjoy a considerable independence.

Of course, if you happened not to belong to the world of champagne and hothouse strawberries, life before 1914 had serious disadvantages. Even today, after two murderous wars, the manual workers throughout most of the world are probably better off, in a physical sense, than they were then. In Britain they are unquestionably better off. But will this still be true after a third world war, this time conducted with atom bombs? Or even after another fifty years of soil erosion and squandering of the world's fuel resources? Before 1914, moreover, people had the inestimable advantage of not knowing that war was coming, or, if they did know it, of not foreseeing what it would be like. Sir Osbert does not claim much more than that life in those days was fun for a privileged minority, and, as anyone who has read *Before the Bombardment* will know, he is perfectly alive to the vulgarity and grotesqueness of the whole epoch. His political outlook, in so far as this book implies one at all, seems to be a mild liberalism. "In those days", he says, "the rich were as much and unjustly revered as they are now reviled". But in the golden summer of 1914 he greatly enjoyed being rich, and he is honest enough to say so.

There is now a widespread idea that nostalgic feelings about the past are inherently vicious. One ought, apparently, to live in a continuous present, a minute-to-minute cancellation of memory, and if one thinks of the past at all it should merely be in order to thank God that we are so much better than we used to be. This seems to me a sort of intellectual face-lifting, the motive behind which is a snobbish terror of growing old. One ought to realize that a human being cannot continue developing indefinitely, and that a writer, in particular, is throwing away his heritage if he repudiates the experience of his early life. In many ways it is a grave handicap to remember that lost paradise "before the war" – that is, before the other war. In other ways it is an advantage. Each generation has its own experience and its own wisdom, and though there is such a thing as intellectual progress, so that the ideas of one age are sometimes demonstrably less silly than those of the last – still, one is likelier to make a good book by sticking to one's early-acquired vision than by a futile effort to "keep up". The great thing is to be your age, which includes being honest about your social origins. In the nineteen-thirties we saw a whole literary generation, or at least the most prominent members of a generation, either pretending to be proletarians or indulging in public orgies of self-hatred because they were not proletarians. Even if they could have kept up this attitude (today, a surprising number of them have either fled to America or found themselves jobs in the B.B.C. or the British Council), it was a stupid one, because their bourgeois origin was not a thing that could be altered. It is to Sir Osbert Sitwell's credit that he has never pretended to be other than he is: a member of the upper classes, with an amused and leisurely attitude which comes out in his manner of writing, and which could only be the product of an expensive upbringing. Probably, so far as his memory serves him, he records his likes and dislikes accurately, which always needs moral courage. How easy it would have been to write of Eton or the Grenadier Guards in a spirit of sneering superiority, with the implication that from earliest youth he was the holder of enlightened sentiments which, in fact, no comfortably-placed person did hold a generation ago. Or how easy, on the other hand, to stand on the defensive and try to argue away the injustice and inequality of the world in which he grew up. He has done neither, with the result that these three volumes (*Left Hand, Right Hand*, *The Scarlet Tree* and *Great Morning*), although the range they cover is narrow, must be among the best autobiographies of our time.

Review of *The Heart of the Matter* by Graham Greene

The New Yorker, 17 July 1948

A fairly large proportion of the distinguished novels of the last few decades have been written by Catholics and have even been describable as Catholic novels. One reason for this is that the conflict not only between this world and the next world but between sanctity and goodness is a fruitful theme of which the ordinary, unbelieving writer cannot make use. Graham Greene used it once successfully, in "The Power and the Glory", and once, with very much more doubtful success, in "Brighton Rock". His latest book, "The Heart of the Matter" (Viking), is, to put it as politely as possible, not one of his best, and gives the impression of having been mechanically constructed, the familiar conflict being set out like an algebraic equation, with no attempt at psychological probability.

Here is the outline of the story: The time is 1942 and the place is a West African British colony, unnamed but probably the Gold Coast. A certain Major Scobie, Deputy Commissioner of Police and a Catholic convert, finds a letter bearing a German address hidden in the cabin of the captain of a Portuguese ship. The letter turns out to be a private one and completely harmless, but it is, of course, Scobie's duty to hand it over to higher authority. However, the pity he feels for the

Portuguese captain is too much for him, and he destroys the letter and says nothing about it. Scobie, it is explained to us, is a man of almost excessive conscientiousness. He does not drink, take bribes, keep Negro mistresses, or indulge in bureaucratic intrigue, and he is, in fact, disliked on all sides because of his uprightness, like Aristides the Just. His leniency toward the Portuguese captain is his first lapse. After it, his life becomes a sort of fable on the theme of "Oh, what a tangled web we weave", and in every single instance it is the goodness of his heart that leads him astray. Actuated at the start by pity, he has a love affair with a girl who has been rescued from a torpedoed ship. He continues with the affair largely out of a sense of duty, since the girl will go to pieces morally if abandoned; he also lies about her to his wife, so as to spare her the pangs of jealousy. Since he intends to persist in his adultery, he does not go to confession, and in order to lull his wife's suspicions he tells her that he has gone. This involves him in the truly fearful act of taking the Sacrament while in a state of mortal sin. By this time, there are other complications, all caused in the same manner, and Scobie finally decides that the only way out is through the unforgivable sin of suicide. Nobody else must be allowed to suffer through his death; it will be so arranged as to look like an accident. As it happens, he bungles one detail, and the fact that he has committed suicide becomes known. The book ends with a Catholic priest's hinting, with doubtful orthodoxy, that Scobie is perhaps not damned. Scobie, however, had not entertained any such hope. White all through, with a stiff upper lip, he had gone to what he believed to be certain damnation out of pure gentlemanliness.

I have not parodied the plot of the book. Even when dressed up in realistic details, it is just as ridiculous as I have indicated. The thing most obviously wrong with it is that Scobie's motives, assuming one could believe in them, do not adequately explain his actions. Another question that comes up is: Why should this novel have its setting in West Africa? Except that one of the characters is a Syrian trader, the whole thing might as well be happening in a London suburb. The Africans exist only as an occasionally mentioned background, and the thing that would actually be in Scobie's mind the whole time – the hostility between black and white, and the struggle against the local nationalist movement – is not mentioned at all. Indeed, although we are shown his thoughts in considerable detail, he seldom appears to think about his work, and then only of trivial aspects of it, and never about the war, although the date is 1942. All he is interested in is his own progress toward damnation. The improbability of this shows up against the colonial setting, but it is an improbability that is present in "Brighton Rock" as well, and that is bound to result from foisting theological preoccupations upon simple people anywhere.

The central idea of the book is that it is better, spiritually higher, to be an erring Catholic than a virtuous pagan. Graham Greene would probably subscribe to the statement of Maritain, made apropos of Léon Bloy, that "there is but one sadness – not to be a saint." A saying of Péguy's is quoted on the title page of the book to the effect that the sinner is "at the very heart of Christianity" and knows more of Christianity than anyone else does, except the saint. All such sayings contain or can be made to contain, the fairly sinister suggestion that ordinary human decency is of no value and that any one sin is no worse than any other sin. In addition, it is impossible not to feel a sort of snobbishness in Mr. Greene's attitude, both here and in his other books written from an explicitly Catholic standpoint. He appears to share the idea, which has been floating around ever since Baudelaire, that there is something rather distingué in being damned; Hell is a sort of high-class night club, entry to which is reserved for Catholics only, since the others, the non-Catholics, are too ignorant to be held guilty, like the beasts that perish. We are carefully informed that Catholics are no better than anybody else; they even, perhaps, have a tendency to be worse, since their temptations are greater. In modern Catholic novels, in both France and England, it is, indeed, the fashion to include bad priests, or at least inadequate priests, as a change from Father Brown. (I imagine that one major objective of young English Catholic writers is not to resemble Chesterton.) But all the while – drunken, lecherous, criminal, or damned outright – the Catholics retain their superiority, since they alone know the meaning of good and evil. Incidentally, it is assumed in "The Heart of the Matter", and in most of Mr. Greene's other books, that no one outside the Catholic Church has the most elementary knowledge of Christian doctrine.

This cult of the sanctified sinner seems to me to be frivolous, and underneath it there probably lies a weakening of belief, for when people really believed in Hell, they were not so fond of striking graceful attitudes on its brink. More to the point, by trying to clothe theological speculations in flesh and blood, it produces psychological absurdities. In "The Power and the Glory", the struggle between this-worldly and other-worldly values is convincing because it is not occurring inside one person. On the one side, there is the priest, a poor creature in some ways but made heroic by his belief in his own thauma-turgic powers; on the other side, there is the lieutenant, repre-senting human justice and material progress, and also a heroic figure after his fashion. They can respect each other, perhaps, but not understand each other. The priest, at any rate, is not credited with any very complex thoughts. In "Brighton Rock", on the other hand, the central situation is incredible, since it presupposes that the most brutishly stupid person can, merely by having been brought up a Catholic, be capable of great intellectual subtlety. Pinkie, the racecourse gangster, is a species of satanist, while his still more limited girl friend under-stands and even states the difference between the categories "right and wrong" and "good and evil". In, for example, Mauriac's "Thérèse" sequence, the spiritual conflict does not outrage probability, because it is not pretended that Thérèse is a normal person. She is a chosen spirit, pursuing her salvation over a long period and by a difficult route, like a patient stretched out on the psychiatrist's sofa. To take an opposite instance, Evelyn Waugh's "Brideshead Revisited", in spite of improbabilities, which are traceable partly to the book's being written in the first person, succeeds because the situation is itself a normal one. The Catholic characters bump up against problems they would meet with in real life; they do not suddenly move on to a different intellectual plane as soon as their religious beliefs are involved. Scobie is incredible because the two halves of him do not fit together. If he were capable of getting into the kind of mess that is described, he would have got into it years earlier. If he really felt that adultery is mortal sin, he would stop committing it; if he persisted in it, his sense of sin would weaken. If he believed in Hell, he would not risk going there merely to spare the feelings of a couple of neurotic women. And one might add that if he were the kind of man we are told he is – that is, a man whose chief characteristic is a horror of causing pain – he would not be an officer in a colonial police force.

There are other improbabilities, some of which arise out of Mr. Greene's method of handling a love affair. Every novelist has his own conventions, and, just as in an E. M. Forster novel there is a strong tendency for the characters to die suddenly without sufficient cause, so in a Graham Greene novel there is a tendency for people to go to bed together almost at sight and with no apparent pleasure to either party. Often this is credible enough, but in "The Heart of the Matter" its effect is to weaken a motive that, for the purposes of the story, ought to be a very strong one. Again, there is the usual, perhaps un-avoidable, mistake of making everyone too highbrow. It is not only that Major Scobie is a theologian. His wife, who is represented as an almost complete fool, reads poetry, while the detective who is sent by the Field Security Corps to spy on Scobie even writes poetry. Here one is up against the fact that it is not easy for most modern writers to imagine the mental processes of anyone who is not a writer.

It seems a pity, when one remembers how admirably he has written of Africa elsewhere, that Mr. Greene should have made just this book out of his wartime African experiences. The fact that the book is set in Africa while the action takes place almost entirely inside a tiny white community gives it an air of triviality. However, one must not carp too much. It is pleasant to see Mr. Greene starting up again after so long a silence, and in postwar England it is a remarkable feat for a novelist to write a novel at all. At any rate, Mr. Greene has not been perma-nently demoralized by the habits acquired during the war, like so many others. But one may hope that his next book will have a different theme, or, if not, that he will at least remember that a perception of the vanity of earthly things, though it may be enough to get one into Heaven, is not sufficient equipment for the writing of a novel.

GEORGE ORWELL

Review of *Portrait of the Anti-Semite* by Jean-Paul Sartre; translated by Erik de Mauny

The Observer, 7 November 1948

Anti-Semitism is obviously a subject that needs serious study, but it seems unlikely that it will get it in the near future. The trouble is that so long as anti-Semitism is regarded simply as a disgraceful aberration, almost a crime, anyone literate enough to have heard the word will naturally claim to be immune from it; with the result that books on anti-Semitism tend to be mere exercises in casting motes out of other people's eyes. M. Sartre's book is no exception, and it is probably no better for having been written in 1944, in the uneasy, self-justifying, quisling-hunting period that followed on the Liberation.

At the beginning, M. Sartre informs us that anti-Semitism has no rational basis: at the end, that it will not exist in a classless society, and that in the meantime it can perhaps be combated to some extent by education and propaganda. These conclusions would hardly be worth stating for their own sake, and in between them there is, in spite of much cerebration, little real discussion of the subject, and no factual evidence worth mentioning.

We are solemnly informed that anti-Semitism is almost unknown among the working class. It is a malady of the bourgeoisie, and, above all, of that goat upon whom all our sins are laid, the "petty bourgeois". Within the bourgeoisie it is seldom found among scientists and engineers. It is a peculiarity of people who think of nationality in terms of inherited culture and of property in terms of land.

Why these people should pick on Jews rather than some other victim M. Sartre does not discuss, except, in one place, by putting forward the ancient and very dubious theory that the Jews are hated because they are supposed to have been responsible for the Crucifixion. He makes no attempt to relate anti-Semitism to such obviously allied phenomena as, for instance, colour prejudice.

Part of what is wrong with M. Sartre's approach is indicated by his title. "The" anti-Semite, he seems to imply all through the book, is always the same kind of person, recognisable at a glance and, so to speak, in action the whole time. Actually one has only to use a little observation to see that anti-Semitism is extremely widespread, is not confined to any one class, and, above all, in any but the worst cases, is intermittent.

But these facts would not square with M. Sartre's atomised vision of society. There is, he comes near to saying, no such thing as a human being, there are only different categories of men, such as "the" worker and "the" bourgeois, all classifiable in much the same way as insects. Another of these insectlike creatures is "the" Jew, who, it seems, can usually be distinguished by his physical appearance. It is true that there are two kinds of Jew, the "Authentic Jew", who wants to remain Jewish, and the "Inauthentic Jew", who would like to be assimilated; but a Jew, of whichever variety, is not just another human being. He is wrong, at this stage of history, if he tries to assimilate himself, and we are wrong if we try to ignore his racial origin. He should be accepted into the national community, not as an ordinary Englishman, Frenchman, or whatever it may be, but as a Jew.

It will be seen that this position is itself dangerously close to anti-Semitism. Race-prejudice of any kind is a neurosis, and it is doubtful whether argument can either increase or diminish it, but the net effect of books of this kind, if they have an effect, is probably to make anti-Semitism slightly more prevalent than it was before. The first step towards serious study of anti-Semitism is to stop regarding it as a crime. Meanwhile, the less talk there is about "the" Jew or "the" anti-Semite, as a species of animal different from ourselves, the better.

Review of *Notes towards the Definition of Culture* by T. S. Eliot

The Observer, 28 November 1948

In his new book, "Notes towards the Definition of Culture", Mr. T. S. Eliot argues that a truly civilised society needs a class system as part of its basis. He is, of course, only speaking negatively. He does not claim that there is any method by which a high civilisation can be created. He maintains merely that such a civilisation is not likely to flourish in the absence of certain conditions, of which class distinctions are one.

This opens up a gloomy prospect, for on the one hand it is almost certain that class distinctions of the old kind are moribund, and on the other hand Mr. Eliot has at the least a strong *prima facie* case.

The essence of his argument is that the highest levels of culture have been attained only by small groups of people – either social groups or regional groups – who have been able to perfect their traditions over long periods of time. The most important of all cultural influences is the family, and family loyalty is strongest when the majority of people take it for granted to go through life at the social level at which they were born. Moreover, not having any precedents to go upon, we do not know what a classless society would be like. We know only that, since functions would still have to be diversified, classes would have to be replaced by "élites", a term Mr. Eliot borrows with evident distaste from the late Karl Mannheim. The élites will plan, organise and administer: whether they can become the guardians and transmitters of culture, as certain social classes have been in the past, Mr. Eliot doubts, perhaps justifiably.

As always, Mr. Eliot insists that tradition does not mean worship of the past; on the contrary, a tradition is alive only while it is growing. A class can preserve a culture because it is itself an organic and changing thing. But here, curiously enough, Mr. Eliot misses what might have been the strongest argument in his case. This is, that a classless society directed by élites may ossify very rapidly, simply because its rulers are able to choose their successors, and will always tend to choose people resembling themselves.

Hereditary institutions – as Mr. Eliot might have argued – have the virtue of being unstable. They must be so, because power is constantly devolving on people who are either incapable of holding it, or use it for purposes not intended by their forefathers. It is impossible to imagine any hereditary body lasting so long, and with so little change, as an adoptive organisation like the Catholic Church. And it is at least thinkable that another adoptive and authoritarian organisation, the Russian Communist Party, will have a similar history. If it hardens into a class, as some observers believe it is already doing, then it will change and develop as classes always do. But if it continues to co-opt its members from all strata of society, and then train them into the desired mentality, it might keep its shape almost unaltered from generation to generation. In aristocratic societies the eccentric aristocrat is a familiar figure, but the eccentric commissar is almost a contradiction in terms.

Although Mr. Eliot does not make use of this argument, he does argue that even the antagonism between classes can have fruitful results for society as a whole. This again is probably true. Yet one continues to have, throughout his book, the feeling that there is something wrong, and that he himself is aware of it. The fact is that class privilege, like slavery, has somehow ceased to be defensible. It conflicts with certain moral assumptions which Mr. Eliot appears to share, although intellectually he may be in disagreement with them.

All through the book his attitude is noticeably defensive. When class distinctions were vigorously believed in, it was not thought necessary to reconcile them either with social justice or with efficiency. The superiority of the ruling classes was held to be self-evident, and in any case the existing order was what God had ordained. The mute inglorious Milton was a sad case, but not remediable on this side of the grave.

This, however, is by no means what Mr. Eliot is saying. He would like, he says, to see in existence both classes *and* élites. It should be normal for the average human being to go through life at his predestined social level, but on the other hand the right man must be able to find his way into the right job. In saying this he seems almost to give away his whole case. For if class distinctions are desirable in themselves, then wastage of talent, or inefficiency in high places, are comparatively unimportant. The social misfit, instead of being directed upwards or downwards, should learn to be contented in his own station.

Mr. Eliot does not say this: indeed, very few people in our time would say it. It would seem morally offensive. Probably, therefore, Mr. Eliot does not believe in class distinctions as our grandfathers believed in them. His approval of them is only negative. That is to say, he cannot see how any civilisation worth having can survive in a society where the differences arising from social background or geographical origin have been ironed out.

It is difficult to make any positive answer to this. To all appearances the old social distinctions are everywhere disappearing, because their economic basis is being destroyed. Possibly new classes are appearing, or possibly we are within sight of a genuinely classless soceity, which Mr. Eliot assumes would be a cultureless society. He may be right, but at some points his pessimism seems to be exaggerated. "We can assert with some confidence", he says, "that our own period is one of decline; that the standards of culture are lower than they were 50 years ago; and that the evidence of this decline is visible in every department of human activity".

This seems true when one thinks of Hollywood films or the atomic bomb, but less true if one thinks of the clothes and architecture of 1898, or what life was like at that date for an unemployed labourer in the East End of London. In any case, as Mr. Eliot himself admits at the start, we cannot reverse the present trend by conscious action. Cultures are not manufactured, they grow of their own accord. Is it too much to hope that the classless society will secrete a culture of its own? And before writing off our own age as irrevocably damned, is it not worth remembering that Matthew Arnold and Swift and Shakespeare – to carry the story back only three centuries – were all equally certain that they lived in a period of decline?

1949

Reflections on Gandhi

Partisan Review, January 1949

Saints should always be judged guilty until they are proved innocent, but the tests that have to be applied to them are not, of course, the same in all cases. In Gandhi's case the questions one feels inclined to ask are: to what extent was Gandhi moved by vanity – by the consciousness of himself as a humble, naked old man, sitting on a praying-mat and shaking empires by sheer spiritual power – and to what extent did he compromise his own principles by entering into politics, which of their nature are inseparable from coercion and fraud? To give a definite answer one would have to study Gandhi's acts and writings in immense detail, for his whole life was a sort of pilgrimage in which every act was significant. But this partial autobiography, which ends in the nineteen-twenties, is strong evidence in his favour, all the more because it covers what he would have called the unregenerate part of his life and reminds one that inside the saint, or near-saint, there was a very shrewd, able person who could, if he had chosen, have been a brilliant success as a lawyer, an administrator or perhaps even a business man.

At about the time when the autobiography first appeared I remember reading its opening chapters in the ill-printed pages of some Indian newspaper. They made a good impression on me, which Gandhi himself, at that time, did not. The things that one associated with him – homespun cloth, "soul forces" and vegetarianism – were unappealing, and his medievalist programme was obviously not viable in a backward, starving, over-populated country. It was also apparent that the British were making use of him, or thought they were making use of him. Strictly speaking, as a Nationalist, he was an enemy, but since in every crisis he would exert himself to prevent violence – which, from the British point of view, meant preventing any effective action whatever – he could be regarded as "our man." In private this was sometimes cynically admitted. The attitude of the Indian millionaires was similar. Gandhi called upon them to repent, and naturally they preferred him to the Socialists and Communists who, given the chance, would actually have taken their money away. How reliable such calculations are in the long run is doubtful; as Gandhi himself says, "in the end deceivers deceive only themselves"; but at any rate the gentleness with which he was nearly always handled was due partly to the feeling that he was useful. The British Conservatives only became really angry with him when, as in 1942, he was in effect turning his non-violence against a different conqueror.

But I could see even then that the British officials who spoke of him with a mixture of amusement and disapproval also genuinely liked and admired him, after a fashion. Nobody ever suggested that he was corrupt, or ambitious in any vulgar way, or that anything he did was actuated by fear or malice. In judging a man like Gandhi one seems instinctively to apply high standards, so that some of his virtues have passed almost unnoticed. For instance, it is clear even from the autobiography that his natural physical courage was quite outstanding: the manner of his death was a later illustration of this, for a public man who attached any value to his own skin would have been more adequately guarded. Again, he seems to have been quite free from that maniacal suspiciousness which, as E. M. Forster rightly says in *A Passage to India*, is the besetting Indian vice, as hypocrisy is the British vice. Although no doubt he was shrewd enough in detecting dishonesty, he seems wherever possible to have believed that other people were acting in good faith and had a better nature through which they could be approached. And though he came of a poor middle-class family, started life rather unfavourably, and was probably of unimpressive physical appearance, he was not afflicted by envy or by the feeling of inferiority. Colour feeling, when he first met it in its worst form in South Africa, seems rather to have astonished him. Even when he was fighting what was in effect a colour war, he did not think of people in terms of race or status. The governor of a province, a cotton millionaire, a half-starved Dravidian coolie, a British private soldier, were all equally human beings, to be approached in much the same way. It is noticeable that even in the worst possible circumstances, as in South Africa when he was making himself unpopular as the champion of the Indian community, he did not lack European friends.

Written in short lengths for newspaper serialization, the autobiography is not a literary masterpiece, but it is the more impressive because of the commonplaceness of much of its material. It is well to be reminded that Gandhi started out with the normal ambitions of a young Indian student and only adopted his extremist opinions by degrees and, in some cases, rather unwillingly. There was a time, it is interesting to learn, when he wore a top hat, took dancing lessons, studied French and Latin, went up the Eiffel Tower and even tried to learn the violin – all this with the idea of assimilating European civilization as thoroughly as possible. He was not one of those saints who are marked out by their phenomenal piety from childhood onwards, nor one of the other kind who forsake the world after sensational debaucheries. He makes full confession of the misdeeds of his youth, but in fact there is not much to confess. As a frontispiece to the book there is a photograph of Gandhi's possessions at the time of his death. The whole outfit could be purchased for about £5, and Gandhi's sins, at least his fleshly sins, would make the same sort of appearance if placed all in one heap. A few cigarettes, a few mouthfuls of meat, a few annas pilfered in childhood from the maidservant, two visits to a brothel (on each occasion he got away without "doing anything"), one narrowly escaped lapse with his landlady in Plymouth, one outburst of temper – that is about the whole collection. Almost from childhood onwards he had a deep earnestness, an attitude ethical rather than religious, but, until he was about thirty, no very definite sense of direction. His first entry into anything describable as public life was made by way of vegetarianism. Underneath his less ordinary qualities one feels all the time the solid middle-class business men who were his ancestors. One feels that even after he had abandoned personal ambition he must have been a resourceful, energetic lawyer and a hardheaded political organizer, careful in keeping down expenses, an adroit handler of committees and an indefatigable chaser of subscriptions. His character was an extraordinarily mixed one, but there was almost nothing in it that you can put your finger on and call bad, and I believe that even Gandhi's worst enemies would admit that he was an interesting and unusual man who enriched the world simply by being alive. Whether he was also a lovable man, and whether his teachings can have much value for those who do not accept the religious beliefs on which they are founded, I have never felt fully certain.

Of late years it has been the fashion to talk about Gandhi as though he were not only sympathetic to the Western leftwing movement, but were even integrally part of it. Anarchists and pacifists, in particular, have claimed him for their own, noticing only that he was opposed to centralism and State violence and ignoring the otherworldly, anti-humanist tendency of his doctrines. But one should, I think, realize that Gandhi's teachings cannot be squared with the belief that Man is the measure of all things, and that our job is to make life worth living on this earth, which is the only earth we have. They make sense only on the assumption that God exists and that the world of solid objects is an illusion to be escaped from. It is worth considering the disciplines which Gandhi imposed on himself and which – though he might not insist on every one of his followers observing every detail – he considered indispensable if one wanted to serve either God or humanity. First of all, no meat-eating, and if possible no animal food in any form. (Gandhi himself, for the sake of his health, had to compromise on milk, but seems to have felt this to be a backsliding.) No alcohol or tobacco, and no spices or condiments, even of a vegetable kind, since food should be taken not for its own sake but solely in order to preserve one's strength. Secondly, if possible, no sexual intercourse. If sexual intercourse must happen, then it should be for the sole purpose of begetting children and presumably at long intervals. Gandhi himself, in his middle thirties, took the vow of *bramahcharya*, which means not only complete chastity but the elimination of sexual desire. This condition, it seems, is difficult to attain without a special diet and frequent fasting. One of the dangers of milk-drinking is that it is apt to arouse sexual desire. And finally – this is the cardinal point – for the seeker after goodness there must be no close friendships and no exclusive loves whatever.

Close friendships, Gandhi says, are dangerous, because "friends react on one another" and through loyalty to a friend one can be led into wrong-doing. This is unquestionably true.

Moreover, if one is to love God, or to love humanity as a whole, one cannot give one's preference to any individual person. This again is true, and it marks the point at which the humanistic and the religious attitude cease to be reconcilable. To an ordinary human being, love means nothing if it does not mean loving some people more than others. The autobiography leaves it uncertain whether Gandhi behaved in an inconsiderate way to his wife and children, but at any rate it makes clear that on three occasions he was willing to let his wife or a child die rather than administer the animal food prescribed by the doctor. It is true that the threatened death never actually occurred, and also that Gandhi – with, one gathers, a good deal of moral pressure in the opposite direction – always gave the patient the choice of staying alive at the price of committing a sin: still, if the decision had been solely his own, he would have forbidden the animal food, whatever the risks might be. There must, he says, be some limit to what we will do in order to remain alive, and the limit is well on this side of chicken broth. This attitude is perhaps a noble one, but, in the sense which – I think – most people would give to the word, it is inhuman. The essence of being human is that one does not seek perfection, that one *is* sometimes willing to commit sins for the sake of loyalty, that one does not push asceticism to the point where it makes friendly intercourse impossible, and that one is prepared in the end to be defeated and broken up by life, which is the inevitable price of fastening one's love upon other human individuals. No doubt alcohol, tobacco and so forth are things that a saint must avoid, but sainthood is also a thing that human beings must avoid. There is an obvious retort to this, but one should be wary about making it. In this yogi-ridden age, it is too readily assumed that "non-attachment" is not only better than a full acceptance of earthly life, but that the ordinary man only rejects it because it is too difficult: in other words, that the average human being is a failed saint. It is doubtful whether this is true. Many people genuinely do not wish to be saints, and it is probable that some who achieve or aspire to sainthood have never felt much temptation to be human beings. If one could follow it to its psychological roots, one would, I believe, find that the main motive for "non-attachment" is a desire to escape from the pain of living, and above all from love, which, sexual or non-sexual, is hard work. But it is not necessary here to argue whether the other-worldly or the humanistic ideal is "higher." The point is that they are incompatible. One must choose between God and Man, and all "radicals" and "progressives," from the mildest Liberal to the most extreme Anarchist, have in effect chosen Man.

However, Gandhi's pacifism can be separated to some extent from his other teachings. Its motive was religious, but he claimed also for it that it was a definite technique, a method, capable of producing desired political results. Gandhi's attitude was not that of most Western pacifists. *Satyagraha*, first evolved in South Africa, was a sort of non-violent warfare, a way of defeating the enemy without hurting him and without feeling or arousing hatred. It entailed such things as civil disobedience, strikes, lying down in front of railway trains, enduring police charges without running away and without hitting back, and the like. Gandhi objected to "passive resistance" as a translation of *Satyagraha*: in Gujarati, it seems, the word means "firmness in the truth." In his early days Gandhi served as a stretcher-bearer on the British side in the Boer War, and he was prepared to do the same again in the war of 1914–18. Even after he had completely abjured violence he was honest enough to see that in war it is usually necessary to take sides. He did not – indeed, since his whole political life centred round a struggle for national independence, he could not – take the sterile and dishonest line of pretending that in every war both sides are exactly the same and it makes no difference who wins. Nor did he, like most Western pacifists, specialize in avoiding awkward questions. In relation to the late war, one question that every pacifist had a clear obligation to answer was: "What about the Jews? Are you prepared to see them exterminated? If not, how do you propose to save them without resorting to war?" I must say that I have never heard, from any Western pacifist, an honest answer to this question, though I have heard plenty of evasions, usually of the "you're another" type. But it so happens that Gandhi was asked a somewhat similar question in 1938 and that his answer is on record in Mr. Louis Fischer's *Gandhi and Stalin*. According to Mr. Fischer, Gandhi's view was that the German Jews ought to commit collective suicide, which "would have aroused the world and the people of Germany to Hitler's violence." After the war he justified himself: the Jews had been killed anyway, and might as well have died significantly. One has the impression that this attitude staggered even so warm an admirer as Mr. Fischer, but Gandhi was merely being honest. If you are not prepared to take life, you must often be prepared for lives to be lost in some other way. When, in 1942, he urged non-violent resistance against a Japanese invasion, he was ready to admit that it might cost several million deaths.

At the same time there is reason to think that Gandhi, who after all was born in 1869, did not understand the nature of totalitarianism and saw everything in terms of his own struggle against the British government. The important point here is not so much that the British treated him forbearingly as that he was always able to command publicity. As can be seen from the phrase quoted above, he believed in "arousing the world," which is only possible if the world gets a chance to hear what you are doing. It is difficult to see how Gandhi's methods could be applied in a country where opponents of the regime disappear in the middle of the night and are never heard of again. Without a free press and the right of assembly, it is impossible not merely to appeal to outside opinion, but to bring a mass movement into being, or even to make your intentions known to your adversary. Is there a Gandhi in Russia at this moment? And if there is, what is he accomplishing? The Russian masses could only practise civil disobedience if the same idea happened to occur to all of them simultaneously, and even then, to judge by the history of the Ukraine famine, it would make no difference. But let it be granted that non-violent resistance can be effective against one's own government, or against an occupying power: even so, how does one put it into practice internationally? Gandhi's various conflicting statements on the late war seem to show that he felt the difficulty of this. Applied to foreign politics, pacifism either stops being pacifist or becomes appeasement. Moreover the assumption, which served Gandhi so well in dealing with individuals, that all human beings are more or less approachable and will respond to a generous gesture, needs to be seriously questioned. It is not necessarily true, for example, when you are dealing with lunatics. Then the question becomes: Who is sane? Was Hitler sane? And is it not possible for one whole culture to be insane by the standards of another? And, so far as one can gauge the feelings of whole nations, is there any apparent connection between a generous deed and a friendly response? Is gratitude a factor in international politics?

These and kindred questions need discussion, and need it urgently, in the few years left to us before somebody presses the button and the rockets begin to fly. It seems doubtful whether civilization can stand another major war, and it is at least thinkable that the way out lies through non-violence. It is Gandhi's virtue that he would have been ready to give honest consideration to the kind of question that I have raised above; and, indeed, he probably did discuss most of these questions somewhere or other in his innumerable newspaper articles. One feels of him that there was much that he did not understand, but not that there was anything that he was frightened of saying or thinking. I have never been able to feel much liking for Gandhi, but I do not feel sure that as a political thinker he was wrong in the main, nor do I believe that his life was a failure. It is curious that when he was assassinated, many of his warmest admirers exclaimed sorrowfully that he had lived just long enough to see his life work in ruins, because India was engaged in a civil war which had always been foreseen as one of the by-products of the transfer of power. But it was not in trying to smooth down Hindu–Moslem rivalry that Gandhi had spent his life. His main political objective, the peaceful ending of British rule, had after all been attained. As usual, the relevant facts cut across one another. On the one hand, the British did get out of India without fighting, an event which very few observers indeed would have predicted until about a year before it happened. On the other hand, this was done by a Labour government, and it is certain that a Conservative government, especially a government headed by Churchill, would have acted differently. But if, by 1945, there had grown up in Britain a large body of opinion sympathetic to Indian independence, how far was this due to Gandhi's personal influence? And if, as may happen, India and Britain finally settle down into a decent and friendly relationship, will this be partly because Gandhi, by keeping up his struggle obstinately and without hatred, disinfected the political air? That one even thinks of asking such questions indicates his stature. One may feel, as I do, a sort of aesthetic distaste for Gandhi, one may reject the claims of sainthood made on his behalf (he never made any such claim himself, by the way), one may also reject sainthood as an ideal and therefore feel that Gandhi's basic aims were anti-human and reactionary: but regarded simply as a politician, and compared with the other leading political figures of our time, how clean a smell he has managed to leave behind!

Evelyn Waugh
Unfinished essay; April(?) 1949 Typescript with handwritten notes

Within the last few decades, in countries like Britain or the United States, the literary intelligentsia has grown large enough to constitute a world in itself. One important result of this is that the opinions which a writer feels frightened of expressing are not those which are disapproved of by society as a whole. To a great extent, what is still loosely thought of as heterodoxy has become orthodoxy. It is nonsense to pretend, for instance, that at this date there is something daring and original in proclaiming yourself an anarchist, an atheist, a pacifist, etc. The daring thing, or at any rate the unfashionable thing, is to believe in God or to approve of the capitalist system. In 1895, when Oscar Wilde was jailed, it must have needed very con-siderable moral courage to defend homosexuality. Today it would need no courage at all: today the equivalent action would be, perhaps, to defend antisemitism. But this example that I have chosen immediately reminds one of something else – namely, that one cannot judge the value of an opinion simply by the amount of courage that is required in holding it. There is still such a thing as truth and falsehood, it is possible to hold true beliefs for the wrong reasons, and – though there may be no advance in human intelligence – the prevailing ideas of one age are sometimes demonstrably less silly than those of another.

In our own day, the English novelist who has most con-spicuously defied his contemporaries is Evelyn Waugh.

Waugh's outlook on life is, I should say, false and to some extent perverse, but at least it must be said for him that he adopted it at a time when it did not pay to do so, and his literary reputation has suffered accordingly. It is true, of course, that he has had immense *popular* success (a thing that does not seem to have any connection, positive or negative, with critical acclaim), and also that he has been underrated partly because he is a "light" writer whose special gift is for something not far removed from low farce. But his main offence in the eyes of his fellow-writers has always been the reactionary political tendency which was already clearly apparent even in such light-hearted books as *Decline and Fall* and *Vile Bodies*. Chronologically Waugh belongs to the generation of Auden and Spender, though he would be about five years older than most of the leading members of the group. This generation, almost en bloc, was politically "left," in a Popular-Front style, with Communist leanings. There were, of course, a few writers of about the same age who did not fit into the pattern – for instance, there were William Empson, William Plomer, V. S. Pritchett and Graham Greene. But of these, the first three were merely lacking in political zeal and not in any way hostile to the Popular-Front orthodoxy, while Graham Greene – the fact has passed almost unnoticed, no doubt because of the unjustified assumption that a Catholic is the same thing as a Conservative – was himself politically "left," in an ill-defined, unobtrusive way. In the whole of this age-group, the only loudly discordant voice was Waugh's. Even his first book, the life of Rossetti, published in 1927, displays a sort of defiant Conservatism, which expresses itself, as was natural at that date, in aesthetic rather than political terms.

Waugh is the latest, perhaps the last, of a long line of English writers whose real driving force is a romantic belief in aristocracy. At a casual glance, *Decline and Fall*, *Vile Bodies*, and considerable passages, at least, in nearly all the subsequent books, appear to consist of nothing but a sort of high-spirited foolery, owing something to Norman Douglas and perhaps a little to "Saki," and tinged by the kind of innocent snobbishness that causes people to wait twenty-four hours on the pavement to get a good view of a royal wedding. If one looks only a little way below the surface, however, one sees that though the approach is at the level of farce, the essential theme is serious. What Waugh is trying to do is to use the feverish, cultureless modern world as a set-off for his own conception of a good and stable way of life. The seeming immoralism of these books (the jokes turn not merely upon adultery but upon prostitution, homosexuality, suicide, lunacy and cannibalism) is merely a reversion to the older tradition of English humour, according to which any event can be funny provided that it either didn't happen or happened a long time ago. In *Decline and Fall*, for instance, the funniest episode is the sawing-off of a clergyman's head. If one were asked to believe this it would be merely disgusting, but being impossible it is acceptable, like the events in, for instance, the *Miller's Tale*, which would seem by no means funny if they happened in real life. Waugh's books certainly owe some of their popularity to their air of naughtiness, but none of them (except, perhaps, to some small extent, *Decline and Fall*) is intended to be morally subversive. They are really sermons in farcical shape, and kept in farcical shape by avoidance of comment. In *Decline and Fall*, *Vile Bodies*, *Scoop* and, to a less extent, *A Handful of Dust* the central character is a passive figure who simply lets things happen to him and hardly appears to notice the difference between good and evil, or even between pain and pleasure: in *Black Mischief* and *The Loved One* he is not passive, but his motives are unexplained. The general outline of these books resembles that of *Candide*, and in very broad terms the "moral" is also the same: "Look, this is what the world is like. Is it really necessary to behave quite so foolishly?" But, of course, Waugh's notion of reasonable conduct is very different from Voltaire's.

In all Waugh's books up to *Brideshead Revisited*, which perhaps indicates a new departure, the idea of sanity and moral integrity is mixed up with the idea of country life – upper-class country life – as it was lived a couple of generations ago. Already in *Vile Bodies* there is an irrelevant outburst in favour of the older kind of minor aristocracy, the people who still have, or used to have, a sense of obligation and a fixed code of behaviour, as against the mob of newspaper peers, financiers, politicians and playboys with whom the book deals:

> . . . a great concourse of pious and honourable people (many of whom made the Anchorage House reception the one

outing of the year), their women-folk well gowned in rich and durable stuffs, their men-folk ablaze with orders; people who had represented their country in foreign places and sent their sons to die for her in battle, people of decent and temperate life, uncultured, unaffected, unembarrassed, unassuming, unambitious people, of independent judgement and marked eccentricities, kind people who cared for animals and the deserving poor, brave and rather unreasonable people, that fine phalanx of the passing order, approaching, as one day at the Last Trump they hoped to meet their Maker, with decorous and frank cordiality to shake Lady Anchorage by the hand at the top of her staircase. . . .

Here "animals and the deserving poor" may perhaps be meant ironically, but the note of affection and esteem, out of tune with most of the rest of the book, is unmistakeable. In *A Handful of Dust* the theme is made more explicit. On the one side the foolish, glittering life of fashionable London: on the other the country house, the succession that must be maintained, the fields and woods that must not be allowed to decay. As an earlier writer in the *Partisan Review* has pointed out, whenever the action of Waugh's books takes place in England, a house, an old house, always plays an important part in it. In *Decline and Fall* the house, in process of being ravaged, is already there. In *A Handful of Dust* – this time a somewhat ridiculous house but beautiful in its owner's eyes – it is the pivot of the story. In *Brideshead Revisited* it appears in more magnificent form. But it is probably as it appears in *Scoop* and *Vile Bodies* that it corresponds most closely with Waugh's private ideal. Everyone knows, at least traditionally, the kind of house that is there described – the middle-sized country house which required, in the days of its glory, about ten servants, and which has now, if it is not merely derelict, been turned into a hotel, a boarding school or a lunatic asylum. All the familiar scenery is there, whether or not Waugh mentions it in detail: the "wet, bird-haunted lawns" and the walled garden with its crucified pear-trees; the large untidy porch with its litter of raincoats, waders, landing-nets and croquet mallets; the plastery smell of the flagged passage leading to the gunroom; the estate map on the library wall; the case of stuffed birds over the staircase. To Waugh, this is magic, or used to be magic, and it would be a waste of time to try to exorcise it from his mind merely by pointing out that

The typescript breaks off at this point.

A Prize for Ezra Pound
Partisan Review, May 1949

On 14 February 1949, Ezra Pound was awarded the Bollingen Prize for Poetry. Pound (1885–1972) had supported Mussolini in the 1930s. During World War II he had lived in Italy and from 1941 had broadcast in support of the Fascist powers. He was arrested by U.S. forces in 1945, but was declared insane at his trial for treason and was confined to St. Elizabeth's Hospital in Washington, D.C., until 1958. In its issue for April 1949, *Partisan Review* published a Comment by William Barrett. This began:

The awarding of a prize is a public act usually surrounded with many difficulties. When the prize is literary, there are not only all the difficulties that attend literary judgement, but the further complications from the fact that the judges, because of the public nature of the award, act both as citizens and literary critics.

The Bollingen Foundation has recently announced that the Bollingen Prize for Poetry, the first of an annual series, has been awarded to Ezra Pound for *The Pisan Cantos* as the best book of poetry published during 1948. The judges were the Fellows in American Letters of the Library of Congress, among whom are T. S. Eliot, W. H. Auden, Allen Tate, Robert Penn Warren, Katherine Anne Porter, and Robert Lowell. In the public statement accompanying the award the judges tell us that they were aware that the choice of Pound was likely to pro-voke objections, and their brief statement implies that they have given these objections careful consideration, ending with something like an affirmation of a general principle:

"To permit other considerations than that of poetic achieve-ment to sway the decision would destroy the significance of the award and would in principle deny the validity of that objective perception of value on which any civilized society must rest."

The sentiments behind this declaration seem to us admirable. Our only interest here is to insist on the application of this principle....

Several writers, one of them George Orwell, were asked to discuss the issues connected with this award. These were published in the May issue of *Partisan Review*. This was Orwell's response:

I think the Bollingen Foundation were quite right to award Pound the prize, if they believed his poems to be the best of the year, but I think also that one ought to keep Pound's career in memory and not feel that his ideas are made respectable by the mere fact of winning a literary prize.

Because of the general revulsion against Allied war propaganda, there has been – indeed, there was, even before the war was over – a tendency to claim that Pound was "not really" a fascist and an antisemite, that he opposed the war on pacifist grounds and that in any case his political activities only belonged to the war years. Some time ago I saw it stated in an American periodical that Pound only broadcast on the Rome radio when "the balance of his mind was upset," and later (I think in the same periodical) that the Italian government had blackmailed him into broadcasting by threats to relatives. All this is plain falsehood. Pound was an ardent follower of Mussolini as far back as the nineteen-twenties, and never concealed it. He was a contributor to Mosley's review, the *British Union Quarterly*, and accepted a professorship from the Rome government before the war started. I should say that his enthusiasm was essentially for the Italian form of fascism. He did not seem to be very strongly pro-Nazi or anti-Russian, his real underlying motive being hatred of Britain, America and "the Jews." His broadcasts were disgusting. I remember at least one in which he approved the massacre of the East European Jews and "warned" the American Jews that their turn was coming presently. These broadcasts – I did not hear them, but only read them in the BBC monitoring report – did not give me the impression of being the work of a lunatic.

Incidentally I am told that in delivering them Pound used to put on a pronounced American accent which he did not normally have, no doubt with the idea of appealing to the isolationists and playing on anti-British sentiment.

None of this is a reason against giving Pound the Bollingen Prize. There are times when such a thing might be undesirable – it would have been undesirable when the Jews were actually being killed in the gas vans, for instance – but I do not think this is one of them. But since the judges have taken what amounts to the "art for art's sake" position, that is, the position that aesthetic integrity and common decency are two separate things, then at least let us keep them separate and not excuse Pound's political career on the ground that he is a good writer. He *may* be a good writer (I must admit that I personally have always regarded him as an entirely spurious writer), but the opinions that he has tried to disseminate by means of his works are evil ones, and I think that the judges should have said so more firmly when awarding him the prize.

Author's Notes

1   (p. 179) Dickens turned Miss Mowcher into a sort of heroine because
the real woman whom he had caricatured had read the earlier chapters
and was bitterly hurt. He had previously meant her to play a villainous
part. But *any* action by such a character would seem incongruous.

2   (p. 183) From a letter to his youngest son (in 1868): 'You will remember
that you have never at home been harassed about religious observances,
or mere formalities. I have always been anxious not to weary my
children with such things, before they are old enough to form opinions
respecting them. You will therefore understand the better that I now
most solemnly impress upon you the truth and beauty of the Christian
Religion, as it came from Christ Himself, and the impossibility of your
going far wrong if you humbly but heartily respect it . . . Never abandon
the wholesome practice of saying your own private prayers, night and
morning. I have never abandoned it myself, and I know the comfort
of it.'

3   (p. 193) There are several corresponding girls' papers. The *Schoolgirl*
is a companion-paper to the *Magnet* and has stories by 'Hilda Richards'.
The characters are interchangeable to some extent. Bessie Bunter,
Billy Bunter's sister, figures in the *Schoolgirl*.

4   (p. 261) 'The mind, that Ocean where each kind
Doth straight its own resemblance find;
Yet it creates, transcending these,
Far other worlds, and other seas' etc.
                    [From Andrew Marvell, 'The Garden,' lines 43–46].

5   (p. 265) The idea is that the demons will come down on you for
being too self-confident. Thus children believe that if you hook a fish
and say 'Got him' before he is landed, he will escape. That if you put
your pads on before it is your turn to bat you will be out first ball etc.
Such beliefs often survive in adults. Adults are only less superstitious than
children in proportion as they have more power over their
environment. In predicaments where everyone is powerless (eg. war,
gambling) everyone is superstitious.

6   (p. 267) I once began making a list of writers whom the critics called
'sentimental'. In the end it included nearly every English writer.
The word is in fact a meaningless symbol of hatred, like the bronze
tripods in Homer which were given to guests as a symbol of
friendship.

7   (p. 296) For example:

> I don't want to join the bloody Army,
> I don't want to go unto the war;
> I want no more to roam,
> I'd rather stay at home
> Living on the earnings of a whore.

But it was not in that spirit that they fought.

8   (p. 343) Written before the outbreak of the war in Greece.

9   (p. 344) It is interesting to notice that Mr. Kennedy, U.S.A. Ambassador in London, remarked on his return to New York in October, 1940, that as a result of the war, 'democracy is finished'. By 'democracy', of course, he meant private capitalism.

10   (p. 718) *Raffles*, *A Thief in the Night* and *Mr. Justice Raffles*, by E. W. Hornung. The third of these is definitely a failure, and only the first has the true Raffles atmosphere. Hornung wrote a number of crime stories, usually with a tendency to take the side of the criminal. A successful book in rather the same vein as *Raffles* is *Stingaree*.

11   (p. 720) 1945. Actually Raffles does kill one man and is more or less consciously responsible for the death of two others. But all three of them are foreigners and have behaved in a very reprehensible manner. He also, on one occasion, contemplates murdering a blackmailer. It is, however, a fairly well-established convention in crime stories that murdering a blackmailer 'doesn't count'.

12   (p. 722) 1945. Another reading of the final episode is possible. It may mean merely that Miss Blandish is pregnant. But the interpretation I have given above seems more in keeping with the general brutality of the book.

13   (p. 724) They are said to have been imported into this country as ballast, which accounted for their low price and crumpled appearance. Since the war the ships have been ballasted with something more useful, probably gravel.

14   (p. 836) *Assignment to Berlin*, by Harry W. Flannery. (Michael Joseph, 1942).

15   (p. 843) *P. G. Wodehouse*, by John Hayward. (*The Saturday Book*, 1942.) I believe this is the only full-length critical essay on Wodehouse.

16   (p. 865) Nations, and even vaguer entities such as the Catholic Church or the proletariat, are commonly thought of as individuals and often referred to as 'she'. Patently absurd remarks such as 'Germany is naturally treacherous' are to be found in any newspaper one opens, and reckless generalisations about national character ('The Spaniard is a natural aristocrat' or 'Every Englishman is a hypocrite') are uttered by almost everyone. Intermittently these generalisations are seen to be unfounded, but the habit of making them persists, and people of professedly international outlook, e.g. Tolstoy or Bernard Shaw, are often guilty of them.

17 (p. 867) A few writers of conservative tendency, such as Peter Drucker, foretold an agreement between Germany and Russia, but they expected an actual alliance or amalgamation which would be permanent. No Marxist or other left-wing writer, of whatever colour, came anywhere near foretelling the Pact.

18 (p. 868) The military commentators of the popular press can mostly be classified as pro-Russian or anti-Russian, pro-blimp or anti-blimp. Such errors as believing the Maginot Line impregnable, or predicting that Russia would conquer Germany in three months, have failed to shake their reputation, because they were always saying what their own particular audience wanted to hear. The two military critics most favoured by the intelligentsia are Captain Liddell Hart and Major-General Fuller, the first of whom teaches that the defence is stronger than the attack, and the second that the attack is stronger than the defence. This contradiction has not prevented both of them from being accepted as authorities by the same public. The secret reason for their vogue in left-wing circles is that both of them are at odds with the War Office.

19 (p. 870) Certain Americans have expressed dissatisfaction because 'Anglo-American' is the normal form of combination for these two words. It has been proposed to substitute 'Americo-British'.

20 (p. 873) The *News Chronicle* advised its readers to visit the news film at which the entire execution could be witnessed, with close-ups. The *Star* published with seeming approval photographs of nearly naked female collaborationists being baited by the Paris mob. These photographs had a marked resemblance to the Nazi photographs of Jews being baited by the Berlin mob.

21 (p. 874) An example is the Russo-German Pact, which is being effaced as quickly as possible from public memory. A Russian correspondent informs me that mention of the Pact is already being omitted from Russian year books which table recent political events.

22 (p. 877) A good example is the sunstroke superstition. Until recently it was believed that the white races were much more liable to sunstroke than the coloured, and that a white man could not safely walk about in tropical sunshine without a pith helmet. There was no evidence whatever for this theory, but it served the purpose of accentuating the difference between 'natives' and Europeans. During the present war the theory has been quietly dropped and whole armies manœuvre in the tropics without pith helmets. So long as the sunstroke superstition survived, English doctors in India appear to have believed in it as firmly as laymen.

23 (p. 921) HOMINIDAE: A family of mammals represented by the single genus Homo (man).

24 (p. 921) PHYLUM: A race of organisms descended from common ancestral form.

NOTES

25 (p. 931) It is fair to say that the P.E.N. Club celebrations, which lasted a
    week or more, did not always stick at quite the same level. I happened to
    strike a bad day. But an examination of the speeches (printed under the
    title *Freedom of Expression*) shows that almost nobody in our own day is
    able to speak out as roundly in favour of intellectual liberty as Milton
    could do 300 years ago – and this in spite of the fact Milton was writing
    in a period of civil war.

26 (p. 958) An interesting illustration of this is the way in which the
    English flower names which were in use till very recently are being
    ousted by Greek ones, *snapdragon* becoming *antirrhinum*, *forget-me-not*
    becoming *myosotis*, etc. It is hard to see any practical reason for this
    change of fashion: it is probably due to an instinctive turning-away
    from the more homely word and a vague feeling that the Greek
    word is scientific.

27 (p. 959) Example: 'Comfort's catholicity of perception and image,
    strangely Whitmanesque in range, almost the exact opposite in
    aesthetic compulsion, continues to evoke that trembling atmospheric
    accumulative hinting at a cruel, an inexorably serene timelessness
    ... Wrey Gardiner scores by aiming at simple bullseyes with precision.
    Only they are not so simple, and through this contented sadness runs
    more than the surface bitter-sweet of resignation.' (*Poetry Quarterly*).

28 (p. 965) One can cure oneself of the *not un-* formation by
    memorizing this sentence: *A not unblack dog was chasing a not
    unsmall rabbit across a not ungreen field.*

29 (p. 1060) It is difficult to think of any politician who has lived to
    be eighty and still been regarded as a success. What we call a 'great'
    statesman normally means one who dies before his policy has had
    time to take effect. If Cromwell had lived a few years longer he
    would probably have fallen from power, in which case we should
    now regard him as a failure. If Pétain had died in 1930, France
    would have venerated him as a hero and patriot. Napoleon
    remarked once that if only a cannon ball had happened to hit him
    when he was riding into Moscow, he would have gone down to
    history as the greatest man who ever lived.

30 (p. 1064) Great Britain raised a million volunteers in the earlier part
    of the 1914–18 war. This must be a world's record, but the pressures
    applied were such that it is doubtful whether the recruitment ought
    to be described as voluntary. Even the most 'ideological' wars have
    been fought largely by pressed men. In the English civil war, the
    Napoleonic wars, the American civil war, the Spanish civil war, etc.,
    both sides resorted to conscription or the press gang.

31 (p. 1067) The only exception I am able to think of is Bernard Shaw,
    who, for some years at any rate, declared Communism and Fascism
    to be much the same thing, and was in favour of both of them.
    But Shaw, after all, is not an Englishman, and probably does not feel
    his fate to be bound up with that of Britain.

32 (p. 1068) As late as the autumn of 1945, a Gallup poll taken among the American troops in Germany showed that 51 per cent. 'thought Hitler did much good before 1939'. This was after five years of anti-Hitler propaganda. The verdict, as quoted, is not very strongly favourable to Germany, but it is hard to believe that a verdict equally favourable to Britain would be given by anywhere near 51 per cent. of the American army.

33 (p. 1093) Houyhnhnms too old to walk are described as being carried in 'sledges' or in 'a kind of vehicle, drawn like a sledge'. Presumably these had no wheels.

34 (p. 1095) The physical decadence which Swift claims to have observed may have been a reality at that date. He attributes it to syphilis, which was a new disease in Europe and may have been more virulent than it is now. Distilled liquors, also, were a novelty in the seventeenth century and must have led at first to a great increase in drunkenness.

35 (p. 1100) At the end of the book, as typical specimens of human folly and viciousness, Swift names 'a Lawyer, a Pickpocket, a Colonel, a Fool, a Lord, a Gamester, a Politician, a Whore-master, a Physician, an Evidence, a Suborner, an Attorney, a Traitor, or the like'. One sees here the irresponsible violence of the powerless. The list lumps together those who break the conventional code, and those who keep it. For instance, if you automatically condemn a colonel, as such, on what grounds do you condemn a traitor? Or again, if you want to suppress pickpockets, you must have laws, which means that you must have lawyers. But the whole closing passage, in which the hatred is so authentic, and the reason given for it so inadequate, is somehow unconvincing. One has the feeling that personal animosity is at work.

36 (p. 1183) *Shakespeare and the Drama.* Written about 1903 as an introduction to another pamphlet, *Shakespeare and the Working Classes*, by Ernest Crosby.

37 (p. 1211) These are not public 'national schools', but something quite the opposite: exclusive and expensive residential secondary schools, scattered far apart. Until recently they admitted almost no one but the sons of rich aristocratic families. It was the dream of *nouveau riche* bankers of the nineteenth century to push their sons into a Public School. At such schools the greatest stress is laid on sport, which forms, so to speak, a lordly, tough and gentlemanly outlook. Among these schools, Eton is particularly famous. Wellington is reported to have said that the victory of Waterloo was decided on the playing fields of Eton. It is not so very long ago that an overwhelming majority of the people who in one way or another ruled England came from the Public School.

38 (p. 1220) *The Struggle for the World*, by James Burnham.

TITLES IN EVERYMAN'S LIBRARY

THE NEW TESTAMENT
(King James Version)

THE OLD TESTAMENT
(King James Version)

GEORGE ORWELL
Animal Farm
Nineteen Eighty-Four
Essays

THOMAS PAINE
Rights of Man
and Common Sense

BORIS PASTERNAK
Doctor Zhivago

PLATO
The Republic
Symposium and Phaedrus

EDGAR ALLAN POE
The Complete Stories

MARCEL PROUST
In Search of Lost Time
(4 vols)

ALEXANDER PUSHKIN
The Collected Stories

FRANÇOIS RABELAIS
Gargantua and Pantagruel

JOSEPH ROTH
The Radetzky March

JEAN-JACQUES
ROUSSEAU
Confessions
The Social Contract and
the Discourses

SALMAN RUSHDIE
Midnight's Children

WALTER SCOTT
Rob Roy

WILLIAM SHAKESPEARE
Comedies Vols 1 and 2
Histories Vols 1 and 2
Romances
Sonnets and Narrative Poems
Tragedies Vols 1 and 2

MARY SHELLEY
Frankenstein

ADAM SMITH
The Wealth of Nations

ALEXANDER
SOLZHENITSYN
One Day in the Life of
Ivan Denisovich

SOPHOCLES
The Theban Plays

CHRISTINA STEAD
The Man Who Loved Children

JOHN STEINBECK
The Grapes of Wrath

STENDHAL
The Charterhouse of Parma
Scarlet and Black

LAURENCE STERNE
Tristram Shandy

ROBERT LOUIS STEVENSON
The Master of Ballantrae and
Weir of Hermiston
Dr Jekyll and Mr Hyde
and Other Stories

HARRIET BEECHER STOWE
Uncle Tom's Cabin

ITALO SVEVO
Zeno's Conscience

JONATHAN SWIFT
Gulliver's Travels

JUNICHIRŌ TANIZAKI
The Makioka Sisters

W. M. THACKERAY
Vanity Fair

HENRY DAVID THOREAU
Walden

ALEXIS DE TOCQUEVILLE
Democracy in America

LEO TOLSTOY
Collected Shorter Fiction
(2 vols)
Anna Karenina
Childhood, Boyhood and Youth
The Cossacks
War and Peace

ANTHONY TROLLOPE
Barchester Towers
Can You Forgive Her?
Doctor Thorne
The Eustace Diamonds

This book is set in BEMBO which was cut
by the punch-cutter Francesco Griffo
for the Venetian printer-publisher
Aldus Manutius in early 1495
and first used in a pamphlet
by a young scholar
named Pietro
Bembo.